# Key to map pages

# Collins Road Atlas

# BRITAIN & IRELAND

## CONTENTS


ii - iii Key to map symbols

iv - ix Route planning maps

x - xi Motorway junctions with limited access

xii - xiii Motorway services information

2-203 Road map section

204-219 City & town centre plans

220-223 London urban maps

224-225 London central map

226-243 Urban area maps

244-247 Ireland road maps & city centre plans

248-252 Index to London street names

253-284 Index to place names in Britain / Ireland



**2003 Edition**

Published by Collins
*An imprint of* HarperCollins*Publishers*
77-85 Fulham Palace Road
Hammersmith
London W6 8JB





Mapping generated from Collins/Bartholomew digital databases.

The Collins website address is: www.collins.co.uk





Printed in Italy ISBN 0 00 766455 9 Imp 001 deluxe PC11241 MDU
ISBN 0 00 766457 5 Imp 001 hardback PC11241 MDU

e-mail: roadcheck@harpercollins.co.uk


The mapping in this Collins Road Atlas is also available for use in promotional gifts or for sale as digital data. For details of these and all other HarperCollins/Bartholomew products and services visit our website at:

www.**fire**and**water**.com
or contact us on:


**Promotional gift enquiries:**
Tel: +44 (0) 20 8307 4272
Fax: +44 (0) 20 8307 4899

**Data Sales enquiries:**
Tel: +44 (0) 1242 258154
Fax: +44 (0) 1242 222725
e-mail: bartholomew@harpercollins.co.uk



HarperCollins*Publishers*

# Key to map symbols

## Route planning maps (pages iv-ix)

|  |  |
|---|---|
| full S M25 S limited, Fleet | Motorway with service area |
| full 4 5 limited | Motorway junction |
| dual A82 single | Primary route |
| Oxford | Primary route destination |
| dual A894 single | 'A' Road |
| | 'B' Road |
| | Road under construction |
| | Gradient / Toll / Tunnel |
| | Ferry route / International airport |
| 886 | Summit height in metres |
| | International / National boundary |
| | National / Forest park |

## Road maps (pages 2-203)

### ROAD INFORMATION

|  |  |
|---|---|
| M4 | Motorway |
| 30 29 | Motorway junction with full / limited access |
| Maidstone, Birch, Sarn | Motorway service area with off road / full / limited access |
| A48 | Primary dual / single carriageway |
| | With passing places |
| A30 | 'A' road dual / single carriageway |
| | With passing places |
| B1403 | 'B' road dual / single carriageway |
| | With passing places |
| | Minor road |
| | Restricted access due to road condition or private ownership |
| | Road projected or under construction |
| 24 | Multi-level junction (occasionally with junction number) |
| | Roundabout |
| 10 | Road distance in miles |
| | Road tunnel |
| | Steep hill (arrows point downhill) |
| Toll | Level crossing / Toll |

### OTHER TRANSPORT INFORMATION

|  |  |
|---|---|
| hours, Cherbourg.....2¼-4¼(5¾) | Car ferry route with journey times; daytime and (night-time) |
| | Railway line / Station / Tunnel |
| | Airport with scheduled services |
| H | Heliport |
| P | Park and Ride site* |

### CITIES, TOWNS & VILLAGES

|  |  |
|---|---|
| | Built up area |
| | Town / Village / Other settlement |
| Peterhead | Primary route destination |
| St Ives | Seaside destination |

### OTHER FEATURES

|  |  |
|---|---|
| | National boundary |
| KENT | County / Unitary Authority boundary & name |
| | National / Regional park |
| | Forest park boundary |
| Danger Zone | Military range |
| | Woodland |
| 468 | Spot height in metres |
| 941 | Summit height in metres |
| | Lake / Dam / River / Waterfall |
| | Canal / Dry canal / Canal tunnel |
| | Beach |
| 14 | Adjoining page indicator |

### TOURIST INFORMATION

A selection of tourist detail is shown on the mapping.
It is advisable to check with the local tourist information office regarding opening times and facilities available.

|  |  |
|---|---|
| i i | Tourist information centre (all year / seasonal) |
| | Preserved railway |
| | Ancient monument |
| 1738 | Battlefield |
| | Castle |
| | Country Park |
| | Ecclesiastical building |
| £ | Factory shop village |
| | Garden |
| | Golf course |
| | Historic house (with or without garden) |
| | Major sports venue |
| | Motor racing circuit |
| | Museum / Art gallery |
| | Nature reserve |
| | Racecourse |
| | Theme park |
| | Wildlife park or Zoo |
| | Other interesting feature |
| (NT) (NTS) | National Trust/ National Trust for Scotland property |
| (MNT) | Manx National Trust (Isle of Man) |

| | land below | 0 | 165 | 490 | 985 | 1640 | 2295 | 2950 | feet |
|---|---|---|---|---|---|---|---|---|---|
| water | sea level | 0 | 50 | 150 | 300 | 500 | 700 | 900 | metres |

## City and town centre plans (pages 204-219)

| | | |
|---|---|---|
| Motorway | Restricted access | One way street |
| dual Primary route | Pedestrian street | Tourist information centre |
| dual 'A' road | Tourist building | Car park |
| dual 'B' road | Important building | Park and Ride site* |
| dual Through route | Higher education building | Railway line / Station |
| dual Other road | Hospital | Underground / Metro / Light rail station |
| Footpath / Footbridge | Cemetery | Foot ferry |
| | Recreational area / Open space | Ecclesiastical building |
| | | N North arrow |

## London central map (pages 224-225)

| | | |
|---|---|---|
| Dual A4 Primary route | Main / Other railway station | Tourist information centre |
| Dual A302 'A' road | LRT / Bus or coach station | Cinema / Theatre |
| B240 'B' road | Leisure and tourism | Major hotel |
| Other road | Shopping | USA Embassy |
| Street market / Pedestrian street | Administration and law | Church |
| Track / Path | Health and welfare | Mosque |
| One way street / Access restriction | Education | Synagogue |
| Ferry | Industry and commerce | Mormon Other place of worship |
| Borough boundary | Public open space | Car park / Public toilet |
| Postal district boundary | Park / Garden / Sports ground | POL Fire Sta PO Police station / Fire station / Post office |

## Urban area maps (pages 220-223 & 226-243)

| | | |
|---|---|---|
| M4 Motorway number | B7078 'B' road number | Railway line / Station / Tunnel |
| 12 13 Motorway junctions with full access | Dual carriageway | Underground station |
| 13 14 Motorway junctions with limited access | Single carriageway | Light rail station |
| BOTHWELL ROWNHAMS CARDIFF GATE Motorway service area with full / limited / off road access | Minor road dual carriageway | Park and Ride site* |
| A316 Primary route number | Minor road single carriageway | Airport with scheduled services |
| Dual carriageway | Road under construction | BRISTOL County / Unitary Authority boundary |
| Single carriageway | Road tunnel | LEEDS Borough / District boundary |
| A4054 'A' road number | Roundabout / Toll | Tourist Information Centre London only |
| Dual carriageway | One way street / Level crossing | Public building |
| Single carriageway | Zeebrugge hours 16 Car ferry with destination | 362 Spot height in metres |
| | | Woodland |
| | | Park |

*PARK AND RIDE SITES SHOWN IN THIS ATLAS OPERATE A MINIMUM OF 5 DAYS A WEEK

To Dublin & Dun Laoghaire
Holyhead
Anglesey
Holy Island
Valley
Moelfre
Llannerch-y-medd
Pentraeth
Llangefni
Beaumaris
Llanfairpwllgwyngyll
Menai Bridge
Bangor
Llandudno
Rhôs-on-Sea
Colwyn Bay
Conwy
Prestatyn
Rhyl
Abergele
Rhuddlan
St Asaph (Llanelwy)
Denbigh
Ruthin
Llangoed
Llanfairfechan
Llansanffraid Glan Conwy
Llanfair Talhaiarn
Llansannan
Holywell
Flint
Connah's Quay
Mold
Buckley
Hawarden
West Kirby
Heswall
Birkenhead
LIVERPOOL
Bebington
Ellesmere Port
Runcorn
Widnes
Warrington
Frodsham
Chester
Northwich
Knutsford
Wilmslow
Macclesfield
Winsford
Middlewich
Sandbach
Congleton
Crewe
Kidsgrove
Nantwich
Newcastle-under-Lyme
Stoke
Bretton
Farndon
Wrexham
Rhosllanerchrugog
Ruabon
Overton
Whitchurch
Audlem
Chirk
Gobowen
Ellesmere
Oswestry
Wem
Market Drayton
Hodnet
Eccleshall
Stafford
Gnosall
Newport
Shrewsbury
Telford
Wellington
Oakengates
Lilleshall
Shifnal
Madeley
Broseley
Much Wenlock
Wolverhampton
Dudley
Bridgnorth
Stourbridge
Halesowen
Kidderminster
Bewdley
Stourport-on-Severn
Bromsgrove
Worcester
Great Malvern
Upton upon Severn
Ledbury
Tewkesbury
Gloucester
Caernarfon
Caernarfon Bay
Llanberis
Snowdon (Yr Wyddfa)
Snowdonia
Capel Curig
Llanrwst
Betws-y-coed
Pentrefoelas
Cerrigydrudion
Corwen
Llangollen
Druid
Llanwnda
Llandwrog
Llanllyfni
Llanaelhaearn
Lleyn Peninsula
Beddgelert
Dolbenmaen
Blaenau Ffestiniog
Ffestiniog
Tremadog
Criccieth
Porthmadog
Tremadog Bay
Nefyn
Pwllheli
Llanbedrog
Abersoch
Aberdaron
Bardsey
Harlech
Trawsfynydd
Bala
Llyn Tegid (Bala Lake)
Llanuwchllyn
Llandrillo
Selattyn
Pen-y-bont-fawr
Llanfyllin
Barmouth
Llanelltyd
Dolgellau
Mallwyd
Llangadfan
Llanfair Caereinion
Welshpool
Llangelynin
Corris
Dyfi
Tywyn
Machynlleth
Aberdyfi
Eglwys Fach
Cardigan Bay
Cambrian Mountains
Llanwnog
Newtown
Montgomery
Chirbury
Church Stretton
Minsterley
Bayston Hill
Clun
Craven Arms
Stokesay
Ludlow
Cleobury Mortimer
Aberystwyth
Llanidloes
Llangurig
Devil's Bridge
Pontrhydfendigaid
Llanrhystud
Rhayader
Llanbister
Knighton
Presteigne
Wigmore
Tenbury Wells
Leominster
Bromyard
Pembridge
Kington
Aberaeron
Cross Inn
Tregaron
New Quay
Llanarth
Synod Inn
Crossgates
Penybont
Llandrindod Wells
Builth Wells
Llanwrtyd Wells
Hay-on-Wye
Clyro
Glasbury
Talgarth
Credenhill
Hereford
Aberporth
Cardigan
Lampeter
Llanybydder
Pumsaint
Llandysul
Newport
Goodwick
Fishguard
Pembrokeshire Coast National Park
Mynydd Preseli
Crymych
Newcastle Emlyn
Llangeler
Llansawel
Llandovery
Sennybridge
Brecon
Black Mountains
Pandy
Pontrilas
Kingsthorne
Ross Spur
Ross-on-Wye
St David's Head
St David's
Ramsey Island
St Bride's Bay
Cynwyl Elfed
Llandissilio
Whitland
Carmarthen
Llanegwad
Llandeilo
Llangadog
Brecon Beacons National Park
Crickhowell
Gilwern
Abergavenny
Skenfrith
Monmouth
Cinderford
Forest of Dean
Haverfordwest
Templeton
Narberth
St Clears
Broad Haven
Johnston
Milford Haven
Neyland
Skomer Island
Pembroke Dock
Pembroke
Tenby
Saundersfoot
Manorbier
Caldey Island
St Govan's Head
To Rosslare
St George's Channel
Kidwelly (Cydweli)
Burry Port
Pembrey
Llanelli
Pont Abraham
Ammanford
Brynamman
Ystalyfera
Glyn-Neath
Hirwaun
Pontardawe
Clydach
Morriston
Swansea
Neath
Briton Ferry
Port Talbot
Swansea Bay
The Mumbles
Llanrhidian
Worms Head
To Cork
Aberdare
Merthyr Tydfil
Ebbw Vale
Tredegar
Brynmawr
Blaenavon
Abertillery
Raglan
Usk
Pontypool
Trelleck
Tintern Parva
Lydney
Blakeney
Chepstow
Caldicot
Magor
Caerleon
Cwmbran
Newport
Blackwood
Newbridge
Gelligaer
Hengoed
Treorchy
Porth
Pontypridd
Risca
Caerphilly
Pyle
Sarn Park
Llantrisant
Bridgend
Porthcawl
Cowbridge
Whitchurch
Cardiff
Cardiff Gate
Penarth
Llantwit Major
Cardiff International
Barry
Sully
Bristol Channel
Portishead
Clevedon
Avonmouth
Gordano
Bristol
Long Ashton
Kingswood
Mangotsfield
Chipping Sodbury
Yate
Patchway
Keynsham
Bath
Melksham
Bradford-on-Avon
Yatton
Chew Magna
Weston-super-Mare
Blagdon
Cheddar
Radstock
Frome
Wells
Shepton Mallet
Sedgemoor
Burnham-on-Sea
Highbridge
Wedmore
Glastonbury
Street
Bridgwater
Westonzoyland
Bridgwater Bay
Lynton
Lynmouth
Porlock
Minehead
Watchet
Williton
Exmoor National Park
Combe Martin
Blackmoor Gate
Ilfracombe
Lundy Island
Croyde
Braunton
Barnstaple
Fremington
Appledore
Barnstaple or Bideford Bay
Westward Ho!
Bideford
Hartland Point
Hartland
South Molton
Dulverton
Wheddon Cross
Bampton
Wiveliscombe
Norton Fitzwarren
Taunton
Taunton Deane
Wellington
Langport
Somerton
Ilchester
Castle Cary
Wincanton
Gillingham
Milborne Port
Sherborne
Yeovil
Stalbridge
Sturminster Newton
South Petherton
Crewkerne
Chard
Blandford Forum
Middlemarsh
Beaminster
Maiden Newton
Puddletown
Charminster
Dorchester
Bridport
Charmouth
Lyme Regis
Burton Bradstock
Abbotsbury
Weymouth
Broadwey
Preston
Chickerell
Fortuneswell
Easton
Bill of Portland
To Channel Islands
Axminster
Honiton
Chardstock
Feniton
Cullompton
Tiverton
Bickleigh
Silverton
Crediton
Copplestone
Witheridge
Chulmleigh
Great Torrington
Stibb Cross
Kilkhampton
Bude
Bude Bay
Stratton
Holsworthy
Highampton
Hatherleigh
Okehampton
Exeter
Sidbury
Colyford
Seaton
Sidmouth
Exminster
Topsham
Exmouth
Starcross
Dawlish
Teignmouth
Kingsteignton
Newton Abbot
Kingskerswell
Babbacombe Bay
Torquay
Paignton
Tor Bay
Berry Head
Brixham
Dartmouth
Totnes
Ashburton
Dartmoor National Park
Widecombe in the Moor
Dartmeet
Moretonhampstead
Whiddon Down
Dartmoor
Lydford
Tavistock
Horrabridge
Callington
Wainhouse Corner
Tintagel
Hallworthy
Launceston
Delabole
Camelford
Bodmin Moor
St Endellion
Padstow
Wadebridge
Bodmin
St Ive
Liskeard
Trenance
Newquay Cornwall
St Columb Major
Newquay
Lostwithiel
Saltash
Plymouth City
Plympton
Ivybridge
Plymouth
Torpoint
Plymstock
Yealmpton
Modbury
Halwell
Kingsbridge
Salcombe
Start Bay
Start Point
Sandplace
East Looe
Polperro
Par
St Austell
Mevagissey
Perranporth
Goonhavern
St Agnes
Portreath
Probus
Truro
Tregony
Redruth
Camborne
St Ives
Zennor
Hayle
Penryn
St Mawes
Falmouth
Pendeen
Marazion
St Just
Penzance
Helston
Sennen
Land's End
Mount's Bay
St Keverne
Lizard Point
Lizard
Isles of Scilly
Hugh Town
St. Mary's
To Santander (summer only)
To Roscoff
CHANNEL ISLANDS
To Poole, Weymouth & Portsmouth
Alderney
Guernsey
St Peter Port
Sark
Jersey
St Helier

V
Lincoln
Chesterfield
Mansfield
Nottingham
Derby
Leicester
Peterborough
Norwich
Great Yarmouth
Lowestoft
Coventry
Northampton
Cambridge
Ipswich
Felixstowe
Harwich
Colchester
Bedford
Milton Keynes
Luton
Oxford
Aylesbury
Chelmsford
Southend-on-Sea
LONDON
Reading
Slough
Watford
Croydon
Guildford
Maidstone
Canterbury
Margate
Dover
Folkestone
Brighton
Hastings
Eastbourne
Portsmouth
Southampton
Bournemouth
Isle of Wight
Salisbury
Winchester
Swindon
Boston
King's Lynn
Skegness
Grantham
Wisbech
The Wash
The Fens
The Broads
North Downs
South Downs
The Weald
Vale of White Horse
River Thames
ENGLISH CHANNEL
Strait of Dover
Channel tunnel
Calais
Dieppe
To Esbjerg
To Hamburg
To Hoek van Holland
To Oostende & Zeebrugge
To Cherbourg, Channel Islands & St. Malo
To Bilbao & Channel Islands
To St. Malo & Cherbourg
To Caen & Le Havre
(summer only)
The Needles
St. Catherine's Point
Selsey Bill
Beachy Head
Dungeness
North Foreland
SCALE
0 10 20 30 40 miles
0 10 20 30 40 50 60 km
1:1,350,000 (approx) 22 miles to 1 inch / 13.5 km to 1 cm

GLASGOW
Edinburgh
SOUTHERN UPLANDS
Galloway Forest Park
Isle of Man
Douglas
IRISH SEA
North Channel
Solway Firth
Firth of Forth
Firth of Clyde
Arran
Kintyre
Islay
Jura
Belfast
Lough Neagh
Ards Peninsula
Mourne Mountains
Dublin (Baile Átha Cliath)
Dun Laoghaire
Wicklow Mts. National Park
Anglesey
Snowdonia National Park
Lleyn Peninsula
Caernarfon Bay
Cardigan Bay
LIVERPOOL
Carlisle
Lake District
Cumbrian Mountains
Blackpool
Preston
Lancaster
Chester
Shrewsbury
Wrexham
Dumfries
Stranraer
Ayr
Kilmarnock
Newry
Drogheda (Droichead Átha)
Wicklow (Cill Mhantáin)
Arklow (An tInbhear Mór)
Barrow-in-Furness
Morecambe
Southport
St Helens
Warrington
Bangor
Douglas (summer only)
Cherbourg (summer only)
To Dublin

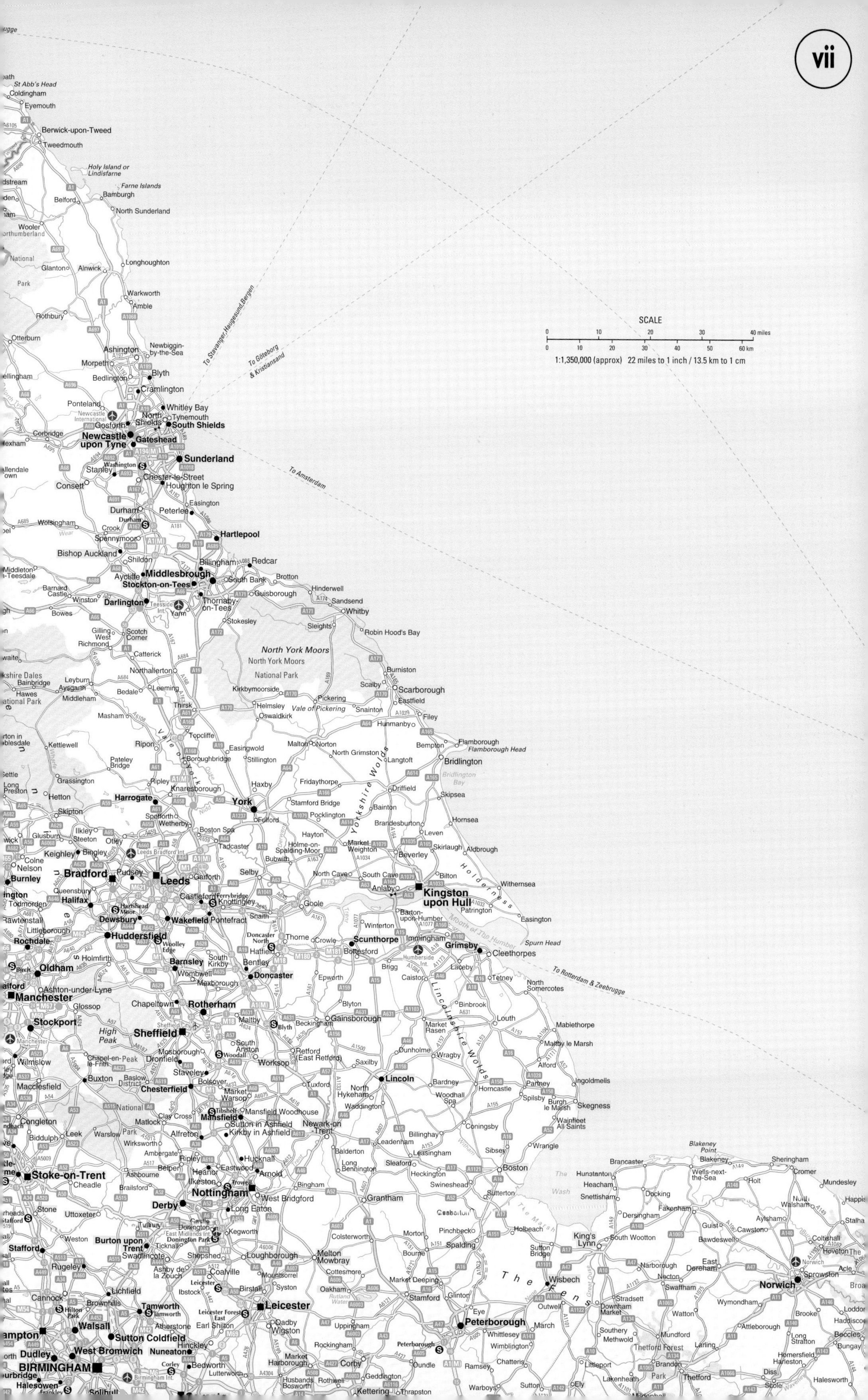
SCALE
0 10 20 30 40 miles
0 10 20 30 40 50 60 km
1:1,350,000 (approx) 22 miles to 1 inch / 13.5 km to 1 cm
To Stavanger, Haugesund, Bergen
To Göteborg & Kristiansand
To Amsterdam
To Rotterdam & Zeebrugge
St Abb's Head
Coldingham
Eyemouth
Berwick-upon-Tweed
Tweedmouth
Holy Island or Lindisfarne
Farne Islands
Bamburgh
Belford
North Sunderland
Wooler
Northumberland National Park
Glanton
Alnwick
Longhoughton
Warkworth
Amble
Rothbury
Otterburn
Ashington
Newbiggin-by-the-Sea
Morpeth
Bedlington
Blyth
Cramlington
Ponteland
Newcastle International
Whitley Bay
Tynemouth
North Shields
South Shields
Gosforth
Corbridge
Hexham
Newcastle upon Tyne
Gateshead
Washington
Sunderland
Stanley
Chester-le-Street
Consett
Houghton le Spring
Easington
Durham
Peterlee
Wolsingham
Crook
Hartlepool
Spennymoor
Bishop Auckland
Shildon
Billingham
Redcar
Middleton-in-Teesdale
Aycliffe
Middlesbrough
South Bank
Brotton
Stockton-on-Tees
Guisborough
Hinderwell
Barnard Castle
Winston
Darlington
Teesside Int.
Thornaby-on-Tees
Yarm
Sandsend
Whitby
Bowes
Stokesley
Sleights
Robin Hood's Bay
Gilling West
Scotch Corner
Richmond
Catterick
North York Moors
North York Moors National Park
Northallerton
Burniston
Yorkshire Dales National Park
Bainbridge
Leyburn
Aysgarth
Hawes
Middleham
Bedale
Leeming
Kirkbymoorside
Scalby
Scarborough
Eastfield
Thirsk
Helmsley
Pickering
Vale of Pickering
Snainton
Oswaldkirk
Masham
Filey
Hunmanby
Topcliffe
Kettlewell
Ripon
Easingwold
Malton
Norton
Flamborough
Flamborough Head
Bempton
North Grimston
Boroughbridge
Stillington
Langtoft
Bridlington
Bridlington Bay
Pateley Bridge
Vale of York
Settle
Grassington
Ripley
Knaresborough
Haxby
Fridaythorpe
Driffield
Yorkshire Wolds
Long Preston
Hetton
Harrogate
York
Stamford Bridge
Skipsea
Skipton
Spofforth
Wetherby
Fulford
Pocklington
Bainton
Brandesburton
Hornsea
Ilkley
Otley
Boston Spa
Hayton
Leven
Glusburn
Steeton
Tadcaster
Holme-on-Spalding-Moor
Market Weighton
Skirlaugh
Aldbrough
Keighley
Bingley
Leeds Bradford Int.
Bubwith
Beverley
Holderness
Colne
Nelson
Bradford
Pudsey
Leeds
Garforth
Selby
North Cave
South Cave
Bilton
Withernsea
Burnley
Queensbury
Halifax
Castleford
Ferrybridge
Knottingley
Goole
Anlaby
Kingston upon Hull
Todmorden
Hartshead Moor
Snaith
Barton-upon-Humber
Patrington
Rawtenstall
Dewsbury
Wakefield
Pontefract
Winterton
Easington
Littleborough
Mouth of The Humber
Rochdale
Huddersfield
Woolley Edge
Doncaster North
Thorne
Crowle
Scunthorpe
Immingham
Grimsby
Spurn Head
Cleethorpes
Holmfirth
Barnsley
South Kirkby
Hatfield
Bottesford
Humberside Int.
Oldham
Wombwell
Bentley
Doncaster
Brigg
Caistor
Laceby
Tetney
Mexborough
Epworth
North Somercotes
Ashton-under-Lyne
Lincolnshire Wolds
Manchester
Glossop
Chapeltown
Rotherham
Blyton
Binbrook
Stockport
High Peak
Sheffield City
Maltby
Blyth
Beckingham
Gainsborough
Market Rasen
Louth
Mablethorpe
Sheffield
South Anston
Mosborough
Woodall
Retford (East Retford)
Maltby le Marsh
Wilmslow
Chapel-en-le-Frith
Peak District
Dronfield
Worksop
Dunholme
Wragby
Saxilby
Alford
Staveley
Buxton
Baslow
Lincoln
Bardney
Partney
Ingoldmells
Macclesfield
Chesterfield
Bolsover
Market Warsop
Tuxford
North Hykeham
Horncastle
Spilsby
Woodhall Spa
Burgh le Marsh
Skegness
Tibshelf
Mansfield Woodhouse
Waddington
Mansfield
Matlock
Clay Cross
Sutton in Ashfield
Newark-on-Trent
Coningsby
Wainfleet All Saints
Congleton
Alfreton
Kirkby in Ashfield
Billinghay
Leek
Biddulph
Warslow
Wirksworth
Ambergate
Hucknall
Leadenham
Wrangle
Ripley
Balderton
Leasingham
Sibsey
Blakeney Point
Blakeney
Sheringham
Stoke-on-Trent
Belper
Heanor
Eastwood
Arnold
Long Bennington
Sleaford
Heckington
Boston
Brancaster
Hunstanton
Wells-next-the-Sea
Cromer
Cheadle
Ashbourne
Ilkeston
Trowell
Nottingham
Bingham
Swineshead
The Wash
Heacham
Holt
Mundesley
Brailsford
Derby
West Bridgford
Grantham
Sutterton
Snettisham
Docking
North Walsham
Happisburgh
Stone
Long Eaton
Fakenham
Dersingham
Aylsham
Uttoxeter
Castle Donington
Kegworth
East Midlands Int.
Donington Park
Morton
Pinchbeck
Holbeach
Guist
Cawston
Stalham
Tutbury
Colsterworth
Spalding
King's Lynn
South Wootton
Coltishall
Weston
Burton upon Trent
Ticknall
Swadlincote
Shepshed
Loughborough
Melton Mowbray
Bourne
Sutton Bridge
Bawdeswell
Hoveton
Stafford
Ashby de la Zouch
Coalville
Narborough
East Dereham
Norwich
Rugeley
Leicester Forest East
Mountsorrel
Syston
Cottesmore
Market Deeping
Wisbech
Necton
Sprowston
Acle
Lichfield
Ibstock
Birstall
Oakham
Rutland Water
Stamford
Glinton
The Fens
Swaffham
Cannock
Brownhills
Leicester
Outwell
Stradsett
Downham Market
Wymondham
Brooke
Loddon
Hilton Park
Tamworth
Walsall
Atherstone
Earl Shilton
Oadby
Wigston
Uppingham
Eye
Peterborough
March
Watton
Attleborough
Haddiscoe
Wolverhampton
Sutton Coldfield
Hinckley
Nuneaton
Rockingham
Whittlesey
Wimblington
Southery
Methwold
Mundford
Thetford Forest
Long Stratton
Beccles
Bungay
Dudley
West Bromwich
Bedworth
Market Harborough
Corby
Oundle
Chatteris
Littleport
Brandon
Homersfield
Harleston
Diss
BIRMINGHAM
Corley
Lutterworth
Husbands Bosworth
Rothwell
Geddington
Ramsey
Lakenheath
Thetford
Halesworth
Stourbridge
Halesowen
Birmingham Int.
Solihull
Frankley
Kettering
Thrapston
Warboys
Sutton
Ely
Scole

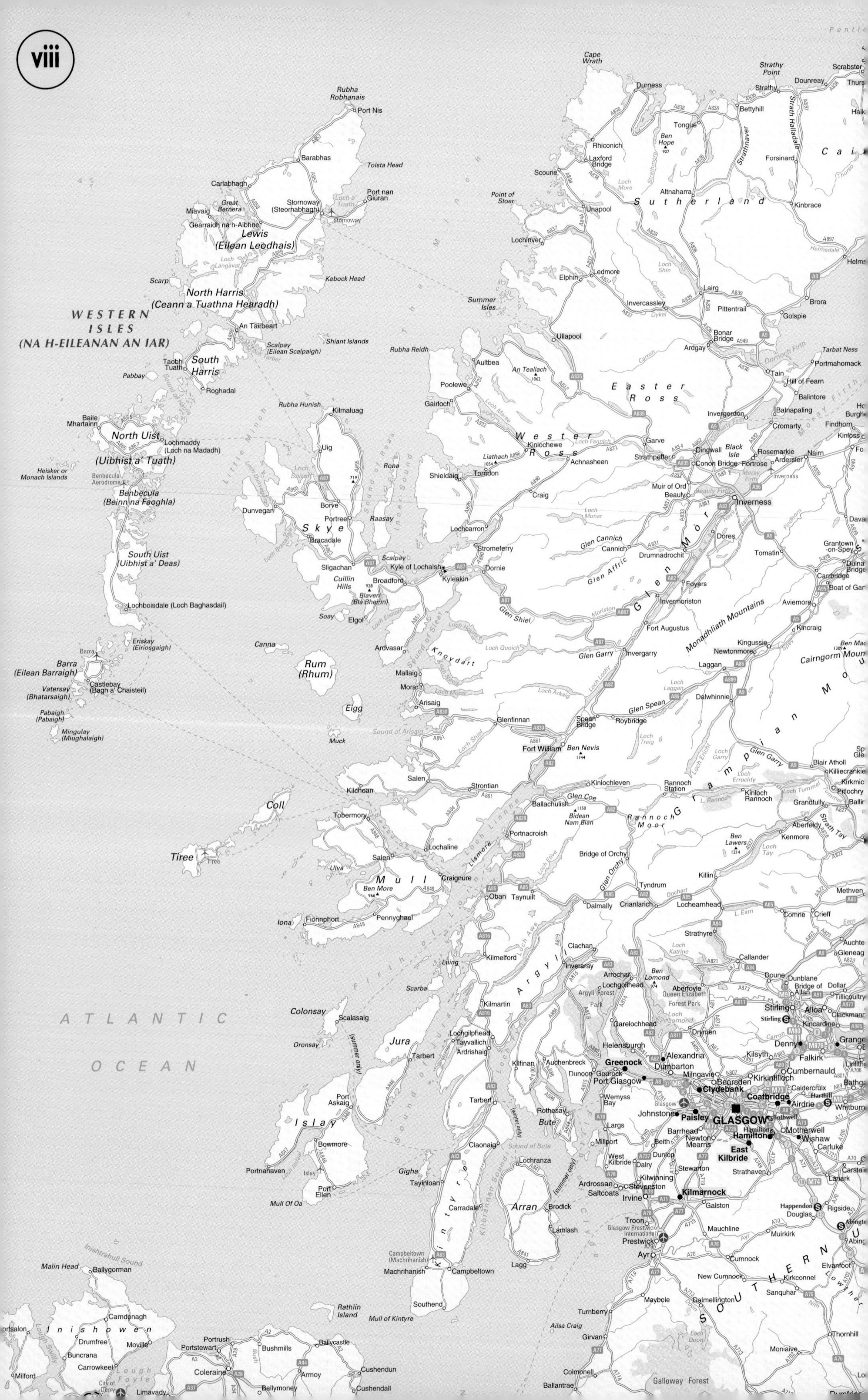

WESTERN ISLES (NA H-EILEANAN AN IAR)
ATLANTIC OCEAN
Rubha Robhanais
Port Nis
Barabhas
Tolsta Head
Carlabhagh
Great Bernera
Miavaig
Gearraidh na h-Aibhne
Stornoway (Steornabhagh)
Port nan Giuran
Lewis (Eilean Leodhais)
Scarp
Kebock Head
North Harris (Ceann a Tuathna Hearadh)
An Tairbeart
Shiant Islands
Scalpay (Eilean Scalpaigh)
Taobh Tuath
South Harris
Pabbay
Roghadal
Rubha Hunish
Baile Mhartainn
North Uist
Lochmaddy (Loch na Madadh)
(Uibhist a' Tuath)
Heisker or Monach Islands
Benbecula Aerodrome
Benbecula (Beinn na Faoghla)
South Uist (Uibhist a' Deas)
Lochboisdale (Loch Baghasdail)
Eriskay (Eiriosgaigh)
Barra (Eilean Barraigh)
Castlebay (Bagh a' Chaisteil)
Vatersay (Bhatarsaigh)
Pabaigh (Pabaigh)
Mingulay (Miughalaigh)
Little Minch
Kilmaluag
Uig
Dunvegan
Skye
Portree
Raasay
Rona
Bracadale
Sligachan
Cuillin Hills
Broadford
Kyle of Lochalsh
Kyleakin
Blaven (Bla Bheinn)
Soay
Elgol
Canna
Rum (Rhum)
Eigg
Muck
Ardvasar
Sound of Sleat
Knoydart
Mallaig
Morar
Arisaig
Sound of Arisaig
Glenfinnan
Fort William
Ben Nevis 1344
Salen
Kilchoan
Strontian
Coll
Tiree
Tobermory
Lochaline
Mull
Ben More 966
Craignure
Ulva
Iona
Fionnphort
Pennyghael
Oban
Taynuilt
Lismore
Loch Linnhe
Kilmelford
Luing
Scarba
Firth of Lorn
Colonsay
Scalasaig
Oronsay
Jura
Tarbert
Sound of Jura
Islay
Port Askaig
Bowmore
Portnahaven
Port Ellen
Mull Of Oa
Gigha
Tayinloan
Kintyre
Carradale
Campbeltown
Machrihanish
Southend
Mull of Kintyre
Rathlin Island
Kilbrannan Sound
Arran
Brodick
Lamlash
Lagg
Lochranza
Ailsa Craig
Cape Wrath
Durness
Tongue
Ben Hope 927
Rhiconich
Laxford Bridge
Scourie
Point of Stoer
Unapool
Lochinver
Sutherland
Altnaharra
Strathy Point
Strathy
Bettyhill
Dounreay
Scrabster
Forsinard
Kinbrace
Ledmore
Elphin
Lairg
Invercassley
Pittentrail
Brora
Golspie
Bonar Bridge
Ardgay
Dornoch Firth
Tain
Tarbat Head
Portmahomack
Hill of Fearn
Balintore
Summer Isles
Ullapool
Rubha Reidh
Aultbea
An Teallach 1062
Poolewe
Gairloch
Easter Ross
Wester Ross
Kinlochewe
Liathach 1054
Torridon
Achnasheen
Shieldaig
Craig
Lochcarron
Stromeferry
Dornie
Garve
Strathpeffer
Dingwall
Conon Bridge
Black Isle
Invergordon
Balnapaling
Cromarty
Rosemarkie
Fortrose
Ardersier
Nairn
Moray Firth
Muir of Ord
Beauly
Inverness
Glen Cannich
Cannich
Drumnadrochit
Dores
Glen Affric
Glen Mòr
Foyers
Invermoriston
Fort Augustus
Glen Shiel
Invergarry
Glen Garry
Monadhliath Mountains
Tomatin
Grantown-on-Spey
Carrbridge
Boat of Garten
Aviemore
Kincraig
Kingussie
Newtonmore
Cairngorm Mountains
Laggan
Dalwhinnie
Glen Spean
Spean Bridge
Roybridge
Grampian Mountains
Blair Atholl
Killiecrankie
Pitlochry
Kinloch Rannoch
Rannoch Station
Kinlochleven
Glen Coe
Ballachulish
Bidean Nam Bian 1150
Rannoch Moor
Portnacroish
Bridge of Orchy
Ben Lawers 1214
Aberfeldy
Kenmore
Killin
Tyndrum
Dalmally
Crianlarich
Lochearnhead
Comrie
Crieff
Strathyre
Callander
Clachan
Inveraray
Arrochar
Ben Lomond 974
Aberfoyle
Queen Elizabeth Forest Park
Argyll Forest Park
Argyll
Kilmartin
Lochgilphead
Tayvallich
Ardrishaig
Garelochhead
Helensburgh
Dunblane
Doune
Bridge of Allan
Stirling
Alloa
Falkirk
Kilsyth
Cumbernauld
Alexandria
Dumbarton
Greenock
Gourock
Port Glasgow
Dunoon
Kilfinan
Auchenbreck
Rothesay
Bute
Wemyss Bay
Largs
Millport
West Kilbride
Dalry
Kilwinning
Stevenston
Ardrossan
Saltcoats
Irvine
Kilmarnock
Troon
Prestwick
Ayr
Clydebank
Paisley
Johnstone
GLASGOW
Coatbridge
Airdrie
Motherwell
Hamilton
East Kilbride
Wishaw
Carluke
Lanark
Strathaven
Galston
Mauchline
Muirkirk
Douglas
Cumnock
New Cumnock
Dalmellington
Maybole
Turnberry
Girvan
Ballantrae
Colmonell
Galloway Forest
Sanquhar
Kirkconnel
Thornhill
Moniaive
SOUTHERN UPLANDS
Malin Head
Ballygorman
Inishowen
Carndonagh
Drumfree
Buncrana
Moville
Carrowkeel
Milford
Lough Foyle
Lough Swilly
Portrush
Portstewart
Bushmills
Ballycastle
Coleraine
Armoy
Cushendun
Cushendall
Ballymoney
Limavady
City of Derry

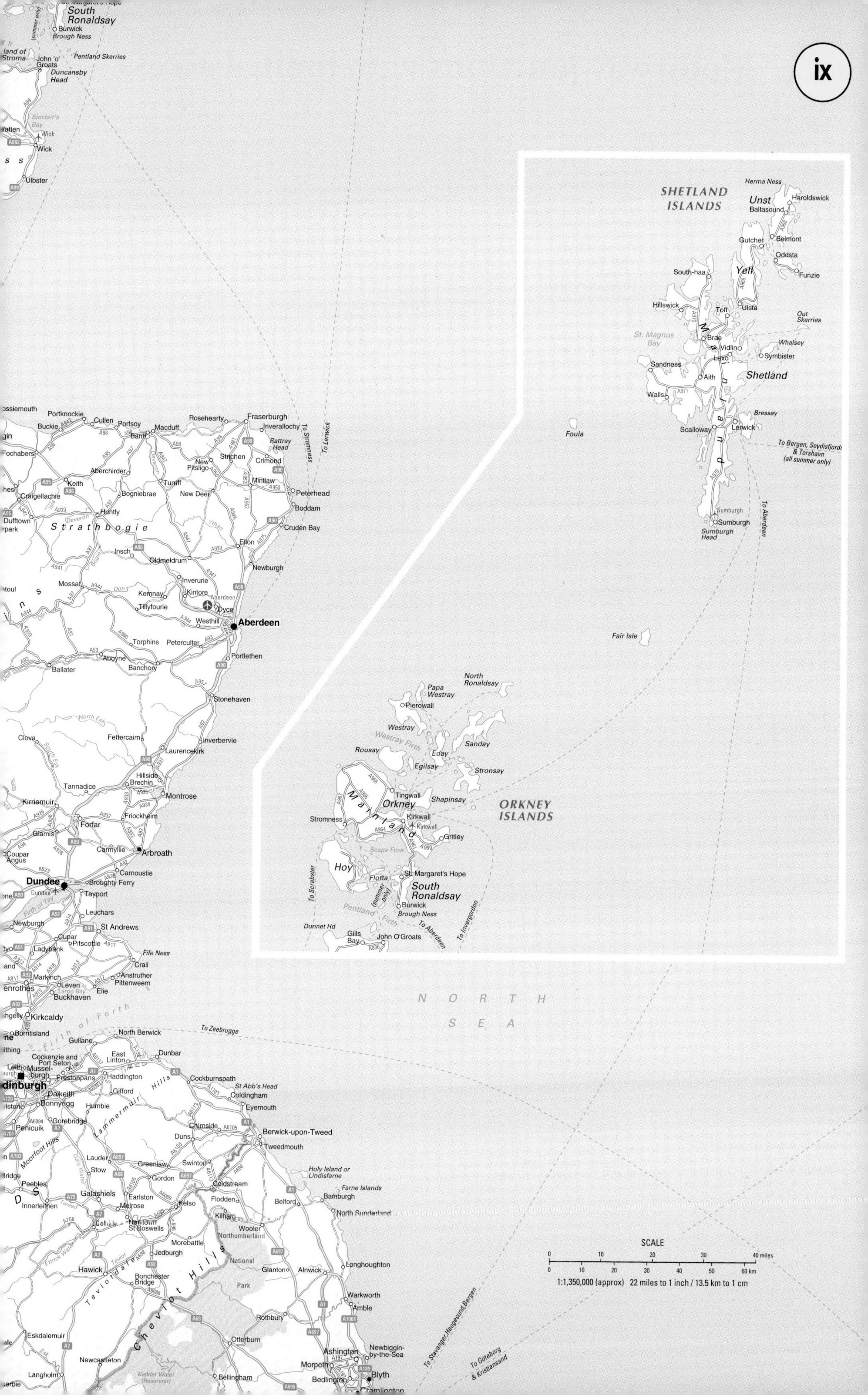
SHETLAND ISLANDS
Herma Ness
Unst
Haroldswick
Baltasound
Gutcher
Belmont
Oddsta
Funzie
Yell
South-haa
Hillswick
Toft
Ulsta
Out Skerries
St. Magnus Bay
Brae
Vidlin
Whalsey
Symbister
Laxo
Sandness
Aith
Shetland
Mainland
Walls
Bressay
Scalloway
Lerwick
Foula
To Bergen, Seydisfjordur & Torshavn (all summer only)
Sumburgh
Sumburgh Head
To Aberdeen
Fair Isle
ORKNEY ISLANDS
North Ronaldsay
Papa Westray
Pierowall
Westray
Westray Firth
Rousay
Eday
Sanday
Egilsay
Stronsay
Tingwall
Shapinsay
Orkney
Mainland
Stromness
Kirkwall
Gritley
Scapa Flow
Hoy
Flotta
St. Margaret's Hope
South Ronaldsay
Burwick
Brough Ness
Pentland Firth
To Scrabster
Dunnet Hd
Gills Bay
John O'Groats
To Aberdeen
To Invergordon
To Stromness
To Lerwick
Pentland Skerries
Island of Stroma
John 'o' Groats
Duncansby Head
Sinclair's Bay
Wick
Ulbster
Fraserburgh
Rosehearty
Inverallochy
Rattray Head
Portknockie
Cullen
Portsoy
Buckie
Banff
Macduff
Fochabers
Aberchirder
New Pitsligo
Strichen
Crimond
Mintlaw
Peterhead
Boddam
Keith
Turriff
New Deer
Craigellachie
Bogniebrae
Huntly
Dufftown
Strathbogie
Cruden Bay
Ellon
Insch
Oldmeldrum
Newburgh
Inverurie
Kintore
Mossat
Kemnay
Tillyfourie
Dyce
Westhill
Aberdeen
Torphins
Peterculter
Aboyne
Ballater
Banchory
Portlethen
Stonehaven
North Esk
Clova
Fettercairn
Inverbervie
Laurencekirk
Tannadice
Hillside
Brechin
Montrose
Kirriemuir
Forfar
Friockheim
Glamis
Carmyllie
Arbroath
Coupar Angus
Carnoustie
Dundee
Broughty Ferry
Tayport
Firth of Tay
Leuchars
Newburgh
St Andrews
Cupar
Pitscottie
Fife Ness
Ladybank
Crail
Markinch
Anstruther
Pittenweem
Leven
Largo Bay
Elie
Buckhaven
Kirkcaldy
Firth of Forth
Burntisland
North Berwick
To Zeebrugge
Gullane
East Linton
Dunbar
Cockenzie and Port Seton
Leith
Musselburgh
Edinburgh
Prestonpans
Haddington
Cockburnspath
St Abb's Head
Dalkeith
Gifford
Coldingham
Bonnyrigg
Humbie
Eyemouth
Lammermuir Hills
Gorebridge
Penicuik
Chirnside
Duns
Berwick-upon-Tweed
Tweedmouth
Moorfoot Hills
Lauder
Stow
Greenlaw
Swinton
Holy Island or Lindisfarne
Peebles
Gordon
Coldstream
Farne Islands
Galashiels
Earlston
Kelso
Flodden
Belford
Bamburgh
Innerleithen
Melrose
Newtown St Boswells
Kilham
North Sunderland
Wooler
Northumberland National Park
Morebattle
Jedburgh
Hawick
Teviotdale
Glanton
Alnwick
Longhoughton
Bonchester Bridge
Cheviot Hills
Warkworth
Amble
Rothbury
Eskdalemuir
Otterburn
Ashington
Newbiggin-by-the-Sea
Newcastleton
Morpeth
Blyth
Langholm
Kielder Water (Reservoir)
Bellingham
Bedlington
Cramlington
To Stavanger, Haugesund, Bergen
To Göteborg & Kristiansand
NORTH SEA
SCALE
0 10 20 30 40 miles
0 10 20 30 40 50 60 km
1:1,350,000 (approx) 22 miles to 1 inch / 13.5 km to 1 cm

# Motorway junctions with limited access

### A1(M) LONDON TO NEWCASTLE
(2)
Northbound : No access
Southbound : No exit
(3)
Southbound : No access
(5)
Northbound : No exit
Southbound : No access
: No exit
(44)
Northbound : No exit to M1 Westbound
Dishforth
Southbound : No access from A168 Eastbound
(57)
Northbound : No access
: Exit only to A66(M) Northbound
Southbound : Access only from A66(M) Southbound
: No exit
(65)
Northbound : No access from A1
Southbound : No exit from A1

### A3(M) PORTSMOUTH
(1)
Northbound : No exit
Southbound : No access
(4)
Northbound : No access
Southbound : No exit

### A38(M) BIRMINGHAM
Victoria Road
Northbound : No exit
Southbound : No access

### A48(M) CARDIFF
M4 (29)
Westbound : No access from M4 (29) Eastbound
Eastbound : No exit to M4 (29) Westbound
(29A)
Westbound : No exit to A48 Eastbound
Eastbound : No access to A48 Westbound

### A57(M) MANCHESTER
Brook Street
Westbound : No exit
Eastbound : No access

### A58(M) LEEDS
Westgate
Southbound : No access
Woodhouse Lane
Westbound : No exit

### A64(M) LEEDS
Claypit Lane
Eastbound : No access

### A66(M) DARLINGTON
A1(M)
Northbound : No access from A1(M) Southbound
: No exit
Southbound : No access
: No exit to A1(M) Northbound

### A167(M) NEWCASTLE
Campden Street
Northbound : No exit
Southbound : No access
: No exit

### M1 LONDON TO LEEDS
(2)
Northbound : No exit
Southbound : No access
(4)
Northbound : No exit
Southbound : No access
(6A)
Northbound : Access only from M25 (21)
: No exit
Southbound : No access
: Exit only to M25 (21)
(7)
Northbound : Access only from M10
: No exit
Southbound : No access
: Exit only to M10
(17)
Northbound : No access
: Exit only to M45
Southbound : Access only from M45
: No exit
(19)
Northbound : Exit only to M6
Southbound : Access only from M6
(21A)
Northbound : No access
Southbound : No exit
(23A)
Northbound : No access from A453
Southbound : No exit to A453
(24A)
Northbound : No exit
Southbound : No access
(35A)
Northbound : No access
Southbound : No exit
(43)
Northbound : No access
: Exit only to M621
Southbound : No exit
: Access only from M621
(48)
Northbound : No exit to A1 Southbound
: Access only from A1
Northbound
Southbound : Exit only to A1 Southbound
: No access

### M2 ROCHESTER TO CANTERBURY
(1)
Westbound : No exit to A2 Eastbound
Eastbound : No access from A2 Westbound

### M3 LONDON TO WINCHESTER
(8)
Westbound : No access
Eastbound : No exit
(10)
Northbound : No access
Southbound : No exit
(13)
Southbound : No exit A335 Eastbound
: No access
(14)
Westbound : No access
Eastbound : No exit

### M4 LONDON TO SWANSEA
(1)
Westbound : No access from A4 Eastbound
Eastbound : No exit to A4 Westbound
(2)
Westbound : No access from A4 Eastbound
: No exit to A4 Eastbound
Eastbound : No access from A4 Westbound
: No exit to A4 Westbound
(21)
Westbound : No access M48 Eastbound
Eastbound : No exit M48 Westbound
(23)
Westbound : No exit M48 Eastbound
Eastbound : No access M48 Westbound
(25)
Westbound : No access
Eastbound : No exit
(25A)
Westbound : No access
Eastbound : No exit
(29)
Westbound : No access
: Exit only to A48(M)
Eastbound : Access only from A48(M)
Eastbound
: No exit
(38)
Westbound : No access
(39)
Westbound : No exit
Eastbound : No access
: No exit
(41)
Westbound : No exit
Eastbound : No access
(42)
Westbound : No exit to A48
Eastbound : No access from A48
(46)
Westbound : No access
Eastbound : No exit

### M5 BIRMINGHAM TO EXETER
(10)
Northbound : No exit
Southbound : No access
(11A)
Northbound : No access from A417
Eastbound
Southbound : No exit to A417
Westbound

### M6 COVENTRY TO CARLISLE
M1
Northbound : No access from M1 (19)
Southbound
Southbound : No exit to M1 (19) Northbound
(4)
Northbound : No exit to M42 Northbound
: No access from M42 Southbound
Southbound : No exit to M42
: No access from M42 Southbound
(4A)
Northbound : No access from M42 (8)
Northbound
: No exit
Southbound : No access
: Exit only to M42 (8)
(5)
Northbound : No access
Southbound : No exit
(10A)
Northbound : No access
: Exit only to M54
Southbound : Access only from M54
: No exit
(20)
Northbound : No exit to M56 Eastbound
Southbound : No access from M56
Westbound
(20A)
Northbound : No exit
: No access
(24)
Northbound : No exit
Southbound : No access
(25)
Northbound : No access
Southbound : No exit
(30)
Northbound : Access only from M61 Northbound
: No exit
Southbound : No access
: Exit only to M61 Southbound
(31A)
Northbound : No access
Southbound : No exit

### M8 EDINBURGH TO GLASGOW
(8)
Westbound : No access from M73 (2) Southbound
: No access from A8 Eastbound
: No access from A89 Eastbound
Eastbound : No access from A89 Westbound
: No exit to M73 (2) Northbound
(9)
Westbound : No exit
Eastbound : No access
(13)
Westbound : Access only from M80
Eastbound : Exit only to M80
(14)
Westbound : No exit
Eastbound : No access
(16)
Westbound : No access
Eastbound : No exit
(17)
Eastbound : Access only from A82,
not central Glasgow
: Exit only to A82, not central
Glasgow
(18)
Westbound : No access
Eastbound : No access
(19)
Westbound : Access only from A814
Eastbound
Eastbound : Exit only to A814 Westbound,
not central Glasgow
(20)
Westbound : No access
Eastbound : No exit
(21)
Westbound : No exit
Eastbound : No access
(22)
Westbound : No access
: Exit only to M77 Southbound
Eastbound : Access only from M77
Northbound
: No exit
: No exit to M77
(23)
Westbound : No access
Eastbound : No exit
(25)
Westbound : No access from A739
Northbound
: No exit to A739 Southbound
Eastbound : No access from A739
Northbound
: No exit to A739 Southbound
(25A)
Eastbound : No exit
Westbound : No access
(28)
Westbound : No access
Eastbound : No exit
(28A)
Westbound : No access
Eastbound : No exit

### M9 EDINBURGH TO STIRLING
(1A)
Westbound : No access
Eastbound : No exit
(2)
Westbound : No exit
Eastbound : No access
(3)
Westbound : No access
Eastbound : No exit
(6)
Westbound : No exit
Eastbound : No access
(8)
Westbound : No access
: No access from M876 Eastbound
Eastbound : No access to M876 Westbound
: No exit

### M10 ST ALBANS
M1
Northbound : No access
: Exit only to M1 (7) Northbound
Southbound : Access only from M1 (7)
Southbound
: No exit

### M11 LONDON TO CAMBRIDGE
(4)
Northbound : No access from A1400
Westbound
: No exit
Southbound : No access
: No exit to A1400 Eastbound
(5)
Northbound : No access
Southbound : No exit
(9)
Northbound : No access
Southbound : No exit
(13)
Northbound : No access
Southbound : No exit
(14)
Northbound : No access from A428
Eastbound
: No exit to A428 Westbound
: No exit to A1307
Southbound : No access from A428 Eastbound
: No access from A1307
: No exit

### M20 LONDON TO FOLKESTONE
(2)
Westbound : No exit
Eastbound : No access
(3)
Westbound : No access
: Exit only to M26 Westbound
Eastbound : Access only from M26 Eastbound
: No exit
(11A)
Westbound : No exit
Eastbound : No access

### M23 LONDON TO CRAWLEY
(7)
Northbound : No exit to A23 Southbound
Southbound : No access from A23
Northbound
(10A)
Southbound : No access from *B2036*
Northbound : No exit to *B2036*

### M25 LONDON ORBITAL MOTORWAY
(1B)
Northbound : No exit
Southbound : No access

(5)
Clockwise : No exit to M26 Eastbound
Anticlockwise : No access from M26 Westbound

Spur of M25 (5)
Clockwise : No access from M26 Westbound
Anticlockwise : No exit to M26 Eastbound

(19)
Clockwise : No access
Anticlockwise : No exit

(21)
Clockwise : No access from M1 (6A) Northbound
: No exit to M1 (6A) Southbound
Anticlockwise : No access from M1 (6A) Northbound
: No exit to M1 (6A) Southbound

(31)
Clockwise : No exit
Anticlockwise : No access

## M26 SEVENOAKS

M25 (5)
Westbound : No exit to M25 Anticlockwise
: No exit to M25 spur
Eastbound : No access from M25 Clockwise
: No access from M25 spur

M20
Westbound : No access from M20 (3) Eastbound
Eastbound : No exit to M20 (3) Westbound

## M27 SOUTHAMPTON TO PORTSMOUTH

(4) West
Westbound : No exit
Eastbound : No access

(4) East
Westbound : No access
Eastbound : No exit

(10)
Westbound : No access
Eastbound : No exit

(12) West
Westbound : No exit
Eastbound : No access

(12) East
Westbound : No access from A3
Eastbound : No exit

## M40 LONDON TO BIRMINGHAM

(3)
Westbound : No access
Eastbound : No exit

(7)
Eastbound : No exit

(13)
Northbound : No access
Southbound : No exit

(14)
Northbound : No exit
Southbound : No access

(16)
Northbound : No exit
Southbound : No access

## M42 BIRMINGHAM

(1)
Northbound : No exit
Southbound : No access

(7)
Northbound : No access
: Exit only to M6 Northbound
Southbound : Access only from M6 Northbound
: No exit

(7A)
Northbound : No access
: Exit only to M6 Eastbound
Southbound : No access
: No exit

(8)
Northbound : Access only from M6 Southbound
: No exit
Southbound : Access only from M6 Southbound
: Exit only to M6 Northbound

## M45 COVENTRY

M1
Westbound : No access from M1 (17) Southbound
Eastbound : No exit to M1 (17) Northbound

Junction with A45
Westbound : No exit
Eastbound : No access

## M48 CHEPSTOW

M4
Westbound : No exit to M4 Eastbound
Eastbound : No access from M4 Westbound

## M49 BRISTOL

(18A)
Northbound : No access from M5 Southbound
Southbound : No access from M5 Northbound

## M53 BIRKENHEAD TO CHESTER

(11)
Northbound : No access from M56 (15) Eastbound
: No exit to M56 (15) Westbound
Southbound : No access from M56 (15) Eastbound
: No exit to M56 (15) Westbound

## M54 WOLVERHAMPTON TO TELFORD

M6
Westbound : No access from M6 (10A) Southbound
Eastbound : No exit to M6 (10A) Northbound

## M56 STOCKPORT TO CHESTER

(1)
Westbound : No access from M60 Eastbound
: No access from A34 Northbound
Eastbound : No exit to M60 Westbound
: No exit to A34 Southbound

(2)
Westbound : No access
Eastbound : No exit

(3)
Westbound : No exit
Eastbound : No access

(4)
Westbound : No access
Eastbound : No exit

(7)
Westbound : No access
Eastbound : No exit

(8)
Westbound : No exit
Eastbound : No access

(9)
Westbound : No exit to M6 Southbound
Eastbound : No access from M6 Northbound

(15)
Westbound : No access
: No access from M53 (11)
Eastbound : No exit
: No exit to M53 (11)

## M57 LIVERPOOL

(3)
Northbound : No exit
Southbound : No access

(5)
Northbound : Access only from A580 Westbound
: No exit
Southbound : No access
: Exit only to A580 Eastbound

## M58 LIVERPOOL TO WIGAN

(1)
Westbound : No access
Eastbound : No exit

## M60 MANCHESTER

(2)
Westbound : No exit
Eastbound : No access

(3)
Westbound : No access from M56 (1)
: No access from A34 Southbound
: No exit to A34 Northbound
Eastbound : No access from A34 Southbound
: No exit to M56 (1)
: No exit to A34 Northbound

(4)
Westbound : No access
Eastbound : No exit to M56

(5)
Westbound : No access from A5103 Southbound
: No exit to A5103 Southbound
Eastbound : No access from A5103 Northbound
: No exit to A5103 Northbound

(7)
Westbound : No access from A56 Southbound
: No exit to A56 Northbound
Eastbound : No exit to A56 Southbound
: No access from A56 Northbound

(14)
Westbound : No access from A580
: No exit to A580 Eastbound
Eastbound : No access from A580 Westbound
: No exit to A580

(16)
Westbound : No access
Eastbound : No exit

(20)
Westbound : No access
Eastbound : No exit

(22)
Westbound : No access

(25)
Westbound : No access

(26)
Eastbound : No access
: No exit

(27)
Westbound : No exit
Eastbound : No access

## M61 MANCHESTER TO PRESTON

(2)
Northbound : No access from A580 Eastbound
: No access from A666
Southbound : No exit to A580 Westbound

(3)
Northbound : No access from A580 Eastbound
: No access from A666
Southbound : No exit to A580 Westbound

M6
Northbound : No exit to M6 (30) Southbound
Southbound : No access from M6 (30) Northbound

## M62 LIVERPOOL TO HULL

(23)
Westbound : No exit
Eastbound : No access

## M65 BURNLEY

(9)
Westbound : No exit
Eastbound : No access

(11)
Westbound : No access
Eastbound : No exit

## M66 MANCHESTER TO EDENFIELD

(1)
Northbound : No access
Southbound : No exit

## M67 MANCHESTER

(1)
Westbound : No exit
Eastbound : No access

(2)
Westbound : No access
Eastbound : No exit

## M69 COVENTRY TO LEICESTER

(2)
Northbound : No exit
Southbound : No access

## M73 GLASGOW

(1)
Northbound : No access from A721 Eastbound
Southbound : No exit to A721 Eastbound

(2)
Northbound : No access from M8 (8) Eastbound
Southbound : No exit to M8 (8) Westbound

(3)
Northbound : No exit to A80 Southbound
Southbound : No access from A80 Northbound

## M74 GLASGOW

(2)
Westbound : No access
Eastbound : No exit

(3)
Westbound : No exit
Eastbound : No access

(7)
Northbound : No exit
Southbound : No access

(9)
Northbound : No access
: No exit
Southbound : No access

(10)
Southbound : No exit

(11)
Northbound : No exit
Southbound : No access

(12)
Northbound : Access only from A70 Northbound
Southbound : Exit only to A70 Southbound

(18)
Northbound : No access
Southbound : No exit

## M77 GLASGOW

M8
Northbound : No exit to M8 (22) Westbound
Southbound : No access from M8 (22) Eastbound

(4)
Northbound : No exit
Southbound : No access

Junction with A77
Northbound : No access from A77 Southbound
Southbound : No exit to A77 Northbound

## M80 STIRLING

(3)
Southbound : No access

(5)
Northbound : No access
: No access from M876
Southbound : No exit
: No exit to M876

## M90 EDINBURGH TO PERTH

(2A)
Northbound : No access
Southbound : No exit

(7)
Northbound : No exit
Southbound : No access

(8)
Northbound : No access
Southbound : No exit

(10)
Northbound : No access from A912
: No exit to A912 Southbound
Southbound : No access from A912 Northbound
: No exit to A912

## M180 SCUNTHORPE

(1)
Westbound : No exit
Eastbound : No access

## M606 BRADFORD

Straithgate Lane
Northbound : No access

## M621 LEEDS

(2A)
Northbound : No exit
Southbound : No access

(4)
Southbound : No access

(5)
Northbound : No access
Southbound : No exit

(6)
Northbound : No exit
Southbound : No access

## M876 FALKIRK

M80
Westbound : No exit to M80 (5) Northbound
Eastbound : No access from M80 (5) Southbound

M9
Westbound : No access
: No access from M9 (7) (8) Eastbound
Eastbound : No exit
: No exit to M9 (7) (8) Westbound

(2)
Northbound : No access
Southbound : No exit

# Motorway services information

| Motorway Number | Junction | Service Provider | Service Name | On-site Services | On-site Services | On-site Services | On-site Services | On-site Services | On-site Services | On-site Services | On-site Services |
|---|---|---|---|---|---|---|---|---|---|---|---|
| A1(M) | 1 | Welcome Break | South Mimms | ● | ● | ● | £ | | ● | ● | ● |
| A1(M) | 10 | Extra | Baldock | ● | ● | ● | £ | i | ● | ● | ● |
| A1(M) | 17 | Extra | Peterborough | ● | ● | ● | £ | i | ● | ● | ● |
| A1(M) | 34 | Moto | Blyth | ● | ● | ● | £ | i | ● | ● | |
| A1(M) | 61 | RoadChef | Durham | ● | ● | ● | £ | | ● | | |
| A1(M) | 64 | Moto | Washington | ● | ● | ● | £ | i | ● | ● | |
| M1 | 2–4 | Welcome Break | London Gateway | ● | ● | ● | £ | | ● | | ● |
| M1 | 11–12 | Moto | Toddington | ● | ● | ● | £ | i | ● | ● | |
| M1 | 14–15 | Welcome Break | Newport Pagnell | ● | ● | ● | £ | | ● | | ● |
| M1 | 15A | RoadChef | Rothersthorpe | ● | ● | ● | £ | | | | |
| M1 | 16–17 | RoadChef | Watford Gap | ● | ● | ● | £ | | ● | | |
| M1 | 21–21A | Welcome Break | Leicester Forest East | ● | ● | ● | £ | | ● | | ● |
| M1 | 22 | Moto | Leicester | ● | ● | ● | £ | i | ● | ● | |
| M1 | 23A | Moto | Donington Park | ● | ● | ● | £ | i | ● | ● | ● |
| M1 | 25–26 | Moto | Trowell | ● | ● | ● | £ | i | ● | ● | |
| M1 | 28–29 | RoadChef | Tibshelf | ● | ● | ● | £ | | ● | ● | |
| M1 | 30–31 | Welcome Break | Woodall | ● | ● | ● | £ | | ● | | ● |
| M1 | 38–39 | Moto | Woolley Edge | ● | ● | ● | £ | i | ● | ● | |
| M2 | 4–5 | Moto | Medway | ● | ● | ● | £ | i | ● | ● | |
| M3 | 4A–5 | Welcome Break | Fleet | ● | ● | ● | £ | | ● | | ● |
| M3 | 8–9 | RoadChef | Winchester | ● | ● | ● | £ | | ● | ● | |
| M4 | 3 | Moto | Heston | ● | ● | ● | £ | i | ● | ● | ● |
| M4 | 11–12 | Moto | Reading | ● | ● | ● | £ | i | ● | ● | ● |
| M4 | 13 | Moto | Chieveley | ● | ● | ● | £ | i | ● | ● | |
| M4 | 14–15 | Welcome Break | Membury | ● | ● | ● | £ | | ● | | ● |
| M4 | 17–18 | Moto | Leigh Delamere | ● | ● | ● | £ | i | ● | ● | ● |
| M4 | 23A | First Motorway | Magor | ● | ● | ● | £ | i | ● | | |
| M4 | 30 | Moto | Cardiff Gate | ● | ● | ● | £ | | ● | | |
| M4 | 33 | Moto | Cardiff | ● | ● | ● | £ | i | ● | ● | ● |
| M4 | 36 | Welcome Break | Sarn Park | ● | ● | ● | £ | | ● | | ● |
| M4 | 47 | Moto | Swansea | ● | ● | ● | £ | i | ● | ● | |
| M4 | 49 | RoadChef | Pont Abraham | ● | ● | ● | £ | i | | ● | |
| M5 | 3–4 | Moto | Frankley | ● | ● | ● | £ | i | ● | ● | |
| M5 | 8 | RoadChef | Strensham (South) | ● | ● | ● | £ | | | | |
| M5 | 8 | RoadChef | Strensham (North) | ● | ● | ● | £ | | ● | ● | |
| M5 | 13–14 | Welcome Break | Michael Wood | ● | ● | ● | £ | | ● | | ● |
| M5 | 19 | Welcome Break | Gordano | ● | ● | ● | £ | | ● | | ● |
| M5 | 21–22 | RoadChef | Sedgemoor (South) | ● | ● | ● | £ | | | | |
| M5 | 21–22 | Welcome Break | Sedgemoor (North) | ● | ● | ● | £ | | ● | | ● |
| M5 | 24 | Moto | Bridgwater | ● | ● | ● | £ | | ● | | |
| M5 | 25–26 | RoadChef | Taunton Deane | ● | ● | ● | £ | | ● | ● | |
| M5 | 28 | Margram | Cullompton | ● | ● | ● | £ | | | | |
| M5 | 29–30 | Moto | Exeter | ● | ● | ● | £ | i | ● | ● | ● |

**On-site Services:** Fuel · Disabled facilities · Food · Service shops · Information · Accommodation · Other shops · Conference facilities

| Motorway Number | Junction | Service Provider | Service Name | On-site Services |
|---|---|---|---|---|
| M6 | 3–4 | Welcome Break | Corley | Fuel, Disabled facilities, Food, Service shops, Accommodation |
| M6 | 10–11 | Moto | Hilton Park | Fuel, Disabled facilities, Food, Service shops, Information, Accommodation, Other shops |
| M6 | 14–15 | RoadChef | Stafford (South) | Fuel, Disabled facilities, Food, Service shops, Accommodation, Other shops |
| M6 | 14–15 | Moto | Stafford (North) | Fuel, Disabled facilities, Food, Service shops, Information, Other shops, Conference facilities |
| M6 | 15–16 | Welcome Break | Keele | Fuel, Disabled facilities, Food, Service shops |
| M6 | 16–17 | RoadChef | Sandbach | Fuel, Disabled facilities, Food, Service shops |
| M6 | 18–19 | Moto | Knutsford | Fuel, Disabled facilities, Food, Service shops, Information, Other shops |
| M6 | 27–28 | Welcome Break | Charnock Richard | Fuel, Disabled facilities, Food, Service shops, Accommodation |
| M6 | 32–33 | Moto | Lancaster | Fuel, Disabled facilities, Food, Service shops, Information, Accommodation, Other shops |
| M6 | 35A–36 | Moto | Burton-in-Kendal (North) | Fuel, Disabled facilities, Food, Service shops, Information, Accommodation, Other shops |
| M6 | 36–37 | RoadChef | Killington Lake (South) | Fuel, Disabled facilities, Food, Service shops, Accommodation |
| M6 | 38–39 | Westmorland | Tebay | Fuel, Disabled facilities, Food, Service shops, Accommodation, Conference facilities |
| M6 | 41–42 | Moto | Southwaite | Fuel, Disabled facilities, Food, Service shops, Information, Accommodation, Other shops |
| M8 | 4–5 | RoadChef | Harthill | Fuel, Disabled facilities, Food, Service shops, Conference facilities |
| M9 | 9 | Moto | Stirling | Fuel, Disabled facilities, Food, Service shops, Information, Accommodation, Other shops |
| M11 | 8 | Welcome Break | Birchanger Green | Fuel, Disabled facilities, Food, Service shops, Accommodation, Conference facilities |
| M18 | 5 | Moto | Doncaster North | Fuel, Disabled facilities, Food, Service shops, Information, Accommodation, Other shops |
| M20 | 8 | RoadChef | Maidstone | Fuel, Disabled facilities, Food, Service shops, Information, Accommodation |
| M23 | 11 | Moto | Pease Pottage | Fuel, Disabled facilities, Food, Service shops, Information, Accommodation, Other shops |
| M25 | 5–6 | RoadChef | Clacket Lane | Fuel, Disabled facilities, Food, Service shops, Information, Accommodation |
| M25 | 23 | Welcome Break | South Mimms | Fuel, Disabled facilities, Food, Service shops, Accommodation, Other shops, Conference facilities |
| M25 | 30 | Moto | Thurrock | Fuel, Disabled facilities, Food, Service shops, Information, Accommodation, Other shops |
| M27 | 3–4 | RoadChef | Rownhams | Fuel, Disabled facilities, Food, Service shops, Accommodation |
| M40 | 8 | Welcome Break | Oxford | Fuel, Disabled facilities, Food, Service shops, Accommodation, Conference facilities |
| M40 | 10 | Moto | Cherwell Valley | Fuel, Disabled facilities, Food, Service shops, Information, Accommodation, Other shops, Conference facilities |
| M40 | 12–13 | Welcome Break | Warwick | Fuel, Disabled facilities, Food, Service shops, Accommodation, Conference facilities |
| M42 | 2 | Welcome Break | Hopwood Park | Fuel, Disabled facilities, Food, Service shops, Other shops |
| M42 | 10 | Moto | Tamworth | Fuel, Disabled facilities, Food, Service shops, Information, Accommodation, Other shops, Conference facilities |
| M48 | 1 | Moto | Severn View | Fuel, Disabled facilities, Food, Service shops, Information, Accommodation, Other shops |
| M50 | 4 | Welcome Break | Ross Spur | Fuel, Disabled facilities, Food, Service shops |
| M56 | 14 | RoadChef | Chester | Fuel, Disabled facilities, Food, Service shops, Information, Accommodation |
| M61 | 6–7 | First Motorway | Bolton West | Fuel, Disabled facilities, Food, Service shops, Accommodation, Conference facilities |
| M62 | 7–9 | Welcome Break | Burtonwood | Fuel, Disabled facilities, Food, Service shops, Accommodation |
| M62 | 18–19 | Moto | Birch | Fuel, Disabled facilities, Food, Service shops, Information, Accommodation, Other shops, Conference facilities |
| M62 | 25–26 | Welcome Break | Hartshead Moor | Fuel, Disabled facilities, Food, Service shops, Accommodation, Conference facilities |
| M62 | 33 | Moto | Ferrybridge | Fuel, Disabled facilities, Food, Service shops, Information, Other shops |
| M65 | 4 | Supermart | Blackburn Interchange | Fuel, Disabled facilities, Food, Service shops, Accommodation |
| M74 | 4–5 | RoadChef | Bothwell (South) | Fuel, Disabled facilities, Food, Service shops |
| M74 | 5–6 | RoadChef | Hamilton (North) | Fuel, Disabled facilities, Food, Service shops, Information, Accommodation, Conference facilities |
| M74 | 11–12 | Cairn Lodge | Happendon | Fuel, Disabled facilities, Food, Service shops, Conference facilities |
| M74 | 12–13 | Welcome Break | Abington | Fuel, Disabled facilities, Food, Service shops, Accommodation, Conference facilities |
| A74(M) | 16 | RoadChef | Annandale Water | Fuel, Disabled facilities, Food, Service shops, Accommodation |
| A74(M) | 22 | Welcome Break | Gretna Green | Fuel, Disabled facilities, Food, Service shops, Accommodation, Conference facilities |
| M90 | 6 | Moto | Kinross | Fuel, Disabled facilities, Food, Service shops, Information, Accommodation, Other shops |

2
A
B
C
D
1
2
3
4
5
0 2 4 6 8 10 miles
0 2 4 6 8 10 km
Crane Islands
Godrevy Island
Navax Point
Gwithian
Kehelland
Tuck
Cambo
Roseworthy
Barbara Hepworth Museum
The Island
Tate St Ives
St Ives
St Ives Bay
Carn Naun Pt
The Carrack's
Gurnard's Head
Trendrine Hill
247
Halsetown
Zennor
Towednack
Carbis Bay
A3074
Phillack
Hayle
Connor Downs
Angarrack
Barripper
Porthmeor
Amalebra
Cripplesease
Lelant
Gwinear
Rosewarne
Carnhell Green
Praze
Pendeen Watch
Chysauster Ancient Village
Trencrom Hill
Fort (NT)
Lower Boscaswell
Morvah
Nancledra
252
Canon's Town
St Erth
St Erth Praze
Fraddam
Leedstown
Levant Steam Engine (NT)
Bojewyan
Pendeen
Whitecross
New Mill
Botallack
Trewellard
Carnyorth
Ludgvan
Crowlas
Townshend
Cape Cornwall
St Just
Madron
Trengwainton (NT)
Gulval
Heamoor
Penzance
Godolphin House
The Brisons
A3071
Newbridge
Longrock
St Hilary
Relubbus
Godolphin Cross
Carn Leskys
Bosavern
Tremethick Cross
Chyandour
Marazion
Goldsithney
Trescowe
Kelynack
Carn Euny Ancient Village
Sancreed
Drift Resr.
Penzance
St Michael's Mount (NT)
Perranuthnoe
Germoe
Tregonning Hill
Buryas Bridge
Tredavoe
Land's End
Brane
Catchall
Lower Drift
Newlyn
Breage
Ashton
Whitesand Bay
Sennen Cove
A30
Crows-an-wra
Kerris
Paul
Cudden Point
Praa Sands
Rinsey
Mousehole
Trewavas Head
Porthleven
Land's End
Longships
Sennen
St Clement's Isle
B3283
St Buryan
MOUNT'S BAY
Land's End
Trevescan
B3315
Boleigh
Burial Chamber
Minack Theatre Visitor Centre
Lamorna Cove
Porthcurno
Treen
St Levan
Cribba Head
Logan Rock
Gwennap Head
Wolf Rock
B3306
B3311
B3309
B3301
B3280
B3302
A394
Hayle
Red

D
E
F
G
3
Newquay Cornwall
Columb Major
Tregonetha
Castle-an-Dinas
Victoria
Roche
Towan Head
Newquay Bay
Newquay
Sea Life Centre
Fistral Bay
Porth
Porth Resr
Trebudannon
Colan
Mountjoy
Ruthvoes
Trevarren
St Columb Road
Pentire
West Pentire
Crantock
Holywell Bay
Quintrell Downs
Newquay Pearl
Kestle Mill
Retyn
Indian Queens
Fraddon
Blue Anchor
St Dennis
Bugle
Bilberry
Stenalees
Penhale Point
Holywell
Cubert
Carines
Ligger Pt
Holywell Bay Fun Park
Trerice (NT)
Penhale Sands
Mount
Newlyn East
Lappa Valley Rly
St Enoder
Retew
Hensbarrow Downs
Nanpean
Carthew
Ruddlemoor
Ligger or Perran Bay
Rose
Rejerrah
Newlyn Downs
Carland Cross
Chapel Town
Summercourt
Treviscoe
Perranporth
Mitchell
Brighton
Scarcewater
Foxhole
Wheal Martyn
Bawden Rocks or Man and his Man
Goonhavern
Bolingey
Trelassick
New Mills
St Stephen
High Street
Trewoon
Boscoppa
St Agnes Head
Trevellas
Zelah
Perranzabuloe
Coombe
St Mewan
ST AUSTELL
St Agnes
Penhallow
Callestock Cider Farm
Truthan
Tregear
Trispen
Ladock
Grampound Road
Sticker
Polgoot
St. Agnes Leisure Park
Mithian
Callestick
St Allen
St Erme
Hewas Water
Goonbell
Shortlanesend
Probus
Grampound
Trewithen
Creed
Mount Hawke
Porthtowan
Three Burrows
Tregavethan
Tresillian
St Ewe
Lost Gardens of Heligan
Pentewan
Penare
Mawla
Portreath
Blackwater
Kenwyn
Polmassick
Bridge
Illogan
Threemilestone
Gloweth
Cathedral
Truro
Merther
Tregony
Cornwall County Mus
Scorrier
Chacewater
Trewarthenick
Trevarrick
St Day
Baldhu
St Clement
St Michael Caerhays
Redruth
Malpas
Ruan Lanihorne
Twelveheads
Cross Lanes
Kea
Lamorran
St Michael Penkevil
Portholland
Gorran Churchtown
Gorran Haven
Cornish Engines (NT)
Carn Brea
Bissoe
Playing Place
Carharrack
Carnon Downs
Old Kea
Boswinger
Maenease
Pennance
Gwennap
Perranwell Sta.
Lanner
Trelissick
Philleigh
Penare
Penpol
Trelissick (NT)
Veryan
Portloe
Veryan Bay
Dodman Point
Four Lanes
Perranarworthal
Devoran
Carclew
Penhalvean
Ponsanooth
Feock
Carne
Gerrans Bay
Stithians
Mylor Bridge
Carrick Roads
St Just in Roseland
Trewithian
Nare Head
Stithian's Resr
Burras
Beacon
Penryn
Mylor
Flushing
St. Just in Roseland
Portscatho
Gerrans
Rame
Long Downs
Mabe Burnthouse
St. Mawes Castle
Greeb Point
Porkellis
Falmouth
Pt
St Mawes
Edgcumbe
Budock Water
Pendennis
St Anthony
Bohortha
Wendron
Seworgan
Treverva
Pendennis Point
Penjerrick
National Maritime Museum Cornwall
Zone Point
Brill
Falmouth Bay
Constantine
Mawnan Smith
Maen Porth
Helston
Cornish Seal Sanctuary
Porth Navas
Glendurgan (NT)
Trebah Garden
Rosemullion Head
Mawnan
Gweek
Helford
Trelowarren
Mawgan
Manaccan
St Anthony
Nare Point
Garras
St Martin
Tunnel
Tregidden
Newtown in St Martin
Porthallow
Porthoustock
St. Winwaloe
Crosslanes
St Keverne
Manacle Point
Cury
Tumuli
Traboe
The Manacles
Goonhilly Downs
Lowland Pt
Penhale
Gwenter
Coverack
Ruan Major
Kuggar
Ruan Minor
Cadgwith
Black Head
Grade
Toll
Landewednack
Lizard
Hot Point
Lizard Point
2
4
5
I
A30
A392
A3058
A3075
A3076
A39
A390
A391
A3047
A393
A394
A3083
A3078
B3285
B3284
B3277
B3298
B3297
B3289
B3292
B3293
B3296
B3280
B3275
B3287
B3273
B3274
B3279
B3276
B3300

A
B
C
D
1
2
3
4
5
ISLES OF SCILLY
same scale as main map
St Helen's
White Island
Tean
St Martin's
King Charles's
Old Grimsby
Lower Town
Middle Town
Cromwell's
Higher Town
Bryher
New Grimsby
Blockhouse
Tresco
Abbey & Gdns
Eastern Isles
Samson
Crow Sound
North West Channel
Bant's Carn
Chambered Cairns
The Road
A3110
St Mary's
Maypole
Hugh Town
Porth Hellick Down Burial Chamber
Star
Garrison Walls
Old Town
St Mary's
Crim Rocks
St Mary's Sound
Broad Sound
Annet
Gugh
Smith Sound
Western Rocks
St Agnes
Bishop Rock
Rumps Point
Newland
Pentire Point
Pentireglaze
Gulland Rock
New Polzeath
Padstow Bay
Trevose Head
Gunver Head
Crugmeer
Prideaux Place
Harlyn Bay
Quies
Trevone
Constantine Bay
B3276
Padstow
Shop
St Merryn
Treyarnon
A389
Porthcothan Beach
Tregolds
St Issey
Porthcothan
Little Petherick
Penrose
Park Head
Rumford
St Ervan
Tredinnick
Bedruthan Steps
15
St Eval
B3274
Trenance
Mawgan Porth
Berryl's Point
Vale of Mawgan or Lanherne
St Mawgan
Watergate Bay
Tregurrian
Talskiddy
St Columb Major
Newquay Cornwall
A39
Newquay Bay
B3276
Towan Head
Porth
Newquay
Sea Life Centre
A3059
Porth Resr
Fistral Bay
St Columb Minor
Trebudannon
Kelsey Head
Pentire
Newquay Zoo
A3058
Colan
Ruthvoes
West Pentire
Mountjoy
Black Cross
Holywell Bay
Crantock
Quintrell Downs
A392
White Cross
Trevarren
St Columb
Newquay Pearl
Penhale Point
Kestle Mill
Retyn
Indian Queens
Holywell
Carines
A3075
Fraddon
Ligger Pt
Trerice (NT)
A3058
Blue Anchor
Holywell Bay Fun Park
Cubert
St Enoder
Penhale Sands
Mount
Newlyn East
A3076
Retew
Ligger or Perran Bay
Lappa Valley Rly
Chapel Town
Summercourt
Trevisco
Rejerrah
Rose
Newlyn Downs
Carland Cross
Perranporth
16
Mitchell
Brighton
Scarcewater
Bawden Rocks or Man and his Man
Goonhavern
A30
A3058
New Mills
B3285
Bolingey
B3285
Trelassick
Zelah
St Agnes Head
Trevellas
Perranzabuloe
A39
St Agnes
Penhallow
Truthan
Tregear
Ladock
St. Agnes Leisure Park
Callestock Cider Farm
Trispen
Grampound Road
Mithian
B3284
Callestick
St Allen
Goonbell
St Erme
13
A30
B3275
B3277
B3284
Shortlanesend
Porthtowan
Mount Hawke
Three Burrows
Probus
Trewithen
Creed
Tregavethan
Mawla
Kenwyn
Tresillian
Blackwater
A30
A390
A390
Portreath
Threemilestone
Gloweth
Cathedral
B3300
Bridge
Cornwall County Mus
Crane Islands
Illogan
Scorrier
Chacewater
Truro
Merther
Tregony
Godrevy Island
Navax Point
A3047
St Day
A39
St Clement
Trewarthenick
Tehidy
Cornish Goldsmiths
Baldhu
Malpas
Ruan Lanihorne
A3078
B3301
Coombe
Pool
Redruth
B3298
Twelveheads
Cross Lanes
Kea
Gwithian
A3047
Carn Brea
Bissoe
Playing Place
Lamorran
Kehelland
Tuckingmill
Carharrack
Carnon Downs
Old Kea
St Michael Penkevil
A30
Camborne
Pennance
Gwennap
Perranwell Sta.
B3289
13
Cornish Engines (NT)
Lanner
A393
Trelissick
Philleigh
Connor Downs
Roseworthy
Penpol
Veryan
3
Four Lanes
Perranarworthal
Devoran
Trelissick (NT)
Angarrack
Barripper
Carclew
Feock
10
Carne
B3303
Troon
Pennalvean
Ponsanooth
A39
Gerrans Bay
Gwinear
Carnhell Green
Mylor Bridge
St Just in Roseland
Trewithian
Nare Head
Rosewarne
Praze-an-Beeble
B3280
Stithians
Carrick Roads
Portscatho
Crowan Beacon

D
E
F
G
5
Tresparrett Posts
Fire Beacon Point
Collamoor Head
Langdon
South Wheatley
Caudworthy
West Curry
Clubworthy
Maxworthy
Troswell
Bennacott
B3263
Marshgate
Boscastle Pottery
Boscastle
Lesnewth
Otterham
Treneglos
Canworthy Water
Brazacott
Tintagel Head
Trevalga
Tintagel Old Post Office (NT)
Bossiney
Tintagel
Treknow
Trewarmett
B3266
B3262
Hallworthy
Tremaine
Treneglos
North Petherwin
Ladycross
Davidstow
Trewassa
Tremail
Tresmeer
Egloskerry
Langore
St Stephens
Start Point
Trebarwith
B3263
B3314
A39
Kensey
Tregeare
Launceston Steam Rly
Red Down
17
A395
Delabole
Rockhead
Camelford
Inny
St Clether
Laneast
Downhead
Pipers Pool
Treligga
Westdowns
Valley Truckle
Lower Moor
New Park
Trewen
Tregadillett
Kennards House
Port Isaac Bay
B3314
B3267
Trewalder
Lanteglos
Tresinney
Buttern Hill
346
Bray Down
346
Polyphant
Port Isaac
Port Quin
Port Gaverne
Helstone
Rough Tor
400
Altarnun
Fivelanes
Lewannick
South Petherwin
Long Cross Victorian Gdns
B3267
St Teath
Brown Willy
420
B3254
B3257
Trelights
Pendoggett
Tregeare Rounds
Michaelstow
Garrow Tor
369
A30
St Endellion
B3314
Codda
Congdon's Shop
Lezant
Trekenner
Allen
11
A39
Trelill
St Kew
St Breward
De Lank
BODMIN MOOR
Coad's Green
Trebartha
Bolventor
St Tudy
13
Row
North Hill
Inny
St Kew Highway
Windmill
Chapel Amble
Trewornan
Smallacombe Downs
Kilmar Tor
390
15
B3257
CORNWALL
Bodieve
Kelly
St Mabyn
B3266
Dozmary Pool
Bathpool
Trevanson
Blisland
Temple
Brown Gelly Downs
342
Henwood
Rilla Mill
Linkinhorne
Wadebridge
Egloshayle
St Breock
21
Camel
Cardinham Moor
Colliford Reservoir
Siblyback Resr
Hurlers Stone Circle
Upton
Upton Cross
A389
Pencarrow
Hellandbridge
Inscribed Stone
Helland
Maidenwell
Common Moor
Minions
Caradon Hill
B3254
Burlawn
7
Washaway
Warleggan
Darite
Lane-end
Trethevy Quoit
Middlehill
Cardinham
King Doniert's Stone
Dunmere
Mount
St Neot
Tremar
Ruthernbridge
Bodmin
Nanstallon
St Cleer
St Ive
A390
St Lawrence
Ley
Dobwalls Family Adventure Park
Withiel
Bodmin & Wenford Rly
B3268
1
12
Liskeard
8
Merrymeet
A38
A389
Bodmin Parkway Sta.
Doublebois
Dobwalls
Seaton
Pengover Green
Lanivet
A30
West Taphouse
East Taphouse
Trevelmond
Trebyan
Lanhydrock House
12
St Pinnock
East Looe
A38
Menheniot
13
Victoria
B3268
Fowey
Restormel
A390
Braddock Down 1643
B3359
Liskeard
A30
Lockengate
Sweetshouse
Bodwen
Redmoor
Boconnoc
Horningtops
Roche
6
Bilberry
St Keyne
Herodsfoot
B3254
Trewidland
B3251
A38
Lostwithiel
Bridgend
Bugle
B3274
Lanlivery
Luxulyan
Couch's Mill
Bocaddon
Duloe
Bylane End
Trerulefoot
11
A387
Widegates
4
Tredinnick
Hensbarrow Downs
B3269
Stenalees
Lerryn
West Looe
Lanreath
Sandplace
Morval
9
Hessenford
Nanpean
Carthew
Penwithick
A390
Penpillick
Muchlarnick
B3247
A391
Trethurgy
Tywardreath Highway
B3253
Ruddlemoor
St Blazey
B3274
Eden Project
St Veep
Golant
Pelynt
St Martin
Sea
Foxhole
Wheal Martyn
St Blazey Gate
Tywardreath
Penpoll
7
4
Looe
Looe Bay
4
High Street
Boscoppa
Par
A3082
Lescrow
Trenewan
Downderry
Holmbush
A3082
A387
East Looe
Trewoon
5
Bodinnick
Porthallow
St Mewan
ST AUSTELL
Carlyon Bay
Polkerris
Fowey
Lansallos
St George's or Looe Island
A390
A390
Charlestown
St Austell Bay
Menabilly
Polruan
Polperro
Lantivet Bay
Sticker
Polgooth
Porthpean
St. Catherine's
Pencarrow Head
Hewas Water
Gribbin Head
5
Trenarren
B3273
Black Head
Pentewan
St Ewe
Lost Gardens of Heligan
Penare Point
Mevagissey Bay
0
2
4
6
8
10 miles
0
2
4
6
8
10 km
5
Mevagissey
Trevarrick
St Michael Caerhays
Chapel Point
Gorran Churchtown
Gorran Haven
Maenease Point
Boswinger
Penare
Veryan Bay
Dodman Point
D
E
F
G
6
6
1
2
3
4
5

6
A
B
C
D
20
1
2
3
4
5
Helebridge
Marhamchurch
Widemouth Bay
Bridgerule
Pyworthy
Rydon
Yeomadon
Coppathorne
Week Orchard
Dizzard Point
Poundstock
Tregole
Treskinnick Cross
Whitstone
Tinney
Herdic
Corfcott Green
Crackington Haven
Cambeak
St Gennys
Trewint
Week St Mary
North Tamerton
Crackington
Jacobstow
Wainhouse Corner
Trebarrow
Tamar
Tresparrett Posts
Fire Beacon Point
South Wheatley
West Curry
Chapma
Collamoor Head
Langdon
Caudworthy
Maxworthy
Clubworthy
Trespareett
Marshgate
Troswell
Bennacott
Boyton
Boscastle Pottery
Lesnewth
Otterham
Trelash
Warbstow
Canworthy Water
Brazacott
Giles
Boscastle
Trevalga
Tintagel Head
Tintagel Old Post Office (NT)
Bossiney
Tintagel
Tremaine
North Petherwin
Ladycross
Polapi Tama
Hallworthy
Treneglos
Treknow
Trewarmett
Davidstow
Trewassa
Tremail
Tresmeer
Kensey
Egloskerry
Ottery
Yeolmb
Start Point
Trebarwith
Tregeare
Langore
Launceston Steam Rly
St Stephens
Newport
Inny
Red Down
Delabole
Rockhead
St Clether
Laneast
Downhead
Pipers Pool
Launceston
Camelford
Trewen
Tregadillett
Treligga
Westdowns
Port Isaac Bay
Valley Truckle
Lower Moor
New Park
Bray Down
Polyphant
Kennards House
Port Isaac
Trewalder
Lanteglos
Buttern Hill
Tresinney
Port Quin
Long Cross Victorian Gdns
Port Gaverne
Helstone
Rough Tor
Altarnun
Fivelanes
Lewannick
South Petherwin
St Teath
Brown Willy
Trelights
Pendoggett
Tregeare Rounds
Michaelstow
Garrow Tor
Lezar
St Endellion
Codda
Congdon's Shop
Trekenn
Allen
De Lank
BODMIN
Trelill
St Kew
St Breward
Bolventor
Trebartha
Coad's Green
St Tudy
MOOR
North Hill
St Kew Highway
Row
Smallacombe Downs
Kilmar Tor
Chapel Amble
CORNWALL
Dozmary Pool
Bathpool
Bodieve
Kelly
St Mabyn
Blisland
Temple
Henwood
Trevanson
Wadebridge
Egloshayle
Brown Gelly Downs
Rilla Mill
Linkinhorne
St Breock
Camel
Pencarrow
Cardinham Moor
Colliford Reservoir
Siblyback Resr
Upton
Upton Cross
A389
Hellandbridge
Hurlers Stone Circle
Inscribed Stone
Helland
Maidenwell
Common Moor
Minions
Caradon Hill
Burlawn
Washaway
Warleggan
Darite
Pensilva
Monolith
Lane-end
Trethevy Quoit
Cardinham
King Doniert's Stone
Middlehill
Dunmere
Mount
St Neot
Tremar
Bodmin
Rutherbridge
Nanstallon
St Cleer
St Ive
St Lawrence
Dobwalls Family Adventure Park
Ley
Withiel
Bodmin & Wenford Rly
Liskeard
Merrymeet
Quethioc
A38
Pengover Green
Lanivet
Bodmin Parkway Sta.
Doublebois
Dobwalls
East Taphouse
West Taphouse
Trevelmond
Seaton
Lanhydrock House
Trebyan
St Pinnock
Menheniot
Victoria
Restormel
Braddock Down
East Looe
Lamellion
A390
Lockengate
Sweetshouse
Roche
Bodwen
Redmoor
Boconnoc
Horningtops
St Keyne
Bilberry
Lostwithiel
Bridgend
Herodsfoot
Trewidland
Bylane End
Bugle
Lanlivery
Couch's Mill
Bocaddon
Duloe
Trerulefoot
Luxulyan
West Looe
Widegates
Hensbarrow Downs
Stenalees
Lerryn
Tredinnick
Hessenford
Dennis
Lanreath
Sandplace
Morval
Nanpean
Carthew
Penwithick
Penpillick
Muchlarnick
Trethurgy
St Blazey
Tywardreath Highway
St Veep
Pelynt
Seaton
Eden Project
Golant
St Martin
Wheal Martyn
St Blazey Gate
Tywardreath
Penpoll
Par
Lescrow
Trenewan
Looe
Downderry
High Street
Boscoppa
A3082
Holmbush
Trewoon
Polkerris
Bodinnick
Porthallow
Looe Bay
St Mewan
ST AUSTELL
Carlyon Bay
Charlestown
Fowey
Lansallos
St George's or Looe Island
St Austell Bay
Menabilly
Polruan
Polperro
Lantivet Bay
Sticker
Polgooth
Porthpean
St Catherine's
Pencarrow Head
Hewas Water
Gribbin Head
Trenarren
Pentewan
St Ewe
Lost Gardens of Heligan
Penare Point
Mevagissey Bay
A39
A395
A30
A387
B3263
B3262
B3266
B3314
B3267
B3254
B3257
B3268
B3269
B3274
B3359
B3253
B3251
B3247
B3273

7
21
D
E
F
G
I
2
3
4
5
8
10
Anvil Corner
Dunsland Cross
Brandis Corner
Highampton
Hatherleigh
Lydacott
A3072
Basset's Cross
Graddon Moor
Halwill Forest
Exbourne
Jacobstowe
Honeychurch
North Tawton
Sampford Courtenay
A3072
Nymet Tracey
Leigh
A3079
Halwill Junction
Halwill
Beaworthy
A386
Inwardleigh
Oak Cross
Northlew
Ashbury
Upcott
Quoditch
Broadbury
Folly Gate
Belstone Corner
Itton
Taw Green
Spreyton
Okehampton
Ashwater
Eworthy
Germansweek
Southcott
B3260
A30
South Tawton
Sticklepath
Thorndon Cross
Yelland
Boasley Cross
Hewton
Belstone
Okehampton Camp
Finch Foundry
South Zeal
Whiddon Down
Virginstow
Roadford Resr
Bratton Clovelly
Meldon
Cawsand Hill 550
Throwleigh
Yes Tor 619
High Willhays 621
Gridley Corner
A30
Bridestowe
Sourton
Wonson
Castle
Gidleigh
413
Broadwoodwidger
Cross Green
Thrushelton
Bridestowe & Stourton Common
Okement Hill
Murchington
Easton
Chagford
A382
Stowford
Lewdown
Hangingstone Hill 604
Shortacombe
Great Kneeset 568
Cranmere Pool
Frenchbeer
Lewtrenchard
Portgate
Amicombe Hill
Lifton
Tinhay
Allerford
D E V O N
Lydford
Danger Zone
Black Ridge
601
Whitehorse Hill
Moretonhampstead
Downton
Coryton
Lydford Gorge (NT)
Fernworthy Resr
Lettaford
Beardon
Sittaford Tor 537
Marystow
Cut Hill 604
B3212
Kelly
North Brentor
Chillaton
Black Down
White Ridge
Easdon Tor
Lawhitton
Settlements
Warren House
Willsworthy
Grimspound
Bradstone
Brent Tor 335
A386
Horndon
Lynch Tor 517
D A R T M O O R
Hameldown Tor
South Brentor
Cowsic Head
Blackdown
Cocks Hill 501
Postbridge
Hamel Down
Milton Abbot
Longcross
Mary Tavy
Cudlipptown
Rough Tor
Higher White Tor
Bonehill Down
Rezare
Lamerton
Peter Tavy
Widecombe in the Moor
Bellever
Cator Court
Church House (NT)
Sydenham Damerel
Cox Tor 442
Great Mis Tor
Horsebridge
Cholwell
B3362
Merrivale
Rundlestone
Two Bridges
B3357
Babeny
Corndon Tor
Stoke Climsland
Tavistock
Merrivale Prehistoric Settlement
436
Luckett
Latchley
Gulworthy
A390
Sampford Spiney
Princetown
High Moorland Visitor Centre
Ponsworthy
Royal Hill 407
Dartmeet
Buckland in the Moor
Whitchurch
Chilsworthy
Hingston Down
Gunnislake
Walkhampton Common
445
Hexworthy
Poundsgate
Kit Hill
Harrowbarrow
Higher Walreddon
Whiteworks
St Ann's Chapel
Albaston
DARTMOOR
Morwellham Quay Mus.
Horrabridge
Ryder's Hill
Dupath Well
Morwellham
Walkhampton
NATIONAL
River Dart
Holne
Cotehele (NT)
Buckland Monachorum
Dousland
Cater's Beam
Burrator Resr
Calstock
The Garden House
Yelverton
PARK
Scorriton
Ashton
St Dominick
Sheepstor
Buckfast
Buckland Abbey (NT)
Crapstone
Meavy
Dean Moor
St Mellion
Bere Alston
Buckfastleigh
Milton Combe
Maristow House
Clearbrook
468
480
A388
Pillaton
A386
Cadover Bridge
Shaugh Prior
Brent Moor
Shell Top 475
Stall Moor
Harford Moor
Ugborough Moor
Shipley Bridge
Bere Ferrers
Penn Moor
Cargreen
Hatt
Bickleigh
Harbourneford
Landulph
Tamerton Foliot
Roborough
Didworthy
Botusfleming
Lee Moor
A38
Carkeel
Plymouth City
South Brent
Landrake
B3373
PLYMOUTH
Trematon
Plym Forest
Cornwood
Harford
Saltash
Toll
Lincombe
Markwell
St Stephens
A3064
Crownhill
Lutton
B3147
Plym Bridge
Drakeland Corner
Dartmoor Wildlife Park
Ugborough Beacon
Avonwick
St Budeaux
B3432
Egg Buckland
St Germans
Antony Ho. (NT)
A386
Sparkwell
Bittaford
Crabtree
B3416
Lee Mill Bridge
Ivybridge
B3213
Ugborough
North Huish
A374
Devonport
Plympton
A38
Sheviock
Torpoint
Royal Citadel
A374
Saltram (NT)
A3121
Crafthole
Antony
Stonehouse
PLYMOUTH
St John
St John's Lake
Cremyll
National Marine Aquarium
Westlake
Gara Bridge
Oreston
Elburton
Brownston
Danger Zone
B3247
Drake's Island
Turnchapel
Plymstock
A379
Brixton
Sequer's Bridge
Ermington
Freathy
Millbrook
Mount Edgcumbe
Hooe
Goosewell
Yealmpton
Dunstone
Modbury
Topsham Bridge
The Sound
Kitley
Flete
Kingsand
Cawsand Bay
Staddiscombe
Torr
Ford
Plymouth Breakwater
Rame
Cawsand
Down Thomas
Knighton
Holbeton
A379
Ashford
Penlee Point
Heybrook Bay
B3186
Wembury
Wembury Bay
Battisborough Cross
Loddiswell
Rame Head
St Ann's Chapel
Great Mew Stone
Worswell
Newton Ferrers
Noss Mayo
Kingston
Aveton Gifford
Gara Pt
Houghton
B3392
Ringmore
Bigbury
Netton
Venn
Stoke Point
Beacon
Churchstow

8
A
B
C
D
1
2
3
4
5
7
Stoke Climsland
Lockett
Latchley
Tavistock
Gulworthy
A390
Merrivale
Prehistoric Settlement
Sampford Spiney
Princetown
High Moorland Visitor Centre
Royal Hill
407
445
Walkhampton Common
Bridges
Hexworthy
Dartmeet
Ponsworthy
Poundsgate
Chilsworthy
Hingston Down
Kit Hill
Gunnislake
Whitchurch
Higher Walreddon
Harrowbarrow
St Ann's Chapel
Albaston
Morwellham Quay
Morwellham
Horrabridge
Walkhampton
Whiteworks
DARTMOOR
NATIONAL
PARK
Ryder's Hill
Cater's Beam
River Dart
Holne
Dupath Well
Cotehele (NT)
Calstock
Buckland Monachorum
The Garden House
Dousland
Yelverton
Burrator Resr
Sheepstor
Meavy
Scorriton
Buckfast
Ashton
St Dominick
St Mellion
Buckland Abbey (NT)
Bere Alston
Crapstone
Dean Moor
Buckfastleigh
Milton Combe
Maristow House
Clearbrook
468
480
A388
Pillaton
A386
Cadover Bridge
Shaugh Prior
Shell Top
475
Stall Moor
Harford Moor
Ugborough Moor
Brent Moor
Penn Moor
Shipley Bridge
Cargreen
Bere Ferrers
Hatt
Tamerton Foliot
Bickleigh
Roborough
Didworthy
Harbourneford
Landulph
Botusfleming
Lee Moor
South Brent
A38
Carkeel
Landrake
Trematon
Plymouth City
PLYMOUTH
DEVON
B3373
Saltash
Toll
A3064
B3413
Crownhill
Plym Forest
Plym Bridge
B3432
B3417
Cornwood
Harford
Lutton
Dartmoor Wildlife Park
Drakeland Corner
Ugborough Beacon
Markwell
St Stephens
St Budeaux
Egg Buckland
Sparkwell
Bittaford
Avonwick
St Germans
St Germans or Lynher
Antony Ho. (NT)
A386
Crabtree
Lee Mill Bridge
Ivybridge
B3213
Ugborough
North Huish
A374
Devonport
Torpoint
Plympton
B3416
Saltram (NT)
Royal Citadel
PLYMOUTH
National Marine Aquarium
Antony
St John
St John's Lake
Stonehouse
Cremyll
A3121
Westlake
Danger Zone
B3247
Oreston
Elburton
Plymstock
A379
Turnchapel
Drake's Island
Millbrook
Freathy
Brixton
Yealmpton
Sequer's Bridge
Ermington
Brownston
Gara Bridge
Hooe
Goosewell
Staddiscombe
Kitley
Torr
Dunstone
Flete
Modbury
Kingsand
Cawsand Bay
The Sound
Mount Edgcumbe
Ford
Cawsand
Rame
Plymouth Breakwater
Down Thomas
Knighton
Holbeton
A379
Ashford
Loddiswell
Aveton Gifford
Rame Head
Penlee Point
Heybrook Bay
Wembury
Wembury Bay
B3186
Newton Ferrers
Battisborough Cross
Kingston
St Ann's Chapel
B3392
Great Mew Stone
Worswell
Noss Mayo
Gara Pt
Netton
Stoke Point
Houghton
Ringmore
Bigbury
Venn
Churchstow
Beacon Pt
Bigbury-on-Sea
Burgh Island
Bantham
Cookworthy
Buckland
Upton
West Alvington
hours
Roscoff....................................6-7½
Santander (Summer Only)..........24
Thurlestone
South Milton
South Huish
Bigbury Bay
Galmpton
A381
Bolt Tail
Hope
Malborough
Bolberry
Soar
Overbeck's Garden (NT)
Overbeck's Museum (NT)
Bolt
CHANNEL ISLANDS
location map
Alderney
Guernsey
Herm
Sark
Jersey
same scale as main map
JERSEY
Grosnez (ruins)
Plemont Pt
Greve de Lecq Bay
St John
149
B55
B33
Bouley Bay
St Ouen
Battle of Flowers Museum
56
Dolmen
B31
La Mielle de Morville
Carrefour Selous
B27
Zoo
St Martin
St Ouen's Bay
St Peter
German Underground Hosp
A8
St Catherine's Bay
B35
B41
A12
A10
A9
Dolmen
Maufant
Mt Orgueil
Jersey
A11
67
A6
A2
A1
Five Oaks
B28
Gorey
Corbière Lighthouse
A13
St Brelade
St Aubin
St Aubin's Bay
Peoples Park
La Hougue Bie
Grouville
A3
A5
La Cotte
Elizabeth
ST HELIER
A4
hours
Poole.......................................3¾
Portsmouth...............................10
St Malo....................................1¼
St Peter Port.............................1
Weymouth................................3¼
Noirmont Pt
La Rocque Pt
A
B
C
D

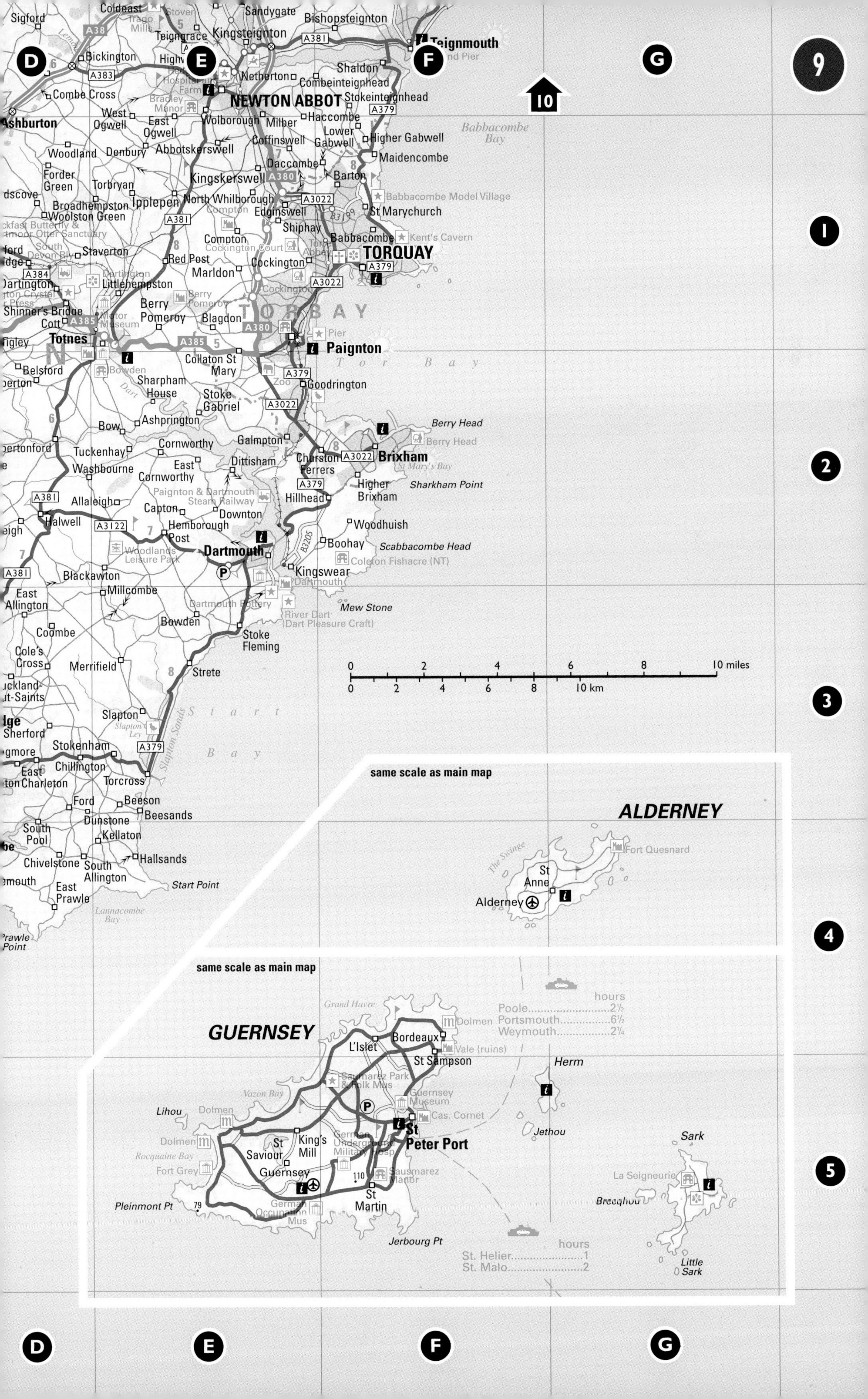
9
10
D
E
F
G
1
2
3
4
5
Sigford
Coldeast
Stover
Trago Mills
Sandygate
Bishopsteignton
Kingsteignton
Teigngrace
Teignmouth
Bickington
A38
A381
A383
Highweek
Netherton
Shaldon
Combeinteignhead
Combe Cross
Bradley Manor
NEWTON ABBOT
Stokeinteignhead
A379
Ashburton
West Ogwell
East Ogwell
Wolborough
Milber
Haccombe
Lower Gabwell
Higher Gabwell
Babbacombe Bay
Woodland
Denbury
Abbotskerswell
Coffinswell
Maidencombe
Forder Green
Torbryan
Kingskerswell
A380
Daccombe
Barton
Broadhempston
Ipplepen
North Whilborough
A3022
Babbacombe Model Village
Woolston Green
Compton
Edginswell
St Marychurch
B3199
Shiphay
Babbacombe
Kent's Cavern
Staverton
Compton
Cockington Court
TORQUAY
Red Post
Cockington
Marldon
A384
Dartington
Littlehempston
Berry Pomeroy
Shinner's Bridge
Blagdon
TORBAY
Cott
A385
Totnes
Motor Museum
Pier
Paignton
Belsford
Bowden
Collaton St Mary
Tor Bay
Sharpham House
Zoo
Goodrington
Stoke Gabriel
Ashprington
Bow
Berry Head
Cornworthy
Galmpton
Tuckenhay
Churston Ferrers
Brixham
Washbourne
East Cornworthy
Dittisham
St Mary's Bay
Higher Brixham
Sharkham Point
Paignton & Dartmouth Steam Railway
Hillhead
Allaleigh
Capton
Downton
Halwell
A3122
Hemborough Post
Woodhuish
B3205
Woodlands Leisure Park
Dartmouth
Boohay
Scabbacombe Head
Coleton Fishacre (NT)
Blackawton
Kingswear
Dartmouth
East Allington
Millcombe
Dartmouth Pottery
Mew Stone
River Dart (Dart Pleasure Craft)
Bowden
Coombe
Stoke Fleming
Cole's Cross
Merrifield
Strete
0 2 4 6 8 10 miles
0 2 4 6 8 10 km
Start Bay
Slapton
Slapton Ley
Slapton Sands
Sherford
Stokenham
A379
Chillington
East Charleton
Torcross
Ford
Beeson
Beesands
Dunstone
South Pool
Kellaton
Chivelstone
South Allington
Hallsands
East Prawle
Start Point
Lannacombe Bay
Prawle Point
same scale as main map
ALDERNEY
Fort Quesnard
The Swinge
St Anne
Alderney
same scale as main map
hours
Poole 2½
Portsmouth 6½
Weymouth 2¼
Grand Havre
GUERNSEY
Dolmen
Bordeaux
L'Islet
Vale (ruins)
St Sampson
Herm
Saumarez Park & Folk Mus
Vazon Bay
Guernsey Museum
Lihou
Dolmen
Cas. Cornet
Dolmen
St Saviour
King's Mill
German Underground Military Hosp
St Peter Port
Jethou
Sark
Rocquaine Bay
Fort Grey
Guernsey
Sausmarez Manor
La Seigneurie
Pleinmont Pt
German Occupation Mus
St Martin
Jerbourg Pt
hours
St. Helier 1
St. Malo 2
Little Sark

10
Clapworthy
George Nympton
Alswear
A
Crooked Oak
Bishop's Nympton
Ash Mill
Mariansleigh
A361
Knowstow
B
22
Rackenford Moor
End
12
17
B3227
Morebath
Exe
Shillingford
Bathern
Petton
C
Bampton
Clayhanger
D
Oakfordbridge
Oakford
A396
Huntsham
Romansleigh
King's Nympton
Rowley
Meshaw
Creacombe
Stoodleigh
Cove
Hockworthy
Head Bridge
Newhouse Moor
B3137
Rackenford
Stoodleigh Beacon
Exe Valley
Cadbury Barton
Week
Kings Nympton Sta.
Elstone
East Mere
Pitt
Little Dart
Knightshayes Court (NT)
Uplowman
Washfield
Loxbeare
Chevithorne
Whitnage
1
Bolham
Chettiscombe
East Worlington
Calverleigh
Witheridge
Dalch
Templeton Bridge
Templeton
A361
Cheldon
West Worlington
Nomansland
Sampford Peverell
Tiverton Parkway Sta.
B3096
Chawleigh
Thelbridge Barton
Washford Pyne
B3137
B3391
Lowman
Tiverton
Halberton
Withleigh
Cruwys Morchard
Ash Thomas
Grand Western Housebeat Co.
B3042
Hele Lane
Puddington
Pennymoor
Eggesford Barton
21
Filleigh
Way Village
Brithem Bottom
Forches Cross
Eastington
Black Dog
Well Town
A396
Coldridge
Lapford
Poughill
Nymet Rowland
Woolfardisworthy
Upham
Cadeleigh
Bickleigh
Butterleigh
Morchard Bishop
Kennerleigh
28
B3220
Taw Bridge
Oldborough
D
E
V
Cullompton
A377
Stockleigh English
Cheriton Fitzpaine
Bickleigh Castle
Colebrook
Morchard Road Sta.
Ash Bullayne
East Village
Fursdon
Ravenshayes
2
A3072
Cadbury
East Leigh
Down St Mary
Upton Hellions
A396
Mutterton
Bradninch
Westcott
Stockleigh Pomeroy
Silverton
Zeal Monachorum
Copplestone Sta.
Copplestone
Sandford
Up Exe
Hele
Langford
North Tawton
Bow
Clannaborough Barton
Creedy Park
Thorverton
14
B3181
20
13
A3072
Broadnymett
Knowle
Efford
Killerton (NT)
Crediton
Shobrooke
Nymet Tracey
Coleford
Colebrooke
Budlake
Nether Exe
Rewe
Clyst St Lawrence
Newton St Cyres
Brampford Speke
Yeoford
Uton
Westwood
Hookway
Itton
Troney
B3219
10
Clyst
Stoke Canon
Upton Pyne
M5
Broadclyst
Court Barton
Oldridge
Spreyton
A377
Poltimore
Dog Village
8
3
Tedburn St Mary
Hittisleigh
A396
Cowley
Rockbeare
Pinhoe
Clyst Honiton
Exeter
Exwick
Whipton
Cheriton Bishop
A30
Whitestone
B3212
Whiddon Down
Cheriton Cross
15
Pathfinder Village
EXETER
B3183
29
Sowton
Crockernwell
A30
Aylesbeare
Longdown
Crealy Park
30
Pocombe Bridge
B3182
Countess Wear
Farringdon
Drewsteignton
Clyst St Mary
Castle Drogo (NT)
B3212
Ide
White Cross
Alphington
Teign
Wonson
6
12
Westpoint Exhibition Centre
Woodbury Salterton
Easton
Dunsford
Clyst St George
Shillingford St George
Kenn
A379
Topsham
Murchington
B3192
B3212
31
Ebford
Woodbury
Chagford
Doccombe
Dunchideock
Exminster
Exton
A382
Bridford
Doddiscombsleigh
Kennford
Moretonhampstead
A38
Exe
A376
Black
4
Higher Ashton
Kenn
Christow
Kennick Resr
Bickham House
Powderham
Great Haldon
North Bovey
Coombe
Lower Ashton
Lettaford
Tottiford Resr
Powderham Castle
Lympstone
B3212
Sanduck
Devon and Exeter
Kenton
A La Ronde
Withycombe Raleigh
Easdon Tor
A382
Trusham
Starcross
Canonteign Falls
Manaton
Trenchford Resr
A38
A380
Grimspound
Lustleigh
Mamhead
EXMOUTH
Becky Falls
Hennock
Cockwood
7
Hameldown Tor
Chudleigh
Ashcombe
Langdon House
Hamel Down
Hound Tor Medieval Village
Yarner Wood
Bonehill Down
Bovey Tracey
House of Marbles & Teign Valley Glass
Devon Guild of Craftsmen
Ugbrooke
Dawlish Water
Dawlish Warren
Dawlish Warren Sta.
Widecombe in the Moor
Haytor Vale
B3344
Chudleigh Knighton
Ideford
Little Haldon
Dawlish
Church House (NT)
B3387
Brimley
Luton
Heathfield
B3192
Cardew Design
Ilsington
A380
5
Dunstone
Rippon Tor
B3193
Liverton
Preston
Holcombe
A379
Horridge
Sigford
Coldeast
Stover
Sandygate
Bishopsteignton
Ponsworthy
Trago Mills
A38
Teigngrace
Kingsteignton
A381
Teignmouth
Grand Pier
Buckland in the Moor
Dartmeet
Poundsgate
A382
Bickington
Highweek
Caton
A383
Netherton
Shaldon
Combeinteignhead
Rew
Combe Cross
Bradley Manor
NEWTON ABBOT
Stokeinteignhead
West Ogwell
East Ogwell
Haccombe
A379
River Dart
Ashburton
Wolborough
Milber
Babbacombe Bay
9
Higher Gabwell
Holne
Abbey
Coffinswell
Lower Gabwell
Scorriton
Woodland
Denbury
Abbotskerswell
Maidencombe
A
B
C
D
Daccombe
Buckfast
Kingskerswell
Barton
Dean Moor
Forder Green
Torbryan
A380
Landscove
Buckfastleigh
Broadhempston
Ipplepen
North Whilborough
Compton
A3022
Babbacombe Model Village
Woolston Green
A381
Edginswell
B3199
St Marychurch

11
D
E
F
G
1
2
3
4
5
TAUNTON
Bishop's Hull
Rumwell
Wilton
Ruishton
Henlade
Thornfalcon
Greenway
Moor
A378
Drayton
Bathealton
Chipley
Langford Budville
Runnington
Appley
Thorne St Margaret
Greenham
Wellington
West Buckland
Bradford-on-Tone
Trull
Taunton Deane
Portman
Thurlbear
Holywell Lake
Rockwell Green
26
M5
A38
Sampford Arundel
Blackmoor
Wrangway
Ford Street
Angersleigh
Wellington Monument (NT)
Pitminster
Poundisford Park
Corfe
Blagdon Hill
Luxhay Resr
Staple Fitzpaine
Bickenhall
Hatch Beauchamp
West Hatch
Wrantage
A358
23
Curry Mallet
Beercrocombe
Hatch Green
Swell
Isle Abbotts
Isle Brewers
Hambridge
Westport
East Lambrook
West Lambrook
South Petherton
Barrington Court (NT)
Barrington
Puckington
Ilton
Stocklinch
Shepton Beauchamp
A303
Burlescombe
Nicholashayne
Black Down Hills
Clayhidon
Rosemary Lane
Churchstanton
SOMERSET
Staple Hill
Curland
Windmill Hill
Ashill
Broadway
Horton Cross
Horton
Fyfett
Ding
16
Ilminster
Whitelackington
Seavington St Mary
Lopen
Appledore
Culmstock
B3391
Culm Valley
Stapley
Hemyock
Buckland St Mary
Donyatt
A358
Crock Street
Kingstone
Dinnington
Merriott
Uffculme
Craddock
Hackpen Hill
Ashill
Bolham Water
Churchingford
Bishopswood
Northay
Combe St Nicholas
Cricket Malherbie
Dowlish Wake
Hinton St George
Chillington
Madford
Smeatharpe
Marsh
Whitestaunton
Wadeford
Cudworth
Crewkerne
Blackborough
Sheldon
Newcott
Howley
A30
Chaffcombe
Cricket St Thomas
Hewish
Kentisbeare
Dunkeswell
Yarcombe
A303
Chard
Cricket Bottom
Wambrook
B3162
Forton
Wayford
Clapton Court
Clapton
Winsham
Tatworth
Upottery
Luppitt
Rawridge
Beacon
13
Kerswell
Broadhembury
Stockland
Furley
South Chard
Chardstock
Forde Abbey
Chard Junction
Axe
B3165
B3167
Colliton
A373
Combe Raleigh
Monkton
A30
Tytherleigh
Thorncombe
Blackdown
Burstock
Broadwindsor
Pilsdon Pen
Luton
Upton
Membury
Alston
A358
Holditch
Stockland Hill
Payhembury
Godford Cross
Awliscombe
Cotleigh
Dalwood
Smallridge
Weycroft
Birdsmoor Gate
Marshwood
B3164
12
Colestocks
Higher Cheriton
Buckerell
Hamlet
Honiton
Wilmington
Widworthy
Loughwood Meeting Ho (NT)
Hawkchurch
Bettiscombe
B3165
South Bowood
Feniton
Gittisham
Offwell
A35
Axminster
Fishpond Bottom
Escot
Fenny Bridges
Alfington
Shute
Kilmington
B3261
Marshwood Vale
A375
Church Green
Coly
Umborne Brook
Offwell Brook
Fairmile
A358
Raymond's Hill
Broadoak
Cadhay
Ottery St Mary
Putts Corner
Seaton Junction
Whitford
Wootton Fitzpaine
Whitchurch Canonicorum
Farway
Northleigh
Ryall
Wiggaton
Musbury
Morcombelake
Farway
Southleigh
Colyton
Seaton Tramway
A35
Charmouth
Symondsbury
West Hill
Broad Down
Colyford
Combpyne
Uplyme
Golden Cap
191
Chideock
Tipton St John
Sand
Blackbury Camp
A3052
Rousdon
Seatown
Venn Ottery
Sidbury
Axmouth
Lyme Regis
Harpford
Sidford
A3052
B3174
Dowlands
Pinhay
Bowd
Harcombe
Old Bakery (NT)
Beer
Seaton
B3172
Newton Poppleford
B3176
B3175
Salcombe Regis
Weston
Vicarage
Marine House
Seaton Bay
Donkey Sanctuary
Branscombe
Beer Head
Colaton Raleigh
Pinn
Sidmouth
B3178
Bicton Park
Otterton
LYME BAY
Fairlynch Arts Centre & Museum
Budleigh Salterton
0
2
4
6
8
10 miles
10 km

12
A
B
C
D
1
2
3
4
5
24
11
Drayton
Long Load
Thorne
Kingsbury Episcopi
Witcombe
Stapleton
Ash
Coat
Martock
Isle Brewers
Hambridge
Westport
Barrington Court (NT)
East Lambrook
East Lambrook Manor
West Lambrook
Bower Hinton
Barrington
Shepton Beauchamp
Stocklinch
South Petherton
Seavington St Michael
Seavington St Mary
Kingstone
Dinnington
Lopen
Over Stratton
Merriott
Norton-sub-Hamdon
Chiselborough
Hinton St George
Cricket Malherbie
Chillington
Cudworth
Crewkerne
Cricket St Thomas
Hewish
Crinkley Bottom
Wayford
Winsham
Clapton
Clapton Court
Misterton
Seaborough
Drimpton
South Perrott
Mosterton
Whetley Cross
Chedington
Corscombe
Blackdown
Burstock
Broadwindsor
Pilsdon Pen
Birdsmoor Gate
Pilsdon
Stoke Abbott
Netherbury
Beaminster
Parnham
Mapperton
Melplash
South Bowood
Waytown
Salwayash
Marshwood Vale
Char
Broadoak
Dottery
Whitchurch Canonicorum
Ryall
Morcombelake
Symondsbury
Charmouth
Chideock
Bridport
Watton
Eype
Seatown
Golden Cap
West Bay
Bothenhampton
Bradpole
Walditch
Shipton Gorge
North Hill
Burton Bradstock
Chilcombe
Loders
Uploders
Nettlecombe
Powerstock
West Milton
North Poorton
Eggardon Hill
Askerswell
Ilchester
Northover
Bridgehampton
Fleet Air Arm Museum
Tintinhull
Tintinhull Ho. (NT)
Chilthorne Domer
Stoke sub Hamdon
Ham Hill
Montacute
Montacute Ho. (NT)
Preston Plucknett
Odcombe
West Coker
North Coker
East Coker
West Chinnock
East Chinnock
Haselbury Plucknett
Hardington Mandeville
Pendomer
Sutton Bingham Res.
Hardington Marsh
North Perrott
Halstock
Closworth
Ashington
Yeovil Marsh
YEOVIL
Mudford
Chilton Cantelo
Marston Magna
Queen Camel
Sutton Montis
Rimpton
Charlton Horethorne
Corton Denham
Adber
Sandford Orcas
Trent
Nether Compton
Over Compton
Compton House
Barwick
Stoford
Bradford Abbas
Thornford
Yetminster
Ryme Intrinseca
Lillington
Beer Hackett
Melbury Osmond
Stockwood
Melbury Sampford
Melbury Bubb
East Chelborough
West Chelborough
Evershot
Holywell
Toller Down Gate
Benville Lane
Uphall
Rampisham
Toller Whelme
Chalmington
Lower Wraxall
Cattistock
Hooke
Higher Kingcombe
Lower Kingcombe
Chilfrome
Maiden Newton
Toller Porcorum
Toller Fratrum
Wynford Eagle
West Compton
Compton Valence
Kingston Russell
Long Bredy
Litton Cheney
Poor Lot Barrows
Littlebredy
Puncknowle
Swyre
Kingston Russell Stone Circle
West Bexington
White Hill
Abbotsbury
Abbey
Abbotsbury Swannery
Abbotsbury Sub-tropical Gardens
St Catherine's Chapel
West Fleet
Chesil Beach
East Fleet
Sherborne
Old Castle
Abbey
Milborne Wick
Poyntington
Oborne
Milborne Port
Stowell
Templecombe
Horsington
Abbas Combe
Yenston
Henstridge Ash
Henstridge
Purse Caundle
Goathill
Haydon
North Wootton
Alweston
Folke
Caundle Marsh
Stourton Caundle
Bishop's Caundle
Longburton
Holwell
Sandhills
Crouch Hill
BLACKMOOR
Holnest
Pulham
Glanvilles Wootton
Leigh
Chetnole
Hermitage
Middlemarsh
Lyon's Gate
Buckland Newton
Duntish
Mappowder
Hilfield
Batcombe
Minterne Magna
Minterne
Up Cerne
Alton Pancras
Plush
Folly
Frome St Quentin
Up Sydling
The Giant (NT)
Cerne Abbas
Sydling St Nicholas
Piddletrenthide
White Lackington
Nether Cerne
Piddlehinton
Godmanstone
Forston
Frampton
Grimstone
Stratton
Charminster
Bradford Peverell
Wolfeton
Burton
Dorset County Mus
Tutankhamun Exhibition
Winterbourne Abbas
Nine Stones
Winterbourne Steepleton
Dorchester
Stinsford
Lower Bockhampton
Maiden Castle
Winterborne Came
Whitcombe
Martinstown
Hardy Monument
Black Down
Bronkham Hill
Portesham
Winterborne Monkton
Upwey
Bincombe
White Horse
Broadwey
Sutton Poyntz
Osmington
Upwey Sta.
Jordan Hill Roman Temple
Preston
Rodden
Langton Herring
Radipole
Overcombe
Osmington Mills
Chickerell
Sea Life Centre
Melcombe Regis
Weymouth Bay
Charlestown
Westham
WEYMOUTH
Brewers Quay
Nothe Fort
The Timewalk
Wyke Regis
Ferry Bridge
Portland Harbour
Guernsey
Jersey
St Malo
(summer only)
West Bay
Portland
Fortuneswell
Grove
Easton
Isle of Portland
Weston
Southwell
Bill of Portland
SOMERSET
DORSET
A378
A303
A356
A3088
A37
A30
A359
A352
A357
A3030
A3066
A35
A354
B3165
B3168
B3151
B3148
B3145
B3162
B3164
B3163
B3143
B3146
B3157
B3159
B3142
0
2
4
6
8
10 miles
0
2
4
6
8
10 km

13
D
E
F
G
1
2
3
4
5
26
14
Knap Corner
West
East Stour
Shaftesbury
Donhead St Mary
A30
Alvediston
Ebbesborne Wake
Woodminton
Bowerchalk
A354
Ludwell
Cann
Cann Common
Charlton
Stour Provost
Stour Row
Fifehead Magdalen
Guy's Marsh
Todber
Marnhull
Margaret Marsh
Twyford
Melbury Abbas
Ashmore
Chase
Cranborne
Tollard Royal
Deanland
Sixpenny Handley
Woodyates
Martin Drove End
Martin
Tidpit
Whitsbury
Rockbourne
Rockbourne Roman Villa
A350
B3091
Bedchester
Compton Abbas
East Orchard
Sutton Waldron
West Orchard
Fontmell Magna
Hinton St Mary
Manston
Sturminster Newton
Iwerne Minster
Hammoon
Fiddleford Manor
Woodcutts
Dean
Farnham
Minchington
Pentridge
Pentridge Hill
Damerham
Lower Burgate
Boveridge
Monkton Up Wimborne
Sandleheath
Fordingbridge
Cranborne Manor
Cranborne
Daggons
Ashford
Alderholt
Stubhampton
Tarrant Gunville
Chettle
Cashmoor
Gussage St Michael
Gussage All Saints
Church & Earthworks
Wimborne St Giles
Edmondsham House
Edmondsham
Cranborne Common
B3078
B3081
Child Okeford
Shroton (Iwerne Courtney)
Common
Fifehead Neville
Shillingstone
Okeford Fitzpaine
A357
Hod Hill
Stourpaine
Tarrant Hinton
Pimperne Down
Long Crichel
Knowlton
Sutton Holms
Romford
Harbridge
Ringwood Forest
Tarrant Launceston
Pimperne
Durweston
Ibberton
Turnworth
Blandford Forum
Blandford Camp
Tarrant Monkton
Manswood
Moor Crichel
Horton Inn
Woodlands
Whitmore
Verwood
Horton Common
Ellingham
Horton
Tarrant Rawston
Witchampton
Uppington
Chalbury Common
Mannington
Moors Valley Railway
Ashley Heath
Tarrant Rushton
Hinton Martell
Gaunt's Common
Three Legged Cross
Bryanston
Blandford St Mary
Langton Long Blandford
Bulbarrow Hill
Winterborne Stickland
Winterborne Houghton
Tarrant Keyneston
Charlton Marshall
Badbury Rings (NT)
Stanbridge
Holt
Holt Heath
Moors Valley
St Leonards
Highbury
Tarrant Crawford
Hilton
Milton Abbas
Milton Abbey
Winterborne Clenston
Thornicombe
Spetisbury
Broom Hill
West Moors
Shapwick
Clapgate
Colehill
Tadden
Canford Bottom
Ferndown
A31
Avon Heath
Kingston Lacy (NT)
Higher Whatcombe
Charlton Down
Trickett's Cross
A338
Pamphill
Stapehill
Knoll Gardens
Winterborne Whitechurch
Sturminster Marshall
Wimborne Minster
Stapehill Abbey Crafts & Garden
Hampreston
Dewlish
Winterborne Kingston
Almer
Winterborne Zelston
East End
Canford Magna
Longham
Dudsbury
Parley Cross
West Parley
Bournemouth International
Milborne St Andrew
Anderson
Corfe Mullen
A349
A341
A347
Bearwood
Kinson
Hurn
Alice in Wonderland Maze
Lytchett Matravers
POOLE
Canford Heath
Holdenhurst
Athelhampton House
A35
Tolpuddle
Bere Regis
Bloxworth
Morden
Hill View
Broadstone
A348
A3049
Wallisdown
Moordown
Burleston
Affpuddle
East Morden
Beacon Hill
Waterloo
Newtown
Winton
Slepe
Briantspuddle
Turners Puddle
Lytchett Minster
Upton
Upton Park
B3067
A3040
Branksome
CHRISTCHURCH
Pokesdown
Southbourne
Lane End
Bloxworth Heath
Gore Heath
A351
Longfleet
BOURNEMOUTH
Hamworthy
Parkstone
Westbourne
Boscombe
Woodsford
Clouds Hill (NT)
Gallows Hill
Wareham Forest
Holton Heath
Poole Arts Centre
Branksome Park
Russell-Cotes Art Gallery & Museum
Trigon Hill
Holton Heath Sta.
Guildhall
Lilliput
Moreton Sta.
Moreton
Bovington Camp
Tank Museum
Sandford
Pottery
Compton Acres
Canford Cliffs
Monkey World Ape Rescue Centre
B3369
Crossways
Wareham
Arne
Poole Harbour
East Burton
A352
Stokeford
Winfrith Heath
Hartland Moor
Brownsea Island
Sandbanks
Wool
Holmebridge
Stoborough
Bindon Abbey
East Stoke
Ridge
Poole Bay
Owermoigne
West Holme
Stoborough Green
Toll
East Knighton
Coombe Keynes
B3070
Middlebere Heath
Wytch Heath
Studland Bay
Winfrith Newburgh
Norden
Newton Heath
Isle of Purbeck
East Creech
Hills
Church Knowle
Corfe (NT)
Corfe Castle
Studland
The Foreland or Handfast Point
Chaldon Herring or East Chaldon
Lulworth
B3071
Danger Zone
Grange Heath
Purbeck
Ballard Down
Lulworth Camp
East Lulworth
Corfe Castle Mus
Harman's Cross
Nine Barrow Down
Ulwell
Ballard Point
Chaldon Down
199
Steeple
B3351
West Lulworth
Tyneham
Swanage Rly
Swanage Bay
Lulworth Cove Heritage Cen
Lulworth Cove
Worbarrow Bay
Kimmeridge
Kingston
B3069
Peveril Point
Toll
Swanage
Smedmore
Langton Matravers
Herston
Durlston Bay
Broad Bench
Worth Matravers
Durlston Country Park Visitor Centre
Durlston
Durlston Head
Tilly Whim Caves
Seacombe Cliff
St Aldhelm's or St Alban's Head
hours
Cherbourg..................2¼-4¼ (5¾)
Guernsey..................2½
Jersey..................3¾
St Malo (Summer Only)..........4½

14
A
B
C
D
1
2
3
4
5
26
13
A354
A36
A27
A3090
M27
M3
M271
A3057
A33
A35
A337
A36
A326
A336
A338
A31
A347
A3060
A3049
A3040
A326
B3078
B3080
B3079
B3081
B3072
B3347
B3073
B3063
B3058
B3055
B3056
B3054
B3055
B3332
B3399
B3401
Wick
Downton
Redlynch
Morgan's Vale
Woodfalls
Lover
Newtown
Newton
Melchet Court
Newhouse
Awbridge
Earls
Abbotswood
Ampfield
Romsey
Sherfield English
East Wellow
West Wellow
North Baddesley
Chandler's Ford
Chilworth
Broadlands
Toothill
Lee
Rownhams
Nursling
Bassett
Upton
Hamptworth
Landford
Plaitford
Canada
Nomansland
Bramshaw
Newbridge
Ower
Paulton's Park
Calmore
Testwood
Copythorne
Totton
Winsor
Cadnam
Brook
Fritham
Millbrook
Shirley
Freemantle
SOUTHAMPTON
Eling
Toll
Hounsdown
Netley Marsh
Bartley
Minstead
Woodlands
Colbury
Ashurst
Lyndhurst Rd. Sta.
Pooksgreen
Marchwood
Stoney Cross
Furzey
Newtown
Emery Down
Lyndhurst
Bank
New Forest Museum & Information Centre
Dibden
Hythe
Dibden Purlieu
Beaulieu
Beaulieu Rd. Sta.
Beaulieu Heath
Hardley
Holbury
Hill Top
Blackfield
National Motor Museum
Abbey
Beaulieu
Buckler's Hard Maritime Museum
Exbury
Bucklers Hard
St Leonards Grange
East Boldre
Balmerlawn
Brockenhurst
Setley
Beaulieu Heath
Battramsley
Pilley
Norleywood
East End
Portmore
Walhampton
Lymington Pier Sta.
LYMINGTON
Boldre
Spinners
Sway
Wootton
Tiptoe
Bashley
New Milton
Hordle
Ashley
Everton
Lower Pennington
Downton
Lymore
Keyhaven
Milford on Sea
Hurst
Fort Victoria
Sconce Point
Yarmouth
Cranmore
Newtown
Shalfleet
Ningwood
Newbridge
Norton
Norton Green
Thorley
Thorley Street
Wellow
Freshwater
Totland
Colwell Bay
Totland Bay
Needles Pleasure Park
Alum Bay
Easton
Freshwater Bay
The Needles
The Needles Old Battery (NT)
Compton Bay
Brook Down
Brook
Shalcombe
Brighstone Forest
Mottistone
Brighstone
Limerstone
The Undercliff
Brighstone Bay
Atherfield
Newtown Bay
½hr
Christchurch Bay
Hengistbury Head
Barton on Sea
Highcliffe
Hinton
Hinton Admiral
Mudeford
Christchurch
Tumuli
CHRISTCHURCH
Purewell
Wick
Southbourne
Pokesdown
Boscombe
Russell-Cotes Art Gallery & Museum
BOURNEMOUTH
Branksome Park
Canford Cliffs
Poole Bay
The Foreland or Handfast Point
Burton
Winkton
Sopley
Neacroft
Bransgore
Macpenny's
Shirley
Thorney Hill
Ripley
Avon
Bisterne
Kingston
Crow
Ringwood
Burley Street
Burley
Bisterne Close
Picket Post
Poulner
Linford
Moyles Court
Linwood
Ellingham
Blashford
THE NEW FOREST
Bolderwood
Ibsley
South Gorley
North Gorley
Hungerford
Frogham
Blissford
Stuckton
Godshill
Fordingbridge
Sandleheath
Ashford
Bickton
Alderholt
Daggons
Lower Burgate
Upper Burgate
Deadman Hill
Hale
Woodgreen
Breamore
Upper Street
North Charford
Whitsbury
Rockbourne
Rockbourne Roman Villa
Rockbourne Down
Tidpit
Martin
Damerham
Cranborne
Edmondsham House
Edmondsham
Cranborne Common
Sutton Holms
Romford
Harbridge
Verwood
Ringwood Forest
Whitmore
Horton Common
Three Legged Cross
Moors Valley Railway
Moors Valley
Ashley Heath
St Ives
St Leonards
Highbury
Holt Heath
St Moors
Avon Heath
Ferndown
Trickett's Cross
Stapehill
Knoll Gardens
Hampreston
Ferndown Common
Dudsbury
Parley Cross
West Parley
Bournemouth International
Hurn
Alice in Wonderland Maze
Holdenhurst
Kinson
Winton
Moordown
Avon
Breamore
Wick Down
0
2
4
6
8
10 miles
0
2
4
6
8
10 km
hours
Cherbourg.................2¼-4¼ (5¾)
Guernsey...............................2½
Jersey.....................................3¾
St Malo (Summer Only)..........4½

D
E
F
G
1
2
3
4
5
28
16
HAMPSHIRE
WEST SUSSEX
Owslebury
Fisher's Pond
Crowdhill
Bishopstoke
Fair Oak
Marwell Zoo
Upham
Lower Upham
Corhampton Down
Corhampton
Dean
Exton
West Meon
Warnford
A32
Meonstoke
Droxford
Brockbridge
Chidden
Clanfield
Langrish
Stroud
Petersfield
A272
Rogate
Weston
Ramsdean
Butser Hill
270
War Down
Queen Elizabeth
Nursted
Buriton
West Harting
South Harting
East Harting
Elsted
Treyford
Uppark (NT)
North Marden
Compton
Up Marden
West Marden
East Marden
Chalton
Newtown
Horton Heath
Wintershill
Bishop's Waltham
Swanmore
Durley
Hillpound
Long Common
Waltham Chase
Shirrell Heath
Soberton
Soberton Heath
Hoe Gate
Hambledon
Catherington
Anthill Common
Horndean
Blendworth
Finchdean
Forestside
Curdridge
Shedfield
Botley
A334
A3051
Hedge End
Manor Farm
Curbridge
Burridge
Wickham
Hundred Acres
Newtown
Worlds End
Denmead
Lovedean
Cowplain
Forest of Bere
Meon Valley
WATERLOOVILLE
A3(M)
Red Hill
Rowland's Castle
Walderton
Stoughton
Kingley Vale
Stansted Park
Bursledon
Swanwick
Lower Swanwick
Hound
Sarisbury
Park Gate
Whiteley
M27
Titchfield Abbey
Funtley
North Boarhunt
Boarhunt
Southwick
Ports Down
Purbrook
Bedhampton
HAVANT
Denvilles
New Brighton
Westbourne
Funtington
Woodmancote
East Ashling
West Ashling
West Stoke
Woodend
Locks Heath
Warsash
Hamble-le-Rice
Titchfield
FAREHAM
Wallington
A27
Portchester
Port Solent
Wymering
Cosham
Horsea Island
Drayton
Langstone
Emsworth
Hermitage
Hambrook
Southbourne
Nutbourne
A259
Broadbridge
Fishbourne
Bosham
Chidham
Meon
Fawley
Calshot
Stubbington
Hill Head
Lee-on-the-Solent
Bridgemary
Rowner
Brockhurst
Hardway
PORTSMOUTH
Portsmouth Harbour
Whale Island
M275
Hilsea
North End
A288
A2030
Portsea Island
Fratton
Portsea
Historic Dockyard
Langstone Harbour
A3023
Northney
North Hayling
Thorney Island
West Thorney
Stoke
Hayling Island
West Town
South Hayling
Eastoke
Hayling Bay
Chichester Harbour
West Itchenor
B2179
West Wittering
East Wittering
Earnley
Birdham
Highleigh
Somerley
Bracklesham Bay
GOSPORT
Alverstoke
Stokes Bay
Gilkicker Point
Southsea
Eastney
PORTSMOUTH
1hr
THE SOLENT
Cowes Roads
Cowes
East Cowes
Gurnard
Osborne
Osborne Bay
Northwood
Whippingham
A3021
Fishbourne
Quarr Hill
½ hr
Ryde Roads
RYDE
Nettlestone Point
Seaview
Nettlestone
Binstead
Wootton Bridge
A3054
A3020
Parkhurst
Parkhurst Forest
Wootton Common
Havenstreet
Haylands
Isle of Wight Steam Rly
Flamingo Park
NEWPORT
Hunny Hill
Gunville
Staplers
Robin Hill
East Ashey
St Helens
Bembridge Point
Bembridge
Foreland
A3055
B3330
Windmill (NT)
Nunwell
Brading
Downend
Arreton
Carisbrooke Castle & Mus
Roman Villa
Hillway
Whitecliff Bay
B3395
Isle of Wight Zoo
Yaverland
Culver Cliff
Geology Mus
Gatcombe
Blackwater
Merstone
Newchurch
Alverstone
Isle of Wight (Sandown)
Sandown
Chillerton
Rookley
A3056
Branstone
A3020
Shorwell
ISLE OF WIGHT
Apse Heath
Sandown Bay
Kingston
Godshill
Sandford
Whiteley Bank
Shanklin
Shanklin Chine
Chale Green
Appuldurcombe
Roud
Wroxall
235
Luccombe Village
Dunnose
Stenbury Down
Pyle
Bierley
Whitwell
Bonchurch
Ventnor
B3399
B3327
Chale
Niton
St Lawrence
236
Blackgang
Blackgang Chine
Ventnor Botanic Gardens
The Undercliff
Rocken End
St. Catherine's Point
hours
Bilbao.........................35
Caen..............................6
Cherbourg.........2¾-5 (7)
Guernsey....................6½
Jersey..........................10
Le Havre......................5½
St. Malo...........8¾(10½)

16
A
B
C
D
29
15
1
2
3
4
5
WEST SUSSEX
Whitehill
Passfield
Bramshott
Haslemere
Educational Museum
Ramsnest Common
Alfold
Bucks Green
Rudgwick
Danger Zone
Conford
Shottermill
Hammer
Liphook
Camelsdale
Lythe Hill
Longmoor Camp
Linchmere
Fisherstreet
Loxwood
Ifold
The Haven
Slinfold
Liss Forest
Liss
Langley
Black Down
Northchapel
Plaistow
Buckman Corner
Roundstreet Common
Five Oaks
Itchingfield
East Liss
Rake
Fernhurst
Newpound Common
Barns Green
Lurgashall
Kirdford
Fishers Farm Park
Milland
Balls Cross
Wisborough Green
Billingshurst
Hill Brow
Redford
Lickfold
Henley
Petersfield
Rogate
Robins
Strood Green
Coneyhurst
Chithurst
Woolbeding
Lodsworth
Upperton
Gunter's Bridge
Adversane
Burdocks
West Harting
Trotton
Iping
Stedham
Easebourne
River
Petworth House (NT)
Coolham
Tillington
Petworth
North Heath
Broadford Bridge
Nyewood
Midhurst
Cowdray House (Ruins)
South Harting
East Harting
South Ambersham
Selham
Byworth
Egdean
Codmore Hill
Gay Street
West Lavington
Coultershaw Bridge
Stopham
Elsted
Fittleworth
Nutbourne
West Chiltington
Treyford
Didling
Bepton
Coates
Pulborough
Uppark (NT)
Heyshott
Graffham
Pulborough Brooks R.S.P.B. Nature Reserve
Hardham
Wiggonholt
West Chiltington Common
Warminghurst
Thakeham
Cocking
Linch Down
Duncton
Coldwaltham
North Marden
East Lavington
Watersfield
Abingworth
East Marden
Barlavington
Greatham
Rackham
Storrington
Chilgrove
Sutton
Cootham
Up Marden
Bignor
Parham
West Marden
Compton
Bury
Singleton
Charlton
East Dean
Upwaltham
West Burton
Amberley
Sullington
Kithurst Hill
Washington
Forestside
West Dean
Weald & Downland Open Air Museum
Houghton
Amberley Museum
Amberley Sta.
Stansted Park
Goodwood
Slindon Estate (NT)
Walderton
Stoughton
Bow Hill
Madehurst
North Stoke
SOUTH
Kingley Vale
Halnaker Hill
Dale Park
South Stoke
Harrow Hill
North End
Findon
Goodwood House
Eartham
Arundel Park
Burpham
Woodend
Mid Lavant
Slindon
St. Nicholas
Wildfowl Trust
Funtington
West Stoke
Halnaker
Priory
Wepham
Woodmancote
East Ashling
East Lavant
Strettington
Denmans
Cathedral
Arundel
Warningcamp
Clapham
High Salvington
Westbourne
West Ashling
Boxgrove
Fontwell
Crossbush
Patching
Emsworth
Hambrook
Westhampnett
Tangmere
Walberton
Binsted
Poling
Hammerpot
CHICHESTER
Norton
Fontwell Park
Priory
Durrington
Nutbourne
Aldingbourne
Nyton
Eastergate
Tortington
Poling Corner
Broadbridge
Oving
Westergate
Lyminster
Body Shop Visitor Cen.
Highdown Hill (NT)
Fishbourne
Tangmere Military Aviation Museum
Woodgate
Angmering
West Tarring
Chidham
Bosham
Roman Palace
Apuldram
Barnham
Yapton
Ford
Wick
Burndell
Merston
Berri Court
Toddington
Goring-by-Sea
West Thorney
Donnington
Runcton
Colworth
Climping
East Preston
Ferring
North Mundham
Shripney
Bilsham
Rustington
Kingston
Hunston
Flansham
Ancton
Harbour Park Amusements
Littlehampton
West Itchenor
South Mundham
North Bersted
Shipton Green
Birdham
South Bersted
Middleton-on-Sea
Street End
Felpham
West Wittering
Highleigh
Windmill
Butlins Family Entertainment Resort, Bognor Regis
Somerley
Nyetimber
Aldwick
BOGNOR REGIS
Sidlesham
East Wittering
Earnley
Pagham
Norton
Church Norton
Bracklesham Bay
Selsey
Selsey Bill
A3
A27
A29
A259
A272
A280
A283
A284
A285
A286
A2032
B2070
B2131
B2133
B2138
B2139
B2140
B2141
B2145
B2146
B2147
B2166
B2178
B2179
B2187
B2198
B2201
B2132
B2233
B3004
Stane Street
280
255
238

17
D
E
F
G
1
2
3
4
5
A264
Buchan
Holmbush
Colgate
Roffey
Pease Pottage
St Leonard's Forest
High Beeches
Selsfield Common
Millennium Seed Bank
Wakehurst Place (NT)
West Hoathly
Sharpthorne
Weir Wood Resr
Spring Hill Wildfowl Park
Kidbrooke Park
Coleman's Hatch
Hartfield
Crowborough
Friar's Gate
Steel Cross
Jarvis Brook
30
Ashdown Forest
Balcombe
Highbrook
Handcross
Nymans (NT)
Ashfold Crossways
Horsted Keynes Sta.
Horsted Keynes
Chelwood Gate
Duddleswell
Poundgate
A26
Denne Park
Mannings Heath
Monk's Gate
Lower Beeding
Staplefield
Slaugham
Ardingly
Ardingly Resr
Danehill
Nutley
Heron's Ghyll
Brook Street
Borde Hill
Paxhill Park
A275
Fairwarp
High Hurstwood
Nuthurst
Warninglid
Leonardslee
Lindfield
Bluebell Railway
Sheffield Green
Sheffield Park (NT)
Sheffield Park Sta.
Maresfield
Five Ash Down
Copsale
Crabtree
Whitemans Green
Cuckfield
Haywards Heath
A272
Pound Green
Maplehurst
Bolney
Ansty
A273
Scayne's Hill
Fletching
Buxted
Piltdown
Ringles Cross
Cowfold
Sandrocks
North Chailey
Newick
Uckfield
Blackboys
New Town
Framfield
A281
Wineham
Hickstead
A2300
Twineham
Wivelsfield Sta.
Wivelsfield
Beeches Farm
West Grinstead
Partridge Green
A23
Burgess Hill
Wivelsfield Green
Chailey
Ridgewood
South Street
Ditchling Common
Newick Park
Horsted Place
Little Horsted
Sayers Common
Albourne
Plumpton Green
South Common
Spithurst
Bines Green
Henfield
Hurstpierpoint
Isfield
Halland
Blackstone
Keymer
Hassocks
Plumpton
Bentley Motor Museum
EAST
Shortgate
Ashurst
Streat
Barcombe Cross
Woodmancote
Muddleswood
Ditchling
East Chiltington
Barcombe
Wildfowl Park
New Hall
Oreham Common
Clayton
Westmeston
Cookbridge
Whitesmith
Laughton
Danny
Pyecombe
(NT)
248
Ditchling Beacon
Plumpton
SUSSEX
Holme's Hill
Small Dole
Poynings
Offham
Hamsey
Ringmer
A2037
Fulking
Mount Harry
South Malling
Cliffe Hill
Glyndebourne
Steyning
Edburton
Lewes 1264
Lewes
Bramber
Upper Beeding
18
St Mary's
DOWNS
Stanmer
Mount Caburn
Glynde Place
Upper
The Dicker
Botolphs
Patcham
A27
Glynde
Chalvington
Coldean
Falmer
Mus. of Sussex Archaeology
Middle Farm & English Farm Cider Centre
Coombes
Foredown Tower
Hollingbury
A270
Kingston near Lewes
Beddingham
British Engineerium
Iford
Moulsecoomb
West Firle
Berwick Sta.
A283
Kingston by Sea
Hangleton
Preston
Newmarket Hill
Rodmell
Firle Place
Charleston Farmhouse
Selmeston
Lancing
Bevendean
Preston Manor
Portslade
West Blatchington
Woodingdean
Monk's House
Firle Beacon
Alciston
Shoreham
Marlipins
Southwick
Royal Pavilion
Brighton
Southease
Berwick
A259
Shoreham-by-Sea
Portslade-by-Sea
HOVE
Kemp Town
Tarring Neville
Drusillas Park
South Lancing
BRIGHTON
Ovingdean
Alfriston
WORTHING
Rottingdean
Telscombe
South Heighton
Old Clergy House
BRIGHTON & HOVE
Palace Pier
Volks Electric Rly
Grange Art Gal. & Mus.
Piddinghoe
Paradise Family Leisure Park
Denton
Saltdean
Newhaven
Litlington
Telscombe Cliffs
Bishopstone
Charleston Manor
Peacehaven
East Blatchington
Westdean
Seaford
Seven Sisters
East
hours
Dieppe (Summer Only)..................2
0
2
4
6
8
10 miles
0
2
4
6
8
10 km

18
A
B
C
D
1
2
3
4
5
31
17
Hartfield
Friar's Gate
Boarshead
Crowborough
Steel Cross
Mark Cross
Town Row
Rotherfield
Jarvis Brook
Poundgate
Heron's Ghyll
Fairwarp
High Hurstwood
Five Ash Down
Buxted
Ringles Cross
Uckfield
New Town
Framfield
Blackboys
Stonebridge
Pound Green
Hadlow Down
Five Ashes
Butcher's Cross
Mayfield
Coggins Mill
Tidebrook
Beech Hill
Sparrow's Green
Cousley Wood
Durgates
Wadhurst
Three Leg Cross
Shover's Green
Ticehurst
Stonegate
Stonegate Sta.
Bewl Water
Bedgebury National Pinetum
Bedgebury Forest
Flimwell
Gill's Green
Benenden
Rolvenden
Iden Green
Hawkhurst
Great Maytham
Four Throws
High Street
Boarzell
Swiftsden
The Moor
Cooper's Corner
Sandhurst
Linkhill
Hurst Green
Silver Hill
Bodiam
Bodiam (NT)
Kent & East Sussex Rly
Great Dixter
Northiam
Ewhurst
Haremere Hall
Etchingham
Witherenden Hill
Witherhurst
Burwash
Bateman's (NT)
Burwash Weald
Burwash Common
Salehurst
Robertsbridge
Darvell
Oxley's Green
Staplecross
Millcorner
Horns Cross
Broad Oak
Cross in Hand
Heathfield
Chapel Cross
Cade Street
Punnett's Town
Dudwell
Brightling
Darwell Resr.
John's Cross
Vinehall Street
Cripp's Corner
Mountfield
Broad Oak
Brede
Sedlescombe
Sedlescombe Street
Cackle Street
Possingworth Park
Little London
Waldron
Maynard's Green
Three Cups Corner
Dallington
Netherfield
Whatlington
Vine's Cross
Warbleton
Rushlake Green
Foxhunt Green
Horam
Halland
Bentley Motor Museum
East Hoathly
Shortgate
Penhurst
Bodle Street Green
Buckley
Yesterday's World
Battle
Battle Abbey
Hastings 1066
Telham
Beauport Park
Kent Street
Westfield
The Moor
Ponts Green
Ashburnham Place
Burlow
Foul Mile
Cowbeech
Catsfield
Henley's Down
Crowhurst
Baldslow
Hollington
St Helen's
Chiddingly
Muddles Green
Whitesmith
Laughton
Holme's Hill
Golden Cross
Lealands
Stunts Green
Windmill Hill
Lower Street
Ninfield
Hellingly
Herstmonceux
Herstmonceux Castle
Lower Horsebridge
Lower Dicker
Upper Dicker
Magham Down
Boreham Street
Hooe Common
Hooe
Lunsford's Cross
Sidley
Bulverhythe
Silverhill
Hastings Fisherman's Museum
Amusement Park
St Leonards
HASTINGS
Glynde Place
Glynde
Ripe
Chalvington
The Dicker
Upper Horsebridge
Hailsham
Michelham Priory
Middle Farm & English Farm Cider Centre
Arlington Resr
Berwick Sta.
Arlington
Wartling
Waller's Haven
Little Common
Cooden
BEXHILL
Pevensey Levels
Norman's Bay
West Firle
Firle Place
Charleston Farmhouse
Selmeston
Alciston
Berwick
Polegate
Hankham
Westham
Pevensey
Pevensey Bay
Wilmington
Priory
Folkington
Drusillas Park
Alfriston
Stone Cross
Wannock
Friday Street
Willingdon
Langney
Old Clergy House
Filching Manor
Lullington Heath
Litlington
Jevington
Hampden Park
Sovereign Harbour
Langney Point
Fort Fun
Charleston Manor
201
Willingdon Hill
Cuckmere
South Heighton
Paradise Family Leisure Park
Denton
Newhaven
Bishopstone
Seaford
Westdean
Seven Sisters
Friston
Eastbourne Pier & Glass Studio
EASTBOURNE
East Dean
Holywell
Birling Gap
Beachy Head
Glyndebourne
Ringmer
Wildfowl
Isfield
Maresfield
Framfield
Pevensey Bay
EAST SUSSEX
A22
A26
A267
A272
A265
A21
A268
A229
A2100
A28
A271
A295
A269
A2036
A2101
A27
A259
A2270
A2021
B2026
B2100
B2099
B2101
B2102
B2192
B2203
B2096
B2204
B2095
B2104
B2191
B2103
B2182
B2092
B2093
B2165
B2089
B2244
B2086
B2124
hours
Dieppe (Summer Only)..................2
0 2 4 6 8 10 miles
0 2 4 6 8 10 km

# CHANNEL TUNNEL MAPS

## Eurotunnel: Access from the UK

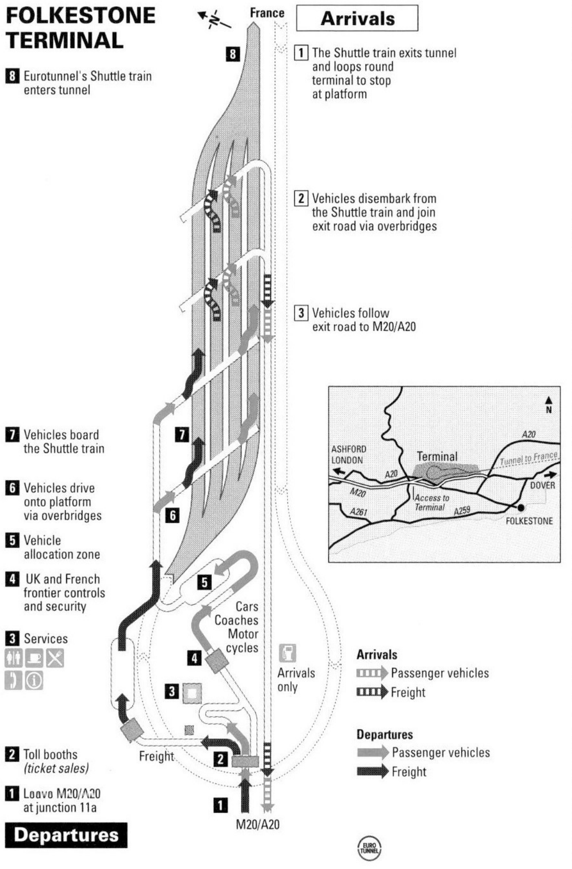


## Eurotunnel: Access from France

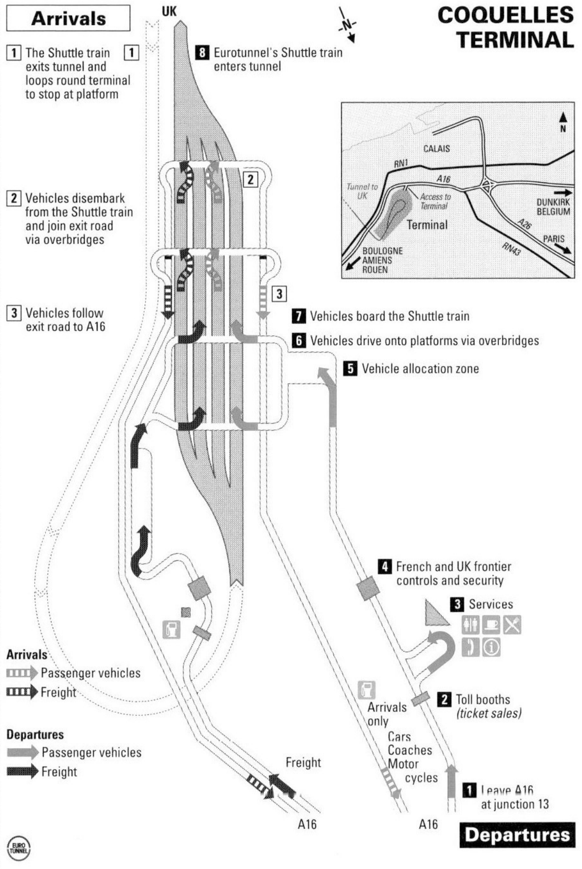

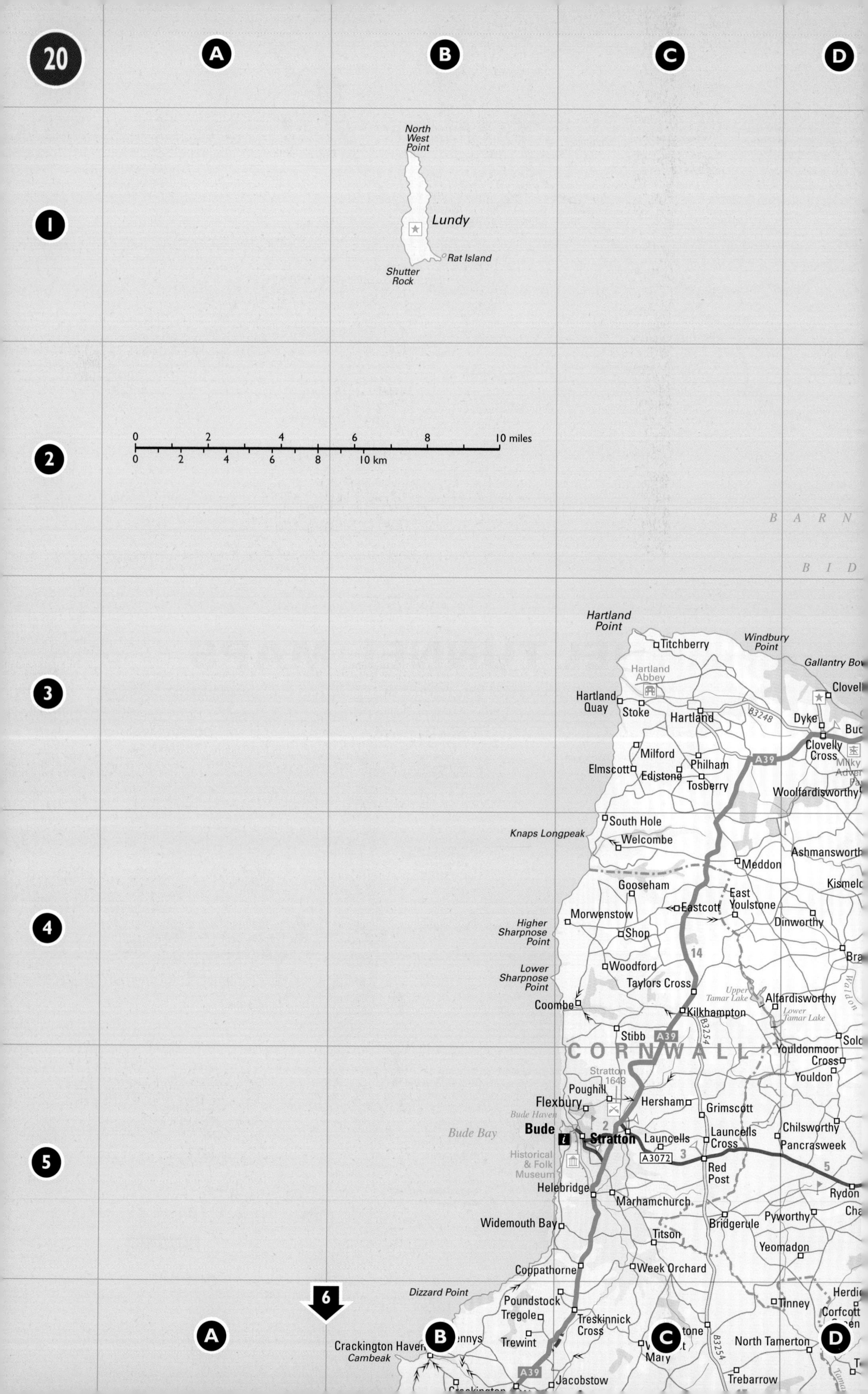
A
B
C
D
1
2
3
4
5
North West Point
Lundy
Rat Island
Shutter Rock
0 2 4 6 8 10 miles
0 2 4 6 8 10 km
B A R N
B I D
Hartland Point
Titchberry
Windbury Point
Gallantry Bo
Hartland Abbey
Clovell
Hartland Quay
Stoke
Hartland
B3248
Dyke
Buc
Clovelly Cross
Milford
Philham
A39
Elmscott
Edistone
Tosberry
Woolfardisworthy
South Hole
Knaps Longpeak
Welcombe
Ashmansworth
Meddon
Gooseham
Kismelo
East Youlstone
Eastcott
Morwenstow
Dinworthy
Higher Sharpnose Point
Shop
14
Bra
Woodford
Lower Sharpnose Point
Taylors Cross
Upper Tamar Lake
Alfardisworthy
Coombe
Kilkhampton
Lower Tamar Lake
B3254
Stibb
A39
Sold
CORNWALL
Youldonmoor Cross
Stratton 1643
Youldon
Poughill
Flexbury
Hersham
Grimscott
Bude Haven
Chilsworthy
Bude Bay
Bude
Stratton
Launcells
Launcells Cross
Pancrasweek
Historical & Folk Museum
A3072
3
Red Post
5
Helebridge
Rydon
Marhamchurch
Cha
Bridgerule
Pyworthy
Widemouth Bay
Titson
Yeomadon
Coppathorne
Week Orchard
Dizzard Point
Herdi
Poundstock
Tinney
Tregole
Corfcott
Treskinnick Cross
Trewint
North Tamerton
Crackington Haven
Cambeak
B3254
Trebarrow
A39
Jacobstow
6

D
E
F
G
The Valley of Rocks
Lynmouth
Cliff Rly
Lynton
Woody Bay
Heddon's Mouth
Trentishoe
Martinhoe
Hunter's Inn
Heale
Barbrook
Hillsford Bridge
Cheriton
Furze
Shallowford
Widmouth Head
Watermouth Castle
Combe Martin Bay
Ilfracombe
Hele
Berrynarbor
Bull Point
Lee Bay
Lee
Rockham Bay
Morte Point
Mortehoe
Slade
A361
A399
Combe Martin
Combe Martin Wildlife & Dinosaur Park
Sterridge
Chambercombe Manor
Mullacott Cross
Trimstone
Woolacombe
Morte Bay
B3343
A3123
Parracombe
Churchtown
Berry Down Cross
Kentisbury
Blackmoor Gate
Hoaroak Hill
West Down
Patchole
Kentisbury Ford
Challacombe Common
Pinkworthy Pond
Baggy Point
Pickwell
North Buckland
Putsborough
Bittadon
East Down
Arlington Beccott
Arlington
Challacombe
B3358
Croyde Bay
Croyde
Georgeham
B3230
Arlington Court (NT)
Milltown
Loxhore
Knightacott
Halsinger
Muddiford
Bratton Fleming
Leworthy
B3231
Knowle
Marwood
Marwood Hill
Shirwell Cross
Shirwell
Saunton
Pippacott
Kingsheanton
Span Head
Saunton Sands
Braunton
Heanton Punchardon
Prixford
Benton
Lydcott
Wrafton
A39
Stoke Rivers
Brayford
Toll
Ashford
Goodleigh
Braunton Burrows
Pilton
St. Anne's Chapel Heritage Centre
High Bray
Barnstaple
Northleigh
Gunn
North Heasley
Charles
Heasley Mill
Newport
The Neck
Bickington
Fremington
West Buckland
East Buckland
Yelland
Northam Burrows
Landkey
Appledore
Swimbridge Newland
Yarnacott
North Devon Maritime Mus.
Instow
Bickleton
Tawstock
Westward Ho!
St John's Chapel
Bishop's Tawton
Tapeley Park
Tapeley
Swimbridge
A386
Northam
Westleigh
Filleigh
A377
Burton Art Gallery
Eastleigh
Horwood
Newton Tracey
Cobbaton
Abbotsham
East-the-Water
Lower Lovacott
Herner
Bideford
Ensis
Hiscott
South Molton
Big Sheep
Woodtown
Alverdiscott
Chittlehampton
B3227
Gammaton Moor
Fishleigh Barton
Hudscott
Clapworthy
Fairy Cross
Ford
Yarnscombe
Umberleigh
Orns Cross
Littleham
Yeo Vale
Landcross
Atherington
Goldworthy
Langridgeford
Langridge
Warkleigh
Satterleigh
George Nympton
Alswear
Buckland Brewer
Huntshaw Cross
B3226
Parkham
Weare Giffard
Parkham Ash
Monkleigh
High Bullen
Chittlehamholt
Romansleigh
Great Torrington
Sherwood Green
High Bickington
Portsmouth Arms Sta.
King's Nympton
Melbury
Frithelstock Stone
Frithelstock
Dartington Crystal
St Giles in the Wood
Head Bridge
Taddiport
Rosemoor
Kingscott
Northcote Manor
East Putford
Cadbury Barton
Little Torrington
Roborough
Burrington
Kings Nympton Sta.
A388
Week
Langtree
Elstone
West Putford
Villavin
Colleton Mills
Beaford
B3217
DEVON
Stibb Cross
Chulmleigh
Bulkworthy
Riddlecombe
B3220
Peters Marland
Winswell
Ashreigney
Copy Lake
Cheldon
Abbots Bickington
B3096
Woollaton
Dolton
Chawleigh
Newton St Petrock
Merton
Heanton Satchville
Ashley
B3042
Milton Damerel
Huish
Hollacombe
Eggesford Barton
North Town
Dowland
Wembworthy
Forches Cross
Shebbear
Buckland Filleigh
Torridge
Thornbury
Petrockstow
Ash Barton
Iddesleigh
Winkleigh
Brushford
Coldridge
Nymet Rowland
Bradford
Meeth
Sheepwash
Taw Bridge
Cookbury
Black Torrington
Hele Bridge
Okement
Broadwood Kelly
Monkokehampton
Bondleigh
East Leigh
Down St Mary
Anvil Corner
Highampton
Hatherleigh
Zeal Monachorum
Dunsland Cross
Brandis Corner
A3072
Lydacott
Bassett's Cross
B3216
Graddon Moor
Honeychurch
North Tawton
Bow
Halwill Forest
Exbourne
Jacobstowe
B3219
Broadnymett
A3079
Halwill Junction
Shilstone
Sampford Courtenay
Nymet Tracey
Halwill
Beaworthy
Inwardleigh
Oak
Northlew
Belstone Corne
Itton
Ashbury
Upcott
Folly Gate
B3215
Quoditch
Taw Green
Spreyton
Okehampton
22
10
7

A
B
C
D
1
2
3
4
5
0 2 4 6 8 10 miles
0 2 4 6 8 10 km
Ugmore-by-Sea
Tusker Rock
Southerndown
St Brides Major
Pitcot
Llysworney
Cowbridge
Llanblethian
A48
Llandow
Wick
Llandough
Broughton
37
Llanmihangel
St Mary Church
Treguff
B4265
B4270
Marcross
Llanmaes
Flemingston
Eglwys-Br
Llantwit Major
Boverton
St Donats
Nash Point
Gileston
St Athan
West Aberthaw
Breakse
B R I S T O L C H A
Foreland Point
Countisbury Cove
Lynton & Lynmouth Cliff Rly
Lynmouth Bay
The Valley of Rocks
Woody Bay
Lynmouth
Countisbury
Lynton
Toll
Watersmeet Ho (NT)
Hunter's Inn
Barbrook
Hillsford Bridge
Brendon
Malmsmead
Oare
387
A39
Culbone Hill
Culbone
Porlock Weir
Porlock Bay
West Porlock
Bossington
Selworthy Beacon
308
Allerford
North Hill
Porlock
Selworthy
Minehead
Butlins Family Entertainment Resort
Dunster Sta.
Blue Anchor Bay
Tippacott
Cheriton
Furzehill
B3223
Brendon Common
South Common
Luccombe
Wootton Courtenay
Alcombe
Marsh Street
Dunster
Dunster Castle & Mill (NT)
Carhampton
Shallowford
Hoaroak Hill
E X M O O R
473
480
Challacombe Common
Pinkworthy Pond
Dry Hill
444
Dunkery Hill
Dunkery Beacon
519
Timberscombe
Withycombe
Bilbrook
Cleeve Abbey
A399
Challacombe
21
Dure Down
B3358
Codsend Moors
A396
Cutcombe
Wheddon Cross
Croydon Hill
Rodhuish
Shoulsbarrow Common
Barle
Simonsbath
B3223
EXMOOR
B3224
Exford
Luckwell Bridge
Lype Hill
423
Luxborough
Roadwater
Kingsbridge
Leworthy
Lydcott
Span Head
439
Kinsford Water
409
NATIONAL PARK
B R E N D O N H I L L S
Treborough
Long Holcombe
Withypool Common
Withypool
Winsford
Winsford Hill
Exton
Withiel Florey
Raleigh's Cross
High Bray
North Radworthy
Worth Hill
S O M E R
Charles
North Heasley
Heasley Mill
South Radworthy
Dane's Brook
Liscombe
Bridgetown
Brompton Regis
Clatworthy Reservoir
East Buckland
Molland Common
Hawkridge
Twitchen
317
Huish C
North Molton
A361
Molland
Dulverton
B3222
Wimbleball Lake
Haddon Hill
Bury
B3190
Upton
D E V O N
West Anstey
Battleton
Skilgate
South Molton
Bish Mill
B3227
East Anstey
Nightcott
Brushford
Chipstab
Quince Honey Farm
Oldways End
Exebridge
Morebath
Petton
Clapworthy
Bishop's Nympton
Shillingford
Satterleigh
George Nympton
Alswear
Crooked Oak
Ash Mill
Knowstone
Bampton
Clayhanger
B3226
Mariansleigh
Rose Ash
Oakfordbridge
Mole
Romansleigh
Rackenford Moor
Oakford
Huntsham
King's Nympton
Rowley
Meshaw
10
Creacombe
Stoodleigh
Cove
Hockworth
Head Bridge
Newhouse Moor
B3137
Rackenf
Stoodleigh Beacon
Cadbury Barton
Kings Nympton Sta.
Elstone
Week
Knightshayes Court (NT)
East Mere
Washfield
Uplowman
Pitt

23
38
24
11
D
E
F
G
I
2
3
4
5
Grangetown
Twyn-yr-odyn
St Nicholas
Leckwith
Wenvoe
St Lythans
Michaelston-le-Pit
Dinas Powys
St Andrews Major
St. Lythans Burial Chamber
Wales Millennium Centre
Cogan
PENARTH
Pleasure Steamers Waverley & Balmoral
Lower Penarth
Cosmeston
Lavernock
Lavernock Point
Palmerstown
Merthyr Dyfan
Colcot
Cadoxton
Sully
Swanbridge
Sully Island
Rhoose
Porthkerry
Porthkerry Park
Barry Island Pleasure Park
BARRY
Barry Island
Whitmore Bay
A4232
A4160
A4055
A4050
A4226
B4267
Clevedon
Clevedon Pier
Manor House
Clevedon Court (NT)
Kenn
Kingston Seymour
North End
Yatton
Middle Hope (NT)
Woodspring Priory
Sand Point
Icelton
Wick St Lawrence
Sand Bay
Kewstoke
Toll
Bourton
St Georges
Hewish
Puxton
Milton
Worle
West Wick
East Rolstone
NORTH SOMERSET
WESTON-SUPER-MARE
Steep Holm
Flat Holm
Weston Bay
B3440
A370
A371
A368
Locking
Sandford
Churchill
Banwell
Sidcot
Hutton
Uphill
Brean Down
Bleadon
Bleadon Hill
Christon
Loxton
Winscombe
Compton Bishop
Cross
Axbridge
Brean
Berrow Flats
Eastertown
Lympsham
Lower Weare
Weare
Biddisham
Tarnock
Badgworth
Sedgemoor
M5
A38
Berrow
Gore Sand
East Brent
Rooks Bridge
Brent Knoll Hillfort
Brent Knoll
Stone Allerton
Clewer
Edithmead
Chapel Allerton
West Stoughton
Burnham-on-Sea
B3140
Mark Causeway
Mark
Blackford
Wedmore
Stert Island
Highbridge
B3139
Watchfield
Westham
Heath House
Hinkley Pt
Stert Flats
Steart
Huntspill
Bason Bridge
River Bridge
Stolford
Lilstock
Shurton
Stockland Bristol
West Huntspill
East Huntspill
Cote
Watchet
Doniford
St Audries
East Quantoxhead
Kilton
Knighton
Burton
Kilve
Stogursey
Otterhampton
Stretcholt
Huntspill Level
B3141
Burtle
Westhay
Stringston
Williton
West Quantoxhead
Holford
QUANTOCK HILLS
Dodington
Coleridge Cottage
Combwich
Pawlett
Down End
Dunball
Puriton
Woolavington
Knowle Hall
Cossington
Coultings
Fiddington
Rodway
Cannington
Chilton Polden
Bawdrip
Edington
Catcott
Stawell
Shapwick
Sampford Brett
Bicknoller
Nether Stowey
Over Stowey
A39
Chilton Trinity
Vellow
Halsway Manor
A358
Monksilver
Stogumber
Four Forks
Charlinch
Wembdon
Chedzoy
Spaxton
BRIDGWATER
Sutton Mallet
Moorlinch
Greinton
Crowcombe
Quantock Forest
Hawkridge Res
Durleigh Res
Lower Aisholt
Admiral Blake Mus
Sedgemoor 1685
Flaxpool
Bagborough Hill
384
Barford Park
Enmore
Durleigh
Westonzoyland
Lower Vexford
Willett
West Bagborough
Goathurst
Merridge
Courtway
Huntworth
Woolmersdon
Northmoor Green or Moorland
Middlezoy
Greylake
A361
A372
North Petherton
Tolland
Lydeard St Lawrence
Cothelstone
Fyne Court (NT)
Broomfield
Thorngrove
Othery
Henley
Gaulden Manor
East Combe
Toulton
Thurloxton
Pitsford Hill
Tarr
B3224
Combe Florey
Cushuish
North Newton
Maunsel
Burrow Bridge
Pathe
High Ham
Langley Marsh
Bishop's Lydeard
Fulford
Kingston St Mary
Lyng
Aller
Low Ham
Ford
Fitzhead
Ash Priors
Hestercombe
Adsborough
Hedging
Athelney
Stathe
Wearne
Halse
West Monkton
Durston
West Lyng
Curload
VALE OF TAUNTON DEANE
Heathfield
Cheddon Fitzpaine
Monkton Heathfield
Creech Heathfield
Stoke St Gregory
Langport
Huish
Norton Fitzwarren
Staplegrove
A3259
Mare Green
West Curry Rivel
Milverton
B3227
Somerset County Mus
Bathpool
Creech St Michael
Oake
Hillfarrance
A3065
Ham
Knapp
North Curry
Sedge Moor
A378
Much Drayton
Priest's House
Bathealton
Bishop's Hull
TAUNTON
Ruishton
Henlade
Thornfalcon
Greenway
Chipley
Wilton
Langford Budville
Rumwell
Nynehead
B3187
Stoke St Mary
Swell
Trull
Bradford-on-Tone
A358
Wrantage
Fivehead
Thorne
Kittisford
Appley
Runnington
Orchard Portman
West Hatch
Hatch Court
Curry Mallet
Isle Abbotts
Hambridge
Kingsbury Episcopi
Thorne St Margaret
West Buckland
Taunton Deane
Thurlbear
Isle Brewers
Greenham
Wellington
Hatch Beauchamp
Beercrocombe
Holywell Lake
Rockwell Green
M5
Poundisford Park
Corfe
Westport
East Lambrook
Barrington Court (NT)
Blackmoor
Pitminster
Staple Fitzpaine
Bickenhall
West Lambrook
Sampford Arundel
Wrangway
Ford Street
Angersleigh
Blagdon Hill
Curland
Barrington
South Petherton
Burlescombe
Nicholashayne
Windmill Hill
Ashill
Stocklinch
Shepton Beauchamp
B3168
Luxhay Resr
Staple Hill
Horton
A303
B3170
MOUTH OF THE SEVERN
BRIDGWATER BAY

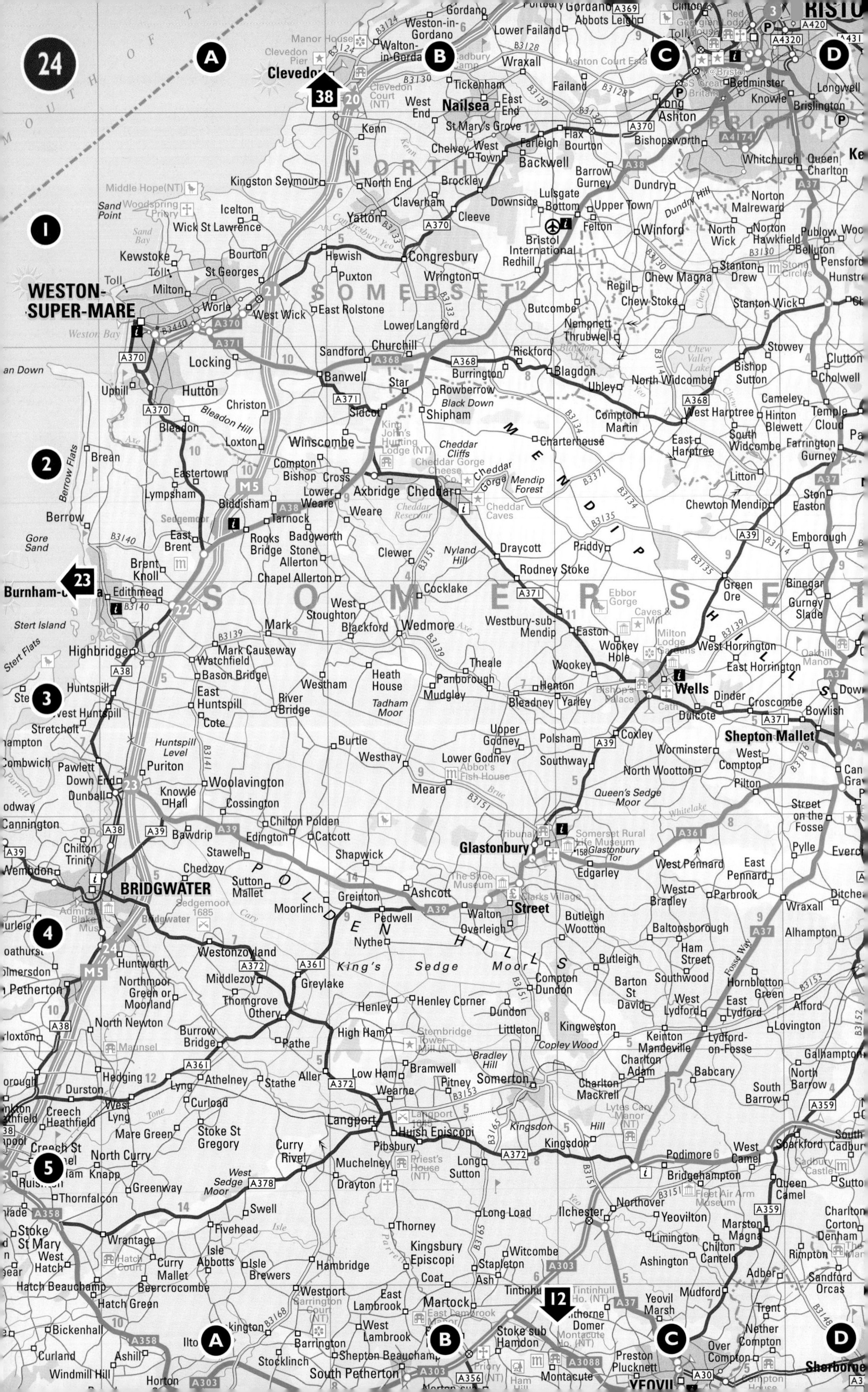
24
A
B
C
D
1
2
3
4
5
38
23
12
MOUTH OF THE
Clevedon
Clevedon Pier
Manor House
Walton-in-Gordano
Weston-in-Gordano
Gordano
Portbury
Gordano
Abbots Leigh
Clifton
Red Lodge
Georgian House
Toll
BRISTOL
A369
A420
A4320
A431
Cadbury Camp
Lower Failand
Wraxall
Ashton Court Estate
Failand
Bedminster
Long Ashton
Knowle
Brislington
Longwell
Clevedon Court (NT)
B3124
B3128
B3130
SS Great Britain
@Bristol
Tickenham
West End
Nailsea
East End
St Mary's Grove
Kenn
Chelvey
West Town
Farleigh
Flax Bourton
A370
Bishopsworth
A4174
Whitchurch
Queen Charlton
Backwell
Barrow Gurney
A38
Dundry
Kingston Seymour
North End
Brockley
Lulsgate Bottom
Upper Town
Dundry Hill
Norton Malreward
NORTH
Middle Hope (NT)
Sand Point
Woodspring Priory
Icelton
Wick St Lawrence
Claverham
Yatton
Cleeve
Downside
Bristol International
Felton
Winford
North Wick
Norton Hawkfield
Publow
Belluton
Pensford
Sand Bay
Kewstoke
Bourton
Hewish
Congresbury
Redhill
Toll
St Georges
Puxton
Wrington
Stanton Drew
Stone Circles
Toll
Milton
Worle
Regil
Chew Magna
WESTON-SUPER-MARE
West Wick
SOMERSET
Chew Stoke
Stanton Wick
Weston Bay
A370
B3440
A371
East Rolstone
Butcombe
Nempnett Thrubwell
Lower Langford
Blagdon Lake
Chew Valley Lake
Stowey
Clutton
Sandford
Churchill
Rickford
Bishop Sutton
Cholwell
Locking
A368
Burrington
Blagdon
Ubley
North Widcombe
Banwell
Star
Rowberrow
Cameley
Temple Cloud
Uphill
Hutton
A371
Sidcot
Black Down
Shipham
Compton Martin
West Harptree
Hinton Blewett
Christon
Bleadon Hill
Bleadon
King John's Hunting Lodge (NT)
MENDIP
South Widcombe
Farrington Gurney
Loxton
Winscombe
Cheddar Cliffs
Charterhouse
East Harptree
Brean
Berrow Flats
Compton Bishop
Cross
Cheddar Gorge Cheese Co.
Cheddar Gorge
Mendip Forest
Litton
Eastertown
Lower Weare
Axbridge
Cheddar
B3371
Ston Easton
Lympsham
Biddisham
Weare
Cheddar Reservoir
Cheddar Caves
B3134
Chewton Mendip
Berrow
Sedgemoor
Tarnock
B3135
Gore Sand
East Brent
Rooks Bridge
Badgworth
Stone Allerton
Clewer
Nyland Hill
Draycott
Priddy
Emborough
Brent Knoll
Chapel Allerton
Rodney Stoke
Burnham-on-Sea
Edithmead
Cocklake
Green Ore
Binegar
Gurney Slade
West Stoughton
Ebbor Gorge
Caves & Mill
Stert Island
Mark
Blackford
Wedmore
Westbury-sub-Mendip
Easton
Milton Lodge Gardens
West Horrington
Stert Flats
Highbridge
Mark Causeway
Watchfield
Wookey Hole
East Horrington
Oakhill Manor
Bason Bridge
Theale
Wookey
Wells
Huntspill
East Huntspill
Westham
Heath House
Panborough
Henton
Bishop's Palace
Dinder
Croscombe
West Huntspill
River Bridge
Mudgley
Bleadney
Yarley
Cath.
Dulcote
Bowlish
Stretcholt
Cote
Tadham Moor
Shepton Mallet
Burtle
Upper Godney
Polsham
Coxley
Worminster
West Compton
Pawlett
Huntspill Level
Westhay
Lower Godney
Southway
North Wootton
Pilton
Combwich
Puriton
Abbot's Fish House
Down End
Dunball
Woolavington
Meare
Knowle Hall
Cossington
Brue
Queen's Sedge Moor
Whitelake
Street on the Fosse
Cannington
Chilton Polden
Catcott
Bawdrip
Edington
Glastonbury
Somerset Rural Life Museum
Glastonbury Tor
Tribunal
Pylle
Evercreech
Chilton Trinity
Stawell
Shapwick
West Pennard
East Pennard
Wembdon
Chedzoy
Sutton Mallet
POLDEN HILLS
Edgarley
BRIDGWATER
Sedgemoor 1685
The Shoe Museum
Clarks Village
Parbrook
West Bradley
Ditcheat
Moorlinch
Greinton
Ashcott
Street
Butleigh Wootton
Admiral Blake Museum
Pedwell
Walton
Overleigh
Wraxall
Durleigh
Bridgwater
Cary
Baltonsbury
Alhampton
Nythe
Ham Street
Fosse Way
Huntworth
Westonzoyland
King's Sedge Moor
Butleigh
Hornblotton Green
Middlezoy
Greylake
Compton Dundon
Barton St David
Southwood
Northmoor Green or Moorland
Othery
Thorngrove
Henley
Henley Corner
Dundon
West Lydford
East Lydford
Alford
North Petherton
North Newton
Burrow Bridge
Pathe
High Ham
Stembridge Tower Mill (NT)
Littleton
Kingweston
Keinton Mandeville
Lydford-on-Fosse
Lovington
Maunsel
Copley Wood
Galhampton
Bradley Hill
Charlton Adam
Babcary
North Barrow
Hedging
Athelney
Stathe
Aller
Low Ham
Bramwell
Pitney
Somerton
Charlton Mackrell
South Barrow
Lyng
Curload
Wearne
Durston
Creech Heathfield
West Lyng
Tone
Langport
Lytes Cary Manor (NT)
Mare Green
Stoke St Gregory
Huish Episcopi
Kingsdon
Hill
Sparkford
South Cadbury
Creech St Michael
North Curry
Curry Rivel
Pibsbury
Long Sutton
Podimore
West Camel
Bridgehampton
Cadbury Castle
Ruishton
Knapp
Greenway
West Sedge Moor
Muchelney
Priest's House (NT)
Drayton
Queen Camel
Thornfalcon
Fleet Air Arm Museum
Northover
Yeovilton
Ilchester
Swell
Long Load
Charlton Horethorne
Stoke St Mary
Fivehead
Thorney
Isle
Wrantage
Isle Abbotts
Kingsbury Episcopi
Witcombe
Limington
Marston Magna
Corton Denham
West Hatch
Hatch Court
Curry Mallet
Isle Brewers
Hambridge
Stapleton
Ashington
Chilton Cantelo
Rimpton
Hatch Beauchamp
Beercrocombe
Coat
Ash
Adber
Sandford Orcas
Westport
Barrington Court (NT)
East Lambrook
Martock
Tintinhull
Tintinhull Ho. (NT)
Yeovil Marsh
Mudford
Trent
Hatch Green
West Lambrook
East Lambrook Manor
Stoke sub Hamdon
Montacute Ho. (NT)
Nether Compton
Bickenhall
Barrington
Over Compton
Curland
Ashill
Ilton
Stocklinch
Shepton Beauchamp
Preston Plucknett
Windmill Hill
Horton
South Petherton
Montacute
Compton House
YEOVIL
Sherborne
M5
A39
A361
A372
A378
A358
A303
A3088
A356
A37
A359
A30
B3139
B3140
B3141
B3151
B3153
B3165
B3168
B3148
B3114
B3133

25
D
E
F
G
D
E
F
G
1
2
3
4
5
40
13
26
Chippenham
Calne
Corsham
Melksham
Devizes
Trowbridge
Bradford-on-Avon
Bath
Westbury
Frome
Warminster
Radstock
Mere
Shaftesbury
Gillingham
Wincanton
Tisbury
Wilton
Bath and North East Somerset
Somerset
Wiltshire
Dorset
Danger Zone
Salisbury Plain
Marshfield
Wick
Warmley
Bridgeyate
Oldland
Bitton
Saltford
Kelston
Upton Cheyney
North Stoke
Lansdown
Langridge
Woolley
Charlcombe
Swainswick
Northend
Batheaston
Bathampton
Bathford
Box
Colerne
Thickwood
Slaughterford
Biddestone
Ditteridge
Hawthorn
Neston
Gastard
Notton
Lacock
Bowden Hill
Bewley Common
Atworth
Whitley
Shaw
Beanacre
Melksham Forest
Bowerhill
Seend Cleeve
Seend
Sells Green
Rowde
Roundway
St Edith's Marsh
Bromham
Netherstreet
Heddington
Stockley
Sandy Lane
Derry Hill
Studley
Bremhill
Tytherton Lucas
Quemerford
Calstone Wellington
Blackland
Potterne
Potterne Wick
Worton
Marston
Poulshot
Bulkington
Keevil
Great Hinton
Steeple Ashton
Ashton Common
Hilperton
Staverton
Semington
Holt
Bradford Leigh
Monkton Farleigh
South Wraxall
Claverton
Monkton Combe
Combe Down
Winsley
Limpley Stoke
Freshford
Westwood
Farleigh Hungerford
Trowle Common
Wingfield
Southwick
North Bradley
Yarnbrook
West Ashton
Heywood
Hawkeridge
Bratton
Edington
Erlestoke
Coulston
Great Cheverell
Little Cheverell
Littleton Panell
Easterton
West Lavington
Gore Cross
Westbury Leigh
Dilton Marsh
Berkley
Chapmanslade
Corsley
Corsley Heath
Upton Scudamore
Boreham
Bishopstrow
Norton Bavant
Heytesbury
Knook
Upton Lovell
Codford St Peter
Codford St Mary
Chitterne
Sutton Veny
Crockerton
Crockerton Green
Longbridge Deverill
Tytherington
Corton
Boyton
Sherrington
Stockton
Fisherton de la Mere
Wylye
Deptford
Hanging Langford
Brixton Deverill
Monkton Deverill
Kingston Deverill
Horningsham
Longleat
Maiden Bradley
Gare Hill
Witham Friary
Upton Noble
Batcombe
Westcombe
Wanstrow
Cloford
Leighton
Nunney
Trudoxhill
Tytherington
West Woodlands
Holwell
Chantry
Whatley
Mells
Great Elm
Buckland Dinham
Vobster
Coleford
Highbury
Holcombe
Leigh upon Mendip
Downhead
East Cranmore
Chesterblade
Kilmersdon
Charlton
Writhlington
Faulkland
Hemington
Hardington
Woolverton
Laverton
Rode
Beckington
Lullington
Rudge
Oldford
Tellisford
Norton St Philip
Shoscombe
Wellow
Peasedown St John
Camerton
Dunkerton
Carlingcott
Twinhoe
Hinton Charterhouse
Midford
Combe Hay
South Stoke
Odd Down
Englishcombe
Inglesbatch
Priston
Stanton Prior
Newton St Loe
Corston
Twerton
Weston
North Brewham
South Brewham
Kilmington
Kilmington Street
Norton Ferris
Stourhead
Stourton
White Sheet Hill
Keysley Down
Chicklade
Berwick St Leonard
Hindon
Fonthill Bishop
Fonthill Gifford
Chilmark
Teffont Magna
Teffont Evias
Ridge
Dinton
Fovant
Sutton Mandeville
Newtown
East Hatch
Swallowcliffe
Ansty
Fifield Bavant
Ebbesbourne Wake
Alvediston
Berwick St John
Bowerchalke
Woodminton
Donhead St Andrew
Donhead St Mary
Semley
Ludwell
Charlton
Cann
Cann Common
Melbury Abbas
Compton Abbas
Fontmell Magna
Ashmore
Tollard Royal
Deanland
Sixpenny Handley
Woodcutts
Woodyates
Pentridge
West Knoyle
The Green
East Knoyle
Barrow Street
Sedgehill
Huntingford
Zeals
Bourton
Penselwood
Stoney Stoke
Redlynch
Hardway
Bruton
Cole
Shepton Montague
Barrow
Charlton Musgrove
Leigh Common
Bayford
Stoke Trister
Silton
Milton on Stour
Cucklington
Peacemarsh
Wyke
Coppleridge
Motcombe
Madjeston
Buckhorn Weston
Kington Magna
West Stour
East Stour
Stour Row
Stour Provost
Fifehead Magdalen
Guy's Marsh
Todber
Margaret Marsh
Twyford
East Orchard
West Orchard
Sutton Waldron
Hinton St Mary
Marnhull
Stalbridge Weston
Henstridge
Henstridge Marsh
Henstridge Ash
Yenston
Templecombe
Stowell
Horsington
Abbas Combe
South Cheriton
North Cheriton
Lattiford
Holton
Maperton
Milborne Port
Purse Caundle
Bratton Seymour
Hadspen House
Blackmore Vale
Cranborne Chase
River Wylye
Kennet & Avon Canal
Pump Room and Roman Baths
The Oval
Abbey
Lansdown Hill 1643
No. 1, Royal Cres
Bath Spa Project
Bath Skyline (NT)
Claverton Manor
The Courts (NT)
Great Chalfield Manor (NT)
Westwood Manor (NT)
Iford Manor
Stoney Littleton Long Barrow
Corsham Court
Bowood
Lacock Abbey (NT)
Fox Talbot Museum (NT)
Bratton Camp & White Horse
Black Swan Guild
East Somerset Rly
Stavordale Priory
Wincanton
Pythouse
Old Wardour Castle
Fitz House
Philipps House (NT)
Gartell Light Rly
Stowell Hill
Roundway Down
Great Ridge
Warminster Down
Summer Down
West Lavington Down
Littleton Down
Cley Hill
Tytherington Hill
A4
A46
A420
A36
A367
A39
A431
A4175
A3062
A362
A366
A361
A363
A365
A350
A342
A3102
A3098
A303
A30
A357
A371
A359
A354
A360
B3109
B3107
B3098
B3099
B3090
B3092
B3095
B3414
B390
B3089
B3081
B3110
B3115
B3139
B3116
B3353
B3145
B3091
M4

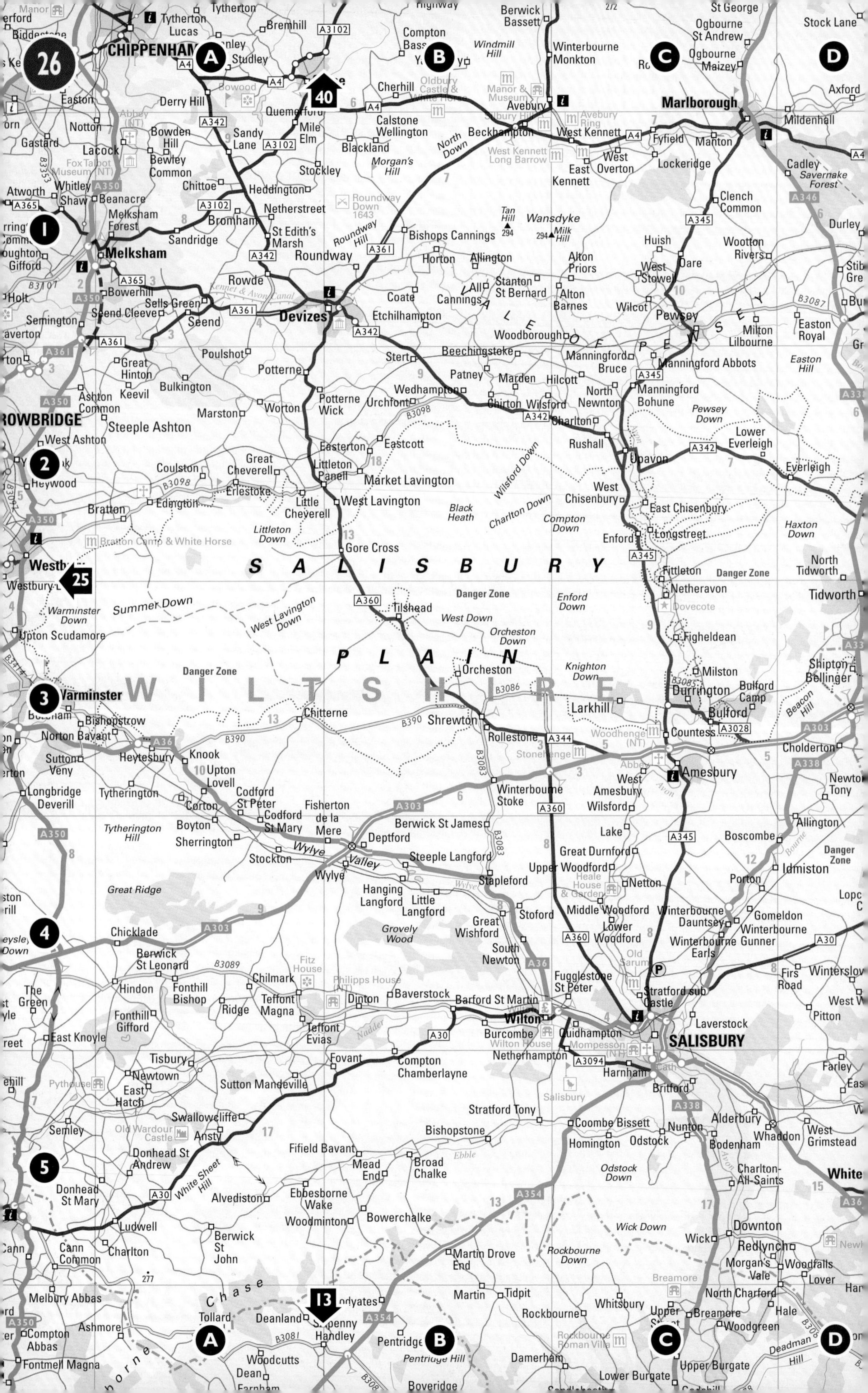
26
40
25
13
A
B
C
D
1
2
3
4
5
Manor
Biddestone
CHIPPENHAM
Tytherton
Tytherton Lucas
Bremhill
A3102
Compton Bassett
Windmill Hill
Berwick Bassett
Winterbourne Monkton
St George
Ogbourne St Andrew
Ogbourne Maizey
Stock Lane
Studley
Bowood
Derry Hill
Quemerford
Cherhill
Oldbury Castle & White Horse
Manor & Museum
Avebury
Avebury Ring
Marlborough
Axford
Mildenhall
Easton
Notton
Lacock
Gastard
Fox Talbot Museum (NT)
Abbey (NT)
Bowden Hill
Bewley Common
Sandy Lane
Mile Elm
Calstone Wellington
Blackland
Beckhampton
West Kennett
West Kennett Long Barrow
North Down
Fyfield
Manton
Cadley
Savernake Forest
Atworth
Whitley
Shaw
Beanacre
Chittoe
Heddington
Stockley
Morgan's Hill
East Kennett
West Overton
Lockeridge
Melksham Forest
Melksham
Bromham
Netherstreet
Roundway Down 1643
Roundway Hill
Clench Common
Durnley
Gifford
Sandridge
St Edith's Marsh
Roundway
Bishops Cannings
Tan Hill
Wansdyke
Milk Hill
Huish
Wootton Rivers
Horton
Allington
Alton Priors
West Stowell
Oare
Holt
Bowerhill
Rowde
Kennet & Avon Canal
Coate
All Cannings
Stanton St Bernard
Alton Barnes
Wilcot
Pewsey
Milton Lilbourne
Easton Royal
Semington
Sells Green
Seend Cleeve
Seend
Devizes
Etchilhampton
Woodborough
Vale of Pewsey
Poulshot
Stert
Beechingstoke
Manningford Bruce
Manningford Abbots
Easton Hill
Great Hinton
Keevil
Bulkington
Potterne
Patney
Marden
Hilcott
North Newnton
Manningford Bohune
Ashton Common
Marston
Worton
Potterne Wick
Urchfont
Wedhampton
Chirton
Wilsford
Charlton
Pewsey Down
TROWBRIDGE
Steeple Ashton
West Ashton
Easterton
Eastcott
Rushall
Upavon
Lower Everleigh
Everleigh
Heywood
Coulston
Great Cheverell
Littleton Panell
Market Lavington
Wilsford Down
West Chisenbury
Erlestoke
Edington
Little Cheverell
West Lavington
Black Heath
Charlton Down
Compton Down
East Chisenbury
Haxton Down
Bratton
Bratton Camp & White Horse
Littleton Down
Gore Cross
Enford
Longstreet
Westbury
SALISBURY PLAIN
North Tidworth
Fittleton
Danger Zone
Netheravon
Tidworth
Dovecote
Enford Down
Warminster Down
Summer Down
West Lavington Down
Tilshead
West Down
Orcheston Down
Upton Scudamore
Figheldean
Knighton Down
Orcheston
Milston
Shipton Bellinger
WILTSHIRE
Warminster
Durrington
Bulford Camp
Bulford
Beacon Hill
Larkhill
Chitterne
Shrewton
Bishopstrow
Norton Bavant
Rollestone
Woodhenge (NT)
Countess
Stonehenge
Cholderton
Heytesbury
Knook
Sutton Veny
Upton Lovell
Abbey
West Amesbury
Amesbury
Longbridge Deverill
Tytherington
Codford St Peter
Corton
Codford St Mary
Fisherton de la Mere
Winterbourne Stoke
Wilsford
Newton Tony
Tytherington Hill
Boyton
Sherrington
Berwick St James
Lake
Allington
Stockton
Wylye Valley
Deptford
Steeple Langford
Great Durnford
Boscombe
Wylye
Upper Woodford
Heale House & Garden
Netton
Porton
Idmiston
Great Ridge
Hanging Langford
Little Langford
Stapleford
Middle Woodford
Winterbourne Dauntsey
Gomeldon
Grovely Wood
Great Wishford
Stoford
Lower Woodford
Winterbourne Earls
Winterbourne Gunner
Chicklade
South Newton
Old Sarum
Berwick St Leonard
Fitz House
Hindon
Fonthill Bishop
Chilmark
Philipps House (NT)
Fugglestone St Peter
Firs Road
Winterslow
The Green
Fonthill Gifford
Ridge
Teffont Magna
Dinton
Baverstock
Barford St Martin
Stratford sub Castle
West Winterslow
Pitton
East Knoyle
Teffont Evias
Wilton
Burcombe
Wilton House
Quidhampton
Laverstock
Mompesson (NT)
SALISBURY
Tisbury
Fovant
Compton Chamberlayne
Netherhampton
Harnham
Farley
Pythouse
Newtown
East Hatch
Sutton Mandeville
Britford
Salisbury
Stratford Tony
Swallowcliffe
Semley
Old Wardour Castle
Ansty
Coombe Bissett
Nunton
Alderbury
Whaddon
West Grimstead
Bishopstone
Homington
Odstock
Bodenham
Donhead St Andrew
Fifield Bavant
Ebble
Mead End
Broad Chalke
White Sheet Hill
Odstock Down
Charlton-All-Saints
Donhead St Mary
Alvediston
Ebbesborne Wake
Woodminton
Bowerchalke
Wick Down
Ludwell
Cann
Cann Common
Charlton
Berwick St John
Martin Drove End
Rockbourne Down
Wick
Downton
Redlynch
Morgan's Vale
Woodfalls
Lover
Breamore
Melbury Abbas
Chase
Martin
Tidpit
Whitsbury
North Charford
Tollard
Deanland
Sixpenny Handley
Rockbourne
Upper Street
Breamore
Hale
Woodgreen
Ashmore
Compton Abbas
Pentridge
Pentridge Hill
Rockbourne Roman Villa
Damerham
Upper Burgate
Lower Burgate
Deadman Hill
Fontmell Magna
Woodcutts
Dean
Farnham
Boveridge
A4
A342
A3102
A350
A365
A361
A3098
A360
A345
A344
A3028
A303
A338
A36
A30
A3094
A354
B3098
B3086
B390
B3083
B3089
B3087
B3081
B3114
A346

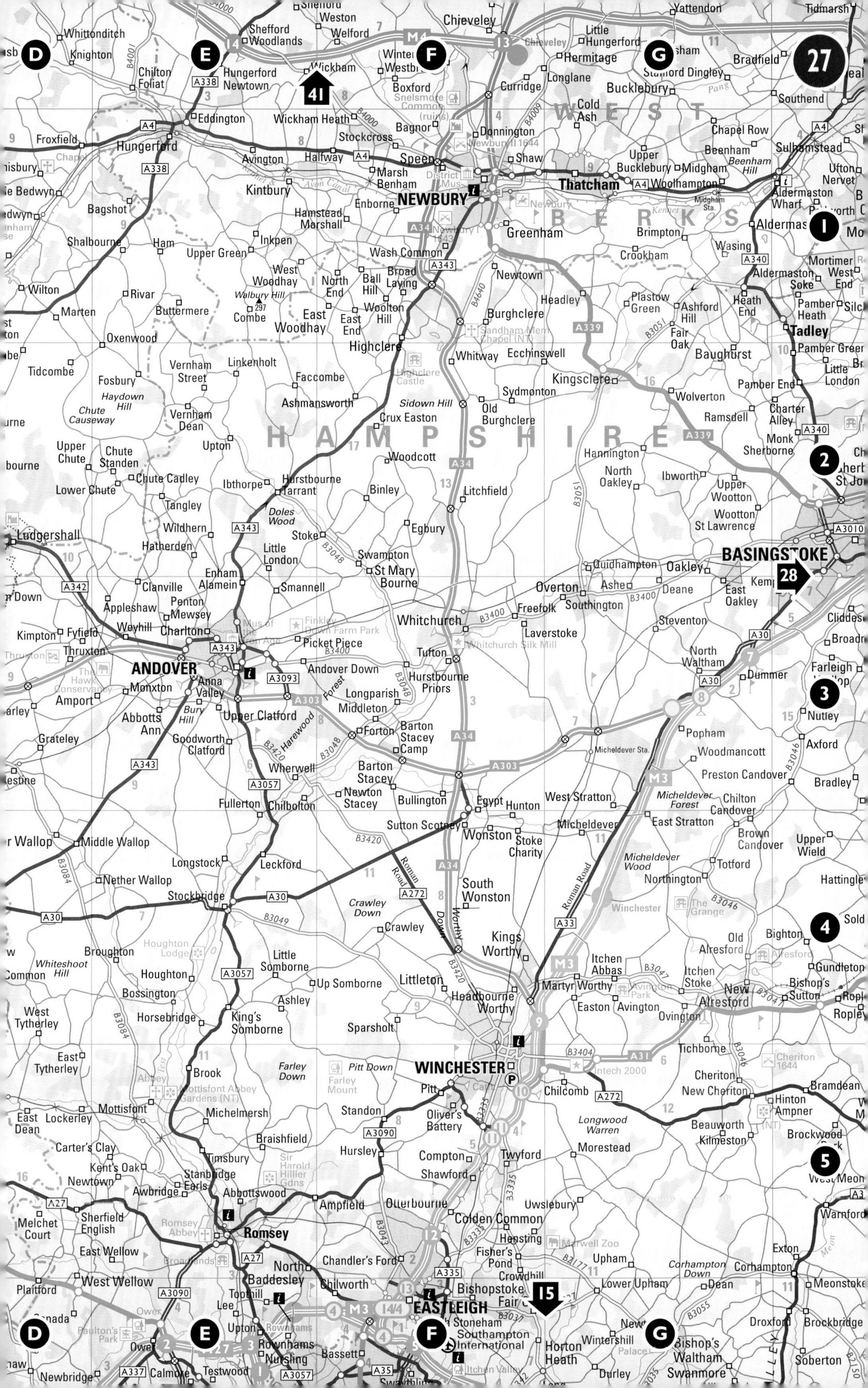

D
E
F
G
14
Shefford Woodlands
Weston
Welford
Chieveley
13
Yattendon
Tidmarsh
Whittonditch
Knighton
Chilton Foliat
B4001
Hungerford Newtown
A338
Wickham
41
Winterbourne
Westbrook
M4
Little Hungerford
Hermitage
Longlane
Curridge
Boxford
Snelsmore Common
Bradfield
Stanford Dingley
Bucklebury
Pang
Southend
WEST
Cold Ash
Eddington
Wickham Heath
B4000
Bagnor
Donnington
B4009
A4
Froxfield
Hungerford
Chapel
Stockcross
Newbury II 1644
Shaw
Chapel Row
Beenham
Beenham Hill
Sulhamstead
Avington
Halfway
Speen
Marsh Benham
District Mus
Upper Bucklebury
Midgham
Thatcham
Woolhampton
Midgham Sta.
Ufton Nervet
Aldermaston Wharf
Kintbury
Kennet & Avon Canal
Enborne
NEWBURY
Newbury
Bagshot
Shalbourne
Ham
Inkpen
Upper Green
Hamstead Marshall
A34
Newbury I 1643
Greenham
BERKS
Brimpton
Aldermaston
Wasing
Crookham
Wash Common
A343
A340
Mortimer West End
Aldermaston Soke
Wilton
Rivar
West Woodhay
Walbury Hill 297
Combe
Buttermere
Marten
North End
Ball Hill
Broad Laying
Woolton Hill
East Woodhay
East End
Newtown
Headley
Plastow Green
Ashford Hill
Heath End
Pamber Heath
Tadley
Oxenwood
Burghclere
B4640
Sandham Mem Chapel (NT)
A339
B3051
Fair Oak
Baughurst
Pamber Green
Little London
Tidcombe
Fosbury
Vernham Street
Linkenholt
Faccombe
Highclere
Highclere Castle
Whitway
Ecchinswell
Kingsclere
Pamber End
Haydown Hill
Chute Causeway
Vernham Dean
Ashmansworth
Sidown Hill
Sydmonton
Old Burghclere
Wolverton
Ramsdell
Charter Alley
Crux Easton
HAMPSHIRE
Upper Chute
Chute Standen
Upton
Monk Sherborne
Hannington
North Oakley
Ibworth
Upper Wootton
Wootton St Lawrence
Woodcott
Chute Cadley
Lower Chute
Ibthorpe
Hurstbourne Tarrant
Binley
Litchfield
Tangley
Wildhern
Doles Wood
Egbury
Ludgershall
Hatherden
A343
Little London
Stoke
B3048
Swampton
St Mary Bourne
Quidhampton
Oakley
BASINGSTOKE
28
Kempshott
Clanville
Enham Alamein
Smannell
Overton
Ashe
Deane
East Oakley
A342
Penton Mewsey
Appleshaw
Weyhill
Charlton
Finkley Down Farm Park
Whitchurch
B3400
Freefolk
Southington
Laverstoke
Steventon
Kimpton
Fyfield
Thruxton
Picket Piece
Whitchurch Silk Mill
A30
North Waltham
Dummer
Farleigh Wallop
ANDOVER
A3093
Andover Down
Tufton
Hurstbourne Priors
Monxton
Anna Valley
Amport
Abbotts Ann
Bury Hill
Upper Clatford
A303
Forest
Longparish
Middleton
Harewood
Forton
Barton Stacey
Camp
Popham
Nutley
Axford
Grateley
Goodworth Clatford
B3420
Wherwell
Barton Stacey
Micheldever Sta.
Woodmancott
Preston Candover
B3046
Bradley
A3057
Newton Stacey
Chilbolton
Fullerton
Bullington
Egypt
Hunton
West Stratton
Micheldever Forest
Chilton Candover
M3
Sutton Scotney
Wonston
Stoke Charity
Micheldever
East Stratton
Brown Candover
Upper Wield
Middle Wallop
B3084
Longstock
Leckford
Roman Road
Micheldever Wood
Northington
Totford
Nether Wallop
Stockbridge
A272
South Wonston
Hattingley
Worthy Down
Roman Road
Winchester
The Grange
Crawley Down
Crawley
B3049
A33
Sold
Bighton
Old Alresford
Alresford
Gundleton
Houghton Lodge
Broughton
Whiteshoot Hill
Little Somborne
Kings Worthy
Itchen Abbas
B3047
Avington Park
Itchen Stoke
Bishop's Sutton
Ropley
Houghton
Up Somborne
Littleton
Headbourne Worthy
Martyr Worthy
New Alresford
Bossington
Ashley
Easton
Avington
Ovington
West Tytherley
Horsebridge
King's Somborne
Sparsholt
East Tytherley
Tichborne
B3404
A31
Cheriton 1644
Intech 2000
Brook
Farley Down
Pitt Down
Farley Mount
WINCHESTER
Cheriton
New Cheriton
Bramdean
Mottisfont Abbey Gardens (NT)
Pitt
Chilcomb
Hinton Ampner
Mottisfont
Oliver's Battery
Longwood Warren
East Dean
Lockerley
Michelmersh
Standon
A3090
Beauworth
Kilmeston
Brockwood Park
Braishfield
Hursley
Twyford
Morestead
Carter's Clay
Timsbury
Sir Harold Hillier Gdns
Compton
Kent's Oak
Stanbridge Earls
Shawford
West Meon
Newtown
Awbridge
Abbotswood
Ampfield
Otterbourne
Uwslebury
Warnford
Melchet Court
Sherfield English
Romsey Abbey
Romsey
Colden Common
B3043
B3335
Hensting
Marwell Zoo
Exton
East Wellow
Broadlands
A27
North Baddesley
Chandler's Ford
Fisher's Pond
Upham
Corhampton Down
Corhampton
Meonstoke
West Wellow
Crowdhill
B2177
A335
Plaitford
A3090
Toothill
Chilworth
Bishopstoke
15
Lower Upham
Dean
Lee
Ower
Rownhams
M3
EASTLEIGH
Fair Oak
B3037
B3055
Droxford
Brockbridge
Canada
Paulton's Park
Upton
Rownhams
Nursling
North Stoneham
Southampton International
Newtown
Wintershill
Bishop's Waltham
Palace
Soberton
Newbridge
A337
Calmore
Testwood
A3057
Bassett
A35
Itchen Valley
Horton Heath
Durley
Swanmore
B2150

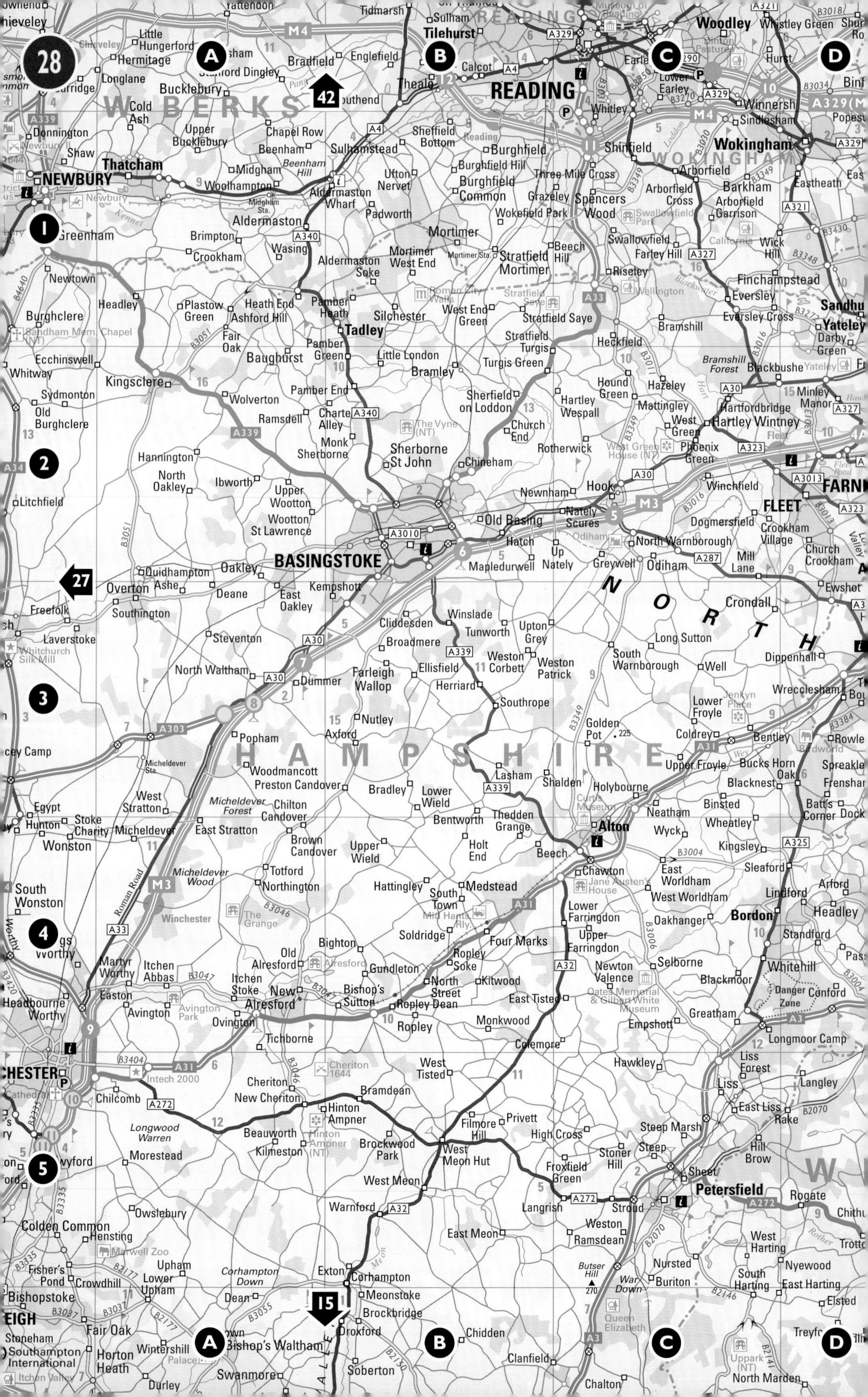
28
42
27
15
A
B
C
D
1
2
3
4
5
W BERKS
READING
WOKINGHAM
HAMPSHIRE
NORTH
M4
M3
A4
A30
A31
A32
A33
A34
A303
A339
A340
A3010
A329
A327
A321
A323
A3013
A287
A325
A3
A272
Yattendon
Chieveley
Little Hungerford
Hermitage
Longlane
Curridge
Bucklebury
Cold Ash
Upper Bucklebury
Donnington
Shaw
Thatcham
NEWBURY
Greenham
Midgham
Woolhampton
Midgham Sta.
Brimpton
Crookham
Wasing
Aldermaston
Aldermaston Wharf
Padworth
Bradfield
Englefield
Stanford Dingley
Southend
Chapel Row
Beenham
Beenham Hill
Sulhamstead
Ufton Nervet
Tidmarsh
Sulham
Tilehurst
Calcot
Theale
Sheffield Bottom
Burghfield
Burghfield Hill
Burghfield Common
Three Mile Cross
Grazeley
Spencers Wood
Wokefield Park
Mortimer
Mortimer West End
Mortimer Sta.
Stratfield Mortimer
Beech Hill
Shinfield
Whitley
Earley
Lower Earley
Woodley
Whistley Green
Hurst
Dinton Pastures
Winnersh
Sindlesham
Wokingham
Arborfield
Arborfield Cross
Barkham
Arborfield Garrison
Eastheath
California
Wick Hill
Finchampstead
Eversley
Eversley Cross
Yateley
Sandhurst
Darby Green
Swallowfield
Swallowfield Park
Farley Hill
Riseley
Wellington
Stratfield Saye
Stratfield Turgis
Turgis Green
Heckfield
Bramshill
Bramshill Forest
Blackbushe
Hazeley
Hound Green
Mattingley
Hartley Wespall
West Green
West Green House (NT)
Hartfordbridge
Hartley Wintney
Minley Manor
Phoenix Green
Rotherwick
Winchfield
FLEET
Crookham Village
Church Crookham
Dogmersfield
Hook
Newnham
Nately Scures
Old Basing
Hatch
Up Nately
Mapledurwell
Greywell
North Warnborough
Odiham
Mill Lane
Crondall
Ewshot
Newtown
Headley
Burghclere
Sandham Mem. Chapel (NT)
Ecchinswell
Whitway
Sydmonton
Old Burghclere
Kingsclere
Plastow Green
Heath End
Ashford Hill
Fair Oak
Baughurst
Pamber Heath
Tadley
Silchester
Pamber Green
Little London
Bramley
Aldermaston Soke
Roman City Walls
West End Green
Sherfield on Loddon
Church End
Pamber End
Wolverton
Ramsdell
Charter Alley
Monk Sherborne
The Vyne (NT)
Sherborne St John
Chineham
Hannington
North Oakley
Ibworth
Upper Wootton
Wootton St Lawrence
Litchfield
BASINGSTOKE
Quidhampton
Oakley
Overton
Ashe
Deane
East Oakley
Kempshott
Freefolk
Southington
Laverstoke
Whitchurch Silk Mill
Steventon
North Waltham
Dummer
Cliddesden
Broadmere
Farleigh Wallop
Winslade
Tunworth
Upton Grey
Ellisfield
Herriard
Weston Corbett
Weston Patrick
Southrope
South Warnborough
Long Sutton
Well
Dippenhall
Wrecclesham
Lower Froyle
Jenkyn Place
Coldrey
Bentley
Upper Froyle
Bucks Horn Oak
Golden Pot
225
Nutley
Axford
Popham
Micheldever Sta.
Woodmancott
Preston Candover
Bradley
Lower Wield
Lasham
Shalden
Holybourne
Curtis Museum
Alton
Neatham
Wyck
Binsted
Blacknest
Spreakley
Frensham
Batt's Corner
Dockenfield
Wheatley
Kingsley
Rowledge
Birdworld
Micheldever
Micheldever Forest
Chilton Candover
Brown Candover
West Stratton
East Stratton
Upper Wield
Bentworth
Thedden Grange
Holt End
Beech
Chawton
Jane Austen's House
East Worldham
West Worldham
Oakhanger
Sleaford
Lindford
Arford
Headley
Bordon
Standford
Egypt
Hunton
Stoke Charity
Wonston
South Wonston
Worthy
Kings Worthy
Roman Road
Micheldever Wood
Winchester
Totford
Northington
The Grange
Hattingley
Medstead
South Town
Mid Hants Rly.
Four Marks
Soldridge
Lower Farringdon
Upper Farringdon
Selborne
Newton Valence
Oates Memorial & Gilbert White Museum
Blackmoor
Whitehill
Danger Zone
Conford
Martyr Worthy
Itchen Abbas
Easton
Avington
Avington Park
Itchen Stoke
Bighton
Old Alresford
Alresford
Gundleton
Ropley
Ropley Soke
North Street
Kitwood
New Alresford
Bishop's Sutton
Ropley Dean
East Tisted
Ovington
Tichborne
Monkwood
Colemore
Empshott
Greatham
Longmoor Camp
Headbourne Worthy
WINCHESTER
Cathedral
Intech 2000
Cheriton 1644
Cheriton
New Cheriton
West Tisted
Hawkley
Liss Forest
Liss
Langley
East Liss
Rake
Chilcomb
Longwood Warren
Morestead
Bramdean
Hinton Ampner
Beauworth
Kilmeston
Hinton Ampner (NT)
Brockwood Park
Filmore Hill
Privett
High Cross
Steep Marsh
Steep
Stoner Hill
Hill Brow
Froxfield Green
West Meon Hut
West Meon
Sheet
Petersfield
Rogate
Twyford
Owslebury
Colden Common
Hensting
Marwell Zoo
Warnford
Langrish
Stroud
Weston
Ramsdean
East Meon
West Harting
Nyewood
Fisher's Pond
Crowdhill
Upham
Lower Upham
Corhampton Down
Exton
Corhampton
Butser Hill
270
War Down
Nursted
Buriton
South Harting
East Harting
Elsted
Bishopstoke
EASTLEIGH
Dean
Meonstoke
Brockbridge
Queen Elizabeth
Fair Oak
Stoneham
Southampton International
Horton Heath
Wintershill
Bishop's Waltham
Palace
Droxford
Chidden
Clanfield
Chalton
Uppark (NT)
North Marden
Treyford
Durley
Swanmore
Soberton
Itchen Valley

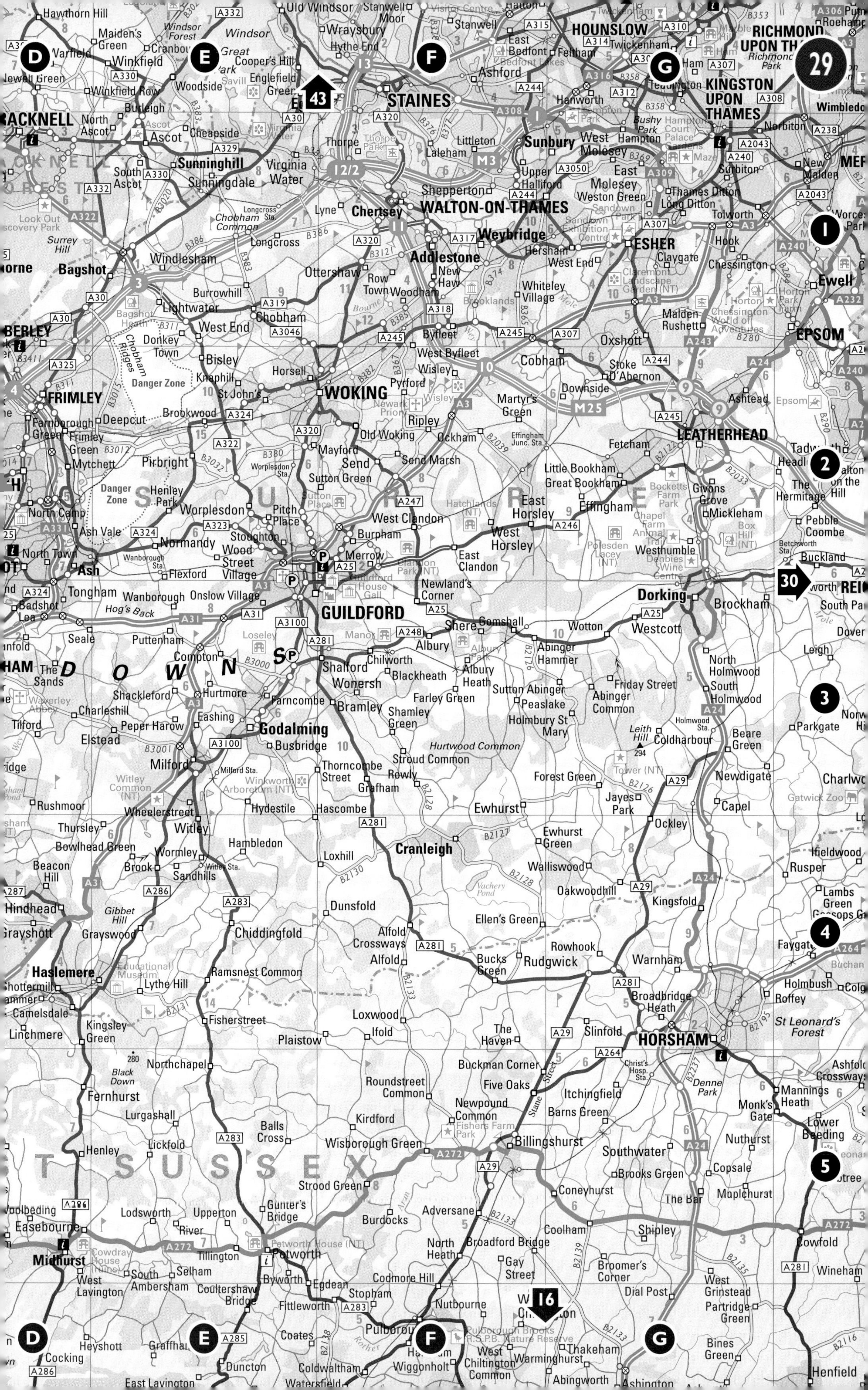
29
30
43
16
D
E
F
G
D
E
F
G
1
2
3
4
5
Hawthorn Hill
Maiden's Green
Windsor Forest
Windsor
Warfield
Winkfield
Cranbourne
Great Cooper's Hill
Park
Englefield Green
Savill
Woodside
Winkfield Row
Jewell Green
Burleigh
BRACKNELL
North Ascot
Ascot
Cheapside
Sunninghill
Sunningdale
South Ascot
Virginia Water
Thorpe
Thorpe Park
Old Windsor
Wraysbury
Hythe End
Stanwell Moor
Stanwell
Visitor Centre
STAINES
Egham
East Bedfont
Bedfont Lakes
Feltham
Ashford
HOUNSLOW
Twickenham
Hanworth
Kempton Park
Sunbury
Littleton
Laleham
Shepperton
Upper Halliford
West Molesey
Hampton
Bushy Park
Hampton Court Palace
East Molesey
Teddington
Ham
RICHMOND UPON THAMES
Richmond Park
KINGSTON UPON THAMES
Wimbledon
Norbiton
Surbiton
New Malden
Thames Ditton
Long Ditton
Weston Green
Sandown Park
Sandown Exhibition Centre
Tolworth
Worcester Park
ESHER
Claygate
Hook
Chessington
Claremont Landscape Garden (NT)
Horton Park Farm
Chessington World of Adventures
Ewell
EPSOM
Malden Rushett
Oxshott
Stoke D'Abernon
Cobham
Downside
Ashtead
Epsom
LEATHERHEAD
Fetcham
Tadworth
Headley
Walton on the Hill
The Hermitage
Givons Grove
Mickleham
Box Hill (NT)
Pebble Coombe
Betchworth Sta.
Buckland
Reigate
South Park
Dover
Leigh
Norwood Hill
Parkgate
Charlwood
Gatwick Zoo
Ifieldwood
Rusper
Lambs Green
Faygate
Holmbush
Roffey
St Leonard's Forest
Colgate
Ashfold Crossways
Mannings Heath
Monk's Gate
Lower Beeding
Nuthurst
Copsale
Maplehurst
Cowfold
Wineham
Henfield
Chertsey
WALTON-ON-THAMES
Weybridge
Hersham
West End
Addlestone
New Haw
Ottershaw
Row Town
Woodham
Whiteley Village
Brooklands
Byfleet
West Byfleet
Wisley
Pyrford
WOKING
Horsell
Chobham
Lyne
Longcross
Longcross Sta.
Chobham Common
Windlesham
Bagshot
Lightwater
Burrowhill
Surrey Hill
Look Out Discovery Park
Bagshot Heath
West End
Donkey Town
Chobham Ridges
Danger Zone
Bisley
Knaphill
St John's
Brookwood
CAMBERLEY
FRIMLEY
Farnborough Green
Deepcut
Frimley Green
Mytchett
Pirbright
Worplesdon
Worplesdon Sta.
Mayford
Send
Send Marsh
Sutton Green
Sutton Place
Old Woking
Ripley
Ockham
Newark Priory
Effingham Junc. Sta.
Martyr's Green
Little Bookham
Great Bookham
Bocketts Farm Park
Effingham
East Horsley
West Horsley
Hatchlands (NT)
West Clandon
Burpham
Merrow
East Clandon
Clandon Park (NT)
Newland's Corner
Polesden Lacey (NT)
Chapel Farm Animal Trail
Westhumble
Denbies Wine Centre
Dorking
Brockham
Westcott
Wotton
Abinger Hammer
Gomshall
Shere
Albury
Albury Park
Chilworth
GUILDFORD
Guildford House Gall.
Merrow
Stoughton
Pitch Place
Wood Street Village
Normandy
Flexford
Wanborough
Wanborough Sta.
Onslow Village
Hog's Back
Henley Park
Danger Zone
North Camp
Ash Vale
Ash
North Town
Tongham
Badshot Lea
Seale
Puttenham
Compton
Loseley
Manor
Shalford
Wonersh
Blackheath
Albury Heath
Farley Green
Sutton Abinger
Peaslake
Holmbury St Mary
Abinger Common
Friday Street
North Holmwood
South Holmwood
Holmwood Sta.
Leith Hill
294
Coldharbour
Tower (NT)
Beare Green
Newdigate
Capel
Forest Green
Jayes Park
Ockley
Ewhurst
Ewhurst Green
Walliswood
Oakwoodhill
Kingsfold
Ellen's Green
Rowhook
Rudgwick
Bucks Green
Warnham
Broadbridge Heath
HORSHAM
Denne Park
Christ's Hosp. Sta.
Slinfold
The Haven
Buckman Corner
Five Oaks
Itchingfield
Barns Green
Stane Street
Newpound Common
Fishers Farm Park
Billingshurst
Southwater
Brooks Green
Coneyhurst
The Bar
Shipley
Coolham
Broadford Bridge
Adversane
North Heath
Gay Street
Broomer's Corner
Dial Post
West Grinstead
Partridge Green
Bines Green
Thakeham
Warminghurst
Abingworth
Ashington
West Chiltington
West Chiltington Common
Pulborough
Pulborough Brooks R.S.P.B. Nature Reserve
Hardham
Wiggonholt
Nutbourne
Codmore Hill
Stopham
Fittleworth
Coates
Coldwaltham
Watersfield
Egdean
Byworth
Petworth
Petworth House (NT)
Tillington
Coultershaw Bridge
Duncton
Graffham
Heyshott
Cocking
East Lavington
South Ambersham
Selham
West Lavington
Midhurst
Cowdray House (ruins)
Easebourne
Woolbeding
Lodsworth
Upperton
River
Gunter's Bridge
Burdocks
Strood Green
Wisborough Green
Kirdford
Balls Cross
Lickfold
Henley
Lurgashall
Fernhurst
Black Down
280
Northchapel
Plaistow
Fisherstreet
Kingsley Green
Linchmere
Camelsdale
Shottermill
Haslemere
Educational Museum
Lythe Hill
Ramsnest Common
Chiddingfold
Grayswood
Grayshott
Hindhead
Gibbet Hill
Beacon Hill
Bowlhead Green
Thursley
Brook
Wormley
Witley
Witley Sta.
Sandhills
Hambledon
Wheelerstreet
Rushmoor
Witley Common (NT)
Milford
Milford Sta.
Winkworth Arboretum (NT)
Hydestile
Hascombe
Busbridge
Godalming
Farncombe
Eashing
Hurtmore
Shackleford
Peper Harow
Elstead
Charleshill
Waverley Abbey
Tilford
The Sands
Thorncombe Street
Bramley
Shamley Green
Stroud Common
Hurtwood Common
Rowly
Grafham
Cranleigh
Vachery Pond
Loxhill
Dunsfold
Alfold Crossways
Alfold
Loxwood
Ifold
Roundstreet Common
SURREY
NORTH DOWNS
WEST SUSSEX
M3
M25
A332
A330
A30
A329
A322
A325
A331
A324
A323
A320
A319
A3046
A318
A317
A308
A315
A314
A310
A307
A316
A312
A306
A238
A2043
A240
A3050
A309
A244
A245
A307
A243
A232
A24
A246
A247
A3
A25
A31
A3100
A281
A248
A29
A283
A286
A272
A264
A285
A287
B3000
B2126
B2127
B2128
B2130
B2133
B2135
B2139
B2237
B2195
B2116
B2138
B2131
B2039
B2122
B2033
B3032
B3012
B3015
B3411
B311
B386
B383
B3020
B3121
B385
B367
B382
B380
B374
B365
B376
B375
B369
B358
B280
B284
B290
B3001
12/2
13
11
10
9
3
4

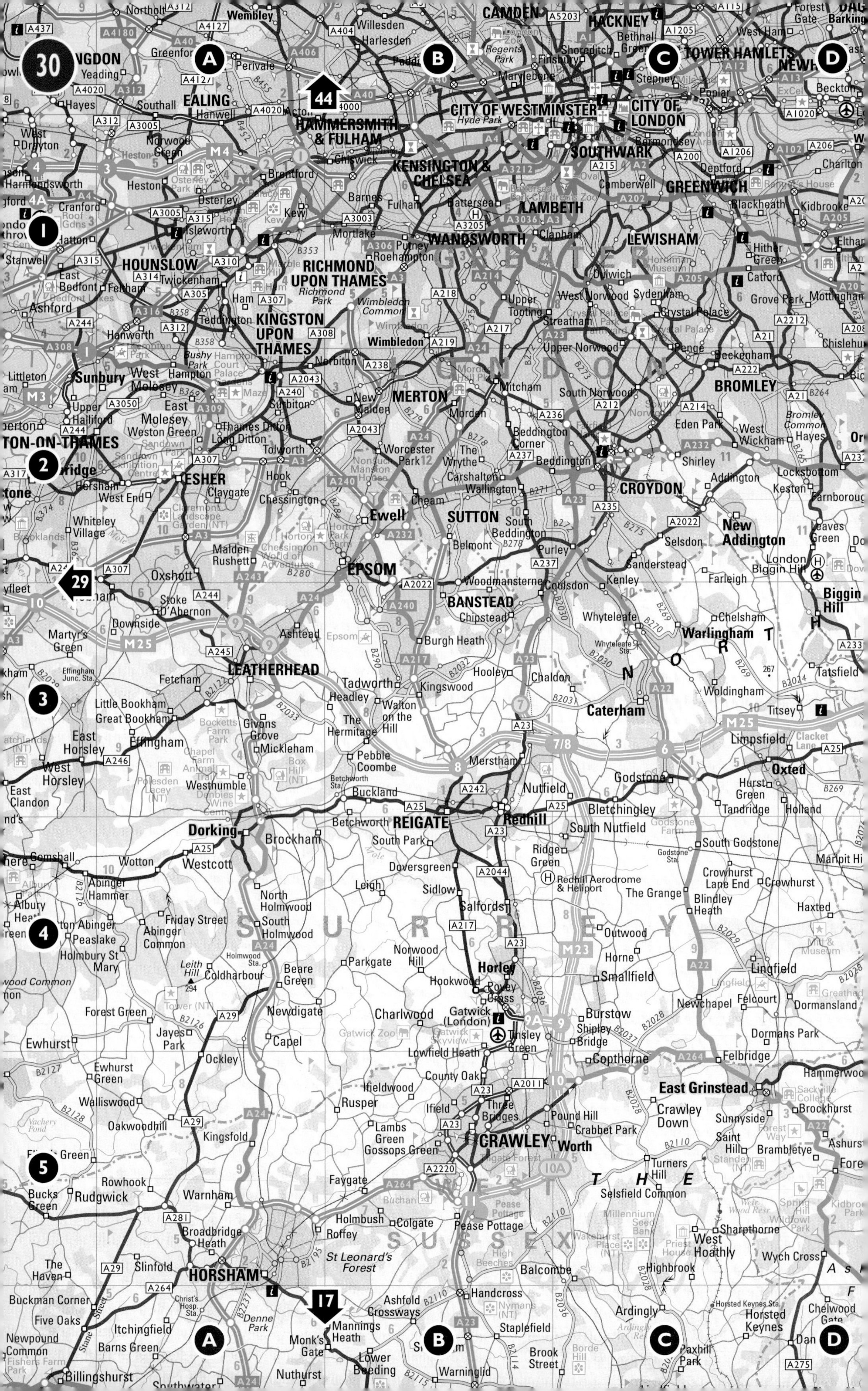
30
44
29
17
A
B
C
D
1
2
3
4
5
Northolt
Wembley
Willesden
Harlesden
CAMDEN
HACKNEY
Bethnal Green
Shoreditch
Finsbury
TOWER HAMLETS
Forest Gate
Barking
West Ham
Greenford
Perivale
Regents Park
Marylebone
Stepney
Poplar
Beckton
Yeading
Hayes
Southall
EALING
Hanwell
Acton
HAMMERSMITH & FULHAM
CITY OF WESTMINSTER
Hyde Park
CITY OF LONDON
West Drayton
Norwood Green
Heston
Chiswick
Brentford
KENSINGTON & CHELSEA
SOUTHWARK
Bermondsey
Deptford
Charlton
Harmondsworth
Osterley Park
Osterley
Barnes
Fulham
Battersea
LAMBETH
Camberwell
GREENWICH
Blackheath
Kidbrooke
Cranford
Kew
Mortlake
Putney
Roehampton
WANDSWORTH
Clapham
LEWISHAM
Hither Green
Eltham
Hatton
Isleworth
Stanwell
HOUNSLOW
Twickenham
RICHMOND UPON THAMES
Richmond Park
GREATER LONDON
Dulwich
Catford
East Bedfont
Feltham
Ham
Wimbledon Common
Upper Tooting
Streatham
West Norwood
Sydenham
Crystal Palace
Grove Park
Mottingham
Ashford
Teddington
KINGSTON UPON THAMES
Hanworth
Wimbledon
Upper Norwood
Penge
Beckenham
Chislehurst
Littleton
Sunbury
West Molesey
Hampton
Bushy Park
Hampton Court Palace
Norbiton
Mitcham
Morden
South Norwood
BROMLEY
Upper Halliford
Molesey
East Molesey
Surbiton
New Malden
MERTON
Weston Green
Thames Ditton
Long Ditton
Tolworth
Worcester Park
The Wrythe
Beddington Corner
Eden Park
West Wickham
Hayes
Bromley Common
Sandown Park
WALTON-ON-THAMES
Weybridge
Hersham
West End
ESHER
Hook
Claygate
Nonsuch Mansion House
Carshalton
Wallington
Beddington
Shirley
Addington
Locksbottom
Keston
CROYDON
Farnborough
Chessington
Cheam
Ewell
SUTTON
South Beddington
Belmont
Purley
Selsdon
New Addington
Whiteley Village
Brooklands
Malden Rushett
Chessington World of Adventures
Horton Park Farm
EPSOM
Sanderstead
London Biggin Hill
Leaves Green
Oxshott
Stoke D'Abernon
Woodmansterne
Coulsdon
Kenley
Farleigh
Biggin Hill
BANSTEAD
Chipstead
Whyteleafe
Chelsham
Downside
Martyr's Green
Ashtead
Epsom
Burgh Heath
Warlingham
NORTH
Effingham Junc. Sta.
Fetcham
LEATHERHEAD
Tadworth
Kingswood
Hooley
Chaldon
Woldingham
Tatsfield
Little Bookham
Great Bookham
Headley
Walton on the Hill
Caterham
Titsey
Effingham
Bocketts Farm Park
Givons Grove
Mickleham
The Hermitage
Limpsfield
Clacket Lane
East Horsley
West Horsley
Box Hill (NT)
Pebble Coombe
Merstham
Oxted
East Clandon
Polesden Lacey (NT)
Westhumble
Denbies Wine Centre
Betchworth Sta.
Buckland
Nutfield
Godstone
Hurst Green
Tandridge
Holland
Bletchingley
Dorking
Brockham
Betchworth
REIGATE
Redhill
South Nutfield
South Godstone
Gomshall
Wotton
Westcott
South Park
Ridge Green
Marlpit Hill
Abinger Hammer
Doversgreen
Redhill Aerodrome & Heliport
Crowhurst Lane End
Crowhurst
Leigh
Sidlow
The Grange
Blindley Heath
Albury Heath
North Holmwood
Salfords
Haxted
Friday Street
South Holmwood
Abinger Common
SURREY
Outwood
Peaslake
Holmbury St Mary
Norwood Hill
Horne
Parkgate
Lingfield
Leith Hill
294
Holmwood Sta.
Coldharbour
Beare Green
Hookwood
Horley
Smallfield
Povey Cross
Felcourt
Dormansland
Forest Green
Newdigate
Charlwood
Gatwick (London)
Burstow
Shipley Bridge
Newchapel
Tower (NT)
Jayes Park
Tinsley Green
Dormans Park
Ewhurst
Capel
Gatwick Zoo
Lowfield Heath
Copthorne
Felbridge
Ockley
County Oak
Hammerwood
Ewhurst Green
Ifieldwood
East Grinstead
Walliswood
Rusper
Ifield
Three Bridges
Pound Hill
Crawley Down
Sackville College
Brockhurst
Oakwoodhill
Kingsfold
Lambs Green
Gossops Green
CRAWLEY
Worth
Crabbet Park
Sunnyside
Saint Hill
Brambletye
Ashurst
Forest
Turners Hill
Faygate
WEST
Selsfield Common
THE
Rowhook
Bucks Green
Rudgwick
Warnham
Buchan
Pease Pottage
Millennium Seed Bank
Weir Wood Resr.
Spring Hill Wildfowl Park
Kidbrooke Park
Holmbush
Colgate
Broadbridge Heath
Roffey
SUSSEX
Wakehurst Place (NT)
Priest House
West Hoathly
Sharpthorne
The Haven
Slinfold
High Beeches
Balcombe
St Leonard's Forest
HORSHAM
Highbrook
Wych Cross
Buckman Corner
Christ's Hosp. Sta.
Handcross
Nymans (NT)
Ashfold Crossways
Ardingly
Horsted Keynes Sta.
Horsted Keynes
Chelwood Gate
Five Oaks
Itchingfield
Denne Park
Mannings Heath
Staplefield
Newpound Common
Fishers Farm Park
Barns Green
Monk's Gate
Brook Street
Borde Hill
Paxhill Park
Billingshurst
Lower Beeding
Nuthurst
Warninglid
Southwater
M25
M4
M3
M23
A3
A23
A24
A25
A264
A29
A22

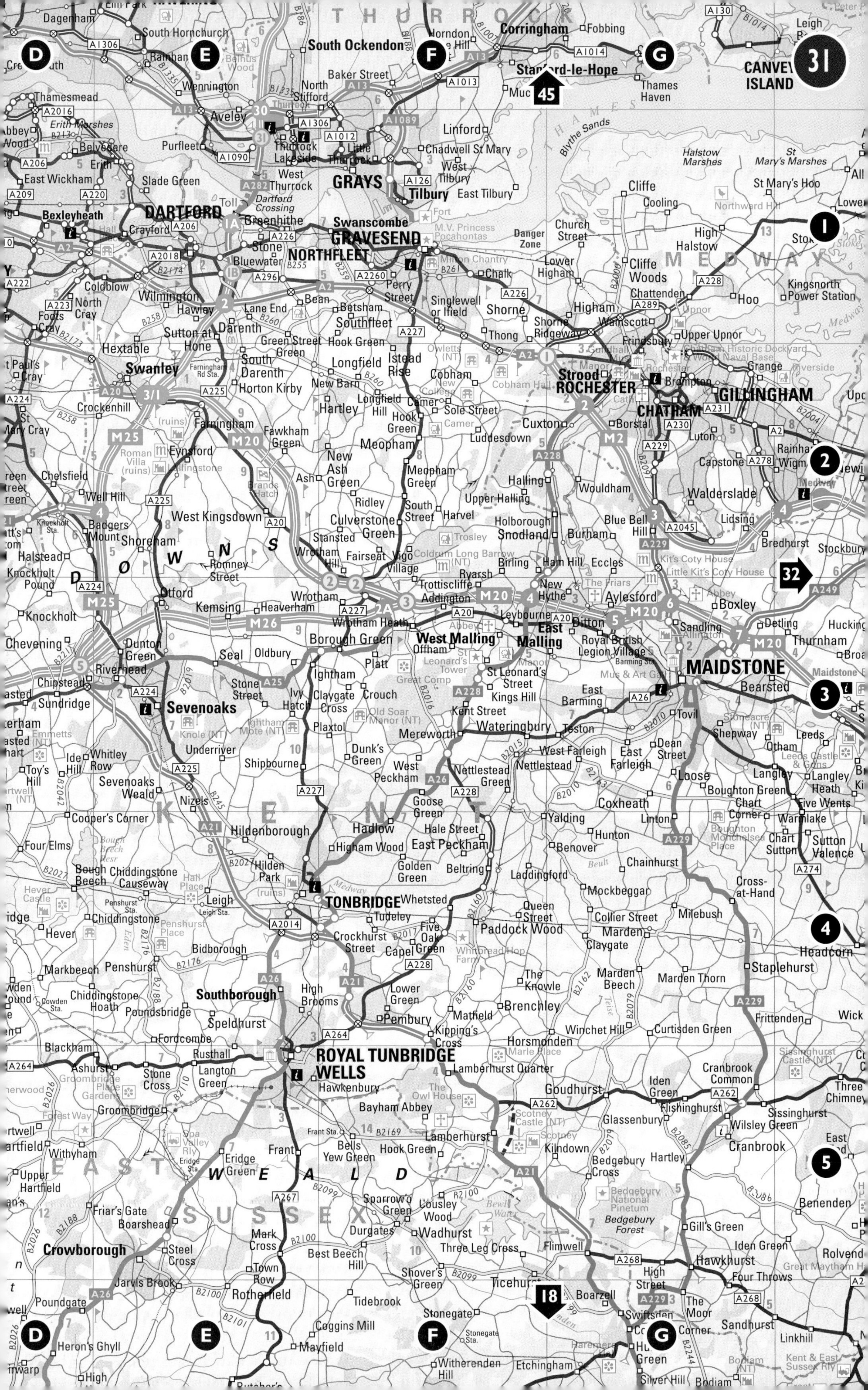
THURROCK
Dagenham
South Hornchurch
Rainham
South Ockendon
Corringham
Fobbing
Stanford-le-Hope
Thames Haven
CANVEY ISLAND
45
32
18
Wennington
Aveley
Baker Street
North Stifford
Thamesmead
Erith Marshes
Belvedere
Erith
Purfleet
Thurrock Lakeside
Little Thurrock
Linford
Chadwell St Mary
West Tilbury
GRAYS
Tilbury
East Tilbury
West Thurrock
Dartford Crossing
East Wickham
Slade Green
Bexleyheath
Crayford
DARTFORD
Greenhithe
Swanscombe
GRAVESEND
NORTHFLEET
Stone
Bluewater
M.V. Princess Pocahontas
Danger Zone
Church Street
Lower Higham
Halstow Marshes
St Mary's Marshes
Cliffe
Cooling
Northward Hill
St Mary's Hoo
High Halstow
MEDWAY
Cliffe Woods
Kingsnorth Power Station
Hoo
Chattenden
Upnor
Upper Upnor
Frindsbury
Wainscott
Higham
Shorne
Shorne Ridgeway
Chalk
Milton Chantry
Coldblow
Wilmington
Hawley
North Cray
Foots Cray
Lane End
Bean
Betsham
Perry Street
Singlewell or Ifield
Southfleet
Green Street Green
Hook Green
Darenth
Sutton at Hone
Hextable
Swanley
South Darenth
Horton Kirby
Longfield
Istead Rise
New Barn
Cobham
Owletts (NT)
Thong
Cobham Hall
Strood
ROCHESTER
Chatham Historic Dockyard & World Naval Base
Grange
Riverside
Brompton
GILLINGHAM
CHATHAM
Crockenhill
Farningham
Eynsford
Lullingstone
Roman Villa (ruins)
Fawkham Green
Hartley
Longfield Hill
Camer
Hook Green
Sole Street
Cuxton
Borstal
Luddesdown
Luton
Capstone
Rainham
Wigmore
Meopham
New Ash Green
Ash
Meopham Green
Halling
Upper Halling
Wouldham
Walderslade
Chelsfield
Well Hill
Badgers Mount
Shoreham
West Kingsdown
Brands Hatch
Ridley
South Street
Harvel
Culverstone Green
Holborough
Snodland
Burham
Blue Bell Hill
Lidsing
Bredhurst
Stockbury
Halstead
Knockholt Pound
Romney Street
DOWNS
Stansted
Wrotham Hill
Fairseat
Vigo Village
Trosley
Coldrum Long Barrow (NT)
Birling
Ham Hill
Eccles
Kit's Coty House
Little Kit's Coty House
Ryarsh
Trottiscliffe
Addington
New Hythe
The Friars
Aylesford
Boxley
Otford
Kemsing
Heaverham
Wrotham
Wrotham Heath
Knockholt
Chevening
Dunton Green
Riverhead
Seal
Oldbury
Borough Green
West Malling
Offham
St Leonard's Tower
Leybourne
East Malling
Ditton
Royal British Legion Village
Sandling
Allington
Detling
Thurnham
Hucking
Chipstead
Sundridge
Sevenoaks
Stone Street
Ivy Hatch
Ightham
Platt
Great Comp
St Leonard's Street
Kings Hill
Barming Sta
Mus & Art Gal
MAIDSTONE
Bearsted
Ightham Mote (NT)
Knole (NT)
Claygate Cross
Crouch
Old Soar Manor (NT)
Kent Street
East Barming
Plaxtol
Mereworth
Wateringbury
Teston
Tovil
Dean Street
Shepway
Stoneacre (NT)
Leeds
Otham
Leeds Castle & Gdns
Emmetts
Ide Hill
Whitley Row
Toy's Hill
Underriver
Dunk's Green
Shipbourne
West Peckham
West Farleigh
Nettlestead
Nettlestead Green
East Farleigh
Loose
Langley
Boughton Green
Chart Corner
Langley Heath
Five Wents
Sevenoaks Weald
Nizels
KENT
Goose Green
Coxheath
Linton
Warmlake
Cooper's Corner
Hildenborough
Hadlow
Hale Street
East Peckham
Yalding
Hunton
Boughton Monchelsea Place
Chart Sutton
Sutton Valence
Four Elms
Bough Beech Resr
Higham Wood
Golden Green
Beltring
Benover
Chainhurst
Bough Beech
Chiddingstone Causeway
Hall Place
Hilden Park
Laddingford
Mockbeggar
Cross-at-Hand
Hever Castle
Penshurst Sta.
Leigh
Leigh Sta.
TONBRIDGE
Whetsted
Queen Street
Collier Street
Milebush
Chiddingstone
Penshurst Place
Tudeley
Five Oak Green
Paddock Wood
Marden
Claygate
Hever
Crockhurst Street
Capel
Whitbread Hop Farm
Headcorn
Bidborough
Markbeech
Penshurst
The Knowle
Marden Beech
Marden Thorn
Staplehurst
Chiddingstone Hoath
Poundsbridge
Southborough
High Brooms
Lower Green
Brenchley
Matfield
Pembury
Speldhurst
Kipping's Cross
Winchet Hill
Curtisden Green
Frittenden
Wick
Fordcombe
Blackham
Rusthall
Horsmonden
Marle Place
Sissinghurst Castle (NT)
ROYAL TUNBRIDGE WELLS
Ashurst
Stone Cross
Langton Green
Lamberhurst Quarter
Groombridge Place Gardens
Hawkenbury
The Owl House
Goudhurst
Iden Green
Cranbrook Common
Three Chimneys
Groombridge
Bayham Abbey
Scotney Castle (NT)
Flishinghurst
Glassenbury
Sissinghurst
Wilsley Green
Forest Way
Frant Sta.
Bells Yew Green
Lamberhurst
Spa Valley Rly
Withyham
Frant
Hook Green
Kilndown
Bedgebury Cross
Hartley
Cranbrook
East End
Upper Hartfield
Eridge Green
Eridge Sta
EAST
WEALD
Bedgebury National Pinetum
Bedgebury Forest
Benenden
SUSSEX
Friar's Gate
Boarshead
Mark Cross
Sparrow's Green
Cousley Wood
Wadhurst
Bewl Water
Durgates
Gill's Green
Crowborough
Steel Cross
Best Beech Hill
Three Leg Cross
Flimwell
Iden Green
Rolvenden
Great Maytham Hall
Town Row
Shover's Green
Ticehurst
High Street
Hawkhurst
Four Throws
Jarvis Brook
Rotherfield
Tidebrook
Boarzell
The Moor
Poundgate
Stonegate
Swiftsden
Sandhurst
Heron's Ghyll
Coggins Mill
Mayfield
Stonegate Sta.
Cripp's Corner
Linkhill
Witherenden Hill
Etchingham
Haremere
Hurst Green
Silver Hill
Bodiam
Bodiam (NT)
Kent & East Sussex Rly
High Hurstwood
Crowborough Warren
M25
M20
M26
M2
A13
A2
A20
A21
A26
A25
A227
A228
A229
A264
A262
A268
A267
A224
A225
A2014
A1306
A1090
A1089
A1012
A1013
A1014
A126
A206
A220
A222
A223
A226
A2260
A296
A2018
A2016
A209
A130
A231
A230
A278
A2045
A249
A274
B2174
B258
B260
B2027
B2176
B2188
B2110
B2026
B2169
B2099
B2100
B2101
B2160
B2015
B2010
B2163
B2079
B2085
B2086
B2244
B2042
B245
B2016
B2017
B2162
B2009
B2097
B2004
B261
B255
B2259
B1007
B1014
B186
B188
B1335
B2213
B2173
B2212
B2000

Peter Pan's Adventure Island
Southend Pier
Sea Life Centre
B1016
Chapman Sands
Shoebury Ness
Leigh Beck
A130
B1014
CANVEY ISLAND
SOUTHEND-ON-SEA
A
B
C
D
46
Allhallows-on-Sea
Halstow Marshes
St Mary's Marshes
Allhallows
Isle of Grain
St Mary's Hoo
Northward Hill
Lower Stoke
Grain
B2001
Sheerness
Stoke
Stoke Saltings
Wallend
A250
West Minster
A228
Kingsnorth Power Station
Hoo
Queenborough
Halfway Houses
Minster
B2008
Warden Point
Warden
Eastchurch
B2231
Leysdown-on-Sea
MEDWAY
Medway
Chetney Marshes
Long Reach
A249
ISLE OF SHEPPEY
Upper Upnor
Chatham Historic Dockyard & World Naval Base
Grange
Riverside
Swale Sta.
Elmley Island
Kingshill
Eastchurch Marshes
Isle of Harty
Shell Ness
WHITSTABLE
Swalecliffe
B2205
GILLINGHAM
Upchurch
Iwade
A231
B2004
Lower Halstow
The Swale
Chestfield
Luton
A2
Kemsley
Seasalter
Rainham
Bobbing
A278
Wigmore
Newington
Milton Regis
Sittingbourne & Kemsley Lt Rly
Conyer
Uplees
Murston
Walderslade
Medway
Hartlip
SITTINGBOURNE
Teynham Sta.
Oare
Graveney
Yorkletts
Clapham Hill
A290
Pean Hill
Lidsing
Borden
Luddenham Court
A299
Dargate
Tyler Hill
Bredhurst
Oad Street
Bapchild
Teynham
Rodmersham
Faversham
Goodnestone
Honey Hill
Blean
Stockbury
Tunstall
Lynsted
Hernhill
Highsted
Preston
Bredgar
Maison Dieu
Ospringe
Boughton Street
Rough Common
31
Boxley
A249
Bicknor
Whitehill
North Street
Dunkirk
M2
Detling
Hucking
Milstead
Brogdale Horticultural Trust
Oversland
Harbledown
Thurnham
M20
Wormshill
Newnham
Chartham Hatch
Thanington
Broad Street
Frinsted
Doddington
Sheldwich
MAIDSTONE
Maidstone
Eyhorne Manor
Wichling
Eastling
Selling
Bearsted
Hollingbourne
Frith
Old Wives Lees
Throwley
Eyhorne Street
West Street
Otterden Place
Badlesmere
Shottenden
Chilham
Shalmsford Street
Chartham
Stoneacre (NT)
Leaveland
Street End
Shepway
Leeds
Warren Street
Chilham Castle
Otham
Harrietsham
A252
Leeds Castle & Gdns
Lenham
Stalisfield Green
A251
Petham
Langley
Broomfield
Molash
Boughton Green
Langley Heath
Kingswood
Sandway
Godmersham
Upper Hardres Court
Chart Corner
Five Wents
A20
Lenham Heath
Challock
Bilting
A28
Boughton Monchelsea Place
Warmlake
Liverton Street
Charing
Eastwell Park
Boughton Aluph
Crundale
Sole Street
Waltham
Chart Sutton
Sutton Valence
Ulcombe
Grafty Green
Boughton Malherbe
Charing Heath
Westwell Leacon
Westwell
Boughton Lees
NORTH DOWNS
Great Stour
Hassell Street
Bodsham Green
B2068
A274
Egerton
A251
Wye
Cross-at-Hand
Little Chart
Ram Lane
M20
Kennington
Stone Street
Egerton Forstal
Pluckley
Pluckley Thorne
National Nature Trails
Brook
Hastingleigh
Lymbridge Green
Hothfield
A20
ASHFORD
Headcorn
Staplehurst
Pluckley Sta.
Willesborough Lees
Stowting
Smarden
Maltman's Hill
Great Chart
Hinxhill
A229
Haffenden Quarter
B2229
Willesborough
Brabourne
Frittenden
Wick Hill
McArthur Glen
South Willesborough
Sevington
Brabourne Lees
Standen
Bethersden
Mersham
A20
Smeeth
Sissinghurst Castle (NT)
Curteis' Corner
Kingsnorth
Bull Green
A28
Cranbrook Common
Three Chimneys
Biddenden
Cheeseman's Green
Swanton Mill
East Stour
Sellindge
Stanford
A262
High Halden
Stonestreet Green
Westenhanger Sta.
Folkestone
Sissinghurst
A262
Shadoxhurst
Aldington
Wilsley Green
A2070
East End
Hengherst
Bromley Green
Stone Cross
Court-at-Street
Cranbrook
London Beach
A28
Redbrook Street
Sugarloaf
Bonnington
B2067
Lympne
St Michaels
Bilsington
Port Lympne
West Hythe
Hole Park
B2086
B2067
Brook Street
Woodchurch
Lympne
Benenden
Tenterden
The Leacon
Ruckinge
A259
Gill's Green
Hole Park
Rolvenden Sta.
Leigh Green
Hamstreet
Romney Marsh
Iden Green
Ashenden
B2080
Shirley Moor
Kenardington
Warehorne
Newchurch
Burmarsh
Rolvenden
Reading Street
Hawkhurst
Great Maytham Hall
Smallhythe Place (NT)
Appledore Heath
Romney, Hythe & Dymchurch
Four Throws
A28
Rolvenden Layne
Small Hythe
Snave
A268
Appledore Sta.
19
Dymchurch
Martello Tower
A2070
St Mary in the Marsh
Appledore
Snargate
Wittersham Rd. Sta.
Sandhurst
Brenzett
Ivychurch
St Mary's Bay
B2082
Stone
Linkhill
Kent & East Sussex Rly
Bodiam (NT)
Wittersham
The Stocks
Brookland
New Romney
Bodiam

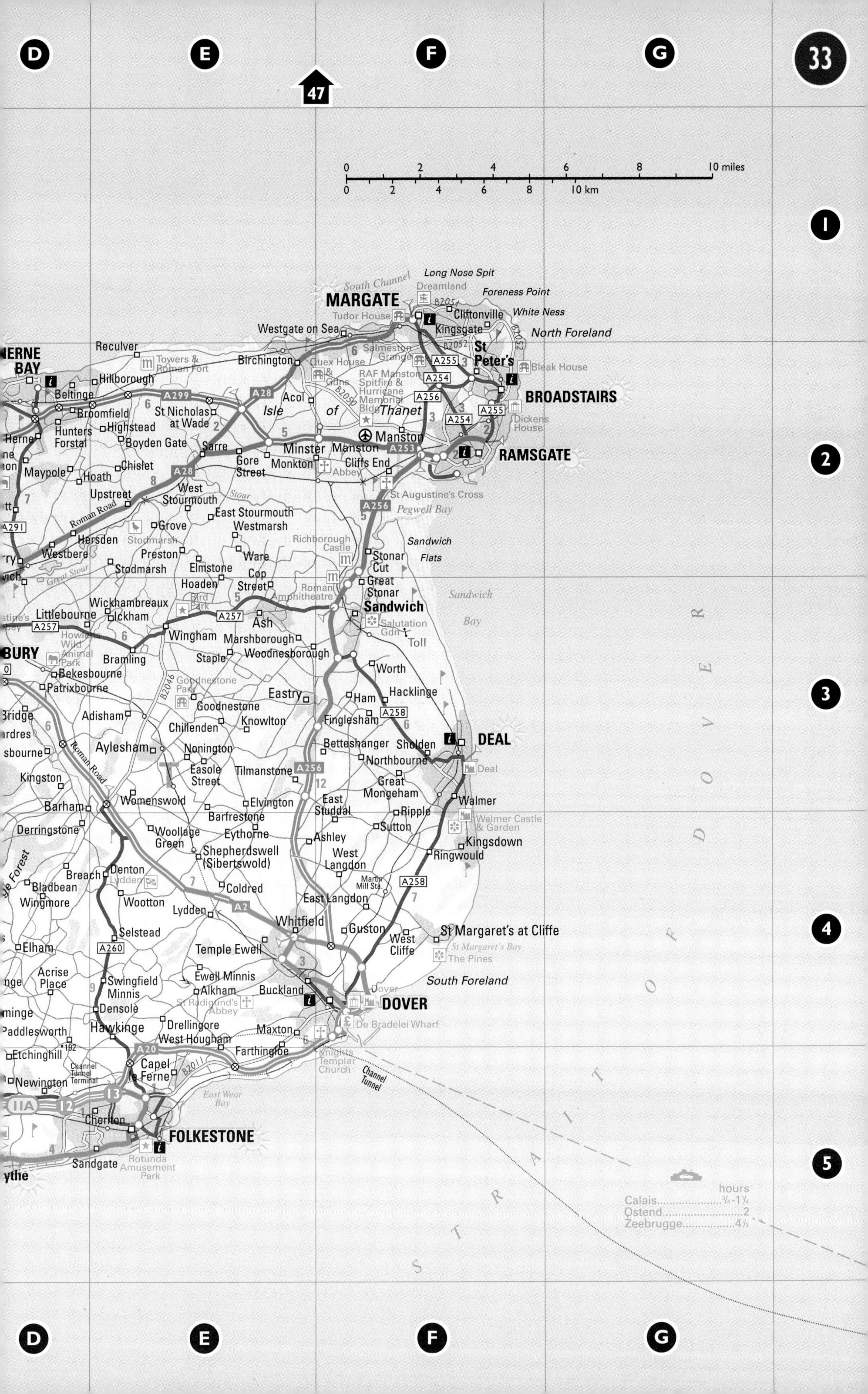
D
E
F
G
47
0 2 4 6 8 10 miles
0 2 4 6 8 10 km
1
2
3
4
5
Long Nose Spit
South Channel
Dreamland
Foreness Point
MARGATE
Tudor House
Cliftonville
White Ness
Westgate on Sea
Kingsgate
North Foreland
Reculver
Salmeston Grange
St Peter's
HERNE BAY
Towers & Roman Fort
Birchington
Quex House & Guns
Bleak House
Hillborough
RAF Manston Spitfire & Hurricane Memorial Bldg
BROADSTAIRS
Beltinge
Acol
Broomfield
St Nicholas at Wade
Isle of Thanet
Dickens House
Hunters Forstal
Highstead
Herne
Boyden Gate
Manston
Sarre
Minster
RAMSGATE
Maypole
Chislet
Gore Street
Monkton
Cliffs End
Hoath
Abbey
Upstreet
West Stourmouth
St Augustine's Cross
Stour
Roman Road
East Stourmouth
Pegwell Bay
Grove
Westmarsh
Hersden
Stodmarsh
Sandwich Flats
Richborough Castle
Westbere
Preston
Stonar Cut
Ware
Stodmarsh
Elmstone
Cop Street
Great Stonar
Great Stour
Hoaden
Bird Park
Roman Amphitheatre
Sandwich Bay
Sandwich
Wickhambreaux
Littlebourne
Ickham
Ash
Salutation Gdn
Toll
Howletts Wild Animal Park
Wingham
Marshborough
BURY
Staple
Woodnesborough
Bramling
Worth
Bekesbourne
Goodnestone Park
Patrixbourne
Eastry
Hacklinge
Ham
Goodnestone
Bridge
Adisham
Knowlton
Finglesham
Chillenden
DEAL
Betteshanger
Sholden
Aylesham
Nonington
Northbourne
Easole Street
Deal
Tilmanstone
Kingston
Great Mongeham
Barham
East Studdal
Womenswold
Elvington
Walmer
Barfrestone
Ripple
Walmer Castle & Garden
Derringstone
Woollage Green
Eythorne
Sutton
Ashley
Kingsdown
Shepherdswell (Sibertswold)
West Langdon
Ringwould
Denton
Breach
Lydden
Martin Mill Sta.
Bladbean
Coldred
Wootton
East Langdon
Wingmore
Lydden
Whitfield
Selstead
Guston
St Margaret's at Cliffe
West Cliffe
Elham
Temple Ewell
St Margaret's Bay
The Pines
Acrise Place
Swingfield Minnis
Ewell Minnis
Alkham
Buckland
South Foreland
Densole
St Radigund's Abbey
Dover
DOVER
Hawkinge
Drellingore
Maxton
De Bradelei Wharf
Paddlesworth
West Hougham
Etchinghill
Farthingloe
Knights Templar Church
Channel Tunnel
Channel Tunnel Terminal
Capel le Ferne
Newington
East Wear Bay
Cheriton
FOLKESTONE
Rotunda Amusement Park
Sandgate
Hythe
STRAIT OF DOVER
hours
Calais........................¾-1¼
Ostend.............................2
Zeebrugge.....................4½
A299
A28
A253
A254
A255
A256
A257
A258
A260
A20
A2
A291
B2050
B2051
B2052
B2046
B2011

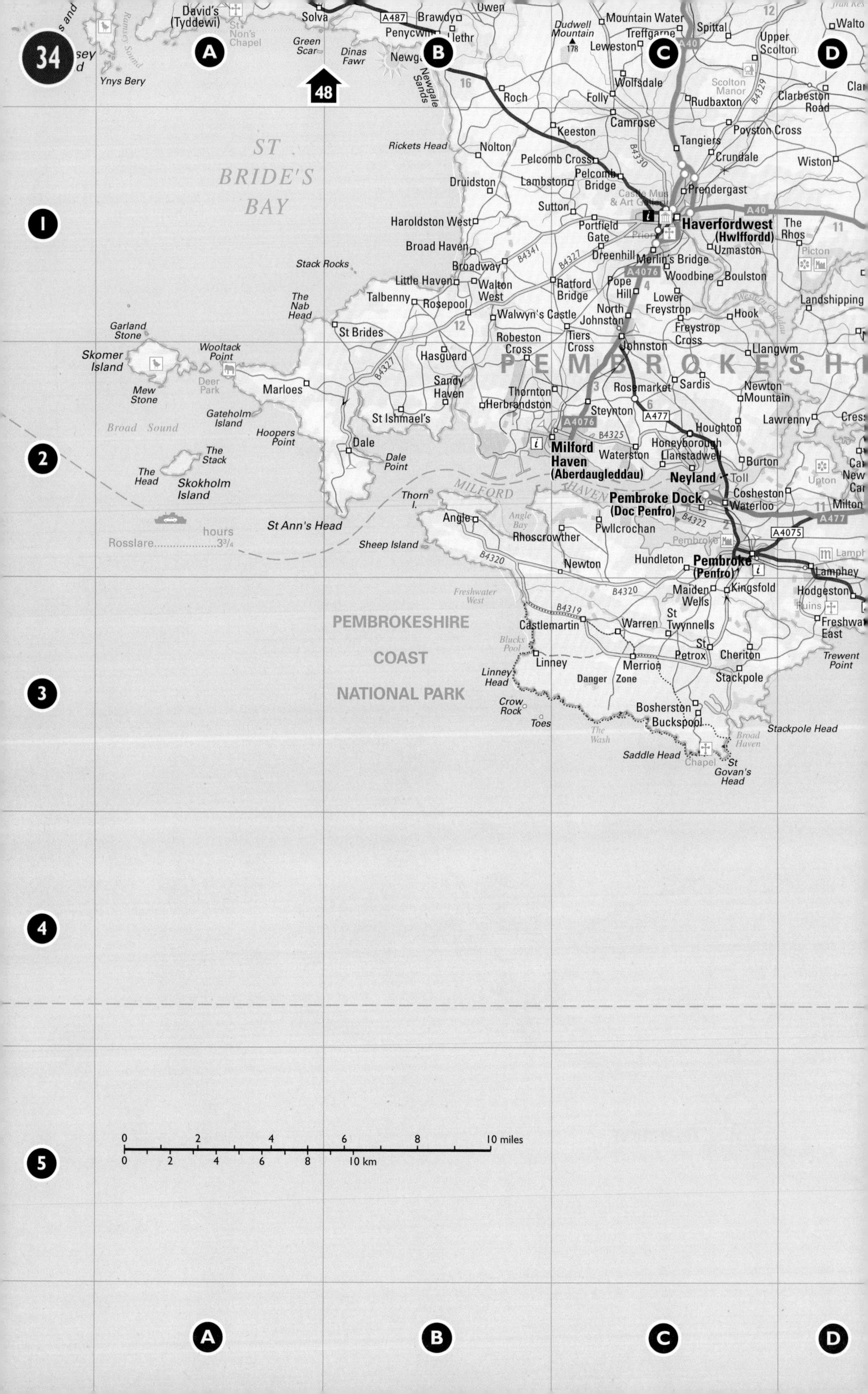
A
B
C
D
1
2
3
4
5
48
David's (Tyddewi)
St Non's Chapel
Ynys Bery
Ramsey Sound
Solva
Green Scar
Dinas Fawr
A487
Brawdy
Penycwm
Llethr
Newgale
Newgale Sands
Dudwell Mountain
178
Mountain Water
Treffgarne
Leweston
A40
Spittal
Upper Scolton
Scolton Manor
Wolfsdale
Folly
Rudbaxton
B4329
Clarbeston Road
Roch
16
Camrose
Keeston
Poyston Cross
Tangiers
Crundale
Wiston
ST BRIDE'S BAY
Rickets Head
Nolton
Pelcomb Cross
Pelcomb Bridge
B4330
Druidston
Lambston
Prendergast
Castle Mus & Art Gallery
Sutton
Haroldston West
Portfield Gate
Haverfordwest (Hwlffordd)
The Rhos
11
Priory
Broad Haven
B4341
B4327
Dreenhill
Merlin's Bridge
Uzmaston
Picton
Stack Rocks
Broadway
A4076
Woodbine
Boulston
Little Haven
Walton West
Ratford Bridge
Pope Hill
Lower Freystrop
Talbenny
Rosepool
The Nab Head
Walwyn's Castle
North Johnston
Western Cleddau
Landshipping
Hook
Garland Stone
St Brides
12
Freystrop Cross
Robeston Cross
Tiers Cross
Johnston
Llangwm
Skomer Island
Wooltack Point
Hasguard
PEMBROKESHIRE
Deer Park
Marloes
Sandy Haven
Rosemarket
Sardis
Newton Mountain
Mew Stone
Thornton
Herbrandston
Steynton
A477
Lawrenny
Gateholm Island
St Ishmael's
Broad Sound
Hoopers Point
Houghton
B4325
Dale
Milford Haven (Aberdaugleddau)
Waterston
Honeyborough
Llanstadwell
Burton
The Stack
Dale Point
Upton
Neyland
Toll
The Head
Skokholm Island
MILFORD HAVEN
Thorn I.
Pembroke Dock (Doc Penfro)
Cosheston
Waterloo
Milton
Angle
Angle Bay
B4322
A4075
hours
Rosslare............3¾
St Ann's Head
Rhoscrowther
Pwllcrochan
Sheep Island
Pembroke
Lamphey
B4320
Newton
Hundleton
Pembroke (Penfro)
Freshwater West
Maiden Wells
Kingsfold
Hodgeston
B4319
PEMBROKESHIRE COAST NATIONAL PARK
Castlemartin
Warren
St Twynnells
Freshwater East
Blucks Pool
St Petrox
Cheriton
Trewent Point
Linney
Merrion
Linney Head
Danger Zone
Stackpole
Crow Rock
Bosherston
Toes
Buckspool
The Wash
Stackpole Head
Broad Haven
Saddle Head
Chapel
St Govan's Head
0 2 4 6 8 10 miles
0 2 4 6 8 10 km

D
E
F
G
49
36
1
2
3
4
5
Llanycefn
Login
Mynach
Maesgwynne
Llanboidy
Gellywen
Abernant
Newchurch
Llandissilio
Henllan Amgoed
Rhydywrach
Clynderwen
Llanfallteg
Llanfallteg West
Cwmfelin Boeth
Castell Gorfod
Meidrim
Llangynin
Merthyr
Tre-vaughan
Carmarthen (Caerfyrddin)
Johnstown
Pensarn
Sarnau
Bron-y-Gaer
Bancyfelin
Llanllwch
Gelly
Bethesda
Llanddewi Velfrey
Whitland Abbey
Whitland
Pwll Trap
St Clears
Llangynog
Llangain
Cwmffrwd
Croesyceiliog
Redstone Bank
Narberth (Arberth)
Canaston Bridge
Crinow
Lampeter Velfrey
Trevaughan
Llwyn-y-brain
CARMARTHENSHIRE
Llanddowror
Brandy Hill
Cold Blow
Princes Gate
Tavernspite
Llandeilo Abercywyn
Cwmllyfri
Llanybri
Oakwood Leisure Park
Cross Hands
Templeton
Red Roses
Llandawke
Laugharne
Llansteffan
Ferryside
Cliff
Lanteg
Ludchurch
Llansadurnen
Broadway
Reynalton
Folly Farm
Loveston
Thomas Chapel
Colby Woodland Garden (NT)
Amroth
Marros
Brook
Wharley Point
Broadlay
Llansaint
Pendine
Llanmiloe
East Marsh
Laugharne Burrows
Ginst Point
St Ishmael
Kidwelly (Cydweli)
Begelly
Kilgetty
Stepaside
Pendine Sands
Laugharne Sands
Jeffreyston
Pentlepoir
Saundersfoot
Saundersfoot Bay
East Williamston
Redberth
Monkstone Point
Welsh Motor Sports Centre
Pembrey Forest
Cefn Sidan Sands
New Hedges
Tenby Roads
Gumfreston
Tenby (Dinbych-y-Pysgod)
St Catherine's Island
Pembrey
St Florence
Manorbier Sta.
Tudor Merchant's House (NT)
Penally
Lydstep
Giltar Point
Caldey Sound
Monastery
St Margaret's Island
Caldey Island
Priory
Old Castle Head
Chapel Point
CARMARTHEN BAY
Llanmadoc
Burry Holms
Rhossili Bay
Rhossili Downs
Rhossili
Middleton
Worms Head
(NT)
Cork to Swansea (Summer only)..........10 hours
A478
A40
A4075
A4115
A477
A4066
A484
A4075
A478
B4328
B4314
B4315
B4316
B4318
B4585
B4586
B4298
B4299
B4312
B4317

36
A
B
C
D
1
2
3
4
5
50
35
Carmarthen (Caerfyrddin)
Johnstown
Llanllwch
Ffynnon-ddrain
Tanerdy
Abergwili
White Mill
Llangunnor
Pensarn
Llanfihangel uwch-gwili
Nantgaredig
Pontargothi
Llanegwad
Llanarthney
Dryslwyn
Capel Dewi
Nantycaws
Court Henry
Pentrefelin
Llandeilo
Broadoak
Felindre
Llangathen
Dinefwr Park (NT)
Ffairfach
Gelli Aur
Maerdy
Golden Grove
National Botanic Garden of Wales
Penrhiwgoch
Trap
Carreg Cennen
Trichrung
Capel Gwynfe
Pont Clydach
Tair Carn Isaf
Derwydd
Blaengweche
Pentre Gwenlais
Carmel
Maesybont
Llandybie
Cwmffrwd
Llangain
Croesyceiliog
Llanddarog
Cwmisfael
Porthyrhyd
Heol-ddu
Llyn Llech Owain
Gorslas
Penygroes
Brynamman
Lower Brynamman
Glanaman
Tir-y-dail
Garnant
Tairgwaith
Gwaun-Cae-Gurwen
Cwmgors
CARMARTHENSHIRE
BLACK MOUNTAIN
Llangendeirne
Crwbin
Mynydd Cerrig
Drefach
Cefneithin
Cross Hands
Tumble
Pontantwn
Llandefaelog
Bancffosfelen
Meinciau
Pontyberem
Saron
Ammanford (Rhydaman)
Pontamman
Betws
Mynydd y Betws
Banc Cwmhelen
Capel Hendre
Tycroes
Pantyffynnon
Ferryside
Cliff
Broadway
Llansaint
Mynydd-y-Garreg
Four Roads
Pontyates
Pont-Henri
Llannon
Mynydd Sylen
Pont Abraham
Garnswllt
Mynydd y Gwair
Kidwelly (Cydweli)
Cynheidre
Sylen
Graig Fawr
Mynydd Garn-fach
Gwendraeth
Llandyry
Carway
Five Roads
Horeb
Fforest
Pentrebach
Cefn Drum
Rhyd-y-fro
Llangiwg
Godre'r-graig
Ynysmeudwy
Pontardawe
Welsh Motor Sports Centre
Waun y Clyn
Trimsaran
Hendy
Pontarddulais
Craig-cefn-parc
Trebanos
Pembrey Forest
Cefn Sidan Sands
Mynydd Pen-bre
Burry Port
Felinfoel
Bolgoed
Felindre
Vardre
Pembrey
Dyfatty
Pwll
Dafen
Llangennech
Pontlliw
Clydach
Bryn
Pant-lasau
Ynystawe
Glais
Llwynhendy
Grovesend
Swansea
Cefn Padrig
Llanelli Coastal Park
Bynea
LLANELLI
Gorseinon
Penllergaer
Llangyfelach
Llansamlet
Birchgrove
Skewen
Loughor
Tirdeunaw
Cadle
Morriston
Treboeth
Whitford Point
Llanrhidian Sands
Gowerton
Fforest-fach
Landore
Winsh-wen
Bon-y-maen
Pentre-Dwr
Crofty
Llanmorlais
Pen-clawdd
Waunarlwydd
Broughton Bay
Whitford Burrows
Poundffald
Three Crosses
Dunvant
Cockett
Pentre-chwyth
Kilvey Hill
Llanmadoc
Landimore
Killay
Sketty
Bury Holms
Cheriton
Llanrhidian
Upper Killay
Clyne Valley
Llangennith
Fairyhill
Oldwalls
Weobley
GOWER
SWANSEA
Ilston
SWANSEA (Abertawe)
Rhossili Bay
Rhossili Downs
Reynoldston
Cefn Bryn
Parc Le Breos Burial Chamber
Pennard
Clyne Common
PORT TALBOT
Llanddewi
Knelston
Penmaen
Parkmill
Bishopston
Black Pill
West Cross
Rhossili
Penrice
Nicholaston
Oystermouth
Newton
The Mumbles
Mumbles Head
Worms Head
Middleton
Scurlage
Southgate
Oxwich Bay
Langland Bay
SWANSEA BAY
Oxwich
Oxwich Green
Pwlldu Head
Port Eynon
Horton
Port Eynon Bay
Overton
Culver Hole
Port Eynon Point
hours
Cork (Summer only)....................10
0 2 4 6 8 10 miles
0 2 4 6 8 10 km

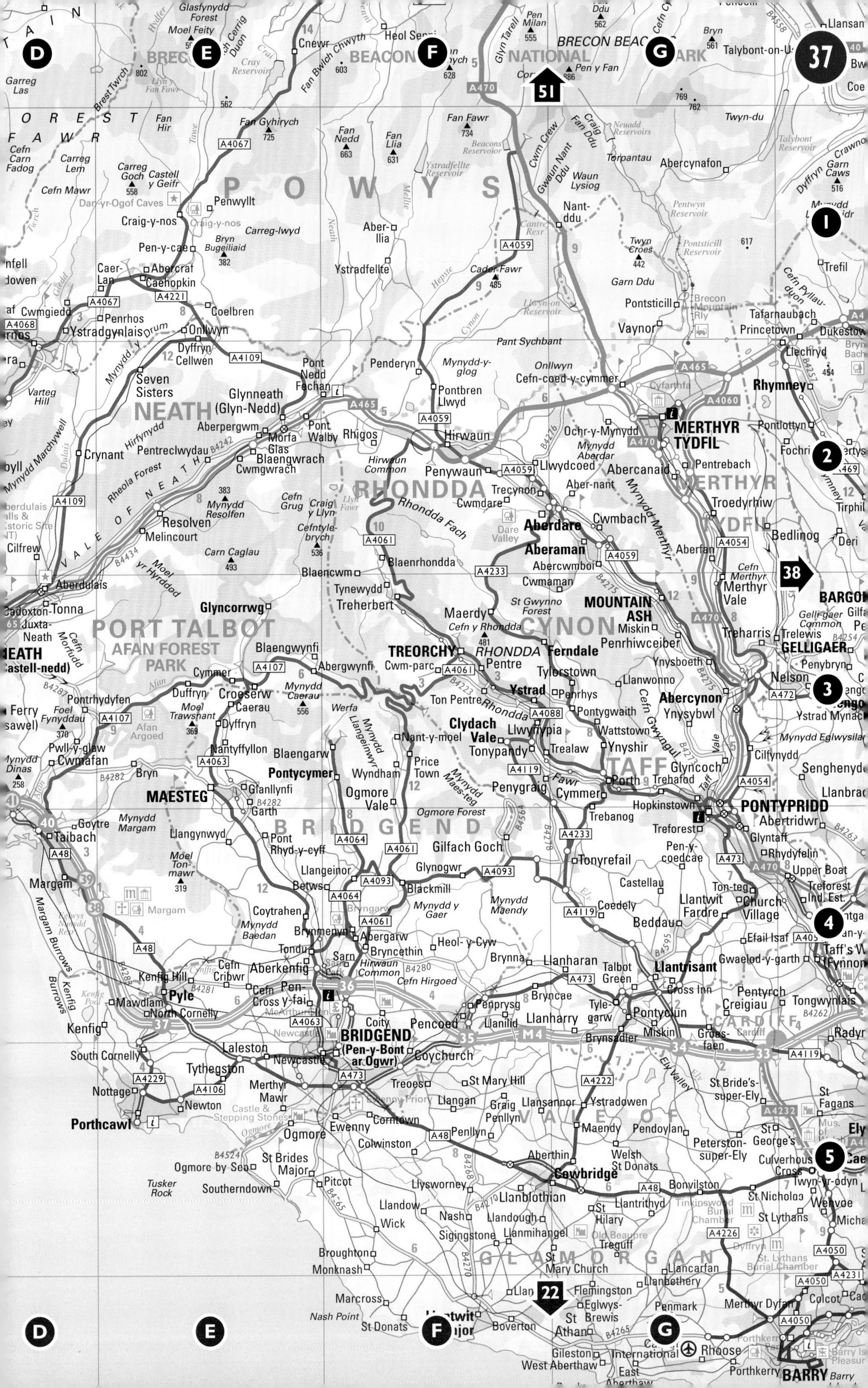
37
51
38
22
D
E
F
G
1
2
3
4
5
BRECON BEACONS NATIONAL PARK
P O W Y S
NEATH
RHONDDA
CYNON
TAFF
MERTHYR TYDFIL
PORT TALBOT
AFAN FOREST PARK
B R I D G E N D
VALE OF NEATH
V A L E O F
G L A M O R G A N
CARDIFF
FOREST FAWR
Glasfynydd Forest
Moel Feity
Cerrig Duon
Cray Reservoir
Heol Senni
Cnewr
Fan Bwlch Chwyth
Pen Milan
555
Glyn Tarell
Pen y Fan
886
Bryn
561
Talybont-on-Usk
Llansantffraed
Garreg Las
Brest Twrch
802
603
628
562
A470
769
762
Twyn-du
Fan Hir
Fan Gyhirych
725
Fan Nedd
663
Fan Llia
631
Fan Fawr
734
Beacons Reservoir
Ystradfellte Reservoir
Cwm Crew
Fan Ddu
Craig
Neuadd Reservoirs
Torpantau
Abercynafon
Talybont Reservoir
Garn
Caws
516
Cefn Carn Fadog
Carreg Lem
Carreg Goch
558
Castell y Geifr
Cefn Mawr
Dan-yr-Ogof Caves
Penwyllt
Craig-y-nos
Bryn Bugeiliaid
382
Carreg-lwyd
Aber-llia
Gwaun Nant Ddu
Waun Lysiog
Nant-ddu
Pentwyn Reservoir
Cantref Resr
A4059
Twyn Croes
442
Pontsticill Reservoir
617
Trefil
Pen-y-cae
Caer-Lan
Abercraf
Caehopkin
Ystradfellte
Cader Fawr
485
Garn Ddu
A4067
A4221
Coelbren
Llwyn-on Reservoir
Pontsticill
Brecon Mountain Rly
Tafarnaubach
Cwmgiedd
Penrhos
A4068
Ystradgynlais
Onllwyn
Dyffryn Cellwen
A4109
Vaynor
Princetown
Dukestown
Pant Sychbant
Llechryd
454
Pont Nedd Fechan
Penderyn
Mynydd-y-glog
Onllwyn
Cefn-coed-y-cymmer
Cyfarthfa
A465
Rhymney
Seven Sisters
Glynneath (Glyn-Nedd)
Pontbren Llwyd
A4060
Varteg Hill
Aberpergwm
Morfa Glas
Pont Walby
Rhigos
Hirwaun
Ochr-y-Mynydd
Mynydd Aberdar
Pontlottyn
Fochriw
Crynant
Pentreclwydau
Blaengwrach
Cwmgwrach
Hirwaun Common
Penywaun
Llwydcoed
Abercanaid
Pentrebach
Rheola Forest
Trecynon
Aber-nant
Cwmdare
Dare Valley
Aberdare
Cwmbach
Mynydd Merthyr
Troedyrhiw
383
Mynydd Resolfen
Cefn Grug
Craig y Llyn
Rhondda Fach
Resolven
Melincourt
Cefntyle-brych
536
A4061
Aberaman
Aberfan
A4054
Bedlinog
Deri
Cilfrew
Carn Caglau
493
Blaenrhondda
Abercwmboi
Cefn Merthyr
Merthyr Vale
Moel yr Hyrddod
Blaencwm
A4233
Cwmaman
Aberdulais
Tynewydd
Treherbert
St Gwynno Forest
Maerdy
Cefn y Rhondda
481
MOUNTAIN ASH
Miskin
Penrhiwceiber
BARGOED
Gelli-gaer Common
Trelewis
Treharris
GELLIGAER
Penybryn
Cadoxton-Juxta-Neath
Glyncorrwg
NEATH (Castell-nedd)
Cefn Morfudd
Blaengwynfi
TREORCHY
RHONDDA
Ferndale
Ynysboeth
Nelson
Cymmer
A4107
Abergwynfi
Cwm-parc
Pentre
Tylorstown
Llanwonno
Abercynon
Ynysybwl
A472
Ystrad Mynach
Pontrhydyfen
Duffryn
Croeserw
Caerau
Mynydd Caerau
556
Werfa
Ton Pentre
Ystrad
Penrhys
Ferry
Foel Fynyddau
370
Moel Trawsnant
369
Afan Argoed
Dyffryn
Mynydd Llangeinwyr
A4088
Pontygwaith
Clydach Vale
Llwynypia
Wattstown
Cefn Gwyngul
Mynydd Eglwysilan
Pwll-y-glaw
Cwmafan
Nantyffyllon
Blaengarw
Nant-y-moel
Tonypandy
Trealaw
Ynyshir
Cilfynydd
Mynydd Dinas
258
A4063
Bryn
Pontycymer
Wyndham
Price Town
Mynydd Maes-teg
A4119
Penygraig
Dinas
Porth
Trehafod
Glyncoch
Senghenydd
B4282
Glanllynfi
Ogmore Vale
Cymmer
A4054
MAESTEG
Garth
Ogmore Forest
Hopkinstown
PONTYPRIDD
Llanbradach
Goytre
Taibach
Mynydd Margam
Llangynwyd
Pont Rhyd-y-cyff
A4064
A4061
Gilfach Goch
Trebanog
A4233
Treforest
Abertridwr
Glyntaff
A48
Moel Ton-mawr
319
Llangeinor
Glynogwr
Tonyrefail
Pen-y-coedcae
A473
Rhydyfelin
Margam
Betws
A4093
Blackmill
Castellau
Ton-teg
Upper Boat
Treforest Ind. Est.
Margam Burrows
Mynydd y Gaer
Mynydd Maendy
Llantwit Fardre
Church Village
Coytrahen
Mynydd Baedan
Bryngarw
Coedely
Beddau
Tondu
Brynmenyn
Aberkenfig
Abergarw
Bryncethin
Heol-y-Cyw
Efail Isaf
Taff's Well (Ffynnon Taf)
Kenfig Burrows
Cefn Cribwr
Kenfig Hill
Sarn
Hirwaun Common
Cefn Hirgoed
Brynna
Llanharan
Talbot Green
Llantrisant
Gwaelod-y-garth
Pyle
Cefn Cross
Pen-y-fai
Bryncae
Cross Inn
Pentyrch
Mawdlam
North Cornelly
A4063
Coity
Penprysg
Llanilid
Llanharry
Tyle-garw
Pontyclun
Creigiau
Tongwynlais
Kenfig
BRIDGEND (Pen-y-Bont ar Ogwr)
Pencoed
M4
Brynsadler
Miskin
Groes-faen
Radyr
South Cornelly
Laleston
Newcastle
Coychurch
Tythegston
A4229
A4106
A473
Treoes
St Mary Hill
A4222
St Bride's-super-Ely
St Fagans
Nottage
Merthyr Mawr
Newton
Ewenny Priory
Llangan
Graig Penllyn
Llansannor
Ystradowen
Porthcawl
Castle & Stepping Stones
Corntown
Ewenny
Ogmore
A48
Penllyn
Maendy
Pendoylan
Peterston-super-Ely
St George's
Colwinston
Aberthin
Welsh St Donats
Culverhouse Cross
Ogmore by Sea
St Brides Major
Cowbridge
Bonvilston
Twyn-yr-odyn
Tusker Rock
Southerndown
Pitcot
Llysworney
Llanblethian
Llantrithyd
St Nicholas
Wenvoe
Llandow
Nash
Llandough
St Hilary
Tinkinswood Burial Chamber
St Lythans
Wick
Sigingstone
Llanmihangel
Old Beaupre
Trerguff
A4226
Dyffryn
St Lythans Burial Chamber
A4050
Broughton
Monknash
St Mary Church
Llancarfan
Llanbethery
A4231
Marcross
Llan
Flemingston
Merthyr Dyfan
Colcot
Nash Point
St Donats
Boverton
Eglwys-Brewis
St Athan
Penmark
Gileston
West Aberthaw
Rhoose
Porthkerry
BARRY
Barry Island Pleasure

A
B
C
D
NATIONAL PARK
52
37
23
Llansantffraed
Cwmdu
Pen Cerrig-calch
701
Patrishow
Cwmyoy
Hoaldalbert
Bwlch
Gaer
Tretower
Llanfihangel Crucorney
Coed-yr-ynys
Myarth
Llanbedr
Llangattock Lingoed
Graig Syfyrddin
762
Twyn-du
Mynydd Pen-y-fal
Blaenawey
Sugar Loaf
596
Bryn arw
Bont
Cross Ash
Llangynidr
B4558
Crickhowell
Llangenny
Rholben
Deri
Ysgyryd Fawr
486
Upper Green
Talybont Reservoir
Ffawyddog
Mynydd Llanwenarth
Llanvetherine
Newcastle
rcynafon
Dyffryn Crawnon
POWYS
Llangattock
Cwrt-y-gollen
Glangrwyney
Cefn Onneu
White
Llangattock-Vibon-Avel
516
Garn Caws
541
A40
Llantilio Pertholey
Hen Gwrt
A4077
Mardy
Llanelly
Gilwern
Abergavenny (Y Fenni)
Llantilio Crossenny
550
Mynydd Llangynidr
Mynydd Llangatwg
A465
B4233
Pontsticill Resr
617
Trefil
Govilon
Croes Hywel
Llanvapley
BLAENAU
Clydach
Llanfoist
Llanddewi Rhydderch
Blackrock
Blorenge
559
Wernyrheolydd
Cefn Pyllau-duon
Rassau
Beaufort
A4047
Brynmawr
Llanelly Hill
B4246
B4269
B4598
Coed Morgan
Penrhos
Tafarnaubach
Dukestown
Pontypool & Blaenavon Steam Rly
Blaenavon Ironworks
Llanellen
Llanarth
Tregare
Princetown
Sirhowy
EBBW VALE
Newtown
Nantyglo
B4248
Great Oak
Brecon Mountain Rly.
Llechryd
Bryn Bach
B4486
Mynydd Carn-y-Cefn
550
Coalbrookvale
Blaenavon
Coedcae
The Bryn
Llanvihangel Gobion
Bryngwyn
Raglan
Tredegar
454
Visitors Cen.
Big Pit Mining Museum
A4042
Maerdy
A469
Festival Pk.
Blaina
A4043
Clytha Hill
A4060
Rhymney
A4048
Coity Mountain
544
Rhyd-y-meirch
Llanover
MERTHYR TYDFIL
Pontlottyn
Mynydd Bedwellte
Cefn Manmoel
Ebbw Vale
Cefn yr Arail
GWENT
Varteg
Pen-groes-oped
Nant-y-derry
Twyn-y-Sheriff
A449
Gwastad
Cwmtillery
Betws Newydd
Sirhowy Valley
Cwm
Goetre
Fochriw
Abertysswg
Mynydd Garnclochdy
Penperlleni
Kemeys Commander
Gwehelog
Rhymney Valley
A4046
ABERTILLERY
B4598
Llandenny
MERTHYR TYDFIL
Manmoel
Croes y pant
Troedyrhiw
New Tredegar
Abersychan
Mamhilad
Monkswood
MONMOUTHSHIRE
Tirphil
Hollybush
Llanhilleth
Llancayo
A467
Little Mill
Bedlinog
Deri
A4049
Aberbeeg
Cwm Ffrwd-oer
Pontnewynydd
Trevethin
Glascoed
Gwernesney
St Illtyd
A472
Usk
A469
Markham
Glandwr
B4285
A470
Bedwellty
Tranch
The Valley Inheritance
Llanbadoc
Llangwm-isaf
Argoed
Trinant
PONTYPOOL
Aber Bargoed
Oakdale
B4471
Swffryd
Griffithstown
Llandegfedd Resr.
BARGOED
Rock
Crumlin
New Inn
Gelli-gaer Common
Gilfach
Croespenmaen
Mynydd Maen
A4042
Coed-y-paen
Llanllywel
A4054
Trelewis
Pengam
B4254
Newbridge (Cefn Bychan)
Sebastopol
472
Upper Cwmbran
Pontrhydyrun
B4235
Treharris
GELLIGAER
Blackwood
Llantrisant
A469
Fleur-de-lis
Greenmeadow Community Farm
Croesyceiliog
Llangybi
Penybryn
A472
Cefn Hengoed
Pontllanfraith
Pontnewydd
Gaerllwyd
Nelson
A467
Abercarn
Cefn Rhyswg
Llandegveth
A449
Pen-y-cae-mawr
Hengoed
Maesycwmmer
CWMBRAN
Tredunnock
Newbridge-on-Usk
Ystrad Mynach
B4459
Wentwood
Taff Vale
Wyllie
Cwmcarn
Henllys
Llantarnam
Llanfrechfa
CAERPHILLY
A4048
Pontywaun
Ponthir
Llanhennock
Cilfynydd
Mynydd Eglwysilan
Sirhowy
Ynysddu
Ebbw Vale
Castell-y-bwch
Croes-y-mwyalch
B4236
Kemeys Inferior
Parc-Seymour
A4054
Cwmfelinfach
Crosskeys
A4051
Llanvaches
Senghenydd
Rhymney Valley
Risca
Caerleon
A48
Penhow
Wattsville
Malpas
Roman Fort
Llanbeder
St Brides Netherwent
Llanbradach
Sirhowy Valley
A467
Pontymister
Bettws
Christchurch
B4245
Llanmartin
Abertridwr
A469
Bedwas
Machen
B4591
26
25A
25
B4596
24
Glyntaff
B4263
Rogerstone
A4042
Milton
Underwood
Llanwern
Rhydyfelin
A468
Lower Machen
A48
A455
Wilcrick
23A
Magor
A470
Upper Boat
CAERPHILLY
A468
Rhiwderin
27
Liswerry
Bishton
A473
Ton-teg
Treforest Ind. Est.
Draethen
Pentre-Poeth
Bassaleg
Gaer
NEWPORT (Casnewydd)
Steel Works
Llandevenny
Nantgarw
Rudry
28
Maesglas
A4042
Toll
Pye Corner
Broadstreet Common
Caldicot Level
Efail Isaf
Glan-y-llyn
Parc Cefn Onn
Michaelston-y-Fedw
M4
Tredegar
Redwick
A4054
Thornhill
Began
29
Coedkernew
NEWPORT
Whitson
Gwaelod-y-garth
Taff's Well (Fynnon Taf)
A48(M)
Nash
Castell Coch
30
Lisvane
Castleton
Goldcliff
A48
Marshfield
St Brides Wentlooge
Pentyrch
Tongwynlais
A469
Cardiff Gate
Llanedeyrn
B4562
Pentwyn
29A
Blacktown
B4262
32
Llanishen
St Mellons
B4239
Creigiau
Llanrumney
Groes-faen
A4119
Radyr
Birchgrove
B4487
Rumney
Peterstone Wentlooge
33
A4119
Whitchurch
Llandaff North
A470
A48
A4232
CARDIFF
A469
Roath
St Fagans
Llandaff
A4161
CARDIFF (Caerdydd)
Peterston-super-Ely
Ely
Canton
Welsh Mus
St George's
Caerau
A4232
Grangetown
Wales Millennium Centre
Redcliff Bay
Twyn-yr-odyn
A48
St Nicholas
Leckwith
A4160
A4232
Wenvoe
Llandough
Manor House
B3124
Walton-in-Gordano
A4226
St Lythans
Michaelston-le-Pit
A4055
Clevedon Pier
Dinas Powys
Cogan
Clevedon
A4050
Pleasure Steamers Waverley and Balmoral
St Lythans Burial Chamber
St Andrews Major
PENARTH
Clevedon Court (NT)
Lower Penarth
20
Colcot
A4231
Palmerstown
Merthyr Dyfan
Cadoxton
B4267
Kenn
MOUTH OF THE SEVERN
Cardiff International
A4050
Sully
Lavernock
Lavernock Point
Swanbridge
Rhoose
Porthkerry
BARRY
Barry Island Pleasure Pk.
Sully Island
Barry Island
Middle Hope (NT)
Sand Point
Woodspring Priory
Kingston Seymour
Icelton
North End
Yatton
Clav

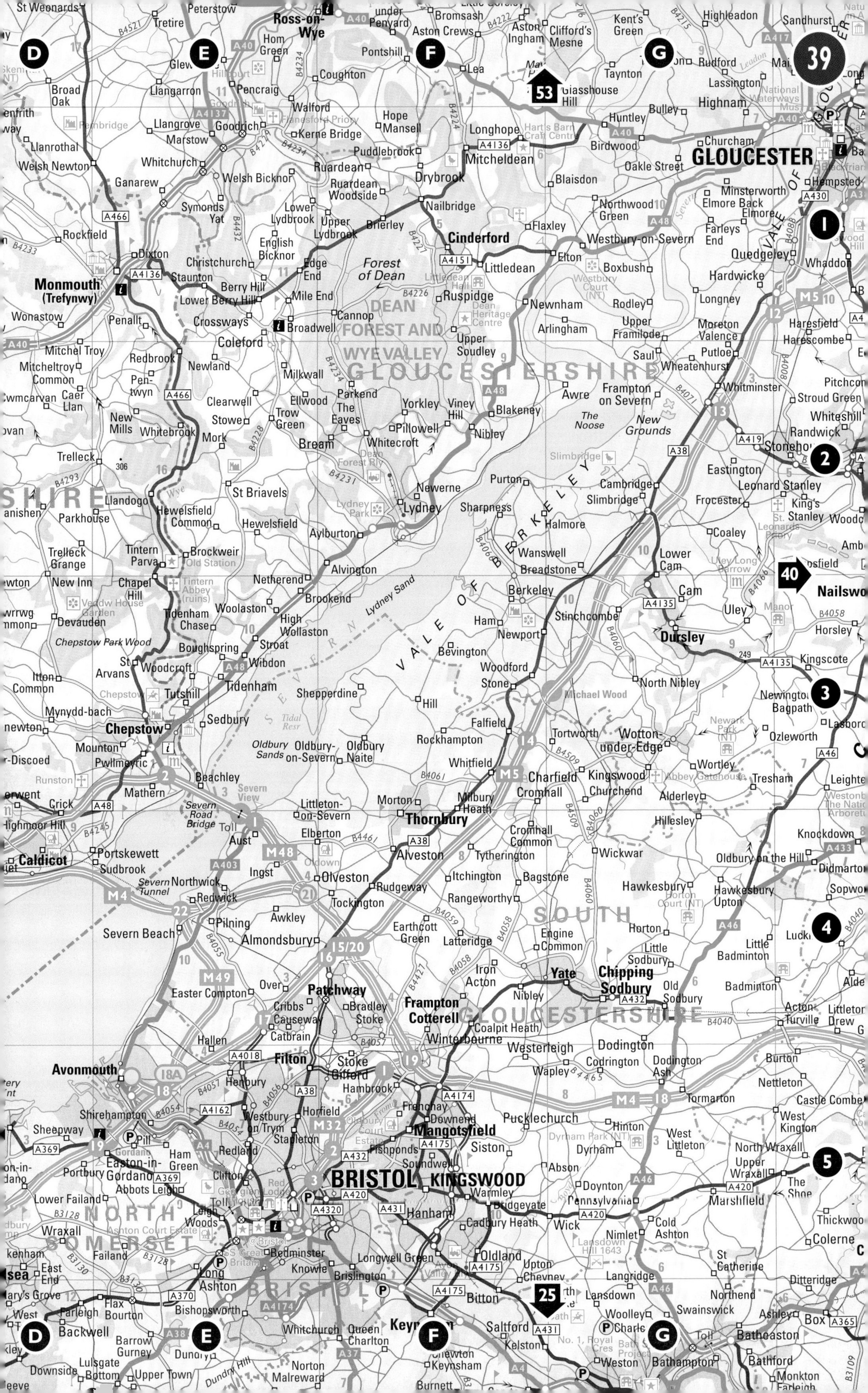
D
E
F
G
53
40
25
St Weonards
Peterstow
Tretire
Ross-on-Wye
Weston under Penyard
Bromsash
Aston Crews
Aston Ingham
Clifford's Mesne
Kent's Green
Highleadon
Sandhurst
Hom Green
Pontshill
Glewstone
Llangarron
Pencraig
Coughton
Lea
May Hill
Glasshouse Hill
Taynton
Rudford
Lassington
Highnam
National Waterways Museum
Broad Oak
Walford
Hope Mansell
Longhope
Huntley
Bulley
Pembridge
Goodrich
Llangrove
Flanesford Priory
Kerne Bridge
Hart's Barn Craft Centre
Birdwood
Churcham
GLOUCESTER
Llanrothal
Marstow
Puddlebrook
Mitcheldean
Oakle Street
Welsh Newton
Whitchurch
Ruardean
Drybrook
Blaisdon
Ganarew
Welsh Bicknor
Ruardean Woodside
Minsterworth
Elmore Back
Hempsted
Symonds Yat
Lower Lydbrook
Upper Lydbrook
Nailbridge
Northwood Green
Elmore
Rockfield
English Bicknor
Brierley
Flaxley
Farleys End
VALE OF GLOUCESTER
Cinderford
Westbury-on-Severn
Quedgeley
Dixton
Christchurch
Edge End
Forest of Dean
Littledean
Elton
Whaddon
Monmouth (Trefynwy)
Staunton
Berry Hill
Littledean Hall
Boxbush
Hardwick
Lower Berry Hill
Mile End
Ruspidge
Westbury Court (NT)
Wonastow
Penallt
Cannop
DEAN FOREST AND WYE VALLEY
Dean Heritage Centre
Newnham
Rodley
Longney
Crossways
Broadwell
Arlingham
Upper Framilode
Moreton Valence
Haresfield
Mitchel Troy
Coleford
Upper Soudley
Saul
Putloe
Harescombe
Mitcheltroy Common
Redbrook
Newland
GLOUCESTERSHIRE
Wheatenhurst
Cwmcarvan
Caer Llan
Pen-twyn
Milkwall
Frampton on Severn
Whitminster
Pitchcombe
Clearwell
Ellwood
Parkend
Awre
Stroud Green
New Mills
Stowe
Trow Green
The Eaves
Yorkley
Viney Hill
Blakeney
The Noose
New Grounds
Whiteshill
Whitebrook
Mork
Pillowell
Randwick
Bream
Whitecroft
Nibley
Stonehouse
Trelleck
Dean Forest Rly
Slimbridge
Eastington
Purton
Cambridge
Leonard Stanley
Newerne
Llandogo
St Briavels
Lydney Park
Lydney
Sharpness
Slimbridge
Frocester
King's Stanley
Parkhouse
Hewelsfield Common
Hewelsfield
BERKELEY
Halmore
Woodchester
Aylburton
Coaley
Trelleck Grange
Tintern Parva
Brockweir Old Station
Wanswell
Lower Cam
Leonards Stanley Priory
Amberley
Alvington
Breadstone
Uley Long Barrow
Nailsworth
New Inn
Chapel Hill
Tintern Abbey (ruins)
Netherend
Lydney Sand
Cam
Veddw House Garden
Brookend
Berkeley
Woolaston
Tidenham Chase
Stinchcombe
Uley
Horsley
Devauden
High Woolaston
Ham
Newport
Dursley
Chepstow Park Wood
Stroat
Bevington
Boughspring
VALE OF BERKELEY
Kingscote
Itton Common
St Arvans
Woodcroft
Wibdon
Woodford
Stone
North Nibley
Tidenham
Michael Wood
Newington Bagpath
Mynydd-bach
Tutshill
Shepperdine
Hill
Lasborough
Sedbury
Falfield
Newark Park (NT)
Chepstow
Tidal Resr
Rockhampton
Tortworth
Wotton-under-Edge
Ozleworth
Mounton
Oldbury Sands
Oldbury-on-Severn
Oldbury Naite
Pwllmeyric
Whitfield
Charfield
Kingswood
Wortley
Tresham
Abbey Gatehouse
Leighterton
Runston
Beachley
Cromhall
Churchend
Mathern
Severn View
Morton
Milbury Heath
Alderley
Westonbirt The National Arboretum
Crick
Severn Road Bridge
Littleton-on-Severn
Hillesley
Highmoor Hill
Aust
Toll
Thornbury
Cromhall Common
Knockdown
Elberton
Caldicot
Portskewett
Alveston
Tytherington
Wickwar
Oldbury on the Hill
Sudbrook
Oldown
Didmarton
Severn Tunnel
Northwick
Ingst
Olveston
Itchington
Bagstone
Hawkesbury
Hawkesbury Upton
Sopworth
Redwick
Rudgeway
Horton Court (NT)
Rangeworthy
Tockington
SOUTH
Pilning
Awkley
Earthcott Green
Horton
Luckington
Severn Beach
Almondsbury
Latteridge
Engine Common
Little Sodbury
Little Badminton
Iron Acton
Yate
Chipping Sodbury
Badminton
Alderton
Over
Patchway
Old Sodbury
Easter Compton
Bradley Stoke
Frampton Cotterell
Acton Turville
Littleton Drew
Cribbs Causeway
Catbrain
Coalpit Heath
GLOUCESTERSHIRE
Hallen
Winterbourne
Westerleigh
Dodington
Filton
Stoke Gifford
Avonmouth
Wapley
Codrington
Dodington Ash
Burton
Henbury
Hambrook
Nettleton
Frenchay
Tormarton
Castle Combe
Shirehampton
Horfield
Downend
Pucklechurch
Westbury on Trym
Hinton
West Kington
Sheepway
Pill
Stapleton
Mangotsfield
Dyrham Park (NT)
West Littleton
North Wraxall
Ham Green
Redland
Fishponds
Siston
Dyrham
Upper Wraxall
Easton-in-Gordano
Soundwell
Abson
The Shoe
Portbury
Gordano
Clifton
BRISTOL
KINGSWOOD
Doynton
Abbots Leigh
Red Lodge
Warmley
Pennsylvania
Marshfield
Lower Failand
Leigh Woods
Georgian House
Bridgeyate
Wick
Cold Ashton
NORTH SOMERSET
Hanham
Nimlet
Thickwood
Wraxall
Ashton Court Estate
@Bristol
Cadbury Heath
Lansdown Hill 1643
Colerne
Failand
SS Great Britain
Bedminster
Oldland
St Catherine
Knowle
Longwell Green
Upton Cheyney
Long Ashton
Avon Valley
Langridge
Ditteridge
East End
Brislington
Bitton
Lansdown
Northend
Flax Bourton
Bishopsworth
Swainswick
Ashley
Box
Parleigh
Backwell
Whitchurch
Queen Charlton
Keynsham
Saltford
Woolley
Charlcombe
Batheaston
West Town
Barrow Gurney
Dundry
Chewton Keynsham
Kelston
No. 1 Royal Cres
Bath Postal Museum
Bathampton
Bathford
Downside
Lulsgate Bottom
Upper Town
Dundry Hill
Norton Malreward
Weston
Monkton Farleigh
Burnett
M4
M5
M32
M48
M49
A38
A40
A46
A48
A417
A420
A430
A431
A432
A4018
A4136
A4151
A4162
A4174
A4175
A4320
A369
A370
A403
A419
A433
A466
A4135
A365
A37
A4
B4521
B4222
B4215
B4234
B4224
B4228
B4229
B4226
B4231
B4233
B4293
B4432
B4245
B4066
B4060
B4061
B4461
B4509
B4058
B4059
B4055
B4056
B4057
B4054
B4465
B4427
B4008
B4071
B4040
B3128
B3130
B3109
B4088
Severn
Wye
Frome
Boyd
Leadon

40
54
39
25
A
B
C
D
1
2
3
4
5
Highleadon
Sandhurst
Nature in Art
Norton
Staverton
Down Hatherley
Staverton Bridge
Golden Valley
Prestbury
CHELTENHAM
Charlton Abbots
Brockhampton
Hawling
Naunton
Maisemore
Longford
Gloucestershire
Up Hatherley
Sevenhampton
Whittington
Syreford
Highnam
National Waterways Mus
Churchdown
Leckhampton
Charlton Kings
Dowdeswell
Andoversford
Salperton
Notgrove
Churcham
GLOUCESTER
Badgeworth
Shurdington
Pilley
Kilkenny
Shipton
Hazleton
Turkdean
Barnwood
Hucclecote
Blackfriars
Crickley Hill
Foxcote
Hempsted
Brockworth
Bentham
Seven Springs
Compton Abdale
Minsterworth
Elmore Back
Elmore
Matson
Upton St Leonards
Roman Villa
Great Witcombe
Little Witcombe
Ullenwood
Coberley
Upper Coberley
Withington
Hampnett
Northleach
Tuffley
Robinswood Hill
Prinknash Abbey
Prinknash Park
Pottery
Birdlip
Cowley
Withington Woods
Chedworth Roman Villa (NT)
Yanworth
Quedgeley
Whaddon
Cranham
Colesbourne
Chedworth Woods
Stowell
Eastington
Hardwicke
Brimpsfield
Elkstone
Chedworth
Longney
Brookthorpe
Syde
Roman Road
Fossebridge
Coln St Dennis
Fosse Way
Moreton Valence
Haresfield
Harescombe
Whiteway
Rendcomb
Foss Cross
Putloe
Rococo
Sheepscombe
Edge
Painswick
The Camp
Winstone
Coln Rogers
GLOUCESTERSHIRE
Miserden
Misarden Park Gardens
Woodmancote
Calmsden
Winson
Whitminster
Pitchcombe
Slad
Sudgrove
Duntisbourne Leer
Duntisbourne Abbots
North Cerney
Ablington
Stroud Green
Whiteshill
Randwick
Edgeworth
Bagendon
Ermin Way
Arlington Mill
Bibury
Arlington
Stonehouse
STROUD
Bisley
Duntisbourne Rouse
Barnsley
Coln St Aldwyn
Barnsley House
Leonard Stanley
Rodborough
Eastcombe
Bournes Green
Daglingworth
Baunton
Frocester
King's Stanley
Thrupp
Bussage
Oakridge Lynch
Sapperton
Stratton
St John Baptist Church
Ampney Crucis
Sunhill
Woodchester
Chalford
Frampton Mansell
Cirencester
Corinium
Amphitheatre
Ampney St Mary
Coaley
St. Leonards Priory
Brimscombe
Hyde
Poulton
Ampney St Peter
Fairford
Amberley
Coates
Preston
Uley Long Barrow
Nympsfield
Minchinhampton
Siddington
Harnhill
Meysey Hampton
Box
Tarlton
Source of The Thames
Driffield
Cam
Nailsworth
Cherington
Uley
Manor
Horsley
Barton End
Avening
Rodmarton
Ewen
Down Ampney
Kemble
South Cerney
Dursley
Tiltups End
Tetbury Upton
Culkerton
Shorncote
Marston Meysey
Kingscote
Poole Keynes
Keynes Park
Cotswold Water Park
Cerney Wick
Latton
Chavenage
Newington Bagpath
Ashley
Somerford Keynes
Beverstone
Chelworth
Ashton Keynes
Newark Park (NT)
Ozleworth
Lasborough
Tetbury
Chedglow
Crudwell
Oakney
Cricklade
Seven
Wortley
Long Newnton
Eastcourt
Leigh
Tresham
Wortley Gatehouse
Leighterton
Doughton
Upper Minety
Purton Stoke
Blunsdon St Andrew
Westonbirt The National Arboretum
Hankerton
Minety
Swindon & Cricklade Rly
Westonbirt
Brokenborough
Charlton Park
Charlton
Knockdown
Willesley
Shipton Moyne
Garsdon
Purton
Oldbury on the Hill
Didmarton
Easton Grey
Malmesbury
WILTSHIRE
Nine Elms
SWINDON
Hawkesbury Upton
Sopworth
Foxley
Lea
Cleverton
Callow Hill
Lydiard Millicent
Shaw
Sherston
Norton
Hook
Lydiard Mansion
Little Badminton
Luckington
Corston
Little Somerford
Brinkworth
Rodbourne
Great Somerford
Grittenham
Wootton Bassett
Badminton
Alderton
Startley
Dauntsey
Tockenham Wick
Hullavington
Lower Seagry
Elcombe
Acton Turville
Littleton Drew
Lower Stanton St Quintin
Upper Seagry
Grittleton
Leigh Delamere
Stanton St Quintin
Lyneham
Tockenham
Sutton Benger
Bradenstoke
Burton
Church End
Preston
Broad Town
Nettleton
Leigh Delamere
Kington St Michael
Christian Malford
Tormarton
Castle Combe
Foxham
Goatacre
Bushton
Clyffe Pypard
Uffcott
West Kington
Yatton Keynell
Kington Langley
Broad Hinton
Clevancy
North Wraxall
Langley Burrell
Charlcutt
Spirthill
Hilmarton
Winterbourne Bassett
Hackpen Hill
Upper Wraxall
Ford
Hardenhuish
East Tytherton
Highway
Sheldon Manor
Berwick Bassett
Marshfield
The Shoe
Slaughterford
Tytherton Lucas
Bremhill
Biddestone
Compton Bassett
Windmill Hill
Winterbourne Monkton
Thickwood
CHIPPENHAM
Stanley
Studley
Yatesbury
Colerne
Cross Keys
Corsham
Corsham Court
Bowood
Calne
St Catherine
Easton
Derry Hill
Cherhill
Oldbury Castle & White Horse
Manor & Museum
Avebury
Ditteridge
Quemerford
Northend
Hawthorn
Abbey (NT)
Mile Elm
Calstone Wellington
Silbury Hill
Avebury Ring
Swainswick
Ashley
Box
Gastard
Lacock
Bowden Hill
Sandy Lane
Blackland
Beckhampton
West Kennett
Batheaston
Fox Talbot Museum (NT)
Bewley Common
Morgan's Hill
North Down
West Kennett Long Barrow
East Kennett
Bathford
Atworth
Whitley
Shaw
Chittoe
Stockley
Heddington
Monkton Farleigh
Beanacre
Melksham
Netherstreet
Roundway Down 1643
Tan Hill
Wansdyke
Bromham
A417
A4019
A40
A38
A430
A46
A4173
A419
A4135
A433
A429
A436
A435
A350
A4
A342
A3102
A365
A420
A4361
M5
M4
B4063
B4008
B4070
B4073
B4058
B4014
B4040
B4042
B4069
B4039
B3109
B3353
B4425
B4696
B4553
B4068
B4534
B4005
295
297
249
272

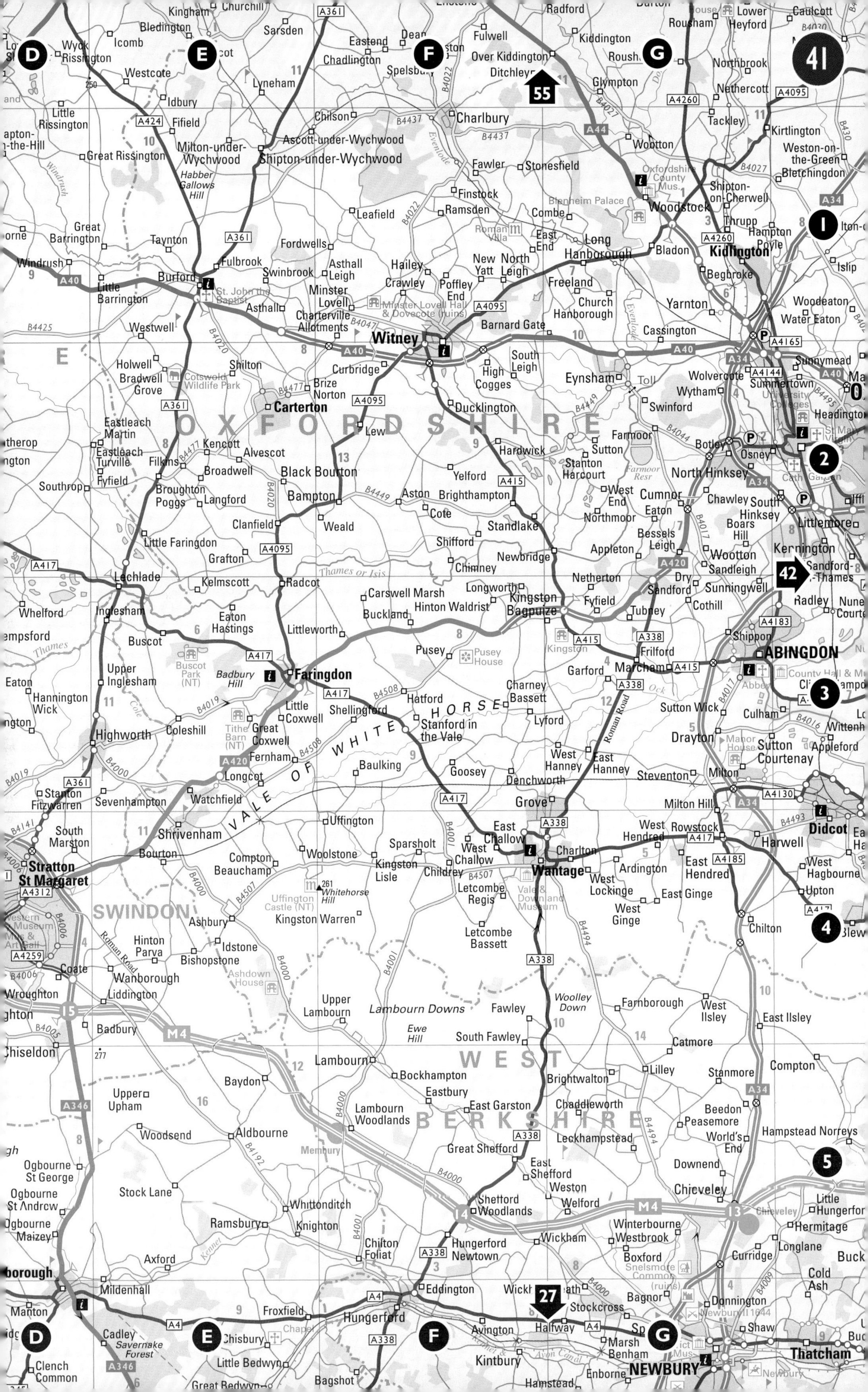
41
D
E
F
G
I
2
3
4
5
55
42
27
Kingham
Churchill
Bledington
Sarsden
A361
Eastend
Dean
Radford
Rousham
Lower Heyford
Caulcott
Wyck Rissington
Icomb
Chadlington
Spelsbury
Fulwell
Over Kiddington
Kiddington
Ditchley
Roush
Northbrook
Westcote
Lyneham
Glympton
Nethercott
A4095
Idbury
A4260
Little Rissington
Fifield
Chilson
Charlbury
B4437
Tackley
Kirtlington
A424
Milton-under-Wychwood
Ascott-under-Wychwood
Shipton-under-Wychwood
Great Rissington
A44
Wootton
Weston-on-the-Green
Bletchingdon
B4027
Habber Gallows Hill
Fawler
Stonesfield
Oxfordshire County Mus.
Shipton-on-Cherwell
Windrush
Evenlode
Finstock
Blenheim Palace
Woodstock
A34
Leafield
Ramsden
Combe
Thrupp
Great Barrington
Taynton
A361
Roman Villa
East End
Long Hanborough
A4260
Hampton Poyle
Kidlington
Fordwells
Asthall Leigh
Hailey
New Yatt
North Leigh
Bladon
Islip
Windrush
A40
Fulbrook
Burford
Swinbrook
Minster Lovell
Crawley
Poffley End
Freeland
Begbroke
St. John the Baptist
Little Barrington
Asthall
Charterville Allotments
Minster Lovell Hall & Dovecote (ruins)
A4095
Church Hanborough
Yarnton
Woodeaton
Water Eaton
B4425
Westwell
B4047
Witney
Barnard Gate
Cassington
A4165
E
B4020
A40
South Leigh
High Cogges
A40
Holwell
Shilton
Curbridge
Eynsham
Toll
Wolvercote
Summertown
Sunnymead
Bradwell Grove
Cotswold Wildlife Park
B4477
Brize Norton
A4095
Wytham
A4144
University Colleges
Headington
A361
Carterton
Ducklington
Swinford
B4449
B4495
OXFORDSHIRE
Eastleach Martin
Lew
Farmoor
St Mary Virgin
Eastleach Turville
Kencott
Alvescot
Hardwick
Sutton
B4044
Botley
Osney
Filkins
B4477
13
Stanton Harcourt
Farmoor Resr
North Hinksey
Fyfield
Broadwell
Black Bourton
Yelford
A415
Cath
Southrop
Broughton Poggs
Langford
Bampton
B4449
Aston
Brighthampton
West End
Cumnor
Chawley
South Hinksey
Cote
Eaton
Northmoor
Boars Hill
Littlemore
Clanfield
Weald
Standlake
Bessels Leigh
B4017
Little Faringdon
Shifford
Appleton
Kennington
A4095
Newbridge
Wootton
Sandford-on-Thames
A417
Grafton
Thames or Isis
Chimney
A420
Sandleigh
Lechlade
Kelmscott
Radcot
Carswell Marsh
Longworth
Netherton
Dry Sandford
Sunningwell
Hinton Waldrist
Kingston Bagpuize
Radley
Nuneham Courtenay
Whelford
Inglesham
Eaton Hastings
Buckland
Fyfield
Tubney
Cothill
A4183
Kempsford
Littleworth
8
Shippon
A338
Buscot
Thames
Pusey
Pusey House
Kingston
A415
Frilford
ABINGDON
Upper Inglesham
Buscot Park (NT)
Badbury Hill
A417
Faringdon
Garford
Marcham
A415
County Hall & Museum
Eaton
Hannington Wick
B4508
Hatford
Charney Bassett
A338
Ock
Abbey
Little Coxwell
A417
Shellingford
HORSE
Lyford
Roman Road
Sutton Wick
Culham
B4017
B4016
Wittenham
B4019
Tithe Barn (NT)
Great Coxwell
Stanford in the Vale
WHITE
Drayton
Manor House
Sutton Courtenay
Appleford
Highworth
Coleshill
Fernhalm
B4508
OF
West Hanney
East Hanney
B4000
A420
Baulking
Goosey
Steventon
Milton
B4019
Longcot
Denchworth
A361
Stanton Fitzwarren
Sevenhampton
Watchfield
VALE
A417
Grove
Milton Hill
A4130
B4141
South Marston
Shrivenham
Uffington
East Challow
A338
Rowstock
West Hendred
Didcot
B4493
Bourton
Sparsholt
West Challow
Charlton
A417
Harwell
Stratton St Margaret
Compton Beauchamp
Woolstone
Kingston Lisle
Childrey
Wantage
Ardington
East Hendred
A4185
West Hagbourne
A4312
B4000
B4507
261 Whitehorse Hill
Uffington Castle (NT)
Letcombe Regis
Vale & Downland Museum
West Lockinge
East Ginge
Upton
Western Museum
SWINDON
Kingston Warren
West Ginge
A417
Ashbury
B4494
Chilton
B4006
Letcombe Bassett
Blewbury
Art Gall
Roman Road
Hinton Parva
Idstone
A4259
Bishopstone
A338
B4006
Coate
Ashdown House
B4000
B4001
Wanborough
Woolley Down
Farnborough
West Ilsley
Wroughton
Liddington
Upper Lambourn
Lambourn Downs
Fawley
East Ilsley
M4
Badbury
Ewe Hill
South Fawley
B4005
Catmore
Chiseldon
277
WEST
Lambourn
Lilley
Compton
Baydon
Bockhampton
Brightwalton
Stanmore
Upper Upham
Eastbury
A34
A346
B4000
East Garston
Chaddleworth
Beedon
Lambourn Woodlands
BERKSHIRE
Peasemore
B4494
Woodsend
Aldbourne
World's End
Hampstead Norreys
Membury
A338
Leckhampstead
Ogbourne St George
B4192
Great Shefford
East Shefford
Downend
B4000
Weston
Ogbourne St Andrew
Stock Lane
Chieveley
Little Hungerford
Whittonditch
Shefford Woodlands
Welford
M4
Chieveley
Ogbourne Maizey
Ramsbury
Knighton
B4001
Winterbourne
Westbrook
Hermitage
Wickham
Chilton Foliat
Hungerford Newtown
Boxford
Longlane
A338
Curridge
Kennet
Snelsmore Common
Bucklebury
Axford
Cold Ash
Marlborough
Mildenhall
Eddington
Wickham Heath
B4000
Bagnor
Donnington
A4
Stockcross
Newbury 1644
B4009
Manton
Froxfield
Hungerford
Halfway
Shaw
A4
Avington
Speen
Chapel
A4
Marsh Benham
Thatcham
Cadley
Chisbury
Savernake Forest
A338
Kintbury
Avon Canal
NEWBURY
A346
Clench Common
Little Bedwyn
Enborne
Bagshot
Great Bedwyn
Hamstead

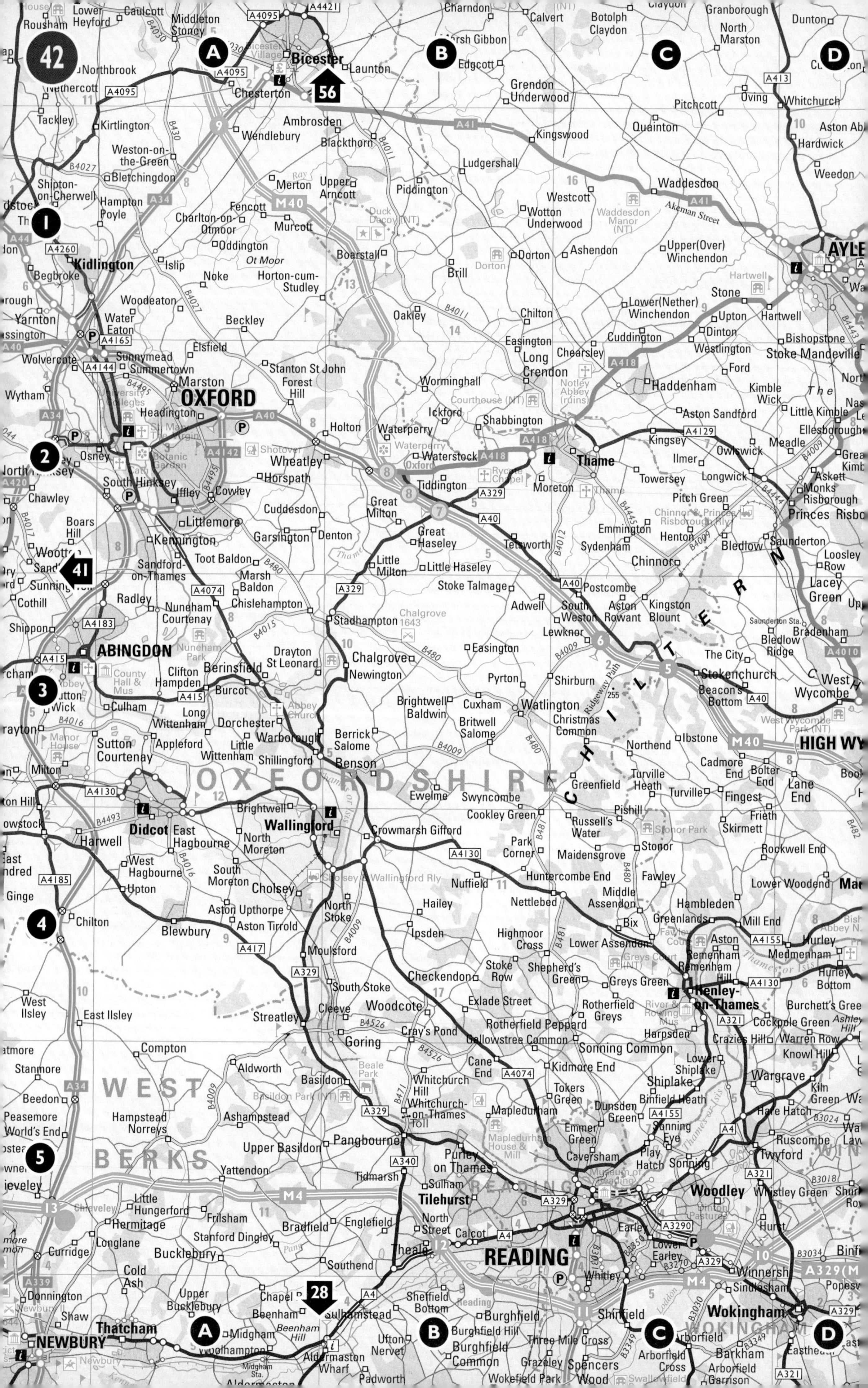

Rousham
Lower Heyford
Caulcott
Middleton Stoney
Bicester
Bicester Village
Launton
Charndon
Calvert
Botolph Claydon
Granborough
North Marston
Dunton
Marsh Gibbon
Edgcott
Northbrook
Nethercott
Chesterton
Grendon Underwood
Pitchcott
Oving
Whitchurch
Tackley
Kirtlington
Ambrosden
Wendlebury
Blackthorn
Kingswood
Quainton
Aston Abbotts
Hardwick
Weston-on-the-Green
Ludgershall
Weedon
Bletchingdon
Shipton-on-Cherwell
Hampton Poyle
Merton
Upper Arncott
Piddington
Westcott
Waddesdon
Akeman Street
Fencott
Charlton-on-Otmoor
Murcott
Duck Decoy (NT)
Wotton Underwood
Waddesdon Manor (NT)
Oddington
Ot Moor
Boarstall
Dorton
Ashendon
Upper(Over) Winchendon
Aylesbury
Kidlington
Begbroke
Islip
Noke
Horton-cum-Studley
Brill
Hartwell
Stone
Woodeaton
Water Eaton
Yarnton
Beckley
Oakley
Chilton
Lower(Nether) Winchendon
Upton
Dinton
Hartwell
Wolvercote
Sunnymead
Summertown
Elsfield
Stanton St John
Forest Hill
Easington
Long Crendon
Chearsley
Cuddington
Westlington
Bishopstone
Stoke Mandeville
Wytham
Marston
OXFORD
University Colleges
Headington
Worminghall
Courthouse (NT)
Notley Abbey (ruins)
Haddenham
Ford
Kimble Wick
Osney
North Hinksey
St Mary the Virgin
Botanic Garden
Holton
Waterperry
Ickford
Shabbington
Aston Sandford
Little Kimble
Ellesborough
Chawley
South Hinksey
Iffley
Cowley
Shotover
Wheatley
Horspath
Waterstock
Rycote Chapel
Thame
Kingsey
Ilmer
Owlswick
Meadle
Longwick
Askett
Monks Risborough
Princes Risborough
Boars Hill
Wootton
Sandford-on-Thames
Kennington
Littlemore
Cuddesdon
Garsington
Denton
Great Milton
Tiddington
Moreton
Towersey
Pitch Green
Chinnor & Princes Risborough Rly
Emmington
Henton
Bledlow
Saunderton
Toot Baldon
Marsh Baldon
Great Haseley
Little Milton
Little Haseley
Tetsworth
Sydenham
Chinnor
Loosley Row
Lacey Green
Cothill
Radley
Nuneham Courtenay
Chislehampton
Stoke Talmage
Postcombe
Adwell
South Weston
Aston Rowant
Kingston Blount
Shippon
ABINGDON
Stadhampton
Chalgrove 1643
Lewknor
Saunderton Sta.
Bradenham
Bledlow Ridge
County Hall & Mus
Nuneham Park
Drayton St Leonard
Chalgrove
Newington
Easington
The City
Stokenchurch
West Wycombe
Clifton Hampden
Berinsfield
Burcot
Pyrton
Shirburn
Beacon's Bottom
Sutton Wick
Culham
Long Wittenham
Dorchester
Abbey Church
Brightwell Baldwin
Cuxham
Britwell Salome
Watlington
Christmas Common
Ridgeway Path
West Wycombe Park (NT)
Drayton
Manor House
Sutton Courtenay
Appleford
Little Wittenham
Warborough
Shillingford
Berrick Salome
Benson
Northend
Ibstone
HIGH WYCOMBE
Milton
OXFORDSHIRE
CHILTERN
Ewelme
Swyncombe
Greenfield
Turville Heath
Turville
Cadmore End
Bolter End
Lane End
Fingest
Didcot
East Hagbourne
Brightwell
Wallingford
Cookley Green
Russell's Water
Pishill
Stonor Park
Frieth
Skirmett
Harwell
North Moreton
Crowmarsh Gifford
Park Corner
Maidensgrove
Stonor
Rockwell End
West Hagbourne
South Moreton
Cholsey
Cholsey & Wallingford Rly
Nuffield
Huntercombe End
Fawley
Lower Woodend
Ginge
Upton
Aston Upthorpe
Aston Tirrold
North Stoke
Hailey
Nettlebed
Middle Assendon
Hambleden
Chilton
Blewbury
Ipsden
Highmoor Cross
Bix
Greenlands
Lower Assendon
Mill End
Aston
Remenham
Hurley
Medmenham
Moulsford
Stoke Row
Shepherd's Green
Greys Court (NT)
Greys Green
Remenham Hill
Henley-on-Thames
Hurley Bottom
Checkendon
South Stoke
West Ilsley
East Ilsley
Streatley
Cleeve
Woodcote
Exlade Street
Rotherfield Greys
River & Rowing Mus
Burchett's Green
Goring
Cray's Pond
Rotherfield Peppard
Gallowstree Common
Harpsden
Cockpole Green
Crazies Hill
Warren Row
Compton
Sonning Common
Lower Shiplake
Knowl Hill
Aldworth
Beale Park
Cane End
Kidmore End
Shiplake
Wargrave
Stanmore
WEST BERKS
Basildon
Whitchurch Hill
Tokers Green
Binfield Heath
Kiln Green
Beedon
Basildon Park (NT)
Whitchurch-on-Thames Toll
Mapledurham
Dunsden Green
Hare Hatch
Peasemore
World's End
Hampstead Norreys
Ashampstead
Mapledurham House & Mill
Emmer Green
Sonning Eye
Ruscombe
Upper Basildon
Pangbourne
Purley on Thames
Caversham
Museum of Reading
Play Hatch
Sonning
Twyford
Yattendon
Tidmarsh
Sulham
Tilehurst
READING
Woodley
Dinton Pastures
Whistley Green
Chieveley
Little Hungerford
Hermitage
Frilsham
Bradfield
Englefield
North Street
Calcot
Earley
Hurst
Curridge
Longlane
Stanford Dingley
Bucklebury
Theale
Lower Earley
Winnersh
Cold Ash
Southend
Whitley
Sindlesham
Donnington
Upper Bucklebury
Chapel Row
Sheffield Bottom
Shinfield
Wokingham
Shaw
Thatcham
Beenham
Sulhamstead
Burghfield
Burghfield Hill
NEWBURY
Midgham
Woolhampton
Beenham Hill
Ufton Nervet
Burghfield Common
Three Mile Cross
Arborfield
Arborfield Cross
Barkham
Arborfield Garrison
Eastheath
Midgham Sta.
Aldermaston Wharf
Padworth
Grazeley
Spencers Wood
Wokefield Park
Swallowfield
WOKINGHAM
M40
M4
A34
A40
A41
A418
A4129
A4010
A329
A4074
A415
A4183
A4130
A4185
A417
A4155
A321
A4
A340
A339
A3290
A4095
A4421
A4260
A4165
A4144
A4142
A413
B4027
B4011
B4009
B4480
B4015
B4016
B4493
B4526
B4445
B4444
B4443
B3024
B3018
B3034
B3030
B3349
B3270
B3350
A
B
C
D
1
2
3
4
5


56
41
28

43
STEVENAGE
LUTON
57
London Luton
Leighton Buzzard
Houghton Regis
DUNSTABLE
HARPENDEN
Welwyn
Wheathampstead
HEMEL HEMPSTEAD
Berkhamsted
Tring
ST ALBANS
London Colney
Kings Langley
Abbots Langley
CHESHAM
AMERSHAM
WATFORD
Radlett
Borehamwood
Elstree
44
Bushey
Rickmansworth
Chorleywood
Beaconsfield
HARROW
Wembley
BRENT
UXBRIDGE
HILLINGDON
EALING
HAMMERSMITH & FULHAM
MAIDENHEAD
SLOUGH
WINDSOR
Eton
London Heathrow
HOUNSLOW
RICHMOND UPON THAMES
KINGSTON UPON THAMES
STAINES
Egham
Ascot
BRACKNELL
Chertsey
WALTON-ON-THAMES
Shepperton
29
Hazlemere
Wendover
Aylesbury
Great Missenden
Gerrards Cross
Denham
Cookham
Marlow
Wooburn
Burnham
Twickenham
Teddington
Surbiton
Harefield
Northwood
Pinner
Ruislip
Stanmore
Edgware
Hendon
Kingsbury
Willesden
Harlesden
Greenford
Southall
Hayes
Yiewsley
Iver
Langley
Datchet
Colnbrook
Ashford
Feltham
Isleworth
Brentford
Kew
Chiswick
Barnes
Hampton
East Molesey
West Molesey
Sunbury
B E D S
H E R T S
B U C K S
M25
M1
M4
M40
M10
M3
A1(M)
A41
A5
A40
A413
A404
A4
A30
A308
A316
A312
A406

44
LUTON
London Luton
Limbury
Leagrave
Stopsley
Cockernhoe
Breachwood Green
King's Walden
St Paul's Walden
Langley
STEVENAGE
Whitwell
Knebworth House
Bendish
Aston
Shephall End
Benington
Hebing End
Haultwick
Great Munden
Nasty
Braughing
Puckeridge
Standon
Collier's End
Dane End
Broadwater
Bragbury End
58
A
B
C
D
Peter's Green
New Mill End
Slip End
Kimpton
Codicote
The Node
Old Knebworth
Knebworth
Datchworth
Woolmer Green
Datchworth Green
Sacombe
Watton at Stone
High Cross
Much Hadham
Hadham Cross
Perry Green
Wadesmill
Thundridge
Baker's End
Widford
East Hyde
Kinsbourne Green
Blackmore End
Ayot St Lawrence
Shaw's Corner (NT)
Welwyn
Oaklands
Bull's Green
Burnham Green
Stapleford
Tonwell
Chapmore End
Paynes Hall
Woodside Farm
Luton Hoo
HARPENDEN
Marshall's Heath
The Folly
Ayot St Peter
Harmer Green
Digswell
Tewin
Bramfield
Waterford
Bengeo
Ware
Wareside
Hunsdon
Trowley Bottom
Hatching Green
Wheathampstead
Cromer Hyde
WELWYN GARDEN CITY
HERTFORD
Little Amwell
Hertford Heath
St Margarets
Great Amwell
Stanstead Abbotts
Eastwick
Gilston Park
Redbourn
Church End
Childwick Green
Sandridge
Lemsford
Stanborough
Hatfield Hyde
Cole Green
Hertingfordbury
Letty Green
Bayfordbury
Hailey
Rye Park
Roydon
Little Parndon
Great Parndon
HEMEL HEMPSTEAD
M1
Verulamium Roman Town
Verulamium Museum
Gorhambury
Activity World
Hatfield
Mill Green Museum
Hatfield House
Essendon
Bayford
Little Berkhamsted
Hoddesdon
Broxbourne
Spitalbrook
Roydon Hamlet
Broadley
ST ALBANS
Colney Heath
Leverstock Green
St Stephens
M10
Potters Crouch
Chiswell Green
Woodside
Welham Green
Wildhill
Epping Green
Newgate Street
Paradise Wildlife Park
Wormley
Lower Nazeing
Nazeing
Epping Green
Bumble's Green
Great Wood
Park Street
Frogmore
London Colney
Water End
Bell Bar
Hammond Street
Goff's Oak
Turnford
Bedmond
Langley
M25
21/6A
21A
22
Smug Oak
Bricket Wood
Colney Street
A1(M)
Brookmans Park
Cuffley
Churchgate
Flamstead End
Cheshunt
Lee Valley
Upshire
Huntonbridge
Abbots Langley
Shenleybury
South Mimms
Northaw
Potters Bar
Waltham Cross
Waltham Abbey
Radlett
Shenley
Green Street
Ridge
23/1
24
25
26
43
Aldenham
Wrotham Park
Enfield Chase
Botany Bay
Capel Manor
Forty Hill
Cassiobury Park
WATFORD
Letchmore Heath
Borehamwood
Hadley Wood
Trent Park
ENFIELD
Sewardstone
High Beach
Epping Forest
Loughton
Monken Hadley
Cockfosters
Ponders End
Bushey
Aldenham Reservoir
Elstree
Arkley
New Barnet
BARNET
East Barnet
Winchmore Hill
Merry Hill
Bushey Heath
Batchworth
Chingford
Buckhurst Hill
London Gateway
Totteridge
Southgate
South Oxhey
Eastbury
Stanmore
Mill Hill
Friern Barnet
Edmonton
Hatch End
Edgware
Woodford Green
Woodford
Woodford Bridge
Northwood
Pinner Green
Harrow Weald
Wealdstone
Harrow Museum
R.A.F. Mus
Finchley
Wood Green
Tottenham
WALTHAM FOREST
Barking
Pinner
Ruislip Common
Bayhurst Wood
Eastcote
HARROW
Kingsbury
Hendon
Golders Green
Hornsey
HARINGEY
Walthamstow
Wanstead
Ruislip
Greenhill
Highgate Cemetery
Kenwood
Leyton
Ickenham
Harrow on the Hill
Wembley Complex
Sudbury
BRENT
Watling Street
Fenton House (NT)
Hampstead
ISLINGTON
Stoke Newington
Northolt
Wembley
Willesden
Harlesden
CAMDEN
HACKNEY
Forest Gate
HILLINGDON
Greenford
Perivale
London Zoo
Regents Park
Shoreditch
Bethnal Green
Finsbury
TOWER HAMLETS
NEWHAM
West Ham
Yeading
Paddington
Marylebone
Stepney
Poplar
Hayes
Southall
EALING
Hanwell
Acton
Beckton
ExCeL
West Drayton
Norwood Green
HAMMERSMITH & FULHAM
CITY OF WESTMINSTER
Hyde Park
CITY OF LONDON
Bermondsey
Heston
Osterley Park
Chiswick
Brentford
KENSINGTON & CHELSEA
SOUTHWARK
Deptford
Charlton
GREENWICH
Harmondsworth
Cranford
Osterley
Barnes
Fulham
Battersea
Battersea Park Children's Zoo
Camberwell
Blackheath
Kidbrooke
Kew
Isleworth
Mortlake
WANDSWORTH
LAMBETH
Clapham
LEWISHAM
Stanwell
HOUNSLOW
Twickenham
East Bedfont
Feltham
Putney
Roehampton
RICHMOND UPON THAMES
Richmond Park
Hither Green
Catford
Ashford
Ham
Teddington
Wimbledon Common
Upper Tooting
Dulwich
West Norwood
Sydenham
Horniman Museum
Grove Park
Mottingham
Hanworth
KINGSTON UPON THAMES
Wimbledon
Streatham
Crystal Palace
Upper Norwood
Penge
Beckenham
Chislehurst
Sunbury
West Molesey
Hampton
Bushy Park
Hampton Court Palace
30
Morden Hall Park
Mitcham
South Norwood
BROMLEY
Littleton
Upper Halliford
East Molesey
Surbiton
New Malden
MERTON
Morden
Beddington Corner
Eden Park
West Wickham
Bromley Common
Hayes
Weston Green
Thames Ditton
Long Ditton
Tolworth
Worcester Park
WALTON-ON-THAMES

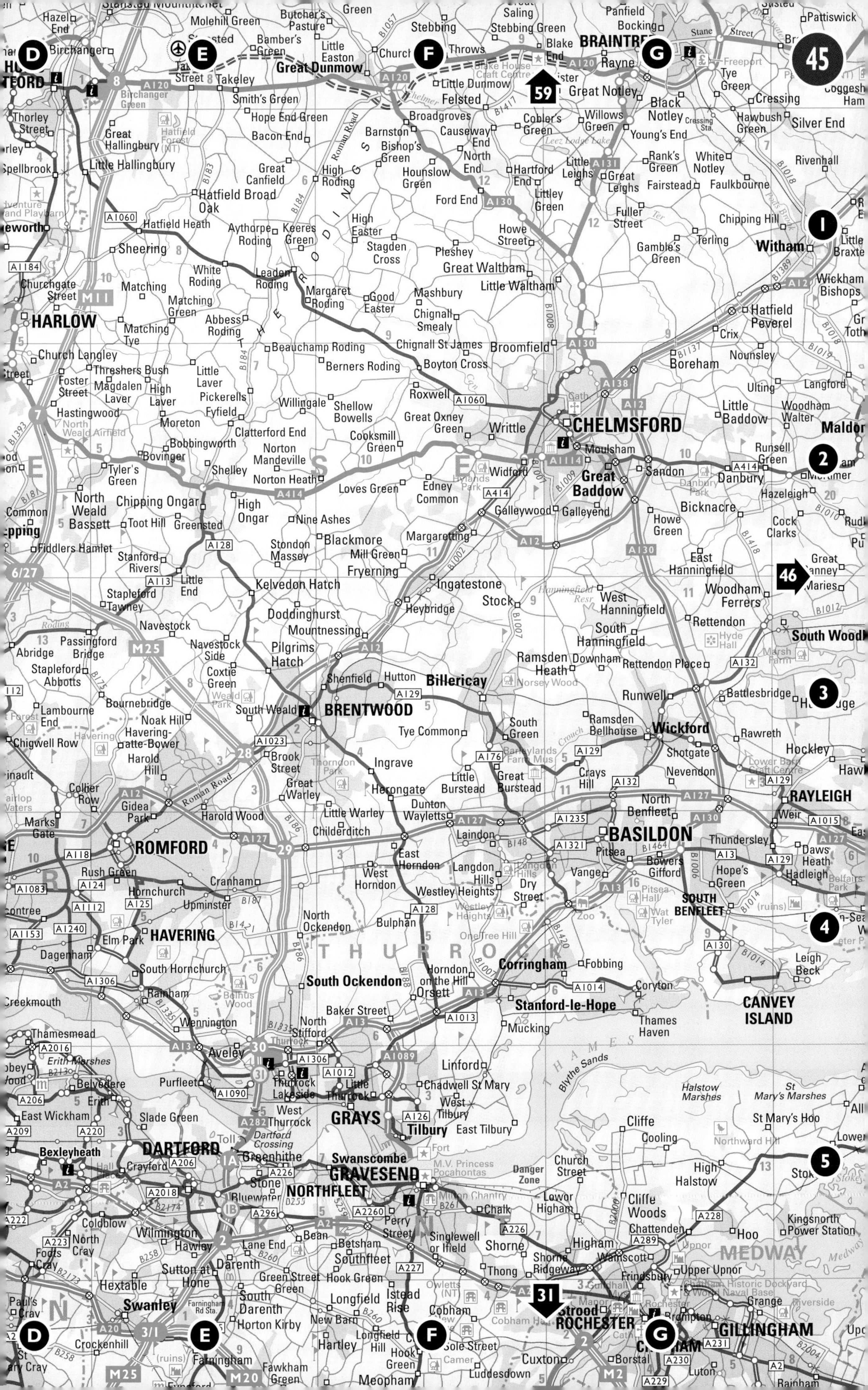

Hazel End
Birchanger
Molehill Green
Stansted
Takeley Street
Takeley
Bamber's Green
Butcher's Pasture
Little Easton
Great Dunmow
Church End
Stebbing
Throws
Saling
Stebbing Green
Blake End
Blake House Craft Centre
Little Dunmow
Felsted
Panfield
Bocking
BRAINTREE
Rayne
Freeport
Tye Green
Great Notley
Black Notley
Cressing
Coggeshall Hamlet
Hawbush Green
Silver End
59
BISHOP'S STORTFORD
Birchanger Green
Thorley Street
Spellbrook
Great Hallingbury
Hatfield Forest (NT)
Little Hallingbury
Smith's Green
Hope End Green
Bacon End
Barnston
Bishop's Green
Broadgroves
Causeway End
North End
Cobler's Green
Willows Green
Young's End
Rank's Green
White Notley
Rivenhall
Great Canfield
High Roding
Hounslow Green
Hartford End
Little Leighs
Great Leighs
Fairstead
Faulkbourne
Hatfield Broad Oak
Ford End
Littley Green
Fuller Street
Chipping Hill
Witham
Little Braxted
Sawbridgeworth
Hatfield Heath
Aythorpe Roding
Keeres Green
High Easter
Stagden Cross
Howe Street
Pleshey
Terling
Gamble's Green
Sheering
White Roding
Leaden Roding
Great Waltham
Little Waltham
Wickham Bishops
Churchgate Street
Matching
Matching Green
Margaret Roding
Good Easter
Mashbury
Chignall Smealy
Hatfield Peverel
HARLOW
Matching Tye
Abbess Roding
THE RODINGS
Beauchamp Roding
Chignall St James
Broomfield
Crix
Boreham
Nounsley
Church Langley
Threshers Bush
Little Laver
Berners Roding
Boyton Cross
Ulting
Langford
Foster Street
Magdalen Laver
High Laver
Pickerells
Roxwell
Little Baddow
Woodham Walter
Hastingwood
North Weald Airfield
Moreton
Fyfield
Willingale
Shellow Bowells
Great Oxney Green
Writtle
CHELMSFORD
Maldon
Bobbingworth
Clatterford End
Cooksmill Green
Moulsham
Runsell Green
Bovinger
Norton Mandeville
Tyler's Green
Shelley
Norton Heath
Widford
Hylands Park
Great Baddow
Sandon
Danbury
Danbury Park
Mortimer
Hazeleigh
Loves Green
Edney Common
North Weald Bassett
Chipping Ongar
High Ongar
Galleywood
Galleyend
Bicknacre
Cock Clarks
Toot Hill
Greensted
Nine Ashes
Howe Green
Epping
Fiddlers Hamlet
Stondon Massey
Blackmore
Margaretting
Mill Green
Fryerning
East Hanningfield
Great Canney
Stanford Rivers
Little End
Kelvedon Hatch
Ingatestone
Stock
Hanningfield Resr
West Hanningfield
Woodham Ferrers
Maries
Stapleford Tawney
Heybridge
Doddinghurst
Navestock
Mountnessing
South Hanningfield
Rettendon
Hyde Hall
South Woodham
Passingford Bridge
Navestock Side
Pilgrims Hatch
Ramsden Heath
Downham
Rettendon Place
Marsh Farm
Abridge
Stapleford Abbotts
Coxtie Green
Weald Park
Norsey Wood
Billericay
Shenfield
Hutton
Runwell
Battlesbridge
Hullbridge
Lambourne End
Bournebridge
South Weald
BRENTWOOD
Ramsden Bellhouse
Wickford
Rawreth
Chigwell Row
Noak Hill
Havering-atte-Bower
Tye Common
South Green
Shotgate
Hockley
Hawkwell
Harold Hill
Brook Street
Thorndon Park
Ingrave
Barleylands Farm Mus
Crays Hill
Nevendon
Lower Barn Craft Centre
Collier Row
Gidea Park
Roman Road
Harold Wood
Great Warley
Herongate
Little Burstead
Great Burstead
North Benfleet
RAYLEIGH
Marks Gate
Little Warley
Childerditch
Dunton Wayletts
Laindon
BASILDON
Weir
ROMFORD
Pitsea
Thundersley
Daws Heath
Rush Green
Cranham
East Horndon
West Horndon
Langdon Hills
Dry Street
Vange
Bowers Gifford
Hope's Green
Hadleigh
Belfairs Park
Hornchurch
Upminster
Westley Heights
Pitsea Hall
Wat Tyler
SOUTH BENFLEET
Leigh-on-Sea
HAVERING
North Ockendon
Bulphan
Zoo
Elm Park
One Tree Hill
Dagenham
THURROCK
Corringham
Fobbing
Leigh Beck
South Hornchurch
South Ockendon
Horndon on the Hill
Orsett
Coryton
CANVEY ISLAND
Creekmouth
Rainham
Belhus Wood
Stanford-le-Hope
Baker Street
Thames Haven
Wennington
North Stifford
Mucking
Thamesmead
Erith Marshes
Aveley
Thurrock
Linford
Blythe Sands
Halstow Marshes
St Mary's Marshes
Abbey Wood
Belvedere
Purfleet
Thurrock Lakeside
Little Thurrock
Chadwell St Mary
West Tilbury
Erith
East Wickham
Slade Green
West Thurrock
GRAYS
Tilbury
East Tilbury
Cliffe
St Mary's Hoo
Dartford Crossing
Cooling
Northward Hill
Lower Stoke
Bexleyheath
DARTFORD
Greenhithe
Fort
M.V. Princess Pocahontas
Danger Zone
Church Street
High Halstow
Stoke
Crayford
Swanscombe
GRAVESEND
Stone
NORTHFLEET
Milton Chantry
Lower Higham
Cliffe Woods
Kingsnorth Power Station
Bluewater
Chalk
Perry Street
Chattenden
Hoo
Coldblow
Wilmington
Singlewell or Ifield
Shorne
Higham
MEDWAY
North Cray
Hawley
Lane End
Bean
Betshan
Southfleet
Thong
Shorne Ridgeway
Wainscott
Upnor
Upper Upnor
Foots Cray
Darenth
Green Street Green
Hook Green
Frindsbury
Chatham Historic Dockyard
World Naval Base
Riverside
Sutton at Hone
Hextable
South Darenth
Longfield
Istead Rise
Owletts (NT)
Strood
Grange
St Paul's Cray
Swanley
Farningham Rd Sta.
Horton Kirby
New Barn
Cobham
Cobham Hall
ROCHESTER
Brompton
GILLINGHAM
Crockenhill
Farningham
Hartley
Longfield Hill
Hook Green
Sole Street
Camer
CHATHAM
St Mary Cray
Fawkham Green
Meopham
Cuxton
Luddesdown
Borstal
Luton
Rainham
31
46

BRAINTREE
Saling
Stebbing Green
Panfield
Bocking
Stane Street
Pattiswick
Bradwell
Little Tey
Marks Tey
Stanway
COLCHESTER
Old Heath
Blake End
Rayne
Freeport
Broad Green
Coggeshall
A1124
Beacon
Shrub End
Bannister Green
Great Notley
Tye Green
Paycocke's (NT)
Coggeshall Hamlet
Copford Green
Heckfordbridge
Easthorpe
St Botolph's Priory
Rowhedge
Blackheath
Felsted
Black Notley
Hawbush Green
Silver End
Feering
Hardy's Green
Birch
Grymes Dyke
Danger Zone
Layer de la Haye
Cobler's Green
Willows Green
Crossing Sta.
Young's End
Messing
Kelvedon
Birch Green
Abberton
Causeway End
North End
Leez Lodge Lake
Little Leighs
Rank's Green
White Notley
Rivenhall
Smythe's Green
Layer Breton
Langenhoe
Hartford End
Great Leighs
Fairstead
Faulkbourne
Inworth
Shalom Hall
Layer Marney Tower
Layer Marney
Abberton Reservoir
Peldon
Littley Green
Fuller Street
Rivenhall End
Tiptree
A130
Chipping Hill
Great Braxted
Tiptree Heath
Tolleshunt Knights
Great Wigborough
Mersea Island
Gamble's Green
Terling
Witham
Little Braxted
Oxley Green
Virley
Great Waltham
Little Waltham
Salcott Channel
Salcott
Wickham Bishops
Great Totham
Little Totham
Tolleshunt D'Arcy
Cobmarsh Island
West Mersea
Hatfield Peverel
Great Totham
Tolleshunt Major
Great Cob I.
Tollesbury Fleet
Virley Channel
Crix
Broomfield
Boreham
Nounsley
Broad Street Green
Tollesbury
The Nass
A1060
Ulting
Langford
Heybridge
Goldhanger
Bradwell Waterside
Writtle
CHELMSFORD
Little Baddow
Woodham Walter
Maldon
Heybridge Basin
Northey Island
Osea Island
Blackwater
Ramsey Island
Bradwell-on-Sea
Moulsham
Runsell Green
Sandon
Great Baddow
Danbury
Woodham Mortimer
Maldon 991
St Lawrence
Tillingham
Hylands Park
A414
Galleywood
Galleyend
Hazeleigh
Bicknacre
Howe Green
Cock Clarks
Rudley Green
Mundon
Maylandsea
Steeple
Dengie
Purleigh
Mayland
Asheldham
Dengie Marshes
E S S E X
East Hanningfield
Great Canney
Latchingdon
Cold Norton
Southminster
45
Ingatestone
Stock
West Hanningfield
Woodham Ferrers
Stow Maries
Althorne
Mangapps Farm Railway Museum
Old Montsale
Deal Hall
Stoneyhills
South Hanningfield
Rettendon
Hyde Hall
South Woodham Ferrers
Bridgemarsh Island
Ostend
Burnham-on-Crouch
Holliwell Point
Ramsden Heath
Downham
Rettendon Place
Marsh Farm
South Fambridge
Norsey Wood
A132
Runwell
Battlesbridge
Hullbridge
Crouch
Courtsend
Canewdon
Wallasea Island
South Green
Ramsden Bellhouse
Wickford
Rawreth
Paglesham Churchend
Churchend
Ashingdon
Foulness Island
Shotgate
Hockley
Barleylands Farm Mus
A176
A129
Great Burstead
Little Burstead
Crays Hill
Nevendon
Lower Barn Craft Centre
Hawkwell
Great Stambridge
Ballards Gore
Paglesham Eastend
Potton Island
North Benfleet
RAYLEIGH
A127
A1235
Laindon
BASILDON
Weir
A1015
Rochford
Barling
Maplin Sands
London Southend
Havengore Island
Little Wakering
Thundersley
Eastwood
A1321
Pitsea
Vange
Bowers Gifford
Hope's Green
Daws Heath
Hadleigh
SOUTHEND
Prittlewell Priory
Kids Kingdom
Mr B's Amusements
Great Wakering
Langdon Hills
Dry Street
Belfairs Park
Prittlewell
A13
Central Mus
Southchurch
North Shoebury
Laindon Heights
Pitsea Hall
Wat Tyler
SOUTH BENFLEET
(ruins)
Thorpe Bay
Shoeburyness
Zoo
Leigh-on-Sea
Westcliff-on-Sea
Peter Pan's Adventure Island
Southend Pier
Sea Life Centre
Shoebury Ness
Corringham
Fobbing
Leigh Beck
Chapman Sands
Coryton
SOUTHEND-ON-SEA
Stanford-le-Hope
A1014
CANVEY ISLAND
Mucking
Thames Haven
A1013
THAMES
Blythe Sands
Allhallows-on-Sea
Halstow Marshes
St Mary's Marshes
Allhallows
East Tilbury
Cliffe
St Mary's Hoo
Isle of Grain
Cooling
Northward Hill
Lower Stoke
Grain
Sheerness
Church Street
Danger Zone
High Halstow
Stoke
Stoke Saltings
Wallend
A250
West Minster
Chalk
Lower Higham
Cliffe Woods
Kingsnorth Power Station
Halfway Houses
Minster
Eastchurch
Warden
Shorne
Higham
Chattenden
Hoo
Queenborough
Shorne Ridgeway
Wainscott
Upnor
MEDWAY
Chetney Marshes
B2231
Thong
Upper Upnor
Frindsbury
Chatham Historic Dockyard
World Naval Base
Grange
Riverside
A249
K E N T
ISLE OF SHEPPEY
Strood
ROCHESTER
Cobham Hall
Brompton
GILLINGHAM
Upchurch
Lower Halstow
32
Iwade
Swale Sta.
Elmley Island
Eastchurch Marshes
Isle of Harty
CHATHAM
A231
Cuxton
Borstal
Luton
Luddesdown
The Swale
Kemsley
Rainham
A229
A230
A2
M2
59

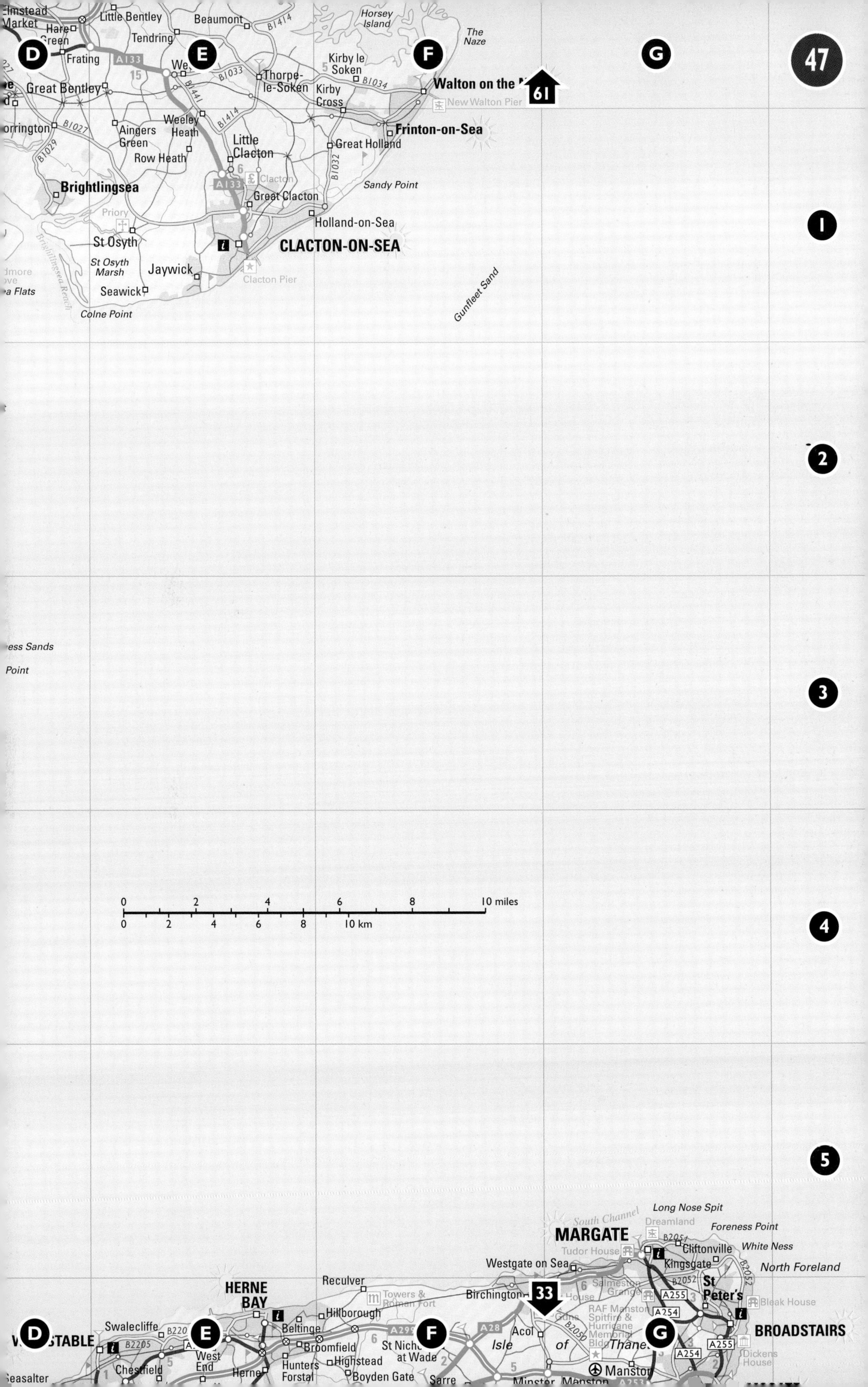
D
E
F
G
I
2
3
4
5
61
33
Elmstead Market
Hare Green
Little Bentley
Beaumont
Tendring
Frating
A133
B1414
Horsey Island
The Naze
Kirby le Soken
Thorpe-le-Soken
B1033
B1034
B1441
Walton on the Naze
New Walton Pier
Great Bentley
Kirby Cross
Frinton-on-Sea
B1027
B1029
Aingers Green
Weeley Heath
B1414
Little Clacton
Great Holland
Row Heath
Brightlingsea
Clacton
B1032
Sandy Point
Great Clacton
Priory
Holland-on-Sea
St Osyth
CLACTON-ON-SEA
St Osyth Marsh
Jaywick
Clacton Pier
Brightlingsea Reach
Seawick
Gunfleet Sand
Colne Point
Point
0
2
4
6
8
10 miles
0
2
4
6
8
10 km
Long Nose Spit
South Channel
Dreamland
Foreness Point
MARGATE
B2051
Cliftonville
White Ness
Tudor House
Westgate on Sea
Kingsgate
North Foreland
B2052
Reculver
B2052
St Peter's
HERNE BAY
Towers & Roman Fort
Birchington
Salmestone Grange
A255
Bleak House
Hillborough
RAF Manston Spitfire & Hurricane Memorial Bldg
A254
BROADSTAIRS
Swalecliffe
B2220
Beltinge
A28
Acol
B2050
STABLE
B2205
Broomfield
A299
St Nicholas at Wade
Isle
of
Thanet
A255
A254
Dickens House
West End
Hunters Forstal
Highstead
Manston
Seasalter
Chestfield
Herne
Boyden Gate
Sarre
Minster
Manston

A
B
C
D
1
2
3
4
5
0 2 4 6 8 10 miles
0 2 4 6 8 10 km
hours
Rosslare.............1¾-3½
PEMBROKESHIRE
COAST
NATIONAL PARK
PEMBROKESHIRE
Strumble Head
Tresinwen
Carregwastad Point
Crincoed Point
Fishguard Bay
Dinas Head
Dinas Island
Cwm-y
Bryn-henllan
Dinas Cross
Pen Brush
Pen Caer
Llanwnda
Goodwick (Wdig)
Fishguard (Abergwaun)
A487
Trefasser
Penbwchdy
Dyffryn
Lower Town
Mynydd Melyn
307
St Nicholas
Manorowen
Llanychaer Bridge
Cilrhedyn Bridge
Pontfaen
Penmorfa
Ynys Deullyn
Granston
Scleddau
Abercastle
Jordanston
Trecwn
Mynydd Cilciffeth
334
Penclegyr
Porthgain
Trevine
Mathry
Castle Morris
Newbridge
Llanrhian
A40
Abereiddy
Penparc
B4331
Berea
Croesgoch
Letterston
Little Newcastle
Puncheston
Mynydd Cas
347
Carreg-gwylan-fach
Penclegyr
Penllechwen
Llanreithan
Tre-ddiog
Castlebythe
St David's Head
Treleddyd-fawr
Tretio
Treglemais
Treffynnon
Welsh Hook
St Dogwells
North Bishop
Rhodiad-y-Brenin
B4330
Whitesands Bay or Porth-mawr
Caerfarchell
Newton
Wolf's Castle
Rinaston
Wallis
B4583
Point St John
Cathedral
Bishop's Palace
Whitchurch
Middle Mill
Llandeloy
Ford
Ambleston
Carreg
Rhosson
St David's (Tyddewi)
Trefgarn Owen
Hayscastle
Hayscastle Cross
Llys-y-fran Re
Bishops and Clerks
St Non's Chapel
Solva
Brawdy
Mountain Water
Spittal
Ramsey Sound
Penycwm
Llethr
Dudwell Mountain
178
Treffgarne
Upper Scolton
Ramsey Island
Green Scar
Dinas Fawr
Newgale
Leweston
Ynys Bery
Newgale Sands
Wolfsdale
Scolton Manor
Clarbeston Road
Roch
Folly
Rudbaxton
B4329
Camrose
Keeston
Poyston Cross
34
Tangiers
ST BRIDE'S BAY
Rickets Head
Nolton
Pelcomb Cross
Crundale
Wis
Druidston
Lambston
Pelcomb Bridge
Prendergast
Castle Mus & Art Gallery
Sutton
B4330
10
8
6
15
14
12
16

D
E
F
G
I
New Quay Head
New Quay
(Ceinewydd)
New Quay Bay
Llwyn-onn
Ffos-y-
Gilfachrheda
B4342
Llanarth
Cwmtudu
Nanternis
Cross Inn
A486
A487
Ynys-Lochtyn
Llwyndafydd
Synod Inn
Llangranog
B4321
Wervil Brook
Plwmp
Pencribach
Penbryn
Pentregat
Cardigan Island
Parcllyn
Aberporth
Tresaith
Brynhoffnant
B4338
Talgarreg
Cemaes Head
Sarnau
Wstrws
50
Gwbert
Ferwig
Blaenannerch
Tan-y-groes
Pen-yr-afr
B4548
Tremain
Glynarthen
Capel Cynon
Pwllygranant
Cippyn
Blaenporth
B4334
Castell Howell
Cardigan
(Aberteifi)
Penparc
Bettws Evan
Rhydlewis
Ffostrasol
Ceibwr Bay
St Dogmaels
CEREDIGION
Tre-Rhys
Llangoedmor
Noyadd Trefawr
Beulah
Hawen
Penrhiw-pal
Abbey
B4570
Pantgwyn
Brongest
Maesllyn
Tre-groes
Moylgrove
Monington
Ponthirwaun
Troedyraur
Croes-lan
A475
Cardigan
A484
Llechryd
Llandygwydd
Capel Tygwydd
Pren-gw
(NT)
Teifi
Glanrhyd
Cilgerran
Manordeifi
Pont Ceri
B4571
Teifi Valley
Aber-banc
Penrhiw-llan
Horeb
B4476
Berry Hill
Llantood
Bridell
Cwmcoy
Llandyfriog
Trewilym
B4582
Pentre Mansion
Cenarth
Newcastle Emlyn
(Castell Newydd Emlyn)
Llanfair-Orllwyn
Bangor Teifi
Llandysul
Nevern
Rhos-hill
Abercych
Aberarad
Pentrecagal
Henllan
Llangeler
Pontwelly
Velindre
Newchapel
Clynfyw
Penrherber
Welsh Woollen Industry
Drefach
Felindre
Pentre-cwrt
Eglwyswrw
B4332
Cilwendeg
Boncath
Glynteg
Saron
Banc-y-ffordd
Ifan Burial Chamber
Llanfair-Nant-Gwyn
Cwmpengraig
Cilgwyn
Crosswell
Blaenffos
Glaspant
Capel Iwan
Moelfre
Whitechurch
A478
Freni-fawr
395
Bwlch-y-groes
335
Penboyr
Bwlch-clawdd
257
Brynberian
B4329
Star
Clydey
Cilrhedyn
Cwm-Morgan
Rhos
Tafarn-y-bwlch
Crymych
326
Gorllwyn
PRESCELLY MTS (MYNYDD PRESELI)
Tegryn
B4333
B4299
Foel Eryr
468
Foel Cwmcerwyn
536
Hermon
Cwmduad
Mynachlogddu
Foel Drych
368
262
Llanfyrnach
Trelech
Hermon
Duad
Greenway
Pentre Galar
Rosebush
Dinas
Glandwr
Esgair
Llanpumsaint
Hebron
Blaen-y-coed
Cynwyl Elfed
B4301
Maenclochog
Llangolman
Blaenwaun
Post House
Trelech a'r Betws
Gwili
New Moat
Llanglydwen
Llanwinio
A484
B4313
Efailwen
Cwmbach
Ialog
Bwlchnewydd
Newchurch
Cefn-y-pant
Via Julia
Cwmfelin Mynach
Gellywen
A478
Llanycefn
Login
Maesgwynno
Llandre
Llanboidy
Abernant
Pen-ffordd
Nant Cynnen
Ffynnon-ddrain
CARMARTHENSHIRE
Tre-vaughan
Llandissilio
Henllan Amgoed
Castell Gorfod
Meidrim
Merthyr
Tanerdy
Carmarthen
(Caerfyrddin)
Rhydywrach
B4298
Johnstown
Clynderwen
Llanfallteg
Llangynin
35
Sarnau
A40
Pensarn
Gelly
Llanfallteg West
Cwmfelin Boeth
Bron-y-Gaer
Llanllwch
Llanddewi Velfrey
Whitland Abbey
Bancyfelin
A484
Cwmffrwd
Whitland
A40
Pwll Trap
Llangynog
Llangain
B4312
Croesyceiliog
Trevaughan
St Clears
Redstone Bank
Robeston Wathen

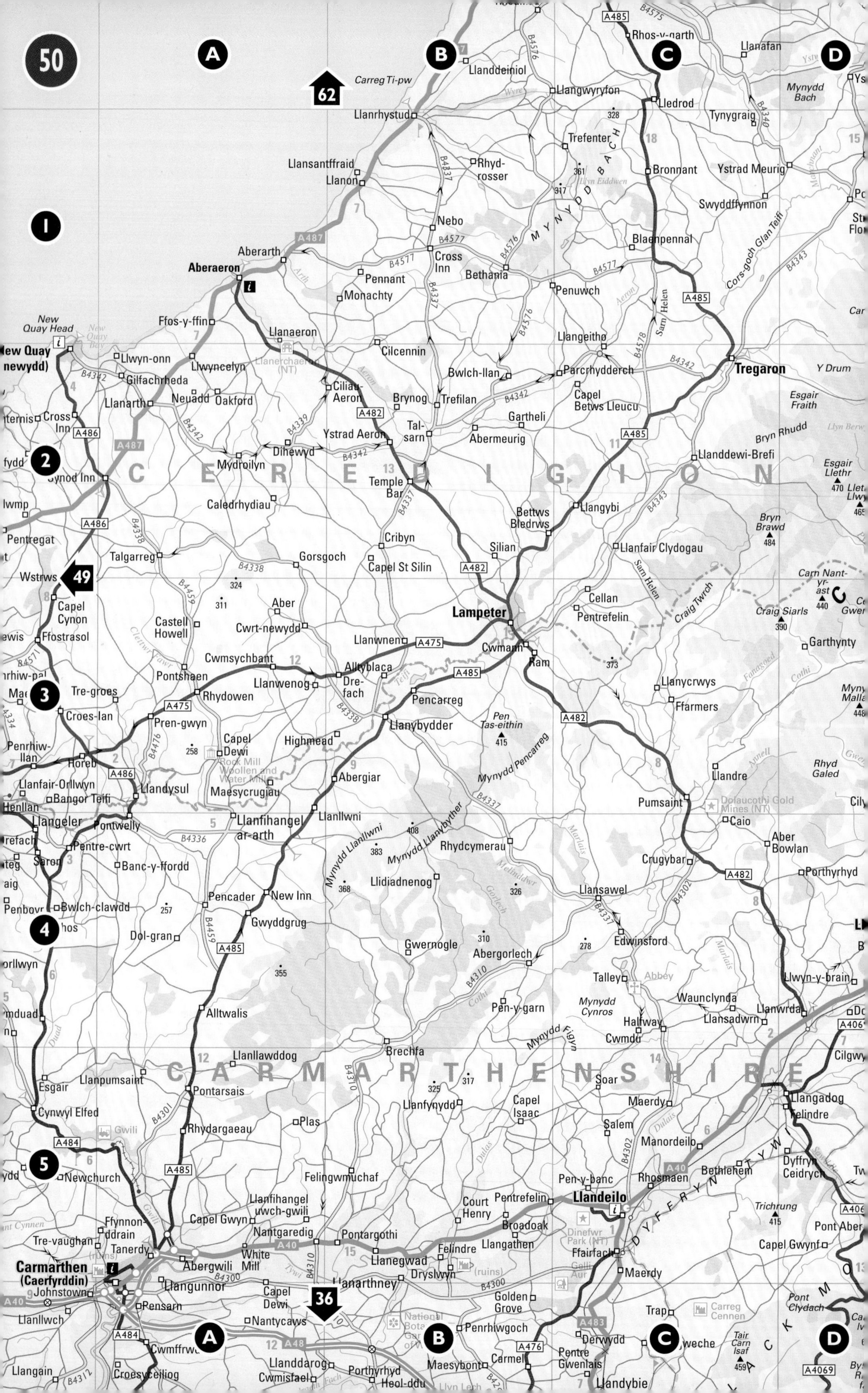
A
B
C
D
62
Carreg Ti-pw
Llanddeiniol
Rhos-y-garth
Llanafan
Llangwyryfon
Lledrod
Mynydd Bach
Llanrhystud
Tynygraig
328
Trefenter
Llansantffraid
Llanon
Rhyd-rosser
Bronnant
Ystrad Meurig
361
317
Llyn Eiddwen
MYNYDD BACH
Swyddffynnon
Nebo
Blaenpennal
Cross Inn
Aberarth
Aberaeron
Pennant
Bethania
Penuwch
Cors-goch Glan Teifi
Monachty
New Quay Head
Ffos-y-ffin
Llanaeron
Llangeitho
Sarn Helen
Tregaron
Y Drum
New Quay (Ceinewydd)
Llwyn-onn
Llwyncelyn
Llanerchaeron (NT)
Cilcennin
Bwlch-llan
Parcrhydderch
Gilfachrheda
Ciliau-Aeron
Capel Betws Lleucu
Esgair Fraith
Llanarth
Neuadd
Oakford
Brynog
Trefilan
Gartheli
Cross Inn
Tal-sarn
Abermeurig
Bryn Rhudd
Ystrad Aeron
Dihewyd
Mydroilyn
Llanddewi-Brefi
Synod Inn
CEREDIGION
Temple Bar
Esgair Llethr
470
Caledrhydiau
Llangybi
Bettws Bledrws
Bryn Brawd
484
Cribyn
Pentregat
Talgarreg
Gorsgoch
Capel St Silin
Silian
Llanfair Clydogau
Wstrws
49
324
Carn Nant-yr-ast
440
Capel Cynon
311
Aber
Lampeter
Cellan
Castell Howell
Cwrt-newydd
Pentrefelin
Craig Twrch
Craig Siarls
390
Ffostrasol
Llanwnen
Cwmann
Garthynty
Cwmsychbant
Alltyblaca
Ram
373
Pontshaen
Llanwenog
Dre-fach
Llanycrwys
Tre-groes
Rhydowen
Pencarreg
Ffarmers
Croes-lan
Pren-gwyn
Llanybydder
Pen Tas-eithin
415
Penrhiw-llan
Capel Dewi
Highmead
258
Mynydd Pencarreg
Horeb
Rock Mill Woollen and Water Mill (NT)
Abergiar
Llandre
Rhyd Galed
Llanfair-Orllwyn
Bangor Teifi
Llandysul
Maesycrugiau
Pumsaint
Dolaucothi Gold Mines (NT)
Henllan
Llangeler
Pontwelly
Llanfihangel-ar-arth
Llanllwni
Caio
Pentre-cwrt
408
Mynydd Llanllwni
Mynydd Llanybyther
Rhydcymerau
Aber Bowlan
Saron
Banc-y-ffordd
383
Crugybar
Porthyrhyd
Llidiadnenog
368
326
Pencader
New Inn
Llansawel
Bwlch-clawdd
257
Gwyddgrug
Edwinsford
Dol-gran
Gwernogle
310
278
Abergorlech
355
Talley
Abbey
Llwyn-y-brain
Mynydd Cynros
Waunclynda
Pen-y-garn
Llansadwrn
Llanwrda
Alltwalis
Halfway
Cwmdu
Mynydd Figyn
Brechfa
Llanllawddog
CARMARTHENSHIRE
Llanpumsaint
325
317
Soar
Esgair
Pontarsais
Llanfynydd
Capel Isaac
Maerdy
Llangadog
Cynwyl Elfed
Felindre
Gwili
Plas
Rhydargaeau
Salem
Manordeilo
Newchurch
Felingwmuchaf
Dyffryn Ceidrych
Pen-y-banc
Rhosmaen
Bethlehem
Llanfihangel uwch-gwili
Court Henry
Pentrefelin
Llandeilo
DYFFRYN TYWI
Trichrung
415
Ffynnon-ddrain
Capel Gwyn
Broadoak
Tre-vaughan
Nantgaredig
Pontargothi
Dinefwr Park (NT)
Pont Aber
Tanerdy
Llangathen
Capel Gwynfe
Carmarthen (Caerfyrddin)
Abergwili
White Mill
Llanegwad
Felindre
Ffairfach
Johnstown
Llangunnor
Capel Dewi
Llanarthney
Dryslwyn
Maerdy
Golden Grove
Pensarn
36
Trap
Carreg Cennen
Pont Clydach
Llanllwch
Nantycaws
National Botanic Garden of Wales
Penrhiwgoch
Derwydd
Tair Carn Isaf
459
Cwmffrwd
Llanddarog
Maesybont
Carmel
Pentre Gwenlais
Llangain
Croesyceiliog
Cwmisfael
Porthyrhyd
Heol-ddu
Llandybie
A485
A487
A482
A486
A475
A484
A40
A48
A476
A483
A4069
A406
B4577
B4576
B4337
B4342
B4339
B4338
B4459
B4476
B4336
B4310
B4301
B4300
B4302
B4343
B4578
B4340
B4571
1
2
3
4
5

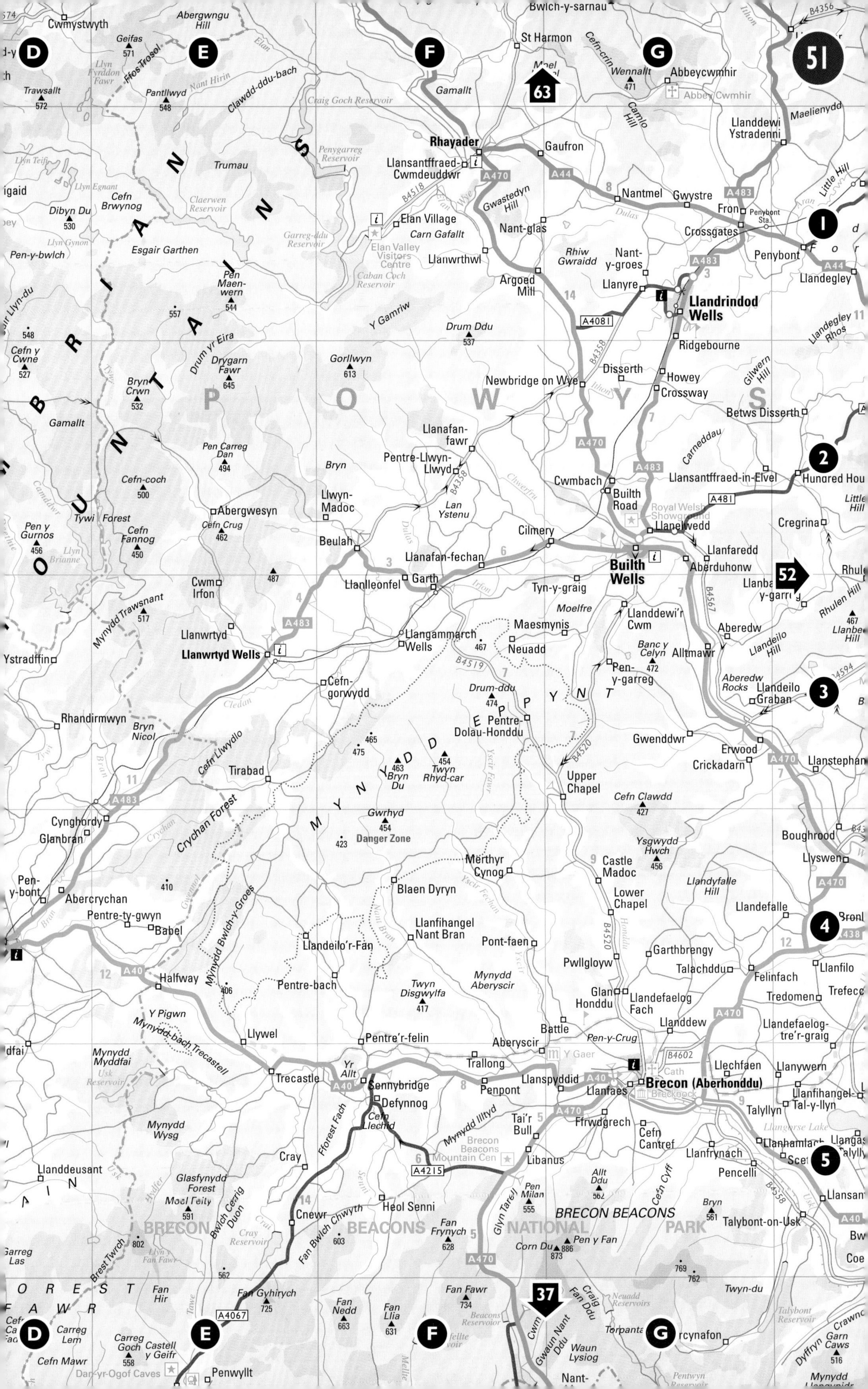
Bwlch-y-sarnau
Cwmystwyth
Abergwngu Hill
St Harmon
Cefn-crin
Ithon
B4356
D
E
F
G
Geifas 571
Ffos Trosol
Elan
Maen Serth
63
Wennallt 471
Abbeycwmhir
Abbey Cwmhir
Llyn Fyrddon Fawr
Trawsallt 572
Pantllwyd 548
Nant Hirin
Clawdd-ddu-bach
Craig Goch Reservoir
Gamallt
Camlo Hill
Llanddewi Ystradenni
Maelienydd
Rhayader
Gaufron
Penygarreg Reservoir
Llansantffraed-Cwmdeuddwr
Llyn Teifi
Trumau
A470
A44
Little Hill
Llyn Egnant
Cefn Brwynog
Claerwen Reservoir
B4518
Gwastedyn Hill
Nantmel
Gwystre
A483
Fron
Penybont Sta.
Dibyn Du 530
Elan Village
Carn Gafallt
Dulas
Aran
Crossgates
I
Llyn Gynon
Garreg-ddu Reservoir
Nant-glas
Pen-y-bwlch
Esgair Garthen
Elan Valley Visitors Centre
Llanwrthwl
Rhiw Gwraidd
Nant-y-groes
Penybont
Caban Coch Reservoir
Argoed Mill
Llanyre
Llandegley
Pen Maen-wern 544
Llandrindod Wells
Llyn-du
557
Y Gamriw
A4081
548
Drum Ddu 537
Llandegley Rhos
Drum yr Eira
B4358
Ridgebourne
Cefn y Cwne 527
Drygarn Fawr 645
Gorllwyn 613
Disserth
Howey
Gilwern Hill
Newbridge on Wye
Ithon
Crossway
Bryn Crwn 532
Betws Disserth
Llanafan-fawr
Gamallt
Pen Carreg Dan 494
Pentre-Llwyn-Llwyd
Carneddau
2
Bryn
Chwefru
Cwmbach
Llansantffraed-in-Elvel
Hundred House
Cefn-coch 500
Builth Road
A481
Llwyn-Madoc
Lan Ystenu
Little Hill
Camddwr
Abergwesyn
Royal Welsh Showground
Tywi Forest
Cefn Crug 462
Llanelwedd
Cregrina
Pen y Gurnos 456
Cefn Fannog 450
Cilmery
Beulah
Llyn Brianne
Llanafan-fechan
Llanfaredd
Builth Wells
Aberduhonw
52
Rhulen
487
Cwm Irfon
Garth
Llanlleonfel
Irfon
Tyn-y-graig
Llanbadarn-y-garreg
Mynydd Trawsnant 517
Moelfre
Llanddewi'r Cwm
Rhulen Hill
B4567
Llanwrtyd
Maesmynis
Aberedw
Llanbedr Hill 467
Llangammarch Wells
Neuadd
467
Llandeilo Hill
Llanwrtyd Wells
Banc y Celyn 472
Alltmawr
Ystradffin
B4519
Pen-y-garreg
Cefn-gorwydd
Cledan
Drum-ddu 474
Aberedw Rocks
Llandeilo Graban
3
B4594
EPPYNT
Pentre-Dolau-Honddu
Rhandirmwyn
Bryn Nicol
Gwenddwr
Erwood
Tywi
Cefn Llwydlo
465
475
463 Bryn Du
454 Twyn Rhyd-car
B4520
Crickadarn
Llanstephan
Bran
Ysgir Fawr
Tirabad
Upper Chapel
Cefn Clawdd 427
MYNYDD EPPYNT
Crychan Forest
Cynghordy
Glanbran
Crychan
Gwrhyd 454
423
Danger Zone
Boughrood
Ysgwydd Hwch 456
Merthyr Cynog
Castle Madoc
Llyswen
Pen-y-bont
Abercrychan
410
Gwenol
Blaen Dyryn
Llandyfalle Hill
Ysgir Fechan
Lower Chapel
Llandefalle
4
Bronllys
Pentre-ty-gwyn
Babel
Mynydd Bwlch-y-Groes
Nant Bran
Llanfihangel Nant Bran
Honddu
A438
Llandeilo'r-Fan
Pont-faen
Garthbrengy
Ysgir
Talachddu
Llanfilo
A40
Halfway
Pentre-bach
406
Pwllgloyw
Felinfach
Mynydd Aberyscir
Twyn Disgwylfa 417
Glan Honddu
Llandefaelog Fach
Tredomen
Trefecca
Y Pigwn
Llanddew
Llandefaelog-tre'r-graig
Battle
Mynydd-bach Trecastell
Llywel
Pentre'r-felin
Pen-y-Crug
Aberyscir
Mynydd Myddfai
Y Gaer
B4602
Llechfaen
Llanywern
Usk Reservoir
Yr Allt
Trallong
Cath
Trecastle
Sennybridge
Penpont
Llanspyddid
Llanfaes
Brecon (Aberhonddu)
Brecknock
Llanfihangel-Tal-y-llyn
Talyllyn
Defynnog
Tai'r Bull
Ffrwdgrech
Cefn Llechid
Mynydd Illtyd
Mynydd Wysg
Cefn Cantref
Llangorse Lake
Llangasty-Talyllyn
Llanhamlach
Ffrorest Fach
Brecon Beacons Mountain Centre
Llanfrynach
Scethrog
5
Cray
A4215
Libanus
Llanddeusant
Glasfynydd Forest
Senni
Hydfer
Allt Ddu 562
Cefn Cyff
Pencelli
B4558
Moel Feity 591
Llansantffraed
Bwlch Cerrig Duon
Cnewr
Heol Senni
Pen Milan 555
Bryn 561
Glyn Tarell
Fan Bwlch Chwyth
BRECON BEACONS NATIONAL PARK
Talybont-on-Usk
Crai
Fan Frynych 628
Cray Reservoir
802
603
Llyn y Fan Fawr
Corn Du 873
Pen y Fan 886
Garreg Las
Brest Twrch
562
769
762
Coed
FOREST FAWR
Fan Hir
Fan Gyhirych 725
Fan Fawr 734
37
Craig Fan Ddu
Neuadd Reservoirs
Twyn-du
Tawe
Beacons Reservoir
Talybont Reservoir
Crawnon
Cefn Cul
Carreg Lem
A4067
Fan Nedd 663
Fan Llia 631
Cwm
Gwaun Nant Ddu
Torpantau
Pontsticill... Garn Caws 516
Dyffryn Crawnon
Carreg Goch 558
Castell y Geifr
Waun Lysiog
Cefn Mawr
Dan-yr-Ogof Caves
Penwyllt
Nant-ddu
Pentwyn Reservoir
Mellte
Mynydd Llangynidr

52
A
B
C
D
64
51
38
1
2
3
4
5
Brynmelyn
Llanbister
B4356
Lanllue
Llangynllo Sta.
Crug
Llanbister Rd Sta.
Llangunllo
Knighton
Stowe
Panpunton
Bucknell
Buckton
Leintwardine
Milebrook
A4113
Bucknell
Brampton Bryan
Walford
Adforton
Burrington
Abbey Cwmhir
Maelienydd
Llanddewi Ystradenni
Glog Hill
A488
Rhos-y-Meirch
B4355
B4357
Llan-wen Hill
Letton
Birtley
Newton
Wigmore
Harley's Mtn
Bleddfa
B4356
Pilleth
Whitton
Lingen
Ongar Street
Leinthall
Little Hill
A488
Fforest-fach
Dolau
Llanfihangel Rhydithon
Black Mixen
Pentre
Cascob
Pilleth 1402
Norton
Lower Lye
Yatton
A483
Penybont Sta.
Aran
Radnor Forest
Great Rhos 660
Maes-Treylow
Stapleton
Presteigne
Kinsham
A4110
Aymestrey
Penybont
Esgairnantau
Bache Hill 610
Kinnerton
Discoed
Offa's Dyke
B4356
Byton
Combe
Mortimer's Cross
Lucton
A483
Llandegley
A44
Llandrindod Wells
Fron Hill
New Radnor
B4372
B4357
Rodd
Nash
Coombes Moor
B4362
Wapley Hill
Shobdon
Ledicot
Kingsland
Llandegley Rhos
Evenjobb
B4362
Knill
Titley
Stansbatch
Staunton on Arrow
Ridgebourne
Walton
Eywood
Shirl Heath
Gilwern Hill
Wolfpits
Old Radnor
Burlingjobb
Bradnor Hill
B4355
Pembridge
Eardisland
Burton Court
Llanfihangel-nant-Melan
Yardro
Dolyhir
Marston
Lower Barewood
Betws Disserth
Bryn-y-maen
Gwaithla
Hergest Ridge
Hergest Croft
Kington
A44
Sollers Dilwyn
A481
Gwaunceste Hill 542
Gladestry
Lower Hergest
Moorcot
Barewood
Lyonshall
Luntley
Colva Hill
Upper Hergest
Kingswood
Holme Marsh
Broxwood
Haven
Dilwyn
Llansantffraed-in-Elvel
Hundred House
Glascwm
Colva
Hengoed
Huntington
A480
A4112
Knapton Green
Little Hill
Glascwm Hill 524
Brilley Mountain
Woonton
Cregrina
Veaullt
Upper Welson
Almeley
Weobley
Weobley Marsh
POWYS
HEREFORDSHIRE
Llanfaredd
Michaelchurch-on-Arrow
Newchurch
Lower Welson
A4111
Upcott
Sarnesfield
Aberduhonw
Rhulen
Red Hill 509
Llanbadarn-y-garreg
Bryngwyn
Dolleycanney
Brilley
Hurstway Common
Eardisley
Kinnersley
Ledgemoor
B4230
B4567
Rhosgoch
Norton Wood
Ailey
Calver Hill
Norton Canon
Wormsley
Rhulen Hill
Llanbedr Hill 467
Aberedw
Llandeilo Hill
Clyro Hill
Rhydspence
Whitney
A438
Winforton
Willersley
Letton Lake
Yarsop
Foxley
Builth Wells
Llanbedr
B4594
Painscastle
Toll
Letton
Moorhampton
Staunton on Wye
Yazor
Mansel Lacy
A480
Aberedw Rocks
Llandeilo Graban
Motte & Bailey
Bronydd
Clifford
B4352
Merbach
Bredwardine
Mansell Gamage
The Begwns
Priory Wood
B4350
Pen-y-Park
Brobury
Portway
Bishopstone
Monnington on Wye
Clyro
B4348
Hardwicke
Arthur's Stone
Moccas Court
A438
Erwood
Hay-on-Wye
The Bage
Moccas
Byford
Bridge Sollers
Crickadarn
A470
Llanstephan
Llowes
B4350
Cusop
Dorstone
Preston on Wye
Ploughfield
The Weir (NT)
Lulham
A438
B4348
Blakemere
Cwmbach
Snodhill
Boughrood
B4350
Glasbury
Llanigon
Cefn Hill 486
Tyberton
B4352
Madley
Pipton
Tregoyd
Hinton
Golden Valley
Peterchurch
Llyswen
A4079
Vagar Hill
Urishay Common
Craswall Priory (ruins)
Shenmore
Three Cocks
Llandyfalle Hill
A470
Hay Bluff 677
Turnastone
Vowchurch
B4348
B4349
Kingstone
Llandefalle
A4078
Velindre
Upper Maes-coed
Webton
Bronllys
Twmpa 690
Craswall
B4348
Talgarth
A438
Llanelieu
Michaelchurch Escley
Escley Brook
St Margarets
B4347
Kerry's Gate
Rhos Dirion 713
Olchon
Middle Maes-coed
Whitfield
Talachddu
Felinfach
Llanfilo
Llyfni
Olchon Valley
Monnow
Dore
Bacton
Tredomen
Trefecca
A479
Pen y Manllwyn
Capel-y-ffin
Llanveynoe
Abbey Dore Court
A470
Llandefaelog-tre'r-graig
Grwyne Fawr Res
Honddu
Abbey Dore
Lower Maes-coed
Abbey (ruins)
Wormbridge
Pengenffordd
Waun Fach 811
BLACK
BRECON
BEACONS
Longtown
Heol Lly Goden
Mynydd Troed
Priory
Ewyas Harold
Howton
Kenderchurch
Llanywern
800
Grwyne Fechan
Grwyne Fawr
Mynydd Merddin
Llechfaen
Llanfihangel-Tal-y-llyn
Llangorse
15
Mynydd Llysiau
Llanthony
Clodock
Pontrilas
Talyllyn
Pen Twyn Mawr
Rowlstone
Llanhamlach
Llangorse Lake
B4560
Mynydd Llangorse
MOUNTAINS
Hatterrall Hill
Llangua
Kentchurch
Llangasty-Talyllyn
Walterstone
Scethrog
Cathedine
Pen Allt-mawr
Pen Gwyllt Meirch
Oldcastle
A465
Grosmont
Cwmdu
NATIONAL
PARK
Cwmyoy
Bryn 561
Talybont-on-Usk
Usk
Llansantffraed
Rhiangoll
A479
Pen Cerrig-calch 701
Crug Mawr 550
Hoaldalbert
Pandy
Graig Syfyrddin
A40
Bwlch
Gaer
Tretower
Patrishow
Llanfihangel Crucorney
B4558
Tretower Court
Llanbedr
Bryn arw
Llanfihangel Court
Llangattock Lingoed
B4347
Coed-yr-ynys
Myarth
762
Twyn-du
Mynydd Pen-y-fal
Blaenawey
Sugar Loaf 596
Bont
Cross Ash
Upper Green
Llangynidr
B4558
Ffawyddog
Crickhowell
MONMOUTHSHIRE
Talybont Reservoir
Llangattock
Llanbedr
Llangenny
Llantilio Pertholey
Ysgyryd Fawr 486
B4521
Crawnon
Garn Caws 516
Cefn Onneu
Cwrt-y-gollen
Glangrwyne
Rholben
Mynydd Llanwenarth
Llanvetherine
White Castle
Dyffryn
Mynydd
A4077
A40
Mardy
Hen Gwrt
Llangattock

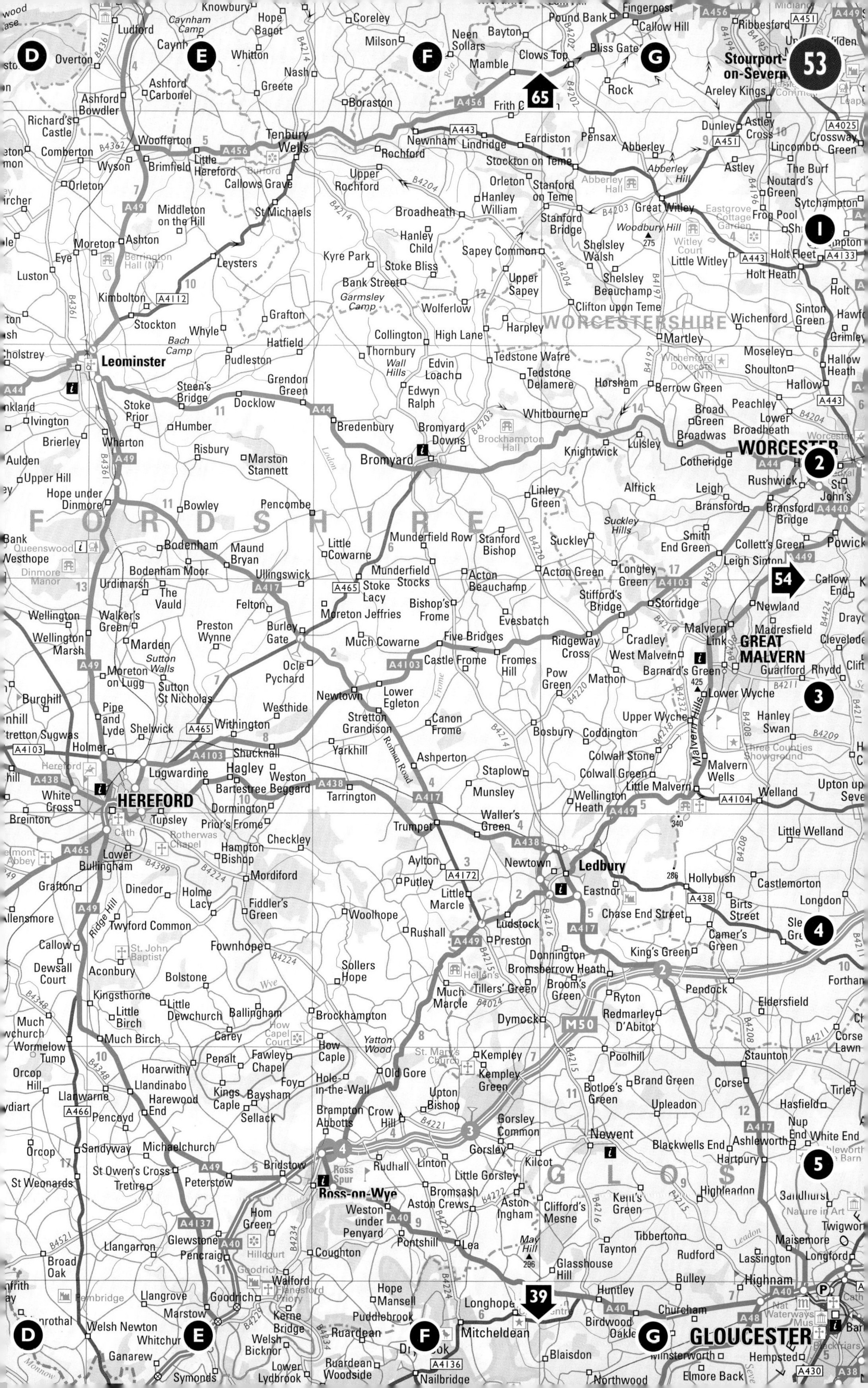
D
E
F
G
53
65
54
39
2
3
4
5
I
Ludford
Caynham Camp
Knowbury
Hope Bagot
Coreley
Milson
Neen Sollars
Bayton
Mamble
Clows Top
Pound Bank
Fingerpost
Callow Hill
Bliss Gate
Rock
Ribbesford
Stourport-on-Severn
Areley Kings
Overton
Whitton
Nash
Greete
Ashford Carbonel
Ashford Bowdler
Boraston
Frith C
Richard's Castle
Woofferton
Comberton
Wyson
Brimfield
Little Hereford
Burford
Tenbury Wells
Newnham
Lindridge
Eardiston
Pensax
Abberley
Dunley
Astley Cross
Lincomb
Crossway Green
The Burf
Astley
Noutard's Green
Sytchampton
Orleton
Callows Grave
Rochford
Upper Rochford
Stockton on Teme
Orleton
Stanford on Teme
Abberley Hall
Abberley Hill
Middleton on the Hill
St Michaels
Broadheath
Hanley William
Stanford Bridge
Great Witley
Eastgrove Cottage Garden
Frog Pool
Woodbury Hill
Moreton
Ashton
Eye
Berrington Hall (NT)
Leysters
Kyre Park
Hanley Child
Sapey Common
Shelsley Walsh
Witley Court
Little Witley
Holt Fleet
Holt Heath
Luston
Stoke Bliss
Bank Street
Upper Sapey
Shelsley Beauchamp
Holt
Kimbolton
Garmsley Camp
Wolferlow
Clifton upon Teme
Wichenford
Sinton Green
Stockton
Grafton
Whyle
Bach Camp
Collington
High Lane
Harpley
WORCESTERSHIRE
Martley
Grimley
Leominster
Hatfield
Pudleston
Thornbury
Wall Hills
Edvin Loach
Tedstone Wafre
Tedstone Delamere
Wichenford Dovecote (NT)
Moseley
Shoulton
Hallow Heath
Hallow
Steen's Bridge
Grendon Green
Docklow
Edwyn Ralph
Horsham
Berrow Green
Stoke Prior
Peachley
Lower Broadheath
Whitbourne
Broad Green
Broadwas
Ivington
Humber
Bredenbury
Bromyard Downs
Brockhampton Hall
Knightwick
Lulsley
WORCESTER
Brierley
Wharton
Risbury
Marston Stannett
Bromyard
Cotheridge
Aulden
Upper Hill
Rushwick
St John's
Hope under Dinmore
Bowley
Pencombe
Linley Green
Alfrick
Leigh
Bransford
Bransford Bridge
Suckley Hills
FORDSHIRE
Bank
Queenswood
Westhope
Dinmore Manor
Bodenham
Maund Bryan
Little Cowarne
Munderfield Row
Stanford Bishop
Suckley
Smith End Green
Collett's Green
Powick
Bodenham Moor
Ullingswick
Munderfield Stocks
Acton Green
Longley Green
Leigh Sinton
Callow End
Urdimarsh
The Vauld
Felton
Stoke Lacy
Acton Beauchamp
Stifford's Bridge
Storridge
Newland
Wellington
Walker's Green
Preston Wynne
Moreton Jeffries
Bishop's Frome
Evesbatch
Malvern Link
Madresfield
Wellington Marsh
Marden
Burley Gate
Much Cowarne
Five Bridges
Ridgeway Cross
Cradley
GREAT MALVERN
Sutton Walls
Castle Frome
Fromes Hill
West Malvern
Guarlford
Rhydd
Moreton on Lugg
Ocle Pychard
Pow Green
Mathon
Barnard's Green
Sutton St Nicholas
Newtown
Lower Egleton
Lower Wyche
Burghill
Pipe and Lyde
Westhide
Stretton Grandison
Canon Frome
Bosbury
Coddington
Upper Wyche
Hanley Swan
Stretton Sugwas
Shelwick
Withington
Malvern Hills
Holmer
Shucknall
Yarkhill
Roman Road
Ashperton
Colwall Stone
Three Counties Showground
Hagley
Weston Beggard
Staplow
Colwall Green
Malvern Wells
Lugwardine
Bartestree
Tarrington
Munsley
Little Malvern
Welland
Upton upon Severn
White Cross
HEREFORD
Tupsley
Dormington
Wellington Heath
Breinton
Prior's Frome
Trumpet
Waller's Green
Little Welland
Rotherwas Chapel
Hampton Bishop
Checkley
Lower Bullingham
Aylton
Newtown
Ledbury
Hollybush
Castlemorton
Grafton
Dinedor
Mordiford
Putley
Little Marcle
Eastnor
Longdon
Holme Lacy
Fiddler's Green
Woolhope
Chase End Street
Birts Street
Allensmoore
Ridge Hill
Twyford Common
Ludstock
Rushall
Preston
Camer's Green
Callow
St. John Baptist
Fownhope
Donnington
King's Green
Dewsall Court
Aconbury
Sollers Hope
Hellens
Bromsberrow Heath
Bolstone
Tillers' Green
Broom's Green
Pendock
Forthampton
Kingsthorne
Little Birch
Little Dewchurch
Ballingham
Much Marcle
Ryton
Eldersfield
Much Dewchurch
Brockhampton
Dymock
Redmarley D'Abitot
Wormelow Tump
Much Birch
How Capel Court
Carey
Yatton Wood
How Caple
St. Mary's Church
Kempley
Poolhill
Corse Lawn
Orcop Hill
Hoarwithy
Penalt
Fawley Chapel
Kempley Green
Staunton
Llandinabo
Foy
Hole-in-the-Wall
Old Gore
Botloe's Green
Brand Green
Corse
Tirley
Llanwarne
Harewood End
Kings Caple
Baysham
Upton Bishop
Upleadon
Hasfield
Pencoyd
Sellack
Brampton Abbotts
Crow Hill
Gorsley Common
Newent
Nup End
White End
Orcop
Sandyway
Michaelchurch
Bridstow
Gorsley
Blackwells End
Ashleworth
St Owen's Cross
Tretire
Peterstow
Ross Spur
Rudhall
Linton
Little Gorsley
Kilcot
GLOS
Hartpury
St Weonards
Ross-on-Wye
Bromsash
Aston Crews
Aston Ingham
Clifford's Mesne
Kent's Green
Highleadon
Sandhurst
Nature in Art
Weston under Penyard
Hom Green
Twigworth
Llangarron
Glewstone
Hillcourt
Pontshill
Lea
May Hill
Tibberton
Maisemore
Pencraig
Broad Oak
Coughton
Taynton
Rudford
Lassington
Longford
Goodrich
Flanesford Priory
Walford
Glasshouse Hill
Bulley
Highnam
Pembridge
Llangrove
Hope Mansell
Huntley
Churcham
Marstow
Kerne Bridge
Puddlebrook
Longhope
Birdwood
Oakle
GLOUCESTER
Nat Waterways Mus
Blackfriars
Welsh Newton
Whitchurch
Welsh Bicknor
Ruardean
Mitcheldean
Ganarew
Symonds
Lower Lydbrook
Ruardean Woodside
Nailbridge
Blaisdon
Minsterworth
Hempsted
Elmore Back
Northwood
Monnow
Wye
Leadon
Frome
Lodon
A456
A451
A443
A4025
A4133
A49
A4112
A44
A417
A465
A4103
A438
A4104
A449
A4172
A466
A40
A4137
A4136
A48
A430
A38
A4440
M50
B4361
B4362
B4214
B4204
B4203
B4202
B4194
B4195
B4196
B4197
B4220
B4219
B4503
B4424
B4211
B4232
B4218
B4208
B4209
B4399
B4224
B4215
B4216
B4221
B4222
B4234
B4228
B4229
B4348
B4521
B4213
275
425
340
286
296

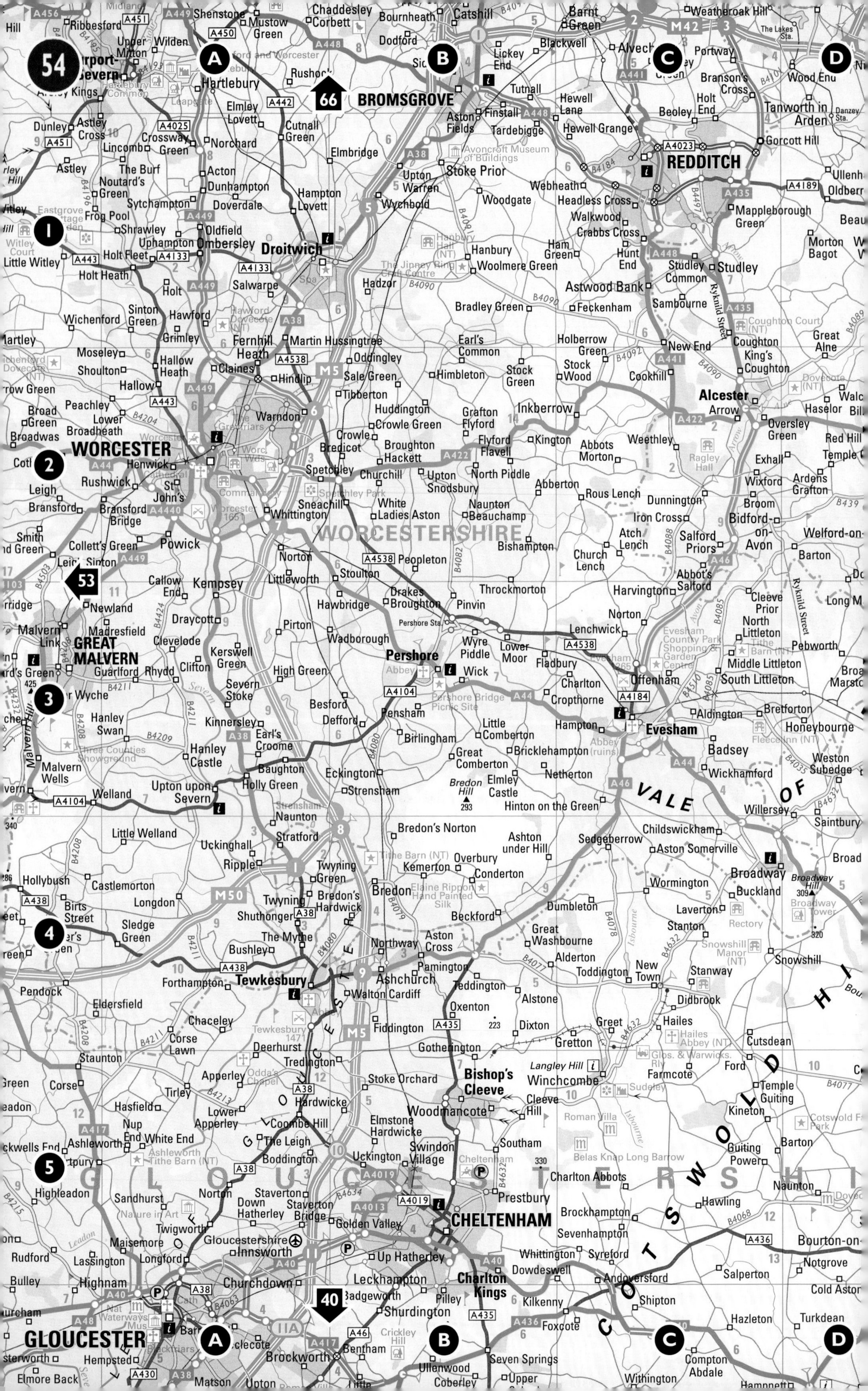
54
66
BROMSGROVE
Shenstone
Mustow Green
Chaddesley Corbett
Bournheath
Catshill
Barnt Green
Weatheroak Hill
M42
The Lakes Sta.
Ribbesford
Upper Mitton
Wilden
Dodford
Blackwell
Lickey End
Alvechurch
Portway
Hartlebury
Rushock
Tutnall
Hewell Lane
Branson's Cross
Wood End
Elmley Lovett
Aston Fields
Finstall
Tardebigge
Beoley
Holt End
Tanworth in Arden
Danzey Sta.
Dunley
Astley Cross
Crossway Green
Norchard
Cutnall Green
Hewell Grange
REDDITCH
Gorcott Hill
Lincomb
Astley
The Burf
Acton
Elmbridge
Avoncroft Museum of Buildings
Upton Warren
Stoke Prior
Webheath
Headless Cross
Ullenhall
Oldberrow
Noutard's Green
Dunhampton
Hampton Lovett
Wychbold
Woodgate
Walkwood
Crabbs Cross
Mappleborough Green
Sytchampton
Doverdale
Eastgrove Cottage Garden
Frog Pool
Shrawley
Oldfield
Ombersley
Uphampton
Droitwich
Hanbury Hall (NT)
Hanbury
Ham Green
Hunt End
Morton Bagot
Witley Court
Little Witley
Holt Fleet
Holt Heath
The Jinney Ring Craft Centre
Woolmere Green
Studley Common
Studley
Salwarpe
Hadzor
Astwood Bank
Holt
Sambourne
Wichenford
Sinton Green
Hawford
Hawford Dovecote (NT)
Bradley Green
Feckenham
Coughton Court (NT)
Great Alne
Ryknild Street
Martley
Grimley
Fernhill Heath
Martin Hussingtree
Earl's Common
Holberrow Green
New End
Coughton
King's Coughton
Moseley
Hallow Heath
Claines
Oddingley
Stock Green
Stock Wood
Shoulton
Hallow
Hindlip
Sale Green
Himbleton
Cookhill
Dovecote (NT)
Peachley
Lower Broadheath
Warndon
Tibberton
Huddington
Grafton Flyford
Inkberrow
Alcester
Arrow
Haselor
Broad Green
Broadwas
The Greyfriars
Crowle Green
Crowle
Oversley Green
Bredicot
Broughton Hackett
Flyford Flavell
Kington
Abbots Morton
Weethley
Red Hill
Temple Grafton
WORCESTER
Henwick
Worcester Cathedral
Rushwick
St John's
Commandery
Spetchley
Spetchley Park
Churchill
Upton Snodsbury
North Piddle
Abberton
Ragley Hall
Exhall
Wixford
Ardens Grafton
Leigh
Bransford
Bransford Bridge
Worcester 1651
Sneachill
Whittington
White Ladies Aston
Naunton Beauchamp
Rous Lench
Dunnington
Iron Cross
Broom
Bidford-on-Avon
Welford-on-
WORCESTERSHIRE
Smith End Green
Collett's Green
Powick
Norton
Bishampton
Atch Lench
Church Lench
Salford Priors
Barton
Leigh Sinton
53
Newland
Callow End
Kempsey
Littleworth
Stoulton
Peopleton
Throckmorton
Harvington
Abbot's Salford
Cleeve Prior
Long Marston
Malvern Link
Madresfield
Draycott
Drakes Broughton
Pinvin
Norton
Lenchwick
North Littleton
GREAT MALVERN
Clevelode
Pirton
Hawbridge
Pershore Sta.
Wyre Piddle
Lower Moor
Fladbury
Evesham Country Park Shopping & Garden Centre
Middle Littleton
Tithe Barn (NT)
Pebworth
Guarlford
Rhydd
Clifton
Kerswell Green
Wadborough
Pershore
Pershore Abbey
Wick
Charlton
Evesham 1265
Offenham
South Littleton
Broad Marston
Wyche
Severn Stoke
High Green
Pershore Bridge Picnic Site
Cropthorne
Aldington
Bretforton
Hanley Swan
Besford
Defford
Little Comberton
Hampton
Evesham
Honeybourne
Three Counties Showground
Kinnersley
Earl's Croome
Pensham
Birlingham
Bricklehampton
Great Comberton
Abbey (ruins)
Badsey
Fleece Inn (NT)
Malvern Wells
Hanley Castle
Baughton
Holly Green
Eckington
Strensham
Elmley Castle
Netherton
Bredon Hill 293
Wickhamford
Weston Subedge
Upton upon Severn
Welland
Hinton on the Green
VALE OF
Willersey
Saintbury
Little Welland
Strensham Naunton
Stratford
Bredon's Norton
Ashton under Hill
Sedgeberrow
Childswickham
Aston Somerville
Uckinghall
Ripple
Twyning Green
Tithe Barn (NT)
Kemerton
Overbury
Conderton
Broadway
Broadway Hill 309
Broadway Tower
Hollybush
Castlemorton
M50
Twyning
Bredon
Bredon's Hardwick
Elaine Rippon Hand Painted Silk
Beckford
Dumbleton
Wormington
Buckland
Laverton
Birts Street
Longdon
Shuthonger
Stanton
Rectory
Sledge Green
The Mythe
Northway
Aston Cross
Great Washbourne
Snowshill Manor (NT)
Snowshill
Bushley
Pamington
Alderton
Toddington
New Town
Stanway
Pendock
Forthampton
Tewkesbury
Ashchurch
Walton Cardiff
Teddington
Alstone
Didbrook
Eldersfield
Oxenton
223
Dixton
Greet
Hailes
Hailes Abbey (NT)
Cutsdean
Chaceley
Corse Lawn
Tewkesbury 1471
Fiddington
Gotherington
Gretton
Staunton
Deerhurst
Tredington
Langley Hill
Glos. & Warwicks. Rly
Ford
Apperley
Odda's Chapel
Stoke Orchard
Bishop's Cleeve
Winchcombe
Farmcote
Temple Guiting
Corse
Tirley
Sudeley
Hasfield
Lower Apperley
Hardwicke
Woodmancote
Cleeve Hill
Kineton
Nup End
White End
Coombe Hill
Elmstone Hardwicke
Roman Villa
Cotswold Farm Park
Ashleworth
Ashleworth Tithe Barn (NT)
The Leigh
Boddington
Uckington
Swindon Village
Southam
Belas Knap Long Barrow
Guiting Power
Barton
330
Hartpury
GLOUCESTERSHIRE
COTSWOLD HILLS
Highleadon
Sandhurst
Nature in Art
Norton
Staverton
Down Hatherley
Staverton Bridge
Cheltenham
Charlton Abbots
Naunton
Prestbury
Hawling
Twigworth
Golden Valley
CHELTENHAM
Brockhampton
Sevenhampton
Bourton-on-
Rudford
Maisemore
Lassington
Gloucestershire
Innsworth
Up Hatherley
Whittington
Syreford
Dowdeswell
Notgrove
Salperton
Bulley
Highnam
Longford
Churchdown
Leckhampton
Charlton Kings
Andoversford
Cold Aston
40
Badgeworth
Shurdington
Pilley
Kilkenny
Shipton
Hazleton
Turkdean
GLOUCESTER
Nat Waterways Mus
Blackfriars
Barnwood
Hucclecote
Brockworth
Bentham
Crickley Hill
Foxcote
Seven Springs
Compton Abdale
Hempsted
Ullenwood
Coberley
Upper
Withington
Elmore Back
Matson
Upton
A B C D
1 2 3 4 5
A456 A451 A449 A450 A448 A442 A4025 A38 A4184 A4023 A441 A435 A4189 A443 A4133 B4090 A4538 A422 M5 A44 A4440 B4082 B4088 A46 A4104 A4184 B4085 A417 A4019 A4013 A40 A436 A430 B4063 B4632 B4077 B4068

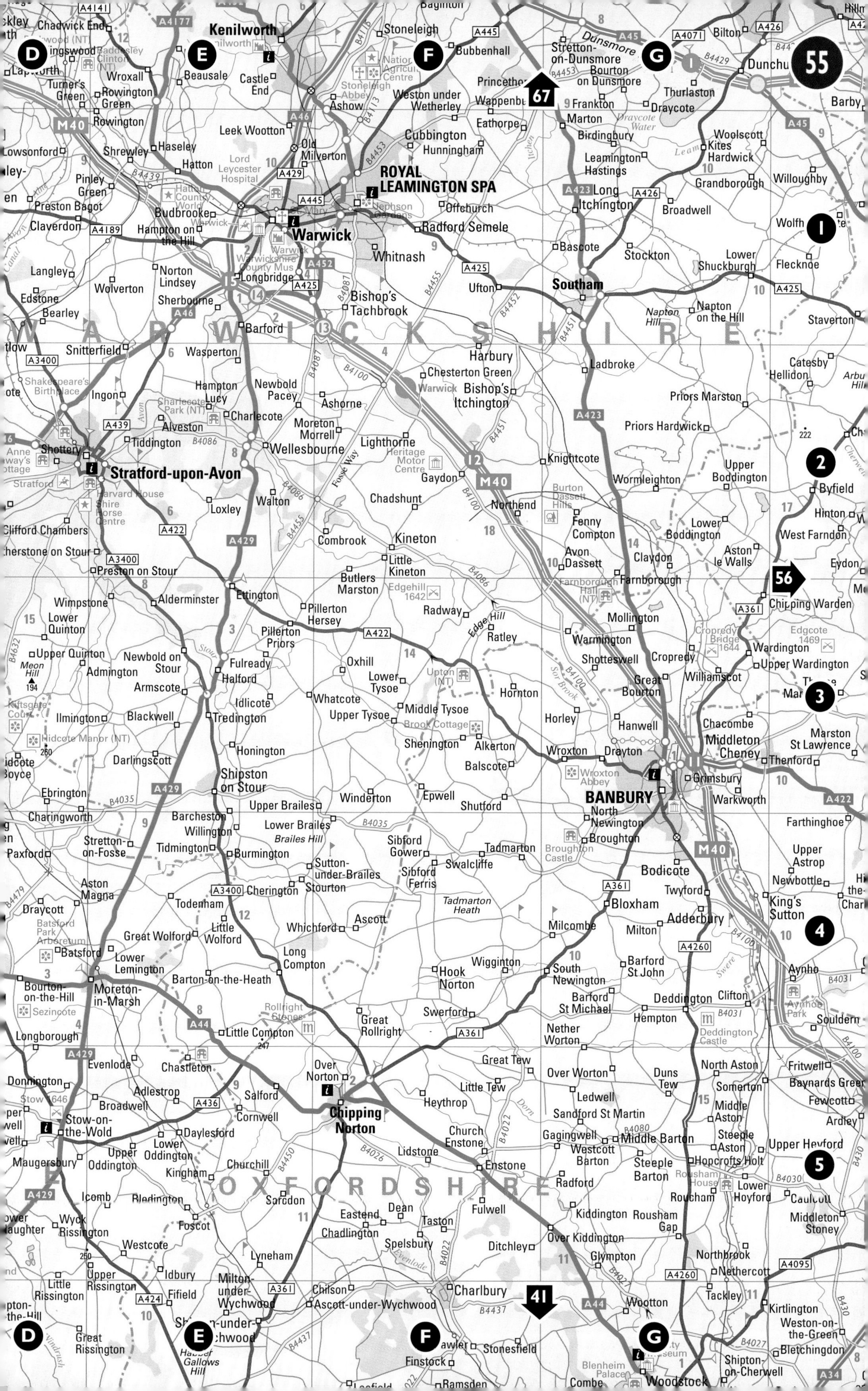
55
56
67
41
Kenilworth
Chadwick End
Baddesley Clinton (NT)
Lapworth
Turner's Green
Wroxall
Rowington Green
Rowington
Beausale
Castle End
Stoneleigh
Stoneleigh Abbey
National Agricultural Centre
Ashow
Bubbenhall
Weston under Wetherley
Princethorpe
Wappenbury
Eathorpe
Stretton-on-Dunsmore
Dunsmore
Bourton on Dunsmore
Frankton
Draycote
Draycote Water
Thurlaston
Dunchurch
Bilton
Barby
Marton
Birdingbury
Leamington Hastings
Woolscott
Kites Hardwick
Grandborough
Willoughby
Lowsonford
Shrewley
Haseley
Hatton
Leek Wootton
Old Milverton
Lord Leycester Hospital
Cubbington
Hunningham
ROYAL LEAMINGTON SPA
Jephson Gardens
Offchurch
Radford Semele
Long Itchington
Broadwell
Wolfhampcote
Pinley Green
Preston Bagot
Claverdon
Hatton Country World
Budbrooke
Hampton on the Hill
Warwick
St Mary
Warwick Castle
Warwickshire County Mus
Whitnash
Bascote
Stockton
Lower Shuckburgh
Flecknoe
Langley
Wolverton
Norton Lindsey
Longbridge
Edstone
Bearley
Sherbourne
Barford
Bishop's Tachbrook
Ufton
Southam
Napton Hill
Napton on the Hill
Staverton
WARWICKSHIRE
Snitterfield
Wasperton
Harbury
Chesterton Green
Bishop's Itchington
Ladbroke
Catesby
Hellidon
Shakespeare's Birthplace
Ingon
Hampton Lucy
Newbold Pacey
Ashorne
Charlecote Park (NT)
Charlecote
Moreton Morrell
Priors Marston
Priors Hardwick
Alveston
Tiddington
Shottery
Anne Hathaway's Cottage
Stratford-upon-Avon
Wellesbourne
Lighthorne
Lighthorne Heritage Motor Centre
Fosse Way
Gaydon
Knightcote
Upper Boddington
Byfield
Stratford
Harvard House
Shire Horse Centre
Loxley
Walton
Chadshunt
Northend
Burton Dassett Hills
Wormleighton
Hinton
West Farndon
Clifford Chambers
Atherstone on Stour
Combrook
Kineton
Little Kineton
Fenny Compton
Lower Boddington
Avon Dassett
Claydon
Aston le Walls
Eydon
Preston on Stour
Ettington
Alderminster
Butlers Marston
Edgehill
Radway
Farnborough Hall (NT)
Farnborough
Chipping Warden
Wimpstone
Lower Quinton
Pillerton Hersey
Pillerton Priors
Edge Hill
Ratley
Mollington
Warmington
Cropredy Bridge 1644
Edgcote 1469
Wardington
Upper Wardington
Upper Quinton
Meon Hill
Newbold on Stour
Admington
Armscote
Fulready
Halford
Oxhill
Lower Tysoe
Upton House (NT)
Shotteswell
Cropredy
Williamscot
Great Bourton
Idlicote
Tredington
Whatcote
Middle Tysoe
Upper Tysoe
Hornton
Kiftsgate Court
Ilmington
Blackwell
Hidcote Manor (NT)
Brook Cottage
Shenington
Alkerton
Horley
Hanwell
Chacombe
Middleton Cheney
Marston St Lawrence
Thenford
Hidcote Boyce
Darlingscott
Honington
Shipston on Stour
Balscote
Wroxton
Wroxton Abbey
Drayton
Grimsbury
Warkworth
BANBURY
Ebrington
Charingworth
Barcheston
Willington
Upper Brailes
Winderton
Epwell
Shutford
North Newington
Broughton
Broughton Castle
Farthinghoe
Paxford
Stretton-on-Fosse
Tidmington
Burmington
Lower Brailes
Brailes Hill
Sibford Gower
Sibford Ferris
Swalcliffe
Tadmarton
Tadmarton Heath
Upper Astrop
Aston Magna
Sutton-under-Brailes
Stourton
Cherington
Todenham
Bodicote
Twyford
Newbottle
King's Sutton
Draycott
Batsford Park Arboretum
Batsford
Great Wolford
Little Wolford
Whichford
Ascott
Bloxham
Adderbury
Milcombe
Milton
Lower Lemington
Long Compton
Wigginton
Hook Norton
South Newington
Barford St John
Aynho
Bourton-on-the-Hill
Moreton-in-Marsh
Sezincote
Barton-on-the-Heath
Rollright Stones
Great Rollright
Swerford
Barford St Michael
Deddington
Deddington Castle
Clifton
Hempton
Aynhoe Park
Souldern
Longborough
Little Compton
Nether Worton
Great Tew
Over Worton
Evenlode
Chastleton
Donnington
Over Norton
Little Tew
Duns Tew
North Aston
Fritwell
Baynards Green
Adlestrop
Salford
Heythrop
Ledwell
Somerton
Fewcott
Middle Aston
Ardley
Stow-on-the-Wold
Broadwell
Cornwell
Chipping Norton
Sandford St Martin
Gagingwell
Middle Barton
Westcott Barton
Steeple Aston
Upper Heyford
Maugersbury
Upper Oddington
Lower Oddington
Daylesford
Kingham
Churchill
Lidstone
Church Enstone
Enstone
Steeple Barton
Hopcrofts Holt
Rousham House
Lower Heyford
Caulcott
Radford
OXFORDSHIRE
Icomb
Bledington
Sarsden
Rousham
Kiddington
Rousham Gap
Middleton Stoney
Wyck Rissington
Foscot
Eastend
Dean
Chadlington
Taston
Fulwell
Spelsbury
Evenlode
Over Kiddington
Ditchley
Glympton
Northbrook
Nethercott
Westcote
Lyneham
Idbury
Upper Rissington
Little Rissington
Fifield
Milton-under-Wychwood
Chilson
Ascott-under-Wychwood
Charlbury
Tackley
Kirtlington
Wootton
Weston-on-the-Green
Great Rissington
Shipton-under-Wychwood
Habber Gallows Hill
Finstock
Fawler
Stonesfield
Blenheim Palace
Bletchingdon
Shipton-on-Cherwell
Combe
Woodstock
Ramsden
M40
M40
M40
A4141
A4177
A445
A45
A4071
A426
A45
A46
A429
A445
A4189
A452
A425
A425
A423
A426
A425
A46
A3400
A439
A422
A423
A429
A3400
A422
A361
A429
A3400
A361
A4260
A422
A44
A429
A436
A361
A429
A424
A361
A44
A4260
A4095
A34
B4439
B4087
B4100
B4086
B4455
B4451
B4452
B4453
B4113
B4115
B4429
B4632
B4035
B4479
B4450
B4026
B4022
B4080
B4027
B4030
B4031
B4437
B4430
B4100
Learn
Itchen
Avon
Stour
Sor Brook
Swere
Dorn
Evenlode
Windrush
Canal
Alne
194
222
247
250
260
1642
1469

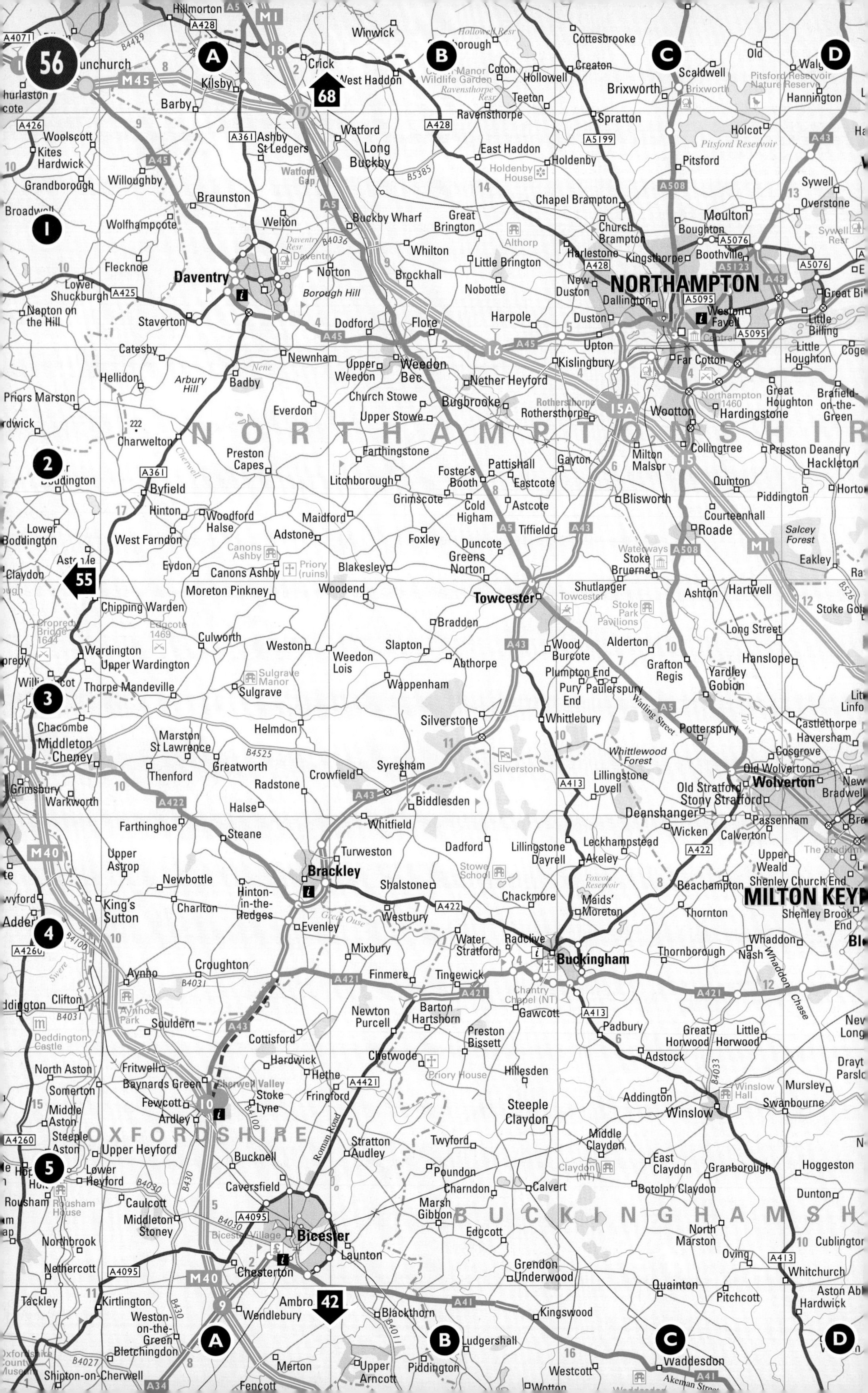

56
68
55
42
A
B
C
D
1
2
3
4
5
NORTHAMPTONSHIRE
OXFORDSHIRE
BUCKINGHAMSHIRE
NORTHAMPTON
MILTON KEYNES
Hillmorton
Winwick
Cottesbrooke
Old
Dunchurch
Kilsby
Crick
West Haddon
Coton
Hollowell
Creaton
Scaldwell
Brixworth
Hannington
Barby
Teeton
Ravensthorpe
Spratton
Woolscott
Kites Hardwick
Ashby St Ledgers
Watford
Long Buckby
East Haddon
Holdenby
Holdenby House
Pitsford
Holcot
Pitsford Reservoir
Grandborough
Willoughby
Braunston
Watford Gap
Chapel Brampton
Sywell
Overstone
Moulton
Broadwell
Wolfhampcote
Welton
Buckby Wharf
Great Brington
Church Brampton
Boughton
Althorp
Whilton
Harlestone
Kingsthorpe
Boothville
Flecknoe
Daventry
Norton
Little Brington
Brockhall
Nobottle
New Duston
Lower Shuckburgh
Borough Hill
Dallington
Great Billing
Napton on the Hill
Staverton
Dodford
Flore
Harpole
Duston
Weston Favell
Little Billing
Catesby
Newnham
Upper Weedon
Weedon Bec
Upton
Kislingbury
Far Cotton
Little Houghton
Hellidon
Arbury Hill
Badby
Nether Heyford
Priors Marston
Church Stowe
Everdon
Upper Stowe
Bugbrooke
Rothersthorpe
Wootton
Great Houghton
Hardingstone
Brafield-on-the-Green
Charwelton
Preston Capes
Farthingstone
Milton Malsor
Collingtree
Preston Deanery
Hackleton
Byfield
Litchborough
Foster's Booth
Pattishall
Eastcote
Gayton
Quinton
Piddington
Grimscote
Cold Higham
Astcote
Blisworth
Courteenhall
Hinton
Woodford Halse
Maidford
Tiffield
Roade
Salcey Forest
Lower Boddington
West Farndon
Adstone
Foxley
Duncote
Canons Ashby
Priory (ruins)
Greens Norton
Stoke Bruerne
Eakley
Claydon
Eydon
Blakesley
Waterways
Moreton Pinkney
Woodend
Shutlanger
Towcester
Ashton
Hartwell
Chipping Warden
Bradden
Stoke Park Pavilions
Stoke Goldington
Edgcote 1469
Cropredy Bridge 1644
Culworth
Long Street
Wardington
Weston
Slapton
Wood Burcote
Alderton
Upper Wardington
Weedon Lois
Abthorpe
Grafton Regis
Hanslope
Sulgrave Manor
Sulgrave
Plumpton End
Yardley Gobion
Thorpe Mandeville
Wappenham
Pury End
Paulerspury
Chacombe
Helmdon
Silverstone
Whittlebury
Watling Street
Castlethorpe
Haversham
Middleton Cheney
Marston St Lawrence
Potterspury
Whittlewood Forest
Cosgrove
Greatworth
Syresham
Lillingstone Lovell
Old Wolverton
Wolverton
Thenford
Crowfield
Old Stratford
Stony Stratford
New Bradwell
Grimsbury
Warkworth
Radstone
Biddlesden
Halse
Whitfield
Deanshanger
Passenham
Farthinghoe
Steane
Wicken
Calverton
Turweston
Dadford
Lillingstone Dayrell
Leckhampstead
Upper Astrop
Akeley
Upper Weald
Brackley
Stowe School
Foxcote Reservoir
Beachampton
Shenley Church End
Newbottle
Shalstone
Chackmore
Maids' Moreton
Hinton-in-the-Hedges
Thornton
Shenley Brook End
King's Sutton
Charlton
Westbury
Evenley
Water Stratford
Radclive
Buckingham
Whaddon
Nash
Thornborough
Mixbury
Aynho
Croughton
Finmere
Tingewick
Chantry Chapel (NT)
Clifton
Aynhoe Park
Gawcott
Whaddon Chase
Newton Purcell
Barton Hartshorn
Souldern
Preston Bissett
Padbury
Great Horwood
Little Horwood
Deddington Castle
Cottisford
Adstock
North Aston
Fritwell
Hardwick
Hethe
Chetwode
Priory House
Hillesden
Somerton
Baynards Green
Cherwell Valley
Stoke Lyne
Fringford
Winslow Hall
Mursley
Middle Aston
Fewcott
Ardley
Steeple Claydon
Addington
Winslow
Swanbourne
Steeple Aston
Upper Heyford
Roman Road
Stratton Audley
Twyford
Middle Claydon
Lower Heyford
Bucknell
Poundon
East Claydon
Granborough
Hoggeston
Rousham
Rousham House
Caulcott
Caversfield
Charndon
Calvert
Claydon (NT)
Botolph Claydon
Dunton
Middleton Stoney
Bicester Village
Bicester
Marsh Gibbon
Edgcott
North Marston
Cublington
Northbrook
Launton
Oving
Nethercott
Chesterton
Grendon Underwood
Quainton
Whitchurch
Tackley
Kirtlington
Ambrosden
Wendlebury
Blackthorn
Pitchcott
Aston Abbotts
Hardwick
Weston-on-the-Green
Kingswood
Bletchingdon
Ludgershall
Merton
Upper Arncott
Piddington
Waddesdon
Westcott
Shipton-on-Cherwell
Fencott
Wotton
Akeman Street
M1
M40
M45
A5
A43
A45
A361
A413
A421
A422
A428
A4421
A508
A5199
A5076
A5095
A5123
A4095
A4260
A426
A425
A41
A34
A4071
B4036
B4525
B4031
B4100
B4030
B4027
B4011
B4033
B5385
B430
B526

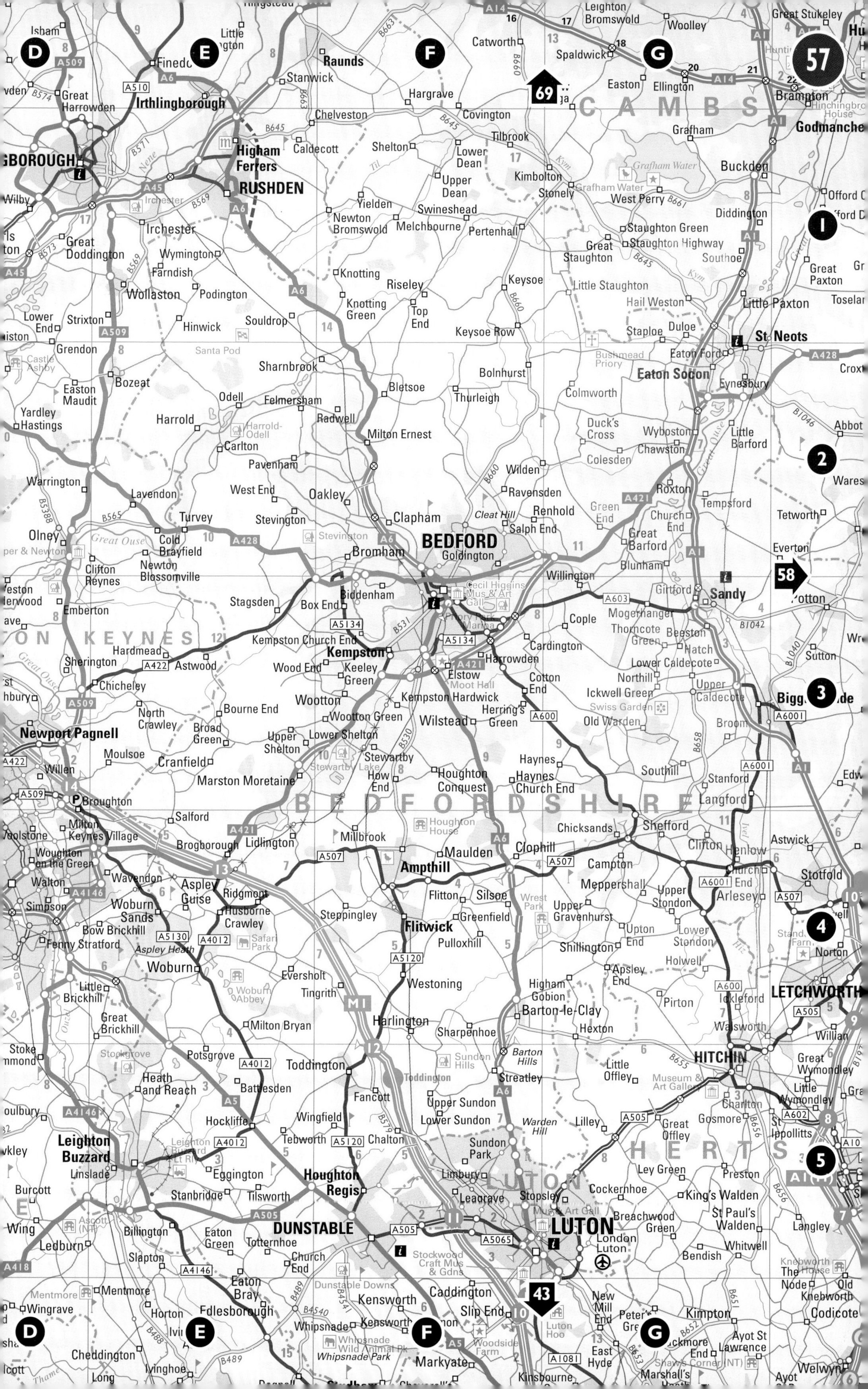

57
69
58
43
D
E
F
G
I
2
3
4
5
CAMBS
BEDFORDSHIRE
HERTS
Isham
Little
Finedon
Raunds
Stanwick
Catworth
Leighton Bromswold
Woolley
Great Stukeley
Spaldwick
Easton
Ellington
Brampton
Hinchingbrooke House
Godmanchester
Great Harrowden
Irthlingborough
Hargrave
Covington
Tilbrook
Grafham
Chelveston
Caldecott
Shelton
Lower Dean
Upper Dean
Kimbolton
Stonely
Grafham Water
West Perry
Buckden
Higham Ferrers
RUSHDEN
Irchester
Yielden
Newton Bromswold
Melchbourne
Swineshead
Pertenhall
Staughton Green
Staughton Highway
Great Staughton
Southoe
Diddington
Offord
Great Paxton
Little Paxton
Toseland
Great Doddington
Wymington
Farndish
Wollaston
Podington
Knotting
Knotting Green
Riseley
Top End
Keysoe
Keysoe Row
Little Staughton
Hail Weston
Staploe
Duloe
St Neots
Eaton Ford
Eaton Socon
Eynesbury
Bushmead Priory
Lower End
Strixton
Hinwick
Souldrop
Santa Pod
Grendon
Castle Ashby
Easton Maudit
Bozeat
Sharnbrook
Bletsoe
Bolnhurst
Thurleigh
Colmworth
Yardley Hastings
Odell
Felmersham
Harrold
Harrold-Odell
Radwell
Milton Ernest
Carlton
Pavenham
Duck's Cross
Wyboston
Chawston
Colesden
Little Barford
Abbotsley
Warrington
Lavendon
West End
Oakley
Wilden
Ravensden
Renhold
Salph End
Cleat Hill
Green End
Roxton
Church End
Great Barford
Tempsford
Tetworth
Olney
Turvey
Cold Brayfield
Newton Blossomville
Stevington
Clapham
BEDFORD
Goldington
Great Ouse
Clifton Reynes
Bromham
Biddenham
Willington
Blunham
Everton
Potton
Girtford
Sandy
Emberton
Stagsden
Box End
Cecil Higgins Mus & Art Gall
Priory Park Marina
Cople
Mogerhanger
Thorncote Green
Beeston
Hatch
Sutton
Hardmead
Kempston Church End
Kempston
Astwood
Sherington
Wood End
Keeley Green
Elstow
Harrowden
Cardington
Cotton End
Moot Hall
Northill
Lower Caldecote
Upper Caldecote
Ickwell Green
Swiss Garden
Chicheley
Wootton
Kempston Hardwick
Herring's Green
Wilstead
Old Warden
Biggleswade
North Crawley
Bourne End
Wootton Green
Broom
Newport Pagnell
Broad Green
Upper Shelton
Lower Shelton
Stewartby
Stewartby Lake
Moulsoe
Cranfield
Willen
Marston Moretaine
How End
Houghton Conquest
Haynes
Haynes Church End
Southill
Stanford
Langford
Edworth
Broughton
Salford
Milton Keynes Village
Millbrook
Houghton House
Chicksands
Shefford
Woolstone
Woughton on the Green
Brogborough
Lidlington
Maulden
Clophill
Clifton
Henlow
Astwick
Walton
Wavendon
Aspley Guise
Ridgmont
Ampthill
Campton
Church End
Arlesey
Stotfold
Simpson
Woburn Sands
Husborne Crawley
Flitton
Silsoe
Wrest Park
Meppershall
Upper Stondon
Bow Brickhill
Steppingley
Upper Gravenhurst
Fenny Stratford
Aspley Heath
Safari Park
Flitwick
Greenfield
Pulloxhill
Shillington
Upton End
Lower Stondon
Holwell
Norton
Woburn
Eversholt
Woburn Abbey
Tingrith
Westoning
Higham Gobion
Apsley End
Little Brickhill
Barton-le-Clay
Pirton
Ickleford
LETCHWORTH
Great Brickhill
Milton Bryan
Harlington
Sharpenhoe
Hexton
Walsworth
Willian
Stoke Hammond
Stockgrove
Potsgrove
Toddington
Sundon Hills
Barton Hills
Little Offley
HITCHIN
Great Wymondley
Heath and Reach
Battlesden
Streatley
Museum & Art Gallery
Little Wymondley
Fancott
Upper Sundon
Charlton
Hockliffe
Wingfield
Lower Sundon
Warden Hill
Lilley
Great Offley
Gosmore
St Ippollitts
Leighton Buzzard
Tebworth
Chalton
Sundon Park
Linslade
Eggington
Houghton Regis
Limbury
LUTON
Ley Green
Preston
Burcott
Stanbridge
Tilsworth
Leagrave
Stopsley
Cockernhoe
King's Walden
St Paul's Walden
Wing
Ascott (NT)
Billington
DUNSTABLE
Mus & Art Gall
Breachwood Green
Ledburn
Eaton Green
Totternhoe
London Luton
Whitwell
Langley
Slapton
Church End
Stockwood Craft Mus & Gdns
Bendish
Knebworth House
Mentmore
Eaton Bray
Dunstable Downs
Kensworth
Caddington
New Mill End
Kimpton
The Node
Old Knebworth
Wingrave
Horton
Edlesborough
Slip End
Peter's Green
Codicote
Ivinghoe
Whipsnade
Whipsnade Wild Animal Pk
Whipsnade Park
Woodside Farm
Luton Hoo
East Hyde
Ayot St Lawrence
Cheddington
Markyate
Shaw's Corner (NT)
Kinsbourne
Marshall's
Welwyn
Ayot
Long
A14
A1
A6
A45
A509
A510
A428
A421
A422
A603
A5134
A600
A6001
A507
A4146
A5130
A4012
A5120
A505
A5065
A5
A418
A602
A1081
B645
B663
B660
B661
B571
B569
B573
B574
B565
B5388
B531
B530
B658
B1040
B1042
B1046
B655
B656
B579
B489
B4540
B4541
B488
B652
B653
B651
B197
M1

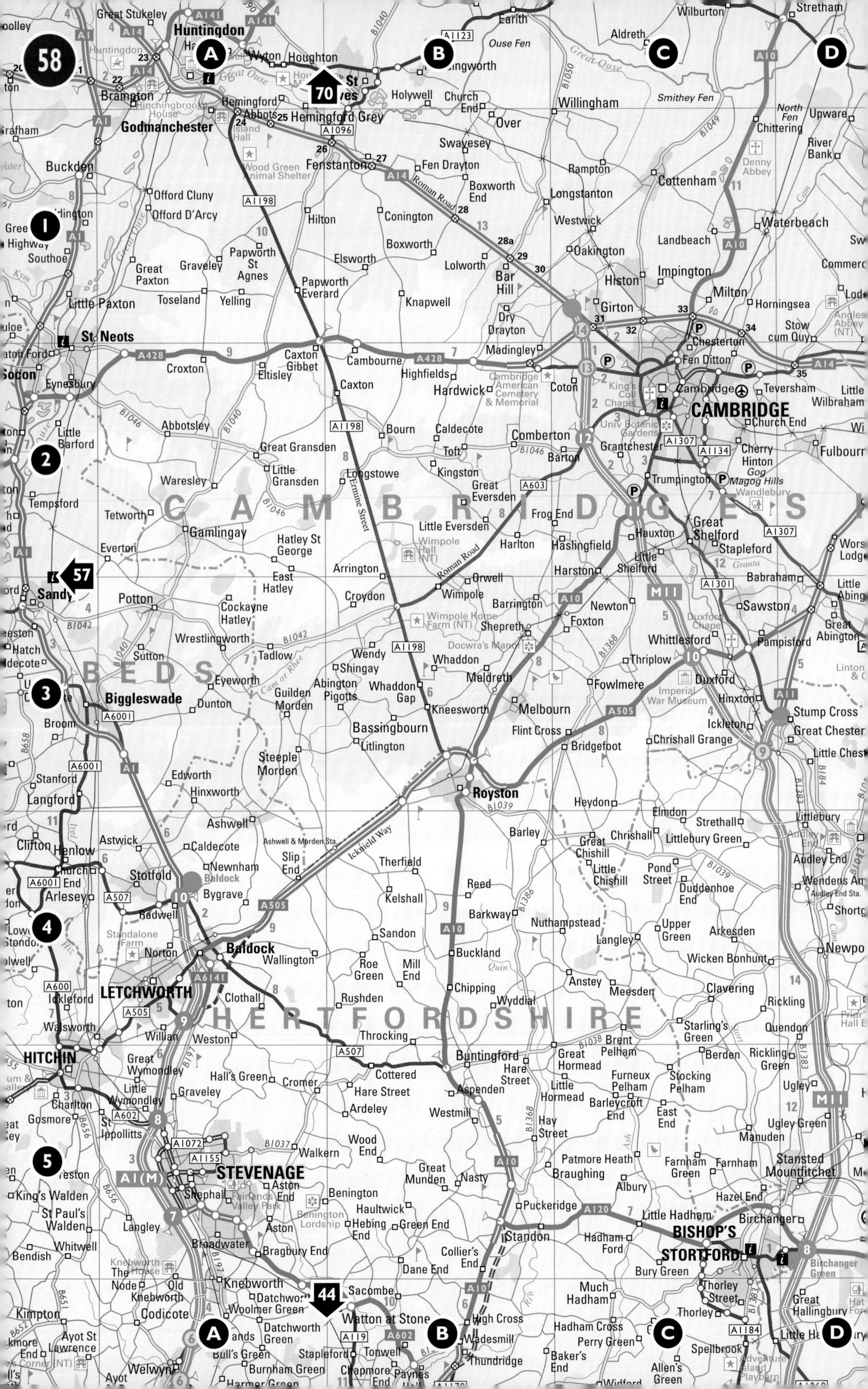
58
70
57
44
A
B
C
D
1
2
3
4
5
Huntingdon
Godmanchester
St Ives
Hemingford Grey
Fenstanton
Buckden
St. Neots
Eynesbury
Little Paxton
Great Paxton
Papworth Everard
Caxton Gibbet
Cambourne
Bar Hill
Cottenham
Waterbeach
Histon
Impington
Girton
Milton
CAMBRIDGE
Fen Ditton
Trumpington
Great Shelford
Sawston
Madingley
Hardwick
Comberton
Gamlingay
Sandy
Potton
Biggleswade
Royston
Melbourn
Bassingbourn
Duxford
Baldock
LETCHWORTH
HITCHIN
STEVENAGE
Buntingford
Standon
Puckeridge
BISHOP'S STORTFORD
Stansted Mountfitchet
Knebworth
Codicote
Watton at Stone
Welwyn
C A M B R I D G E S H I R E
B E D S
H E R T F O R D S H I R E
A1
A14
A10
A428
A1198
A505
A507
A603
A1307
A120
A602
A6001
A600
A1(M)
M11
Ermine Street
Icknield Way
Roman Road
Great Ouse

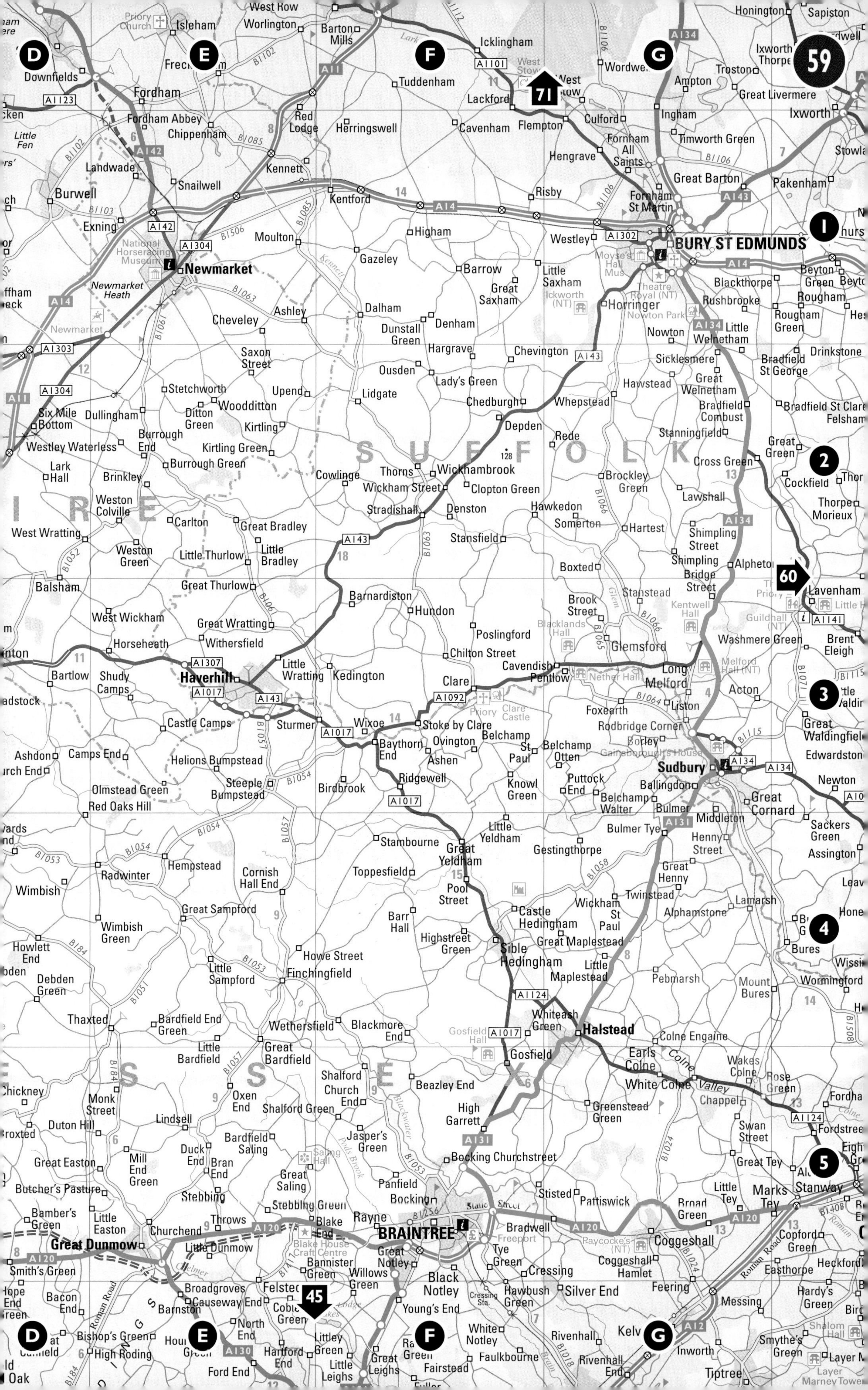
59
D
E
F
G
Priory Church
West Row
Worlington
Isleham
Barton Mills
Icklingham
Honington
Sapiston
Ixworth Thorpe
Downfields
Freckenham
Tuddenham
West Stow
Wordwell
Troston
Ampton
Great Livermere
Fordham
Fordham Abbey
Chippenham
Red Lodge
Herringswell
Lackford
Cavenham
Flempton
Culford
Ingham
Ixworth
Timworth Green
Fornham All Saints
Hengrave
Stowlangtoft
Little Fen
Landwade
Kennett
Snailwell
Burwell
Kentford
Risby
Great Barton
Pakenham
Fornham St Martin
Exning
Moulton
Higham
Westley
BURY ST EDMUNDS
National Horseracing Museum
Newmarket
Gazeley
Barrow
Little Saxham
Great Saxham
Moyse's Hall Mus
Theatre Royal (NT)
Ickworth (NT)
Beyton
Beyton Green
Blackthorpe
Rushbrooke
Rougham
Rougham Green
Newmarket Heath
Newmarket
Cheveley
Ashley
Dalham
Dunstall Green
Denham
Horringer
Nowton Park
Nowton
Little Welnetham
Saxon Street
Hargrave
Chevington
Sicklesmere
Drinkstone
Bradfield St George
Ousden
Lady's Green
Hawstead
Great Welnetham
Stetchworth
Upend
Lidgate
Chedburgh
Whepstead
Bradfield Combust
Bradfield St Clare
Felsham
Six Mile Bottom
Dullingham
Ditton Green
Woodditton
Kirtling
Depden
Burrough End
Burrough Green
Kirtling Green
Rede
Stanningfield
Great Green
Westley Waterless
SUFFOLK
128
Cross Green
Lark Hall
Brinkley
Cowlinge
Thorns
Wickhambrook
Wickham Street
Clopton Green
Brockley Green
Cockfield
Thorpe Morieux
Weston Colville
Stradishall
Denston
Hawkedon
Somerton
Lawshall
West Wratting
Carlton
Great Bradley
Hartest
Shimpling Street
Shimpling
Stansfield
Weston Green
Little Thurlow
Little Bradley
Boxted
Alpheton
Bridge Street
Balsham
Great Thurlow
Barnardiston
Hundon
Brook Street
Stanstead
Kentwell Hall
Lavenham
Little Hall
60
West Wickham
Great Wratting
Poslingford
Blacklands Hall
Guildhall (NT)
Withersfield
Horseheath
Chilton Street
Glemsford
Washmere Green
Brent Eleigh
Bartlow
Shudy Camps
Haverhill
Little Wratting
Kedington
Clare
Cavendish
Pentlow
Nether Hall
Long Melford
Melford Hall (NT)
Acton
Little Waldingfield
Priory
Clare Castle
Liston
Foxearth
Castle Camps
Sturmer
Wixoe
Stoke by Clare
Rodbridge Corner
Great Waldingfield
Ashdon
Camps End
Baythorn End
Ovington
Belchamp St Paul
Belchamp Otten
Borley
Gainsborough's House
Edwardstone
Church End
Helions Bumpstead
Ashen
Sudbury
Steeple Bumpstead
Ridgewell
Puttock End
Knowl Green
Belchamp Walter
Ballingdon
Bulmer
Newton
Olmstead Green
Birdbrook
Great Cornard
Red Oaks Hill
Middleton
Sackers Green
Little Yeldham
Bulmer Tye
Henny Street
Stambourne
Great Yeldham
Gestingthorpe
Assington
Hempstead
Radwinter
Cornish Hall End
Toppesfield
Great Henny
Wimbish
Pool Street
Twinstead
Lamarsh
Great Sampford
Castle Hedingham
Wickham St Paul
Alphamstone
Barr Hall
Bures
Wimbish Green
Highstreet Green
Great Maplestead
Howlett End
Sible Hedingham
Howe Street
Little Maplestead
Little Sampford
Finchingfield
Pebmarsh
Wormingford
Debden Green
Mount Bures
Thaxted
Bardfield End Green
Wethersfield
Blackmore End
Whiteash Green
Halstead
Gosfield Hall
Colne Engaine
Little Bardfield
Great Bardfield
Gosfield
Earls Colne
Colne
Wakes Colne
Rose Green
ESSEX
Shalford Church End
Beazley End
White Colne
Colne Valley
Chappel
Chickney
Monk Street
Oxen End
Shalford Green
High Garrett
Greenstead Green
Fordham
Duton Hill
Lindsell
Jasper's Green
Swan Street
Fordstreet
Great Easton
Mill End Green
Duck End
Bran End
Bardfield Saling
Saling Hall
Bocking Churchstreet
Great Tey
Butcher's Pasture
Great Saling
Panfield
Stisted
Pattiswick
Little Tey
Marks Tey
Stanway
Bamber's Green
Little Easton
Stebbing
Stebbing Green
Bocking
Broad Green
Throws
Blake End
Rayne
Bradwell
Freeport
Copford Green
Churchend
Blake House Craft Centre
BRAINTREE
Paycocke's (NT)
Coggeshall
Great Dunmow
Little Dunmow
Great Notley
Tye Green
Coggeshall Hamlet
Smith's Green
Bannister Green
Willows Green
Cressing
Easthorpe
Heckford
Hope End Green
Broadgroves
Felsted
Black Notley
Cressing Sta.
Hawbush Green
Silver End
Feering
Messing
Hardy's Green
Bacon End
Causeway End
Barnston
Cobler's Green
45
Young's End
Birch
North End
White Notley
Rivenhall
Kelvedon
Shalom Hall
Bishop's Green
Hounslow Green
Littley Green
Rayne Green
Smythe's Green
Great Canfield
High Roding
Hartford End
Great Leighs
Faulkbourne
Rivenhall End
Inworth
Layer Marney
Fairstead
Little Leighs
Tiptree
Layer Marney Tower
Ford End
Oak
71
A11
A1101
A134
A1123
A142
A14
A1304
A1302
A143
A1303
A1307
A1017
A1092
A1141
A131
A1124
A120
A130
A12
B1102
B1085
B1103
B1506
B1063
B1061
B1106
B1066
B1065
B1064
B1115
B1071
B1057
B1054
B1053
B1051
B1058
B1024
B1508
B1417
B1256
B1018
B1408
B184
B1052
Roman Road
Kennett
Glem
Colne
Blackwater
Pods Brook
Chelmer
Brain

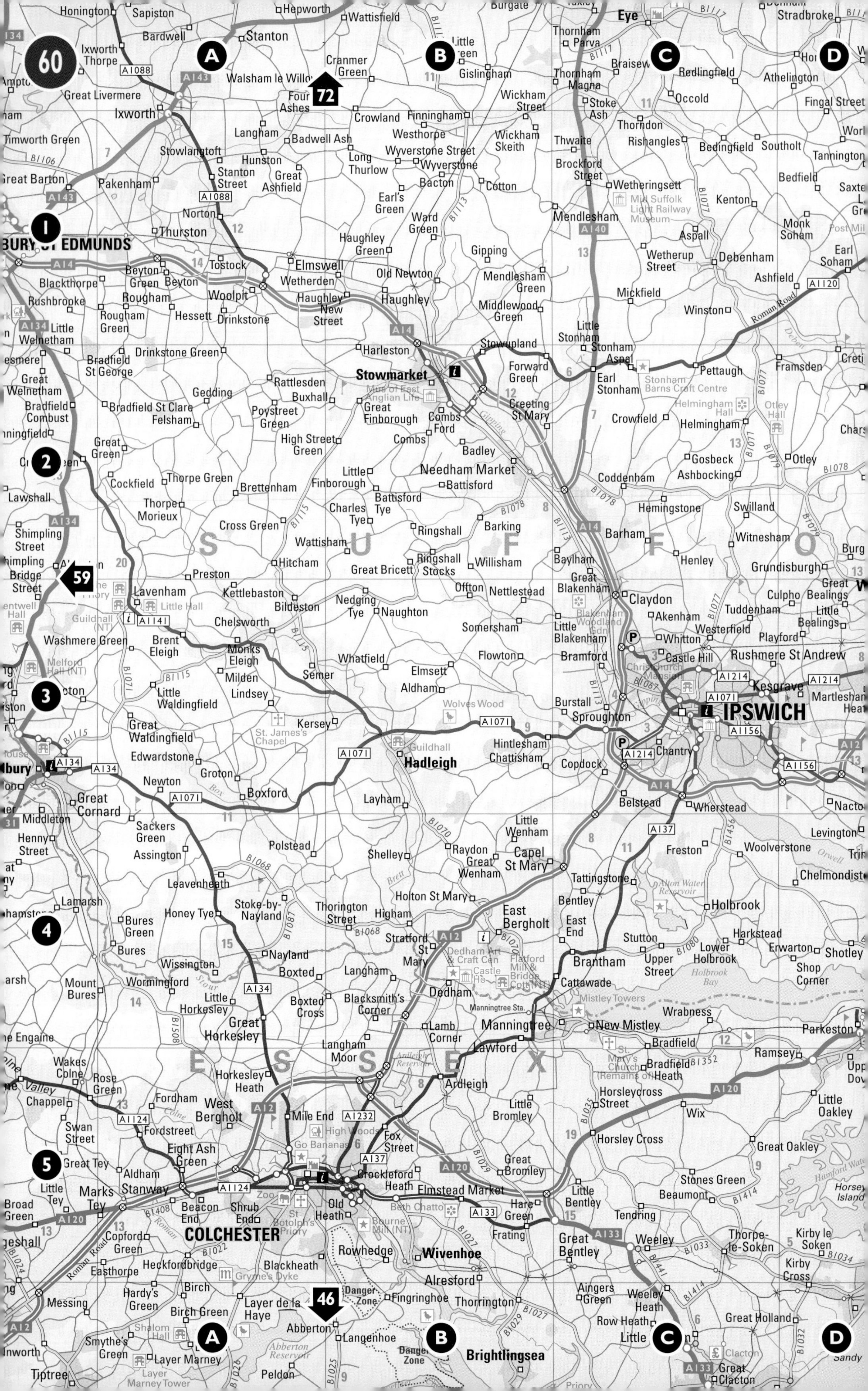
A
B
C
D
72
59
46
1
2
3
4
5
Honington
Sapiston
Hepworth
Wattisfield
Burgate
Eye
Stradbroke
Bardwell
Stanton
Ixworth Thorpe
Little Green
Thornham Parva
Braisewort
Redlingfield
Athelington
Cranmer Green
Walsham le Willows
Gislingham
Thornham Magna
Occold
Fingal Street
Great Livermere
Ixworth
Four Ashes
Wickham Street
Stoke Ash
Crowland
Finningham
Thorndon
Langham
Badwell Ash
Westhorpe
Wickham Skeith
Thwaite
Rishangles
Bedingfield
Southolt
Tannington
Timworth Green
Stowlangtoft
Hunston
Long Thurlow
Wyverstone Street
Wyverstone
Brockford Street
Stanton Street
Great Ashfield
Bacton
Cotton
Wetheringsett
Mid Suffolk Light Railway Museum
Bedfield
Great Barton
Pakenham
Kenton
Earl's Green
Norton
Ward Green
Mendlesham
Monk Soham
Thurston
Aspall
BURY ST EDMUNDS
Haughley Green
Gipping
Wetherup Street
Debenham
Earl Soham
Tostock
Elmswell
Beyton Green
Beyton
Wetherden
Old Newton
Mendlesham Green
Ashfield
Blackthorpe
Woolpit
Haughley
Mickfield
Rushbrooke
Rougham
Hessett
Drinkstone
Haughley New Street
Middlewood Green
Winston
Roman Road
Rougham Green
Little Welnetham
Little Stonham
Drinkstone Green
Harleston
Stowupland
Stonham Aspal
Pettaugh
Framsden
Bradfield St George
Forward Green
Earl Stonham
Stonham Barns Craft Centre
Great Welnetham
Rattlesden
Stowmarket
Bradfield Combust
Gedding
Buxhall
Mus of East Anglian Life
Creeting St Mary
Helmingham Hall
Otley Hall
Bradfield St Clare
Felsham
Poystreet Green
Great Finborough
Combs Ford
Crowfield
Helmingham
High Street Green
Combs
Gipping
Great Green
Badley
Gosbeck
Otley
Ashbocking
Little Finborough
Needham Market
Cockfield
Thorpe Green
Battisford
Coddenham
Brettenham
Battisford Tye
Lawshall
Thorpe Morieux
Charles Tye
Hemingstone
Swilland
Shimpling Street
Cross Green
Ringshall
Barking
Barham
Witnesham
Wattisham
Baylham
Henley
Hitcham
Ringshall Stocks
Willisham
Bridge Street
Great Bricett
Grundisburgh
Preston
Great Blakenham
Offton
Nettlestead
Claydon
Culpho
Great Bealings
Lavenham
Little Hall
Kettlebaston
Bildeston
Nedging Tye
Naughton
Akenham
Tuddenham
Little Bealings
Guildhall (NT)
Chelsworth
Little Blakenham
Blakenham Woodland Gdn
Westerfield
Somersham
Whitton
Playford
Washmere Green
Brent Eleigh
Monks Eleigh
Bramford
Flowton
Castle Hill
Rushmere St Andrew
Melford Hall (NT)
Whatfield
Semer
Christchurch Mansion
Milden
Elmsett
Kesgrave
Little Waldingfield
Lindsey
Aldham
Martlesham Heath
Wolves Wood
Burstall
Sproughton
IPSWICH
Kersey
Great Waldingfield
St. James's Chapel
Hintlesham
Chattisham
Guildhall
Copdock
Chantry
Edwardstone
Hadleigh
Groton
Newton
Boxford
Great Cornard
Layham
Belstead
Wherstead
Middleton
Sackers Green
Little Wenham
Nacton
Henny Street
Levington
Assington
Polstead
Shelley
Raydon
Great Wenham
Capel St Mary
Freston
Woolverstone
Tattingstone
Chelmondiston
Leavenheath
Alton Water Reservoir
Holton St Mary
Bentley
Lamarsh
Honey Tye
Stoke-by-Nayland
Thorington Street
Higham
East Bergholt
Holbrook
Bures Green
East End
Harkstead
Stratford St Mary
Stutton
Lower Holbrook
Erwarton
Shotley
Bures
Nayland
Dedham Art & Craft Cen
Flatford Mill & Bridge Cott (NT)
Brantham
Upper Street
Shop Corner
Wissington
Holbrook Bay
Mount Bures
Wormingford
Boxted
Langham
Castle Ho
Cattawade
Little Horkesley
Boxted Cross
Blacksmith's Corner
Dedham
Mistley Towers
Wrabness
Great Horkesley
Manningtree Sta.
Lamb Corner
Manningtree
New Mistley
Parkeston
Langham Moor
Bradfield
Wakes Colne
Rose Green
Horkesley Heath
Lawford
St. Mary's Church (Remains of)
Bradfield Heath
Ramsey
Colne Valley
Ardleigh Reservoir
Ardleigh
Chappel
Fordham
West Bergholt
Horsleycross Street
Little Oakley
Little Bromley
Mile End
Swan Street
Fordstreet
High Woods
Fox Street
Wix
Eight Ash Green
Go Bananas
Horsley Cross
Great Tey
Great Oakley
Aldham
Great Bromley
Stanway
Crockleford Heath
Stones Green
Little Tey
Marks Tey
Elmstead Market
Little Bentley
Beaumont
Beacon End
Shrub End
Zoo
Old Heath
Beth Chatto
Hare Green
Tendring
Broad Green
St Botolph's Priory
Bourne Mill (NT)
Frating
COLCHESTER
Great Bentley
Thorpe-le-Soken
Kirby le Soken
Copford Green
Rowhedge
Wivenhoe
Weeley
Heckfordbridge
Blackheath
Kirby Cross
Easthorpe
Gryme's Dyke
Alresford
Birch
Aingers Green
Weeley Heath
Messing
Hardy's Green
Layer de la Haye
Danger Zone
Fingringhoe
Thorrington
Birch Green
Row Heath
Great Holland
Shalom Hall
Abberton
Langenhoe
Little Clacton
Smythe's Green
Abberton Reservoir
Brightlingsea
Inworth
Layer Marney
Clacton
Tiptree
Layer Marney Tower
Peldon
Great Clacton
S U F F O
E S S E X
A1088
A143
A14
A134
A140
A1120
A1141
A1071
A1214
A1156
A137
A12
A1124
A1232
A120
A133
B1106
B1113
B1077
B1078
B1115
B1070
B1068
B1087
B1508
B1035
B1029
B1027
B1022
B1408
B1024
B1025
B1026
B1033
B1441
B1414
B1032
B1034
B1352
B1080
B1456
B1079
B1117

D
E
F
G
73
47
1
2
3
4
5
Huntingfield
Walpole
Blackheath
Thorington
Walberswick
Bramfield
A144
Laxfield
Heveningham
Ubbeston Green
Poys Street
Dunwich
Darsham Sta.
Brundish
Peasenhall
Sibton
A1120
Darsham
Westleton
Badingham
Yoxford
Middleton
Alde
A12
Dunwich Heath (NT)
Bruisyard
Bruisyard Street
Vineyard & Winery
Theberton
East Bridge
Kelsale
Brabling Green
Cransford
Rendham
Carlton
Leiston Abbey
B1119
B1121
B1122
Sweffling
Saxmundham
Sizewell
Leiston
Great Glemham
Sternfield
Knodishall
Coldfair Green
B1116
B1120
B1353
Parham
Farnham
Friston
Aldringham
Thorpe Ness
Kettleburgh
Glemham Hall
Stratford St Andrew
Thorpeness
Easton
Hacheston
The Meare
Easton Farm Park
Marlesford
Gromford
Church Common
A1094
Little Glemham
Snape
Moot Hall
Campsey Ash
Blaxhall
B1069
Aldeburgh
Wickham Market
Wickham Market Sta.
B1078
Iken
High Street
Pettistree
Tunstall
Slaughden
Aldeburgh Bay
Rendlesham
Tunstall Forest
Sudbourne
Ufford
A1152
Chillesford
B1438
K
Butley
B1084
Eyke
Melton
Bromeswell
Orford
Rendlesham Forest
Orford Ness
Sutton Hoo
Tumuli
B1083
Tide Mill
Capel St Andrew
Gedgrave Hall
Boyton
Orford Beach
Sutton
Shottisham
Waldringfield
Hollesley
Shingle Street
Hollesley Bay
0 2 4 6 8 10 miles
0 2 4 6 8 10 km
Newbourne
Hemley
Ramsholt
Alderton
Kirton
Bawdsey
Falkenham
A14
Felixstowe Ferry
Walton
Old Felixstowe
FELIXSTOWE
Manning's Amusement Park
Harwich Harbour
Landguard Fort
Landguard Point
hours
Esbjerg....................................19
Hamburg..................................20
Hook of Holland.......................3¾
The Naze
Walton Pier

A
B
C
D
75
1
2
3
4
5
50
CARDIGAN BAY
Barmouth Bay
Llanenddwyn
Ystumgwern
Dyffryn Ardudwy Sta.
Dyffryn Ardudwy
Dyffryn Burial Chamber
Llanddwywe
Tal-y-bont
A496
Diffwys
750
589
Craig-y-cae
Y Garn
629
Ganllwyd
Uwch-mynydd
Taicynhaeaf
Llanelltyd
Bontddu
Pen-y-bryn
Toll
A470
Caerdeon
Llanaber
461
Panorama Walk
Abergwynant
Penmaenpool
Dolgellau
Cutiau
A493
Islawr-dref
Barmouth (Abermaw)
The Bar
Mawddach
GWYNEDD
Arthog
Morfa Mawddach Sta.
SNOWDONIA
CADAIR IDRIS
Mynydd Moel
855
Penygadair
893
Llyn Cau
Fairbourne & Barmouth Rly
Fairbourne
Friog
661
622
Pen y Garn
459
Mynydd Pennant
Mynydd Pencoed
Tal-y-llyn Lake
Llwyngwril
Llanfihangel-y-pennant
Tal-y-llyn
Esgair Berfa
Castell y Bere (Ruin)
Craig Goch
Llangelynin
390
Dysynni
Abergynolwyn
PARK
Tarren-y-Gesail
Rhoslefain
Llanegryn
B4405
Mynydd Tan-y-coed
666
Llanfendigaid
Peniarth
Foel Wyllt
Dolgoch
Foel y-Geifr
313
Tarrenhendre
Pantperthog
Tonfanau
Bryncrug
633
Aber Dysynni
Pandy
Pen Trum-gwr
Rhyd-yr-onnen
Trum Gelli
535
Tywyn
Talyllyn Rly
Pennal
Cwrt
DYFI
Caethle Farm
Derwenlas
Glaspwll
279
Aberdyfi Bar
Eglwys Fach
Aberdovey (Aberdyfi)
Ysgubor-y-coed
Furnace
Dyfi Furnace
Pen Carreg Gopa
447
Twyni Bach
Traeth Maelgwyn
Dyfi (Dovey)
Fochno
Cwm Einion
Ynyslas
B4353
Foel Goch
475
Angler's Retreat
Llancynfelyn
Tre'r-ddol
Moel-y-Llyn
521
Cors
Leri
Cletwr
Taliesin
Cwm Ceulan
Borth
Talybont
Upper Borth
Dolybont
Nant-y-moch Resr
A487
Llandre
CEREDIGION
Bont-goch (Elerch)
Sarn Cynfelyn
B4572
Bow Street
Penrhyn-coch
Salem
Llyn Syfydrin
Llangorwen
Great Aberystwyth Camera Obscura
Clarach
Plas Gogerddan
Cwmsymlog
Cliff Railway
Aberystwyth Arts Centre
Pen-bont Rhydybeddau
National Library of Wales
Capel Dewi
Aberystwyth
Waun Fawr
A4159
Old Goginan
Goginan
The Bar
Llanbadarn Fawr
Capel Bangor
A44
Ponterwyd
Ceredigion
Penparcau
Vale of Rheidol Rly
Cwmbrwyno
(Summer Only)
Rheidol Falls
Rhydyfelin
Capel Seion
Aberffrwd
A4120
Llanfarian
Rheidol
Allt Wen
Gors
New Cross
Devil's Bridge (Pontarfynach)
Abermad
Llanfihangel-y-Creuddyn
Blaenplwyf
Llanilar
Ystwyth
B4340
Cnwch Coch
Rhodmad
A485
B4575
B4576
Rhos-y-garth
Llanafan
A487
Ystwyth
Llanddeiniol
Carreg Ti-pw
Wyre
Llangwyryfon
Mynydd Bach
Lledrod
Llanrhystud
328
Tynygraig
B4340
Trefenter
18
Llansantffraid
Rhyd-rosser
Llanon
361
317
Llyn Eiddwen
Ystrad Meurig
Swyddffynnon
Meurig
15
7
9
12
14
10
20
11

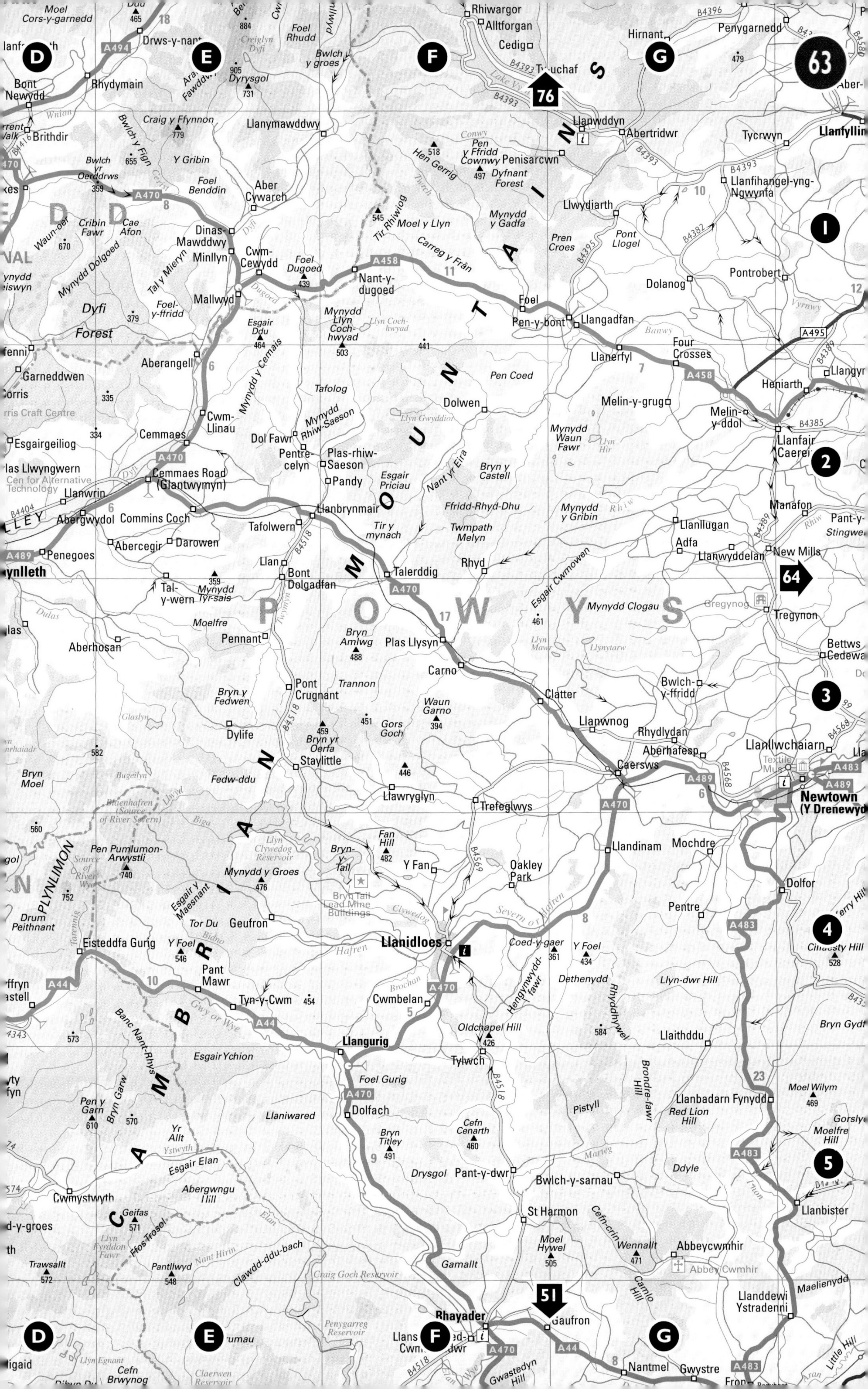
63
76
64
51
D
E
F
G
I
2
3
4
5
Moel Cors-y-garnedd
Drws-y-nant
Bont Newydd
Rhydymain
Brithdir
Creiglyn Dyfi
Dyrysgol
Foel Rhudd
Bwlch y groes
Rhiwargor
Alltforgan
Cedig
Ty-uchaf
Lake Vyrnwy
Hirnant
Penygarnedd
Aber-
Craig y Ffynnon
Bwlch y Fign
Y Gribin
Bwlch yr Oerddrws
Llanymawddwy
Hen Gerrig
Pen y Ffridd Cownwy
Penisarcwn
Dyfnant Forest
Llanwddyn
Abertridwr
Tycrwyn
Llanfyllin
Llanfihangel-yng-Ngwynfa
Foel Benddin
Aber Cywarch
Tir Rhiwiog
Moel y Llyn
Mynydd y Gadfa
Llwydiarth
Pont Llogel
Cribin Fawr
Cae Afon
Waun-oer
Mynydd Dolgoed
Dinas-Mawddwy
Minllyn
Cwm-Cewydd
Foel Dugoed
Carreg y Frân
Pren Croes
Dolanog
Pontrobert
Tal y Mieryn
Mallwyd
Nant-y-dugoed
Foel
Pen-y-bont
Llangadfan
Dyfi Forest
Foel-y-ffridd
Esgair Ddu
Mynydd Llyn Coch-hwyad
Llyn Coch-hwyad
Banwy
Vyrnwy
Aberangell
Garneddwen
Corris
Corris Craft Centre
Mynydd y Cemais
Tafolog
Llanerfyl
Four Crosses
Heniarth
Llangyn
Pen Coed
Dolwen
Melin-y-grug
Melin-y-ddol
Llanfair Caereinion
Cwm-Llinau
Esgairgeiliog
Cemmaes
Dol Fawr
Mynydd Rhiw-Saeson
Llyn Gwyddior
Mynydd Waun Fawr
Llyn Hir
Plas Llwyngwern
Centre for Alternative Technology
Cemmaes Road (Glantwymyn)
Pentre-celyn
Plas-rhiw-Saeson
Pandy
Esgair Priciau
Nant yr Eira
Bryn y Castell
Llanwrin
Commins Coch
Llanbrynmair
Ffridd-Rhyd-Dhu
Mynydd y Gribin
Rhiw
Manafon
Pant-y-
Stingwern
Abergwydol
Abercegir
Darowen
Tafolwern
Tir y mynach
Twmpath Melyn
Llanllugan
Adfa
Llanwyddelan
New Mills
Penegoes
Machynlleth
Llan
Bont Dolgadfan
Talerddig
Rhyd
Esgair Cwmowen
Tal-y-wern
Mynydd Tyr-sais
POWYS
Mynydd Clogau
Gregynog
Tregynon
Dulas
Moelfre
Pennant
Bryn Amlwg
Plas Llysyn
Llyn Mawr
Llynytarw
Bettws Cedewain
Aberhosan
Carno
Clatter
Bwlch-y-ffridd
Bryn y Fedwen
Pont Crugnant
Trannon
Waun Garno
Glaslyn
Dylife
Gors Goch
Llanwnog
Rhydlydan
Bryn yr Oerfa
Aberhafesp
Llanllwchaiarn
Bryn Moel
Bugeilyn
Staylittle
Caersws
Textile Museum
Newtown (Y Drenewydd)
Fedw-ddu
Llawryglyn
Trefeglwys
Blaenhafren Source of River Severn
Biga
Llyn Clywedog Reservoir
Fan Hill
Llandinam
Mochdre
PLYNLIMON
Pen Pumlumon-Arwystli
Source of River Wye
Mynydd y Groes
Bryn-y-Tail
Y Fan
Oakley Park
Dolfor
Bryn Tail Lead Mine Buildings
Drum Peithnant
Esgair y Maesnant
Tor Du
Geufron
Clywedog
Severn or Hafren
Pentre
Kerry Hill
Eisteddfa Gurig
Y Foel
Llanidloes
Coed-y-gaer
Y Foel
Cilfaesty Hill
Hafren
Pant Mawr
Hengynwydd-fawr
Dethenydd
Rhyddhywel
Llyn-dwr Hill
Ffrwd Fawr
Brochan
Tyn-y-Cwm
Cwmbelan
Banc Nant-Rhys
Gwy or Wye
Oldchapel Hill
Llaithddu
Bryn Gydfa
Llangurig
Esgair Ychion
Tylwch
Brondre-fawr Hill
CAMBRIAN MOUNTAINS
Foel Gurig
Moel Wilym
Pen y Garn
Bryn Garw
Dolfach
Llaniwared
Pistyll
Llanbadarn Fynydd
Red Lion Hill
Gorsley
Moelfre Hill
Yr Allt
Ystwyth
Bryn Titley
Cefn Cenarth
Marteg
Esgair Elan
Drysgol
Pant-y-dwr
Bwlch-y-sarnau
Ddyle
Ithon
Abergwngu Hill
Cwmystwyth
St Harmon
Cefn-crin
Llanbister
Geifas
Ffos Trosol
Llyn Fyrddon Fawr
Nant Hirin
Elan
Moel Hywel
Wennallt
Abbeycwmhir
Clawdd-ddu-bach
Trawsallt
Pantllwyd
Craig Goch Reservoir
Gamallt
Abbey Cwmhir
Camlo Hill
Maelienydd
Llanddewi Ystradenni
Rhayader
Gaufron
Penygarreg Reservoir
Llansantffraed-Cwmdeuddwr
Llyn Egnant
Cefn Brwynog
Claerwen Reservoir
Gwastedyn Hill
Nantmel
Gwystre
Fron
Little Hill
Aran
A494
A470
A458
A495
A489
A483
A44
B4393
B4395
B4382
B4389
B4385
B4404
B4518
B4569
B4568
B4396
B4580
B4416
B4343

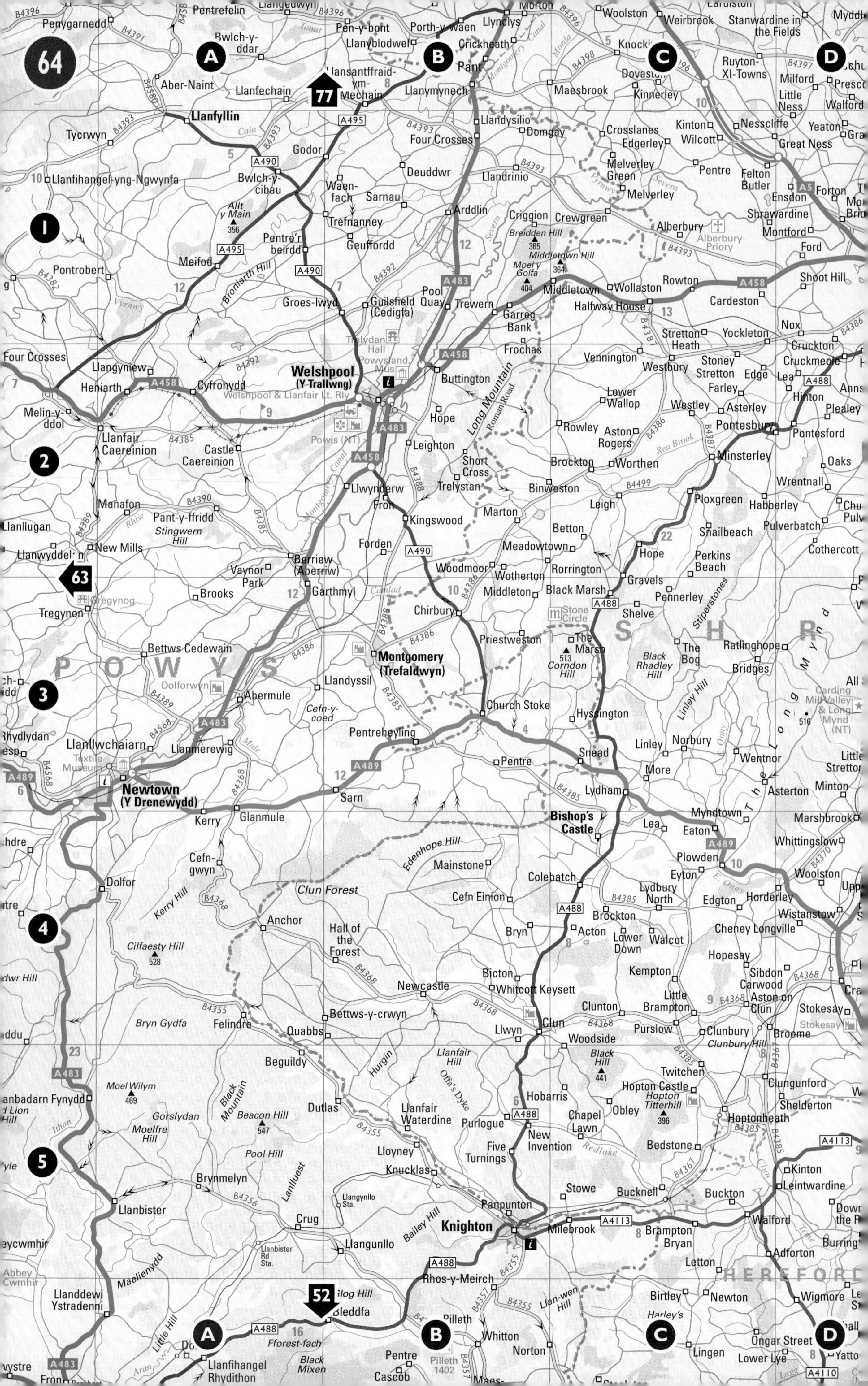

Penygarnedd
Pentrefelin
Llangedwyn
Pen-y-bont
Porth-y-waen
Llynclys
Morton
Woolston
Weirbrook
Stanwardine in the Fields
Bwlch-y-ddar
Llanyblodwel
Crickheath
Montgomery Canal
Knockin
Ruyton-XI-Towns
Milford
Llansantffraid-ym-Mechain
77
Aber-Naint
Llanfechain
Pant
Llanymynech
Maesbrook
Dovaston
Kinnerley
Little Ness
Walford
Llanfyllin
A495
B4393
Llandysilio
Domgay
Crosslanes
Edgerley
Kinton
Wilcott
Nesscliffe
Yeaton
Great Ness
Tycrwyn
Cain
Godor
Four Crosses
A490
Bwlch-y-cibau
Deuddwr
Llandrinio
Melverley Green
Melverley
Pentre
Felton Butler
Ensdon
Forton
Llanfihangel-yng-Ngwynfa
Waen-fach
Sarnau
Severn
Vyrnwy
Shrawardine
Allt y Main
356
Trefnanney
Arddlin
Criggion
Crewgreen
Alberbury
Alberbury Priory
Montford
Pentre'r beirdd
Geuffordd
Breidden Hill
365
Middletown Hill
364
B4393
Ford
Pontrobert
Meifod
Broniarth Hill
B4392
Moel y Golfa
404
Middletown
Wollaston
Rowton
A458
Shoot Hill
Groes-lwyd
Guilsfield (Cegidfa)
Pool Quay
Trewern
Garreg Bank
Halfway House
Cardeston
Stretton Heath
Yockleton
Nox
Cruckton
Four Crosses
Llangyniew
Trelydan Hall
Powysland Mus
Frochas
Vennington
Westbury
Stoney Stretton
Edge
Cruckmeole
Lea
A488
Heniarth
Cyfronydd
Welshpool (Y Trallwng)
Welshpool & Llanfair Lt. Rly
Buttington
Long Mountain
Roman Road
Lower Wallop
Farley
Hinton
Annscroft
Melin-y-ddol
Llanfair Caereinion
B4385
Castle Caereinion
Powis (NT)
A483
Hope
Leighton
Rowley
Aston Rogers
Westley
Asterley
Pontesbury
Pontesford
Pleal
Short Cross
Brockton
Worthen
Rea Brook
Minsterley
Oaks
Llwynderw
Fron
Trelystan
Binweston
Wrentnall
Manafon
B4390
Pant-y-ffridd
Stingwern Hill
Rhiw
Llanllugan
Kingswood
Marton
Leigh
Ploxgreen
Habberley
Pulverbatch
Betton
Snailbeach
New Mills
Llanwyddelan
Berriew (Aberriw)
Vaynor Park
Forden
Meadowtown
Hope
Perkins Beach
Cothercott
63
Brooks
Woodmoor
Wotherton
Rorrington
Gravels
Gregynog
Garthmyl
Camlad
Middleton
Black Marsh
Pennerley
Tregynon
Chirbury
Stone Circle
Shelve
Stiperstones
Bettws Cedewain
B4386
Priestweston
The Marsh
Black Rhadley Hill
The Bog
Ratlinghope
P O W Y S
S H R
Montgomery (Trefaldwyn)
Corndon Hill
513
Bridges
Long Mynd
Dolforwyn
Llandyssil
Carding Mill Valley & Long Mynd (NT)
Abermule
Cefn-y-coed
Church Stoke
Linley Hill
Hyssington
516
B4389
Pentreheyling
Rhydlydan
Llanllwchaiarn
B4568
Llanmerewig
Mule
Linley
Norbury
Snead
Wentnor
Little Stretton
Textile Museum
A489
Pentre
More
Asterton
Minton
Newtown (Y Drenewydd)
Sarn
Lydham
B4368
Kerry
Glanmule
Bishop's Castle
Myndtown
Lea
Eaton
Marshbrook
Edenhope Hill
Whittingslow
Cefn-gwyn
Mainstone
Plowden
Dolfor
Clun Forest
Colebatch
Eyton
Woolston
Lydbury North
Kerry Hill
Cefn Einion
B4385
Edgton
Horderley
Anchor
Brockton
Wistanstow
Hall of the Forest
Bryn
Acton
Lower Down
Walcot
Cheney Longville
Cilfaesty Hill
528
Hopesay
Kempton
Sibdon Carwood
Bicton
Newcastle
Whitcott Keysett
Little Brampton
Aston on Clun
Stokesay
B4355
Felindre
Bettws-y-crwyn
Clunton
Bryn Gydfa
Quabbs
Llwyn
Clun
Purslow
Clunbury
Clunbury Hill
Broome
Woodside
Beguildy
Llanfair Hill
Black Hill
441
Twitchen
Hurgin
Offa's Dyke
Hopton Castle
Clungunford
Moel Wilym
469
Black Mountain
Hobarris
Hopton Titterhill
396
Shelderton
Llanbadarn Fynydd
Dutlas
Llanfair Waterdine
Chapel Lawn
Obley
Hoptonheath
Ithon
Gorslydan
Beacon Hill
547
Purlogue
New Invention
Moelfre Hill
Redlake
Bedstone
A4113
Pool Hill
Lloyney
Five Turnings
Knucklas
Kinton
Leintwardine
Brynmelyn
Lanlluest
Stowe
Bucknell
Buckton
B4367
Llanbister
B4356
Llangynllo Sta.
Panpunton
Walford
Crug
Bailey Hill
Knighton
Milebrook
Brampton Bryan
Llanbister Rd Sta.
Llangunllo
Burrington
Maelienydd
A488
B4355
Adforton
Rhos-y-Meirch
Letton
HEREFORD
Llanddewi Ystradenni
52
Glog Hill
B4357
Llan-wen Hill
Birtley
Newton
Wigmore
Bleddfa
Pilleth
Harley's
Little Hill
Fforest-fach
Whitton
Norton
Lingen
Ongar Street
Black Mixen
Pentre
Pilleth 1402
Lower Lye
Llanfihangel Rhydithon
Aran
Cascob
Fron
A4110
Lugg

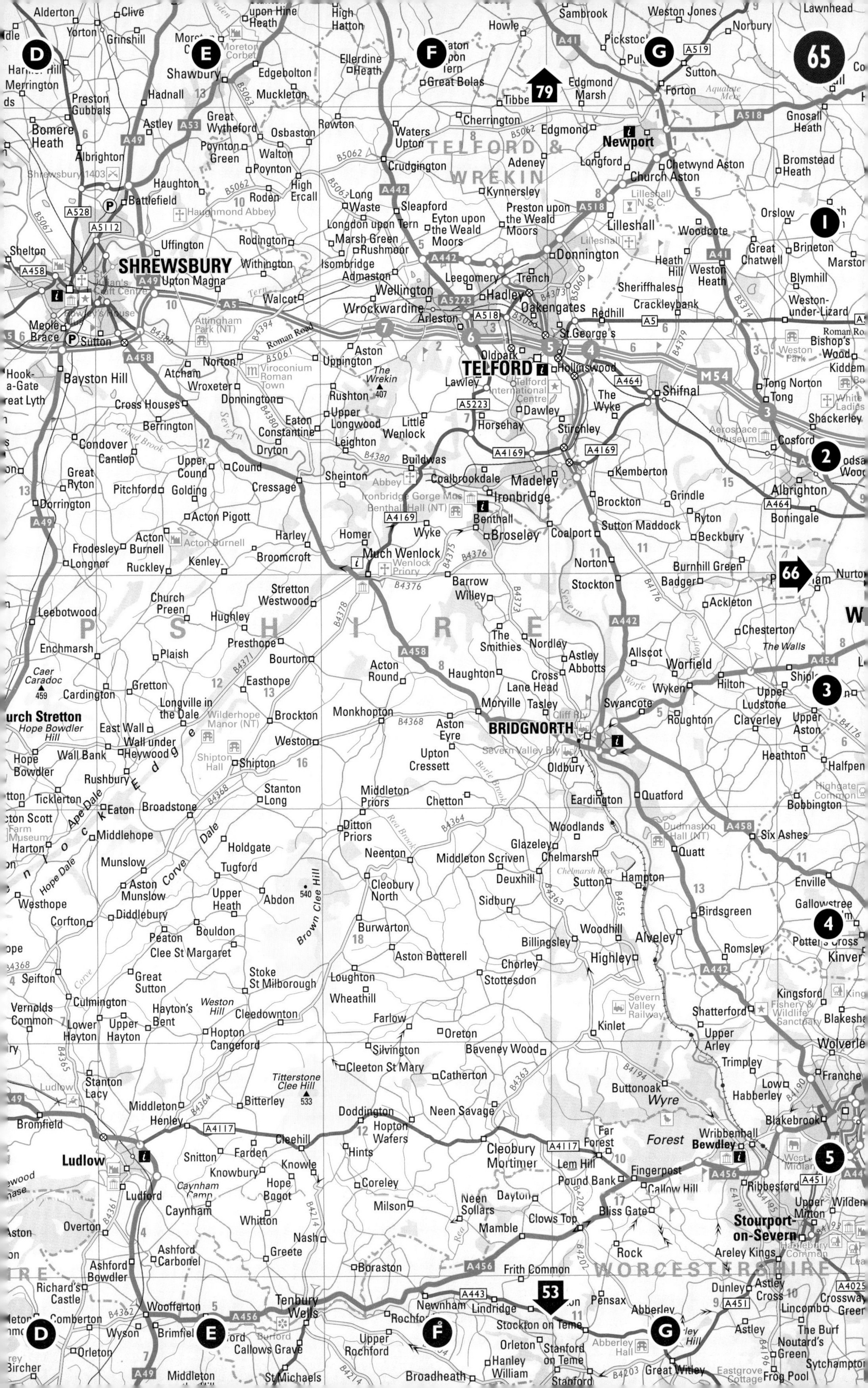
D
E
F
G
79
66
53
I
Alderton
Clive
Yorton
Grinshill
Shawbury
Moreton Corbet
High Hatton
Ellerdine Heath
Howle
Sambrook
Weston Jones
Norbury
Lawnhead
Pickstock
Sutton
Forton
Edgmond Marsh
Tibberton
Great Bolas
Hadnall
Edgebolton
Muckleton
Preston Gubbals
Merrington
Bomere Heath
Albrighton
Astley
Great Wytheford
Poynton Green
Rowton
Osbaston
Walton
Poynton
Waters Upton
Cherrington
Edgmond
Newport
TELFORD & WREKIN
Crudgington
Adeney
Longford
Church Aston
Chetwynd Aston
Gnosall Heath
Bromstead Heath
Haughton
Battlefield
Roden
High Ercall
Long Waste
Sleapford
Kynnersley
Lilleshall N.S.C.
Eyton upon the Weald Moors
Preston upon the Weald Moors
Lilleshall
Woodcote
Orslow
Haughmond Abbey
Shrewsbury 1403
Longdon upon Tern
Marsh Green
Rushmoor
Rodington
Uffington
SHREWSBURY
Withington
Isombridge
Admaston
Donnington
Heath Hill
Weston Heath
Great Chatwell
Brineton
Marston
Blymhill
Shelton
Upton Magna
Walcot
Wellington
Leegomery
Trench
Hadley
Sheriffhales
Crackleybank
Weston-under-Lizard
Meole Brace
Sutton
Attingham Park (NT)
Wrockwardine
Arleston
Oakengates
Redhill
St. George's
Bishop's Wood
Roman Road
Shrewsbury Castle
St Julian's Craft Centre
Rowley's House
Aston
Uppington
The Wrekin 407
Oldpark
TELFORD
Hollinswood
Weston Park
Hook-a-Gate
Great Lyth
Bayston Hill
Atcham
Norton
Wroxeter
Viroconium Roman Town
Lawley
Telford International Centre
Shifnal
The Wyke
Tong Norton
Tong
White Ladies
Cross Houses
Donnington
Rushton
Upper Longwood
Eaton Constantine
Little Wenlock
Dawley
Horsehay
Stirchley
Aerospace Museum
Shackerley
Cosford
Berrington
Condover
Cantlop
Dryton
Leighton
Buildwas
Kemberton
Great Ryton
Pitchford
Golding
Upper Cound
Cound
Cressage
Sheinton
Abbey
Coalbrookdale
Madeley
Ironbridge
Ironbridge Gorge Mus
Benthall Hall (NT)
Brockton
Grindle
Albrighton
Boningale
Dorrington
Acton Pigott
Benthall
Broseley
Coalport
Sutton Maddock
Ryton
Beckbury
Frodesley
Acton Burnell
Harley
Homer
Wyke
Much Wenlock
Wenlock Priory
Longnor
Ruckley
Kenley
Broomcroft
Barrow
Willey
Norton
Stockton
Burnhill Green
Badger
Ackleton
Church Preen
Stretton Westwood
Leebotwood
Hughley
SHROPSHIRE
The Smithies
Nordley
Astley Abbotts
Chesterton
The Walls
Enchmarsh
Plaish
Presthope
Bourton
Acton Round
Haughton
Cross Lane Head
Allscot
Worfield
Hilton
Caer Caradoc 459
Cardington
Gretton
Easthope
Longville in the Dale
Wilderhope Manor (NT)
Brockton
Monkhopton
Morville
Tasley
Swancote
Wyken
Upper Ludstone
Claverley
Upper Aston
Church Stretton
Hope Bowdler Hill
East Wall
Wall under Heywood
Wall Bank
Hope Bowdler
Rushbury
Shipton Hall
Shipton
Weston
Aston Eyre
Upton Cressett
BRIDGNORTH
Severn Valley Rly
Oldbury
Roughton
Heathton
Halfpenny
Wenlock Edge
Ticklerton
Acton Scott Farm Museum
Harton
Eaton
Broadstone
Stanton Long
Middleton Priors
Chetton
Eardington
Quatford
Highgate Common
Bobbington
Ape Dale
Middlehope
Holdgate
Ditton Priors
Woodlands
Dudmaston Hall (NT)
Quatt
Six Ashes
Hope Dale
Munslow
Corve Dale
Tugford
Neenton
Glazeley
Middleton Scriven
Chelmarsh
Chelmarsh Resr
Hampton
Aston Munslow
Upper Heath
Abdon
540
Brown Clee Hill
Cleobury North
Deuxhill
Sutton
Enville
Westhope
Diddlebury
Corfton
Sidbury
Birdsgreen
Gallowstree Elm
Peaton
Bouldon
Clee St Margaret
Burwarton
Woodhill
Alveley
Billingsley
Highley
Potters Cross
Romsley
Kinver
Seifton
Great Sutton
Stoke St Milborough
Aston Botterell
Loughton
Chorley
Stottesdon
Culmington
Hayton's Bent
Weston Hill
Cleedownton
Wheathill
Kingsford
Fishery & Wildlife Sanctuary
Severn Valley Railway
Shatterford
Blakeshall
Vernolds Common
Lower Hayton
Upper Hayton
Hopton Cangeford
Farlow
Oreton
Kinlet
Upper Arley
Wolverley
Silvington
Baveney Wood
Trimpley
Cleeton St Mary
Catherton
Titterstone Clee Hill 533
Stanton Lacy
Ludlow Racecourse
Bitterley
Buttonoak
Wyre Forest
Low Habberley
Franche
Bromfield
Middleton
Henley
Doddington
Hopton Wafers
Neen Savage
Blakebrook
Cleehill
Ludlow
Snitton
Farden
Knowle
Hints
Cleobury Mortimer
Far Forest
Lem Hill
Wribbenhall
Bewdley
West Midland Safari Park
Knowbury
Caynham Camp
Hope Bagot
Coreley
Pound Bank
Fingerpost
Callow Hill
Ribbesford
Ludford
Caynham
Whitton
Milson
Neen Sollars
Dayton
Bliss Gate
Upper Mitton
Wilden
Overton
Mamble
Clows Top
Stourport-on-Severn
Hartlebury Common
Nash
Rock
Areley Kings
Ashford Carbonel
Greete
Frith Common
WORCESTERSHIRE
Ashford Bowdler
Boraston
Richard's Castle
Tenbury Wells
Newnham
Lindridge
Pensax
Abberley
Dunley
Astley Cross
Crossway Green
Comberton
Wooferton
Rochford
Stockton on Teme
Lincomb
The Burf
Wyson
Brimfield
Burford
Callows Grave
Upper Rochford
Orleton
Stanford on Teme
Abberley Hall
Astley
Noutard's Green
Orleton
Hanley William
Great Witley
Eastgrove Cottage
Frog Pool
Sytchampton
Birchers
Middleton
St Michaels
Broadheath
Stanford

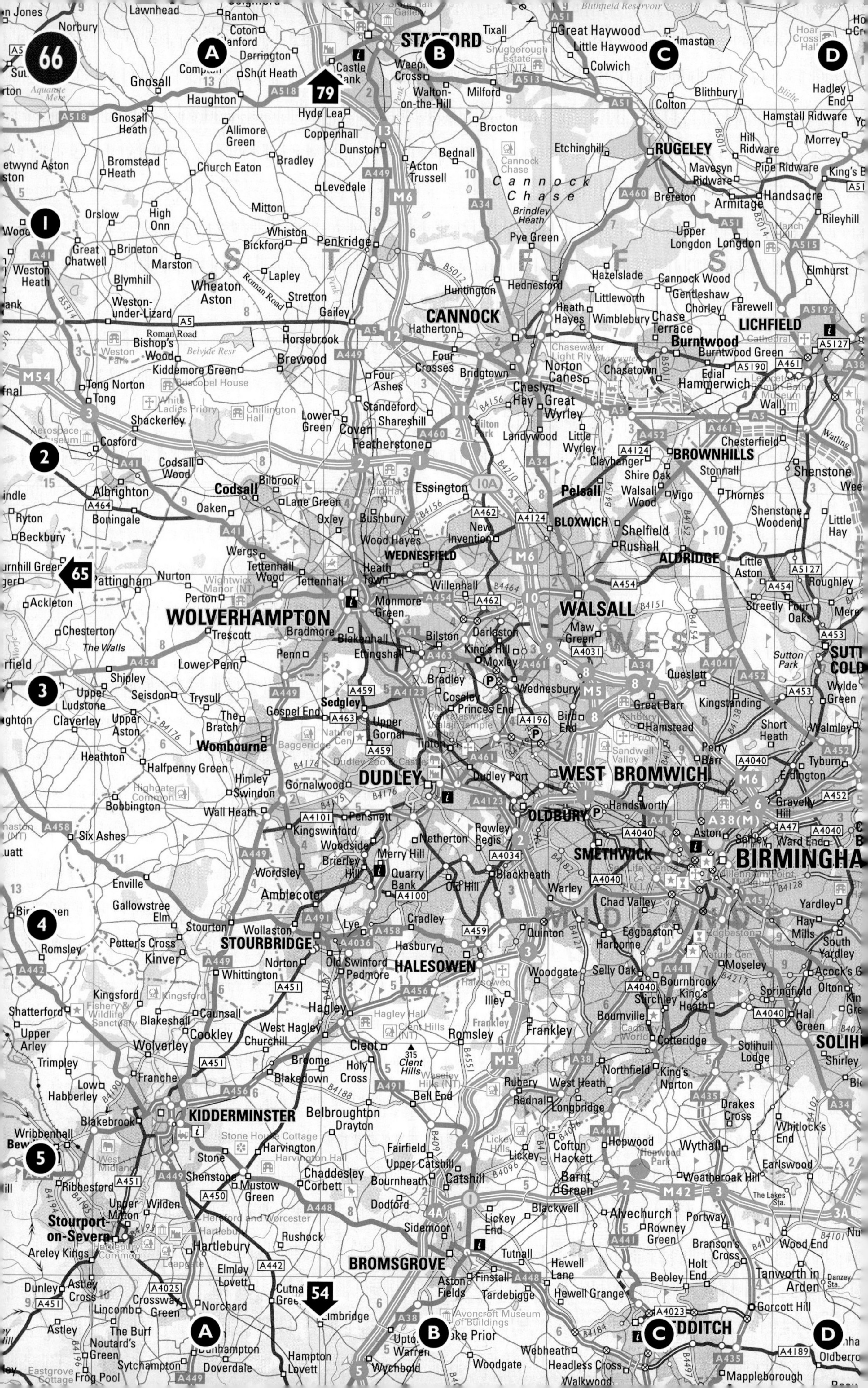

66
Lawnhead
Norbury
Ranton
Coton
Derrington
Compton
Shut Heath
Gnosall
Haughton
Castle Bank
79
STAFFORD
Tixall
Great Haywood
Little Haywood
Colwich
Shugborough Estate (NT)
Admaston
Weeping Cross
Walton-on-the-Hill
Milford
Blithfield Reservoir
Blithbury
Colton
Hadley End
Hamstall Ridware
Gnosall Heath
Allimore Green
Hyde Lea
Coppenhall
Dunston
Brocton
Bednall
Cannock Chase
Etchinghill
RUGELEY
Hill Ridware
Morrey
Mavesyn Ridware
Pipe Ridware
King's Bromley
Bromstead Heath
Church Eaton
Bradley
Acton Trussell
Brindley Heath
Brereton
Armitage
Handsacre
Levedale
Mitton
Orslow
High Onn
Whiston
Bickford
Penkridge
Pye Green
Upper Longdon
Longdon
Rileyhill
Great Chatwell
Brineton
Marston
Weston Heath
Blymhill
Wheaton Aston
Lapley
Roman Road
Stretton
Huntington
Hednesford
Hazelslade
Littleworth
Cannock Wood
Gentleshaw
Chorley
Farewell
Elmhurst
Weston-under-Lizard
Gailey
CANNOCK
Heath Hayes
Wimblebury
Chase Terrace
LICHFIELD
Bishop's Wood
Belvide Resr
Horsebrook
Hatherton
Burntwood
Burntwood Green
Weston Park
Kiddemore Green
Brewood
Four Crosses
Bridgtown
Norton Canes
Chasetown
Edial
Hammerwich
M54
Tong Norton
Tong
Boscobel House
White Ladies Priory
Chillington Hall
Four Ashes
Cheslyn Hay
Great Wyrley
Wall
Shackerley
Aerospace Museum
Cosford
Standeford
Shareshill
Lower Green
Coven
Featherstone
Hilton Park
Landywood
Little Wyrley
Chesterfield
Clayhanger
BROWNHILLS
Stonnall
Shenstone
Codsall Wood
Albrighton
Bilbrook
Codsall
Essington
Pelsall
Shire Oak
Walsall Wood
Vigo
Thornes
Shenstone Woodend
Little Hay
Ryton
Boningale
Oaken
Lane Green
Oxley
Bushbury
New Invention
BLOXWICH
Shelfield
Rushall
Beckbury
Wood Hayes
WEDNESFIELD
ALDRIDGE
Little Aston
Wergs
Tettenhall Wood
Tettenhall
Heath Town
Willenhall
Nurton
Pattingham
65
Wightwick Manor (NT)
Perton
Ackleton
WOLVERHAMPTON
Monmore Green
WALSALL
Streetly
Four Oaks
Roughley
Chesterton
Trescott
Bradmore
Blakenhall
Bilston
Darlaston
Maw Green
The Walls
Penn
Ettingshall
King's Hill
Moxley
WEST MIDLANDS
Queslett
Sutton Park
SUTTON COLDFIELD
Shipley
Lower Penn
Upper Ludstone
Seisdon
Trysull
Sedgley
Bradley
Coseley
Wednesbury
Great Barr
Kingstanding
Wylde Green
Claverley
Upper Aston
The Bratch
Gospel End
Upper Gornal
Princes End
Bird End
Hamstead
Short Heath
Walmley
Heathton
Wombourne
Baggeridge
Tipton
Sandwell Valley
Perry Barr
Tyburn
Halfpenny Green
Highgate Common
Himley
Swindon
Bobbington
Dudley Zoo & Castle
DUDLEY
Dudley Port
WEST BROMWICH
Erdington
Gornalwood
Handsworth
Gravelly Hill
Wall Heath
Pensnett
OLDBURY
Six Ashes
Kingswinford
Netherton
Rowley Regis
Aston
Salford
Ward End
Woodside
Brierley Hill
Merry Hill
SMETHWICK
BIRMINGHAM
Enville
Wordsley
Quarry Bank
Blackheath
Old Hill
Warley
Millennium Point
Yardley
Gallowstree Elm
Amblecote
Cradley
Chad Valley
Hay Mills
Stourton
Wollaston
Lye
Quinton
Edgbaston
South Yardley
Romsley
Potter's Cross
STOURBRIDGE
Hasbury
Harborne
Kinver
Norton
Old Swinford
Pedmore
HALESOWEN
Woodgate
Selly Oak
Moseley
Acock's Green
Whittington
Bournbrook
Stirchley
King's Heath
Springfield
Olton
Kingsford
Caunsall
Hagley
Illey
Bournville
Cadbury World
Hall Green
Shatterford
Fishery & Wildlife Sanctuary
Blakeshall
West Hagley
Hagley Hall
Clent Hills (NT)
Frankley
Upper Arley
Cookley
Churchill
Clent
Romsley
Cotteridge
Solihull Lodge
SOLIHULL
Wolverley
Broome
Holy Cross
315 Clent Hills
Northfield
King's Norton
Shirley
Trimpley
Franche
Blakedown
Rubery
West Heath
Low Habberley
Bell End
Rednal
Longbridge
Drakes Cross
Blakebrook
KIDDERMINSTER
Belbroughton
Drayton
Whitlock's End
Wribbenhall
Bewdley
Stone House Cottage
Harvington
Lickey Hills
Cofton Hackett
Hopwood
Wythall
Stone
Harvington Hall
Fairfield
Upper Catshill
Lickey
Earlswood
Ribbesford
Shenstone
Mustow Green
Chaddesley Corbett
Bournheath
Catshill
Barnt Green
Weatheroak Hill
M42
The Lakes Sta.
Upper Mitton
Wilden
Dodford
Blackwell
Alvechurch
Portway
Stourport-on-Severn
Hereford and Worcester
Rushock
Sidemoor
Lickey End
Rowney Green
Hartlebury
Hartlebury Common
Areley Kings
Tutnall
Hewell Lane
Branson's Cross
Wood End
BROMSGROVE
Elmley Lovett
Holt End
Beoley
Tanworth in Arden
Danzey Sta.
Astley Cross
Dunley
Aston Fields
Finstall
Tardebigge
Hewell Grange
Crossway Green
Cutnall Green
54
Lincomb
Norchard
Gorcott Hill
Astley
The Burf
Elmbridge
Avoncroft Museum of Buildings
REDDITCH
Noutard's Green
Ombersley
Doverdale
Hampton Lovett
Upton Warren
Stoke Prior
Webheath
Headless Cross
Oldberrow
Sytchampton
Eastgrove Cottage
Frog Pool
Wychbold
Woodgate
Walkwood
Mappleborough

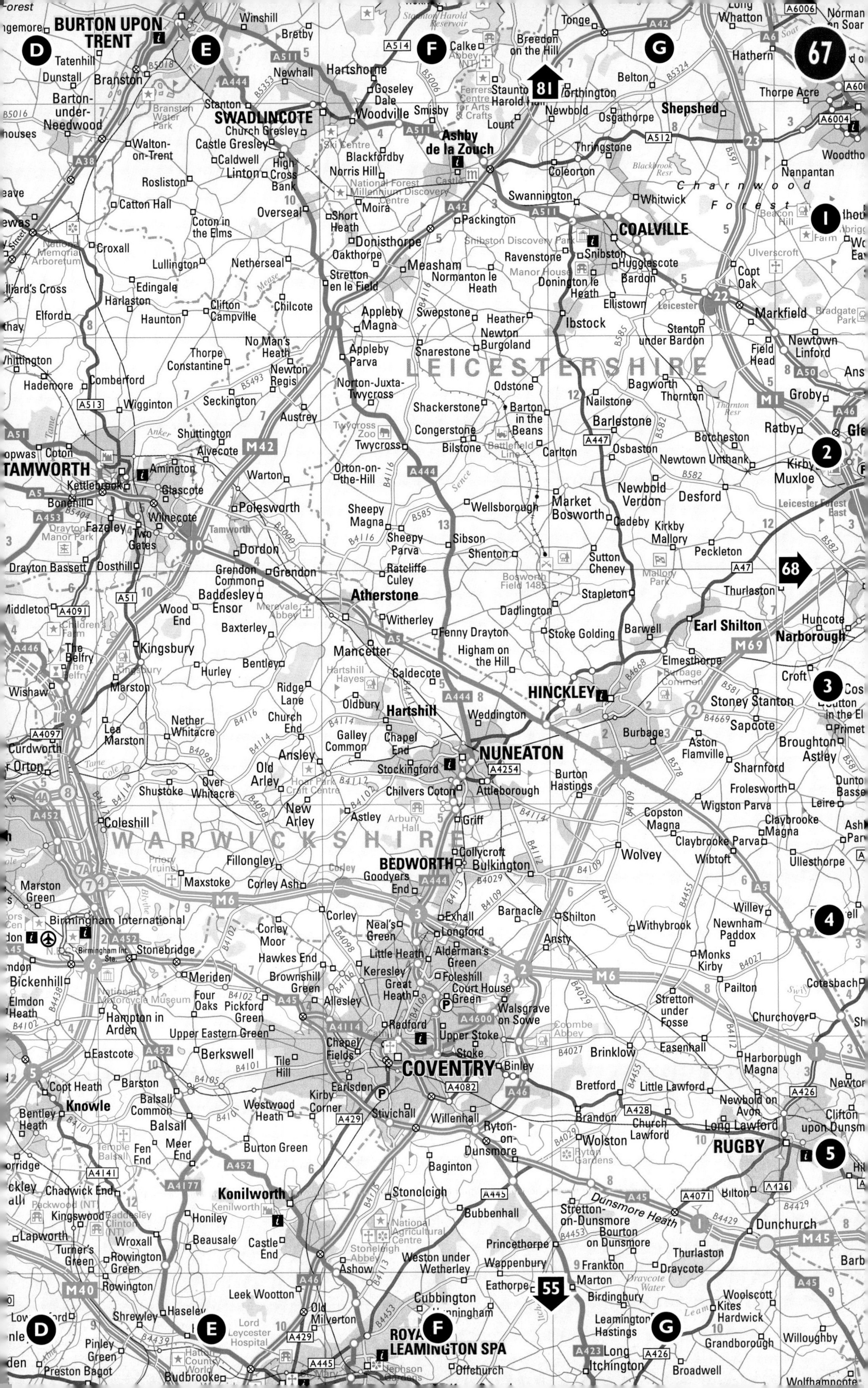

67
BURTON UPON TRENT
Tatenhill
Dunstall
Branston
Barton-under-Needwood
Winshill
Bretby
Newhall
Hartshorne
Stanton
SWADLINCOTE
Church Gresley
Castle Gresley
Walton-on-Trent
Caldwell
Linton
High Cross Bank
Rosliston
Catton Hall
Coton in the Elms
Overseal
Croxall
Lullington
Netherseal
National Memorial Arboretum
Edingale
Harlaston
Elford
Haunton
Clifton Campville
Chilcote
No Man's Heath
Thorpe Constantine
Newton Regis
Comberford
Hademore
Wigginton
Seckington
Austrey
Shuttington
Alvecote
Amington
TAMWORTH
Kettlebrook
Glascote
Bonehill
Wilnecote
Fazeley
Two Gates
Drayton Manor Park
Dosthill
Drayton Bassett
Polesworth
Dordon
Grendon
Grendon Common
Baddesley Ensor
Wood End
Baxterley
Kingsbury
Hurley
Bentley
Marston
Middleton
Wishaw
Lea Marston
Nether Whitacre
Over Whitacre
Shustoke
Curdworth
Coleshill
WARWICKSHIRE
Fillongley
Maxstoke
Corley Ash
Marston Green
Birmingham International
Stonebridge
Meriden
Corley Moor
Hawkes End
Bickenhill
Elmdon Heath
Hampton in Arden
Four Oaks
Pickford Green
Upper Eastern Green
Eastcote
Berkswell
Tile Hill
Barston
Balsall Common
Balsall
Copt Heath
Knowle
Bentley Heath
Temple Balsall
Fen End
Meer End
Chadwick End
Packwood (NT)
Kingswood
Baddesley Clinton (NT)
Lapworth
Turner's Green
Wroxall
Rowington Green
Rowington
Beausale
Honiley
Kenilworth
Castle End
Shrewley
Haseley
Pinley Green
Preston Bagot
Budbrooke
Hatton Country World
Lord Leycester Hospital
Leek Wootton
Old Milverton
ROYAL LEAMINGTON SPA
Jephson Gardens
Offchurch
Cubbington
Weston under Wetherley
Ashow
Stoneleigh Abbey
National Agricultural Centre
Stoneleigh
Bubbenhall
Baginton
Ryton-on-Dunsmore
Willenhall
Stivichall
Kirby Corner
Westwood Heath
Burton Green
Earlsdon
COVENTRY
Chapel Fields
Radford
Upper Stoke
Stoke
Binley
Coombe Abbey
Walsgrave on Sowe
Court House Green
Foleshill
Great Heath
Keresley
Allesley
Brownshill Green
Little Heath
Alderman's Green
Neal's Green
Longford
Exhall
Barnacle
Shilton
Ansty
Goodyers End
BEDWORTH
Collycroft
Bulkington
Corley
Hartshill
Chapel End
Galley Common
Ansley
Old Arley
New Arley
Astley
Arbury Hall
Chilvers Coton
Griff
Stockingford
NUNEATON
Attleborough
Burton Hastings
Weddington
Caldecote
Mancetter
Hartshill Hayes
Oldbury
Ridge Lane
Church End
Atherstone
Merevale Abbey
Witherley
Fenny Drayton
Higham on the Hill
Ratcliffe Culey
Sheepy Parva
Sheepy Magna
Sibson
Shenton
Bosworth Field 1485
Dadlington
Stoke Golding
Stapleton
Sutton Cheney
Wellsborough
Market Bosworth
Cadeby
Kirkby Mallory
Mallory Park
Peckleton
Orton-on-the-Hill
Twycross
Twycross Zoo
Norton-Juxta-Twycross
Appleby Parva
Appleby Magna
Snarestone
Swepstone
Stretton en le Field
Measham
Oakthorpe
Donisthorpe
Short Heath
Moira
National Forest Millennium Discovery Centre
Norris Hill
Blackfordby
Ski Centre
Woodville
Goseley Dale
Smisby
Ashby de la Zouch
Castle
Calke Abbey (NT)
Ferrers Centre for Arts & Crafts
Staunton Harold Hall
Lount
Breedon on the Hill
Tonge
Worthington
Newbold
Osgathorpe
Belton
Shepshed
Thorpe Acre
Hathern
Long Whatton
Normanton on Soar
Thringstone
Coleorton
Swannington
Whitwick
COALVILLE
Snibston
Snibston Discovery Park
Ravenstone
Manor House
Donington le Heath
Hugglescote
Bardon
Ellistown
Ibstock
Heather
Newton Burgoland
Normanton le Heath
Packington
Odstone
Shackerstone
Barton in the Beans
Congerstone
Bilstone
Battlefield Line
Carlton
Nailstone
Barlestone
Osbaston
Newbold Verdon
Desford
Bagworth
Thornton
Thornton Resr
Stanton under Bardon
Markfield
Copt Oak
Ulverscroft
Charnwood Forest
Nanpantan
Field Head
Newtown Linford
Bradgate Park
Groby
Ratby
Botcheston
Newtown Unthank
Kirby Muxloe
Leicester Forest East
LEICESTERSHIRE
Thurlaston
Earl Shilton
Barwell
Elmesthorpe
HINCKLEY
Burbage Common
Burbage
Aston Flamville
Sapcote
Stoney Stanton
Croft
Huncote
Narborough
Broughton Astley
Sharnford
Frolesworth
Wigston Parva
Copston Magna
Wolvey
Claybrooke Parva
Claybrooke Magna
Wibtoft
Ullesthorpe
Leire
Willey
Withybrook
Newnham Paddox
Monks Kirby
Pailton
Cotesbach
Stretton under Fosse
Churchover
Brinklow
Easenhall
Harborough Magna
Little Lawford
Bretford
Brandon
Church Lawford
Wolston
Ryton Gardens
Newbold on Avon
Long Lawford
RUGBY
Clifton upon Dunsmore
Bilton
Dunchurch
Dunsmore Heath
Stretton-on-Dunsmore
Bourton on Dunsmore
Princethorpe
Wappenbury
Frankton
Thurlaston
Draycote
Draycote Water
Eathorpe
Marton
Birdingbury
Leamington Hastings
Long Itchington
Broadwell
Woolscott
Kites Hardwick
Grandborough
Willoughby
Wolfhampcote
81
55
68
M1
M6
M42
M40
M45
M69
A5
A38
A42
A444
A447
A45
A46
A47
A50
A51
A426
A428
A429
A445
A452
A4091
A4097
A4114
A4141
A4177
A4254
A4600
A4071
A4082
A423
A511
A512
A513
A514

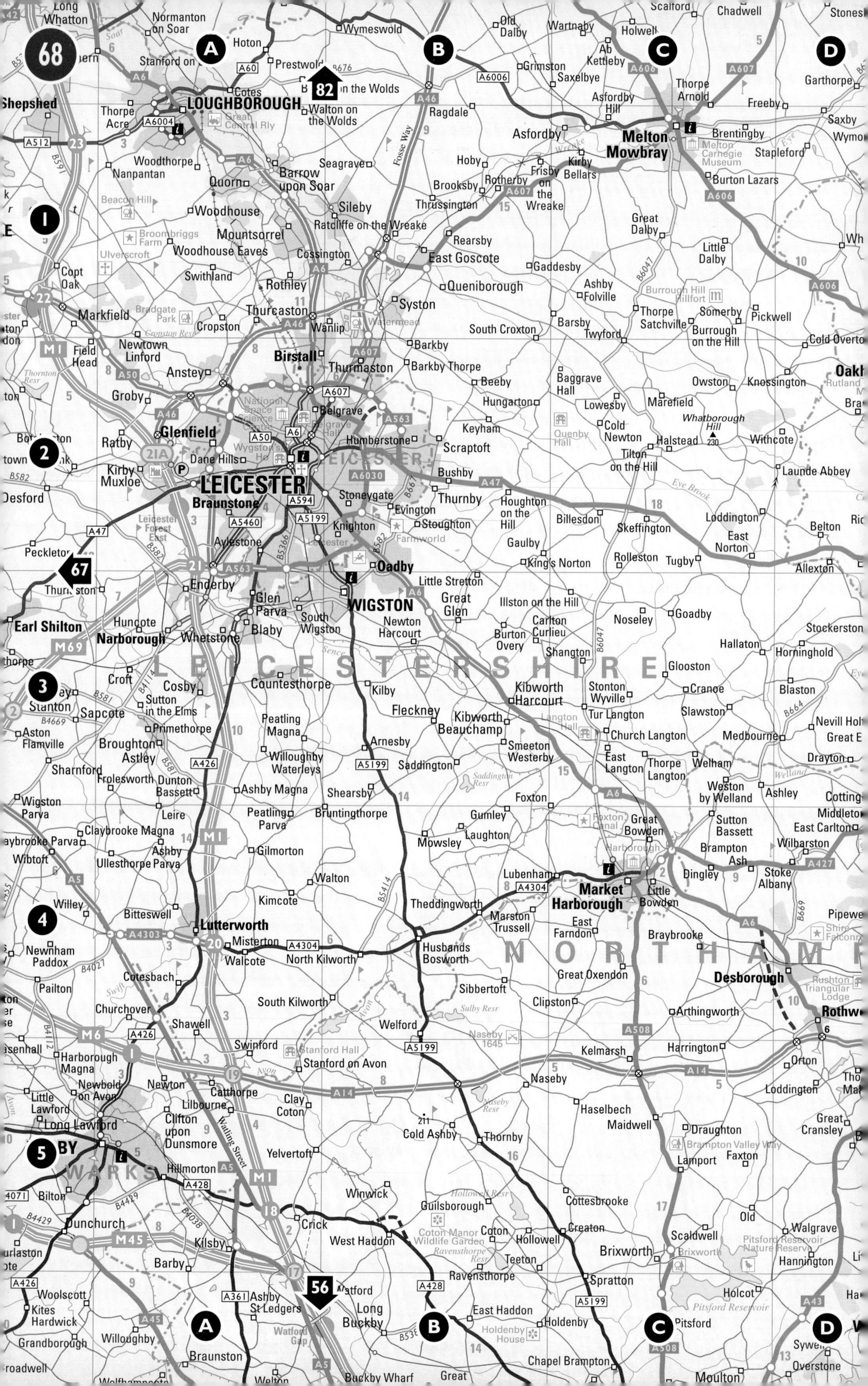
A
B
C
D
1
2
3
4
5
82
67
56
LOUGHBOROUGH
LEICESTER
WIGSTON
Oadby
Birstall
Glenfield
Braunstone
Melton Mowbray
Market Harborough
Lutterworth
Desborough
LEICESTERSHIRE
NORTHAM
WARKS
Long Whatton
Normanton on Soar
Hoton
Wymeswold
Old Dalby
Wartnaby
Holwell
Scalford
Chadwell
Stonesby
Shepshed
Stanford on Soar
Prestwold
Cotes
Thorpe Acre
Walton on the Wolds
Grimston
Saxelbye
Ab Kettleby
Asfordby Hill
Asfordby
Thorpe Arnold
Freeby
Garthorpe
Saxby
Brentingby
Melton Carnegie Museum
Stapleford
Burton Lazars
Great Central Rly
Woodthorpe
Nanpantan
Ragdale
Seagrave
Barrow upon Soar
Quorn
Hoby
Rotherby
Brooksby
Frisby on the Wreake
Kirby Bellars
Thrussington
Beacon Hill
Woodhouse
Sileby
Ratcliffe on the Wreake
Broombriggs Farm
Mountsorrel
Woodhouse Eaves
Ulverscroft
Cossington
Rearsby
East Goscote
Great Dalby
Little Dalby
Copt Oak
Swithland
Rothley
Gaddesby
Queniborough
Ashby Folville
Burrough Hill Hillfort
Markfield
Bradgate Park
Thurcaston
Syston
Wanlip
Watermead
Cropston
Cropston Resr
South Croxton
Barsby
Twyford
Thorpe Satchville
Somerby
Burrough on the Hill
Pickwell
Cold Overton
Field Head
Newtown Linford
Barkby
Thurmaston
Barkby Thorpe
Thornton Resr
Anstey
Beeby
Baggrave Hall
Owston
Knossington
Oakham
Rutland
Groby
National Space Science Centre
Belgrave
Belgrave Hall
Hungarton
Lowesby
Marefield
Whatborough Hill
230
Keyham
Quenby Hall
Cold Newton
Halstead
Withcote
Ratby
Humberstone
Scraptoft
Tilton on the Hill
Launde Abbey
Kirby Muxloe
Dane Hills
Wygston's Ho
Bushby
Desford
Stoneygate
Thurnby
Houghton on the Hill
Billesdon
Eye Brook
Skeffington
Loddington
Belton
Evington
Stoughton
Knighton
Farmworld
Leicester Forest East
Gaulby
East Norton
Peckleton
Aylestone
King's Norton
Rolleston
Tugby
Allexton
Thurlaston
Enderby
Little Stretton
Glen Parva
Great Glen
Illston on the Hill
Carlton Curlieu
Noseley
Goadby
Stockerston
Earl Shilton
Huncote
Narborough
Whetstone
Blaby
South Wigston
Newton Harcourt
Burton Overy
Shangton
Hallaton
Horninghold
Glooston
Croft
Cosby
Countesthorpe
Kilby
Kibworth Harcourt
Stonton Wyville
Cranoe
Blaston
Stanton
Sapcote
Sutton in the Elms
Fleckney
Kibworth Beauchamp
Langton Hall
Tur Langton
Slawston
Nevill Holt
Aston Flamville
Primethorpe
Peatling Magna
Church Langton
Medbourne
Great Easton
Broughton Astley
Arnesby
Smeeton Westerby
East Langton
Thorpe Langton
Welham
Drayton
Sharnford
Willoughby Waterleys
Saddington
Saddington Resr
Frolesworth
Dunton Bassett
Weston by Welland
Ashley
Cottingham
Wigston Parva
Ashby Magna
Shearsby
Foxton
Middleton
Leire
Peatling Parva
Bruntingthorpe
Gumley
Foxton Canal
Great Bowden
Sutton Bassett
East Carlton
Claybrooke Magna
Laughton
Mowsley
Brampton Ash
Wilbarston
Claybrooke Parva
Ashby Parva
Gilmorton
Harborough
Wibtoft
Ullesthorpe
Walton
Lubenham
Dingley
Stoke Albany
Little Bowden
Willey
Kimcote
Theddingworth
Marston Trussell
Pipewell
Bitteswell
East Farndon
Braybrooke
Misterton
Walcote
North Kilworth
Husbands Bosworth
Newnham Paddox
Cotesbach
Great Oxendon
Rushton Triangular Lodge
Pailton
Sibbertoft
Clipston
Churchover
South Kilworth
Sulby Resr
Arthingworth
Rothwell
Shawell
Welford
Naseby 1645
Harborough Magna
Swinford
Stanford Hall
Stanford on Avon
Kelmarsh
Harrington
Orton
Little Lawford
Newbold on Avon
Newton
Catthorpe
Naseby
Loddington
Long Lawford
Lilbourne
Clay Coton
Naseby Resr
Haselbech
Clifton upon Dunsmore
Watling Street
211
Cold Ashby
Maidwell
Draughton
Great Cransley
Thornby
Brampton Valley Way
Faxton
Lamport
Yelvertoft
Hillmorton
Bilton
Winwick
Hollowell Resr
Cottesbrooke
Dunchurch
Guilsborough
Crick
Old
Scaldwell
Walgrave
Coton Manor Wildlife Garden
Coton
Creaton
Brixworth
Pitsford Nature Reserve
Kilsby
West Haddon
Ravensthorpe Resr
Hollowell
Hannington
Barby
Teeton
Ravensthorpe
Spratton
Watford
Holcot
Woolscott
Kites Hardwick
Ashby St Ledgers
Long Buckby
East Haddon
Pitsford Reservoir
Pitsford
Grandborough
Willoughby
Watford Gap
Holdenby
Holdenby House
Sywell
Overstone
Braunston
Chapel Brampton
Moulton
Buckby Wharf
Great
Welton
A6
A60
A6004
A512
A6006
A46
A606
A607
A50
A607
A563
A6030
A47
A594
A5460
A5199
B5366
A426
A5
M1
M69
M6
A4303
A4304
A14
A508
A428
A45
M45
A361
A43
A427
A6
B6047
B664
B581
B4114
B582
B4669
B5414
B4027
B4112
B4429
B4038
B669
B676
B591
Fosse Way
Wreake
Soar
Avon
Sence
Welland
Swift
Eye

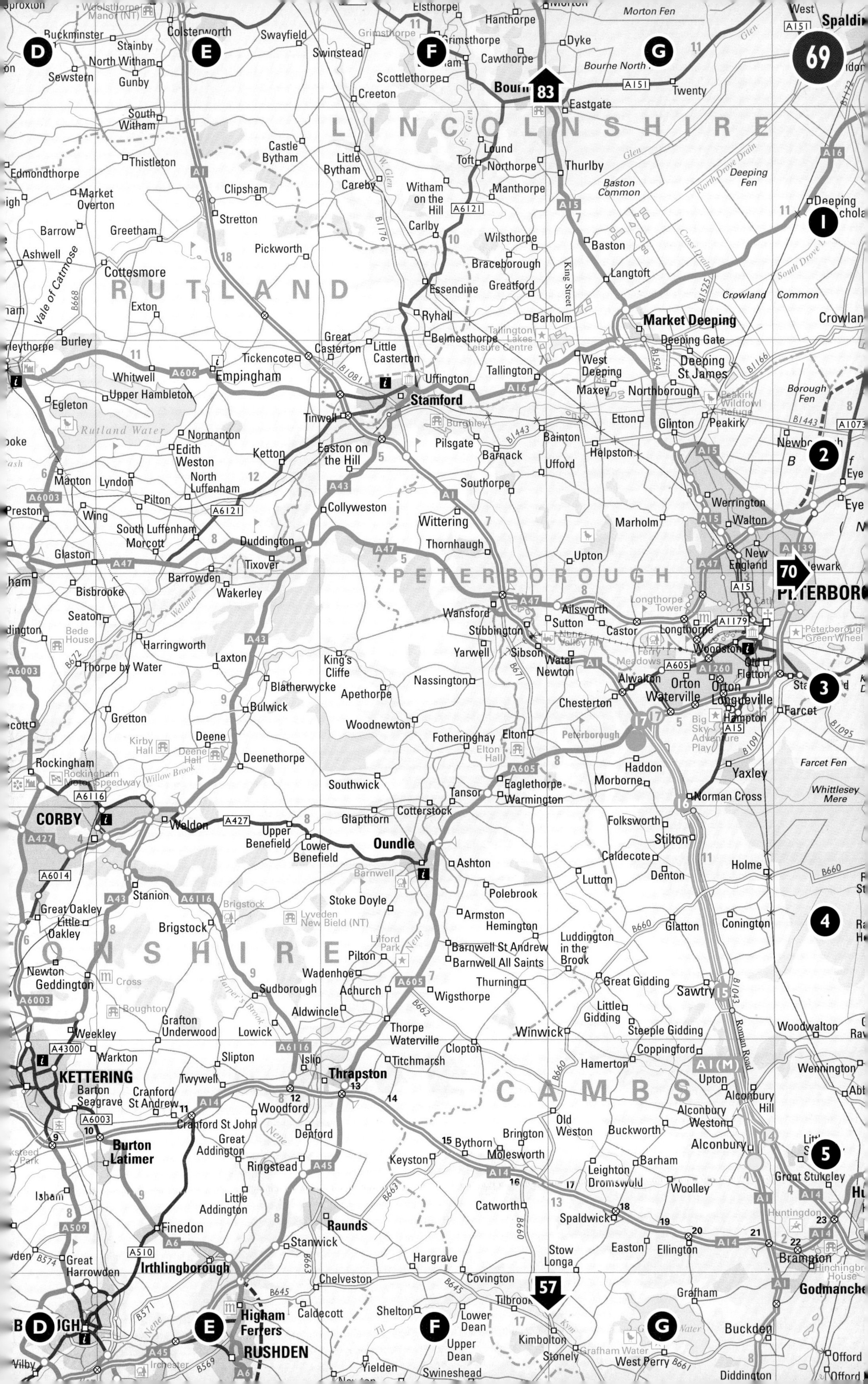
69
83
70
57
LINCOLNSHIRE
RUTLAND
PETERBOROUGH
CAMBS
ONSHIRE
Woolsthorpe Manor (NT)
Colsterworth
Buckminster
Stainby
North Witham
Sewstern
Gunby
South Witham
Swayfield
Swinstead
Grimsthorpe
Elsthorpe
Hanthorpe
Morton Fen
Dyke
Cawthorpe
Bourne North Fen
Twenty
Eastgate
West
Spalding
Scottlethorpe
Creeton
Castle Bytham
Little Bytham
Careby
Witham on the Hill
Carlby
Lound
Toft
Northorpe
Manthorpe
Thurlby
Baston Common
Deeping Fen
Deeping St Nicholas
Thistleton
Edmondthorpe
Market Overton
Clipsham
Stretton
Barrow
Greetham
Pickworth
Wilsthorpe
Braceborough
Greatford
Baston
Langtoft
King Street
Crowland
Common
Ashwell
Cottesmore
Exton
Vale of Catmose
Burley
Essendine
Ryhall
Belmesthorpe
Barholm
Tallington Lakes Leisure Centre
Market Deeping
Deeping Gate
Deeping St James
West Deeping
Maxey
Northborough
Great Casterton
Little Casterton
Tickencote
Whitwell
Empingham
Upper Hambleton
Egleton
Rutland Water
Uffington
Tallington
Stamford
Tinwell
Burghley
Peakirk Wildfowl Refuge
Peakirk
Borough Fen
Etton
Glinton
Newborough
Normanton
Edith Weston
Ketton
Easton on the Hill
Pilsgate
Barnack
Bainton
Helpston
Ufford
Manton
Lyndon
North Luffenham
Pilton
Southorpe
Wittering
Thornhaugh
Werrington
Walton
Marholm
Eye
Preston
Wing
South Luffenham
Morcott
Duddington
Collyweston
Glaston
Tixover
Barrowden
Wakerley
Upton
New England
Newark
PETERBOROUGH
Bisbrooke
Seaton
Bede House
Harringworth
Thorpe by Water
Laxton
King's Cliffe
Wansford
Stibbington
Ailsworth
Sutton
Castor
Longthorpe Tower
Longthorpe
Nene Valley Rly
Peterborough Green Wheel
Yarwell
Sibson
Water Newton
Ferry Meadows
Woodston
Old Fletton
Stanground
Blatherwycke
Apethorpe
Nassington
Alwalton
Orton Waterville
Orton Longueville
Bulwick
Gretton
Woodnewton
Chesterton
Hampton
Farcet
Kirby Hall
Deene
Deene Hall
Deenethorpe
Fotheringhay
Elton
Elton Hall
Peterborough
Big Sky Adventure Play
Farcet Fen
Rockingham
Rockingham Motor Speedway
Willow Brook
Southwick
Tansor
Eaglethorpe
Warmington
Haddon
Morborne
Yaxley
Norman Cross
Whittlesey Mere
CORBY
Weldon
Upper Benefield
Lower Benefield
Glapthorn
Cotterstock
Oundle
Folksworth
Stilton
Caldecote
Denton
Holme
Barnwell
Ashton
Lutton
Stanion
Brigstock
Great Oakley
Little Oakley
Stoke Doyle
Lyveden New Bield (NT)
Polebrook
Armston
Hemington
Glatton
Conington
Lilford Park
Pilton
Barnwell St Andrew
Barnwell All Saints
Luddington in the Brook
Newton
Geddington
Cross
Boughton
Wadenhoe
Sudborough
Achurch
Aldwincle
Thurning
Wigsthorpe
Great Gidding
Sawtry
Little Gidding
Steeple Gidding
Woodwalton
Weekley
Grafton Underwood
Lowick
Thorpe Waterville
Clopton
Winwick
Coppingford
Warkton
Slipton
Islip
Titchmarsh
Hamerton
Roman Road
Wennington
KETTERING
Barton Seagrave
Cranford St Andrew
Twywell
Thrapston
Upton
Alconbury Hill
Woodford
Cranford St John
Great Addington
Denford
Old Weston
Buckworth
Alconbury Weston
Alconbury
Burton Latimer
Ringstead
Keyston
Bythorn
Brington
Molesworth
Barham
Leighton Bromswold
Woolley
Great Stukeley
Isham
Little Addington
Catworth
Spaldwick
Huntingdon
Finedon
Raunds
Stanwick
Easton
Ellington
Brampton
Hinchingbrooke House
Great Harrowden
Irthlingborough
Hargrave
Stow Longa
Godmanchester
Chelveston
Covington
Tilbrook
Grafham
Higham Ferrers
Caldecott
Shelton
Lower Dean
Upper Dean
Kimbolton
Grafham Water
Buckden
RUSHDEN
Irchester
Yielden
Swineshead
Stonely
West Perry
Diddington
Offord
A1
A15
A16
A151
A6121
A606
A6003
A47
A43
A605
A1179
A1260
A1073
A427
A6116
A6014
A4300
A14
A1(M)
A45
A509
A510
A6
B1176
B1081
B1443
B1524
B1525
B1166
B1091
B1095
B1043
B660
B662
B663
B645
B571
B574
B569
B661
B668
B672
B671
D
E
F
G
I
2
3
4
5

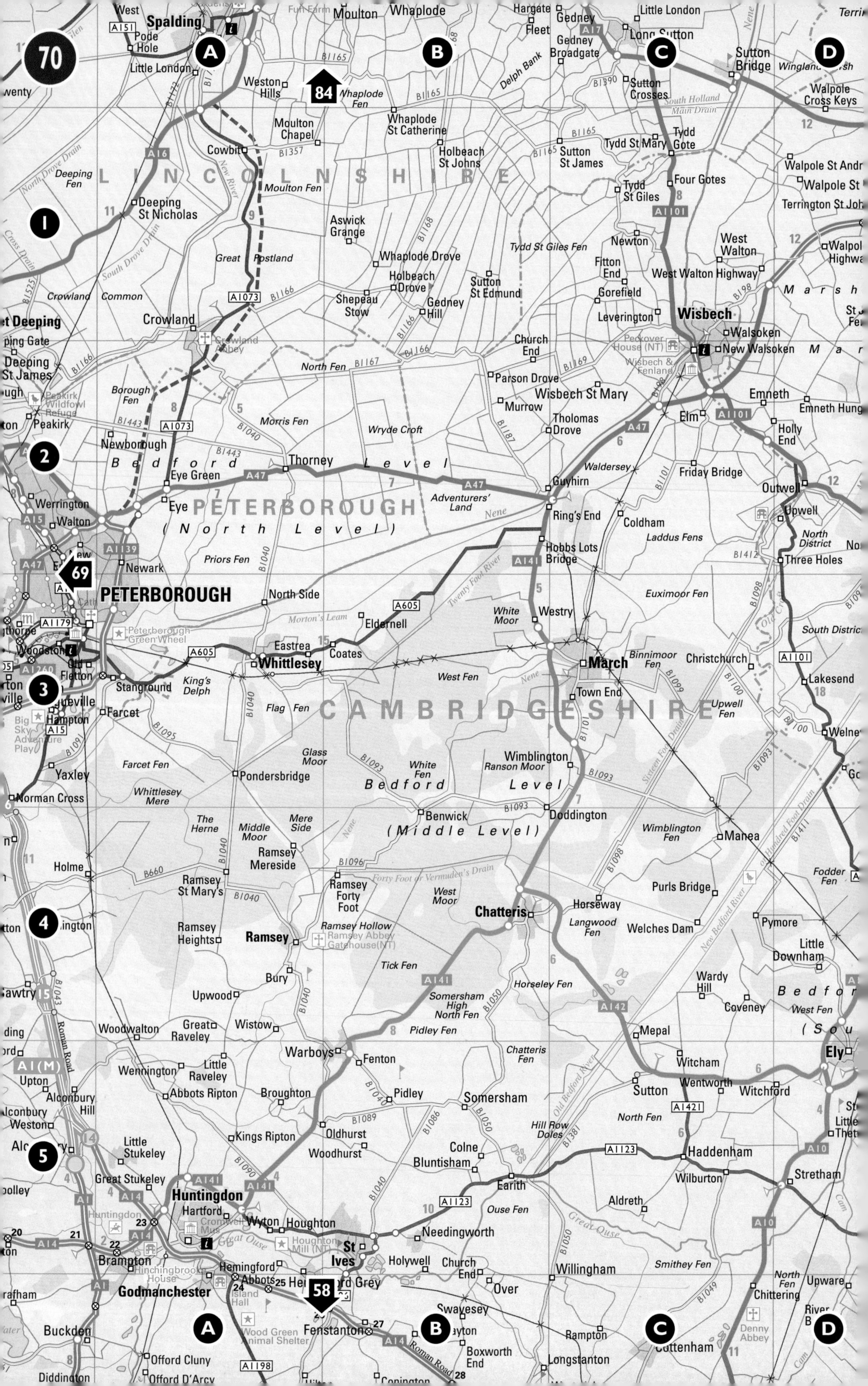
70
A
B
C
D
West
Spalding
Pode Hole
A151
Little London
Moulton
Whaplode
Hargate
Fleet
Gedney
Little London
Long Sutton
A17
Gedney Broadgate
Delph Bank
Sutton Bridge
Wingland Marsh
Terrington
Weston Hills
84
Whaplode Fen
B1165
B1390
Sutton Crosses
South Holland Main Drain
Walpole Cross Keys
Moulton Chapel
Whaplode St Catherine
Cowbit
B1357
Holbeach St Johns
B1165
Sutton St James
Tydd St Mary
Tydd Gote
Deeping Fen
North Drove Drain
LINCOLNSHIRE
New River
Moulton Fen
Four Gotes
Walpole St Andrew
Walpole St Peter
Terrington St John
Deeping St Nicholas
Tydd St Giles
A1101
Aswick Grange
B1168
Newton
West Walton
Cross Drain
South Drove Drain
Great Postland
Whaplode Drove
Tydd St Giles Fen
Fitton End
West Walton Highway
Walpole Highway
Holbeach Drove
Sutton St Edmund
Gorefield
B1525
Crowland
Common
A1073
B1166
Shepeau Stow
Gedney Hill
Leverington
Wisbech
Marsh
Market Deeping
Deeping Gate
Crowland
Crowland Abbey
Church End
Peckover House (NT)
Walsoken
New Walsoken
Deeping St James
B1166
North Fen
B1167
B1166
B1169
Wisbech & Fenland
Parson Drove
Borough Fen
Peakirk Wildfowl Refuge
Peakirk
Wisbech St Mary
Emneth
Emneth Hungate
Murrow
Tholomas Drove
Morris Fen
Wryde Croft
B1443
A1073
B1040
B1187
B1198
Elm
A1101
A47
Holly End
Newborough
B1443
Thorney
Bedford Level
Waldersey
Friday Bridge
Eye Green
A47
A47
Adventurers' Land
Guyhirn
B1101
Outwell
Werrington
Eye
PETERBOROUGH
(North Level)
Nene
Ring's End
Upwell
A15
Walton
Coldham
Laddus Fens
North District
A1139
Priors Fen
Hobbs Lots Bridge
A141
B1412
Three Holes
A47
69
Newark
B1040
Twenty Foot River
PETERBOROUGH
North Side
A605
Euximoor Fen
B1098
Morton's Leam
Eldernell
White Moor
Westry
Old Croft River
A1179
Peterborough Green Wheel
South District
Eastrea
A605
Coates
Binnimoor Fen
Christchurch
A1101
Woodston
Whittlesey
March
Fletton
West Fen
Nene
B1099
Lakesend
Stanground
King's Delph
Town End
B1100
A1260
Flag Fen
CAMBRIDGESHIRE
Upwell Fen
Hampton
Farcet
B1040
Sixteen Foot Drain
B1100
Welney
Big Sky Adventure Play
A15
B1095
B1101
B1093
Glass Moor
B1093
Farcet Fen
White Fen
Wimblington
Ranson Moor
B1093
Yaxley
Pondersbridge
Bedford Level
Whittlesey Mere
Norman Cross
Doddington
B1093
Benwick
Hundred Foot Drain
B1411
The Herne
Middle Moor
Mere Side
Nene
(Middle Level)
Wimblington Fen
Manea
Ramsey Mereside
B1040
B1098
Holme
B660
B1096
Forty Foot or Vermuden's Drain
Fodder Fen
Ramsey St Mary's
Ramsey Forty Foot
West Moor
Purls Bridge
B1040
Chatteris
Horseway
New Bedford River
Conington
Ramsey Hollow
Ramsey Abbey Gatehouse (NT)
Ramsey Heights
Ramsey
Langwood Fen
Welches Dam
Pymore
Little Downham
Tick Fen
A141
Horseley Fen
Sawtry
Bury
Somersham High North Fen
B1050
Wardy Hill
B1043
Upwood
B1040
Bedford
Coveney
West Fen
Roman Road
A142
(South Level)
Woodwalton
Great Raveley
Wistow
Pidley Fen
Mepal
Ely
Warboys
Fenton
Chatteris Fen
Little Raveley
Witcham
A1(M)
Wennington
Old Bedford River
Upton
Abbots Ripton
Broughton
Pidley
Sutton
Wentworth
Witchford
Alconbury Hill
B1040
Somersham
Alconbury Weston
B1089
B1086
B1050
North Fen
A1421
Stretham
Little Thetford
Kings Ripton
Oldhurst
Hill Row Doles
B1381
Alconbury
Little Stukeley
Woodhurst
Colne
A1123
Haddenham
A10
Bluntisham
Wilburton
B1090
A141
B1040
Great Stukeley
A141
Earith
Aldreth
Huntingdon
A1123
Ouse Fen
Hartford
Cromwell Mus
Wyton
Houghton
Great Ouse
A10
Great Ouse
Houghton Mill (NT)
Needingworth
B1050
Brampton
Hinchingbrooke House
St Ives
Holywell
Church End
Willingham
Smithey Fen
North Fen
Upware
A14
Hemingford Abbots
Hemingford Grey
Over
B1049
Chittering
Godmanchester
Island Hall
58
Swavesey
Denny Abbey
River Bank
Buckden
Wood Green Animal Shelter
Fenstanton
Conington
Boxworth End
Rampton
Cottenham
Offord Cluny
A1198
A14
Roman Road
Longstanton
Offord D'Arcy
Diddington

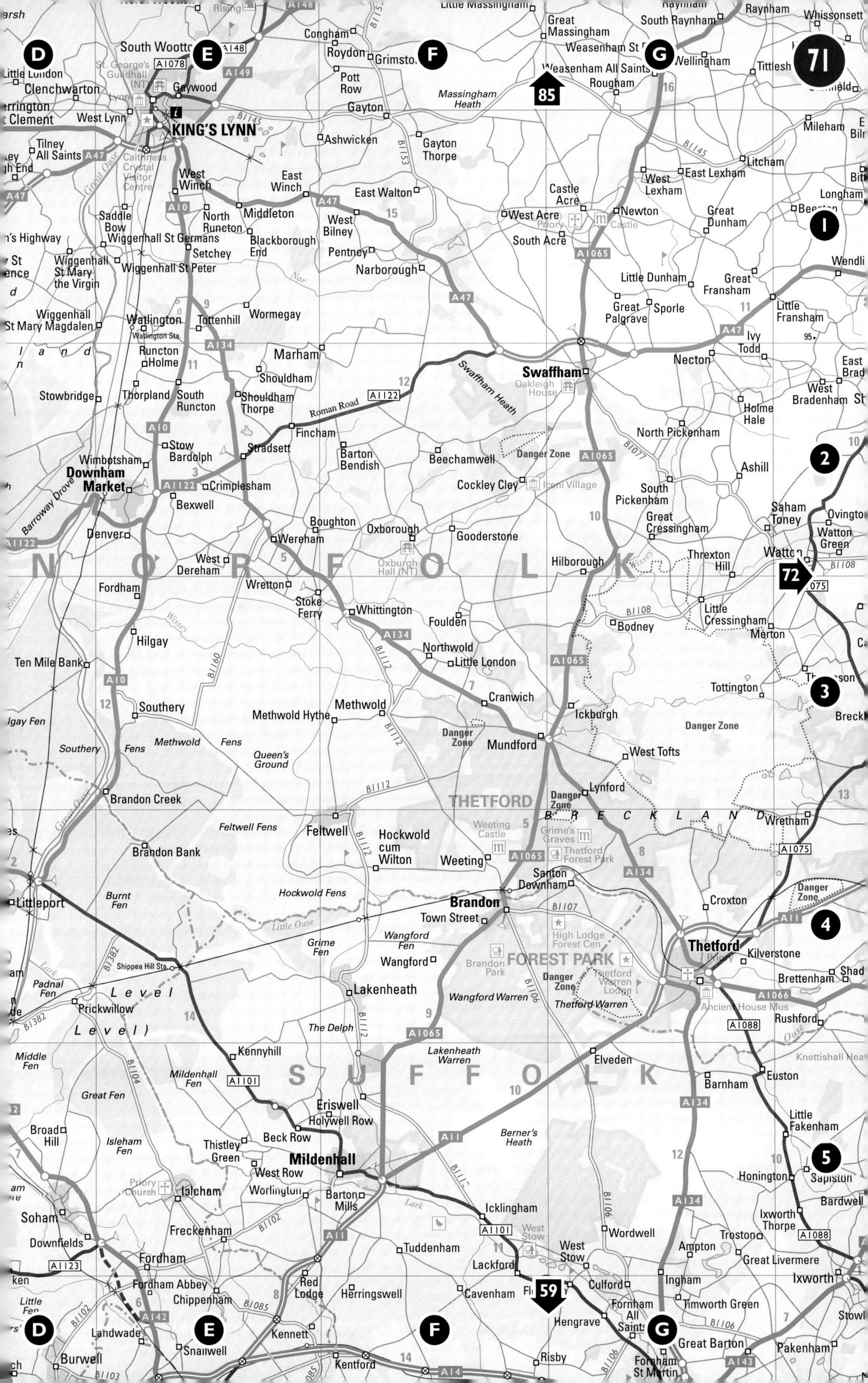
D
E
F
G
Rising
A148
Congham
Little Massingham
Great Massingham
South Raynham
Raynham
Whissonsett
South Wootton
A148
Roydon
Grimston
Weasenham St Peter
Wellingham
Tittleshall
Little London
A1078
St. George's Guildhall (NT)
Gaywood
A149
Pott Row
Weasenham All Saints
85
Rougham
Clenchwarton
Massingham Heath
Terrington St Clement
West Lynn
Gayton
KING'S LYNN
B1145
Mileham
Tilney All Saints
A47
Caithness Crystal Visitor Centre
Ashwicken
Gayton Thorpe
B1153
B1145
Litcham
West Winch
East Winch
West Lexham
East Lexham
A47
A10
East Walton
Castle Acre
Longham
Great Ouse
Saddle Bow
North Runcton
Middleton
A47
Newton
Great Dunham
Wiggenhall St Germans
West Bilney
15
West Acre
Priory
Castle
Setchey
Blackborough End
South Acre
I
Wiggenhall St Mary the Virgin
Wiggenhall St Peter
Pentney
A1065
Narborough
Nar
Little Dunham
Great Fransham
Wendling
9
Wormegay
A47
Great Palgrave
Sporle
11
Little Fransham
Wiggenhall St Mary Magdalen
Watlington
Watlington Sta.
Tottenhill
A47
Ivy Todd
A134
Runcton Holme
11
Marham
Swaffham Heath
Swaffham
Necton
East Bradenham
Shouldham
12
Oakleigh House
Stowbridge
Thorpland
South Runcton
Shouldham Thorpe
A1122
Roman Road
West Bradenham
Holme Hale
A10
Fincham
North Pickenham
Stow Bardolph
Stradsett
Barton Bendish
Beechamwell
Danger Zone
A1065
B1077
Ashill
2
Wimbotsham
Downham Market
3
A1122
Crimplesham
Cockley Cley
Iceni Village
South Pickenham
Barroway Drove
Bexwell
Saham Toney
Ovington
10
Great Cressingham
Boughton
Oxborough
Gooderstone
Watton Green
A1122
Denver
Wereham
Oxburgh Hall (NT)
Watton
Threxton Hill
Hilborough
Wissey
B1108
N O R F O L K
West Dereham
5
72
A1075
Fordham
Wretton
Stoke Ferry
B1108
Little Cressingham
Whittington
Foulden
Bodney
Merton
Wissey
A134
Hilgay
Northwold
Little London
A1065
B1112
B1160
Ten Mile Bank
7
Tottington
A10
Cranwich
3
12
Southery
Methwold
Ickburgh
Methwold Hythe
Danger Zone
Danger Zone
Mundford
Methwold Fens
Southery Fens
West Tofts
Queen's Ground
B1112
Lynford
Danger Zone
THETFORD
B R E C K L A N D
13
Brandon Creek
B1112
Wretham
Feltwell Fens
Weeting Castle
5
Grime's Graves
A1075
Feltwell
Hockwold cum Wilton
B1112
Brandon Bank
Thetford Forest Park
8
Weeting
A1065
Great Ouse
A134
Burnt Fen
Santon Downham
Danger Zone
Littleport
Hockwold Fens
Brandon
Croxton
B1107
Town Street
Little Ouse
A11
4
Wangford Fen
Grime Fen
High Lodge Forest Centre
Thetford
Kilverstone
Wangford
B1382
Shippea Hill Sta.
Brandon Park
FOREST PARK
Priory
Lark
Shadwell
Thetford Warren Lodge
Brettenham
Padnal Fen
Level
Lakenheath
Danger Zone
A1066
Wangford Warren
B1106
Prickwillow
Thetford Warren
Ancient House Mus
A1088
B1382
14
9
Rushford
Level)
The Delph
B1112
Ouse
A1065
Middle Fen
Kennyhill
Lakenheath Warren
Knettishall Heath
Elveden
Mildenhall Fen
S U F F O L K
Euston
A1101
Barnham
B1104
Great Fen
10
A134
Eriswell
Little Fakenham
Broad Hill
Isleham Fen
Holywell Row
Berner's Heath
Thistley Green
Beck Row
A11
12
10
5
Mildenhall
West Row
B1112
Honington
Sapiston
Priory Church
Isleham
Worlington
Barton Mills
B1106
Bardwell
Soham
Lark
A134
Ixworth Thorpe
Freckenham
B1102
Icklingham
A1101
West Stow
Wordwell
Troston
A1088
Downfields
A11
Tuddenham
West Stow
Ampton
Great Livermere
A1123
Fordham
11
Lackford
Ixworth
Fordham Abbey
Red Lodge
Herringswell
Cavenham
59
Culford
Ingham
Little Fen
6
Chippenham
B1085
8
Fornham All Saints
Timworth Green
Stowlangtoft
A142
Hengrave
B1106
B1102
Landwade
Kennett
Great Barton
Pakenham
Burwell
Snailwell
Kentford
14
Risby
B1106
Fornham St Martin
A143
B1103
A14

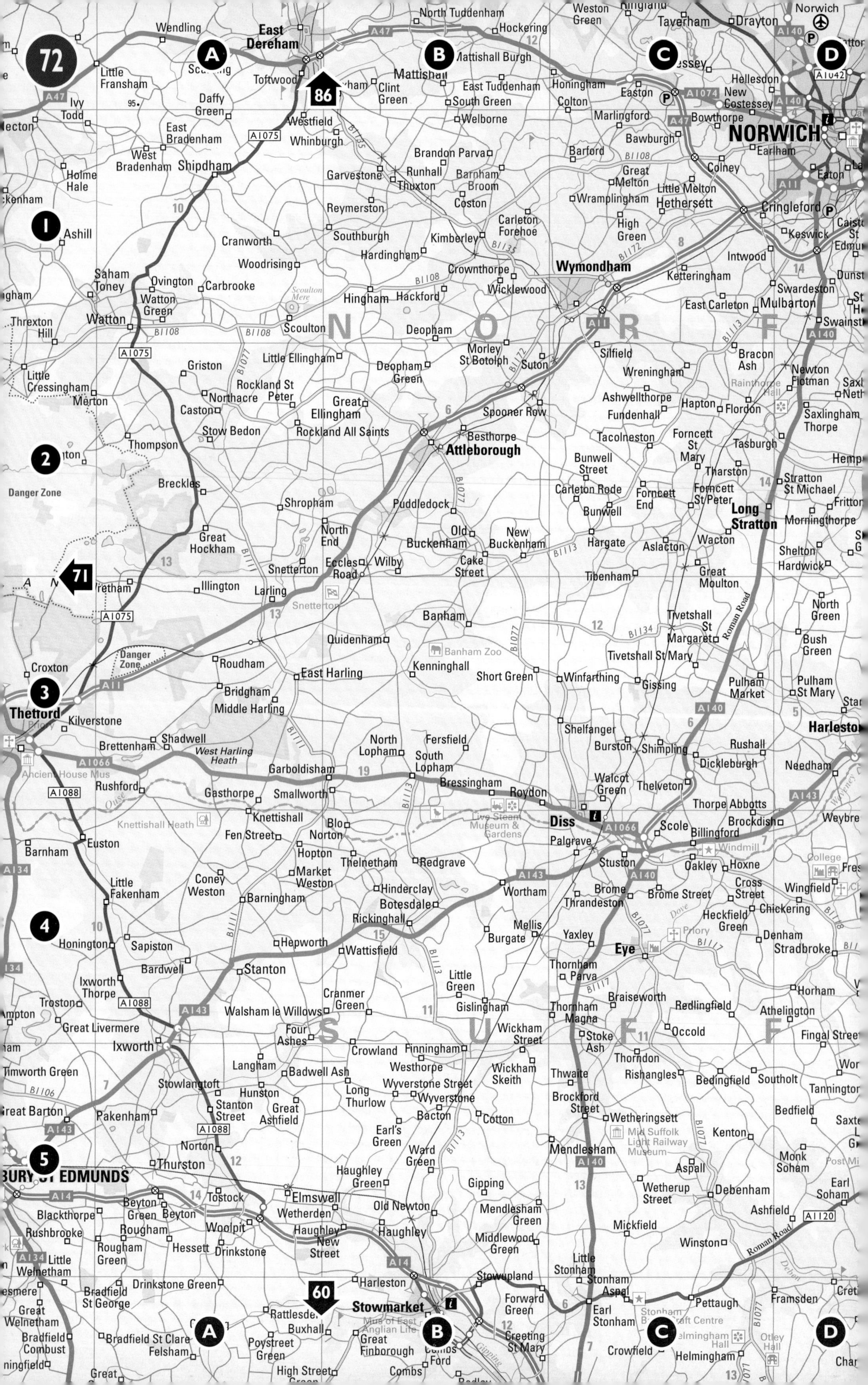
72
A
B
C
D
86
71
60
1
2
3
4
5
Wendling
East Dereham
North Tuddenham
Hockering
Weston Green
Taverham
Drayton
Norwich
Little Fransham
Scarning
Toftwood
Mattishall
Mattishall Burgh
East Tuddenham
Honingham
Easton
New Costessey
Hellesdon
Ivy Todd
Daffy Green
Clint Green
South Green
Welborne
Colton
Marlingford
Bowthorpe
NORWICH
East Bradenham
West Bradenham
Westfield
Whinburgh
Brandon Parva
Barford
Bawburgh
Earlham
Shipdham
Garvestone
Runhall
Thuxton
Barnham Broom
Great Melton
Colney
Eaton
Holme Hale
Reymerston
Coston
Wramplingham
Little Melton
Hethersett
Cringleford
Ashill
Cranworth
Southburgh
Hardingham
Kimberley
Carleton Forehoe
High Green
Keswick
Intwood
Woodrising
Crownthorpe
Wicklewood
Wymondham
Ketteringham
Saham Toney
Ovington
Watton Green
Carbrooke
Scoulton Mere
Hingham
Hackford
Swardeston
East Carleton
Mulbarton
Threxton Hill
Watton
Scoulton
Deopham
Silfield
Bracon Ash
Little Cressingham
Merton
Griston
Little Ellingham
Morley St Botolph
Suton
Wreningham
Newton Flotman
Rockland St Peter
Northacre
Deopham Green
Ashwellthorpe
Rainthorpe Hall
Caston
Great Ellingham
Spooner Row
Fundenhall
Hapton
Flordon
Saxlingham Thorpe
Stow Bedon
Rockland All Saints
Besthorpe
Attleborough
Tacolneston
Forncett St Mary
Tasburgh
Thompson
Danger Zone
Bunwell Street
Tharston
Breckles
Carleton Rode
Forncett St Peter
Forncett End
Stratton St Michael
Shropham
Puddledock
Bunwell
Long Stratton
Morningthorpe
Fritton
Great Hockham
North End
Old Buckenham
New Buckenham
Hargate
Aslacton
Wacton
Shelton
Hardwick
Snetterton
Eccles Road
Wilby
Cake Street
Tibenham
Great Moulton
Illington
Larling
Snetterton
Banham
Tivetshall St Margaret
Roman Road
North Green
Bush Green
Quidenham
Banham Zoo
Croxton
Roudham
Kenninghall
East Harling
Short Green
Winfarthing
Tivetshall St Mary
Gissing
Pulham Market
Pulham St Mary
Bridgham
Middle Harling
Thetford
Kilverstone
Priory
Shadwell
Brettenham
West Harling Heath
North Lopham
South Lopham
Fersfield
Shelfanger
Burston
Shimpling
Rushall
Dickleburgh
Harleston
Needham
Ancient House Mus
Rushford
Garboldisham
Bressingham
Roydon
Walcot Green
Thelveton
Thorpe Abbotts
Gasthorpe
Smallworth
Knettishall Heath
Knettishall
Live Steam Museum & Gardens
Diss
Scole
Brockdish
Billingford
Weybread
Fen Street
Blo Norton
Palgrave
Windmill
Euston
Barnham
Hopton
Thelnetham
Redgrave
Stuston
Oakley
Hoxne
Market Weston
Coney Weston
Little Fakenham
Hinderclay
Wortham
Brome
Brome Street
Cross Street
Wingfield
Botesdale
Thrandeston
Chickering
Barningham
Rickinghall
Heckfield Green
Mellis
Burgate
Yaxley
Priory
Denham
Honington
Sapiston
Hepworth
Wattisfield
Eye
Stradbroke
Bardwell
Stanton
Little Green
Thornham Parva
Ixworth Thorpe
Cranmer Green
Braiseworth
Redlingfield
Horham
Troston
Walsham le Willows
Gislingham
Thornham Magna
Athelington
Great Livermere
Four Ashes
Wickham Street
Occold
Stoke Ash
Fingal Street
Ixworth
Crowland
Finningham
Thorndon
Langham
Westhorpe
Wickham Skeith
Thwaite
Rishangles
Bedingfield
Southolt
Timworth Green
Badwell Ash
Wyverstone Street
Stowlangtoft
Long Thurlow
Wyverstone
Brockford Street
Tannington
Hunston
Stanton Street
Great Ashfield
Bacton
Wetheringsett
Great Barton
Pakenham
Cotton
Mid Suffolk Light Railway Museum
Bedfield
Kenton
Earl's Green
Ward Green
Mendlesham
Norton
Thurston
Monk Soham
BURY ST EDMUNDS
Aspall
Haughley Green
Gipping
Wetherup Street
Debenham
Earl Soham
Tostock
Elmswell
Beyton Green
Beyton
Blackthorpe
Wetherden
Old Newton
Mendlesham Green
Ashfield
Rushbrooke
Rougham
Woolpit
Haughley New Street
Haughley
Middlewood Green
Mickfield
Winston
Rougham Green
Hessett
Drinkstone
Little Welnetham
Little Stonham
Stowupland
Stonham Aspal
Drinkstone Green
Harleston
Bradfield St George
Forward Green
Pettaugh
Framsden
Great Welnetham
Stowmarket
Earl Stonham
Stonham Barns Craft Centre
Rattlesden
Mus of East Anglian Life
Buxhall
Bradfield Combust
Bradfield St Clare
Felsham
Poystreet Green
Great Finborough
Combs Ford
Creeting St Mary
Crowfield
Helmingham Hall
Helmingham
Otley Hall
High Street Green
Combs
N O R F O L K
S U F F O L K
A47
A1075
A11
A1066
A1088
A134
A143
A140
A14
A1074
A1042
A1120
B1135
B1108
B1172
B1077
B1111
B1113
B1134
B1106
B1117
B1118

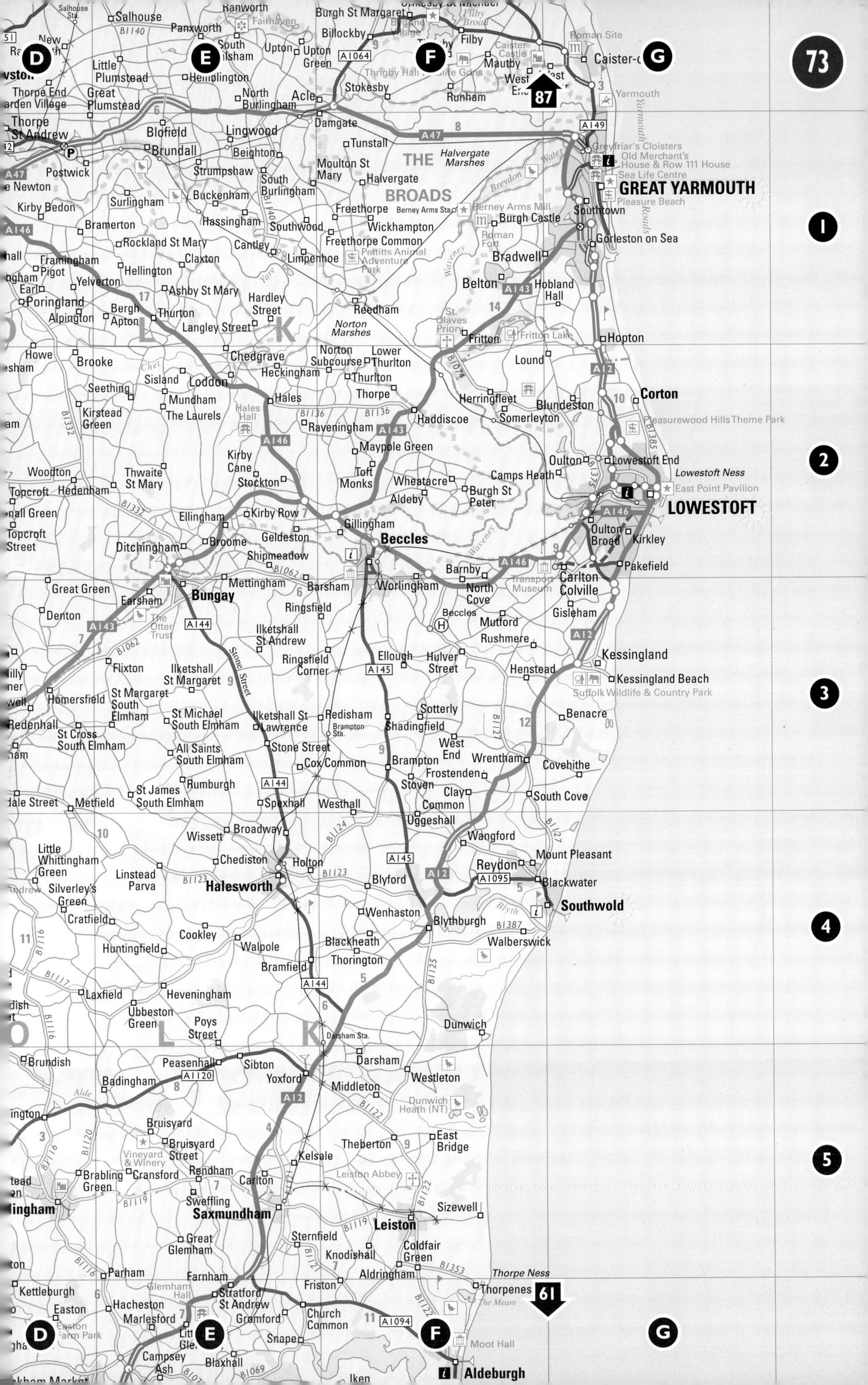

Salhouse
Ranworth
Burgh St Margaret
Billockby
Filby
Roman Site
Caister-on-Sea
Panxworth
South Walsham
Upton
Upton Green
A1064
Thrigby Hall Wildlife Gdns
Mautby
Caister Castle
West End
Little Plumstead
Great Plumstead
Hemblington
North Burlingham
Acle
Stokesby
Runham
87
Yarmouth
Thorpe End Garden Village
Thorpe St Andrew
Blofield
Damgate
A47
A149
Lingwood
Tunstall
THE BROADS
Halvergate Marshes
Brundall
Beighton
Greyfriar's Cloisters
Old Merchant's House & Row 111 House
Sea Life Centre
Postwick
Strumpshaw
Moulton St Mary
Halvergate
Breydon Water
GREAT YARMOUTH
Newton
South Burlingham
Pleasure Beach
Surlingham
Buckenham
Freethorpe
Berney Arms Sta.
Berney Arms Mill
Kirby Bedon
Bramerton
Hassingham
Southwood
Wickhampton
Burgh Castle
Southtown
Rockland St Mary
Cantley
Freethorpe Common
Roman Fort
Gorleston on Sea
Claxton
Limpenhoe
Pettitts Animal Adventure Park
Bradwell
Framingham Pigot
Hellington
Yelverton
Belton
A143
Hobland Hall
Ashby St Mary
Hardley Street
Poringland
Bergh Apton
Thurton
Reedham
St. Olaves Priory
Alpington
Langley Street
Norton Marshes
Fritton
Fritton Lake
Hopton
Howe
Brooke
Chedgrave
Norton Subcourse
Lower Thurlton
Lound
Sisland
Loddon
Heckingham
Thurlton
A12
Seething
Mundham
Hales
Thorpe
Herringfleet
Blundeston
Corton
Kirstead Green
The Laurels
Hales Hall
B1136
Haddiscoe
Somerleyton
Pleasurewood Hills Theme Park
Raveningham
A146
Maypole Green
Kirby Cane
Toft Monks
Oulton
Lowestoft End
Woodton
Thwaite St Mary
Stockton
Wheatacre
Camps Heath
Lowestoft Ness
Topcroft
Hedenham
Aldeby
Burgh St Peter
East Point Pavilion
Topcroft Street
Ellingham
Kirby Row
Gillingham
LOWESTOFT
Broome
Geldeston
Beccles
Oulton Broad
Kirkley
Ditchingham
Shipmeadow
Barnby
Pakefield
Great Green
Mettingham
Barsham
Worlingham
North Cove
Transport Museum
Carlton Colville
Earsham
Bungay
Ringsfield
Denton
The Otter Trust
A144
Beccles
Mutford
Gisleham
Ilketshall St Andrew
Rushmere
Stone Street
Ringsfield Corner
Ellough
Hulver Street
Kessingland
Flixton
Ilketshall St Margaret
A145
Henstead
Kessingland Beach
Suffolk Wildlife & Country Park
Homersfield
St Margaret South Elmham
St Michael South Elmham
Ilketshall St Lawrence
Redisham
Brampton Sta.
Sotterly
Shadingfield
Benacre
Redenhall
St Cross South Elmham
All Saints South Elmham
Stone Street
West End
Wrentham
Covehithe
Cox Common
Brampton
Frostenden
Stoven
Clay Common
South Cove
Rumburgh
St James South Elmham
Metfield
Spexhall
Westhall
Uggeshall
Wissett
Broadway
Wangford
Mount Pleasant
Little Whittingham Green
Chediston
Holton
Reydon
Blackwater
Linstead Parva
Halesworth
Blyford
A1095
Southwold
Silverley's Green
Wenhaston
Blythburgh
Cratfield
Cookley
Walberswick
Huntingfield
Walpole
Blackheath
Thorington
Bramfield
Laxfield
Heveningham
Ubbeston Green
Poys Street
Dunwich
Darsham Sta.
Brundish
Peasenhall
Sibton
Darsham
Westleton
Badingham
A1120
Yoxford
Middleton
Dunwich Heath (NT)
Bruisyard
Theberton
East Bridge
Vineyard & Winery
Bruisyard Street
Kelsale
Leiston Abbey
Brabling Green
Cransford
Rendham
Carlton
Sweffling
Saxmundham
Leiston
Sizewell
Great Glemham
Sternfield
Knodishall
Coldfair Green
Parham
Aldringham
Thorpe Ness
Kettleburgh
Glemham Hall
Farnham
Friston
Thorpeness
The Meare
61
Hacheston
Stratford St Andrew
Easton
Marlesford
Easton Farm Park
Gromford
Church Common
A1094
Snape
Moot Hall
Campsey Ash
Blaxhall
Aldeburgh
Iken

A
B
C
D
1
2
3
4
5
88
0 2 4 6 8 10 miles
0 2 4 6 8 10 km
CAERNARFON
BAY
Cymyran Bay
Rhosneigr
A4080
Ty Newydd Burial Chamber
Burial Chamber
Barclodiad y Gawres Chambered Cairn
Cerrigceinwen
B4422
Bethel
Trefdraeth
Llyn Coron
Llangadwaladr
Aberffraw
Hermon
Malltraeth
Aberffraw Bay
Bodorgan
Malltraeth Sands
Newborough (Niwbwrch)
Malltraeth Bay
Newborough Warren
Llanddwyn Island
Llanddwyn Bay
Abermenai
The Bar
Dinas Dinlle
Pontllyfni
Trwyn Maen Dylan
Aberdesach
Capeluchaf
Clynnog-fawr
Gyrn Goch
Bwlch Mawr 509
Gyrn Ddu 522
Trefor
Trwyn y Gorlech
A499
Yr Eifl 564
Llanaelhaearn
Pen-sarn
B4417
Llithfaen
Cefn-Ferch
Carreg Ddu
Porth Dinllaen
Pistyll
Pencaenewydd
Llwyndyrys
Llangybi
Morfa Nefyn
Nefyn
LLEYN PENINSULA
Groesffordd
Edern
B4412
Garn Boduan
Fron
Y Ffôr
B4354
Rhos-fawr
Chwilog
Tan-y-graig
Porth Ysgadan
Rhos-y-llan
Ceidio Fawr
Bodfuan
Llannor
Abererch
A497
Tudweiliog
Efailnewydd
Denio
Dinas
Carn Fadryn 371
Penllech
Garnfadryn
B4415
Rhyd-y-clafdy
Pwllheli
Carreg yr Imbill
Porth Colmon
Llaniestyn
Penrhos
Porth Colmon
Llangwnnadl
Sarn-Meyllteyrn
Penrhyn Mawr
Rhedyn
B4413
Y Gamlas
Porth Oer
Bryncroes
Llanbedrog
Ty-hen
Botwnnog
Nanhoron
Methlem
Rhydlios
Llandegwning
Mynytho
Trwyn Llanbedrog
Capel Carmel
Rhoshirwaun
Mynydd Rhiw 305
Llangian
Braich Anelog
Rhiw
Llawr-y-dref
Abersoch
Anelog
Plas-yn-Rhiw (NT)
Rhydolion
St Tudwal's Road
Mynydd Anelog 191
Llanengan
Pwlldefaid
Aberdaron
Llanfaelrhys
Porth Neigwl or Hell's Mouth
Sarn Bach
Braich y Pwll
Aberdaron Bay
Bwlchtocyn
St Tudwal's Islands
Uwchmynydd
Ynys Gwylan-fawr
Porth Ceiriad
Trwyn yr Wylfa
Pen y Cil
Cilan Uchaf
Bardsey Sound (Swnt Enlli)
Trwyn Cilan
Bardsey Island (Ynys Enlli)
St. Mary's Abbey

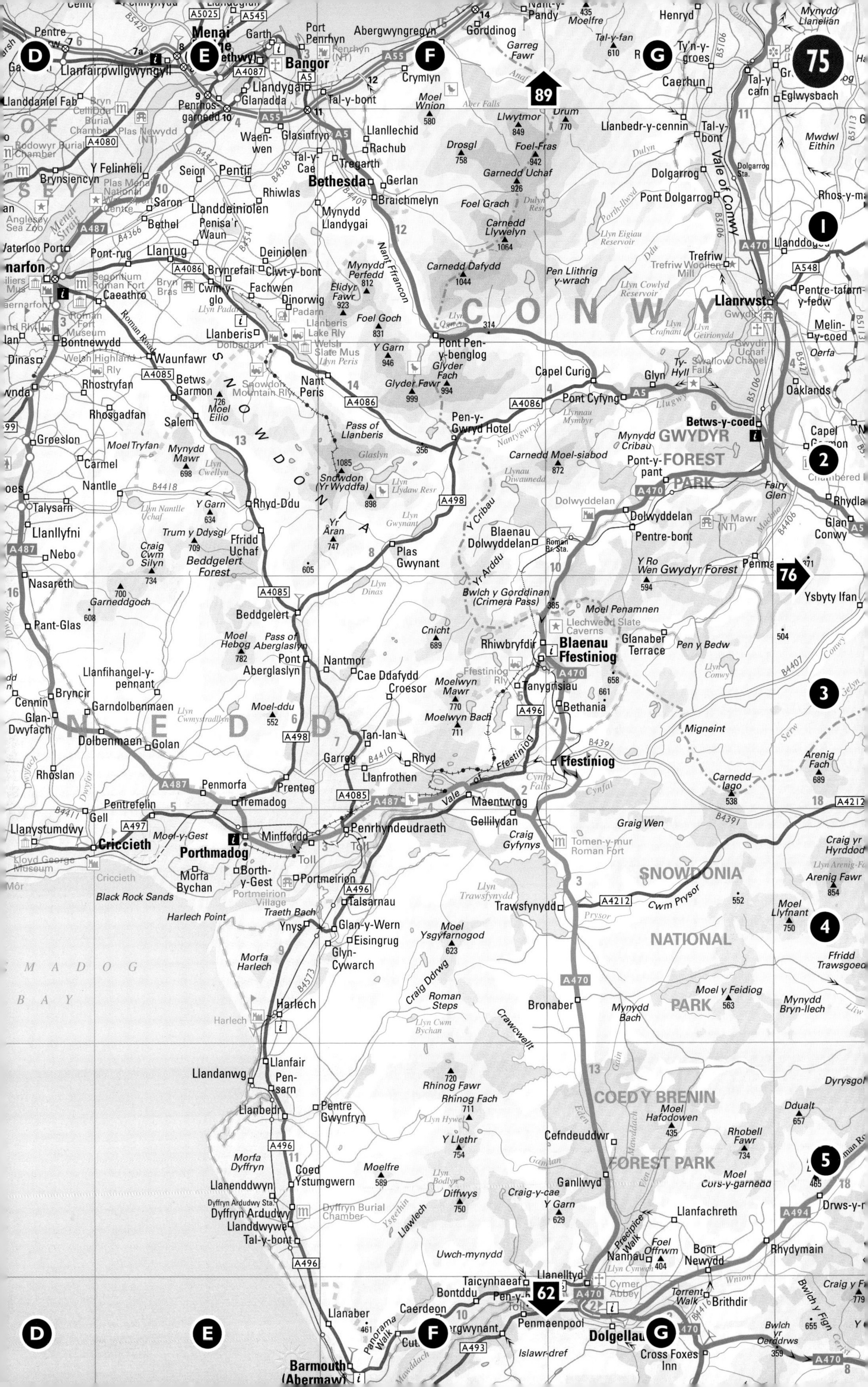
75
D
E
F
G
89
76
62
I
2
3
4
5
Menai Bridge
Pentre Berw
Llanfairpwllgwyngyll
Gaerwen
Llanddaniel Fab
Bryn Celli Ddu Burial Chamber
Plas Newydd (NT)
Bodowyr Burial Chamber
Brynsiencyn
Anglesey Sea Zoo
Y Felinheli
Plas Menai National Watersports Centre
Menai Strait
Bangor
Port Penrhyn
Penrhyn Castle (NT)
Garth
Llandygai
Glanadda
Penrhosgarnedd
Abergwyngregyn
Crymlyn
Tal-y-bont
Moel Wnion
Aber Falls
Gorddinog
Garreg Fawr
Nant-y-Pandy
Moelfre
Tal-y-fan
Henryd
Ty'n-y-groes
Caerhun
Tal-y-cafn
Eglwysbach
Mynydd Llanelian
Llanbedr-y-cennin
Tal-y-bont
Mwdwl Eithin
Dolgarrog
Dolgarrog Sta.
Pont Dolgarrog
Vale of Conwy
Rhos-y-mawn
Llanddoged
Waen-wen
Glasinfryn
Llanllechid
Rachub
Tal-y-Cae
Tregarth
Bethesda
Gerlan
Braichmelyn
Seion
Pentir
Rhiwlas
Saron
Llanddeiniolen
Bethel
Penisa'r Waun
Mynydd Llandygai
Nant Ffrancon
Llwytmor
Drum
Drosgl
Foel-Fras
Garnedd Uchaf
Foel Grach
Dulyn Resr
Carnedd Llywelyn
Carnedd Dafydd
Pen Llithrig y-wrach
Llyn Eigiau Reservoir
Llyn Cowlyd Reservoir
Trefriw
Trefriw Woollen Mill
Llanrwst
Pentre-tafarn-y-fedw
Gwydir
Gwydir Uchaf Chapel
Melin-y-coed
Oerfa
Waterloo Port
Caernarfon
Pont-rug
Llanrug
Brynrefail
Clwt-y-bont
Deiniolen
Fachwen
Dinorwig
Cwm-y-glo
Llyn Padarn
Padarn
Llanberis Lake Rly
Llanberis
Dolbadarn
Welsh Slate Mus
Llyn Peris
Segontium Roman Fort
Caeathro
Bryn Bras
Roman Road
Bontnewydd
Dinas
Waunfawr
Welsh Highland Rly
Snowdon Mountain Rly
SNOWDONIA
CONWY
Mynydd Perfedd
Elidyr Fawr
Foel Goch
Y Garn
Glyder Fach
Glyder Fawr
Llyn Ogwen
Pont Pen-y-benglog
Capel Curig
Llyn Crafnant
Llyn Geirionydd
Ty-Hyll
Swallow Falls
Glyn
Pont Cyfyng
Llynnau Mymbyr
Llugwy
Betws-y-coed
Oaklands
Capel Garmon
Chambered Tomb
Fairy Glen
Rhydlanfair
Glan Conwy
Rhostryfan
Betws Garmon
Moel Eilio
Nant Peris
Pass of Llanberis
Pen-y-Gwryd Hotel
Glaslyn
Snowdon (Yr Wyddfa)
Llyn Llydaw Resr
Nantygwryd
Mynydd Cribau
GWYDYR FOREST PARK
Carnedd Moel-siabod
Llynnau Diwaunedd
Pont-y-pant
Dolwyddelan
Ty Mawr (NT)
Pentre-bont
Machno
Groeslon
Rhosgadfan
Salem
Moel Tryfan
Mynydd Mawr
Llyn Cwellyn
Carmel
Nantlle
Llyn Nantlle Uchaf
Y Garn
Rhyd-Ddu
Talysarn
Penygroes
Llanllyfni
Nebo
Trum y Ddysgl
Ffridd Uchaf
Craig Cwm Silyn
Beddgelert Forest
Yr Aran
Llyn Gwynant
Plas Gwynant
Y Cribau
Blaenau Dolwyddelan
Roman Br. Sta.
Y Ro Wen
Gwydyr Forest
Penmachno
Ysbyty Ifan
Nasareth
Garneddgoch
Pant-Glas
Llyn Dinas
Beddgelert
Yr Arddu
Bwlch y Gorddinan (Crimea Pass)
Moel Penamnen
Llechwedd Slate Caverns
Moel Hebog
Pass of Aberglaslyn
Pont Aberglaslyn
Nantmor
Cnicht
Rhiwbryfdir
Blaenau Ffestiniog
Glanaber Terrace
Pen y Bedw
Llyn Conwy
Llanfihangel-y-pennant
Bryncir
Cae Ddafydd
Croesor
Moelwyn Mawr
Ffestiniog Rly
Tanygrisiau
Bethania
Cennin
Garndolbenmaen
Llyn Cwmystradllyn
Moel-ddu
Moelwyn Bach
Glan-Dwyfach
Dolbenmaen
Golan
EIFIONYDD
Tan-lan
Migneint
Garreg
Rhyd
Llanfrothen
Vale of Ffestiniog
Ffestiniog
Cynfal Falls
Arenig Fach
Carnedd Iago
Rhoslan
Penmorfa
Prenteg
Tremadog
Maentwrog
Gellilydan
Craig Gyfynys
Pentrefelin
Gell
Llanystumdwy
Criccieth
Lloyd George Museum
Moel-y-Gest
Porthmadog
Minffordd
Penrhyndeudraeth
Toll
Tomen-y-mur Roman Fort
Graig Wen
Craig yr Hyrddod
Llyn Arenig Fawr
Arenig Fawr
Borth-y-Gest
Morfa Bychan
Portmeirion
Portmeirion Village
Black Rock Sands
Harlech Point
Traeth Bach
Talsarnau
Ynys
Glan-y-Wern
Eisingrug
Glyn-Cywarch
Llyn Trawsfynydd
Trawsfynydd
Cwm Prysor
SNOWDONIA NATIONAL PARK
Moel Llyfnant
Ffridd Trawsgoed
Moel Ysgyfarnogod
Craig Ddrwg
Roman Steps
Morfa Harlech
TREMADOG BAY
Harlech
Bronaber
Mynydd Bach
Moel y Feidiog
Mynydd Bryn-llech
Llyn Cwm Bychan
Crawcwellt
Llanfair
Llandanwg
Pen-sarn
Llanbedr
Rhinog Fawr
Rhinog Fach
Llyn Hywel
Pentre Gwynfryn
COED Y BRENIN FOREST PARK
Moel Hafodowen
Dyrysgol
Dduallt
Cefndeuddwr
Rhobell Fawr
Y Llethr
Morfa Dyffryn
Coed Ystumgwern
Moelfre
Llyn Bodlyn
Diffwys
Llanenddwyn
Ganllwyd
Moel Cors-y-garnedd
Craig-y-cae
Y Garn
Dyffryn Ardudwy Sta.
Dyffryn Ardudwy
Dyffryn Burial Chamber
Ysgethin
Llawlech
Precipice Walk
Llanfachreth
Drws-y-nant
Llanddwywe
Foel Offrwm
Nannau
Llyn Cynwch
Bont Newydd
Rhydymain
Tal-y-bont
Uwch-mynydd
Taicynhaeaf
Llanelltyd
Cymer Abbey
Torrent Walk
Brithdir
Craig y Ffynnon
Bontddu
Pen-y-bryn
Caerdeon
Llanaber
Panorama Walk
Cutiau
Abergwynant
Penmaenpool
Dolgellau
Islawr-dref
Cross Foxes Inn
Bwlch yr Oerddrws
Bwlch y Fign
Barmouth (Abermaw)
Mawddach
A5025
A545
A4087
A5
A55
A4080
A487
A4086
A4085
A498
A470
A496
A497
A493
A494
A4212
A548
B5420
B4547
B4366
B4409
B4418
B4410
B4411
B4391
B4407
B4406
B5106
B5427
B5113
B4573
B4416

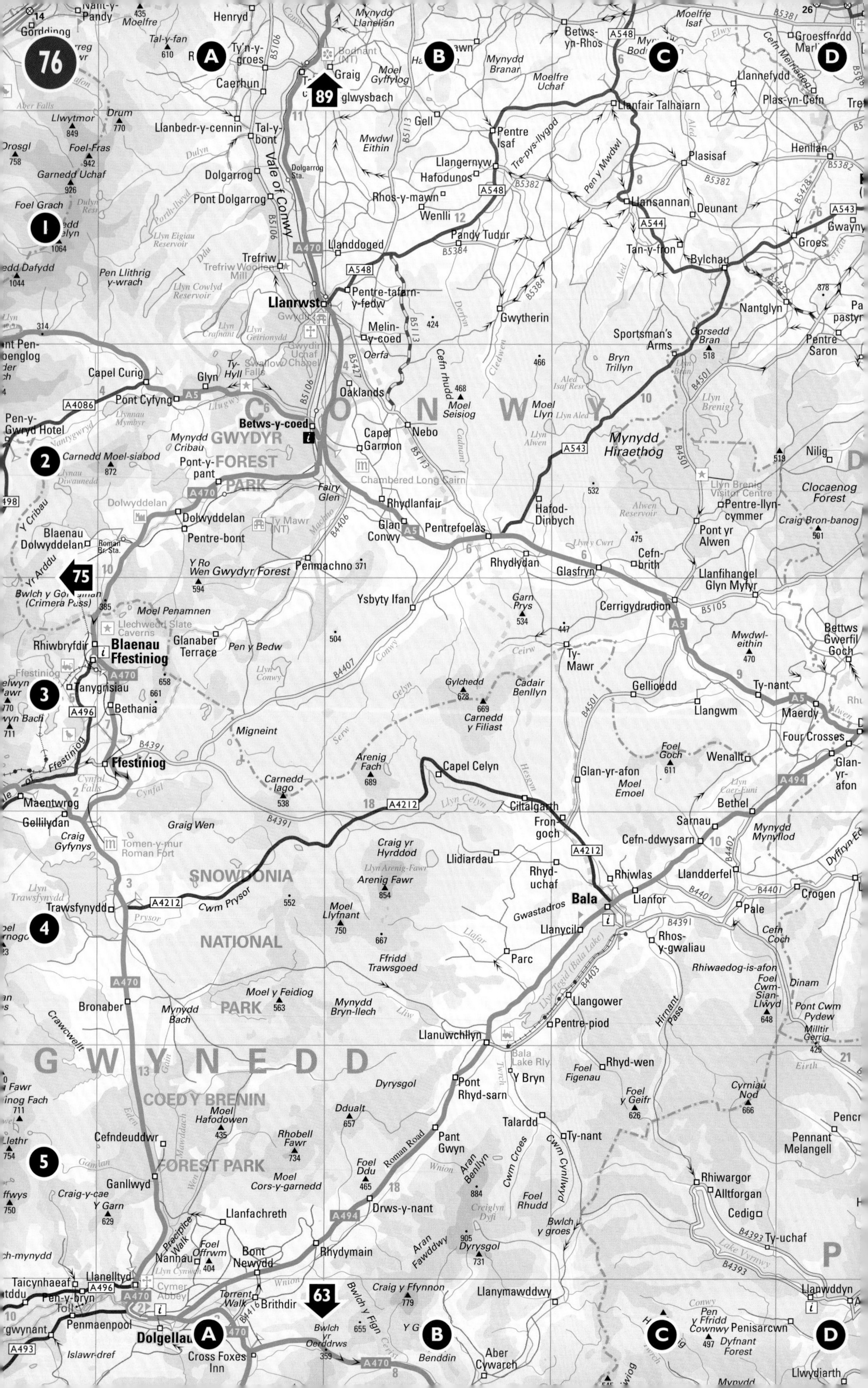
76
89
75
63
A
B
C
D
1
2
3
4
5
CONWY
GWYNEDD
SNOWDONIA
NATIONAL
PARK
GWYDYR
FOREST
PARK
COED Y BRENIN
FOREST PARK
Henryd
Moelfre
Tal-y-fan
610
Ty'n-y-groes
Caerhun
Bodnant (NT)
Graig
Mynydd Llanelian
Moel Gyffylog
Betws-yn-Rhos
Mynydd Branar
Moelfre Uchaf
Moelfre Isaf
Groesffordd Marli
Llannefydd
Llanfair Talhaiarn
Plas-yn-Cefn
Drum
770
Llwytmor
849
Foel-Fras
942
Garnedd Uchaf
926
Foel Grach
1064
Aber Falls
Llanbedr-y-cennin
Tal-y-bont
Dolgarrog
Dolgarrog Sta.
Pont Dolgarrog
Vale of Conwy
Gell
Mwdwl Eithin
Pentre Isaf
Tre-pys-llygod
Llangernyw
Hafodunos
Rhos-y-mawn
Wenlli
Pen y Mwdwl
Llansannan
Plasisaf
Deunant
Henllan
Gwaenysgor
Groes
Llyn Eigiau Reservoir
Trefriw
Trefriw Woollen Mill
Llanddoged
Pandy Tudur
Tan-y-fron
Bylchau
Nantglyn
Pen Llithrig y-wrach
Llyn Cowlyd Reservoir
Llanrwst
Gwydir
Pentre-tafarn-y-fedw
Melin-y-coed
Gwytherin
Sportsman's Arms
Gorsedd Bran
518
Pentre Saron
Llyn Crafnant
Llyn Geirionydd
Gwydir Uchaf Chapel
Swallow Falls
Ty-Hyll
Oerfa
Oaklands
Cefn rhudd
468
Moel Seisiog
466
Bryn Trillyn
Aled Isaf Resr
Llyn Brenig
Capel Curig
Glyn
Pont Cyfyng
Llugwy
Pen-y-Gwryd Hotel
Llynnau Mymbyr
Betws-y-coed
Capel Garmon
Nebo
Moel Llyn
Llyn Aled
Llyn Alwen
Mynydd Hiraethog
Nilig
519
Carnedd Moel-siabod
872
Mynydd Cribau
Pont-y-pant
Chambered Long Cairn
Fairy Glen
Rhydlanfair
532
Hafod-Dinbych
Llyn Brenig Visitor Centre
Clocaenog Forest
Pentre-llyn-cymmer
Alwen Reservoir
Craig Bron-banog
501
Dolwyddelan
Ty Mawr (NT)
Glan Conwy
Pentrefoelas
Pont yr Alwen
Blaenau Dolwyddelan
Pentre-bont
Roman Br. Sta.
Y Cribau
475
Cefn-brith
Rhydlydan
Glasfryn
Llyn y Cwrt
Penmachno
371
Y Ro Wen
Gwydyr Forest
594
Yr Arddu
Bwlch y Gorddinan (Crimera Pass)
385
Llanfihangel Glyn Myfyr
Ysbyty Ifan
Garn Prys
534
Cerrigydrudion
Moel Penamnen
Llechwedd Slate Caverns
Glanaber Terrace
Pen y Bedw
504
447
Bettws Gwerfil Goch
Mwdwl-eithin
470
Rhiwbryfdir
Blaenau Ffestiniog
Ty-Mawr
Ceirw
Llyn Conwy
658
661
Ffestiniog
Tanygrisiau
Bethania
Gylchedd
628
Cadair Benllyn
669
Carnedd y Filiast
Gellioedd
Ty-nant
Llangwm
Maerdy
Four Crosses
Migneint
Serw
Gelyn
Ffestiniog
Arenig Fach
689
Capel Celyn
Foel Goch
611
Wenallt
Glan-yr-afon
Glan-yr-afon
Carnedd Iago
538
Cynfal Falls
Cynfal
Maentwrog
Llyn Celyn
Ciltalgarth
Moel Emoel
Bethel
Gellilydan
Craig Gyfynys
Graig Wen
Tomen-y-mur Roman Fort
Craig yr Hyrddod
Llyn Arenig-Fawr
Arenig Fawr
854
Fron-goch
Llidiardau
Rhyd-uchaf
Sarnau
Cefn-ddwysarn
Mynydd Mynyllod
Llandderfel
Dyffryn Edeirnion
Crogen
Llyn Trawsfynydd
Trawsfynydd
Cwm Prysor
Prysor
552
Moel Llyfnant
750
667
Rhiwlas
Bala
Llanfor
Pale
Gwastadros
Llanycil
Rhos-y-gwaliau
Cefn Coch
Ffridd Trawsgoed
Parc
Llafar
Rhiwaedog-is-afon
Foel Cwm-Sian-Llwyd
648
Dinam
Llyn Tegid (Bala Lake)
Bronaber
Crawcwellt
Mynydd Bach
Moel y Feiddiog
563
Mynydd Bryn-llech
Lliw
Llangower
Pentre-piod
Hirnant Pass
Pont Cwm Pydew
Milltir Gerrig
425
Llanuwchllyn
Bala Lake Rly.
Twrch
Y Bryn
Rhyd-wen
Foel Figenau
Eirth
Dyrysgol
Pont Rhyd-sarn
Foel y Geifr
626
Cyrniau Nod
666
Moel Hafodowen
435
Dduallt
657
Rhobell Fawr
734
Talardd
Ty-nant
Pant Gwyn
Roman Road
Aran Benllyn
Cwm Croes
Cwm Cynllwyd
Pennant Melangell
Cefndeuddwr
Gamlan
Foel Ddu
465
Moel Cors-y-garnedd
Wnion
884
Creiglyn Dyfi
Foel Rhudd
Rhiwargor
Alltforgan
Cedig
Ganllwyd
Craig-y-cae
Y Garn
629
Drws-y-nant
Bwlch y groes
Llanfachreth
Precipice Walk
Foel Offrwm
404
Bont Newydd
Rhydymain
Aran Fawddwy
905
Dyrysgol
731
Ty-uchaf
Lake Vyrnwy
Nannau
Llyn Cynwch
Taicynhaeaf
Llanelltyd
Cymer Abbey
Torrent Walk
Brithdir
Craig y Ffynnon
779
Bwlch y Fign
Llanymawddwy
Llanwddyn
Penmaenpool
Pen-y-bryn
Toll
Dolgellau
Bwlch yr Oerddrws
359
655
Benddin
Aber Cywarch
Conwy
Pen y Ffridd Cownwy
Penisarcwn
497
Dyfnant Forest
Cross Foxes Inn
Islawr-dref
Llwydiarth
A470
A5
A548
A543
A544
A4086
A496
A4212
A494
A493
B5106
B5113
B5427
B5382
B5384
B5381
B5428
B4406
B4407
B4391
B4501
B5105
B4402
B4401
B4403
B4393
B4416

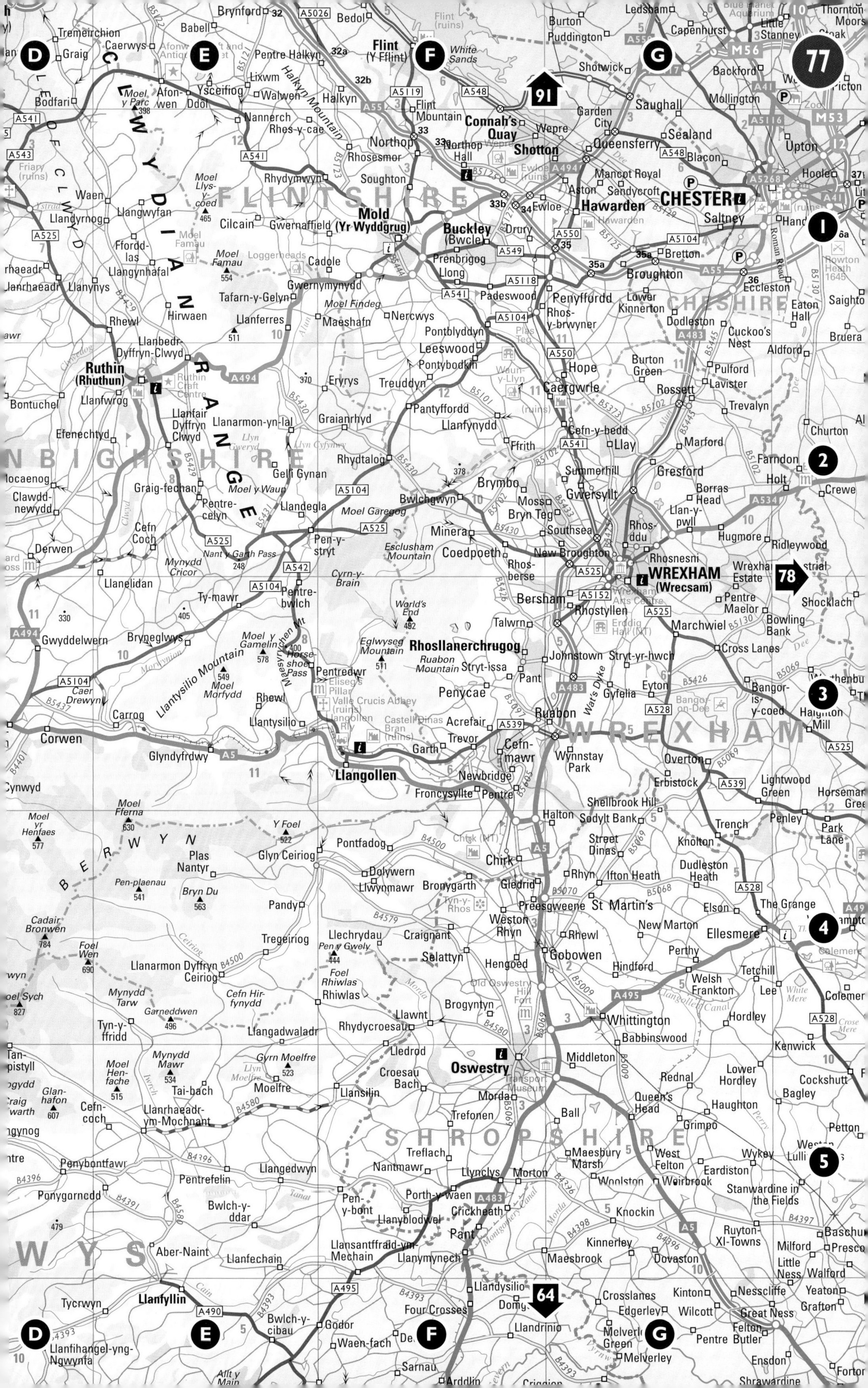
77
D
E
F
G
91
78
64
I
2
3
4
5
Brynford
Babell
Tremeirchion
Caerwys
Graig
Bodfari
Afonwen
Ysceifiog
Ddol
Pentre Halkyn
Lixwm
Walwen
Halkyn
Halkyn Mountain
Flint (Y Fflint)
White Sands
Flint (ruins)
Flint Mountain
Northop
Northop Hall
Rhosesmor
Soughton
Nannerch
Rhes-y-cae
Rhydymwyn
Connah's Quay
Wepre
Shotton
Garden City
Queensferry
Sealand
Blacon
Saughall
Shotwick
Burton
Puddington
Ledsham
Capenhurst
Backford
Mollington
Upton
Hoole
Little Stanney
Thornton
Moors
Stoak
Picton
Blue Planet Aquarium
Zoo
Mancot Royal
Sandycroft
Aston
Ewloe
Hawarden
CHESTER
Saltney
Handbridge
Bretton
Broughton
Eccleston
Rowton Heath 1645
Roman Road
Saighton
Eaton Hall
CHESHIRE
FLINTSHIRE
Mold (Yr Wyddgrug)
Buckley (Bwcle)
Drury
Prenbrigog
Llong
Padeswood
Penyffordd
Lower Kinnerton
Dodleston
Cuckoo's Nest
Pulford
Lavister
Rossett
Trevalyn
Aldford
Bruera
Churton
Farndon
Holt
Crewe
Rhos-y-brwyner
Hope
Caergwrle
Burton Green
Cefn-y-bedd
Llay
Marford
Gresford
Summerhill
Gwersyllt
Borras Head
Llan-y-pwll
Rhosddu
Hugmore
Ridleywood
Wrexham Industrial Estate
WREXHAM (Wrecsam)
Rhosnesni
Pentre Maelor
Shocklach
Marchwiel
Bowling Bank
Cross Lanes
Bangor-is-y-coed
Bangor-on-Dee
Eyton
Halghton Mill
Overton
Erbistock
Lightwood Green
Horseman's Green
Penley
Park Lane
Trench
Knolton
Shellbrook Hill
Sodylt Bank
Street Dinas
Dudleston Heath
Elson
The Grange
Ellesmere
Welsh Frankton
Lee
White Mere
Colemere
Tetchill
Hordley
Kenwick
Crose Mere
Whittington
Babbinswood
Middleton
Lower Hordley
Cockshutt
Bagley
Rednal
Queen's Head
Haughton
Grimpo
Petton
Wykey
West Felton
Eardiston
Weston Lullingfields
Stanwardine in the Fields
Woolston
Weirbrook
Knockin
Ruyton-XI-Towns
Baschurch
Prescott
Milford
Little Ness
Walford
Nesscliffe
Yeaton
Grafton
Great Ness
Kinton
Wilcott
Felton Butler
Pentre
Ensdon
Shrawardine
Forton
Kinnerley
Dovaston
Maesbrook
Crosslanes
Edgerley
Melverley Green
Melverley
Llandrinio
Domgay
Llandysilio
Four Crosses
Maesbury Marsh
Morton
Llynclys
Porth-y-waen
Crickheath
Pant
Llanymynech
Llansantffraid-ym-Mechain
Llanyblodwel
Pen-y-bont
Nantmawr
Treflach
Trefonen
Morda
Oswestry
Transport Museum
Ball
SHROPSHIRE
Old Oswestry Hill Fort
Hengoed
Gobowen
Rhewl
Weston Rhyn
Preesgweene
St Martin's
New Marton
Perthy
Hindford
Rhyn
Ifton Heath
Gledrid
Chirk
Chirk (NT)
Halton
Bronygarth
Tyn-y-Rhos
Craignant
Selattyn
Llawnt
Brogyntyn
Rhydycroesau
Lledrod
Croesau Bach
Llansilin
Moelfre
Gyrn Moelfre 523
Llyn Moelfre
Tai-bach
Llanrhaeadr-ym-Mochnant
Llangedwyn
Pentrefelin
Bwlch-y-ddar
Penybontfawr
Ponygarnedd
Aber-Naint
Llanfechain
Llanfyllin
Tycrwyn
Llanfihangel-yng-Ngwynfa
Bwlch-y-cibau
Godor
Waen-fach
Sarnau
Arddlin
Criggion
Allt y Main
Mynydd Mawr 534
Moel Hen-fache 515
Glan-hafon 607
Cefn-coch
Tyn-y-ffridd
Llangadwaladr
Garneddwen 496
Mynydd Tarw
Cefn Hir-fynydd
Rhiwlas
Foel Rhiwlas
Pen y Gwely 444
Llechrydau
Tregeiriog
Llanarmon Dyffryn Ceiriog
Pandy
Dolywern
Llwynmawr
Pontfadog
Glyn Ceiriog
Y Foel 522
Plas Nantyr
Bryn Du 563
Pen-plaenau 541
Moel Fferna 630
Moel yr Henfaes 577
BERWYN
Cadair Bronwen 784
Foel Wen 690
Moel Sych 827
Cynwyd
Corwen
Carrog
Glyndyfrdwy
Llangollen
Froncysyllte
Pentre
Newbridge
Cefn-mawr
Trevor
Garth
Acrefair
Castell Dinas Bran (ruins)
Valle Crucis Abbey (ruins)
Eliseg's Pillar
Pentredwr
Llantysilio
Rhewl
Horseshoe Pass
Maesyrychen Mt
Moel Morfydd
Llantysilio Mountain
Moel y Gamelin 578
Bryneglwys
Gwyddelwern
Caer Drewyn
Llanelidan
Derwen
Clawdd-newydd
Cefn Coch
Mynydd Cricor
Nant y Garth Pass 248
Ty-mawr
Pentre-bwlch
Cyrn-y-Brain
World's End 492
Eglwyseg Mountain 511
Ruabon Mountain
Rhosllanerchrugog
Stryt-issa
Penycae
Pant
Johnstown
Stryt-yr-hwch
Gyfelia
Ruabon
Wynnstay Park
Wat's Dyke
WREXHAM
Rhostyllen
Erddig Hall (NT)
Bersham
Talwrn
Rhosberse
Coedpoeth
New Broughton
Southsea
Bryn Teg
Moss
Brymbo
Minera
Bwlchgwyn
Esclusham Mountain
Moel Garegog
Pen-y-stryt
Llandegla
Gelli Gynan
Rhydtalog
Pentre-celyn
Graig-fechan
Moel y Waun
Llanarmon-yn-Ial
Llyn Gweryd
Llyn Cyfynwy
Graianrhyd
Eryrys
Treuddyn
Pantyffordd
Llanfynydd
Ffrith
Leeswood
Pontybodkin
Pontblyddyn
Nercwys
Maeshafn
Moel Findeg
Gwernymynydd
Cadole
Gwernaffield
Cilcain
Moel Famau 554
Loggerheads
Tafarn-y-Gelyn
Llanferres
Hirwaen
Llangynhafal
Llangwyfan
Moel Llys-y-coed 465
Moel y Parc 398
CLWYDIAN RANGE
VALE OF CLWYD
Llandyrnog
Waen
Ffordd-las
Llanynys
Llanrhaeadr
Rhewl
Llanbedr-Dyffryn-Clwyd
Ruthin (Rhuthun)
Ruthin Craft Centre
Llanfwrog
Bontuchel
Efenechtyd
Llanfair Dyffryn Clwyd
DENBIGHSHIRE
Friary (ruins)
Plas Teg
Waun-y-Llyn
Hawarden
Ewloe (ruins)
Brynford
M56
M53
A5026
A5119
A548
A55
A541
A543
A525
A494
A550
A549
A5118
A5104
A483
A534
A5152
A528
A539
A5
A495
A490
B4393
B4396
B4391
B4580
B4500
B4579
B4398
B4397
B5069
B5070
B5009
B5130
B5426
B5102
B5101
B5430
B5431
B5429
B5373
B5445
B5125
B5129
B5123
B4401
B5437
B5605
B5097
B5433
B4336
B4396

A
B
C
D
1
2
3
4
5
91
77
64
Burton
Ledsham
Little Stanney
Thornton-le-Moors
Hapsford
Alvanley
Kingsley
Crowton
Weaverham
NORTH
Puddington
Capenhurst
Stoak
Dunham-on-the-Hill
DELAMERE
Shotwick
Backford
Wervin
Hatchmere
Norley
Cuddington
Sandiway
Connah's Quay
Saughall
Picton
Bridge Trafford
Manley
Mouldsworth
Vale Royal
Mollington
Delamere Sta
Whitegate
Wepre
Garden City
Sealand
Upton
Mickle Trafford
Ashton
FOREST PARK
Blakemere Craft Cen
Northop Hall
Shotton
Queensferry
Blacon
Great Barrow
Eddisbury Hill
Delamere
Foxwist Green
Ewloe (ruins)
Guilden Sutton
Aston
Mancot Royal
Sandycroft
Cathedral
Hoole
Roman Road
Tarvin
Kelsall
Willington Corner
Salterswall
Ewloe
Littleton
Tarvin Sands
Oscroft
Hawarden
FLINTSHIRE
CHESTER
Christleton
Little Budworth Common
Buckley
Hawarden
Saltney
Handbridge
Rowton
Quarrybank
Cotebrook
Little Budworth
Hebden Green
Prenbrigog
Bretton
Waverton
Duddon
Clotton
Oulton Park
Rushton
Llong
Broughton
Rowton Heath 1645
Burton
Eaton
Padeswood
Penyffordd
Lower Kinnerton
Eccleston
Hargrave
Tarporley
CHESHIRE
Rhos-y-brwyner
Eaton Hall
Saighton
Hatton Heath
Birch Heath
Wettenhall
Dodleston
Huxley
Tilstone Fearnall
Cuckoo's Nest
Bruera
Tiverton
Plas Teg
Gatesheath
Cheshire Farm Ice Cream
Newton
Beeston (ruins)
Alpraham
Calveley
Hope
Pulford
Aldford
Milton Green
Beeston
Waun-y-Llyn
Burton Green
Lavister
Tattenhall
Newtown
Peckforton
Bunbury
Caergwrle
Rossett
Handley
Cheshire Candle Workshops
Spurstow
Aston Mon
Llanfynydd
Cefn-y-bedd
Trevalyn
Aldersey Green
Peckforton Hills
Ffrith
Llay
Alun
Churton
Chowley
Burwardsley
Wardle
Haughton Moss
Marford
Coddington
Harthill
Farndon
Summerhill
Gresford
Barton
Broxton
Fuller's Moor
Bulkeley
Burland
Brymbo
Gwersyllt
Borras Head
Clutton
Bickerton Hill
Gallantry Bank
Croxton Green
Moss
Crewe
Holt
Bryn Teg
Llan-y-pwll
Stretton
Bickerton
Egerton Green
Faddiley
Acton
Coedpoeth
Southsea
Rhos-ddu
Hugmore
Duckington
Larden Green
Nantwich 1644
New Broughton
Rhosnesni
Ridleywood
Tilston
Cholmondeley Castle
Chorley
WREXHAM (Wrecsam)
Wrexham Industrial Estate
Ravensmoor
Shocklach
Hampton Heath
Bickley Town
Rhostyllen
Pentre Maelor
Horton Green
Chorlton Lane
Bickley Moss
Talwrn
Erddig Hall (NT)
Marchwiel
Bowling Bank
Malpas
No Man's Heath
Wrenbury
Rhosllanerchrugog
Johnstown
Stryt-yr-hwch
Cross Lanes
Cuddington Heath
Norbury
Aston
Stryt-issa
Pant
Worthenbury
Marbury
Marley Green
Newhall
Acrefair
Gyfelia
Eyton
Bangor-is-y-coed
Threapwood
Oldcastle Heath
Wat's Dyke
Bangor-on-Dee
Tallarn Green
Wirswall
Ruabon
Halghton Mill
Higher Wych
Burleydam
Trevor
WREXHAM
Cefn-mawr
Newbridge
Wynnstay Park
Overton
WHITCHURCH
Erbistock
Horseman's Green
Broughall
Pentre
Shellbrook Hill
Sodylt Bank
Lightwood Green
Eglwys Cross
The Chequer
Edgeley
Wilkes
Halton
Penley
Hanmer
Alkington
Park Lane
Street Dinas
Knolton
Trench
Arowry
Bronington
Ash Magna
Chirk
Rhyn
Dudleston Heath
Gredington
Ightfield
Gledrid
Ifton Heath
Fenn's Moss
Tilstock
Calverhall
Preesgweene
St Martin's
The Grange
Platt Lane
Prees Higher Heath
Hollinwood
Elson
Welshampton
Bettisfield
Welsh End
Roman Road
Moreton Say
Rhewl
New Marton
Ellesmere
The Mere
Llangollen Canal
Millenheath
Gobowen
Perthy
Whixall
Prees
Prees Sta.
Hengoed
Tetchill
Northwood
Quina Brook
Darliston
Bletchley
Hindford
Welsh Frankton
Lyneal
Lee
White Mere
Colemere
Fauls
Old Oswestry Hill Fort
Paddolgreen
Newtown
Prees Green
Ternhill
Brogyntyn
Whittington
Hordley
Crose Mere
Wolverley
Edstaston
Babbinswood
Transport Museum
Kenwick
English Frankton
Wollerton
Oswestry
Middleton
Rednal
Lower Hordley
Cockshutt
Loppington
Wem
Aston
Marchamley
Hodnet
Hodnet Hall
Morda
Haughton
Bagley
Tilley
Weston
Bury Walls
SHROPSHIRE
Trefonen
Ball
Queen's Head
Grimpo
Noneley
Lee Brockhurst
Hopton
Petton
Burlton
Maesbury Marsh
West Felton
Weston Lullingfields
Preston Brockhurst
Besford
Booley
Morton
Wykey
Stanton upon Hine Heath
Llynclys
Woolston
Eardiston
Stanwardine in the Fields
Myddlewood
Alderton
Clive
High Hatton
Weirbrook
Myddle
Yorton
Grinshill
Moreton Corbet
Crickheath
Knockin
Montgomery Canal
Ruyton-XI-Towns
Baschurch
Harmer Hill
Merrington
Pant
Maesbrook
Dovaston
Kinnerley
Milford
Prescott
Shawbury
Ellerdine Heath
Edgebolton
Little Ness
Walford
Old Woods
Preston Gubbals
Hadnall
Muckleton
Llandysilio
Domgay
Crosslanes
Kinton
Nesscliffe
Yeaton
Grafton
Bomere Heath
Astley
Great Wytheford
Rowton
Edgerley
Wilcott
Great Ness
Osbaston
Walton
Melverley Green
Pentre
Felton Butler
Albrighton
Poynton
Llandrinio
Shrewsbury 1403
The Isle
Haughton
Roden
High Ercall
Melverley
Ensdon
Forton
Montford Bridge
Battlefield
Long Waste
Arddlin
Shrawardine
Haughmond Abbey

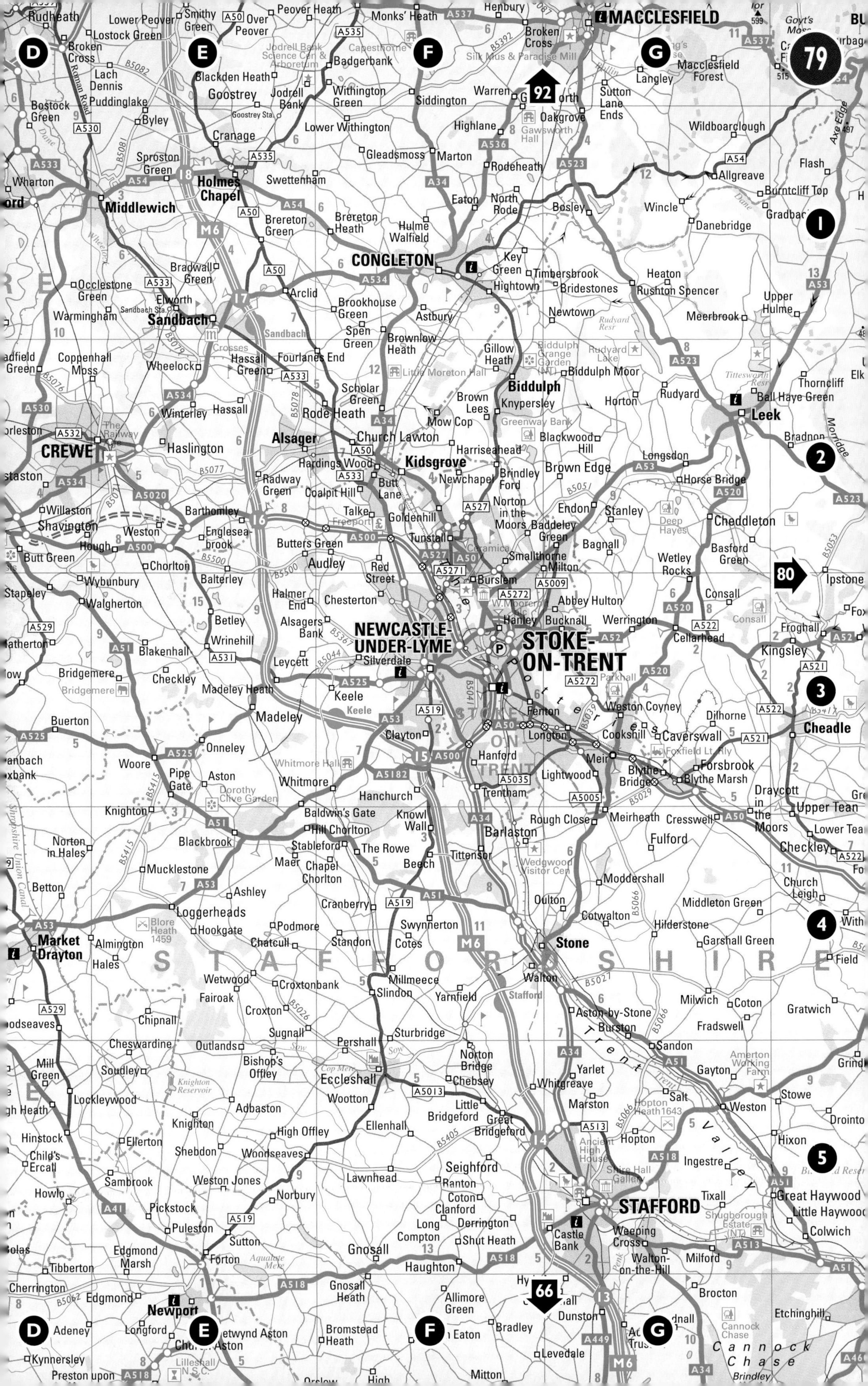

MACCLESFIELD
CONGLETON
Holmes Chapel
Middlewich
Sandbach
CREWE
Alsager
Kidsgrove
Biddulph
Leek
NEWCASTLE-UNDER-LYME
STOKE-ON-TRENT
Cheadle
Market Drayton
Stone
Eccleshall
STAFFORD
Newport
STAFFORDSHIRE
Rudheath
Lower Peover
Smithy Green
Over Peover
Peover Heath
Monks' Heath
Henbury
Broken Cross
Lostock Green
Jodrell Bank Science Cen & Arboretum
Capesthorne
Badgerbank
Silk Mus & Paradise Mill
Langley
Macclesfield Forest
Lach Dennis
Blackden Heath
Goostrey
Jodrell Bank
Withington Green
Siddington
Warren
Oakgrove
Sutton Lane Ends
Bostock Green
Puddinglake
Byley
Cranage
Lower Withington
Highlane
Gawsworth Hall
Wildboarclough
Gleadsmoss
Marton
Rodeheath
Flash
Sproston Green
Wharton
Swettenham
Allgreave
Burntcliff Top
Brereton Green
Brereton Heath
Eaton
North Rode
Bosley
Wincle
Gradbach
Danebridge
Hulme Walfield
Bradwall Green
Key Green
Timbersbrook
Hightown
Bridestones
Heaton
Rushton Spencer
Occlestone Green
Elworth
Arclid
Brookhouse Green
Astbury
Newtown
Upper Hulme
Warmingham
Meerbrook
Spen Green
Brownlow Heath
Gillow Heath
Biddulph Grange Garden
Rudyard Lake
Coppenhall Moss
Wheelock
Hassall Green
Fourlanes End
Little Moreton Hall
Biddulph Moor
Tittesworth Resr
Thorncliff
Scholar Green
Rudyard
Horton
Ball Haye Green
Winterley
Hassall
Rode Heath
Brown Lees
Knypersley
Mow Cop
Haslington
Church Lawton
Greenway Bank
Blackwood Hill
Harriseahead
Bradnop
Hardings Wood
Brindley Ford
Brown Edge
Longsdon
Radway Green
Coalpit Hill
Butt Lane
Newchapel
Horse Bridge
Norton in the Moors
Willaston
Shavington
Barthomley
Talke
Goldenhill
Endon
Stanley
Cheddleton
Weston
Englesea-brook
Baddeley Green
Deep Hayes
Hough
Butters Green
Tunstall
Bagnall
Butt Green
Chorlton
Audley
Red Street
Smallthorne
Milton
Wetley Rocks
Basford Green
Ipstone
Wybunbury
Balterley
Burslem
Stapeley
Halmer End
Chesterton
Abbey Hulton
Consall
Walgherton
Betley
Alsagers Bank
Hanley
Bucknall
Werrington
Cellarhead
Froghall
Wrinehill
Blakenhall
Leycett
Silverdale
Kingsley
Bridgemere
Checkley
Madeley Heath
Keele
Parkhall
Weston Coyney
Dilhorne
Madeley
Fenton
Buerton
Clayton
Longton
Cookshill
Caverswall
Onneley
Foxfield Lt Rly
Forsbrook
Woore
Pipe Gate
Aston
Dorothy Clive Garden
Whitmore Hall
Whitmore
Hanford
Trentham
Lightwood
Meir
Blythe Bridge
Blythe Marsh
Draycott in the Moors
Upper Tean
Knighton
Hanchurch
Baldwin's Gate
Knowl Wall
Rough Close
Meirheath
Cresswell
Lower Tean
Norton in Hales
Blackbrook
Hill Chorlton
Barlaston
Fulford
Checkley
Stableford
The Rowe
Maer
Chapel Chorlton
Beech
Tittensor
Wedgwood Visitor Cen
Mucklestone
Betton
Ashley
Moddershall
Church Leigh
Cranberry
Oulton
Middleton Green
Loggerheads
Blore Heath 1459
Hookgate
Podmore
Swynnerton
Cotwalton
Hilderstone
Almington
Chatcull
Standon
Cotes
Garshall Green
Hales
Wetwood
Millmeece
Walton
Fairoak
Croxtonbank
Slindon
Yarnfield
Milwich
Coton
Gratwich
Croxton
Aston-by-Stone
Burston
Chipnall
Sugnall
Sturbridge
Fradswell
Cheswardine
Outlands
Pershall
Sandon
Bishop's Offley
Norton Bridge
Amerton Working Farm
Mill Green
Soudley
Knighton Reservoir
Chebsey
Yarlet
Gayton
Lockleywood
Wootton
Whitgreave
Salt
Stowe
Adbaston
Little Bridgeford
Marston
Hopton Heath 1643
Weston
Knighton
Great Bridgeford
Hinstock
Ellerton
High Offley
Ellenhall
Hopton
Hixon
Drointon
Child's Ercall
Shebdon
Woodseaves
Ancient High House
Ingestre
Seighford
Shire Hall Gallery
Sambrook
Weston Jones
Lawnhead
Ranton
Howle
Norbury
Coton Clanford
Tixall
Great Haywood
Little Haywood
Pickstock
Shugborough Estate (NT)
Colwich
Puleston
Long Compton
Derrington
Sutton
Shut Heath
Castle Bank
Weeping Cross
Edgmond Marsh
Gnosall
Walton-on-the-Hill
Milford
Forton
Aqualate Mere
Tibberton
Haughton
Brocton
Cherrington
Gnosall Heath
Edgmond
Allimore Green
Dunston
Etchinghill
Newport
Adeney
Longford
Chetwynd Aston
Church Aston
Bromstead Heath
Bradley
Cannock Chase
Kynnersley
Lilleshall N.S.C.
Levedale
Preston upon
High
Mitton
Brindley
Trent
Trent Valley
Shropshire Union Canal
92
80
66

80
MACCLESFIELD
BUXTON
93
A
B
C
D
CHESHIRE
PEAK
DISTRICT
NATIONAL
PARK
STAFFORDSHIRE
STOKE-ON-TRENT
Leek
Cheadle
Uttoxeter
Ashbourne
Stone
STAFFORD
BURTON UPON TRENT
RUGELEY
79
66
1
2
3
4
5
Henbury
Broken Cross
Paradise Mill
Warren
Gawsworth
Gawsworth Hall
Oakgrove
Highlane
Rodeheath
Eaton
North Rode
Bosley
Key Green
Timbersbrook
Hightown
Bridestones
Newtown
Gillow Heath
Biddulph Grange Garden (NT)
Biddulph
Biddulph Moor
Brown Lees
Knypersley
Greenway Bank
Blackwood Hill
Brown Edge
Brindley Ford
Norton in the Moors
Baddeley Green
Endon
Stanley
Bagnall
Milton
Burslem
Abbey Hulton
Hanley
Bucknall
Werrington
Fenton
Longton
Weston Coyney
Meir
Cookshill
Caverswall
Foxfield Lt Rly
Blythe Bridge
Blythe Marsh
Forsbrook
Dilhorne
Hanford
Lightwood
Trentham
Rough Close
Meirheath
Barlaston
Wedgwood Visitor Cen
Tittensor
Moddershall
Oulton
Cotwalton
Hilderstone
Walton
Aston-by-Stone
Burston
Sandon
Norton Bridge
Yarlet
Chebsey
Whitgreave
Marston
Little Bridgeford
Great Bridgeford
Hopton
Ancient High House
Shire Hall Gallery
Derrington
Castle Bank
Shut Heath
Weeping Cross
Walton-on-the-Hill
Milford
Hyde Lea
Coppenhall
Dunston
Bradley
Levedale
Mitton
Brocton
Cannock Chase
Langley
Macclesfield Forest
Sutton Lane Ends
Wildboarclough
Allgreave
Wincle
Danebridge
Heaton
Rushton Spencer
Meerbrook
Rudyard
Horton
Longsdon
Horse Bridge
Cheddleton
Deep Hayes
Basford Green
Wetley Rocks
Consall
Cellarhead
Kingsley
Froghall
Goyt's Moss
Cat and Fiddle Inn
Burbage
Flash
Burntcliff Top
Gradbach
Upper Hulme
Tittesworth Resr
Thorncliff
Ball Haye Green
Bradnop
Morridge
Onecote
Butterton
Winkhill
Ipstones
Foxt
Whiston
Near Cotton
Harpur Hill
Axe Edge
Hollinsclough
Longnor
Fawfieldhead
Newtown
Upper Elkstone
Warslow
Pilsbury
Sheen
Brund
Hartington
Hulme End
Ecton
Wetton
Alstonefield
Grindon
Thor's Cave
Waterfall
Waterhouses
Calton
Cauldon
Ilam
Thorpe
Blore
Swinscoe
Mapleton
Fairfield
Micrarium
Wormhill
Miller's Dale
King Sterndale
Blackwell
Taddington
Chelmorton
Flagg
Earl Sterndale
Crowdecote
Monyash
Sheldon
Little Longstone
Great Longstone
Rowland
Ashford in the Water
Bakewell
Over Haddon
Youlgreave
Alport
Arbor Low Stone Circle & Gib Hill Barrow
Nine Ladies Stone Circle
Middleton
Elton
Winster
Heathcote
Biggin
Pikehall
Market House (NT)
Grangemill
Aldwark
Longcliffe
Alsop en le Dale
Ballidon
Brassington
Parwich
Bradbourne
Tissington
Fenny Bentley
Kniveton
Atlow
Dove Dale
Hanging Bridge
Mayfield
Stanton
Weaver Hills
Ramshorn
Oakamoor
Farley
Alton Towers Leisure Park
Alton
Wootton
Ellastone
Snelston
Clifton
Osmaston
Edlaston
Wyaston
Norbury
Roston
Denstone
Croxden Abbey
Croxden
Bradley in the Moors
Greatgate
Upper Tean
Lower Tean
Draycott in the Moors
Cresswell
Fulford
Checkley
Hollington
Rocester
Marston Montgomery
Great Cubley
Little Cubley
Alkmonton
Longford
Yeaveley
Rodsley
Shirley
Beamhurst
Stramshall
Fole
Church Leigh
Middleton Green
Withington
Garshall Green
Field
Waldley
Somersal Herbert
Doveridge
Bramshall
Blount's Green
Sudbury
Sudbury Hall (NT)
Foston
Scropton
Marchington
Hatton
Tutbury
Coton in the Clay
Draycott in the Clay
Hanbury
Hanbury Woodend
Marchington Woodlands
Kingstone
Grindley
Bagot's Park
Abbots Bromley
Newborough
Needwood Forest
Anslow
Anslow Gate
Horninglow
Hoar Cross
Hoar Cross Hall
Rangemore
Tatenhill
Dunstall
Branston
Barton-under-Needwood
Yoxall
Hadley End
Hamstall Ridware
Hill Ridware
Pipe Ridware
Mavesyn Ridware
Morrey
Woodhouses
King's Bromley
Orgreave
Handsacre
Armitage
Brereton
Blithbury
Colton
Admaston
Newton
Blithfield Reservoir
Gratwich
Milwich
Coton
Fradswell
Gayton
Amerton Working Farm
Stowe
Drointon
Hixon
Weston
Salt
Hopton Heath 1643
Ingestre
Tixall
Great Haywood
Little Haywood
Shugborough Estate (NT)
Colwich
Trent Valley
Church Broughton
Sutton on the Hill
Boylestone
Longford
Thurvaston
Hollington
Ednaston
Commonside
Hulland
Bradley
Roslisto
Catton Hall
Walton-on-Trent
M6
A50
A52
A53
A54
A515
A523
A520
A521
A522
A518
A51
A513
A34
A6
A5012
B5053
B5032
B5017
Weaver Hills

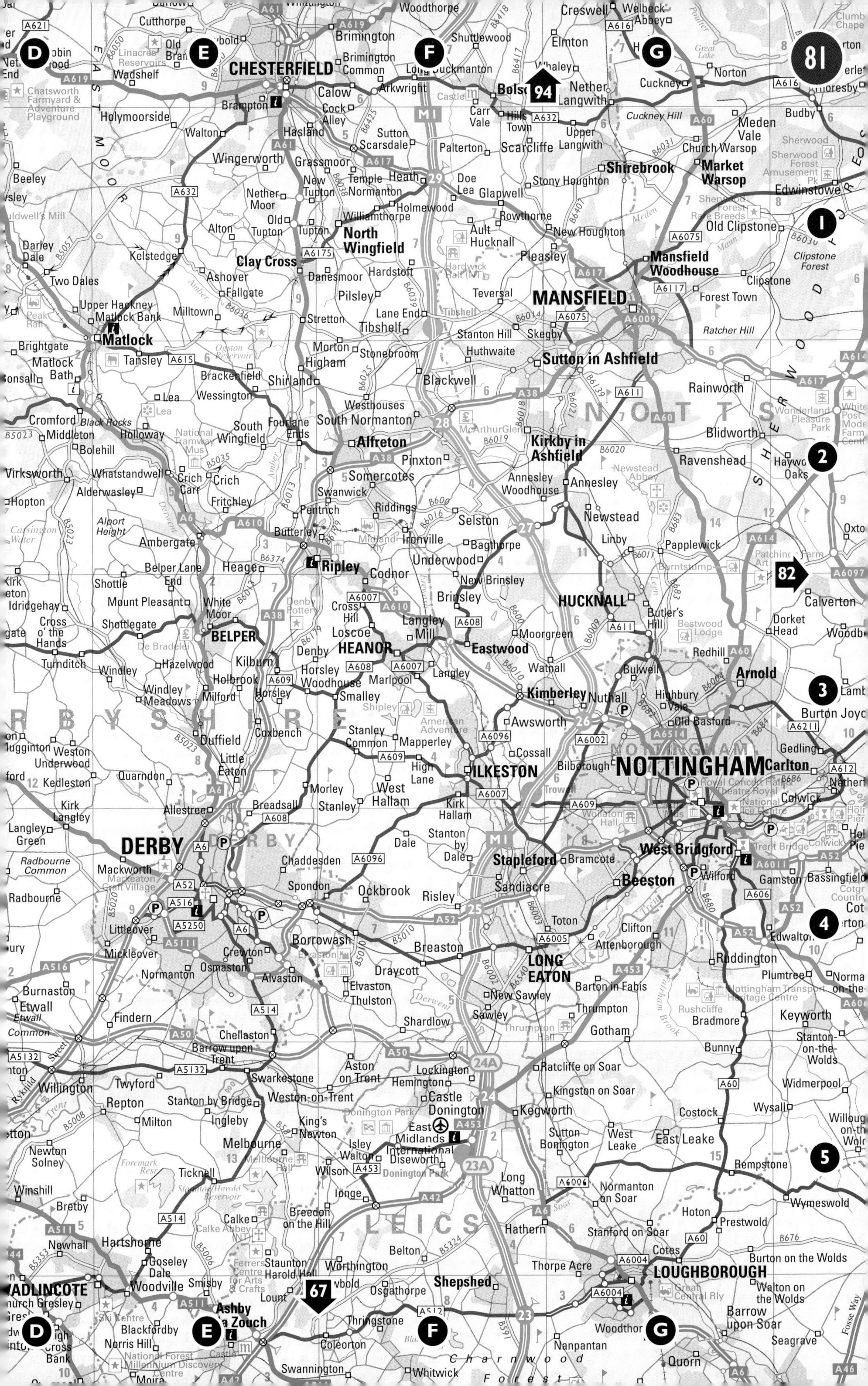

94
82
67
D
E
F
G
I
2
3
4
5
CHESTERFIELD
MANSFIELD
NOTTINGHAM
DERBY
LOUGHBOROUGH
Cutthorpe
Old Brampton
Linacre Reservoirs
Wadshelf
Chatsworth Farmyard & Adventure Playground
Holymoorside
Brampton
Walton
Brimington
Brimington Common
Woodthorpe
Calow
Cock Alley
Hasland
Arkwright
Long Duckmanton
Shuttlewood
Bolsover
Carr Vale
Hills Town
Sutton Scarsdale
Palterton
Scarcliffe
Creswell
Welbeck Abbey
Elmton
Whaley
Nether Langwith
Upper Langwith
Cuckney
Cuckney Hill
Norton
Budby
Meden Vale
Church Warsop
Market Warsop
Sherwood
Sherwood Forest Amusement Pk
Edwinstowe
Sherwood Forest Rare Breeds
Old Clipstone
Clipstone Forest
Clipstone
Forest Town
Ratcher Hill
Shirebrook
Stony Houghton
Glapwell
Doe Lea
Heath
Temple Normanton
Holmewood
Williamthorpe
Grassmoor
Wingerworth
New Tupton
Nether Moor
Old Tupton
Tupton
North Wingfield
Clay Cross
Danesmoor
Hardstoft
Pilsley
Ault Hucknall
Hardwick Hall
Rowthorne
New Houghton
Pleasley
Mansfield Woodhouse
Teversal
Tibshelf
Lane End
Stanton Hill
Skegby
Sutton in Ashfield
Huthwaite
Blackwell
Stretton
Morton
Higham
Shirland
Stonebroom
Westhouses
South Normanton
Alfreton
Pinxton
Kirkby in Ashfield
Annesley
Annesley Woodhouse
Newstead
Newstead Abbey
Rainworth
Blidworth
Ravenshead
Haywood Oaks
Wonderland Pleasure Park
Papplewick
Linby
Hucknall
Calverton
Dorket Head
Arnold
Redhill
Bestwood Lodge
Butler's Hill
Bulwell
Highbury Vale
Old Basford
Nuthall
Kimberley
Awsworth
Watnall
Moorgreen
Eastwood
Brinsley
New Brinsley
Underwood
Bagthorpe
Selston
Ironville
Riddings
Somercotes
Swanwick
Pentrich
Butterley
Ripley
Codnor
Langley Mill
Heanor
Loscoe
Cross Hill
Denby
Denby Pottery
Kilburn
Belper
Heage
Ambergate
Crich
Fritchley
South Wingfield
Fourlane Ends
Wessington
Brackenfield
Ogston Reservoir
Milltown
Ashover
Fallgate
Kelstedge
Upper Hackney
Matlock Bank
Matlock
Two Dales
Darley Dale
Beeley
Tansley
Lea
Holloway
Cromford
Middleton
Bolehill
Black Rocks
Wirksworth
Whatstandwell
Alderwasley
Hopton
Carsington Water
Alport Height
Shottle
Belper Lane End
Mount Pleasant
White Moor
Idridgehay
Cross o' the Hands
Shottlegate
Turnditch
Windley
Hazelwood
Holbrook
Milford
Duffield
Horsley
Horsley Woodhouse
Smalley
Marlpool
Langley
Shipley
American Adventure
Stanley Common
Mapperley
Coxbench
Little Eaton
Quarndon
Weston Underwood
Kedleston
Kirk Langley
Allestree
Breadsall
Morley
Stanley
West Hallam
High Lane
Ilkeston
Cossall
Kirk Hallam
Dale
Stanton by Dale
Stapleford
Sandiacre
Bramcote
Trowell
Bilborough
Wollaton Hall
Carlton
Gedling
Colwick
Netherfield
West Bridgford
Beeston
Wilford
Gamston
Bassingfield
Edwalton
Ruddington
Clifton
Attenborough
Toton
Long Eaton
Barton in Fabis
Thrumpton
Gotham
Bunny
Bradmore
Keyworth
Plumtree
Stanton-on-the-Wolds
Widmerpool
Wysall
Costock
East Leake
West Leake
Rempstone
Wymeswold
Hoton
Prestwold
Burton on the Wolds
Walton on the Wolds
Barrow upon Soar
Seagrave
Quorn
Woodthorpe
Nanpantan
Thorpe Acre
Cotes
Stanford on Soar
Normanton on Soar
Hathern
Long Whatton
Kegworth
Sutton Bonington
Kingston on Soar
Ratcliffe on Soar
East Midlands International
Castle Donington
Donington Park
Lockington
Hemington
Diseworth
Isley Walton
Wilson
Tonge
Breedon on the Hill
Belton
Shepshed
Osgathorpe
Thringstone
Coleorton
Whitwick
Charnwood Forest
Worthington
Staunton Harold Hall
Staunton Harold Reservoir
Melbourne
Melbourne Hall
King's Newton
Weston-on-Trent
Aston on Trent
Swarkestone
Barrow upon Trent
Chellaston
Stanton by Bridge
Ingleby
Ticknall
Calke Abbey
Ferrers Centre for Arts & Crafts
Smisby
Ashby de la Zouch
Lount
Norris Hill
Blackfordby
Woodville
Goseley Dale
Hartshorne
Newhall
Bretby
Winshill
Newton Solney
Repton
Milton
Twyford
Willington
Findern
Etwall
Burnaston
Mickleover
Littleover
Radbourne
Radbourne Common
Mackworth
Markeaton Craft Village
Langley Green
Normanton
Osmaston
Crewton
Alvaston
Borrowash
Elvaston
Elvaston Castle
Thulston
Spondon
Ockbrook
Chaddesden
Risley
Breaston
Draycott
Shardlow
Sawley
New Sawley
Swadlincote
Church Gresley
Moira
Swannington
NOTTS
LEICS
DERBYSHIRE
EAST MOOR
SHERWOOD FOREST

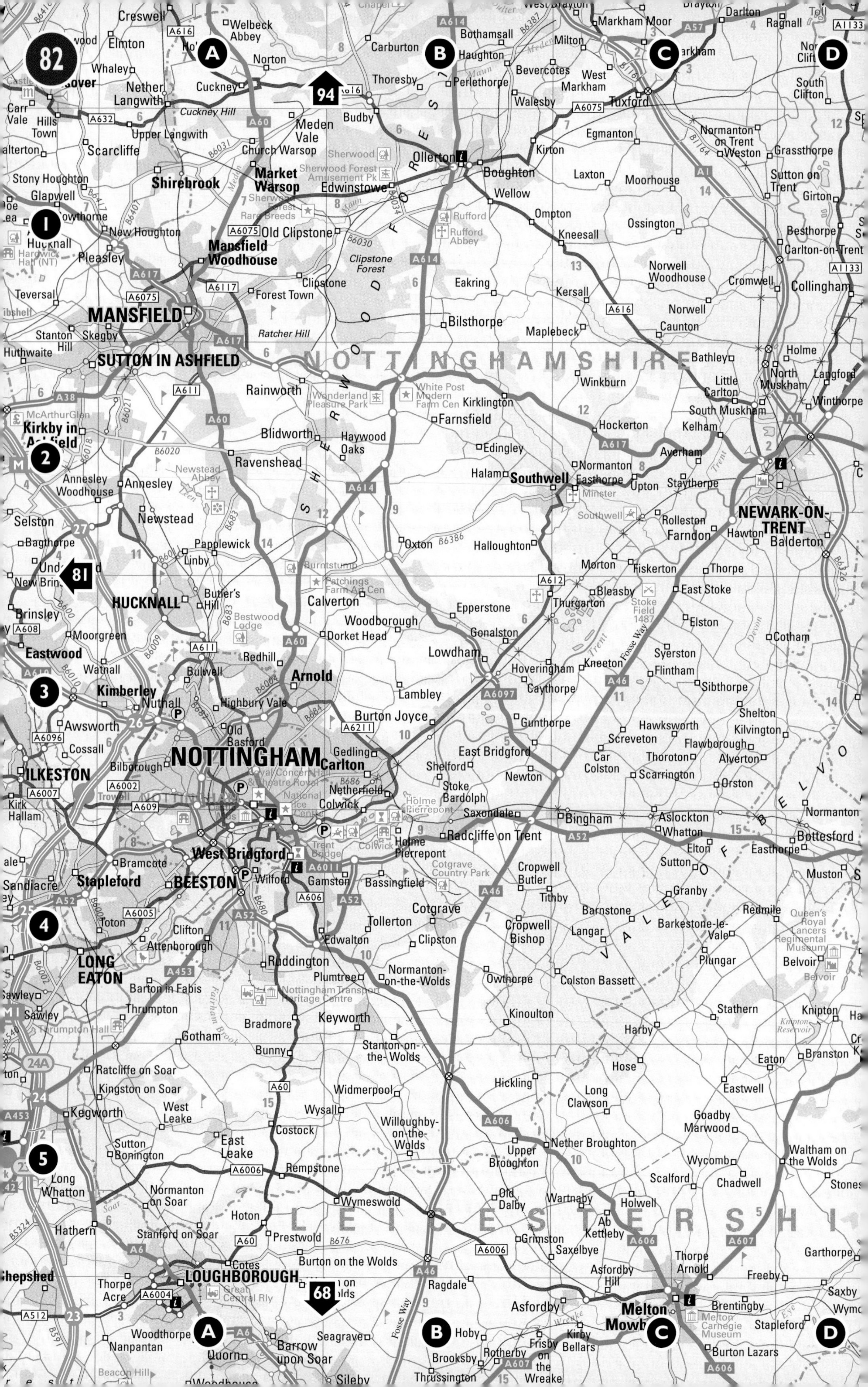

82
Creswell
Welbeck Abbey
Elmton
Whaley
Norton
Carburton
Bothamsall
Haughton
Markham Moor
Milton
Darlton
Ragnall
Dunham
Nether Langwith
Cuckney
Cuckney Hill
94
Thoresby
Perlethorpe
Beverotes
West Markham
Markham
Tuxford
South Clifton
Carr Vale
Hills Town
Upper Langwith
Meden Vale
Budby
Walesby
Egmanton
Normanton on Trent
Weston
Grassthorpe
Scarcliffe
Church Warsop
Sherwood
Sherwood Forest Amusement Pk
Ollerton
Boughton
Kirton
Laxton
Moorhouse
Sutton on Trent
Stony Houghton
Shirebrook
Market Warsop
Edwinstowe
Wellow
Girton
Glapwell
Sherwood Forest Rare Breeds
Rufford
Rufford Abbey
Ompton
Ossington
Besthorpe
Rowthorne
Ault Hucknall
Hardwick Hall (NT)
New Houghton
Pleasley
Old Clipstone
Kneesall
Carlton-on-Trent
Mansfield Woodhouse
Clipstone Forest
Norwell Woodhouse
Cromwell
Collingham
Teversall
Clipstone
Forest Town
Eakring
Kersall
MANSFIELD
Bilsthorpe
Norwell
Caunton
Maplebeck
Stanton Hill
Skegby
Ratcher Hill
Huthwaite
SUTTON IN ASHFIELD
NOTTINGHAMSHIRE
Bathley
Holme
North Muskham
Langford
Winkburn
Little Carlton
Rainworth
Wonderland Pleasure Park
White Post Modern Farm Cen
Kirklington
South Muskham
Winthorpe
McArthurGlen
Farnsfield
Hockerton
Kelham
Kirkby in Ashfield
Blidworth
Haywood Oaks
Edingley
Averham
Annesley Woodhouse
Annesley
Ravenshead
Newstead Abbey
Normanton
Eakring
Halam
Southwell
Easthorpe
Minster
Upton
Staythorpe
Newstead
Southwell
Rolleston
NEWARK-ON-TRENT
Selston
Farndon
Hawton
Balderton
Bagthorpe
Papplewick
Oxton
Halloughton
Underwood
81
Linby
Burntstump
Morton
Fiskerton
Thorpe
New Brinsley
Patchings Farm Art Cen
Bleasby
East Stoke
Brinsley
HUCKNALL
Butler's Hill
Calverton
Epperstone
Thurgarton
Stoke Field 1487
Bestwood Lodge
Woodborough
Elston
Moorgreen
Dorket Head
Gonalston
Cotham
Eastwood
Lowdham
Syerston
Redhill
Watnall
Bulwell
Arnold
Hoveringham
Kneeton
Flintham
Kimberley
Caythorpe
Sibthorpe
Nuthall
Highbury Vale
Lambley
Awsworth
Burton Joyce
Gunthorpe
Shelton
Old Basford
Hawksworth
Kilvington
Cossall
Screveton
Flawborough
Gedling
East Bridgford
Car Colston
Thoroton
Alverton
Bilborough
NOTTINGHAM
Carlton
Shelford
Newton
Scarrington
Orston
ILKESTON
Royal Concert Hall & Theatre Royal
Netherfield
Stoke Bardolph
Kirk Hallam
Trowell
National Ice Centre
Colwick
Holme Pierrepont
Saxondale
Bingham
Aslockton
Normanton
Whatton
Bottesford
Radcliffe on Trent
Elton
Easthorpe
Dale
Holme Pierrepont
West Bridgford
Trent Bridge
Colwick
Cotgrave Country Park
Cropwell Butler
Bramcote
Sutton
Muston
Sandiacre
Stapleford
BEESTON
Wilford
Gamston
Bassingfield
Tithby
Granby
Toton
Cotgrave
Barnstone
Redmile
Queen's Royal Lancers Regimental Museum
Clifton
Tollerton
Cropwell Bishop
Langar
Barkestone-le-Vale
Attenborough
Edwalton
Clipston
VALE OF BELVOIR
LONG EATON
Ruddington
Normanton-on-the-Wolds
Plungar
Belvoir
Plumtree
Owthorpe
Colston Bassett
Barton in Fabis
Nottingham Transport Heritage Centre
Sawley
Thrumpton
Stathern
Knipton
Thrumpton Hall
Keyworth
Kinoulton
Knipton Reservoir
Bradmore
Harby
Gotham
Stanton-on-the-Wolds
Eaton
Branston
Bunny
Hose
Ratcliffe on Soar
Hickling
Kingston on Soar
Widmerpool
Long Clawson
Eastwell
West Leake
Kegworth
Wysall
Willoughby-on-the-Wolds
Goadby Marwood
Costock
Sutton Bonington
East Leake
Nether Broughton
Upper Broughton
Wycomb
Waltham on the Wolds
Rempstone
Long Whatton
Scalford
Chadwell
Normanton on Soar
Old Dalby
Wartnaby
Holwell
Stonesby
Wymeswold
Hoton
LEICESTERSHIRE
Ab Kettleby
Hathern
Stanford on Soar
Prestwold
Grimston
Saxelbye
Thorpe Arnold
Garthorpe
Cotes
Burton on the Wolds
Asfordby Hill
Freeby
Shepshed
LOUGHBOROUGH
68
Ragdale
Brentingby
Saxby
Thorpe Acre
Great Central Rly
Asfordby
Melton Mowbray
Melton Carnegie Museum
Stapleford
Woodthorpe
Fosse Way
Hoby
Kirby Bellars
Nanpantan
Barrow upon Soar
Seagrave
Frisby on the Wreake
Burton Lazars
Quorn
Brooksby
Rotherby
Beacon Hill
Woodhouse
Sileby
Thrussington
Wreake
Trent
Maun
Meden
Soar
Devon
Fairham Brook
A616
A614
A57
A1133
A632
A60
A6075
A1
A617
A6117
A6075
A38
A611
A6097
A612
A46
A6211
A608
A610
A6096
A6002
A6007
A609
A6011
A606
A52
A6005
A453
A6006
A6004
A6
A512
A607
B6417
B6407
B6031
B6030
B6034
B6387
B1164
B6021
B6018
B6020
B683
B6011
B6009
B6010
B6004
B684
B686
B680
B6002
B6540
B676
B5324
B591
B6386
B6326
M1
24A
24
25
26
27
23

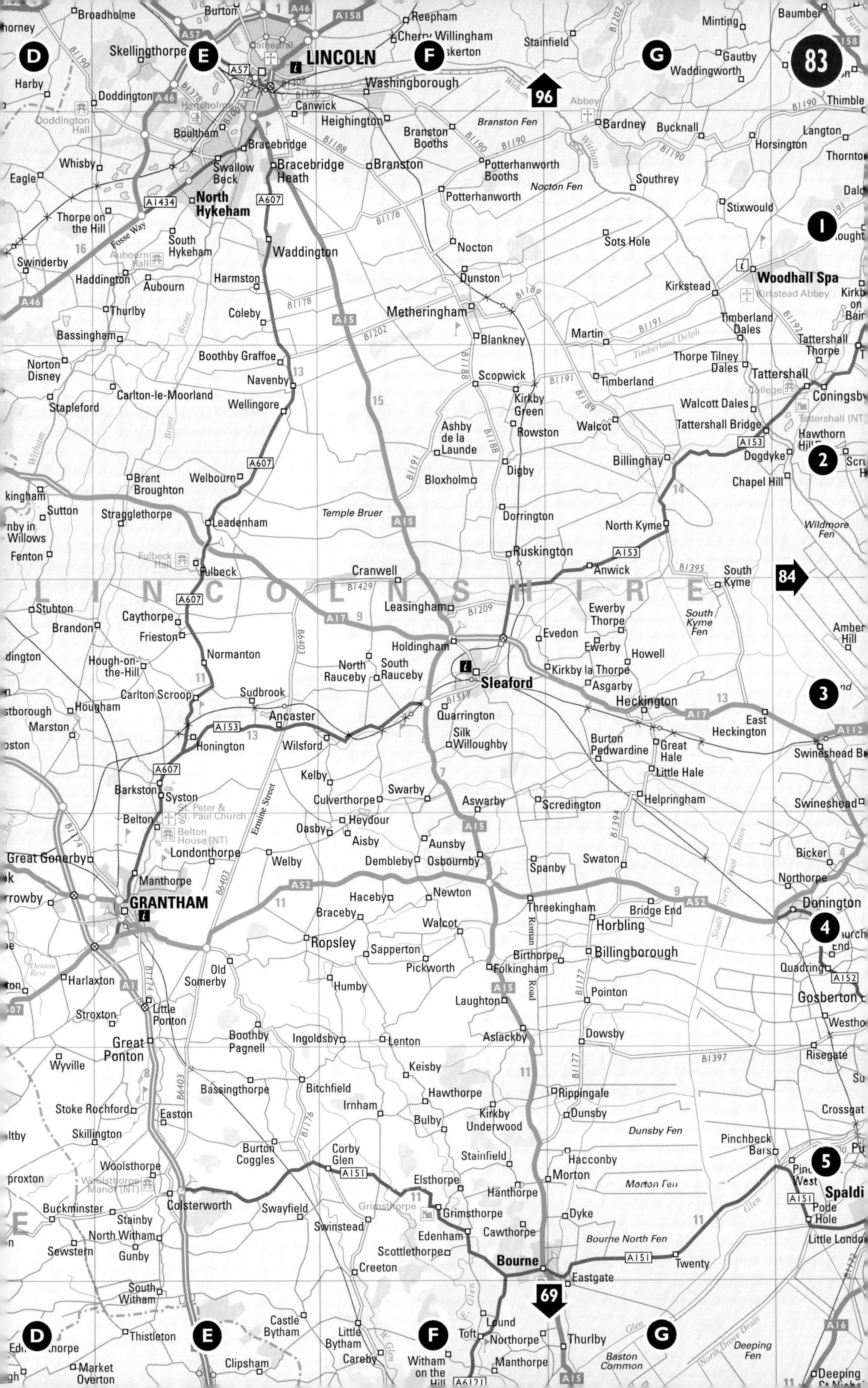
D
E
F
G
Broadholme
Burton
LINCOLN
Reepham
Cherry Willingham
Minting
Baumber
Skellingthorpe
Stainfield
Gautby
Waddingworth
Harby
Doddington
Washingborough
96
Thimble
Doddington Hall
Hartsholme
Canwick
Abbey
Boultham
Heighington
Branston Fen
Bardney
Bucknall
Langton
Whisby
Bracebridge
Branston Booths
Horsington
Thornton
Eagle
Swallow Beck
Bracebridge Heath
Branston
Potterhanworth Booths
Southrey
North Hykeham
Potterhanworth
Nocton Fen
Stixwould
Thorpe on the Hill
South Hykeham
Nocton
Sots Hole
I
Swinderby
Aubourn Hall
Waddington
Haddington
Aubourn
Harmston
Dunston
Kirkstead
Woodhall Spa
Kirkstead Abbey
Thurlby
Coleby
Metheringham
Timberland Dales
Bassingham
Blankney
Martin
Timberland Delph
Tattershall Thorpe
Norton Disney
Boothby Graffoe
Thorpe Tilney Dales
Tattershall
Navenby
Scopwick
Timberland
Coningsby
Carlton-le-Moorland
Kirkby Green
College
Stapleford
Wellingore
Walcott Dales
Tattershall (NT)
Ashby de la Launde
Rowston
Walcot
Tattershall Bridge
Hawthorn Hill
Dogdyke
2
Billinghay
Brant Broughton
Welbourn
Bloxholm
Digby
Chapel Hill
Sutton
Stragglethorpe
Temple Bruer
Dorrington
North Kyme
Wildmore Fen
Leadenham
Fenton
Fulbeck Hall
Fulbeck
Ruskington
Cranwell
Anwick
South Kyme
84
LINCOLNSHIRE
Stubton
Leasingham
Ewerby Thorpe
South Kyme Fen
Amber Hill
Brandon
Caythorpe
Frieston
Holdingham
Evedon
Ewerby
Howell
Normanton
North Rauceby
South Rauceby
Hough-on-the-Hill
Sleaford
Kirkby la Thorpe
Asgarby
Carlton Scroop
Sudbrook
Quarrington
Heckington
3
Hougham
Ancaster
Silk Willoughby
East Heckington
Marston
Honington
Wilsford
Burton Pedwardine
Great Hale
Swineshead Bridge
Little Hale
Kelby
Barkston
Syston
Swarby
Culverthorpe
Aswarby
Scredington
Helpringham
Swineshead
St. Peter & St. Paul Church
Belton
Heydour
Belton House (NT)
Oasby
Aisby
Ermine Street
Aunsby
Bicker
Great Gonerby
Londonthorpe
Welby
Dembleby
Osbournby
Spanby
Swaton
Northorpe
Manthorpe
Newton
Haceby
Donington
GRANTHAM
Braceby
Threekingham
Bridge End
4
Walcot
Horbling
Sapperton
Ropsley
Birthorpe
Billingborough
Denton Resr
Harlaxton
Old Somerby
Pickworth
Folkingham
Quadring
Humby
Pointon
Gosberton
Stroxton
Little Ponton
Laughton
Westhorpe
Great Ponton
Boothby Pagnell
Ingoldsby
Lenton
Aslackby
Dowsby
Risegate
Wyville
Keisby
Bassingthorpe
Bitchfield
Hawthorpe
Rippingale
Stoke Rochford
Easton
Irnham
Kirkby Underwood
Dunsby
Crossgate
Skillington
Bulby
Dunsby Fen
Burton Coggles
Corby Glen
Pinchbeck Bars
5
Woolsthorpe
Stainfield
Hacconby
Pinchbeck West
Woolsthorpe Manor (NT)
Elsthorpe
Morton
Morton Fen
Colsterworth
Swayfield
Grimsthorpe
Hanthorpe
Spalding
Buckminster
Stainby
Swinstead
Grimsthorpe
Dyke
Pode Hole
North Witham
Edenham
Cawthorpe
Sewstern
Gunby
Scottlethorpe
Bourne North Fen
Little London
Creeton
Bourne
Twenty
South Witham
Eastgate
69
Castle Bytham
Lound
Thistleton
Little Bytham
Toft
Northorpe
Thurlby
Deeping Fen
Market Overton
Clipsham
Carby
Witham on the Hill
Manthorpe
Baston Common
North Drove Drain
Deeping
Fosse Way
Roman Road
A46
A57
A158
A1434
A607
A15
A153
A17
A52
A1
A151
A16
A6121
B1190
B1378
B1003
B1308
B1188
B1178
B1202
B1189
B1191
B1192
B1395
B1429
B1209
B6403
B1517
B1394
B1177
B1397
B1176
B1174

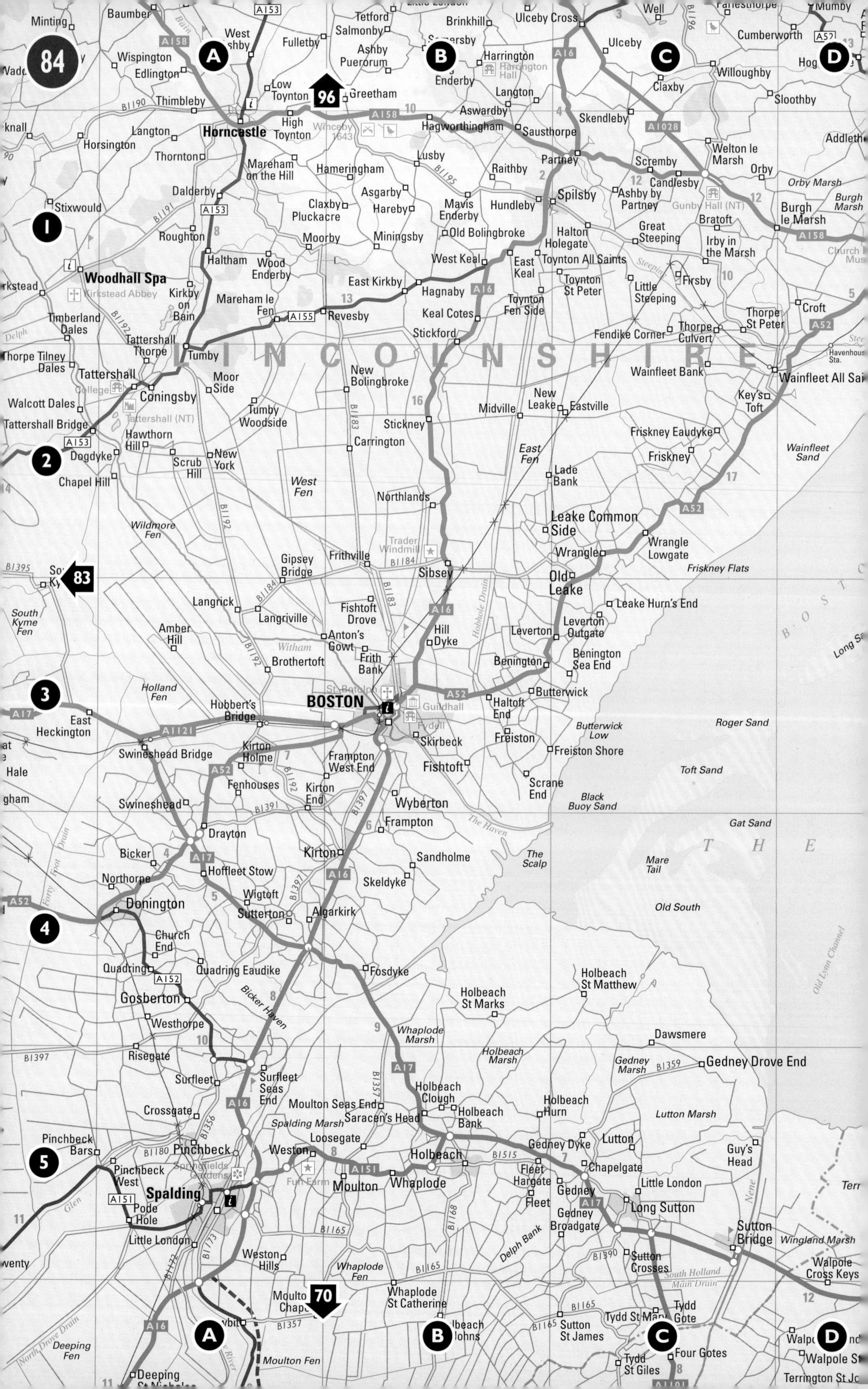

96
83
70
A
B
C
D
1
2
3
4
5
LINCOLNSHIRE
Minting
Baumber
A153
Tetford
Brinkhill
Ulceby Cross
Well
Mumby
West Ashby
Fulletby
Salmonby
Somersby
Ulceby
Cumberworth
A52
A158
Wispington
Edlington
Ashby Puerorum
Harrington
Harrington Hall
Enderby
Claxby
Willoughby
Hog
Low Toynton
Greetham
Langton
Sloothby
B1190
Thimbleby
High Toynton
Winceby 1643
A158
Aswardby
Skendleby
A1028
A16
Langton
Horsington
Horncastle
Hagworthingham
Sausthorpe
Welton le Marsh
Addleth
Thornton
Mareham on the Hill
Hameringham
Lusby
Raithby
Partney
Scremby
Orby
B1195
Candlesby
Orby Marsh
Dalderby
Asgarby
Spilsby
Ashby by Partney
Gunby Hall (NT)
Burgh le Marsh
Burgh Marsh
Stixwould
A153
Claxby Pluckacre
Hareby
Mavis Enderby
Hundleby
Bratoft
B1191
Old Bolingbroke
Halton Holegate
Great Steeping
Irby in the Marsh
A158
Roughton
Moorby
Miningsby
Church
Haltham
Wood Enderby
West Keal
East Keal
Toynton All Saints
Steeping
Firsby
Woodhall Spa
East Kirkby
Toynton St Peter
Little Steeping
Kirkstead
Kirkstead Abbey
Kirkby on Bain
Hagnaby
Mareham le Fen
Toynton Fen Side
Croft
Thorpe St Peter
Timberland Dales
B1192
A155
Revesby
Keal Cotes
Thorpe Culvert
Delph
Stickford
Fendike Corner
A52
Tattershall Thorpe
Havenhouse Sta.
Thorpe Tilney Dales
Tumby
Tattershall
Moor Side
New Bolingbroke
Wainfleet Bank
Wainfleet All Saints
College
Coningsby
Key's Toft
Walcott Dales
Tumby Woodside
New Leake
Eastville
Midville
Tattershall (NT)
Tattershall Bridge
A153
Hawthorn Hill
Stickney
Friskney Eaudyke
Dogdyke
New York
Carrington
East Fen
Friskney
Wainfleet Sand
Scrub Hill
Chapel Hill
West Fen
Lade Bank
B1183
Northlands
A52
Wildmore Fen
B1192
Leake Common Side
Trader Windmill
Wrangle
Wrangle Lowgate
Frithville
B1184
Gipsey Bridge
Sibsey
Friskney Flats
B1395
South Kyme
South Kyme Fen
Old Leake
Langrick
B1184
Fishtoft Drove
B1183
Leake Hurn's End
A16
Langriville
Hobhole Drain
Amber Hill
Hill Dyke
Leverton
Leverton Outgate
Witham
Anton's Gowt
Frith Bank
Long Sand
B1192
Brothertoft
Benington
Benington Sea End
Holland Fen
A52
Butterwick
St Botolph
BOSTON
Guildhall
Haltoft End
3
Hubbert's Bridge
East Heckington
A17
A1121
Pydell
Skirbeck
Freiston
Butterwick Low
Roger Sand
Swineshead Bridge
Kirton Holme
Frampton West End
Freiston Shore
Hale
A52
Fishtoft
Toft Sand
B1192
Fenhouses
Kirton End
Scrane End
Swineshead
B1391
Wyberton
Black Buoy Sand
B1397
Frampton
The Haven
Gat Sand
Drayton
THE
Kirton
The Scalp
Mare Tail
Bicker
Sandholme
Forty Foot Drain
A17
Hoffleet Stow
A16
Skeldyke
Northorpe
A52
Wigtoft
B1397
Old South
Donington
Sutterton
Algarkirk
Church End
Quadring
Quadring Eaudike
Fosdyke
Old Lynn Channel
A152
Holbeach St Matthew
Bicker Haven
Holbeach St Marks
Gosberton
Westhorpe
Whaplode Marsh
Dawsmere
B1397
Risegate
Holbeach Marsh
A17
Gedney Marsh
B1359
Gedney Drove End
Surfleet
Surfleet Seas End
B1357
Holbeach Clough
Holbeach Hurn
Crossgate
A16
Moulton Seas End
Holbeach Bank
Lutton Marsh
B1356
Spalding Marsh
Saracen's Head
Pinchbeck Bars
Loosegate
Gedney Dyke
Lutton
Guy's Head
Pinchbeck
B1180
Weston
Holbeach
B1515
Fleet Hargate
Chapelgate
Pinchbeck West
Springfields Gardens
Fun Farm
A151
Moulton
Whaplode
Fleet
Gedney
Little London
Nene
A151
Spalding
A17
Long Sutton
Glen
Pode Hole
B1168
Gedney Broadgate
Delph Bank
Sutton Bridge
Wingland Marsh
Little London
B1173
B1165
B1390
Sutton Crosses
Walpole Cross Keys
B1172
Weston Hills
Whaplode Fen
B1165
South Holland Main Drain
North Drove Drain
Moulton Chapel
Whaplode St Catherine
Tydd Gote
Deeping Fen
A16
B1357
Holbeach St Johns
B1165
Sutton St James
Tydd St Mary
Four Gotes
Walpole St Andrew
Walpole St
Moulton Fen
Tydd St Giles
Deeping St Nicholas
Terrington St

D
E
F
G
97
Ingoldmells
Ingoldmells Point
Fantasy Island
Butlins Family Entertainment Resort, Skegness
A52
Skegness
Skegness Natureland Seal Sanctuary
Gibraltar Point
Gibraltar
0 2 4 6 8 10 miles
0 2 4 6 8 10 km
1
2
3
4
5
LYNN DEEPS
DEEPS
Brancaster Bay
Holkham Bay
Norton Creek
Holme next the Sea
Thornham
A149
Brancaster
Titchwell
Burnham Deepdale
Burnham Norton
Overy Staithe
Holkham
Wells-n
Burnham Market
Burnham Overy
B1155
Holkham Hall
Burnham Thorpe
Sea Life Centre
Hunstanton
Ringstead
Creake Abbey
Summerfield
Wells & Walsingham Lt Rly
Heacham
Norfolk Lavender
B1454
Docking
B1155
Stanhoe
North Creake
Shirehall Museum
Egmere
Shrine of Our Lady of Walsingham
Sedgeford
South Creake
North Barsham
East Barsham
West Barsham
Fring
Snettisham
Barmer
A149
Southgate
Bircham Newton
Shernborne
Ingoldisthorpe
Great Bircham
Bircham Tofts
Bagthorpe
Syderstone
Sculthorpe
Peter Black Sand
N O R F O L K
Dersingham
Anmer
Tattersett
A148
Dunton
86
Fakenh
Shereford
Sandringham House
Sandringham
Houghton Hall
Hempton
Fakenham
Bulldog Sand
Wolferton
West Newton
St Mary Magdalene Chapel
New Houghton
East Rudham
West Rudham
Tatterford
Helhoughton
Toftrees
Colkirk
Flitcham
Harpley
A1065
Castle Rising
Trinity Hospital
Castle Rising
Ongar Hill
North Wootton
A148
Hillington
Little Massingham
West Raynham
East Raynham
South Raynham
Whissonsett
Great Massingham
Congham
South Wootton
A148
A1078
Roydon
Grimston
Weasenham St Peter
Wellingham
Horningtoft
St. George's Guildhall (NT)
Gaywood
A149
Weasenham All Saints
Tittleshall
Little London
Clenchwarton
Pott Row
Rougham
Stanfield
Terrington St Clement
West Lynn
Massingham Heath
Gayton
KING'S LYNN
B1145
71
Mileham
Tilney All Saints
A47
Ashwicken
Gayton
Caithness Crystal Visitor Centre
Great Ouse
West Winch
East Winch
B1153
Litcham
East Lexham
Lexham
Castle Acre
East Walton
A47
A10
North
Middleton
West Acre
Newton
Great
Longham
Beeston

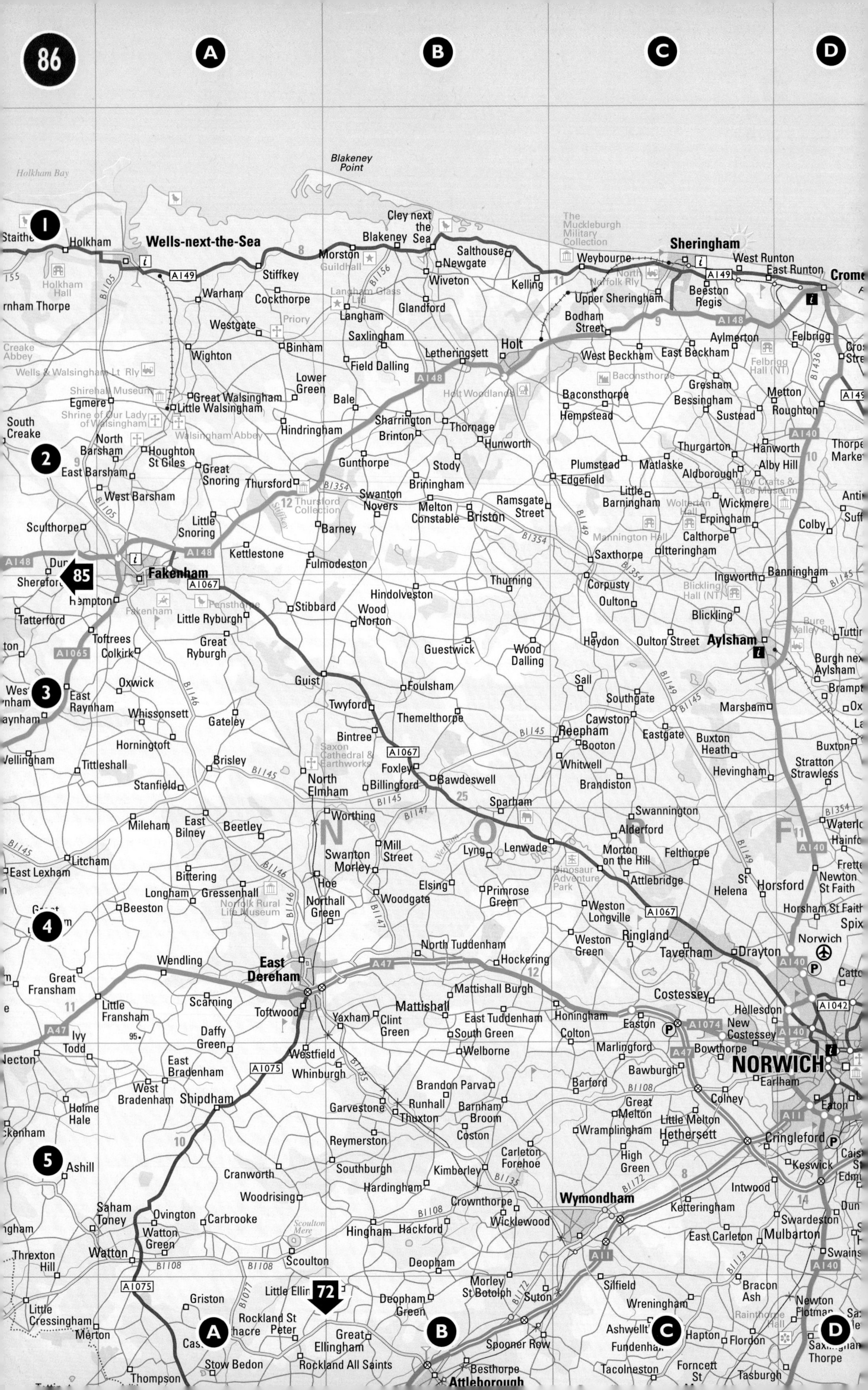
A
B
C
D
1
2
3
4
5
Blakeney Point
Holkham Bay
Staithe
Holkham
Wells-next-the-Sea
Holkham Hall
Cley next the Sea
Blakeney
Morston
Stiffkey
Salthouse
Newgate
Wiveton
Glandford
Guildhall
Langham Glass Ltd
The Muckleburgh Military Collection
Weybourne
Sheringham
West Runton
East Runton
Cromer
North Norfolk Rly
Kelling
Upper Sheringham
Beeston Regis
A149
B1105
B1156
A148
Warham
Cockthorpe
Westgate
Priory
Langham
Saxlingham
Binham
Wighton
Field Dalling
Letheringsett
Holt
Bodham Street
West Beckham
East Beckham
Aylmerton
Felbrigg
Felbrigg Hall (NT)
Creake Abbey
Wells & Walsingham Lt Rly
Shirehall Museum
Egmere
Shrine of Our Lady of Walsingham
Great Walsingham
Little Walsingham
Walsingham Abbey
Lower Green
Bale
Holt Woodlands
Baconsthorpe
Gresham
Bessingham
Metton
Roughton
Sustead
Hempstead
South Creake
North Barsham
Houghton St Giles
Hindringham
Sharrington
Brinton
Thornage
Hunworth
Thurgarton
Hanworth
Thorpe Market
East Barsham
Great Snoring
Thursford
Gunthorpe
Stody
Briningham
Plumstead
Matlaske
Alby Hill
Aldborough
Edgefield
Alby Crafts & Lace Museum
West Barsham
B1354
Thursford Collection
Swanton Novers
Melton Constable
Briston
Ramsgate Street
Little Barningham
Wolterton Hall
Wickmere
Antingham
Suffield
Sculthorpe
Little Snoring
Barney
B1149
Erpingham
Calthorpe
Colby
Mannington Hall
Itteringham
Saxthorpe
A148
Kettlestone
Fulmodeston
Dunton
Shereford
85
Fakenham
A1067
Hempton
Pensthorpe
Hindolveston
Thurning
Corpusty
Oulton
Ingworth
Banningham
Blickling Hall (NT)
Blickling
Tatterford
Little Ryburgh
Stibbard
Wood Norton
Great Ryburgh
Toftrees
Colkirk
A1065
Guestwick
Wood Dalling
Heydon
Oulton Street
Aylsham
Bure Valley Rly
Tuttington
Burgh next Aylsham
West Raynham
East Raynham
Oxwick
Guist
Foulsham
Sall
Southgate
Marsham
Brampton
Oxnead
Whissonsett
B1146
Gateley
Twyford
Themelthorpe
Cawston
Reepham
Eastgate
Buxton Heath
Buxton
Horningtoft
Bintree
Saxon Cathedral & Earthworks
Booton
Whitwell
Hevingham
Stratton Strawless
Wellingham
Tittleshall
Brisley
B1145
Foxley
Stanfield
North Elmham
Billingford
Bawdeswell
Brandiston
Sparham
Swannington
Waterloo
Hainford
Mileham
East Bilney
Beetley
Worthing
B1147
Alderford
Lyng
Lenwade
Morton on the Hill
Felthorpe
Frettenham
Litcham
Swanton Morley
Mill Street
East Lexham
Bittering
Hoe
Elsing
Dinosaur Adventure Park
Attlebridge
St Helena
Horsford
Newton St Faith
Longham
Gressenhall
Norfolk Rural Life Museum
Beeston
Northall Green
Woodgate
Primrose Green
Weston Longville
Horsham St Faith
Spixworth
Great Dunham
Weston Green
Ringland
Taverham
Drayton
Norwich
North Tuddenham
Hockering
Wendling
East Dereham
A47
Mattishall Burgh
Catton
Great Fransham
Little Fransham
Scarning
Toftwood
Mattishall
Yaxham
Clint Green
East Tuddenham
Honingham
Easton
Costessey
Hellesdon
A1042
A1074
New Costessey
A140
Necton
Ivy Todd
Daffy Green
South Green
Colton
Marlingford
Bowthorpe
East Bradenham
Westfield
Welborne
Bawburgh
NORWICH
A1075
Whinburgh
B1135
Earlham
West Bradenham
Shipdham
Brandon Parva
Barford
B1108
Great Melton
Colney
Eaton
Holme Hale
Garvestone
Runhall
Thuxton
Barnham Broom
Little Melton
Necton
Wramplingham
Hethersett
A11
Cringleford
Caistor St Edmund
Reymerston
Coston
Carleton Forehoe
High Green
Keswick
Ashill
Cranworth
Southburgh
Kimberley
Intwood
Hardingham
B1172
Wymondham
Woodrising
Crownthorpe
Ketteringham
Swardeston
Saham Toney
Ovington
Carbrooke
Scoulton Mere
Hingham
Hackford
Wicklewood
East Carleton
Mulbarton
Watton Green
Watton
Threxton Hill
Scoulton
Deopham
Swainsthorpe
Griston
B1077
Little Ellingham
72
Deopham Green
Morley St Botolph
Suton
Silfield
Wreningham
Bracon Ash
Newton Flotman
Little Cressingham
Merton
Caston
Rockland St Peter
Great Ellingham
Ashwellthorpe
Rainthorpe Hall
Fundenhall
Hapton
Flordon
Saxlingham Thorpe
Stow Bedon
Rockland All Saints
Spooner Row
Besthorpe
Tacolneston
Forncett St
Tasburgh
Thompson
Attleborough
B1113
Norwich

D
E
F
G
1
2
3
4
5
0 2 4 6 8 10 miles
0 2 4 6 8 10 km
Sidestrand
Trimingham
Gimingham
Mundesley
Trunch
Knapton
Paston
Bacton
Edingthorpe
Keswick
Bradfield
Swafield
Walcott
North Walsham
Witton Bridge
Ridlington
Happisburgh
Spa Common
Whimpwell Green
Crostwight
Happisburgh Common
Hempstead
Lessingham
Sea Palling
Waxham
Bengate
Honing
East Ruston
Worstead
A149
Stalham
Ingham
Dilham
Smallburgh
Stalham Green
Low Street
Sutton
Hickling
Sloley
A1151
Sutton Broad
Hickling Green
Fairstead
Barton Common
A149
Hickling Heath
Horsey
Market Street
Beeston St Lawrence
Beeston Hall
Barton Turf
Clearwater 2000
Horsey Mere
Horsey Windpump (NT)
Ruston
Tunstead
Hickling Broad
Catfield
Barton Broad
Hundred Stream
Ashmanhaugh
Wroxham Barns
Neatishead
Irstead
Potter Heigham
Martham Broad
West Somerton
East Somerton
Winterton-on-Sea
Hoveton
NORFOLK
Thurne
Hemsby Hole
Belaugh
Ludham
Bastwick
Wroxham
Horning
A1062
Martham
Hemsby
Newport
Upper Street
Repps
BROADS
Thurne
Ormesby St Margaret
B1152
Rollesby
A149
Scratby
California
Rackheath
Woodbastwick
St. Helen
Clippesby
Ormesby St Michael
Salhouse Sta.
Ranworth
Burgh St Margaret
Filby Broad
Salhouse
Fairhaven
Billockby
Thrigby
Filby
Roman Site
Panxworth
Caister Castle
New Rackheath
South Walsham
Upton
Upton Green
A1064
Mauthy
Caister-on-Sea
Little Plumstead
Hemblington
Thrigby Hall Wildlife Gdns
West End
West Caister
Thorpe End
Great Plumstead
North Burlingham
Acle
Stokesby
Runham
Yarmouth
Yarmouth Roads
Thorpe St Andrew
Blofield
Lingwood
Damgate
A149
A47
Brundall
Beighton
Tunstall
Greyfriar's Cloisters
Old Merchant's House & Row 111 House
Sea Life Centre
Postwick
Strumpshaw
Moulton St Mary
THE BROADS
Halvergate Marshes
Halvergate
Breydon Water
Newton
South Burlingham
GREAT YARMOUTH
Kirby Bedon
Surlingham
Buckenham
B1140
Freethorpe
Berney Arms Sta.
Berney Arms Mill
Pleasure Beach
Southtown
Bramerton
Hassingham
Southwood
Wickhampton
Burgh Castle
Rockland St Mary
Cantley
Freethorpe Common
Roman Fort
Gorleston on Sea
Framingham Pigot
Claxton
Limpenhoe
Pettitts Animal Adventure Park
Bradwell
Yare
Waveney
Yelverton
Belton
A143
Hobland Hall
Poringland
Ashby St Mary
Hardley Street
Alpington
Bergh Apton
Thurton
Reedham
Langley Street
Norton Marshes
St. Olaves Priory
Fritton
Fritton Lake
Hopton
Howe
Brooke
Chedgrave
Norton Subcourse
Lower Thurlton
Thurlton
B1074
A12
Heckingham
Seething
Sisland
Loddon
Hales
Thorpe
Herringfleet
Blundeston
Kirstead Green
Hales Hall
B1136
Haddiscoe
Somerleyton
Pleasurewood Hills Theme Park
B1332
Raveningham
A143
A146
Maypole Green
B1385
73

A
B
C
D
1
2
3
4
5
The Skerries
West Mouse
Middle Mouse
Carmel Head
Cemlyn Bay
Cemaes Bay
Porth Wen Bay
Bull Bay
Point Lynas
Llanbadrig
Amlwch
Amlwch Port
Cemaes
Neuadd
Burwen
Tregele
Llaneilian
Pengorffwysfa
Llanfairynghornwy
Llanfechell
Bodewryd
Pen-y-sarn
Nebo
Ynys Dulas
Dulas
Dulas Bay
Lligwy Bay
A5025
B5111
Parys Mountain
Llanrhyddlad
Carreg-lefn
Llanfflewyn
Rhos-goch
Rhos-y-bol
Rhyd-wyn
Church Bay
HOLYHEAD BAY
ISLE OF ANGLESEY
ANGLESEY
(YNYS MÔN)
Llanfaethlu
Llanbabo
Capel Parc
City Dulas
Brynrefail
Capel Lligwy
Moelfre
Llyn Alaw
Ceidio
Llandyfrydog
Llanallgo
Windmill
Elim
Llanddeusant
Llannerch-y-medd
Maenaddwyn
Marian-Glas
hours
Dublin.......................1¾-3
Dún Laoghaire............1¾
Llanfwrog
North Stack
Holyhead Mountain
220
Holyhead (Caergybi)
Roman Fort
Salt Island
South Stack
Llaingoch
Llanfigael
Llanfachraeth
Pen-llyn
Standing Stone
Carmel
Capel Coch
Bryn-teg
Benllech
B5112
B5111
B5110
B5108
Hut Circles
Kingsland
Standing Stones
Penrhos
Llanynghenedl
B5109
Llyn Llywenan
Llechcynfarwy
Llanbedrgoch
Red Wharf
Burial Chamber
Bodedern
Burial Chambers
Trefor
Tregaian
Llangwyllog
A5
A55
Trearddur
Valley (Dyffryn)
Caergeiliog
Penrhyn Mawr
Llynfaes
Rhosmeirch
Llanddyfnan
B4545
Four Mile Bridge
Llanfair-yn-neubwll
Bryngwran
Llyn Frogwy
Cefni Resr
Talwrn
HOLY ISLAND
Bodior
Rhoscolyn
Capel Gwyn
Gwalchmai
Bodffordd
Heneglwys
Llangefni
B4422
A5114
A4080
Ceint
B5420
Penmynydd
Braint
Tywyn Trewan
Cymyran Bay
Ty Newydd Burial Chamber
Cerrigceinwen
Llangristiolus
Rhosneigr
Llanfaelog
Ty Croes Sta.
Pentre Berw
Gaerwen
Llanfairpwllgwyngyll
Menai (Porthaethwy)
Barclodiad y Gawres Chambered Cairn
Cefni
Malltraeth Marsh
B4419
Bethel
Trefdraeth
Llanddaniel Fab
Llyn Coron
Bryn Celli Ddu Burial Chamber
Plas Newydd (NT)
Bodowyr Burial Chamber
Castell Bryn-gwyn
74
Aberffraw
Llangadwaladr
Hermon
Malltraeth
Llangaffo
Aberffraw Bay
Bodorgan
Malltraeth Sands
Newborough (Niwbwrch)
B4421
Dwyran
Brynsiencyn
Llanddeiniol
A487
(NT)
17
6
7
7a
1
2
3
4
5

D
E
F
G
0 2 4 6 8 10 miles
0 2 4 6 8 10 km
1
2
3
4
5
Liverpool to... hours
Belfast....7½
Dublin....4-8
Douglas, Isle of Man....2½-4
hours
Mostyn to Dublin....6-8
90
Great Ormes Head
Great Orme
Cable Car
North Wales Theatre
Toll
Llandudno
Little Ormes Head
Gogarth
Great Orme Tramway
Penrhyn-side
Penrhyn Bay (Bae Penrhyn)
Rhôs-on-Sea
Llandrillo-yn-Rhôs
COLWYN BAY (Bae Colwyn)
Conwy Sands
Suspension Bridge (NT)
Llanrhos
Deganwy
Mochdre
Aberconwy House (NT)
Conwy
Gyffin
Llandudno Junction
Llansanffraid Glan Conwy
Dwygyfylchi
Foel Lus
Capelulo
Penmaenmawr
Puffin Island (Priestholm)
St. Seirol's Well
Penmon
Llanddona
Llangoed
Llan-faes
Beaumaris
Beaumaris (Biwmaris)
CONWY BAY
Penmaen Swatch
Llanfairfechan
Nant-y-Pandy
Moelfre
Henryd
Pentrefelin
Bryn-y-maen
Old Colwyn
Llanelian-yn-Rhôs
Llysfaen
Gwrych
Rhyd-y-foel
Dolwen
Betws-yn-Rhos
Llanddulas
Abergele
Abergele Roads
Kinmel
Mynydd Llanelian
Dawn
Hafod-lom
Mynydd Branar
Bodnant (NT)
Graig
Moel Gyffylog
Tal-y-cafn
Eglwysbach
Gorddinog
Garreg Fawr
Abergwyngregyn
Tal-y-fan
Rowen
Ty'n-y-groes
Caerhun
Crymlyn
Port Penrhyn
Penrhyn (NT)
Bangor
Llandygai
Glanadda
Tal-y-bont
Moel Wnion
Aber Falls
Drum
Llwytmor
Llanllechid
Waen-
Glasinfryn
Tal-y-Cae
Tregarth
Rachub
Bethesda
Gerlan
Braichmelyn
Pentir
Rhiwlas
Mynydd
Drosgl
Foel-Fras
Garnedd Uchaf
SNOWDONIA
Foel Grach
Dulyn Resr
Porth-llwyd
Dolgarrog
Pont Dolgarrog
Dolgarrog Sta.
Llanbedr-y-cennin
Tal-y-bont
Vale of Conwy
76
Mwdwl Eithin
Gell
Rhos-y-mawn
Llanfair Talhaiarn
Pentre Isaf
Tre-pys-llygod
Pen y Mwdwl
GWYNEDD
CONWY
A55
A5
A545
A546
A547
A470
A548
A544
B5109
B5115
B5113
B5381
B5383
B5106
B4409
B5382
Anafon
Roe
Conwy

A
B
C
D
1
2
3
4
5
0 2 4 6 8 10 miles
0 2 4 6 8 10 km
hours
Belfast..........7½
Dublin..........4-8
Douglas, Isle of Man..........2½-4
89
L I V E R P O O L B A
hours
Dublin..........6-8
East Hoyle Bank
Meols Sta.
Hoylake
Manor Rd. Sta.
Saughall Mas
Hilbre Island
West Kirby
Frank
Caldy
Thurstast
The Wirral
Dawpool Bank
Welsh Channel
Point of Ayr
Talacre
Mostyn Bank
Prestatyn
Gronant
Gwespyr
Ffynnongroyw
RHYL
Sky Tower
Sea Life Centre
Ocean Beach Amusement Park
A548
A547
Llanasa
Gwaenysgor
Gyrn
Mostyn Quay
Bae Penrhyn)
on-Sea
yn-Rhôs
COLWYN BAY
(Bae Colwyn)
Kinmel Bay (Bae Cinmel)
Towyn
Meliden (Gallt Melyd)
Gop Hill
Trelogan
Mostyn
Glan-y-don
Llannerch-y-Môr
A525
B5119
Trelawnyd
Maen Achwyfaen
Downing
Holywell Bank
Abergele Roads
Pensarn
23
23a
A55
Llanddulas
Abergele
Morfa Rhuddlan
Plas Llwyd
Rhuddlan
Dyserth
Bodrhyddan Hall
Marian Cwm
Whitford (Chwitffordd)
Mertyn
Basingwerk Abbey
Greenfield Valley
Old
Llysfaen
Gwrych
24
Castle & Twt Hill
Cwm
A5151
Llyn Helyg
Lloc
A5026
Carmel
Greenfield
Llanelian-yn-Rhôs
B5383
Rhyd-y-foel
Gele
24a
DENBIGHSHIRE
Pengwern
29
30
Gorsedd
St Winefride's Holy Well
Walwen
Dolwen
Betws-yn-Rhos
St George
25
Bodelwyddan
B5429
27a
28
Rhuallt
Roman Road
31
14
Pantasaph
Holywell (Treffynnon)
32
CLWYD
Moelfre Isaf
Groesffordd Marli
26
27
St Asaph (Llanelwy)
Pen-y-cefn
B5122
Brynford
Bagillt
Bedol
B5381
A548
Mynydd Bodrochwyn
Elwy
Cefn Meiriadog
Tremeirchion
Babell
B5121
A5026
Mynydd Branar
CONWY
Llannefydd
VALE
B5429
Graig
Llannerch
Caerwys
Afonwen Craft & Antique Centre
FLINTSHIRE
Pentre Halkyn
Flint (Y Fflint)
32a
32b
Halkyn Mountain
Halkyn
Plas-yn-Cefn
Afon-wen
Llanfair Talhaiarn
Trefnant
A541
Moel y Parc
398
Ddôl
Ysceifiog
Lixwm
Walwen
A544
Aled
76
B5428
A525
Bodfari
OF
Nannerch
Rhes-y-cae
North
Pentre Isaf
Tre-pys-llygod
Henllan
A543
Plasisaf
B5382
Pen y Mwdwl
Friary (ruins)
B5123
Rhydymwyn
Llansannan
Deunant
B5428
B5382
Denbigh (Dinbych)
Waen
Llangwyfan
Moel Llys-y-coed
A541
A548
A543
Ystrad

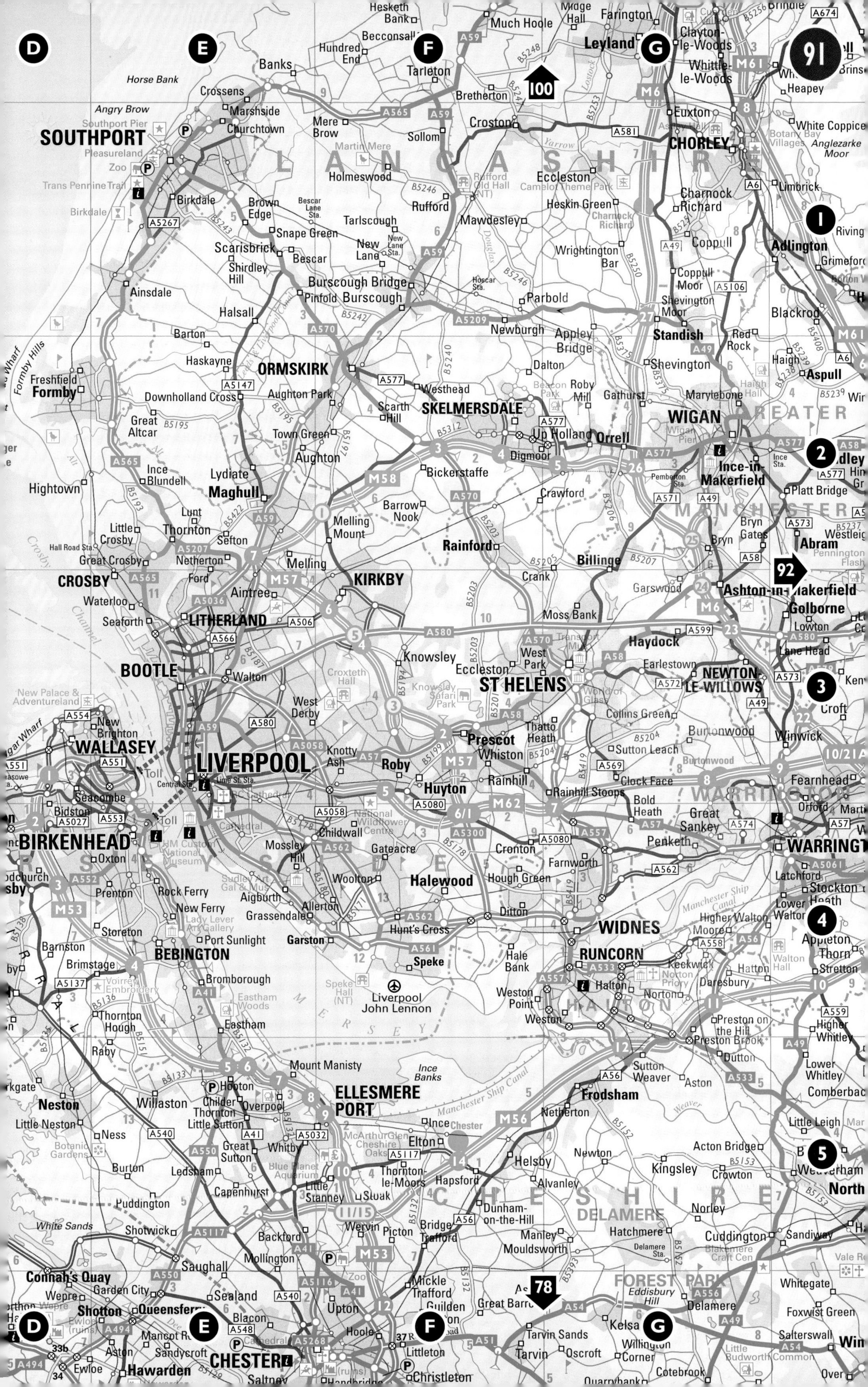
91
D
E
F
G
100
92
78
I
2
3
4
5
SOUTHPORT
Horse Bank
Angry Brow
Southport Pier
Pleasureland
Zoo
Trans Pennine Trail
Birkdale
Crossens
Marshside
Churchtown
Banks
Hesketh Bank
Becconsall
Hundred End
Tarleton
Much Hoole
Midge Hall
Farington
Leyland
Clayton-le-Woods
Whittle-le-Woods
Heapey
Bretherton
Croston
Mere Brow
Sollom
Martin Mere
LANCASHIRE
Euxton
White Coppice
CHORLEY
Botany Bay Villages
Anglezarke Moor
Holmeswood
Rufford
Rufford Old Hall (NT)
Eccleston
Camelot Theme Park
Limbrick
Charnock Richard
Heskin Green
Birkdale
Brown Edge
Bescar Lane Sta.
Tarlscough
Mawdesley
Adlington
Rivington
Scarisbrick
Snape Green
New Lane
New Lane Sta.
Coppull
Wrightington Bar
Grimeford
Shirdley Hill
Bescar
Burscough Bridge
Pinfold
Burscough
Hoscar Sta.
Parbold
Coppull Moor
Ainsdale
Halsall
Shevington Moor
Blackrod
Barton
Newburgh
Appley Bridge
Standish
Red Rock
Haskayne
Formby Hills
Freshfield
Formby
ORMSKIRK
Dalton
Shevington
Haigh
Aspull
Downholland Cross
Aughton Park
Westhead
Beacon Park
Roby Mill
Gathurst
Marylebone
Haigh Hall
Great Altcar
Scarth Hill
SKELMERSDALE
WIGAN
GREATER
Town Green
Up Holland
Orrell
Wigan Pier
Aughton
Digmoor
Ince-in-Makerfield
Ince Sta.
Hindley
Ince Blundell
Lydiate
Bickerstaffe
Pemberton Sta.
Platt Bridge
Hightown
Maghull
Crawford
MANCHESTER
Lunt
Barrow Nook
Bryn Gates
Little Crosby
Thornton
Melling Mount
Bryn
Abram
Westleigh
Sefton
Rainford
Hall Road Sta.
Great Crosby
Netherton
Melling
Billinge
Pennington Flash
CROSBY
Ford
KIRKBY
Crank
Garswood
Ashton-in-Makerfield
Waterloo
Aintree
Golborne
Seaforth
LITHERLAND
Moss Bank
Lowton
Haydock
Lane Head
Knowsley
BOOTLE
Walton
Croxteth Hall
Knowsley Safari Park
Eccleston
West Park
ST HELENS
Earlestown
NEWTON-LE-WILLOWS
Kenyon
New Palace & Adventureland
West Derby
World of Glass
Croft
New Brighton
WALLASEY
Thatto Heath
Collins Green
Winwick
Knotty Ash
Roby
Prescot
Whiston
Sutton Leach
Burtonwood
LIVERPOOL
Toll
Central Sta.
Lime St. Sta.
Huyton
Rainhill
Clock Face
Fearnhead
Seacombe
Bidston
RC Cathedral
Rainhill Stoops
Bold Heath
WARRINGTON
Orford
Martinscroft
BIRKENHEAD
Cathedral
HM Customs National Museum
Childwall
National Wildflower Centre
Great Sankey
Penketh
Oxton
Mossley Hill
Gateacre
Cronton
Farnworth
Latchford
Prenton
Rock Ferry
Sudley Art Gal & Mus
Woolton
Halewood
Hough Green
Stockton Heath
Aigburth
Allerton
Manchester Ship Canal
Lower Walton
Higher Walton
New Ferry
Lady Lever Art Gallery
Grassendale
Ditton
Moore
Storeton
Hunt's Cross
WIDNES
Appleton Thorn
Barnston
Port Sunlight
Garston
RUNCORN
Walton Hall
Brimstage
BEBINGTON
Speke
Hale Bank
Keckwick
Hatton
Stretton
Bromborough
Speke Hall (NT)
Liverpool John Lennon
Halton
Norton Priory
Daresbury
Voirrey Embroidery
Eastham Woods
Weston Point
Norton
Thornton Hough
Weston
HALTON
Preston on the Hill
Higher Whitley
Eastham
MERSEY
Preston Brook
Raby
Dutton
Lower Whitley
Mount Manisty
Ince Banks
Sutton Weaver
Aston
Hooton
Neston
Willaston
Childer Thornton
Overpool
ELLESMERE PORT
Frodsham
Comberbach
Little Neston
Little Sutton
Ince
Netherton
Little Leigh
Ness
Great Sutton
Whitby
McArthurGlen Cheshire Oaks
Elton
Chester
Botanic Gardens
Blue Planet Aquarium
Helsby
Newton
Acton Bridge
Burton
Ledsham
Thornton-le-Moors
Kingsley
Crowton
Weaverham
Little Stanney
Hapsford
Alvanley
Northwich
Capenhurst
Stoak
CHESHIRE
Puddington
DELAMERE
Dunham-on-the-Hill
Norley
White Sands
Shotwick
Backford
Wervin
Picton
Bridge Trafford
Hatchmere
Cuddington
Sandiway
Manley
Mouldsworth
Delamere Sta.
Blakemere Craft Cen
Saughall
Mollington
Connah's Quay
Zoo
Mickle Trafford
FOREST PARK
Eddisbury Hill
Whitegate
Wepre
Garden City
Sealand
Guilden Sutton
Great Barrow
Delamere
Foxwist Green
Shotton
Queensferry
Blacon
Upton
Hoole
Kelsa
Ewloe (ruins)
Mancot
Sandycroft
Cathedral
Littleton
Tarvin Sands
Oscroft
Willington Corner
Salterswall
Aston
Ewloe
Hawarden
CHESTER
Tarvin
Little Budworth Common
Saltney
Handbridge
Christleton
Quarrybank
Cotebrook
Over
Winsford
M6
M61
M58
M57
M62
M53
M56
A59
A565
A581
A5209
A570
A577
A5147
A49
A5106
A58
A573
A571
A5207
A506
A566
A580
A599
A572
A5036
A554
A551
A553
A5027
A552
A5058
A57
A5080
A5300
A562
A561
A574
A5061
A557
A533
A558
A56
A5137
A41
A540
A550
A5032
A5117
A5116
A494
A548
A5268
A51
A54
A556
A6
A674
A559
A5267
B5195
B5242
B5240
B5312
B5203
B5204
B5419
B5178
B5180
B5171
B5132
B5133
B5136
B5138
B5151
B5152
B5153
B5393
B5248
B5253
B5250
B5246
B5375
B5206
B5207
B5201
B5199
B5194
B5187
B5422
B5193
B5243
B5239
B5238
B5408
B5237
B5256
B5129

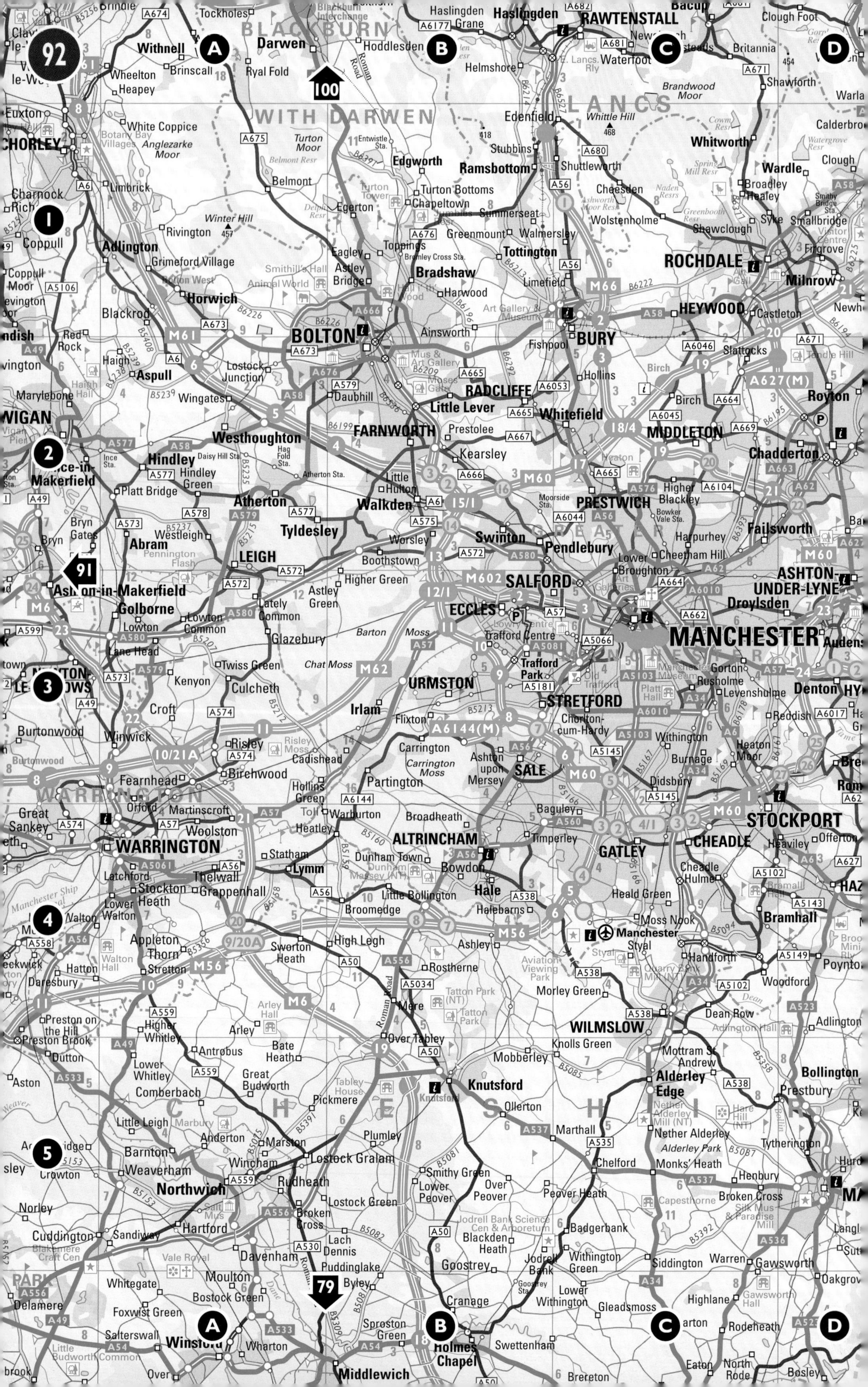
92
A
B
C
D
100
91
79
1
2
3
4
5
BLACKBURN WITH DARWEN
LANCS
GREATER MANCHESTER
WARRINGTON
CHESHIRE
Withnell
Tockholes
Darwen
Hoddlesden
Haslingden
Grane
RAWTENSTALL
Waterfoot
Clough Foot
Britannia
Shawforth
Brinscall
Wheelton
Heapey
Ryal Fold
Helmshore
Brandwood Moor
Whittle Hill
468
Euxton
CHORLEY
White Coppice
Botany Bay Villages
Anglezarke Moor
Turton Moor
Entwistle Sta.
Edgworth
Edenfield
Stubbins
Ramsbottom
Shuttleworth
Whitworth
Wardle
Calderbrook
Clough
Broadley
Healey
Belmont
Belmont Resr
Turton Tower
Turton Bottoms
Chapeltown
Cheesden
Naden Resrs
Limbrick
Charnock Richard
Coppull
Winter Hill
457
Rivington
Egerton
Delph Resr
Summerseat
Wolstenholme
Greenbooth Resr
Syke
Smallbridge
Shawclough
Adlington
Grimeford Village
Eagley
Toppings
Bromley Cross Sta.
Greenmount
Walmersley
Tottington
ROCHDALE
Firgrove
Milnrow
Coppull Moor
Smithill's Hall
Animal World
Astley Bridge
Bradshaw
Harwood
Limefield
Rivington
Horwich
Blackrod
Art Gallery & Museum
HEYWOOD
Castleton
Newhey
Red Rock
Haigh
Aspull
BOLTON
Ainsworth
BURY
Fishpool
Slattocks
Tandle Hill
Lostock Junction
Mus & Art Gallery
Moses Gate
RADCLIFFE
Hollins
Birch
Royton
Marylebone
Haigh Hall
Wingates
Daubhill
Little Lever
Whitefield
Westhoughton
FARNWORTH
Prestolee
MIDDLETON
WIGAN
Hindley
Daisy Hill Sta.
Hag Fold Sta.
Kearsley
Chadderton
Heaton
Ince-in-Makerfield
Hindley Green
Atherton Sta.
Little Hulton
Higher Blackley
Platt Bridge
Atherton
Walkden
Moorside Sta.
PRESTWICH
Bowker Vale Sta.
Failsworth
Bryn Gates
Abram
Westleigh
Tyldesley
Worsley
Swinton
Pendlebury
Harpurhey
Bryn
Pennington Flash
LEIGH
Boothstown
Lower Broughton
Cheetham Hill
Higher Green
SALFORD
ASHTON-UNDER-LYNE
Ashton-in-Makerfield
Golborne
Lately Common
Astley Green
ECCLES
Droylsden
Lowton
Lowton Common
Trafford Centre
MANCHESTER
Audenshaw
Glazebury
Barton
Moss
Lane Head
Twiss Green
Chat Moss
Trafford Park
Gorton
Kenyon
Culcheth
URMSTON
Old Trafford
Manchester Museum
Rusholme
Denton
NEWTON-LE-WILLOWS
Platt Hall
Levenshulme
STRETFORD
Croft
Irlam
Flixton
Chorlton-cum-Hardy
Reddish
Burtonwood
Winwick
Risley
Risley Moss
Withington
Heaton Moor
Cadishead
Carrington
Carrington Moss
Ashton upon Mersey
Burnage
Fearnhead
Birchwood
SALE
Didsbury
Hollins Green
Partington
Great Sankey
Orford
Martinscroft
Toll
Warburton
Broadheath
Baguley
STOCKPORT
Woolston
Heatley
ALTRINCHAM
Timperley
CHEADLE
Heaviley
Offerton
WARRINGTON
Statham
Lymm
Dunham Town
Dunham Massey (NT)
Bowdon
GATLEY
Latchford
Thelwall
Cheadle Hulme
Stockton Heath
Grappenhall
Little Bollington
Hale
Heald Green
Lower Walton
Walton
Broomedge
Halebarns
Bramhall
Manchester Ship Canal
Moss Nook
Appleton Thorn
Swinton Heath
High Legh
Ashley
Manchester
Styal
Handforth
Walton Hall
Hatton
Stretton
Rostherne
Aviation Viewing Park
Quarry Bank Mill (NT)
Poynton
Daresbury
Woodford
Tatton Park (NT)
Morley Green
Preston on the Hill
Preston Brook
Arley Hall
Mere
Dean Row
Adlington
Higher Whitley
Arley
WILMSLOW
Adlington Hall
Bate Heath
Over Tabley
Knolls Green
Dutton
Antrobus
Mobberley
Mottram St Andrew
Lower Whitley
Great Budworth
Tabley House
Knutsford
Alderley Edge
Bollington
Aston
Comberbach
Pickmere
Ollerton
Prestbury
Nether Alderley Mill (NT)
Hare Hill (NT)
Little Leigh
Marbury
Anderton
Marston
Plumley
Marthall
Nether Alderley
Tytherington
Alderley Park
Barnton
Wincham
Lostock Gralam
Smithy Green
Chelford
Monks' Heath
Weaverham
Northwich
Rudheath
Lower Peover
Over Peover
Peover Heath
Henbury
Crowton
Broken Cross
Norley
Salt Mus
Lostock Green
Capesthorne
Silk Mus & Paradise Mill
Hartford
Broken Cross
Jodrell Bank Science Cen & Arboretum
Badgerbank
Cuddington
Sandiway
Blakemere Craft Cen
Lach Dennis
Blackden Heath
Vale Royal
Davenham
Puddinglake
Goostrey
Jodrell Bank
Withington Green
Siddington
Warren
Gawsworth
Moulton
Byley
Goostrey Sta.
Lower Withington
Oakgrove
Whitegate
Bostock Green
Gawsworth Hall
Highlane
Delamere
Cranage
Gleadsmoss
Foxwist Green
Sproston Green
Marton
Rodeheath
Salterswall
Winsford
Wharton
Holmes Chapel
Swettenham
Little Budworth Common
Over
Middlewich
Eaton
North Rode
Bosley
Brereton
M6
M61
M60
M62
M66
M602
M56
A6144(M)
A627(M)
A580
A56
A34
A6
A49
A57
A62
A58
A666
A676
A673
A674
A675
A680
A681
A6177
A6053
A6044
A6045
A6010
A6046
A665
A667
A664
A669
A663
A6104
A5103
A5145
A5181
A5081
A5066
A5106
A5061
A5102
A5143
A5149
A5034
A5022
A538
A560
A559
A556
A533
A530
A535
A537
A54
A50
A523
A536
A574
A573
A572
A575
A577
A578
A579
A599
A558
A671
A6017
B6222
B6226
B6213
B6214
B6527
B6196
B6292
B6209
B6536
B6199
B5239
B5238
B5408
B5235
B5237
B5215
B5207
B5212
B5213
B5160
B5159
B5158
B5166
B5167
B5169
B6178
B6167
B5094
B5358
B5085
B5081
B5087
B5392
B5082
B5075
B5391
B5152
B5153
B5356
B5309
B5080
B6391
B6195
B6194
B6393
Roman Road

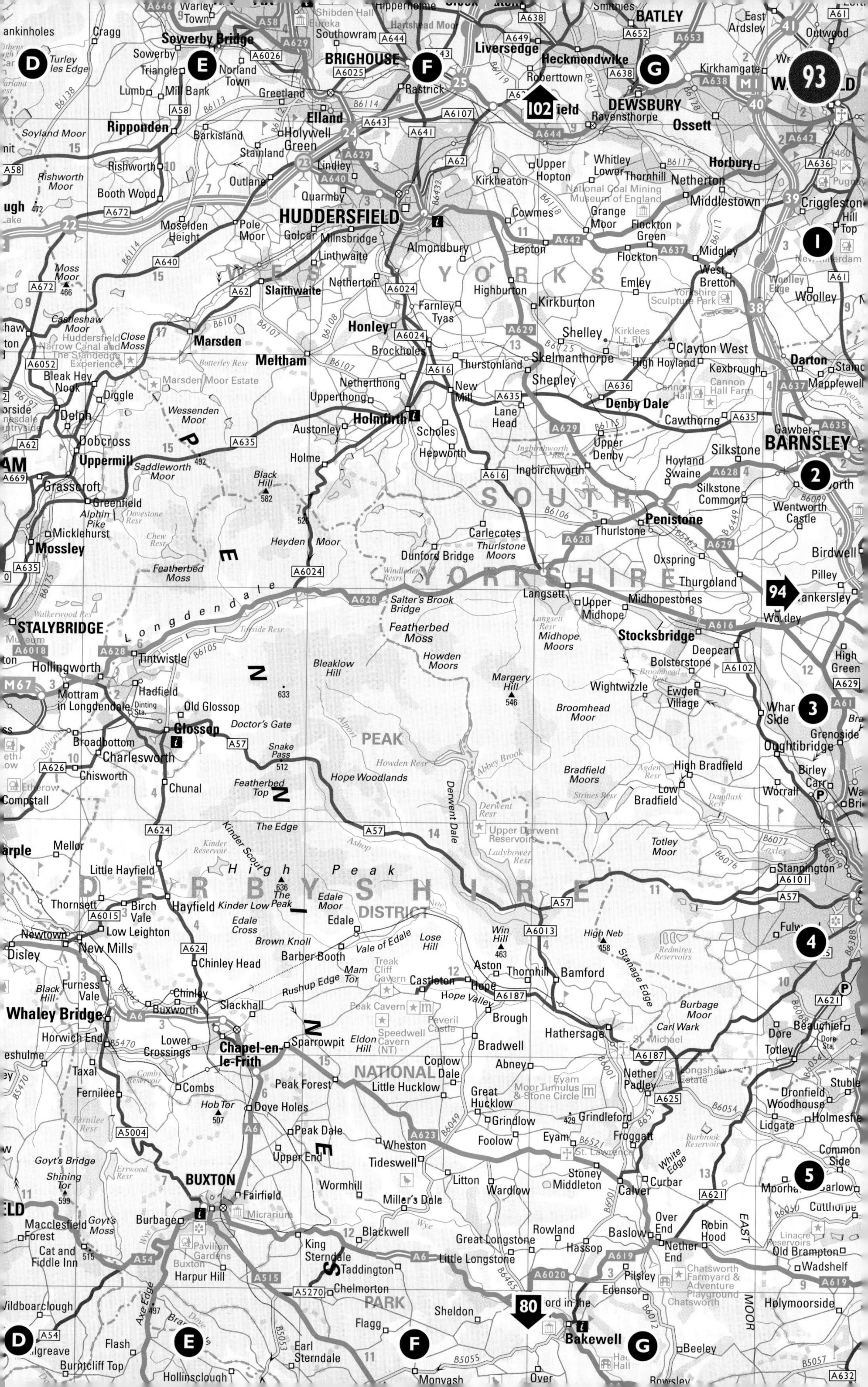

Sowerby Bridge
Sowerby
Triangle
Norland Town
Mill Bank
Lumb
Cragg
Turley Holes Edge
Ripponden
Barkisland
Soyland Moor
Rishworth
Rishworth Moor
Booth Wood
Moselden Height
Pole Moor
Outlane
Stainland
Holywell Green
Greetland
Elland
BRIGHOUSE
Southowram
Shibden Hall
Eureka
Hipperholme
Hartshead Moor
Rastrick
Liversedge
Heckmondwike
Roberttown
BATLEY
East Ardsley
Outwood
Kirkhamgate
DEWSBURY
Ravensthorpe
Ossett
Horbury
Whitley Lower
Thornhill
Netherton
Middlestown
Crigglestone
Hill Top
Upper Hopton
Kirkheaton
National Coal Mining Museum of England
Grange Moor
Flockton Green
Flockton
Midgley
Cowmes
Lepton
HUDDERSFIELD
Lindley
Quarmby
Golcar
Milnsbridge
Linthwaite
Almondbury
Slaithwaite
Netherton
Highburton
Kirkburton
Emley
West Bretton
Yorkshire Sculpture Park
Woolley
Woolley Edge
Moss Moor
Castleshaw Moor
Huddersfield Narrow Canal and The Standedge Experience
Close Moss
Marsden
Meltham
Honley
Farnley Tyas
Brockholes
Shelley
Kirklees Lt. Rly
Clayton West
High Hoyland
Kexbrough
Darton
Mapplewell
Skelmanthorpe
Shepley
Thurstonland
Netherthong
Upperthong
Holmfirth
New Mill
Lane Head
Denby Dale
Cannon Hall Farm
Cawthorne
Gawber
BARNSLEY
Bleak Hey Nook
Diggle
Delph
Dobcross
Uppermill
Marsden Moor Estate
Wessenden Moor
Butterley Resr
Saddleworth Moor
Austonley
Scholes
Hepworth
Holme
Black Hill
Ingbirchworth
Upper Denby
Hoyland Swaine
Silkstone
Silkstone Common
Wentworth Castle
Grasscroft
Greenfield
Alphin Pike
Dovestone Resr
Chew Resr
Micklehurst
Mossley
Heyden Moor
Carlecotes
Thurlstone Moors
Dunford Bridge
Thurlstone
Penistone
Oxspring
Thurgoland
Birdwell
Pilley
Featherbed Moss
Longdendale
Salter's Brook Bridge
Windleden Resrs
Langsett
Upper Midhope
Midhopestones
Tankersley
Wortley
STALYBRIDGE
Walkerwood Res
Torside Resr
Featherbed Moss
Howden Moors
Langsett Resr
Midhope Moors
Stocksbridge
Deepcar
Bolsterstone
Broomhead Resr
High Green
Hollingworth
Tintwistle
Bleaklow Hill
Margery Hill
Wightwizzle
Ewden Village
Mottram in Longdendale
Hadfield
Dinting Sta.
Old Glossop
Broomhead Moor
Whar Side
Grenoside
Glossop
Broadbottom
Charlesworth
Doctor's Gate
Snake Pass
PEAK
Oughtibridge
Bradfield Moors
Agden Resr
High Bradfield
Low Bradfield
Birley Carr
Chisworth
Chunal
Featherbed Top
Hope Woodlands
Howden Resr
Derwent Dale
Abbey Brook
Strines Resr
Damflask Resr
Worrall
Compstall
Etherow
The Edge
Kinder Scout
Derwent Resr
Upper Derwent Reservoirs
Ladybower Resr
Totley Moor
Loxley
Mellor
Kinder Reservoir
Ashop
Little Hayfield
High Peak
Stannington
DERBYSHIRE
Thornsett
Birch Vale
Hayfield
Kinder Low
The Peak
Edale Moor
DISTRICT
Newtown
Low Leighton
Edale Cross
Edale
Win Hill
High Neb
Disley
New Mills
Brown Knoll
Vale of Edale
Lose Hill
Stanage Edge
Redmires Reservoirs
Fulwood
Chinley Head
Barber Booth
Mam Tor
Treak Cliff Cavern
Aston
Thornhill
Bamford
Black Hill
Furness Vale
Chinley
Rushup Edge
Castleton
Hope
Hope Valley
Whaley Bridge
Buxworth
Slackhall
Peak Cavern
Peveril Castle
Brough
Burbage Moor
Carl Wark
Beauchief
Dore
Horwich End
Lower Crossings
Chapel-en-le-Frith
Sparrowpit
Eldon Hill
Speedwell Cavern (NT)
Bradwell
Hathersage
St. Michael
Totley
eshulme
Taxal
Combs Reservoir
Combs
NATIONAL
Coplow Dale
Little Hucklow
Abney
Nether Padley
Longshaw Estate
Dronfield Woodhouse
Fernilee
Peak Forest
Hob Tor
Dove Holes
Great Hucklow
Grindlow
Eyam Moor Tumulus & Stone Circle
Grindleford
Lidgate
Holmesfield
Fernilee Resr
Peak Dale
Foolow
Eyam
Froggatt
Barbrook Reservoir
Goyt's Bridge
Shining Tor
Errwood Resr
Upper End
Wheston
Tideswell
St. Lawrence
White Edge
Common Side
BUXTON
Fairfield
Wormhill
Litton
Wardlow
Stoney Middleton
Calver
Curbar
Moorhall
Barlow
Macclesfield Forest
Goyt's Moss
Burbage
Micrarium
Miller's Dale
Over End
Robin Hood
Cutthorpe
Cat and Fiddle Inn
Pavilion Gardens
Blackwell
Rowland
Hassop
Baslow
Nether End
Linacre Reservoirs
Old Brampton
King Sterndale
Great Longstone
Little Longstone
Wadshelf
Buxton
Harpur Hill
Axe Edge
Taddington
Chatsworth Farmyard & Adventure Playground
Chatsworth
Pilsley
Edensor
Holymoorside
Wildboarclough
Chelmorton
PARK
Sheldon
Bakewell
EAST MOOR
Flagg
Flash
Earl Sterndale
Beeley
Burntcliff Top
Hollinsclough
Monyash
Over Haddon
Hassop Hall
Rowsley
SOUTH YORKSHIRE
WEST YORKS
PEAK
DERBYSHIRE
94
80
102

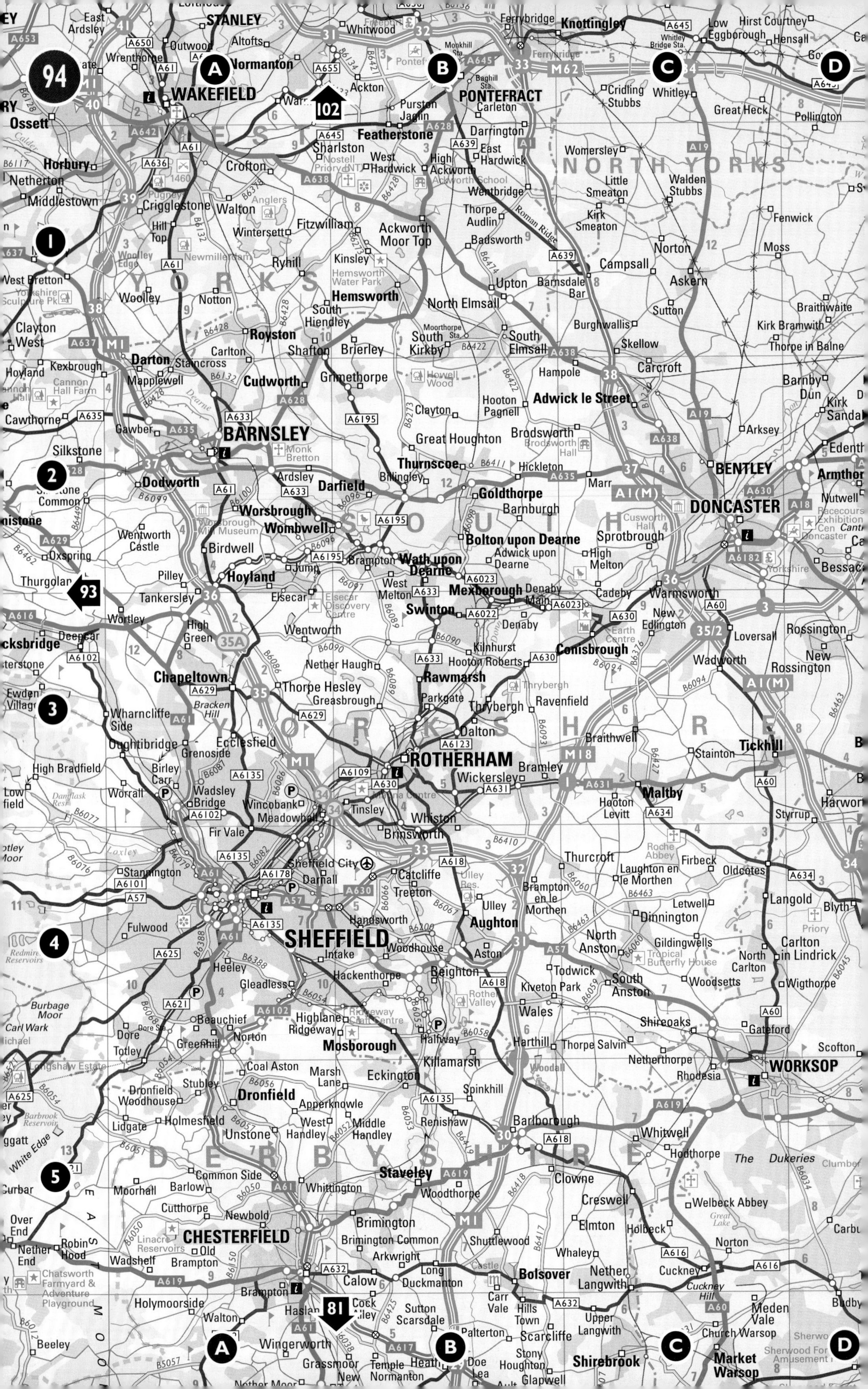

94
102
93
81
A
B
C
D
1
2
3
4
5
WAKEFIELD
STANLEY
Normanton
Altofts
Outwood
East Ardsley
Wrenthorpe
Ossett
Horbury
Netherton
Middlestown
Crigglestone
Walton
Crofton
Sharlston
Nostell Priory
Featherstone
Ackton
Whitwood
Pontefract
PONTEFRACT
Carleton
Ferrybridge
Knottingley
Low Eggborough
Hirst Courtney
Hensall
Whitley Bridge Sta.
Whitley
Cridling Stubbs
Great Heck
Pollington
Darrington
East Hardwick
High Ackworth
Ackworth School
West Hardwick
Purston Jaglin
Wentbridge
Thorpe Audlin
Badsworth
Womersley
Little Smeaton
Kirk Smeaton
Walden Stubbs
NORTH YORKS
Fenwick
Moss
Norton
Campsall
Askern
Roman Ridge
Fitzwilliam
Ackworth Moor Top
Kinsley
Hemsworth Water Park
Hemsworth
Ryhill
Wintersett
Anglers
Newmillerdam
Woolley Edge
Hill Top
Woolley
Notton
West Bretton
Yorkshire Sculpture Pk
Clayton West
Upton
Barnsdale Bar
North Elmsall
South Elmsall
South Kirkby
Moorthorpe Sta.
South Hiendley
Royston
Shafton
Brierley
Burghwallis
Skellow
Carcroft
Sutton
Braithwaite
Kirk Bramwith
Thorpe in Balne
Barnby Dun
Kirk Sandal
Arksey
Hampole
Adwick le Street
Hooton Pagnell
Howell Wood
Grimethorpe
Cudworth
Carlton
Staincross
Darton
Mapplewell
Kexbrough
Hoyland
Cannon Hall Farm
Cawthorne
Gawber
BARNSLEY
Monk Bretton
Silkstone
Silkstone Common
Dodworth
Ardsley
Darfield
Clayton
Great Houghton
Brodsworth
Brodsworth Hall
Thurnscoe
Billingley
Hickleton
Marr
Goldthorpe
Barnburgh
BENTLEY
DONCASTER
Armthorpe
Edenthorpe
Nutwell
Racecourse Exhibition Cen
Doncaster
Cantley
Bessacarr
Cusworth Hall
Sprotbrough
High Melton
Cadeby
Bolton upon Dearne
Adwick upon Dearne
Worsbrough
Worsbrough Mill Museum
Wombwell
Wentworth Castle
Birdwell
Oxspring
Thurgoland
Pilley
Tankersley
Hoyland
Jump
Brampton
Wath upon Dearne
Elsecar
Elsecar Discovery Centre
West Melton
Mexborough
Denaby Main
Denaby
Swinton
Warmsworth
New Edlington
Earth Centre
Conisbrough
Loversall
Rossington
New Rossington
Wadworth
Wortley
High Green
Deepcar
Stocksbridge
Wentworth
Kilnhurst
Hooton Roberts
Nether Haugh
Chapeltown
Thorpe Hesley
Greasbrough
Rawmarsh
Parkgate
Thrybergh
Ravenfield
Bracken Hill
Ewden Village
Wharncliffe Side
Oughtibridge
Grenoside
Ecclesfield
Dalton
ROTHERHAM
Bramley
Wickersley
Braithwell
Stainton
Tickhill
Maltby
Hooton Levitt
Harworth
Styrrup
High Bradfield
Birley Carr
Low Bradfield
Damflask Resr.
Worrall
Wadsley Bridge
Wincobank
Meadowhall
Tinsley
Whiston
Brinsworth
Fir Vale
Roche Abbey
Firbeck
Oldcotes
Thurcroft
Laughton en le Morthen
Brampton en le Morthen
Langold
Blyth
Letwell
Dinnington
Stannington
Sheffield City
Darnall
Catcliffe
Treeton
Ulley Res.
Ulley
Aughton
Fulwood
Handsworth
SHEFFIELD
Intake
Woodhouse
Aston
North Anston
Gildingwells
Tropical Butterfly House
North Carlton
Carlton in Lindrick
Wigthorpe
Woodsetts
South Anston
Todwick
Kiveton Park
Wales
Redmires Reservoirs
Heeley
Gleadless
Hackenthorpe
Beighton
Rother Valley
Burbage Moor
Carl Wark
Beauchief
Dore Sta.
Dore
Totley
Greenhill
Norton
Highlane
Ridgeway
Ridgeway Craft Centre
Mosborough
Halfway
Harthill
Thorpe Salvin
Shireoaks
Gateford
Netherthorpe
Rhodesia
WORKSOP
Scofton
Longshaw Estate
Coal Aston
Marsh Lane
Eckington
Killamarsh
Woodall
Dronfield Woodhouse
Stubley
Dronfield
Apperknowle
Spinkhill
Barbrook Reservoir
Lidgate
Holmesfield
Unstone
West Handley
Middle Handley
Renishaw
Barlborough
Whitwell
Hodthorpe
The Dukeries
Clumber
White Edge
Common Side
DERBYSHIRE
Barlow
Whittington
Staveley
Clowne
Creswell
Welbeck Abbey
Great Lake
Curbar
Moorhall
Cutthorpe
Newbold
Woodthorpe
Brimington
Brimington Common
Shuttlewood
Elmton
Holbeck
Norton
Carburton
Over End
Nether End
Robin Hood
Linacre Reservoirs
CHESTERFIELD
Old Brampton
Wadshelf
Arkwright
Whaley
Nether Langwith
Cuckney
Cuckney Hill
Chatsworth Farmyard & Adventure Playground
Brampton
Calow
Long Duckmanton
Bolsover
Castle
Carr Vale
Hills Town
Upper Langwith
Meden Vale
Budby
Holymoorside
Walton
Hasland
Cock Alley
Sutton Scarsdale
Palterton
Scarcliffe
Church Warsop
Sherwood Forest Amusement Park
Beeley
Wingerworth
Grassmoor
Temple Normanton
Heath
Doe Lea
Stony Houghton
Shirebrook
Market Warsop
Glapwell
New
Nether Moor
EAST MOOR
YORKSHIRE
SOUTH YORKSHIRE
WEST
M1
M62
M18
A1(M)
A1
A61
A638
A628
A635
A630
A631
A57
A619
A616
A60

95
104
96
83
D
E
F
G
I
2
3
4
5
EAST RIDING
OF YORKSHIRE
NORTH
LINCOLNSHIRE
LINCOLNSHIRE
NOTTINGHAMSHIRE
Humber
Redcliff Channel
South Channel
Read's Island
Rawcliffe
Goole
Saltmarshe
Yokefleet
Faxfleet
Whitton
Reedness
Swinefleet
Whitgift
Ousefleet
Alkborough
Winteringham
South Ferriby
Rawcliffe Bridge
Adlingfleet
West Halton
Coleby
Goole Fields
Marshland
Garthorpe
Fockerby
Burton upon Stather
Thealby
Winterton
Horkstow
Normanby Hall
Roxby
Goole Moors
Luddington
Normanby
Saxby All Saints
Moorends
Thorne Waste or Moors
Eastoft
Flixborough
Low Risby
High Risby
Appleby
Bonby
Risby Warren
Worlaby Carrs
Amcotts
Crosby Warren
Low Santon
Worlaby
Thorne
Crowle
Keadby
Frodingham
Elsham Hall
Elsham Sta.
Ealand
Gunness
Crosby
SCUNTHORPE
Hatfield Chase
Althorpe
Burringham
Derrythorpe
Ashby
Broughton
Hatfield Woodhouse
Sandtoft
Yaddlethorpe
Bottesford
Brigg
Wrawby
Westgate
Belton
Beltoft
West Butterwick
Bottesford Beck
Hatfield Moors
Isle of Axholme
Scawby
Epworth
Old Rectory
Messingham
Howsham
Wroot
Low Burnham
Manton
Cadney
Susworth
Scotterthorpe
Hibaldstow
North Kelsey
Kelfield
Scotter
Blaxton
Owston Ferry
East Lound
Redbourne
Westwoodside
Haxey
East Ferry
Scotton
Graiseland
Kirton in Lindsey
South Kelsey
Wildsworth
Laughton
Northorpe
Waddingham
Brandy Wharf
Misterton
West Stockwith
Blyton
Grayingham
Snitterby
Misterton Carr
Misson
East Stockwith
Blyborough
Pilham
Willoughton
Walkerith
Atterby
Aisby
Walkeringham
Bishop Norton
Scaftworth
Harwell
Gringley on the Hill
Corringham
Hemswell
Spital in the Street
Bishopbridge
Everton
Glentham
Morton
Beckingham
Old Hall
Gainsborough
Harpswell
Caenby Corner
Normanby-by-Spital
Caenby
Wiseton
Mattersey
Mattersey Priory
Springthorpe
Heapham
Glentworth
Clayworth
Saundby
Bole
Upton
Owmby-by-Spital
Torworth
Lea
Kexby
North Wheatley
South Wheatley
Fillingham
Saxby
Lound
Knaith
Ermine Street
Spridlington
Sutton
Hayton
Sturton le Steeple
Willingham
Coates
Ingham
Cold Hanworth
Gate Burton
Normanby by Stow
Clarborough
North Leverton with Habblesthorpe
Littleborough
Hackthorn
Welham
Stow
Cammeringham
Marton
Snarford
Retford (East Retford)
South Leverton
Cottam
Brattleby
Thorpe in the Fallows
Aisthorpe
Sturton by Stow
Welton
Ryland
Sundown Kiddies Adventureland
Brampton
Scampton
Dunholme
Ordsall
Grove
Treswell
Rampton
Torksey
Roman Road
Bransby
Broxholme
Eaton
Ingleby
Stainton by Langworth
Woodbeck
North Carlton
Nether Headon
Headon
Stokeham
Gamston
Upton
Laneham
Laughterton
Fenton
South Carlton
Sudbrooke
East Drayton
Saxilby
Elkesley
Askham
Dunham
Toll
Kettlethorpe
Burton
Nettleham
Newton on Trent
Broadholme
West Drayton
Markham Moor
Darlton
Ragnall
Thorney
Reepham
Cherry Willingham
Milton
East Markham
North Clifton
Skellingthorpe
Bevercotes
West Markham
Cath.
Walesby
Tuxford
South Clifton
Harby
LINCOLN
Washingborough
Wigsley
Doddington
Canwick
Doddington Hall
Hartsholme
Heighington
Normanton on Trent
Spalford
Egmanton
Boultham
Kirton
Grassthorpe
Bracebridge
Weston
Whisby
Branston
Swallow Beck
Bracebridge Heath
Laxton
Sutton on Trent
Eagle
Wellow
Moorhouse
Girton
North Hykeham
Trent
Don
Idle
Old Ancholme
New Ancholme
Weir Dike
North Kelsey Beck
Eau
Till
Meden
Poulter
M62
M18
M180
M181
A614
A161
A1077
A18
A1146
A1029
A1084
A15
A159
A631
A620
A638
A156
A1500
A1133
A57
A6075
A1
A46
A158
A607
A1434
B1430
B1392
B1216
B1450
B1207
B1204
B1218
B1208
B1206
B1398
B1400
B1396
B1205
B1403
B1433
B1241
B1190
B1378
B1003
B1131
B1308
B1188
B6045
B6420
B6387
B1164

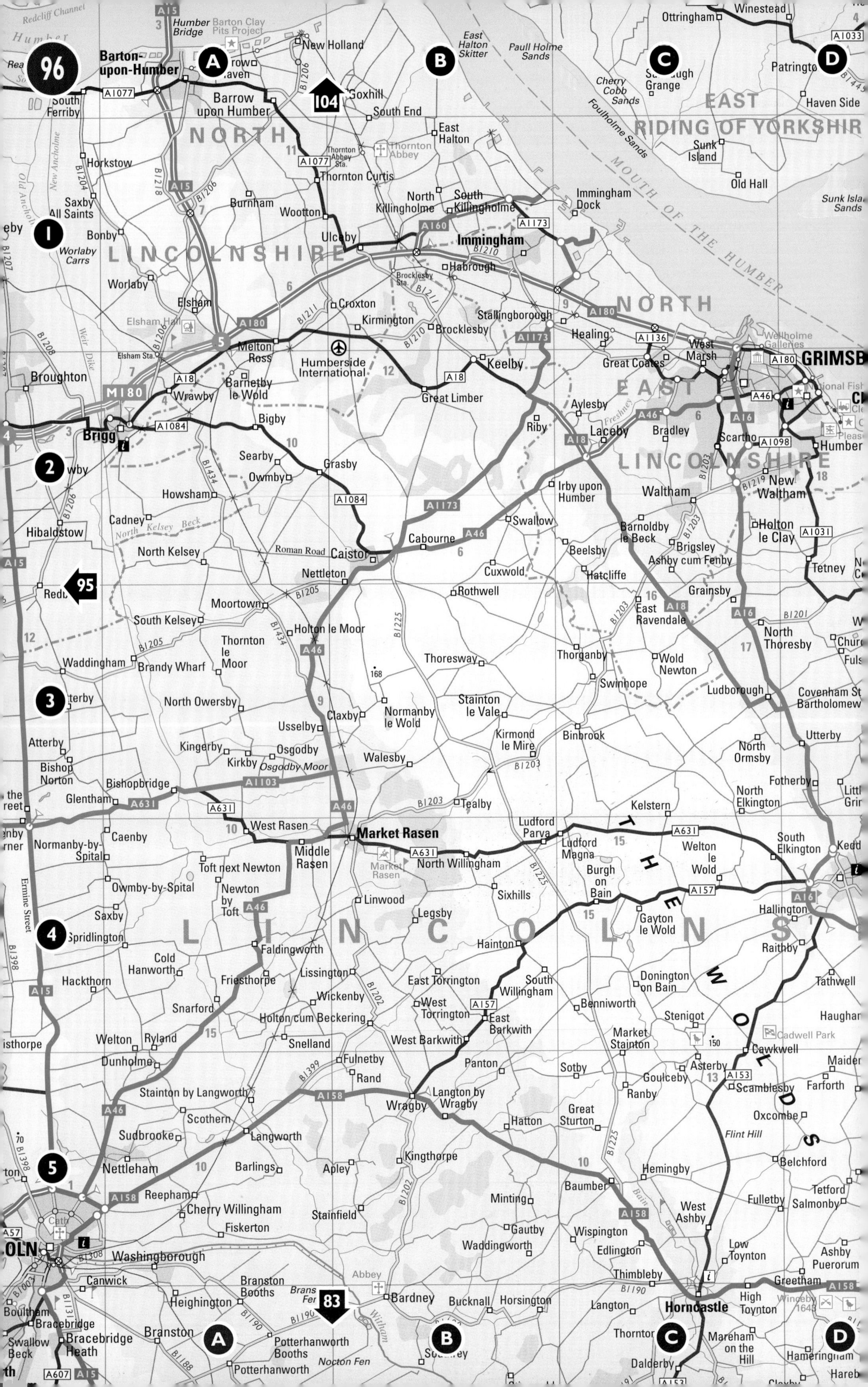

96
104
95
83
A
B
C
D
1
2
3
4
5
Humber
Redcliff Channel
Barton-upon-Humber
Humber Bridge
Barton Clay Pits Project
New Holland
Barrow Haven
Barrow upon Humber
East Halton Skitter
Paull Holme Sands
Cherry Cobb Sands
Foulholme Sands
Sunk Island
Old Hall
Sunk Island Sands
Ottringham
Winestead
Patrington
Haven Side
EAST RIDING OF YORKSHIRE
MOUTH OF THE HUMBER
South Ferriby
Goxhill
South End
East Halton
Thornton Abbey
Thornton Curtis
Horkstow
Saxby All Saints
Burnham
Wootton
North Killingholme
South Killingholme
Immingham Dock
Immingham
Ulceby
Habrough
Bonby
Worlaby
Worlaby Carrs
LINCOLNSHIRE
NORTH
Elsham
Elsham Hall
Elsham Sta.
Croxton
Kirmington
Brocklesby
Stallingborough
Healing
Melton Ross
Humberside International
Keelby
Great Coates
West Marsh
GRIMSBY
Broughton
Wrawby
Barnetby le Wold
Great Limber
Aylesby
Laceby
Bradley
Scartho
Humber
Brigg
Bigby
Riby
Searby
Owmby
Grasby
Howsham
Irby upon Humber
Waltham
New Waltham
Hibaldstow
Cadney
Kelsey Beck
Swallow
Barnoldby le Beck
Holton le Clay
Brigsley
Ashby cum Fenby
Tetney
Cabourne
Caistor
Roman Road
North Kelsey
Beelsby
Cuxwold
Hatcliffe
Nettleton
Rothwell
Grainsby
East Ravendale
Moortown
South Kelsey
Holton le Moor
North Thoresby
Thornton le Moor
Thoresway
Thorganby
Wold Newton
Waddingham
Brandy Wharf
Swinhope
Ludborough
Covenham St Bartholomew
North Owersby
Stainton le Vale
Normanby le Wold
Claxby
Usselby
Kirmond le Mire
Binbrook
Utterby
North Ormsby
Atterby
Bishop Norton
Kingerby
Osgodby
Kirkby
Osgodby Moor
Walesby
Bishopbridge
Glentham
Tealby
Fotherby
North Elkington
Kelstern
Ludford Parva
Ludford Magna
West Rasen
Market Rasen
Middle Rasen
North Willingham
Caenby
Normanby-by-Spital
Toft next Newton
Welton le Wold
South Elkington
Owmby-by-Spital
Newton by Toft
Burgh on Bain
Linwood
Sixhills
Saxby
Spridlington
Legsby
Gayton le Wold
Hallington
Ermine Street
LINCOLNS
THE WOLDS
Faldingworth
Hainton
Raithby
Cold Hanworth
Hackthorn
Friesthorpe
Lissington
East Torrington
South Willingham
Donington on Bain
Tathwell
Snarford
Wickenby
West Torrington
East Barkwith
Benniworth
Holton cum Beckering
Stenigot
Welton
Ryland
Snelland
West Barkwith
Market Stainton
Cadwell Park
Dunholme
Fulnetby
Rand
Panton
Sotby
Cawkwell
Asterby
Goulceby
Scamblesby
Farforth
Ranby
Stainton by Langworth
Langton by Wragby
Wragby
Great Sturton
Hatton
Oxcombe
Scothern
Sudbrooke
Langworth
Flint Hill
Nettleham
Barlings
Apley
Kingthorpe
Hemingby
Belchford
Reepham
Cherry Willingham
Minting
Baumber
Fulletby
Tetford
Salmonby
West Ashby
Stainfield
Fiskerton
Gautby
Wispington
Waddingworth
Edlington
Low Toynton
Ashby Puerorum
Washingborough
Thimbleby
Greetham
Canwick
Branston Booths
Abbey
Bardney
Brans Fer
Bucknall
Horsington
Langton
Horncastle
High Toynton
Winceby 1643
Heighington
Branston
Bracebridge
Bracebridge Heath
Boultham
Swallow Beck
Potterhanworth Booths
Potterhanworth
Nocton Fen
Witham
Thornton
Mareham on the Hill
Dalderby
Hameringham
Bain
A15
A1077
A160
A1173
A180
A18
A1084
M180
A1136
A46
A16
A1098
A1031
A1103
A631
A157
A153
A158
A607
B1206
B1204
B1218
B1210
B1211
B1208
B1207
B1434
B1205
B1225
B1203
B1219
B1201
B1202
B1399
B1398
B1308
B1190
B1188
B1131
B1003
168
150

D
E
F
G
105
Holmpton
Out Newton
Weeton
Skeffling
Easington
Skeffling Clays
Kilnsea
Kilnsea Clays
Spurn Head
0 2 4 6 8 10 miles
0 2 4 6 8 10 km
1
2
3
4
5
RPES
Coast Light Rly
Discovery Centre
Kingston upon Hull to... hours
Rotterdam................................14
Zeebrugge...............................14
Marsh Chapel
Eskham
Wragholme
Donna Nook
Meals
North Somercotes
Ludney
Conisholme
Church End
A1031
South Somercotes
Saltfleet
Skidbrooke
Saltfleetby St Clements
Alvingham
Saltfleetby All Saints
North
South
Saltfleetby St Peter
Theddlethorpe St Helen
Grimoldby
B1200
Theddlethorpe All Saints
Manby
Little Carlton
Great Carlton
Great Eau
Mablethorpe
Legbourne
South Reston
Gayton le Marsh
A1104
Trusthorpe
North Reston
Strubby
Thorpe
A52
Withern
A157
Authorpe
Tothill
Maltby le Marsh
Sutton on Sea
B1373
Sandilands
Beesby
Sutton le Marsh
Claythorpe
Belleau
Markby
Hannah
Aby
Saleby
A1111
White Pit
Swaby
A1104
South Thoresby
Bilsby
B1449
Huttoft
Alford
Rigsby
A1104
Anderby
Farlesthorpe
Mumby
Well
Driby
Authorpe Row
Ulceby Cross
Cumberworth
A52
Harrington
Ulceby
Harrington Hall
B1196
Hogsthorpe
Chapel St Leonards
A16
Willoughby
Langton
Claxby
Sloothby
Skendleby
A1028
Welton le Marsh
Sausthorpe
Addlethorpe
85
Fantasy Island
Ingoldmells Point
Partney
A158
Ashby by Partney
Orby
Hundleby
Spilsby
Candlesby
Orby Marsh
Butlins Family Entertainment Resort, Skegness
Gunby Hall (NT)
Burgh Marsh
Burgh
Winthorpe
16
11
8
15
9
13
3
4
2
12

A B C D

ISLE OF MAN
1
2
3
4
5
Point of Ayre
The Ayres
A16
Rue Point
Visitors Centre
Smeale Farm
Glentruan
Cranstal
The Lhen
A10
Bride
Dhowin
A17
A19
Andreas
Sartfield
Jurby Head
Jurby West
Jurby
Jurby East
B3
A9
Shellag Point
Ballasalla
Sandygate
A17
B14
B7
Regaby
Ballachurry Fort
A13
Crawyn
A14
St Judes
Dhoor
Ramsey Bay
The Cronk
The Curraghs
A13
B9
Sulby
A3
B14
Ramsey
A10
Churchtown
Orrisdale
A3
Ballaugh
Glen Auldyn
A18
Port e Vullen
Orrisdale Head
Ravensdale
A15
Maughold Head & Brooghs (MNT)
Maughold Head
T.T. Course
Dreemskerry
Maughold
Kirk Michael
Glen Auldyn
North Barrule
565
Slieau Curn
I S L E
Ballajora
Port Mooar
Corrany
Slieau Dhoo
Slieau Managh
T.T. Course
Clagh Ouyr
Ballacarnane Beg
A3
Sileau Freoaghane
A14
Manx Electric Rly
488
Sulby Resr
Snaefell
Glen Mona
Barregarrow
Sartfell
621
A2
Gob y Deigan
Slieau Lhean
Port Cornaa
Shoughlaige-e-Caine
B10
Dhoon
Knocksharry
A4
Little London
Beinn-y-Phott
Laxey Wheel
St. German's Cath
Cronk-y-Voddy
546
O F
Snaefell Mountain Rly
Bulgham Bay
Peel
Ballagyr
Injebreck
Laxey Glen
St Patrick's Isle
Lambfell Moar
Colden
Injebreck Resr
B11
Peel Castle & Round Tower
Neb
487
Ballaheannagh
Laxey
House of Manannan
A20
Laxey Head
Contrary Head
A1
Ballig
Sileau Ruy
B22
A18
B12
Ballacannell
Tynwald
478
Laxey Bay
Knockaloe Moar
Greeba Mountain
Baldwin
Baldrine
Patrick
A30
St John's
M A N
B20
Garwick Bay
A27
T.T. Course
B21
333
A3
A1
A23
Hillberry
Clay Head
Glenmaye
Crosby
A22
A2
Dalby Point
Glen Vine
Strang
Dalby
Foxdale
Eairy
Garth
B35
Onchan
A11
Port Groudle
Niarbyl Island
Dalby Mountain
A36
A24
Union Mills
Niarbyl Bay
A26
B32
Onchan Head
South Barrule
B36
Manx Mus
Douglas Bay
483
Close Clark
Stuggadhoo
Braaid
A24
13
B39
B35
B37
A41
DOUGLAS
Stroin Vuigh
341
A27
Quine's Hill
A37
Douglas Head
Ballamodha
Newtown
B29
A3
St Mark's
Ronague
Lingague
B44
Grenaby
A26
Ballaveare
Little Ness
Fleshwick Bay
A36
Ballakilpheric
B40
A5
A25
Isle of Man Steam Rly
Bradda
Colby
Ballabeg
B25
Bradda Head
A32
Ballafesson
A7
Ballasalla
Santon Head
Port Erin
Croit e Caley
A3
B53
Port Grenaugh
Meayl Circle
Balladoole
Nautical Mus
Isle of Man
Derbyhaven
Calf of Man
Cregneash
The Howe
Port St Mary
Bay ny Carrickey
Rushen
Derby Fort
A31
Perwick Bay
Castletown
St Michael's Island
Castletown Bay
Spanish Head
Langness
Dreswick Point
hours
Belfast (Summer Only) 2¾
Dublin (Summer Only) 2¾-4¾
Heysham 3½
Liverpool 2½-4
same scale as main map


A B C D

D
E
F
G
Dalton-in-Furness
Great Urswick
Little Urswick
Bardsea
Stainton with Adgarley
Hawcoat
Baycliff
Humphrey Head Point
Scales
A590
Furness Abbey
Dendron
Aldingham
Gleaston
A5087
107
Newbarns
North Scale
Furness Mus
Leece
Dock Museum
Roosecote
Newbiggin
Vickerstown
BARROW-IN-FURNESS
MORECAMBE
Lancaster Sound
Cartmel Wharf
BAY
Tummer Hill Scar
CUMBRIA
Biggar
Rampside
Mort Bank
Roa Island
ISLE OF WALNEY
Sheep Island
Foulney Island
MORECAMBE
West End
A5105
Yeoman Wharf
Piel
Piel Island
Sandylands
South End
Piel Bar
Oxcliffe
Hilpsford Point
HEYSHAM
Heaton
A683
Heysham Lake
Middleton
hours
Belfast....4
Douglas, Isle of Man....3½
Overton
Sunderland Bank
Sunderland Point
2
Cockersand Abbey
hours
Larne....8
Bernard Wharf
North Wharf
Pilling Lane
100
Rossall Point
Pilling
Knott End-on-Sea
Preesall
Fisher's Row
FLEETWOOD
Stake Pool
Freeport
Stalmine
Wyre
Burn Naze
LANCS
3
A587
Staynall
A588
Cleveleys
Trunnah
Hambleton Moss Side
Thornton
Hambleton
Little Bispham
Out Rawcliffe
Norbreck
Whin Lane End
Toll
Bispham
Carleton
A585
Great Eccleston
A586
North Shore
A587
Poulton-le-Fylde
Singleton
BLACKPOOL
A584
A587
Thistleton
Elswick
B5266
Normoss
BLACKPOOL
Staining
A585
Esprick
B5260
Blackpool Tower
Blackpool Zoo
Greenhalgh
Sea Life Centre
Great Marton
Weeton
4
South Shore
A5073
A583
South Pier
Common Edge
M55
Great Plumpton
Wesham
Pleasure Beach
B5262
A583
Kirkham
A5230
Squires Gate
Westby
Blackpool
Wrea Green
B5261
B5259
Higher Ballam
Moss Side
St Anne's
LYTHAM ST ANNE'S
Ansdell
Saltcotes
Warton
Lytham
Lytham
Salter's Bank
Ribble
0
2
4
6
8
10 miles
0
2
4
6
8
10 km
Banks Sands
5
Hesketh Bank
Becconsall
Hundred End
Banks
Horse Bank
Crossens
Marshside
Churchtown
91
Mere Brow
SOUTHPORT
Pleasureland
Martin Mere
Zoo
G
Holmeswood
Trans Pennine Trail
Birkdale
Brown
Bescar Lane
D
E
F

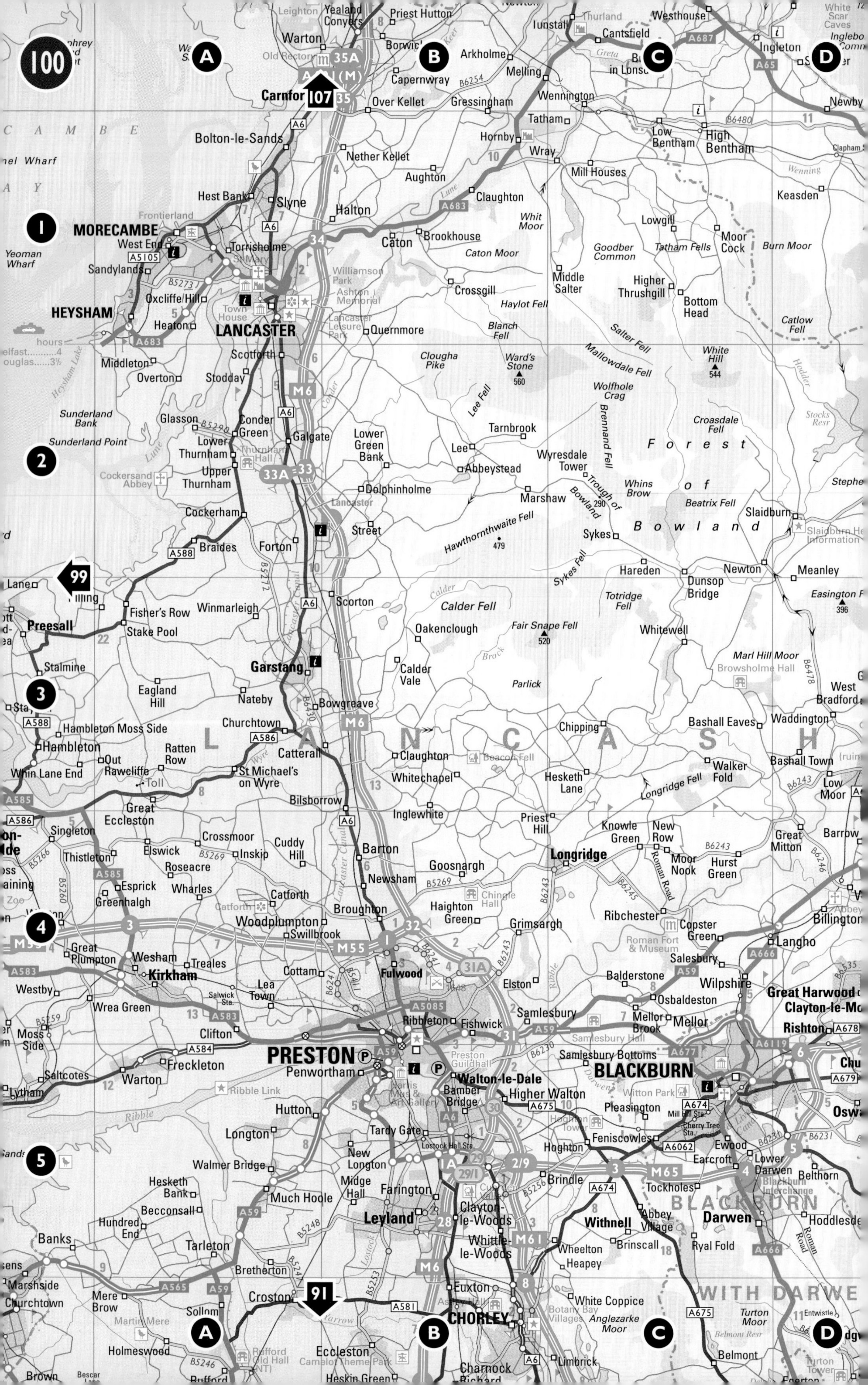

100
A
B
C
D
107
99
91
1
2
3
4
5
Leighton
Yealand Conyers
Priest Hutton
Warton
Old Rectory
Borwick
Arkholme
Tunstall
Thurland
Cantsfield
Westhouse
Ingleton
White Scar Caves
Newby
Carnforth
Capernwray
Melling
Over Kellet
Gressingham
Wennington
Tatham
Low Bentham
High Bentham
Hornby
Wray
Bolton-le-Sands
Nether Kellet
Aughton
Mill Houses
Keasden
Hest Bank
Slyne
Halton
Claughton
Whit Moor
Lowgill
Moor Cock
Burn Moor
MORECAMBE
Frontierland
West End
Torrisholme
Caton
Brookhouse
Caton Moor
Goodber Common
Tatham Fells
Yeoman Wharf
Sandylands
Williamson Park
Ashton Memorial
Middle Salter
Higher Thrushgill
Bottom Head
Oxcliffe Hill
Crossgill
Haylot Fell
HEYSHAM
Town House
Heaton
LANCASTER
Lancaster Leisure Park
Quernmore
Blanch Fell
Salter Fell
Catlow Fell
Middleton
Overton
Scotforth
Stodday
Clougha Pike
Ward's Stone
560
Mallowdale Fell
White Hill
544
Heysham Lake
Sunderland Bank
Sunderland Point
Glasson
Conder Green
Lower Thurnham
Thurnham Hall
Upper Thurnham
Galgate
Lower Green Bank
Lee Fell
Tarnbrook
Wolfhole Crag
Brennand Fell
Croasdale Fell
Stocks Resr
Forest of Bowland
Lee
Abbeystead
Wyresdale Tower
Cockersand Abbey
Dolphinholme
Marshaw
Trough of Bowland
290
Whins Brow
Beatrix Fell
Slaidburn
Cockerham
Street
Hawthornthwaite Fell
479
Sykes
Braides
Forton
Hareden
Newton
Meanley
Sykes Fell
Dunsop Bridge
Easington Fell
396
Winmarleigh
Scorton
Calder Fell
Totridge Fell
Preesall
Fisher's Row
Stake Pool
Oakenclough
Fair Snape Fell
520
Whitewell
Stalmine
Garstang
Calder Vale
Marl Hill Moor
Browsholme Hall
West Bradford
Eagland Hill
Nateby
Bowgreave
Parlick
Churchtown
Hambleton Moss Side
Chipping
Bashall Eaves
Waddington
Hambleton
Ratten Row
Catterall
Claughton
Beacon Fell
Bashall Town
Whin Lane End
Out Rawcliffe
Toll
St Michael's on Wyre
Whitechapel
Hesketh Lane
Longridge Fell
Walker Fold
Low Moor
Great Eccleston
Bilsborrow
Inglewhite
Priest Hill
Knowle Green
New Row
Great Mitton
Barrow
Singleton
Crossmoor
Cuddy Hill
Barton
Longridge
Thistleton
Elswick
Inskip
Roseacre
Goosnargh
Moor Nook
Hurst Green
Esprick
Greenhalgh
Wharles
Newsham
Chingle Hall
Catforth
Haighton Green
Broughton
Grimsargh
Ribchester
Copster Green
Billington
Woodplumpton
Swillbrook
Roman Fort & Museum
Langho
Great Plumpton
Wesham
Treales
Kirkham
Cottam
Fulwood
Elston
Salesbury
Balderstone
Wilpshire
Great Harwood
Clayton-le-Moors
Westby
Wrea Green
Salwick Sta.
Lea Town
Ribbleton
Fishwick
Samlesbury
Osbaldeston
Mellor Brook
Mellor
Rishton
Moss Side
Clifton
Samlesbury Hall
PRESTON
Preston Guildhall
Samlesbury Bottoms
BLACKBURN
Freckleton
Penwortham
Walton-le-Dale
Saltcotes
Lytham
Warton
Ribble Link
Harris Mus & Art Gallery
Bamber Bridge
Higher Walton
Witton Park
Pleasington
Mill Hill Sta.
Cherry Tree Sta.
Hutton
Tardy Gate
Hoghton Tower
Feniscowles
Ewood
Longton
Lostock Hall Sta.
Hoghton
Earcroft
Lower Darwen
Belthorn
Walmer Bridge
New Longton
Brindle
Tockholes
Blackburn Interchange
Hesketh Bank
Midge Hall
Farington
Much Hoole
Becconsall
Clayton-le-Woods
Withnell
Abbey Village
Darwen
Hoddlesden
Hundred End
Leyland
Whittle-le-Woods
Banks
Tarleton
Wheelton
Brinscall
Ryal Fold
Roman Road
Heapey
Marshside
Churchtown
Bretherton
Euxton
Mere Brow
Croston
White Coppice
Botany Bay Villages
Anglezarke Moor
BLACKBURN WITH DARWEN
Turton Moor
Entwistle
Martin Mere
Sollom
CHORLEY
Belmont Resr
Holmeswood
Rufford Old Hall (NT)
Eccleston
Camelot Theme Park
Charnock Richard
Limbrick
Belmont
Turton Tower
Heskin Green
Brown
Bescar Lane
Rufford
M6
M55
M61
M65
A6
A65
A683
A687
A5105
A588
A586
A585
A583
A584
A59
A5085
A675
A674
A6062
A6119
A678
A679
A666
A565
A581
B6254
B6480
B5273
B5290
B5272
B6430
B6243
B6245
B6246
B5269
B5266
B5260
B5259
B6241
B5411
B6230
B6231
B5256
B5248
B5247
B5253
B6478
B6235
B5246

NORTH YORKSHIRE
PENNINE
WEST YORKSHIRE
NATIONAL PARK
109
102
93
D
E
F
G
D
E
F
G
2
3
4
5
I
New Houses
Pen-y-Ghent
694
Nether Heselden
Littondale
Kettlewell
703
Riggs Moor
Stean
Lofthouse
How Stean
Ribblesdale
Fountains Fell
668
Darnbrook Fell
Arn
Skirfare
Hawkswick
Great Whernside Moor
Meugher
Stean Moor
Ramsgill
Moughton Fell
Studfold
Arncliffe Cote
Wharfe
Helwith Bridge
538
Grassington Moor
Austwick
Feizor
Stainforth Bridge (NT)
Stainforth
Malham Tarn
Kilnsey
Conistone
Heathfield Moor
Hebden Moor
B6160
Appletreewick
Eldroth
Stackhouse
Watershed Mill Visitor Centre
Langcliffe
Bordley
Pateley
Green Hill
Moor
Giggleswick
Settle
553
Kirkby Fell
Threshfield
Grassington
Grimwith Resr
B6265
Giggleswick Sta.
Malham
Grassington National Park Centre
Linton
Hebden
Wham
Malham National Park Centre
Burnsall
Cleatop
Winterburn Resr
Threapland
Thorpe
Dibb
Pock Stones Moor
Black Hill
Hanlith
Kirkby Malham
Way Gill
Cracoe
Appletreewick
Rathmell
Mearbeck
Howgill
Simon's Seat
Airton
506
Calton
Drebley
Thruscross Resr
Long Gill
Long Preston
Hetton
Rylstone
Barden Fell
Brown Bank Head
Otterburn
Winterburn
Earl Seat
410
West End
Hellifield
Eshton
Barden Resrs
Eller Beck
Wigglesworth
Bell Busk
Flasby
Embsay Moor
A65
Priory (rems. of)
Hill End
Halton West
Coniston Cold
Eastby
Halton East
Bolton Abbey Estate
A59
Round Hill
Embsay Steam Rly
Bolton Abbey
409
Nappa
Gargrave
Stirton
Embsay
Bolton Bridge
Beamsley Beacon
Paythorne Moor
Bank Newton
Thorlby
Draughton
Beamsley
Chelker Resr
March Ghyll Resr
Paythorne
Newsholme
East Marton
Broughton
A6069
Holy Trinity
Langbar
Horton
Skipton
A682
West Marton
A6131
Carleton
Addingham
Middleton
Holden
Bolton by Bowland
A56
Elslack
Ravenshaw
Low Bradley
Gisburn
Bracewell
A629
13
Ilkley
B6251
Thornton-in-Craven
Pinhaw
388
Cononley
B6382
Sawley
B6252
Earby
Silsden
Manor House
Sawley Abbey
Newby
Barnoldswick
Rombalds Moor
Ilkley Moor
402
Rimington
Salterforth
Lothersdale
Kildwick
A6034
B6383
Downham
Weets Hill
Kelbrook
Cross Hills
Glusburn
Airedale
Greystone
Whitemoor Resr
Steeton
Sutton-in-Craven
Worston
Riddlesden
Foulridge
Cowling
East Morton
Pendle Hill
557
Blacko
Laneshaw Resr
Cliffe Cas. Art Gall & Mus
Utley
East Riddlesden Hall (NT)
Barley
Roughlee
B6247
A6068
KEIGHLEY
Laycock
Eldwick
Ogden Resrs
Barrowford
Colne
Laneshawbridge
Pendleton
Newchurch
Wheatley Lane
Pendle Heritage Centre
B6250
Winewall
Ingrow
Keighley & Worth Valley Rly
BINGLEY
The Forest of Pendle
Wycoller
443
Keighley Moor
Oakworth
1853 Gallery
Sabden
Sabden Brook
Trawden
Oldfield
Harden
Fence
NELSON
The Forest of Trawden
B6143
Haworth
B6429
Higham
A6068
Worth
Bronte Weaving Shed
A650
Stanbury
Cullingworth
Brierfield
Catlow
Boulsworth Hill
518
Haworth Moor
Penistone Hill
Bronte Parsonage
Wilsden
Simonstone
Gawthorpe Hall (NT)
Haggate
B6144
Read
Calder
Harle Syke
Oxenhope
B6146
Sandy Lane
Padiham
Denholme
A6114
Widdop
Walshaw Dean Resrs
A6033
Leeming
BRADFORD
Forest of Burnley
Worsthorne
Wadsworth Moor
B6141
B6145
A678
BURNLEY
Hurstwood Resr
Gorple Resrs
Denholme Clough
Thornton
Hapton
Towneley Hall Art Gall & Mus
Hurstwood
Hebden Water
451
Warley Moor Resr
Ogden Water
Clayton
Huncoat
Hardcastle Crags
Heptonstall Moor
Ogden
Queensbury
Great Hameldon
409
A679
Walk Mill
A682
A646
Calder
Pecket Well
B6380
Buttershaw
Hameldon Hill
479
High Gate
Wainstalls
Illingworth
Shelf
A644
Dunnockshaw
Clowbridge Resr
A671
Holme Chapel
Redmires Dam
Old Grammar School Mus
Blackshaw Head
Heptonstall
Hebden Bridge
Mount Tabor
Holmfield
A647
Ovenden
Northowram
A680
Baxenden
Love Clough
Forest of Rossendale
Heald Moor
Cornholme
Mytholm
Walkley Clogs
Midgley
Boothtown
Lydgate
Eastwood
Walkley's Canalside Mill
Luddenden
A56
Crawshawbooth
Water
B6238
Weir
Mytholmroyd
Acre
Warley Town
HALIFAX
Shibden
Haslingden
A682
RAWTENSTALL
Bacup
A681
Todmorden
Clough Foot
Mankinholes
Cragg
Eureka
Southowram
Newchurch
Stacksteads
Lumbutts
Gorpley Resr
Withens Clough Resr
Turley Holes Edge
Sowerby Bridge
A6026
BRIGHOUSE
A681
Waterfoot
Britannia
E. Lancs. Rly
Rochdale Canal Restoration
454
Sowerby
A6025
Helmshore
A671
Triangle
Norland Town
Walsden
B6138
Greetland
Brandwood Moor
Shawforth
Warland Resr
Lumb
Mill Bank
B6114
Warland
A58
B6113
Elland
B6214
B6527
A6033
Edenfield
Whittle Hill
468
Cowm Resr
Calderbrook
Soyland Moor
Ripponden
Barkisland
Holywell Green
418
Whitworth
Summit
Stainland
Lindley
Watergrove Resr
A629
A680
A58
Rishworth
Outlane
Shuttleworth
Spring Mill Resr
Clough
Rishworth Moor
A640
Ramsbottom
Wardle
Booth Wood
M62
Quarmby
Broadley
Littleborough
472
Cheesden
Naden Resrs
Healey
A672
HUDDERSFIELD
Ashworth Moor Resr
A58
Smithy Bridge
Hollingworth Lake
Moselden
Pole

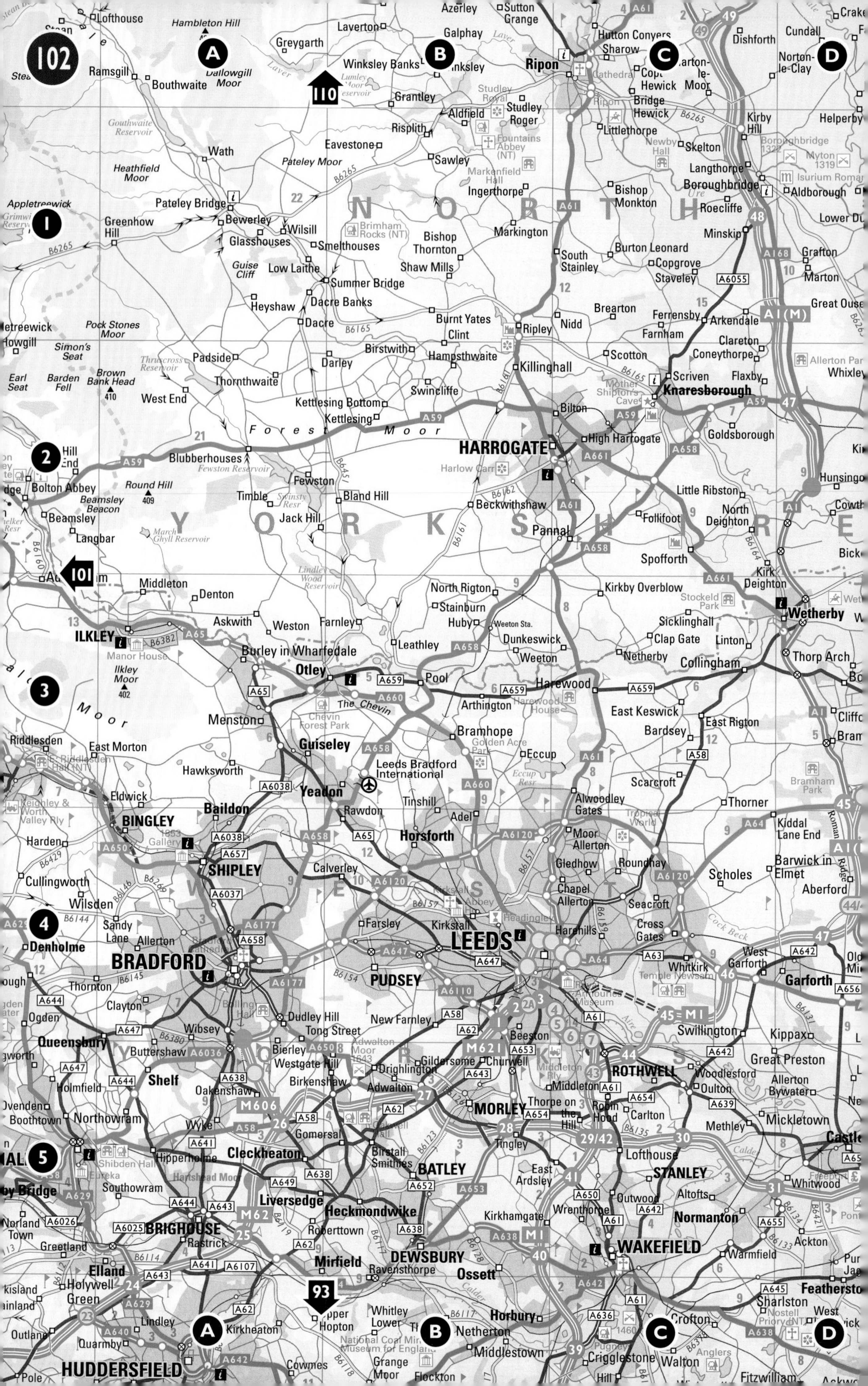

110
101
93
A
B
C
D
1
2
3
4
5
Lofthouse
Hambleton Hill
Ramsgill
Bouthwaite
Dallowgill Moor
Laverton
Greygarth
Winksley Banks
Winksley
Azerley
Sutton Grange
Galphay
Lumley Moor Reservoir
Grantley
Ripon
Hutton Conyers
Sharow
Copt Hewick
Marton-le-Moor
Cundall
Norton-le-Clay
Dishforth
Cathedral
Bridge Hewick
Studley Royal
Studley Roger
Aldfield
Risplith
Fountains Abbey (NT)
Littlethorpe
Kirby Hill
Helperby
Skelton
Newby Hall
Boroughbridge
Langthorpe
Myton
Isurium Roman
Aldborough
Gouthwaite Reservoir
Eavestone
Sawley
Wath
Heathfield Moor
Pateley Moor
Markenfield Hall
Ingerthorpe
Bishop Monkton
Roecliffe
Lower Dunsforth
Minskip
Appletreewick
Grimwith Reservoir
Pateley Bridge
Greenhow Hill
Bewerley
Glasshouses
Wilsill
Brimham Rocks (NT)
Bishop Thornton
Markington
Smelthouses
Burton Leonard
Grafton
Marton
South Stainley
Copgrove
Staveley
Guise Cliff
Low Laithe
Shaw Mills
Summer Bridge
Dacre Banks
Heyshaw
Dacre
Burnt Yates
Brearton
Nidd
Ferrensby
Arkendale
Great Ouseburn
Clint
Ripley
Farnham
Clareton
Coneythorpe
Pock Stones Moor
Simon's Seat
Thruscross Reservoir
Padside
Birstwith
Darley
Hampsthwaite
Killinghall
Scotton
Allerton Park
Whixley
Scriven
Knaresborough
Flaxby
Mother Shipton's Cave
Earl Seat
Barden Fell
Brown Bank Head
Thornthwaite
West End
Swincliffe
Kettlesing Bottom
Kettlesing
Bilton
Goldsborough
Forest Moor
Hill End
Blubberhouses
Fewston Reservoir
HARROGATE
High Harrogate
Bolton Abbey
Round Hill
Fewston
Harlow Carr
Hunsingore
Little Ribston
Beamsley Beacon
Beamsley
Langbar
Timble
Swinsty Resr
Bland Hill
Beckwithshaw
North Deighton
Cowthorpe
Jack Hill
Follifoot
March Ghyll Reservoir
Pannal
Spofforth
Kirk Deighton
Middleton
Denton
Lindley Wood Reservoir
North Rigton
Kirkby Overblow
Stockeld Park
Stainburn
Huby
Weeton Sta.
Wetherby
Sicklinghall
Clap Gate
Linton
Askwith
Weston
Farnley
Dunkeswick
ILKLEY
Manor House
Leathley
Weeton
Netherby
Thorp Arch
Collingham
Ilkley Moor
Burley in Wharfedale
Otley
Pool
Harewood
Arthington
Harewood House
The Chevin
Chevin Forest Park
Menston
East Keswick
East Rigton
Bardsey
Bramham
Riddlesden
East Morton
Guiseley
Bramhope
Golden Acre Park
Eccup
Eccup Resr
Leeds Bradford International
Hawksworth
Scarcroft
Bramham Park
Keighley & Worth Valley Rly
Eldwick
Yeadon
Tinshill
Alwoodley Gates
Thorner
BINGLEY
Baildon
Rawdon
Adel
Tropical World
Kiddal Lane End
1853 Gallery
Harden
Horsforth
Moor Allerton
SHIPLEY
Calverley
Gledhow
Roundhay
Barwick in Elmet
Scholes
Cullingworth
Chapel Allerton
Aberford
Wilsden
Kirkstall Abbey
Seacroft
Headingley
Sandy Lane
Allerton
Farsley
Kirkstall
Cross Gates
Denholme
LEEDS
Harehills
BRADFORD
PUDSEY
Whitkirk
West Garforth
Temple Newsam
Garforth
Thornton
Clayton
Royal Armouries Museum
Ogden
Bolling Hall
Dudley Hill
Tong Street
New Farnley
Swillington
Kippax
Queensbury
Wibsey
Adwalton Moor 1643
Beeston
Buttershaw
Bierley
Westgate Hill
Gildersome
Churwell
ROTHWELL
Great Preston
Woodlesford
Allerton Bywater
Holmfield
Shelf
Birkenshaw
Drighlington
Middleton Rly
Middleton
Oulton
Adwalton
Oakenshaw
Ovenden
Northowram
Boothtown
Wyke
MORLEY
Thorpe on the Hill
Robin Hood
Carlton
Methley
Mickleton
Gomersal
Tingley
Hipperholme
Cleckheaton
Birstall
Smithies
Lofthouse
STANLEY
Whitwood
Shibden Hall
Eureka
Halifax Moor
BATLEY
East Ardsley
Southowram
Liversedge
Heckmondwike
Altofts
Outwood
Normanton
Norland Town
BRIGHOUSE
Rastrick
Roberttown
Kirkhamgate
Wrenthorpe
Greetland
DEWSBURY
WAKEFIELD
Warmfield
Ackton
Elland
Mirfield
Ravensthorpe
Ossett
Holywell Green
Featherstone
Sharlston
Lindley
Upper Hopton
Whitley Lower
Horbury
Crofton
Nostell Priory (NT)
West Hardwick
Outlane
Quarmby
Kirkheaton
Netherton
National Coal Mining Museum for England
Middlestown
Pugney
Crigglestone
Walton
Anglers
HUDDERSFIELD
Cowmes
Grange Moor
Flockton
Fitzwilliam
Pole
N O R T H
Y O R K S H I R E
W E S T
Y O R K S
A61
A59
A65
A658
A659
A660
A661
A6055
A168
A1(M)
A1
A64
A6120
A6038
A657
A650
A6037
A6177
A647
A6110
A58
A62
A653
A643
A654
A642
A639
A656
A655
A645
A636
A638
A6036
A641
A629
A6026
A6025
A644
A649
A652
A6107
A640
M1
M62
M606
M621
B6265
B6165
B6161
B6162
B6451
B6160
B6382
B6164
B6157
B6159
B6154
B6146
B6429
B6144
B6145
B6380
B6135
B6123
B6128
B6117
B6118
B6114
B6119
B6134
B6133
B6421
B6131
B6378
410
409
402
1319
1322
1460

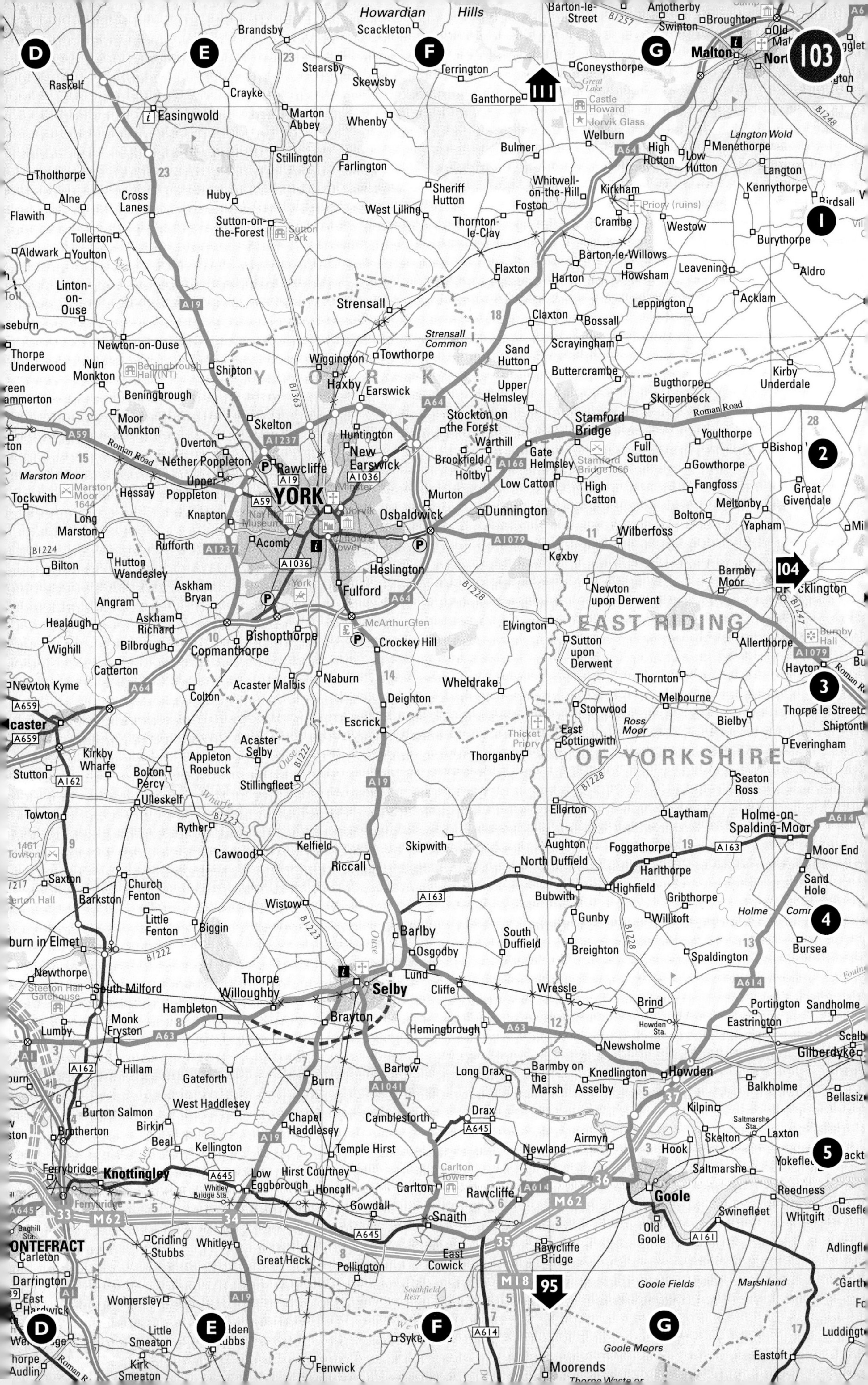
Howardian Hills
Barton-le-Street
B1257
Amotherby
Swinton
Broughton
Old Malton
Malton
Norton
A64
D
E
F
G
Brandsby
Scackleton
Stearsby
Skewsby
Terrington
Coneysthorpe
Great Lake
Castle Howard
Jorvik Glass
Ganthorpe
Raskelf
Crayke
Easingwold
Marton Abbey
Whenby
Welburn
Bulmer
Stillington
Farlington
High Hutton
Low Hutton
Menethorpe
Langton Wold
Langton
B1248
Tholthorpe
Alne
Flawith
Cross Lanes
Huby
Sheriff Hutton
Whitwell-on-the-Hill
Kirkham
Priory (ruins)
Kennythorpe
Birdsall
Sutton-on-the-Forest
Sutton Park
West Lilling
Thornton-le-Clay
Foston
Crambe
Westow
Burythorpe
Tollerton
Aldwark
Youlton
Kyle
Linton-on-Ouse
Barton-le-Willows
Harton
Howsham
Leavening
Aldro
Flaxton
Acklam
Leppington
A19
Strensall
Claxton
Bossall
Strensall Common
Newton-on-Ouse
Thorpe Underwood
Nun Monkton
Beningbrough Hall (NT)
Shipton
Wigginton
Towthorpe
Sand Hutton
Scrayingham
Buttercrambe
Kirby Underdale
YORK
Haxby
Earswick
Upper Helmsley
Bugthorpe
Skirpenbeck
Green Hammerton
Beningbrough
B1363
A64
Stockton on the Forest
Stamford Bridge
Roman Road
Moor Monkton
Skelton
Huntington
Warthill
Youlthorpe
Bishop Wilton
Overton
A1237
New Earswick
Gate Helmsley
Full Sutton
A59
Roman Road
Nether Poppleton
Rawcliffe
Brockfield
A166
Stamford Bridge 1066
Gowthorpe
Marston Moor
Upper Poppleton
A19
A1036
Holtby
Low Catton
Fangfoss
Great Givendale
Tockwith
Marston Moor 1644
Hessay
YORK
Minster
Murton
High Catton
Meltonby
Long Marston
Knapton
Nat Rly Museum
Jorvik
Osbaldwick
Dunnington
Bolton
Yapham
Rufforth
A1237
Acomb
Clifford's Tower
A1079
Wilberfoss
B1224
Bilton
Hutton Wandesley
A1036
Heslington
Kexby
Barmby Moor
104
Pocklington
Askham Bryan
York
Fulford
B1228
Newton upon Derwent
Angram
A64
McArthurGlen
Elvington
EAST RIDING
Healaugh
Askham Richard
Bishopthorpe
Crockey Hill
Sutton upon Derwent
Allerthorpe
Burnby Hall
Wighill
Bilbrough
Copmanthorpe
A1079
Hayton
Roman Road
Catterton
Acaster Malbis
Naburn
Thornton
Wheldrake
Newton Kyme
A64
Colton
Deighton
Melbourne
A659
Tadcaster
Escrick
Storwood
Bielby
Thorpe le Street
Shiptonthorpe
A659
Acaster Selby
East Cottingwith
Ross Moor
Thicket Priory
Kirkby Wharfe
Appleton Roebuck
Thorganby
OF YORKSHIRE
Everingham
Stutton
A162
Bolton Percy
Ouse
B1222
Stillingfleet
A19
B1228
Seaton Ross
Ulleskelf
Wharfe
Towton
B1223
Ellerton
Laytham
Holme-on-Spalding-Moor
A614
Ryther
Towton 1461
Cawood
Kelfield
Skipwith
Aughton
Foggathorpe
A163
Moor End
North Duffield
Harlthorpe
Riccall
Saxton
Church Fenton
Barkston
Bubwith
Highfield
Sand Hole
A163
Gribthorpe
Wistow
B1223
Holme
Gunby
Willitoft
Little Fenton
Biggin
Barlby
South Duffield
B1228
Sherburn in Elmet
B1222
Osgodby
Breighton
Spaldington
Bursea
Ouse
Newthorpe
Thorpe Willoughby
Lund
Selby
Cliffe
Wressle
A614
Steeton Hall Gatehouse
South Milford
Hambleton
Brind
Portington
Sandholme
Monk Fryston
Brayton
Hemingbrough
A63
Howden Sta.
Eastrington
Lumby
A63
Newsholme
Gilberdyke
A1
A162
Hillam
Barlow
Long Drax
Barmby on the Marsh
Knedlington
Howden
Gateforth
Burn
A1041
Asselby
Balkholme
West Haddlesey
Burton Salmon
Kilpin
Bellasize
Chapel Haddlesey
Camblesforth
Drax
A645
Saltmarshe Sta.
Brotherton
Birkin
Laxton
Beal
A19
Temple Hirst
Airmyn
Skelton
Kellington
Aire
Newland
Hook
Ferrybridge
Knottingley
A645
Low Eggborough
Hirst Courtney
Carlton Towers
Whitley Bridge Sta.
Hensall
Carlton
Rawcliffe
A614
M62
Saltmarshe
Goole
Reedness
Ferrybridge
Gowdall
Swinefleet
Whitgift
Ousefleet
A645
M62
Snaith
Old Goole
Baghill Sta.
Cridling Stubbs
Whitley
A645
East Cowick
Rawcliffe Bridge
A161
Adlingfleet
PONTEFRACT
Carleton
Great Heck
Pollington
Darrington
M18
Southfield Resr
95
Goole Fields
Marshland
East Hardwick
A1
Womersley
A19
Wentbridge
Little Smeaton
Norton
Balne
Sykehouse
A614
Goole Moors
Luddington
Kirk Smeaton
Fenwick
Moorends
Thorne Waste or Moors
Eastoft
Roman Road
Thorpe Audlin
1
2
3
4
5
11
12
13
14
15
17
18
19
23
28

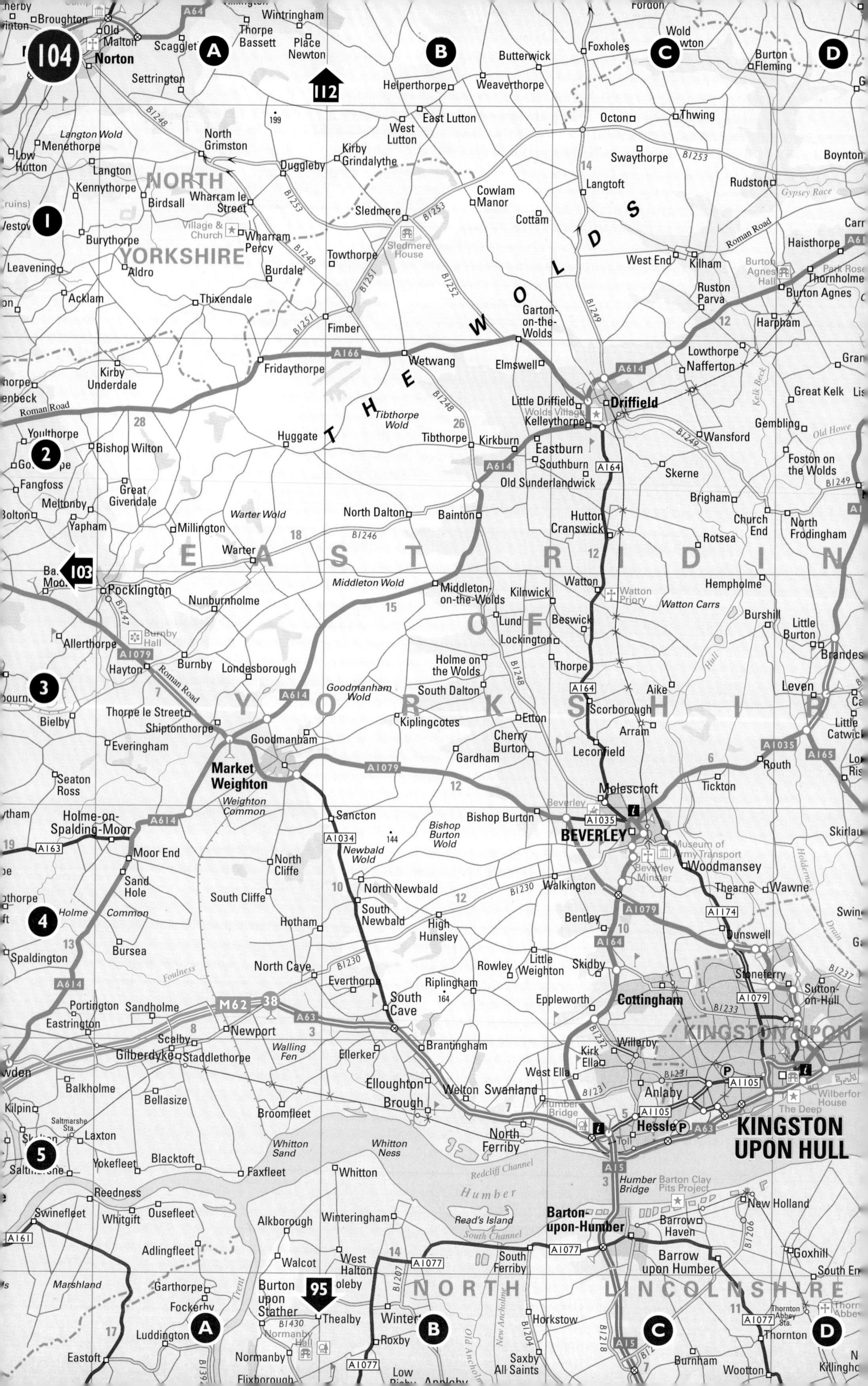
104
112
103
95
A
B
C
D
1
2
3
4
5
Broughton
Old Malton
Malton
Norton
Scagglethorpe
Thorpe Bassett
Wintringham
Place Newton
Settrington
Helperthorpe
Weaverthorpe
Butterwick
Foxholes
Wold Newton
Burton Fleming
East Lutton
West Lutton
Octon
Thwing
North Grimston
Menethorpe
Langton Wold
Low Hutton
Langton
Kennythorpe
Birdsall
NORTH YORKSHIRE
Duggleby
Kirby Grindalythe
Wharram le Street
Wharram Percy
Village & Church
Sledmere
Sledmere House
Cowlam Manor
Cottam
Swaythorpe
Langtoft
Rudston
Boynton
Gypsey Race
Roman Road
Burythorpe
Aldro
Leavening
Towthorpe
Burdale
West End
Kilham
Haisthorpe
Burton Agnes Hall
Thornholme
Burton Agnes
Ruston Parva
Acklam
Thixendale
Fimber
Garton-on-the-Wolds
Harpham
THE WOLDS
Kirby Underdale
Fridaythorpe
Wetwang
Elmswell
Lowthorpe
Nafferton
Grange
Little Driffield
Driffield
Wolds Village
Kelleythorpe
Great Kelk
Kelk Beck
Youlthorpe
Bishop Wilton
Huggate
Tibthorpe Wold
Tibthorpe
Kirkburn
Eastburn
Southburn
Wansford
Gembling
Old Howe
Foston on the Wolds
Fangfoss
Great Givendale
Old Sunderlandwick
Skerne
Meltonby
Bolton
Yapham
Millington
Warter Wold
North Dalton
Bainton
Hutton Cranswick
Brigham
Church End
North Frodingham
Rotsea
EAST RIDING OF YORKSHIRE
Warter
Pocklington
Middleton Wold
Middleton-on-the-Wolds
Kilnwick
Watton
Watton Priory
Watton Carrs
Hempholme
Nunburnholme
Lund
Beswick
Burshill
Little Burton
Burnby Hall
Allerthorpe
Lockington
Brandesburton
Hayton
Burnby
Londesborough
Holme on the Wolds
Thorpe
Hull
Roman Road
Goodmanham Wold
South Dalton
Aike
Leven
Bielby
Thorpe le Street
Kiplingcotes
Scorborough
Etton
Arram
Little Catwick
Shiptonthorpe
Everingham
Goodmanham
Cherry Burton
Gardham
Leconfield
Routh
Market Weighton
Seaton Ross
Weighton Common
Molescroft
Tickton
Holme-on-Spalding-Moor
Sancton
Bishop Burton
Beverley
BEVERLEY
Bishop Burton Wold
Newbald Wold
Museum of Army Transport
Moor End
North Cliffe
Beverley Minster
Woodmansey
Skirlaugh
Sand Hole
South Cliffe
North Newbald
Walkington
Thearne
Wawne
Holme Common
South Newbald
High Hunsley
Bentley
Hotham
Dunswell
Spaldington
Bursea
Foulness
North Cave
Rowley
Little Weighton
Skidby
Stoneferry
Sutton-on-Hull
Everthorpe
Riplingham
South Cave
Eppleworth
Cottingham
Portington
Sandholme
Newport
Walling Fen
Eastrington
KINGSTON UPON HULL
Scalby
Brantingham
Willerby
Gilberdyke
Staddlethorpe
Ellerker
Kirk Ella
West Ella
Howden
Balkholme
Elloughton
Welton
Swanland
Bellasize
Brough
Anlaby
Wilberforce House
The Deep
Kilpin
Broomfleet
Humber Bridge
Hessle
Saltmarshe Sta.
Laxton
Whitton Sand
Whitton Ness
North Ferriby
Blacktoft
Yokefleet
Faxfleet
Redcliff Channel
Whitton
Humber Bridge
Barton Clay Pits Project
Reedness
Humber
New Holland
Swinefleet
Whitgift
Ousefleet
Alkborough
Winteringham
Read's Island
South Channel
Barton-upon-Humber
Barrow Haven
Adlingfleet
West Halton
South Ferriby
Goxhill
Marshland
Walcot
Barrow upon Humber
South End
Garthorpe
Burton upon Stather
Coleby
NORTH LINCOLNSHIRE
Trent
Fockerby
Thealby
Winterton
Horkstow
Thornton Abbey
Thornton Abbey Sta.
Normanby Hall
Roxby
New Ancholme
Old Ancholme
Thornton
Luddington
Normanby
Saxby All Saints
Burnham
Wootton
Killingholme
Eastoft
Flixborough
Low Risby
Appleby
A64
A166
A614
A164
A1079
A1035
A1034
A163
A63
M62
A1174
A1105
A15
A1077
A161
A165
A61
B1248
B1253
B1251
B1252
B1249
B1246
B1247
B1230
B1233
B1237
B1231
B1232
B1206
B1207
B1204
B1218
B1430
B1392
38
199
144
164

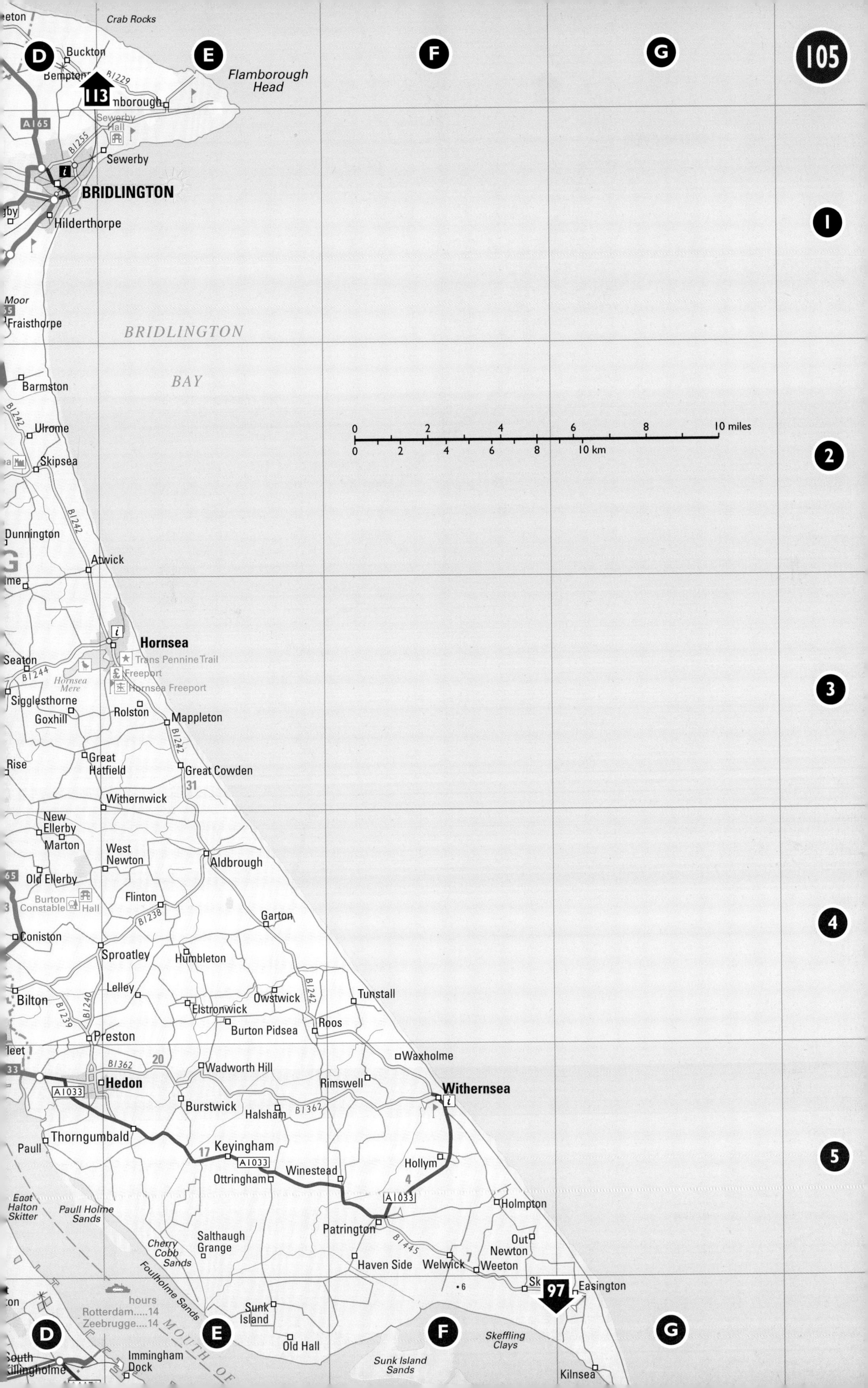
Crab Rocks
D
E
F
G
Buckton
Bempton
113
B1229
Flamborough Head
A165
Sewerby Hall
B1255
Sewerby
BRIDLINGTON
Hilderthorpe
1
Moor
Fraisthorpe
BRIDLINGTON
BAY
Barmston
B1242
Ulrome
Skipsea
0 2 4 6 8 10 miles
0 2 4 6 8 10 km
2
B1242
Dunnington
Atwick
Hornsea
Trans Pennine Trail
Freeport
Hornsea Freeport
Seaton
B1244
Hornsea Mere
Sigglesthorne
Goxhill
Rolston
Mappleton
B1242
Great Hatfield
Rise
Great Cowden
31
3
Withernwick
New Ellerby
Marton
West Newton
Aldbrough
Old Ellerby
Burton Constable Hall
Flinton
B1238
Garton
Coniston
4
Sproatley
Humbleton
Lelley
Bilton
B1239
B1240
Elstronwick
Owstwick
B1242
Tunstall
Roos
Burton Pidsea
Preston
Waxholme
B1362
20
Wadworth Hill
Hedon
A1033
Rimswell
Withernsea
Burstwick
Halsham
B1362
Thorngumbald
Paull
17
Keyingham
A1033
Hollym
Winestead
Ottringham
4
A1033
Holmpton
5
East Halton Skitter
Paull Holme Sands
Patrington
Salthaugh Grange
Cherry Cobb Sands
B1445
Out Newton
7
Haven Side
Welwick
Weeton
Foulholme Sands
6
97
Easington
hours
Rotterdam.....14
Zeebrugge....14
Sunk Island
MOUTH OF
Skeffling Clays
Old Hall
South Killingholme
Immingham Dock
Sunk Island Sands
Kilnsea

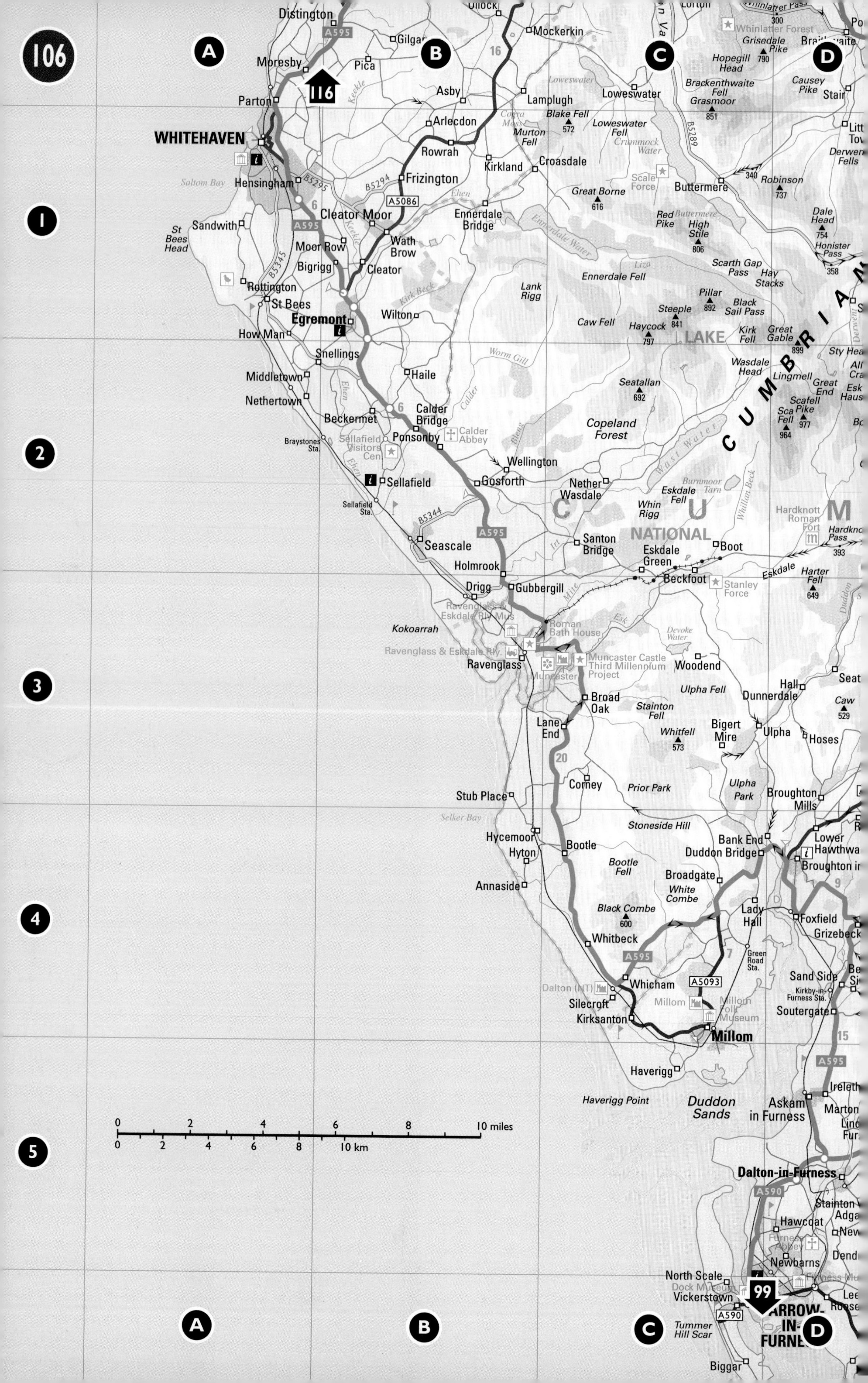
A
B
C
D
1
2
3
4
5
116
Distington
A595
Gilgarran
Mockerkin
Moresby
Pica
Asby
Lamplugh
Loweswater
Parton
Arlecdon
Blake Fell
572
WHITEHAVEN
Rowrah
Kirkland
Croasdale
Murton Fell
Loweswater Fell
Crummock Water
Saltom Bay
Hensingham
B5295
B5294
Frizington
A5086
Ehen
Scale Force
Buttermere
Great Borne
616
Cleator Moor
Ennerdale Bridge
Ennerdale Water
Sandwith
St Bees Head
Keekle
Wath Brow
Moor Row
Cleator
Bigrigg
B5345
Rottington
St Bees
Egremont
Wilton
How Man
Snellings
Middletown
Nethertown
Haile
Beckermet
Calder Bridge
Ponsonby
Calder Abbey
Sellafield Visitors Cen
Braystones Sta.
Sellafield
Sellafield Sta.
Gosforth
Wellington
B5344
Seascale
Holmrook
Drigg
Gubbergill
Ravenglass & Eskdale Rly Mus
Kokoarrah
Ravenglass & Eskdale Rly.
Ravenglass
Roman Bath House
Muncaster Castle
Third Millennium Project
Muncaster
Broad Oak
Lane End
20
Corney
Stub Place
Selker Bay
Hycemoor
Hyton
Annaside
Bootle
Bootle Fell
Black Combe
600
Whitbeck
A595
Whicham
Dalton (NT)
Silecroft
Kirksanton
Millom
Millom Folk Museum
A5093
Haverigg
Haverigg Point
Duddon Sands
Askam in Furness
Dalton-in-Furness
A590
Hawcoat
Furness Abbey
Newbarns
North Scale
Dock Museum
Vickerstown
99
BARROW-IN-FURNESS
Tummer Hill Scar
Biggar
Whinlatter Pass
300
Whinlatter Forest
Grisedale Pike
790
Hopegill Head
Brackenthwaite Fell
Grasmoor
851
Causey Pike
B5289
Robinson
737
Dale Head
754
Honister Pass
358
Red Pike
High Stile
806
Scarth Gap Pass
Hay Stacks
Liza
Ennerdale Fell
Lank Rigg
Pillar
892
Black Sail Pass
Steeple
841
Caw Fell
Haycock
797
LAKE
Kirk Fell
Great Gable
899
Worm Gill
Wasdale Head
Lingmell
Great End
Scafell Pike
977
Sca Fell
964
Seatallan
692
Copeland Forest
Wast Water
CUMBRIA
Burnmoor Tarn
Nether Wasdale
Eskdale Fell
Whin Rigg
NATIONAL
Hardknott Roman Fort
Hardknott Pass
393
Santon Bridge
Eskdale Green
Boot
Beckfoot
Stanley Force
Eskdale
Harter Fell
649
Mite
Esk
Devoke Water
Woodend
Ulpha Fell
Stainton Fell
Hall
Dunnerdale
Caw
529
Whitfell
573
Bigert Mire
Ulpha
Hoses
Prior Park
Ulpha Park
Broughton Mills
Stoneside Hill
Bank End
Duddon Bridge
Lower Hawthwaite
Broughton in Furness
Broadgate
White Combe
Lady Hall
Foxfield
Grizebeck
Green Road Sta.
Sand Side
Kirkby-in-Furness Sta.
Soutergate
15
Ireleth
Marton
Stainton
Adgarley
Dendron
Roose
0
2
4
6
8
10 miles
10 km

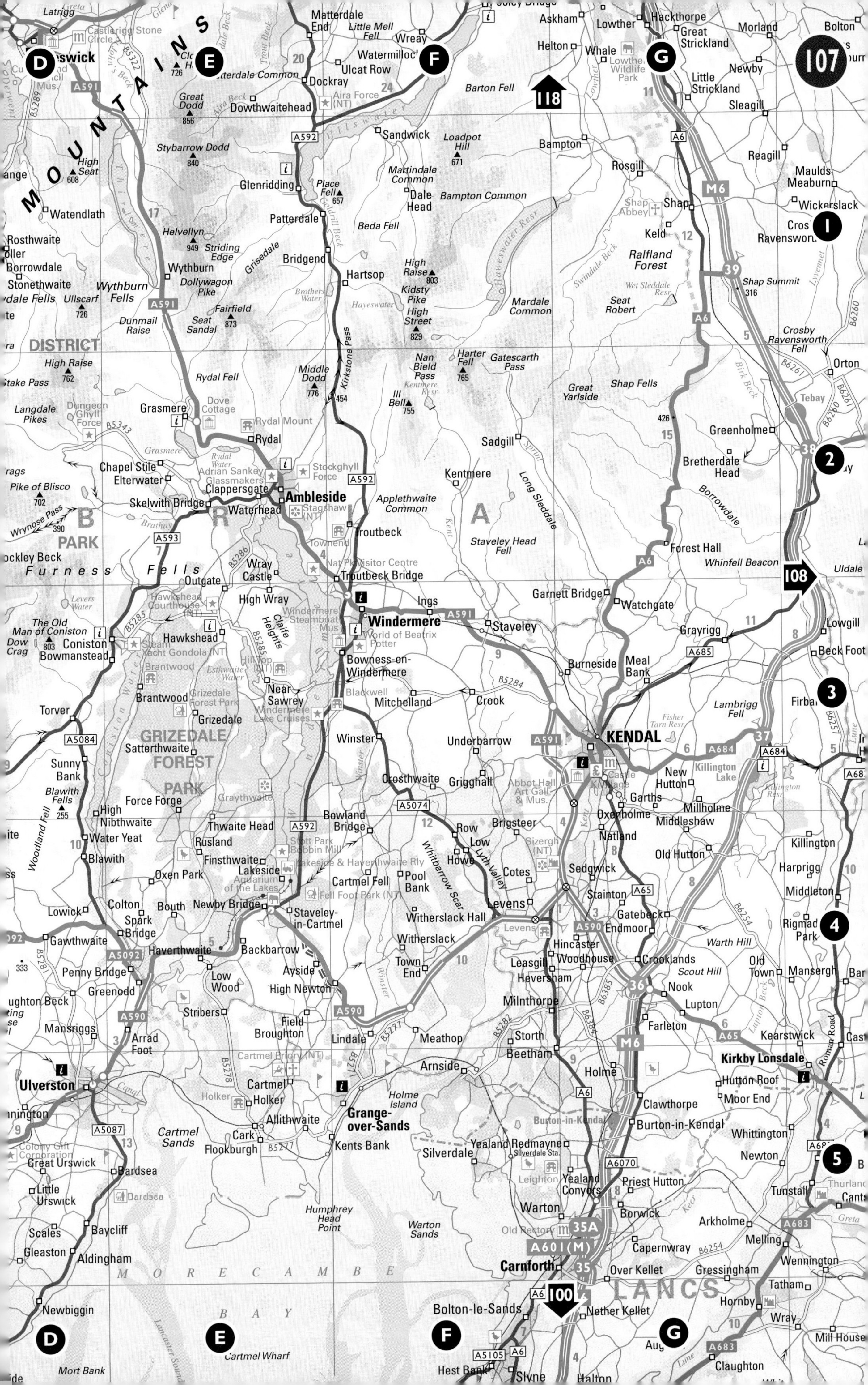

107
Latrigg
Castlerigg Stone Circle
Keswick
MOUNTAINS
Great Dodd
856
Dowthwaitehead
Stybarrow Dodd
840
High Seat
608
Watendlath
Rosthwaite
Borrowdale
Stonethwaite
Ullscarf
726
Wythburn Fells
Helvellyn
949
Striding Edge
Wythburn
Dollywagon Pike
Grisedale
Fairfield
873
Seat Sandal
Dunmail Raise
DISTRICT
High Raise
762
Stake Pass
Rydal Fell
Langdale Pikes
Dungeon Ghyll Force
Grasmere
Dove Cottage
Rydal Mount
Rydal
Chapel Stile
Elterwater
Pike of Blisco
702
Wrynose Pass
390
Skelwith Bridge
Clappersgate
Ambleside
Waterhead
Stagshaw (NT)
Stockghyll Force
Adrian Sankey Glassmakers
B
R
PARK
Cockley Beck
Furness Fells
Brathay
Outgate
Wray Castle
High Wray
Hawkshead Courthouse (NT)
Hawkshead
Claife Heights
Levers Water
The Old Man of Coniston
803
Dow Crag
Coniston
Bowmanstead
Steam Yacht Gondola (NT)
Brantwood
Esthwaite Water
Hill Top
Near Sawrey
Grizedale Forest Park
Grizedale
Windermere Lake Cruises
Torver
GRIZEDALE FOREST PARK
Satterthwaite
Sunny Bank
Blawith Fells
255
High Nibthwaite
Force Forge
Graythwaite
Woodland Fell
Water Yeat
Blawith
Thwaite Head
Rusland
Finsthwaite
Lakeside
Aquarium of the Lakes
Oxen Park
Lakeside & Haverthwaite Rly
Stott Park Bobbin Mill
Colton
Spark Bridge
Bouth
Newby Bridge
Lowick
Gawthwaite
Haverthwaite
Backbarrow
Penny Bridge
Greenodd
Low Wood
Ayside
High Newton
Stribers
Staveley-in-Cartmel
Broughton
Field Broughton
Lindale
Meathop
Mansriggs
Arrad Foot
Ulverston
Canal
Cartmel Priory (NT)
Cartmel
Holker
Allithwaite
Cark
Flookburgh
Grange-over-Sands
Kents Bank
Holme Island
Arnside
Cartmel Sands
Colony Gift Corporation
Great Urswick
Bardsea
Little Urswick
Dardsea
Scales
Baycliff
Gleaston
Aldingham
Newbiggin
Humphrey Head Point
Warton Sands
MORECAMBE BAY
Cartmel Wharf
Mort Bank
Lancaster Sound
Matterdale End
Little Mell Fell
Wreay
Watermillock
Ulcat Row
Dockray
Aira Force (NT)
Ullswater
Sandwick
Loadpot Hill
671
Glenridding
Place Fell
657
Martindale Common
Dale Head
Patterdale
Beda Fell
Bridgend
Hartsop
Brothers Water
Hayeswater
High Raise
803
Kidsty Pike
High Street
829
Kirkstone Pass
454
Middle Dodd
776
Nan Bield Pass
Kentmere Resr
Harter Fell
765
Ill Bell
755
Troutbeck
Townend
Applethwaite Common
Nat Pk Visitor Centre
Troutbeck Bridge
Windermere
World of Beatrix Potter
Windermere Steamboat Mus
Ings
Bowness-on-Windermere
Blackwell
Mitchelland
Crook
Winster
Underbarrow
Crosthwaite
Grigghall
Bowland Bridge
Row
Low
Howe
Lyth Valley
Whitbarrow Scar
Cartmel Fell
Pool Bank
Fell Foot Park (NT)
Witherslack Hall
Witherslack
Town End
Askham
Lowther
Helton
Whale
Lowther Wildlife Park
Barton Fell
118
Bampton
Rosgill
Bampton Common
Haweswater Resr
Shap Abbey
Shap
Keld
Ralfland Forest
Swindale Beck
Wet Sleddale Resr
Seat Robert
Mardale Common
Gatescarth Pass
Great Yarlside
Shap Fells
Sadgill
Kentmere
Long Sleddale
Staveley Head Fell
A
Kent
Garnett Bridge
Watchgate
Staveley
Burneside
Meal Bank
Grayrigg
KENDAL
Castle
K Village
Abbot Hall Art Gall & Mus.
Brigsteer
Sizergh (NT)
Garths
Oxenholme
Natland
Sedgwick
Stainton
Cotes
Levens
Gatebeck
Endmoor
Hincaster
Woodhouse
Leasgill
Heversham
Crooklands
Milnthorpe
Storth
Beetham
Holme
Clawthorpe
Burton-in-Kendal
Yealand Redmayne
Silverdale
Silverdale Sta.
Leighton
Yealand Conyers
Warton
Priest Hutton
Borwick
Old Rectory
Capernwray
Carnforth
Over Kellet
Nether Kellet
Bolton-le-Sands
Hest Bank
Slyne
Halton
LANCS
Hackthorpe
Great Strickland
Morland
Bolton
Little Strickland
Newby
Sleagill
Reagill
Maulds Meaburn
Wickerslack
Crosby Ravensworth
Shap Summit
316
Crosby Ravensworth Fell
Birk Beck
Orton
Tebay
Greenholme
Bretherdale Head
Borrowdale
426
Forest Hall
Whinfell Beacon
108
Uldale
Lowgill
Beck Foot
Lambrigg Fell
Fisher Tarn Resr
New Hutton
Killington Lake
Killington Resr
Millholme
Middleshaw
Old Hutton
Killington
Harprigg
Middleton
Rigmaden Park
Warth Hill
Old Town
Mansergh
Scout Hill
Nook
Lupton
Farleton
Kearstwick
Roman Road
Kirkby Lonsdale
Hutton Roof
Moor End
Whittington
Newton
Tunstall
Thurland
Arkholme
Melling
Gressingham
Wennington
Tatham
Hornby
Wray
Mill House
Claughton
Aughton
Lune
Greta
M6
A6
A591
A592
A593
A5084
A5092
A590
A5087
A5074
A685
A684
A65
A6070
A601(M)
A683
A5105
B5289
B5322
B5343
B5285
B5286
B5284
B5278
B5277
B5271
B5282
B6385
B6384
B6254
B6257
B6261
B6260
D
E
F
G
I
1
2
3
4
5

108
118
107
100
CUMBRIA
LANCS
YORKS
A
B
C
D
1
2
3
4
5
Askham
Lowther
Hackthorpe
Great Strickland
Morland
Bolton
Brampton
Crackenthorpe
Kings Meaburn
Appleby-in-Westmorland
Murton
Little Fell 745
Danger Zone
Burton Fell
Warcop Fell
Lune Forest
Helton
Whale
Lowther Wildlife Park
Little Strickland
Newby
Sleagill
Colby
Hilton
Brackenber
Burrells
Coupland
Hoff
Great Ormside
Iron Band 562
Stainmore Common
Bampton
Reagill
Rosgill
Maulds Meaburn
Sandford
Warcop
Hillbeck
Brough
North
Haweswater Resr
Shap
Shap Abbey
Wickerslack
Drybeck
Crosby Ravensworth
Keld
Ralfland Forest
Swindale Beck
Wet Sleddale Resr
Shap Summit 316
Great Asby
Bleatarn
Little Musgrave
Great Musgrave
Verteris Roman Fort
Brough Sowerby
Argill Beck
Mardale Common
Seat Robert
Soulby
Kaber
Winton
Harter Fell
Gatescarth Pass
Crosby Ravensworth Fell
Grange Scar
Crosby Garrett
Waitby
Kirkby Stephen
Hartley
Orton
Raisbeck
Tebay
Great Yarlside
Shap Fells
Birk Beck
Nettle Hill
Smardale
Winton Fell
Begin Hill
Nateby
Bastifell
Nine Standards Rigg 662
426
Greenholme
Newbiggin-on-Lune
Tailbridge Hill
Sadgill
Long Sleddale
Bretherdale Head
Kelleth
Ash Fell
Southwaite
Borrowdale
Ravenstonedale
West Fell
Birkdale
Staveley Head Fell
Forest Hall
Langdale Fell
Simon's Seat 587
Ravenstonedale Common
Harter Fell 522
Outhgill
High Seat 710
Whinfell Beacon
Uldale Head
Burneside Bridge
Watchgate
Wild Boar Fell 708
Staveley
Yarlside
Mallerstang Common
Angram
Grayrigg
Lowgill
The Calf 676
Uldale House
Bluecaster
Beck Foot
Swarth Fell
Burneside
Meal Bank
Low Haygarth
Brant Fell
West Baugh Fell
Holmes Moss
Abbotside Common
Firbank
Cautley
Lambrigg Fell
Fisher Tarn Resr
KENDAL
Baugh Fell
Cotterdale
Ingmire Hall
Garsdale Head
Knoutberry Haw 676
Killington Lake
Sedbergh
Clough
Garsdale Sta.
Mid Mossdale
New Hutton
East Baugh Fell
Millthrop
Garsdale
Abbot Hall Art Gall. & Mus.
Castle
Kirkby Village
Garths
Killington Resr
West Mostard
Mossdale Moor
Oxenholme
Millholme
Middleshaw
Brigsteer
Natland
Aye Gill Pike 556
Killington
Sizergh (NT)
Lyth Valley
Old Hutton
Harprigg
Gawthrop
Great Knoutberry Hill 672
Widdale Fell
Cotes
Sedgwick
Middleton Fell
Dent
Dentdale
Cowgill
Dent Sta.
Lea Yeat
Levens
Stainton
Middleton
Calf Top 609
Gatebeck
Endmoor
Rigmaden Park
Stone House
Wold Fell 557
Hincaster
Warth Hill
Crag Hill 682
Deepdale
Leasgill
Woodhouse
Crooklands
Old Town
Heversham
Scout Hill
Mansergh
Barbon
Blea Moor
Milnthorpe
Nook
Bullpot Farm
Oughtershaw Moss
Lupton
Whernside 736
Gayle Moor
Storth
Farleton
Kearstwick
Casterton
Far Gearstones
Cam Fell
Beetham
Roman Road
Lupton Beck
Kirkby Lonsdale
627
Langstrothdale
Holme
Hutton Roof
Leck Beck
Ribblehead Sta.
Sike Moor
NATIONAL
Moor End
Leck Fell
Weathercote
Clawthorpe
Scales Moor
Burton-in-Kendal
Leck
Chapel-le-Dale
Cam Beck
High Birkwith
Redmayne
Whittington
Cowan Bridge
Ireby
Silverdale Sta.
Newton
White Scar Caves
Ingleborough 724
Selside
Horton Moor
Leighton
Yealand Conyers
Nether Burrow
Simon Fell
Pen-y-Ghent 694
Priest Hutton
Thurland
Westhouse
Skirwith
New Houses
Warton
Tunstall
Cantsfield
Ingleborough Common
Borwick
Greta
Burton in Lonsdale
Ingleton
Old Rectory
Arkholme
Keer
Slatenber
Horton in Ribblesdale
Capernwray
Melling
Moughton Fell
Carnforth
Over Kellet
Wennington
Low Bentham
Studfold
Gressingham
Newby
Helwith Bridge
Hornby
High Bentham
Clapham
Wharfe
Sands
Nether Kellet
Wray
Austwick
Clapham Sta.
Aughton
Mill Houses
Wenning
Feizor
Slyne
Halton
Claughton
Keasden
Lawkland
Stainforth
M6
A6
A66
A685
A683
A684
A591
A590
A65
A6070
A601(M)
A687
B6260
B6261
B6276
B6259
B6270
B6257
B6254
B6385
B6384
B5282
B6255
B6479
B6480
B5284
B5105
36
35A
35
37
38
39

109
D
E
F
G
119
110
101
Thringarth
Lunedale
Grassholme
Selset Reservoir
Mickleton Moor
Romaldkirk
Hunderthwaite
Hury
Hunderthwaite Moor
Blackton Resr
Hury Resr
Baldersdale
Balderhead Resr
Clove Lodge
Cotherstone Moor
Cotherstone
Lartington
Barnard Castle
Startforth
Bowes Museum
Westwick
Egglestone
Stainton
Cleatlam
Little Newsham
Staindrop
Raby
Burnt Houses
Hilton
Bolam
Redworth
Ingleton
Killerby
Langton
Headlam
Summerhouse
Denton
Dere Street
Winston
Gainford
Piercebridge
High Coniscliffe
Whorlton
Ovington
Wycliffe
Caldwell
Eppleby
Forcett
Manfield
Cleasby
Deep Dale
Deepdale Beck
Beldoo Hill
Boldron
Bowes
Gilmonby
Greta Bridge
Hutton Magna
Lane Head
Brignall
Aldbrough St John
Stanwick Camp
Barningham
West Layton
East Layton
Scargill
Newsham
Bowes Moor
DURHAM
Stainmore Forest
Scargill High Moor
Barningham Moor
Dalton
Ravensworth
Roman Road
Melsonby
A1(M)
Sleightholme Moor
Taylor Rigg
Tan Hill
Cleasby Hill
Hope Moor
Gayles
Kirby Hill
Whashton
Gilling West
Arkle Beck
Arkengarthdale Moor
Water Crag
668
Rogan's Seat
671
Stonesdale Moor
Kexwith Moor
Holgate Moor
Whaw
Hurst Moor
Markse Moor
High Moor
Skeeby
Great Pinseat
583
Gunnerside Gill
Hard Level Gill
Langthwaite
Arkengarthdale
Washfold
Hurst
Georgian Theatre
Richmond
West Stonesdale
Melbecks Moor
Keld
Marrick Moor
Calver Hill
Skelton
Marske
A6108
Hudswell
A6136
Brompton
Catterick
Kearton
Reeth
Fremington
Thwaite
Gunnerside
Blades
Healaugh
Low Row
Feetham
Grinton
Harkerside Moor
Marrick
Downholme
Catterick Camp
Hipswell Moor
Ivelet
Muker
B6270
Ellerton Priory
Stainton
Scotton
Tunstall
Butter Tubs Pass
478
526
675
Crackpot
Oxnop Ghyll
Gibbon Hill
Stainton Moor
Redmire Moor
565
Barden
East Hauxwell
East Bolton Moor
Preston Moor
Bellerby Moor
Leyburn Moor
Bellerby
Arrathorne
Hunton
NORTH
High Shaw
Askrigg
Common
Bolton
Castle Bolton
Burton Hall
Sedbusk
Askrigg
Newbiggin
Redmire
Preston-under-Scar
Leyburn
A684
Constable Burton
Patrick Brompton
Wensleydale
Ropemaker
Bainbridge
Woodhall
Carperby
Low Bolton
Aysgarth Falls
National Park Centre
Swinithwaite
Wensley
Harmby
Finghall
Newton-le-Willows
Burtersett
Wensleydale Cheese Visitor Centre
Thornton Rust
Aysgarth
West Witton
Spennithorne
Thornton Resr
Cowling
Countersett
West Burton
Middleham
Abbey (rems. of)
Thornton Steward
Rookwith
Wether Fell
614
Marsett
Semer Water
Thoralby
Penhill
546
Agglethorpe
Braithwaite Hall (NT)
Stake Fell
Newbiggin
Coverham
East Witton
Thirn
Stalling Busk
Bishopdale Beck
Melmerby
Jervaulx Abbey
Brymor High Jervaulx Farm
RKSHIRE
Carlton
Caldbergh
Fleet Moss
Harland Hill
Carlton Moor
Cover
Ellingstring
High Ellington
Black Sheep Brewery Visitors Centre
High Burton
Walden
Coverdale
West Scrafton
Cragdale Moor
Gammersgill
DALES
Kidstones
Colsterdale
Fearby
Oughtershaw
Middle Tongue
643
564
Horsehouse
Colsterdale Moor
Masham
Walden Head
Braidley
Arkleside
Healey
Deepdale
Langstrothdale Chase
Cover Head Bents
Hindlethwaite Moor
Great Haw
544
Leighton
Ilton
Swinton
Yockenthwaite
Cray
Buckden Pike
702
PARK
Hubberholme
Woodale
Masham Moor
Leighton Resr
Buckden
Little Whernside
605
Scar House Reservoir
Brown Ridge
429
Roundhill Resr
Halton Gill
B6160
Wharfe
Starbotton
Angram Resr
Nidderdale
Litton
Great Whernside
703
Middlesmoor
How Stean Beck
Kirkby Malzeard Moor
Nether Heselden
Littondale
Lofthouse
Hambleton Hill
406
Laverton
Rigg Moor
Stean
Kettlewell
Arncliffe
Skirfare
Dallowgill Moor
Greygarth
Darnbrook Fell
Wharfedale
Stean Moor
Ramsgill
Bouthwaite
Lumley Moor Resr
Hawkswick
Conistone Moor
Meugher
Grantley
Arncliffe Cote
Gouthwaite Resr
Eavestone
538
Malham Tarn
Kilnsey
Conistone
Grassington Moor
Heathfield Moor
Pateley Moor
Pateley Bridge
Appletreewick Moor
B6265

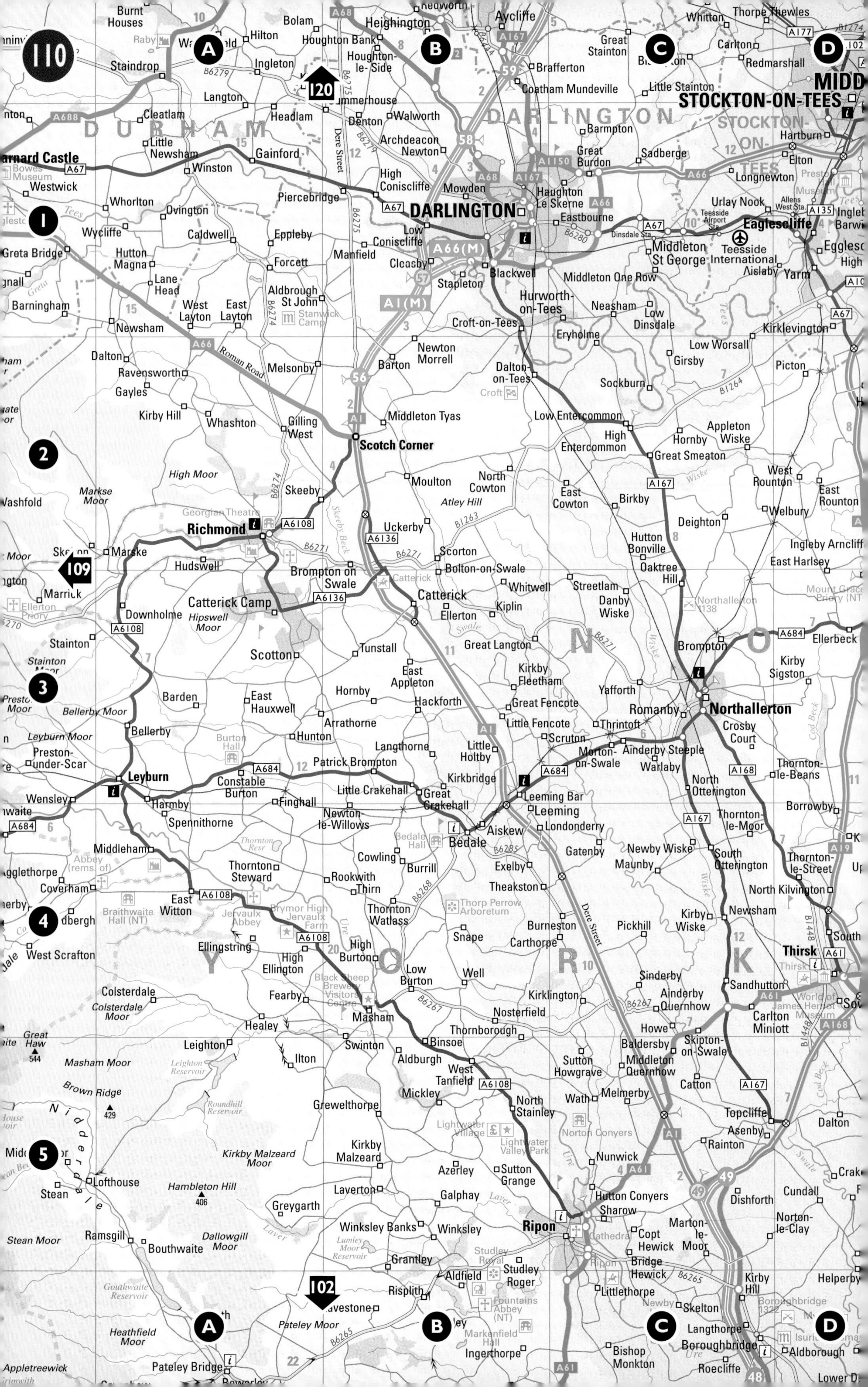

A
B
C
D
1
2
3
4
5
120
109
102
DURHAM
DARLINGTON
STOCKTON-ON-TEES
N
O
R
T
H
Y
O
R
K
Burnt Houses
Raby
Staindrop
Hilton
Bolam
Ingleton
Houghton Bank
Heighington
Houghton-le-Side
Aycliffe
Great Stainton
Whitton
Thorpe Thewles
Carlton
Redmarshall
Brafferton
Coatham Mundeville
Little Stainton
MIDD
Summerhouse
Walworth
Denton
Archdeacon Newton
Langton
Cleatlam
Headlam
Little Newsham
Gainford
Winston
Barnard Castle
Bowes Museum
Westwick
Whorlton
Ovington
Piercebridge
High Coniscliffe
Mowden
DARLINGTON
Haughton Le Skerne
Great Burdon
Barmpton
Sadberge
Hartburn
Elton
Longnewton
Preston Hall Museum
Urlay Nook
Allens West Sta
Teesside Airport Sta
Eaglescliffe
Eastbourne
Dinsdale Sta
Middleton St George
Teesside International
Aislaby
Yarm
Egglescliffe
Tees
Wycliffe
Greta Bridge
Hutton Magna
Caldwell
Eppleby
Forcett
Low Coniscliffe
Manfield
Cleasby
Stapleton
Blackwell
Middleton One Row
Lane Head
Barningham
West Layton
East Layton
Aldbrough St John
Stanwick Camp
Hurworth-on-Tees
Neasham
Low Dinsdale
Croft-on-Tees
Eryholme
Newsham
Dalton
Ravensworth
Gayles
Roman Road
Melsonby
Barton
Newton Morrell
Dalton-on-Tees
Croft
Sockburn
Low Worsall
Girsby
Kirklevington
Picton
Kirby Hill
Whashton
Gilling West
Middleton Tyas
Scotch Corner
Low Entercommon
High Entercommon
Hornby
Appleton Wiske
Great Smeaton
West Rounton
East Rounton
High Moor
Marske Moor
Washfold
Skeeby
Moulton
North Cowton
Atley Hill
East Cowton
Birkby
Welbury
Georgian Theatre
Richmond
Uckerby
Deighton
Hutton Bonville
Ingleby Arncliffe
Marske
Hudswell
Brompton on Swale
Scorton
Bolton-on-Swale
Oaktree Hill
East Harlsey
Marrick
Ellerton Priory
Catterick
Whitwell
Streetlam
Mount Grace Priory (NT)
Downholme
Catterick Camp
Hipswell Moor
Ellerton
Kiplin
Danby Wiske
Northallerton
Stainton
Stainton Moor
Scotton
Tunstall
Great Langton
Brompton
Ellerbeck
Kirby Sigston
East Appleton
Kirby Fleetham
Yafforth
Barden
East Hauxwell
Hornby
Hackforth
Great Fencote
Romanby
Northallerton
Crosby Court
Bellerby Moor
Bellerby
Arrathorne
Little Fencote
Thrintoft
Leyburn Moor
Burton Hall
Hunton
Langthorne
Little Holtby
Scruton
Morton-on-Swale
Ainderby Steeple
Warlaby
Preston-under-Scar
Patrick Brompton
Kirkbridge
Thornton-le-Beans
Leyburn
Constable Burton
Little Crakehall
Great Crakehall
Leeming Bar
North Otterington
Wensley
Harmby
Finghall
Newton-le-Willows
Leeming
Thornton-le-Moor
Borrowby
Spennithorne
Bedale Hall
Bedale
Aiskew
Londonderry
Middleham
Thornton Resr
Abbey (rems. of)
Cowling
Burrill
Exelby
Gatenby
Newby Wiske
Maunby
South Otterington
Thornton-le-Street
Agglethorpe
Thornton Steward
Rookwith
Thirn
Theakston
North Kilvington
Coverham
East Witton
Braithwaite Hall (NT)
Jervaulx Abbey
Brymor High Jervaulx Farm
Thornton Watlass
Thorp Perrow Arboretum
Newsham
Kirby Wiske
Carlton Moor
West Scrafton
Ellingstring
High Burton
Snape
Burneston
Carthorpe
Pickhill
South
Thirsk
High Ellington
Low Burton
Well
Sinderby
Sandhutton
Colsterdale
Colsterdale Moor
Fearby
Black Sheep Brewery Visitors Centre
Masham
Kirklington
Ainderby Quernhow
Carlton Miniott
Healey
Nosterfield
Howe
Great Haw
544
Leighton
Swinton
Thornborough
Binsoe
Baldersby
Skipton-on-Swale
Ilton
Aldburgh
Sutton Howgrave
Middleton Quernhow
Masham Moor
Leighton Reservoir
West Tanfield
Catton
Brown Ridge
429
Roundhill Reservoir
Mickley
North Stainley
Wath
Melmerby
Topcliffe
Dalton
Nidderdale
Grewelthorpe
Lightwater Village
Norton Conyers
Asenby
Rainton
Kirkby Malzeard Moor
Kirkby Malzeard
Lightwater Valley Park
Nunwick
Azerley
Sutton Grange
Lofthouse
Stean
Hambleton Hill
406
Laverton
Galphay
Hutton Conyers
Dishforth
Cundall
Greygarth
Sharow
Norton-le-Clay
Stean Moor
Ramsgill
Bouthwaite
Dallowgill Moor
Winksley Banks
Winksley
Ripon
Cathedral
Copt Hewick
Marton-le-Moor
Lumley Moor Reservoir
Grantley
Studley Royal
Studley Roger
Bridge Hewick
Helperby
Gouthwaite Reservoir
Aldfield
Risplith
Ripon
Littlethorpe
Kirby Hill
Boroughbridge 1322
Fountains Abbey (NT)
Newby
Skelton
Pateley Moor
Markenfield Hall
Langthorpe
Heathfield Moor
Boroughbridge
Bishop Monkton
Ingerthorpe
Aldborough
Roecliffe
Appletreewick
Pateley Bridge
Lower D
A68
A167
A688
A67
A66
A1150
A66(M)
A1(M)
A1
A6108
A6136
A684
A168
A19
A61
A135
A177
B6279
B6275
B6274
B6271
B6280
B1264
B1263
B6285
B6268
B6267
B6265
B1448
B6444
Dere Street
57
56
58
59
49
48
Skeeby Beck
Swale
Wiske
Cod Beck
Ure
Laver
Greta

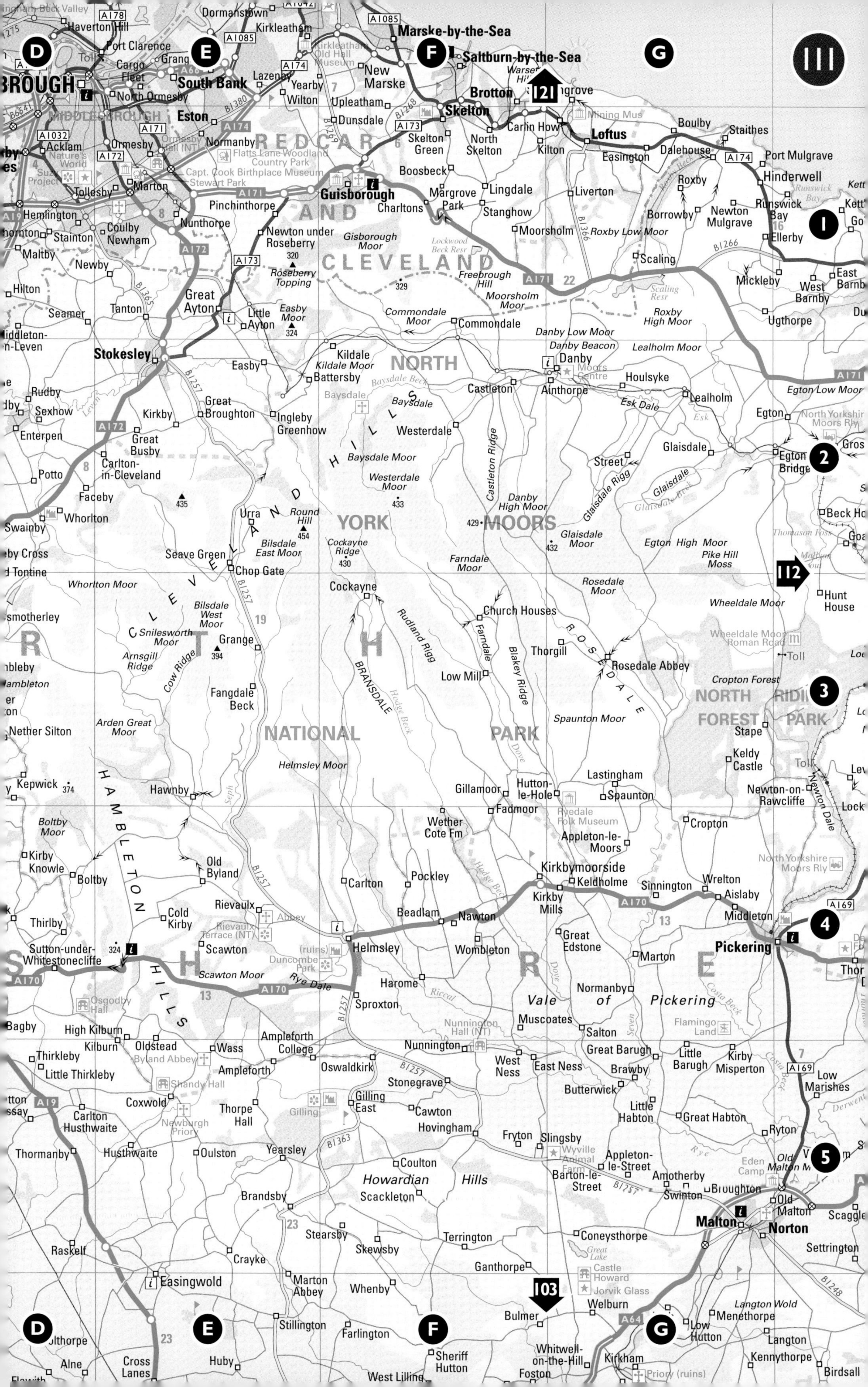
D
E
F
G
Dormanstown
Kirkleatham
A1085
Marske-by-the-Sea
Saltburn-by-the-Sea
Haverton Hill
Port Clarence
Cargo Fleet
Grangetown
Kirkleatham Old Hall Museum
New Marske
Warsett Hill
121
Skinningrove
South Bank
Lazenby
Yearby
A174
Wilton
Upleatham
Brotton
Skelton
Mining Mus
North Ormesby
Eston
MIDDLESBROUGH
A1032
A171
Dunsdale
A173
Carlin How
Loftus
Boulby
Staithes
Acklam
Ormesby
Normanby
REDCAR
Skelton Green
North Skelton
Kilton
Easington
Dalehouse
A174
Port Mulgrave
Nature's World
A172
Ormesby Hall (NT)
Flatts Lane Woodland Country Park
Capt. Cook Birthplace Museum
Stewart Park
Boosbeck
Hinderwell
Tollesby
Marton
Guisborough
Margrove Park
Lingdale
Liverton
Roxby
Runswick Bay
Kettleness
Hemlington
Coulby Newham
Pinchinthorpe
AND
Charltons
Stanghow
Newton Mulgrave
Borrowby
Stainton
Nunthorpe
Newton under Roseberry
Gisborough Moor
Lockwood Beck Resr
Moorsholm
Roxby Low Moor
Ellerby
I
Maltby
A172
320
Roseberry Topping
CLEVELAND
B1366
Scaling
B1266
Mickleby
East Barnby
Newby
A173
Freebrough Hill
A171
22
Scaling Resr
West Barnby
Hilton
329
Moorsholm Moor
Roxby High Moor
Tanton
Great Ayton
Little Ayton
Easby Moor
324
Commondale Moor
Commondale
Ugthorpe
Seamer
B1365
Danby Low Moor
Hilton
Middleton-on-Leven
Danby Beacon
Lealholm Moor
Stokesley
Kildale
Kildale Moor
NORTH
Danby
Moors Centre
A171
Easby
B1257
Battersby
Baysdale Beck
Castleton
Ainthorpe
Houlsyke
Egton Low Moor
Rudby
Baysdale
Lealholm
Great Broughton
Esk Dale
Sexhow
Kirkby
Ingleby Greenhow
Baysdale
HILLS
Esk
Egton
North Yorkshire Moors Rly
Westerdale
Enterpen
A172
Great Busby
Castleton Ridge
Glaisdale
Egton Bridge
2
Carlton-in-Cleveland
Baysdale Moor
Street
8
Potto
Westerdale Moor
Glaisdale Rigg
Glaisdale
Glaisdale Beck
Faceby
433
Danby High Moor
435
Whorlton
Round Hill
454
YORK
429
MOORS
Beck Hole
Swainby
Urra
Cockayne Ridge
430
Glaisdale Moor
432
Egton High Moor
Thomason Foss
Goathland
Bilsdale East Moor
Pike Hill Moss
Seave Green
Farndale Moor
Mallyan Spout
Chop Gate
112
Whorlton Moor
Cockayne
Rosedale Moor
Hunt House
Bilsdale West Moor
19
Church Houses
Wheeldale Moor
Osmotherley
CLEVELAND
Rudland Rigg
Snilesworth Moor
Grange
Farndale
ROSEDALE
Wheeldale Moor Roman Road
Arnsgill Ridge
394
Thorgill
Toll
Cow Ridge
BRANSDALE
Blakey Ridge
Rosedale Abbey
Low Mill
Hodge Beck
Crropton Forest
Fangdale Beck
NORTH RIDING FOREST PARK
3
Arden Great Moor
Spaunton Moor
Nether Silton
NATIONAL
PARK
Stape
Helmsley Moor
Keldy Castle
Dove
Toll
Kepwick
374
Lastingham
HAMBLETON
Hawnby
Gillamoor
Hutton-le-Hole
Spaunton
Newton-on-Rawcliffe
Seph
Fadmoor
Newton Dale
Boltby Moor
Ryedale Folk Museum
Cropton
Wether Cote Fm
Appleton-le-Moors
North Yorkshire Moors Rly
Kirby Knowle
Old Byland
Kirkbymoorside
Boltby
B1257
Pockley
Keldholme
Sinnington
Wrelton
Carlton
Hodge Beck
Kirkby Mills
Aislaby
A169
Rievaulx
A170
Middleton
Cold Kirby
Beadlam
Nawton
13
4
Thirlby
Rievaulx Abbey
Rievaulx Terrace (NT)
Great Edstone
Scawton
Helmsley
Pickering
324
(ruins)
Wombleton
Marton
Sutton-under-Whitestonecliffe
Duncombe Park
Dove
A170
Scawton Moor
Rye Dale
A170
Harome
Riccal
Normanby
13
Osgodby Hall
HILLS
Spaunton
Costa Beck
B1257
Vale of Pickering
Muscoates
Flamingo Land
Bagby
High Kilburn
Ampleforth College
Nunnington Hall (NT)
Salton
Seven
Kilburn
Oldstead
Wass
Nunnington
Great Barugh
Little Barugh
Kirby Misperton
Thirkleby
Byland Abbey
West Ness
East Ness
7
Little Thirkleby
Ampleforth
Oswaldkirk
B1257
Brawby
A169
Low Marishes
Shandy Hall
Stonegrave
Butterwick
Coxwold
Gilling East
Cawton
Derwent
A19
Carlton Husthwaite
Thorpe Hall
Newburgh Priory
Gilling
Little Habton
Great Habton
Hovingham
Fryton
Slingsby
Ryton
Thormanby
Husthwaite
Oulston
Yearsley
B1363
Wyville Animal Farm
Appleton-le-Street
Rye
Eden Camp
Old Malton
5
Coulton
Barton-le-Street
Howardian Hills
B1257
Amotherby
Brandsby
Scackleton
Broughton
Swinton
23
Old Malton
Malton
Norton
Scagglethorpe
Raskelf
Stearsby
Terrington
Coneysthorpe
Skewsby
Great Lake
Settrington
Crayke
Ganthorpe
Castle Howard
Easingwold
Marton Abbey
103
B1248
Whenby
Jorvik Glass
Langton Wold
Welburn
Menethorpe
Bulmer
A64
Low Hutton
Stillington
Farlington
23
Langton
Sheriff Hutton
Whitwell-on-the-Hill
Kirkham
Kennythorpe
Cross Lanes
Huby
Alne
Foston
Priory (ruins)
West Lilling
Birdsall

112
A
B
C
D
1
2
3
4
5
Brotton
Skelton
Skinningrove
Carlin How
Mining Mus
Loftus
North Skelton
Kilton
Easington
Boulby
Staithes
Dalehouse
A174
Port Mulgrave
Hinderwell
Runswick Bay
Kettle Ness
Kettleness
Goldsborough
REDCAR AND CLEVELAND
Lingdale
Liverton
Roxby
Newton Mulgrave
Runswick Bay
Borrowby
Ellerby
Moorsholm
Roxby Low Moor
Scaling
B1266
B1366
Lythe
Sandsend
Sandsend Ness
Freebrough Hill
A171
22
Moorsholm Moor
Scaling Resr
Roxby High Moor
Mickleby
East Barnby
West Barnby
Ugthorpe
Dunsley
Newholm
Whitby
Lifeboat Mus
St. Mary's
Abbey
Saltwick Bay
Capt.Cook Memorial Museum
Commondale
Danby Low Moor
Danby Beacon
Lealholm Moor
Danby
Moors Centre
Castleton
Ainthorpe
Houlsyke
Lealholm
Esk Dale
Egton Low Moor
Aislaby
Ruswarp
Stainsacre
Sleights
Sneaton
High Hawsker
Ugglebarnby
Low Hawkser
Egton
North Yorkshire Moors Rly
Grosmont
Glaisdale
Egton Bridge
Sneatonthorpe
Ness Point or North Cheek
Robin Hood's Bay
B1447
Raw
Fylingthorpe
Littlebeck
B1416
Street
Glaisdale Rigg
Glaisdale
Castle Ridge
Danby High Moor
Sleights Moor
Falling Foss
Low Moor
Old Peak or South Cheek
Ravenscar
429
432
Glaisdale Moor
Beck Hole
NORTH YORK MOORS
Thomason Foss
Goathland
A169
Egton High Moor
Pike Hill Moss
Mallyan Spout
Flask Inn
20
Farndale Moor
111
Rosedale Moor
NATIONAL PARK
Fylingdales Moor
Hunt House
292
Burn Howe Rigg
Staintondale
Church Houses
Wheeldale Moor
N O R T H
Farndale
Wheeldale Moor Roman Road
Toll
Lockton High Moor
Allerston High Moor
Harwood Dale
Thorgill
ROSEDALE
Rosedale Abbey
Blakey Ridge
Crompton Forest
Cloughton
NORTH RIDING FOREST PARK
Saltergate
Broxa Forest
Lockton Low Moor
Cloughton
Spaunton Moor
Stape
Keldy Castle
North Riding Forest Park
Silpho
Burniston
Toll
Levisham
Broxa
Suffield
Lastingham
Langdale End
Toll
A165
Gillamoor
Hutton-le-Hole
Spaunton
Newton-on-Rawcliffe
Newton Dale
Hackness
Fadmoor
Ryedale Folk Museum
Lockton
Stain Dale
Everley
Scalby
Crompton
Appleton-le-Moors
NORTH RIDING FOREST PARK
Dalby Forest
Wykeham Forest
A171
Irton Moor
Kirkbymoorside
North Yorkshire Moors Rly
Falsgrave
Keldholme
Kirkby Mills
Sinnington
Wrelton
Aislaby
West Ayton
East Ayton
A170
13
Middleton
A169
Toll
Sawdon
Hutton Buscel
Y O R K S H I R E
Great Edstone
Pickering
Dalby Forest Drive
Ebberston Hall
Ruston
Wombleton
Marton
Wilton
Wykeham
Thornton-le-Dale
Allerston
Ebberston
17
Irton
Normanby
Snainton
A170
Wykeham Abbey
Vale of Pickering
B1415
Brompton
Costa Beck
Wilton Carr
Muscoates
Salton
Flamingo Land
Priory
A64
West Ness
East Ness
Great Barugh
Little Barugh
Kirby Misperton
Yedingham
THE CARRS
Staxton
Brawby
A169
Low Marishes
East Heslerton
Sherburn
Willerby
Butterwick
B1258
Ganton
Little Habton
Great Habton
Derwent
East Knapton
A64
16
Fryton
Slingsby
Ryton
West Knapton
West Heslerton
Wyville Animal Farm
Scampston
Appleton-le-Street
Wykeham
Barton-le-Street
Eden Camp
Old Malton Moor
Rillington
Sherburn Wold
B1249
B1257
Amotherby
Broughton
A64
Wintringham
Swinton
Old Malton
Thorpe Bassett
Place Newton
Foxholes
Malton
Norton
Scagglethorpe
Butterwick
Coneysthorpe
Settrington
Helperthorpe
Weaverthorpe
Great Lake
Ganthorpe
Castle Howard
B1248
199
104
East Lutton
Octon
Jorvik Glass
West Lutton
Welburn
Langton Wold
North Grimston
Kirby Grindalythe
Bulmer
A64
Menethorpe
Low Hutton
Duggleby
Langtoft
Whitwell-on-the-Hill
Langton
Kirkham
Kennythorpe
Cowlam Manor
Foston
Priory (ruins)
Birdsall
Wharram le Street
B1253
Sledmere

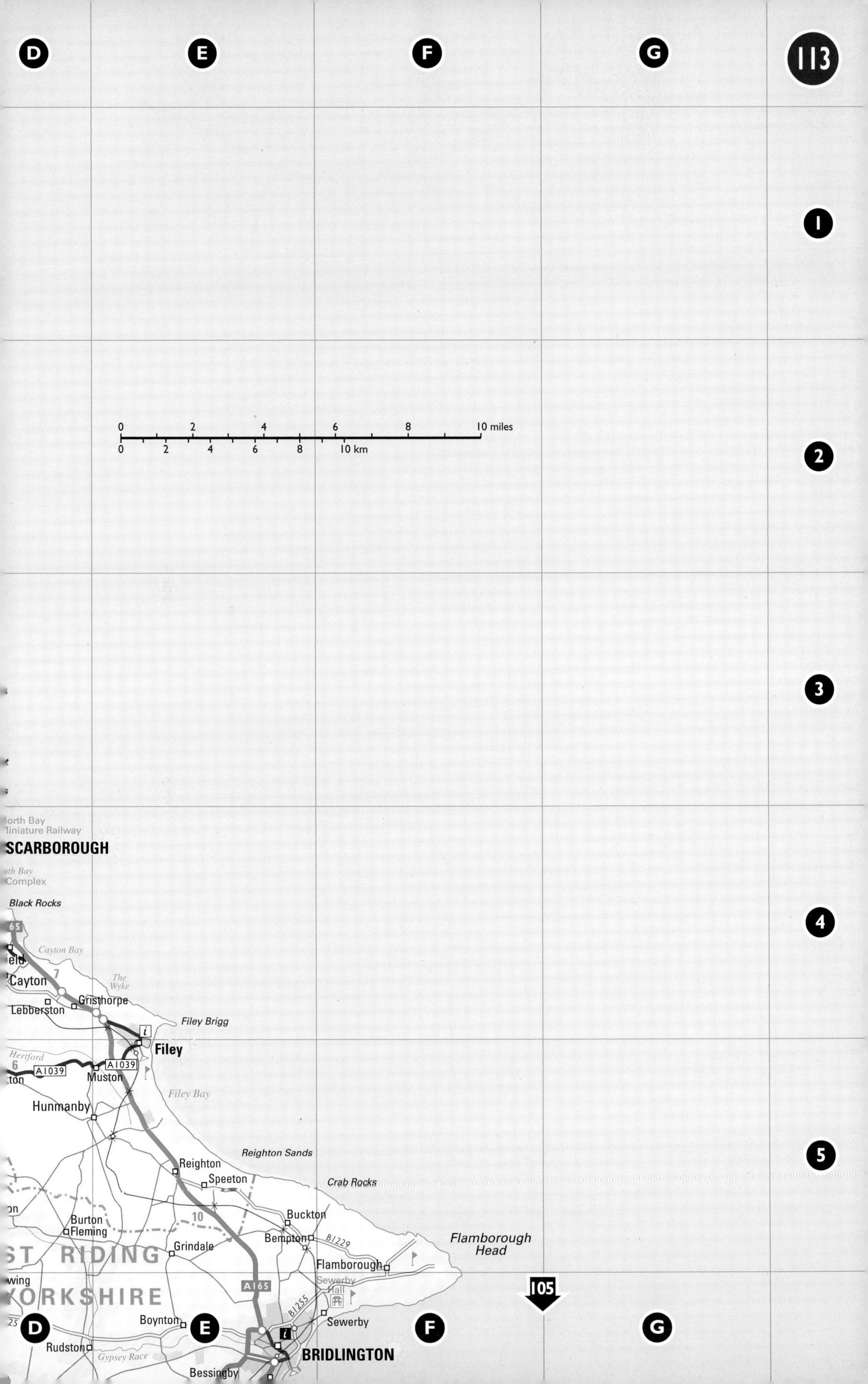
D
E
F
G
1
2
3
4
5
0 2 4 6 8 10 miles
0 2 4 6 8 10 km
SCARBOROUGH
Black Rocks
Cayton Bay
Cayton
The Wyke
Gristhorpe
Lebberston
Filey Brigg
Filey
Hertford
A1039
A1039
Muston
Filey Bay
Hunmanby
Reighton Sands
Reighton
Speeton
Crab Rocks
10
Buckton
Burton Fleming
Bempton
B1229
Grindale
Flamborough Head
Flamborough
A165
Sewerby Hall
B1255
Sewerby
Boynton
Rudston
Gypsey Race
BRIDLINGTON
Bessingby
105

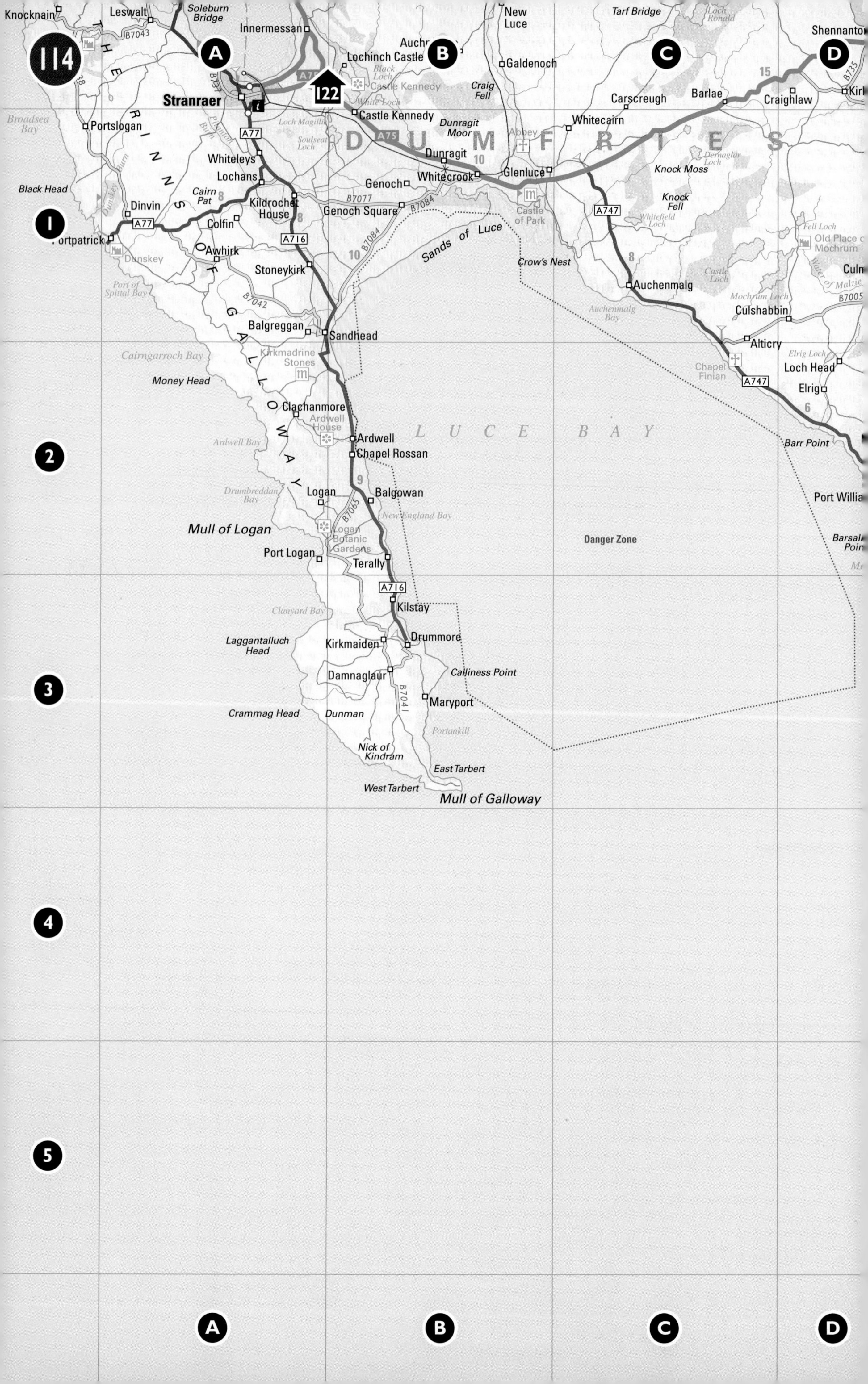
114
A
B
C
D
1
2
3
4
5
122
Knocknain
Leswalt
Soleburn Bridge
Innermessan
New Luce
Tarf Bridge
Loch Ronald
Shennanton
Auchr
Lochinch Castle
Galdenoch
Black Loch
Castle Kennedy
Craig Fell
Stranraer
Carscreugh
Barlae
Craighlaw
Kirk
White Loch
Castle Kennedy
Dunragit Moor
Whitecairn
Broadsea Bay
Portslogan
Loch Magillie
Soulseat Loch
Abbey
D U M F R I E S
A75
A77
B7043
B737
THE RINNS OF GALLOWAY
Dunragit
Dernaglar Loch
Whiteleys
Knock Moss
Lochans
Whitecrook
Glenluce
Genoch
Black Head
Cairn Pat
Kildrochet House
B7077
B7084
Genoch Square
Castle of Park
Knock Fell
A747
Whitefield Loch
Fell Loch
Old Place of Mochrum
Dinvin
Colfin
Portpatrick
A716
Sands of Luce
Awhirk
Dunskey
Stoneykirk
Crow's Nest
Water of Malzie
Culn
Castle Loch
Auchenmalg
Port of Spittal Bay
B7042
Auchenmalg Bay
Mochrum Loch
B7005
Culshabbin
Balgreggan
Sandhead
Alticry
Cairngarroch Bay
Kirkmadrine Stones
Elrig Loch
Chapel Finian
Loch Head
Money Head
Elrig
Clachanmore
Ardwell House
L U C E   B A Y
Ardwell Bay
Ardwell
Barr Point
Chapel Rossan
Drumbreddan Bay
Logan
Balgowan
B7065
Port William
New England Bay
Mull of Logan
Logan Botanic Gardens
Danger Zone
Barsalloch Point
Port Logan
Terally
Kilstay
Clanyard Bay
Laggantalluch Head
Drummore
Kirkmaiden
Damnaglaur
Cailiness Point
B7041
Crammag Head
Dunman
Maryport
Portankill
Nick of Kindram
East Tarbert
West Tarbert
Mull of Galloway

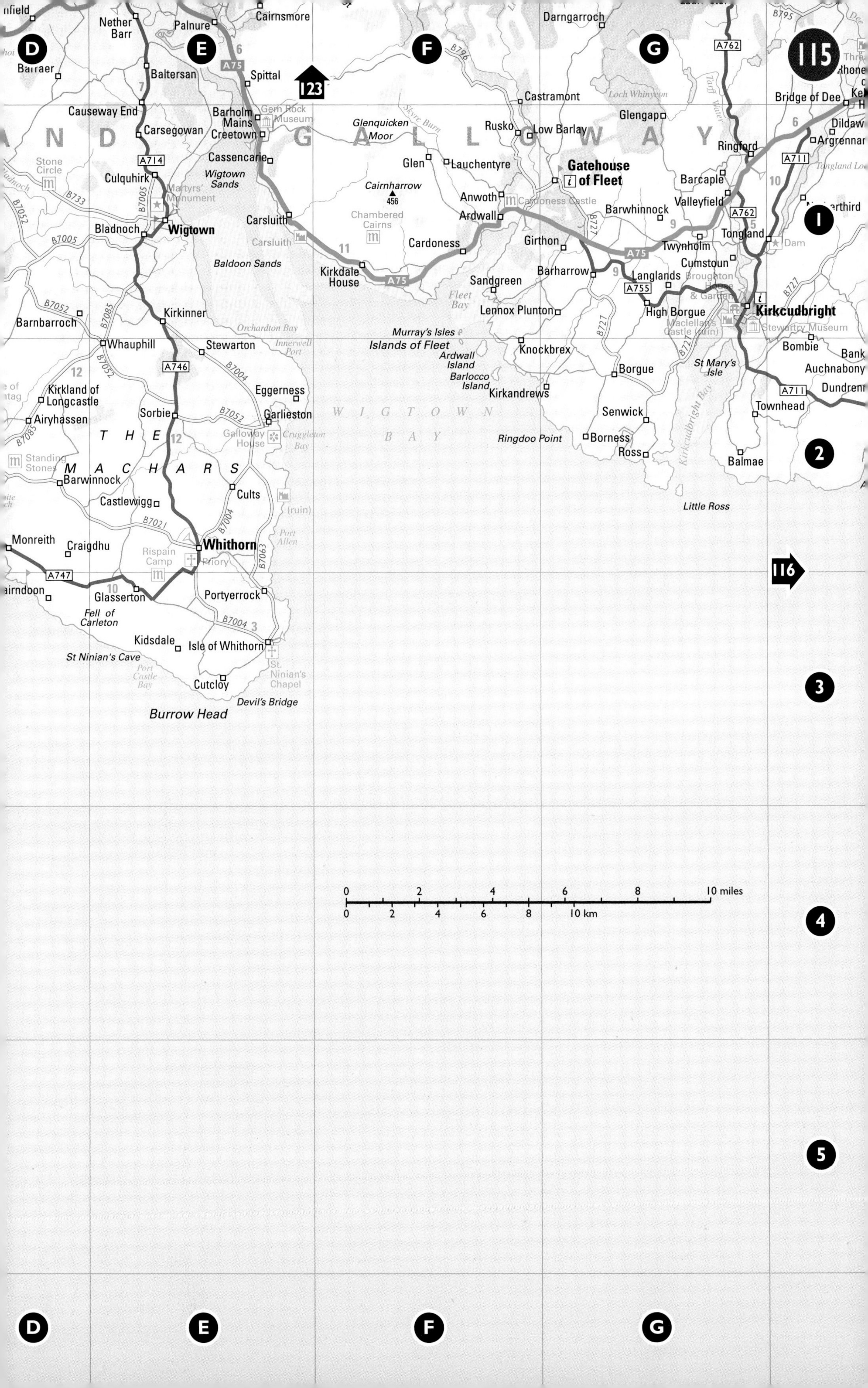
D
E
F
G
D
E
F
G
1
2
3
4
5
123
116
nfield
Nether Barr
Palnure
Cairnsmore
Darngarroch
B795
A762
Barraer
Baltersan
Spittal
A75
B796
Castramont
Loch Whinyeon
Bridge of Dee
Causeway End
Barholm Mains
Creetown
Gem Rock Museum
Glenquicken Moor
Skyre Burn
Rusko
Low Barlay
Glengap
Tarff Water
Dildawn
Argrennan
Carsegowan
A N D G A L L O W A Y
Ringford
A714
Stone Circle
Cassencarie
Glen
Lauchentyre
Gatehouse of Fleet
A711
Tongland Loch
Culquhirk
Wigtown Sands
Martyrs' Monument
Cairnharrow
456
Barcaple
B733
B7005
Anworth
Cardoness Castle
Valleyfield
B7052
Chambered Cairns
Ardwall
Barwhinnock
A762
Bladnoch
Wigtown
Carsluith
B727
Tongland
B7005
Carsluith
Cardoness
Girthon
Twynholm
Dam
Baldoon Sands
Cumstoun
Kirkdale House
A75
Barharrow
Langlands
Broughton House & Garden
B727
B7052
Sandgreen
A755
Fleet Bay
Lennox Plunton
High Borgue
Kirkcudbright
Barnbarroch
B7085
Kirkinner
Orchardton Bay
Maclellan's Castle (ruin)
Stewartry Museum
Murray's Isles
Whauphill
Stewarton
Innerwell Port
Islands of Fleet
Knockbrex
B727
Bombie
Bank
12
B7052
A746
B7004
Ardwall Island
Borgue
St Mary's Isle
Auchnabony
Barlocco Island
Kirkland of Longcastle
Eggerness
Kirkandrews
A711
Dundrenn
Airyhassen
Sorbie
B7052
Garlieston
W I G T O W N
Senwick
Townhead
Kirkcudbright Bay
B7085
T H E
12
Galloway House
Cruggleton Bay
B A Y
Ringdoo Point
Borness
Standing Stones
M A C H A R S
Ross
Balmae
Barwinnock
Cults
Castlewigg
(ruin)
Little Ross
B7021
B7004
Port Allen
Monreith
Craigdhu
Whithorn
Rispain Camp
Priory
B7063
A747
10
airndoon
Glasserton
Portyerrock
Fell of Carleton
B7004
3
Kidsdale
Isle of Whithorn
St Ninian's Cave
Port Castle Bay
St. Ninian's Chapel
Cutcloy
Devil's Bridge
Burrow Head
0 2 4 6 8 10 miles
0 2 4 6 8 10 km

A713
B795
Threave
Hillowton
Motte of Urr
B794
A711
Loch Kindar
Cuil Hill
Blacks Ban
Castle Douglas
Buchan
Carlingwark Loch
Threave (NTS)
124
A745
Craignair
Dalbeattie
Loch Fern
Southwick Burn
Criffel
569
A710
Carse Bay
Bridge of Dee
Tarff Water
Rhonehouse or Kelton Hill
B736
B727
Breoch
Gelston
Dildawn
Argrennan
A75
Ringford
Barcaple
Valleyfield
A762
Twynholm
Cumstoun
Langlands
Broughton House & Garden
Maclellan's Castle (ruin)
Kirkcudbright
Stewartry Museum
Tongland Loch
A711
Netherthird
Tongland
Dam
Airieland
Screel Hill
Bengairn
391
DUMFRIES & GALLOWAY
B727
B736
Palnackie
A711
A710
Dalbeattie Forest
B793
Barnbarroch
Kippford or Scaur
Orchardton Tower
Rough Firth
(NTS)
Rockcliffe
White Loch
Colvend
Fairgirth
Douglas Hall
Port o' Warren
Caulkerbush
Mainsriddle
Kirkbean
Carsethorn
Cavens
Borron Point
Arbigland
Preston Merse
Gillfoot Bay
Southerness
Southerness Point
Mersehead Sands
Barnhourie Sands
Castlehill Point
Almorness Point
Hestan Island
Auchencairn
Auchencairn Bay
Balcary Point
Bombie
Bankhead
Hazlefield
Rascarrel
Auchnabony
Dundrennan
St Mary's Isle
Kirkcudbright Bay
Townhead
Abbey
Orroland
Rascarrel Bay
Barlocco Bay
Port Mary
Balmae
Little Ross
Abbey Head
SOLWAY FIRTH
115
Maryport
Ellenborough
Flimby
A596
Camerton
Seaton
Great
A66
WORKINGTON
A597
A596
Westfield
High Harrington
Distington
A595
Moresby
Pica
Keekle
Parton
WHITEHAVEN
Saltom Bay
Hensingham
B5295
B5294
Sandwith
St Bees Head
Cleator Moor
A595
Moor Row
Bigrigg
Cleator
B5345
Rottington
St Bees
Egremont
How Man
Snellings
Middletown
Nethertown
Ehen
Beckermet
Braystones
Sellafield Visitors
0 2 4 6 8 10 miles
0 2 4 6 8 10 km
A B C D
1 2 3 4 5

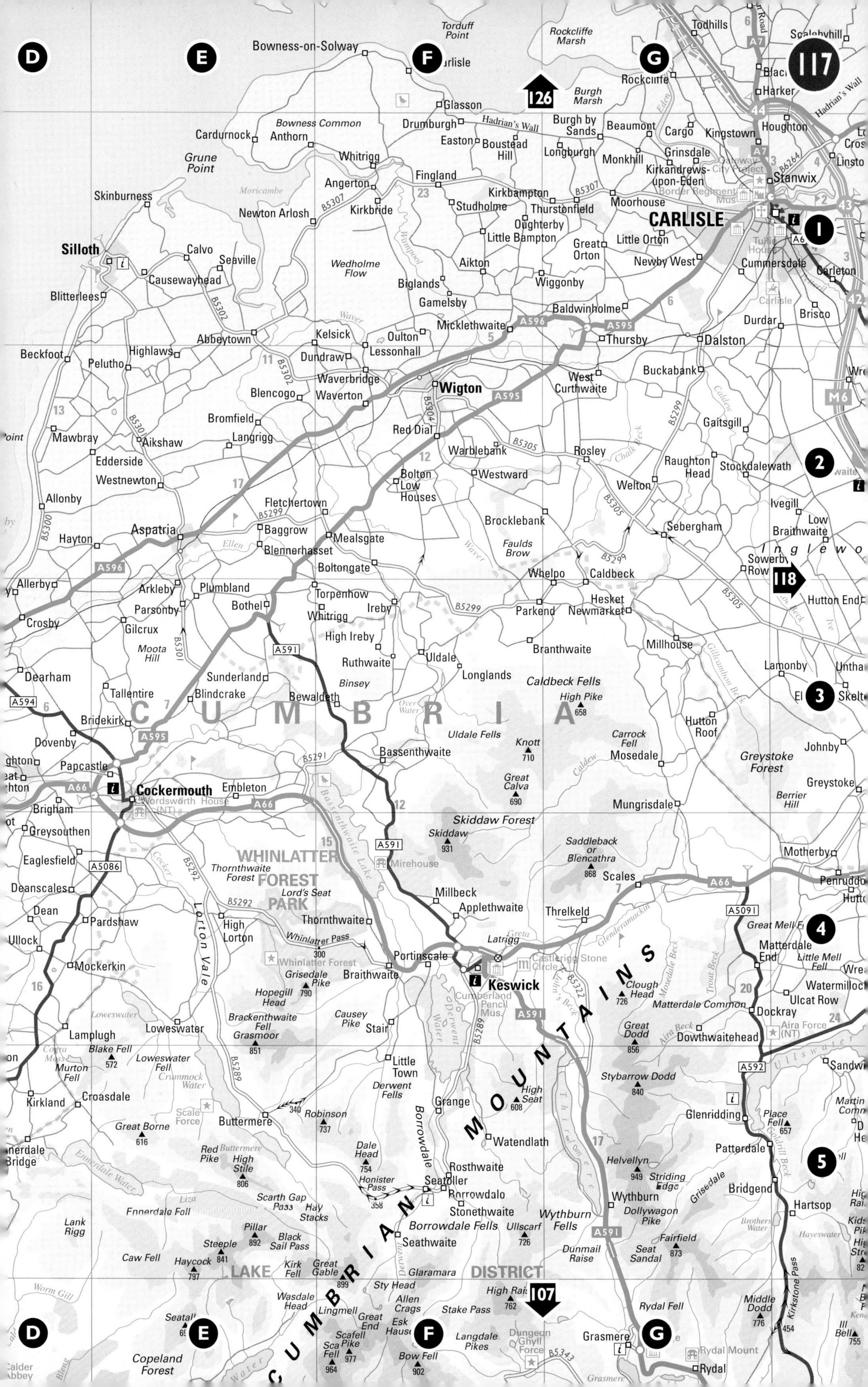

117
126
118
107
D
E
F
G
D
E
F
G
1
2
3
4
5
CUMBRIA
CUMBRIAN MOUNTAINS
LAKE DISTRICT
Torduff Point
Rockcliffe Marsh
Todhills
Scalebyhill
Bowness-on-Solway
Port Carlisle
Rockcliffe
Harker
Hadrian's Wall
Burgh Marsh
Glasson
Drumburgh
Bowness Common
Cardurnock
Anthorn
Burgh by Sands
Beaumont
Cargo
Kingstown
Houghton
Easton
Boustead Hill
Longburgh
Monkhill
Grinsdale
Kirkandrews-upon-Eden
Gateway City Project
Border Regiment Mus
Stanwix
Linstock
Grune Point
Whitrigg
Fingland
Angerton
Moricambe
Skinburness
Kirkbampton
Moorhouse
Newton Arlosh
Kirkbride
Studholme
Thurstonfield
CARLISLE
Oughterby
Little Bampton
Great Orton
Little Orton
Tullie House
Silloth
Calvo
Seaville
Wedholme Flow
Wampool
Aikton
Newby West
Cummersdale
Carleton
Causewayhead
Biglands
Wiggonby
Blitterlees
Gamelsby
Baldwinholme
Carlisle
Brisco
Waver
Micklethwaite
Durdar
Kelsick
Oulton
Thursby
Dalston
Beckfoot
Abbeytown
Highlaws
Lessonhall
Dundraw
Pelutho
Waverbridge
Wigton
Buckabank
Blencogo
Waverton
West Curthwaite
Caldew
M6
Bromfield
Langrigg
Red Dial
Gaitsgill
Mawbray
Aikshaw
Warblebank
Rosley
Chalk Beck
Edderside
Raughton Head
Stockdalewath
Westnewton
Bolton Low Houses
Westward
Welton
Allonby
Fletchertown
Ivegill
Low Braithwaite
Aspatria
Baggrow
Brocklebank
Sebergham
Hayton
Mealsgate
Ellen
Blennerhasset
Faulds Brow
Inglewood
Sowerby Row
Boltongate
Whelpo
Caldbeck
Allerby
Arkleby
Plumbland
Torpenhow
Hutton End
Parsonby
Bothel
Ireby
Parkend
Hesket Newmarket
Crosby
Gilcrux
Whitrigg
High Ireby
Millhouse
Moota Hill
Branthwaite
Uldale
Gillcambon Beck
Dearham
Sunderland
Ruthwaite
Longlands
Lamonby
Unthank
Tallentire
Blindcrake
Binsey
Bewaldeth
Caldbeck Fells
High Pike 658
Skelton
Over Water
Uldale Fells
Hutton Roof
Bridekirk
Dovenby
Carrock Fell
Knott 710
Johnby
Greystoke Forest
Papcastle
Bassenthwaite
Mosedale
Greystoke
Cockermouth
Embleton
Wordsworth House (NT)
Great Calva 690
Berrier Hill
Mungrisdale
Brigham
Bassenthwaite Lake
Skiddaw Forest
Greysouthen
WHINLATTER FOREST PARK
Skiddaw 931
Saddleback or Blencathra 868
Motherby
Eaglesfield
Thornthwaite Forest
Mirehouse
Deanscales
Lord's Seat
Millbeck
Scales
Penruddock
Dean
Applethwaite
Threlkeld
Pardshaw
Thornthwaite
Lorton Vale
High Lorton
Great Mell Fell
Ullock
Whinlatter Pass
Latrigg
Greta
Glenderamackin
Matterdale End
Mockerkin
Portinscale
Castlerigg Stone Circle
Little Mell Fell
Whinlatter Forest
Grisedale Pike 790
Braithwaite
Keswick
Clough Head 726
Watermillock
Hopegill Head
Cumberland Pencil Mus.
St John's Beck
Mosedale Beck
Trout Beck
Ulcat Row
Matterdale Common
Dockray
Loweswater
Brackenthwaite Fell
Causey Pike
Derwent Water
Great Dodd 856
Aira Force (NT)
Lamplugh
Loweswater
Grasmoor 851
Stair
Aira Beck
Dowthwaitehead
Cogra Moss
Blake Fell 572
Loweswater Fell
Crummock Water
Little Town
Stybarrow Dodd 840
Ullswater
Sandwick
Murton Fell
Derwent Fells
High Seat 608
Kirkland
Croasdale
Scale Force
Buttermere
Robinson 737
Grange
Thirlmere
Glenridding
Martindale Common
Place Fell 657
Great Borne 616
Watendlath
Borrowdale
Ennerdale Bridge
Red Pike
Buttermere
High Stile 806
Dale Head 754
Helvellyn 949
Patterdale
Ennerdale Water
Rosthwaite
Striding Edge
Goldrill Beck
Honister Pass 358
Seatoller
Wythburn
Grisedale
Bridgend
Scarth Gap Pass
Hay Stacks
Borrowdale
Dollywagon Pike
Hartsop
Ennerdale Fell
Liza
Stonethwaite
Wythburn Fells
Brothers Water
Lank Rigg
Pillar 892
Borrowdale Fells
Ullscarf 726
Hayeswater
Steeple 841
Black Sail Pass
Seathwaite
Fairfield 873
Caw Fell
Haycock 797
Kirk Fell
Great Gable 899
Dunmail Raise
Seat Sandal
Glaramara
Kirkstone Pass 454
Worm Gill
Sty Head
High Raise 762
Wasdale Head
Allen Crags
Rydal Fell
Middle Dodd 776
Lingmell
Great End
Stake Pass
Seatallan
Esk Hause
Scafell Pike 977
Sca Fell 964
Langdale Pikes
Dungeon Ghyll Force
Grasmere
Rydal Mount
Ill Bell 755
Copeland Forest
Bow Fell 902
Rydal
Calder Abbey
A7
A6
A595
A596
A591
A66
A5086
A594
A5091
A592
B5307
B5302
B5300
B5301
B5299
B5304
B5305
B6264
B5291
B5292
B5289
B5322
B5343

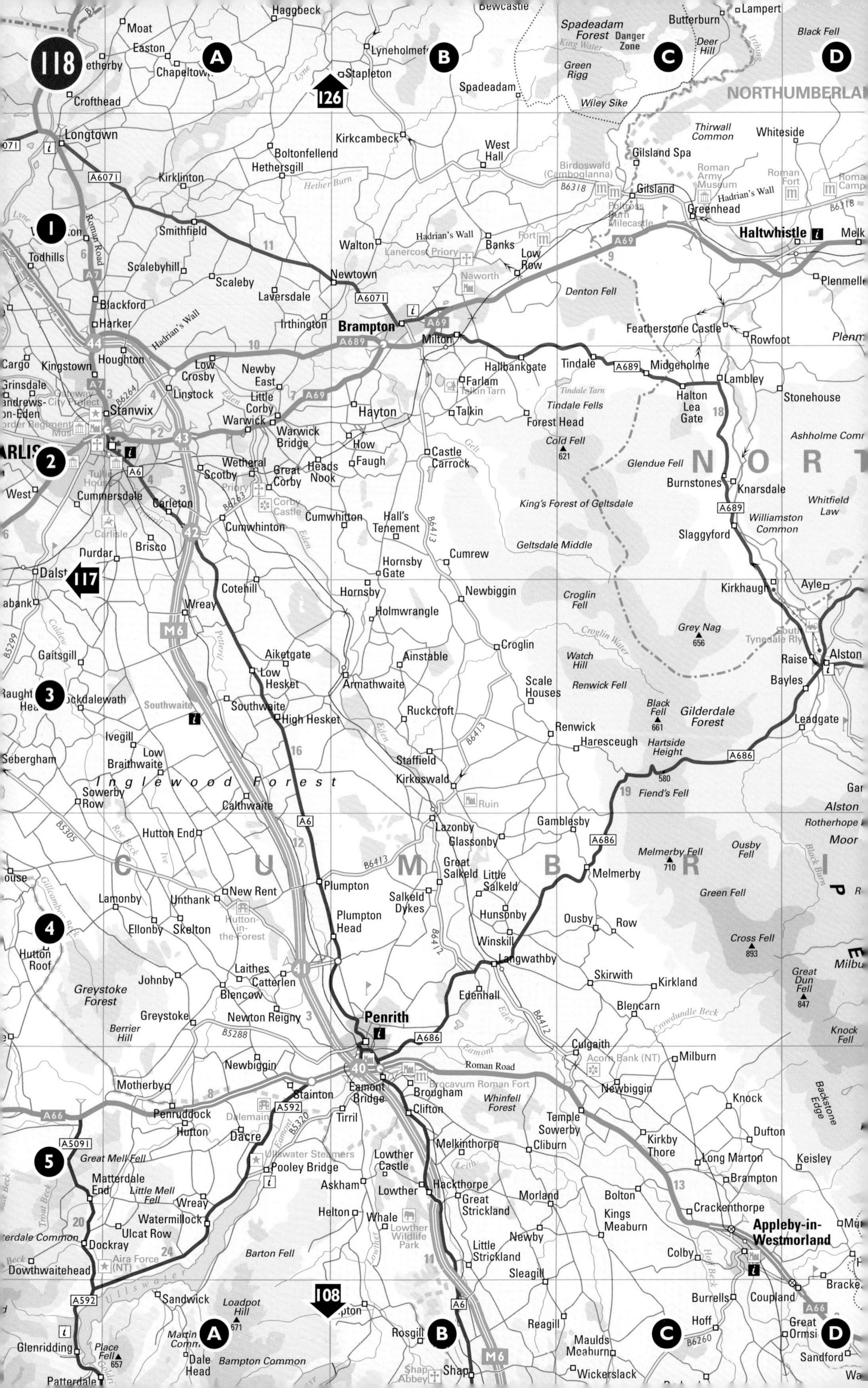

118
126
117
108
A
B
C
D
1
2
3
4
5
Haggbeck
Bewcastle
Moat
Easton
Chapeltown
Lyneholmeford
Stapleton
Spadeadam Forest Danger Zone
King Water
Butterburn
Lampert
Deer Hill
Irthing
Black Fell
Green Rigg
Spadeadam
Wiley Sike
NORTHUMBERLAND
Crofthead
Longtown
Kirkcambeck
West Hall
Thirwall Common
Whiteside
Gilsland Spa
Boltonfellend
Hethersgill
Hether Burn
A6071
Kirklinton
Birdoswald (Camboglanna)
B6318
Roman Army Museum
Roman Fort
Roman Camp
Gilsland
Hadrian's Wall
Greenhead
Poltross Burn Milecastle
Smithfield
Roman Road
Todhills
Walton
Hadrian's Wall
Banks
Lanercost Priory
Low Row
Haltwhistle
Melkridge
A69
Scalebyhill
Scaleby
Laversdale
Newtown
Naworth
Denton Fell
Plenmeller
Blackford
Harker
Hadrian's Wall
Irthington
Brampton
Featherstone Castle
Rowfoot
A689
Milton
Cargo
Kingstown
Houghton
Low Crosby
Newby East
Hallbankgate
Tindale
Midgeholme
Lambley
Grinsdale
Linstock
Farlam
Talkin Tarn
Tindale Tarn
Gateway City Project
Little Corby
Tindale Fells
Halton Lea Gate
Stonehouse
Stanwix
Talkin
Hayton
Warwick
Forest Head
Border Regiment Mus
Warwick Bridge
How
Castle Carrock
Cold Fell 621
Ashholme Common
Tullie House
Faugh
Glendue Fell
Wetheral
Great Corby
Heads Nook
Scotby
Priory
Burnstones
Knarsdale
West
Cummersdale
Carleton
Corby Castle
King's Forest of Geltsdale
Whitfield Law
Williamston Common
Cumwhitton
Hall's Tenement
Carlisle
Cumwhinton
Slaggyford
Brisco
Geltsdale Middle
Durdar
B6413
Cumrew
Dalston
Hornsby Gate
Cotehill
Hornsby
Newbiggin
Croglin Fell
Kirkhaugh
Ayle
Wreay
Holmwrangle
M6
Croglin Water
Grey Nag 656
South Tynedale Rly
Caldew
Petteril
B5299
Gaitsgill
Aiketgate
Ainstable
Croglin
Watch Hill
Alston
Raise
Low Hesket
Armathwaite
Scale Houses
Renwick Fell
Bayles
Raughton Head
Rockcliffe
Southwaite
Southwaite
High Hesket
Ruckcroft
Black Fell 661
Gilderdale Forest
Leadgate
Ivegill
Renwick
Haresceugh
Hartside Height
Low Braithwaite
Sebergham
Staffield
A686
Inglewood Forest
Kirkoswald
580
Fiend's Fell
Sowerby Row
Calthwaite
Ruin
Garrigill
Alston
Hutton End
Gamblesby
Rotherhope Moor
B5305
Lazonby
Glassonby
Melmerby Fell 710
Ousby Fell
Roe Beck
Ive
CUMBRIA
B6413
Great Salkeld
Little Salkeld
Melmerby
Black Burn
Gillcambon Beck
Plumpton
New Rent
Green Fell
Lamonby
Unthank
Salkeld Dykes
Hunsonby
Ellonby
Skelton
Hutton-in-the-Forest
Plumpton Head
Ousby
Row
Hutton Roof
B6412
Winskill
Cross Fell 893
Langwathby
Milburn
Johnby
Laithes
Catterlen
Skirwith
Kirkland
Great Dun Fell 847
Greystoke Forest
Blencow
Edenhall
Blencarn
Crowdundle Beck
Greystoke
Newton Reigny
Penrith
Berrier Hill
B5288
Knock Fell
A686
Eamont
Culgaith
Acorn Bank (NT)
Milburn
Newbiggin
Roman Road
Brougham
Brocavum Roman Fort
Backstone Edge
Motherby
Stainton
Eamont Bridge
Whinfell Forest
Knock
A66
Penruddock
Hutton
Dalemain
A592
Clifton
Temple Sowerby
Tirril
B5320
Dacre
Dufton
A5091
Kirkby Thore
Cliburn
Melkinthorpe
Great Mell Fell
Ullswater Steamers
Lowther Castle
Leith
Long Marton
Keisley
Pooley Bridge
Matterdale End
Little Mell Fell
Askham
Hackthorpe
Brampton
Wreay
Lowther
Great Strickland
Morland
Bolton
Watermillock
Helton
Whale
Lowther Wildlife Park
Crackenthorpe
Kings Meaburn
Appleby-in-Westmorland
Ulcat Row
Trout Beck
Matterdale Common
Dockray
Newby
Little Strickland
Colby
Barton Fell
Aira Force (NT)
Hoff Beck
Dowthwaitehead
Lowther
Sleagill
Ullswater
Bracken
A592
Sandwick
Loadpot Hill 671
Burrells
Coupland
A6
Reagill
Hoff
Great Ormside
Glenridding
Martindale Common
Rosgill
Maulds Meaburn
B6260
Place Fell 657
Dale Head
Bampton Common
Shap Abbey
Shap
Sandford
Patterdale
Wickerslack

119
D
E
F
G
128
120
109
1
2
3
4
5
Haughton Common
Simonburn
Nunwick
Barrasford
Choll
Humshaugh
Chollerford
Walwick
Low Brunton
Chesters (Cilurnvm)
Turret
Brocolitia
Wall
Hadrian's Wall
Ryal
Grindstonelaw
Bingfield
Great Whittington
Fenwick
Heugh
Stamfordham
Hawkwell
Ouston
High
Dar
Little Whittington
Hadrian's Wall (Course of)
Harlow Hill
Callerton
Rudchester
Heddon-on-the-Wall
Broomlee Lough
Housesteads (Vercovicium)
Stanegate
Once Brewed Visitor Centre
Chesterholm (Vindolanda)
Newbrough
Fourstones
Warden
Acomb
Stagshaw Bank
Halton
Sandhoe
Aydon
Bardon Mill
Haydon Bridge
Henshaw
South Tyne
Low Gate
Hexham
Tyne Green
Corstopitum
Corbridge
Newton
Horsley
Stephenson's Birthplace
Wylam
Ovington
Ovingham
Crawcrook
Prudhoe
Dilston
Riding Mill
Mickley Square
Stocksfield
Coalburns
Sunnyside
Linnels
Newbiggin
Hexham Levels
Hexham
West Dipton Burn
Dipton Wood
Broomhaugh
Painshawfield
Leadgate
High Spen
Hedley on the Hill
Dotland
Dalton
Catton
Whitley Chapel
Slaley
Healey
Dere Street
Whittonstall
Chopwell
Hamsterley
Slaley Forest
Allendale Town
NORTHUMBERLAND
Barleyhill
Kiln Pit Hill
Newlands
Ebchester
Medomsley
Studdon
Ninebanks
Hexhamshire Common
Broadwell House
Blanchland Moor
Derwent Resr
Shotleyfield
Shotley Bridge
Derwent Walk
Sinderhope
Allendale Common
Hangman Hill
Devil's Water
Hope Fell
Blanchland
Pow Hill
Ruffside
Edmundbyers
Abbey
Muggleswick
Carterway Heads
CONSETT
Allensford
Delves
Hartley Moor
West Allen
Spartylea
Hunstanworth
Nookton Fell
Cross Rigg
Castleside
Healeyfield
Rowley
Knitsley
Carr Shield
Green Hill
Beldon Burn
Muggleswick Common
Smiddy Shaw Resr
Butsfield
Coalcleugh
Allenheads
Bolt's Law
Redburn Common
Skaylock Hill
Waskerley
Waskerley Resr
Waskerley Beck
Satley
Nenthead
Killhope Moor
Killhope Lead Mining Centre
Rookhope
Rookhope Burn
Middlehope Moor
Stanhope Common
Collier Law
Wolsingham Park Moor
Tunstall Resr
Cornriggs
Cowshill
Crawleyside
Stanhope
Tow Law
Wearhead
Burnhope Reservoir
Eastgate
Ireshopeburn
Westgate
Weardale
Frosterley
Wolsingham
Thornley
Burnhope Seat
St John's Chapel
Daddry Shield
Brotherlee
Ireshope Moor
Chapel Fell
Hill End
Harvey Hill
Chapelfell Top
Westernhope Moor
Snowhope Hill
Knitsley Fell
Three Pikes
Viewing Hill
Bollihope
Common
Harwood
Langdon Common
DURHAM
Outberry Plain
Pikeston Fell
St Johns Hall
Pawlaw Pike
Langdon Beck
Newbiggin Common
Middleton Common
Bedburn
Redford
Hamsterley
Witton-le-Wear
Cow Green Reservoir
Widdybank Fell
Carrs Hill
Hamsterley Common
Forest-in-Teesdale
Monks Moor
Euden Beck
Newbiggin
High Force
Bowlees Picnic Area
Hamsterley Forest
Morley
Tees
Holwick Fell
Holwick
Middleton-in-Teesdale
Eggleston Common
Woodland
Butterknowle
Cronkley Fell
Woodland Fell
Copley
Mickle Fell
Lune Forest
Lune Moor
Bowbank
Mickleton
Eggleston
Langleydale Common
Thringarth
Lunedale
Burnt Houses
Fish Lake
Little Fell
Danger Zone
Grassholme
Grassholme Resr
Romaldkirk
Kinninvie
Raby
Selset Reservoir
Mickleton Moor
Hury
Hunderthwaite
Balder
Staindrop
Warcop Fell
Hunderthwaite Moor
Blackton Resr
Hury Resr
Cotherstone
Cleatlam
Iron Band
Baldersdale
Stainton
Little Newsham
Balderhead Resr
Stainmore Common
Barnard Castle
Bowes Museum
Startforth
Cotherstone Moor
Westwick
Hillbeck
North Stainmore
Deep Dale
A68
A69
A6079
A695
A686
A692
A689
A688
A67
B6318
B6320
B6319
B6321
B6309
B6528
B6306
B6307
B6530
B6395
B6305
B6295
B6278
B6277
B6297
B6276
B6262
B6282
B6279
B6274
B6296
561
516
627
746
699
675
790
745
562
1464

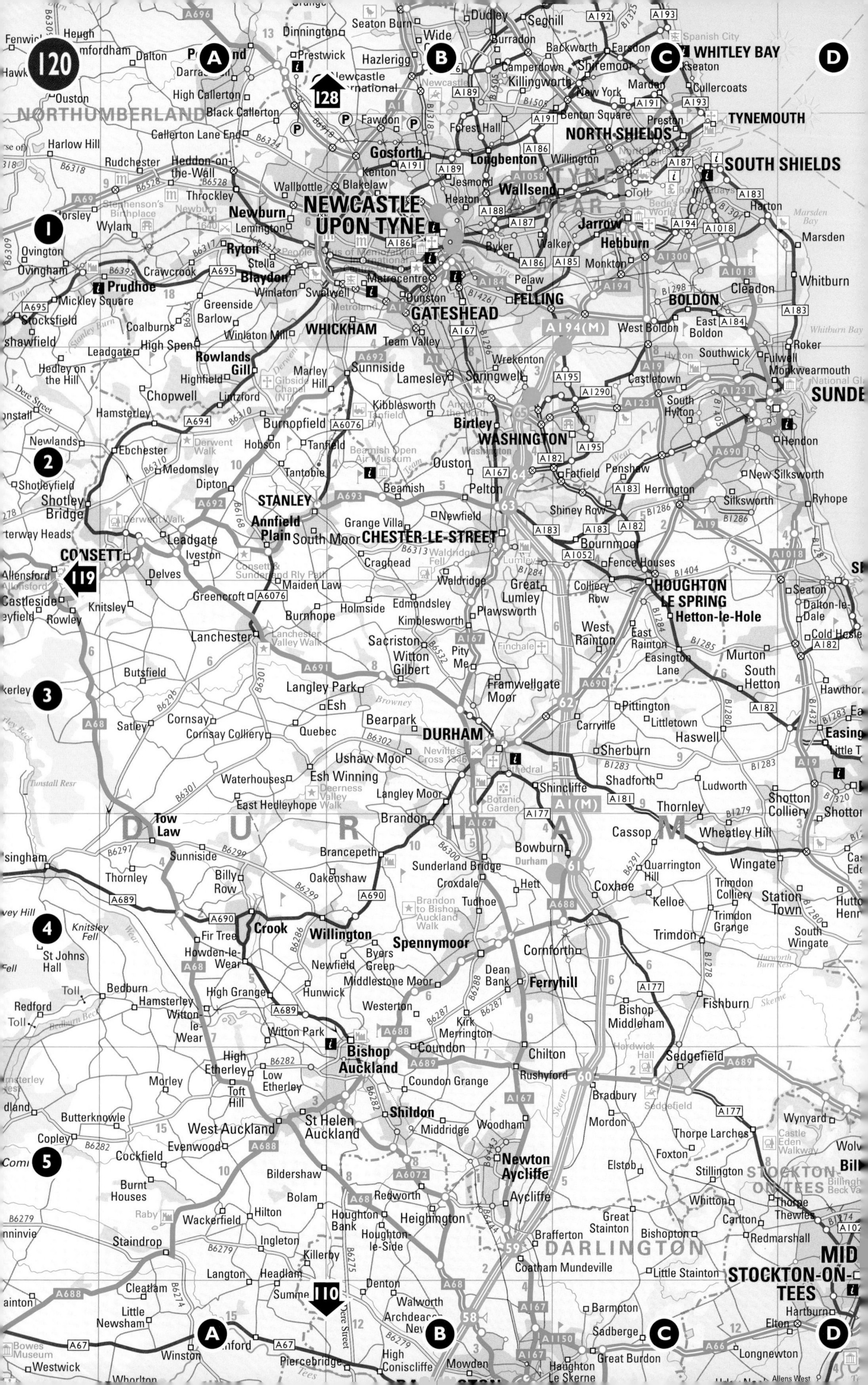
A
B
C
D
1
2
3
4
5
NORTHUMBERLAND
DURHAM
TYNE AND WEAR
128
119
110
NEWCASTLE UPON TYNE
GATESHEAD
NORTH SHIELDS
SOUTH SHIELDS
TYNEMOUTH
WHITLEY BAY
SUNDE
WASHINGTON
CHESTER-LE-STREET
STANLEY
CONSETT
DURHAM
HOUGHTON LE SPRING
DARLINGTON
STOCKTON-ON-TEES
MID
Fenwick
Heugh
Dalton
Ponteland
Darras Hall
Ouston
High Callerton
Black Callerton
Callerton Lane End
Harlow Hill
Rudchester
Heddon-on-the-Wall
Throckley
Newburn
Lemington
Ovington
Ovingham
Wylam
Horsley
Stephenson's Birthplace
Ryton
Stella
Crawcrook
Prudhoe
Mickley Square
Stocksfield
Blaydon
Winlaton
Swalwell
Metrocentre
Dunston
Whickham
Greenside
Barlow
Coalburns
Winlaton Mill
High Spen
Rowlands Gill
Leadgate
Hedley on the Hill
Highfield
Chopwell
Lintzford
Hamsterley
Newlands
Ebchester
Medomsley
Dipton
Shotleyfield
Shotley Bridge
Leadgate
Iveston
Delves
Allensford
Castleside
Rowley
Knitsley
Greencroft
Lanchester
Butsfield
Cornsay
Cornsay Colliery
Satley
Quebec
Waterhouses
Esh Winning
Esh
Langley Park
East Hedleyhope
Tow Law
Sunniside
Thornley
Billy Row
Crook
Fir Tree
Howden-le-Wear
Willington
Oakenshaw
Brancepeth
Brandon
Langley Moor
Ushaw Moor
Bearpark
Dinnington
Prestwick
Seaton Burn
Wideopen
Hazlerigg
Newcastle International
Fawdon
Gosforth
Kenton
Blakelaw
Wallbottle
Jesmond
Heaton
Longbenton
Forest Hall
Killingworth
Camperdown
Dudley
Seghill
Burradon
Backworth
Earsdon
Shiremoor
New York
Benton Square
Marden
Preston
Cullercoats
Whitley Bay
Seaton Sluice
Spanish City
Wallsend
Willington
Walker
Byker
Jarrow
Hebburn
Monkton
Felling
Pelaw
Harton
Marsden
Whitburn
Cleadon
Boldon
East Boldon
West Boldon
Roker
Fulwell
Monkwearmouth
Southwick
Castletown
South Hylton
Hendon
New Silksworth
Silksworth
Ryhope
Herrington
Penshaw
Fatfield
Shiney Row
Bournmoor
Fence Houses
Colliery Row
West Rainton
East Rainton
Easington Lane
Hetton-le-Hole
Murton
South Hetton
Haswell
Seaton
Dalton-le-Dale
Cold Hesledon
Hawthorn
Easington
Team Valley
Sunniside
Marley Hill
Lamesley
Springwell
Wrekenton
Kibblesworth
Birtley
Burnopfield
Hobson
Tanfield
Tantobie
Beamish Open Air Museum
Ouston
Pelton
Beamish
Grange Villa
Newfield
Annfield Plain
South Moor
Craghead
Waldridge
Maiden Law
Burnhope
Holmside
Edmondsley
Kimblesworth
Sacriston
Witton Gilbert
Pity Me
Plawsworth
Great Lumley
Framwellgate Moor
Pittington
Littletown
Carrville
Sherburn
Shadforth
Ludworth
Shincliffe
Thornley
Shotton Colliery
Wheatley Hill
Wingate
Cassop
Bowburn
Quarrington Hill
Kelloe
Coxhoe
Trimdon Colliery
Trimdon Grange
Trimdon
Station Town
South Wingate
Hett
Croxdale
Sunderland Bridge
Tudhoe
Spennymoor
Byers Green
Newfield
Middlestone Moor
Cornforth
Dean Bank
Ferryhill
Bishop Middleham
Fishburn
Sedgefield
Hunwick
High Grange
Westerton
Kirk Merrington
Witton Park
Witton-le-Wear
Hamsterley
Bedburn
Bishop Auckland
Coundon
Coundon Grange
Chilton
Rushyford
Bradbury
Mordon
High Etherley
Low Etherley
Toft Hill
Morley
Butterknowle
Copley
Cockfield
Evenwood
West Auckland
St Helen Auckland
Shildon
Middridge
Woodham
Newton Aycliffe
Aycliffe
Bildershaw
Bolam
Redworth
Heighington
Houghton Bank
Houghton-le-Side
Killerby
Burnt Houses
Raby
Wackerfield
Hilton
Ingleton
Staindrop
Langton
Headlam
Summerhouse
Denton
Walworth
Archdeacon Newton
High Coniscliffe
Piercebridge
Mowden
Cleatham
Little Newsham
Winston
Gainford
Westwick
Whorlton
Bowes Museum
Wynyard
Thorpe Larches
Foxton
Stillington
Whitton
Carlton
Thorpe Thewles
Redmarshall
Bishopton
Great Stainton
Brafferton
Coatham Mundeville
Little Stainton
Barmpton
Sadberge
Great Burdon
Haughton Le Skerne
Hartburn
Elton
Longnewton
Elstob
Billingham
A1
A1(M)
A19
A68
A69
A167
A688
A689
A690
A691
A692
A693
A694
A695
A696
A6076
A194(M)
A184
A185
A186
A187
A188
A189
A191
A192
A193
A1018
A1058
A1231
A1290
A1300
A177
A181
A182
A183
A195
A1052
A66
A67
A1150
A6072
A1027

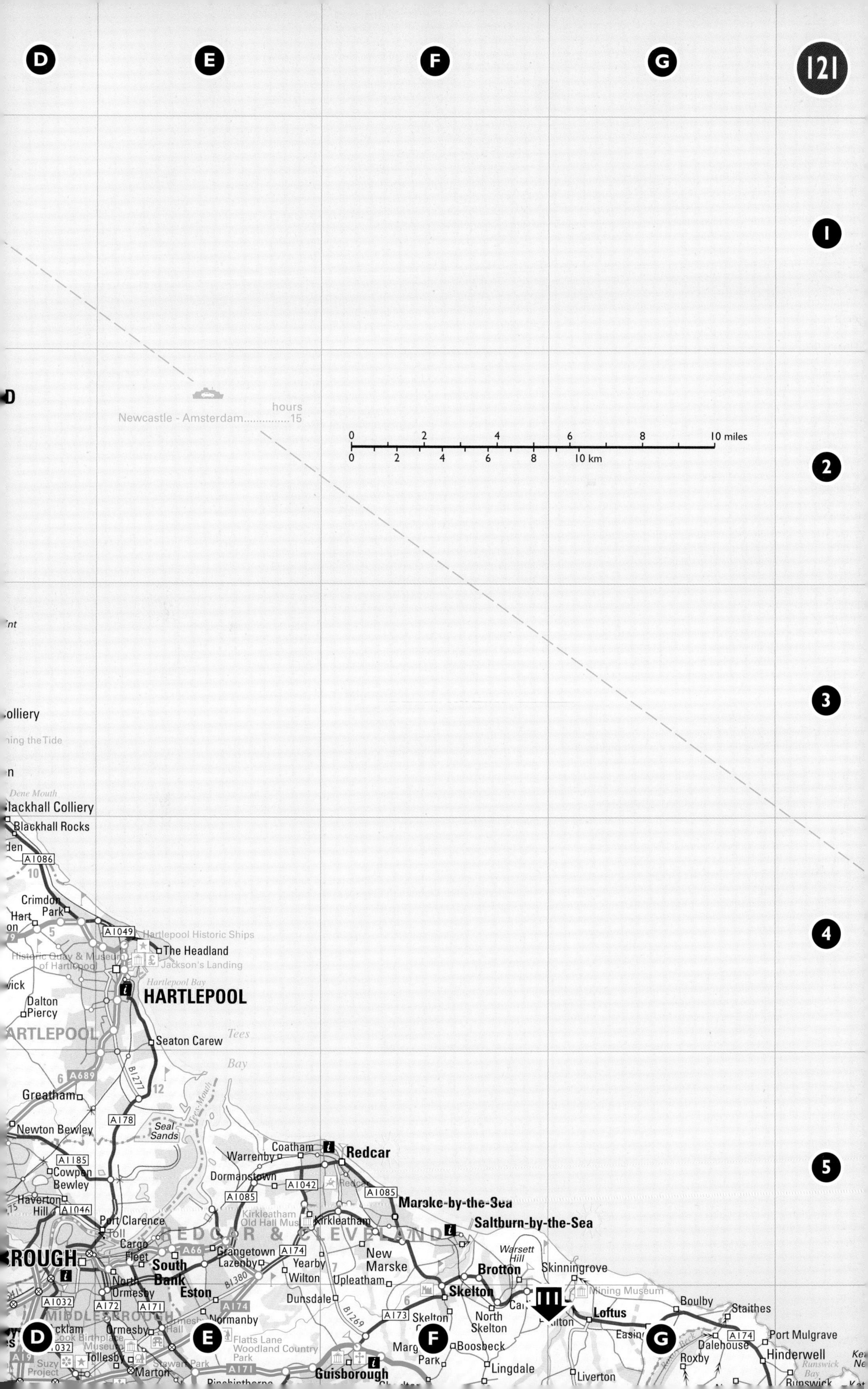
D
E
F
G
1
2
3
4
5
Newcastle - Amsterdam..............15
hours
0 2 4 6 8 10 miles
0 2 4 6 8 10 km
olliery
ning the Tide
Dene Mouth
lackhall Colliery
Blackhall Rocks
den
A1086
Crimdon Park
Hart
A1049
Hartlepool Historic Ships
The Headland
Historic Quay & Museum of Hartlepool
Jackson's Landing
Hartlepool Bay
HARTLEPOOL
Dalton Piercy
ARTLEPOOL
Seaton Carew
Tees Bay
A689
B1277
Greatham
A178
Seal Sands
Newton Bewley
Tees Mouth
Coatham
Redcar
Warrenby
Dormanstown
A1042
A1185
Cowpen Bewley
A1085
Haverton Hill
A1046
Kirkleatham Old Hall Museum
Kirkleatham
Marske-by-the-Sea
Saltburn-by-the-Sea
Port Clarence
REDCAR & CLEVELAND
Cargo Fleet
A66
Grangetown
A174
Yearby
New Marske
Warsett Hill
Skinningrove
ROUGH
South Bank
Lazenby
Wilton
Upleatham
Brotton
North Ormesby
Eston
B1380
Mining Museum
Dunsdale
Skelton
A1032
A172
A171
MIDDLESBROUGH
A174
Normanby
A173
Skelton
North Skelton
Loftus
Boulby
Staithes
Ormesby
B1269
Easington
A174
Port Mulgrave
Cook Birthplace Museum
Flatts Lane Woodland Country Park
Margrove Park
Boosbeck
Dalehouse
Hinderwell
Tollesby
Stewart Park
Roxby
Runswick Bay
Suzy Project
Marton
A171
Guisborough
Lingdale
Liverton
Runswick

A
B
C
D
131
Ailsa Craig
0 2 4 6 8 10 miles
0 2 4 6 8 10 km
1
2
3
4
5
Turnberry
A77
Dipple
Low
Craighead
Chapeldonan
Grangeston
Girvan
Saugh Hill
Glendoune
Black Neuk
Glendrissaig
Ardwell
Pinminnoch
Kennedy's Pass
Grey Hill
297
A77
A714
13
Pinmore
Lendalfoot
Motte
Water of Lendal
Aldons
Carleton Fishery
Daljarrock
Poundland
Pinwherry
Bennane Head
Colmonell
B734
Dalreoch
Glenduisk
Ballantrae Bay
Stinchair
Craigneil
Knockdolian
B734
Ballochmor
B7044
Mains of Tig
Water of Tig
Ballantrae
Auchairne
Balkissock
Barrhill
Glenapp Castle
Smyrton
Shiel Hill
Downan Point
Kilantringan Loch
Craigie Fell
Beneraird
439
Cross Water
Carlock Hill
Milljoan Hill
Chirmorrie
Altimeg Hill
hours
Larne....................1-2 1/4
Belfast...............1 1/2-3 3/4
Finnarts Point
Glen App
Markdhu
Milleur Point
A77
Miltonise
Corsewall Point
Barnhills
Dalnigap
Glenwhilly
North Cairn
DUMFRI
17
Corsewall
Cairnryan
South Cairn
B738
Cairn Point
Dounan Bay
Kirkcolm
Main Water of Luce
Cross Water of Luce
Airies
Ervie
Loch Connell
Artfield Fell
A718
Portobello
B798
Sole Burn
St Mary's Croft
LOCH RYAN
Beoch Burn
Braid Fell
B738
7
Knocknain
Leswalt
Soleburn Bridge
New Luce
Tarf Br
THE RINNS OF GALLOWAY
B7043
Innermessan
Auchmantle
Lochnaw
Lochinch Castle
Galdenoch
B738
A751
Black Loch
Castle Kennedy
Craig Fell
B737
Stranraer
White Loch
Carsc
Castle Kennedy
Broadsea Bay
Loch Magillie
Dunragit Moor
Whitecairn
Piltanton Burn
A77
Soulseat Loch
Portslogan
Abbey
A75
Dunragit
10
Whiteleys
Whitecrook
Glenluce
Lochans
Genoch
Black Head
Cairn Pat
8
Kildrochet House
B7077
Dunskey Burn
A747
Dinvin
Genoch Square
B7084
Castle of Park
A77
Colfin
Portpatrick
A716
Sands of Luce
Dunskey
Awhirk
B7084
10
Crow's Nest
Stoneykirk
Port of Spittal Bay
B7042
Auchenmalg Bay
Balgreggan
Sandhead
Cairngarroch Bay
Kirkmadrine Stone
114
Money Head
Clachanmore
Ardwell House
Ardwell
LUCE BA

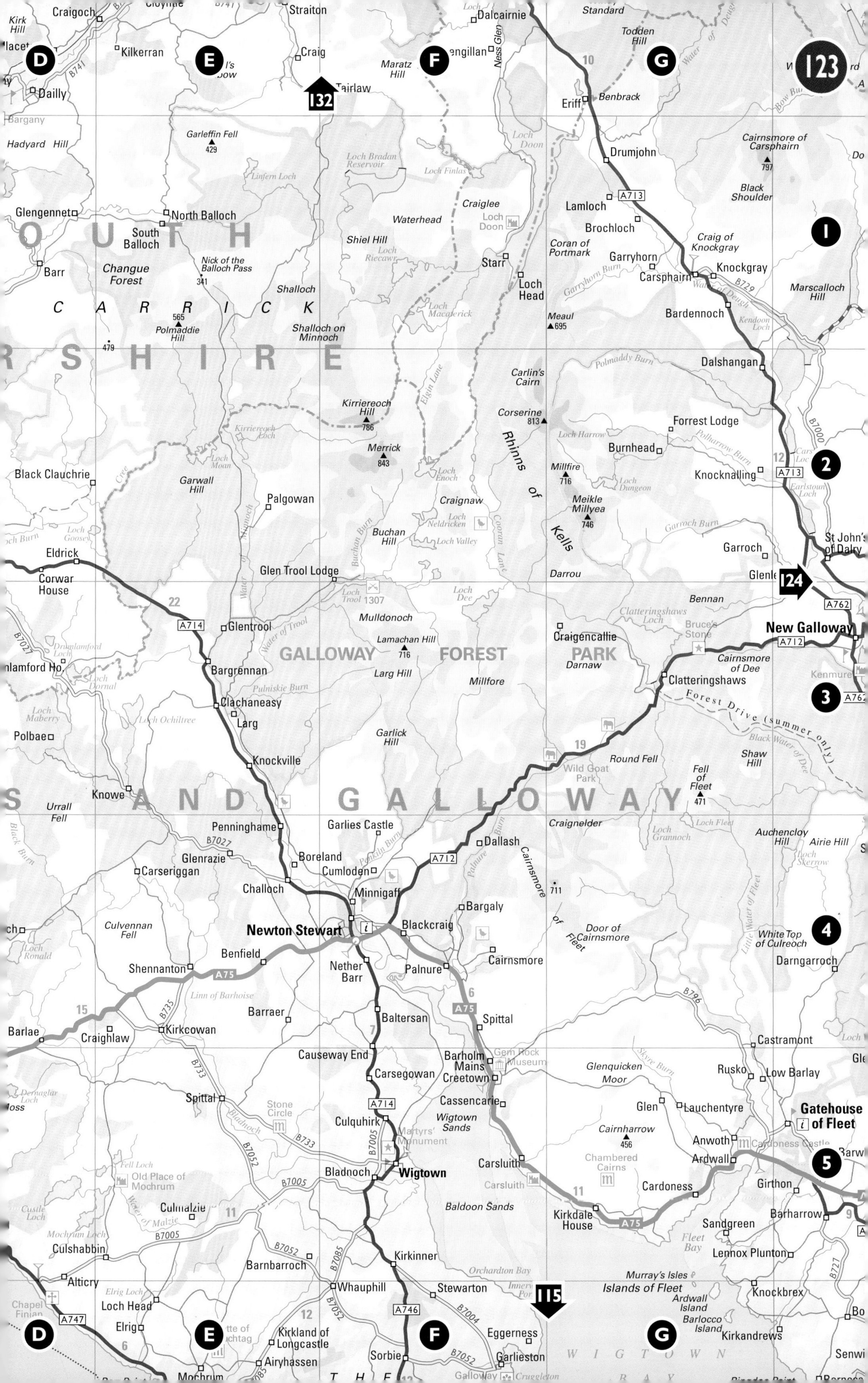

Kirk Hill
Craigoch
Straiton
Dalcairnie
Standard
Todden Hill
Kilkerran
Craig
Maratz Hill
Dailly
Tairlaw
132
Eriff
Benbrack
Bargany
Hadyard Hill
Garleffin Fell
429
Loch Doon
Drumjohn
Cairnsmore of Carsphairn
797
Loch Bradan Reservoir
Linfern Loch
Loch Finlas
A713
Black Shoulder
Glengennet
North Balloch
South Balloch
SOUTH
Craiglee
Loch Doon
Lamloch
Waterhead
Brochloch
Shiel Hill
Loch Riecawr
Coran of Portmark
Craig of Knockgray
Barr
Change Forest
Nick of the Balloch Pass
341
Starr
Garryhorn
Carsphairn
Knockgray
Loch Head
Garryhorn Burn
B729
Marscalloch Hill
Shalloch
Water of Deugh
CARRICK
Loch Macaterick
Bardennoch
565
Polmaddie Hill
Shalloch on Minnoch
Meaul
695
Kendoon Loch
479
SHIRE
Dalshangan
Polmaddy Burn
Carlin's Cairn
Elgin Lane
Kirriereoch Hill
786
Corserine
813
Forrest Lodge
Kirriereoch Loch
B7000
Loch Harrow
Merrick
843
Rhinns of Kells
Burnhead
Polharrow Burn
Loch Moan
Black Clauchrie
Garwall Hill
Loch Enoch
Millfire
716
Knocknalling
A713
Earlstoun Loch
Craignaw
Loch Dungeon
Palgowan
Meikle Millyea
746
Loch Neldricken
Garroch Burn
Loch Goosey
Buchan Hill
Buchan Burn
Loch Valley
Cooran Lane
St John's of Dalry
Eldrick
Garroch
Glen Trool Lodge
Darrou
Glenlee
124
Corwar House
Loch Trool
1307
Loch Dee
Bennan
A762
22
Mulldonoch
Clatteringshaws Loch
A714
Glentrool
Water of Trool
Craigencallie
Bruce's Stone
New Galloway
Drumlamford Loch
Lamachan Hill
716
A712
Drumlamford Ho.
GALLOWAY FOREST PARK
Cairnsmore of Dee
Darnaw
Loch Dornal
Bargrennan
Larg Hill
Millfore
Clatteringshaws
Kenmure
Pulniskie Burn
Loch Maberry
Clachaneasy
Forest Drive (summer only)
A762
Larg
Loch Ochiltree
Black Water of Dee
Polbae
Garlick Hill
Shaw Hill
19
Knockville
Round Fell
Wild Goat Park
Fell of Fleet
471
Knowe
AND GALLOWAY
Urrall Fell
Black Burn
Craignelder
Penninghame
Garlies Castle
Loch Grannoch
Loch Fleet
Auchencloy Hill
Airie Hill
B7027
Dallash
Glenrazie
Boreland
A712
Palnure Burn
Loch Skerrow
Carseriggan
Cumloden
Penkiln Burn
Cairnsmore of Fleet
711
Challoch
Minnigaff
Bargaly
Culvennan Fell
Newton Stewart
Blackcraig
Door of Cairnsmore
White Top of Culreoch
Little Water of Fleet
Loch Ronald
Benfield
Nether Barr
Cairnsmore
Darngarroch
Shennanton
A75
Palnure
6
A75
B796
Linn of Barhoise
15
B735
Barraer
Spittal
Baltersan
Barlae
Craighlaw
Kirkcowan
7
Castramont
B733
Causeway End
Barholm Mains
Gem Rock Museum
Skyre Burn
Glenquicken Moor
Rusko
Low Barlay
Dernaglar Loch
Carsegowan
Creetown
Spittal
Stone Circle
Cassencarie
Glen
Lauchentyre
Gatehouse of Fleet
A714
Wigtown Sands
Cairnharrow
456
B733
Culquhirk
Martyrs' Monument
Anwoth
Cardoness Castle
B7052
B7005
Chambered Cairns
Ardwall
Fell Loch
Bladnoch
Wigtown
Carsluith
5
Old Place of Mochrum
Carsluith
Girthon
B7005
Cardoness
Water of Malzie
Culmalzie
11
11
Castle Loch
Baldoon Sands
Kirkdale House
A75
Barharrow
Mochrum Loch
B7052
Sandgreen
B7005
B7085
Fleet Bay
Culshabbin
Lennox Plunton
Kirkinner
Barnbarroch
Orchardton Bay
Murray's Isles
B727
Alticry
Whauphill
Stewarton
Islands of Fleet
Knockbrex
Chapel Finian
Elrig Loch
115
Ardwall Island
Loch Head
12
A747
B7052
A746
B7004
Barlocco Island
D
E
F
G
Elrig
Kirkland of Longcastle
Eggerness
Kirkandrews
Airyhassen
6
Sorbie
Garlieston
WIGTOWN BAY
Mochrum
Galloway
Cruggleton
I
2
3
4
5

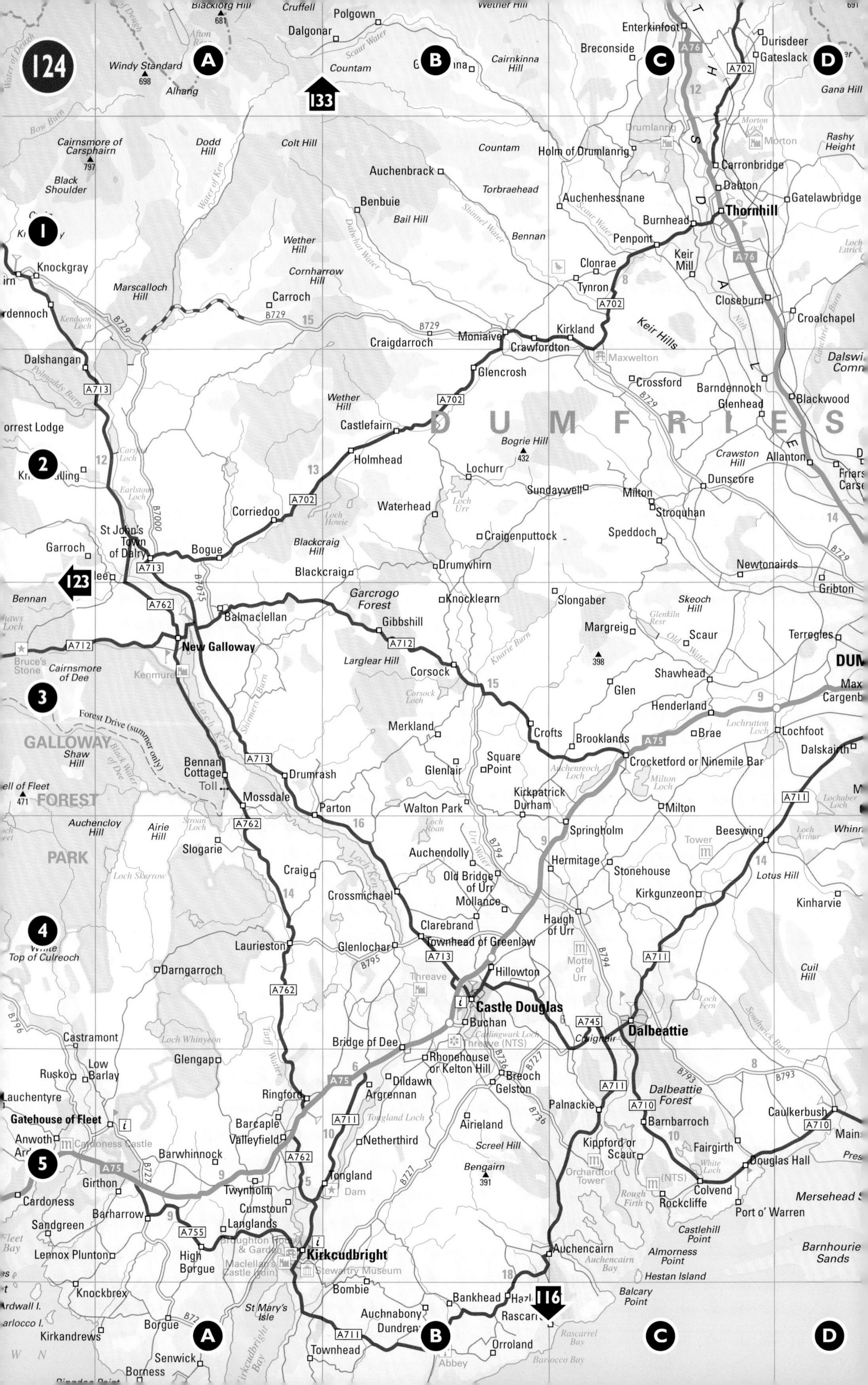
124
133
123
116
A
B
C
D
1
2
3
4
5
Blackiorg Hill
681
Cruffell
Polgown
Wether Hill
Dalgonar
Enterkinfoot
Durisdeer
Gateslack
Windy Standard
698
Alhang
Afton
Scaur Water
Countam
Cairnkinna Hill
Breconside
A76
A702
Gana Hill
Bow Burn
Cairnsmore of Carsphairn
797
Dodd Hill
Colt Hill
Countam
Holm of Drumlanrig
Drumlanrig
Morton Loch
Morton
Rashy Height
Black Shoulder
Water of Ken
Auchenbrack
Torbraehead
Carronbridge
Dabton
Gatelawbridge
Benbuie
Bail Hill
Auchenhessnane
Burnhead
Thornhill
Wether Hill
Dalwhat Water
Shinnel Water
Bennan
Penpont
Keir Mill
Knockgray
Cornharrow Hill
Clonrae
Tynron
Marscalloch Hill
Carroch
Closeburn
Kendoon Loch
B729
Craigdarroch
Moniaive
Kirkland
Crawfordton
Keir Hills
Croalchapel
Dalshangan
A713
Polmaddy Burn
Glencrosh
Maxwelton
Crossford
Barndennoch
Glenhead
Blackwood
Wether Hill
A702
Castlefairn
DUMFRIES
Bogrie Hill
432
Crawston Hill
Allanton
Friars Carse
Holmhead
Lochurr
Loch Urr
Dunscore
Sundaywell
Milton
Stroquhan
Carsfad Loch
Earlstoun Loch
B7000
Corriedoo
Waterhead
Loch Howie
Craigenputtock
Speddoch
St John's Town of Dalry
Bogue
Blackcraig Hill
Drumwhirn
Newtonairds
Garroch
Blackcraig
Gribton
Bennan
B7075
A762
Garcrogo Forest
Knocklearn
Slongaber
Skeoch Hill
Balmaclellan
Gibbshill
Glenkiln Resr
Margreig
Scaur
Old Water
Terregles
A712
New Galloway
Larglear Hill
Corsock
Knarie Burn
398
Shawhead
Bruce's Stone
Cairnsmore of Dee
Kenmure
Corsock Loch
Glen
Cargenbridge
Forest Drive (summer only)
Shirmers Burn
Loch Ken
Henderland
Lochrutton Loch
Lochfoot
GALLOWAY
Shaw Hill
Black Water of Dee
Merkland
Crofts
Brooklands
A75
Brae
Dalskairth
Bennan Cottage
Toll
A713
Drumrash
Glenlair
Square Point
Auchenreoch Loch
Crocketford or Ninemile Bar
Milton Loch
471
FOREST
Mossdale
Parton
Walton Park
Kirkpatrick Durham
Milton
A711
Lochaber Loch
Auchencloy Hill
Airie Hill
Stroan Loch
A762
Loch Roan
Springholm
Beeswing
Loch Arthur
Slogarie
Urr Water
B794
Tower
PARK
Loch Skerrow
Auchendolly
Hermitage
Stonehouse
Lotus Hill
Craig
Old Bridge of Urr
Kirkgunzeon
Crossmichael
Mollance
Kinharvie
Top of Culreoch
Clarebrand
Haugh of Urr
Laurieston
Glenlochar
Townhead of Greenlaw
Motte of Urr
A711
Darngarroch
B795
A713
Hillowton
Cuil Hill
Threave
A762
Castle Douglas
Loch Fern
B796
Buchan
A745
Dalbeattie
Castramont
Loch Whinyeon
Bridge of Dee
Carlingwark Loch
Threave (NTS)
Craignair
Southwick Burn
Low Barlay
Glengap
Rhonehouse or Kelton Hill
B736
B727
Rusko
Tarff Water
Breoch
B793
B793
Dildawn
Gelston
A711
Dalbeattie Forest
Lauchentyre
Ringford
Argrennan
Palnackie
A710
Caulkerbush
Gatehouse of Fleet
Barcaple
A711
Tongland Loch
Airieland
Barnbarroch
A710
Anwoth
Cardoness Castle
Valleyfield
Netherthird
Kippford or Scaur
Fairgirth
Barwhinnock
A762
Screel Hill
Douglas Hall
A75
B727
Tongland
Bengairn
391
Orchardton Tower
(NTS)
White Loch
Girthon
Twynholm
Dam
Colvend
Cardoness
Cumstoun
Rough Firth
Rockcliffe
Port o' Warren
Mersehead
Barharrow
Langlands
Castlehill Point
Sandgreen
A755
Broughton House & Garden
Fleet Bay
Lennox Plunton
High Borgue
Kirkcudbright
Auchencairn
Almorness Point
Barnhourie Sands
Maclellan's Castle (HS)
Stewartry Museum
Auchencairn Bay
Hestan Island
Knockbrex
Bombie
Bankhead
Balcary Point
St Mary's Isle
Auchnabony
Rascarrel
Borgue
Dundrennan
Rascarrel Bay
Kirkandrews
A711
Townhead
Orroland
Kirkcudbright Bay
Senwick
Abbey
Barlocco Bay
Borness

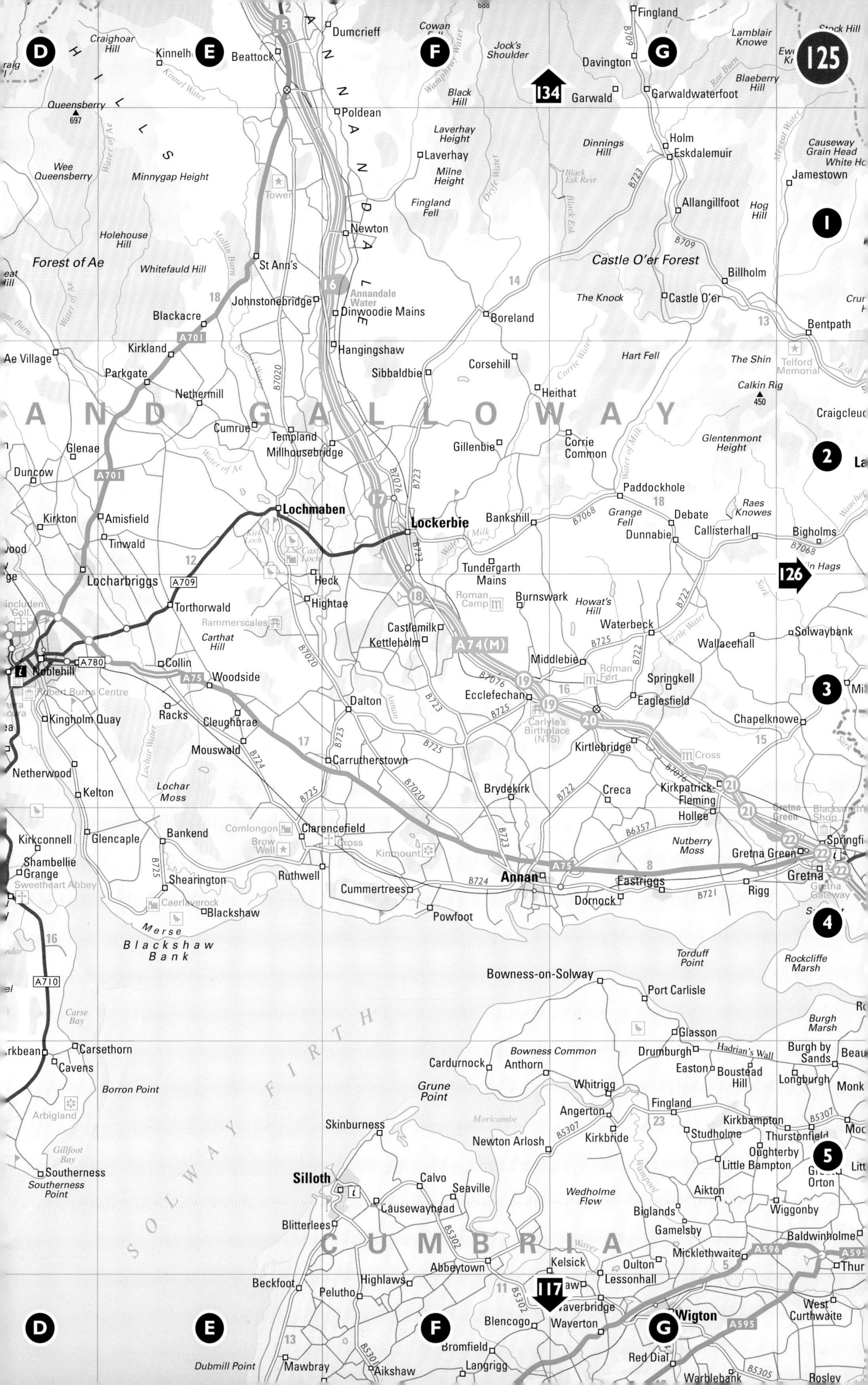
125
134
126
117
D
E
F
G
I
2
3
4
5
Craighoar Hill
Kinnelhead
Beattock
Dumcrieff
Cowan Fell
Jock's Shoulder
Fingland
Davington
Lamblair Knowe
Stock Hill
Garwald
Garwaldwaterfoot
Blaeberry Hill
Queensberry
697
Poldean
Black Hill
Laverhay Height
Laverhay
Milne Height
Fingland Fell
Dinnings Hill
Holm
Eskdalemuir
Black Esk Resr
Causeway Grain Head
White Hope
Jamestown
Wee Queensberry
Minnygap Height
Tower
Newton
Allangillfoot
Hog Hill
Holehouse Hill
Forest of Ae
Whitefauld Hill
St Ann's
Castle O'er Forest
Billholm
Johnstonebridge
Annandale Water
Dinwoodie Mains
The Knock
Castle O'er
Blackacre
Boreland
Bentpath
Ae Village
Kirkland
Hangingshaw
Parkgate
Sibbaldbie
Corsehill
Hart Fell
The Shin
Telford Memorial
Calkin Rig
450
Heithat
Nethermill
Craigcleuch
Cumrue
Templand
Millhousebridge
Gillenbie
Corrie Common
Glentenmont Height
Glenae
Duncow
Paddockhole
Raes Knowes
Kirkton
Amisfield
Lochmaben
Lockerbie
Bankshill
Grange Fell
Debate
Dunnabie
Callisterhall
Bigholms
Tinwald
Tundergarth Mains
Locharbriggs
Heck
Hightae
Torthorwald
Roman Camp
Burnswark
Howat's Hill
Waterbeck
Solwaybank
Rammerscales
Castlemilk
Kettleholm
Wallacehall
Carthat Hill
Middlebie
Noblehill
Collin
Woodside
Robert Burns Centre
Roman Fort
Springkell
Ecclefechan
Eaglesfield
Kingholm Quay
Racks
Cleughbrae
Dalton
Carlyle's Birthplace (NTS)
Chapelknowe
Mouswald
Carrutherstown
Kirtlebridge
Cross
Netherwood
Lochar Moss
Brydekirk
Creca
Kirkpatrick-Fleming
Kelton
Hollee
Gretna Green
Kirkconnell
Glencaple
Bankend
Comlongon
Clarencefield
Brow Well
Cross
Kinmount
Nutberry Moss
Springfield
Shambellie Grange
Sweetheart Abbey
Shearington
Ruthwell
Annan
Eastriggs
Gretna
Rigg
Gretna Gateway
Cummertrees
Dornock
Caerlaverock
Blackshaw
Powfoot
Merse
Blackshaw Bank
Torduff Point
Rockcliffe Marsh
Bowness-on-Solway
Port Carlisle
Carse Bay
Glasson
Burgh Marsh
Carsethorn
Cavens
Cardurnock
Bowness Common
Anthorn
Drumburgh
Hadrian's Wall
Burgh by Sands
Easton
Boustead Hill
Longburgh
Borron Point
Whitrigg
Grune Point
Arbigland
Angerton
Fingland
Kirkbampton
Thurstonfield
Skinburness
Moricambe
Newton Arlosh
Kirkbride
Studholme
Oughterby
Gillfoot Bay
Little Bampton
Great Orton
Southerness
Southerness Point
Silloth
Calvo
Seaville
Wedholme Flow
Aikton
Causewayhead
Biglands
Wiggonby
Blitterlees
Gamelsby
Baldwinholme
SOLWAY FIRTH
CUMBRIA
DUMFRIES AND GALLOWAY
ANNANDALE
HILLS
Micklethwaite
Abbeytown
Kelsick
Oulton
Thursby
Beckfoot
Highlaws
Lessonhall
Pelutho
Waverbridge
West Curthwaite
Wigton
Blencogo
Waverton
Bromfield
Red Dial
Dubmill Point
Mawbray
Aikshaw
Langrigg
Warblebank
Rosley
A701
A709
A780
A75
A74(M)
A710
A596
A595
B7020
B7076
B723
B709
B7068
B722
B725
B724
B6357
B721
B5307
B5302
B5301
B5305

A
B
C
D
A
B
C
D
1
2
3
4
5
135
125
118
Ettrick
James Hogg Monument
Buccleuch
Law Kneis
Coutlair Knowe
Borthwickbrae
Burnfoot
Bridgend
Deanburnhaugh
Drumlanrig's Tower
Kirkton
Bodesbeck Law
Black Knowe
Glenkerry
Nether Dalgliesh
Craik Forest
Redcleuch Edge
Newmill
Hott Hill
Harwood on Teviot
High Seat
Crib Law
Craik
The Pike
Cross Hill
Ettrick Pen
692
Black Knowe
Moodlaw Loch
Foulbog
Tima Water
Howpasley
Borthwick Water
Broadhaugh
Northhouse
Dryden Fell
Capel Fell
Wind Fell
Stell Hill
Pike Hill
S C O T T I
Berry
Slitrig Water
B6399
Glendearg
Langshawburn
Craik Cross Hill
Shankend
Teviothead
Castleweary
The Pike
Fingland
Davington
Stock Hill
Lamblair Knowe
Skelfhill Pen
Allan Water
Jock's Shoulder
Garwald
Garwaldwaterfoot
Blaeberry Hill
Rae Burn
Eweslees Knowe
Linhope
Cauldcleuch Head
608
Maiden Paps
Sandy Edge
Comb Hill
Millstone Edge
Greatmoor Hill
B O R D
Wisp Hill
Mosspaul Hotel
Tudhope Hill
Holm
Eskdalemuir
Dinnings Hill
Black Esk Reservoir
Causeway Grain Head
White Hope Edge
Faw Side
Hermitage
Jamestown
Geordie's Hill
Din Fell
Hermitage Water
Arnton Fell
Hermitage
Allangillfoot
Black Esk
B723
B709
Hog Hill
Meggat Water
Broad Head
Pike Fell
Newlands
Hartsgarth Fell
Castle O'er Forest
Castle O'er
Billholm
Longgrain Head
Roan Fell
567
North Birny Fell
Steele
Dryfe Water
The Knock
Crumpton Hill
Arkleton Hill
Watch Hill
Boreland
Kirkstile
Arkleton
Ewes Water
Dinlabyre
Corrie Water
D U M F R I E S
Bentpath
Castleton
Hart Fell
The Shin
Telford Memorial
Esk
Hog Fell
Black Edge
Corsehill
Heithat
Calkin Rig
450
B709
L I D D E S D A L E
Newcastleton
A N D
Corrie Common
Craigcleuch
A7
Newcastleton Forest
Tinnis Hill
Glentenmont Height
Langholm
Blinkbonny Height
Water of Milk
Tarras Water
Kershope Burn
G A L L O W A Y
Paddockhole
Wauchope Water
B6357
Bankshill
Debate
Raes Knowes
Earshaw Hill
B6318
Bruntshiel Hill
Kershopefoot
B7068
Grange Fell
Callisterhall
Bigholms
Dunnabie
B7068
Tundergarth Mains
Collin Hags
Auchenrivock
Caulside
K e r s h o p e
F o r e s t
Arthur Seat
Nook
Roman Camp
Burnswark
Howat's Hill
B722
Kirtle Water
Sark
Tower
Liddel Water
Waterbeck
Wallacehall
Solwaybank
B720
Rowanburn
B6357
Catlowdy
B6318
Blackpool Gate
Wakey Hill
B725
Middlebie
B722
Roman Fort
Evertown
Canonbie
Oakshaw Ford
B7076
Springkell
B6357
Milltown
Haggbeck
Roadhead
Ecclefechan
Eaglesfield
B7201
Moat
B725
Carlyle's Birthplace (NTS)
Chapelknowe
Easton
Lyneholme
Kirtlebridge
A74(M)
Cross
Sark
Netherby
Chapeltown
Stapleton
B7076
Lyne
Brydekirk
B722
Kirkpatrick-Fleming
Solway Moss 1542
Crofthead
Blacksmith's Shop
C U M B R
Creca
Hollee
Longtown
Boltonfellend
Kirkcambeck
B6357
Nutberry Moss
Gretna Green
Springfield
A6071
B723
Gretna Green
A6071
Hethersgill
Annan
A75
B72
Gretna
Hether Burn
B724
Eastriggs
Rigg
Gretna Gateway
Kirklinton
Dornock
Lyne
Smithfield
A74
Sarkfoot Point
Westlinton
Walton
Torduff Point
Rockcliffe Marsh
Todhills
Roman Road
Scalebyhill
Lanercost
Bowness-on-Solway
Scaleby
Newtown
Port Carlisle
Laversdale
A6071
Rockcliffe
Blackford
Irthington
Brampton
Burgh Marsh
Harker
Hadrian's Wall
Glasson
Bowness Common
Drumburgh
Hadrian's Wall
Burgh by Sands
Beaumont
Houghton
A689
Anthorn
Easton
Boustead Hill
Cargo
Kingstown
Low Crosby
Newby East
Eden
M6
Linstock
Whitrigg
Longburgh
Monkhill
Grinsdale
Kirkandrews-upon-Eden
Gateway City Project
Eden
A69
Moricambe
Angerton
Studholme
Kirkbampton
Stanwix
Warwick Bridge
Warwick
Little Corby
How
B5307
Kirkbride
Thurstonfield
Moorhouse
Border Regiment Mus
Newton Arlosh
CARLISLE

D
E
F
G
136
Hallrule
Faw Hill
Abbotrule
Mervinslaw
Camptown
Falla
Beefstand Hill
Bloodybush Edge
Cushat Law
Bonchester Hill
Woden Law
Philip Law
Windburn
Nettlehope Hill
Hobkirk
Cleuch Head
Wolfelee
Chesters
Southdean
A6088
A68
Leithope Forest
Bell Hill
Makendon
Wolfelee Hill
Huntford
Deerlee Knowe
Arks Edge
Grindstone Law
Chew Green
Woolbist Law
Shillmoor
Linbriggs
Alwinton
Hyndlee
Carter Bar
418
Redeswire Fray 1575
Leap Hill
Hungry Law
Ravens Knowe
Danger Zone
Crigdon Hill
Linshiels
I
Harbottle
Green Law
Catcleugh Shin
Windy Crag
Blackkip
Note o' the Gate
376
Wauchope Forest
Carter Fell
Catcleugh
Catcleugh Resr
Carlin Tooth
Knox Knowe
Byrness
NORTHUMBERLAND NATIONAL PARK
Fanna Hill
Singdean
Needs Law
Hartshorn Pike
Girdle Fell
Ellis Crag
Redesdale Forest
Toll
Corby Pike
Sills
North Yardhope
Kielderhead Moor
Peel Fell
Oh Me Edge
13
Rochester
Rushy Knowe
CHEVIOT HILLS
REDESDALE
Blackman's Law
Hindhope Law
Horsley
Davyshiel Common
Forest Drive
Kielder Burn
Wether Lair
Tarset Burn
Elishaw
Blakeman's Law
Otterburn Camp
2
Foulmire Heights
Emblehope Moor
Monkside
513
Brownrigg Head
Blakehope Fell
Otterburn 1388
Loch Knowe
Toll
Wainhope
Blackburn Common
Dargues
Otterburn
Troughend
B6341
Kielder
Earl's Seat
Padon Hill
Otterburn Mill
KIELDER FOREST PARK
Highfield
Highgreen Manor
Old Town
Black Knowe
Kielder Forest
Troughend Common
Rayleees
A696
128
NORTHUMBERLAND
A68
Hawkhope
White Hill
B6320
Caplestone Fell
Falstone
Greenhaugh
West Woodburn
East Woodburn
Kielder Water (Resr)
Stannersburn
Glendhu Hill
514
Kielder Water Experience
Rough Pike
Lanehead
Charlton
15
3
Gill Pike
Jock's Pike
Hesleyside
Bellingham
Ridsdale
The Rigg
Reeker Pike
Bower
Redesmouth
Christianbury Crag
Sighty Crag
518
Bolt's Law
White Lyne
Black Knowe
Chirdon Burn
Blacka Burn
The Flatt
Paddaburn Moor
Clintburn
Dere Street
Colt Crag Resr
North Tyne
Churnside Lodge
Wark
Hetherington
Wark
Birtley
White Preston
Round Top
Barron's Pike
Spy Rigg
Forest
Warks Burn
Whygate
Stonehaugh
Chipchase Castle
Park End
4
Bewcastle
Lampert
Shepherdshield
Nunwick
Barrasford
A6079
Danger Zone
Butterburn
Simonburn
Spadeadam Forest
Black Fell
Deer Hill
Irthing
Haughton Common
Green Rigg
Spadeadam
Wiley Sike
B6318
Greenlee Lough
Brocolitia
Chollerford
Walwick
Chesters (Cilurnvm)
Thirwall Common
Whiteside
Housesteads (Vercovicivm)
Broomlee Lough
West Hall
Crag Lough
Stanegate
Newbrough
Wall
Gilsland Spa
Roman Army Museum
Roman Fort
Roman Camps
Once Brewed Visitor Centre
Fourstones
Warden
Birdoswald (Camboglanna)
Gilsland
Hadrian's Wall
Chesterholm (Vindolanda)
A69
Poltross Burn Milecastle
Greenhead
Bardon Mill
Haydon Bridge
B6319
Banks
Fort
Haltwhistle
Melkridge
12
Henshaw
South Tyne
Low Gate
Hexham
Low Row
9
Plenmeller
Willimontswick
A686
Denton Fell
Allen
B6305
Hexham
West Dipton Burn
Plenmeller Common
Featherstone Castle
Rowfoot
Fellhouse Fell
B6295
119
Tindale
A689
Lambley
Midgeholme
Dotland
Dalton
Forest Head
Tindale Tarn
Whitfield
A686
Catton
Tindale Fells
Stonehouse
18
15
Cold Fell
Ashholme Common
Allendale Town

Beefstand Hill
Bloodybush Edge
Cushat Law
Pike
Great Ryle
Bolton
A
B
C
D
Nettlehope Hill
High Knowes
Prendwick
Whittingham
136
Blindburn
Wether Cairn
Hazeltonrig Hill
Alnham
Little Ryle
Thrunton
Callaly Castle
Bell Hill
Yetlington
Callaly
Thrunton Wood
Edlingham
Makendon
Scrainwood
Elilaw
Woolbist Law
Chew Green
Biddlestone
Lorbottle Hall
Netherton
A697
Ravens Knowe
Shillmoor
Linbriggs
Long Crag
Bigges' Pillar
Lorbottle
Alwinton
Danger Zone
Crigdon Hill
Linshiels
Burradon
High Trewhitt
Newton-on-
Cartington
Blackkip
Harbottle
Shirlaw Pike
Forest
Sharperton
Warton
Snitter
Lady's Well (NT)
NORTHUMBERLAND NATIONAL PARK
Cragside (NT)
Nelly's Moss Lakes
Corby Pike
Holystone Common
Holystone
Flotterton
Thropton
Rothbury
Caistron
North
Toll
Sills
Whitton
Great Tosson
Newtown
North Yardhope
Hepple
Longframlington
13
REDESDALE
Rede
Pauperhaugh
B6344
Rushy Knowe
Rochester
Simonside
Rothbury
Brinkburn
Hindhope Law
A68
Davyshiel Common
Horsley
Tosson Hill
Low Hesleyhurst
B6341
Otterburn Camp
Billsmoor Park
Forestburn Gate
Elishaw
Blakeman's Law
2
Brownrigg Head
Otterburn 1388
Dough Crag
Wingates
Coldrife
Blakehope Fell
14
Blackburn Common
Dargues
Otterburn
Harwood Forest
Troughend
Elsdon
Fontburn Resr
Padon Hill
Otterburn Mill
Fallowlees Burn
Highgreen Manor
Old Town
B6342
Troughend Common
Raylees
Ewesley Burn
127
A696
Rothley Lakes
Stanton
Netherwitton
Raylees Common
B6320
Ottercops Moss
Longwitton
Greenhaugh
Rothley
West Woodburn
East Woodburn Common
Hart Burn
Raechester
19
Scots' Gap
Hartburn
Lanehead
15
Ray Fell
Knowesgate
Cambo
3
Charlton
B6343
Middleton
Kirkwhelpington
Meldon
Hesleyside
Bellingham
Ridsdale
Wallington Grounds (NT)
Middleton Bank Top
Wansbeck
Bower
Redesmouth
Bolam Lake
Kirkharle
Sweethope Loughs
NORTHUMBERLAND
Capheaton
Blacka Burn
Great Bavington
Colt Crag Resr
Dere Street
Thockrington
Hetherington
North Tyne
B6342
Belsay
Little Swinburne
Belsay Hall & Gardens
Wark
Birtley
Kirkheaton
A696
Stonehaugh
Great Swinburne
Kearsley Fell
Black Heddon
Whygate
Hallington
B6309
Park End
Chipchase Castle
Gunnerton
Hallington Reservoir
Milbourne
4
Colwell
Ingoe
Blackheddon Burn
Nunwick
Barrasford
A6079
Ryal
Simonburn
Grindstonelaw
Fenwick
Haughton Common
Chollerton
A68
Heugh
Dalton
Stamfordham
Bingfield
Matfen
Hawkwell
Chollerford
Humshaugh
Great Whittington
Ouston
B6318
Brocolitia
Walwick
Low Brunton
Chesters (Cilurnvm)
9
Broomlee Lough
Little Whittington
Turret
Hadrian's Wall Vallum
Harlow Hill
Wall
B6318
15
Hadrian's Wall (Course of)
Newbrough
Stanegate
Stagshaw Bank
B6318 Vallum
Rudchester
Once Brewed Visitor Centre
Fourstones
A6079
Halton
Warden
B6528
Chesterholm (Vindolanda)
B6319
A69
Acomb
Sandhoe
Aydon
B6321
Stephenson's Birthplace
Bardon Mill
5
Horsley
Haydon Bridge
Tyne Green
Corstopitum
Newton
A69
Wylam
Low Gate
B6531
Corbridge
Ovington
Crawcrook
South Tyne
A686
Hexham
A695
Dilston
Ovingham
B6395
Prudhoe
A695
B6306
B6307
B6530
Riding Mill
Tyne
Allen
B6305
Sunnyside
Hexham
Mickley Square
Coalburns
Linnels
Stocksfield
West Dipton Burn
Newbiggin
Hexham Levels 1464
Broomhaugh
Painshawfield
Stanley Burn
Leadgate
B6295
Dipton Wood
120
A68
Hedley on the Hill
Dotland
Chopwell
A686
Dalton
Healey
Catton
Whitley Chapel
Slaley
Dere Street
Hamsterley
Kiln Pit Hill
Newlands
Allendale Town
Slaley

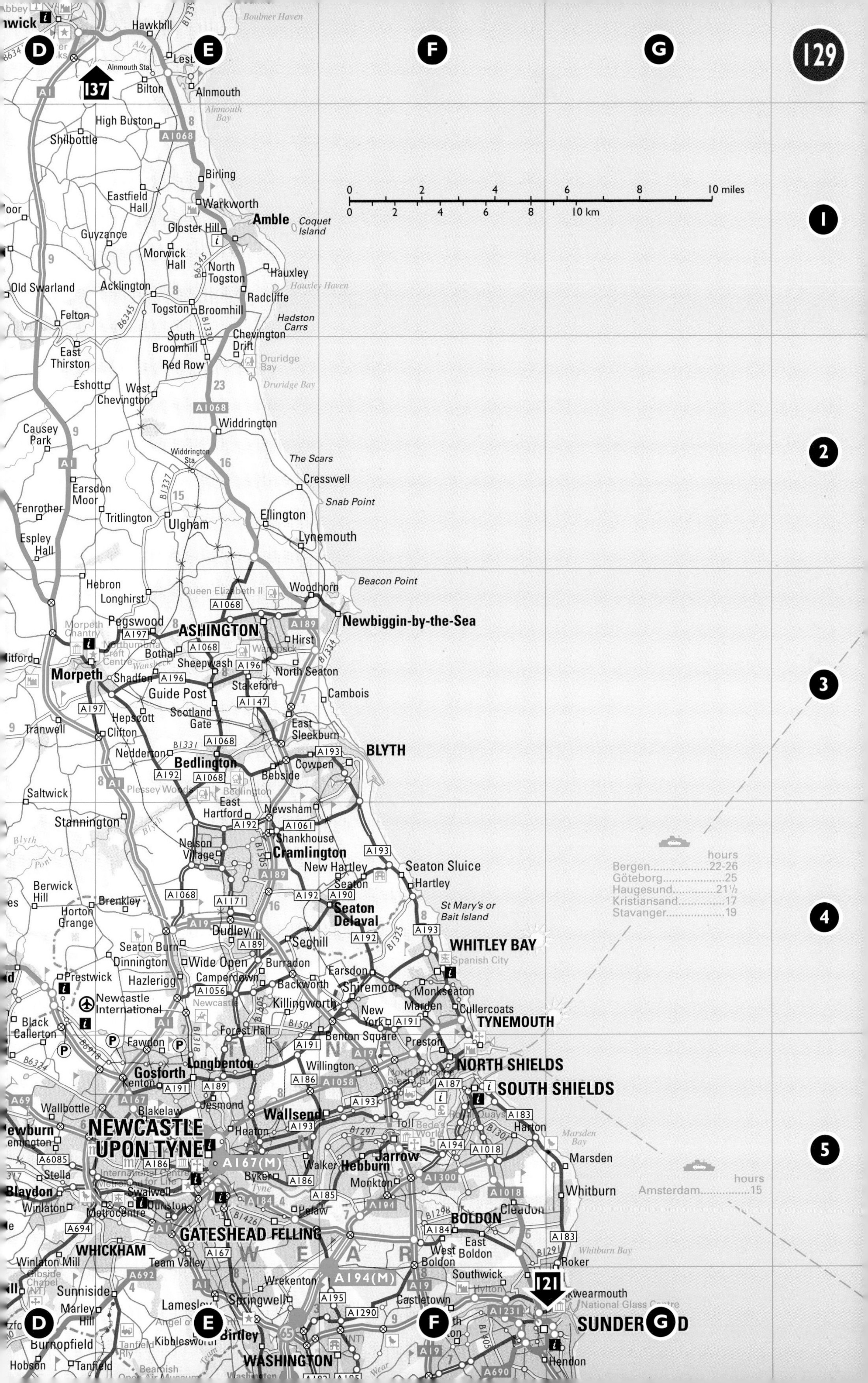
D
E
F
G
137
1
2
3
4
5
121
0 2 4 6 8 10 miles
0 2 4 6 8 10 km
Boulmer Haven
Hawkhill
Lesbury
Alnmouth Sta
Bilton
Alnmouth
Alnmouth Bay
High Buston
Shilbottle
A1068
Birling
Eastfield Hall
Warkworth
Amble
Coquet Island
Gloster Hill
Guyzance
Morwick Hall
North Togston
Hauxley
Hauxley Haven
Old Swarland
Acklington
Radcliffe
Togston
Broomhill
Hadston Carrs
Felton
South Broomhill
Chevington Drift
East Thirston
Red Row
Druridge Bay
Eshott
West Chevington
Druridge Bay
Widdrington
Causey Park
Widdrington Sta
The Scars
Cresswell
Earsdon Moor
Snab Point
Fenrother
Tritlington
Ulgham
Ellington
Espley Hall
Lynemouth
Hebron
Longhirst
Queen Elizabeth II
Woodhorn
Beacon Point
Pegswood
ASHINGTON
Newbiggin-by-the-Sea
Morpeth Chantry
Hirst
Bothal
Mitford
Morpeth
Sheepwash
North Seaton
Shadfen
Guide Post
Stakeford
Cambois
Hepscott
Scotland Gate
Tranwell
Clifton
East Sleekburn
Nedderton
Bedlington
Cowpen
BLYTH
Bebside
Saltwick
Plessey Woods
East Hartford
Stannington
Newsham
Nelson Village
Shankhouse
Cramlington
Seaton Sluice
New Hartley
Hartley
Berwick Hill
Seaton
Brenkley
Horton Grange
Seaton Delaval
St Mary's or Bait Island
Dudley
Seghill
WHITLEY BAY
Seaton Burn
Dinnington
Wide Open
Burradon
Spanish City
Earsdon
Prestwick
Hazlerigg
Camperdown
Backworth
Shiremoor
Monkseaton
Newcastle International
Killingworth
New York
Marden
Cullercoats
Black Callerton
TYNEMOUTH
Forest Hall
Benton Square
Preston
Fawdon
Longbenton
NORTH SHIELDS
Gosforth
Kenton
Willington
SOUTH SHIELDS
Wallbottle
Blakelaw
Jesmond
Wallsend
Royal Quays
Harton
Newburn
NEWCASTLE UPON TYNE
Heaton
Toll Bede's World
Marsden Bay
Jarrow
Marsden
Stella
A167(M)
Byker
Walker
Hebburn
Monkton
Whitburn
Blaydon
Swalwell
Winlaton
Metrocentre
Dunston
Pelaw
BOLDON
Cleadon
GATESHEAD
FELLING
East Boldon
WHICKHAM
West Boldon
Whitburn Bay
Winlaton Mill
Team Valley
Roker
Wrekenton
A194(M)
Southwick
Sunniside
Springwell
Castletown
Monkwearmouth
Lamesley
National Glass Centre
Marley Hill
SUNDERLAND
Burnopfield
Kibblesworth
Birtley
Hobson
Tanfield
Beamish
WASHINGTON
Hendon
hours
Bergen 22-26
Göteborg 25
Haugesund 21½
Kristiansand 17
Stavanger 19
hours
Amsterdam 15

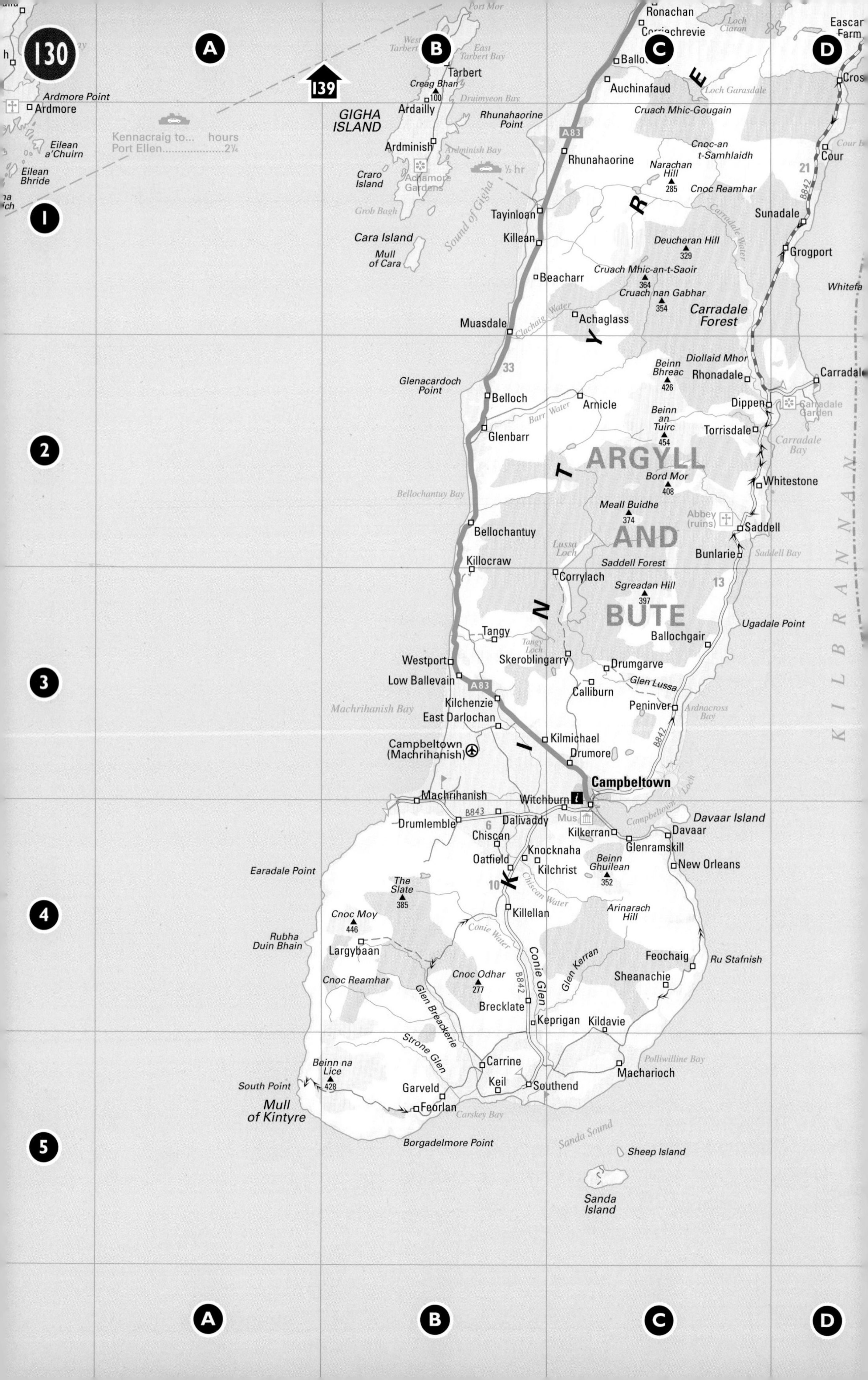
A
B
C
D
1
2
3
4
5
139
Ardmore Point
Ardmore
Eilean a'Chuirn
Eilean Bhride
Kennacraig to... hours
Port Ellen....................2¼
Port Mor
West Tarbert
East Tarbert Bay
Tarbert
Creag Bhan
100
Druimyeon Bay
Ardailly
GIGHA ISLAND
Ardminish
Ardminish Bay
Achamore Gardens
½ hr
Craro Island
Grob Bagh
Sound of Gigha
Cara Island
Mull of Cara
Ronachan
Loch Ciaran
Corriechrevie
Ballochroy
Auchinafaud
Loch Garasdale
Cruach Mhic-Gougain
Eascar Farm
Cross
Rhunahaorine Point
A83
Rhunahaorine
Cnoc-an t-Samhlaidh
Narachan Hill
285
Cnoc Reamhar
Cour
Cour Bay
21
B842
Sunadale
Tayinloan
Killean
Carradale Water
Deucheran Hill
329
Grogport
Whitefarland
Cruach Mhic-an-t-Saoir
364
Beacharr
Cruach nan Gabhar
354
Carradale Forest
Muasdale
Clachaig Water
Achaglass
KINTYRE
33
Diollaid Mhor
Glenacardoch Point
Beinn Bhreac
426
Rhonadale
Carradale
Belloch
Arnicle
Dippen
Carradale Garden
Barr Water
Beinn an Tuirc
454
Glenbarr
Torrisdale
Carradale Bay
ARGYLL AND BUTE
Bord Mor
408
Whitestone
Bellochantuy Bay
Meall Buidhe
374
Abbey (ruins)
Bellochantuy
Saddell
Lussa Loch
Bunlarie
Saddell Bay
Killocraw
Saddell Forest
Corrylach
13
Sgreadan Hill
397
KILBRANNAN
Tangy
Tangy Loch
Ugadale Point
Ballochgair
Skeroblingarry
Westport
Drumgarve
Low Ballevain
Glen Lussa
Calliburn
Kilchenzie
Machrihanish Bay
Peninver
Ardnacross Bay
East Darlochan
Kilmichael
Campbeltown (Machrihanish)
Drumore
Campbeltown
Campbeltown Loch
Machrihanish
Witchburn
Davaar Island
B843
Mus
Drumlemble
Dalivaddy
6
Kilkerran
Davaar
Chiscan
Glenramskill
Knocknaha
Oatfield
Kilchrist
New Orleans
Earadale Point
Beinn Ghuilean
352
10
The Slate
385
Chiscan Water
Killellan
Arinarach Hill
Cnoc Moy
446
Conie Water
Rubha Duin Bhain
Largybaan
Glen Kerran
Feochaig
Ru Stafnish
Conie Glen
Cnoc Odhar
277
Sheanachie
Cnoc Reamhar
Glen Breackerie
Brecklate
Keprigan
Kildavie
Strone Glen
Polliwilline Bay
Beinn na Lice
428
Carrine
Machariochi
South Point
Keil
Southend
Garveld
Mull of Kintyre
Feorlan
Carskey Bay
Sanda Sound
Borgadelmore Point
Sheep Island
Sanda Island

131
140
132
122
D
E
F
G
1
2
3
4
5
SOUND OF BUTE
½ hr
1½ hrs (Winter only)
1¾ hrs (Summer only)
1 hr
NORTH ARRAN
AYRSHIRE
FIRTH OF CLYDE
Newton
Loch Ranza
Lochranza
A841
Catacol Bay
Rubha Airigh Bheirg
Glen Catacol
Glen Chalmadale
North Glen Sannox
Craw
Lenimore
Thundergay
Beinn Bhreac 573
Beinn Tarsuinn
Beinn Bhreac 711
Caisteal Abhail 859
Cir Mhor 798
Glen Sannox
Cioch-na-h-Oighe
Mid Sannox
Sannox Bay
Corrie
Pirnmill
Mullach Buidhe 721
Loch Tanna
Goat Fell 874
Imachar
Beinn Bharrain
Beinn Tarsuinn 825
Glen Rosa
Balliekine
Beinn Nuis 792
Brodick (NTS)
Merkland Point
Glen Iorsa
Iorsa Water
Brodick Garden (NTS)
Brodick Castle (NTS)
Dougarie
Brodick Bay
Heritage Museum
Brodick
Glencloy
361
An Tunna
Auchagallon Stone Circle
Chambered Cairn
Strathwhillan
Glaister
Tarrnacraig
South Corrygills
Machrie
A'Chruach 512
Machrie Bay
Machrie Water
B880
Ard Bheinn 512
Clauchlands Point
Machrie Moor Stone Circles
Beinn Bhreac 503
Margnaheglish
Tormore
Ballymichael
Benlister Glen
Lamlash
Lamlash Bay
Holy Island
King's Cave
Cnoc a'Chapuill 417
Glenkiln
Hut Circles
Shiskine
Torbeg
Fort
Tighvein 458
Kingscross Point
Kingscross
Blackwaterfoot
Drumadoon Bay
Knockenkelly
Whiting Bay
Kilpatrick
Brown Head
Glen Scorrodale
Glen Ashdale
Kiscadale
Largymore
Corriecravie
Largybeg
Largybeg Point
Torr a' Chaisteal
Sliddery
Dippin
Dippin Head
Levencorroch
Lagg
Kilmory Water
Shannochie
Kildonan
Chambered Cairns
Bennan Head
Sound of Pladda
Pladda
Cock of Arran
St Blane's Church
B881
Dunagoil Bay
Torr Mor
Garrochty
Garroch Head
Little Cumbrae
Millport Bay
Fairlie Roads
Kaim Hill 387
Inner Brigurd Point
Hunterston
A78
Crosbie
Gull Point
Portencross
B7048
West Kilbride
Farland Head
Ardneil Bay
Seamill
Munnoch Reservoir
B781
Ardrossan
Horse Isle
Saltcoats
0 2 4 6 8 10 miles
0 2 4 6 8 10 km
Troon to... hours
Belfast...2½
Larne...4
Dunure
Culzean Bay
Culzean Castle & Country Park (NTS)
Maidenhead Bay
Morriston
Maidens
Turnberry
Turnberry Bay
A77
Dowhill
Dipple
Low Craighead
Chapeldonan
Grangeston
Ailsa Craig
Girvan
Saugh Hill
Glendoune
Black Neuk

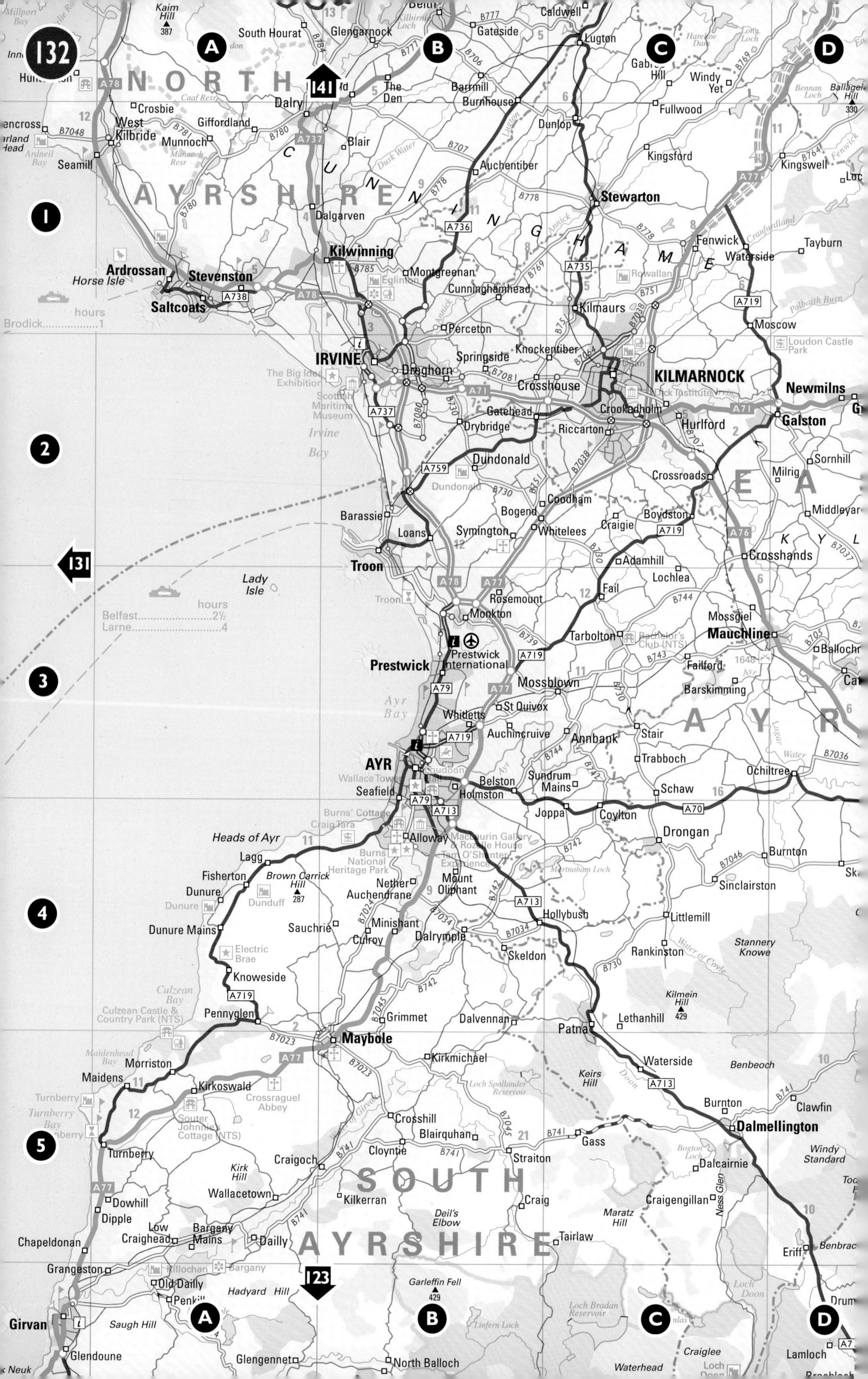

A
B
C
D
1
2
3
4
5
141
131
123
NORTH AYRSHIRE
CUNNINGHAME
EAST AYRSHIRE
KYLE
SOUTH AYRSHIRE
Kaim Hill 387
South Hourat
Glengarnock
Kilbirnie Loch
Beith
Gateside
Caldwell
Lugton
Gabroc Hill
Windy Yet
Long Loch
Harelaw Dam
Ballageich Hill 330
Bennan Loch
Hunterston
Crosbie
West Kilbride
Fairlie
Portencross
Farland Head
Ardneil Bay
Seamill
Giffordland
Munnoch
Munnoch Resr
Caaf Resr
Dalry
Blair
The Den
Barrmill
Burnhouse
Dunlop
Fullwood
Kingsford
Kingswell
Auchentiber
Dusk Water
Stewarton
Dalgarven
Kilwinning
Montgreenan
Eglinton
Cunninghamhead
Annick
Fenwick
Waterside
Tayburn
Craufurdland
Rowallan
Kilmaurs
Polbaith Burn
Moscow
Loudon Castle Park
Ardrossan
Horse Isle
Stevenston
Saltcoats
Brodick hours 1
Perceton
Springside
Knockentiber
IRVINE
The Big Idea Exhibition
Scottish Maritime Museum
Dreghorn
Crosshouse
KILMARNOCK
Dick Institute
Irvine
Newmilns
Galston
Crookedholm
Hurlford
Gatehead
Drybridge
Riccarton
Irvine Bay
Dundonald
Sornhill
Milrig
Crossroads
Coodham
Bogend
Boydston
Middleyard
Barassie
Symington
Whitelees
Craigie
Loans
Troon
Adamhill
Lochlea
Crosshands
Lady Isle
Belfast 2½
Larne 4
hours
Rosemount
Monkton
Fail
Mossgiel
Mauchline
Ballochmyle
Tarbolton
Bachelor's Club (NTS)
Prestwick
Prestwick International
Failford
Mossblown
Barskimming
Catrine
St Quivox
Ayr Bay
Whitletts
Auchincruive
Annbank
Stair
AYR
Wallace Tower
Loudoun Hall
Seafield
Belston
Holmston
Sundrum Mains
Trabboch
Schaw
Ochiltree
Lugar Water
Joppa
Coylton
Drongan
Burns' Cottage
Craig Tara
Heads of Ayr
Alloway
Maclaurin Gallery & Rozelle House
Tam O'Shanter Experience
Burns National Heritage Park
Martnaham Loch
Burnton
Sinclairston
Lagg
Fisherton
Brown Carrick Hill 287
Dunure
Dunduff
Nether Auchendrane
Mount Oliphant
Hollybush
Littlemill
Dunure Mains
Sauchrie
Minishant
Culroy
Dalrymple
Skeldon
Rankinston
Water of Coyle
Stannery Knowe
Electric Brae
Knoweside
Culzean Bay
Culzean Castle & Country Park (NTS)
Pennyglen
Grimmet
Dalvennan
Patna
Lethanhill
Kilmein Hill 429
Maybole
Maidenhead Bay
Morriston
Maidens
Kirkmichael
Waterside
Keirs Hill
Doon
Benbeoch
Kirkoswald
Crossraguel Abbey
Souter Johnnie's Cottage (NTS)
Loch Spallander Reservoir
Turnberry
Turnberry Bay
Crosshill
Blairquhan
Burnton
Clawfin
Dalmellington
Gass
Bogton Loch
Windy Standard
Cloyntie
Straiton
Craigoch
Kirk Hill
Dalcairnie
Ness Glen
Wallacetown
Kilkerran
Craig
Craigengillan
Deil's Elbow
Maratz Hill
Dowhill
Dipple
Low Craighead
Bargany Mains
Dailly
Tairlaw
Eriff
Benbrack
Chapeldonan
Grangeston
Killochan
Bargany
Old Dailly
Penkill
Hadyard Hill
Garleffin Fell 429
Loch Doon
Loch Bradan Reservoir
Girvan
Saugh Hill
Linfern Loch
Glendoune
Glengennet
North Balloch
Waterhead
Craiglee
Lamloch
Drumjohn
A78
A737
A736
A735
A738
A719
A77
A71
A759
A79
A713
A70
A76
B7048
B781
B780
B784
B777
B706
B707
B778
B769
B785
B751
B7038
B7064
B7081
B7080
B730
B744
B739
B743
B705
B742
B7024
B7034
B7045
B7023
B741
B7036
B7046
B764
B7037
B7073

133
KILBRIDE
Meikle Earnock
Low Waters
Chatelherault
B754
Auchter
Hare Hill
Forth
Jackton
Calder Glen
Eddlewood
Overtown
Waterloo
Polnoon
Crutherland
A723
Quarter
A72
Law
Fairholm
B7011
B7056
Larkhall
142
Carluke
Netherton
Dunwan Dam
Auldhouse
A726
Limekilnburn
Machan
Shawtonhill
Rutherend
Ashgill
Rosebank
A721
Melowther Hill
Chapelton
Milton Lockhart
Kilncadzow
Netherburn
Braidwood
Harelaw
Glassford
Corse Hill
376
Ardochrig
Udstonhead
Stonehouse
Craignethan
Crossford
Cleghorn
Laird's Seat
Netherfield
A71
B7078
Draffan
Hazelbank
A73
A706
A70
Strathaven
Blackwood
B7086
Jerviswood
Black Hill Fort
Nemphlar
Auchenheath
Lanark
Sandford
Kirkmuirhill
Kirkfieldbank
A72
New Lanark
Boghead
B7018
New Lanark World Heritage Village
Falls of Clyde
Hyndford Bridge
Caldermill
Hareshaw
Deadwaters
B7086
West Cauldcoats
SOUTH
Lesmahagow
Hawksland
A71
Drumclog
B743
Kype Muir
Kype Water
Birkwood
A70
Harleyho
arvel
Priestland
A71
1307
Dungavel
B745
Logan Water
Auchlochan
Stone Hill
LANARKSHIRE
Auchingilloch
Glengavel
Douglas Water
Changue Hill
Mill Rig
Goodbush Hill
B7078
Cumberhead
Rigside
Glengavel Reservoir
Nutberry Hill
522
Coalburn
Braehead
Bankend
Happendon
Uddington
Distinkhorn
B7055
Priesthill Height
Robert Law
Garf Water
Newton
Wedder Hill
434
St Bride's Church
New Mains
Scaur Hill
Dung
Middlefield Law
Douglas
Mid Hill
Dun Rig
Poneil Burn
134
Glenbuck
Hazelside
A70
Black Hill
Parish Holm
Glespin
Redshaw
Netherwood
M74
Wildshaw Hill
Robertor
Greenock Water
Muirkirk
B743
Smallburn
B7078
Nethershield
Carmacoup
Nether Wellwood
Kames
Abington
Gilmilnscroft
Glentaggart
Airds Moss
Boghead
1680
Cairn Table
593
Dryrigs Hill
Crawfordjohn
Duneaton Water
A70
HIRE
Wardlaw Hill
B740
Glespin Burn
Cronberry
Carbellow
Drake Law
A702
Lugar
Stony Hill
B797
Gass Water
Lettershaws
Logan
Duneaton Water
Cumnock
Netherthird
Mount Stuart
Dalblair
Glenmuir Water
LOWTHER
Wellgrain Dod
Fingland
Spango Water
Snar Water
B7040
A76
Craigdullyeart Hill
Cocker Hill
Corsebank
Wanlock Water
Lochhill
Hallmerk Hill
Leadhills
Elvan Water
Pathhead
Kirkland
Lagrae
Carco
Wanlock Dod
Crawick Water
New Cumnock
DUMFRIES
Wanlockhead
468
Museum of Scottish Lead Mining
Connel Park
Kirkconnel
A76
Beam Engine
732
Afton Bridgend
B740
Green Lowther
Burnside
B741
Willowgrain Hill
Laight
Kelloholm
Crawick
Mennock Pass
329
Lowther Hill
Drumbuie
B797
Sanquhar
Hare Hill
Kello Water
Mennock Water
Enterkin Burn
Ulzieside
Mennock
Dalveen Pass
Blackcraig Hill
700
AND
Eliock
A702
Craigdarroch
Glengenny Muir
NITHSDALE
Euchan Water
Cloud Hill
Ardoch
Blacklorg Hill
681
Wether Hill
Afton Resr
Cruffell
Polgown
Enterkinfoot
Durisdeer
Dalgonar
A76
Gateslack
Breconside
Scaur Water
Wedder Law
Cairnkinna Hill
Windy Standard
698
Countam
Glenmanna
A702
Alhang
Bow Burn
GALLOWAY
Gan
124
Drumlanrig
Morton Loch
Cairnsmore of Carsphairn
797
Colt Hill
Countam
Morton
Rashy Height
Black Shoulder
Auchenbrack
Torbraehead
Dabton
Gatelawbridge
Benbuie
Shinnel Water
Auchenhessnane
Scaur Water
Burnhead
Thornhill
Bail Hill
D
E
F
G
I
2
3
4
5

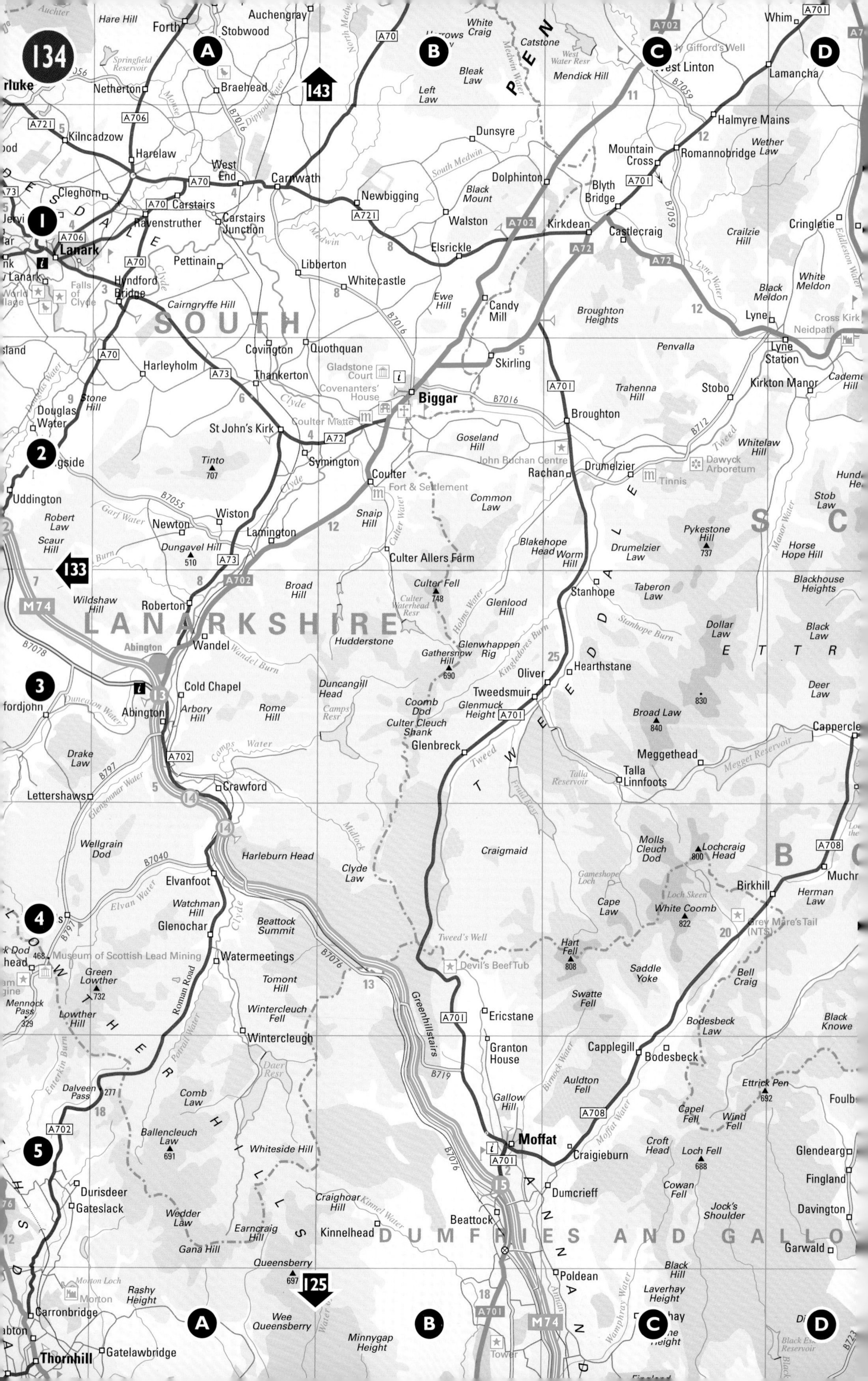
134
143
133
125
A
B
C
D
1
2
3
4
5
SOUTH LANARKSHIRE
DUMFRIES AND GALLOWAY
PENTLAND
LOWTHER HILLS
TWEEDDALE
CLYDESDALE
ETTRICK
Hare Hill
Forth
Auchengray
Stobwood
Springfield Reservoir
Netherton
Braehead
Carluke
Kilncadzow
Harelaw
West End
Carnwath
Newbigging
Cleghorn
Carstairs
Ravenstruther
Carstairs Junction
Lanark
Falls of Clyde
New Lanark World Heritage Village
Pettinain
Hyndford Bridge
Cairngryffe Hill
Libberton
Whitecastle
Covington
Quothquan
Harleyholm
Thankerton
Gladstone Court
Covenanters' House
Biggar
Coulter Motte
St John's Kirk
Symington
Coulter
Fort & Settlement
Tinto 707
Stone Hill
Douglas Water
Uddington
Robert Law
Scaur Hill
Newton
Wiston
Lamington
Dungavel Hill 510
Wildshaw Hill
Roberton
Abington
Wandel
Cold Chapel
Arbory Hill
Rome Hill
Crawford
Drake Law
Lettershaws
Wellgrain Dod
Elvanfoot
Watchman Hill
Glenochar
Museum of Scottish Lead Mining
Green Lowther 732
Mennock Pass 329
Lowther Hill
Dalveen Pass 277
Ballencleuch Law 691
Durisdeer
Gateslack
Wedder Law
Gana Hill
Carronbridge
Thornhill
Gatelawbridge
Morton Loch
Morton
Rashy Height
Comb Law
Whiteside Hill
Earncraig Hill
Queensberry 697
Wee Queensberry
Craighoar Hill
Kinnelhead
Minnygap Height
Harleburn Head
Beattock Summit
Watermeetings
Tomont Hill
Wintercleuch Fell
Wintercleugh
Daer Resr
Greenhillstairs
Clyde Law
Hudderstone
Duncangill Head
Camps Resr
Coomb Dod
Culter Cleuch Shank
Glenbreck
Culter Fell 748
Culter Waterhead Resr
Culter Allers Farm
Snaip Hill
Broad Hill
Gathersnow Hill 690
Glenwhappen Rig
Glenmuck Height
Tweedsmuir
Oliver
Hearthstane
Glenlood Hill
Blakehope Head
Worm Hill
Stanhope
Common Law
Goseland Hill
John Buchan Centre
Rachan
Drumelzier
Tinnis
Dawyck Arboretum
Whitelaw Hill
Broughton
Skirling
Candy Mill
Broughton Heights
Ewe Hill
Elsrickle
Walston
Black Mount
Dolphinton
Dunsyre
Left Law
Bleak Law
White Craig
Catstone
West Water Resr
Mendick Hill
West Linton
Lady Gifford's Well
Whim
Lamancha
Halmyre Mains
Wether Law
Romannobridge
Mountain Cross
Blyth Bridge
Kirkdean
Castlecraig
Crailzie Hill
Cringletie
White Meldon
Black Meldon
Lyne
Cross Kirk
Neidpath
Lyne Station
Penvalla
Trahenna Hill
Stobo
Kirkton Manor
Pykestone Hill 737
Drumelzier Law
Stob Law
Horse Hope Hill
Blackhouse Heights
Taberon Law
Dollar Law
Black Law
Deer Law
830
Broad Law 840
Meggethead
Talla Linnfoots
Talla Reservoir
Fruid Resr
Megget Reservoir
Cappercleuch
Craigmaid
Molls Cleuch Dod
Lochcraig Head 800
Gameshope Loch
Loch Skeen
Cape Law
White Coomb 822
Grey Mare's Tail (NTS)
Birkhill
Herman Law
Tweed's Well
Devil's Beef Tub
Hart Fell 808
Saddle Yoke
Bell Craig
Swatte Fell
Ericstane
Granton House
Capplegill
Bodesbeck
Bodesbeck Law
Auldton Fell
Gallow Hill
Moffat
Craigieburn
Dumcrieff
Beattock
Poldean
Ettrick Pen 692
Capel Fell
Wind Fell
Croft Head
Loch Fell 688
Cowan Fell
Jock's Shoulder
Black Hill
Laverhay Height
Black Knowe
Glendearg
Fingland
Davington
Garwald
Black Esk Reservoir
Tower
Clyde
Tweed
Medwin
South Medwin
Lyne Water
Manor Water
Elvan Water
Camps Water
Culter Water
Holms Water
Kingledores Burn
Stanhope Burn
Potrail Water
Enterkin Burn
Birnock Water
Moffat Water
Wamphray Water
Annan
Kinnel Water
Glengonnar Water
Duneaton Water
Garf Water
Wandel Burn
Midlock
Dippool Water
Mouse
Eddleston Water
M74
A70
A71
A72
A73
A701
A702
A706
A708
A721
B7016
B7040
B7055
B7059
B7076
B7078
B712
B719
B797
13
14
15

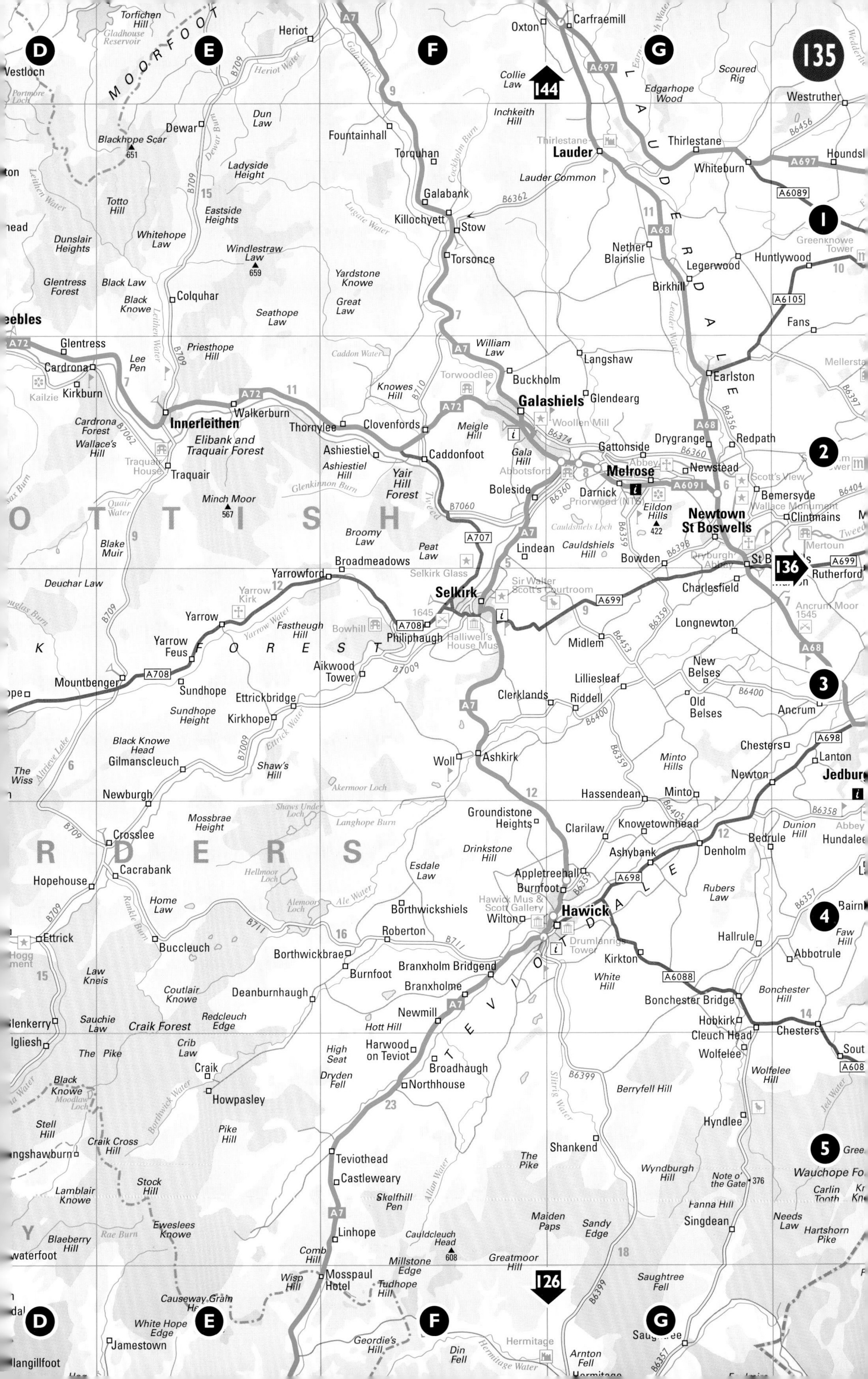
D
E
F
G
Torfichen Hill
Gladhouse Reservoir
MOORFOOT
Heriot
A7
Oxton
Carfraemill
Westloch
Portmore Loch
B709
Heriot Water
Gala Water
Collie Law
144
A697
Earn's Water
Edgarhope Wood
Scoured Rig
Westruther
Dun Law
Dewar
Fountainhall
Inchkeith Hill
Blackhope Scar
651
Dewar Burn
Torquhan
Thirlestane
Lauder
Thirlestane
Whiteburn
B6456
Houndslow
A697
Ladyside Height
Lauder Common
A6089
Leithen Water
Totto Hill
Eastside Heights
Galabank
Cockholm Burn
B6362
Killochyett
Stow
Lugate Water
Dunslair Heights
Whitehope Law
Windlestraw Law
659
Torsonce
Nether Blainslie
A68
Greenknowe Tower
Huntlywood
Legerwood
Birkhill
Glentress Forest
Black Law
Yardstone Knowe
Black Knowe
Colquhar
Great Law
Seathope Law
Leader Water
A6105
Fans
LAUDERDALE
Peebles
A72
Glentress
Priesthope Hill
Caddon Water
William Law
Langshaw
Cardrona
Lee Pen
Torwoodlee
Buckholm
Earlston
Mellerstain
Kailzie
Kirkburn
Walkerburn
Knowes Hill
B710
Galashiels
Glendearg
B6397
Innerleithen
Thornylee
Clovenfords
Meigle Hill
Woollen Mill
B6356
Cardrona Forest
Elibank and Traquair Forest
B6374
Gattonside
Drygrange
Redpath
Wallace's Hill
B7062
Ashiestiel
Gala Hill
Abbey
B6360
Newstead
Traquair House
Traquair
Ashiestiel Hill
Caddonfoot
Yair Hill Forest
Abbotsford
Melrose
Scott's View
Glenkinnon Burn
Boleside
Darnick
A6091
Bemersyde
B6404
Quair Water
Minch Moor
567
Tweed
B7060
Priorwood (NTS)
Eildon Hills
422
Wallace Monument
Clintmains
Newtown St Boswells
Mertoun
SCOTTISH
Blake Muir
Broomy Law
Peat Law
A707
A7
Cauldshiels Loch
B6359
Lindean
Cauldshiels Hill
Bowden
B6398
Dryburgh Abbey
St Boswells
136
A699
Rutherford
Broadmeadows
Selkirk Glass
Deuchar Law
Yarrowford
Sir Walter Scott's Courtroom
Yarrow Kirk
Selkirk
Charlesfield
Douglas Burn
Yarrow
Yarrow Water
1645
Fastheugh Hill
Bowhill
A708
Philiphaugh
Halliwell's House Mus
A699
Longnewton
Ancrum Moor
1545
Yarrow Feus
FOREST
Midlem
B6453
B6359
A68
Aikwood Tower
B7009
New Belses
Mountbenger
Sundhope
Ettrickbridge
Clerklands
Lilliesleaf
Riddell
B6400
Old Belses
Ancrum
Sundhope Height
Kirkhope
Ettrick Water
Black Knowe Head
Gilmanscleuch
B7009
Altrieve Lake
The Wiss
Shaw's Hill
Woll
Ashkirk
B6400
B6359
Minto Hills
Chesters
A698
Lanton
Newton
Jedburgh
Akermoor Loch
Newburgh
Hassendean
Minto
Shaws Under Loch
Mossbrae Height
Langhope Burn
Groundistone Heights
B6405
Clarilaw
Knowetownhead
B6358
Dunion Hill
Abbey
B709
Crosslee
Denholm
Bedrule
Hundalee
RDERS
Drinkstone Hill
Ashybank
Hopehouse
Cacrabank
Hellmoor Loch
Esdale Law
Appletreehall
A698
Burnfoot
B6359
Rubers Law
Home Law
Rankle Burn
Alemoor Loch
Ale Water
Borthwickshiels
Hawick Mus & Scott Gallery
Wilton
Hawick
B6357
Bairnkine
B709
B711
Faw Hill
Ettrick
Roberton
B711
Drumlanrig's Tower
Hallrule
Hogg Monument
Buccleuch
Borthwickbrae
Branxholm Bridgend
Kirkton
Abbotrule
Law Kneis
Burnfoot
TEVIOTDALE
White Hill
A6088
Coutlair Knowe
Deanburnhaugh
Branxholme
Bonchester Hill
Bonchester Bridge
Glenkerry
Sauchie Law
Craik Forest
Redcleuch Edge
Newmill
A7
Hott Hill
Hobkirk
Chesters
Ingliesh
Crib Law
Cleuch Head
Southdean
The Pike
Harwood on Teviot
High Seat
Wolfelee
A6088
Craik
Broadhaugh
Black Knowe
Moodlaw Loch
Dryden Fell
Northhouse
Wolfelee Hill
Jed Water
Howpasley
Borthwick Water
Slitrig Water
B6399
Berryfell Hill
Stell Hill
23
Hyndlee
Craik Cross Hill
Pike Hill
Langshawburn
Teviothead
The Pike
Shankend
Greenriggs
Wauchope Forest
Stock Hill
Castleweary
Allan Water
Wyndburgh Hill
Note o' the Gate
376
Carlin Tooth
Lamblair Knowe
Skelfhill Pen
Fanna Hill
Knox Knowe
A7
Maiden Paps
Sandy Edge
Needs Law
Hartshorn Pike
Eweslees Knowe
Singdean
Blaeberry Hill
Rae Burn
Linhope
Cauldcleuch Head
608
Ettrickwaterfoot
Comb Hill
Millstone Edge
Greatmoor Hill
18
Wisp Hill
Mosspaul Hotel
Tudhope Hill
126
B6399
Saughtree Fell
Causeway Grain Head
White Hope Edge
Saughtree
Jamestown
Geordie's Hill
Hermitage
Din Fell
Arnton Fell
Hermitage Water
Hermitage
B6357
Langillfoot
1
2
3
4
5
I
7
9
11
12
14
15
16
6
8
10

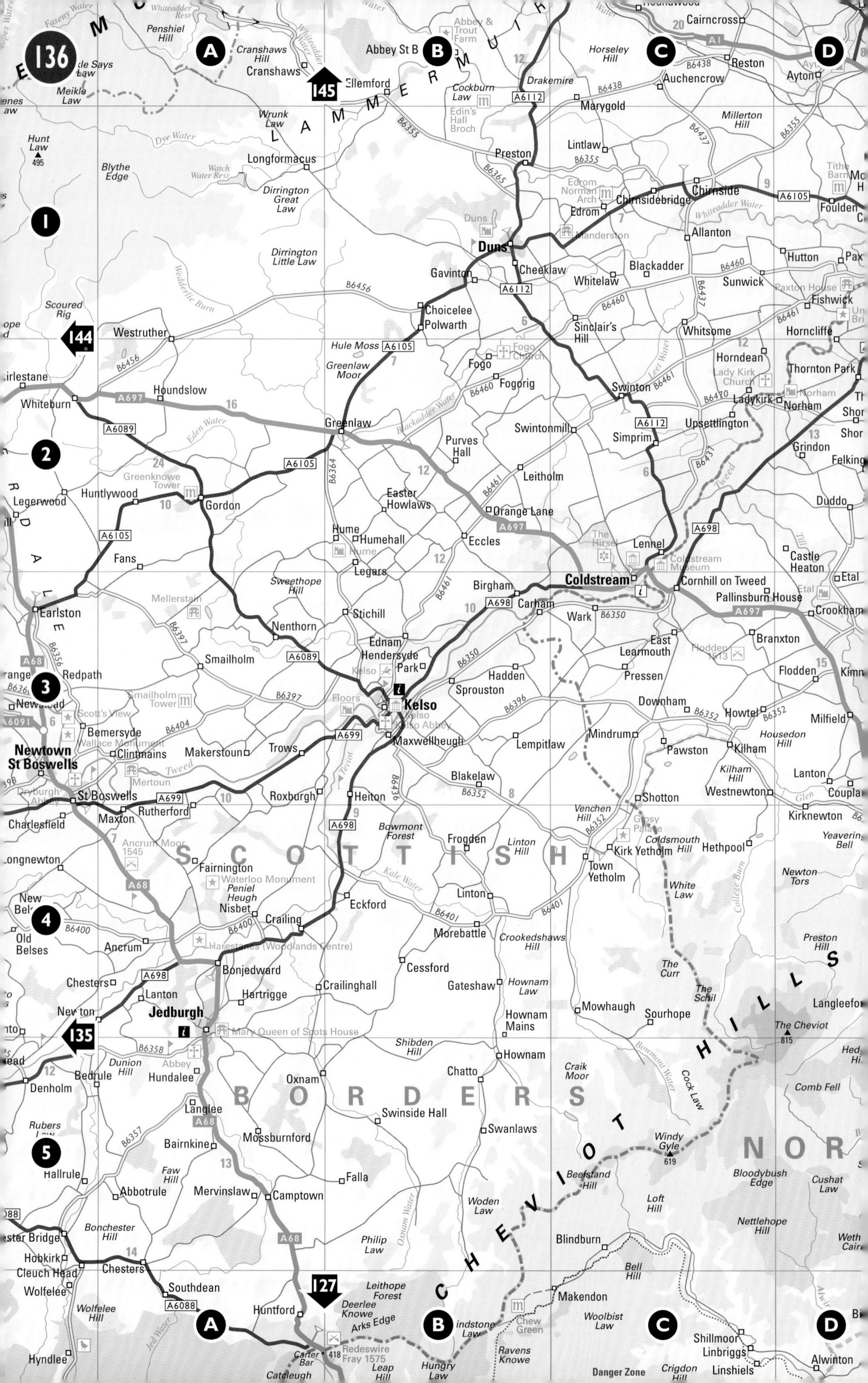
A
B
C
D
1
2
3
4
5
145
144
135
127
L A M M E R M U I R
S C O T T I S H
B O R D E R S
C H E V I O T   H I L L S
Penshiel Hill
Cranshaws Hill
Cranshaws
Meikle Says Law
Meikle Law
Abbey St B
Abbey & Trout Farm
Ellemford
Cairncross
Reston
Auchencrow
Ayton
Horseley Hill
Drakemire
Cockburn Law
Edin's Hall Broch
Marygold
Millerton Hill
Wrunk Law
Dye Water
Hunt Law
495
Blythe Edge
Watch Water Resr
Longformacus
Dirrington Great Law
Dirrington Little Law
Lintlaw
Preston
Edrom
Norman Arch
Chirnsidebridge
Chirnside
Whiteadder Water
Foulden
Duns
Manderston
Allanton
Hutton
Blackadder
Sunwick
Paxton House
Fishwick
Cheeklaw
Whitelaw
Gavinton
Choicelee
Polwarth
Sinclair's Hill
Whitsome
Horncliffe
Scoured Rig
Westruther
Wedderlie Burn
Hule Moss
Greenlaw Moor
Fogo
Fogo Church
Fogorig
Horndean
Lady Kirk Church
Thornton Park
Ladykirk
Norham
Swinton
Houndslow
Whiteburn
Eden Water
Greenlaw
Blackadder Water
Swintonmill
Upsettlington
Simprim
Purves Hall
Grindon
Felking
Greenknowe Tower
Huntlywood
Gordon
Legerwood
Easter Howlaws
Leitholm
Orange Lane
Duddo
Hume
Humehall
Eccles
Lennel
The Hirsel
Coldstream Museum
Coldstream
Castle Heaton
Fans
Legars
Sweethope Hill
Birgham
Cornhill on Tweed
Pallinsburn House
Etal
Crookham
Mellerstain
Earlston
Stichill
Carham
Wark
Nenthorn
Ednam
Hendersyde Park
East Learmouth
Branxton
Smailholm
Redpath
Hadden
Sprouston
Pressen
Flodden 1513
Flodden
Smailholm Tower
Floors
Kelso
Kelso Abbey
Downham
Howtel
Milfield
Scott's View
Bemersyde
Wallace Monument
Clintmains
Makerstoun
Trows
Maxwellheugh
Lempitlaw
Mindrum
Pawston
Kilham
Housedon Hill
Newtown St Boswells
Mertoun
Tweed
Dryburgh Abbey
St Boswells
Roxburgh
Heiton
Blakelaw
Shotton
Kilham Hill
Westnewton
Lanton
Charlesfield
Maxton
Rutherford
Bowmont Forest
Vencheh Hill
Gipsy Palace
Kirknewton
Ancrum Moor 1545
Frogden
Linton Hill
Kirk Yetholm
Coldsmouth Hill
Hethpool
Yeavering Bell
Longnewton
Fairnington
Waterloo Monument
Peniel Heugh
Town Yetholm
Newton Tors
Kale Water
New Belses
Nisbet
Crailing
Eckford
Linton
White Law
Old Belses
Ancrum
Harestanes (Woodlands Centre)
Morebattle
Crookedshaws Hill
Preston Hill
Cessford
The Curr
Chesters
Bonjedward
Crailinghall
Gateshaw
Hownam Law
The Schil
Langleeford
Lanton
Hartrigge
Jedburgh
Newton
Mary Queen of Scots House
Hownam Mains
Mowhaugh
Sourhope
The Cheviot
815
Dunion Hill
Abbey
Shibden Hill
Hownam
Bedrule
Hundalee
Oxnam
Chatto
Craik Moor
Bowmont Water
Cock Law
Denholm
Comb Fell
Langlee
Swinside Hall
Rubers Law
Mossburnford
Swanlaws
Windy Gyle
619
Bairnkine
Beefstand Hill
Bloodybush Edge
Cushat Law
Hallrule
Faw Hill
Loft Hill
Abbotrule
Mervinslaw
Camptown
Falla
Woden Law
Oxnam Water
Nettlehope Hill
Bonchester Bridge
Bonchester Hill
Philip Law
Blindburn
Hobkirk
Cleuch Head
Chesters
Bell Hill
Wolfelee
Southdean
Leithope Forest
Deerlee Knowe
Makendon
Woolbist Law
Wolfelee Hill
Huntford
Arks Edge
Chew Green
Shillmoor
Linbriggs
Redeswire Fray 1575
Carter Bar
418
Ravens Knowe
Hyndlee
Catcleugh
Leap Hill
Hungry Law
Danger Zone
Crigdon Hill
Linshiels
Alwinton
Jed Water
A1
A6112
A6105
A697
A6089
A68
A698
A699
A6088
B6438
B6437
B6355
B6365
B6456
B6460
B6461
B6470
B6364
B6350
B6396
B6352
B6397
B6404
B6356
B6400
B6401
B6436
B6358
B6357

D
E
F
G
1
2
3
4
5
0 2 4 6 8 10 miles
0 2 4 6 8 10 km
Hilton Bay
Lamberton Beach
Needles Eye
Sharper's Head
Ravensdown Barracks
Berwick-upon-Tweed
Berwick (ruins)
East Ord
Tweedmouth
Spittal
Redshin Cove
A1167
Scremerston
Cheswick Black Rocks
Allerdeannill Burn
Cheswick
West Allerdean
Goswick
Ancroft
Berrington
Haydon Dean
B6525
Bowsden
A1
Beal
West Mains
14
Emmanuel Head
St. Mary
Holy Island or Lindisfarne
St. Aidan's Winery
Lindisfarne (NT)
Holy Island
Priory
Holy Island Sands
Castle Point
Burrows Hole
Guile Point
Fenham Flats
Barmoor Lane End
B6353
West Kyloe
Fenwick
Lowick
Kyloe Hills
Buckton
Longstone
Staple Sound
Farne Islands
Farne Island
Ross
Budle Bay
Budle Point
Grace Darling Museum
Bamburgh
Inner Sound
Holburn
Detchant
Middleton
Elwick
Easington
Budle
B1342
Cockenheugh
211
Waren Mill
Glororum
Bamburgh
9
B1340
Monks House Rocks
Seahouses
Fenton
North Hazelrigg
Belford
Spindlestone
Burton
Roman Road
Nesbit
Doddington
South Hazelrigg
B6349
Bradford
B1341
North Sunderland
Ewart Newtown
East Horton
10
Bellshill
Elford
West Horton
Warenton
Adderstone
Lucker
Newham Hall
Beadnell
Humbleton Hill
1402
B6348
Twizell House
Warenford
Swinhoe Burn
Benthall
B6348
Newham
West Fleetham
Swinhoe
Beadnell Bay
Wandon
Chatton
Greendykes
Wooler
Newstead
Chathill
Earle
Haugh Head
Chillingham
Chillingham Park
Rosebrough
High Newton by-the-Sea
Snook Point
Tughall
Middleton Hall
Ellingham
Preston
Newtown
315
Wandylaw
Preston Tower
Newton Haven or St Mary's
Lilburn Tower
Hepburn
Brownieside
Brunton
B1339
Low Newton-by-the-Sea
East Lilburn
Cateran Hill
Embleton Bay
A697
Middle Moor
Christon Bank
Embleton
Ilderton
Old Bewick
Bewick Moor
North Charlton
14
B6347
Dunstanburgh (NT)
Roseden
West Ditchburn
South Charlton
Roddam
17
Rock
Dunstan
Craster
Wooperton
New Bewick
B6346
Rennington
Stamford
1464
15
Eglingham
B6347
B6341
Cullernose Point
Beanley
Howick Hall
Howick
Brandon
East Bolton
B6346
B1340
Reaveley
Shipley
Littlehoughton
Powburn
Hulne Priory
Howick Haven
Branton
A1
Ingram
Longhoughton Steel
UMBERLAND
Aln
1093
Hulne Park
Denwick
Longhoughton
Glanton
Boulmer
Cochrane Pike
Alnwick Abbey
Great Ryle
Abberwick
Bolton
Alnwick
Hawkhill
B1339
Boulmer Haven
High Knowes
Prendwick
Whittingham
Broome Wood
Barter Books
B6341
Aln
Lesbury
Little Ryle
8
Alnmouth Sta.
Thrunton
Alnham
Yetlington
Callaly Castle
A1
Bilton
Alnmouth
Alnwick Moor
Alnmouth Bay
Scrainwood
Callaly
Thrunton Wood
Edlingham
128
Buston
Lorbottle Hall
8
Shilbottle
A1068
Long Crag
A697
Bigges' Pillar
Lorbottle
Eastfield Hall
Burradon
High Trewhitt
Newton-on-the-Moor
Warkworth

A
B
C
D
1
2
3
4
5
146
0
2
4
6
8
10 miles
0
2
4
6
8
10 km
Port Mor
Machrins
B8086
B8085
Scalasaig
Loch Staosnaig
Baleromindubh
Rubha Dubh
Garvard
Balerominmore
Eilean Mhucaig
Priory
Rubha Ban
Dubh Eilean
Oronsay
Eilean nan Ron
Caolas Mor
Eilean Ghaoideamal
Sgeir Mhor a'Bhrein-phuirt
1¼ hrs
(Summer only)
Rubh' an t-Sailein
Loch Tarbert
Rubh' a'Chrois-aoinidh
Shian Bay
Glenbat
Scrinadle
Rubh a'Mhail
Rubha Bholsa
Sgarbh Breac
364
Jura Forest
Beinn an Oir
785
Beinn Shiantaidh
755
Na Peileirean
Nave Island
Ardnave Point
Gortantaoid Point
Margadale Hill
Bunnahabhainn Bay
Beinn a'Chaolais
734
Paps of Jura
Loch a'Chnuic Bhric
Loch an t-Siob
Ardnave
Tayovullin
Killinallan Point
Killinallan
Bunnahabhainn
316
Giur-bheinn
Carraig Bhan
Ton Mhor
Kilnave
Beinn Bhreac
286
Ardnahoe
Loch Staoisha
Gleann Asdale
Leargybreck
Sanaigmore
Ardnave Loch
Loch Gruinart
Glas Bheinn
561
Eilean Mor
A R G Y L L
Balulive
Feolin
Braigo
Leckgruinart
Port Askaig
Feolin Ferry
Keils
Rubha Lamanais
Smaull
Keills
Dubh Bheinn
Loch Finlaggan
Craighouse
Ballinaby
Carnduncan
B8017
Aoradh
Craigens
Brat Bheinn
342
Saligo Bay
Grainel
Gruinart Flats
Ballygrant
Loch Ballygrant
Crackaig
Loch Gorm
B8018
I S L A Y
Loch Cam
A846
8
Loch Lossit
Cabrach
Sannaig
Coul Point
Machrie
Aruadh
Foreland
Lyrabus
Moin'a'choire
Esknish
Beinn Dubh
Ardfin
Jura Ho.
Rockside
Blackrock
Redhouses
Machir Bay
Kilchoman
Islay Ho.
Am Fraoch Eilean
Rubha na Traille
Conisby
Bridgend
Brosdale Island
Sgorr nam Faoileann
Loch Indaal
Cachlaidh Mhor
Bruichladdich
Barr
Kilchiaran
Gartnatra
Neriby
Beinn na Caillich
Kilchiaran Bay
Bowmore
Cattadale
Glas Bheinn
471
McArthur's Head
15
Rinns of Islay
Tormisdale
Gearach
Port Charlotte
Ronnachmore
Cluanach
Gartbreck
Cruach
Kilennan
Proaig
Carn
Beinn Tart a'Mhill
232
Lossit
Kelsay
Laggan
Laggan
Beinn Bhan
471
Beinn Bheigeir
491
Nerabus
Rubha Liath
Duich
Ardtalla
Easter Ellister
A847
Beinn Uraraidh
454
Loch Uraraidh
13
B8016
11
Claggain Bay
Portnahaven
A846
Trudernish
Kintour
Laggan Bay
Port Wemyss
Islay
Orsay
Rinns Point
Glenegedale
Sgorr Bhogachain
Loch Uigeadail
Kintour
Ardmore Point
Kildalton Church & Crosses
Ardmore
Machrie
Beinn Sholum
347
Leorin
2¼ h
Kintra
Machrie
Eilean a'Chuirn
Rubha Mor
Leorin Lochs
Eilean Bhride
Maol Buidhe
165
Cornabus
Port Ellen
Lagavulin
Ardbeg
Rubha na Gainmhich
Carnmore
Laphroaig
THE OA
The Ard
Caolas an Eilein
Risabus
Lower Killeyan
Port Chubaird
Texa
Inerval
Mull Of Oa
Loch Kinnabus
Rubha nan Leacan

D
E
F
G
I
147
Crinan
Ardnoe Point
Kilmichael Glassary
Craigans
Bridgend
Dunadd Fort
Cup & Ring Marks
Moine Mhor
Bellanoch
Cnoc Reamhar
265
Rubha nan Barr
Achnashelloch
Achnabreck Cup & Ring Marks
Cairnbaan
Ardnackaig
Arichonan
Craigglas
A816
Badden
Lochgair
Loch Gair
Gallchoille
Arinafad Beg
Garioh
Knapdale Forest
Auchindarrach
Lochgilphead
Middle Kames
Carsaig Island
Carsaig Bay
Scotnish
Seafield
Eilean Dubh
Tayvallich
Achnamara
Cruach Breacain
360
Brackley
Carrick
Achnaba
Kilmichael of Inverlussa
Cam Loch
Ardrishaig
Loch Gilp
Turbiskill
Eilean Loain
Ashfield
Castleton
Silvercraigs
Otter Ferry
Kilmory
Beinn Bheag
Caolard Rubha
Eilean Mor
Ballimore
Barrahormid
Daltote
Cruach Lusach
466
Taynish
Ulva Islands
Auchbraad
Inverneil
B8000
Keillmore
New Ulva
Dunrostan
Fearnoch
B8025
Loch Sween
Loch na Cille
Sween
Abhainn Mor
Achahoish
B8024
Srondoire
Rubha Beag
Otter
Loch Fuar Bheinne
Kilfinan Bay
St Columba's Cave
14
A83
Cruach a'Phubuill
477
Port Leathan
12
Chapel
Ellary
Clachbreck
Erines
2
Kilmory
Stob Odham
562
Meall Mor
Auchalick Bay
Lower Auchalick
Ballyaurgan
Kilmory Bay
Loch Caolisport
Baile Boidheach
Cnoc a Bharaille
Point of Knap
Loch Chaorunn
Stonefield
Barmore Island
Ashens
Druimdrishaig
Dubh Chreag
480
Derybruich
140
Larach na Gaibhre
Meall Reamhar
Barfad
East Loch Tarbert
Tarbert
½ hr
Dubhchladach
Cretshengan
Loch nan Torran
Meall Reamhar
Loch a'Chaorainn
Mealdarroch Point
West Tarbert
Escart
1½ hrs (Winter only)
Asgog Bay
Coulaghailtro
Corranbuie
Cruach an t-Sorchain
3
Kilberry
Kilberry Head
Crosses
Cruach Airde
Achadacaie
Cruach Doire Leithe
422
377
Rubha Laggan
Camas na Ceardaich
Achaglachgach Forest
5
Kennacraig
Carse
Dunmore
Redhouse
Cnoc a'Bhaile-shios
Rubha Cruitiridh
Loch Stornoway
Ardpatrick
Whitehouse
Coire nan Capull
Achadh-chaorrunn
West Loch Tarbert
Gartnagrenach
B8001
Glenrisdell
Culindrach
Gartavaich
Skipness
Skipness Point
Ardpatrick Point
Portachoillan
Cruach nam Fiadh
269
Claonaig
Auchameanach
2 hr
Quinhill
Ronachan Point
Clachan
B842
Rockfield
4
Sound
Port Mor
Ronachan
Corriechrevie
Loch Ciaran
Eascart Farm
Port Fada
West Tarbert Bay
East Tarbert Bay
Ballochroy
Tarbert
Creag Bhan
100
Auchinafaud
Loch Garasdale
Crossaig
Loch Ranza
Druimyeon Bay
Ardailly
Gigha Island
Rhunahaorine Point
Cruach Mhic-Gougain
Kilbrannan Sound
Lochranza
Catacol Bay
Rubha Airigh Bheirg
Glen Catacol
Ardminish
Ardminish Bay
A83
Rhunahaorine
Cnoc-an t-Samhlaidh
Cour Bay
Cour
Craw
Craro Island
Achamore Gardens
Narachan Hill
285
Cnoc Reamhar
21
Lenimore
Thundergay
Grob Bagh
Sound of Gigha
Tayinloan
Sunadale
Carradale Water
5
Cara Island
Killean
Deucheran Hill
329
Grogport
Beinn Bhreac
711
Pirnmill
Mull of Cara
Beacharr
Cruach Mhic-an-t-Saoir
364
Cruach nan Gabhar
354
Whitefarland Point
Mullach Buidhe
721
Loch Tanna
Imachar
Beinn Bharrain
Carradale Forest
Achaglass
Clachaig Water
Muasdale
130
Ballickine
17
33
Diollaid Mhor
Beinn Bhreac
Rhonadale
Carradale
Dougarie Point
A841
Glen Iorsa
Iorsa Water
Belloch
Arnicle
Barr Water
Dippen
Carradale Garden
Dougarie
Glenbarr
Beinn an Tuirc
Torrisdale
Lealt
Lussa
Beinn Bhreac
467
Dubh Bheinn
Jura
Tramaig Bay
Inverlussa
Ardlussa
Cruach Sganadail
453
Lussagiven
Lussa Point
Eilean an Rubha
A846
Beinn Sgaillinish
Gleann Aoistail
Gleann Dorch
Tarbert
Tarbert Bay
Creag Nam Fiadh Mor
Lagg
Rubh' a'Chamais
Gate House
Achamore
Danna Island
Corr Eilean
Eilean Mor
Eilean Mor Chapel
Ardmenish
An Dunan
Rubh 'an Leim
Lowlandman's Bay
Sron Garbh
Rubh 'an Leanachais
Argyll and Bute
Knapdale
Kintyre
Sound of Jura

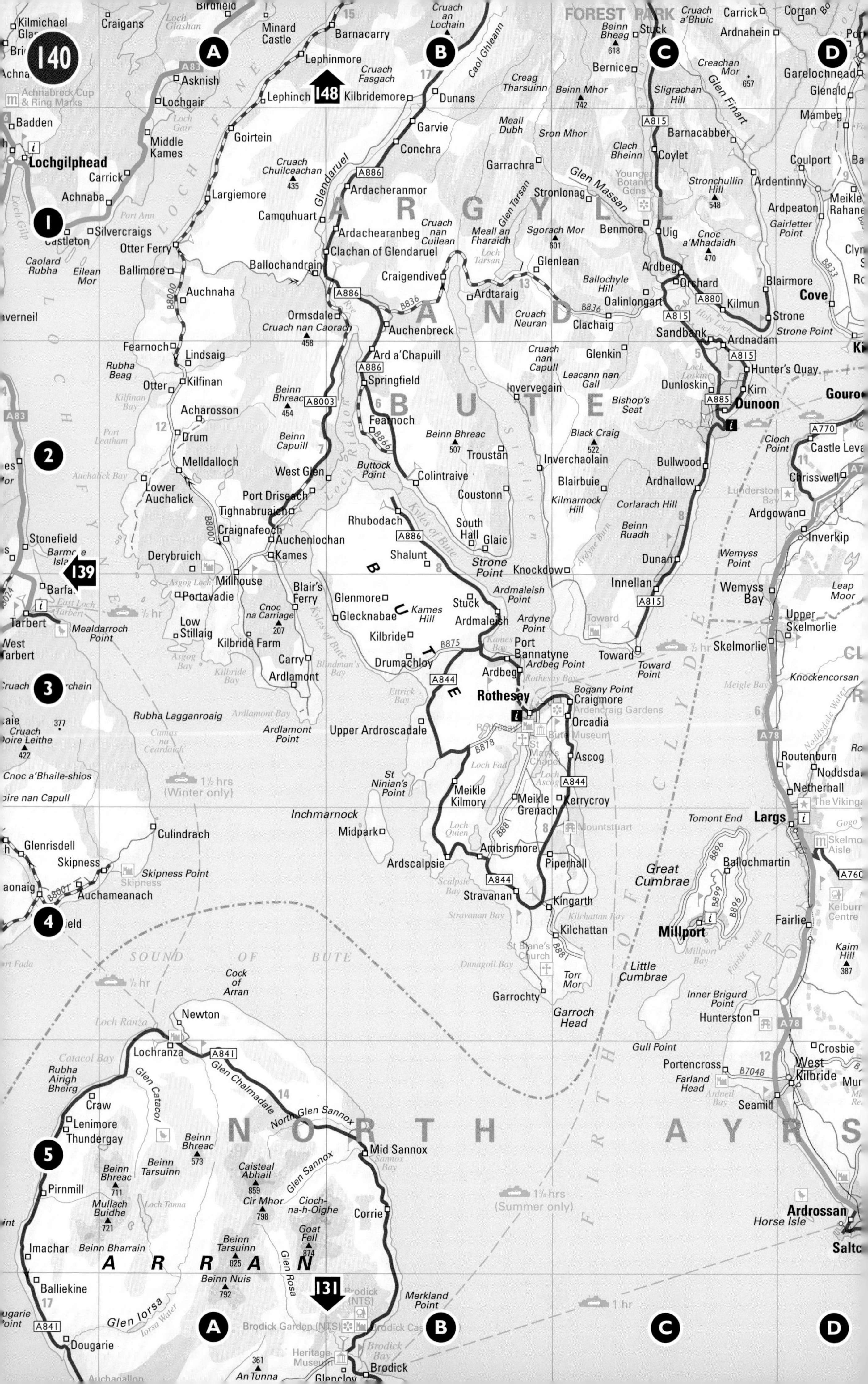

A
B
C
D
1
2
3
4
5
148
139
131
FOREST PARK
Kilmichael Glassary
Craigans
Loch Glashan
Birdfield
Minard Castle
Barnacarry
Cruach an Lochain
Beinn Bheag
618
Stuck
Cruach a'Bhuic
Carrick
Corran Bo
Asknish
Lephinmore
Cruach Fasgach
Caol Ghleann
Bernice
Ardnahein
Creachan Mor
657
Garelochhead
Achnabreck Cup & Ring Marks
Lochgair
Lephinch
Kilbridemore
Dunans
Creag Tharsuinn
Beinn Mhor
742
Sligrachan Hill
Glen Finart
Glenald
Badden
Loch Gair
Goirtein
Garvie
Meall Dubh
Sron Mhor
A815
Mambeg
Lochgilphead
Middle Kames
Conchra
Clach Bheinn
Barnacabber
Coylet
Coulport
Carrick
Cruach Chuilceachan
435
Garrachra
Glen Massan
Younger Botanic Gdns
Stronchullin Hill
548
Ardentinny
Meikle Rahane
Achnaba
Largiemore
A886
Ardacheranmor
Stronlonag
Ardpeaton
Loch Gilp
Glendaruel
ARGYLL
Cruach nan Cuilean
Glen Tarsan
Benmore
Gairletter Point
Port Ann
Camquhuart
Meall an Fharaidh
Sgorach Mor
601
Uig
Cnoc a'Mhadaidh
470
Castleton
Silvercraigs
Ardachearanbeg
Otter Ferry
Clachan of Glendaruel
Loch Tarsan
Glenlean
Caolard Rubha
Eilean Mor
Ballimore
Ballochandrain
Craigendive
Ballochyle Hill
Ardbeg
Orchard
Blairmore
Cove
B8000
Auchnaha
A886
Ardtaraig
B836
Oalinlongart
A880
Kilmun
Inverneil
Ormsdale
Cruach nan Caorach
458
AND
Cruach Neuran
Clachaig
A815
Holy Loch
Strone
Auchenbreck
Sandbank
Strone Point
Ardnadam
Fearnoch
Lindsaig
Ard a'Chapuill
Cruach nan Capull
Glenkin
A815
Hunter's Quay
Rubha Beag
A886
Springfield
Leacann nan Gall
Loch Loskin
Dunloskin
Kirn
Otter
Kilfinan
Invervegain
A885
Dunoon
Gourock
Kilfinan Bay
Beinn Bhreac
454
A8003
BUTE
Bishop's Seat
A83
Acharosson
Fearnoch
B866
A770
Port Leathan
Drum
Beinn Capuill
Beinn Bhreac
507
Troustan
Black Craig
522
Cloch Point
Castle Levan
Melldalloch
Inverchaolain
Bullwood
Auchalick Bay
West Glen
Buttock Point
Colintraive
Blairbuie
Ardhallow
Chrisswell
Lower Auchalick
Port Driseach
Coustonn
Kilmarnock Hill
Corlarach Hill
Lunderston Bay
Tighnabruaich
Rhubodach
Ardgowan
B8000
Craignafeoch
South Hall
Glaic
Beinn Ruadh
Kyles of Bute
Stonefield
Auchenlochan
A886
Inverkip
Barmore Island
Derybruich
Kames
Shalunt
Strone Point
Knockdow
Ardyne Burn
Dunan
Wemyss Point
Loch Riddon
Asgog Loch
Millhouse
Blair's Ferry
Innellan
Leap Moor
Barfad
Portavadie
Glenmore
Stuck
Ardmaleish Point
A815
Wemyss Bay
East Loch Tarbert
Cnoc na Carraige
207
Glecknabae
Kames Hill
Ardmaleish
Ardyne Point
Toward
Upper Skelmorlie
Tarbert
Mealdarroch Point
Low Stillaig
Kilbride
Kames Bay
Port Bannatyne
Toward
Skelmorlie
West Tarbert
Kilbride Farm
B875
Ardbeg Point
Toward Point
Asgog Bay
Carry
Blindman's Bay
Drumachloy
Ardbeg
Rothesay Bay
Kilbride Bay
Ardlamont
A844
Bogany Point
Meigle Bay
Knockencorsan
Cruach Doire Leithe
Ettrick Bay
Rothesay
Craigmore
377
Ardencraig Gardens
422
Rubha Lagganroaig
Ardlamont Bay
Orcadia
Camas na Ceardaich
Ardlamont Point
Upper Ardroscadale
Rothesay
Bute Museum
A78
B878
St Mary's Chapel
Ascog
Routenburn
Noddsdale Water
Cnoc a'Bhaile-shios
Loch Fad
Loch Ascog
A844
Noddsdale
St Ninian's Point
Meikle Kilmory
Netherhall
1½ hrs (Winter only)
Meikle Grenach
Kerrycroy
The Vikingar
Inchmarnock
Tomont End
Largs
Culindrach
Midpark
Loch Quien
B881
Mountstuart
Gogo
Ambrismore
Skelmorlie Aisle
Glenrisdell
B896
Ballochmartin
Skipness
Ardscalpsie
Piperhall
Great Cumbrae
A760
Skipness Point
Scalpsie Bay
A844
B899
B896
Kelburn Centre
Claonaig
B8001
Auchameanach
Stravanan
Kingarth
Millport
Fairlie
Stravanan Bay
Kilchattan Bay
Kilchattan
Millport Bay
Fairlie Roads
Kaim Hill
387
SOUND OF BUTE
St Blane's Church
B881
Dunagoil Bay
Torr Mor
Little Cumbrae
½ hr
Cock of Arran
Garrochty
Inner Brigurd Point
Garroch Head
Newton
Hunterston
Loch Ranza
A78
Lochranza
A841
Gull Point
Crosbie
Catacol Bay
West Kilbride
Rubha Airigh Bheirg
Glen Catacol
Glen Chalmadale
Portencross
B7048
Farland Head
Ardneil Bay
Craw
Seamill
North Glen Sannox
Lenimore
Thundergay
NORTH AYRSHIRE
Beinn Bhreac
573
Mid Sannox
Sannox Bay
Caisteal Abhail
859
Glen Sannox
Pirnmill
Beinn Bhreac
711
Beinn Tarsuinn
Cir Mhor
798
Cioch-na-h-Oighe
1¾ hrs (Summer only)
Mullach Buidhe
721
Loch Tanna
Corrie
Ardrossan
Horse Isle
Goat Fell
874
Beinn Tarsuinn
825
Imachar
Beinn Bharrain
ARRAN
Glen Rosa
Saltcoats
Balliekine
Beinn Nuis
792
Brodick Castle (NTS)
Merkland Point
1 hr
Glen Iorsa
Iorsa Water
A841
Brodick Garden (NTS)
Dougarie
Brodick Bay
Heritage Museum
361
An Tunna
Brodick
Auchagallon
Glencloy
FIRTH OF CLYDE

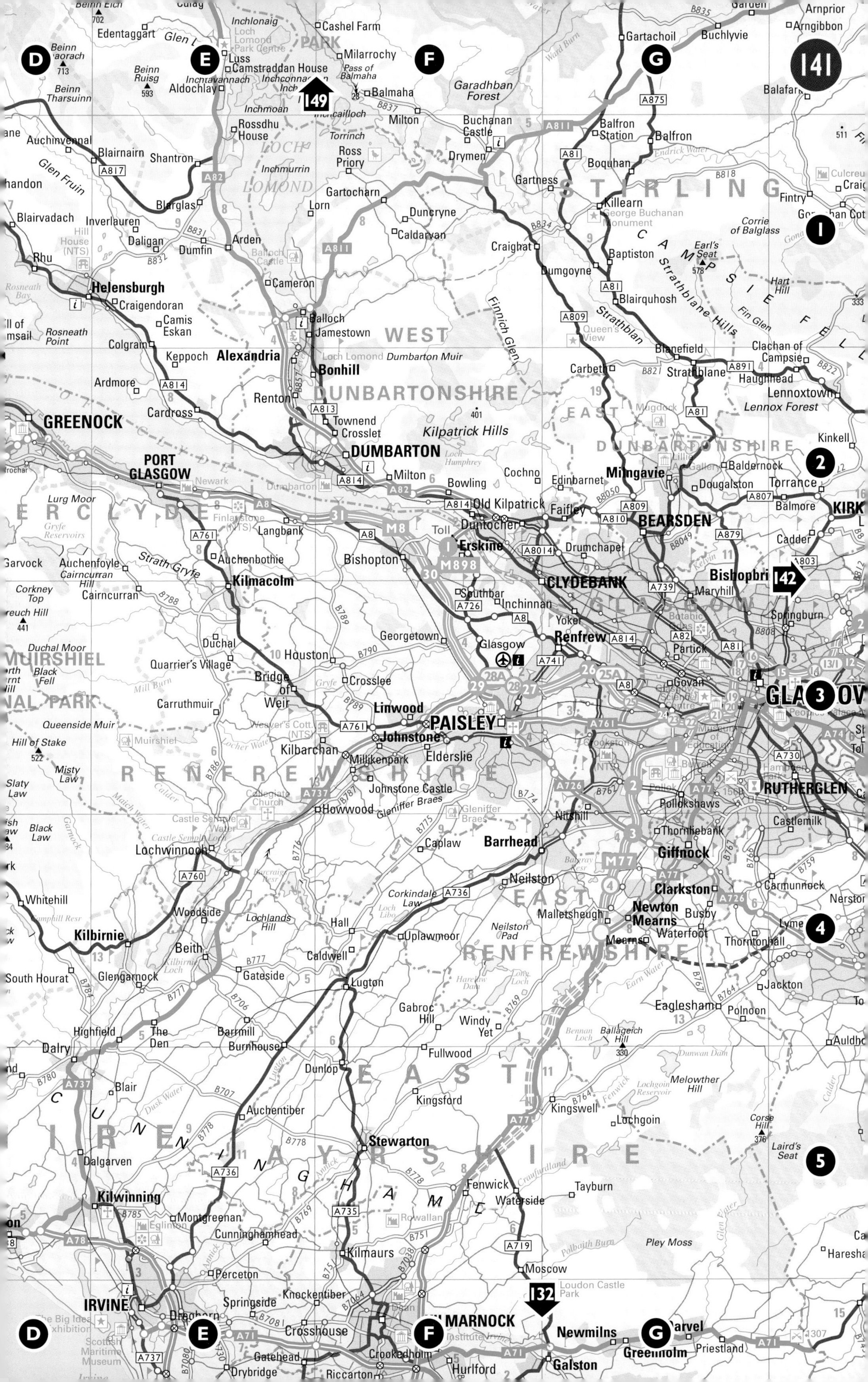
Beinn Eich
702
Edentaggart
Glen Luss
Inchlonaig
Loch Lomond Park Centre
PARK
Cashel Farm
Milarrochy
Pass of Balmaha
Balmaha
Garadhban Forest
Gartachoil
Buchlyvie
Arnprior
Arngibbon
Balafark
Beinn Dubhchraig
Beinn Chaorach
713
Beinn Ruisg
593
Luss
Camstradden House
Inchtavannach
Inchconnachan
Inchfad
Aldochlay
149
Beinn Tharsuinn
Inchmoan
Inchcailloch
B837
Milton
Buchanan Castle
A875
A811
Balfron Station
Balfron
511
Auchinvennal
Blairnairn
Shantron
Rossdhu House
LOCH LOMOND
Torrinch
Ross Priory
Inchmurrin
Drymen
A81
Boquhan
Endrick Water
B818
Culcreuch
Craig
A817
Glen Fruin
A82
Gartocharn
Gartness
STIRLING
Fintry
Blarglas
Lorn
Duncryne
Killearn
George Buchanan Monument
Gonachan Cottage
Blairvadach
Inverlauren
Hill House (NTS)
Daligan
B831
Dumfin
Arden
Caldarvan
B834
Craighat
Corrie of Balglass
Rhu
B832
Balloch Castle
A811
Baptiston
Earl's Seat
578
Rosneath Bay
Helensburgh
Cameron
Dumgoyne
CAMPSIE FELLS
Hart Hill
Craigendoran
A81
Blairquhosh
333
Rosneath Point
Camis Eskan
Balloch
Jamestown
WEST
A809
Finnich Glen
Strathblane Hills
Fin Glen
Colgrain
Queen's View
Strathblane
Blanefield
Clachan of Campsie
Keppoch
Alexandria
Loch Lomond
Dumbarton Muir
Bonhill
Carbeth
B821
Strathblane
A891
B822
Haughhead
Ardmore
A814
DUNBARTONSHIRE
Lennoxtown
Lennox Forest
Renton
B857
A813
Mugdock
A81
Cardross
Townend
Crossley
401
Kilpatrick Hills
EAST
GREENOCK
DUNBARTONSHIRE
Kinkell
PORT GLASGOW
DUMBARTON
Loch Humphrey
Lillie Art Gallery
Baldernock
Newark
A814
Milton
Bowling
Cochno
Edinbarnet
Milngavie
Dougalston
Torrance
Dumbarton
A82
B8050
A807
Lurg Moor
Old Kilpatrick
Faifley
A809
Balmore
KIRK
INVERCLYDE
Finlaystone (NTS)
A8
31
M8
Duntocher
A810
BEARSDEN
Gryfe Reservoirs
A761
Langbank
A8
Toll
Erskine
A8014
Drumchapel
B8049
A879
Cadder
Garvock
Auchenfoyle
Strath Gryfe
Auchenbothie
Bishopton
M898
Bishopbriggs
142
A803
Cairncurran Hill
Kilmacolm
30
CLYDEBANK
A739
Maryhill
Corkney Top
Cairncurran
B788
B789
Southbar
A726
Inchinnan
GLASGOW
Botanic Gardens
Springburn
Creuch Hill
441
A8
Yoker
B808
Duchal Moor
Duchal
Georgetown
Renfrew
A814
A82
Partick
MUIRSHIEL
Houston
B790
Glasgow
A81
Black Fell
Quarrier's Village
A741
26
25A
Govan
REGIONAL PARK
Mill Burn
Bridge of Weir
Crosslee
Gryfe
28A
29
28
27
A8
Glasgow Science Centre
GLASGOW
Carruthmuir
B789
Linwood
A761
PAISLEY
A761
Queenside Muir
Weaver's Cottage (NTS)
Johnstone
People's Palace
Hill of Stake
522
Muirshiel
Kilbarchan
Elderslie
Crookston
Museum of Education
A730
Misty Law
B786
Milliken Park
Pollok House
A74
Slaty Law
RENFREWSHIRE
A737
B787
Johnstone Castle
A726
B761
Pollok
A77
Hamilton
RUTHERGLEN
Collegiate Church
Gleniffer Braes
B774
Pollokshaws
Black Law
Maich Water
Castle Semple Water
Howwood
Gleniffer Braes
Nitshill
Castlemilk
Castle Semple Loch
B775
Thornliebank
Lochwinnoch
B776
Caplaw
Barrhead
Giffnock
B767
B766
Barcraigs Resr
Balgray Resr
M77
B759
A760
Neilston
A77
Carmunnock
Whitehill
Camphill Resr
Corkindale Law
A736
EAST
Clarkston
Nerston
Loch Libo
A726
Woodside
Malletsheugh
Newton Mearns
Busby
Lochlands Hill
Hall
Neilston Pad
Waterfoot
Lyme
Kilbirnie
Uplawmoor
Mearns
Thorntonhall
Beith
Kilbirnie Loch
Caldwell
RENFREWSHIRE
Earn Water
B777
Long Loch
B767
South Hourat
Glengarnock
Gateside
Harelaw Dam
Jackton
B784
B777
Lugton
B764
B769
Eaglesham
Polnoon
B706
Gabroc Hill
Windy Yet
Highfield
The Den
Barrmill
Bennan Loch
Ballageich Hill
330
Auldhouse
Dalry
Burnhouse
Fullwood
Dunwan Dam
B780
A737
Dunlop
EAST
Blair
B707
Melowther Hill
Dusk Water
Lochgoin Reservoir
Calder
Kingsford
B764
Kingswell
Fenwick
Auchentiber
Lochgoin
Corse Hill
376
CUNNINGHAME
IRVINE
B778
Stewarton
AYRSHIRE
Laird's Seat
Dalgarven
A736
Annick
B778
Fenwick
Craufurdland
Tayburn
Kilwinning
B785
Waterside
A735
Rowallan
Montgreenan
Eglinton
B769
B751
A78
Cunninghamhead
Annick
A719
Polbaith Burn
Pley Moss
Glen Water
Haresha
Kilmaurs
B7038
Moscow
Perceton
B751
Loudon Castle Park
Knockentiber
132
IRVINE
Springside
B7064
Dean
The Big Idea Exhibition
Dreghorn
B7081
KILMARNOCK
Newmilns
Darvel
Scottish Maritime Museum
Crosshouse
Burns Institute
A71
A71
Greenholm
Priestland
A71
1307
A737
Gatehead
Crookedholm
A71
A730
B7080
Drybridge
Riccarton
Hurlford
Galston

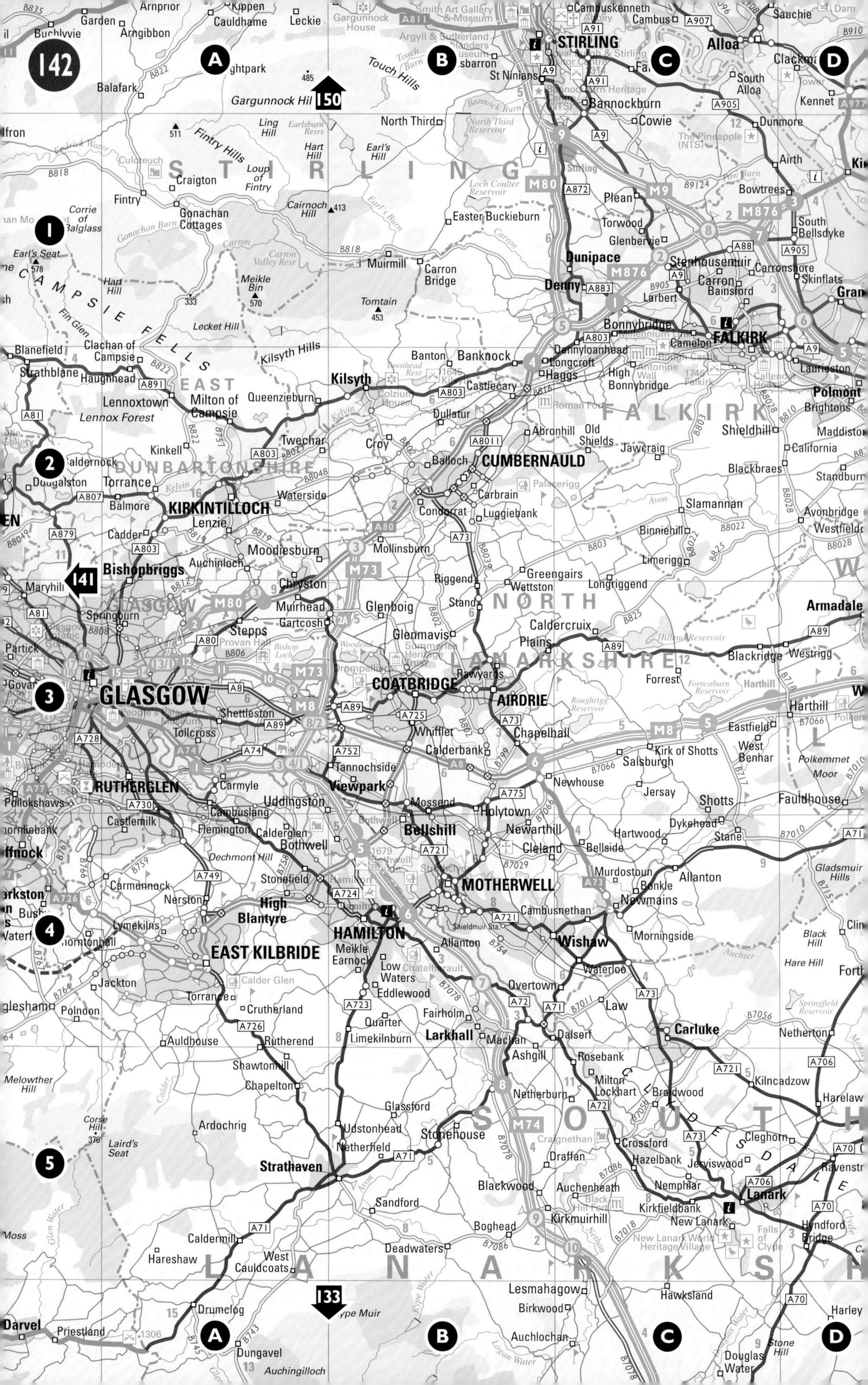
A
B
C
D
1
2
3
4
5
150
141
133
STIRLING
Alloa
Sauchie
Cambuskenneth
Cambus
Clackmannan
South Alloa
Kennet
Dunmore
Airth
Bannockburn
Cowie
St Ninians
Smith Art Gallery & Museum
Argyll & Sutherland Highlanders Museum
Gargunnock House
Touch Hills
Gargunnock Hill
Arnprior
Kippen
Cauldhame
Leckie
Garden
Buchlyvie
Arngibbon
Balafark
North Third
North Third Reservoir
The Pineapple (NTS)
Ling Hill
Earlsburn Resrs
Hart Hill
Earl's Hill
Fintry Hills
Culcreuch
Craigton
Fintry
Loup of Fintry
Gonachan Cottages
Gonachan Burn
Endrick Water
Corrie of Balglass
Earl's Seat
Cairnoch Hill
Loch Coulter Reservoir
Easter Buckieburn
Carron Valley Resr
Meikle Bin
Muirmill
Carron Bridge
Tomtain
Hart Hill
Lecket Hill
CAMPSIE FELLS
Fin Glen
Blanefield
Strathblane
Clachan of Campsie
Haughhead
Lennoxtown
Lennox Forest
Milton of Campsie
Kilsyth Hills
Kilsyth
Queenzieburn
Colzium House
Banton
Banknock
Townhead Resr
Castlecary
Dennyloanhead
Longcroft
Haggs
High Bonnybridge
Bonnybridge
Denny
Dunipace
Plean
Torwood
Glenbervie
Stenhousemuir
Carronshore
Skinflats
Grangemouth
Carron
Bainsford
Larbert
FALKIRK
Camelon
Laurieston
Polmont
Brightons
Callendar House
Rough Castle
Antonine Wall
Bowtrees
South Bellsdyke
Roman Fort
FALKIRK
Shieldhill
Maddiston
California
Blackbraes
Standburn
Avonbridge
Westfield
Slamannan
Binniehill
Limerigg
Jawcraig
Old Shields
Abronhill
Dullatur
CUMBERNAULD
Balloch
Carbrain
Condorrat
Luggiebank
Palacerigg
Twechar
Croy
Kinkell
Baldernock
Dougalston
Torrance
Balmore
KIRKINTILLOCH
Lenzie
Waterside
Cadder
DUNBARTONSHIRE
EAST
Moodiesburn
Auchinloch
Mollinsburn
Bishopbriggs
Maryhill
Springburn
Chryston
Muirhead
Gartcosh
Glenboig
Riggend
Stand
Greengairs
Wattston
Longriggend
NORTH LANARKSHIRE
Caldercruix
Plains
Hillend Reservoir
Armadale
Blackridge
Westrigg
Harthill
Forrest
Forrestburn Reservoir
Roughrigg Reservoir
Glenmavis
Drumpellier
Summerlee Heritage Trust
Rawyards
AIRDRIE
COATBRIDGE
Stepps
Provan Hall
Bishop Loch
Partick
Govan
GLASGOW
Glasgow Botanic Gardens
People's Palace Museum
Shettleston
Tollcross
RUTHERGLEN
Pollokshaws
Giffnock
Carmyle
Tannochside
Viewpark
Uddingston
Cambuslang
Flemington
Castlemilk
Calderglen
Bothwell
Dechmont Hill
Carmunnock
Stonefield
Nerston
High Blantyre
Mossend
Bellshill
Holytown
Newarthill
Cleland
Whifflet
Calderbank
Chapelhall
Newhouse
Eastfield
West Benhar
Kirk of Shotts
Salsburgh
Jersay
Shotts
Fauldhouse
Polkemmet Moor
Dykehead
Stane
Hartwood
Bellside
Murdostoun
Bonkle
Newmains
Allanton
Gladsmuir Hills
MOTHERWELL
Strathclyde
Cambusnethan
Shieldmuir Sta.
Wishaw
Morningside
Waterloo
Overtown
Black Hill
Hare Hill
Forth
HAMILTON
Bothwell Bridge
Lymekilns
EAST KILBRIDE
Thorntonhall
Busby
Jackton
Eaglesham
Polnoon
Calder Glen
Torrance
Crutherland
Meikle Earnock
Low Waters
Chatelherault
Eddlewood
Allanton
Quarter
Limekilnburn
Fairholm
Larkhall
Machan
Dalserf
Law
Carluke
Netherton
Auldhouse
Rutherend
Shawtonhill
Chapelton
Ashgill
Rosebank
Milton Lockhart
Braidwood
Kilncadzow
Harelaw
Netherburn
Melowther Hill
Corse Hill
Laird's Seat
Ardochrig
Glassford
Udstonhead
Netherfield
Stonehouse
Craignethan
Draffan
Crossford
Hazelbank
Cleghorn
Jerviswood
CLYDESDALE
Ravenstruther
Strathaven
Blackwood
Auchenheath
Nemphlar
Lanark
Sandford
Kirkfieldbank
New Lanark
Kirkmuirhill
Black Hill Fort
New Lanark World Heritage Village
Falls of Clyde
Hyndford Bridge
Boghead
Deadwaters
Caldermill
Hareshaw
West Cauldcoats
SOUTH LANARKSHIRE
Lesmahagow
Hawksland
Birkwood
Auchlochan
Harley
Stone Hill
Douglas Water
Darvel
Priestland
Drumclog
Dungavel
Auchingilloch
Kype Muir
M80
M9
M876
M73
M8
M74
A811
A91
A907
A9
A905
A872
A88
A883
A803
A891
A81
A807
A879
A8011
A80
A73
A89
A8
A725
A752
A74
A728
A730
A749
A726
A724
A721
A775
A71
A723
A72
A706
A70
A706
A71
B835
B822
B818
B8048
B8023
B810
B8028
B8022
B803
B825
B802
B8039
B7066
B7070
B7029
B7011
B7056
B7078
B7086
B7018
B743
B745
B764
B767
B766
B759
B758
B754
B816
B9124
B905
B908
B808
B806
B812
B819
B757
B7010
B715
B718
B717
Avon
Kelvin
Calder
Nethan
Kype Water
Logan Water
Glen Water
Douglas Water
Clyde
Auchter
Rowan Burn
Bannock Burn
1645 Kilsyth
1746 Falkirk
1679 Bothwell Bridge
1568
1306
485
511
578
333
570
453
413
376

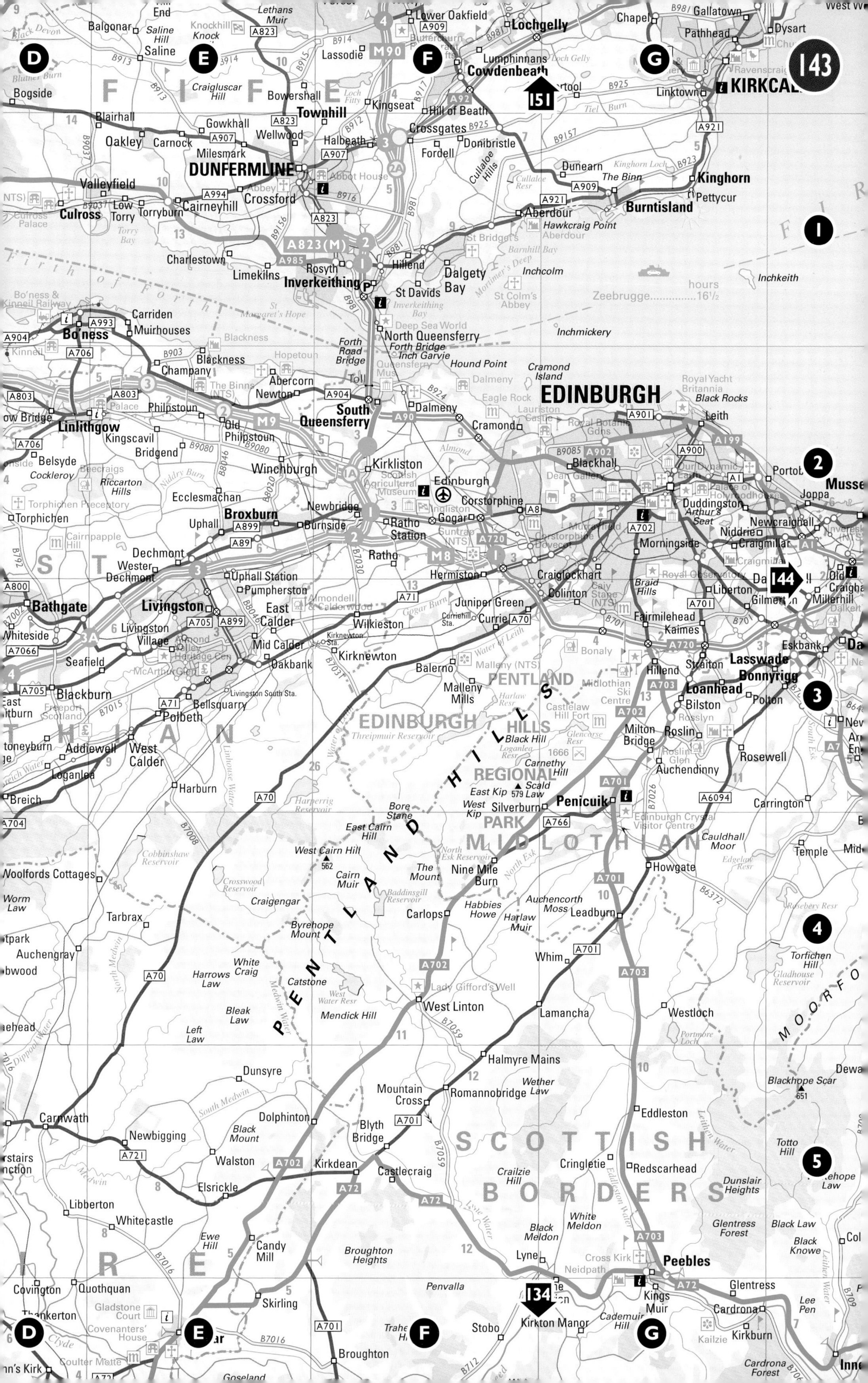
143
D
E
F
G
I
2
3
4
5
151
144
134
FIFE
Firth of Forth
Balgonar
Saline Hill
Saline
Knockhill
Knock
Lethans Muir
A823
Lower Oakfield
A909
Lochgelly
Lassodie
M90
B914
Lumphinnans
Loch Gelly
Cowdenbeath
Chapel
Gallatown
Pathhead
Dysart
Ravenscraig
Linktown
KIRKCALDY
Black Devon
Blairhall Burn
Bogside
Craigluscar Hill
Bowershall
Loch Fitty
Kingseat
Townhill
Hill of Beath
A92
B925
Tiel Burn
Blairhall
Oakley
Carnock
Gowkhall
A907
Wellwood
Halbeath
Crossgates
Donibristle
Fordell
B9157
Cullaloe Hills
Cullaloe Resr
A921
Milesmark
DUNFERMLINE
Abbot House
Abbey
Dunearn
Kinghorn Loch
The Binn
B923
Kinghorn
Pettycur
Valleyfield
A994
Crossford
B916
A909
Burntisland
NTS
Culross Palace
Culross
Low Torry
Torryburn
Cairneyhill
Torry Bay
A823
Aberdour
Hawkcraig Point
Aberdour
B9156
A823(M)
St Bridget's
Barnhill Bay
Charlestown
A985
Limekilns
Rosyth
Hillend
Dalgety Bay
Mortimer's Deep
Inchcolm
St Colm's Abbey
Inverkeithing
St Davids
Inverkeithing Bay
B981
Inchkeith
hours
Zeebrugge..............16½
Bo'ness & Kinneil Railway
Carriden
A993
Bo'ness
Muirhouses
A904
Kinneil
A706
St Margaret's Hope
Blackness
Deep Sea World
North Queensferry
Forth Bridge
Inch Garvie
Forth Road Bridge
Inchmickery
Hopetoun
B903
Blackness
Champany
Queensferry Mus
Hound Point
Cramond Island
The Binns (NTS)
Abercorn
Toll
Dalmeny
Royal Yacht Britannia
Black Rocks
A803
A803
Palace
Newton
A904
Eagle Rock
EDINBURGH
Philpstoun
South Queensferry
Lauriston Castle
A901
Leith
ow Bridge
Linlithgow
Old Philpstoun
M9
B9080
A90
Dalmeny
Cramond
Royal Botanic Gdns
Kingscavil
Bridgend
Almond
B9085
A902
A900
A199
A706
Belsyde
Cockleroy
Beecraigs
Riccarton Hills
B8046
Winchburgh
Kirkliston
Scottish Agricultural Museum
Edinburgh
Blackhall
Dean Gallery
Our Dynamic Earth
A1
Portob
Musse
Niddry Burn
Ecclesmachan
Corstorphine
Palace of Holyroodhouse
Joppa
Torphichen Preceptory
Torphichen
B8020
Broxburn
Newbridge
Ingliston
A8
Duddingston
Arthur's Seat
Uphall
A899
Burnside
Ratho Station
Gogar
Sutran (NTS)
A720
Murrayfield
Corstorphine Dovecot
A702
Niddrie
Newcraighall
Cairnpapple Hill
Dechmont
A89
Ratho
M8
B7030
Morningside
Craigmillar
Craigmillar
Wester Dechmont
Uphall Station
Hermiston
Craiglockhart
Royal Observatory
Da
Old Craighall
A800
Bathgate
Livingston
Pumpherston
Almondell & Calderwood
A71
Colinton
Caiy Stane (NTS)
Braid Hills
Liberton
Gilmerton
Millerhill
Dalkeith
Whiteside
Livingston Village
A705
A899
East Calder
B8046
Gogar Burn
Juniper Green
Curriehill Sta.
Currie
A70
Fairmilehead
A701
Kaimes
B701
A7066
Seafield
Almond Valley Heritage Cen
Mid Calder
Wilkieston
Kirknewton Sta.
Water of Leith
Bonaly
A720
Eskbank
Lasswade
Bonnyrigg
McArthurGlen
Oakbank
Kirknewton
B7031
Balerno
Malleny (NTS)
Hillend
Straiton
A705
Blackburn
Livingston South Sta.
Malleny Mills
PENTLAND
Midlothian Ski Centre
Loanhead
Polton
East
Freeport Scotland
B7015
Bellsquarry
Harlaw Resr
Castlelaw Hill Fort
A703
Bilston
A71
Polbeth
EDINBURGH
HILLS
Glencorse Resr
Rosslyn
Milton Bridge
Roslin
Threipmuir Reservoir
Black Hill
Loganlea Resr
Roslin Glen
Rosewell
Toneyburn
Addiewell
West Calder
Breich Water
Loganlea
Breich
A70
Harburn
Linhouse Water
Water of Leith
26
Carnethy Hill
1666
Auchendinny
REGIONAL
East Kip
579
Scald Law
West Kip
Silverburn
Penicuik
B7026
A6094
Carrington
A704
Harperrig Reservoir
Bore Stane
PARK
A766
Edinburgh Crystal Visitor Centre
B7008
East Cairn Hill
MIDLOTHIAN
Cauldhall Moor
Temple
Cobbinshaw Reservoir
West Cairn Hill
562
North Esk Reservoir
North Esk
Edgelaw Resr
Howgate
Woolfords Cottages
Crosswood Reservoir
Cairn Muir
The Mount
Nine Mile Burn
A701
Worm Law
Craigengar
Baddinsgill Reservoir
Habbies Howe
Auchencorth Moss
Leadburn
B6372
Rosebery Resr
Tarbrax
Carlops
Harlaw Muir
Byrehope Mount
PENTLAND
A701
Whim
Auchengray
North Medwin
White Craig
Harrows Law
A702
A703
Torfichen Hill
Gladhouse Reservoir
A70
Catstone
Lady Gifford's Well
West Water Resr
Medwin Water
West Linton
Lamancha
Westloch
MOORFO
Bleak Law
Mendick Hill
B7059
Portmore Loch
Left Law
Dippool Water
Halmyre Mains
Dunsyre
Wether Law
Mountain Cross
Romannobridge
Blackhope Scar
651
South Medwin
Eddleston
Dewa
Carnwath
Dolphinton
Black Mount
Blyth Bridge
A701
B7059
SCOTTISH
Leithen Water
Newbigging
A721
Walston
Totto Hill
Kirkdean
A702
Crailzie Hill
Cringletie
Redscarhead
Eddleston Water
Castlecraig
Dunslair Heights
Medwin
A72
BORDERS
Elsrickle
A72
Lyne Water
Libberton
Whitecastle
Black Meldon
White Meldon
Glentress Forest
Black Law
Black Knowe
Ewe Hill
Candy Mill
Broughton Heights
Lyne
A703
Cross Kirk
Neidpath
Peebles
Leithen Water
B7016
Gladstone Court
Skirling
Penvalla
Kings Muir
Glentress
Covington
Quothquan
A72
Cardrona
Lee Pen
Covenanters' House
Thankerton
A701
Trahenna Hill
Stobo
Kirkton Manor
Cademuir Hill
Kailzie
Kirkburn
B7016
Clyde
Coulter Motte
Broughton
B712
Cardrona Forest
B709
Goseland

144
A
B
C
D
152
135
143
1
2
3
4
5
FIRTH OF FORTH
Gallatown
West Wemyss
Dysart
Pathhead
Church
KIRKCALDY
A921
B923
Kinghorn
Pettycur
Inchkeith
Rosyth to Zeebrugge............hours 16½
Fidra
Lamb
North Berwick
Craigleith
Bass Rock
Yellowcraig
Scottish Seabird Centre
Tantallon
St Baldred's Boat
Muirfield
Dirleton
Gullane Bay
Gullane Bents
Gullane Point
Gullane
A198
North Berwick Law
Kingston
Auldhame
Whitekirk
B1347
Aberlady Bay
Luffness
Aberlady
EAST LOTHIAN
B1345
B1377
Drem
East Fortune
Tyninghame House
Tyninghame
Craigielaw Point
Friary
Mungoswells
Chesters Hill Fort
Church of Flagpe
Museum of Flight
Preston
Preston Mill & Phantassie Dovecot (NTS)
Gosford House
Gosford Bay
Ballencrieff
Spittal
B1371
A6137
B1343
Athelstaneford
East Linton
Longniddry Bents
Royal Yacht Britannia
Black Rocks
Leith
A900
A199
Cockenzie and Port Seton
Collegiate Church
Longniddry
B1348
Garleton Hills
Traprain
Hailes
Pitcox
Biel Water
Portobello
Prestonpans 1745
Prestonpans
Seton Tower & Hamilton House (NTS)
Meadowmill
Elvingston
St Mary's Church
Church
Stenton
Musselburgh
Palace of Holyroodhouse
Duddingston
Arthur's Seat
Joppa
Levenhall
Cross
A1
Tranent
Gladsmuir
Haddington
Traprain Law Fort
Pressmennan Lake
Newcraighall
Niddrie
Craigmillar
Inveresk
Wallyford
Pinkie 1547
A199
Macmerry
B6414
B6355
B6363
New Winton
Papple
Deuchrie Dod
Whitelaw Hill
Garvald
Lennoxlove
Samuelston
A6093
New Town
Bolton
B6368
B6369
B6370
Nunraw Abbey
Dunbar Common
Clints Dod
Inveresk
Whitecraig
Old Craighall
Gilmerton
Millerhill
Dalkeith
Carberry Tower
Elphinstone
Market Cross
Winton House
Ormiston
Pencaitland
Gifford Church
Gifford
Carfrae
Danskine
White
Rangely Kip
Whiteadder Water
A701
A720
Liberton
B701
Lasswade
Bonnyrigg
Loanhead
Eskbank
Dalkeith
Crossgatehall
Cousland
A6124
West Saltoun
East Saltoun
B6355
Peastonbank
Gilchriston
Longyester
Gifford Water
Birns Water
A68
Newbattle
Straiton
Bilston
Roslin
Rosslyn
Polton
Easthouses
Oxenfoord
Peaston
Newlands Hill
Whiteadder Reservoir
Penshiel Hill
Mayfield
Ford
Pathhead
B6371
Newtongrange
Arniston Engine
Newlandrig
Vogrie
B6482
B6372
B6367
Fala Dam
Humbie
Hopes Water
Faseny Water
Lammer Law 528
Hopes Resr
Meikle Says Law 635
Rosewell
Glencorse
Auchendinny
South Esk
A7
MIDLOTHIAN
Crichton
Fala
B6457
Crib Law
Seenes Law
Meikle Law
LAMMERMUIR
A6094
Carrington
Gorebridge
Borthwick
North Middleton
B6458
Tynehead
West Hill
Soonhope Burn
Edinburgh Crystal Visitor Centre
Cauldhall Moor
Temple
Edgelaw Resr
Middleton
Fala Moor
Dean Burn
Soutra Hill
Dun Law 363
Hunt Law 495
Dye Water
Blythe Edge
Newbigging
B6372
Rosebery Resr
Falahill
Tyne Water
Gilston
B6368
Turf Law
Hogs Law
B7007
MOORFOOT HILLS
Torfichen Hill
Gladhouse Reservoir
Heriot
Oxton
Carfraemill
Earnscleugh Water
Westloch
Portmore Loch
B709
Heriot Water
Gala Water
SCOTTISH BORDERS
Collie Law
A697
Scoured Rig
Inchkeith Hill
Edgarhope Wood
LAUDERDALE
Westruther
B6456
Dun Law
Dewar
Dewar Burn
Blackhope Scar 651
Fountainhall
Torquhan
Thirlestane Castle
Lauder
Thirlestane
Houndslow
Whiteburn
Ladyside Height
Cockholm Burn
Lauder Common
Eddleston
Leithen Water
B709
Totto Hill
Galabank
B6362
Eastside Heights
Killochyett
Stow
Lugate Water
A6089
Nether Blainslie
Greenknowe Tower
Dunslair Heights
Whitehope Law
Windlestraw Law 659
Torsonce
Huntlywood
Legerwood
Glentress Forest
Black Law
Black Knowe
Colquhar
Yardstone Knowe
Great Law
Birkhill
A6105
Leader Water
Seathope Law
Peebles
A72
Glentress
Priesthope Hill
Lee Pen
B709
Fans
William Law
Caddon Water
Langshaw
Cardrona
Kailzie
Kirkburn
Walkerburn
Innerleithen
Thornylee
Knowes Hill
Clovenfords
Torwoodlee
Buckholm
Galashiels
Glendearg
Earlston
Meigle Hill
Woollen Mill
Cardrona Forest
Mellerstain
B6356

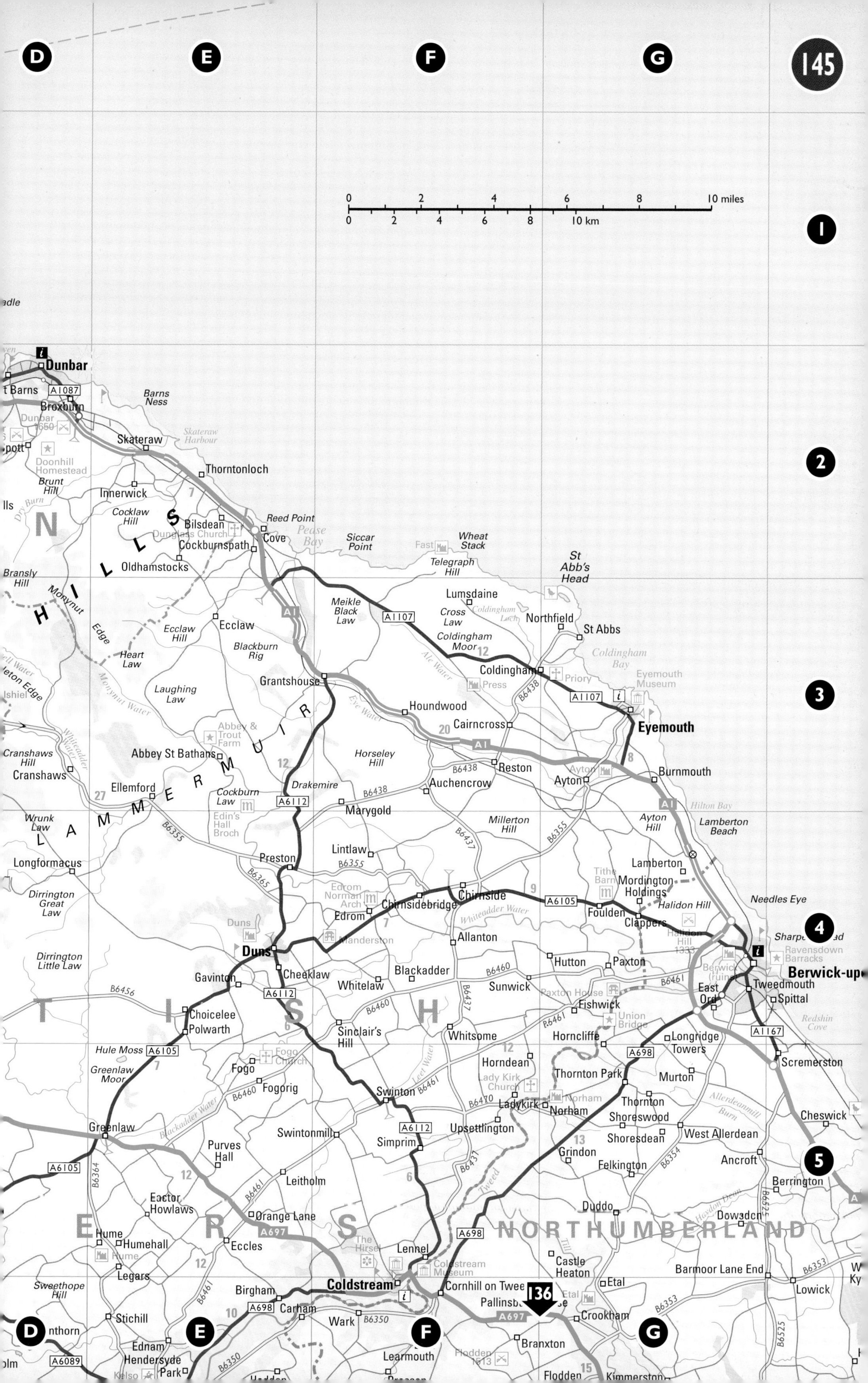
D
E
F
G
1
2
3
4
5
0
2
4
6
8
10 miles
0
2
4
6
8
10 km
Dunbar
Barns
A1087
Broxburn
Barns Ness
Dunbar 1650
Skateraw
Skateraw Harbour
Doonhill Homestead
Brunt Hill
Thorntonloch
Innerwick
Cocklaw Hill
Dry Burn
Bilsdean
Reed Point
Pease Bay
Dunglass Church
Cove
Cockburnspath
Siccar Point
Fast
Wheat Stack
Telegraph Hill
St Abb's Head
Oldhamstocks
Bransly Hill
Monynut Edge
Meikle Black Law
A1107
Lumsdaine
Cross Law
Coldingham Loch
Northfield
St Abbs
Coldingham Moor
Coldingham Bay
Ecclaw Hill
Ecclaw
Blackburn Rig
Heart Law
Coldingham
Priory
Press
B6438
Eyemouth Museum
Grantshouse
Laughing Law
Monynut Water
Eye Water
Ale Water
Houndwood
A1107
Eyemouth
Cairncross
Abbey & Trout Farm
Whiteadder Water
Cranshaws Hill
Cranshaws
Abbey St Bathans
Horseley Hill
A1
Reston
B6438
Burnmouth
Ayton
Ellemford
Drakemire
Cockburn Law
Auchencrow
A6112
Marygold
Hilton Bay
Ayton Hill
Lamberton Beach
Wrunk Law
Edin's Hall Broch
B6355
Millerton Hill
B6437
B6355
Longformacus
Preston
Lintlaw
B6355
B6365
Lamberton
Tithe Barn
Mordington Holdings
Dirrington Great Law
Edrom Norman Arch
Edrom
Chirnside
Chirnsidebridge
A6105
Foulden
Halidon Hill
Needles Eye
Clappers
Halidon Hill 1333
Sharpe... Head
Duns
Manderston
Allanton
Dirrington Little Law
Duns
Cheeklaw
Blackadder
Hutton
Paxton
Ravensdown Barracks
Berwick-up...
Berwick (ruins)
B6456
Gavinton
Whitelaw
B6460
Sunwick
B6461
East Ord
Tweedmouth
Spittal
A6112
B6437
Paxton House
Fishwick
Choicelee
Polwarth
B6460
Union Bridge
Redshin Cove
Sinclair's Hill
Whitsome
Horncliffe
Longridge Towers
A1167
Hule Moss
A6105
Fogo Church
Fogo
Horndean
A698
Scremerston
Greenlaw Moor
Fogorig
B6460
Blackadder Water
Leet Water
Lady Kirk Church
Thornton Park
Murton
Swinton
B6461
B6470
Ladykirk
Norham
Thornton
Allerdeanmill Burn
Greenlaw
Swintonmill
A6112
Upsettlington
Shoreswood
Cheswick
Simprim
Shoresdean
West Allerdean
Purves Hall
B6437
Grindon
Felkington
B6354
Ancroft
A6105
B6364
B6461
Leitholm
Tweed
Berrington
Eccles
Howlaws
Duddo
Haydon Dean
B6525
Orange Lane
Dowsdon
Hume
A697
A698
NORTHUMBERLAND
Humehall
Eccles
The Hirsel
Lennel
Castle Heaton
Hume
Legars
Coldstream Museum
Barmoor Lane End
B6353
Sweethope Hill
B6461
Birgham
Coldstream
Cornhill on Tweed
Etal
Lowick
Pallinsburn House
136
Etal
Crookham
A698
Carham
B6353
Stichill
Wark
B6350
A697
Ednam
Hendersyde Park
Learmouth
Branxton
Flodden 1513
B6525
A6089
Kelso
B6350
Flodden
Kimmerston
L A M M E R M U I R
H I L L S
T I B E R S
R
S
H
E

A
B
C
D
1
2
3
4
5
154
138
Cairn na Burgh More
Cairn na Burgh Beg
t-Suibhein
Port Burg
Loch Tuath
Fanmore
Sgeir a Chaisteil
Fladda
Rubha Chulinish
Lunga
Gometra
Gometra Ho.
Bearnus
Beinn Chreagach
Rubha Maol na Mine
Beinn Eolasary
ULVA
Maisgeir
A'Chranr
Bac Mor or Dutchman's Cap
Bac Beag
Little Colonsay
Staffa
Eilean Dubh
Staffa (NTS)
Fingal's Cave
Inch Kenneth
Erisgeir
Creach Bheinn
491
Ardmeanach
Bearraich
Burg (NTS)
Aird na h-Iolaire
Reidh Eilean
Eilean Chalbha
Rubha nan Cearc
Carraig Mhic Thomais
Dun I
Maclean's Cross
Port an Duine Mhairbh
Iona Abbey
Kintra
Beinn Chladan
Baile Mor
Iona (NTS)
Ardchrishnish
Stac an Aoineidh
Ruanaich
Iona
Fionnphort
Aridhglas
Loch na Lathaich
Eorabus
Ardtun
A849
Bunessan
Lee
Fidden
Sound of Iona
Rubha na Carraig-geire
Loch Assapol
Ross of Mull
Knockvologan
Ardalanish
Uisken
Scoor
Soa Island
Erraid
Eilean Dubh
Torr Fada
Ardchiavaig
Port Mor
Aird Mor
Eilean a'Chalmain
Eilean Mor
Rubh' Ardalanish
Dearg Sgeir
Torran Rocks
Ruadh Sgeir
Na Torrain
West Reef
McPhail's Anvil
Torran Sgoilte
Sgeir Ghobhlach
Otter Rock
Dubh Artach
Balnahard
Kiloran Bay
Port Ceann a'Gharraidh
Kiloran Gardens
Loch an Sgoltaire
COLONSAY
Kiloran
Colonsay
Upper Kilchattan
B8086
B8087
Lower Kilchattan
L. Fada
Scalasaig
Port Mor
Machrins
B8085
Port Lotha
Baleromindubh
Sguide Loinne
Garvard
Balerominmore
Eilean Mhucaig
Port Askaig
Rubha Ban
Priory
Dubh Eilean
Oronsay
Eilean Ghaoideamal
Eilean nan Ron
Caolas Mor
0
2
4
6
8
10 miles
0
2
4
6
8
10 km

D
E
F
G
I
2
3
4
5
155
148
139
MULL
ARGYLL AND BUTE
FIRTH OF LORN
JURA
Salen
Pennygown
A849
Lochaline
Inninbeg
Glais Bheinn
479
Mam a' Chullaich
a' Chaorainn
481
An Sleaghach
513
Eignaig
Lynn of Morven
Lismore
Killiechronan
Kellan
B8073
B8035
Cruach Torran Lochain
Killbeg
Balmeanach
Garmony
Ardtornish Point
Inninmore Bay
Rubha an Ridire
Bernera
Achadun (ruin)
Kilcheran
Loch Fiart
Lagganulva
Killiemor
Gruline
Knock
Loch Na Keal
Loch Ba
Beinn Bhuidhe
412
Glen Forsa
Beinn Chreagach Mhor
579
Salen Forest
Scallastle Bay
Scallastle
Craignure Bay
Craignure
Mull & West Highland Railway
Torosay Castle
Duart Bay
Duart
Duart Point
Lady's Rock
Eilean Musdile
¾ hr
Eorsa
Beinn a'Ghraig
591
Na Binneinean
Gaodhail
Beinn Mheadhon
637
Beinn na Duatharach
Dun da Ghaoithe
766
Maol nan Uan
Clachandhu
Dhiseig
Beinn Fhada
702
Gortenbuie
Beinn Talaidh
761
Sgurr Dearg
741
Lochdon
Ben More
966
Cruachan Dearg
704
Beinn Chaisgidle
504
Corra-bheinn
704
Coirc Bheinn
561
Guibean Uluvailt
Cruach Choireadail
Glen More
Ishriff
Ardachoil
Oakbank
Gorten
Ardnadrochit
Loch Don
Grass Point
Maiden Island
Rubh' a'Bhearnaig
Eilean nan Gamhna
Maol na Coille Moire
Balevulin
Dererach
Uluvalt
Craig
Ardura
Cruach Ardura
Glas Bheinn
Auchnacraig
Carn Ban
Port Donain
Ruba na Lice
Ardantrive
Barr-nam-boc Bay
Balliemore
Kerrera
Upper Gylen
Gylen
Sound of Kerrera
Loch Beg
Aird of Kinloch
Kilfinichen Bay
Cruach nan Con
Creag na h-Iolaire
Loch Airdeglais
Beinn Fhada
Creach Beinn
698
Fellonmore
Loch Spelve
Croggan
Rubha na Faoilinn
Ardmore
Bach Island
Maol nan Uan
Pennyghael
Killunaig
A849
Loch Fuaron
Beinn na Croise
503
Ben Buie
717
Kinlochspelve
Dalnaha
Portfield
Rubha Seanach
Dubh Sgeir
Minard Point
Ardentallan
Lochbuie
Loch Uisg
Creag nam Fitheach
Maol Ban
Brolass
Leidle
Glenbyre
Loch Buie
Druim Fada
405
Barnacarry Bay
Barnacarry
Beinn Chreagach
376
Carsaig
Beinn a'Bhainne
Eilean Duin
Kilninver
Creachan Mor
Nun's Pass
Carsaig Bay
Rubha Dubh
Port Ohirnie
Rubha Garbh Airde
Ardencaple House
B844
Frank Lockwood's Island
Insh Island
Sound of Insh
Ardfad
Clachan-Seil
Malcolm's Point
An Cala Garden
Dun-Mor
Seil
Ardshellach
Folk Museum
Easdale
Balvicar
Henderson's Rock
B8003
Caddleton
Cuan Sound
Seil Sound
Melfort
Garvellachs
Isles of the Sea
Cullipool
Torsay Island
Kilchoan
Ardanstur
Garbh Eileach
Belnahua
Glas Eilean
Ardinamar
Degnish
Degnish Point
Loch Melfort
A'Chuli
Eilean Gamhna
Luing
Kames
Monastery (ruin)
Eilean Dubh Mor
Arduaine Garden (NTS)
Arduaine
Eileach an Naoimh
Lunga
Sound of Luing
Toberonochy
Black Mill Bay
Shuna
Asknish Bay
Barravullin
2¼ hrs
Guirasdeal
Eilean Arsa
Shuna Sound
Craobh Haven
Lunga
Shuna Point
Gemmil
Cruach Scarba
449
Ardfern
Kintraw
Barrackan
Eilean Mhic Chrion
Scarba
Bagh Ban
Bagh Gleann a'Mhaoil
Corranmore
B8002
Tibertich
Rubha Righinn
Str. of Corryvreckan
Reisa Mhic Phaidean
Craignish Sculptured Stones
Eilean Righ
Kirkton
Carnassarie
Old Poltalloch
Beinn nan Capull
Kinuachdrachd
Reisa an t-Sruith
Kilmartin
Sculptured Stones
Stone Circle
Kinuachdrach Harbour
Craignish Point
Island Macaskin
Slockavullin
Ri Cruin Cairn
Glengarrisdale Bay
Bagh Gleann Speireig
Glengarrisdale
Cruach na Seilcheig
Poltalloch
Rubha Garbh-ard
Barsloisnoch
Crinan Loch
Glendebadel Bay
Ben Garrisdale
365
Lealt Burn
Ardnoe Point
Crinan
B8025
Dunadd
Cruach Ionnastail
Lussa
Corpach Bay
Bellanoch
Moine Mhor
Beinn Bhreac
467
Lealt
Rubha nam Barr
Cnoc Reamhar
265
Arichonan
Ardnackaig
B841
Cairnbaan
Gallchoille
Arinafad Beg
Gariob
Craigglass
Dubh Bheinn
Carsaig Island
Knapdale Forest
Tarbert
Tramaig Bay
Rainberg Mor
453
Cruach Sganadail
Ardlussa
Carsaig Bay
Seafield
Auchindrain
Shian Bay
Lussagiven
Inverlussa
Lussa Point
Eilean an Rubha
Eilean Dubh
Tayvallich
Achnamara
Cruach Breacain
360
Aoistail

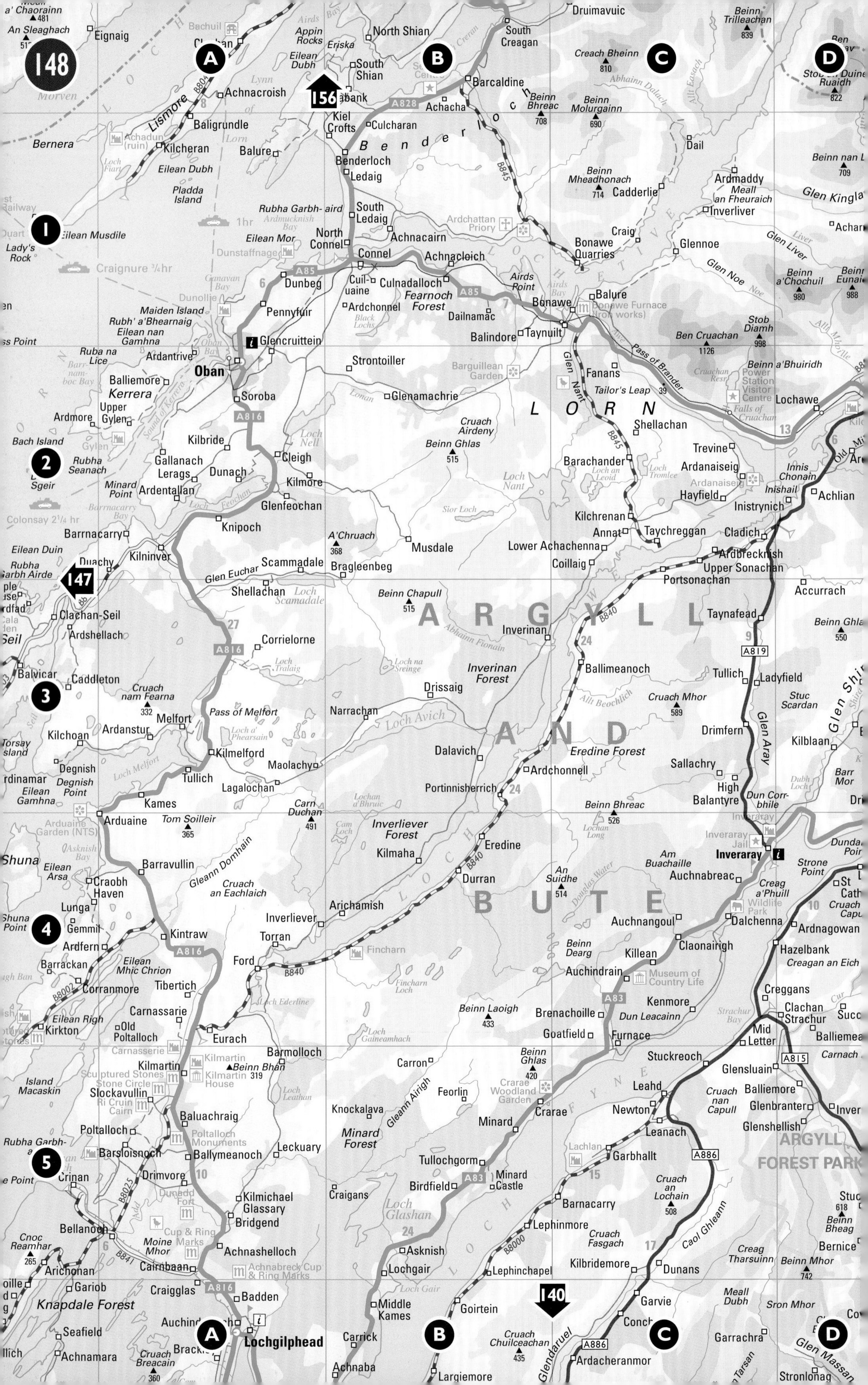
a' Chaorainn
481
An Sleaghach
Eignaig
Bachuil
Clachan
A
B
C
D
Morven
Lismore
B8044
Achnacroish
Appin Rocks
Eriska
Eilean Dubh
156
North Shian
South Shian
Benderloch
Baligrundle
Achadun (ruin)
Kilcheran
Bernera
Loch Fiart
Eilean Dubh
Pladda Island
Balure
Kiel Crofts
Culcharan
Benderloch
Ledaig
South Ledaig
Rubha Garbh-aird
Ardmucknish Bay
Eilean Mor
North Connel
Connel
Achnacairn
Achnacloich
Dunstaffnage
1hr
Eilean Musdile
Lady's Rock
Craignure ¾hr
Railway
Ganavan Bay
Dunbeg
Cuil-uaine
Culnadalloch
Fearnoch Forest
A85
A828
Dunollie
Maiden Island
Rubh' a'Bhearnaig
Eilean nan Gamhna
Pennyfuir
Ardchonnel
Black Lochs
Dailnamac
Glencruittein
Oban
Oban Bay
Ardantrive
Ruba na Lice
Barr-nam-boc Bay
Balliemore
Kerrera
Ardmore
Upper Gylen
Gylen
Sound of Kerrera
Soroba
A816
Strontoiller
Glenamachrie
Loch Nell
Kilbride
Bach Island
Rubha Seanach
Gallanach
Lerags
Dunach
Cleigh
Kilmore
Minard Point
Ardentallan
Loch Feochan
Glenfeochan
Sgeir
Barrnacarry Bay
Colonsay 2¼ hr
Knipoch
Barrnacarry
Eilean Duin
Rubha Garbh Airde
Duachy
Kilninver
147
Glen Euchar
Scammadale
Shellachan
Loch Scamadale
Clachan-Seil
Ardshellach
Seil
Balvicar
Caddleton
Corrielorne
Loch Tralaig
Cruach nam Fearna
332
Melfort
Pass of Melfort
Loch a' Phearsain
Ardanstur
Kilchoan
Torsay Island
Kilmelford
Degnish
Degnish Point
Loch Melfort
Ardinamar
Eilean Gamhna
Tullich
Lagalochan
Kames
Arduaine
Arduaine Garden (NTS)
Asknish Bay
Tom Soilleir
365
Shuna
Eilean Arsa
Barravullin
Craobh Haven
Lunga
Shuna Point
Gemmil
Ardfern
Barrackan
Eilean Mhic Chrion
Kintraw
Gleann Domhain
Cruach an Eachlaich
B8002
Corranmore
Tibertich
Carnassarie
Eilean Righ
Kirkton
Old Poltalloch
Carnasserie
Kilmartin
Kilmartin House
Beinn Bhan
319
Sculptured Stones
Stone Circle
Island Macaskin
Slockavullin
Ri Cruin Cairn
Baluachraig
Poltalloch
Rubha Garbh-
Barsloisnoch
Poltalloch Monuments
Ballymeanoch
Drimvore
Dunadd Fort
B8025
Crinan
Bellanoch
Kilmichael Glassary
Bridgend
Cup & Ring Marks
Moine Mhor
Achnashelloch
B841
Cnoc Reamhar
265
Arichonan
Cairnbaan
Achnabreck Cup & Ring Marks
Gariob
Craigglas
Badden
Knapdale Forest
Auchindrain
Seafield
Brackley
Lochgilphead
Cruach Breacain
360
Achnamara
Druimavuic
South Creagan
Creagan
Sea Life Centre
Barcaldine
Achacha
Benderloch
B845
Creach Bheinn
810
Abhainn Dalach
Allt Easach
Beinn Bhreac
708
Beinn Molurgainn
690
Beinn Trilleachan
839
Ben Starav
Stob Coire an Albannaich
Stob an Duine Ruaidh
822
Dail
Beinn nan Lus
709
Beinn Mheadhonach
714
Cadderlie
Ardmaddy
Meall an Fheuraich
Glen Kinglass
Inverliver
Ardchattan Priory
Craig
Bonawe Quarries
Loch Etive
Glennoe
Glen Liver
Glen Noe
Achara
Beinn a'Chochuil
980
Beinn Eunaich
988
Airds Point
Airds Bay
Bonawe
Balure
Bonawe Furnace (iron works)
Taynuilt
Balindore
Stob Diamh
998
Ben Cruachan
1126
Pass of Brander
River Awe
Glen Nant
Fanans
Tailor's Leap
39
Barguillean Garden
Cruachan Resr
Beinn a'Bhuiridh
Power Station Visitor Centre
Falls of Cruachan
Lochawe
13
L O R N
Cruach Airdeny
Beinn Ghlas
515
Shellachan
B845
Barachander
Loch an Leoid
Loch Tromlee
Trevine
Ardanaiseig
Loch Nant
Sior Loch
Hayfield
Innis Chonain
Inishail
Achlian
Old Military Road
Kilchrenan
Annat
Taychreggan
Inistrynich
Cladich
A'Chruach
368
Musdale
Lower Achachenna
Coillaig
Ardbrecknish
Upper Sonachan
Bragleenbeg
Portsonachan
Accurrach
Beinn Chapull
515
A R G Y L L
B840
Loch Awe
Inverinan
Taynafead
Beinn Ghlas
550
Abhainn Fionain
Loch na Sreinge
9
A819
Inverinan Forest
Ballimeanoch
Tullich
Ladyfield
Allt Beochlich
Cruach Mhor
589
Stuc Scardan
Glen Shira
Drissaig
Narrachan
Loch Avich
A N D
Eredine Forest
Drimfern
Glen Aray
Kilblaan
Dalavich
Ardchonnell
Sallachry
Maolachy
Portinnisherrich
24
High Balantyre
Barr Mor
Dubh Loch
Carn Duchan
491
Lochan a'Bhruic
Cam Loch
Beinn Bhreac
526
Lochan Long
Dun Corr-bhile
Inveraray Castle
Inveraray Jail
Inveraray
Inverliever Forest
Kilmaha
Eredine
Am Buachaille
An Suidhe
514
Douglas Water
Auchnabreac
Strone Point
Dundarave Point
Durran
Creag a'Phuill
Wildlife Park
St Catherines
Cruach Capull
B U T E
Arichamish
Inverliever
Auchnangoul
Dalchenna
Ardnagowan
10
Torran
Fincharn
Beinn Dearg
Killean
Claonairigh
Hazelbank
Creagan an Eich
Ford
B840
Fincharn Loch
Auchindrain
Museum of Country Life
A83
Loch Ederline
Beinn Laoigh
433
Kenmore
Creggans
Brenachoille
Dun Leacainn
Strachur Bay
Clachan Strachur
Succoth
Eurach
Loch Gaineamhach
Goatfield
Furnace
Mid Letter
Balliemeanoch
Barmolloch
Carron
Beinn Ghlas
420
Stuckreoch
A815
Carnach
Loch Leathan
Gleann Airigh
Feorlin
Crarae Woodland Garden
Loch Fyne
Leahd
Glensluain
Knockalava
Minard
Crarae
Newton
Cruach nan Capull
Balliemore
Glenbranter
Inverchapel
Minard Forest
Leanach
Glenshellish
ARGYLL FOREST PARK
Leckuary
Tullochgorm
Lachlan
Garbhallt
A886
Minard Castle
Birdfield
A83
15
Cruach an Lochain
508
Craigens
Loch Glashan
Barnacarry
Caol Ghleann
Stuc
618
Beinn Bheag
24
Lephinmore
Cruach Fasgach
Bernice
Asknish
17
Creag Tharsuinn
Beinn Mhor
742
Lochgair
B8000
Lephinchapel
Kilbridemore
Dunans
Loch Gair
140
Middle Kames
Garvie
Meall Dubh
Sron Mhor
Goirtein
Conchra
Carrick
Cruach Chuileachan
435
Glendaruel
A886
Garrachra
Glen Massan
Achnaba
Ardacheranmor
Largiemore
Stronlonag
1
2
3
4
5
6
7
8
10
27

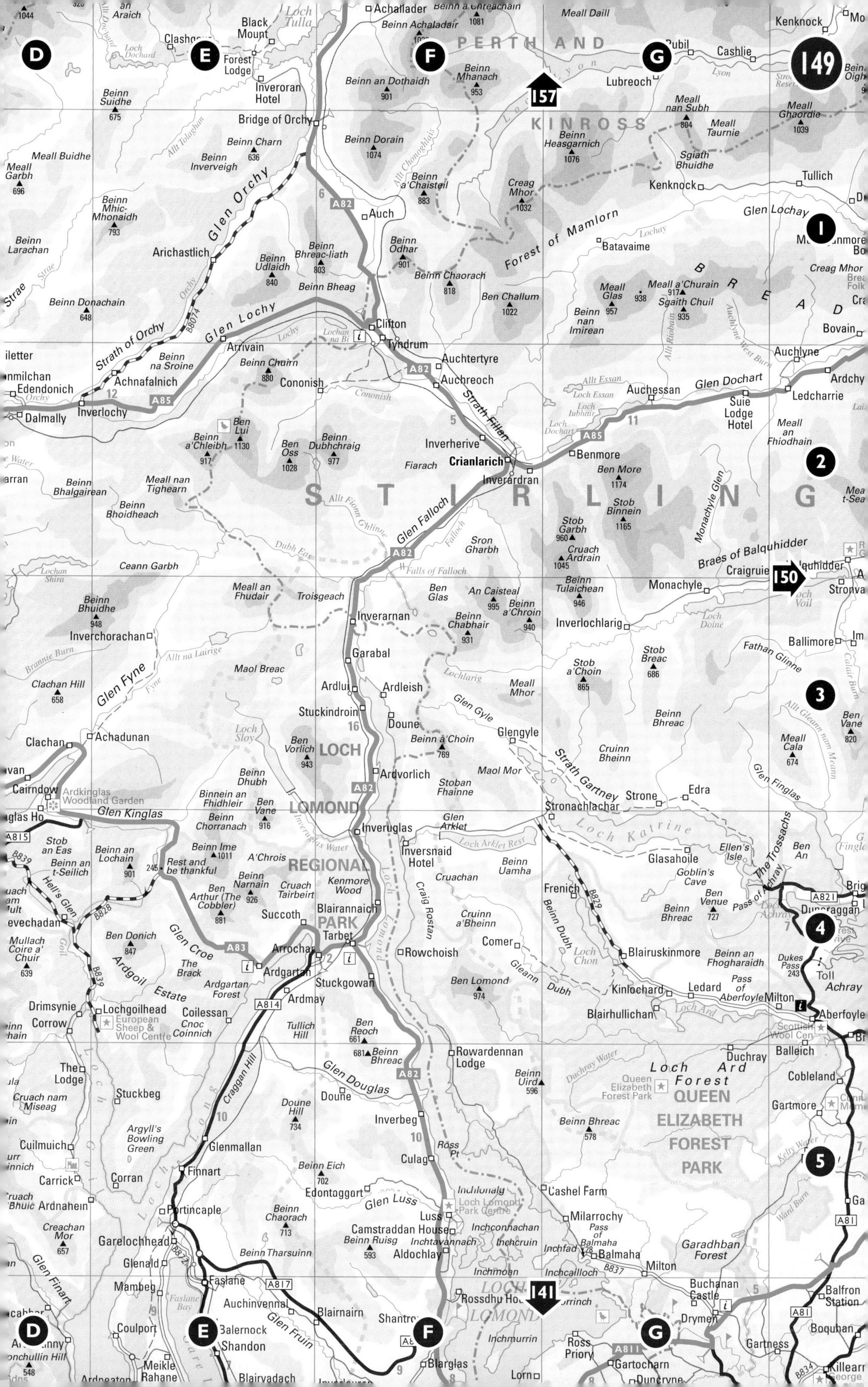
149
157
150
141
D
E
F
G
I
2
3
4
5
PERTH AND
KINROSS
STIRLING
LOCH
LOMOND
REGIONAL
PARK
QUEEN
ELIZABETH
FOREST
PARK
Loch Tulla
Black Mount
Clashgour
Forest Lodge
Inveroran Hotel
Loch Dochard
Achallader
Beinn Achaladair
Beinn a' Chreachain
1081
Meall Daill
Beinn Mhanach
953
Beinn an Dothaidh
901
Pubil
Cashlie
Lubreoch
Kenknock
Lyon
Beinn Suidhe
675
Bridge of Orchy
Beinn Dorain
1074
Meall nan Subh
804
Meall Taurnie
Meall Ghaordie
1039
Beinn Heasgarnich
1076
Sgiath Bhuidhe
Beinn Charn
636
Beinn Inverveigh
Allt Tolaghan
Meall Buidhe
Meall Garbh
696
Glen Orchy
Beinn a' Chaisteil
883
Allt Chonoghlais
Creag Mhor
1032
Kenknock
Tullich
Glen Lochay
Beinn Mhic-Mhonaidh
793
A82
Auch
Forest of Mamlorn
Batavaime
Lochay
Beinn Larachan
Arichastlich
Beinn Udlaidh
840
Beinn Bhreac-liath
803
Beinn Odhar
901
Beinn Chaorach
818
Creag Mhor
Meall Glas
957
938
Meall a' Churain
917
Sgiath Chuil
935
BREADALBANE
Straе
Orchy
B8074
Beinn Donachain
648
Beinn Bheag
Glen Lochy
Clifton
Ben Challum
1022
Beinn nan Imirean
Bovain
Allt Riobain
Auchlyne West Burn
Strath of Orchy
Lochy
Lochan na Bi
Tyndrum
Arrivain
Beinn na Sroine
Beinn Chuirn
880
Auchtertyre
Auchlyne
Achnafalnich
Cononish
Auchreoch
Strath Fillan
Allt Essan
Loch Essan
Loch Iubhair
Auchessan
Glen Dochart
Suie Lodge Hotel
Ardchyle
Ledcharrie
Edendonich
Dalmally
Inverlochy
A85
Ben Lui
1130
Beinn a' Chleibh
917
Ben Oss
1028
Beinn Dubhchraig
977
Loch Dochart
Inverherive
Crianlarich
Inverardran
Benmore
Ben More
1174
Meall an Fhiodhain
Fiarach
Beinn Bhalgairean
Meall nan Tighearn
Beinn Bhoidheach
Allt Fionn Ghlinne
Glen Falloch
Stob Binnein
1165
Stob Garbh
960
Cruach Ardrain
1045
Monachyle Glen
Sron Gharbh
Falloch
Dubh Eas
Ceann Garbh
Lochan Shira
Falls of Falloch
Braes of Balquhidder
Balquhidder
Craigruie
Monachyle
Stronvar
Loch Voil
Beinn Bhuidhe
948
Meall an Fhudair
Troisgeach
Ben Glas
An Caisteal
995
Beinn a' Chroin
940
Beinn Tulaichean
946
Inverlochlarig
Loch Doine
Inverchorachan
Inverarnan
Beinn Chabhair
931
Ballimore
Brannie Burn
Allt na Lairige
Garabal
Stob Breac
686
Fathan Glinne
Maol Breac
Lochlarig
Stob a' Choin
865
Clachan Hill
658
Glen Fyne
Ardlui
Ardleish
Meall Mhor
Glen Gyle
Stuckindroin
Doune
Beinn Bhreac
Ben Vane
820
Clachan
Achadunan
Loch Sloy
Ben Vorlich
943
Beinn a' Choin
769
Glengyle
Strath Gartney
Cruinn Bheinn
Meall Cala
674
Allt Gleann nam Meann
Glen Finglas
Cairndow
Ardkinglas Woodland Garden
Beinn Dhubh
Binnein an Fhidhlein
Ardvorlich
Maol Mor
Stoban Fhainne
Strone
Edra
Glen Kinglas
Ben Vane
916
Stronachlachar
Beinn Chorranach
Inveruglas
Glen Arklet
Loch Katrine
The Trossachs
Ben An
Stob an Eas
Beinn an Lochain
901
Beinn Ime
1011
Inveruglas Water
Loch Arklet Res
Inversnaid Hotel
Glasahoile
Ellen's Isle
Beinn an t-Seilich
245
Rest and be thankful
A'Chrois
Beinn Narnain
926
Kenmore Wood
Beinn Uamha
Goblin's Cave
Hell's Glen
Cruachan
Craig Rostan
Frenich
Ben Venue
727
Pass of Achray
A821
Duncraggan
Ben Arthur (The Cobbler)
881
Cruach Tairbeirt
Blairannaich
Beinn Bhreac
B828
Succoth
Cruinn a' Bheinn
B829
Beinn Dubh
Glen Croe
Ben Donich
847
Arrochar
Tarbet
Comer
Loch Chon
Blairuskinmore
Beinn an Fhogharaidh
Dukes Pass
243
Toll
Achray
Mullach Coire a' Chuir
639
The Brack
A83
Ardgartan
Rowchoish
Gleann Dubh
Ardgoil Estate
Ardgartan Forest
Stuckgowan
Ben Lomond
974
Kinlochard
Ledard
Pass of Aberfoyle
Milton
B839
Ardmay
Drimsynie
Lochgoilhead
European Sheep & Wool Centre
Coilessan
Cnoc Coinnich
A814
Blairhullichan
Loch Ard
Aberfoyle
Corrow
Tullich Hill
Ben Reoch
661
681
Beinn Bhreac
Rowardennan Lodge
Scottish Wool Centre
Balleich
Duchray
Glen Douglas
Duchray Water
Loch Ard Forest
Cobleland
The Lodge
Craggan Hill
Beinn Uird
596
Queen Elizabeth Forest Park
Gartmore
Cruach nam Miseag
Stuckbeg
Doune
Doune Hill
734
Argyll's Bowling Green
Inverbeg
Beinn Bhreac
578
Cuilmuich
Glenmallan
Ross Pt
Kelty Water
Culag
Carrick
Corran
Finnart
Beinn Eich
702
Edentaggart
Cashel Farm
Glen Luss
Inchlonaig
Loch Lomond Park Centre
Ward Burn
Cruach a' Bhuic
Ardnahein
Portincaple
Beinn Chaorach
713
Luss
Milarrochy
Creachan Mor
657
Camstraddan House
Inchconnachan
Pass of Balmaha
Garelochhead
Beinn Ruisg
593
Aldochlay
Inchtavannach
Inchcruin
Inchfad
Balmaha
Garadhban Forest
Glenald
Beinn Tharsuinn
B872
Inchmoan
Inchcailloch
B837
Milton
Glen Finart
Mambeg
Faslane
Faslane Bay
A817
Buchanan Castle
Balfron Station
Auchinvennal
Rossdhu House
Glen Fruin
Blairnairn
Shantron
Drymen
Coulport
Balernock
Shandon
Ross Priory
Gartness
Boquhan
A811
Gartocharn
Duncryne
Inchmurrin
Lorn
Blarglas
Meikle Rahane
Blairvadach
Ardpeaton
Killearn
B834
A81
548

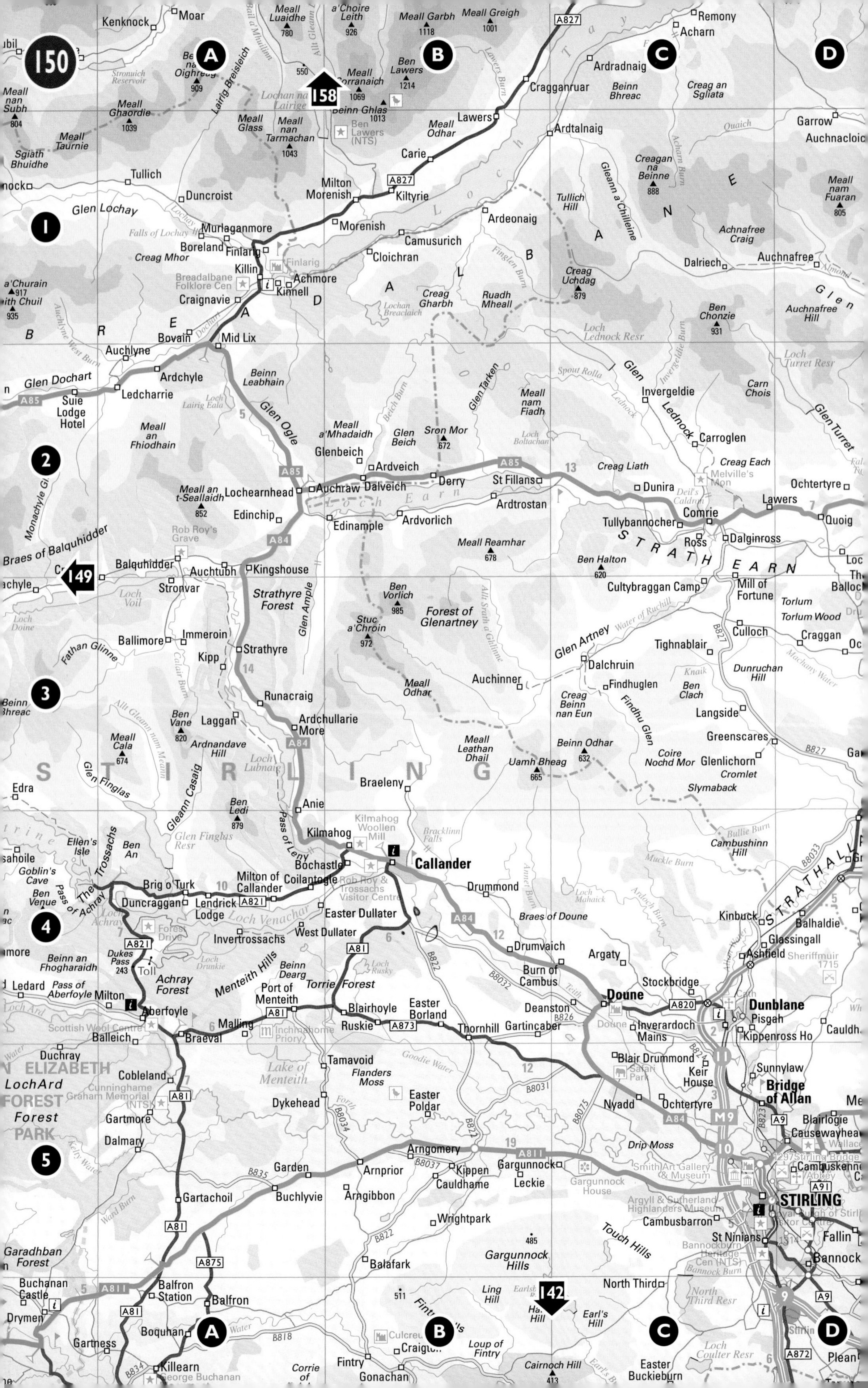
A
B
C
D
1
2
3
4
5
158
149
142
Kenknock
Moar
Meall Luaidhe 780
a'Choire Leith 926
Meall Garbh 1118
Meall Greigh 1001
A827
Remony
Acharn
Ardradnaig
Beinn nan Oighreag 909
Stronuich Reservoir
Lairig Breisleich
Meall Corranaich 1069
Ben Lawers 1214
Beinn Ghlas 1013
Ben Lawers (NTS)
Lochan na Lairige
550
Cragganruar
Beinn Bhreac
Creag an Sgliata
Meall nan Subh 804
Meall Ghaordie 1039
Meall Taurnie
Sgiath Bhuidhe
Meall Glass
Meall nan Tarmachan 1043
Meall Odhar
Lawers
Ardtalnaig
Garrow
Auchnacloich
Quaich
Carie
Creagan na Beinne 888
Acharn Burn
Gleann a'Chilleine
Tullich
Milton Morenish
Kiltyrie
Duncroist
Tullich Hill
Meall nam Fuaran 805
Glen Lochay
Murlaganmore
Falls of Lochay
Morenish
Ardeonaig
Boreland
Finlarig
Camusurich
Creag Mhor
Killin
Cloichran
Breadalbane Folklore Cen
Achmore
Kinnell
Finglen Burn
Dalriech
Auchnafree
Achnafree Craig
Almond
Creag Uchdag 879
Loch Tay
Breadalbane
a'Churain 917
Sgiath Chuil 935
Craignavie
Creag Gharbh
Lochan Breaclaich
Ruadh Mheall
Ben Chonzie 931
Auchnafree Hill
Glen Almond
Auchlyne West Burn
Bovain
Mid Lix
Loch Lednock Resr
Invergeldie Burn
Auchlyne
Loch Turret Resr
Glen Dochart
Ardchyle
Beinn Leabhain
Spout Rolla
Glen Lednock
Carn Chois
Ledcharrie
Loch Lairig Eala
Glen Tarken
Meall nam Fiadh
Invergeldie
A85
Suie Lodge Hotel
Meall an Fhiodhain
Glen Ogle
Meall a'Mhadaidh
Glen Beich
Sron Mor 672
Loch Boltachan
Carroglen
Glen Turret
Beich Burn
Glenbeich
Ardveich
Creag Liath
Creag Each
Melville's Mon
Monachyle Glen
Meall an t-Seallaidh 852
Lochearnhead
Auchraw
Dalveich
Derry
St Fillans
Dunira
Ochtertyre
Deil's Cauldron
Loch Earn
Edinchip
Edinample
Ardvorlich
Ardtrostan
Tullybannocher
Comrie
Lawers
Quoig
Braes of Balquhidder
Rob Roy's Grave
A84
Meall Reamhar 678
Ross
Dalginross
Strath Earn
Balquhidder
Auchtubh
Kingshouse
Ben Halton 620
Monachyle
Stronvar
Loch Voil
Strathyre Forest
Glen Ample
Ben Vorlich 985
Forest of Glenartney
Allt Srath a' Ghlinne
Cultybraggan Camp
Mill of Fortune
Torlum
Torlum Wood
Loch Doine
Water of Ruchill
Glen Artney
B827
Culloch
Craggan
Ballimore
Immeroin
Stuc a'Chroin 972
Tighnablair
Fathan Glinne
Kipp
Strathyre
Calair Burn
Dalchruin
Knaik
Dunruchan Hill
Machany Water
Auchinner
Findhuglen
Ben Clach
Meall Odhar
Creag Beinn nan Eun
Findhu Glen
Langside
Beinn Bhreac
Runacraig
Allt Gleann nam Meann
Ben Vane 820
Laggan
Ardchullarie More
Greenscares
Meall Cala 674
Ardnandave Hill
Meall Leathan Dhail
Beinn Odhar 632
Coire Nochd Mor
Glenlichorn
Cromlet
B827
Loch Lubnaig
Uamh Bheag 665
Stirling
Glen Finglas
Gleann Casaig
Braeleny
Slymaback
Edra
Anie
Ben Ledi 879
Pass of Leny
Glen Finglas Resr
Kilmahog Woollen Mill
Bracklinn Falls
Bullie Burn
Cambushinn Hill
Ellen's Isle
The Trossachs
Ben An
Kilmahog
Callander
Muckle Burn
B8033
Strathallan
Goblin's Cave
Bochastle
Rob Roy & Trossachs Visitor Centre
Ardoch Burn
Ben Venue
Pass of Achray
Brig o'Turk
Milton of Callander
Coilantogle
Drummond
Annet Burn
Loch Mahaick
Duncraggan
Lendrick Lodge
A821
Loch Venachar
Easter Dullater
A84
Braes of Doune
Kinbuck
Balhaldie
Loch Achray
Forest Drive
West Dullater
Invertrossachs
Drumvaich
Glassingall
Allan Water
Beinn an Fhogharaidh
Dukes Pass 243
Toll
Loch Drunkie
Menteith Hills
A81
Loch Rusky
B822
Argaty
Ashfield
Sheriffmuir 1715
Achray Forest
Beinn Dearg
Torrie Forest
B8032
Burn of Cambus
Stockbridge
Ledard
Pass of Aberfoyle
Milton
Port of Menteith
Easter Borland
Teith
Doune
A820
Dunblane
Loch Ard
Aberfoyle
Blairhoyle
Deanston
Pisgah
Scottish Wool Centre
Malling
Ruskie
A873
Thornhill
Gartincaber
B826
Inverardoch Mains
Kippenross Ho
Cauldhame
Balleich
Braeval
Inchmahome Priory
Duchray
Tamavoid
Goodie Water
Blair Drummond
Safari Park
Keir House
Sunnylaw
Queen Elizabeth Forest Park
Loch Ard Forest
Cobleland
Cunninghame Graham Memorial (NTS)
Lake of Menteith
Flanders Moss
Easter Poldar
B8031
Bridge of Allan
Dykehead
Forth
B8034
B8075
Nyadd
Ochtertyre
M9
Gartmore
B822
A9
Blairlogie
Causewayhead
Wallace
Dalmary
Kelty Water
Arngomery
A811
Drip Moss
1297 Stirling Bridge
Cambuskenneth Abbey
Garden
B835
Arnprior
B8037
Kippen
Gargunnock
Leckie
Gargunnock House
Smith Art Gallery & Museum
Gartachoil
Buchlyvie
Arngibbon
Cauldhame
A91
Argyll & Sutherland Highlanders Museum
Stirling
Royal Burgh of Stirling Visitor Centre
Ward Burn
Wrightpark
Cambusbarron
Touch Hills
St Ninians
Fallin
Garadhban Forest
B822
485
Gargunnock Hills
Bannockburn Heritage Cen (NTS)
Bannock Burn
Bannockburn
A875
Balafark
Buchanan Castle
Balfron Station
Balfron
Ling Hill
Earlsburn
North Third
North Third Resr
Drymen
511
Hart Hill
Earl's Hill
Endrick Water
B818
Culcreuch
Craigton
Loup of Fintry
Boquhan
Gartness
Fintry
Gonachan
Corrie of Balglass
Killearn
George Buchanan
B834
Cairnoch Hill 413
Earl's Burn
Easter Buckieburn
Loch Coulter Resr
Stirling
A872
Plean

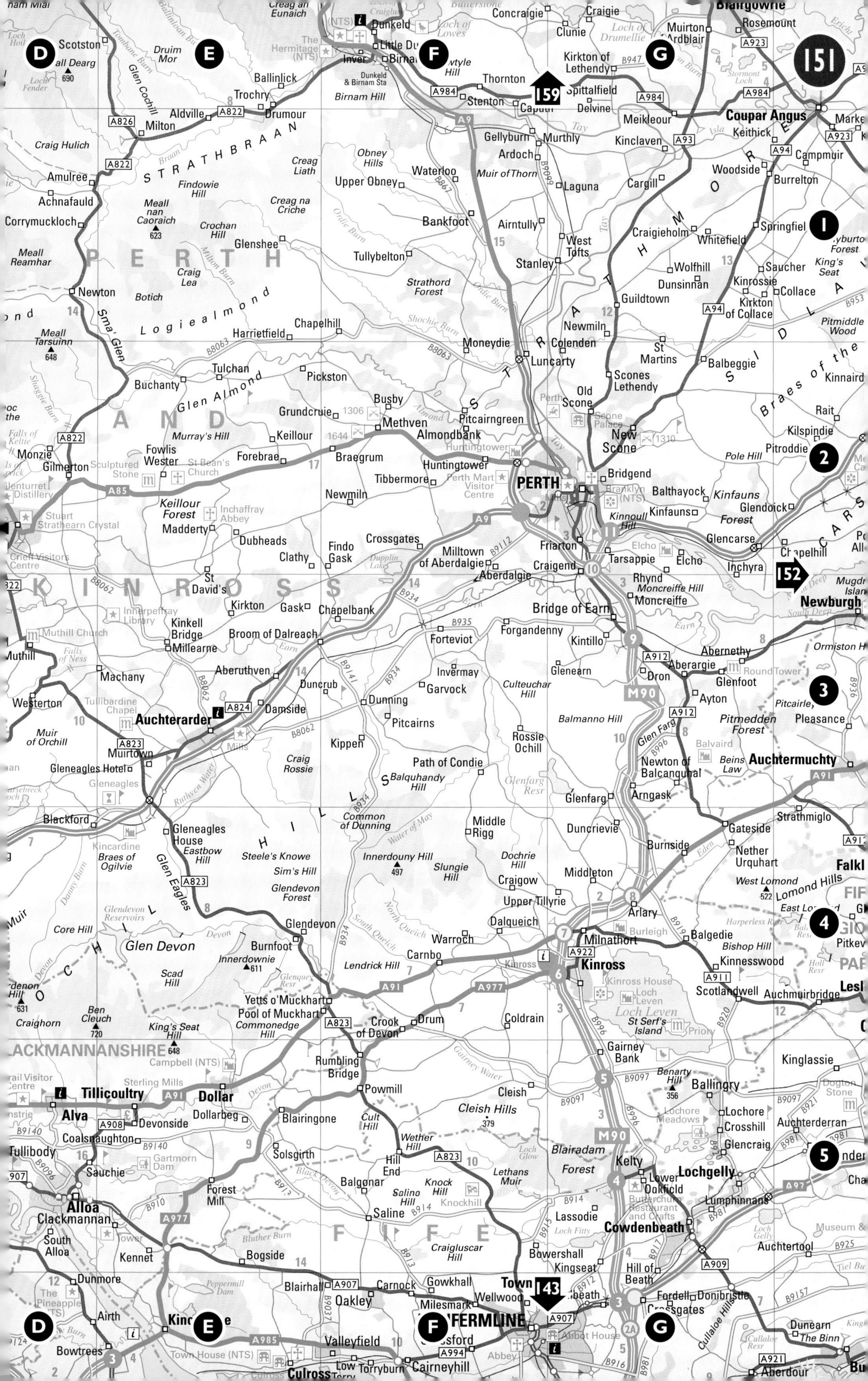
151
Scotston
Creag an Eunaich
Dunkeld
Little Dunkeld
Inver
Birnam
The Hermitage (NTS)
Dunkeld & Birnam Sta
Birnam Hill
Concraigie
Craigie
Clunie
Loch of Lowes
Loch of Drumellie
Muirton
Ardblair
Blairgowrie
Rosemount
A923
Druim Mor
Ballinlick
Trochry
Drumour
Aldville
Milton
A822
A826
Glen Cochill
Craig Hulich
Amulree
Achnafauld
Corrymuckloch
STRATHBRAAN
Findowie Hill
Meall nan Caoraich
623
Creag Liath
Creag na Criche
Crochan Hill
Glenshee
Obney Hills
Upper Obney
Waterloo
Bankfoot
Tullybelton
Thornton
A984
Stenton
Caputh
159
Spittalfield
Delvine
Kirkton of Lethendy
B947
Meikleour
A984
Coupar Angus
Keithick
A923
A94
Campmuir
Gellyburn
Murthly
Ardoch
Muir of Thorn
Kinclaven
A93
Cargill
Laguna
Woodside
Burrelton
Airntully
West Tofts
Stanley
Craigieholm
Whitefield
Springfield
STRATHMORE
Meall Reamhar
PERTH
Craig Lea
Newton
Botich
Logiealmond
Harrietfield
Chapelhill
Meall Tarsuinn
648
Sma' Glen
Strathord Forest
Wolfhill
Dunsinnan
Saucher
Kinrossie
Collace
Kirkton of Collace
King's Seat
Guildtown
Pitmiddle Wood
B953
Moneydie
Colenden
Luncarty
Newmiln
St Martins
Balbeggie
Braes of the
Kinnaird
SIDLAW
Tulchan
Buchanty
Pickston
Glen Almond
B8063
Grundcruie
1306
Busby
Methven
Almondbank
Pitcairngreen
Scones Lethendy
Old Scone
Scone Palace
New Scone
Rait
Kilspindie
Pitroddie
Pole Hill
2
A822
Monzie
Gilmerton
Fowlis Wester
Murray's Hill
Keillour
1644
Forebrae
Braegrum
Huntingtower
Tibbermore
Perth Mart Visitor Centre
PERTH
Bridgend
Branklyn (NTS)
Balthayock
Kinfauns
Glendoick
Kinfauns Forest
Sculptured Stone
St Bean's Church
A85
Glenturret Distillery
Stuart Strathearn Crystal
Crieff Visitors Centre
Keillour Forest
Inchaffray Abbey
Madderty
Dubheads
Newmiln
A9
Crossgates
Findo Gask
Clathy
Dupplin Lake
Milltown of Aberdalgie
B9112
Friarton
Kinnoull Hill
Elcho
Tarsappie
Glencarse
Chapelhill
CARSE
Inchyra
152
Newburgh
Mugdrum Island
St David's
KINROSS
B8062
Kirkton
Gask
Chapelbank
Aberdalgie
Craigend
Rhynd
Moncreiffe Hill
Moncreiffe
Bridge of Earn
Innerpeffray Library
Muthill Church
Muthill
Kinkell Bridge
Millearne
Broom of Dalreach
B934
B935
Forteviot
Forgandenny
Kintillo
Abernethy
Ormiston Hill
Round Tower
Aberargie
A912
Dron
Glenfoot
Ayton
Machany
Aberuthven
Duncrub
B9141
Invermay
Garvock
Culteuchar Hill
Glenearn
M90
Westerton
Tullibardine Chapel
Auchterarder
A824
Damside
Dunning
Pitcairns
Balmanno Hill
Pitcairlie
Pleasance
B936
3
Muir of Orchill
A823
Muirtown
B8062
Kippen
Rossie Ochill
Glen Farg
B996
Pitmedden Forest
Gleneagles Hotel
Craig Rossie
Path of Condie
Newton of Balcanquhal
Balvaird
Beins Law
Auchtermuchty
Gleneagles
Balquhandy Hill
Glenfarg Resr
Glenfarg
Arngask
A91
Blackford
OCHIL HILLS
Common of Dunning
Middle Rigg
Duncrievie
Strathmiglo
Gateside
Gleneagles House
Eastbow Hill
Kincardine
Braes of Ogilvie
Steele's Knowe
Water of May
Innerdouny Hill
497
Slungie Hill
Dochrie Hill
Burnside
Nether Urquhart
Sim's Hill
Glendevon Forest
Craigow
Middleton
West Lomond
522
Lomond Hills
Falkland
A823
Glen Eagles
Upper Tillyrie
Arlary
East Lomond
Glendevon Reservoirs
Core Hill
Glendevon
Dalqueich
Burleigh
Harperleis Resr
B919
Balgedie
4
Glen Devon
Burnfoot
North Queich
South Queich
B934
Warroch
Milnathort
A922
Bishop Hill
Kinross
Kinnesswood
Holl Resr
Scad Hill
Innerdownie
611
Glenquey Resr
Lendrick Hill
Carnbo
A91
A977
Kinross House
A911
Scotlandwell
Auchmuirbridge
Leslie
Ardenon Hill
631
Ben Cleuch
720
Yetts o'Muckhart
Pool of Muckhart
Commonedge Hill
A823
Crook of Devon
Drum
Coldrain
Loch Leven
St Serf's Island
Priory
B920
Craighorn
King's Seat Hill
648
CLACKMANNANSHIRE
Campbell (NTS)
Rumbling Bridge
Gairney Water
B996
Gairney Bank
Kinglassie
Trail Visitor Centre
Tillicoultry
Sterling Mills
A91
Dollar
Devon
Powmill
Cleish
Benarty Hill
356
B9097
Ballingry
Dogton Stone
Alva
Dollarbeg
A908
Devonside
Blairingone
Cult Hill
Cleish Hills
379
Lochore Meadows
Lochore
Crosshill
Auchterderran
B9097
B9140
Coalsnaughton
Tullibody
B9140
Gartmorn Dam
Solsgirth
Wether Hill
A823
Hill End
Blairadam Forest
Loch Glow
Kelty
Glencraig
5
Sauchie
B9096
Lethans Muir
Lochgelly
Lower Oakfield
Forest Mill
Balgonar
Knock Hill
Salino Hill
Knockhill
Alloa
Clackmannan
B910
B914
Butterchurn Restaurant and Crafts
Lumphinnans
A92
Saline
Lassodie
Cowdenbeath
South Alloa
Tower
Kennet
A977
FIFE
Bluther Burn
Bogside
B913
Craigluscar Hill
Loch Fitty
B915
Bowershall
Kingseat
B917
Loch Gelly
Auchtertool
Museum
B925
A909
Hill of Beath
Dunmore
The Pineapple (NTS)
Peppermill Dam
Blairhall
A907
Carnock
Gowkhall
Oakley
B9037
Milesmark
Wellwood
143
Town
Fordell
Donibristle
Crossgates
Cullaloe Hills
B9157
Airth
Kincardine
A985
Valleyfield
FERMLINE
Crossford
A994
A907
Abbot House
Abbey
B916
B981
Town House (NTS)
Culross
Low Torryburn
Cairneyhill
Dunearn
The Binn
A921
Aberdour
Bowtrees
D
E
F
G
I

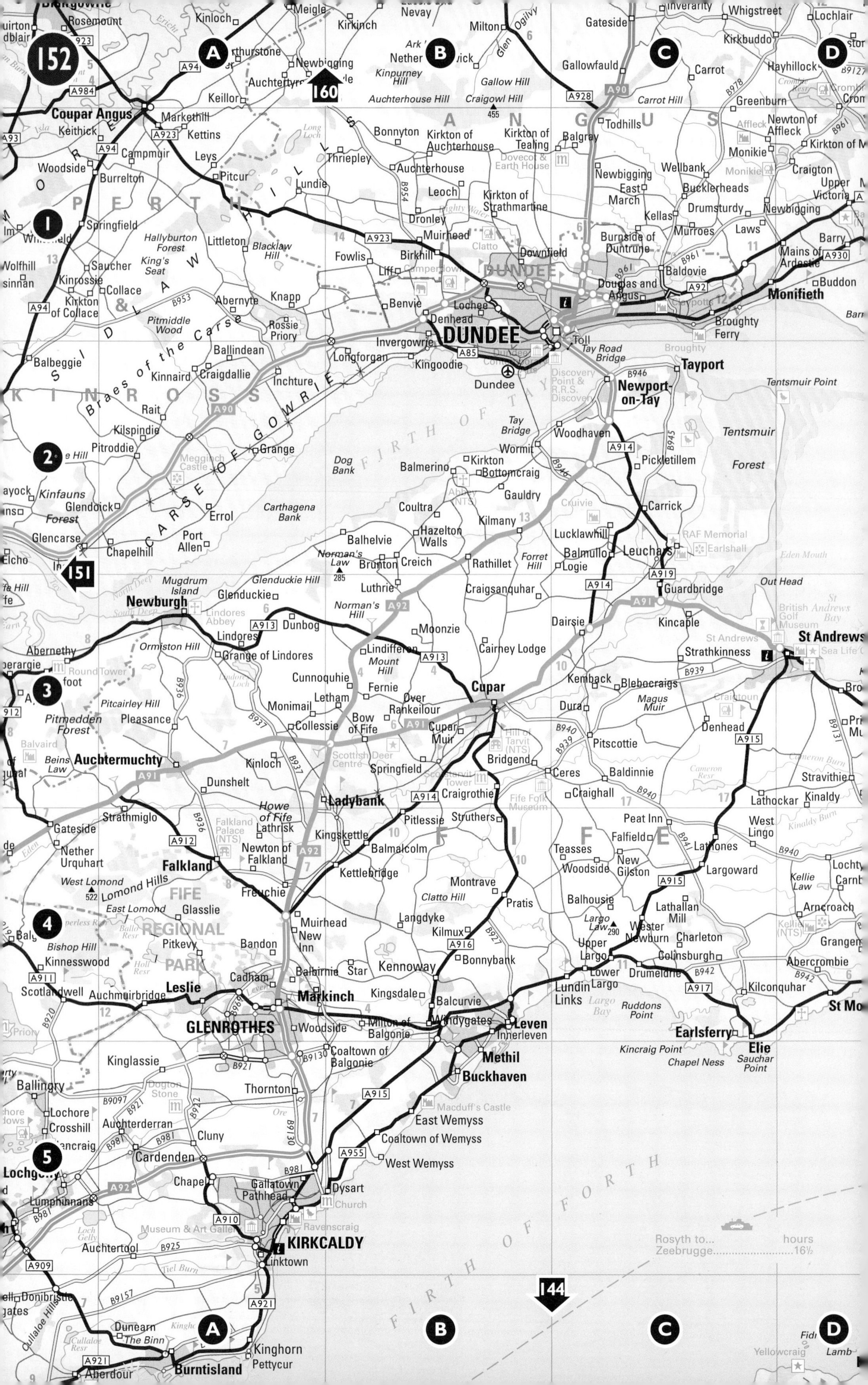
152
160
151
144
A
B
C
D
1
2
3
4
5
Rosemount
Kinloch
Meigle
Kirkinch
Nevay
Milton
Glen Ogilvy
Inverarity
Whigstreet
Lochlair
Gateside
Arthurstone
Newbigging
Ark
Nether
Kinpurney Hill
Gallow Hill
Gallowfauld
Carrot
Kirkbuddo
Hayhillock
Auchtertyre
Keillor
Auchterhouse Hill
Craigowl Hill
455
Carrot Hill
Greenburn
Coupar Angus
Markethill
Keithick
Kettins
Bonnyton
Kirkton of Auchterhouse
Kirkton of Tealing
Balgray
Todhills
Affleck
Newton of Affleck
Kirkton of M
Campmuir
Leys
Thriepley
Dovecot & Earth House
Newbigging
Wellbank
Monikie
Craigton
Woodside
Burrelton
Pitcur
Auchterhouse
Lundie
Leoch
Kirkton of Strathmartine
East March
Bucklerheads
Drumsturdy
Newbigging
Upper Victoria
ANGUS
PERTH
SIDLAW HILLS
Springfield
Dronley
Kellas
Murroes
Laws
Barry
Hallyburton Forest
Littleton
Blacklaw Hill
Fowlis
Muirhead
Birkhill
Clatto
Downfield
Burnside of Duntrune
Mains of Ardestie
King's Seat
Camperdown
Liff
DUNDEE
Baldovie
Douglas and Angus
Buddon
Monifieth
Saucher
Kinrossie
Collace
Kirkton of Collace
Abernyte
Knapp
Benvie
Lochee
Claypotts
Broughty Ferry
Pitmiddle Wood
Rossie Priory
Denhead
Invergowrie
Longforgan
Kingoodie
Dundee
Toll
Tay Road Bridge
Broughty
Tayport
Balbeggie
Ballindean
Braes of the Carse
Kinnaird
Craigdallie
Inchture
Discovery Point & R.R.S. Discovery
Newport-on-Tay
Tentsmuir Point
KINROSS
Rait
Kilspindie
Pitroddie
Tay Bridge
Woodhaven
Wormit
Tentsmuir
Forest
CARSE OF GOWRIE
FIRTH OF TAY
Grange
Megginch Castle
Dog Bank
Balmerino
Kirkton
Bottomcraig
Pickletillem
Kinfauns
Glendoick
Forest
Abbey (NTS)
Gauldry
Coultra
Carthagena Bank
Errol
Kilmany
Carrick
Cruivie
Port Allen
Glencarse
Chapelhill
Balhelvie
Hazelton Walls
Lucklawhill
RAF Memorial
Earlshall
Balmullo
Leuchars
Logie
Norman's Law
285
Brunton
Creich
Rathillet
Forret Hill
Eden Mouth
Mugdrum Island
Glenduckie Hill
Glenduckie
Luthrie
Craigsanquhar
Guardbridge
Out Head
Newburgh
Lindores Abbey
Norman's Hill
Dairsie
Kincaple
St Andrews Bay
British Golf Museum
Dunbog
Lindores
Moonzie
St Andrews
Abernethy
Ormiston Hill
Grange of Lindores
Lindifferon
Mount Hill
Cairney Lodge
Strathkinness
Round Tower
Cunnoquhie
Fernie
Cupar
Kemback
Blebocraigs
Magus Muir
Craigtoun
Pitcairley Hill
Letham
Over Rankeilour
Monimail
Dura
Pitmedden Forest
Pleasance
Collessie
Bow of Fife
Cupar Muir
Hill of Tarvit (NTS)
Denhead
Balvaird
Pitscottie
Beins Law
Auchtermuchty
Kinloch
Scottish Deer Centre
Springfield
Bridgend
Ceres
Baldinnie
Cameron Resr
Stravithie
Dunshelt
Scotstarvit Tower
Craigrothie
Craighall
Fife Folk Museum
Lathockar
Kinaldy
Ladybank
Howe of Fife
Lathrisk
Strathmiglo
Falkland Palace (NTS)
Kingskettle
Pitlessie
Struthers
Peat Inn
West Lingo
Gateside
Falfield
FIFE
Lathones
Nether Urquhart
Newton of Falkland
Balmalcolm
Teasses
Falkland
Kettlebridge
Woodside
New Gilston
Largoward
Kellie Law
West Lomond
522
Lomond Hills
Montrave
Clatto Hill
Balhousie
Lathallan Mill
Arncroach
Freuchie
Pratis
East Lomond
Glasslie
FIFE REGIONAL PARK
Muirhead
Langdyke
Largo Law
290
Wester Newburn
Charleton
Kellie Castle (NTS)
Grangemuir
Bishop Hill
Pitkevy
Bandon
New Inn
Kilmux
Upper Largo
Colinsburgh
Kinnesswood
Bonnybank
Abercrombie
Balbirnie
Star
Kennoway
Lower Largo
Drumeldrie
Kilconquhar
Scotlandwell
Auchmuirbridge
Leslie
Cadham
Markinch
Kingsdale
Balcurvie
Lundin Links
Largo Bay
Ruddons Point
St Monans
GLENROTHES
Woodside
Milton of Balgonie
Windygates
Leven
Innerleven
Earlsferry
Elie
Kinglassie
Coaltown of Balgonie
Methil
Kincraig Point
Chapel Ness
Saucher Point
Buckhaven
Ballingry
Dogton Stone
Thornton
Lochore
Crosshill
Auchterderran
Macduff's Castle
East Wemyss
Cluny
Coaltown of Wemyss
Cardenden
West Wemyss
FIRTH OF FORTH
Chapel
Gallatown
Pathhead
Dysart
Church
Lumphinnans
Ravenscraig
Museum & Art Gallery
Loch Gelly
Auchtertool
KIRKCALDY
Linktown
Rosyth to... hours
Zeebrugge......16½
Donibristle
Dunearn
The Binn
Kinghorn
Pettycur
Burntisland
Aberdour
Yellowcraig
A90
A92
A94
A923
A984
A928
A930
A85
A914
A919
A91
A913
A915
A912
A916
A911
A917
A955
A910
A909
A921
B954
B953
B961
B978
B946
B945
B939
B940
B941
B942
B936
B937
B9131
B9130
B9097
B921
B922
B981
B925
B9157
B920
B969

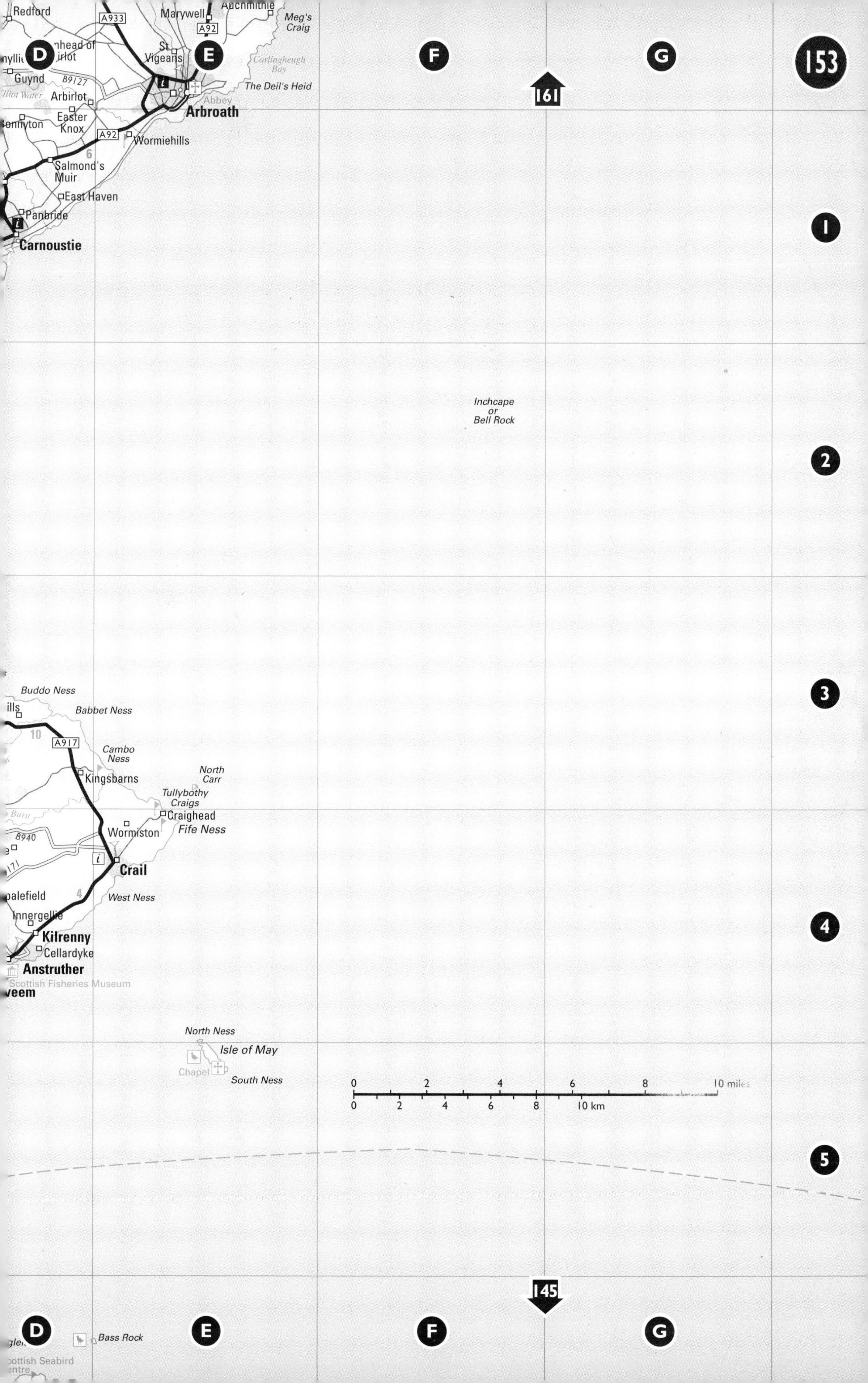

Redford
A933
Marywell
A92
Auchmithie
Meg's Craig
St Vigeans
Carlinghaugh Bay
The Deil's Heid
Guynd
B9127
Arbirlot
Abbey
Arbroath
Easter Knox
A92
Wormiehills
Salmond's Muir
East Haven
Panbride
Carnoustie
161
Inchcape or Bell Rock
Buddo Ness
Babbet Ness
A917
Cambo Ness
North Carr
Kingsbarns
Tullybothy Craigs
Craighead
Fife Ness
B940
Wormiston
Crail
West Ness
Innergellie
Kilrenny
Cellardyke
Anstruther
Scottish Fisheries Museum
North Ness
Isle of May
Chapel
South Ness
0 2 4 6 8 10 miles
0 2 4 6 8 10 km
145
Bass Rock
D E F G
1 2 3 4 5

A
B
C
D
163
SEA OF THE HEBRIDES
Rubha Sgor an t-Snidhe
Ruinsival 528
Ainshval 781
Sgurr nan Gillean 764
Rubha nam Meirleach
SOUND OF
Rubh an Fhasair
Sound of Eigg
1
2
3
4
5
same scale as main map
Calgary Point
Caolas Ban
Gunna
Port a'Mhurain
Urvaig
Miodar
Sgeir Bharrach
Salum Bay
Rubha Dubh
Caolas
Vaul
Balephetrish Bay
Balephetrish Hill
B8069
Ruaig
Brock
Port Ban
The Green
Hough Bay
TIREE
Gott Bay
Rubha Liath
Soa
B8068
Tiree
Scarinish
Kilkenneth
Moss
Crossapoll
B8065
Heanish
Saundaig
Heylipoll
Baugh
Barrapoll
Hynish Bay
Balemartine
B8067
Mannel
Balephuil
Rinn Thorbhais
Hynish
Skerryvore Museum
Eilean nan Each
Godag
Rubh' Leam na Laraich
Beinn Airein 137
Port
Muck
HIG
Sanna Point
Point of Ardnamurchan
Port Min
Grigadale
Oban to... Lochboisdale hours 5-7
Oban to... Castlebay hours 5¼
Eag na Maoile
Eilean Mor
Rubha Mor
Bousd
Rubha Sgor-Innis
Sorisdale
Rubh' a'Bhinnein
B8072
Loch Fada
Torastan
Bagh na Coille
INNER HEBRIDES
Cliad Bay
Arnabost
Grishipoll
Grishipoll Bay
B8071
Clabhach
Ben Hogh 104
73
Ballyhaugh
Loch Cliad
Hogh Bay
Arinagour
Totamore
Totronald
COLL
B8070
Loch Eatharna
Arileod
Acha
Uig
Feall Bay
Port Mine
Eilean Ornsay
Gorton
Calgary Point
Crossapol
Crossapol Bay
Friesland Bay
Gunna
Caolas Ban
Port a'Mhurain
Soa
Loch Breachacha
Rubha Fasachd
Sorne Point
Quinish Point
Oban hours 2¾
Caliach Point
Port na Ba
Quinish
Sunipol
Langamull
Mornish
Croig
Cruach Sleibhe 166
Frachadil
Dervaig
Rubha nan Oirean
Calgary
B8073
Urvaig
Miodar
Rubha Dubh
Caolas
Ruaig
Brock
Port Ban
Gott Bay
Rubha Liath
1¼hrs
ARGYLL AND BUTE
Calgary Bay
Treshnish Point
Ensay
Carn Mor 342
Cruach Ceann a' Ghairbh 261
Treshnish
Beinn Duill 191
Cruachan Odhar 256
Beinn nan Gabhar 315
Rubh' a'Chaoil
Kilninian
Rubh' an t-Suibhein
Tostarie
Normann's Ruh
Port Burg
Cairn na Burgh More
Cairn na Burgh Beg
Loch Tuath
Fanmore
Treshnish Isles
Sgeir a Chaisteil
Fladda
Rubha Chulinish
Ballygown Bay
Eilean Dioghlum
Gometra Ho.
Rubha nan Gall
Lunga
Gometra
Bearnus
Beinn Chreagach
Rubha Maol na Mine
Beinn Eolasary
ULVA
Maisgeir
146
Bac Mor or Dutchman's Cap
Bac Beag
Little Colonsay
Staffa
Eilean Dubh

D
E
F
G
I
164
156
147
2
3
4
5
A830
A861
A884
A848
A849
B8007
B8044
B8073
B8035
B849
Morar
Loch a'Ghille Ghobaich
Stoul
Kylesknoydart
Bracora
Brac
Tarbet
Eilean a'Phidhir
NORTH MORAR
Swordland
Loch Morar
Cleadale
An Cruachan
299
Laig
EIGG
An Sgurr
393
Kildonnan
Galmisdale
Portnaluchaig
Back of Keppoch
Eilean Ighe
Carn a'Mhadaidh-ruaidh
503
Lettermorar
Loch a'Choire Riabhaich
SOUTH MORAR
Druim a' Chuirn
ARISAIG
Luinga Mhor
Loch nan Ceall
Arisaig
Rhumach
Morroch
Rubh' Arisaig
Cruach Doire 'n Dobhrain
103
Druimindarroch
The Prince's Cairn
Sidhean Mor
599
Glen Beasdale
Beinn nan Cabar
574
Meoble
Meith Bheinn
710
Arnipol
Sron Thoraraidh
383
Arienskill
Lochailort
Ranoch
Inverailort
Loch Eilt
Sgurr na
Loch nan Uamh
L. Beag
Loch Doir a'Ghearrain
Loch Ailort
Rubha Chaolais
Ardnish
Eilean nan Gobhar
Sound of Arisaig
Samalaman Island
Glenuig Bay
Roshven
An Stac
814
Druim Fiaclach
869
Smirisary
Glenuig
Rois-Bheinn
882
Cruach Bhrochdadail
357
Sgurr Dhomhnuill Mor
713
Croit Bheinn
663
HIGHLAND
Glenuig Hill
Kylesbeg
Beinn Gaire
666
Eilean Shona
265
Baileronach
Shona Beag
Brunery Hill
MOIDART
Glen Forslan
Gaskan
Rubha Aird Druimnich
Tioram
Kinlochmoidart
Loch Moidart
Glen Moidart
Gorstanvorran
Ockle Point
Carn Mor
Beinn Bhreac
240
Ardmolich
Ardtoe
Newton of Ardtoe
Cruach a' Ghaill
371
Ockle
Shielfoot
Fascadale
Achateny
Kilmory
Swordle
Beinn Bhreac
357
Kentra
Kentra Bay
Cliff
Dalnabreck
Dalelia
Achnaha
Meall nan Con
437
Branault
Gorteneorn
Arivegaig
Acharacle
Polloch
Beinn an Leathaid
Ardshealach
Claish Moss
Achnanellan
Meall an Tarmachain
404
Loch Mudle
SUNART
Kinlochan
ARDNAMURCHAN
Leac Shoilleir
440
Camphouse
313
Beinn nan Losgann
Salen
Beinn Resipol
845
Kilchoan
Lochan nam Fiann
Tarbert
Resipole
Scotstown
Mingary
Ben Hiant
528
Loch Laga
Ardery
Beinn Bhuidhe
278
Glenbeg
Natural History Centre
Ben Laga
512
Loch Sunart
Gearr Chreag
340
Anaheilt
Drumn
Kilchoan Bay
Glenborrodale
Ranachan
Strontian
Woodend
Ardnastang
Maclean's Nose
Ardslignish
Laga
Eilean Mor
½hr
Ardmore Point
Oronsay
Risga
Carna
Glencripesdale
Meall a' Bhroin
Liddesdale
Achleek
Bloody Bay
Auliston Point
Meall an Inbhire
Beinn Ghormaig
452
Taobh Dubh
352
Glas Bheinn
620
Rahoy
Meall a'Chaise
522
Tobermory
Tobermory Bay
Beinn Iadain
571
Achagavel
Lochuisge
Calve Island
Barr
Kinloch
Loch Teacuis
Achleanan
Ardantiobairt
Gleann Dubh
Loch Uisge
Airdhe Beinn
MORVERN
Beinn na h-Uamha
464
Beinn Chlaonleud
475
Beach
Meall a' Chaorainn Loch Uisge
Drimnin
Beinn Bhuidhe
451
Sgurr Shalachain
Mishnish Lochs
Sidhean na Raplaich
550
Durinemast
Loch Arienas
Clounlaid
Aros
Rhemore
Beinn Mheadhoin
739
Caol Lochan
Gleann Geal
Alltachonaich
Sgurr a' Bhuic
569
Speinne Mor
444
Claggan
Ardnacross
Killundine
Beinn an t-Sruthain
267
Ardtornish
Loch Frisa
Lettermore
Creag Bhan Ard
339
Beinn Bhan
400
Larachbeg
Braigh na Glaice Moire
Meall Damh
Achnacraig
Salen Forest
Kinlochaline
Meall na Caorach
Fiunary Forest
Ardtornish
Beinn a'Chaisil
437
Glensanda
Druim an Fhraoich Mhin
318
Loch Teàrnait
Ledmore
Fiunary
Tenga
Glen Aros
Tighachnoic
Loch nan Clach
Aros
Eileanan Glasa
Achnaha
Meall an Fhiar Mhaim
309
Beinn Bhuidhe
387
Salen Bay
Meall a' Chaorainn
481
Glais Bheinn
479
Mam a' Chullaich
462
An Sleaghach
513
Lochaline
Eignaig
Beinn na Drise
424
Inninbeg
Salen
Fishnish Bay
Fishnish Point
Pennygown
Beinn nan Carn
333
MULL
Cruach Torran Lochain
Ardtornish Point
Lynn of Morven
Fishnish
Killbeg
Innimore Bay
Killiechronan
Balmeanach
Kellan
Glen Forsa
Garmony
Killiemor
Beinn Bhuidhe
412
Beinn Chreagach Mhor
579
Rubha an Ridire
Lismore
Gruline
Sound of Mull
Loch Na Keal
Loch Ba
Bernera
Achadun (ruin)
Knock
Gaodhail
Salen Forest
Scallastle
Craignure Bay
Kilcheran
Na Binneinean
Eilean Dubh
Loch Fiart
591
Beinn na Duatharach
Dun da Ghaoithe
Maol nan Uan
Craignure
Mull & West Highland Railway
Plad Islands
18
10
8
12
11
13
7
23
Loch Linnhe

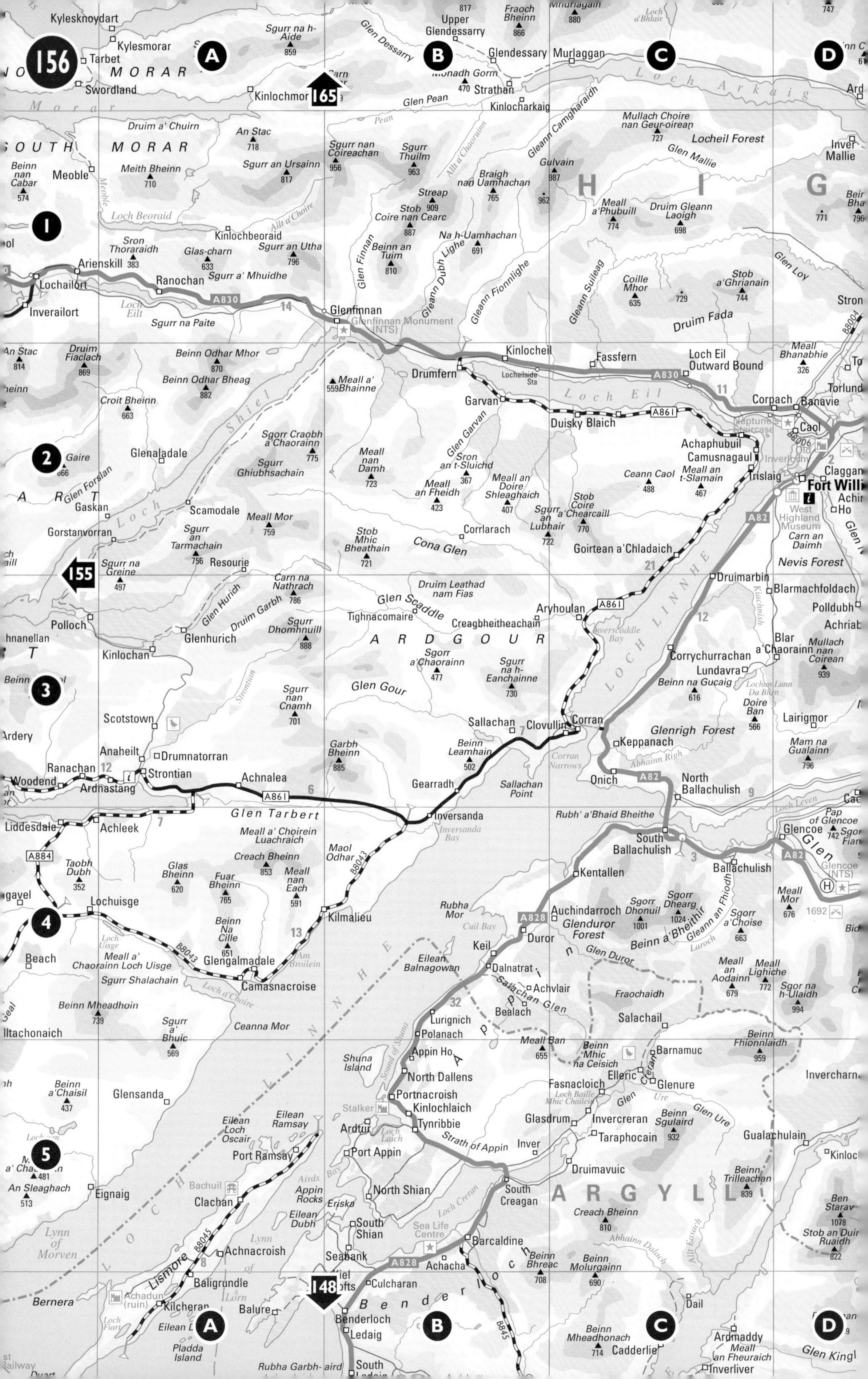
A
B
C
D
1
2
3
4
5
165
155
148
Kylesknoydart
Kylesmorar
Tarbet
Swordland
MORAR
Loch Morar
SOUTH MORAR
Kinlochmorar
Sgurr na h-Aide 859
Glen Dessarry
Upper Glendessarry
Glendessarry
Murlaggan
Monadh Gorm 470
Strathan
Kinlocharkaig
Loch Arkaig
Glen Pean
Druim a' Chuirn
An Stac 718
Sgurr nan Coireachan 956
Sgurr Thuilm 963
Sgurr an Ursainn 817
Meith Bheinn 710
Beinn nan Cabar 574
Meoble
Loch Beoraid
Kinlochbeoraid
Gleann Camgharaidh
Mullach Choire nan Geur-oirean 727
Locheil Forest
Glen Mallie
Inver Mallie
Gulvain 987
962
Braigh nan Uamhachan 765
Streap 909
Stob Coire nan Cearc 887
Meall a'Phubuill 774
Druim Gleann Laoigh 698
771
796
HIGHLAND
Na h-Uamhachan 691
Glen Finnan
Beinn an Tuim 810
Gleann Dubh Lighe
Sron Thoraraidh 383
Glas-charn 633
Sgurr an Utha 796
Arienskill
Lochailort
Ranochan
Sgurr a' Mhuidhe
A830
Loch Eilt
Inverailort
Sgurr na Paite
Glenfinnan
Glenfinnan Monument (NTS)
Gleann Fionnlighe
Gleann Suileag
Coille Mhor 635
729
Stob a'Ghrianain 744
Glen Loy
Druim Fada
Stron
B8004
An Stac 814
Druim Fiaclach 869
Beinn Odhar Mhor 870
Beinn Odhar Bheag 882
Meall a' Bhainne 559
Kinlocheil
Fassfern
Loch Eil Outward Bound
Meall Bhanabhie 326
Torlundy
Drumfern
Locheilside Sta
Loch Eil
A861
Garvan
Duisky
Blaich
Corpach
Banavie
Neptune's Staircase
Caol
Croit Bheinn 663
Loch Shiel
Sgorr Craobh a'Chaorainn 775
Meall nan Damh 723
Glen Garvan
Sron an t-Sluichd 367
Achaphubuil
Camusnagaul
Inverlochy
B8006
Claggan
Fort William
Glenaladale
Gaire 666
Sgurr Ghiubhsachain
Meall an Fheidh 423
Meall an Doire Shleaghaich 407
Ceann Caol 488
Meall an t-Slamain 467
Trislaig
Achintee
West Highland Museum
Glen Forslan
Gaskan
Scamodale
Meall Mor 759
Corrlarach
Stob Coire a'Chearcaill 770
Sgurr an Lubhair 722
A82
Carn an Daimh
Gorstanvorran
Sgurr an Tarmachain 756
Stob Mhic Bheathain 721
Cona Glen
Goirtean a'Chladaich
Nevis Forest
Sgurr na Greine 497
Resourie
Carn na Nathrach 786
Druim Leathad nam Fias
Druimarbin
Blarmachfoldach
Glen Hurich
Druim Garbh
Glen Scaddle
Aryhoulan
Polldubh
Polloch
Tighnacomaire
Creagbheitheachain
Inverscaddle Bay
Achriabhach
Sgurr Dhomhnuill 888
ARDGOUR
LOCH LINNHE
Blar a'Chaorainn
Mullach nan Coirean 939
Glenhurich
Kinlochan
Sgorr a'Chaorainn 477
Sgorr na h-Eanchainne 730
Corrychurrachan
Lundavra
Glen Gour
Beinn na Gucaig 616
Lochan Lunn Da Bhra
Doire Ban 566
Sgurr nan Cnamh 701
Sallachan
Clovullin
Corran
Lairigmor
Scotstown
Glenrigh Forest
Keppanach
Ardery
Garbh Bheinn 885
Beinn Leamhain 502
Corran Narrows
Mam na Gualainn 796
Anaheilt
Drumnatorran
Abhainn Righ
Ranachan
Strontian
Achnalea
Onich
North Ballachulish
Woodend
Ardnastang
A861
Gearradh
Sallachan Point
Loch Leven
Glen Tarbert
Inversanda
Inversanda Bay
Rubh' a'Bhaid Bheithe
Pap of Glencoe 742
Liddesdale
Achleek
Meall a' Choirein Luachraich
South Ballachulish
Glencoe
Maol Odhar
Ballachulish
Glencoe (NTS)
A884
Taobh Dubh 352
Glas Bheinn 620
Creach Bheinn 853
Meall nan Each 591
B8043
Kentallen
Fuar Bheinn 765
Gleann an Fhiodh
Meall Mor 676
1692
Lochuisge
Kilmalieu
Rubha Mor
Auchindarroch
Sgorr Dhonuil 1001
Sgorr Dhearg 1024
Beinn a'Bheithir
Sgurr a'Choise 663
Beinn Na Cille 651
Cuil Bay
A828
Glenduror Forest
Loch Uisge
Meall a' Chaorainn
Loch Uisge
Glengalmadale
Am Broilein
Keil
Duror
Glen Duror
Beach
Eilean Balnagowan
Dalnatrat
Meall an Aodainn 679
Meall Lighiche 772
Sgor na h-Ulaidh 994
Sgurr Shalachain
Camasnacroise
Loch a'Choire
Achvlair
Salachan Glen
Fraochaidh
Beinn Mheadhoin 739
Bealach
Ceanna Mor
Lurignich
Salachail
Altachonaich
Sgurr a' Bhuic 569
Polanach
Meall Ban 655
Beinn Mhic na Ceisich
Beinn Fhionnlaidh 959
Shuna Island
Sound of Shuna
Appin Ho.
Barnamuc
APPIN
Beinn a'Chaisil 437
North Dallens
Elleric
Glenure
Inverchar
Glensanda
Portnacroish
Fasnacloich
Loch Baile Mhic Chailein
Glen Creran
Glen Ure
Stalker
Kinlochlaich
Eilean Loch Oscair
Eilean Ramsay
Tynribbie
Glasdrum
Invercreran
Beinn Sgulaird 932
Gualachulain
Ardtur
Loch Laich
Taraphocain
Port Ramsay
Port Appin
Strath of Appin
Inver
Kinlochetive
a' Chaolain
An Sleaghach 513
Eignaig
Bachuil
Airds Bay
Druimavuic
Beinn Trilleachan 839
Clachan
Appin Rocks
North Shian
South Creagan
ARGYLL
Eriska
Loch Creran
Creach Bheinn 810
Ben Starav 1078
Eilean Dubh
South Shian
Abhainn Dalach
Allt Easach
Lynn of Morven
Lynn of Lorn
Achnacroish
B8045
Sea Life Centre
Barcaldine
Stob an Duine Ruaidh 822
Seabank
A828
Beinn Bhreac 708
Beinn Molurgainn 690
Lismore
Achacha
Baligrundle
Culcharan
Bernera
Achadun (ruin)
Kilcheran
Balure
Benderloch
Dail
Eilean Dubh
Loch Fiart
Ledaig
Beinn Mheadhonach 714
Ardmaddy
Pladda Island
B845
Cadderlie
Meall an Fheuraich
Inverliver
Railway
Rubha Garbh-aird
South Ledaig
Glen Kinglass

D
E
F
G
Turret Bridge
166
Meall na Teanga 917
Letter Finlay
Altura
Glen Gloy
Loch Lochy
Clunes
Bunarkaig
Invergloy
Leana Mhor 685
Leana Mhor
Carn Dearg 834
Glen Roy
Burn of Agie
Loch Sguadaig
Stob Poite Coire Ardair 1053
Creag Meagaidh 1130
Carn Liath 1006
Coille Coire Chrannaig
Aberarder
Ardverikie
A86
Loch Laggan
H
L
A
N
D
Coire Ceirsle Hill 654
Bohuntine Hill
Beinn Teallach 915
Beinn a'Chaorainn 1050
An Cearcallach 993
29
B8005
A82
Rathliesbeag
Stronenaba
Gairlochy
B8004
Bohuntine
Creag Dhubh 658
Moy Forest
Binnein Shuas
I
B
A
E
Commando Memorial
Spean Bridge Woollen Mill
Brackletter
Spean Bridge
Tirindrish
Inverroy
Roybridge
Bohenie
Murlaggan
Braes o' Lochaber
Roughburn
Moy
Craigbeg
Lochan na h-Earba
Creag Pitridh 924
Geal Charn 1049
Cruim Leacainn 228
Killiechanate
Tom an Teine 187
Tulloch Sta
Loch Moy
Forest
8
Leanachan Forest
Spean
GLEN SPEAN
1688
Beinn Chlianaig 721
Meall Liath Mor
Ardverikie
Allt an Loin
Allt Leachdach
Fersit
Beinn a'Chlachair 1087
Allt Cam
An Lairig
Aonach Mor Mountain Gondola & Nevis Range Ski Centre
Sgurr Finnisg-aig 663
Allt Laire
Carn Dearg 1034
Killiechonate Forest
Stob Choire Claurigh 1177
Stob a'Choire Mheadhoin 1106
Stob Coire Sgriodain 976
Chno Dearg 1047
Loch Guilbinn
Aonach Beag 1114
Geal Charn 1132
Loch an Sgoir
2
Ben Alder
Carn Mor Dearg 1223
Aonach Mor 1219
Stob Coire an Laoigh 1115
Stob Ban 977
Stob Coire Easain 1116
Lairig Leacach
Loch Treig
Beinn Eibhinn 1101
Ben Nevis 1344
Aonach Beag 1238
Sgurr Choinnich Mor 1095
Meall a'Bhuirich 840
Garbh Bheinn 858
Strath Ossian
Beinn a'Chumhainn
Ben Alder 1148
Beinn Bheoil 1019
Uisge Labhair
158
Beinn na Lap 937
Corrour Shooting Lodge
Charlie's Cave
Water of Nevis
Abhainn Rath
Binnein Beag 940
Luibeilt
Corrour Forest
Meall a'Bhealaich
Sgor Gaibhre 952
Ben Alder Cottage
An Gearanach 982
Binnein Mor 1128
Loch Ossian
Corrour Sta
Loch na Sgeallaig
Carn Dearg 939
Rannoch Forest
Stob Coire a'Chairn 981
Na Gruagaichean 1005
Sgurr Eilde Mor 1008
Loch Eilde Beag
Ciaran Water
Leum Uilleim 906
Beinn Pharlagain 807
3
Am Bodach 1032
Glas Bheinn 789
Loch Eilde Mor
609
Kinlochmore
Kinlochleven
Meall na Duibhe 570
Allt na Caim
Allt Eigheach
Black Water
Lochan Sron Smeur
Lochan Loin nan Donnlaich
Ericht
Leven
Garbh Bheinn 867
Blackwater Reservoir
PERTH
Garbh Lochan
Black Corries
Bridge of Ericht
The Chancellor
Devil's Staircase
Beinn Bheag
Meall Bhalach 708
Meall nan Ruadhag 646
Stob na Cruaiche 739
Rannoch Sta
B846
Finnart
27
The Study
Altnafeadh
857
Beinn a'Chrulaiste
Black Corries Lodge
Loch Eigheach
Bridge of Gaur
Gaur
Ossian's Cave
Pass of Glen Coe
Coupall
Kingshouse Hotel
A Chruach
Gleann Duibhe
4
Three Sisters
924
Stob Dearg 1022
Loch Laidon
Stob Dubh 958
Buachaille Etive Beag
Royal Forest
955
Buachaille Etive Mor
Lochan Gaineamhach
AND
Glen Etive
Glencoe (Whitecorries) Chairlift & Ski Area
348
Rannoch
Moor
RANNOCH
Beinn Mhic Chasgaig 843
Sròn na Creise 1100
Meall a'Bhuiridh 1108
Beinn Chaorach
Lochan na Stainge
Meall Buidhe 931
Beinn Ceitlein
Clach Leathad 1098
Loch Ba
Abhainn Duibhe
KINROSS
Cam Chreag 860
Meall Garbh 701
Aonach Mor
Coire Chaolain
Ba
Black Mount
Lochan na h-Achlaise
Meall Cruinn
Eas Daimh
Loch an Daimh
Meall Odhar 876
Stob Ghabhar 1087
Stob a'Choire Odhair 947
Water of Tulla
Meall Buidhe 907
Stuchd an Lochain 960
5
Meall nan Eun 926
Meall an Araich
Allt Dochard
Loch Tulla
Achallader
Beinn a'Chreachain 1081
Meall Daill
Kenknock
1044
Black Mount
Beinn Achaladair 1038
Clashgour
Loch Dochard
Forest Lodge
Pubil
Cashlie
AND
Inveroran Hotel
Beinn an Dothaidh 901
Beinn Mhanach 953
Lyon
Lubreoch
Stronuich Reservoir
Beinn Suidhe 675
Loch Lyon
Meall nan Subh 804
Meall Ghaordie 1039
Bridge of Orchy
BUTE
Meall Taurnie
Allt Tolaghan
Beinn Charn 636
Beinn Dorain 1074
149
Beinn Heasgarnich 1076
Sgiath Bhuidhe
696
Allt Chonoghlais
Beinn a'Chaisteil 883
Creag Mhor 1032
Kenknock
Tullich
Orchy
6
A82
Glen Lochay
Beinn Mhic-

Garvamore
Crathie
Balgowan
Spey
Phones
Sherramore
Loch Crunachdan
A
Black Craig
565
B
Falls of Truim
Etteridge
Garbh Mheall Mor
593
C
D
Liath
1006
Allt Crunachdain
Comra
A86
167
Meallach Mor
768
857
Kinloch Laggan
Coille Coire Chrannaig
Loch Caoldair
9
12
Glen Truim
A889
Loch Cuaich
Meall Chuaich
951
Boghacloiche
897
Laggan
Linn of Pattack
Ardverikie
Allt an t-Sluic
Allt Cuaich
Loch an t-Seilich
Allt Bhruin
29
Dalwhinnie
A9
1
Beinn Eilde
HIGHLAND
GRAMPIAN MOUNTAINS
Gaick Lodge
Gaick Forest
912
Lochan na h-Earba
Mashie
Loch Ericht Forest
Carn na Caim
941
Loch Bhrodainn
Allt Gharbh Ghaig
Creag Pitridh
924
Geal Charn
1049
Meall Cruaidh
897
Meall a'Chaorainn
Ardverikie Forest
Pattack
Creagan Mor
Loch an Duin
Cam a Choire
Loch Pattack
Ben Alder Lodge
Geal Charn
917
424
A'Bhuidheanach Bheag
936
Sronphadruig Lodge
Dalnamein Forest
Beinn a'Chlachair
1087
An Lairig
Allt Cam
An Torc
Glas Mheall Mor
928
Sron a'Chleirich
816
Carn Dearg
1034
Ben Alder Forest
Allt a'Chaoil Reidhe
A'Mharconaich
975
Allt Glas Choire
Allt Dearg
Bruar Water
2
1132
Loch an Sgoir
Ericht
Beinn Udlamain
1010
Sow of Atholl
Sgairneach Mhor
991
Dalnacardoch Forest
Forest of Atholl
Glen Bruar
Pass of Drumochter
18
Badnambiast
Allt Glas Choire
Ben Alder
1148
Beinn Bheoil
1019
A9
An Cearcall
Meall na Leitreach
775
Allt a'Chireachain
A
157
Stob an Aonaich Mhoir
855
Craiganour Forest
Glen
Garry
A9
Craig Bhagailteach
Meall a'Bhealaich
Prince Charlie's Cave
Ben Alder Cottage
Loch
Loch Garry
PERTH
Loch Con
Meall a'Chathaidh
Fair Bhuidhe
Allt Shallainn
Duinish
Sron Choin
Falls of the
Beinn Mholach
841
Allt Sleibh
Calvine
Pitagowan
Struan
3
Sron a'Chlaonaidh
Talla Bheith Forest
Allt Ghlas
Creag a'Mhadaidh
Loch Errochty
Trinafour
Dalchalloch
10
B847
Errochty Water
Glen Errochty
Sron Bheag
Aulich Burn
Allt Ruighe nan Saorach
Beinn a'Chuallaich
891
Torr Dubh
TAY
FOREST
Craig nan Caisean
AND
B847
Lochan Loin nan Donnlaich
Killichonan Burn
Erich
Tressait
TAY
Aulich
20
Balmore
Dunalastair
B846
B8019
Loch Tummel
Bridge of Ericht
Talladh-a-Bheith
B846
Kinloch Rannoch
Tummel
4
Tummel Bridge
Dunalastair Resr
B846
Killichonan
Foss
Loch Rannoch
Inverhadden
Tempar
Lassintullich
Finnart
Carie
PARK
Bridge of Gaur
Camghouran
Rannoch School
Braes of Foss
B846
4
Schiehallion
1083
Loch Kinardochy
388
Meall Tairneachan
787
FOREST
PARK
Leagag
Geal Charn
Deer Park
Burn
14
Allt Camghouran
KINROSS
Allt Mor
N O C H
Meall a'Bhobuir
Meall Garbh
968
Carn Mairg
1042
Strath of Appin
Weem Hill
Meall a'Mhuic
745
Keltney
Menzies
Meall Buidhe
931
Beinn Dearg
Carn Gorm
1029
Creag Mhor
981
Camserney
Coshieville
Dull
Cam Chreag
860
B846
Meall Cruinn
GLEN LYON
Invervar
Balintyre
Keltneyburn
Woodend
Ancient Yew
Lyon
Innerwick
Camusvrachan
Drummond Hill
Fortingall
Stix
Tay
Bolfrac
Loch an Daimh
Allt Conait
Lyon
Bridge of Balgie
Taymouth
Urlar Burn
5
Lochain
Gleann Da-ghob
25
Fearnan
Kenmore
Craig Hill
Meall a'Choire Leith
926
Meall Luaidhe
780
Meall Garbh
1118
Meall Greigh
1001
A827
Kenknock
Moar
Allt Gleann Da-Eig
Allt Bail' a'Mhuilinn
Remony
Acharn
Tay
Cashlie
Ben Lawers
1214
Lawers Burn
Falls of Acharn
Lyon
Stronuich Reservoir
Beinn nan Oighreag
909
Lairig Breisleich
550
Meall Corranaich
1069
Ardradnaig
Cragganruar
Beinn Bhreac
Creag an Sgliata
Meall nan Subh
804
Meall Ghaordie
1039
Lochan na Lairige
Beinn Ghlas
1013
Ben Lawers (NTS)
Meall Glass
Meall nan Tarmachan
1043
150
Lawers
Meall Odhar
Ardtalnaig
Quaich
Garrow
Auchnacloich
Meall Taurnie
Sgiath Bhuidhe
A
B
C
D
888
Acharn Burn
Loch
Gleann a' Chilleine
Meall nam Fuaran
Tullich
Duncroist
Milton Morenish
A827
Kiltyrie
Tullich Hill
Glen Lochay

159
168
160
151
D
E
F
G
I
2
3
4
5
Mullach Clach a'Bhlair
1019
Glenfeshie Forest
Beinn Bhrotain
Glen Dee
Sgor Mor
813
Mar Forest
B
R
A
Drochaide
818
617
Inver
Braemar
Allanaquoich
Invercauld Bridge
Creag Bhalg
Linn of Quoich
Mar Lodge (NTS)
Kindrochit
Bridge of Dee
Linn of Dee
Cairn Geldie
623
Dee
Muir
Inverey
Linn of Corriemulzie
Morrone Hill
859
Falls of Garbh Allt
Ballochbuie Forest
Auchallater
Feshie
Carn Liath
818
A B E R D E E N S H I R E
The Colonel's Bed
Newbigging
Cac Carn Beag
Glen Ey Forest
Carn an t-Sagairt Mor
1047
Carn an Fhidhleir (Carn Ealar)
994
An Sgarsoch
1006
Geldie Burn
Carn Bhac
946
Glen Ey
Loch Callater
Creag nan Gabhar
Glen Callater
G L E N C L U N I E
Clunie Water
Carn Bannoch
1012
920
Sgor Mor
887
Beinn Bhreac
Ey Burn
Baddoch Burn
An Socach
944
938
Carn an Tuirc
1019
Falls of Tarf
Allt Garbh Buidhe
16
Loch Mhairc
Tarf Water
Beinn Iutharn Mhor
1045
Beinn Iutharn Bheag
953
Carn Aosda
917
Tolmount
958
Cairn of Claise
1064
Tom Buidhe
957
Braigh Sron Ghorm
879
An Sligearnach
786
Carn an Righ
1029
A93
Glenshee Chairlifts & Ski Centre
933
Carn a'Gheoidh
975
The Cairnwell
665
Glas Maol
1068
Caenlochan
Carn a'Chlamain
963
Glas Tulaichean
1051
Devil's Elbow
Gleann Mor
Monega Hill
Finalty Hill
Beinn a'Chait
899
Loch Loch
Glen Loch
Creag Leacach
987
Caenlochan Forest
Forest Lodge
Carn nan Gabhar
1121
Carn Alt
864
Gleann Beag
A N G U S
Glen Tilt
Braigh Coire Chruinn-bhalgain
1069
Glen Lochsie
Beinn a'Ghlo
Ben Gulabin
Meall a'Choire Bhuidhe
868
Dalmunzie Hotel
Carn an Daimh
755
Fender Burn
Monamenach
807
A T H O L L
Carn Liath
975
Ben Earb
801
Spittal of Glenshee
Auchavan
Croftmore
Loch Beanie
Shee Water
Badandun Hill
Cairn Daunie
Meall Breac
Gleann Fearnach
Meall Uaine
794
G L E N S H E E
Mealna Letter or Duchray Hill
Loch Moraig
Glen Girnaig
Creag an -t Sithein
Finegand
Glen Finlet
Bridge of Tilt
Dalnaglar Castle
Forter
B951
Blair Atholl
Aldclune
Tarvie
Straloch
Lamh Dhearg
Lair
Cray
Mount Blair
744
Folda
Glenisla Forest
12
Garry
Ben Vrackie
841
Dalnacarn
13
Glen Brerachan
Killiecrankie
Pass of Killiecrankie
141
1689
Kindrogan Field Centre
Ennochdhu
Balvarran
Alrick
Bridge of Brewlands
The Soldier's Leap
Linn of Tummel (NTS)
Pass of Killiecrankie Visitor Centre
Creag Dhubh
A924
Meall Mor
B8019
Queen's View Visitor Centre
Craigower
Craigower (NTS)
Badyo
Blacklunans
Kirkton of Glenisla
Falls of Tummel
Moulin
Kirkmichael
S T R A T H A R D L E
B950
Bellaty
Loch Faskally
B8079
View
Cammoch Hill
Port na Craig
Pitlochry
Ballinluig
Dalrulzian
Cairn Gibbs
Druim Dearg
Loch Broom
Knock of Balmyle
Knockton
Eagagach
Hydro-Electric Visitor Centre & Fish Ladder
Edradour Distillery
Meall Reamhar
Forest of Alyth
Alyth Burn
Dunfallandy Stone
Balmyle
Lochbroom Burn
Ballintuim
Tummel
Creag nam Mial
561
Persie House
Drumderg
Strathtay
Pitnacree
Milton of Dalcapon
Bridge of Craigisla
S T R A T H T A Y
Ballechin
Ashmore
Balduff Hill
Grandtully
A827
Ballinluig
Tulliemet
Blackcraig Hill
Netherton
Tullymurdoch
Bamff
Logierait
Little Ballinluig
Balnaguard
Ardle
Bridge of Cally
Bochallie
Forest of Clunie
Loch Ordie
Loch Benachally
B898
Hill of Alyth
Grandtully
Balnaguard Burn
Bishopric
A9
Blackcraig Forest
Balmacneil
Kindallachan
Buckny Burn
Aberfeldy
Guay
Deuchary Hill
Benachally
Cochrage Muir
A93
Tullyfergus
Kincraigie
Alyth
Grandtully Hill
Loch Skiach
Dowally
Lornty Burn
Gatehouse
Elrick More
Riechip
Middleton
New Alyth
A826
Meall Reamhar
Arlick
Dalguise
Craigvinean Forest
Loch Kennard
Butterstone
A926
9
Achalader
Lornty
Parkhill
Loch na Craige
Craig a Barns
A923
Loch of Butterstone
Forneth
Loch of Clunie
Kinloch
Rattray
Monadh nam Mial
Dalmarnock
Creag an Eunaich
Loch of Craiglush
Blairgowrie
Concraigie
Craigie
Dunkeld
Loch of Lowes
Clunie
Loch of Drumellie
Muirton of Ardblair
Rosemount
Ericht
Scotston
The Hermitage (NTS)
Little Dunkeld
Druim Mor
Inver
Birnam
Lunan Burn
A923
Meall Dearg
690
Glen Cochill
Newtyle Hill
Kirkton of Lethendy
B947
Stormont Loch
Loch Fender
Dunkeld & Birnam Sta
Ballinlick
Thornton
Spittalfield
A984
Trochry
Birnam Hill
A984
Stenton
A984
Delvine
Aldville
A822
Drumour
Caputh
Meikleour
Coupar Angus
A826
Milton
S T R A T H B R A A N
Gellyburn
Kinclaven
Keithick
Markethill
Creag Hulich
Tay
Isla
A923
Ardoch
A94
Campmuir
A822
Obney Hills
Creag Liath
Muir of Thorn
Woodside
Amulree
Braan
Upper Obney
B9099
Laguna
Cargill
Burrelton
Achnafauld
Findowie Hill
Creag na Criche
Meall nan
B867
10
11
8
5
4
20
6
12

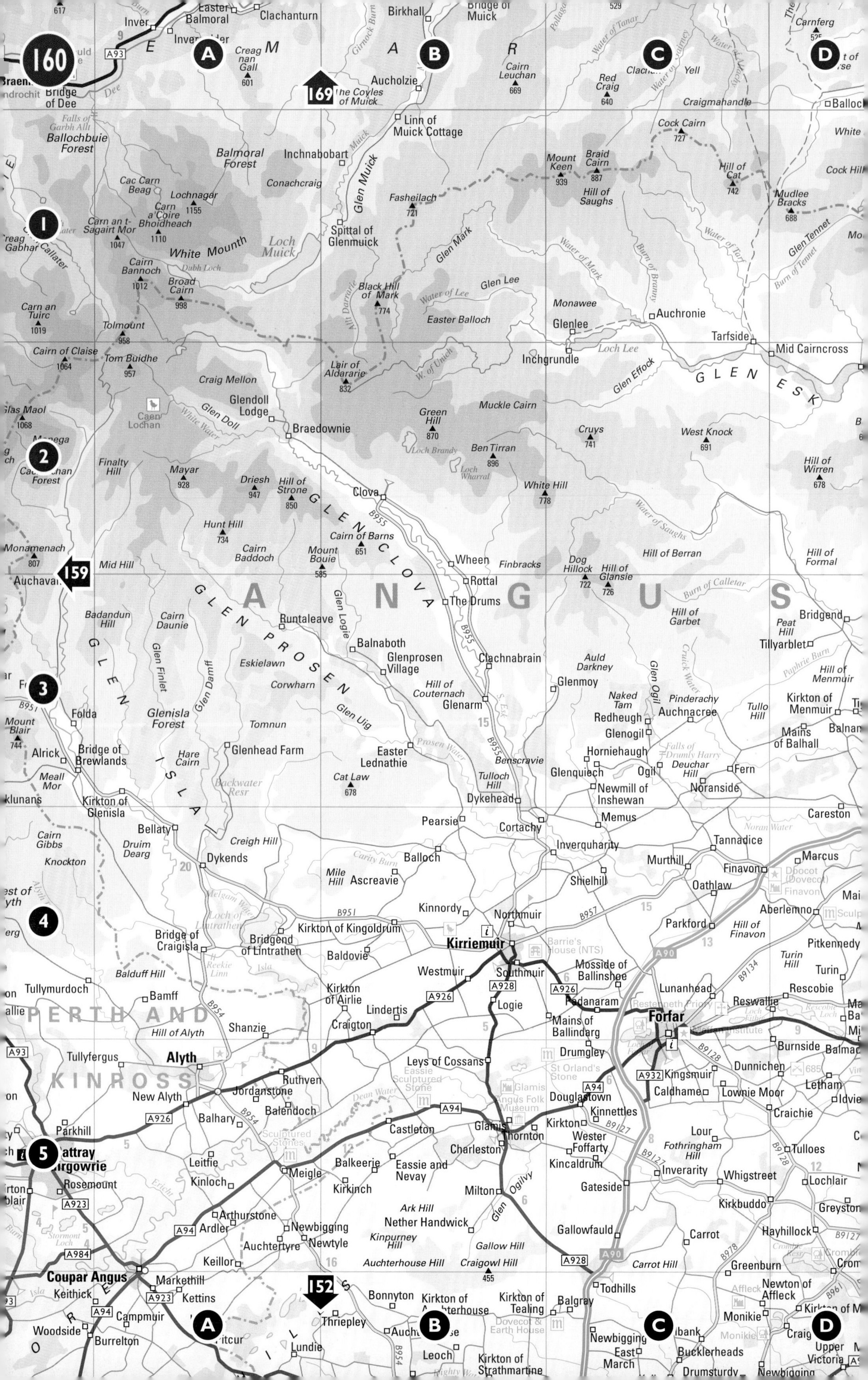
160
169
159
152
A
B
C
D
1
2
3
4
5
A N G U S
PERTH AND KINROSS
Balmoral Forest
Ballochbuie Forest
Lochnagar 1155
White Mounth
Loch Muick
Glen Muick
Spittal of Glenmuick
Inchnabobart
Linn of Muick Cottage
Aucholzie
Birkhall
Bridge of Dee
Inver
Easter Balmoral
Clachanturn
Creag nan Gall 601
Cairn Leuchan 669
Red Craig 640
Clachan Yell
Craigmahandle
Cock Cairn 727
Mount Keen 939
Braid Cairn 887
Hill of Saughs
Hill of Cat 742
Mudlee Bracks 688
Carnferg
Fasheilach 721
Glen Mark
Black Hill of Mark 774
Glen Lee
Water of Lee
Easter Balloch
Monawee
Auchronie
Glenlee
Tarfside
Mid Cairncross
Loch Lee
Inchgrundle
Glen Effock
GLEN ESK
Muckle Cairn
Cruys 741
West Knock 691
Hill of Wirren 678
Green Hill 870
Ben Tirran 896
Loch Brandy
Loch Wharral
White Hill 778
Lair of Aldararie 832
W. of Unich
Craig Mellon
Glendoll Lodge
Braedownie
Glen Doll
Caen Lochan
Mayar 928
Driesh 947
Hill of Strone 850
Clova
GLEN CLOVA
Cairn of Barns 651
Mount Bouie 585
Wheen
Rottal
The Drums
Finbracks
Dog Hillock 722
Hill of Glansie 726
Hill of Berran
Hill of Formal
Water of Saughs
Burn of Calletar
Hill of Garbet
Bridgend
Peat Hill
Tillyarblet
Cac Carn Beag
Carn a'Coire Bhoidheach 1110
Carn an t-Sagairt Mor 1047
Cairn Bannoch 1012
Broad Cairn 998
Dubh Loch
Carn an Tuirc 1019
Tolmount 958
Cairn of Claise 1064
Tom Buidhe 957
Glas Maol 1068
Finalty Hill
Hunt Hill 734
Cairn Baddoch
Monamenach 807
Mid Hill
Auchavan
GLEN PROSEN
Runtaleave
Balnaboth
Glenprosen Village
Glen Logie
Eskielawn
Corwharn
Glen Uig
Tomnun
Badandun Hill
Cairn Daunie
Glen Finlet
Glen Damff
Glenisla Forest
GLEN ISLA
Folda
Mount Blair 744
Alrick
Bridge of Brewlands
Hare Cairn
Glenhead Farm
Backwater Resr
Meall Mor
Kirkton of Glenisla
Bellaty
Cairn Gibbs
Knockton
Druim Dearg
Creigh Hill
Dykends
Easter Lednathie
Cat Law 678
Prosen Water
Hill of Couternach
Glenarm
Clachnabrain
Auld Darkney
Glenmoy
Glen Ogil
Naked Tam
Redheugh
Glenogil
Pinderachy
Auchnacree
Tullo Hill
Kirkton of Menmuir
Mains of Balhall
Hill of Menmuir
Horniehaugh
Falls of Drumly Harry
Deuchar Hill
Fern
Glenquiech
Ogil
Newmill of Inshewan
Noranside
Benscravie
Tulloch Hill
Dykehead
Careston
Pearsie
Cortachy
Memus
Inverquharity
Tannadice
Noran Water
Balloch
Mile Hill
Ascreavie
Carity Burn
Murthill
Shielhill
Finavon
Oathlaw
Marcus
Dovecot
Kinnordy
Northmuir
Kirriemuir
Barrie's House (NTS)
Aberlemno
Parkford
Hill of Finavon
Pitkennedy
Turin Hill
Turin
B951
B957
B955
A90
A926
A928
A93
A94
A923
A984
A932
B954
B9134
B9128
B9127
B978
B961
Bridge of Craigisla
Bridgend of Lintrathen
Loch of Lintrathen
Melgam Water
Kirkton of Kingoldrum
Baldovie
Reekie Linn
Isla
Balduff Hill
Tullymurdoch
Bamff
Westmuir
Southmuir
Mosside of Ballinshoe
Kirkton of Airlie
Logie
Padanaram
Lunanhead
Restenneth Priory
Reswallie
Rescobie
Rescobie Loch
Forfar
Meffan Institute
Lindertis
Craigton
Shanzie
Hill of Alyth
Mains of Ballindarg
Drumgley
Burnside
Tullyfergus
Alyth
Leys of Cossans
Eassie Sculptured Stone
St Orland's Stone
Kingsmuir
Dunnichen
Letham
Ruthven
Jordanstone
New Alyth
Balhary
Balendoch
Dean Water
Glamis Angus Folk Museum
Douglastown
Caldhame
Lownie Moor
Idvies
Craichie
Kinnettles
Glamis
Thornton
Kirkton
Wester Foffarty
Parkhill
Castleton
Charleston
Sculptured Stones
Rattray
Blairgowrie
Leitfie
Kinloch
Rosemount
Meigle
Balkeerie
Kirkinch
Eassie and Nevay
Milton
Glen Ogilvy
Kincaldrum
Fothringham Hill
Inverarity
Gateside
Lour
Tulloes
Whigstreet
Lochlair
Kirkbuddo
Greystone
Arthurstone
Ardler
Newbigging
Newtyle
Auchtertyre
Ark Hill
Nether Handwick
Kinpurney Hill
Gallow Hill
Gallowfauld
Carrot
Hayhillock
Stormont Loch
Keillor
Auchterhouse Hill
Craigowl Hill 455
Carrot Hill
Greenburn
Crombie
Coupar Angus
Markethill
Kettins
Keithick
Woodside
Campmuir
Burrelton
Pitcur
Lundie
Thriepley
Bonnyton
Kirkton of Auchterhouse
Leoch
Kirkton of Tealing
Dovecot & Earth House
Balgray
Todhills
Newbigging
East March
Kirkton of Strathmartine
Bucklerheads
Drumsturdy
Affleck
Newton of Affleck
Monikie
Kirkton of Monikie
Craig
Upper Victoria
Newbigging

D
E
F
G
170
Finzean
Baulds
Drumhead
Blackhall Forest
Goauch
337
Scolty
299
Auchattie
Blackness
Strachan
Invery Ho.
Crossroads
Blairydryi
Darnford
Cairn-mon-earn
378
A957
Durris Forest
Upper Burnhaugh
Borrowfield
Netherley
Cammachmore
Cookney
Craiggie
Muchalls
Meikle Carewe Hill
Newbigging
Bridge of Muchalls
Union Croft
Doonie Point
Castle Rock of Muchalls
Bridge of Bogendreip
Greendams
B974
B976
Westerton
Mongour
376
Craig of Dalfro
Peter Hill
617
Water of Aven
Mergie
Rickarton
Mowtie
A90
15
13
Fetteresso Forest
Kerloch
534
Burn of Sheeoch
Glendye Lodge
Clachnaben
589
Hill of Edendocher
Bridge of Dye
Water of Dye
Tipperweir
Hill of Trusta
321
Hill of Hobseat
New Mains of Ury
Garron Point
Cowie
Redcloak
Cowie Water
Strathlethan Bay
Stonehaven
Tewel
Kirktown of Fetteresso
ABERDEENSHIRE
Leachie Hill
Glen Dye
18
Brae of Glenbervie
Carron Water
Carmont
Castle Haven
Dunnottar
A92
Tannachie
Newmill
Thornyhive Bay
Hill of Fingray
485
Meluncart
525
369
Goyle Hill
464
Tipperty
Mains of Dillavaird
Chapelton
Trelung Ness
Water of Charr
Cairn o' Mount
455
Drumlithie
Bruxie Hill
216
Midtown of Barras
Mill of Uras
Herscha Hill
Glenbervie
Hound Hillock
518
Strath
Finella
Drumtochty
Forest
14
Nether Pitforthie
Crawton
Crawton Bay
Sturdy Hill
544
Clatterin Brig
Glensaugh
Strathfinella Hill
Auchenblae
B966
10
Catterline
Braidon Bay
Fawsyde
Todhead Point
North Esk
Fasque House
Thainston
East Cairnbeg
Fordoun
Bervie Water
Parkneuk
Roadside of Kinneff
Slains Park
Phesdo
Arbuthnott House
B967
Allardice
Kinneff
Auchmull
Howe of the Mearns
Arbuthnott
Fettercairn
Scotston
B9120
Burn Farm
Thornyhill
4
Inverbervie
Bervie Bay
Dalbog
The Burn
A937
Mains of Thornton
Easter Tulloch
Knox Hill
Gannochy
Meikle Strath
Laurencekirk
Garvock
Gourdon
Edzell
Inch of Arnhall
Johnston Mains
Redford
Arnhall
Sauchieburn
227
Benholm
Dunlappie
Luthermuir
Luther Water
Dykelands
Feus of Caldhame
Inglismaldie Forest
11
Brown Caterthun
Caterthun
Johnshaven
Inchbare
Stracathro
Pert
Gallery
Marykirk
Kirktonhill
Ecclesgreig
Newtonmill
Logie Pert
Craigo
Lochside
St Cyrus
Milton Ness
Belliehill
Keithock
Muirton of Ballochy
Morphie
Logie
Templewood
Pathhead
Little Brechin
Trinity
Hillside
Dun's Dish
House of Dun (NTS)
Brechin
Kirkhill
A935
Dun
Tayock
Round Tower
Arrat
Bridge of Dun
Caledonian Rly
9
Montrose
Montrose Basin
Montrose Museum & Art Gallery
Middle Drums
Barnhead
Scurdie Ness
Inchbraoch
Ferryden
Farnell
Bonnyton
Kirkton of Craig
A933
A934
Carcary
Maryton
Montreathmont Moor
Rossie Moor
Fishtown of Usan
12
Westerton
Long Craig
Wuddy Law
Boddin Point
Dubton
Bolshan
Rossie Farm School
Braehead of Lunan
Glasterlaw
Lunan
Lunan Bay
Red Castle
Friockheim
Kinnell
Redcastle
Boysack
Lunan Water
Pitmuies
B965
Inverkeilor
Chapelton
Inchock
Lang Craig
Red Head
Cauldcots
Ethie Mains
Leysmill
Kinblethmont
Drunkendub
0 2 4 6 8 10 miles
0 2 4 6 8 10 km
Parkhill
Colliston
Auchmithie
Redford
Marywell
Meg's Craig
Denhead of Arbirlot
St Vigeans
Carlingheugh Bay
Guynd
B9127
Arbirlot
Abbey
The Deil's Heid
Arbroath
Easter Knox
153
Wormiehills
Salmond's Muir
East Haven
1
2
3
4
5

174
172
A
B
C
D
1
2
3
4
5
Loch Bee
Geirninis
A865
Drimore
Groigearraidh
Stadhlaigearraidh
Loch Sheilavaig
Ben Tarbert
168
B890
Loch Sgioport
Loch Sgioport
Ornish Island
Tobha Mòr
Loch Druidibeg
Loch Spotal
Mol a'Tuath
Snishival
Peighinn nan Aoireann
Rubha Aird-mhicheil
Hecla
606
Staoinebrig
Ben Corodale
527
Loch Corodale
Rubha Rossel
Rubha Bhilidh
Ormacleit
SOUTH UIST
(UIBHIST A DEAS)
620 Beinn Mhor
Prince's Cave
Rubha Hellisdale
Rubha Ardvule
Bornais
Loch Kildonan
Arinambane
Ben na Hoe
Rubha Bolum
WESTERN ISLES
(NA H-EILEANAN AN IAR)
Flora Macdonald's Birthplace
Sheaval
223
Loch Eynort
Gearraidh Bhailteas
Mingearraidh
Arnaval
252
Rubha na Gibhte
A865
Hornary
Stulaval
374
Aisgernis
Loch Stulaval
Stuley
Loch Hallan
Dalabrog
Triuirebheinn
357
Pictish Wheel House
Crois Dughaill
Beinn Ruigh Choinnich
275
Rubha na Creige Mòire
Cille Pheadair
B888
Lochboisdale (Loch Baghasdail)
Rubha na Cruibe
Baghasdal
Loch Baghasdail
Orosay
Taobh a'Deas Loch Baghasdail
Calvay
Leth Meadhanach
Rubha Meall na Hoe
Trosaraidh
Gearraidh na Monadh
Easaval
Oitir na Cudaig
Ceann a' Gharaidh
Poll a'Charra
Cille Bhrighde
Ludag
Loch Moreef
Rubha na h-Ordaig
Roneval
201
Sound of Eriskay
Sound of Barra
Lingay
Haunn
Ben Scrien
185
Sloc Caol
Hartamul
Fiaray
Scurrival Point
Hornish
Eriskay
Ben Stack
122
Heinish
Rubha Liath
Eolaigearraidh
80
102
Cille-Bharra
Fuday
Traigh Eais
Orosay
Oitir Mhor
Stack Islands
hours
Oban..........................5-7
Barra (Tràigh Mhòr)
Greanamul
95
Gighay
Ardmhòr
Cuidhir
207
12
73
Hellisay
BARRA
(EILEAN BARRAIGH)
North Bay
107
Sound of Hellisay
Buaile nam Bodach
Fuiay
Flodday
1³/₄hrs
Ruleos
A888
Bruernish Point
Heaval
383
Earsairidh
Leideag
Kiessimul
Rubha Mòr
153
Muldoanich
hours
Oban..........................5¹/₄
A
B
C
D

163
D
E
F
G
I
2
3
4
5
175
164
154
Ramasaig Bay
Ramasaig
The Hoe
233
Lorgill
468
Orbost
Healabhal Bheag (Macleod's Table South)
488
Roag
Vatten
Harlosh
L. Vatten
Loch Varkasaig
Balmore
Harlosh Point
Ben Connan
244
Beinn na Boineid
371
Harlosh Island
Ben Idrigill
340
Tarner Island
Loch Bracadale
An Dubh Sgeir
MacLeod's Maidens
Idrigill Point
Wiay
Oronsay
Ose
Glen Ose
Loch Connan
Beinn na Cloiche
232
B885
Allt Mor
A863
Dun Beag
Bracadale
Ullinish
Struan
Coillore
S K Y E
Loch Duagrich
Ben Duagrich
304
Beinn Totaig
Tungadal
Ardtreck Point
Portnalong
Loch Harport
Fernilea
Rubha nan Clach
Arnaval
369
Carbost
Drynoch
B8009
Gleann Oraid
Talisker Bay
Talisker
Stockval
416
Biod Mor
383
Beinn Bhreac
445
Eynort
Beinn a'Bhraghad
461
Minginish
Loch Eynort
Beinn Staic
411
Sgurr a'Ghreadaidh
An Cruachan
435
Brittle
965
Sgurr Dearg (Inaccessible Pinnacle)
Glenbrittle
Bualintur
Sgurr Alasdair
Beinn an Eoin
312
Culnamean
Rubha Thearna Sgurr
Ceann na Beinne
Rubh' an Dunain
Soay Sound
INNER HEBRIDES
SEA OF THE HEBRIDES
HIGHLAND
CULLIN SOUND
CANNA
Camas Tharbernish
Carn a'Ghaill
210
Compass Hill
140
A'Chill
Canna (NTS)
Garrisdale Point
Tarbert Bay
Canna Harbour
Sron Ruail
Sanday
Rubha Shamhnan Insir
Sound of Canna
Kilmory
Sgaorishal
278
Mullach Mor
304
Humla
Bloodstone Hill
388
A'Bhrideanach
National Nature Reserve
Kinloch
Orval
571
RUM
Sgor Reidh
An Dornabac
263
Barkeval
591
Hallival
723
Askival
812
Harris
Garbh Sgeir
Oigh-sgeir
Rubha Sgor an t-Snidhe
Ruinsival
528
Ainshval
781
Sgurr nan Gillean
764
Rubha nam Meirleach
SOUND OF

164
176
163
155
A
B
C
D
1
2
3
4
5
Portree
Loch Portree
Raasay
Applecross
Milton
Camusteel
Camusterrach
Culduie
Sron na h-Airde Baine
Poll Creadha
INNER
SOUND
Loch Connan
Am Maol
212
Snizort
Beinn na Greine
417
Penifiler
Ben Tianavaig
413
Balachuirn
385
Glenmore
Glenmore
Mugeary
Stroc-bheinn
400
Loch Duagrich
Ben Duagrich
304
Allt Mor
Coillore
Camastianavaig
Holoman Bay
Oskaig Point
Dun Caan
443
Rubha na' Leac
Toscaig
Oskaig
L. Fada
B883
Tianavaig Bay
Narrows of Raasay
Lower Ollach
Upper Ollach
Clachan
Inverarish
Beinn na'Leac
319
A863
Beinn Totaig
Tungadal
Meall an Fhuarain
Roineval
439
The Braes
Ben Lee
445
Suisnish Point
East Suisnish
Peinchorran
Kyle More
Crowlin Islands
Caolas Mor
Eilean Meadhonach
Rubh' an Lochain
Eilean Mor
Uags
L. Toscaig
Loch Harport
Broc-bheinn
Glen Varragill
A87
Drynoch
A863
Carbost
B8009
Glen Drynoch
Sconser
Loch Sligachan
Meall a' Mhaoil
284
Scalpay
Mullach na Carn
396
Longay
Camas na Fisteodh
Glamaig
775
Sligachan
A87
Beinn Bhreac
370
Allt Dearg Mor
Glen Sligachan
Biod Mor
383
SKYE
Beinn Dearg
Loch Ainort
Luib
Dunan
Caolas Scalpay
Pabay
Kyle of Lochalsh
Kyle Akin
Eynort
Beinn a'Bhraghad
461
Cuillin Hills
Am Basteir
Sgurr nan Gillean
Bruach na Frithe
958
935
965
Glas Bheinn Mhor
570
Strath Mor
Marsco
736
6
A87
Corry
Broadford Bay
Broadford
Lower Breakish
Sgurr Thuilm
879
Sgurr a'Mhadaidh
918
Harta Corrie
Beinn Staic
411
Belig
Beinn Dearg Mhor
709
Beinn na Caillich
732
Broadford
Harrapool
Skulamus
Upper Breakish
An Cruachan
435
Sgurr a'Ghreadaidh
973
Sligachan
Garbh-bheinn
806
Sgurr na Banachdich
965
Sgurr Dearg (Inaccessible Pinnacle)
986
Druim Hain
Bla Bheinn (Blaven)
928
Torrin
Strath Suardal
A851
Cnoc Glac na Luachrach
Glen Arroch
Glenbrittle
Sgurr Mhic Choinnich
948
Brittle
Loch Coruisk
Loch na Creitheach
Loch Cill Chriosd
Ben Suardal
283
Beinn an Eoin
Culnamean
Sgurr Alasdair
993
Sgurr Dubh Mor
944
Sgurr na Stri
497
Kilbride
B8083
Sgurr nan Eag
924
Gars-bheinn
895
Strathaird
Camasunary
Loch Brittle
Loch na Cuilce
Camas Fhionnaigh
Beinn nan Carn
301
HIGH
Beinn na Seamraig
561
Ceann na Beinne
Kilmarie
Kirkibost
Beinn Bhuidhe
277
Heast
Beinn Bhreac
436
Loch Slapin
Rubh' an Dunain
Soay Sound
Beinn Bhreac
141
Loch Scavaig
Ben Meabost
346
Rubha Suisnish
Eilean Heast
Drumfearn
Leac nam Faoileann
Soay
Camas nan Gall
B8083
Drinan
Loch Eishort
Loch na Dal
Ardnamealach
Mol-chlach
Elgol
Spar Cave
Glasnakille
Sgorach Breac
299
Duisdealmor
Ord
Prince Charles's Cave
Rubha na h-Easgainne
Eilean Iarmain (Isleornsay)
Isle Ornsay
Dunsgaith
Ord
Tokavaig
A851
Camascross
Camus Croise
CUILLIN SOUND
SLEAT
Tarskavaig
Sgurr na h-Iolaire
292
Tarskavaig Bay
Teangue
Knock
Rubha Sliseach
Loch nam Uamh
Knock Bay
Achnacloich
Sgurr Breac
249
Kilmore
Kilbeg
Inverguseran
SOUND OF SLEAT
Loch a' Ghlinne
Clan Donald Centre
Inver Dalavil
Airor
Sgorr na h-Insir
Gleann Meadhonach
Armadale Bay
Armadale
Ardvasar
Calligarry
Sgurr nan Caorach
280
Sandaig
Sandaig Bay
Kilmory
Mullach Mor
304
Geur Rubha
Rubha na Roinne
½hr
Aird of Sleat
Kinloch
Kinloch
Ard Thurinish
Point of Sleat
Rubha Raonuill
RUM
Mallaigvaig
Mallaigmore
Sgurr an Eilein Ghiubhais
522
Barkeval
591
Bagh na h-Uamha
Carn a'Ghobhair
547
Mallaig
Glasnacardoch
Hallival
723
Askival
812
Loch an Nostarie
Sgurr Bhuidhe
440
781
A830
Loch a'Ghille Ghobaich
Sgurr nan Gillean
764
SOUND OF RUM
Morar
Bracora
8
Eilean a'Phidhir
Gleann nam Meirleach
Portnaluchaig
Carn a'Mhadaidh-ruaidh
503
Lettermorar
Rubha an Fhasaidh
Bay of Laig
Cleadale
An Cruachan
299
Eilean Ighe
Back of Keppoch
Laig
315
EIGG
ARISAIG
Loch a'Chaol Riabhaich
599
Luinga Mhor
Loch nan Ceall
Arisaig
Rhumach
Kildonnan
Morroch
Glen Beasdale

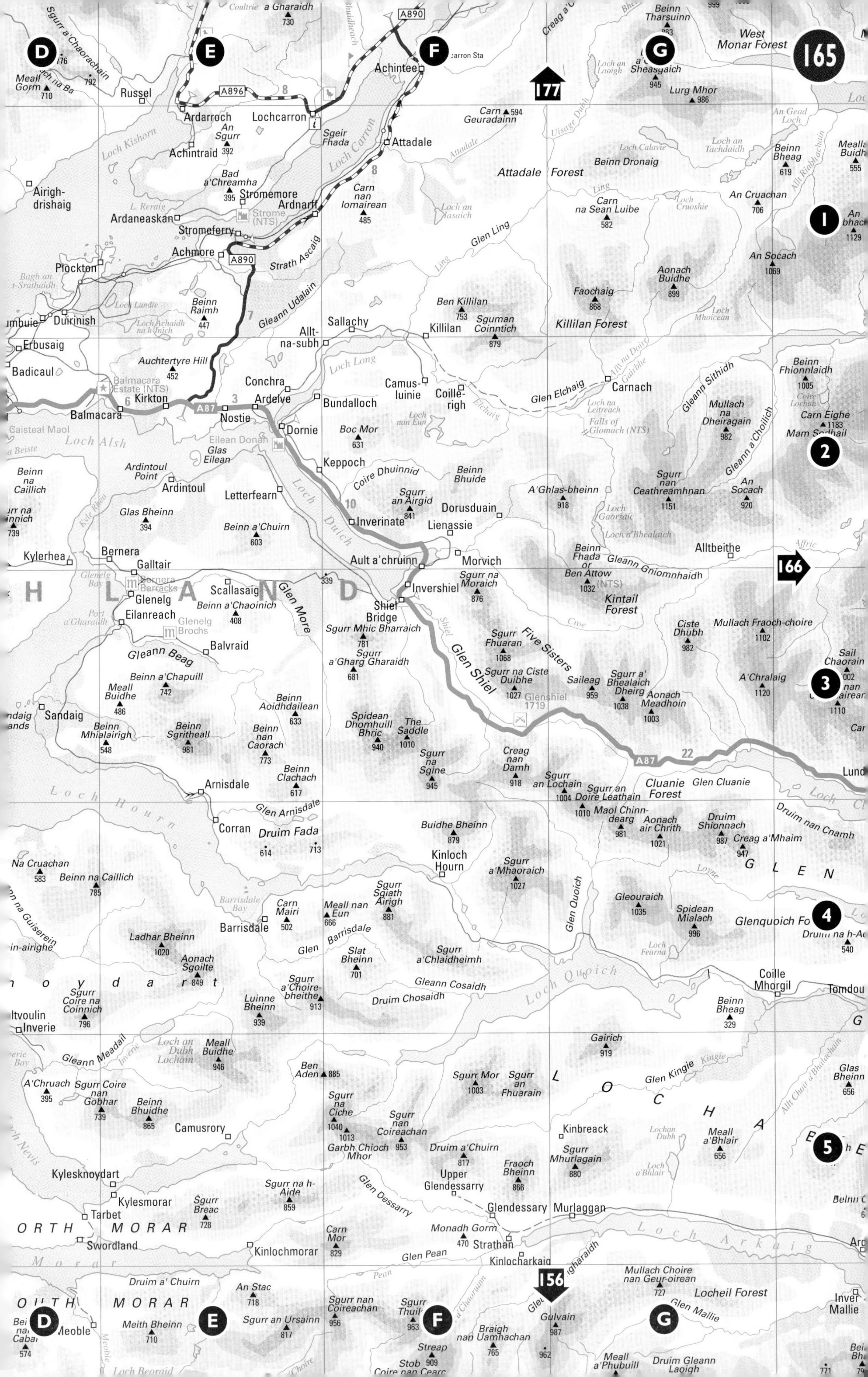
D
E
F
G
177
West Monar Forest
Sgurr a Chaorachain
Meall Gorm 710
Russel
A896
A890
Coultrie
a Gharaidh 730
Achintee
carron Sta
Beinn Tharsuinn 863
Sheasgaich 945
Lurg Mhor 986
Loch an Laoigh
Creag a'
Ardarroch
Lochcarron
An Sgurr 392
Achintraid
Loch Kishorn
Sgeir Fhada
Loch Carron
Attadale
Carn Geuradainn 594
Uisage Dubh
Loch Calavie
Beinn Dronaig
Attadale Forest
Loch an Tachdaidh
An Gead Loch
Beinn Bheag 619
Meall Buidh 555
Airigh-drishaig
Bad a'Chreamha 395
Stromemore
Ardnarff
Carn nan Iomairean 485
L. Reraig
Strome (NTS)
Ardaneaskan
Stromeferry
Achmore
Strath Ascaig
Loch an Iasaich
Glen Ling
Ling
Carn na Sean Luibe 582
Loch Cruoshie
An Cruachan 706
An Socach 1069
1129
Plockton
Bagh an t-Srathaidh
Loch Lundie
Beinn Raimh 447
Loch Achaidh na h-Inich
Gleann Udalain
Ben Killilan 753
Sguman Coinntich 879
Faochaig 868
Aonach Buidhe 899
Killilan Forest
Loch Mhoicean
Duirinish
Erbusaig
Badicaul
Auchtertyre Hill 452
Sallachy
Allt-na-subh
Killilan
Loch Long
Camus-luinie
Coille-righ
Elchaig
Glen Elchaig
Allt na Doire Gairbhe
Carnach
Gleann Sithidh
Beinn Fhionnlaidh 1005
Coire Lochan
Carn Eighe 1183
Mam Sodhail
Balmacara Estate (NTS)
Balmacara
Kirkton
A87
Conchra
Ardelve
Nostie
Bundalloch
Dornie
Eilean Donan
Loch nan Eun
Loch na Leitreach
Falls of Glomach (NTS)
Mullach na Dheiragain 982
Gleann a'Choilich
Caisteal Maol
Loch Alsh
Glas Eilean
Boc Mor 631
Keppoch
Coire Dhuinnid
Beinn Bhuide
Sgurr an Airgid 841
Sgurr nan Ceathreamhnan 1151
An Socach 920
Beinn na Caillich
Ardintoul Point
Ardintoul
Letterfearn
Loch Duich
Kyle Rhea
Glas Bheinn 394
Beinn a'Chuirn 603
Inverinate
Lienassie
Dorusduain
A'Ghlas-bheinn 918
Loch Gaorsaic
Loch a'Bhealaich
Alltbeithe
Affric
Kylerhea
Bernera
Galltair
Bernera Barracks
Glenelg Bay
Ault a'chruinn
Morvich
Beinn Fhada or Ben Attow 1032 (NTS)
Gleann Gniomhnaidh
Kintail Forest
166
H L A N D
Glenelg
Scallasaig
Beinn a'Chaoinich 408
Glen More
339
Inversheil
Shiel Bridge
Sgurr na Moraich 876
Port a'Gharaidh
Eilanreach
Glenelg Brochs
Balvraid
Sgurr Mhic Bharraich 781
Sgurr a'Gharg Gharaidh 681
Glen Shiel
Sgurr Fhuaran 1068
Five Sisters
Croe
Ciste Dhubh 982
Mullach Fraoch-choire 1102
Sail Chaorain
Gleann Beag
Beinn a'Chapuill 742
Meall Buidhe 486
Sgurr na Ciste Duibhe 1027
Glenshiel 1719
Saileag 959
Sgurr a' Bhealaich Dheirg 1038
Aonach Meadhoin 1003
A'Chralaig 1120
1110
Sandaig
Beinn Aoidhdailean 633
Beinn Mhialairigh 548
Beinn Sgritheall 981
Beinn nan Caorach 773
Spidean Dhomhuill Bhric 940
The Saddle 1010
Sgurr na Sgine 945
Creag nan Damh 918
Sgurr an Lochain 1004
A87
22
Lund
Beinn Clachach 617
Sgurr an Doire Leathain 1010
Cluanie Forest
Glen Cluanie
Loch Hourn
Arnisdale
Glen Arnisdale
Corran
Druim Fada 614
713
Maol Chinn-dearg 981
Aonach air Chrith 1021
Druim Shionnach 987
Creag a'Mhaim 947
Druim nan Cnamh
Buidhe Bheinn 879
Kinloch Hourn
Na Cruachan 583
Beinn na Caillich 785
Sgurr a'Mhaoraich 1027
GLEN
Loyne
Barrisdale Bay
Carn Mairi 502
Meall nan Eun 666
Sgurr Sgiath Airigh 881
Glen Quoich
Gleouraich 1035
Spidean Mialach 996
Glenquoich Fo
Barrisdale
Ladhar Bheinn 1020
Glen Barrisdale
Slat Bheinn 701
Sgurr a'Chlaidheimh
Loch Fearna
Druim na h-A 540
Aonach Sgoilte 849
oydart
Sgurr Coire na Coinnich 796
Sgurr a'Choire-bheithe 913
Gleann Cosaidh
Loch Quoich
Coille Mhorgil
Tomdou
Luinne Bheinn 939
Druim Chosaidh
Beinn Bheag 329
Inverie
Loch an Dubh Lochain
Meall Buidhe 946
Gairich 919
Gleann Meadail
Inverie
Ben Aden 885
Sgurr Mor 1003
Sgurr an Fhuarain
Glen Kingie
Kingie
Glas Bheinn 656
A'Chruach 395
Sgurr Coire nan Gobhar 739
Beinn Bhuidhe 865
Sgurr na Ciche 1040
1013
Sgurr nan Coireachan 953
LOCHA
Kinbreack
Lochan Dubh
Allt Choir a'Bhalachain
Camusrory
Garbh Chioch Mhor
Druim a'Chuirn 817
Sgurr Mhurlagain 880
Meall a'Bhlair 656
Loch a'Bhlair
Fraoch Bheinn 866
Upper Glendessarry
Kylesknoydart
Kylesmorar
Sgurr na h-Aide 859
Glen Dessarry
Glendessary
Murlaggan
Tarbet
Sgurr Breac 728
Monadh Gorm 470
Strathan
Loch Arkaig
NORTH MORAR
Swordland
Kinlochmorar
Carn Mor 829
Glen Pean
Kinlocharkaig
Morar
Pean
156
Mullach Choire nan Geur-oirean 727
Locheil Forest
Druim a' Chuirn
An Stac 718
Sgurr nan Coireachan 956
Sgurr Thuilm 963
Glen Mallie
Inver Mallie
SOUTH MORAR
Meith Bheinn 710
Sgurr an Ursainn 817
Gulvain 987
Braigh nan Uamhachan 765
962
Meoble
Beinn na Cabar 574
Streap 909
Stob Coire nan Cearc
Meall a'Phubuill
Druim Gleann Laoigh
Loch Beoraid
771

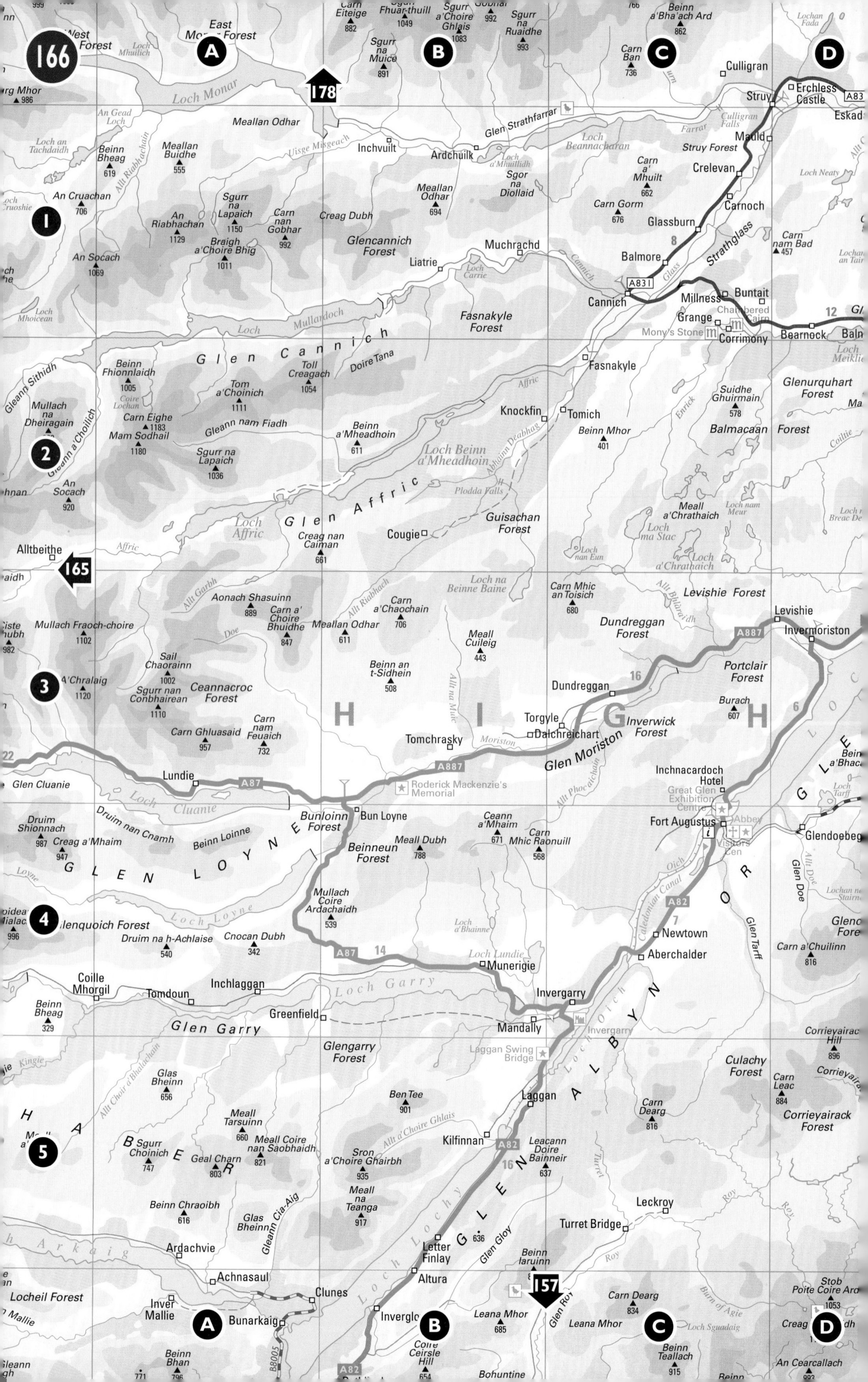
166
178
165
157
A
B
C
D
1
2
3
4
5
East Monar Forest
West Forest
Loch Monar
Sgurr Fhuar-thuill 1049
Carn Eiteige 882
Sgurr a'Choire Ghlais 1083
Sgurr na Ruaidhe 993
Sgurr na Muice 891
Beinn a'Bha'ach Ard 862
Carn Ban 736
Culligran
Struy
Erchless Castle
A831
Eskadale
Glen Strathfarrar
Farrar
Culligran Falls
Mauld
Struy Forest
Loch Beannacharan
Meallan Odhar
Uisge Misgeach
Inchvuilt
Ardchuilk
Loch an Tachdaidh
An Gead Loch
Beinn Bheag 619
Meallan Buidhe 555
Allt Riabhachain
Loch a'Mhuillidh
Sgor na Diollaid
Carn a' Mhuilt 662
Crelevan
Loch Neaty
An Cruachan 706
Sgurr na Lapaich 1150
Carn nan Gobhar 992
Creag Dubh
Meallan Odhar 694
Carn Gorm 676
Carnoch
Glassburn
An Riabhachan 1129
Braigh a'Choire Bhig 1011
Glencannich Forest
Strathglass
Carn nam Bad 457
An Socach 1069
Muchrachd
Liatrie
Loch Carrie
Cannich
Balmore
A831
Glass
Loch Mhoicean
Loch Mullardoch
Fasnakyle Forest
Millness
Buntait
Grange
Chambered Cairn
Mony's Stone
Corrimony
Bearnock
12
Glen Cannich
Gleann Sithidh
Beinn Fhionnlaidh 1005
Tom a'Choinich 1111
Toll Creagach 1054
Doire Tana
Fasnakyle
Affric
Enrick
Suidhe Ghuirmain 578
Glenurquhart Forest
Loch Meiklie
Mullach na Dheiragain
Coire Lochan
Carn Eighe 1183
Mam Sodhail 1180
Gleann nam Fiadh
Beinn a'Mheadhoin 611
Knockfin
Tomich
Beinn Mhor 401
Balmacaan Forest
Gleann a'Choilich
Sgurr na Lapaich 1036
Loch Beinn a'Mheadhoin
Abhainn Deabhag
An Socach 920
Glen Affric
Plodda Falls
Meall a'Chrathaich
Loch nam Meur
Loch Affric
Creag nan Caiman 661
Cougie
Guisachan Forest
Loch ma Stac
Alltbeithe
Loch nan Eun
Loch a'Chrathaich
Aonach Shasuinn 889
Allt Garbh
Allt Riabhach
Loch na Beinne Baine
Carn Mhic an Toisich 680
Levishie Forest
Allt Bhlaraidh
Levishie
Invermoriston
A887
Mullach Fraoch-choire 1102
Carn a' Choire Bhuidhe 847
Carn a'Chaochain 706
Meallan Odhar 611
Meall Cuileig 443
Dundreggan Forest
Doe
Sail Chaorainn 1002
A'Chralaig 1120
Beinn an t-Sidhein 508
Portclair Forest
16
Sgurr nan Conbhairean 1110
Ceannacroc Forest
Allt na Muic
Dundreggan
Burach 607
H
I
G
H
Torgyle
Inverwick Forest
Carn Ghluasaid 957
Carn nam Feuaich 732
Tomchrasky
Dalchreichart
Moriston
Glen Moriston
6
22
Lundie
A87
A887
Glen Cluanie
Loch Cluanie
Roderick Mackenzie's Memorial
Allt Phocaichain
Inchnacardoch Hotel
Great Glen Exhibition Centre
Abbey
Bun Loyne
Bunloinn Forest
Druim Shionnach 987
Druim nan Cnamh
Beinn Loinne
Creag a'Mhaim 947
Ceann a'Mhaim 671
Meall Dubh 788
Carn Mhic Raonuill 568
Beinneun Forest
Fort Augustus
Visitors Cen
Glendoebeg
Glen Doe
Allt Doe
GLEN LOYNE
Loyne
Oich
Caledonian Canal
A82
Mullach Coire Ardachaidh 539
Loch a'Bhainne
7
Newtown
Aberchalder
Glen Tarff
Carn a'Chuilinn 816
Glenquoich Forest
Loch Loyne
Druim na h-Achlaise 540
Cnocan Dubh 342
A87
14
Loch Lundie
Munerigie
Coille Mhorgil
Tomdoun
Inchlaggan
Loch Garry
Invergarry
Beinn Bheag 329
Greenfield
Mandally
Glen Garry
Loch Oich
Glengarry Forest
Laggan Swing Bridge
Corrieyairack Hill 896
Culachy Forest
Kingie
Glas Bheinn 656
Allt Choir a'Bhalachain
Ben Tee 901
Laggan
Carn Leac 884
Carn Dearg 816
Corrieyairack Forest
Meall Tarsuinn 660
Allt a'Choire Ghlais
Kilfinnan
Sgurr Choinich 747
Geal Charn 803
Meall Coire nan Saobhaidh 821
Sron a'Choire Ghairbh 935
A82
Leacann Doire Bainneir 637
Turret
GLEN ALBYN
GREAT GLEN
Meall na Teanga 917
Beinn Chraoibh 616
Glas Bheinn
Gleann Cia-Aig
Loch Lochy
Glen Gloy
636
Leckroy
Turret Bridge
Roy
Loch Arkaig
Ardachvie
Letter Finlay
Beinn Iaruinn
Roy
Achnasaul
Altura
Stob Poite Coire Ardair 1053
Locheil Forest
Clunes
Carn Dearg 834
Burn of Agie
Inver Mallie
Bunarkaig
Invergloy
Leana Mhor 685
Leana Mhor
Glen Roy
Loch Sguadaig
Creag Meagaidh
B8005
Coire Ceirsle Hill 654
Beinn Teallach 915
An Cearcallach
Beinn Bhan 796
A82
Bohuntine
Gleann

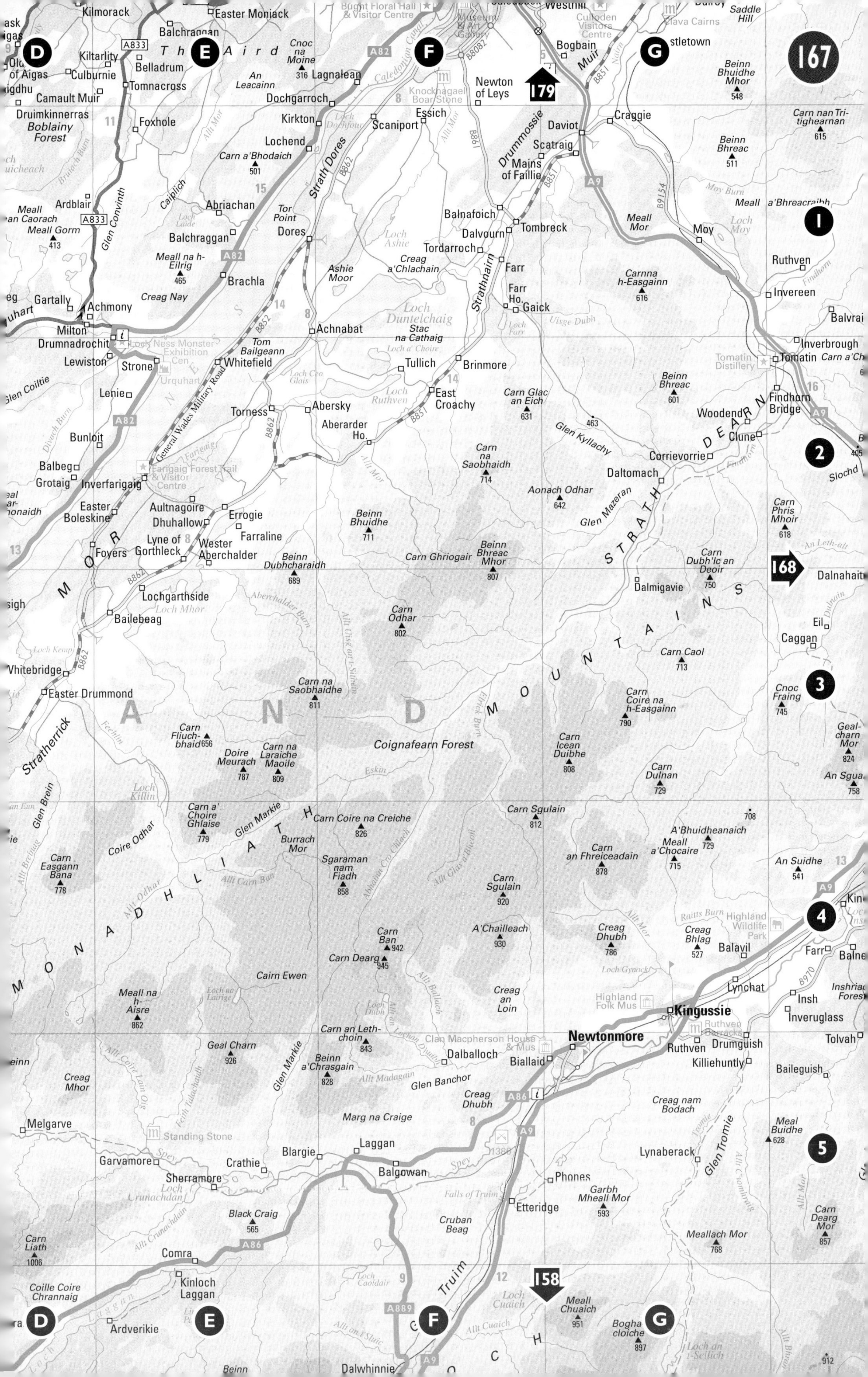
167
Kilmorack
Easter Moniack
Balchraggan
The Aird
Cnoc na Moine 316
Lagnalean
Kiltarlity
Belladrum
Culburnie
Tomnacross
Camault Muir
An Leacainn
Dochgarroch
Caledonian Canal
Museum & Art Gallery
Bught Floral Hall & Visitor Centre
Knockhagael Boar Stone
Newton of Leys
Culloden Visitors Centre
Bogbain
Muir
stletown
Clava Cairns
Saddle Hill
Beinn Bhuidhe Mhor 548
Druimkinnerras
Boblainy Forest
Foxhole
Kirkton
Loch Dochfour
Scaniport
Essich
Drummossie
Daviot
Craggie
Carn nan Tri-tighearnan 615
Lochend
Strath Dores
Carn a'Bhodaich 501
Scatraig
Mains of Faillie
Beinn Bhreac 511
Meall nan Caorach
Ardblair
Glen Convinth
Caiplich
Abriachan
Loch Laide
Tor Point
Dores
Balnafoich
Dalvourn
Tombreck
Moy Burn
Meall a'Bhreacraibh
Meall Gorm 413
Balchraggan
Loch Ashie
Tordarroch
Meall Mor
Moy
Loch Moy
Meall na h-Eilrig 465
Brachla
Ashie Moor
Creag a'Chlachain
Farr
Carnna h-Easgainn 616
Ruthven
Creag Nay
Farr Ho.
Gaick
Strathnairn
Uisge Dubh
Invereen
Findhorn
Gartally
Achmony
Loch Duntelchaig
Achnabat
Stac na Cathaig
Loch Farr
Balvraid
Milton
Drumnadrochit
Loch Ness Monster Exhibition Cen
Tom Bailgeann
Loch a' Choire
Inverbrough
Lewiston
Strone
Urquhart
Whitefield
General Wades Military Road
Tullich
Brinmore
Tomatin Distillery
Tomatin
Carn a'Ch
Glen Coiltie
Lenie
Loch Ceo Glais
Loch Ruthven
East Croachy
Carn Glac an Eich 631
Beinn Bhreac 601
Findhorn Bridge
Woodend
Torness
Abersky
Aberarder Ho.
463
Glen Kyllachy
Clune
Bunloit
Divach Burn
Balbeg
Grotaig
Inverfarigaig
Farigaig Forest Trail & Visitor Centre
Allt Mor
Carn na Saobhaidh 714
Corrievorrie
Daltomach
Slochd
405
Easter Boleskine
Aultnagoire
Errogie
Dhuhallow
Beinn Bhuidhe 711
Aonach Odhar 642
Glen Mazeran
Strath Dearn
Carn Phris Mhoir 618
Foyers
Lyne of Gorthleck
Wester Aberchalder
Farraline
Beinn Dubhcharaidh 689
Carn Ghriogair
Beinn Bhreac Mhor 807
Carn Dubh'Ic an Deoir 750
An Leth-allt
168
Dalnahaitnach
Lochgarthside
Loch Mhor
Aberchalder Burn
Dalmigavie
Bailebeag
Carn Odhar 802
Allt Uisg an t-Sithein
Eil
Caggan
Loch Kemp
Carn Caol 713
Whitebridge
Easter Drummond
Carn na Saobhaidhe 811
Carn Coire na h-Easgainn 790
Cnoc Fraing 745
Stratherrick
Feehlin
Monadhliath Mountains
Coignafearn Forest
Carn Fliuch-bhaid 656
Doire Meurach 787
Carn na Laraiche Maoile 809
Elrick Burn
Carn Icean Duibhe 808
Geal-charn Mor 824
Glen Brein
Loch Killin
Eskin
Carn Dulnan 729
An Sgua 758
Carn a' Choire Ghlaise 779
Glen Markie
Carn Coire na Creiche 826
Carn Sgulain 812
708
Coire Odhar
Burrach Mor
A'Bhuidheanaich 729
Carn Easgann Bana 778
Allt Breinag
Allt Carn Ban
Sgaraman nam Fiadh 858
Abhainn Cro Chlach
Allt Glas a'Bheoil
Carn an Fhreiceadain 878
Meall a'Chocaire 715
An Suidhe 541
Allt Odhar
Carn Sgulain 920
Raitts Burn
Highland Wildlife Park
Kincraig
Carn Ban 942
A'Chailleach 930
Creag Dhubh 786
Creag Bhlag 527
Balavil
Farr
Balnespick
Carn Dearg 945
Cairn Ewen
Loch na Lairige
Allt Bellach
Creag an Loin
Loch Gynack
Lynchat
Meall na h-Aisre 862
Highland Folk Mus
Kingussie
Insh
Inshriach Forest
Inveruglass
Loch Dubh
Carn an Leth-choin 843
Clan Macpherson House & Mus
Newtonmore
Ruthven Barracks
Tolvah
Geal Charn 926
Dalballoch
Biallaid
Ruthven
Drumguish
Killiehuntly
Beinn a'Chrasgain 828
Allt Madagain
Glen Banchor
Baileguish
Creag Mhor
Allt Coire Lain Oig
Feith Talachaidh
Creag Dhubh
Creag nam Bodach
Melgarve
Standing Stone
Marg na Craige
Meal Buidhe 628
Glen Tromie
Spey
Laggan
Blargie
Lynaberack
Garvamore
Crathie
Balgowan
1386
Sherramore
Loch Crunachdan
Phones
Falls of Truim
Garbh Mheall Mor 593
Etteridge
Allt Crunachdain
Black Craig 565
Cruban Beag
Meallach Mor 768
Carn Dearg Mor 857
Carn Liath 1006
Comra
Truim
Kinloch Laggan
Coille Coire Chrannaig
Loch Caoldair
Loch Cuaich
158
Meall Chuaich 951
Bogha cloiche 897
Laggan
Ardverikie
Allt an t-Sluic
Allt Cuaich
Loch an t-Seilich
912
Dalwhinnie
Beinn
A82
A833
A86
A889
A9
B862
B852
B851
B861
B8082
B9154
B970
179
1 2 3 4 5
D E F G

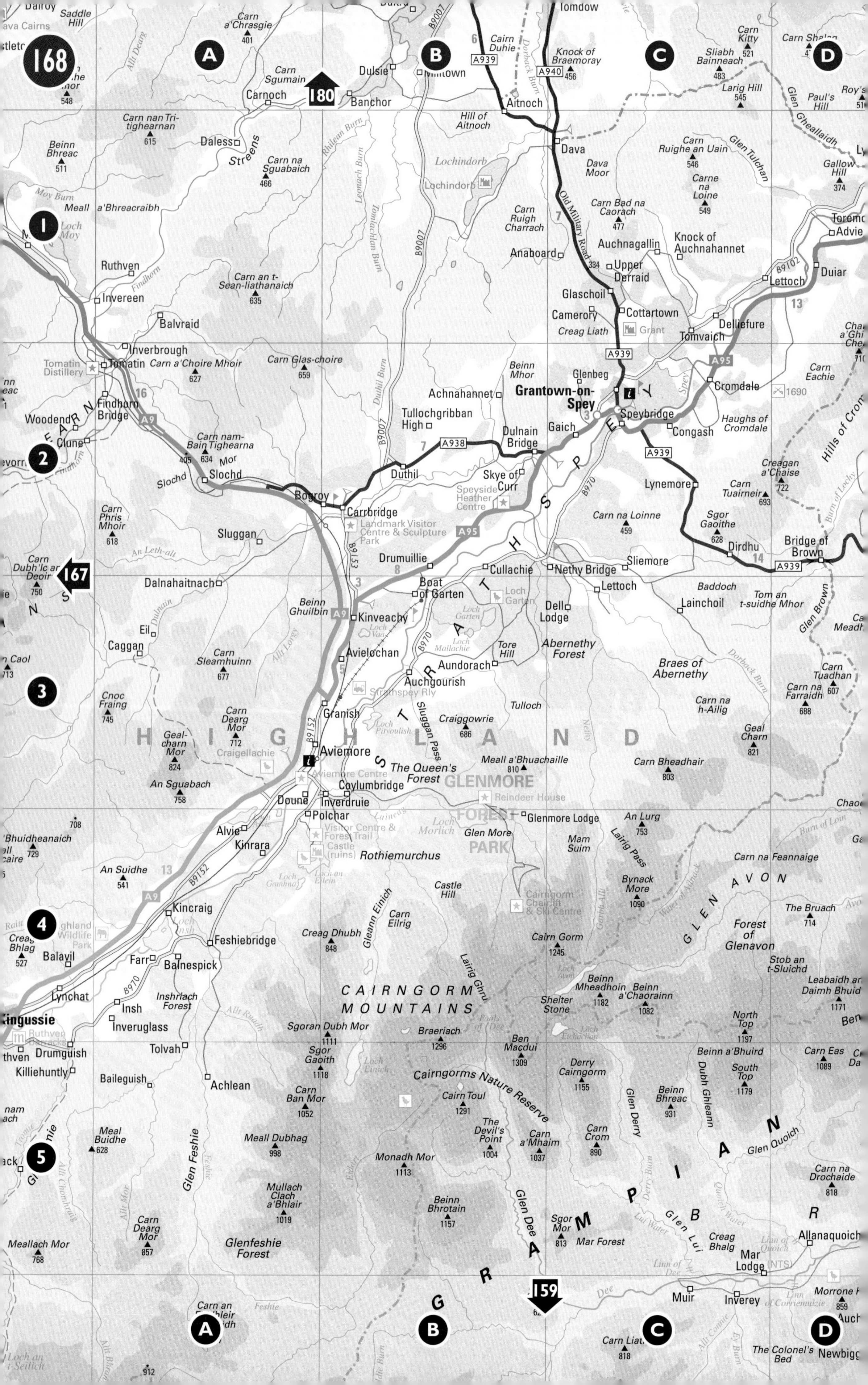
168
Saddle Hill
Carn a'Chrasgie 401
A
B
C
D
Carn Sgumain
180
Dulsie
Milltown
Carnoch
Banchor
Carn Duhie
A939
A940
Tomdow
Knock of Braemoray 456
Carn Kitty 521
Sliabh Bainneach 483
Larig Hill 545
Carn Shalag
Paul's Hill
Roy's Hill
Glen Gheallaidh
Aitnoch
Hill of Aitnoch
Carn nan Tri-tighearnan 615
Daless
Streens
Carn na Sguabaich 466
Rhilean Burn
Lochindorb
Dava
Dava Moor
Carn Ruighe an Uain 546
Glen Tulchan
Carne na Loine 549
Gallow Hill 374
Beinn Bhreac 511
Moy Burn
Meall a'Bhreacraibh
Leonach Burn
Tomlachlan Burn
B9007
Carn Ruigh Charrach
Old Military Road
Carn Bad na Caorach 477
Loch Moy
Ruthven
Findhorn
Carn an t-Sean-liathanaich 635
Anaboard
Auchnagallin
Knock of Auchnahannet
Tormore
Advie
Upper Derraid 334
B9102
Lettoch
Duiar
Invereen
Glaschoil
Balvraid
Camerory
Cottartown
Grant
Creag Liath
Delliefure
Tomvaich
Inverbrough
Tomatin Distillery
Tomatin
Carn a'Choire Mhoir 627
Carn Glas-choire 659
Dulnain Burn
A939
Beinn Mhor
Glenbeg
A95
Carn Eachie
Cromdale
1690
Achnahannet
Grantown-on-Spey
Findhorn Bridge
A9
Woodend
Clune
Tullochgribban High
Dulnain Bridge
Gaich
Speybridge
Congash
Haughs of Cromdale
Hills of Cromdale
A938
Carn nam-Bain Tighearna 634
405
Mor
Slochd
Duthil
Skye of Curr
Speyside Heather Centre
B970
A939
Creagan a'Chaise 722
Lynemore
Carn Tuairneir 693
Bogroy
Carrbridge
Landmark Visitor Centre & Sculpture Park
Carn Phris Mhoir 618
Sluggan
Carn na Loinne 459
Sgor Gaoithe 628
Dirdhu
Bridge of Brown
An Leth-allt
B9153
A95
Drumuillie
Sliemore
Carn Dubh'Ic an Deoir 750
167
Dalnahaitnach
Boat of Garten
Cullachie
Nethy Bridge
Lettoch
Baddoch
Tom an t-suidhe Mhor
Loch Garten
Beinn Ghuilbin
Kinveachy
Dell Lodge
Lainchoil
Glen Brown
Eil
Loch Vaa
Loch Mallachie
Tore Hill
Abernethy Forest
Caggan
Avielochan
Allt Lorgy
Aundorach
Auchgourish
Braes of Abernethy
Dorback Burn
Carn Tuadhan 607
Carn Sleamhuinn 677
Strathspey Rly
Carn na Farraidh 688
Carn na h-Ailig
Cnoc Fraing 745
Carn Dearg Mor 712
Granish
Sluggan Pass
Craiggowrie 686
Tulloch
Loch Pityoulish
Geal-charn Mor 824
Craigellachie
Aviemore
B9152
HIGHLAND
STRATHSPEY
Geal Charn 821
Meall a'Bhuachaille 810
Carn Bheadhair 803
The Queen's Forest
GLENMORE FOREST PARK
An Sguabach 758
Aviemore Centre
Coylumbridge
Reindeer House
Doune
Inverdruie
Polchar
Glenmore Lodge
An Lurg 753
708
Alvie
Kinrara
Loch Morlich
Glen More
Mam Suim
Lairig Pass
Visitor Centre & Forest Trail
Castle (ruins)
Rothiemurchus
Carn na Feannaige
An Suidhe 541
B9152
13
Loch Gamhna
Loch an Eilein
Castle Hill
Bynack More 1090
Water of Ailnack
GLEN AVON
A9
Cairngorm Chairlift & Ski Centre
Kincraig
Highland Wildlife Park
Carn Eilrig
Glen Einich
Creag Dhubh 848
The Bruach 714
Forest of Glenavon
Creag Bhlag 527
Feshiebridge
Loch Insh
Cairn Gorm 1245
Balavil
Farr
Balnespick
Lairig Ghru
Stob an t-Sluichd
Leabaidh an Daimh Bhuidhe 1171
B970
Lynchat
Inshriach Forest
CAIRNGORM MOUNTAINS
Beinn Mheadhoin 1182
Beinn a'Chaorainn 1082
Shelter Stone
Insh
Kingussie
Inveruglass
Allt Ruadh
Sgoran Dubh Mor 1111
Pools of Dee
Loch Etchachan
North Top 1197
Ruthven Barracks
Tolvah
Braeriach 1296
Ben Macdui 1309
Beinn a'Bhuird
Carn Eas 1089
Drumguish
Killiehuntly
Sgor Gaoith 1118
Loch Einich
Derry Cairngorm 1155
South Top 1179
Baileguish
Achlean
Cairngorms Nature Reserve
Glen Derry
Dubh Ghleann
Carn Ban Mor 1052
Cairn Toul 1291
Beinn Bhreac 931
Glen Tromie
Meall Buidhe 628
Glen Feshie
The Devil's Point 1004
Carn a'Mhaim 1037
Carn Crom 890
GRAMPIAN
Glen Quoich
Meall Dubhag 998
Monadh Mor 1113
Carn na Drochaide 818
Allt Chomhraig
Eidart
Derry Burn
Quoich Water
Mullach Clach a'Bhlair 1019
Beinn Bhrotain 1157
Glen Dee
Glen Lui
Lui Water
Carn Dearg Mor 857
Allt Mor
Sgor Mor 813
Mar Forest
Creag Bhalg
Linn of Quoich
Allanaquoich
Meallach Mor 768
Glenfeshie Forest
Linn of Dee
Mar Lodge (NTS)
159
Dee
Muir
Inverey
Morrone
Linn of Corriemulzie
Carn an Fhidhleir
Feshie
Carn Liath 818
Allt Connie
Ey Burn
The Colonel's Bed
Newbigging
Loch an t-Seilich
Allt Bhran
912
1
2
3
4
5
6
7
8
13
14
16

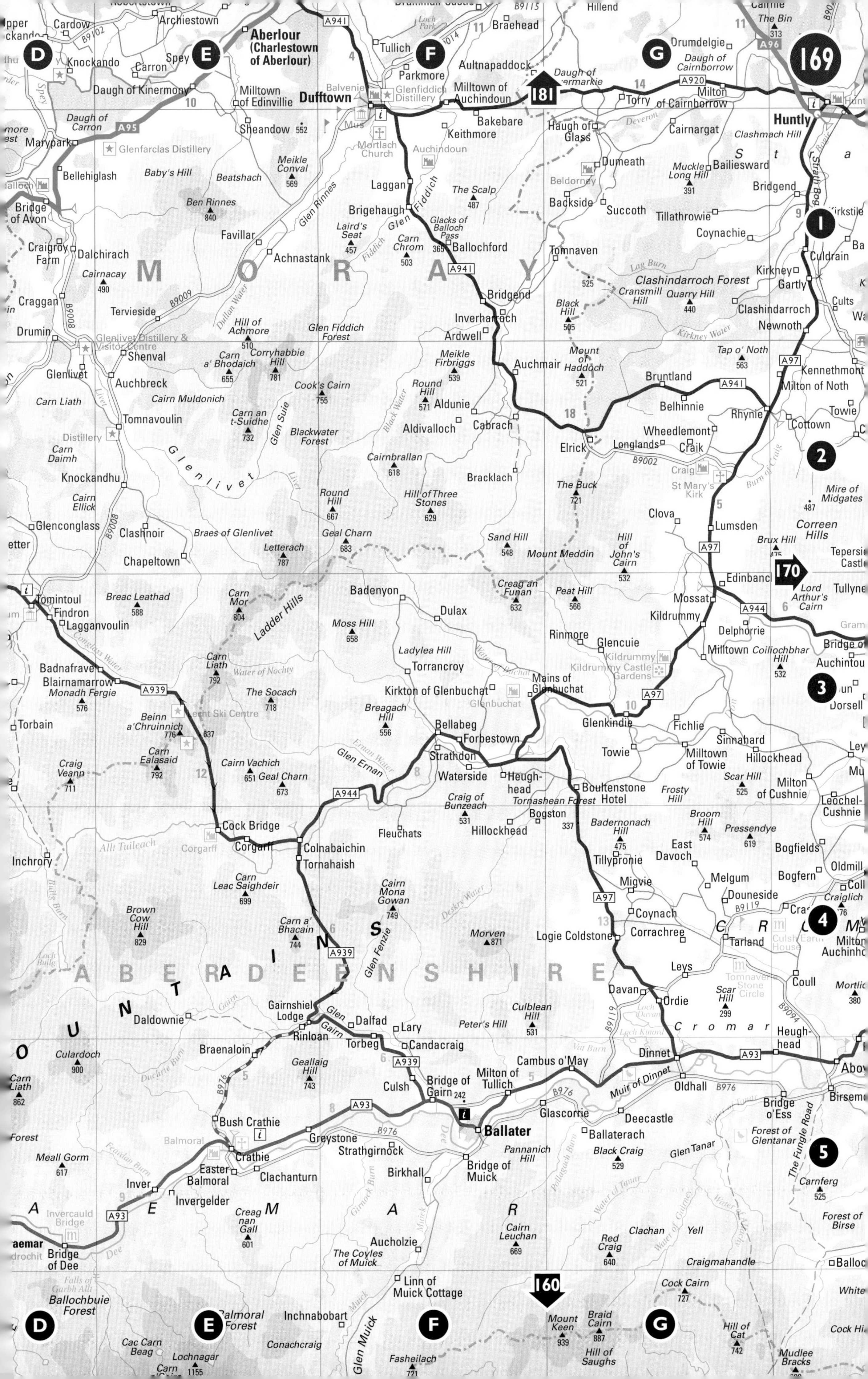

D
E
F
G
I
2
3
4
5
181
170
160
M O R A Y
A B E R D E E N S H I R E
M O U N T A I N S
C R O M A R
E M A R
Aberlour
(Charlestown
of Aberlour)
Archiestown
Cardow
Knockando
Carron
Spey
Daugh of Kinermony
Milltown
of Edinvillie
Dufftown
Balvenie
Glenfiddich
Distillery
Mus
Mortlach
Church
Tullich
Parkmore
Braehead
Aultnapaddock
Milltown of
Auchindoun
Bakebare
Keithmore
Auchindoun
Drumdelgie
Daugh of
Cairnborrow
Torry
Milton
of Cairnborrow
Huntly
Haugh of
Glass
Cairnargat
Clashmach Hill
Deveron
Dumeath
Muckle
Long Hill
391
Bailiesward
Bridgend
Beldorney
Backside
Succoth
Tillathrowie
Coynachie
Culdrain
Kirkney
Gartly
Strath Bogie
Kirkstile
The Bin
313
Hillend
Daugh of
Carron
A95
Marypark
Glenfarclas Distillery
Sheandow
552
Meikle
Conval
569
Baby's Hill
Beatshach
Bellehiglash
Bridge
of Avon
Ben Rinnes
840
Favillar
Achnastank
Glen Rinnes
Laggan
Brigehaugh
Glen Fiddich
Laird's
Seat
457
Carn
Chrom
503
Glacks of
Balloch
Pass
365
Ballochford
The Scalp
487
Tomnaven
Lag Burn
Clashindarroch Forest
Cransmill
Hill
Quarry Hill
440
Clashindarroch
Newnoth
Cults
525
Craigroy
Farm
Dalchirach
Cairnacay
490
Craggan
Tervieside
B9009
B9008
Drumin
Dullan Water
Hill of
Achmore
510
Glenlivet Distillery &
Visitor Centre
Shenval
Glenlivet
Auchbreck
Carn Liath
Tomnavoulin
Distillery
Carn
Daimh
Knockandhu
Cairn
Ellick
Glenconglass
Clashnoir
Chapeltown
Braes of Glenlivet
Carn
a' Bhodaich
655
Corryhabbie
Hill
781
Cairn Muldonich
Carn an
t-Suidhe
732
Glen Suie
Glen Fiddich
Forest
Cook's Cairn
755
Blackwater
Forest
Black Water
Glenlivet
Livet
Meikle
Firbriggs
539
Round
Hill
571
Aldunie
Aldivalloch
Cabrach
Bridgend
Inverharroch
Ardwell
A941
Auchmair
Black
Hill
505
Mount
of
Haddoch
521
Tap o' Noth
563
Kirkney Water
Kennethmont
Milton of Noth
A97
Bruntland
Belhinnie
Rhynie
Towie
Cottown
18
Wheedlemont
Longlands
Craik
Elrick
B9002
Craig
St Mary's
Kirk
Burn of Craig
Bracklach
Cairnbrallan
618
Hill of Three
Stones
629
Round
Hill
667
Geal Charn
683
Letterach
787
The Buck
721
Mire of
Midgates
487
Clova
Lumsden
Correen
Hills
Brux Hill
Tepersie
Castle
Sand Hill
548
Mount Meddin
Hill
of
John's
Cairn
532
Edinbanchory
Lord
Arthur's
Cairn
Tullynessle
Tomintoul
Findron
Lagganvoulin
Breac Leathad
588
Carn
Mor
804
Ladder Hills
Badenyon
Dulax
Moss Hill
658
Creag an
Funan
632
Peat Hill
566
Mossat
Kildrummy
A944
Delphorrie
Rinmore
Glencuie
Kildrummy
Kildrummy Castle
Gardens
Milltown
Coiliochbhar
Hill
532
Bridge of
Auchintoul
Dorsell
Conglass Water
Badnafrave
Blairnamarrow
Monadh Fergie
576
A939
Carn
Liath
792
Water of Nochty
The Socach
718
Ladylea Hill
Torrancroy
Water of Buchat
Mains of
Glenbuchat
Kirkton of Glenbuchat
Glenbuchat
Torbain
Beinn
a'Chruinnich
776
Lecht Ski Centre
637
Breagach
Hill
556
Bellabeg
Forbestown
Glenkindie
Fichlie
Sinnahard
Towie
Milltown
of Towie
Hillockhead
Carn
Ealasaid
792
Craig
Veann
711
Cairn Vachich
651
Geal Charn
673
Glen Ernan
Ernan Water
Strathdon
Waterside
Heugh-
head
Boultenstone
Hotel
Tornashean Forest
Frosty
Hill
Scar Hill
525
Milton
of Cushnie
Leochel-
Cushnie
A944
Craig of
Bunzeach
531
Bogston
337
Hillockhead
Badernonach
Hill
475
Broom
Hill
574
Pressendye
619
Cock Bridge
Corgarff
Allt Tuileach
Colnabaichin
Tornahaish
Fleuchats
Inchrory
Tillypronie
East
Davoch
Bogfields
Oldmill
Bogfern
Melgum
Migvie
Douneside
Craiglich
B9119
Carn
Leac Saighdeir
699
Cairn
Mona
Gowan
749
Deskry Water
Coynach
Corrachree
Tarland
Culsh Earth
House
Milton
Auchinhove
Brown
Cow
Hill
829
Carn a'
Bhacain
744
Glen Fenzie
Morven
871
Logie Coldstone
Builg Burn
Loch
Builg
Leys
Tomnaverie
Stone
Circle
Coull
Davan
Ordie
Loch
Davan
Scar
Hill
299
Mortlich
380
B9094
Gairnshiel
Lodge
Glen Gairn
Dalfad
Lary
Daldownie
Gairn
Culblean
Hill
531
Peter's Hill
B9119
Loch Kinord
Culardoch
900
Braenaloin
Rinloan
Torbeg
Candacraig
Heugh-
head
Geallaig
Hill
743
Vat Burn
Cambus o'May
Dinnet
A93
Aboyne
Carn
Liath
862
Duchrie Burn
B976
Culsh
Bridge of
Gairn
242
Milton of
Tullich
Muir of Dinnet
Oldhall
B976
Bridge
o'Ess
Birse
Forest
Bush Crathie
Greystone
B976
Ballater
Glascorrie
Deecastle
Forest of
Glentanar
The Fungle Road
Water of Tanar
Balmoral
Crathie
Strathgirnock
Dee
Pannanich
Hill
Ballaterach
Black Craig
529
Glen Tanar
Meall Gorm
617
Feardan Burn
Easter
Balmoral
Clachanturn
Birkhall
Bridge of
Muick
Girnock Burn
Pollagach Burn
Carnferg
525
Inver
Invergelder
Water of Tanar
Water of Gairney
Water of Allachy
Forest of
Birse
Invercauld
Bridge
A93
Creag
nan
Gall
601
Muick
Cairn
Leuchan
669
Clachan
Yell
Braemar
Bridge
of Dee
Aucholzie
The Coyles
of Muick
Red
Craig
640
Craigmahandle
Balloch
Falls of
Garbh Allt
Ballochbuie
Forest
Linn of
Muick Cottage
Cock Cairn
727
White
Balmoral
Forest
Inchnabobart
Mount
Keen
939
Braid
Cairn
887
Hill of
Cat
742
Cock Hill
Cac Carn
Beag
Lochnagar
1155
Conachcraig
Glen Muick
Fasheilach
721
Hill of
Saughs
Mudlee
Bracks

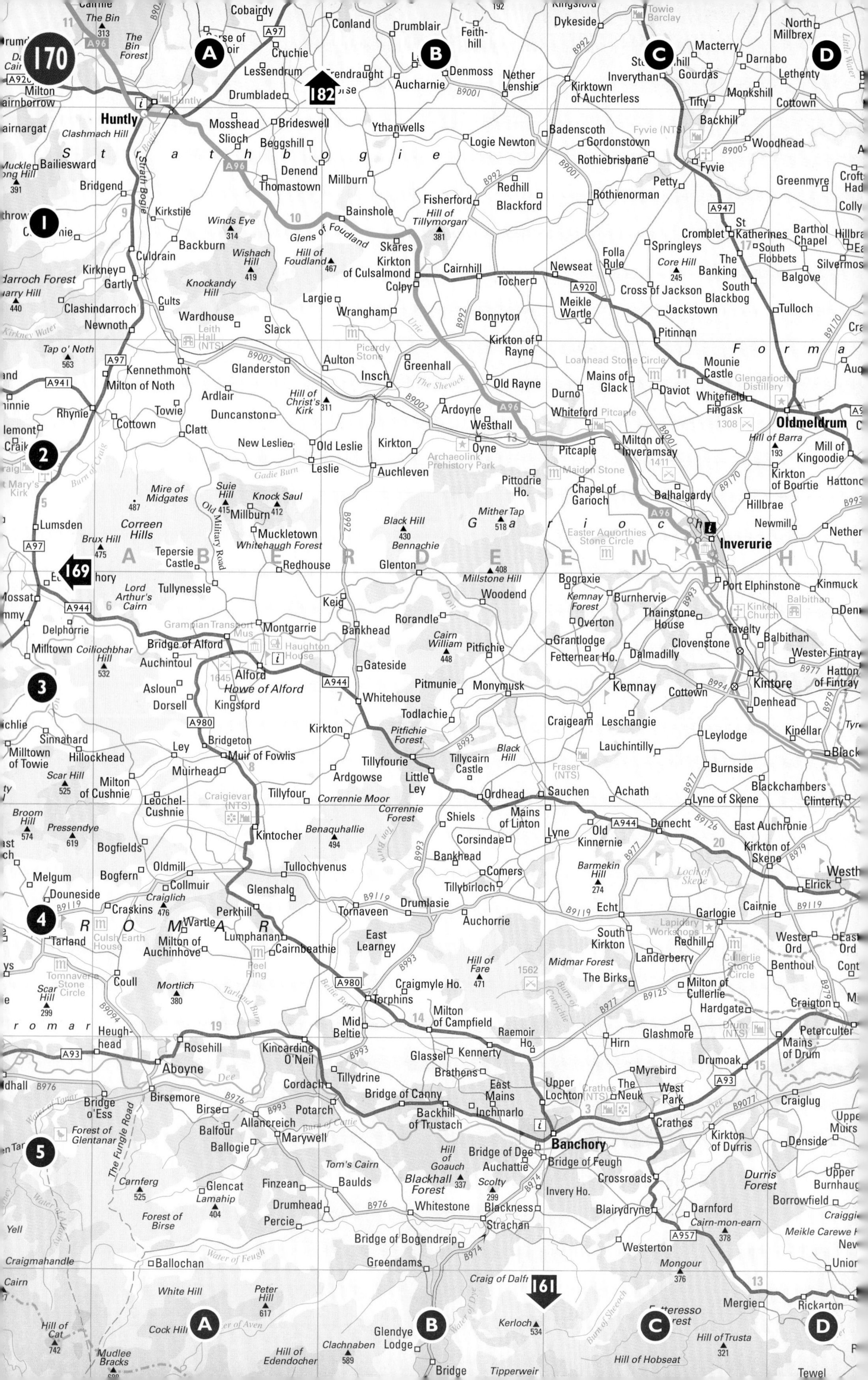
A
B
C
D
The Bin
313
The Bin Forest
A96
Cobairdy
Corse of Kinnoir
A97
Cruchie
Conland
Drumblair
Feith-hill
Dykeside
Towie Barclay
North Millbrex
Macterry
Darnabo
Lessendrum
Frendraught House
182
Denmoss
Nether Lenshie
Aucharnie
B9001
Kirktown of Auchterless
Inveryhan
Gourdas
Lethenty
Milton
A920
Drumblade
Huntly
Monkshill
Tifty
Cottown
Clashmach Hill
Mosshead
Brideswell
Ythanwells
Badenscoth
Gordonstown
Fyvie (NTS)
Backhill
Woodhead
Slioch
Beggshill
Logie Newton
B9005
Strathbogie
Rothiebrisbane
Fyvie
Bailiesward
Denend
Millburn
Thomastown
Bridgend
391
Strath Bogie
B992
Redhill
Petty
Greenmyre
Fisherford
Blackford
Rothienorman
A947
Kirkstile
Bainshole
Hill of Tillymorgan
381
Winds Eye
314
Glens of Foudland
St Katherines
Cromblet
Barthol Chapel
Springleys
South Flobbets
Backburn
Wishach Hill
419
Hill of Foudland
467
Skares
Folla Rule
Core Hill
245
The Banking
Silvermoss
Culdrain
Kirkney
Kirkton of Culsalmond
Cairnhill
Newseat
Balgove
Gartly
Knockandy Hill
Colpy
Tocher
A920
Cross of Jackson
South Blackbog
Clashindarroch Forest
440
Clashindarroch
Cults
Largie
Meikle Wartle
Jackstown
Tulloch
Wardhouse
Wrangham
Bonnyton
Newnoth
Slack
Leith Hall (NTS)
Urie
Pitinnan
Kirkney Water
Picardy Stone
Kirkton of Rayne
Tap o' Noth
563
B9002
Aulton
Loanhead Stone Circle
Mounie Castle
A97
Kennethmont
Glanderston
Greenhall
Mains of Glack
Glengarioch Distillery
A941
Milton of Noth
Insch
The Shevock
Old Rayne
11
Durno
Daviot
Whitefield
Ardlair
Hill of Christ's Kirk
311
Fingask
Rhynie
Towie
Duncanston
Ardoyne
A96
Whiteford
Pitcaple
Oldmeldrum
Cottown
Westhall
1308
Clatt
Milton of Inveramsay
Hill of Barra
193
Mill of Kingoodie
New Leslie
Old Leslie
Kirkton
Oyne
Pitcaple
1411
Leslie
Archaeolink Prehistory Park
Maiden Stone
Kirkton of Bourtie
2
Gadie Burn
Auchleven
Pittodrie Ho.
Chapel of Garioch
Balhalgardy
B9170
Burn of Craig
Mire of Midgates
Suie Hill
415
Knock Saul
412
Hillbrae
Mither Tap
518
487
Millburn
A96
Old Military Road
Black Hill
430
Newmill
Lumsden
Correen Hills
Muckletown
Whitehaugh Forest
B992
Bennachie
Garioch
Inverurie
Brux Hill
475
Easter Aquorthies Stone Circle
A97
Tepersie Castle
ABERDEENSHIRE
169
Redhouse
Glenton
Millstone Hill
408
Bograxie
Port Elphinstone
Kinmuck
Lord Arthur's Cairn
Tullynessle
Woodend
Kemnay Forest
Burnhervie
Keig
Kinkell Church
Balbithan
A944
6
Thainstone House
Rorandle
Overton
Delphorrie
Grampian Transport Mus
Montgarrie
Bankhead
Don
Tavelty
Balbithan
Grantlodge
Milltown
Coiliochbhar Hill
532
Bridge of Alford
Haughton House
Cairn William
448
Pitfichie
Clovenstone
Wester Fintray
Fetternear Ho.
Dalmadilly
Auchintoul
Alford
Gateside
B977
Hatton of Fintray
3
1645
A944
Kemnay
B994
Kintore
Asloun
Howe of Alford
Pitmunie
Monymusk
Cottown
Dorsell
Kingsford
7
Whitehouse
Denhead
Todlachie
Craigearn
Leschangie
A980
Kirkton
Pitfichie Forest
Sinnahard
Bridgeton
Leylodge
Kinellar
B993
Milltown of Towie
Hillockhead
Ley
Muir of Fowlis
Lauchintilly
Black Hill
Tillycairn Castle
Blackburn
Tillyfourie
8
Muirhead
Ardgowse
Burnside
Fraser (NTS)
Scar Hill
525
Milton of Cushnie
Little Ley
B977
Blackchambers
Ordhead
Sauchen
Achath
Leochel-Cushnie
Tillyfour
Corrennie Moor
Lyne of Skene
Clinterty
Craigievar (NTS)
Corrennie Forest
Broom Hill
574
Shiels
Mains of Linton
A944
Dunecht
Pressendye
619
Benaquhallie
494
B9126
East Auchronie
Kintocher
Ton Burn
Lyne
Old Kinnernie
20
Bogfields
Corsindae
Kirkton of Skene
B979
B993
Bankhead
Barmekin Hill
274
Loch of Skene
Melgum
Bogfern
Oldmill
Tullochvenus
Comers
Westhill
Collmuir
Tillybirloch
Elrick
Douneside
Craiglich
476
Glenshalg
B9119
B9119
Echt
Cairnie
B9119
4
Craskins
Perkhill
Tornaveen
Drumlasie
B9119
Garlogie
Auchorrie
CROMAR
Wartle
Lapidary Workshops
Tarland
Culsh Earth House
Milton of Auchinhove
Lumphanan
Cairnbeathie
East Learney
South Kirkton
Redhill
Wester Ord
East Ord
Peel Ring
Midmar Forest
Tomnaverie Stone Circle
Coull
Hill of Fare
471
1562
Landerberry
Cullerlie Stone Circle
Benthoul
B993
The Birks
Scar Hill
299
Mortlich
380
Tarland Burn
A980
Craigmyle Ho.
Burn of Corrichie
Milton of Cullerlie
B9125
Craigton
B9094
Beltie Burn
Torphins
B977
Hardgate
Cromar
19
14
Milton of Campfield
Drum (NTS)
Peterculter
Mid Beltie
Heugh-head
Raemoir Ho.
Glashmore
Mains of Drum
A93
Rosehill
Kincardine O'Neil
Glassel
Kennerty
Hirn
Drumoak
15
Aboyne
B993
Brathens
Myrebird
Tillydrine
Dee
Upper Lochton
East Mains
The Neuk
West Park
A93
B976
B976
Birsemore
Cordach
Bridge of Canny
Crathes (NTS)
Bridge o'Ess
Birse
B993
Potarch
Backhill of Trustach
Inchmarlo
3
B9077
Craiglug
Allancreich
Crathes
Upper Muirs
Forest of Glentanar
Balfour
Burn of Cattie
Marywell
Banchory
Kirkton of Durris
5
Ballogie
Hill of Goauch
Bridge of Dee
Denside
The Fungle Road
Tom's Cairn
Auchattie
Bridge of Feugh
Water of Tanar
Carnferg
525
Glencat
Finzean
Baulds
Blackhall Forest
337
Scolty
299
Crossroads
Durris Forest
Upper Burnhaugh
Lamahip
404
Invery Ho.
Forest of Birse
Drumhead
B976
Whitestone
Blackness
B974
Blairydryne
Darnford
Borrowfield
Yell
Percie
Strachan
A957
Cairn-mon-earn
378
Meikle Carewe Hill
Craigmahandle
Ballochan
Water of Feugh
Bridge of Bogendreip
Westerton
Greendams
B974
Mongour
376
Cairn
Craig of Dalfro
161
White Hill
Peter Hill
617
13
Mergie
Rickarton
Hill of Cat
742
Cock Hill
Water of Aven
Water of Dye
Kerloch
534
Burn of Sheeoch
Fetteresso Forest
Glendye Lodge
Clachnaben
589
Hill of Trusta
321
Mudlee Bracks
Hill of Edendocher
Hill of Hobseat
Bridge
Tipperweir
Tewel

D
E
F
G
1
2
3
4
5
Moss of Belnagoak
Nethermuir
Clola
Little Dens
Burnhaven
Sandford Bay
Knaven
Kinnadie
Skelmuir
Nether
Invernettie
Blackhill
Stirling
Boddam
Cairnorrie
South Upper Barrack
Mill of Elrick
Skelmuir Hill
Kinknockie
Newton
Smallburn
Moss of Cruden
Sandfordhill
183
Monteach
Hill of Skilmafilly
Aldie
Gask
Murdoch Head
Skelmonae
Inkhorn
Loanhead
Upper Hawkhillock
Ardallie
Greenheads
Teuchan
Quilquox
A948
Milton of Coldwells
Hill of Dudwick
174
A952
Auchiries
A90
North Haven
Bullers of Buchan
Methlick
Muirtack
Drumwhindle
Arthrath
Mains of Dudwick
Hatton
Errollston
Cruden Bay
Waterloo
Chapel Hill
Slains (ruins)
B9005
Tanglandford
Blindburn
Port Erroll
Haddo House (NTS)
Craigie Brae
Bearnie
Toll of Birness
Bogbrae
Hilton Croft
Bay of Cruden
The Skares
Inverebrie
Kiplaw Croft
Whinnyfold
Raxton
Cookston
Broomfield
Leask
Ythsie
Kinharrachie
Ellon
Artrochie
Auchmacoy
Meikle Loch
A975
The Veshels
Clochtow
Ythan
Esslemont
Kirkton of Logie Buchan
B9003
Kirktown of Slains
B999
A920
Collieston
Pitmedden (NTS)
Bronie Burn
St Catherine's Dub
Pitmedden
Cairnhill
Tipperty
Meikle Tarty
Waterside
Forvie Ness or Hackley Head
B9000
Udny Green
Old Craig
Tarty Burn
Sands of Forvie
Kincraig
Newburgh
Newburgh Bar
Udny Station
Foveran Burn
Foveran House
Pettymuick
Affleck
Culterculien
Tillycorthie
Minnes
Blairythan Cottage
Tillygreig
Tillery
Drums
Whitlam
Delfrigs
Menie Ho.
A947
Beauty Hill
Causeyend
Newmachar
B979
Craigie
Orrok Ho.
Blackbraes
Whitecairns
Belhelvie
Balmedie
Longdrum
B977
Middleton of Potterton
Millden
Cothall
Potterton
Corby Loch
Skelly Rock
hours
Bergen (Summer Only)................30
Lerwick, Shetland Islands.............13
Stromness, Orkney Islands.......8-14
Blackdog
Blackdog Rock
Mundurno
North Tarbothill
Dyce
B997
ABERDEEN
Cloverhill
Stoneywood
Middleton Park
Aberdeen Exhibition & Conference Centre
Bankhead
Danestone
Bucksburn
Woodside
Bridge of Don
St Machar's Cathedral
A96
Northfield
Old Aberdeen
A956
B9119
Maritime Museum
Kingswells
Mastrick
Aberdeen Art Gallery
Provost Skene's House
Hazlehead
Girdle Ness
Nigg Bay
Gordon Highlanders Regimental Mus
Mannofield
Duthie Park & Winter Gardens
Ruthrieston
Greg Ness
Bridge of Dee
Nigg
Cults
Loirston
Kincorth
Altens
Souter Head
Dee
Banchory-Devenick
Cove Bay
Charlestown
B9077
Heathcot
Storybook Glen
Auchlunies
Marywell
Earnsheugh Bay
Sunnyside
Hillside
Findon
Hill of Auchlee
Findon Ness
Portlethen
Berry Top
Downies
Portlethen Village
0 2 4 6 8 10 miles
0 2 4 6 8 10 km
Cammachmore
Cookney
Newtonhill
Muchalls
Bridge of Muchalls
Doonie Point
Castle Rock of Muchalls
Garron Point
Cowie
Strathlethan Bay
Stonehaven

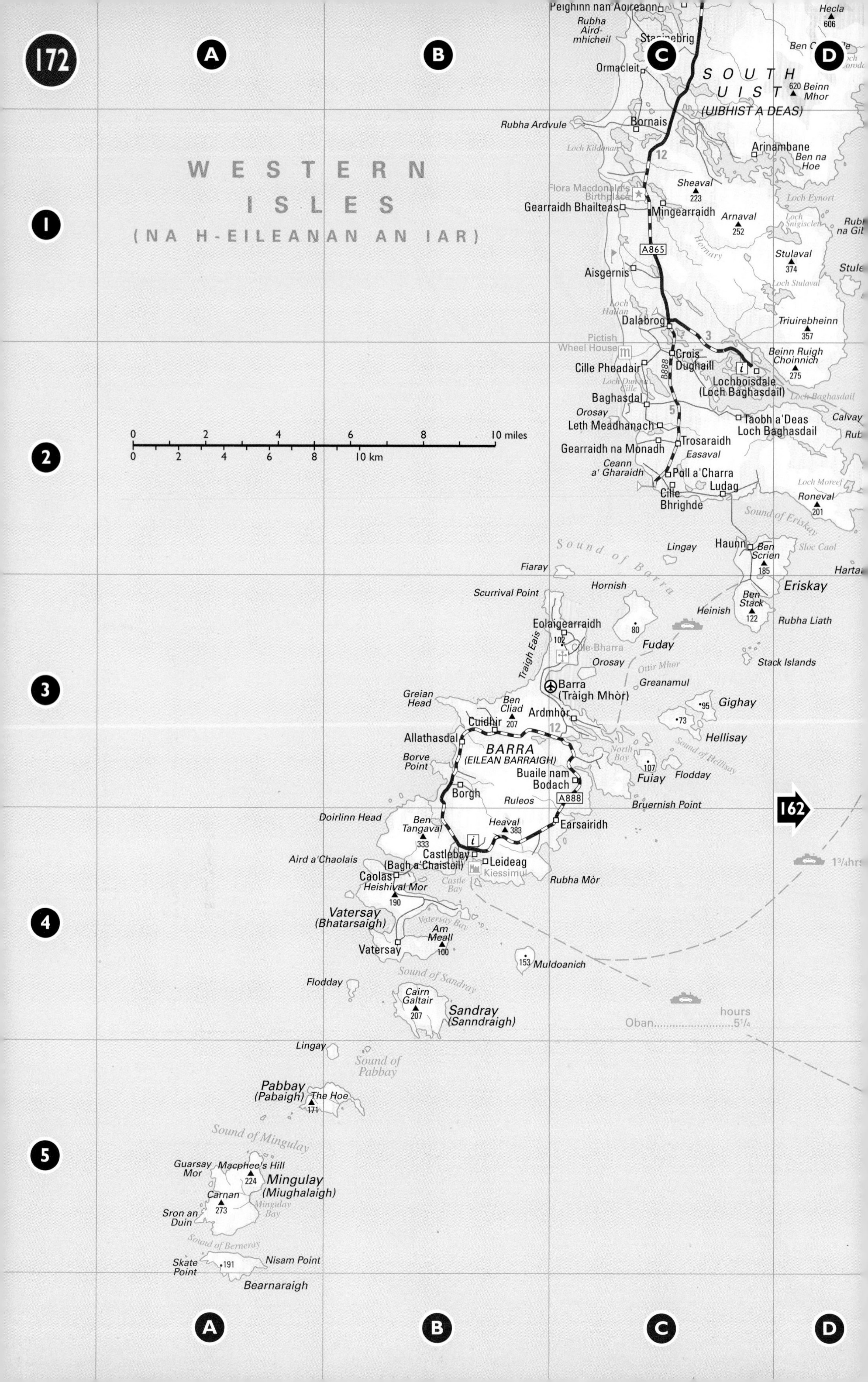
WESTERN ISLES
(NA H-EILEANAN AN IAR)
0 2 4 6 8 10 miles
0 2 4 6 8 10 km
SOUTH UIST
(UIBHIST A DEAS)
Peighinn nan Aoireann
Rubha Aird-mhicheil
Staoinebrig
Ormacleit
Hecla 606
620 Beinn Mhor
Rubha Ardvule
Bornais
Loch Kildonan
Arinambane
Ben na Hoe
Flora Macdonald's Birthplace
Gearraidh Bhailteas
Mingearraidh
Sheaval 223
Arnaval 252
Loch Eynort
Loch Snigisclett
A865
Hornary
Stulaval 374
Loch Stulaval
Aisgernis
Loch Hallan
Dalabrog
Triuirebheinn 357
Pictish Wheel House
Crois Dughaill
Beinn Ruigh Choinnich 275
Cille Pheadair
Loch Dun na Cille
B888
Lochboisdale (Loch Baghasdail)
Loch Baghasdail
Baghasdal
Orosay
Taobh a'Deas Loch Baghasdail
Calvay
Leth Meadhanach
Gearraidh na Monadh
Trosaraidh
Easaval
Ceann a' Gharaidh
Poll a'Charra
Loch Moreef
Cille Bhrighde
Ludag
Roneval 201
Sound of Eriskay
Sound of Barra
Lingay
Haunn
Ben Scrien 185
Sloc Caol
Fiaray
Eriskay
Scurrival Point
Hornish
Ben Stack 122
Heinish
Rubha Liath
Eolaigearraidh
102
80
Cille-Bhàrra
Traigh Eais
Fuday
Orosay
Ottir Mhor
Stack Islands
Barra (Tràigh Mhòr)
Greanamul
Greian Head
Ben Cliad 207
Ardmhòr
Gighay 95
73
Hellisay
Cuidhir
12
Allathasdal
BARRA (EILEAN BARRAIGH)
North Bay
Sound of Hellisay
Borve Point
107
Buaile nam Bodach
Fuiay
Flodday
Borgh
Ruleos
A888
Bruernish Point
162
Doirlinn Head
Ben Tangaval 333
Heaval 383
Earsairidh
Aird a'Chaolais
Castlebay (Bagh a'Chaisteil)
Leideag
Kiessimul
Caolas
Castle Bay
Rubha Mòr
Heishival Mor 190
Vatersay (Bhatarsaigh)
Vatersay Bay
Am Meall 100
Vatersay
153 Muldoanich
Sound of Sandray
Flodday
Cairn Galtair 207
Sandray (Sanndraigh)
hours
Oban 5¼
1¾hrs
Lingay
Sound of Pabbay
Pabbay (Pabaigh)
The Hoe 171
Sound of Mingulay
Guarsay Mor
Macphee's Hill 224
Mingulay (Miughalaigh)
Carnan 273
Sron an Duin
Mingulay Bay
Sound of Berneray
Skate Point
191
Nisam Point
Bearnaraigh

WESTERN ISLES
(NA H-EILEANAN AN IAR)
D
E
F
G
I
2
3
4
5
Shillay
Sound of Shillay
Beinn a'Charnain
196
Baile-na-Cille
Quinish
Pabbay
Sound of Pabbay
Berneray
(Eilean Bhearnaraigh)
Borve Hill
85
Ruisigearraidh
Borgh
Bays Loch
Boreray
Caolas a' Mhorain
Sound of Berneray
Haskeir Island
Haskeir Eagach
Huilish Point
Veilish Point
Lingay
Port nan Long
Baile Mhic Phail
Beinn Mhòr
190
Aird Thorr...
Vallay
Griminis Point
Oronsay
Trumaisge Arraidh
B893
Scolpaig
A865
Vallay Strand
Ceathramh Meadhanach
Greinetobht
Solas
Crogary Mor
180
Maari
171
Balmartin
(Baile Mhartainn)
Balelone
Malacleit
Loch Hosta
Hosta
Botarua
Loch nan Geireann
Keallasay More
Lochportain
Manish Point
Tigh a'Gearraidh
NORTH UIST
(UIBHIST A TUATH)
Blathaisbhal
Keallasay Beg
Loch Fada
174
Hogha Gearraidh
Causamul
Aird an Runair
Marrival
230
Loch Scadavay
Loch Skealtar
Baile Raghaill
Ceann a'Bhàigh
Lochmaddy
(Loch na Madadh)
Rubha Port Scolpaig
Loch nan Eun
Paibeil
Baile Mòr
Cladach a'Chaolais
Loch Hunder
Loch a' Bharpa
Oitir Mhòr
North Lee
250
Deasker
Rubha Raouill
A867
Loch Scadavay
Cladach Chircebost
Sound of Monach
Kirkibost Island
Langais
Loch Euphoirt
Ceann Iar
Hearnish
Stockay
A865
B894
Saighdinis
Shillay
Heisker or Monach Islands
Ceann Ear
Scrot Mòr
Teanamachar
Samhla
Corœna
(Corunna)
Loch Caravat
Loch Obisary
Eaval
347
Eachkamish
9
Teampull na Trionaid
Baleshare
Cairinis
Eigneig
Oitir Mhòr
Floddaybeg
Baile Glas
Grimsay
(Griomasaigh)
Beinn a'Charnain
115
Floddaymore
Benbecula
(Baile a'Mhanaich)
Uachdar
Eilean Flodaigh
Ceallan
Beinn Roagrich
99
Aird
Gramsdal
Balivanich
(Baile a'Mhanaich)
Loch Olavat
Rubha na Rodagrich
Baile nan Cailleach
Garry-a-siar
Rueval
124
BENBECULA
(BEINN NA FAOGHLA)
Griminis
A865
Loch Uisgebhagh
Torlum
Loch Olavat
B892
Uisgebhagh
Lionacleit
Gualann
Creag Ghoraidh
B891
Hornish Point
Baile Gharbhaidh
Rubha Cam nan Gall
Ardivachar Point
Clachan
Iochdar
Aird a'Mhachair
Loch Bee
Bagh Nam Faoileann
102
Wiay
Loch Carnan
Geirninis
A865
Drimore
Ben Sherbert
Loch Sheilavaig
Loch Sgioport
162
Groigearraidh
B890
168
Loch Sgioport
Ornish Island
Loch Druidibeg
Loch Spotal
Tobha Mòr
Mol a'Tuath
SOUTH UIST

A
B
C
D
184
1
2
3
4
5
173
162
Toe Head
Chaipaval
339
365
Traigh na Cleavag
Northton (Taobh Tuath)
Maodal
251
398
Loch Langavat
Shillay
Sound of Shillay
Beinn a'Charnain
196
Baile-na-Cille
Quinish
Pabbay
SOUND OF HARRIS
Carminish Islands
Ensay
Leverburgh (An T-ob)
A859
Cairminis
Strannda
211
Killegray
Sound of Pabbay
Berneray
(Eilean Bhearnaraigh)
Massacamber
Borve Hill
85
Ruisigearraidh
Borgh
Bays Loch
Boreray
Caolas a' Mhorain
1¼ hrs
Groay
Gilsay
Lingay
Scaravay
Sound of Berneray
Huilish Point
Veilish Point
Lingay
Port nan Long
Baile Mhic Phail
B893
Beinn Mhòr
190
Aird Thormaid
Griminis Point
Vallay
Oronsay
Stromay
Scolpaig
Vallay Strand
Ceathramh Meadhanach
Trumaisge Arraidh
A865
Greinetobht
Solas
Malacleit
Crogary Mor
180
Maari
171
Hermetray
Balmartin (Baile Mhartainn)
Balelone
Loch Hosta
Botarua
Loch nan Geireann
Loch Aulasary
Leac na Hoe
Manish Point
Hosta
Keallasay More
Lochportain
Loch na Dubhcha
Tigh a'Gearraidh
NORTH UIST
(UIBHIST A TUATH)
Blathaisbhal
Keallasay Beg
Scarts Rock
Loch Portain
Loch Fada
WESTERN ISLES
Marrival
230
Loch Scadavay
Loch Skealtar
Baile Raghaill
Ceann a'Bhàigh
Lochmaddy (Loch na Madadh)
Loch na Madadh
Rubha Port Scolpaig
Loch nan Eun
Paibeil
Baile Mòr
Oitir Mhòr
Cladach a'Chaolais
Loch Hunda
Loch a' Bharpa
A867
North Lee
250
Rubha Raouill
South Lee
281
Cladach Chircebost
Loch Scadavay
Loch Hunder
Kirkibost Island
Langais
(NA H-EILEANAN AN IAR)
Stockay
Loch Euphoirt
Rubha Mhic Gille-mh'cheil
A865
B894
Saighdinis
Heisker or Monach Islands
Teanamachar
Samhla
Corœna (Corunna)
Loch Caravat
Loch Obisary
Eigneig Mhòr
Eachkamish
Eaval
347
Baleshare
Teampull na Trionaid
Cairinis
Eigneig Bheag
Oitir Mhòr
Baile Glas
Floddaybeg
Grimsay (Griomasaigh)
Floddaymore
Benbecula (Baile a'Mhanaich)
Beinn a'Charnain
115
Uachdar
Eilean Flodaigh
Ceallan
Ronay (Ronaigh)
Gramsdal
Beinn Roagrich
99
Aird
Balivanich (Baile a'Mhanaich)
Loch Olavat
Rueval
124
Rubha na Rodagrich
Baile nan Cailleach
Garry-a-siar
BENBECULA
(BEINN NA FAOGHLA)
Griminis
A865
Torlum
Loch Uisgebhagh
B892
Loch Olavat
Lionacleit
Uisgebhagh
Gualann
Creag Ghoraidh
B891
Hornish Point
Baile Gharbhaidh
Rubha Cam nan Gall
Ardivachar Point
Clachan
Iochdar
Aird a'Mhachair
102
Wiay
Bagh Nam Faoileann
LITTLE MINCH
Loch Bee
Geirninis
Loch Carnan
A865
Drimore
Loch Sheilavaig
168
Groigearraidh
Loch Sgioport
Loch Sgioport
Ornish Island
Tobha Mòr
Loch Druidibeg
Loch Spotal
Mol a'Tuath

Heileasbhal
An Coileach
386
Aird Mhige
Greosabhagh
Leac a'Li
Liceasto
Scadabhagh
Meall Challibost
Rubha Bocaig
Cluer
Loch Grosebay
L. Stocinis
D
E
F
G
185
A R R I S
Aird Leimhe
Manais
Rubha Cluer
Fleoideabhagh
Ard Manish
L. Fleoideabhagh
Cuidhtinis
Rubha Quidnish
Boirseam
Loch Finsbay
Ceann a'Bhàigh
Lingarabay Island
Clement's Church
Tarbert
hours
1¾
I
Fladda-chuain
Gaeilavore Island
Gearran Island
Rubha Hunish
Loch Hunish
Duntulm Bay
Tulm Island
2
Duntulm
Score Bay
Skye Cottage Museum
Ru Bornaskitaig
Kilmuir
Hunglader
Camas Mor
176
Kilvaxter
Balgown
Loch Sheosdal
350
Monkstadt
1¾ hrs
Vaternish Point
Whitewave Activities
Kilbride Point
Linicro
Bioda B
466
A855
Stack of Skudiburgh
3
Sron Ocrhulan
251
Ascrib Islands
Idrigil
Uig
Rubha Idrigil
Balnakn
South Ascrib
Uig Bay
Ben Geary
284
Geary
Rubha Chorachan
Trumpan
Earlish
Aros Bay
LOCH SNIZORT
TROTT
Ardmore Bay
Loch Losait
Cuidrach
Ardmore Point
Halistra
Gillen
Stac a' Bhothain
Poll na h-Ealaidh
Hallin
A87
Peinlich
Glenuac
Biod nan Laogh
Lyndale Point
Dunvegan Head
Isay
Mingay Island
Greshornish Point
Beinn a
452
Rubha Maol
Stein
Lusta
Ben Diubaig
L. Diubaig
Lynedale Ho.
Kingsburgh
VATERNISH
Lovaig Bay
Loch Bay
B886
214
Loch Snizort Beag
4
313
Lampay Islands
Claigan
Greshornish
Loch Greshornish
Treaslane
Galtrigill
Ben Skriaig
Boreraig
Beinn Bhreac
327
Flashader
Eyre
Uig
Loch Dunvegan
A850
The Aird
Carn Lia
Kensal
Husabost
Beinn Chreagach
Loch Pooltiel
Totaig
Edinbane
Milovaig
Ben Horneval
264
Bernisdale
Feriniquarrie
Oisgill Bay
B884
Dunvegan
Colbost Croft Museum
Ben Uigshader
246
Tote
A87
HIGHLAND
Loch Mor
Colbost
Skinidin
Dunvegan
Ben Sca
286
Skeabost
Carbost
296
Waterstein Head
Beinn na Creiche
Uiginish
A850
Neist Point
Moonen Bay
Glen Dale
Kilmuir
Cruachan Beinn a'Chearcaill
271
Lonmore
Ben Aketil
265
Uigshader
B884
A863
Healabhal Mhor (Macleod's Table North)
468
Beinn a'Ghlinne Bhig
208
5
Ben Corkeval
Roskhill
SKYE
Ramasaig Bay
Roag
Vatten
Loch Connan
Ramasaig
Orbost
Am Maol
212
Hoe Rape
The Hoe
233
Lorgill
Healabhal Bheag (Macleod's Table South)
488
Harlosh
Glen Ose
Beinn na Cloiche
232
Balmore
Loch Vatten
Loch Varkasaig
Loch Caroy
Ose
B885
Ben Connan
244
Harlosh Point
Beinn na Boineid
371
163
A863
Dun Beag
Bracadale
Loch Duagrich
Ben Duagrich
304
Harlosh Island
Ullinish
Coillore
Ben Idrig
An Dubh Sgeir
Loch Bracadale
Beinn Totaig
MacLeod's Maidens
Idrigill Point
Wiay
Ardtreck Point

A
B
C
D
1
2
3
4
5
0 2 4 6 8 10 miles
0 2 4 6 8 10 km
Melvaig
Fladda-chuain
Gearran Island
Eilean Trodday
North Erradale
Longa Island
Rubha Hunish
Rubha na h-Aiseig
Loch Hunish
Kilmaluag Bay
Duntulm Bay
The Aird
Duntulm
A855
Kilmaluag
Duntulm
Score Bay
Galta Mor
Sgeir Eirin
Skye Cottage Museum
Flodigarry
Eilean Flodigarry
Kilmuir
Hunglader
Camas Mor
Meall na Suiramach
543
Quirang
175
Kilvaxter
Balgown
Suidh' a'Mhinn
350
Loch Sheosdal
The Needle
Digg
Staffin Island
Staffin Bay
Redpoint
Rubha Garbhaig
Red Point
Monkstadt
Stenscholl
Staffin
Bioda Buidhe
466
Kilbride Point
Linicro
Whitewave Activities
Loch Cleap
Elishader
Maligar
Ben Gorm
Idrigil
Uig
Rubha Idrigil
Uig Bay
Balnaknock
Beinn Edra
611
Marishader
Garros
Culnaknock
Rubha nam Brathairean
Rubha na Fearn
Loch Mealt
Earlish
Lealt
Loch a'Bhraige
TROTTERNISH
Cuidrach
Fearnmore
Fearnbeg
RONA
Poll na h-Ealaidh
A87
Peinlich
Glenuachdarach
Creag a'Lain
608
Baca Ruadh
637
Dry Harbour
125
Leac Tressirnish
Arinacrinachd
Cuaig
Lyndale Point
Beinn a'Sga
452
Hartaval
Rigg
Kingsburgh
13
Callakille
Eilean Tigh
111
The Storr
719
A855
An Garbh-mheall
493
Lynedale
Treaslane
Eyre
Romesdal
Lon Mor
Bearreraig Bay
Loch a'Sguirr
Lonbain
SOUND OF RAASAY
INNER SOUND
Kyle Rona
Eilean Fladday
Beinn na h-Iolaire
254
Meall na Fhuaid
518
The Aird
Carn Liath
Kensaleyre
Haultin
Loch Leathan
Edinbane
Bernisdale
Ben Dearg
552
Ben Uigshader
246
Tote
Borve
A87
Loch Fada
Torran
626
Prince Charles's Cave
Manish Point
Loch Arnish
Arnish
Skeabost
Carbost
Drumuie
Sithean Bhealaich Chumhaing
392
Brochel
Loch nan Eun
Uigshader
Hartfield
Applecross
Beinn a'Ghlinne Bhig
208
Glengrasco
Torvaig
RAASAY
Applecross
Loch Connan
Portree
Loch Portree
SKYE
Am Maol
212
Beinn na Greine
417
Milton
Beinn na Cloiche
232
B885
Penifiler
Ben Tianavaig
413
Camusteel
Glame
385
Camusterrach
Glenmore
Balachuirn
Culduie
Poll Creadha
Loch Duagrich
Stroc-bheinn
400
Dun Caan
443
Sron na h-Airde Baine
Ben Duagrich
304
Mugeary
A87
164
Camastianavaig
Holoman Bay
Rubha na' Leac
Toscaig
Coillore
Beinn Totaig
Lower Ollach
Tianavaig Bay
Narrows of Raasay
Clachan
Beinn na'Leac
319
Upper Ollach
Inverarish
Loch Toscaig
Caolas

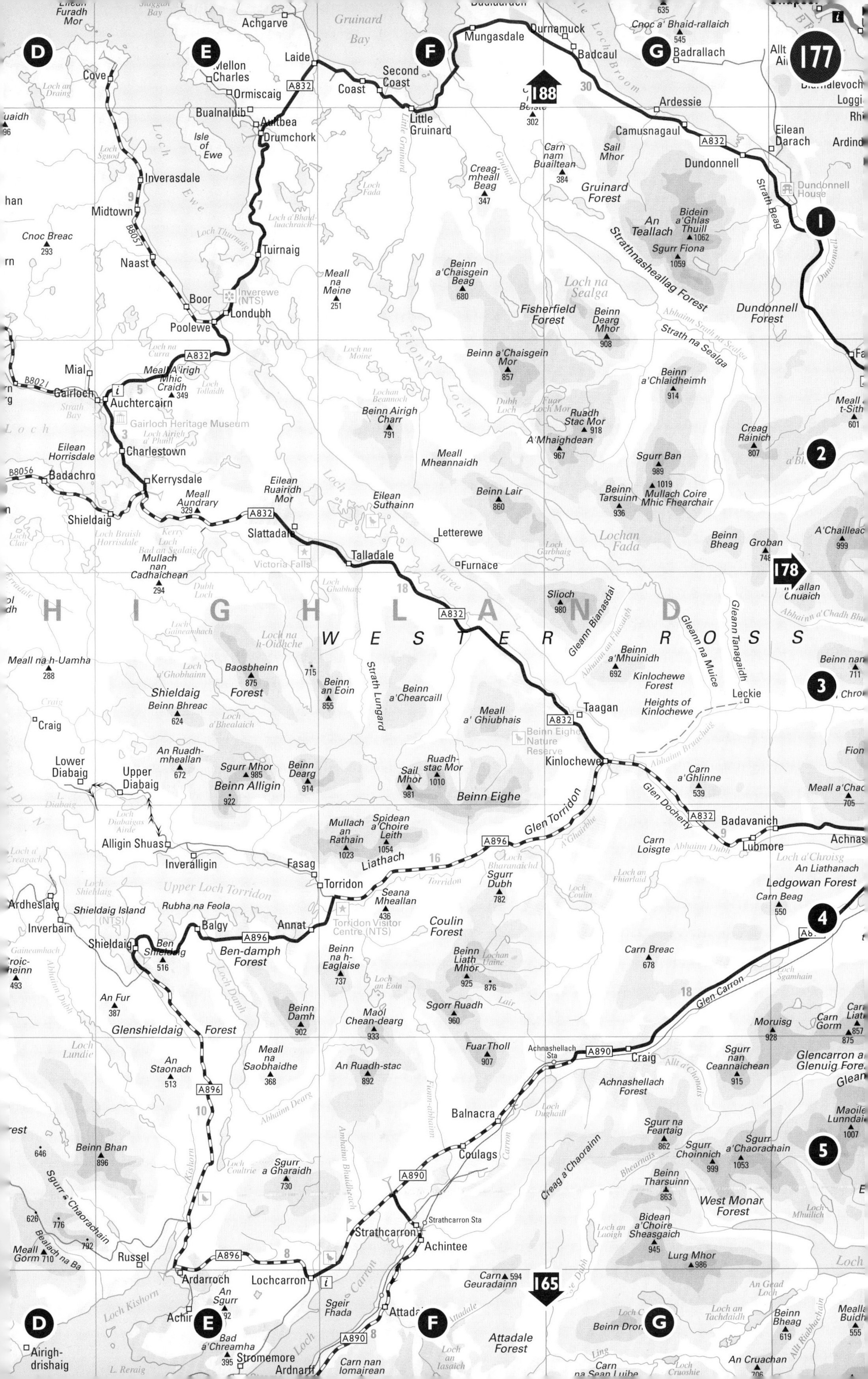
D
E
F
G
D
E
F
G
1
2
3
4
5
188
178
165
Achgarve
Gruinard Bay
Laide
Mungasdale
Durnamuck
Badcaul
Cnoc a' Bhaid-rallaich
545
Badrallach
Loch Broom
Mellon Charles
Cove
Ormiscaig
A832
Second Coast
Coast
Bualnaluib
Aultbea
Drumchork
Isle of Ewe
Loch Ewe
Little Gruinard
Ardessie
Camusnagaul
Dundonnell
Eilean Darach
Dundonnell House
Strath Beag
Inverasdale
Midtown
B8057
Naast
Cnoc Breac
293
Loch Thurnaig
Tuirnaig
Inverewe (NTS)
Boor
Londubh
Poolewe
Loch Fada
Loch a' Bhaid-luachraich
Meall na Meine
251
Creag-mheall Beag
347
Carn nam Buailtean
384
Sail Mhor
Gruinard Forest
An Teallach
Bidein a'Ghlas Thuill
1062
Sgurr Fiona
1059
Strathnasheallag Forest
Beinn a'Chaisgein Beag
680
Loch na Sealga
Fisherfield Forest
Beinn Dearg Mhor
908
Dundonnell Forest
Strath na Sealga
Abhainn Strath na Sealga
Mial
B8021
Gairloch
Strath Bay
Auchtercairn
Meall A'irigh Mhic Craidh
349
Loch Tollaidh
Gairloch Heritage Museum
Loch na Moine
Lochan Beannoch
Beinn Airigh Charr
791
Beinn a'Chaisgein Mor
857
Dubh Loch
Fuar Loch Mor
Ruadh Stac Mor
918
A'Mhaighdean
967
Beinn a'Chlaidheimh
914
Creag Rainich
807
Meall an t-Sith
601
Eilean Horrisdale
Charlestown
B8056
Badachro
Kerrysdale
Meall Aundrary
329
Shieldaig
Loch Braigh Horrisdale
Meall Mheannaidh
Sgurr Ban
989
1019
Mullach Coire Mhic Fhearchair
Beinn Tarsuinn
936
Beinn Lair
860
Eilean Ruairidh Mor
Eilean Suthainn
Letterewe
Slattadale
Talladale
Victoria Falls
Furnace
Loch Garbhaig
Lochan Fada
Beinn Bheag
Groban
748
A'Chailleach
999
Bad an Sgalaig
Mullach nan Cadhaichean
294
Dubh Loch
Loch Maree
18
Slioch
980
Lochan Cnuaich
Abhainn a'Chadh Bhuidhe
H I G H L A N D
WESTER ROSS
Loch Gaineamhach
Loch na h-Oidhche
715
Gleann Bianasdail
Gleann na Muice
Gleann Tanagaidh
Beinn a'Mhuinidh
692
Kinlochewe Forest
Heights of Kinlochewe
Leckie
Beinn nan
711
Meall na h-Uamha
288
Loch a' Ghobhainn
Baosbheinn
875
Shieldaig Forest
Beinn Bhreac
624
Beinn an Eoin
855
Strath Lungard
Beinn a'Chearcaill
Meall a' Ghiubhais
Taagan
Beinn Eighe Nature Reserve
Craig
Loch a'Bhealaich
An Ruadh-mheallan
672
Sgurr Mhor
985
Beinn Alligin
922
Beinn Dearg
914
Sail Mhor
981
Ruadh-stac Mor
1010
Beinn Eighe
Kinlochewe
Abhainn Bruachaig
Carn a'Ghlinne
539
Glen Docherty
Meall a'Chaorainn
705
Lower Diabaig
Upper Diabaig
Loch Diabaigas Airde
Mullach an Rathain
1023
Spidean a'Choire Leith
1054
Liathach
Glen Torridon
A896
16
A832
9
Badavanich
Lubmore
Achnasheen
Carn Loisgte
Abhainn Dubh
Loch a'Chroisg
An Liathanach
Ledgowan Forest
Alligin Shuas
Inveralligin
Fasag
Torridon
Upper Loch Torridon
Loch Bharanaichd
Sgurr Dubh
782
Loch an Fhiarlaid
Loch Coulin
Carn Beag
550
Ardheslaig
Loch Shieldaig
Shieldaig Island (NTS)
Rubha na Feola
Inverbain
Balgy
Annat
Seana Mheallan
436
Torridon Visitor Centre (NTS)
Coulin Forest
Shieldaig
Ben Shieldaig
516
Ben-damph Forest
Beinn na h-Eaglaise
737
Beinn Liath Mhor
925
876
Lochan Uaine
Carn Breac
678
Loch Sgamhain
Croic-bheinn
493
Abhainn Dubh
Loch Damh
Loch an Eoin
An Fur
387
Glenshieldaig Forest
Beinn Damh
902
Maol Chean-dearg
933
Sgorr Ruadh
960
Glen Carron
18
Moruisg
928
Carn Gorm
875
857
Loch Lundie
An Staonach
513
Meall na Saobhaidhe
368
An Ruadh-stac
892
Fuar Tholl
907
Achnashellach Sta
A890
Craig
Allt a'Chonais
Sgurr nan Ceannaichean
915
Glencarron and Glenuig Forest
Achnashellach Forest
10
Abhainn Dearg
Fionn-abhainn
Balnacra
Loch Dughaill
Sgurr na Feartaig
862
Sgurr Choinnich
999
Sgurr a'Chaorachain
1053
Maoile Lunndaidh
1007
Beinn Bhan
896
646
Loch Coultrie
Sgurr a Gharaidh
730
Kishorn
Coulags
Carron
Creag a'Chaorainn
Bhearnais
Beinn Tharsuinn
863
West Monar Forest
Loch Mhuilich
Sgurr a'Chaorachain
626
776
792
Bealach na Ba
Meall Gorm
710
Amhainn Bhuidheach
Strathcarron
Strathcarron Sta
Achintee
Bidean a'Choire Sheasgaich
945
Loch an Laoigh
Lurg Mhor
986
Russel
A896
8
Ardarroch
Lochcarron
Carn Geuradainn
594
An Gead Loch
Loch Kishorn
An Sgurr
392
Achintraid
Sgeir Fhada
Attadale
Loch Carron
Beinn Dronaig
Loch an Tachdaidh
Beinn Bheag
619
Meallan Buidhe
555
Airigh-drishaig
Bad a'Chreamha
395
Stromemore
A890
8
Carn nan Iomairean
Attadale Forest
Loch an Iasaich
Carn na Sean Luibe
An Cruachan
706
Allt Riabhachain
L. Reraig
Ardnarff

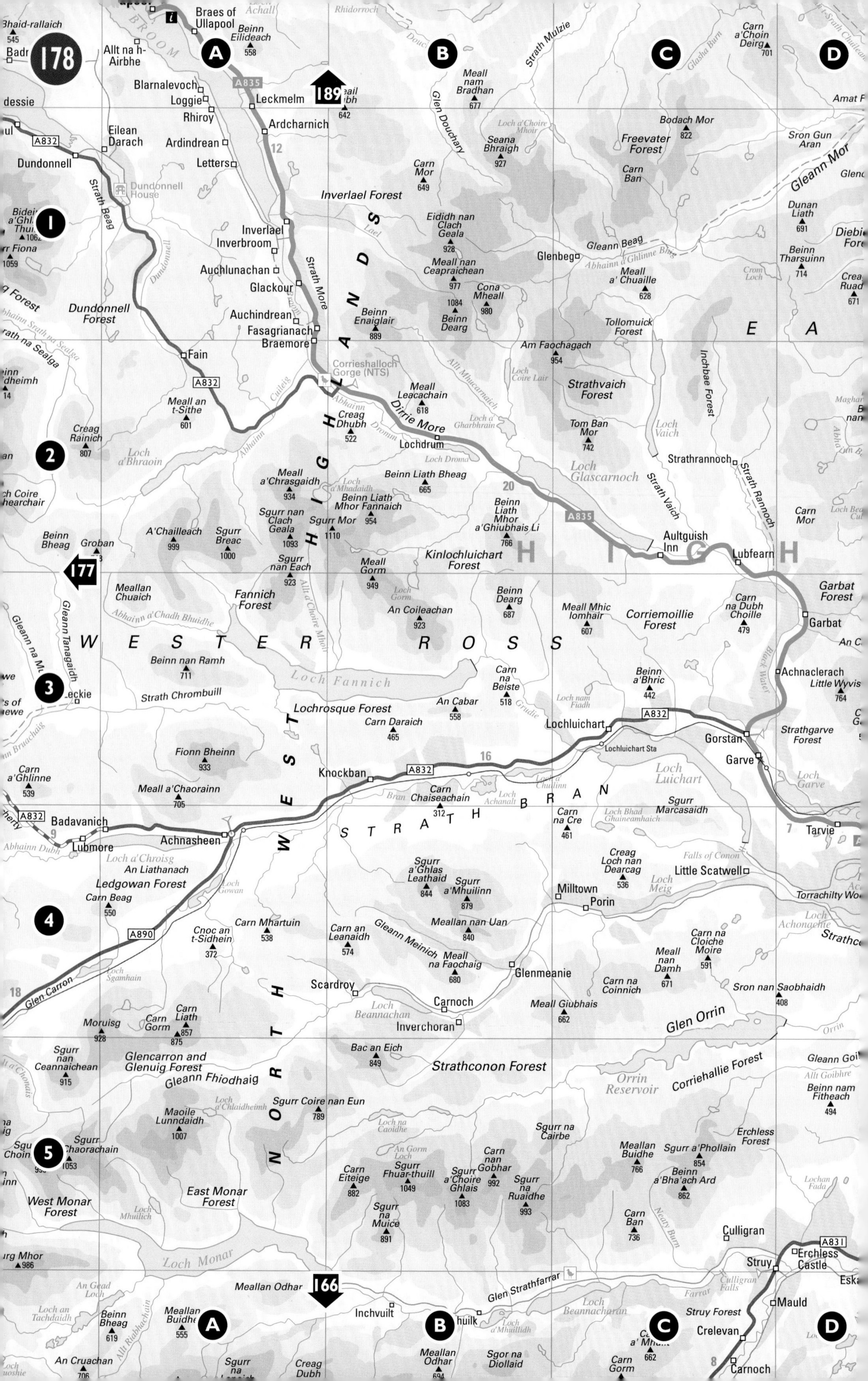
A
B
C
D
1
2
3
4
5
189
177
166
Braes of Ullapool
Beinn Eilideach
558
Allt na h-Airbhe
BROOM
A835
Blarnalevoch
Loggie
Rhiroy
Leckmelm
Ardcharnich
Eilean Darach
Ardindrean
Letters
Dundonnell
A832
Strath Beag
Dundonnell House
Inverlael Forest
Inverlael
Inverbroom
Auchlunachan
Glackour
Strath More
Auchindrean
Fasagrianach
Braemore
Dundonnell Forest
Fain
Corrieshalloch Gorge (NTS)
Meall an t-Sithe
601
Creag Rainich
807
Loch a'Bhraoin
Creag Dhubh
522
Meall Leacachain
618
Dirrie More
Lochdrum
Loch Droma
Meall a'Chrasgaidh
934
Beinn Liath Bheag
665
Beinn Liath Mhor Fannaich
954
Sgurr nan Clach Geala
1093
Sgurr Mor
1110
A'Chailleach
999
Sgurr Breac
1000
Beinn Bheag
Groban
Sgurr nan Each
923
Meall Gorm
949
Meallan Chuaich
Fannich Forest
An Coileachan
923
Kinlochluichart Forest
Strath Mulzie
Meall nam Bradhan
677
Glen Douchary
Seana Bhraigh
927
Carn Mor
649
Eididh nan Clach Geala
928
Meall nan Ceapraichean
977
Cona Mheall
980
1084
Beinn Dearg
Beinn Enaiglair
889
Carn a'Choin Deirg
701
Bodach Mor
822
Freevater Forest
Carn Ban
Glenbeg
Gleann Beag
Meall a' Chuaille
628
Tollomuick Forest
Am Faochagach
954
Strathvaich Forest
Tom Ban Mor
742
Loch Vaich
Loch Glascarnoch
Strath Vaich
Inchbae Forest
Sron Gun Aran
Gleann Mor
Dunan Liath
691
Beinn Tharsuinn
714
Strathrannoch
Strath Rannoch
Carn Mor
Beinn Liath Mhor a'Ghiubhais Li
766
Aultguish Inn
Lubfearn
HIGHLAND
Garbat Forest
Garbat
Beinn Dearg
687
Meall Mhic Iomhair
607
Corriemoillie Forest
Carn na Dubh Choille
479
Achnaclerach
Little Wyvis
764
WESTER ROSS
Beinn nan Ramh
711
Loch Fannich
Leckie
Strath Chrombuill
Lochrosque Forest
Carn Daraich
465
An Cabar
558
Carn na Beiste
518
Beinn a'Bhric
442
Lochluichart
Lochluichart Sta
Gorstan
Garve
Strathgarve Forest
Loch Garve
Loch Luichart
Fionn Bheinn
933
Carn a'Ghlinne
539
Meall a'Chaorainn
705
Knockban
Carn Chaiseachain
312
STRATH BRAN
Carn na Cre
461
Sgurr Marcasaidh
Tarvie
Badavanich
Lubmore
Achnasheen
Loch a'Chroisg
An Liathanach
Ledgowan Forest
Carn Beag
550
A890
Sgurr a'Ghlas Leathaid
844
Sgurr a'Mhuilinn
879
Creag Loch nan Dearcag
536
Little Scatwell
Milltown
Porin
Loch Meig
Torrachilty Wood
Cnoc an t-Sidhein
372
Carn Mhartuin
538
Carn an Leanaidh
574
Gleann Meinich
Meallan nan Uan
840
Meall na Faochaig
680
Glenmeanie
Carn na Cloiche Moire
591
Meall nan Damh
671
Carn na Coinnich
Sron nan Saobhaidh
408
Glen Carron
Scardroy
Carnoch
Loch Beannachan
Inverchoran
Meall Giubhais
662
Glen Orrin
Moruisg
928
Carn Gorm
Carn Liath
857
875
Bac an Eich
849
Strathconon Forest
Sgurr nan Ceannaichean
915
Glencarron and Glenuig Forest
Gleann Fhiodhaig
Orrin Reservoir
Corriehallie Forest
Gleann Goibhre
Beinn nam Fitheach
494
Maoile Lunndaidh
1007
Sgurr Coire nan Eun
789
NORTH WEST HIGHLANDS
Sgurr na Cairbe
Meallan Buidhe
766
Sgurr a'Phollain
854
Erchless Forest
Sgurr a'Chaorachain
1053
Carn Eiteige
882
Sgurr Fhuar-thuill
1049
Sgurr a'Choire Ghlais
1083
Carn nan Gobhar
992
Sgurr na Ruaidhe
993
Beinn a'Bha'ach Ard
862
West Monar Forest
East Monar Forest
Sgurr na Muice
891
Carn Ban
736
Culligran
A831
Erchless Castle
Struy
Loch Monar
Meallan Odhar
Glen Strathfarrar
Loch Beannacharan
Inchvuilt
Mauld
Struy Forest
Crelevan
Carnoch
Beinn Bheag
619
Meallan Buidhe
555
An Cruachan
706
Meallan Odhar
694
Sgor na Diollaid
Creag Dubh
Carn Gorm
662
Sgurr na Lapaich

Strathcarron
Wester Gruinards
The Craigs
Soyal
Bonar Bridge
Tulloch
Migdale
Kyle of Sutherland
Lower Gledfield
Ardgay
Dounie
Kincardine
Ardchronie
Little Creich
Kyloag
Spinningdale
A949
A836
190
Achosnich
Rearquhar
Badninish
Poles
Fourpenny
Creagan Asdale
Clashmore Wood
Evelix
Pitgrudy
Carmore
Clashmore
Whiteface
Skibo
Pulrossie
Craft Centre
Lonemore
Dornoch
Cuthill
Dornoch Sands
Dornoch Point
Whiteness Sands
Carn Bhrain
635
Coire Bog
Wester Fearn Burn
Easter Fearn
Struie Hill
Struie
371
Dounie
Ardmore
Edderton
Ardjachie Point
Morangie
St Duthus's Chapel
Tain
Balcherry
Balnagall
Glen Calvie
Carn Chuinneag
838
Meall Bhenneit
532
Carn Cas nan Gabhar
602
Beinn Clach an Fheadain
477
Cnoc Mugh-bhlaraidh
Aultnamain Inn
Morangie Forest
Lairgs of Tain
Glen Aldie
Aldie
Knockbreck
B9174
A9
T E R
R O S S
Beinn Tharsuinn
692
Cnoc an t-Sabhail
Strath Rory
Braeantra
Kildermorie Lodge
Loch Morie
Strath Rusdale
Black Water
B9176
Lamington
Scotsburn
Cnoc Corr Guinie
Torran
Newfield
Logie Hill
Loandhu
Fearn Sta
Calrossie
Rhynie
Hill of Fearn
Fearn Abbey
Clay of Allan
Inchlumpie
Meall Mor
738
Wyvis Lodge
Loch Glass
Boath
Meall an Tuirc
625
Stittenham
Inchindown
Balnagown Castle
Tullich Muir
Kildary
Milton
Anker
Chapel
Easter Ardross
Dalnavie
Wester Lonvine
Tarbat Ho.
Sands of Nigg
Kilmuir
Wester Lealty
Achandunie
Barbaraville
Nigg
Hill of Nigg
Rhicullen
Delny
Nigg Bay
Wyvis Forest
Bendcallt
Cnoc Ceislein
523
Balnaguisich
Tomich
Balintraid
Balnabruaich
A N D
Meall na Drochaide
Kinloch
Contullich
Achnagarron
Saltburn
B817
180
Balnapaling
Alness
Rosskeen
Castlecraig
North Sutor
Glen Glass
Dalmore
Invergordon
CROMARTY FIRTH
Hugh Miller's Cottage (NTS)
Cromarty
Cromarty Court House
Sutor Stacks
Sutors of Cromarty
Redburn
Black Rock Gorge
Alness Bay
Balblair
Newhall Point
Cromarty Bay
Meall na Speireig
Swordale
Evanton
Drummond
Udale Bay
Shoremill
B9163
Newton
Blue Head
Navity
Cioch Mhor
482
Balconie Point
Cullicudden
Resolis
Newmills
Jemimaville
Strath Sgitheach
Ardullie
The Den
Poyntzfield
Muirton
Upper Eathie
Glenurquhart
Easter Brae
Heights of Brae
Mountgerald
Shoretown
Craighead
Bottacks
Town House
A862
Culbo
Millbuie
Millbuie Forest
B9160
187
A832
Auchterneed
Fodderty
Findon Mains
Balmungie
Castle Leod
A834
Strath Peffer
Dingwall
Urquhart
Culbokie
Mount Eagle
256
Janefield
Whiteness Head
Strathpeffer
Loch Ussie
Maryburgh
Alcaig
Black Isle
Killen
Rosemarkie
Rosemarkie Bay
Fort George
Lochussie
Duncanston
Belmaduthy
Fortrose
Kirkton
Carse of Ardesier
Strathpeffer 1411
Corntown
Knockbain
Cath
Fort George
Conon Bridge
Easter Kinkell
Bogbuie
Easter Suddie
Avoch
Chanonry Point
Ardersier
B9092
Leanaig
Shantullich
Avoch Bay
Black
Gollanfield
Urray
A835
Tore
Munlochy
Munlochy Bay
Moray Firth
B9096
Muir of the Clans
Inverness
Brackley
Balvaird
B9161
Drumderfit
B9039
Fisherton
Drumine
Clephanton
Faebait
Kilcoy
Bogallan
Castle Stuart
Muir of Ord
Newton
Redcastle
Milton
Kilmuir
Alturlie Point
Newton
A96
Tornagrain
Croy
Dallaschyle
Ardnagrask
Windhill
Charlestown
Craigton Point
Dalcross
Cantray
Easter Galcantray
Rheindown
North Kessock
Beauly Firth
Cantraywood
Ruilick
Beauly
Priory
Made in Scotland
South Kessock
Longman Point
Culloden
Balloch
Culloden Forest
Assich Forest
Kirkton of Barevan
Clachnaharry
INVERNESS
Culloden Muir
Kirkhill
B9164
Rhinduie
Bunchrew
Battle of Culloden 1746 (NTS)
Smithton
Cantraydoune
Cumberland Stone
Achnagairn
Drumchardine
Leachkin
Bught Floral Hall and Visitor Cen
Culcabock
Westhill
Leanach
Dalroy
Saddle Hill
Kilmorack
Easter Moniack
Mus & Art Gallery
Culloden Visitors Centre
Clava Cairns
A833
Balchraggan
The Aird
A82
Caledonian Canal
B8082
B9177
Castletown
Kiltarlity
Belladrum
Cnoc na Moine
316
Bogbain
Oldtown of Aigas
Culburnie
An Leacainn
Lagnalean
Knocknagael Boar Stone
Newton of Leys
B851
Beinn Bhuidhe Mhor
548
Tomnacross
Camault Muir
Dochgarroch
B862
Druimkinnerras
Kirkton
Essich
167
Craggie
Carn nan Tri-tighearnan
615
Boblainy Forest
Foxhole
Dores
Scaniport
Loch Ashie
Lochend
Mains of Faillie
Beinn Bhreac
511
Carn a'Bhodaich
501
B861
Glen Convinth
Abriachan
Tor Point
Strath
Ardblair
Moy Burn
Meall a'Bhreacraibh

180
A
B
C
D
191
Fourpenny
Poles
Embo
Embo Street
Carmore
A949
Cath
Craft Centre
Dornoch
Lonemore
Dornoch Sands
Dornoch Point
DORNOCH FIRTH
Whiteness Sands
Innis Mhor
Innis Bheag
Tarbat Ness
Port Mor
Wilkhaven
Hilton
Bindal
Portmahomack
Rockfield
St Duthus's Chapel
Tain
Balcherry
Inver Bay
Inver
Balnagall
Tarrel
B9174
Knockbreck
Aldie
A9
Lochslin
B9165
Rhynie
Baladie
Geanies Ho.
Loandhu
Hill of Fearn
Fearn Sta
Calrossie
Cadboll
Newfield
Fearn
Fearn Abbey
Tullich
Logie Hill
Clay of Allan
B9166
Hilton of Cadboll
Shandwick
Balintore
Invergordon to... hours
Kirkwall............................9
Ankerville
Chapelhill
Tarbat Ho.
Sands of Nigg
B9175
Nigg
Hill of Nigg
Nigg Bay
Balnabruaich
179
Castlecraig
North Sutor
Hugh Miller's Cottage (NTS)
Cromarty
Cromarty Court House
Sutor Stacks
Sutors of Cromarty
B9163
Newton
Blue Head
Upper Eathie
MORAY FIRTH
Burghead Well
Hopeman
Burghead
B9089
Burghead Bay
Roseisle Forest
Findhorn
Hempriggs
Coltfield
Muirhead
Miltonhill
B9011
Findhorn Bay
Culbin Forest
Wellhill
Kinloss
Kintessack
Invererne
Grange Hall
Moy House
Springfield
The Bar
Toreduff
Forres
Sueno's Stone
Mains of Burgie
Brodie (NTS)
Dyke
Falconer Museum
Monaughty Forest
Heldon Hill 234
Whiteness Head
Fort George
Kirkton
Carse of Ardesier
Hilton of Delnies
Nairn
Kingsteps
Macbeth's Hillock
A96
A940
Newton of Dalvey
B9010
Califer
Blervie Castle
Boath Dovecot (NTS)
10
B9092
Tradespark
Househill
Auldearn
Auldearn 1645
Loch of Blairs
Rafford
Tulloch
Ard
Blackcastle
15
B9091
Boghole Farm
Darnaway
Whitemire
Old Military Road
Altyre Woods
Briach
Edinvale
Hill of the Wangie 319
B9006
Gollanfield
B9090
Laiken Forest
Conicavel
Newtyle Forest
Branchill
Muir of the Clans
Moss-side
B9101
Milton
Mains of Sluie
Dallas
Inverness
Brackley
Loch Flemington
Torrich
Phorp
Romach Hill 313
Regoul
A939
Darnaway Forest
Presley
Drumine
Clephanton
Piperhill
Fornighty
Logie
Drumine Forest
Mill Buie 371
Ardoch
Cawdor
Culcharry
Littlemill
Tomnamoon
Craigroy
Tornagrain
Croy
Cawdor
Urchany
Lethen Bar
Randolph's Leap
Hill of Tomechole 344
Dallaschyle
Relugas
Dalcross
Cantray
Easter Galcantray
Achindown
Cantraywood
Redburn
Loch Dallas
Carnachie 359
M
O
Assich Forest
Kirkton of Barevan
Clunas
Mount
B9007
Cantraydoune
Bruachmary
Ardclach Bell Tower
Carn Ghiubhais 430
Balmore
Ferness
Saddle Hill
Daltra
Tomdow
Clava Cairns
Carn a'Chrasgie 401
Carn Duhie
Castletown
HIGHLAND
Riereach Burn
Allt Dearg
Dulsie
Knock of Braemoray 456
Carn Kitty 521
Carn Shalag 470
Dorback Burn
Beinn Bhuidhe Mhor 548
Carn Sgumain
Milltown
Sliabh Bainneach 483
Carnoch
Banchor
Larig Hill 545
Paul's Hill
Hill of Aitnoch
Glen Gheallaidh
Carn nan Tri-tighearnan 615
168
Aitnoch
Daless
Streens
Dava
Carn Ruighe an Uain 546
Beinn Bhreac 511
STRATHDEARN
466
Dava Moor
Glen Tulchan
Carn na Sguabaich
Lochindorb
Carne na Loine 549
Moy Burn
Leonach Burn
Carn Bad na Caorach
Meall a'Bhreacraibh
B9102

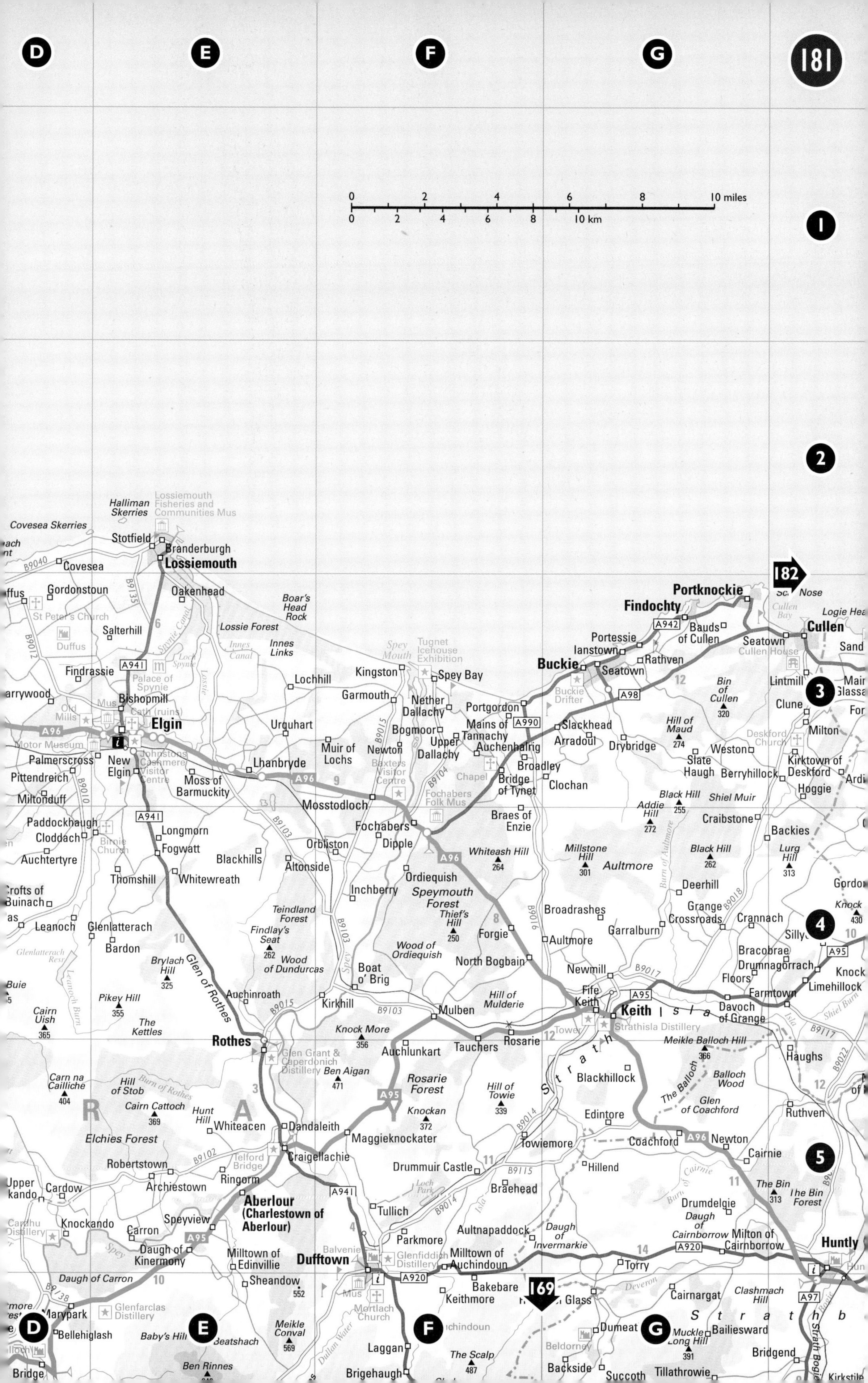
D
E
F
G
0 2 4 6 8 10 miles
0 2 4 6 8 10 km
1
2
3
4
5
Halliman Skerries
Lossiemouth Fisheries and Communities Mus
Covesea Skerries
Stotfield
Branderburgh
Lossiemouth
Covesea
Gordonstoun
Oakenhead
St Peter's Church
Salterhill
Duffus
Boar's Head Rock
Lossie Forest
Innes Links
Spynie Canal
Innes Canal
Findrassie
Palace of Spynie
Bishopmill
Elgin
Old Mills
Mus
Cath (ruins)
Motor Museum
Johnstons Cashmere Visitor Centre
Palmerscross
Pittendreich
Miltonduff
New Elgin
Moss of Barmuckity
Lhanbryde
Lochhill
Urquhart
Kingston
Spey Mouth
Tugnet Icehouse Exhibition
Spey Bay
Garmouth
Nether Dallachy
Portgordon
Bogmoor
Muir of Lochs
Newton
Baxters Visitor Centre
Upper Dallachy
Mains of Tannachy
Auchenhalrig
Chapel
Fochabers Folk Mus
Bridge of Tynet
Broadley
Clochan
Mosstodloch
Fochabers
Dipple
Orbliston
Altonside
Braes of Enzie
Paddockhaugh
Cloddach
Birnie Church
Longmorn
Fogwatt
Auchtertyre
Blackhills
Thomshill
Whitewreath
Ordiequish
Inchberry
Speymouth Forest
Thief's Hill 250
Teindland Forest
Findlay's Seat 262
Wood of Dundurcas
Wood of Ordiequish
Leanoch
Glenlatterach
Bardon
Glenlatterach Resr
Brylach Hill 325
Pikey Hill 355
Glen of Rothes
Boat o' Brig
Forgie
North Bogbain
Auchinroath
Kirkhill
Mulben
Cairn Uish 365
The Kettles
Knock More 356
Rothes
Glen Grant & Caperdonich Distillery
Auchlunkart
Tauchers
Rosarie
Ben Aigan 471
Rosarie Forest
Carn na Cailliche 404
Hill of Stob
Cairn Cattoch 369
Hunt Hill
Whiteacen
Elchies Forest
Dandaleith
Maggieknockater
Knockan 372
Robertstown
Telford Bridge
Craigellachie
Drummuir Castle
Archiestown
Ringorm
Aberlour (Charlestown of Aberlour)
Tullich
Loch Park
Knockando
Cardhu Distillery
Carron
Speyview
Parkmore
Aultnapaddock
Daugh of Kinermony
Milltown of Edinvillie
Balvenie
Dufftown
Glenfiddich Distillery
Milltown of Auchindoun
Daugh of Carron
Sheandow 552
Mus
Mortlach Church
Bakebare
Keithmore
Marypark
Glenfarclas Distillery
Bellehiglash
Baby's Hill
Beatshach
Meikle Conval 569
Laggan
Ben Rinnes
Bridge
Brigehaugh
The Scalp 487
Portknockie
Findochty
Bauds of Cullen
Portessie
Ianstown
Rathven
Buckie
Seatown
Buckie Drifter
Cullen
Seatown
Cullen House
Cullen Bay
Logie Head
Bin of Cullen 320
Lintmill
Clune
Hill of Maud 274
Deskford Church
Milton
Slackhead
Arradoul
Drybridge
Weston
Slate Haugh
Berryhillock
Kirktown of Deskford
Hoggie
Black Hill 255
Addie Hill 272
Shiel Muir
Craibstone
Backies
Whiteash Hill 264
Millstone Hill 301
Aultmore
Black Hill 262
Lurg Hill 313
Deerhill
Broadrashes
Grange Crossroads
Crannach
Aultmore
Garralburn
Newmill
Bracobrae
Drumnagorrach
Floors
Fife Keith
Keith
Isla
Strathisla Distillery
Davoch of Grange
Farmtown
Limehillock
Hill of Mulderie
Meikle Balloch Hill 366
Haughs
Strath Isla
Blackhillock
The Balloch
Balloch Wood
Glen of Coachford
Hill of Towie 339
Edintore
Ruthven
Towiemore
Coachford
Newton
Cairnie
Hillend
Braehead
The Bin 313
The Bin Forest
Drumdelgie
Daugh of Cairnborrow
Milton of Cairnborrow
Daugh of Invermarkie
Torry
Huntly
Deveron
Glass
Cairnargat
Clashmach Hill
Dumeath
Muckle Long Hill 391
Bailiesward
Beldorney
Backside
Succoth
Tillathrowie
Bridgend
Strathbogie
182
169
A96
A941
A95
A920
A98
A942
A990
A97
B9040
B9135
B9012
B9010
B9103
B9015
B9104
B9016
B9018
B9017
B9117
B9022
B9014
B9115
B9102
B9138
B9013

A
B
C
D
1
2
3
4
5
0 2 4 6 8 10 miles
0 2 4 6 8 10 km
181
170
Portknockie
Scar Nose
Cullen Bay
Logie Head
Findlater Castle
Bauds of Cullen
Cullen
Seatown
Cullen House
Sandend Bay
Sandend
Redhythe Point
Portsoy
Boyne Bay
Boyne
Easter Whyntie
Whitehills
Knock Head
Boyndie Bay
Banff Bay
Banff
Macduff
Head of Garness
Crovie Head
Gamrie Bay
Crovie
North
Troup
Lintmill
Mains of Glassaugh
Durn Hill
199
Clune
Fordyce
Fordyce Hill
Milton
Deskford Church
Weston
Slate Haugh
Berryhillock
Kirktown of Deskford
Ardiecow
Hoggie
Shiel Muir
Craibstone
Backies
Canterbury
Black Hill
262
Lurg Hill
313
Deerhill
MORAY
Gordonstown
Knock Hill
430
Crannach
Sillyearn
Bracobrae
Drumnagorrach
Floors
Farmtown
Knock
Limehillock
Wether Hill
Knabbygates
Glen Barry
Crombie
Davoch of Grange
Isla
Meikle Balloch Hill
366
Haughs
Balloch Wood
Glen of Coachford
Ruthven
Moss-side
Old Crombie
Marnoch
Milltown of Rothiemay
Mayen
Hillbrae
Yonder Bognie
Redhill
Fourman Hill
344
Newton
Cairnie
The Bin
313
The Bin Forest
Cobairdy
Corse of Kinnoir
Drumdelgie
Daugh of Cairnborrow
Milton of Cairnborrow
Huntly
Clashmach Hill
Cairnargat
Strathbogie
Bailiesward
Muckle Long Hill
391
Bridgend
Kirkstile
Mosshead
Slioch
Brides
Boggshill
Denend
Thomastown
Millburn
Drumblade
Lessendrum
Cruchie
Conland
Bogniebrae
Glendronach Distillery
Inverkeithny
Auchininna
Fortrie
Feith-hill
Hill of Carlincraig
192
Drumblair
Largue
Frendraught
Corse
Aucharnie
Denmoss
Nether Lenshie
Ythanwells
Badenscoth
Logie Newton
Fisherford
Redhill
Blackford
Bainshole
Boyndie
Auds
Blairshinnoch
Wester Culbeuchly
Duff House
Kirktown of Alvah
Hill of Culbirnie
156
Oldtown of Ord
Cornhill
Park
Milbethill
Fattahead
Weachyburn
Greenlaw
The Pole of Itlaw
Linhead
Kebholes
Finnygaud
Knowes of Elrick
Gallow Hill
226
Culvie
Cranna
Boghead
Auchintoul
Aberchirder
Bogton
Clunie
Carnousie
Kirkton
Laithers
Deveron
Mountblairy
Muirden
Wrae
ABERD
Dounepark
Melrose
Wester Greenskares
Longmanhill
Gardenstown
Gamrie
Dubford
Protstonhill
Cushnie
Minnonie
Netherbrae
Foulzie
Keilhill
Eden
Balgreen
Balchers
Gorrachie
Castleton
Milltown of Craigston
Plaidy
Craigston
Fintry
Brackens
Wester Badentyre
Garmond
Muiryfold
Turriff
1639
Delgatie
Cuminestown
Delgaty Forest
Balthangie
Mill of Colp
Little Idoch
Southend
Gask
Darra
Howe of Teuchar
Braefoot
Hatton Castle
Birkenhills
South Redbriggs
Kingsford
Dykeside
Towie Barclay
Steinmanhill
Gourdas
Macterry
Darnabo
Kirktown of Auchterless
Inverythan
Monkshill
Tifty
Backhill
Fyvie
Gordonstown
Rothiebrisbane
Rothienorman
Petty
Woodhead
Crofts
Greenmyre
Bracklamore
Overbrae
Hill of Fishrie
Brucklay
New Byth
West Cairncake
Northburnhill
Waggle Hill
Muirtack
Deer's Hill
178
North Millbrex
Lethenty
Cottown
A98
A95
A97
A947
A96
A920
B9139
B9121
B9018
B9022
B9023
B9025
B9117
B9001
B9024
B992
B9031
B9123
B9105
B9170
B9027
B9005
B9001

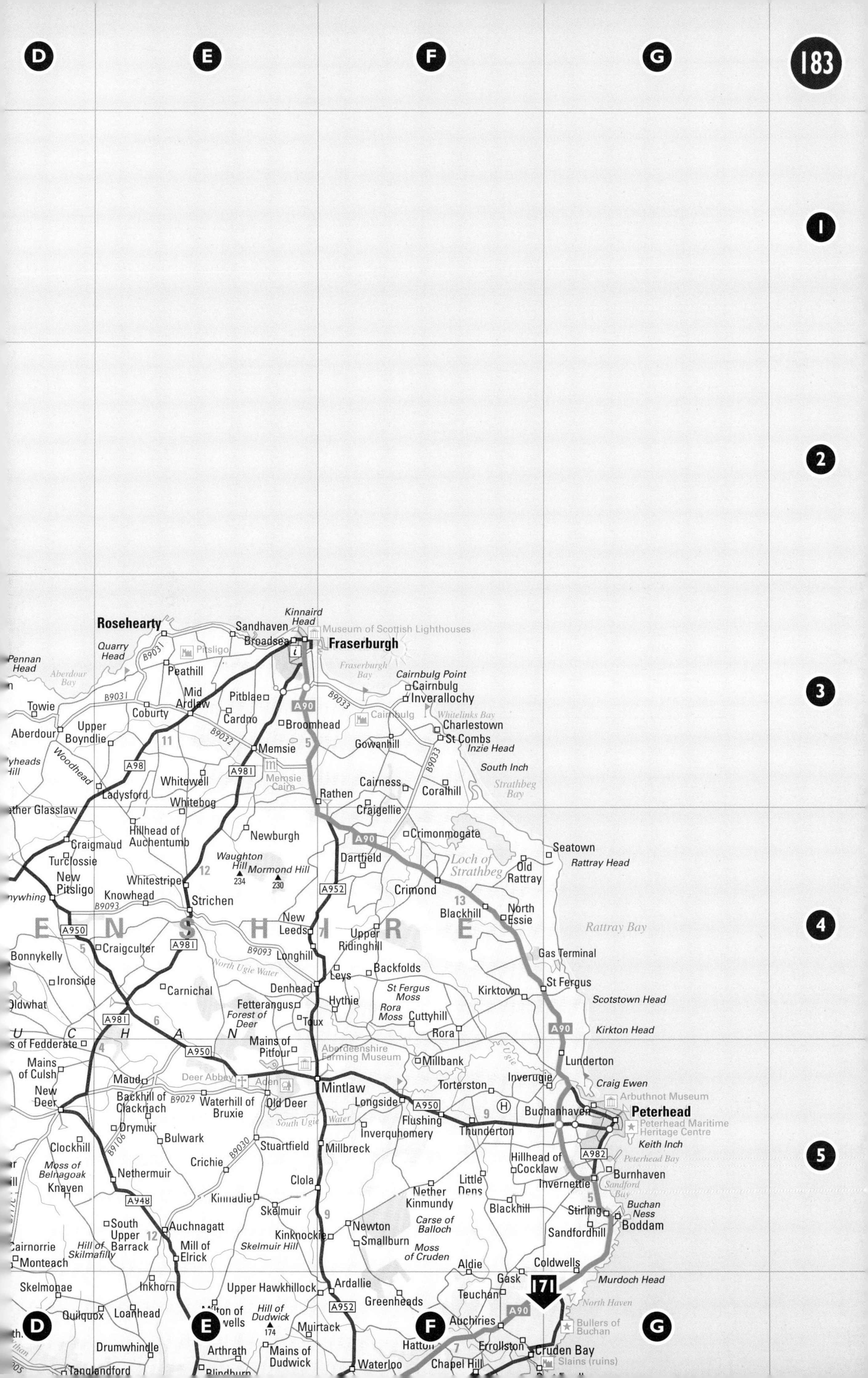
D
E
F
G
1
2
3
4
5
Rosehearty
Quarry Head
Pennan Head
Aberdour Bay
Pitsligo
Peathill
Sandhaven
Broadsea
Kinnaird Head
Museum of Scottish Lighthouses
Fraserburgh
Fraserburgh Bay
Cairnbulg Point
Cairnbulg
Inverallochy
Cairnbulg
Whitelinks Bay
Charlestown
St Combs
Inzie Head
South Inch
Strathbeg Bay
Towie
Aberdour
Upper Boyndlie
Coburty
Mid Ardlaw
Pitblae
Cardno
Broomhead
Memsie
Gowanhill
Woodhead
Ladysford
Whitewell
Whitebog
Memsie Cairn
Rathen
Cairness
Corahill
Craigellie
Crimonmogate
Glasslaw
Hillhead of Auchentumb
Craigmaud
Newburgh
Turclossie
New Pitsligo
Waughton Hill 234
Mormond Hill 230
Dartfield
Loch of Strathbeg
Seatown
Rattray Head
Old Rattray
Whitestripe
Knowhead
Strichen
Crimond
Blackhill
North Essie
Rattray Bay
New Leeds
Upper Ridinghill
Craigculter
Bonnykelly
Ironside
Carnichal
Longhill
North Ugie Water
Leys
Backfolds
Gas Terminal
St Fergus Moss
Kirktown
St Fergus
Denhead
Hythie
Fetterangus
Forest of Deer
Toux
Rora Moss
Cuttyhill
Rora
Scotstown Head
Kirkton Head
Mains of Pitfour
Aberdeenshire Farming Museum
Millbank
Lunderton
Mains of Culsh
Maud
Deer Abbey
Aden
Mintlaw
Torterston
Inverugie
Craig Ewen
Arbuthnot Museum
New Deer
Backhill of Clackriach
Waterhill of Bruxie
Old Deer
Longside
Flushing
Buchanhaven
Peterhead
Peterhead Maritime Heritage Centre
Drymuir
Bulwark
South Ugie Water
Inverquhomery
Thunderton
Keith Inch
Clockhill
Stuartfield
Millbreck
Hillhead of Cocklaw
Peterhead Bay
Moss of Belnagoak
Crichie
Nethermuir
Clola
Little Dens
Burnhaven
Knaven
Kinnadie
Nether Kinmundy
Invernettie
Sandford Bay
Skelmuir
Blackhill
Stirling
Buchan Ness
South Upper Barrack
Auchnagatt
Newton
Carse of Balloch
Boddam
Cairnorrie
Mill of Elrick
Kinknockie
Smallburn
Sandfordhill
Monteach
Hill of Skilmafilly
Skelmuir Hill
Moss of Cruden
Aldie
Coldwells
Skelmonae
Inkhorn
Upper Hawkhillock
Ardallie
Gask
Murdoch Head
Teuchan
Greenheads
North Haven
Quilquox
Loanhead
Hill of Dudwick 174
Auchiries
Bullers of Buchan
Muirtack
Drumwhindle
Arthrath
Mains of Dudwick
Hatton
Errollston
Cruden Bay
Slains (ruins)
Tanglandford
Waterloo
Chapel Hill
171
ABERDEENSHIRE
A90
A98
A981
A950
A952
A948
A982
B9031
B9033
B9032
B9093
B9029
B9106
B9030

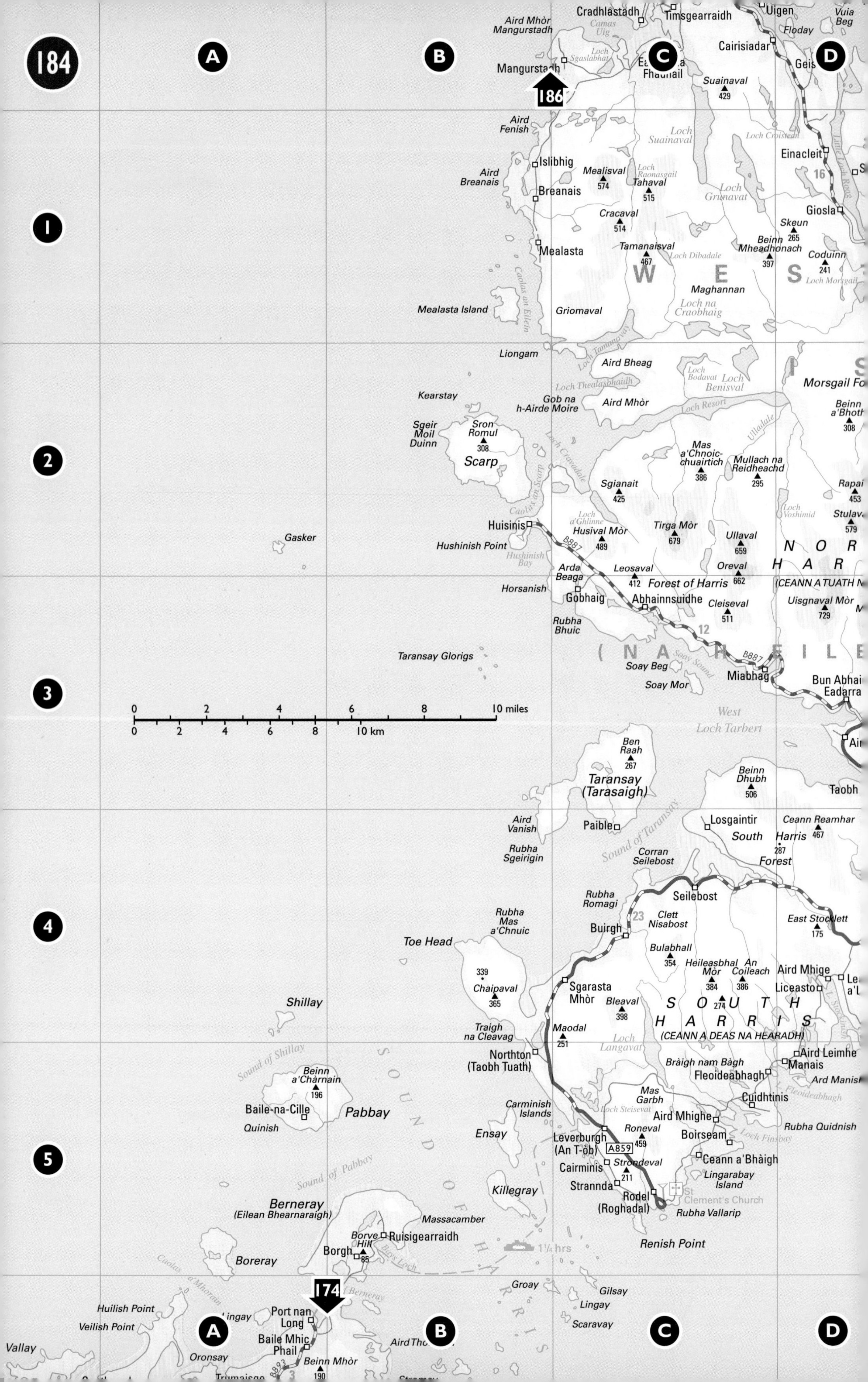
A
B
C
D
1
2
3
4
5
186
174
Cradhlastadh
Timsgearraidh
Uigen
Vuia Beg
Aird Mhòr Mangurstadh
Camas Uig
Floday
Cairisiadar
Mangurstadh
Sgaslabhat
Geis
Suainaval
429
Aird Fenish
Loch Suainaval
Loch Croistean
Einacleit
Islibhig
Aird Breanais
Mealisval
574
Loch Raonasgail
Tahaval
515
Loch Grunavat
16
Breanais
Cracaval
514
Giosla
Skeun
265
Mealasta
Tamanaisval
467
Loch Dibadale
Beinn Mheadhonach
397
Coduinn
241
Loch Morsgail
W E S
Caolas an Eilein
Maghannan
Loch na Craobhaig
Mealasta Island
Griomaval
Liongam
Loch Tamanavay
Aird Bheag
Loch Bodavat
Loch Benisval
Morsgail Fo
Loch Thealasbhaidh
Kearstay
Gob na h-Airde Moire
Aird Mhòr
Loch Resort
Beinn a'Bhoth
308
Sgeir Moil Duinn
Sron Romul
308
Ulladale
Loch Cravadale
Mas a'Chnoic-chuairtich
386
Mullach na Reidheachd
295
Scarp
Caolas an Scarp
Sgianait
425
Rapai
453
Loch Voshimid
Stulava
579
Loch a'Ghlinne
Husival Mòr
489
Tirga Mòr
679
Huisinis
Gasker
Hushinish Point
Hushinish Bay
B887
Ullaval
659
N O R
H A R
Arda Beaga
Leosaval
412
Oreval
662
Horsanish
Forest of Harris
(CEANN A TUATH N
Gobhaig
Abhainnsuidhe
Cleiseval
511
Uisgnaval Mòr
729
Rubha Bhuic
12
( N A H E I L E
Taransay Glorigs
Soay Sound
B887
Soay Beg
Miabhag
Soay Mor
Bun Abhai Eadarra
0 2 4 6 8 10 miles
0 2 4 6 8 10 km
West Loch Tarbert
Ben Raah
267
Taransay (Tarasaigh)
Beinn Dhubh
506
Taobh
Aird Vanish
Paible
Losgaintir
Ceann Reamhar
467
South Harris Forest
287
Rubha Sgeirigin
Sound of Taransay
Corran Seilebost
Seilebost
Rubha Romagi
Clett Nisabost
23
East Stocklett
175
Rubha Mas a'Chnuic
Buirgh
Toe Head
Bulabhall
354
Heileasbhal Mòr
384
An Coileach
386
Aird Mhige
339
Chaipaval
365
Sgarasta Mhòr
Liceasto
274
Shillay
Bleaval
398
S O U T H
H A R R I S
Traigh na Cleavag
Maodal
251
(CEANN A DEAS NA HEARADH)
Sound of Shillay
Northton (Taobh Tuath)
Loch Langavat
Aird Leimhe
Manais
Bràigh nam Bàgh
Fleoideabhagh
Ard Manish
Beinn a'Chàrnain
196
L. Fleoideabhagh
Mas Garbh
Cuidhtinis
Baile-na-Cille
Pabbay
Carminish Islands
Loch Steisevat
Aird Mhighe
Rubha Quidnish
Quinish
Ensay
Roneval
459
Boirseam
Loch Finsbay
Leverburgh (An T-òb)
A859
Cairminis
Strondeval
211
Ceann a'Bhàigh
Sound of Pabbay
Killegray
Strannda
Lingarabay Island
St Clement's Church
Rodel (Roghadal)
Rubha Vallarip
Berneray (Eilean Bhearnaraigh)
Massacamber
Borve Hill
Ruisigearraidh
Borgh
85
Bays Loch
1¼ hrs
Renish Point
Boreray
Caolas a'Mhorain
S O U N D O F H A R R I S
Groay
Gilsay
Lingay
Huilish Point
Lingay
Port nan Long
Veilish Point
Scaravay
Baile Mhic Phail
Aird Tho
Vallay
Oronsay
B893
3
Beinn Mhòr
190
Trumaisge

Kirkibost
Crulabhig
Eilean Kearstay
Callanish (Calanais)
Callanish Standing Stones
Loch Airigh nan Sloc
Loch an Tairbeart
Loch Vatandip
Loch Ceann Thulabhig
A858
Loch Urayal
Beinn nan Surrag
223
200
Eitshal
13
Linsiadar
Griomarstaidh
Teahaval
256
A858
Achadh Mòr
Beinn a'Bhuna
B8011
3
5
Stornoway
Nan Eilean
Melbost
Melbost Pt
Garrabost
Roisnish
Seisiad
Eye Peninsula
Aignis
Cnoc
Creed
Lews Castle
Stornoway Harbour
St Columba's Church
Branahuie Banks
Suardail
Pabail Iarach
Arnish Pt
Rubh a'Bhaigh Uaine
Ceann na Circ
187
Arnish Moor
A859
Loch Orasay
Ullapool hours 2¾
Loch Thota Bridein
Loch nam Falcag
Loch Nisreaval
Loch Cleit Steirmeis
6
Liurbost
Grimsiadar
Loch Grimsiadar
B897
Crosbost
Raerinish Point
Loch an Fhir Mhaoil
Beinn Mohal
207
Loch Airigh na h-Airde
Loch Trealaval
Loch Fada
Loch Leurbost
Tabhaigh Mhor
Loch Fadagoa
Roineval
281
12
Ceos
Eilean Chaluim Chille
Orasaigh
Gleann Ghrabhair
Lacasaigh
A859
Baile Ailein
Loch Erisort
Cearsiadar
Cabharstadh
Torraigh
Gearraidh Bhaird
Tabost
B8060
Loch Strandavat
Sleiteachal Mhòr
248
Kintarvie
Loch Langavat
Airidh a'Bhruaich
Marbhig
13
Loch Sgibacleit
Malasgair
172
B8060
Calbost
Aird an Troim
Ceann Loch Shiphoirt
Rubha Iosal
Kearnaval
378
Glen Ouirn
Loch Shanndabhat
Feirihisval
326
Grabhair
Beinn a' Mhuil
370
Sidhean an Airgid
381
Mòr Mhonadh
401
Tom an Fhuadain
Loch Odhairn
Kebock Head
Liuthaid
492
A859
473
18
Beinn nah-Uamha
424
389
Muaithabhal
Eisgean
Leumrabhagh
Gob na Milaid
Athlinne
Seaforth Island
Aird a'Mhulaidh
Loch Shell
Caolas a' Tuath
Srianach
Beinn Mhòr
572
Beannan Mòr
242
Eilean Iubhard
Corlabhadh
Clett Ard
P a r k
Uisenis
371
Mulhagery
Kenmore
Maruig
A859
470
Crionaig
Mol Truisg
Sgaoth Aird
559
Straiaval
389
Caiteshal
449
Toddun
528
Loch Seaforth
Loch Claidh
Tathas Mhòr
Loch Bhrollum
Gob Rubh'Uisenis
Laxadale Lochs
Reinigeadal
Bhalamus
Rubha Bhrollum
Beinn a'Chaolais
Eilean Mòr a' Bhàigh
Sgeir na h-Eigheach
Rubh a' Bhaird
Urgha
Carragrich
Uieseval
334
Kyles Scalpay (Caolas Scalpaigh)
Sgeotasaigh
Sound of Scalpay
East Loch Tarbert
Ben Scoravick
104
Scalpay (Eilean Scalpaigh)
Kennavay
Meall Challibost
Scadabhagh
Rubha Bocaig
S O U N D O F S H I A N T
Garbh Eilean
161
Eilean Mhuire
Eilean an Tighe
Shiant Islands
Uig hours 1¾
Fladda-chuain
Gaeilavore Island
Gearran Island
175
Eilean Trodday
Rubha Hunish
h-Aiseig
Loch Hunish
Kilmaluag Bay
D
E
F
G
1
2
3
4
5

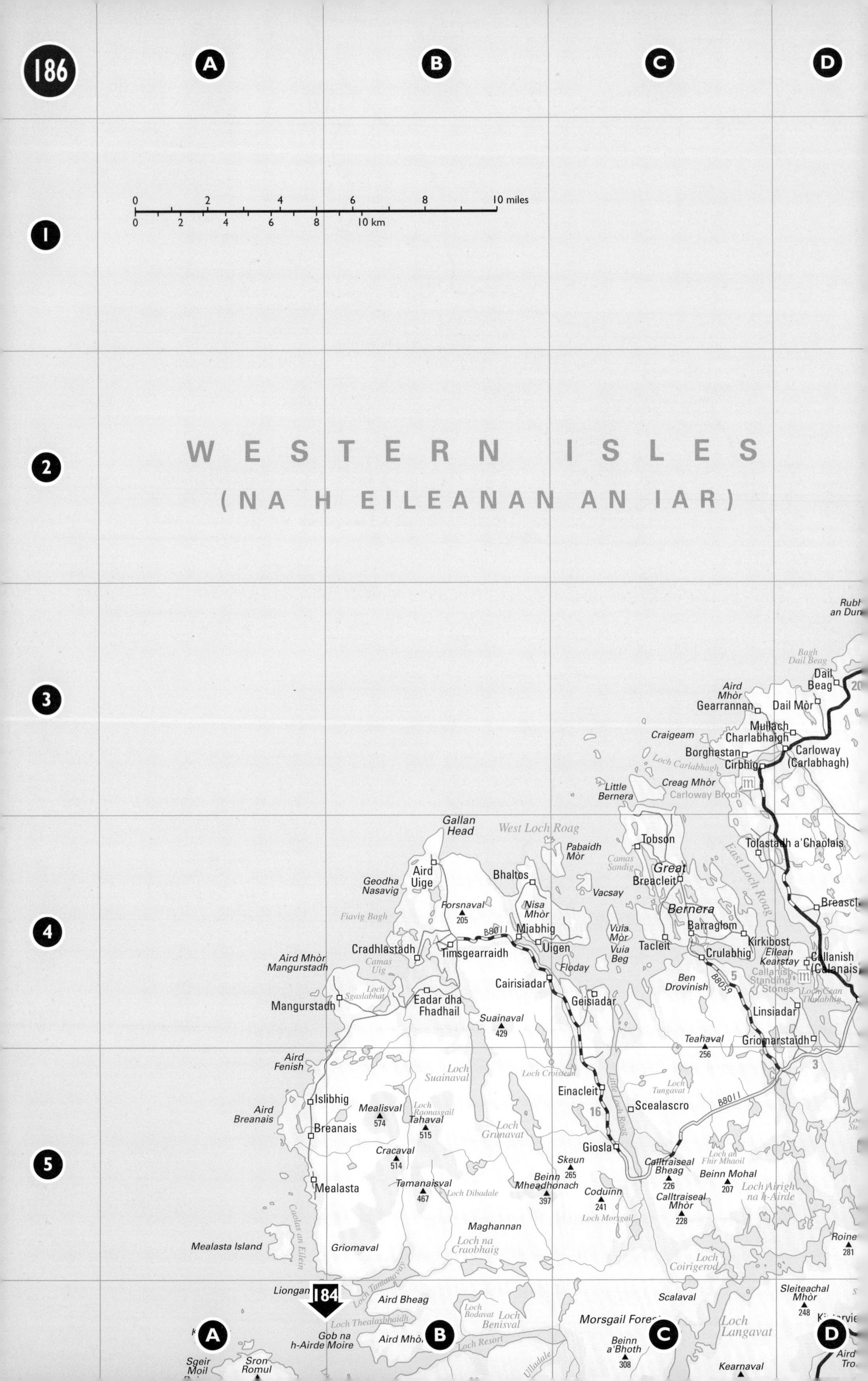
A
B
C
D
1
2
3
4
5
0 2 4 6 8 10 miles
0 2 4 6 8 10 km
WESTERN ISLES
(NA H EILEANAN AN IAR)
Rubh an Dun
Bagh Dail Beag
Dail Beag
Aird Mhòr
Gearrannan
Dail Mòr
Craigeam
Mullach Charlabhaigh
Borghastan
Carloway (Carlabhagh)
Loch Carlabhagh
Cirbhig
Little Bernera
Creag Mhòr
Carloway Broch
Gallan Head
West Loch Roag
Pabaidh Mòr
Tobson
Tolastadh a'Chaolais
Camas Sandig
East Loch Roag
Aird Uige
Geodha Nasavig
Bhaltos
Great Bernera
Breacleit
Vacsay
Breascl
Fiavig Bagh
Forsnaval 205
Nisa Mhòr
B8011
Miabhig
Uigen
Vuia Mòr
Vuia Beg
Barraglom
Kirkibost
Cradhlastadh
Timsgearraidh
Tacleit
Crulabhig
Eilean Kearstay
Callanish (Calanais)
Aird Mhòr Mangurstadh
Camas Uig
Floday
Cairisiadar
Ben Drovinish
B8059
Callanish Standing Stones
Loch Sgaslabhat
Eadar dha Fhadhail
Geisiadar
Loch Ceann Thulabhig
Mangurstadh
Linsiadar
Suainaval 429
Teahaval 256
Griomarstaidh
Aird Fenish
Loch Suainaval
Loch Croistean
Loch Tungavat
Little Loch Roag
Einacleit
Islibhig
Mealisval 574
Loch Raonasgail
Tahaval 515
Scealascro
B8011
Aird Breanais
Breanais
16
Loch Grunavat
Giosla
Cracaval 514
Skeun 265
Calltraiseal Bheag 226
Loch an Fhir Mhaoil
Beinn Mohal 207
Mealasta
Tamanaisval 467
Loch Dibadale
Beinn Mheadhonach 397
Coduinn 241
Calltraiseal Mhòr 228
Loch Airigh na h-Airde
Loch Morsgail
Maghannan
Caolas an Eilein
Mealasta Island
Griomaval
Loch na Craobhaig
Roine 281
Loch Coirigerod
Liongan
184
Loch Tamanavay
Aird Bheag
Scalaval
Sleiteachal Mhòr 248
Loch Bodavat
Loch Benisval
Loch Thealasbhaidh
Morsgail Fore
Loch Langavat
Gob na h-Airde Moire
Aird Mhòr
Loch Resort
Beinn a'Bhoth 308
Sgeir Moil
Sron Romul
Kearnaval
Aird Tro

D
E
F
G
1
2
3
4
5
Butt of Lewis
(Rubha Robhanais)
Port a' Stoth
Cunndal
Teampull Mholuidh
Eoropaidh
Còig Peighinnean
Bad an Fhithich
Port Nis
Lional
Tabost
Suainebost
Eorodal
Port Skigersta
Aird Dhail
Cros
B8015
Sgiogarstaigh
Dail Bho Dheas
Dail Bho Thuath
Ness
Meall Geal
Glen Cross
Toa Galson
A857
Gabhsunn Bho Thuath
Port Alasdair
Gabhsunn Bho Dheas
Cuidhaseadair
Laimhrig
Broch
Mealabost
Roinn a' Bhuic
15
South Galson
Airigh na Glaice
Dell
Ben Dell
Airighean Beinn nan Caorach
Cellar Head
Còig Peighinnean
Siadar Iarach
Airighean Loch Breihavat
Loch Langavat
Siadar Uarach
Rubha Leathann
Baile an Truiseil
Steinacleit Cairn & Standing Stones
Diaval
Loch Mor Sandavat
Geiraha
Glen Shader
Goile Chroic
Rinn Druim Tallig
A857
Port Arnol
Loch Mor Bharabhat
Torray
Loch Gress
Muirneag
248
Port Geiraha
Labost
Bru
Barvas (Barabhas)
Black House
Tolastadh Ùr
Bragar
Arnol
Tolastadh
Tolsta Head
Siabost
Loch Casgro
Loch Urrahag
Gleann Mòr Bharabhais
Loch Mor Sandavat
Gridis
Port nam Bothag
Loch an Tobair
Loch Sgeireach Mor
B895
Loch Breivat
11
Gleann Tholastaidh
Glen Bragar
Gleann Bhruthadail
Beinn Bragar
261
Beinn Choinnich
210
Rahacleit
248
Port Bun a' Ghlinne
12
Griais
Roishal Mòr
174
ISLE OF LEWIS
(EILEAN LEODHAIS)
Creag Fhraoich
Bac
Loch na Scaravat
Col
Col
Beinn Mholach
292
Loch Mor an Stairr
Breibhig
Rubha Bhataisgeir
Col Sands
Tiumpan Head
(Rubha an t-Siumpain)
Portnaguran
(Port nan Giùran)
Stacashal
216
Loch nam Breac
Loch nan Stearnag
A857
Aird Thunga
Rubha Deas
Laxdale
Tunga
Sron Ruadh
Newmarket
B895
Loch a' Tuath
A866
Stornoway
(Steornabhagh)
Laxdale
(Lacasdal)
Melbost Sands
Siulaisiadar
East Roisnish
Seisiadar
Loch Vatandip
A858
Stornoway
Melbost Pt
Garrabost
10
Rubha na Gréine
Loch Airigh nan Sloc
Melbost
Eye Peninsula
(An Rubha)
Loch Uraval
Creed
Lews Castle
Nan Eilean
Sandwick
(Sanndabhaig)
Aignis
Cnoc
St Columba's Church
Pabail Uarach
Rubha na Bearnaich
Beinn nan Surrag
200
13
Stornoway Harbour
Suardail
Bagh Phabail
223
Eitshal
Beinn a'Bhuna
Branahuie Banks
Arnish Pt
Pabail Iarach
A858
Achadh Mòr
Arnish Moor
Rubh a'Bhaigh Uaine
Ceann na Circ
A859
Loch Orasay
Loch Thota Bridein
Loch nam Falcag
6
Loch Nisreaval
B897
Liurbost
Grimsiadar
Loch Grimsiadar
Crosbost
Raerinish Point
hours
Ullapool.................2¾
Loch Fada
Loch Leurbost
Tabhaigh Mhor
Laxay
12
Ceos
Eilean Chaluim Chille
Orasaigh
A859
Lacasaigh
Gleann Ghrabhair
Baile Ailein
Loch Erisort
Cearsiadar
Cabharstadh
Torraigh
Gearraidh Bhaird
Tabost
B8060
13
185
Marbhig
Loch Sgibacleit
B8060
Calbost
Malasgair
172
Ceann Loch Shiphoirt
Rubha Iosal
Glen Ouirn
Grabhair

THE MINCH
Point of Stoer
Cirean Geardail
Culkein
Raffin
Achnacarnin
Cluas Deas
Clashnessie
Balchladich
Stoer
Clachtoll
Achmelvich
Rhicarn
Ardroe
Baddidarach
Lochinver
Strathan
Badnaban
Inverkirkaig
Rhegreanoch
Falls of Kirkaig
Drumbeg
Nedd
Oldany Island
Reiff
Alltan Dubh
Polbain
Isle Ristol
Achiltibuie
Polglass
The Hydroponicum
Ardnagoine
Garadheancal
Tanera Beg
Summer Isles
Priest Island
Bottle Island
Achvraie
Achduart
Culnacraig
Stac Pollaidh
Inverpolly Forest
Ben Mòr Coigach
Ardmair
Rhue
Morefield
Ullapool
Allt na h-Airbhe
Blarnalevoch
Scoraig
Achmore
Carnach
Rhireavach
Badrallach
Badluarach
Mungasdale
Durnamuck
Badcaul
Ardessie
Camusnagaul
Dundonnell
Dundonnell House
Gruinard Island
Gruinard Bay
Second Coast
Coast
Little Gruinard
Laide
Achgarve
Mellon Udrigle
Opinan
Mellon Charles
Ormiscaig
Bualnaluib
Aultbea
Drumchork
Cove
Inverasdale
Greenstone Point
Eilean Furadh Mor
Stornoway hours 2¾
A832
A835
B869
177
10 miles
10 km

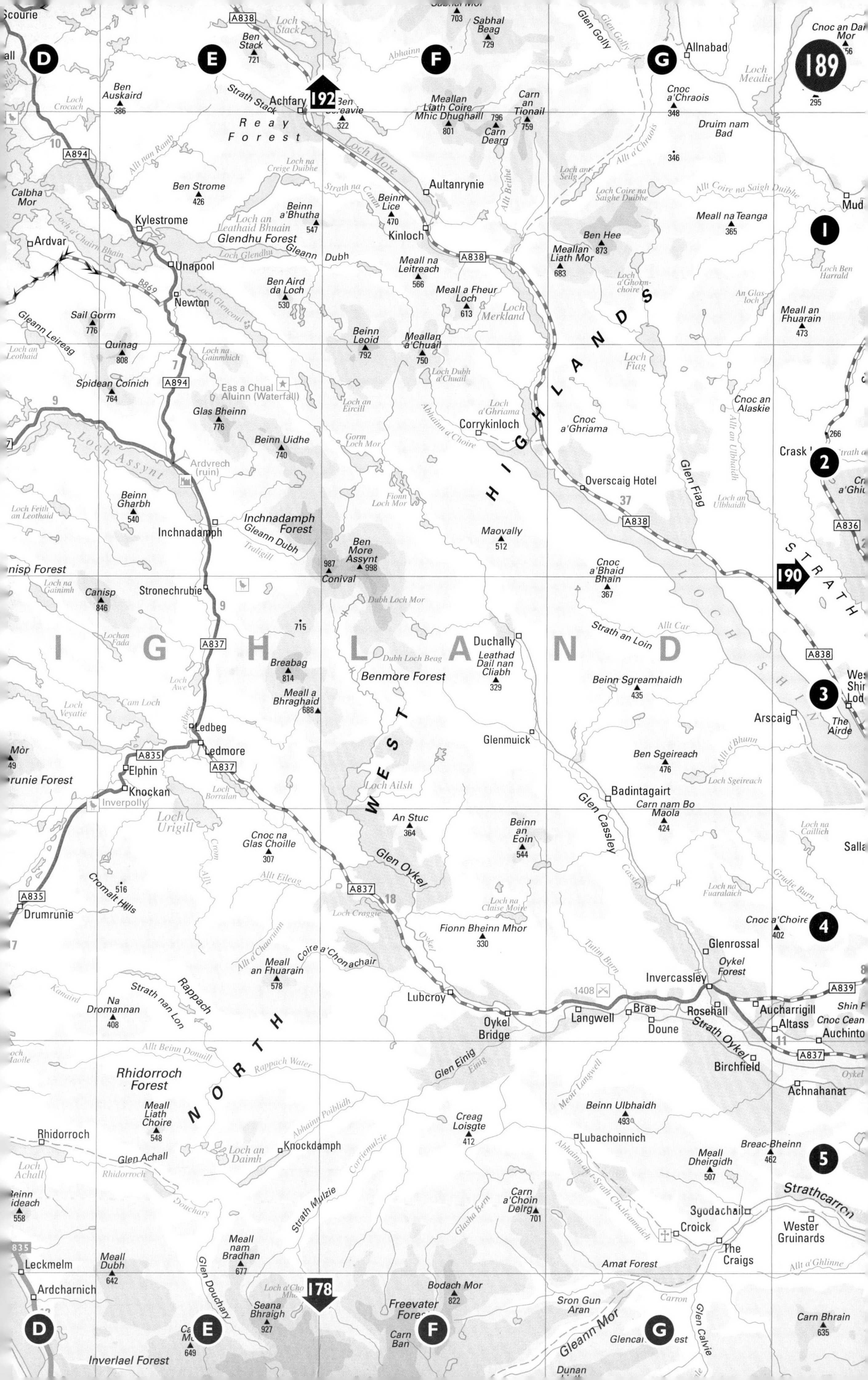
Scourie
D
E
F
G
192
178
190
A838
Loch Stack
Ben Stack
721
Sabhal Beag
729
703
Glen Golly
Allnabad
Loch Meadie
Cnoc an Dai Mor
Ben Auskaird
386
Strath Stack
Achfary
Ben Screavie
322
Reay Forest
Meallan Liath Coire Mhic Dhughaill
801
796
Carn Dearg
Carn an Tionail
759
Cnoc a'Chraois
348
Druim nam Bad
346
295
Loch Crocach
A894
Loch na Creige Duibhe
Loch More
Strath na Caran
Aultanrynie
Allt nan Ramh
Ben Strome
426
Beinn a'Bhutha
547
Beinn Lice
470
Kinloch
Loch an Seilg
Loch Coire na Saighe Duibhe
Allt Coire na Saigh Duibhe
Mud
Meall na Teanga
365
Calbha Mor
Kylestrome
Ardvar
Loch a'Chairn Bhain
Loch an Leathaid Bhuain
Glendhu Forest
Loch Glendhu
Gleann Dubh
Unapool
B869
Newton
Loch Glencoul
Ben Aird da Loch
530
Meall na Leitreach
566
A838
Meall a Fheur Loch
613
Loch Merkland
Ben Hee
873
Meallan Liath Mor
683
Loch a'Ghorm-choire
Loch Ben Harrald
An Glas-loch
Meall an Fhuarain
473
Sail Gorm
776
Gleann Leireag
Quinag
808
Loch an Leothaid
Loch na Gainmhich
Beinn Leoid
792
Meallan a'Chuail
750
Loch Dubh a'Chuail
Loch Fiag
Spidean Coinich
764
A894
Eas a Chual Aluinn (Waterfall)
Loch an Eircill
Loch a'Ghriama
Cnoc an Alaskie
Glas Bheinn
776
Abhainn a'Choire
Corrykinloch
Cnoc a'Ghriama
266
Loch Assynt
Beinn Uidhe
740
Gorm Loch Mor
Crask Inn
Ardvrech (ruin)
Glen Fiag
Allt an Ulbhaidh
Beinn Gharbh
540
Fionn Loch Mor
Overscaig Hotel
Loch an Ulbhaidh
Loch Feith an Leothaid
Inchnadamph Forest
Gleann Dubh
37
A838
A836
Inchnadamph
Ben More Assynt
998
987
Conival
Traligill
Maovally
512
Canisp Forest
Cnoc a'Bhaid Bhain
367
STRATH
Loch na Gainimh
Canisp
846
Stronechrubie
Dubh Loch Mor
9
715
Lochan Fada
Duchally
Allt Car
Strath an Loin
LOCH SHIN
HIGHLAND
HIGHLANDS
A837
Dubh Loch Beag
Leathad Dail nan Cliabh
329
A838
Breabag
814
Benmore Forest
Loch Awe
Meall a Bhraghaid
688
Beinn Sgreamhaidh
435
Loch Veyatie
Cam Loch
West Shin Lodge
Ledbeg
Arscaig
The Airde
WEST
Glenmuick
Mòr
A835
Ledmore
Elphin
Ben Sgeireach
476
Allt a'Bhunn
A837
Loch Borralan
Loch Ailsh
Loch Sgeireach
Knockan
Inverpolly
Badintagairt
Loch Urigill
Carn nam Bo Maola
424
An Stuc
364
Beinn an Eoin
544
Glen Cassley
Loch na Caillich
Cnoc na Glas Choille
307
Salla
Cromalt Hills
516
Allt Eileag
Glen Oykel
Cassley
Loch na Fuaralaich
Grudie Burn
A835
A837
18
Drumrunie
Loch Craggie
Loch na Claise Moire
Fionn Bheinn Mhor
330
Cnoc a'Choire
402
Glenrossal
Allt a'Chaorainn
Meall an Fhuarain
578
Coire a'Chonachair
Oykel
Tutim Burn
Oykel Forest
Invercassley
A839
Strath nan Lon
Rappach
Kanaird
1408
Na Dromannan
408
Lubcroy
Langwell
Brae
Rosehall
Aucharrigill
Shin Forest
Oykel Bridge
Doune
Altass
Cnoc Cean
Achinto
Strath Oykel
11
A837
Loch Maoile
Allt Beinn Donuill
Rappach Water
Birchfield
Oykel
NORTH
Rhidorroch Forest
Glen Einig
Einig
Meoir Langwell
Achnahanat
Meall Liath Choire
548
Creag Loisgte
412
Beinn Ulbhaidh
493
Rhidorroch
Abhainn Poiblidh
Lubachoinnich
Breac-Bheinn
462
Loch an Daimh
Knockdamph
Loch Achall
Glen Achall
Rhidorroch
Corriemulzie
Abhainn an t-Srath Chuileannaich
Meall Dheirgidh
507
Strathcarron
Beinn ideach
558
Douchary
Strath Mulzie
Glasha Burn
Carn a'Choin Deirg
701
Sgodachail
Croick
Wester Gruinards
835
Meall Dubh
642
Meall nam Bradhan
677
Glen Douchary
The Craigs
Amat Forest
Allt a'Ghlinne
Leckmelm
Loch a'Chroisg
Bodach Mor
822
Ardcharnich
Carron
Seana Bhraigh
927
Freevater Forest
Sron Gun Aran
Gleann Mor
Glencalvie Forest
Glen Calvie
Carn Bhrain
635
649
Carn Ban
Inverlael Forest
Dunan

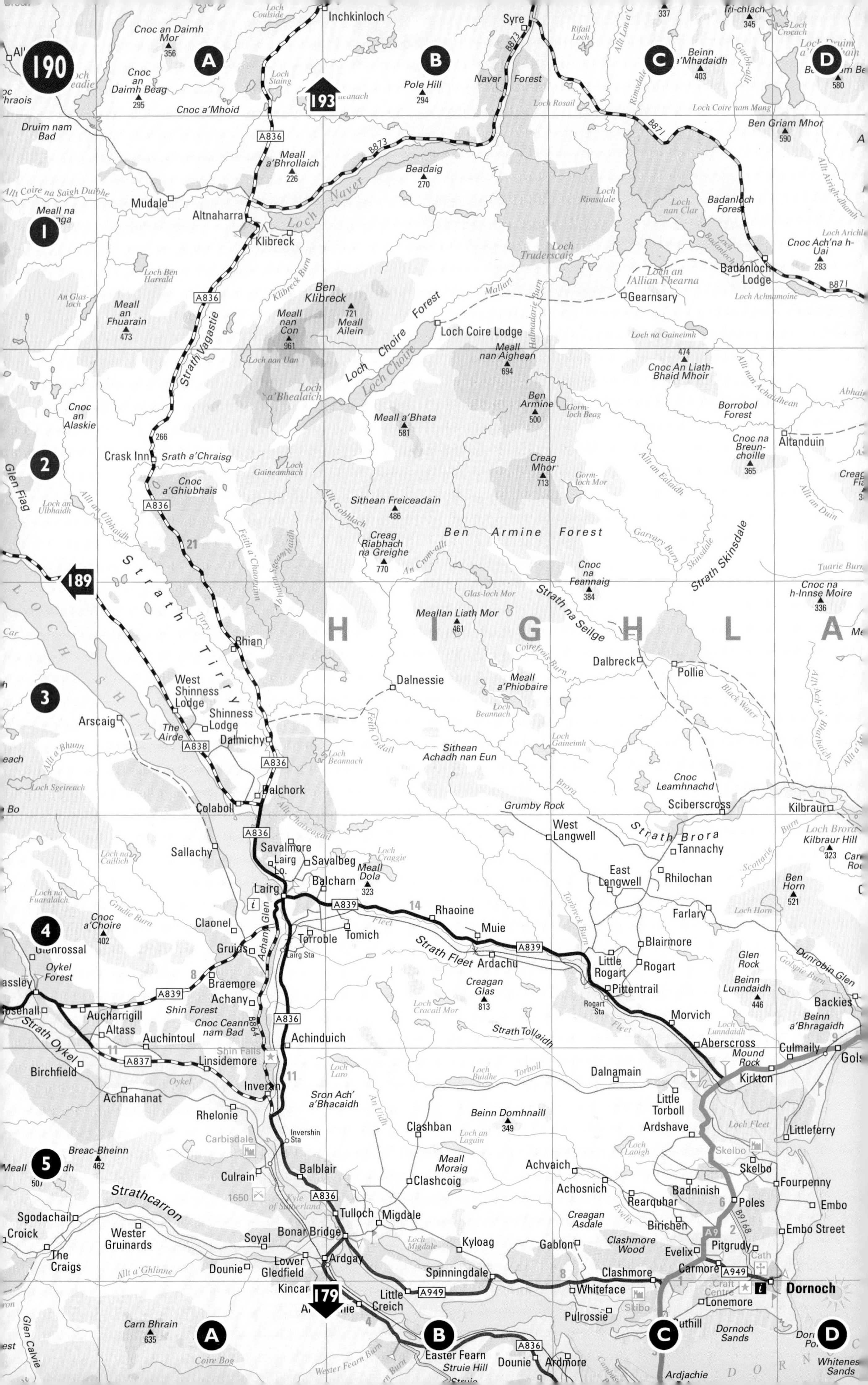

190
A
B
C
D
193
189
179
1
2
3
4
5
Inchkinloch
Loch Coulside
Cnoc an Daimh Mor
356
Cnoc an Daimh Beag
295
Cnoc a'Mhoid
Loch Staing
Syre
Rifail Loch
Pole Hill
294
Naver Forest
Loch Rosail
337
Tri-chlach
345
Loch Crocach
Beinn a'Mhadaidh
403
Rimsdale
Loch Coire nam Mang
Ben Griam Mhor
590
580
Druim nam Bad
A836
B873
B871
Meall a'Bhrollaich
226
Beadaig
270
Loch Naver
Loch Rimsdale
Loch nan Clar
Badanloch Forest
Loch Badanloch
Cnoc Ach'na h-Uai
283
Loch Arichlinie
Allt Airigh-dhamh
Allt Coire na Saigh Duibhe
Mudale
Altnaharra
Klibreck
Meall na
Loch Truderscaig
Loch an Allian Fhearna
Badanloch Lodge
Gearnsary
Loch Achnamoine
Loch Ben Harrald
An Glas-loch
Klibreck Burn
Mallart
Halmadarie Burn
Meall an Fhuarain
473
Ben Klibreck
721
Meall nan Con
961
Meall Ailein
Loch Choire Forest
Loch Coire Lodge
Loch na Gaineimh
Strath Vagastie
Loch nan Uan
Loch Choire
Loch a'Bhealaich
Meall nan Aighean
694
474
Cnoc An Liath-Bhaid Mhoir
Allt nan Achaidhean
Cnoc an Alaskie
Meall a'Bhata
581
Ben Armine
500
Gorm-loch Beag
Borrobol Forest
Abhainn
Altanduin
266
Crask Inn
Strath a'Chraisg
Loch Gaineamhach
Creag Mhor
713
Gorm-loch Mor
Allt an Ealaidh
Cnoc na Breun-choille
365
Glen Fiag
Loch an Ulbhaidh
Allt an Ulbhaidh
Cnoc a'Ghiubhais
Allt Gobhlach
Sithean Freiceadain
486
Creag Riabhach na Greighe
770
An Crom-allt
Ben Armine Forest
Garvary Burn
Skinsdale
Strath Skinsdale
Allt an Duin
Tuarie Burn
21
Strath Tirry
Feith a'Chaoruinn
Abhainn Sgeamhaidh
Cnoc na Feannaig
384
Glas-loch Mor
Strath na Seilge
Cnoc na h-Innse Moire
336
Loch Shin
Meallan Liath Mor
461
HIGHLAND
Rhian
Tirry
Coirefrois Burn
Dalbreck
Pollie
Black Water
West Shinness Lodge
Shinness Lodge
Arscaig
The Airde
A838
Dalmichy
Dalnessie
Meall a'Phiobaire
Loch Beannach
Feith Osdail
Loch Gaineimh
Allt Ach' a' Bhathaich
Allt a'Bhunn
Loch Sgeireach
Sithean Achadh nan Eun
Cnoc Leamhnachd
Brora
Balchork
Colaboll
Allt Chaiseagail
Grumby Rock
Sciberscross
Kilbraur
West Langwell
Strath Brora
Tannachy
Loch Brora
Kilbraur Hill
323
Sallachy
Savalmore
Lairg Lo.
Savalbeg
Loch Craggie
Meall Dola
323
Balcharn
East Langwell
Rhilochan
Scottarie
Ben Horn
521
Loch na Caillich
Loch na Fuaralaich
Lairg
A839
14
Rhaoine
Farlary
Loch Horn
Cnoc a'Choire
402
Grudie Burn
Claonel
Achany Glen
Fleet
Tomich
Muie
Torbreck Burn
Blairmore
Glen Rock
Dunrobin Glen
Glenrossal
Oykel Forest
Gruids
Torroble
Lairg Sta
Strath Fleet
Ardachu
Little Rogart
Rogart
Beinn Lunndaidh
446
Golspie Burn
8
Braemore
Achany
Creagan Glas
813
Pittentrail
Rogart Sta
Backies
Beinn a'Bhragaidh
Cassley
Rosehall
Shin Forest
Cnoc Ceann nam Bad
Loch Cracail Mor
B864
Morvich
Aucharrigill
Altass
Auchintoul
A837
11
Achinduich
Strath Tollaidh
Loch Lunndaidh
Aberscross
Mound Rock
Culmaily
Golspie
9
Strath Oykel
Birchfield
Linsidemore
Shin Falls
Loch Laro
Torboll
Loch Buidhe
Dalnamain
Kirkton
Oykel
Invershin
Achnahanat
Sron Ach' a'Bhacaidh
An Uidh
Beinn Domhnaill
349
Little Torboll
Rhelonie
Carbisdale
Invershin Sta
Clashban
Loch an Lagain
Ardshave
Loch Fleet
Littleferry
Breac-Bheinn
462
507
Meall Moraig
Achvaich
Loch Laoigh
Skelbo
Culrain
Balblair
Clashcoig
Achosnich
Badninish
Fourpenny
Strathcarron
1650
Kyle of Sutherland
Rearquhar
Poles
Embo
Sgodachail
Tulloch
Migdale
Creagan Asdale
Evelix
B9168
6
Croick
Wester Gruinards
Soyal
Bonar Bridge
Loch Migdale
Kyloag
Gablon
Clashmore Wood
Birichen
Embo Street
A9
Pitgrudy
The Craigs
Allt a'Ghlinne
Dounie
Lower Gledfield
Ardgay
Spinningdale
Evelix
Cath
Carmore
A949
Clashmore
Kincardine
Little Creich
Whiteface
Craft Centre
Dornoch
Skibo
Lonemore
Pulrossie
Cuthill
Dornoch Sands
Glen Calvie
Carn Bhrain
635
Coire Bog
Easter Fearn
Wester Fearn Burn
Struie Hill
Dounie
Ardmore
Ardjachie
Whiteness Sands
DORNOCH

191
194
180
Forsinard
Cnoc nan Gall
275
Meall a' Bhealaich
Rumsdale Water
Dalganachan
Loch a' Mhuilinn
Sleach Water
Thurso
Loch Ruard
Lochan Thulachan
Loch Sand
Loch Stemster
Stemster Hill
248
Loch Rangag
Coire na Beinne
226
Sheppardstown
Crofts of Benachielt
Ben-a-chielt
Rumster Forest
Reisgill
Reisgill Burn
Cnoc Cromuillt
365
Ben Alisky
349
Cnocan Conachreag
269
Burn of Houstry
Houstry
Nottingham
Forse
Gillivoan
Latheron
Latheronwheel
Smerral
Badnagie
Laidhay Croft Museum
Heritage Centre
Toremore
Achorn
Dunbeath
Inver
Knockally
Dunbeath
Dunbeath Bay
Ramscraigs
Bannock Burn
Knockfin Heights
438
Cnoc na Saobhaidhe
290
Glutt Water
Dunbeath Water
Achnaclyth
Achentoul
Feith Gaineimh Mhor
Kinbrace Burn
Cnoc Coire na Fearna
437
Gobernuisgeach
Braemore
Burnfoot
Maiden Pap
484
Berriedale Water
Morven
706
A897
Cnoc an Eireannaich
517
Suisgill Burn
Scaraben
626
Meall na Caorach
17
Wag
Langwell Forest
A9
20
Borgue
Strath of Kildonan
Loch Scalabsdale
Garvery Hill
333
Creag Scalabsdale
555
Cnoc Salislade
483
Kildonan Burn
Torrish Burn
Mid Hill
312
330
Blar a'Ghille Dhomhnaich
Aultibea
Langwell Water
Newport
Ceann Leathad nam Bo
Braigh na h-Eaglaise
422
Langwell House
Berriedale
Kildonan Lodge
Beinn Dubhain
414
Craggie
Duible
Ousdale
Badbea
Craggie Water
Kilphedir
Torrish
Creag Thoraraidh
Caen
Ord of Caithness
N
D
The Craggan
482
Ben Uarie
Eldrable Hill
Marrel
Navidale
Beinn Dhorain
628
Helmsdale
East Helmsdale
Meallan Liath Beag
Beinn Mhealaich
592
West Helmsdale
Gartymore
Allt Smeorail
Glen Sletdale
Glen Loth
Portgower
Culgower
Lothmore
Kilmote
Col-bheinn
538
Creag a'Chrionaich
394
Lothbeg
11
Lothbeg Point
Kintradwell
Killin
Achrimsdale
West Clyne
Greenhill
Dalchalm
Clynelish
East Brora
Brora
Brora
Doll
Dunrobin Castle
0 2 4 6 8 10 miles
0 2 4 6 8 10 km
Invergordon to... hours
Kirkwall............................9
2
3
4
5
D
E
F
G
I
F I R T H
Port Mor
Tarbat Ness
Mhor
Hilton
Bindal

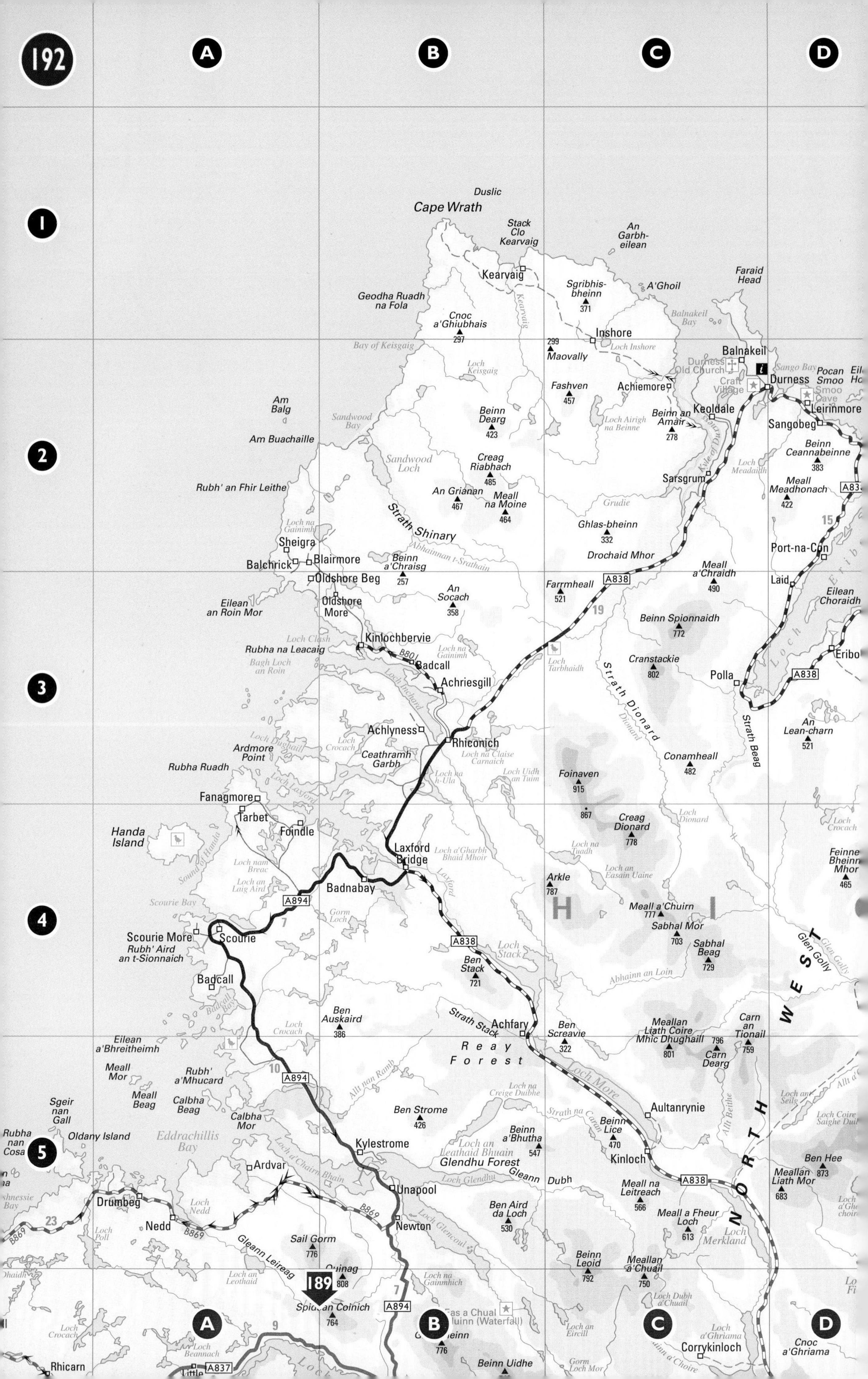
A
B
C
D
1
2
3
4
5
Duslic
Cape Wrath
Stack Clo Kearvaig
An Garbh-eilean
Kearvaig
Sgribhis-bheinn 371
A'Ghoil
Faraid Head
Geodha Ruadh na Fola
Cnoc a'Ghiubhais 297
Balnakeil Bay
Inshore
Bay of Keisgaig
299 Maovally
Loch Inshore
Balnakeil
Loch Keisgaig
Durness Old Church
Craft Village
Sango Bay
Durness
Pocan Smoo
Smoo Cave
Fashven 457
Achiemore
Am Balg
Sandwood Bay
Beinn Dearg 423
Keoldale
Leirinmore
Beinn an Amair 278
Loch Airigh na Beinne
Sangobeg
Am Buachaille
Sandwood Loch
Creag Riabhach 485
Kyle of Durness
Beinn Ceannabeinne 383
Loch Meadaidh
Sarsgrum
Rubh' an Fhir Leithe
An Grianan 467
Meall na Moine 464
Meall Meadhonach 422
Grudie
Strath Shinary
Loch na Gainimh
Ghlas-bheinn 332
15
Sheigra
Abhainn an t-Srathain
Port-na-Con
Balchrick
Blairmore
Beinn a'Chraisg 257
Drochaid Mhor
Meall a'Chraidh 490
Laid
Oldshore Beg
Farrmheall 521
A838
Eilean Choraidh
Eilean an Roin Mor
Oldshore More
An Socach 358
19
Beinn Spionnaidh 772
Loch Clash
Kinlochbervie
Rubha na Leacaig
Loch na Gainimh
B801
Loch Tarbhaidh
Strath Dionard
Cranstackie 802
Eriboll
Bagh Loch an Roin
Badcall
Achriesgill
Polla
A838
Loch Inchard
Dionard
Strath Beag
Achlyness
An Lean-charn 521
Loch Dughaill
Loch Crocach
Rhiconich
Ardmore Point
Ceathramh Garbh
Loch na Claise Carnaich
Conamheall 482
Rubha Ruadh
Loch na h-Ula
Loch Uidh an Tuim
Foinaven 915
Loch Laxford
Fanagmore
867
Loch Dionard
Tarbet
Loch Crocach
Handa Island
Foindle
Creag Dionard 778
Sound of Handa
Laxford Bridge
Loch a'Gharbh Bhaid Mhoir
Loch na Tuadh
Feinne Bheinn Mhor 465
Loch nam Breac
Loch an Easain Uaine
Arkle 787
Loch an Laig Aird
Badnabay
Laxford
Scourie Bay
A894
Gorm Loch
Meall a'Chuirn 777
H
I
7
Sabhal Mor 703
Scourie More
Scourie
A838
Loch Stack
Sabhal Beag 729
Glen Golly
Rubh' Aird an t-Sionnaich
Ben Stack 721
Badcall
Badcall Bay
Abhainn an Loin
Ben Auskaird 386
Strath Stack
Achfary
Ben Screavie 322
Meallan Liath Coire Mhic Dhughaill 801
Carn an Tionail 759
Loch Crocach
Eilean a'Bhreitheimh
Reay Forest
796
Carn Dearg
Meall Mor
Rubh' a'Mhucard
10
A894
Allt nan Ramh
Loch More
Loch a'Chreige Duibhe
Loch an Seilg
Meall Beag
Calbha Beag
Ben Strome 426
Aultanrynie
Allt Beithe
Loch Coire Saighe Duibhe
Sgeir nan Gall
Calbha Mor
Beinn a'Bhutha 547
Strath na Caran
Beinn Lice 470
Rubha nan Cosa
Oldany Island
Eddrachillis Bay
Kylestrome
Loch an Leathaid Bhuain
Kinloch
Ben Hee 873
Glendhu Forest
Ardvar
Loch a'Chairn Bhain
Gleann Dubh
Loch Glendhu
A838
Meallan Liath Mor 683
Drumbeg
Unapool
Meall na Leitreach 566
Loch Nedd
B869
Meall a Fheur Loch 613
Nedd
B869
Newton
Ben Aird da Loch 530
23
Loch Poll
Loch Glencoul
Loch Merkland
Gleann Leireag
Sail Gorm 776
Beinn Leoid 792
Meallan a'Chuail 750
Quinag 808
Loch an Leothaid
189
Loch na Gainmhich
Loch Dubh a'Chuail
Spidean Coinich 764
A894
Eas a Chual Aluinn (Waterfall)
Loch an Eircill
Loch a'Ghriama
Cnoc a'Ghriama
Loch Crocach
9
Loch Beannach
Corrykinloch
Rhicarn
A837
Beinn Uidhe
Gorm Loch Mor
NORTH WEST

D
E
F
G
0
2
4
6
8
10 miles
0
2
4
6
8
10 km
I
Strathy Point
Whiten Head
Rubha Thormaid
Cnoc Ard an t-Siuil
183
Geodh' a'Bhrideoin
Eilean Cluimhrig
Port Vasgo
Ben Hutig
408
Midfield
Rabbit Islands
Eilean nan Ron
Neave or Coomb Island
Farr Point
Kirtomy Point
Ardmore Point
Port Allt a'Mhuilinn
Totegan
Armadale Bay
Brawl
Aultiphurst
2
Lednagullin
Armadale
Kirtomy
Kirtomy Bay
Coal Raineach
Talmine
Skerray
Achtoty
Torrisdale Bay
Farr Bay
Farr
Swordly
Strathnaver Museum
A836
28
Beinn Chuldail
169
Strathy Forest
Armadale Burn
Tongue Bay
Modsarie
Torrisdale
Skullomie
Bettyhill
Achina
A'Mhoine
Strath Melness Burn
Midtown
Inverhope
22
Moine Ho.
Loch Maovally
Coldbackie
Tongue Ho.
Loch Buidhe
Borgie
Invernaver
Leckfurin
Naver Rock
Achnabourin
Beinn nam Bo
229
Loch Buidhe Mor
194
Lochside
262
A838
Achuvoldrach
A836
Loch Meadie
HIGHLANDS
Druim nan Cliar
Kyle of Tongue
Beinn Bhreac
Tongue
Meall Leathad na Craoibhe
310
Clachan Burn
Skelpick Burn
Loch Meala
Ribigill
B871
Borgie Forest
Achargary
3
Loch Mor na Caorach
Creag Riabhach Bheag
463
Lochan Hakel
Cnoc Craggie
318
Loch Slaim
Loch Craggie
Loch na Moine
Lochan nan Carn
Loch nan Clach
Kinloch
Loch na Seilg
Ben Hope
927
Meallan Liath
Ben Hiel
557
Beinn Stumanadh
527
Loch nan Ealachan
Dunviden Lochs
Strathy
Rhifail
Ben Loyal
764
Loch an Dherue
Lettermore
Loch Loyal
Meall an Spothaidh
Strathnaver
Loch Rifa-gil
Loch na Saobhaidhe
Loch Strathy
Altnacaillich
Cnoc nan Cuilean
557
17
Skail
Creagan Dubha Reidhe Bhig
337
4
H
L
A
N
D
Loch Haluim
Loch Syre
A836
B871
Loch Coulside
Inchkinloch
Syre
Cnoc nan Tri-chlach
345
Loch Croeach
Loch Druim a'Chliabhain
Rifail Loch
Allt Lon a' Chuil
Allnabad
Cnoc an Daimh Mor
356
B873
Beinn a'Mhadaidh
403
Ben Griam Beg
580
Loch Meadie
Cnoc an Daimh Beag
295
Loch Staing
Pole Hill
294
Naver Forest
Rimsdale Burn
Loch Eileanach
Loch Rosail
Cnoc a'Mhoid
Loch Coire nam Mang
Druim nam Bad
A836
B871
Ben Griam Mhor
590
Meall a'Bhrollaich
226
B873
Beadaig
270
Meall na Teanga
365
Mudale
Loch Naver
Loch Rimsdale
Loch nan Clar
Badanloch Forest
Altnaharra
Klibreck
5
Loch Truderscaig
Loch Badanloch
Cnoc an h-Uai
203
Loch Ben Harrald
Loch an Alltan Fhearna
Badanloch Lodge
B871
A836
Gearnsary
Loch Achnamoine
Ben Klibreck
Klibreck Burn
Mallart
Meall an Fhuarain
473
Meall nan Con
961
721
Meall Ailein
Loch Choire Forest
Loch Coire Lodge
Loch na Gaineimh
Strath Vagastie
Loch nan Uan
Loch Choire
Meall nan Aighean
694
190
474
Cnoc An Liath-Bhaid Mhoir
Allt nan Achaidhean
D
Cnoc an Alaskie
E
Loch a'Bhealaich
F
Ben Armine
500
Gorm-loch Beag
G
Borrobol Forest
Meall a'Bhata
581
266
Cnoc na Breun-
Altanduin

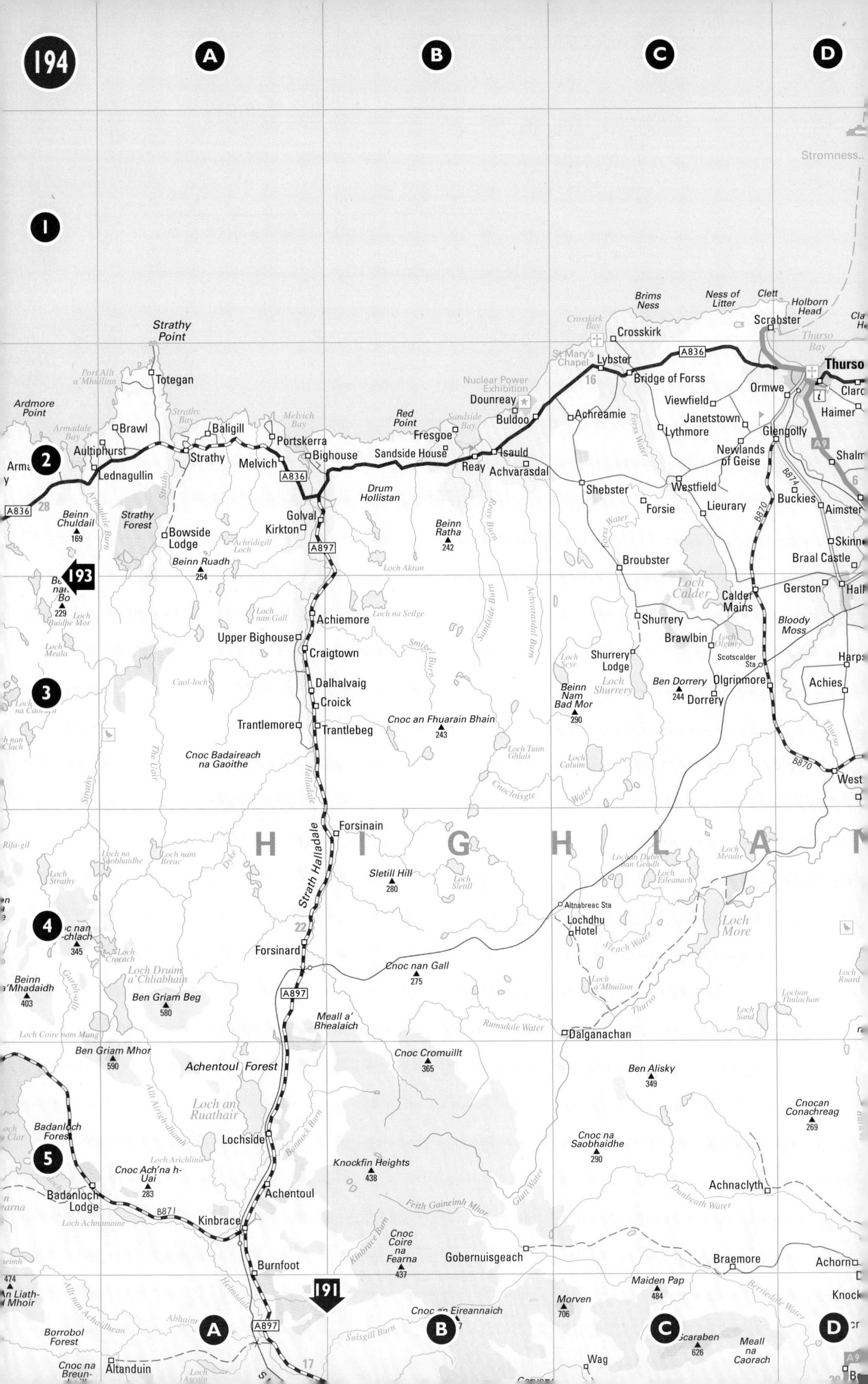
A
B
C
D
1
2
3
4
5
Stromness
Strathy Point
Totegan
Port Allt a'Mhuilinn
Ardmore Point
Armadale Bay
Brawl
Aultiphurst
Strathy Bay
Baligill
Melvich Bay
Portskerra
Strathy
Melvich
Bighouse
Lednagullin
A836
28
Armadale Burn
Beinn Chuldail
169
Strathy Forest
Bowside Lodge
Achridigill Loch
Beinn Ruadh
254
Golval
Kirkton
A897
Red Point
Fresgoe
Sandside Bay
Sandside House
Drum Hollistan
Nuclear Power Exhibition
Dounreay
Buldoo
Isauld
Reay
Achvarasdal
Beinn Ratha
242
Reay Burn
Loch Akran
Brims Ness
Ness of Litter
Clett
Holborn Head
Crosskirk Bay
Crosskirk
St Mary's Chapel
Lybster
16
Scrabster
Thurso Bay
Thurso
A836
Bridge of Forss
Ormwe
Clarc
Viewfield
Achreamie
Janetstown
Haimer
Forss Water
Lythmore
Glengolly
A9
Newlands of Geise
Shalm
Shebster
Westfield
B874
Buckies
Forsie
Lieurary
B870
Aimster
Forss Water
Broubster
Skinn
Braal Castle
Loch Calder
Calder Mains
Gerston
Halk
193
Loch Buidhe Mor
Loch Meala
Loch nan Gall
Achiemore
Loch na Seilge
Upper Bighouse
Craigtown
Smigel Burn
Sandside Burn
Achvarasdal Burn
Shurrery
Brawlbin
Bloody Moss
Loch Olginey
Shurrery Lodge
Loch Scye
Scotscalder Sta
Harps
Caol-loch
Dalhalvaig
Croick
Beinn Nam Bad Mor
290
Loch Shurrery
Ben Dorrery
244
Olgrinmore
Dorrery
Achies
Loch na Caorach
Trantlemore
Trantlebeg
Cnoc an Fhuarain Bhain
243
Loch Tuim Ghlais
Loch Caluim
Thurso
The Uair
Cnoc Badaireach na Gaoithe
Halladale
Cnocloisgte
Water
B870
West
Strathy
Rifa-gil
Loch Strathy
Loch na Saobhaidhe
Loch nam Breac
Dyke
Forsinain
Strath Halladale
H I G H L A N
Sletill Hill
280
Loch Sletill
Lochan Dubh nan Geodh
Loch Eileanach
Loch Meadie
Altnabreac Sta
Lochdhu Hotel
Loch More
Sleach Water
22
Forsinard
Cnoc nan Gall
275
Loch a'Mhuilinn
Loch Ruard
Lochan Thulachan
Thurso
Loch Sand
Cnoc nan Clach
345
Loch Croach
Loch Druim a'Chliabhain
Beinn a'Mhadaidh
403
Garbh-allt
Ben Griam Beg
580
A897
Meall a' Bhealaich
Rumsdale Water
Dalganachan
Loch Coire nam Mang
Ben Griam Mhor
590
Achentoul Forest
Cnoc Cromuillt
365
Ben Alisky
349
Cnocan Conachreag
269
Allt Airigh-dhamh
Loch an Ruathair
Bannock Burn
Badanloch Forest
Lochside
Cnoc na Saobhaidhe
290
Loch Arichlinie
Cnoc Ach'na h-Uai
283
Knockfin Heights
438
Glutt Water
Achnaclyth
Badanloch Lodge
Achentoul
Feith Gaineimh Mhor
Dunbeath Water
B871
Loch Achnamoine
Kinbrace
Kinbrace Burn
Cnoc Coire na Fearna
437
Gobernuisgeach
Braemore
Achorn
Burnfoot
191
Maiden Pap
484
Knock
Helmsdale
Allt nan Achaidhean
Morven
706
Berriedale Water
Abhainn
Cnoc an Eireannaich
A897
Borrobol Forest
Suisgill Burn
Scaraben
626
Meall na Caorach
Cnoc na Breun-
Altanduin
Loch Avaig
17
Wag
A9

D
E
F
G
PENTLAND FIRTH
The Tails of Tarf
Swona
Burwick
B9041
Tomb of the Eagles
Liddel
Old Head
196
Langaton Point
Island of Stroma
Nethertown
Red Head
Mell Head
Uppertown
Inner Sound
hours
St Margaret's Hope........1
(Summer only)
Boars of Duncansby
Muckle Skerry
Pentland Skerries
ours
......2
Dunnet Head
Easter Head
B855
Dunnet Hill
121
Skarfskerry Point
Tang Head
Castle of Mey
Men of Mey
St John's Point
Head of Crees
Ness of Duncansby
Bay of Sannick
Duncansby Head
Stacks of Duncansby
Scarfskerry
Harrow
Loch of Mey
East Mey
Gills Bay
Brough
Ham
St John's Loch
Rattar
Gills
A836
Huna
John o' Groats
The Thirl
Hunspow
20
Whitebridge
Mey
Canisbay
West Dunnet
Barrock
Upper Gills
Dwarwick Head
Dunnet
The Spur
Dunnet Bay
Inkstack
Warth Hill
124
Wife Geo
Murkle Bay
Links of Dunnet
Brabster
Everley
Murkle
Greenland
Loch Heilen
Lochend
Tofts
Skirza
Skirza Head
Gill Burn
Castletown
Thurdistoft
Slickly
Freswick Bay
Freswick
Olrig House
Hayfield
Tain
A99
Ness Head
Lochside
Alterwall
Auckengill
Hilliclay
Reaster
Kirk Burn
ale
Durran
Hoy
Bowermadden
Nybster
B876
Achingills
Lyth
Sortat
17
Brough Head
Stemster
Bowertower
Burn of Lyth
Howe
ockdee
Tister
Keiss
Stemster House
Hastigrow
Mireland
Tang Head
adside
B874
Corsback
Halcro
Stain
Clayock
Gillock
Loch Scarmclate
North Watten
B870
Kirk
rgemas Sta
A882
Loch of Wester
Sinclair's Bay
Lynegar
Quoys of Reiss
Spittal Hill
Loch Watten
Killimster
A99
Oldhall
Mains of Watten
Dunn
B874
B876
Ackergill Tower
Girnigoe
Noss Head
Houstry of Dunn
Wick
Loch of Winless
Reiss
Newton
Watten
Winless
Sinclair
B870
15
Ackergill
tal
Backlass
Whitefield
Wick
Mybster
Bilbster
Sibster
Staxigoe
A882
Caithness Glass
Loch of Toftingall
Strath
Thuster
Haster
North Head
Burn of Acharole
Strath Burn
Milton
Stirkoke House
Wick
Newton
Achairn Burn
South Head
Whiterow
Badlipster
17
Northfield
Puldagon
Castle of Old Wick
Camster Burn
Tannach
Hempriggs House
Loch Hempriggs
17
Toftcarl
acher
Lower Camster
Thrumster
Ires Geo
Stemster
Ballharn Hill
Grey Cairns of Camster
145
Corbiegoe
Loch Stemster
Hill of Yarrows
Loch of Yarrows
Sarclet
Sarclet Head
avanich
Stemster Hill
Whiteleen
213
Upper Camster
Stack of Ulbster
Loch Rangag
248
Cnoc an Earrannaiche
A99
Cairn of Get
Ulbster
Whaligoe
A9
Sheppardstown
Roster
Bruan
East Clyth
Prehistoric Stones
Crofts of Benachielt
Upper Lybster
Ben-a-chielt
Rumster Forest
Reisgill Burn
Mid Clyth
Blackness
Reisgill
Swiney
Occumster
Invergordon to... hours
Kirkwall.................................9
oustry
Nottingham
Lybster
Gillivoan
Forse
Latheron
0 2 4 6 8 10 miles
0 2 4 6 8 10 km
merral
adnagie
Latheronwheel
Heritage Centre
Toremore
Inver
Dunbeath
1
2
3
4
5

A
B
C
D
1
2
3
4
5
198
195
Outshore Point
Isbister
Twatt
Beaquoy
Click
Milldoe 221
Tingwall
Hackland
Gorseness
Isbister
Tor Ness
Broad Taing
Northdyke
Quoyloo
Skeabrae
Mirbister
Bay of Skaill
Skaill
Skara Brae
Corrigall Farm Museum
Settiscarth
Row Head
Loch of Skaill
Aith
Loch of Harray
Brough
Netherbrough
Bay of Isbister
Yesnaby
Ness of Tenston
Bimbister
Loch of Wasdale
Voy
WIDE FIRTH
Hill of Miffia 158
Neban Point
Loch of Stenness
Ring of Brodgar
Maes Howe
Finstown
Bay of Firth
Damsay
Rennibister Earth House
Quholm
Stones of Stenness
Heddle
Chambered Cairn
Wideford Hill 225
Grainbank Earth House
Clouston
Keelylang Hill 221
Outertown
Breck Ness
Stromness
Museum
Pier Arts Centre
Ireland
St Magnus Cathedral
Loch of Kirbister
Ward Hill 268
Kirbister
Greenigo
Hobbister
Clestrain
Clestrain Sound
Hoy Sound
Graemsay
Scapa Bay
Waulkmill Bay
Kame of Hoy
Murra
Orphir
Gyre
Swanbister Bay
Ve Ness
Long G
Houton
St John's Head
Cuilags 433
Linksness
Orphir Round Church and Earl's Bu
Houton Head
Midland Ness
The Sow
Ward Hill 479
Bring Deeps
Old Man of Hoy
Barrel of Butter
SCAPA FL
Dwarfie Stane
Green Head
Cava
Rora Head
Rackwick
Rack Wick
Knap of Trowieglen 399
Lyrawa Burn
Rysa Little
½ hr
Pegal Burn
354
Hunda
Calf of Flotta
Roan Head
ORKNEY
HOY
Fara
Oil Terminal
Flotta
Sneuk Head
2 hrs
Lyness Naval Base and Interpretation Centre
Lyness
Sound of Hoxa
Hoxa
Little Rack Wick
Burn of Ore
Rinnigill
Crock Ness
Bow
Pan
Widewall Bay
Quindry
Heldale Water
Martello Towers
Herston Head
Herston
Longhope
Hackness
Switha
North Bay
Melsetter
Hurliness
Cantick Head
Tor Ness
South Walls
Brims Ness
Garth Head
Swona
The North Head
Barth Head
Burwick
The Tails of Tarf
PENTLAND FIRTH
1 hr (Summer only)
Langaton Point
Nethertown
Island of Stroma
Red Head
Dunnet Head
Easter Head
Mell Head
Uppertown
Boars of Duncansby
Men of Mey
St John's Point
Inner Sound
Skarfskerry Point
Tang Head
Castle of Mey
Head of Crees
Ness of Duncansby
Bay of Sannick
Duncansby Head
Dunnet Hill 121
Scarfskerry
Harrow
Loch of Mey
East Mey
Gills Bay
Stacks of Duncansby
Brough
Ham
Rattar
Gills
Huna
John o' Groats
The Thirl
Hunspow
St John's Loch
Whitebridge
Mey
Ness of Litter
Clett
Holborn Head
West Dunnet
Dwarwick Head
Barrock
Upper Gills
Canisbay
Scrabster
Clardon Head
The Spur
Dunnet
HIGHLAND
Warth Hill 124
Wife Geo
Thurso Bay
Murkle Bay
Dunnet Bay
Inkstack
Links of Dunnet
Brabster
Everley
Thurso
Murkle
Tofts
Skirza Head
Ormwe
Castletown
Greenland
Lochend
Skirza
Freswick Bay
Haimer
Thurdistoft
Freswick
Janetstown
Glengolly
Olrig House
Hayfield
Tain
Slickly
Ness Head
Alterwall
A967
A986
A966
A965
A964
A836
A99
A9
B9056
B9057
B9055
B9047
B9045
B9042
B855
B876

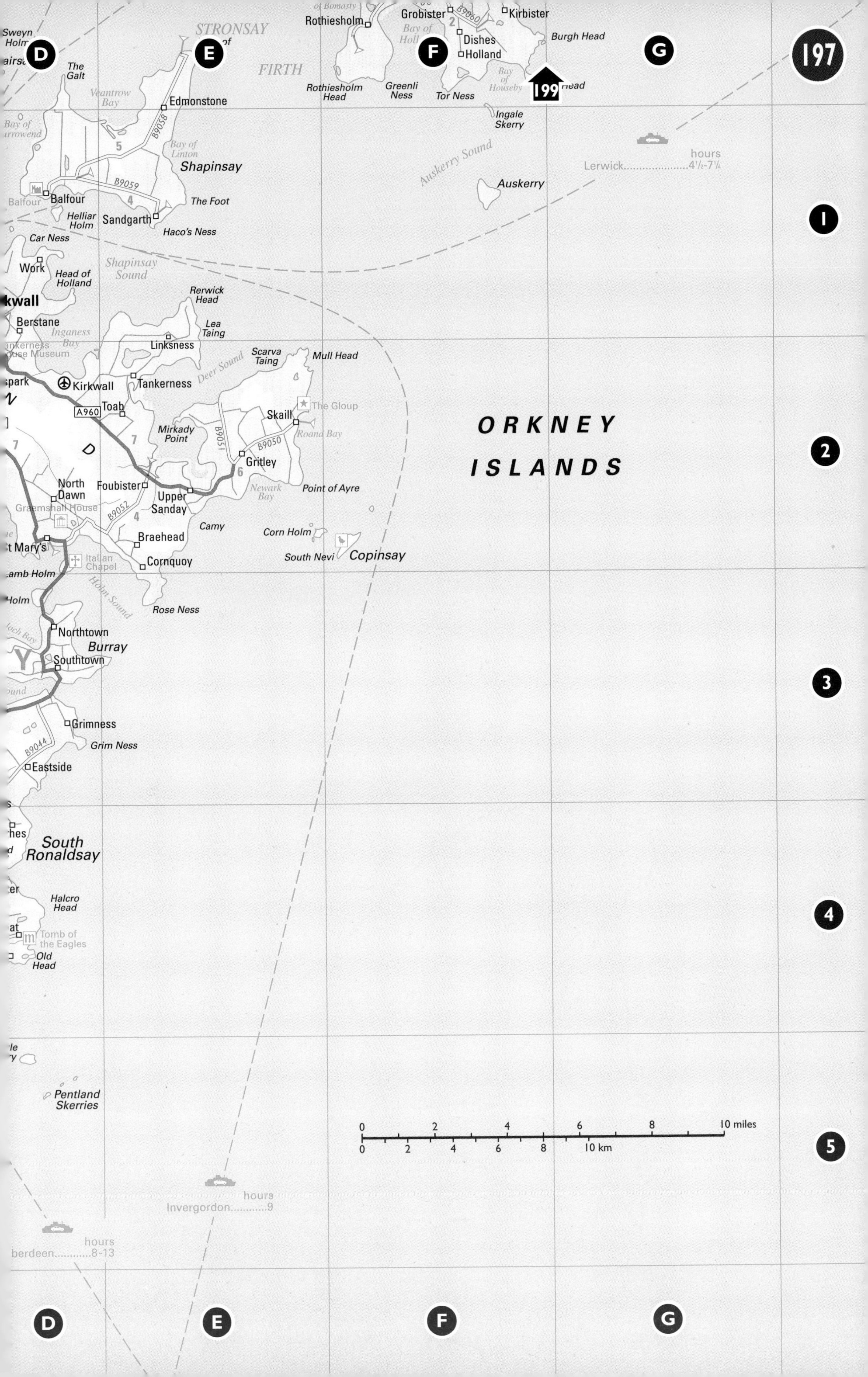
ORKNEY ISLANDS
STRONSAY FIRTH
Sweyn Holm
The Galt
Veantrow Bay
Bay of Carrowend
Edmonstone
B9058
Bay of Linton
Shapinsay
B9059
Balfour
Helliar Holm
Sandgarth
The Foot
Haco's Ness
Car Ness
Work
Head of Holland
Shapinsay Sound
Rerwick Head
Lea Taing
Berstane
Inganess Bay
Linksness
Kirkwall
Tankerness
Deer Sound
Scarva Taing
Mull Head
A960
Toab
The Gloup
Skaill
Roand Bay
Mirkady Point
B9051
B9050
Gritley
North Dawn
Foubister
Upper Sanday
Newark Bay
Point of Ayre
Graemshall House
B9052
Braehead
Camy
Corn Holm
St Mary's
Italian Chapel
Cornquoy
South Nevi
Copinsay
Lamb Holm
Holm Sound
Rose Ness
Northtown
Burray
Southtown
Grimness
Grim Ness
B9044
Eastside
South Ronaldsay
Halcro Head
Tomb of the Eagles
Old Head
Pentland Skerries
Rothiesholm
Grobister
Kirbister
B9060
Bay of Holland
Dishes
Holland
Burgh Head
Rothiesholm Head
Greenli Ness
Tor Ness
Bay of Houseby
199
Ingale Skerry
Auskerry Sound
Auskerry
hours
Lerwick.....................4½-7¼
hours
Invergordon............9
hours
Aberdeen............8-13
D
E
F
G
1
2
3
4
5
0 2 4 6 8 10 miles
0 2 4 6 8 10 km

A
B
C
D
1
2
3
4
5
0 2 4 6 8 10 miles
0 2 4 6 8 10 km
The Bore
Mull Head
Papa Westray
North Hill
Bow Head
St Boniface Kirk
Papa Sound
Aikerness
Papa Westray
Knap of Howar
Holland
Holm of Papa
Chambered Cairn
St Tredwell's Chapel
Westray
Noup Head
Rackwick
Backaskaill
Gentlemens' Cave
Noltland
Ouse Ness
B9066
St.Mary's Medieval Church
Head of Moclett
Pierowall
Broughton
Bis Geos
Braehead
Spo Ness
B9067
Westray
Skelwick
Inga Ness
Midbea
Bay of Tuquoy
Cross Kirk
Stanger Head
Langskaill
B9066
Berst Ness
Twiness
Rapness
Skea Skerries
WESTRAY FIRTH
Point of Huro
Rapness Sound
Faray
Rusk Holm
Sacquoy Head
Saviskaill Head
2½ hrs (Summer only)
Bring Head
Saviskaill Bay
Faraclett Head
Rousay
Wasbister
B9064
Kili Holm
Eday
Sourin
Mae Ness
Costa Head
Muckle Water
Skea
Midhowe Broch and Cairn
St Magnus Church
Eynhallow
Blotchnie Fiold
250
Westness
Egilsay
Brough Head
Brough of Birsay
Costa
Knowe of Yarso Chambered Cairn
Brinian
Rousay Sound
Muckle Green Holm
Earl's Palace
Birsay
A966
Abune-the-Hill
Eynhallow Church
Birsay Bay
Standing Stones
Loch of Swannay
B9064
Broch of Gurness
Eynhallow Sound
Wyre Sound
Marwick Head
Loch of Boardhouse
St Mary's Chapel
Kitchener's Monument
A967
Loch of Hundland
Evie
Aiker Ness
Wyre
Cubbie Roo's Castle
Marwick
Kirbuster
Redland
Twatt
Gairsay Sound
1½ hrs (Summer only)
Outshore Point
Isbister
B9057
Wood Wick
Sweyn Holm
B9056
Beaquoy
Tingwall
Click Mill
ORKNEY
Gairsay
The Galt
A967
A986
Hillside
A966
Veantrow Bay
Northdyke
Quoyloo
Skeabrae
Dounby
Milldoe
221
Hackland
B9058
Mirbister
Bay of Skaill
Skaill
Corrigall Farm Museum
Gorseness
Skara Brae
Settiscarth
Tor Ness
Row Head
Loch of Skaill
B9057
Isbister
Bay of Furrowend
Aith
Loch of Harray
Brough
Broad Taing
Bay of Isbister
Netherbrough
B9059
Yesnaby
B9056
Voy
Ness of Tenston
Bimbister
Balfour
Balfour
B9055
A986
Loch of Wasdale
WIDE FIRTH
Helliar Holm
Sandgarth
A967
Ring of Brodgar
Maes Howe
Bay of Firth
Damsay
Car Ness
Haco's
Neban Point
Hill of Miffia
158
Loch of Stenness
Finstown
Rennibister Earth House
Bay of Kirkwall
Work
Shapinsay Sound
Quholm
A965
Chambered Cairn
Head of Holland
Stones of Stenness
Heddle
Chambered Cairn
Wideford Hill
225
Kirkwall
A965
Clouston
Chambered Cairn
Keelylang Hill
221
Grainbank Earth House
Berstane
Outertown
A965
Inganess Bay
Breck Ness
Ireland
St Magnus Cathedral
Tankerness House Museum
Linksness
Stromness
Museum
Loch of Kirbister
Scapa
Pier Arts Centre
Ward Hill
268
196
Tradespark
Kirkwall
Tankerness
Hoy Sound
Clestrain Sound
A964
Hobbister
Scapa Bay
A960
Toab
Clestrain
A964
Graemsay
Mirkady Point
Kame of Hoy
Murra
Orphir
Waulkmill Bay
Swanbister

D
E
F
G
North Ronaldsay
Point of Sinsoss
Tor Ness
North Ronaldsay
Linklet Bay
Hollandstoun
Bride's Ness
South Bay
Strom Ness
North Ronaldsay Firth
3 hrs (Summer only)
Tofts Ness
Whitemill Point
Holms of Ire
Sandquoy
North Loch
Scuthvie Bay
Scar
Burness
Otters Wick
NORTH SOUND
B9068
B9069
Bay of Lopness
Start Point
North Bay
Newark
Red Head
Grey Head
Broughtown
Sanday
Roadside
Cata Sand
Sanday
Overbister
Calf of Eday
B9070
Kettletoft
Bay of Newark
Calfsound
Backaskail Bay
Sty Wick
Quoy Ness
Stone of Setter
Els Ness
Elsness-Quoyness Chambered Tomb
Tres Ness
Braeswick
Millbounds
Stove
Eday Sound
SANDAY SOUND
Loth
Eday
Spur Ness
Holm of Huip
B9063
Huip Sound
Huip Ness
Papa Stronsay
Links Ness
Veness
Odie
Stronsay
War Ness
Linga Holm
B9062
B9060
Whitehall
Mill Bay
Odness
St Catherine's Bay
Stronsay
Aith
Everbay
Odin Bay
Bay of Bomasty
B9061
Kirbister
Rothiesholm
Grobister
B9060
hours
Lerwick.....................$4^{1}/_{2}$-$7^{1}/_{4}$
ONSAY
Bay of Holland
Dishes
Burgh Head
E
Y
FIRTH
Holland
Bay of Houseby
Lamb Head
Rothiesholm Head
Greenli Ness
Tor Ness
Ingale Skerry
Auskerry Sound
Auskerry
hours
Invergordon.............9
Scarva Taing
Mull Head
The Gloup
Roana Bay
B9050
Gritley
D
E
F
G
1
2
3
4
5

197

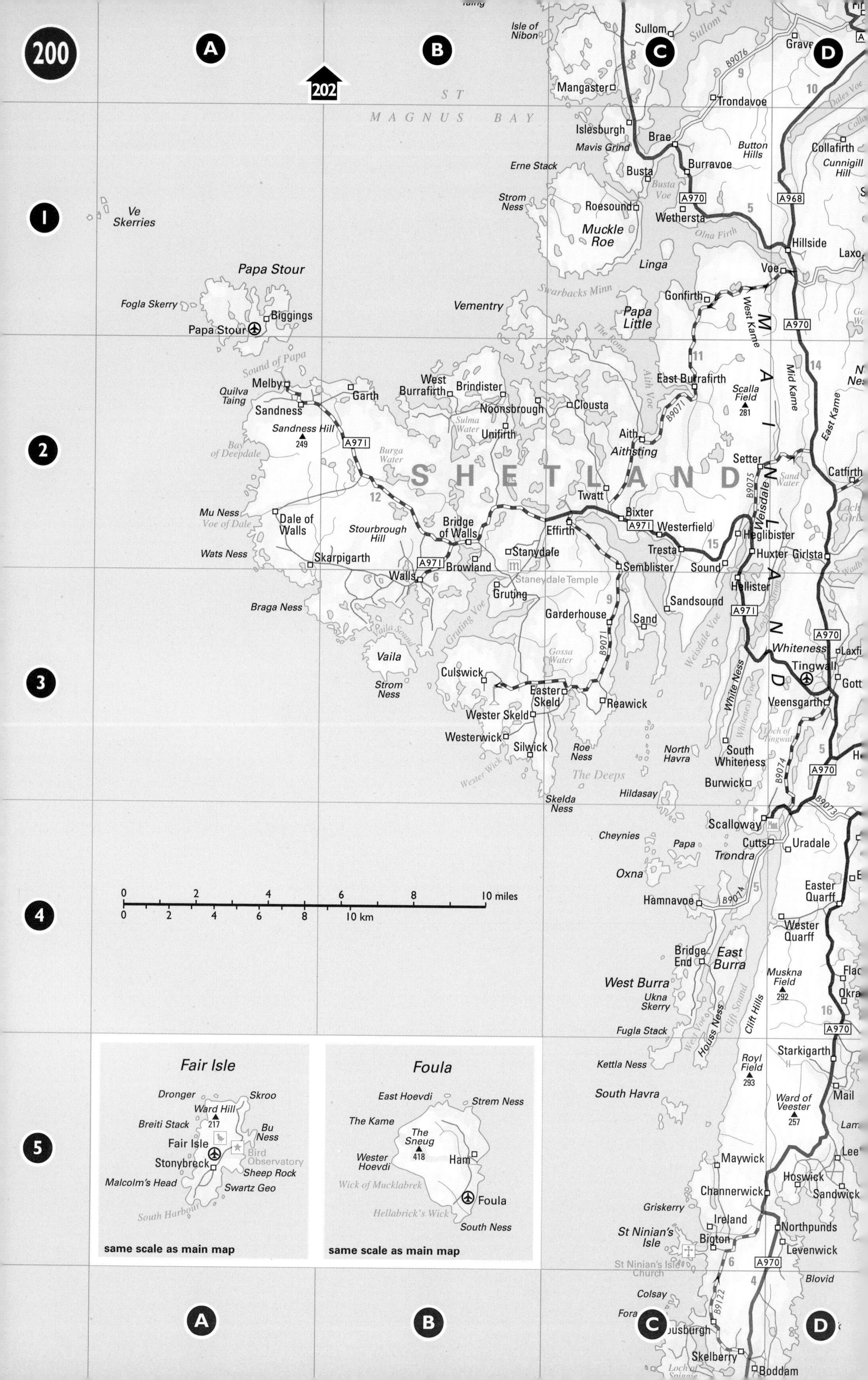

A
B
C
D
1
2
3
4
5
202
ST MAGNUS BAY
Isle of Nibon
Sullom
Sullom Voe
Graven
Mangaster
Trondavoe
B9076
Islesburgh
Brae
Mavis Grind
Button Hills
Collafirth
Cunnigill Hill
Erne Stack
Busta
Burravoe
Busta Voe
Strom Ness
Roesound
A970
A968
Wethersta
Muckle Roe
Olna Firth
Hillside
Laxo
Linga
Voe
Ve Skerries
Papa Stour
Fogla Skerry
Biggings
Swarbacks Minn
Vementry
Gonfirth
Papa Little
West Kame
The Rona
MAINLAND
Mid Kame
East Kame
Sound of Papa
Melby
Quilva Taing
Garth
West Burrafirth
Brindister
Noonsbrough
Clousta
East Burrafirth
Scalla Field
281
Sandness
Sandness Hill
249
Sulma Water
Unifirth
Aith Voe
B9071
Aith
Aithsting
A971
Bay of Deepdale
Burga Water
SHETLAND
Setter
Sand Water
Catfirth
B9075
Weisdale
Twatt
Mu Ness
Voe of Dale
Dale of Walls
Stourbrough Hill
Bridge of Walls
Effirth
Bixter
Westerfield
Heglibister
Wats Ness
Skarpigarth
Stanydale
Tresta
Huxter
Girlsta
Walls
Browland
Staneydale Temple
Semblister
Sound
Hellister
Braga Ness
Gruting
Garderhouse
Sandsound
Gruting Voe
Sand
Vaila Sound
Weisdale Voe
Loch of Strom
Whiteness
Vaila
Gossa Water
Tingwall
Strom Ness
Culswick
White Ness
Easter Skeld
Reawick
Veensgarth
Wester Skeld
Loch of Tingwall
Westerwick
Silwick
Roe Ness
North Havra
South Whiteness
B9074
Wester Wick
The Deeps
Burwick
Skelda Ness
Hildasay
B9073
Scalloway
Cheynies
Papa
Cutts
Uradale
Trondra
Oxna
Easter Quarff
0
2
4
6
8
10 miles
0
2
4
6
8
10 km
Hamnavoe
Wester Quarff
Bridge End
East Burra
West Burra
Muskna Field
292
Ukna Skerry
Fugla Stack
West Voe
Houss Ness
Cliff Sound
Clift Hills
Kettla Ness
Royl Field
293
Starkigarth
South Havra
Mail
Ward of Veester
257
Fair Isle
Dronger
Skroo
Ward Hill
217
Breiti Stack
Bu Ness
Fair Isle
Bird Observatory
Stonybreck
Sheep Rock
Malcolm's Head
Swartz Geo
South Harbour
same scale as main map
Foula
East Hoevdi
Strem Ness
The Kame
The Sneug
418
Wester Hoevdi
Ham
Wick of Mucklabrek
Foula
Hellabrick's Wick
South Ness
same scale as main map
Maywick
Hoswick
Channerwick
Sandwick
Griskerry
Ireland
St Ninian's Isle
Bigton
Northpunds
Levenwick
St Ninian's Isle Church
B9122
Blovid
Colsay
Fora
Skelberry
Boddam

SHETLAND ISLANDS
D
E
F
G
1
2
3
4
5
Fish Holm
Lunna Ness
Hamnavoe
Lunna
Taing of Kelswick
Lunning
3/4 hr
2 1/2 hrs
Challister Ness
Skaw
Skaw Taing
Vidlin
Lunnasting
West Linga
Brough
Marrister
Isbister
Huxter
Symbister
Whalsay
East Linga
Grif Skerry
1/2 hr
Dury Voe
Stava Ness
Clett Head
Muckle Skerry
Out Skerries
Bruray
Housay
Filla
203
Laxfirth
Neap
Bretabister
The Keen
B9075
South Nesting Bay
Skellister
Ling Ness
South Nesting
Moul of Eswick
Gletness
South Isle of Gletness
2 1/2 hrs
Hawks Ness
Kebister Ness
Score Head
Aith Ness
Heogan
Gunnista
Bressay
Loder Head
Maryfield
Setter
Isle of Noss
Shetland Mus
Lerwick
Brough
Fort Charlotte
Sound
Grindiscol
Ward of Bressay
226
Millburn Geo
Feadda Ness
Brei Wick
Kirkabister
Bard Head
hours
Bergen (Summer only)............12 1/2
Seydisfjordur (Summer only).....31
Torshavn (Summer only)...........13
hours
Aberdeen..............13
Kirkwall..........4 1/2-7 1/4
Helli Ness
Mousa
Ireland
Northpunds
St Ninian's Isle
Bigton
Levenwick
No Ness
St Ninian's Isle Church
Blovid
Colsay
B9122
Fora Ness
Troswick Ness
Scousburgh
Skelberry
Boddam
Wick of Shunni
Loch of Spiggie
Hillwell
Voe
Lambhoga Head
Quendale
283
A970
Fitful Head
Bay of Quendale
Exnaboe
Siggar Ness
Toab
Sumburgh
Jarlshof
Grutness
Lady's Holm
Sumburgh
Ness of Burgi
Sumburgh Head
Sumburgh Roost
same scale as main map

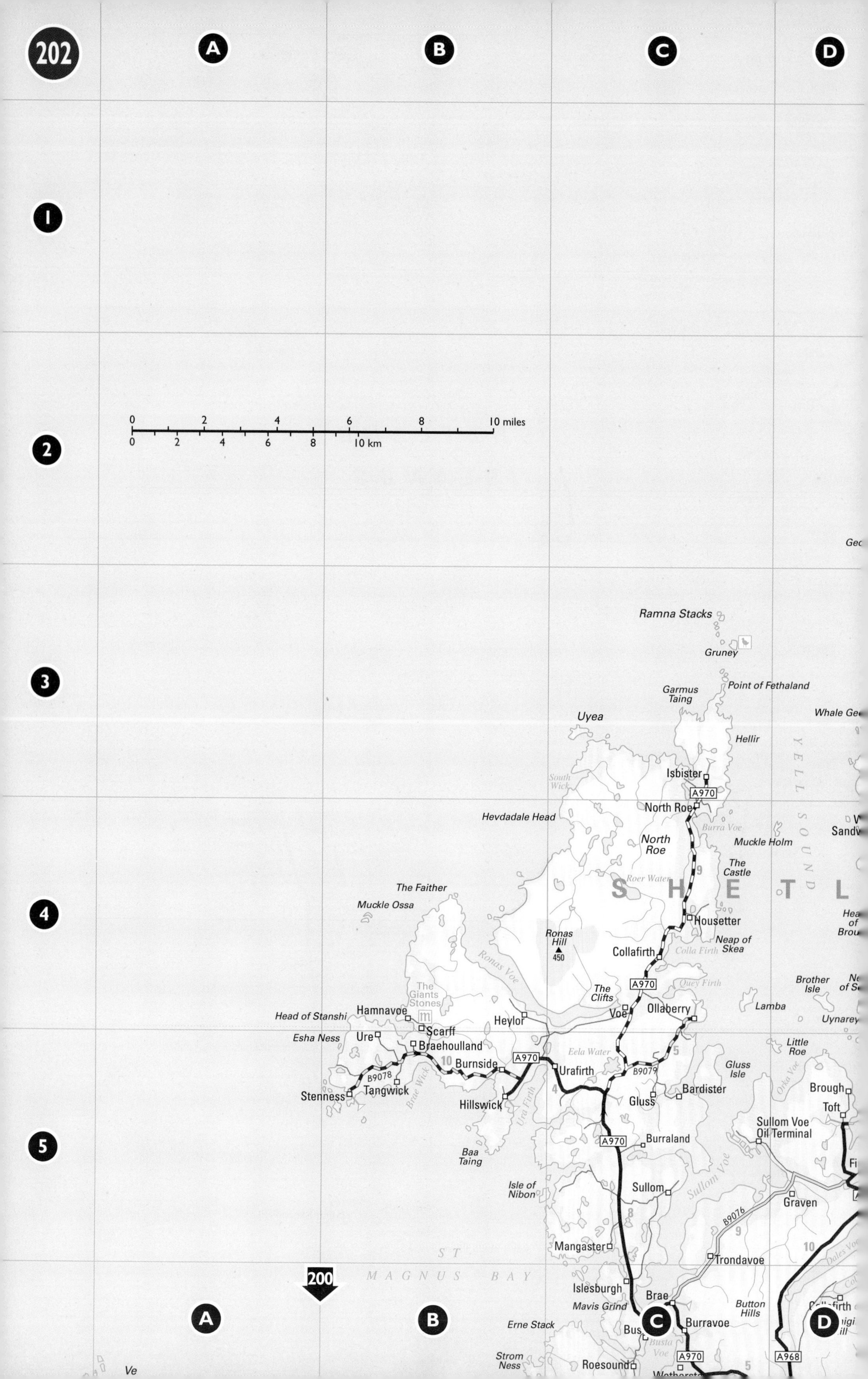
A
B
C
D
1
2
3
4
5
0 2 4 6 8 10 miles
0 2 4 6 8 10 km
Ramna Stacks
Gruney
Garmus Taing
Point of Fethaland
Whale Geo
Uyea
Hellir
YELL SOUND
South Wick
Isbister
A970
North Roe
Hevdadale Head
Burra Voe
North Roe
Muckle Holm
Sandwick
The Castle
Roer Water
SHETLAND
The Faither
Muckle Ossa
Housetter
Head of Brough
Ronas Hill
450
Neap of Skea
Collafirth
Colla Firth
Ronas Voe
Quey Firth
Brother Isle
The Giants Stones
The Clifts
Lamba
Head of Stanshi
Hamnavoe
Heylor
Voe
Ollaberry
Uynarey
Esha Ness
Ure
Scarff
Braehoulland
Little Roe
Eela Water
Burnside
Urafirth
B9079
Gluss Isle
B9078
Tangwick
Brae Wick
Hillswick
Ura Firth
Gluss
Bardister
Brough
Stenness
Toft
Sullom Voe Oil Terminal
Burraland
Baa Taing
Sullom
Sullom Voe
Graven
Isle of Nibon
B9076
ST MAGNUS BAY
Mangaster
Trondavoe
200
Islesburgh
Brae
Button Hills
Mavis Grind
Collafirth
Erne Stack
Busta
Burravoe
Busta Voe
A968
Strom Ness
Roesound
Ve

D
E
F
G
1
2
3
4
5
Out Stack
Muckle Flugga
The Noup
Herma Ness
Saxa Vord
285
Holm of Skaw
Burra Firth
Grunka Hellier
Lamba Ness
Nor Wick
Norwick
Orknagable
Burrafirth
Valsgarth
B9086
B9087
Haroldswick
Loch of Cliff
Quoys
UNST
The Nev
Harold's Wick
South Holms
Baliasta
A968
Baltasound
Buness
Valla Field
Balta
Spoo Ness
A968
Unst
Caldback
10
oup Holm
Gloup Ness
Newgord
Huney
Breakon
Westing
North Neaps
St Olaf's Church
Loch of Watlee
Brough Taing
of Vigon
Gloup
B9083
Bluemull Sound
Underhoull
Lund
The Vere
Cullivoe
Sand Wick
Stonganess
Mu Ness
mouth
Belmont
Uyeasound
Clivocast
Muness
South Garth
Uyea Sound
Skuda Sound
Uyea
Gossa Water
Gutcher
Linga
Nev of Stuis
Sellafirth
Haaf Gruney
Colvister
A968
North Sandwick
Sound Gruney
Lochs of Lumbister
Cunnister
Urie Lingey
Whale Firth
Basta Voe
Burra Ness
Hamars Ness
8
Basta
Oddsta
Vord Hill
158
Strandburgh Ness
Wick of Gruting
Hascosay Sound
Brough Lodge
imister
Camb
Fetlar
Head of Hesta
B9088
Hascosay
6
A968
YELL
Mid Yell
Tresta
Houbie
South Sound
Aith
Funzie
Lamb Hoga
Wick of Tresta
Colgrave Sound
Birrier
Kame of Sandwick
Laxa Burn
The Snap
Aywick
N
D
Rams Ness
Otterswick
B9082
Otters Wick
East Yell
Hill of Arisdale
Vest
ell
Burn of Arisdale
Gossabrough
12
Clothan
Stack of the Horse
Ulsta
Hamnavoe
B9081
Burravoe
Copister
Hamna Voe
Brough
½ hr
Orfasay
Samphrey
Lunna Holm
ssbank
Muckle Skerry
Fish Holm
Linga
Lunna Ness
Out Skerries
Bruray
Out Skerries
Housay
Grunay
Hamnavoe
201
Lunna
Taing of Kelswick
1½ hrs
Filla
¾ hr
D
E
F
G
Challister Ness
Skaw Taing
Lunning
Skaw
hours
Lerwick..............2½

# Aberdeen • Bath

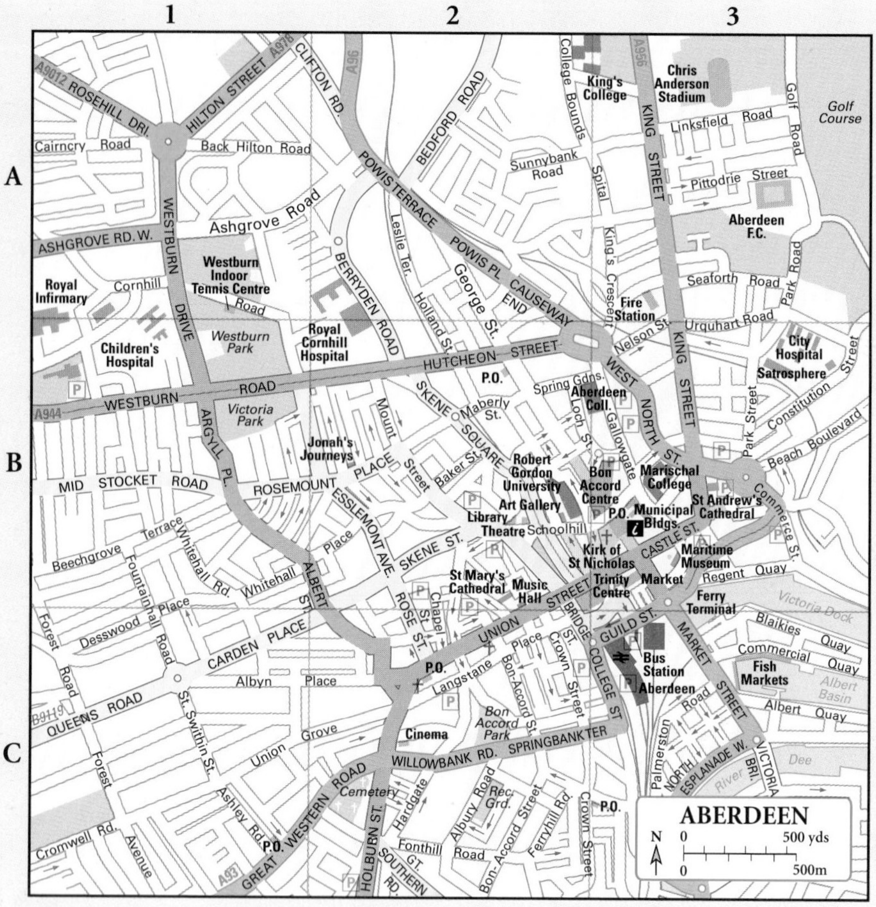


**Information Centre: St. Nicholas House, Broad Street**
**Tel: 01224 632727**

| | | | |
|---|---|---|---|
| Albert Quay | C3 | Leslie Terrace | A2 |
| Albert Street | B2 | Linksfield Road | A3 |
| Albury Road | C2 | Loch Street | B2 |
| Albyn Place | C1 | Maberly Street | B2 |
| Argyll Place | B1 | Market Street | C3 |
| Ashgrove Road | A1 | Mid Stocket Road | B1 |
| Ashgrove Road West | A1 | Mount Street | B2 |
| Ashley Road | C1 | Nelson Street | B3 |
| Back Hilton Road | A1 | North Esplanade West | C3 |
| Baker Street | B2 | Palmerston Road | C3 |
| Beach Boulevard | B3 | Park Road | A3 |
| Bedford Road | A2 | Park Street | B3 |
| Beechgrove Terrace | B1 | Pittodrie Street | A3 |
| Berryden Road | A2 | Powis Place | A2 |
| Blaikie's Quay | C3 | Powis Terrace | A2 |
| Bon-Accord Street | C2 | Queens Road | C1 |
| Bridge Street | B2 | Regent Quay | B3 |
| Cairncry Road | A1 | Rosehill Drive | A1 |
| Carden Place | C1 | Rosemount Place | B1 |
| Castle Street | B3 | Rose Street | B2 |
| Causewayend | A2 | St. Swithin Street | C1 |
| Chapel Street | B2 | Schoolhill | B2 |
| Clifton Road | A1 | Seaforth Road | A3 |
| College Bounds | A2 | Skene Square | B2 |
| College Street | C3 | Skene Street | B2 |
| Commerce Street | B3 | Spital | A3 |
| Commercial Quay | C3 | Springbank Terrace | C2 |
| Constitution Street | B3 | Spring Gardens | B2 |
| Cornhill Road | A1 | Sunnybank Road | A2 |
| Cromwell Road | C1 | Union Grove | C1 |
| Crown Street | C2 | Union Street | C2 |
| Desswood Place | C1 | Urquhart Road | B3 |
| Esslemont Avenue | B2 | Victoria Bridge | C3 |
| Ferryhill Road | C2 | Westburn Drive | A1 |
| Fonthill Road | C2 | Westburn Road | B1 |
| Forest Road | C1 | West North Street | B3 |
| Forest Avenue | C1 | Whitehall Place | B1 |
| Fountainhall Road | B1 | Whitehall Road | B1 |
| Gallowgate | B3 | Willowbank Road | C2 |
| George Street | A2 | | |
| Golf Road | A3 | | |
| Great Southern Road | C2 | | |
| Great Western Road | C1 | | |
| Guild Street | C3 | | |
| Hardgate | C2 | | |
| Hilton Street | A1 | | |
| Holburn Street | C2 | | |
| Holland Street | A2 | | |
| Hutcheon Street | B2 | | |
| King's Crescent | A3 | | |
| King Street | A3 | | |
| Langstane Place | C2 | | |

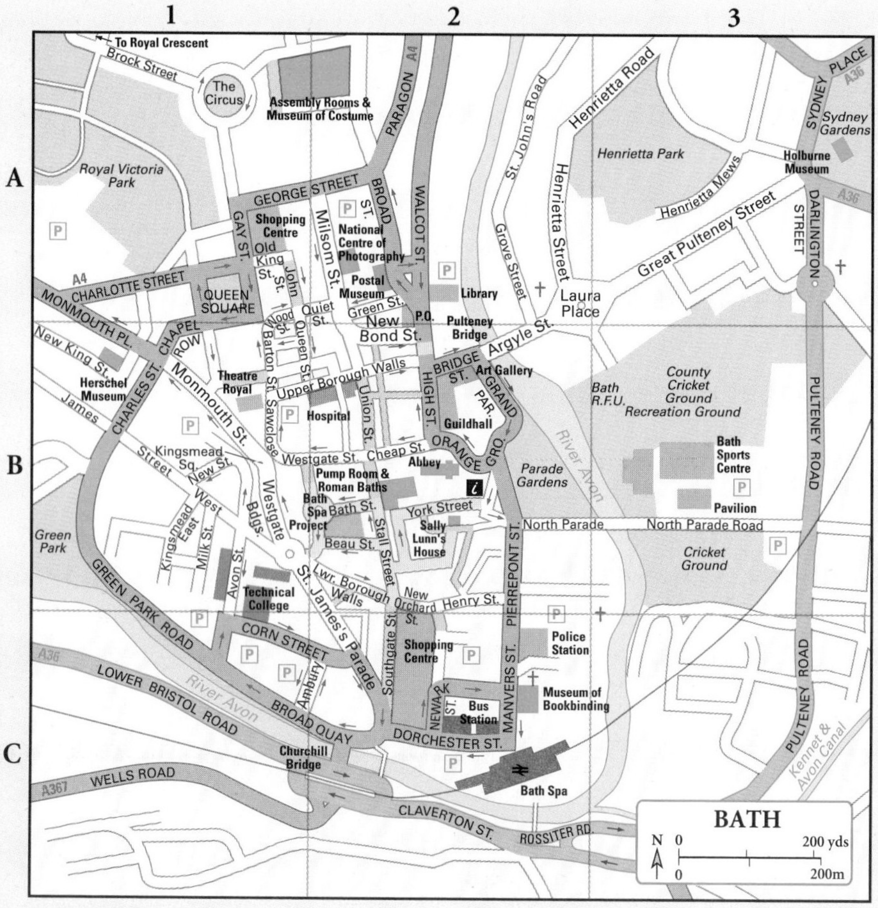


**Information Centre: Abbey Chambers, Abbey Churchyard**
**Tel: 01225 477101**

| | | | |
|---|---|---|---|
| Ambury | C1 | Pulteney Road | B3 |
| Argyle Street | B2 | Queen Street | B1 |
| Avon Street | B1 | Quiet Street | A1 |
| Barton Street | B1 | Rossiter Road | C2 |
| Bath Street | B2 | St. James's Parade | B1 |
| Beau Street | B2 | St. John's Road | A2 |
| Bridge Street | B2 | Sawclose | B1 |
| Broad Quay | C1 | Southgate Street | C2 |
| Broad Street | A2 | Stall Street | B2 |
| Brock Street | A1 | Sydney Place | A3 |
| Chapel Row | B1 | The Circus | A1 |
| Charles Street | B1 | Union Street | B2 |
| Charlotte Street | A1 | Upper Borough Walls | B1 |
| Cheap Street | B2 | Walcot Street | A2 |
| Claverton Street | C2 | Wells Road | C1 |
| Corn Street | C1 | Westgate Buildings | B1 |
| Darlington Street | A3 | Westgate Street | B1 |
| Dorchester Street | C2 | Wood Street | A1 |
| Gay Street | A1 | York Street | B2 |
| George Street | A1 | | |
| Grand Parade | B2 | | |
| Great Pulteney Street | A3 | | |
| Green Park Road | B1 | | |
| Green Street | A2 | | |
| Grove Street | A2 | | |
| Henrietta Mews | A3 | | |
| Henrietta Road | A2 | | |
| Henrietta Street | A2 | | |
| Henry Street | B2 | | |
| High Street | B2 | | |
| James Street West | B1 | | |
| John Street | A1 | | |
| Kingsmead East | B1 | | |
| Laura Place | A2 | | |
| Lower Borough Walls | B2 | | |
| Lower Bristol Road | C1 | | |
| Manvers Street | C2 | | |
| Milk Street | B1 | | |
| Milsom Street | A2 | | |
| Monmouth Place | A1 | | |
| Monmouth Street | B1 | | |
| Newark Street | C2 | | |
| New Bond Street | B2 | | |
| New King Street | B1 | | |
| New Orchard Street | B2 | | |
| New Street | B1 | | |
| North Parade | B2 | | |
| North Parade Road | B3 | | |
| Old King Street | A1 | | |
| Orange Grove | B2 | | |
| Paragon | A2 | | |
| Pierrepont Street | B2 | | |

For Birmingham see page 230

# Blackpool • Bournemouth

**Information Centre: 1 Clifton Street**
**Tel: 01253 478222**

| | |
|---|---|
| Abingdon Street | B1 |
| Adelaide Street | B1 |
| Albert Road | C1 |
| Ascot Road | A3 |
| Bank Hey Street | B1 |
| Beech Avenue West | B3 |
| Birchway Avenue | A3 |
| Bonny Street | C1 |
| Boothley Road | A2 |
| Breck Road | C3 |
| Bryan Road | B3 |
| Buchanan Street | B2 |
| Caunce Street | B2/A3 |
| Central Drive | C1 |
| Chapel Street | C1 |
| Charles Street | B2 |
| Charnley Road | C1 |
| Church Street | B2 |
| Clifton Street | B1 |
| Clinton Avenue | C2 |
| Cocker Square | A1 |
| Cocker Street | A1 |
| Collingwood Avenue | A3 |
| Cookson Street | B2 |
| Coronation Street | C1 |
| Corporation Street | B1 |
| Deansgate | B1 |
| Devonshire Road | A2 |
| Devonshire Square | B3 |
| Dickson Road | A1 |
| Egerton Road | A1 |
| Elizabeth Street | A2 |
| Exchange Street | A1 |
| Forest Gate | B3 |
| George Street | B2/A2 |
| Gloucester Avenue | C3 |
| Gorse Road | C3 |
| Gorton Street | A2 |
| Granville Road | B2 |
| Grosvenor Street | B2 |
| High Street | A1 |
| Hornby Road | C1 |
| Hounds Hill | C1 |
| King Street | B1 |
| Laycock Gate | A3 |
| Layton Road | A3 |
| Leamington Road | B2 |
| Leicester Road | B2 |
| Lincoln Road | B2 |
| Liverpool Road | B2 |
| London Road | A3 |
| Lord Street | A1 |
| Market Street | B1 |
| Mather Street | A3 |
| Mere Road | B3 |
| Newton Drive | B3 |
| Palatine Road | C2 |
| Park Road | C2 |
| Peter Street | B2 |
| Pleasant Street | A1 |
| Portland Road | C3 |
| Princess Parade | B1 |
| Promenade | C1 |
| Queens Square | B1 |
| Queen Street | B1 |
| Rathlyn Avenue | A3 |
| Reads Avenue | C2 |
| Regent Road | B2 |
| Ribble Road | C2 |
| Ripon Road | C2 |
| St. Albans Road | C3 |
| Seaside Way | C1 |
| South King Street | B2 |
| Talbot Road | B1/A2 |
| Topping Street | B1 |
| Victory Road | A2 |
| Wayman Road | B3 |
| Whitegate Drive | B3/C3 |
| Woodland Grove | C3 |
| Woolman Road | C2 |

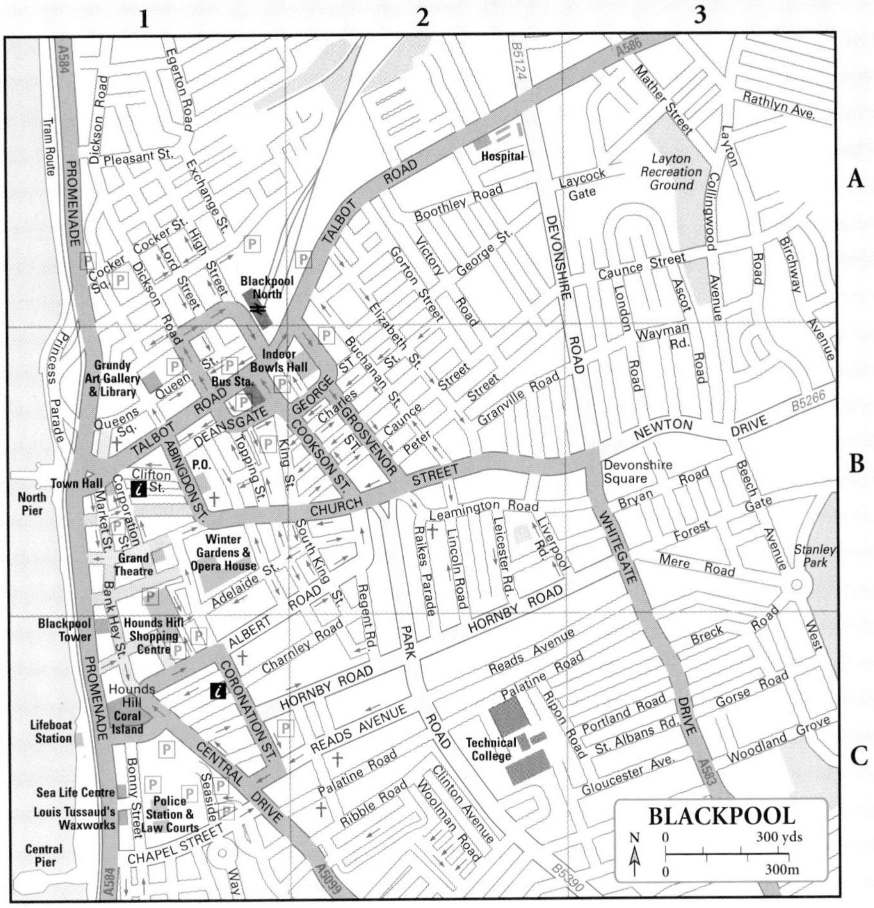


**Information Centre: Westover Road**
**Tel: 0906 802 0234**

| | |
|---|---|
| Avenue Road | B1 |
| Bath Road | C2 |
| Beechey Road | A3 |
| Bennett Road | A3 |
| Bourne Avenue | B1 |
| Braidley Road | B2 |
| Branksome Wood Road | B1 |
| Cavendish Road | A2 |
| Central Drive | A1 |
| Charminster Road | A2 |
| Christchurch Road | B3 |
| Dean Park Road | B2 |
| Durley Chine Road | C1 |
| Durley Chine Road South | C1 |
| Durley Road | C1 |
| East Avenue | A1 |
| East Overcliff Drive | C3 |
| Elgin Road | A1 |
| Exeter Road | C2 |
| Gervis Place | C2 |
| Gervis Road | C3 |
| Grove Road | C3 |
| Hinton Road | C2 |
| Holdenhurst Road | B3 |
| Knyveton Road | B3 |
| Lansdowne Road | A2 |
| Leven Avenue | A1 |
| Lowther Road | A3 |
| Madeira Road | B2 |
| Malmesbury Park Road | A3 |
| Methuen Road | A3 |
| Meyrick Road | B3 |
| Old Christchurch Road | B2 |
| Ophir Road | A3 |
| Oxford Road | B3 |
| Poole Hill | C1 |
| Portchester Road | A3 |
| Priory Road | C1 |
| Queen's Road | B1 |
| Richmond Hill | B2 |
| Russell Cotes Road | C2 |
| St. Augustin's Road | A2 |
| St. Anthony's Road | A2 |
| St. Leonard's Road | A3 |
| St. Michael's Road | C1 |
| St. Pauls' Road | B3 |
| St. Peter's Road | B2 |
| St. Stephen's Road | B1 |
| St. Swithun's Road | B3 |
| St. Swithun's Road South | B3 |
| St. Winifred's Road | A2 |
| St. Valerie Road | A2 |
| Stewart Raod | A3 |
| Surrey Road | B1 |
| The Lansdowne | B3 |
| The Square | B2 |
| The Triangle | B1 |
| Tregonwell Road | C1 |
| Undercliff Drive | C3 |
| Wellington Road | A2 |
| Wessex Way | B1/A3 |
| West Cliff Promenade | C1 |
| West Cliff Road | C1 |
| West Hill Road | C1 |
| West Overcliff Drive | C1 |
| West Promenade | C1 |
| Westover Road | C2 |
| Wimborne Road | B2 |

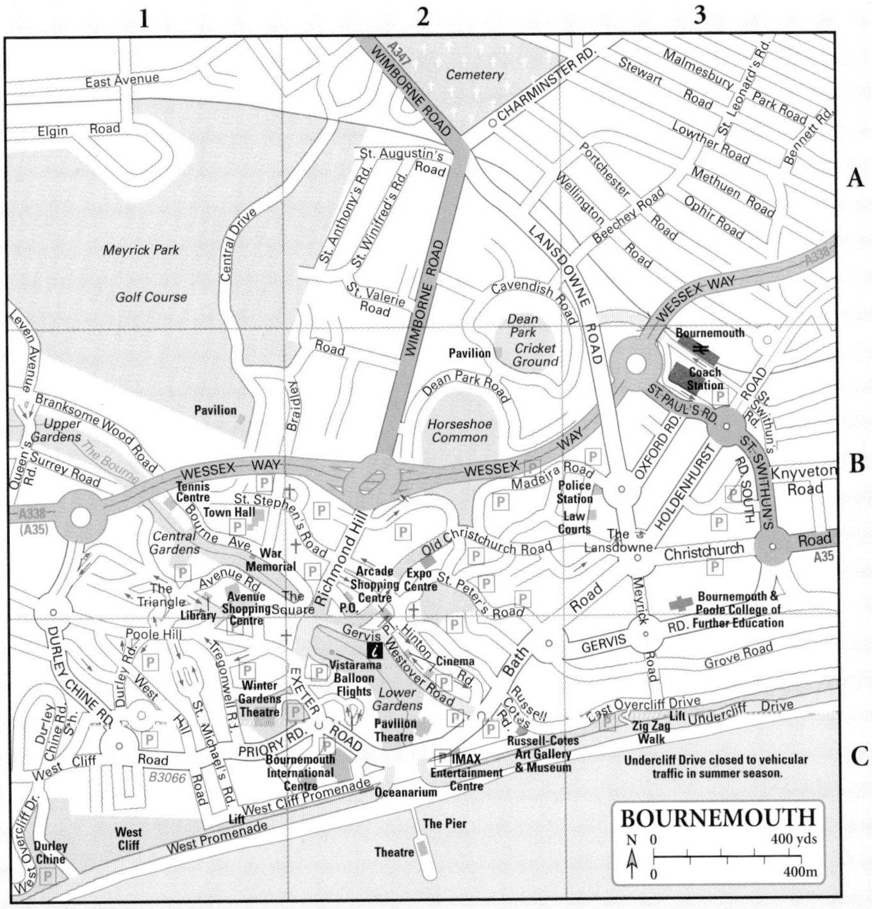


For Bradford see page 238
For Bristol see page 229

# Brighton • Cambridge

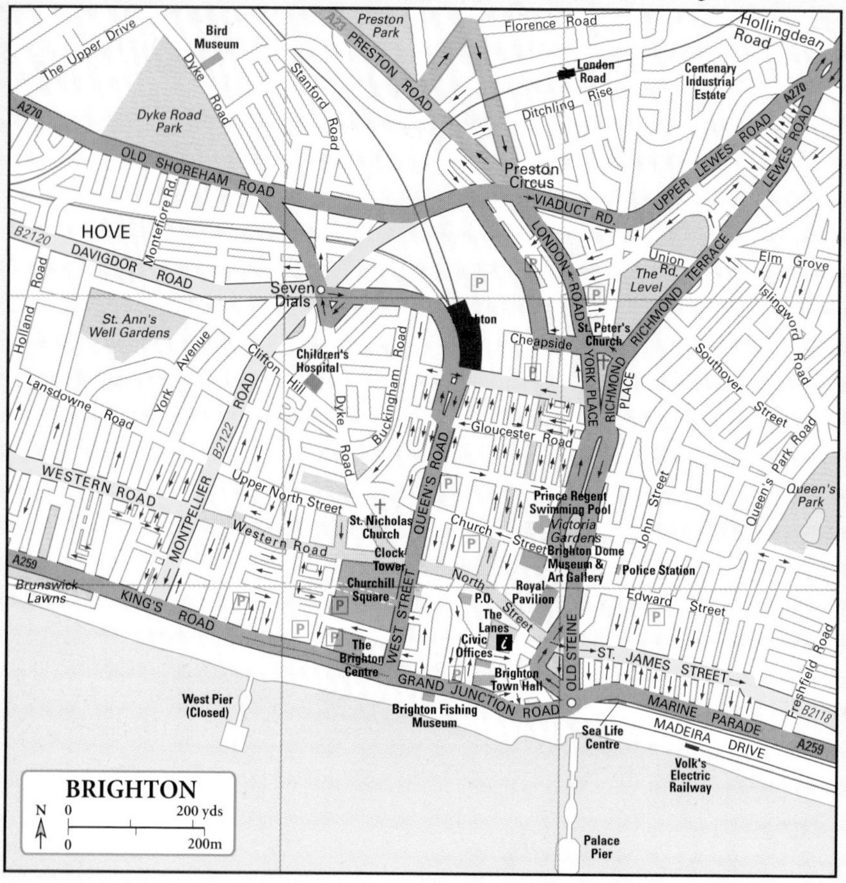


**Information Centre: 10 Bartholomew Square**
**Tel: 0906 711 2255**

| | |
|---|---|
| Buckingham Road | B2 |
| Cheapside | B2 |
| Church Street | B2 |
| Churchill Square | C2 |
| Clifton Hill | B1 |
| Davigdor Road | A1 |
| Ditchling Rise | A2 |
| Dyke Road | B2 |
| Edward Street | C3 |
| Elm Grove | A3 |
| Florence Road | A2 |
| Freshfield Road | C3 |
| Gloucester Road | B2 |
| Grand Junction Road | C2 |
| Holland Road | B1 |
| Hollingdean Road | A3 |
| Islingword Road | A3 |
| John Street | B3 |
| King's Road | C1 |
| Lansdowne Road | B1 |
| Lewes Road | A3 |
| London Road | A2 |
| Madeira Drive | C3 |
| Marine Parade | C3 |
| Montefiore Road | A1 |
| Montpelier Road | B1 |
| North Street | B2 |
| Old Shoreham Road | A1 |
| Old Steine | C3 |
| Preston Circus | A2 |
| Preston Road | A2 |
| Queen's Park Road | B3 |
| Queen's Road | B2 |
| Richmond Place | B3 |
| Richmond Terrace | B3 |
| St. James's Street | C3 |
| Southover Street | B3 |
| Stanford Road | A2 |
| The Lanes | C2 |
| The Upper Drive | A1 |
| Union Road | A3 |
| Upper Lewes Road | A3 |
| Upper North Street | B1 |
| Viaduct Road | A2 |
| West Street | C2 |
| Western Road | B1 |
| York Avenue | B1 |
| York Place | B3 |

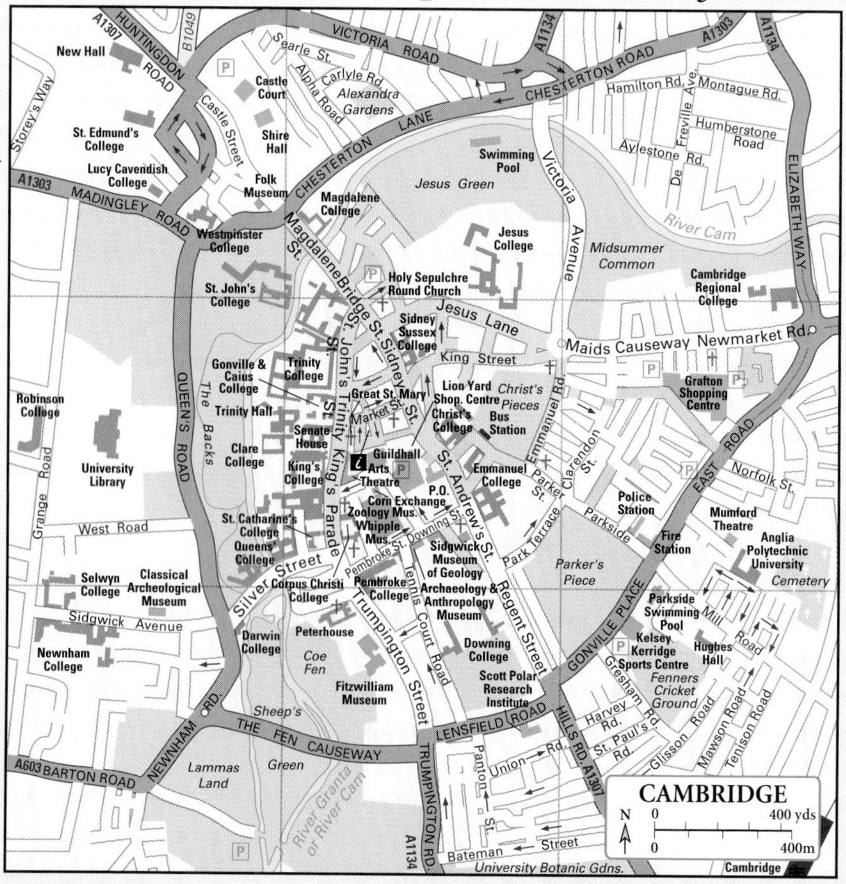


**Information Centre: Wheeler Street**
**Tel: 01223 322640**

| | |
|---|---|
| Alpha Road | A2 |
| Aylestone Road | A3 |
| Barton Road | C1 |
| Bateman Street | C2 |
| Carlyle Road | A2 |
| Castle Street | A1 |
| Chesterton Lane | A2 |
| Chesterton Road | A2 |
| Clarendon Street | B3 |
| De Freville Avenue | A3 |
| Downing Street | B2 |
| East Road | B3 |
| Elizabeth Way | A3 |
| Emmanuel Road | B2 |
| Fen Causeway, The | C1 |
| Glisson Road | C3 |
| Gonville Place | C3 |
| Grange Road | B1 |
| Gresham Road | C3 |
| Hamilton Road | A3 |
| Harvey Road | C3 |
| Hills Road | C3 |
| Humberstone Road | A3 |
| Huntingdon Road | A1 |
| Jesus Lane | B2 |
| King's Parade | B2 |
| King Street | B2 |
| Lensfield Road | C2 |
| Madingley Road | A1 |
| Magdalene Bridge Street | A2 |
| Maids Causeway | B3 |
| Market Street | B2 |
| Mawson Road | C3 |
| Mill Road | C3 |
| Montague Road | A3 |
| Newmarket Road | B3 |
| Newnham Road | C1 |
| Norfolk Street | B3 |
| Panton Street | C2 |
| Parker Street | B2 |
| Parkside | B3 |
| Park Terrace | B2 |
| Pembroke Street | B2 |
| Queen's Road | B1 |
| Regent Street | B2 |
| St. Andrew's Street | B2 |
| St. John's Street | B2 |
| St. Paul's Road | C3 |
| Searce Street | A1 |
| Sidgwick Avenue | C1 |
| Sidney Street | B2 |
| Silver Street | C1 |
| Storey's Way | A1 |
| Tenison Road | C3 |
| Tennis Court Road | B2 |
| Trinity Street | B2 |
| Trumpington Road | C2 |
| Trumpington Street | C2 |
| Union Road | C2 |
| Victoria Avenue | A2 |
| Victoria Road | A2 |
| West Road | B1 |

For Cardiff see page 228

# Cheltenham • Chester

**Information Centre: 77 The Promenade**
**Tel: 01242 522878**

| | |
|---|---|
| Albert Road | A3 |
| Albion Street | B2 |
| All Saints Road | B3 |
| Andover Road | C1 |
| Bath Road | C2 |
| Bayshill Road | B1 |
| Carlton Street | B3 |
| Central Cross Drive | A3 |
| Christchurch Road | B1 |
| Christchurch Terrace | B1 |
| Clarence Road | A2 |
| College Lawn | C2 |
| College Road | C2 |
| Dunnally Street | A2 |
| Eldon Road | B3 |
| Evesham Road | A3 |
| Fairview Road | B3 |
| Folly Lane | A2 |
| Gloucester Road | B1 |
| Grafton Road | C1 |
| Hale's Road | C3 |
| Hanover Street | A2 |
| Henrietta Street | B2 |
| Hewlett Road | B3 |
| High Street | A2 |
| Keynsham Road | C2 |
| King's Road | B3 |
| Lansdown Crescent | C1 |
| Lansdown Road | C1 |
| London Road | C3 |
| Malvern Road | B1 |
| Market Street | A1 |
| Marle Hill Parade | A2 |
| Marle Hill Road | A2 |
| Montpellier Spa Road | B2 |
| Montpellier Street | C1 |
| Montpellier Terrace | C1 |
| Montpellier Walk | C1 |
| New Street | A2 |
| North Place | B2 |
| North Street | B2 |
| Old Bath Road | C3 |
| Oriel Road | B2 |
| Overton Road | B1 |
| Parabola Road | B1 |
| Park Place | C1 |
| Park Street | A1 |
| Pittville Circus | A3 |
| Pittville Circus Road | B3 |
| Portland Street | B2 |
| Prestbury Road | A3 |
| Priory Street | C3 |
| Promenade | B2 |
| St. George's Place | B2 |
| St. George's Road | B1 |
| St. Johns Avenue | B2 |
| St. Margaret's Road | A2 |
| St. Paul's Road | A2 |
| St. Paul's Street North | A2 |
| St. Paul's Street South | A2 |
| St. Stephen's Road | C1 |
| Sandford Road | C2 |
| Sherborne Street | B3 |
| Suffolk Road | C1 |
| Sun Street | A1 |
| Swindon Road | A1 |
| Tewkesbury Road | A1 |
| Thirlestaine Road | C2 |
| Townsend Street | A1 |
| Vittoria Walk | C2 |
| Wellington Road | A3 |
| West Drive | A2 |
| Whaddon Road | A3 |
| Winchcombe Street | B2 |

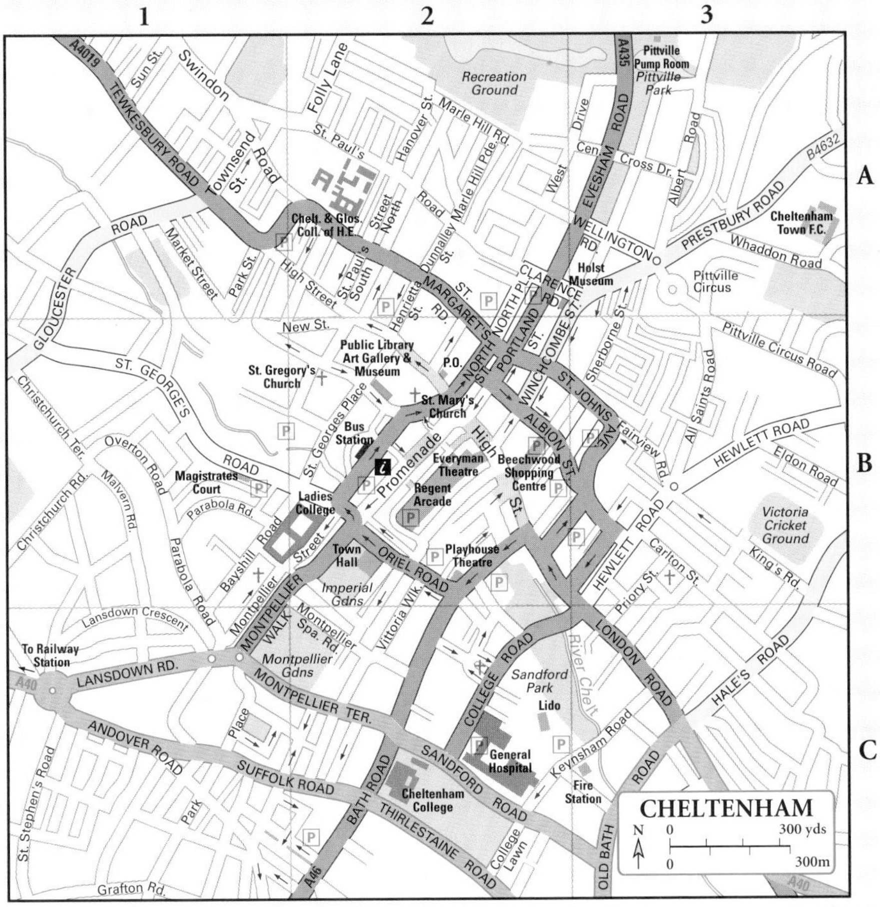


**Information Centre: Town Hall, Northgate Street**
**Tel: 01244 402111**

| | |
|---|---|
| Black Friars | C1 |
| Boughton | B3 |
| Bridge Street | B2 |
| Brook Street | A2 |
| Canal Street | A1 |
| Castle Drive | C1 |
| City Road | B3 |
| City Walls Road | B1 |
| Commonhall Street | B1 |
| Dee Bridge | C2 |
| Dee Lane | B3 |
| Duke Street | C2 |
| Eastgate Street | B2 |
| Foregate Street | B2 |
| Francis Street | A3 |
| Frodsham Street | B2 |
| Garden Lane | A1 |
| George Street | A2 |
| Grosvenor Road | C1 |
| Grosvenor Street | C1 |
| Handbridge | C2 |
| Hoole Road | A2 |
| Hoole Way | A2 |
| Hunter Street | B1 |
| Love Street | B2 |
| Lower Bridge Street | C2 |
| Milton Street | A2 |
| Newgate Street | B2 |
| Nicholas Street | B1 |
| Northgate Street | B1 |
| Nun's Road | C1 |
| Old Dee Bridge | C2 |
| Pepper Street | C2 |
| Princess Street | B1 |
| Queens Park Road | C2 |
| Queen Street | B2 |
| Raymond Street | A1 |
| St. Anne Street | A2 |
| St. John Street | B2 |
| St. Martins Way | A1 |
| St. Oswalds Way | A2 |
| St. Werburgh Street | B2 |
| Souter's Lane | C2 |
| The Bars | B3 |
| The Groves | C2 |
| Union Street | B2 |
| Upper Northgate | A1 |
| Vicar's Lane | B2 |
| Watergate Street | B1 |
| Weaver Street | B1 |
| White Friars | C1 |

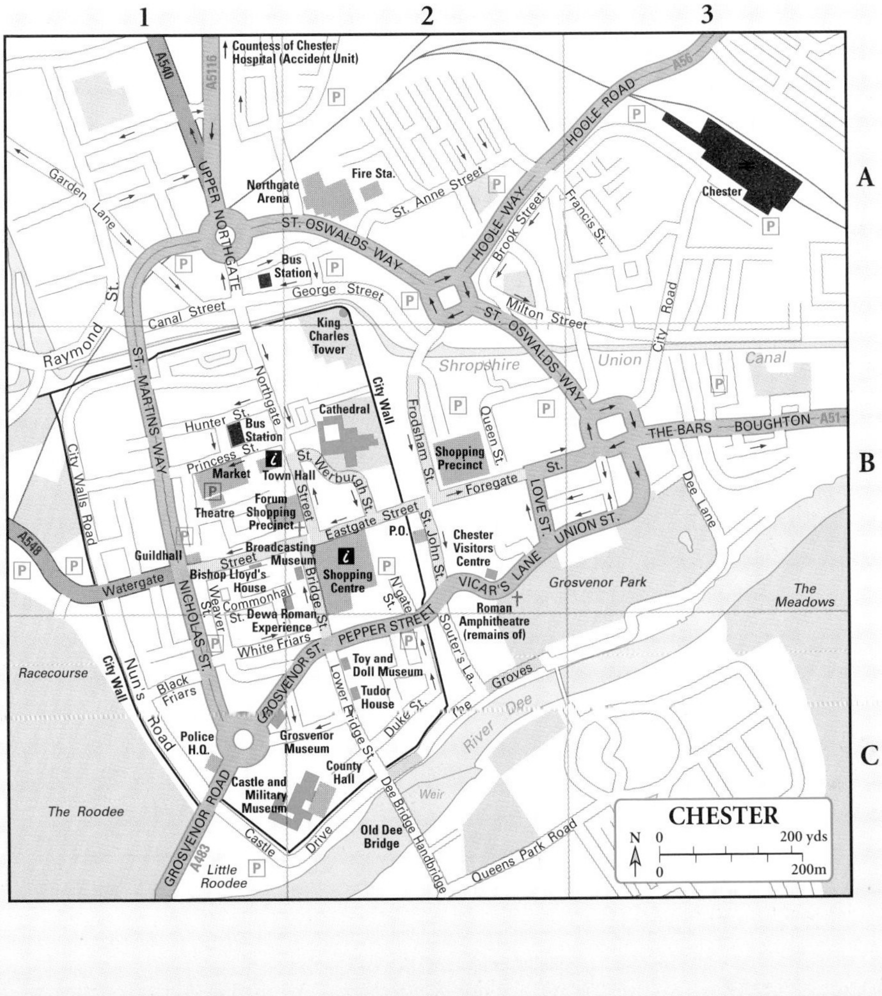

# Coventry • Derby

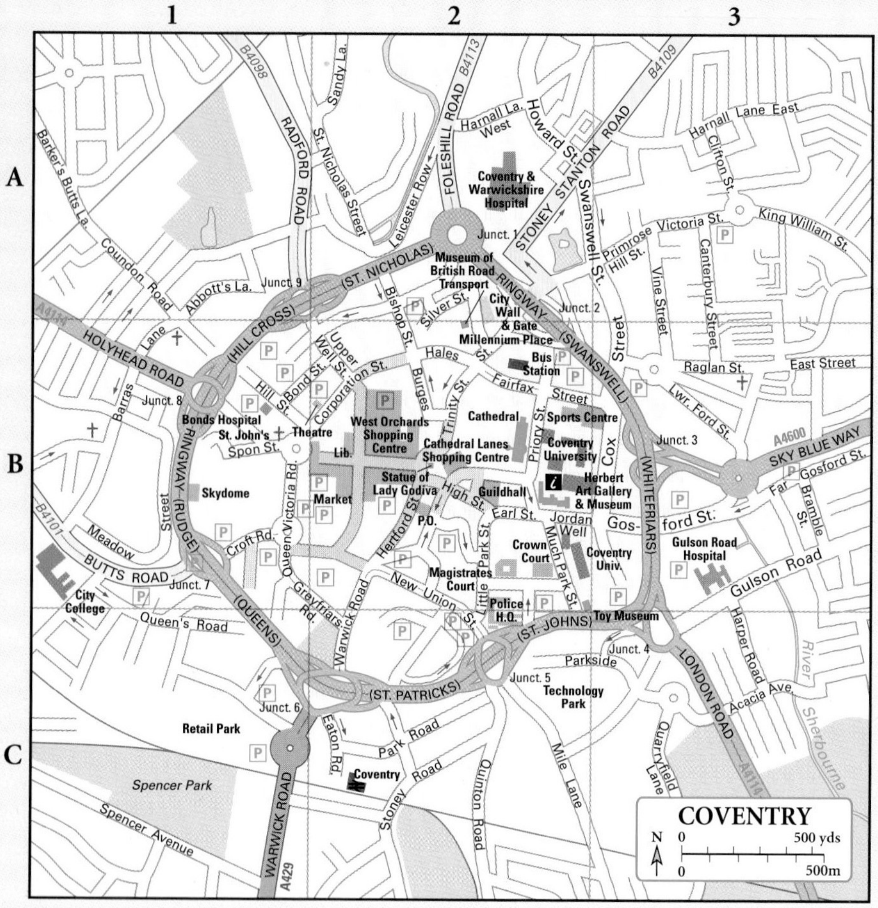


**Information Centre: Bayley Lane**
**Tel: 024 7622 7264**



| | | | |
|---|---|---|---|
| Abbott's Lane | A1 | Raglan Street | B3 |
| Acacia Avenue | C3 | Ringway Hill Cross | B1 |
| Barker's Butts Lane | A1 | Ringway St. Johns | C2 |
| Barras Lane | B1 | Ringway St. Nicholas | A2 |
| Bishop Street | A2 | Ringway St. Patricks | C2 |
| Bond Street | B1 | Ringway Queens | B1 |
| Bramble Street | B3 | Ringway Rudge | B1 |
| Burges | B2 | Ringway Swanswell | B2 |
| Butts Road | B1 | Ringway Whitefriars | B3 |
| Canterbury Street | A3 | St. Nicholas Street | A2 |
| Clifton Street | A3 | Sandy Lane | A2 |
| Corporation Street | B2 | Silver Street | A2 |
| Coundon Road | A1 | Sky Blue Way | B3 |
| Cox Street | B3 | Spencer Avenue | C1 |
| Croft Road | B1 | Spon Street | B1 |
| Earl Street | B2 | Stoney Road | C2 |
| East Street | B3 | Stoney Stanton Road | A2 |
| Eaton Road | C2 | Swanswell Street | A2 |
| Fairfax Street | B2 | Trinity Street | B2 |
| Far Gosford Street | B3 | Upper Well Street | B2 |
| Foleshill Road | A2 | Victoria Street | A3 |
| Gosford Street | B3 | Vine Street | A3 |
| Greyfriars Road | B1 | Warwick Road | C1 |
| Gulson Road | B3 | | |
| Hales Street | B2 | | |
| Harnall Lane East | A3 | | |
| Harnall Lane West | A2 | | |
| Harper Road | C3 | | |
| Hertford Street | B2 | | |
| High Street | B2 | | |
| Hill Street | B1 | | |
| Holyhead Road | B1 | | |
| Howard Street | A2 | | |
| Jordan Well | B2 | | |
| King William Street | A3 | | |
| Leicester Row | A2 | | |
| Little Park Street | C2 | | |
| London Road | C3 | | |
| Lower Ford Street | B3 | | |
| Meadow Street | B1 | | |
| Mile Lane | C2 | | |
| Much Park Street | B2 | | |
| New Union Street | B2 | | |
| Park Road | C2 | | |
| Parkside | C2 | | |
| Primrose Hill Street | A3 | | |
| Priory Street | B2 | | |
| Quarryfield Lane | C3 | | |
| Queen's Road | C1 | | |
| Queen Victoria Road | B1 | | |
| Quinton Road | C2 | | |
| Radford Road | A1 | | |



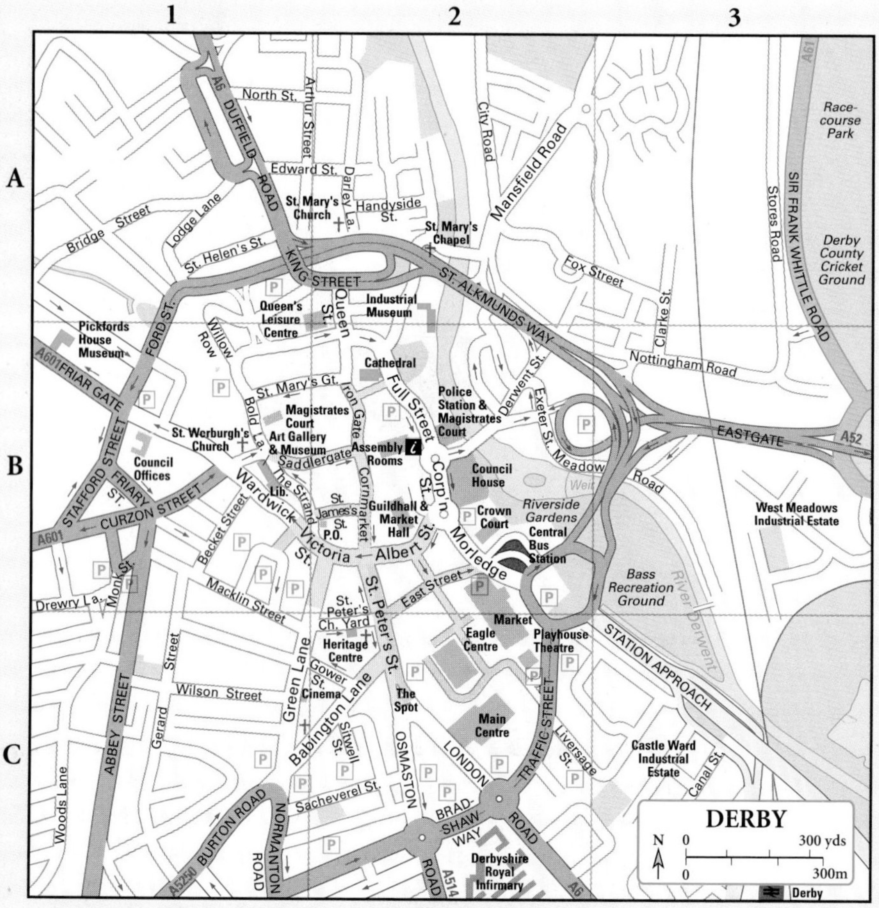


**Information Centre: Assembly Rooms, Market Place**
**Tel: 01332 255802**



| | | | |
|---|---|---|---|
| Abbey Street | C1 | St. James Street | B2 |
| Albert Street | B2 | St. Mary's Gate | B1 |
| Arthur Street | A1 | St. Peter's Church Yard | C2 |
| Babington Lane | C1 | St. Peter's Street | B2 |
| Becket Street | B1 | Sir Frank Whittle Road | A3 |
| Bold Lane | B1 | Sitwell Street | C2 |
| Bradshaw Way | C2 | Stafford Street | B1 |
| Bridge Street | A1 | Station Approach | B3 |
| Burton Road | C1 | Stores Road | A3 |
| Canal Street | C3 | The Strand | B1 |
| City Road | A2 | Traffic Street | C2 |
| Clarke Street | B3 | Victoria Street | B1 |
| Cornmarket | B2 | Wardwick | B1 |
| Corporation Street | B2 | Willow Row | B1 |
| Curzon Street | B1 | Wilson Street | C1 |
| Darley Lane | A2 | Woods Lane | C1 |
| Derwent Street | B2 | | |
| Drewry Lane | B1 | | |
| Duffield Road | A1 | | |
| Eastgate | B3 | | |
| East Street | B2 | | |
| Edward Street | A1 | | |
| Exeter Street | B2 | | |
| Ford Street | B1 | | |
| Fox Street | A2 | | |
| Friar Gate | B1 | | |
| Friary Street | B1 | | |
| Full Street | B2 | | |
| Gerard Street | C1 | | |
| Gower Street | C2 | | |
| Green Lane | C1 | | |
| Handyside Street | A2 | | |
| Iron Gate | B2 | | |
| King Street | A1 | | |
| Liversage Street | C2 | | |
| Lodge Lane | A1 | | |
| London Road | C2 | | |
| Macklin Street | B1 | | |
| Mansfield Road | A2 | | |
| Market Place | B2 | | |
| Meadow Road | B2 | | |
| Monk Street | B1 | | |
| Morledge | B2 | | |
| Normanton Road | C1 | | |
| North Street | A1 | | |
| Nottingham Road | B3 | | |
| Osmaston Road | C2 | | |
| Queen Street | A2 | | |
| Sacheverel Street | C1 | | |
| Saddlergate | B2 | | |
| St. Alkmunds Way | A2 | | |
| St. Helen's Street | A1 | | |

# Dover • Dundee

**Information Centre: Townwall Street**
**Tel: 01304 205108**

| | |
|---|---|
| Astor Avenue | B1 |
| Barton Road | A1 |
| Beaconsfield Avenue | A1 |
| Beaconsfield Road | A1 |
| Biggin Street | B2 |
| Bridge Street | B2 |
| Buckland Avenue | A1 |
| Cannon Street | B2 |
| Canons Gate Road | B2 |
| Castle Hill Road | B2 |
| Castle Street | B2 |
| Cherry Tree Avenue | A1 |
| Connaught Road | A2 |
| Coombe Valley Road | B1 |
| Dover Road | A3 |
| Eaton Road | B1 |
| Folkestone Road | B1 |
| Frith Road | A2 |
| Godwyne Road | B2 |
| Guston Road | A2 |
| High Street | B2 |
| Jubilee Way | A3 |
| Ladywell | B2 |
| Limekiln Street | C2 |
| London Road | A1 |
| Maison Dieu Road | B2 |
| Marine Parade | B2 |
| Military Road | B2 |
| Noah's Ark Road | B1 |
| Northbourne Avenue | B1 |
| North Military Road | B1 |
| Old Charlton Road | A2 |
| Park Avenue | A2 |
| Pencester Road | B2 |
| Priory Hill | B1 |
| Snargate Street | C2 |
| South Road | B1 |
| The Viaduct | C2 |
| Townwall Street | B2 |
| Upper Road | A3 |
| York Street | B2 |

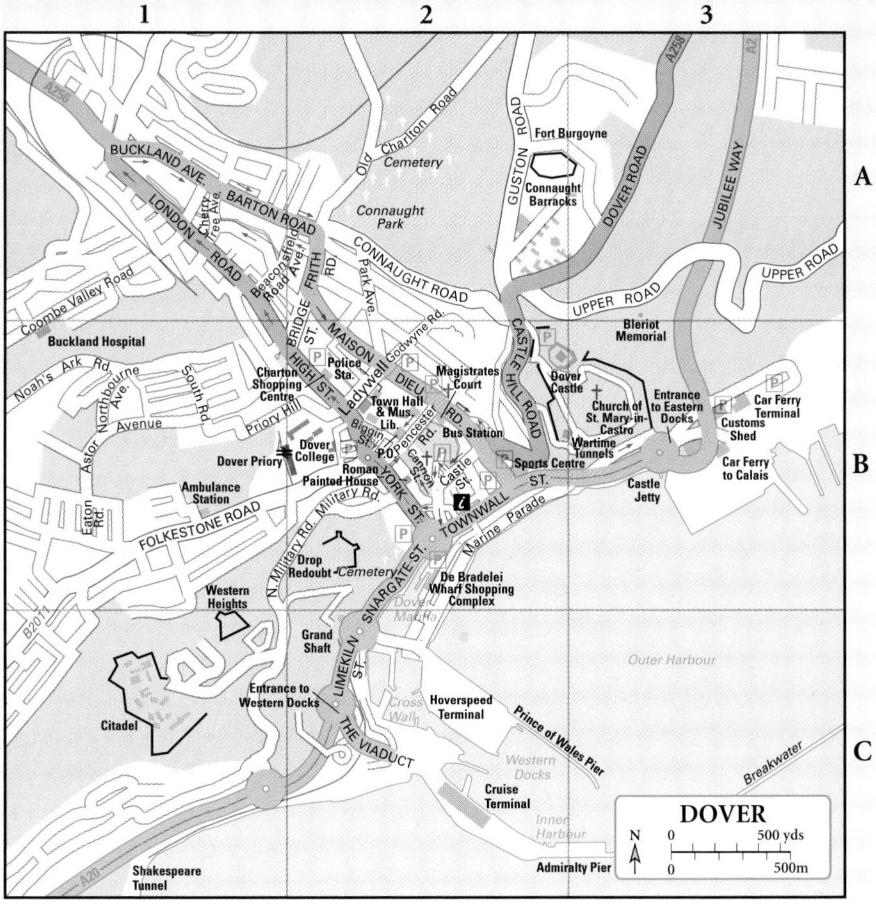


**Information Centre: 21 Castle Street**
**Tel: 01382 527527**

| | | | |
|---|---|---|---|
| Albany Terrace | A1 | Roseangle | C1 |
| Albert Street | B3 | Riverside Drive | C1 |
| Alexander Street | A2 | Seagate | B2 |
| Ann Street | B2 | South Marketgait | C2 |
| Arbroath Road | B3 | South Tay Street | C1 |
| Arklay Street | A3 | Strathmartine Road | A2 |
| Arthurstone Terrace | B3 | Tay Road Bridge | C2 |
| Barrack Road | B1 | Trades Lane | B2 |
| Blackness Road | B1 | Upper Constitution Street | A1 |
| Blackscroft | B3 | | |
| Blinshall Street | B1 | Victoria Road | B2 |
| Brook Street | B1 | Victoria Street | B3 |
| Broughty Ferry Road | B3 | Ward Road | B1 |
| Brown Street | B1 | West Marketgait | B1 |
| Bruce Street | A1 | West Port | B1 |
| Byron Street | A1 | | |
| Canning Street | A2 | | |
| City Square | C2 | | |
| Constitution Road | B2 | | |
| Constitution Street | A2 | | |
| Court Street | A3 | | |
| Cowgate Street | B2 | | |
| Dens Road | A2 | | |
| Douglas Street | B1 | | |
| Dudhope Street | A1 | | |
| Dudhope Terrace | A3 | | |
| Dundonald Street | A3 | | |
| Dura Street | B3 | | |
| East Dock Street | B3 | | |
| East Marketgait | B2 | | |
| Guthrie Street | B1 | | |
| Hawkhill | B1 | | |
| High Street | C2 | | |
| Hill Street | A2 | | |
| Hilltown | A2 | | |
| Kenmore Terrace | A1 | | |
| Killin Avenue | A1 | | |
| Kinghorne Road | A1 | | |
| King Street | B2 | | |
| Larch Street | B1 | | |
| Law Crescent | A1 | | |
| Lawside Avenue | A1 | | |
| Leng Street | A2 | | |
| Lochee Road | B1 | | |
| Mains Road | A2 | | |
| Main Street | A2 | | |
| Meadowside | B2 | | |
| Nelson Street | B2 | | |
| Nethergate | C1 | | |
| North Marketgait | B1 | | |
| Perth Road | C1 | | |
| Princes Street | B3 | | |

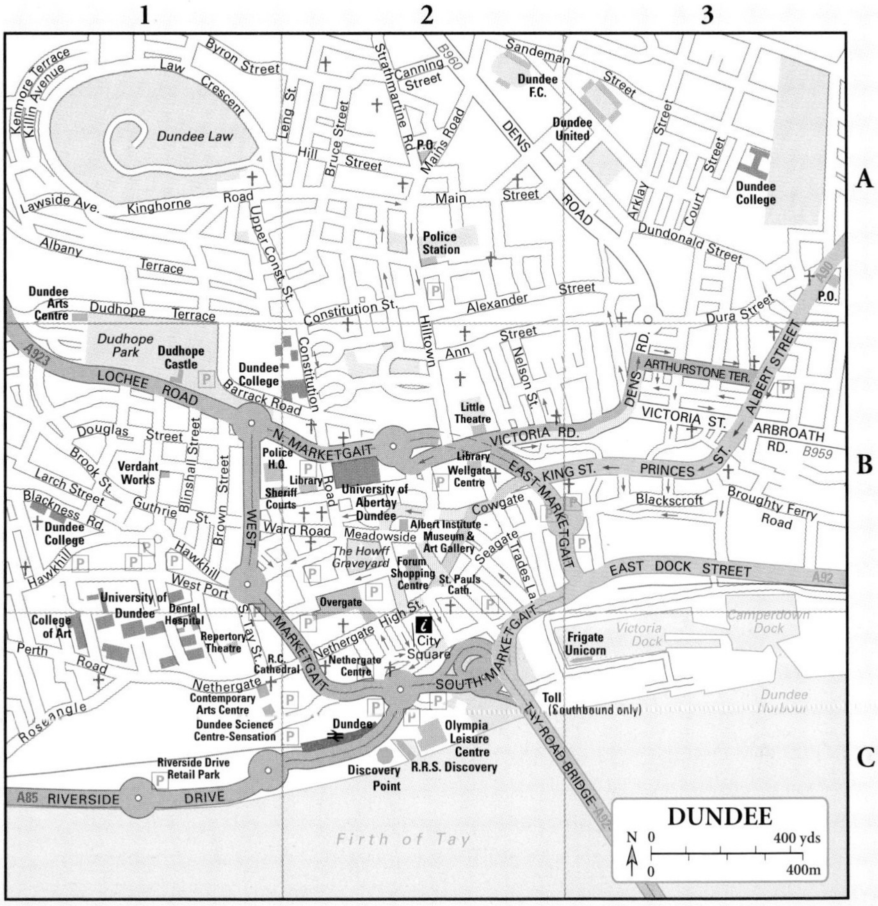

# Durham • Exeter

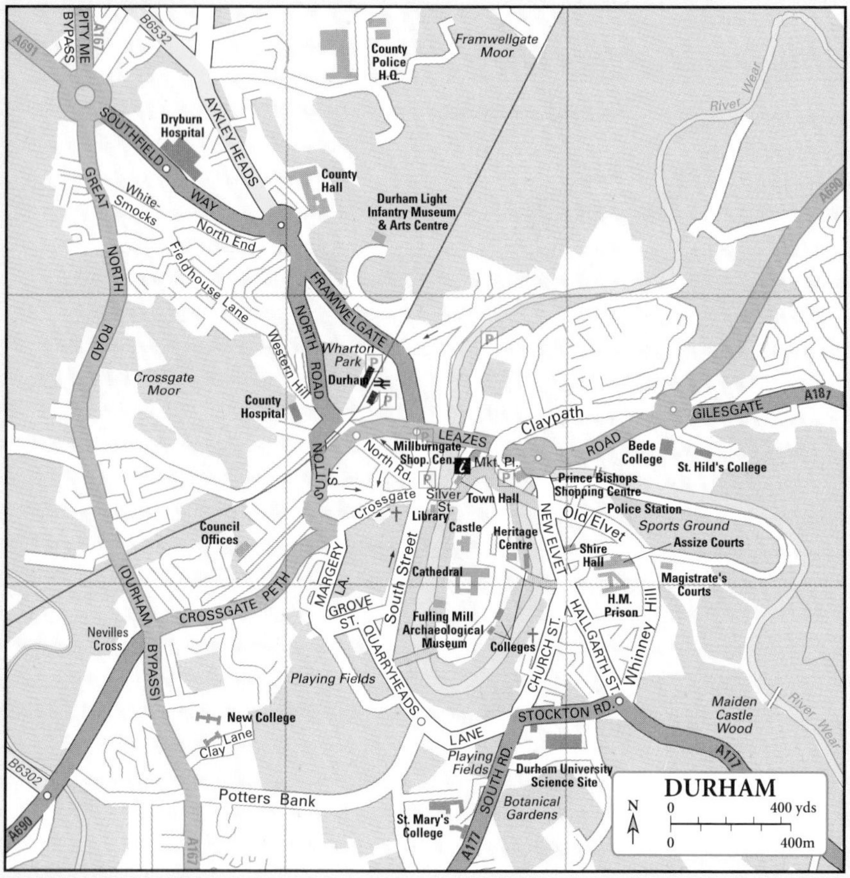


For Edinburgh see page 241

**Information Centre: Market Place**
**Tel: 0191 384 3720**

| | |
|---|---|
| Aykley Heads | A1 |
| Church Street | C2 |
| Clay Lane | C1 |
| Claypath | B2 |
| Crossgate | B2 |
| Crossgate Peth | C1 |
| Durham By-Pass | B1 |
| Fieldhouse Lane | A1 |
| Framwelgate | A2 |
| Gilesgate | B3 |
| Great North Road | A1 |
| Grove Street | C2 |
| Hallgarth Street | C3 |
| Leazes Road | B2 |
| Margery Lane | C2 |
| Market Place | B2 |
| Millburngate Bridge | B2 |
| New Elvet | B2 |
| North End | A1 |
| North Road | B2 |
| Old Elvet | B3 |
| Pity Me By-Pass | A1 |
| Potters Bank | C1 |
| Quarryheads Lane | C2 |
| Silver Street | B2 |
| South Road | C2 |
| South Street | C2 |
| Southfield Way | A1 |
| Stockton Road | C2 |
| Sutton Street | B2 |
| Western Hill | B1 |
| Whinney Hill | C3 |
| Whitesmocks | A1 |

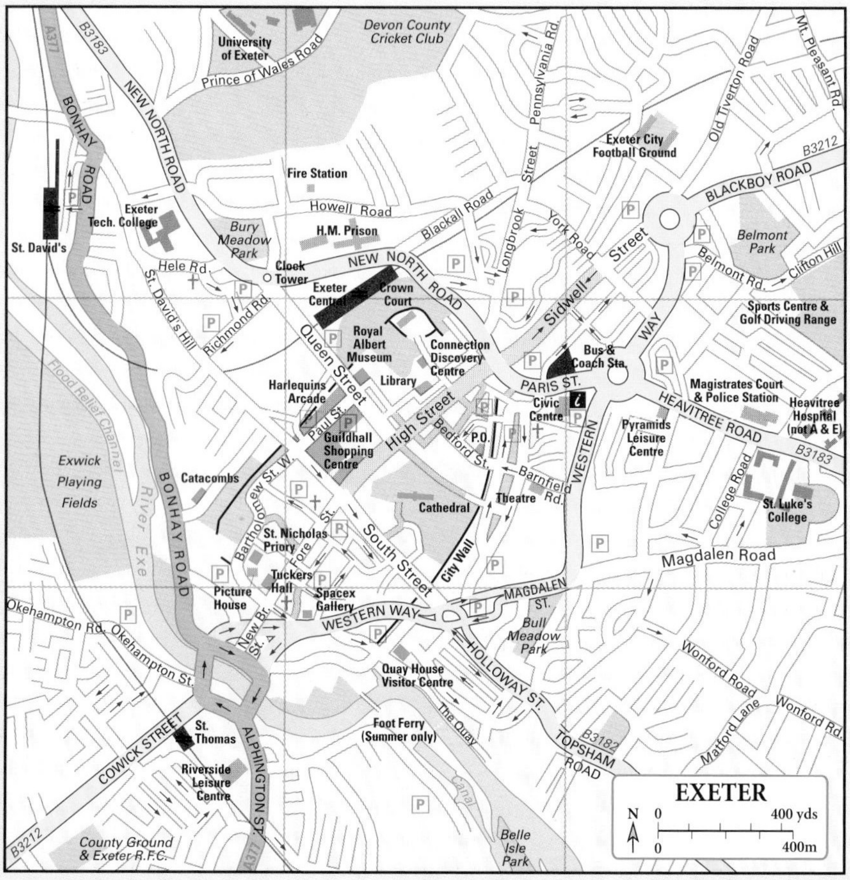


For Glasgow see page 242

**Information Centre: Civic Centre, Paris Street**
**Tel: 01392 265700**

| | |
|---|---|
| Alphington Street | C1 |
| Barnfield Road | B2 |
| Bartholomew Street West | B1 |
| Bedford Street | B2 |
| Belmont Road | A3 |
| Blackboy Road | A3 |
| Blackall Road | A2 |
| Bonhay Road | B1 |
| Clifton Hill | A3 |
| College Road | B3 |
| Cowick Street | C1 |
| Fore Street | B2 |
| Heavitree Road | B3 |
| Hele Road | A1 |
| High Street | B2 |
| Holloway Street | C2 |
| Howell Road | A2 |
| Longbrook Street | A2 |
| Magdalen Road | B3 |
| Magdalen Street | C2 |
| Matford Lane | C3 |
| Mount Pleasant Road | A3 |
| New Bridge Street | C1 |
| New North Road | A1/A2 |
| Okehampton Road | C1 |
| Okehampton Street | C1 |
| Old Tiverton Road | A3 |
| Paris Street | B2 |
| Paul Street | B2 |
| Pennsylvania Road | A2 |
| Prince of Wales Road | A1 |
| Queen Street | B2 |
| Richmond Road | B1 |
| St. David's Hill | A1 |
| Sidwell Street | B2 |
| South Street | B2 |
| The Quay | C2 |
| Topsham Road | C2 |
| Western Way | B2 |
| Wonford Road | C3 |
| York Road | A2 |

**Information Centre: 28 Southgate Street**
**Tel: 01452 421188**

| | | | |
|---|---|---|---|
| Adelaide Street | C2 | Stroud Road | C1 |
| Alma Place | C1 | The Quay | B1 |
| Alvin Street | A2 | Tredworth Road | C2 |
| Archdeacon Street | A1 | Trier Way | C1 |
| Barnwood Road | A3 | Upton Street | C2 |
| Barton Street | B2 | Victoria Street | B2 |
| Black Dog Way | A2 | Wellington Street | B2 |
| Bristol Road | C1 | Westgate Street | A1 |
| Brunswick Road | B2 | Weston Road | C1 |
| Bruton Way | B2 | Wheatstone Road | C2 |
| Calton Road | C2 | Worcester Street | A2 |
| Cheltenham Road | A3 | | |
| Churchill Road | C1 | | |
| Conduit Street | C2 | | |
| Dean's Way | A2 | | |
| Denmark Road | A2 | | |
| Derby Road | B2 | | |
| Estcourt Road | A2 | | |
| Eastern Avenue | C3 | | |
| Eastgate Street | B2 | | |
| Gouda Way | A1 | | |
| Great Western Road | B2 | | |
| Greyfriars | B2 | | |
| Hatherley Road | C2 | | |
| High Street | C2 | | |
| Hopewell Street | C2 | | |
| Horton Road | B3 | | |
| King Edward's Avenue | C2 | | |
| Kingsholm Road | A2 | | |
| Linden Road | C1 | | |
| London Road | A2 | | |
| Lower Westgate Street | A1 | | |
| Merevale Road | A3 | | |
| Metz Way | B2 | | |
| Millbrook Street | B2 | | |
| Northgate Street | B2 | | |
| Oxford Road | A2 | | |
| Oxstalls Lane | A3 | | |
| Painswick Road | C3 | | |
| Park Road | B2 | | |
| Parkend Road | C2 | | |
| Pitt Street | A2 | | |
| Quay Street | B1 | | |
| Ryecroft Street | C2 | | |
| St. Ann Way | C1 | | |
| St. Oswald's Road | A1 | | |
| Secunda Way | C1 | | |
| Severn Road | B1 | | |
| Seymour Road | C1 | | |
| Southgate Street | B1 | | |
| Spa Road | B1 | | |
| Station Road | B2 | | |

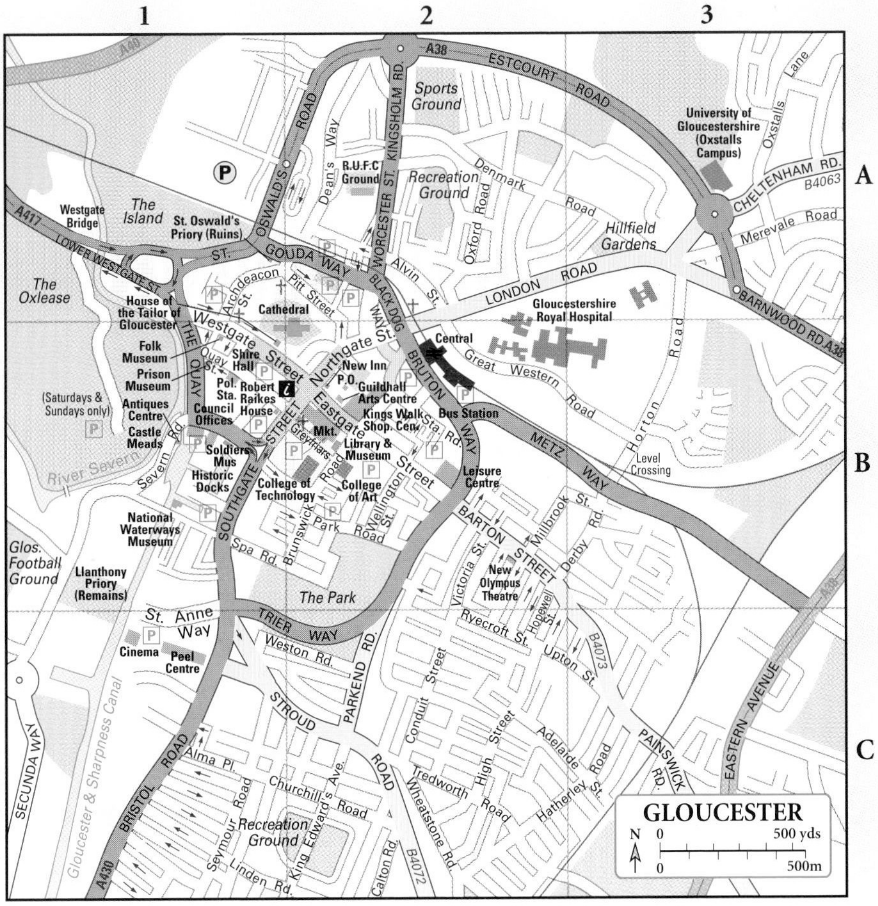


**Information Centre: 1 King Street**
**Tel: 01432 268430**

| | | | |
|---|---|---|---|
| Aubrey Street | B2 | Stonebow Road | A3 |
| Barrs Court Road | A3 | Symonds Street | B3 |
| Barton Road | B1 | The Atrium | A2 |
| Barton Yard | B1 | Turner Street | C3 |
| Bath Street | B3 | Union Street | B2 |
| Berrington Street | B2 | Union Walk | A3 |
| Bewell Street | B2 | Victoria Street | B1 |
| Blackfriars Street | A2 | West Street | B2 |
| Blueschool Street | A2 | Widemarsh Street | B2 |
| Brewers Passage | B2 | Wye Street | C2 |
| Bridge Street | B2 | | |
| Broad Street | B2 | | |
| Canonmoor Street | A1 | | |
| Cantilupe Street | B3 | | |
| Castle Street | B2 | | |
| Catherine Street | A2 | | |
| Central Avenue | B3 | | |
| Church Street | B2 | | |
| Commercial Road | A3 | | |
| Commercial Street | B2 | | |
| Coningsby Street | A2 | | |
| East Street | B2 | | |
| Edgar Street | A2 | | |
| Eign Gate | B2 | | |
| Eign Street | B1 | | |
| Friars Street | B1 | | |
| Fryzer Court | B2 | | |
| Gaol Street | B3 | | |
| Green Street | C3 | | |
| Grenfell Road | C3 | | |
| Greyfriars Avenue | C1 | | |
| Greyfriars Bridge | B2 | | |
| Grove Road | C3 | | |
| Harold Street | C3 | | |
| High Street | B2 | | |
| High Town | B2 | | |
| King Street | B2 | | |
| Kyrle Street | B3 | | |
| Maylord Street | B2 | | |
| Mill Street | C3 | | |
| Moorfield Street | A1 | | |
| Nelson Street | C3 | | |
| Newmarket Street | A2 | | |
| Portland Street | A1 | | |
| Quay Street | B2 | | |
| St. Guthiac Street | B3 | | |
| St. James Road | C3 | | |
| St. Martin's Avenue | C2 | | |
| St. Martin's Street | C2 | | |
| St. Owen Street | B3 | | |
| Station Approach | A3 | | |
| Station Road | B1 | | |

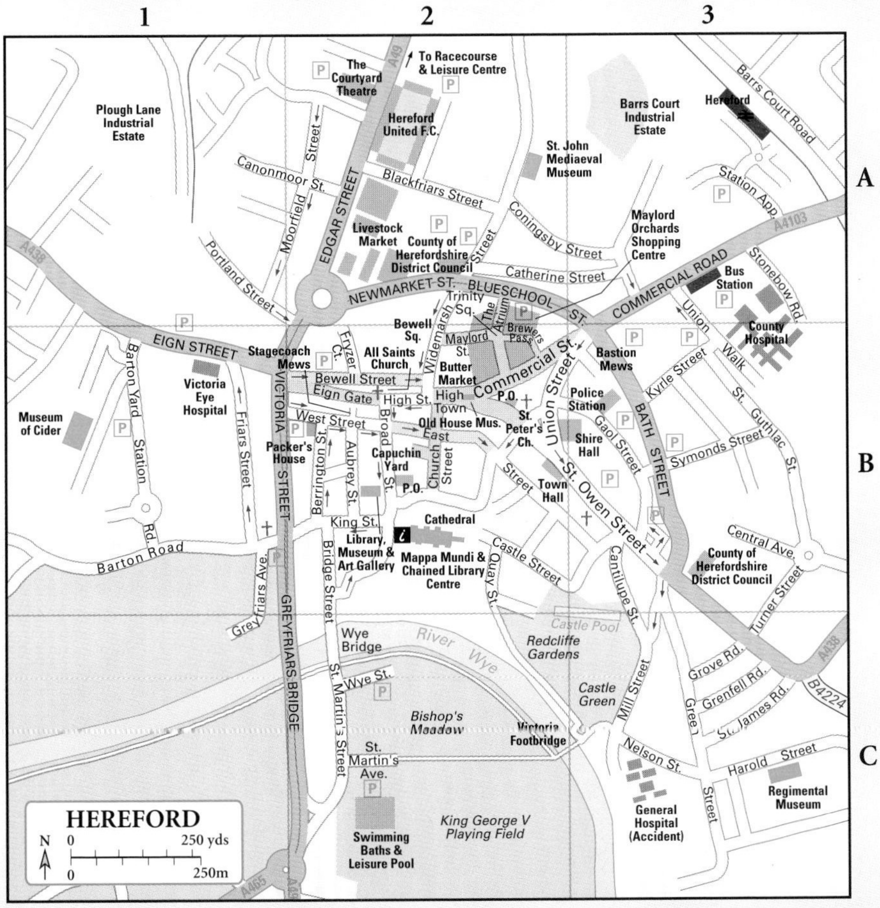

# Kingston upon Hull • Leicester

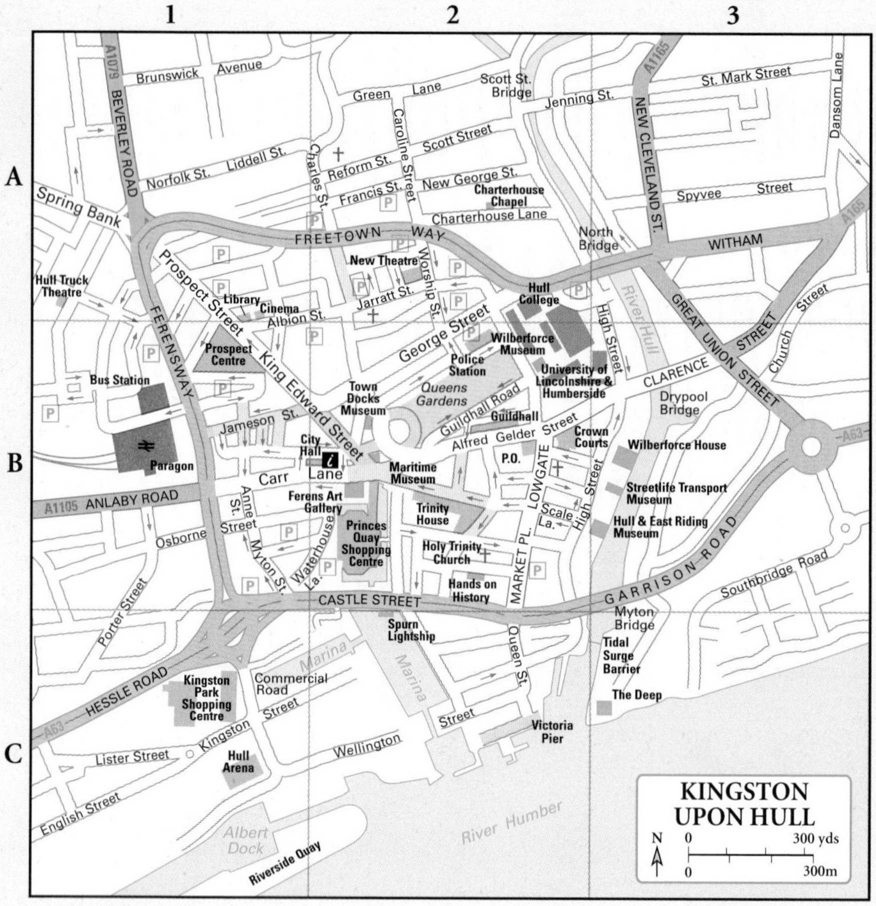


For Leeds see page 238

**Information Centre: 1 Paragon Street**
**Tel: 01482 223559**

| Street | Grid |
|---|---|
| Albion Street | B1 |
| Alfred Gelder Street | B2 |
| Anlaby Road | B1 |
| Anne Street | B1 |
| Beverley Road | A1 |
| Brunswick Avenue | A1 |
| Caroline Street | A2 |
| Carr Lane | B1 |
| Castle Street | B2 |
| Charles Street | A2 |
| Charterhouse Lane | A2 |
| Church Street | B3 |
| Clarence Street | B3 |
| Cleveland Street | A3 |
| Dansom Lane | A3 |
| English Street | C1 |
| Ferensway | A1 |
| Francis Street | A2 |
| Freetown Way | A1 |
| Garrison Road | B3 |
| George Street | B2 |
| Great Union Street | A3 |
| Green Lane | A2 |
| Guildhall Road | B2 |
| Hessle Road | C1 |
| High Street | A3 |
| Jameson Street | B1 |
| Jarratt Street | A2 |
| Jenning Street | A2 |
| King Edward Street | B1 |
| Kingston Street | C1 |
| Liddell Street | A1 |
| Lister Street | C1 |
| Lowgate | B2 |
| Market Place | B2 |
| Myton Street | B1 |
| New Cleveland Street | A3 |
| New George Street | A2 |
| Norfolk Street | A1 |
| North Bridge | A2 |
| Osborne Street | B1 |
| Porter Street | C1 |
| Prospect Street | A1 |
| Queen Street | C2 |
| Reform Street | A2 |
| St. Mark Street | A3 |
| Scale Lane | B2 |
| Scott Street | A2 |
| Scott Street Bridge | A2 |
| Southbridge Road | B3 |
| Spring Bank | A1 |
| Spyvee Street | A3 |
| Waterhouse Lane | B1 |
| Wellington Street | C2 |
| Witham | A3 |
| Worship Street | A2 |

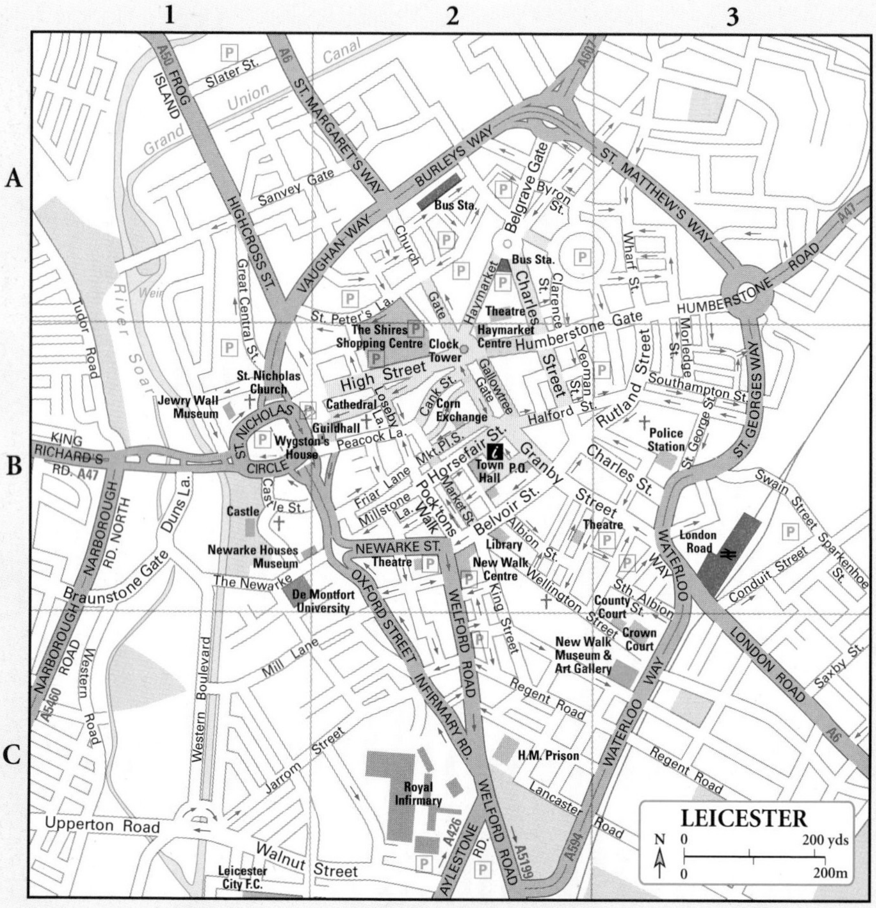


**Information Centre: 7-9 Every Street, Town Hall Square**
**Tel: 0116 299 8888**

| Street | Grid |
|---|---|
| Albion Street | B2 |
| Aylestone Road | C2 |
| Belgrave Gate | A2 |
| Belvoir Street | B2 |
| Braunstone Gate | B1 |
| Burleys Way | A2 |
| Byron Street | A2 |
| Cank Street | B2 |
| Castle Street | B1 |
| Charles Street | B3 |
| Church Gate | A2 |
| Clarence Street | A2 |
| Conduit Street | B3 |
| Duns Lane | B1 |
| Friar Lane | B2 |
| Frog Island | A1 |
| Gallowtree Gate | B2 |
| Granby Street | B2 |
| Great Central Street | A1 |
| Halford Street | B2 |
| Haymarket | A2 |
| High Street | B2 |
| Highcross Street | A1 |
| Horsfair Street | B2 |
| Humberstone Gate | B2 |
| Humberstone Road | A3 |
| Infirmary Road | C2 |
| Jarrom Street | C1 |
| King Richard's Road | B1 |
| King Street | B2 |
| Lancaster Road | C2 |
| London Road | C3 |
| Loseby Lane | B2 |
| Market Place South | B2 |
| Market Street | B2 |
| Mill Lane | C1 |
| Millstone Lane | B2 |
| Morledge Street | B3 |
| Narborough Road | C1 |
| Narborough Road North | B1 |
| Newarke Street | B2 |
| Oxford Street | B2 |
| Peacock Lane | B2 |
| Pocklingtons Walk | B2 |
| Regent Road | C2 |
| Rutland Street | B3 |
| St. George Street | B3 |
| St. George's Way | B3 |
| St. Margaret's Way | A1 |
| St. Matthew's Way | A3 |
| St. Nicholas Circle | B1 |
| St. Peter's Lane | A2 |
| Sanvey Gare | A1 |
| Saxby Street | C3 |
| Slater Street | A1 |
| South Albion Street | B3 |
| Southampton Street | B3 |
| Sparkenhoe Street | B3 |
| Swain Street | B3 |
| The Newarke | B1 |
| Tudor Road | A1 |
| Upperton Road | C1 |
| Vaughan Way | A1 |
| Walnut Street | C1 |
| Waterloo Way | C3 |
| Welford Road | B2 |
| Wellington Street | B2 |
| Western Boulevard | C1 |
| Western Road | C1 |
| Wharf Street | A3 |
| Yeoman Street | B2 |

# Lincoln • Middlesbrough

**Information Centre: 9 Castle Hill**
**Tel: 01522 873213**

| | | | |
|---|---|---|---|
| Bailgate | A2 | Wigford Way | B2 |
| Brayford Way | C1 | Winn Street | B3 |
| Beevor Street | C1 | Wragby Road | B3 |
| Broadgate | B2 | Yarborough Road | A1 |
| Broadway | A2 | | |
| Burton Road | A1 | | |
| Canwick Road | C2 | | |
| Carholme Road | B1 | | |
| Carline Road | A1 | | |
| Church Lane | A2 | | |
| Clasketgate | B2 | | |
| Croft Street | B2 | | |
| Cross Street | C2 | | |
| Drury Lane | B2 | | |
| East Gate | B2 | | |
| Firth Road | C1 | | |
| Great Northern Terrace | C2 | | |
| Greetwell Road | B3 | | |
| Gresham Street | B1 | | |
| High Street | C2 | | |
| Lee Road | A3 | | |
| Lindum Road | B2 | | |
| Lindum Terrace | B3 | | |
| Long Leys Road | A1 | | |
| Milman Road | B3 | | |
| Monks Road | B3 | | |
| Monson Street | C2 | | |
| Nettleham Road | A2 | | |
| Newland | B1 | | |
| Newport | A2 | | |
| Northgate | A2 | | |
| Pelham Bridge | C2 | | |
| Portland Street | C2 | | |
| Rasen Lane | A2 | | |
| Ripon Street | C2 | | |
| Rope Walk | C1 | | |
| Ruskin Avenue | A3 | | |
| St. Anne's Road | B3 | | |
| St. Mark Street | C2 | | |
| Saltergate | B2 | | |
| Sewell Road | B3 | | |
| Silver Street | B2 | | |
| Spa Road | C3 | | |
| Stamp End | C3 | | |
| Steep Hill | B2 | | |
| The Avenue | B1 | | |
| Tritton Road | C1 | | |
| Upper Long Leys Road | A1 | | |
| Waterside North | C2 | | |
| Waterside South | C2 | | |
| West Parade | B1 | | |
| Westgate | A2 | | |

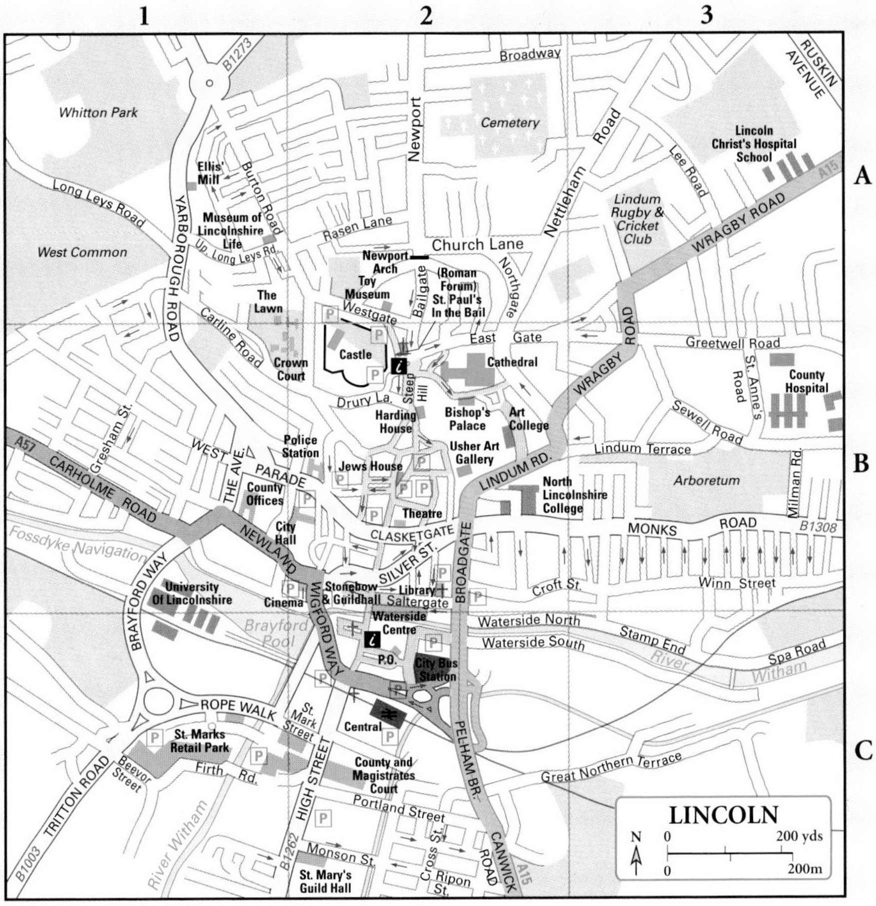


For Liverpool see page 235
For Manchester see page 236

**Information Centre: 99-101 Albert Road**
**Tel: 01642 243425/358086**

| | |
|---|---|
| Abingdon Road | B2 |
| Albert Road | A2 |
| Ayresome Green Lane | B1 |
| Ayresome Street | B1 |
| Belle Vue Grove | C3 |
| Bishopton Road | C2 |
| Borough Road | A2/C3 |
| Bridge Street West | A2 |
| Burlam Road | C1 |
| Cargo Fleet Road | A3 |
| Clairville Road | B2 |
| Corporation Road | A2 |
| Crescent Road | B1 |
| Cumberland Road | C2 |
| Dockside Road | A2/A3 |
| Eastbourne Road | C2 |
| Forty Foot Road | A1 |
| Grange Road | A2 |
| Gresham Road | B1 |
| Hartington Road | A1 |
| Heywood Street | B1 |
| Highfield Road | C3 |
| Holwick Road | A1 |
| Linthorpe Road | C2 |
| Longlands Road | B3 |
| Marton Burn Road | C2 |
| Marton Road | B3/C3 |
| Newport Road | A1/A2 |
| North Ormesby Road | A3 |
| Orchard Road | C1 |
| Park Road North | B2 |
| Park Road South | B2 |
| Park Vale Road | B2 |
| Parliament Road | B1 |
| Riverside Park Road | A1 |
| Roman Road | C1 |
| St. Barnabas Road | B1 |
| Scotts Road | A3 |
| Sheperdson Way | A3 |
| Snowdon Road | A2 |
| Southfield Road | B2 |
| The Avenue | C2 |
| The Crescent | C1 |
| Union Street | B1 |
| Valley Road | C2 |
| Victoria Road | B2 |
| Westbourne Grove | B3 |
| Wilson Street | A2 |
| Woodlands Road | B2 |

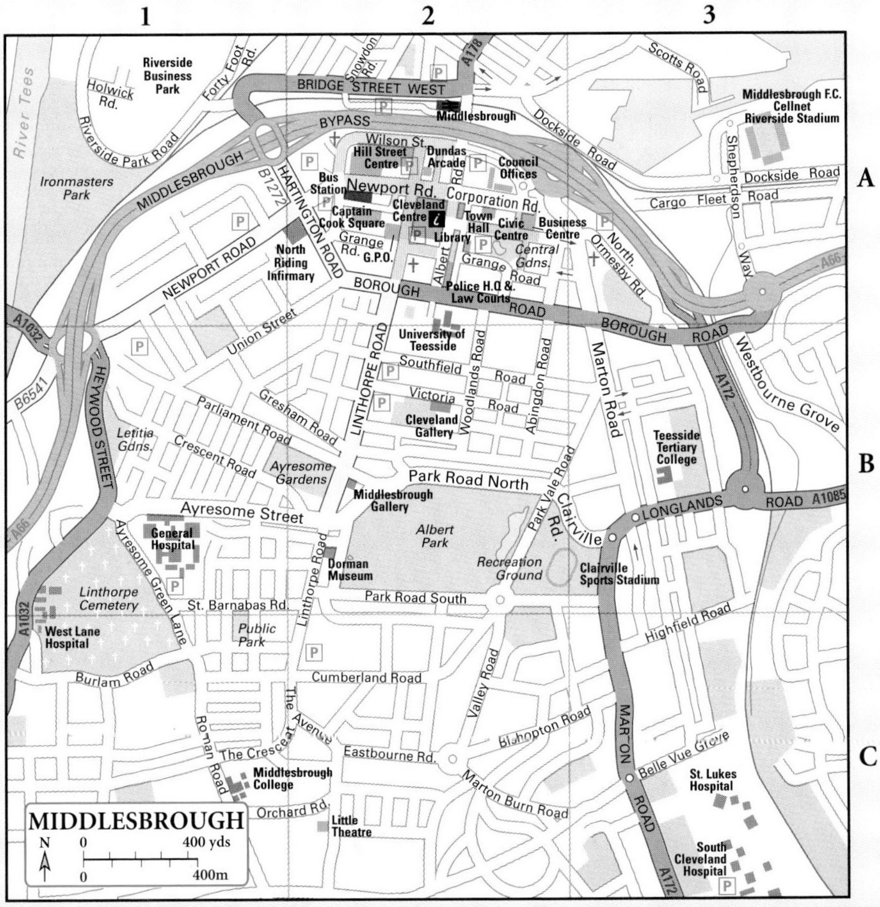


For Newcastle see page 240

# Norwich • Oxford

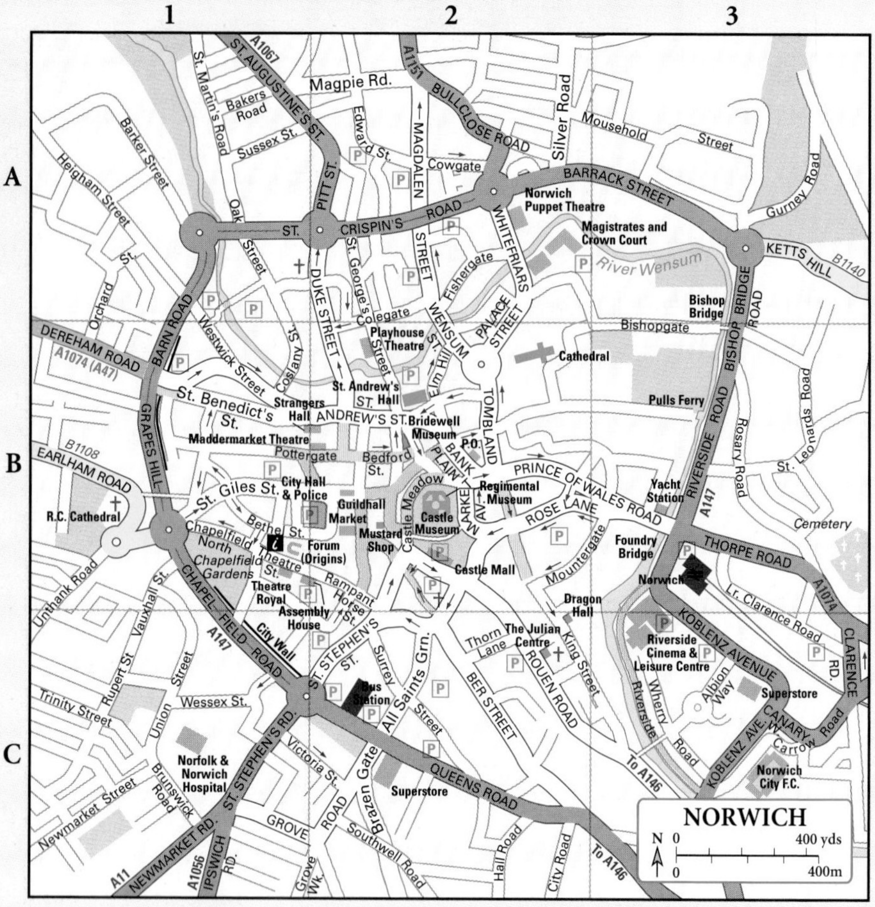


For Nottingham see page 232

**Information Centre: The Forum, Millennium Plain**
**Tel: 01603 666071**

| | | | |
|---|---|---|---|
| Albion Way | C3 | Pitt Street | A2 |
| All Saints Green | C2 | Pottergate | B1 |
| Bakers Road | A1 | Prince of Wales Road | B2 |
| Bank Plain | B2 | Queens Road | C2 |
| Barker Street | A1 | Rampant Horse Street | B2 |
| Barn Road | B1 | Riverside | C3 |
| Barrack Street | A2 | Riverside Road | B3 |
| Bedford Street | B2 | Rosary Road | B3 |
| Ber Street | C2 | Rose Lane | B2 |
| Bethel Street | B1 | Rouen Road | C2 |
| Bishopbridge Road | B3 | Rupert Street | C1 |
| Bishopgate | B3 | St. Andrew's Street | B2 |
| Brazen Gate | C2 | St. Augustine's Street | A1 |
| Brunswick Road | C1 | St. Benedict's Street | B1 |
| Bullclose Road | A2 | St. Crispin's Road | A1 |
| Canary Way | C3 | St. George's Street | A2 |
| Carrow Road | C3 | St. Giles Street | B1 |
| Castle Meadow | B2 | St. Leonards Road | B3 |
| Chapel Field Road | B1 | St. Martin's Road | A1 |
| Chapelfield North | B1 | St. Stephen's Road | C1 |
| City Road | C2 | St. Stephen's Street | C2 |
| Clarence Road | C3 | Silver Road | A2 |
| Colegate | A2 | Southwell Road | C2 |
| Coslany Street | B1 | Surrey Street | C2 |
| Cowgate | A2 | Sussex Street | A1 |
| Dereham Road | B1 | Theatre Street | B1 |
| Duke Street | A2 | Thorn Lane | C2 |
| Earlham Road | B1 | Thorpe Road | B3 |
| Edward Street | A2 | Tombland | B2 |
| Elm Hill | B2 | Trinity Street | C1 |
| Fishergate | A2 | Union Street | C1 |
| Grapes Hill | B1 | Unthank Road | C1 |
| Grove Road | C1 | Vauxhall Street | C1 |
| Grove Walk | C1 | Victoria Street | C1 |
| Gurney Road | A3 | Wensum Street | A2 |
| Hall Road | C2 | Wessex Street | C1 |
| Heigham Street | A1 | Westwick Street | A1 |
| Ipswich Road | C1 | Wherry Road | C3 |
| Ketts Hill | A3 | Whitefriars | A2 |
| King Street | C2 | | |
| Koblenz Avenue | C3 | | |
| Lower Clarence Road | B3 | | |
| Magdalen Street | A2 | | |
| Magpie Road | A2 | | |
| Market Avenue | B2 | | |
| Mountergate | B2 | | |
| Mousehold Street | A3 | | |
| Newmarket Road | C1 | | |
| Newmarket Street | C1 | | |
| Oak Street | A1 | | |
| Orchard Street | A1 | | |
| Palace Street | B2 | | |

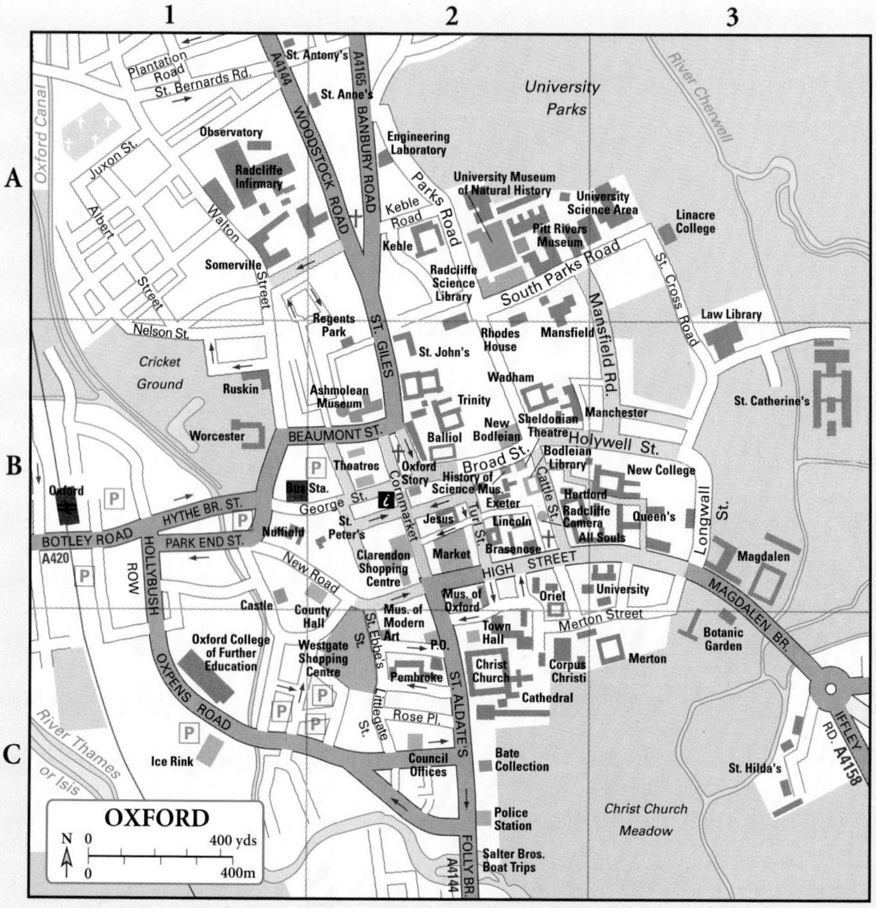


**Information Centre: 15-16 Broad Street**
**Tel: 01865 726871**

| | |
|---|---|
| Albert Street | A1 |
| Banbury Road | A2 |
| Beaumont Street | B1 |
| Botley Road | B1 |
| Broad Street | B2 |
| Cattle Street | B2 |
| Cornmarket | B2 |
| Folly Bridge | C2 |
| George Street | B1 |
| High Street | B2 |
| Hollybush Row | B1 |
| Holywell Street | B2 |
| Hythe Bridge Street | B1 |
| Iffley Road | C3 |
| Juxon Street | A1 |
| Keble Road | A2 |
| Littlegate Street | C2 |
| Longwall Street | B3 |
| Magdalen Bridge | B3 |
| Mansfield Road | A3 |
| Merton Street | C2 |
| Nelson Street | B1 |
| New Road | B1 |
| Oxpens Road | C1 |
| Park End Street | B1 |
| Parks Road | A2 |
| Plantation Road | A1 |
| Rose Place | C2 |
| St. Aldate's | C2 |
| St. Bernards Road | A1 |
| St. Cross Road | A3 |
| St. Ebbe's Street | C2 |
| St. Giles | A2 |
| South Parks Road | A2 |
| Turl Street | B2 |
| Walton Street | A1 |
| Woodstock Road | A1 |

# Plymouth • Reading

**Information Centre: Island House, 9 The Barbican**
**Tel: 01752 264849**

| | | | |
|---|---|---|---|
| Alexandra Road | A3 | North Cross | B2 |
| Alma Road | A1 | North Hill | B2 |
| Armada Way | B2 | North Road East | B2 |
| Ashford Road | A3 | North Road West | B1 |
| Barbican Approach | C3 | North Street | B2 |
| Beaumont Road | B3 | Notte Street | C2 |
| Beechwood Avenue | A2 | Oxford Street | B1 |
| Bretonside | B2 | Pentillie Road | A2 |
| Buckwell Street | C2 | Princess Street | C2 |
| Camden Street | B2 | Queen's Road | A3 |
| Cattledown Road | C3 | Royal Parade | B2 |
| Cecil Street | B1 | Salisbury Road | B3 |
| Central Park Avenue | A1 | Saltash Road | A1 |
| Charles Street | B2 | Seaton Avenue | A2 |
| Citadel Road | C1 | Seymour Avenue | B3 |
| Clarence Place | B1 | Southside Street | C2 |
| Cliff Road | C1 | Stoke Road | B1 |
| Clifton Place | A2 | Stuart Road | A1 |
| Clovelly Road | C3 | Sutton Road | B3 |
| Cobourg Street | B2 | Sydney Street | B1 |
| Cornwall Street | B2 | Teats Hill Road | C3 |
| Dale Road | A2 | The Crescent | C1 |
| Drake Circus | B2 | Tothill Avenue | B3 |
| East Street | C1 | Tothill Road | B3 |
| Eastlake Street | B2 | Union Street | B1 |
| Ebrington Street | B2 | Vauxhall Street | C2 |
| Elliot Street | C1 | West Hoe Road | C1 |
| Embankment Road | B3 | Western Approach | B1 |
| Exeter Street | B2 | Whittington Street | A1 |
| Ford Park Road | A2 | Wilton Street | B1 |
| Gdynia Way | C3 | Wyndham Street | B1 |
| Grand Parade | C1 | | |
| Greenbank Road | A3 | | |
| Grenville Road | B3 | | |
| Harwell Street | B1 | | |
| Hoe Road | C2 | | |
| Houndiscombe Road | A2 | | |
| James Street | B2 | | |
| King Street | B1 | | |
| Lipson Hill | A3 | | |
| Lipson Road | B3 | | |
| Lisson Grove | A3 | | |
| Lockyer Street | C2 | | |
| Looe Street | B2 | | |
| Madeira Road | C2 | | |
| Manor Road | B1 | | |
| Martin Street | C1 | | |
| Mayflower Street | B2 | | |
| Millbay Road | C1 | | |
| Mount Gould Road | A3 | | |
| Mutley Plain | A2 | | |
| New George Street | B1 | | |

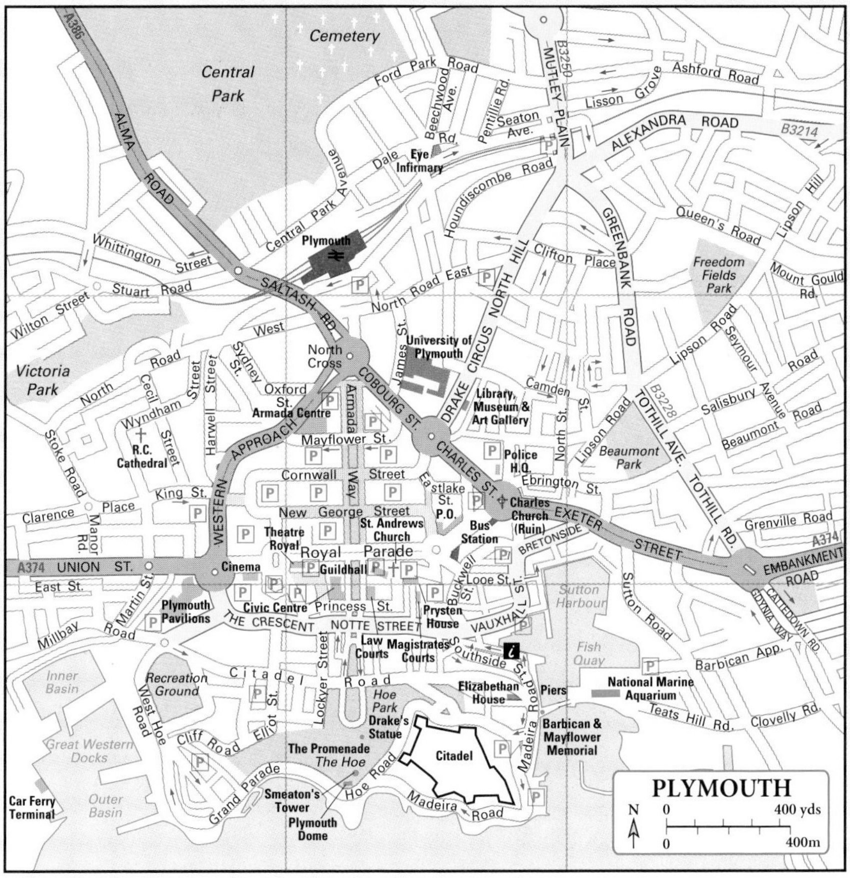


For Portsmouth see page 227

**Information Centre: Town Hall, Blagrave Street**
**Tel: 0118 956 6226**

| | | | |
|---|---|---|---|
| Addington Road | C3 | Hill Street | C2 |
| Addison Road | A1 | Holybrook Road | C1 |
| Alexandra Road | B3 | Kenavon Drive | B3 |
| Allcroft Road | C3 | Kendrick Road | C2 |
| Alpine Street | C2 | King's Road *Caversham* | A2 |
| Amersham Road | A3 | King's Road *Reading* | B2 |
| Amity Road | B1 | London Road | B3 |
| Ardler Road | A2 | London Street | B2 |
| Audley Street | B1 | Lower Henley Road | A3 |
| Basingstoke Road | C2 | Mill Road | A3 |
| Bath Road | C1 | Millford Road | A1 |
| Bedford Road | B1 | Millman Road | C2 |
| Berkeley Avenue | C1 | Minster Street | B2 |
| Blagrave Street | B2 | Morgan Road | C3 |
| Blenheim Road | B3 | Napier Road | B2 |
| Briant's Avenue | A3 | Orts Road | B3 |
| Bridge Street | B2 | Oxford Road | B1 |
| Broad Street | B2 | Pell Street | C2 |
| Cardiff Road | A1 | Portman Road | A1 |
| Castle Hill | B1 | Priest Hill | A2 |
| Castle Street | B2 | Prospect Street *Caversham* | A2 |
| Catherine Street | B1 | Prospect Street *Reading* | B1 |
| Caversham Road | B2 | Queen's Road *Caversham* | A2 |
| Chatham Street | B1 | Queen's Road *Reading* | B2 |
| Cheapside | B2 | Redlands Road | C3 |
| Cholmeley Road | B3 | Richfield Avenue | A1 |
| Christchurch Road | C2 | Rose Kiln Lane | C2 |
| Church Road | A1 | Russell Street | B1 |
| Church Street | A2 | St. Ann's Road | A2 |
| Coley Avenue | C1 | St. John's Road | A3 |
| Cow Lane | B1 | St. Mary's Butts | B2 |
| Craven Road | B3 | St. Peters Avenue | A1 |
| Crown Place | B3 | St. Saviours Road | C1 |
| Crown Street | C2 | Silver Street | C2 |
| Cumberland Road | B3 | South Street | B2 |
| Curzon Street | B1 | Southampton Street | C2 |
| De Beauvoir Road | B3 | South View Road | A2 |
| Donnington Road | B3 | Star Road | A3 |
| Duke Street | B2 | Station Hill | B2 |
| East Street | B2 | Station Road | B2 |
| Eldon Road | B3 | Swansea Road | A2 |
| Eldon Terrace | B3 | Tessa Road | A1 |
| Elgar Road | C2 | The Warren | A1 |
| Elgar Road South | C2 | Tilehurst Road | B1 |
| Erleigh Road | B3 | Upper Redlands Road | C3 |
| Fobney Street | B2 | Vastern Road | A2 |
| Forbury Road | B2 | Waldeck Street | C2 |
| Friar Street | B2 | Waterloo Road | C2 |
| Gas Work Road | B3 | Wensley Road | C1 |
| George Street *Caversham* | A2 | Western Elms Avenue | B1 |
| George Street *Reading* | B1 | Westfield Road | A2 |
| Gosbrook Road | A2 | West Street | B2 |
| Gower Street | B1 | Whitley Street | C2 |
| Great Knollys Street | B1 | Wolsey Road | A2 |
| Greyfriars Road | B2 | York Road | A2 |
| Hemdean Road | A2 | | |

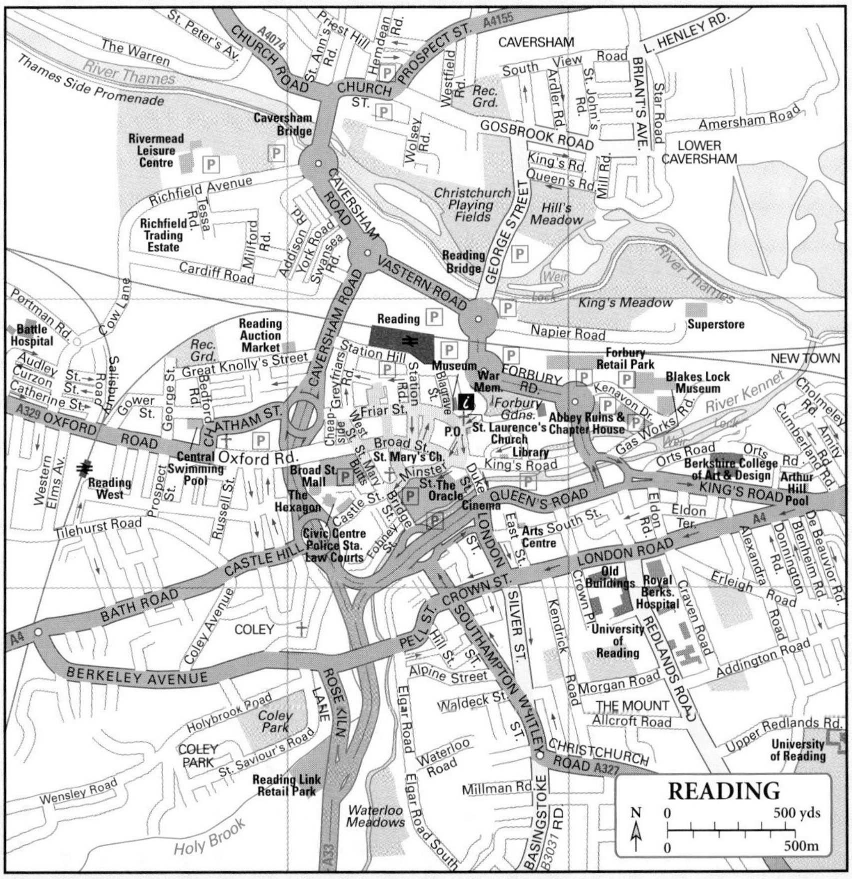


For Sheffield see page 233
For Southampton see page 226

# Stoke-on-Trent • Stratford-upon-Avon

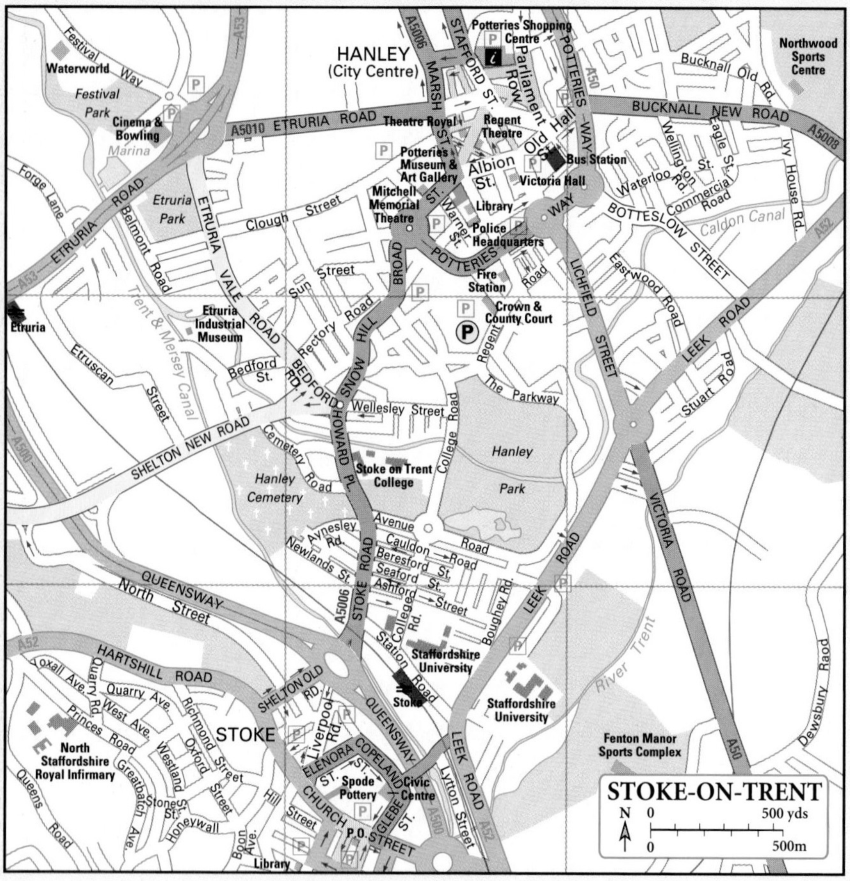


**Information Centre: Potteries Shopping Cen, Quadrant Rd**
**Tel: 01782 236000**

| | |
|---|---|
| Albion Street | A2 |
| Ashford Street | B2 |
| Avenue Road | B2 |
| Aynsley Road | B2 |
| Bedford Road | B2 |
| Bedford Street | B1 |
| Belmont Road | A1 |
| Beresford Street | B2 |
| Boon Avenue | C1 |
| Botteslow Street | A3 |
| Boughey Road | C2 |
| Broad Street | A2 |
| Bucknall New Road | A3 |
| Bucknall Old Road | A3 |
| Cauldon Road | B2 |
| Cemetery Road | B1 |
| Church Street | C2 |
| Clough Street | A1 |
| College Road | B2 |
| Commercial Road | A3 |
| Copeland Street | C2 |
| Dewsbury Road | C3 |
| Eagle Street | A3 |
| Eastwood Road | A3 |
| Elenora Street | C2 |
| Etruria Road | A1 |
| Etruria Vale Road | A1 |
| Etruscan Street | B1 |
| Festival Way | A1 |
| Forge Lane | A1 |
| Glebe Street | C2 |
| Greatbatch Avenue | C1 |
| Hanley | A2 |
| Hartshill Road | C1 |
| Hill Street | C1 |
| Honeywall | C1 |
| Howard Place | B2 |
| Ivy House Road | A3 |
| Leek Road | C2 |
| Lichfield Street | A3 |
| Liverpool Road | C2 |
| Lytton Street | C2 |
| Marsh Street | A2 |
| Newlands Street | B2 |
| North Street | B1 |
| Old Hall Street | A2 |
| Oxford Street | C1 |
| Parliament Row | A2 |
| Potteries Way | A2 |
| Potters Way | A3 |
| Prince's Road | C1 |
| Quarry Avenue | C1 |
| Quarry Road | C1 |
| Queen's Road | C1 |
| Queensway | B1 |
| Rectory Road | B2 |
| Regent Road | B2 |
| Richmond Street | C1 |
| Seaford Street | B2 |
| Shelton New Road | B1 |
| Shelton Old Road | C1 |
| Snow Hill | B2 |
| Stafford Street | A2 |
| Station Road | C2 |
| Stoke | C2 |
| Stoke Road | C2 |
| Stone Street | C1 |
| Stuart Road | B3 |
| Sun Street | A2 |
| The Parkway | B2 |
| Victoria Road | B3 |
| Warner Street | A2 |
| Waterloo Street | A3 |
| Wellesley Street | B2 |
| Wellington Road | A3 |
| West Avenue | C1 |
| Westland Street | C1 |
| Yoxall Avenue | C1 |

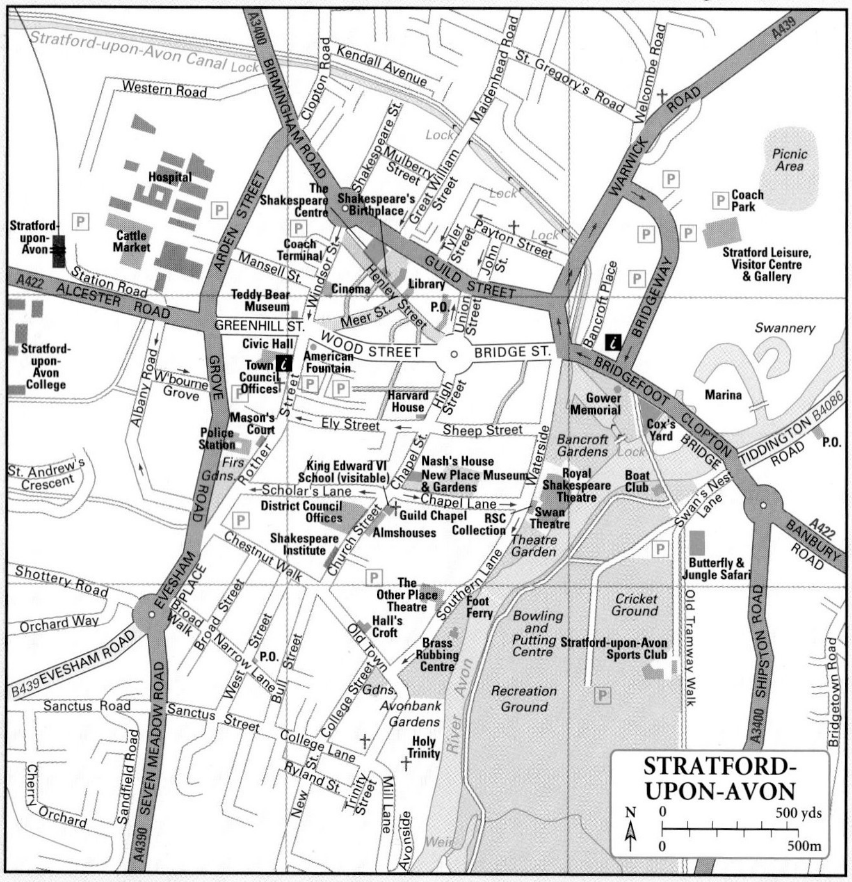


**Information Centre: Bridgefoot**
**Tel: 01789 293127**

| | |
|---|---|
| Albany Road | B1 |
| Alcester Road | A1 |
| Arden Street | A1 |
| Avonside | C2 |
| Banbury Road | B3 |
| Bancroft Place | B3 |
| Birmingham Road | A1 |
| Bridgefoot | B3 |
| Bridge Street | B2 |
| Bridgeway | B3 |
| Bridgetown Road | C3 |
| Broad Street | C1 |
| Broad Walk | C1 |
| Bull Street | C1 |
| Chapel Lane | B2 |
| Chapel Street | B2 |
| Cherry Orchard | C1 |
| Chestnut Walk | B1 |
| Church Street | B2 |
| Clopton Bridge | B3 |
| Clopton Road | A2 |
| College Lane | C2 |
| College Street | C2 |
| Ely Street | B2 |
| Evesham Place | C1 |
| Evesham Road | C1 |
| Great William Street | A2 |
| Greenhill Street | B1 |
| Grove Road | B1 |
| Guild Street | A2 |
| Henley Street | A2 |
| High Street | B2 |
| John Street | A2 |
| Kendall Avenue | A2 |
| Maidenhead Road | A2 |
| Mansell Street | A1 |
| Meer Street | B2 |
| Mill Lane | C2 |
| Mulberry Street | A2 |
| Narrow Lane | C1 |
| New Street | C2 |
| Old Town | C2 |
| Old Tramway Walk | C3 |
| Orchard Way | C1 |
| Payton Street | A2 |
| Rother Street | B1 |
| Ryland Street | C2 |
| St. Andrews Crescent | B1 |
| St. Gregory's Road | A2 |
| Sanctus Road | C1 |
| Sanctus Street | C1 |
| Sandfield Road | C1 |
| Scholar's Lane | B1 |
| Shakespeare Street | A2 |
| Sheep Street | B2 |
| Shipston Road | C3 |
| Shottery Road | B1 |
| Seven Meadow Road | C1 |
| Southern Lane | C2 |
| Station Road | A1 |
| Swans Nest Lane | B3 |
| Tiddington Road | B3 |
| Trinity Street | C2 |
| Tyler Street | A2 |
| Union Street | B2 |
| Warwick Road | A3 |
| Waterside | B2 |
| Welcombe Road | A3 |
| Westbourne Grove | B1 |
| Western Road | A1 |
| West Street | C1 |
| Windsor Street | B2 |
| Wood Street | B2 |

# Swansea • Swindon

**Information Centre: Westway**
**Tel: 01792 468321**

| | |
|---|---|
| Albert Row | C2 |
| Alexandra Road | B2 |
| Argyle Street | C1 |
| Beach Street | C1 |
| Belle Vue Way | B2 |
| Bond Street | C1 |
| Brooklands Terrace | B1 |
| Brynymor Crescent | C1 |
| Brynymor Road | C1 |
| Burrows Place | C3 |
| Cambrian Place | C3 |
| Carmarthen Road | A2 |
| Castle Street | B2 |
| Clarence Terrace | C2 |
| Constitution Hill | B1 |
| Cromwell Street | B1 |
| De La Beche Street | B2 |
| Delhi Street | B3 |
| Dyfatty Street | A2 |
| Dyfed Avenue | B1 |
| East Burrows Road | C3 |
| Fabian Way | B3 |
| Foxhole Road | A3 |
| Glamorgan Street | C2 |
| Gors Avenue | A1 |
| Grove Place | B2 |
| Gwent Road | A1 |
| Hanover Street | B1 |
| High Street | B2 |
| Islwyn Road | A1 |
| King Edward's Road | C1 |
| Llangyfelach Road | A2 |
| Lower Oxford Street | C1 |
| Mackworth Street | B3 |
| Mansel Street | B1 |
| Mayhill Road | A1 |
| Morris Lane | B3 |
| Mount Pleasant | B2 |
| Mumbles Road | C1 |
| Neath Road | A3 |
| New Cut Road | B3 |
| New Orchard Street | A2 |
| North Hill Road | A2 |
| Orchard Street | B2 |
| Oystermouth Road | C1 |
| Page Street | B2 |
| Pentre Guinea Road | A3 |
| Pen-y-Craig Road | A1 |
| Powys Avenue | A1 |
| Princess Way | B2 |
| Rose Hill | B1 |
| St. Helen's Avenue | C1 |
| St. Helen's Road | C1 |
| St. Mary Street | B2 |
| Singleton Street | C2 |
| Somerset Place | C3 |
| South Guildhall Road | C1 |
| Strand | B3 |
| Terrace Road | B1 |
| The Kingsway | B2 |
| Townhill Road | A1 |
| Vincent Street | C1 |
| Walter Road | C1 |
| Waun-Wen Road | A2 |
| Wellington Street | C2 |
| Westbury Street | C1 |
| Western Street | C1 |
| West Way | C2 |

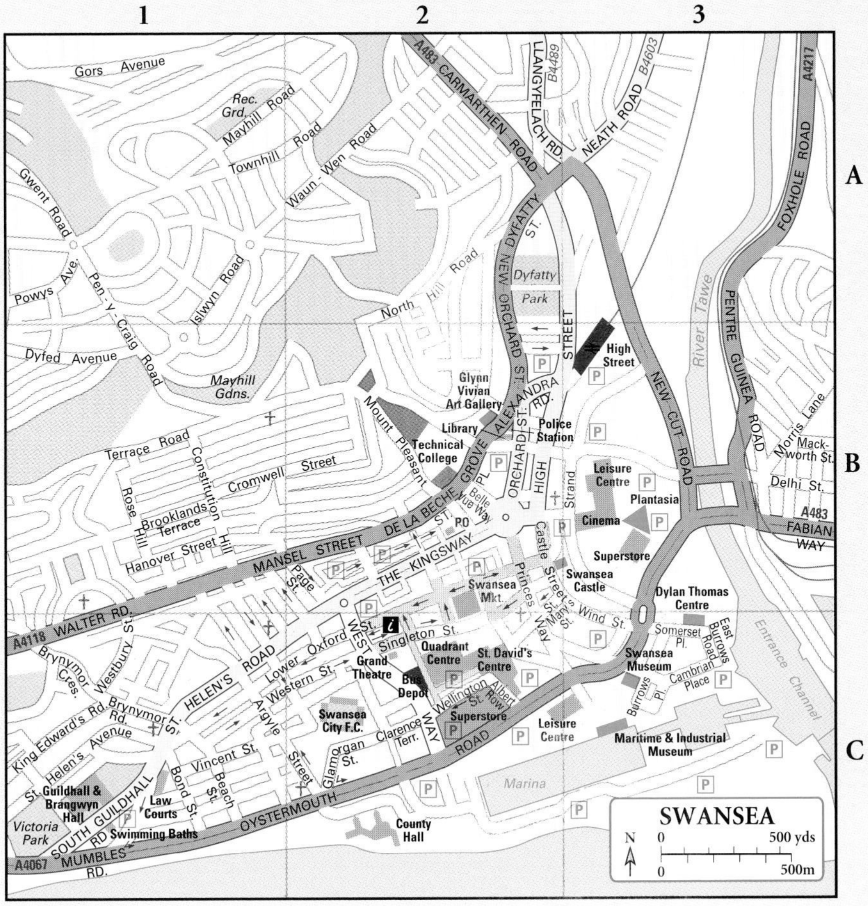


**Information Centre: 37 Regent Street**
**Tel: 01793 530328**

| | |
|---|---|
| Bath Road | C2 |
| Beatrice Street | A2 |
| Birch Street | B1 |
| Bridge Street | B2 |
| Broad Street | A3 |
| Canal Walk | B2 |
| Cirencester Way | A3 |
| Clifton Street | C2 |
| Commercial Road | B2 |
| County Road | A3 |
| Courtsknap Court | B1 |
| Cricklade Street | C3 |
| Curtis Street | B2 |
| Dean Street | B1 |
| Drove Road | C3 |
| Eastcott Hill | C2 |
| Edmund Street | B2 |
| Euclid Street | B3 |
| Faringdon Road | B1 |
| Farnby Street | B2 |
| Fleet Street | B2 |
| Fleming Way | B2 |
| Folkstone Road | C2 |
| Great Western Way | A1 |
| Groundwell Road | B3 |
| Hawksworth Way | A1 |
| High Street | C3 |
| Hythe Road | C2 |
| Jennings Street | B1 |
| Kemble Drive | A1 |
| Kent Road | C2 |
| Kingshill Street | C1 |
| Manchester Road | A2 |
| Market Street | B2 |
| Milford Street | B2 |
| Milton Road | B2 |
| Morris Street | A1 |
| Newburn Crescent | B1 |
| North Star Avenue | A2 |
| Ocotal Way | A3 |
| Okus Road | C1 |
| Park Lane | B1 |
| Penzance Drive | B1 |
| Princes Street | B3 |
| Queen Street | B2 |
| Redcliffe Street | B1 |
| Regent Street | B2 |
| Rodbourne Road | A1 |
| Rosebery Way | A3 |
| Spring Gardens | B3 |
| Stafford Street | C2 |
| Station Road | A2 |
| Swindon Road | C2 |
| The Parade | B2 |
| Upham Road | C3 |
| Victoria Road | B3 |
| Westcott Place | C1 |
| Western Street | C3 |
| William Street | C1 |

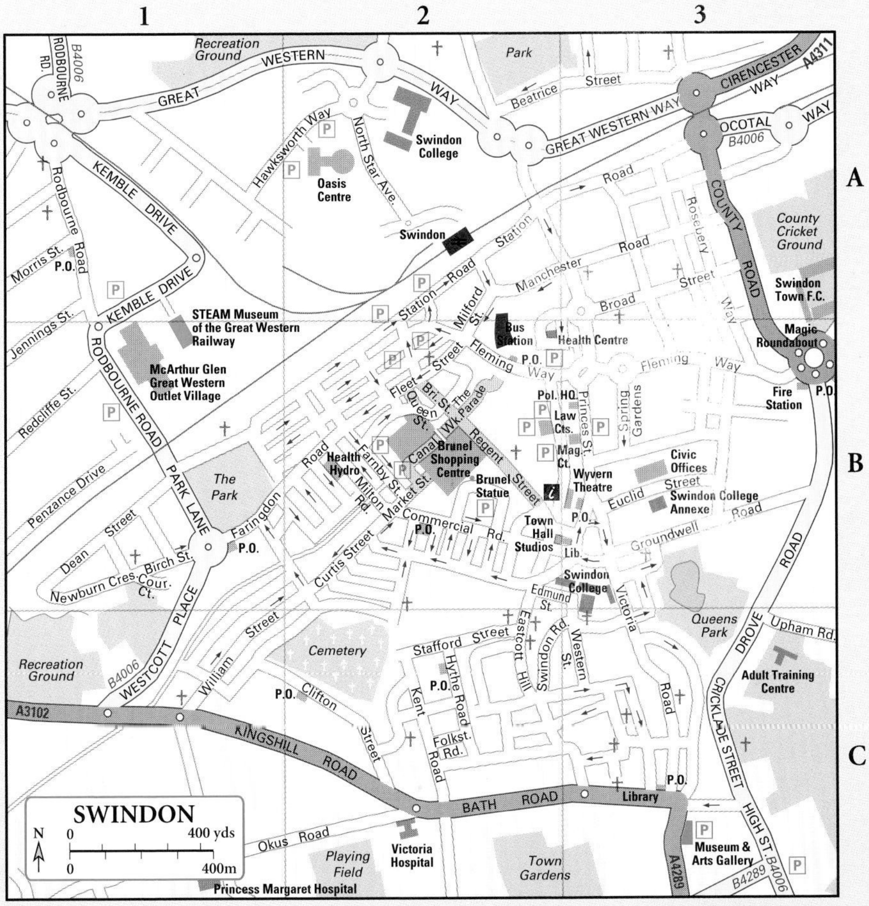

# Torquay • Winchester

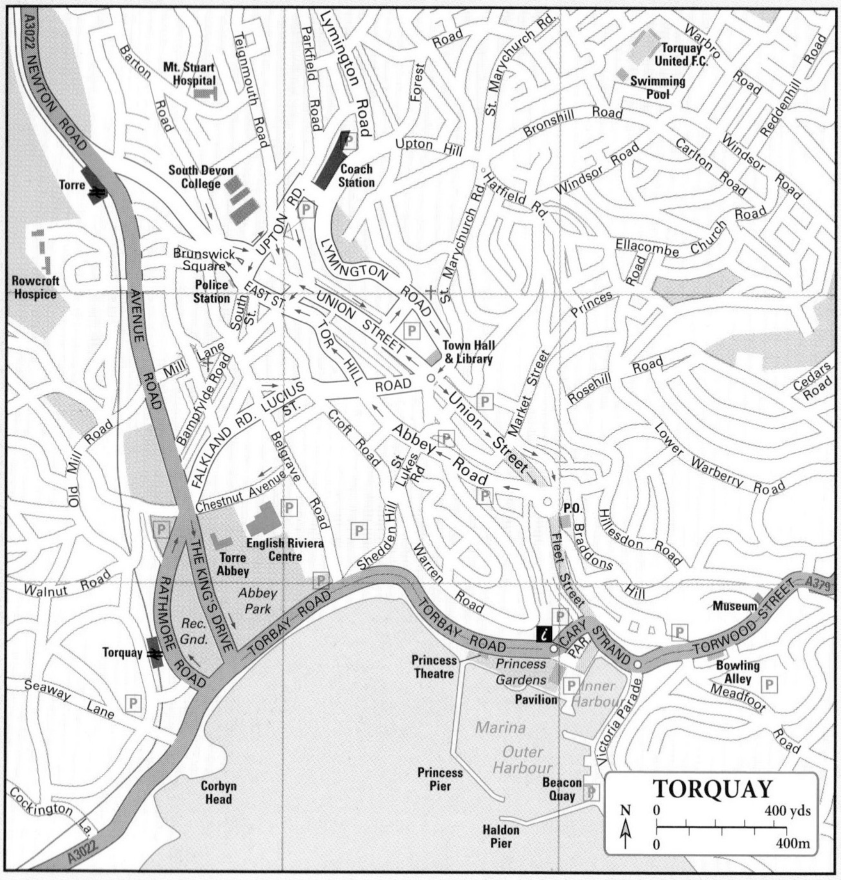


**Information Centre: Vaughan Parade**
**Tel: 01803 297428**

| | | | |
|---|---|---|---|
| Abbey Road | B2 | Warbro Road | A3 |
| Avenue Road | B1 | Warren Road | B2 |
| Bampfylde Road | B1 | Westhill Road | A2 |
| Barton Road | A1 | Windsor Road | A3 |
| Belgrave Road | B1 | | |
| Braddons Hill | B3 | | |
| Bronshill Road | A2 | | |
| Brunswick Square | B1 | | |
| Carlton Road | A3 | | |
| Cary Parade | C3 | | |
| Cedars Road | B3 | | |
| Chestnut Avenue | B1 | | |
| Cockington Lane | C1 | | |
| Croft Road | B2 | | |
| East Street | A1 | | |
| Ellacombe Church Road | A3 | | |
| Falkland Road | B1 | | |
| Fleet Street | B2 | | |
| Forest Road | A2 | | |
| Hatfield Road | A2 | | |
| Hillesdon Road | B3 | | |
| Lower Warberry Road | B3 | | |
| Lucius Street | B1 | | |
| Lymington Road | A2 | | |
| Market Street | B2 | | |
| Meadfoot Road | C3 | | |
| Mill Lane | B1 | | |
| Newton Road | A1 | | |
| Old Mill Road | B1 | | |
| Parkfield Road | A2 | | |
| Prince's Road | B3 | | |
| Rathmore Road | C1 | | |
| Reddenhill Road | A3 | | |
| Rosehill Road | B3 | | |
| St. Lukes Road | B2 | | |
| St. Marychurch Road | B2 | | |
| Seaway Lane | C1 | | |
| Shedden Hill | B2 | | |
| Shiphay Lane | A1 | | |
| South Street | B1 | | |
| Strand | C3 | | |
| Teignmouth Road | A1 | | |
| The King's Drive | B1 | | |
| Torbay Road | C1 | | |
| Tor Hill Road | B2 | | |
| Torwood Street | C3 | | |
| Union Street | B2 | | |
| Upton Hill | A2 | | |
| Upton Road | A1 | | |
| Victoria Parade | C3 | | |
| Walnut Road | C1 | | |

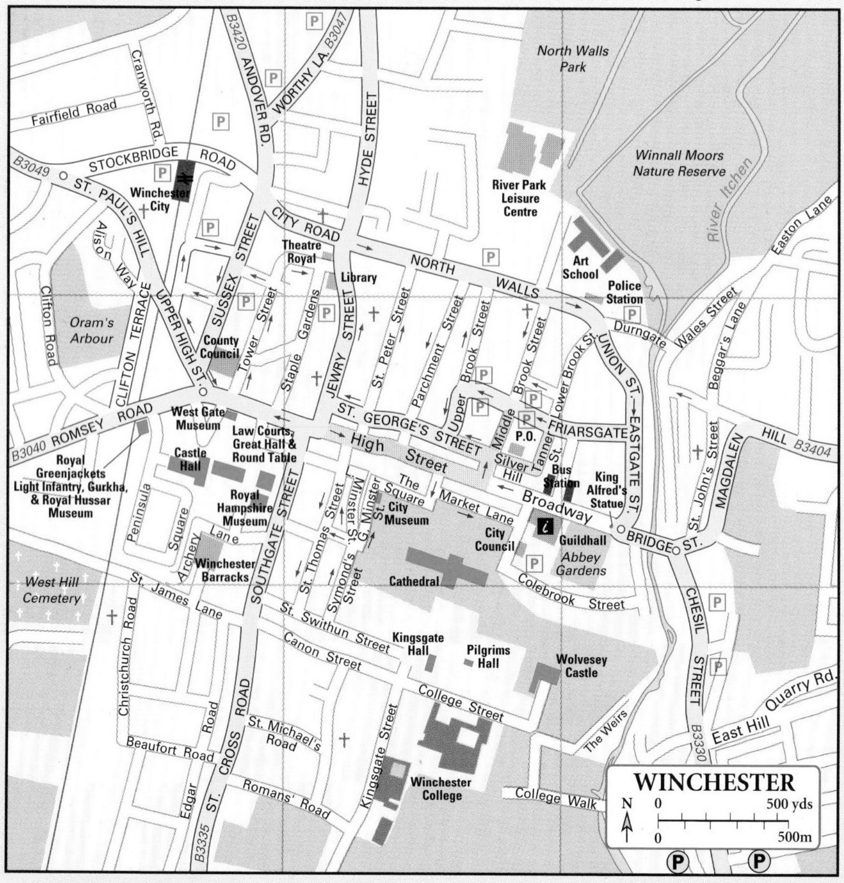


**Information Centre: Guildhall, The Broadway**
**Tel: 01962 840500**

| | | | |
|---|---|---|---|
| Alison Way | A1 | Stockbridge Road | A1 |
| Andover Road | A1 | Sussex Street | B1 |
| Archery Lane | B1 | Symond's Street | C2 |
| Beaufort Road | C1 | Tanner Street | B2 |
| Beggar's Lane | B3 | The Square | B2 |
| Bridge Stret | B3 | Tower Street | B1 |
| Broadway | B2 | Union Street | B3 |
| Canon Street | C2 | Upper Brook Street | B2 |
| Chesil Street | C3 | Upper High Street | B1 |
| Christchurch Road | C1 | Wales Street | B3 |
| City Road | A1 | Worthy Lane | A1 |
| Clifton Road | A1 | | |
| Clifton Terrace | B1 | | |
| Colebrook Street | B2 | | |
| College Street | C2 | | |
| College Walk | C2 | | |
| Cranworth Road | A1 | | |
| Durngate | B3 | | |
| Eastgate Street | B3 | | |
| Easton Lane | A3 | | |
| East Hill | C3 | | |
| Edgar Road | C1 | | |
| Fairfield Road | A1 | | |
| Friarsgate | B2 | | |
| Great Minster Street | B2 | | |
| High Street | B2 | | |
| Hyde Street | A2 | | |
| Jewry Street | B2 | | |
| Kingsgate Street | C2 | | |
| Little Minster Street | B2 | | |
| Lower Brook Street | B2 | | |
| Magdalen Hill | B3 | | |
| Market Lane | B2 | | |
| Middle Brook Street | B2 | | |
| North Walls | A1 | | |
| Parchment Street | B2 | | |
| Peninsula Square | B1 | | |
| Quarry Road | C3 | | |
| Romans' Road | C1 | | |
| Romsey Road | B1 | | |
| St. Cross Road | C1 | | |
| St. George's Street | B2 | | |
| St. James Lane | B1 | | |
| St. John's Street | B3 | | |
| St. Michael's Road | C1 | | |
| St. Paul's Hill | A1 | | |
| St. Peter Street | B2 | | |
| St. Swithun Street | C2 | | |
| St. Thomas Street | C2 | | |
| Silver Hill | B2 | | |
| Southgate Street | C1 | | |
| Staple Gardens | B2 | | |

**Information Centre: 24 High Street**
**Tel: 01753 743900**

| | |
|---|---|
| Alexandra Road | C2 |
| Alma Road | B2 |
| Arthur Road | B2 |
| Barry Avenue | A2 |
| Bolton Avenue | C2 |
| Bolton Road | C2 |
| Bulkeley Avenue | C1 |
| Charles Street | B2 |
| Clarence Road | B1 |
| Datchet Road | A3 |
| Eton & Windsor Relief Road | B1 |
| Frances Road | C2 |
| Goslar Way | B1 |
| Green Lane | B1 |
| Grove Road | B2 |
| High Street (Eton) | A2 |
| High Street (Windsor) | B3 |
| Imperial Road | C1 |
| King Edward VII Avenue | A3 |
| Kings Road | C3 |
| Meadow Lane | A2 |
| Osborne Road | C2 |
| Oxford Road | B2 |
| Parsonage Lane | B1 |
| Peascod Street | B2 |
| St. Leonards Road | C2 |
| Sheet Street | B3 |
| Springfield Road | C1 |
| Stovell Road | A1 |
| Thames Street | A3 |
| The Long Walk | C3 |
| Vansittart Road | B2 |
| Victoria Street | B2 |
| York Avenue | C1 |

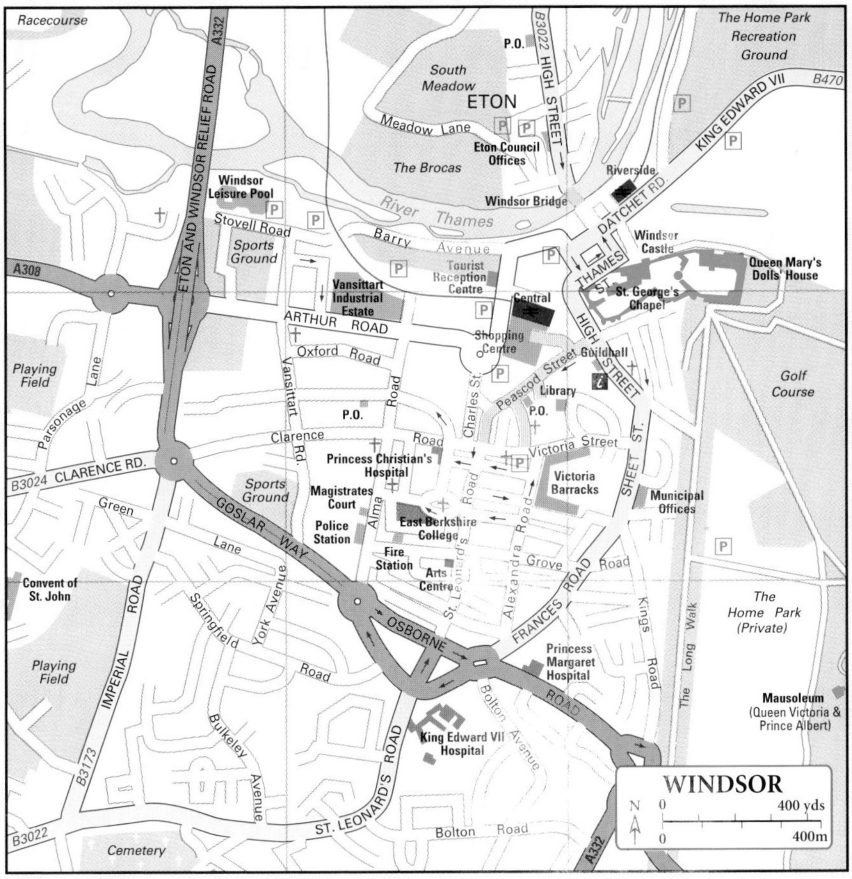


**Information Centre: TIC Travel Office, 20 George Hudson St.**
**Tel: 01904 554488**

| | |
|---|---|
| Albermarle Road | C1 |
| Aldwark | B2 |
| Barbican Road | C3 |
| Bishopthorpe Road | C2 |
| Bishopgate Street | C2 |
| Blossom Street | C1 |
| Bootham | A1 |
| Bull Lane | A3/B3 |
| Burton Stone Lane | A1 |
| Cemetery Road | C3 |
| Church Street | B2 |
| Clarence Street | A2 |
| Clifford Street | B2 |
| Clifton | A1 |
| Coney Street | B2 |
| Dale Street | C1 |
| Dalton Terrace | C1 |
| Dodsworth Avenue | A3 |
| East Parade | A3 |
| Fifth Avenue | A3 |
| Fishergate | C2 |
| Foss Bank | B3 |
| Fossgate | B2 |
| Foss Islands Road | B3 |
| Fourth Avenue | B3 |
| Gillygate | A2 |
| Goodramgate | B2 |
| Grosvenor Road | A1 |
| Grosvenor Terrace | A1 |
| Hallfield Road | B3 |
| Haxby Road | A2 |
| Heslington Road | C3 |
| Heworth Green | A3 |
| Holgate Road | C1 |
| Huntington Road | A3 |
| James Street | B2 |
| Lawrence Street | C3 |
| Layerthorpe | B3 |
| Leeman Road | B1 |
| Lendal | B2 |
| Longfield Terrace | B1 |
| Lord Mayor's Walk | A2 |
| Lowther Street | A2 |
| Malton Road | A3 |
| Marygate | B1 |
| Maurices Road | B2 |
| Micklegate | B1 |
| Monkgate | A2 |
| Moss Street | C1 |
| Mount Vale | C1 |
| Museum Street | B2 |
| North Street | B2 |
| Nunnery Lane | C1 |
| Nunthorpe Road | C1 |
| Ousegate | B2 |
| Paragon Street | C2 |
| Park Grove | A2 |
| Penley's Grove Street | A2 |
| Petergate | B2 |
| Piccadilly | B2 |
| Queen Street | B1 |
| Rougier Street | B1 |
| Church Street | B2 |
| St. Andrewgate | B2 |
| St. John Street | A2 |
| St. Maurice's Road | B2 |
| Scarcroft Hill | C1 |
| Scarcroft Road | C1 |
| Shambles | B2 |
| Sixth Avenue | A3 |
| Skeldergate | B2 |
| Southlands Road | C1 |
| Station Road | B1 |
| Terry Avenue | C2 |
| The Mount | C1 |
| The Stonebow | B2 |
| Tower Street | B2 |
| Walmgate | B2 |
| Wigginton Road | A2 |

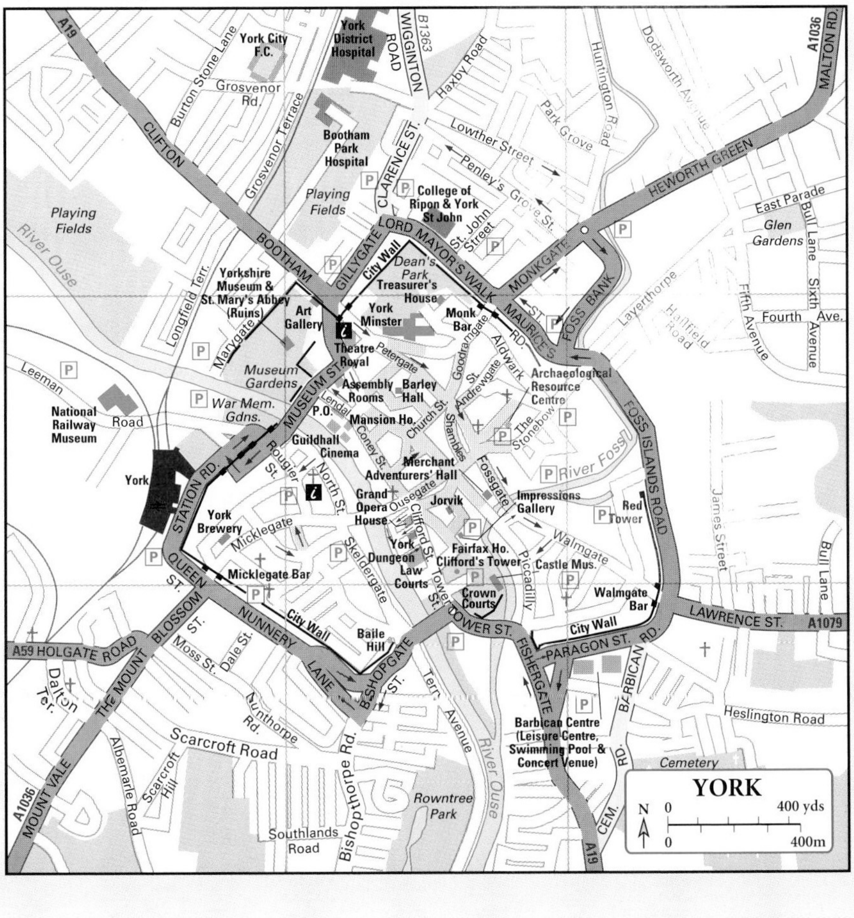

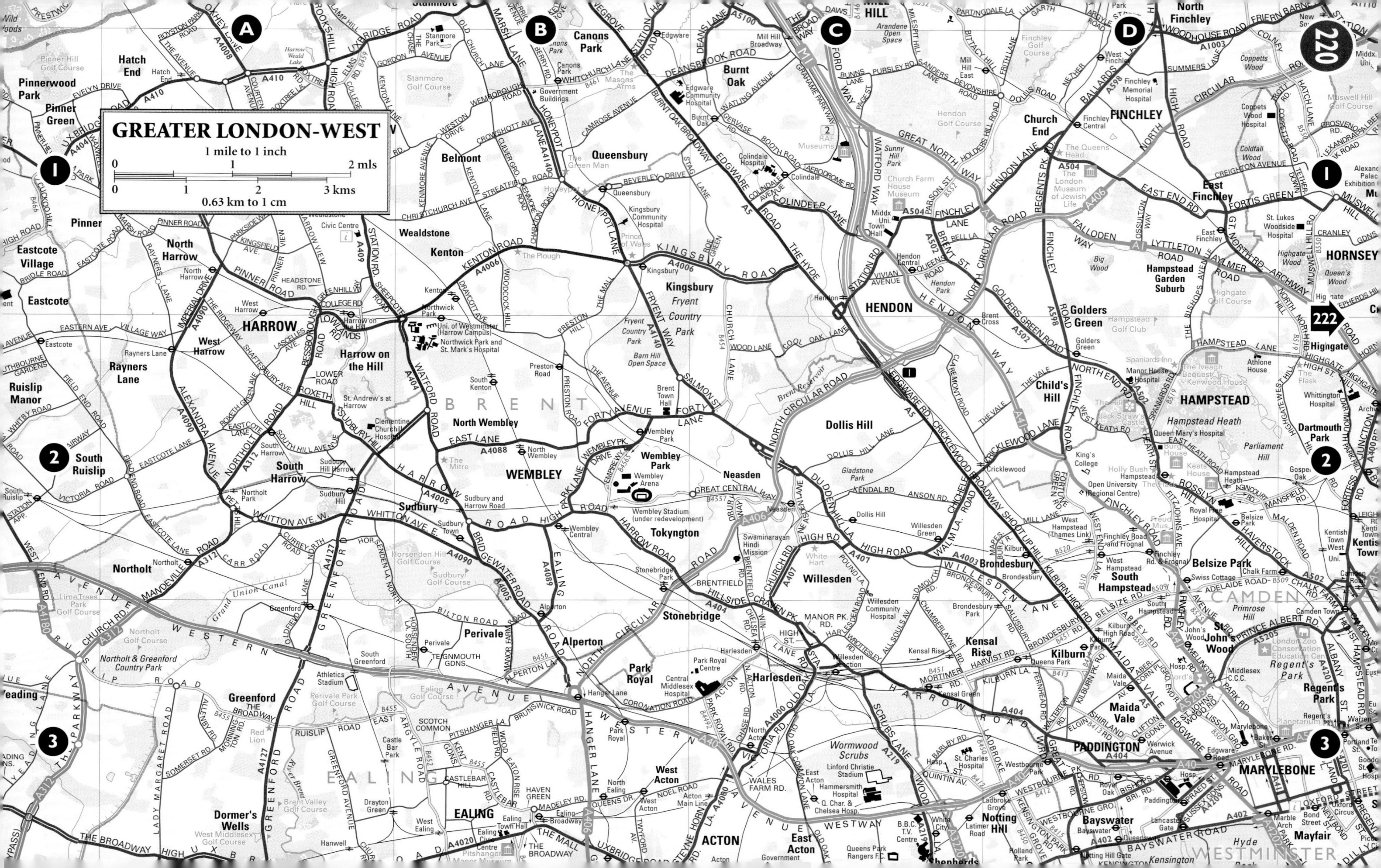

220
GREATER LONDON-WEST
1 mile to 1 inch
0
1
2 mls
0
1
2
3 kms
0.63 km to 1 cm
222
A
B
C
D
1
2
3
Pinnerwood Park
Pinner Green
Hatch End
Pinner
Eastcote Village
Eastcote
Ruislip Manor
Rayners Lane
South Ruislip
North Harrow
West Harrow
HARROW
Harrow on the Hill
South Harrow
Northolt
Greenford
Perivale
Dormer's Wells
EALING
Belmont
Wealdstone
Kenton
Queensbury
Canons Park
Burnt Oak
Kingsbury
North Wembley
WEMBLEY
Wembley Park
Sudbury
Alperton
Tokyngton
Stonebridge
Park Royal
West Acton
ACTON
East Acton
Neasden
Dollis Hill
Willesden
Harlesden
Kensal Rise
Kilburn
Maida Vale
PADDINGTON
MARYLEBONE
Bayswater
Mayfair
Notting Hill
HENDON
Church End
FINCHLEY
North Finchley
East Finchley
Golders Green
Child's Hill
Hampstead Garden Suburb
HAMPSTEAD
South Hampstead
Belsize Park
St. John's Wood
Regent's Park
Dartmouth Park
Highgate
HORNSEY
CAMDEN
BRENT
EALING
WESTMINSTER
Wormwood Scrubs
Hampstead Heath
Primrose Hill
Parliament Hill
Hyde Park
Kensington
Grand Union Canal
Brent Reservoir
River Brent
WATFORD WAY
EDGWARE ROAD
NORTH CIRCULAR ROAD
WESTERN AVENUE
HARROW ROAD
KINGSBURY ROAD
WATFORD ROAD
HANGER LANE
Wembley Stadium (under redevelopment)

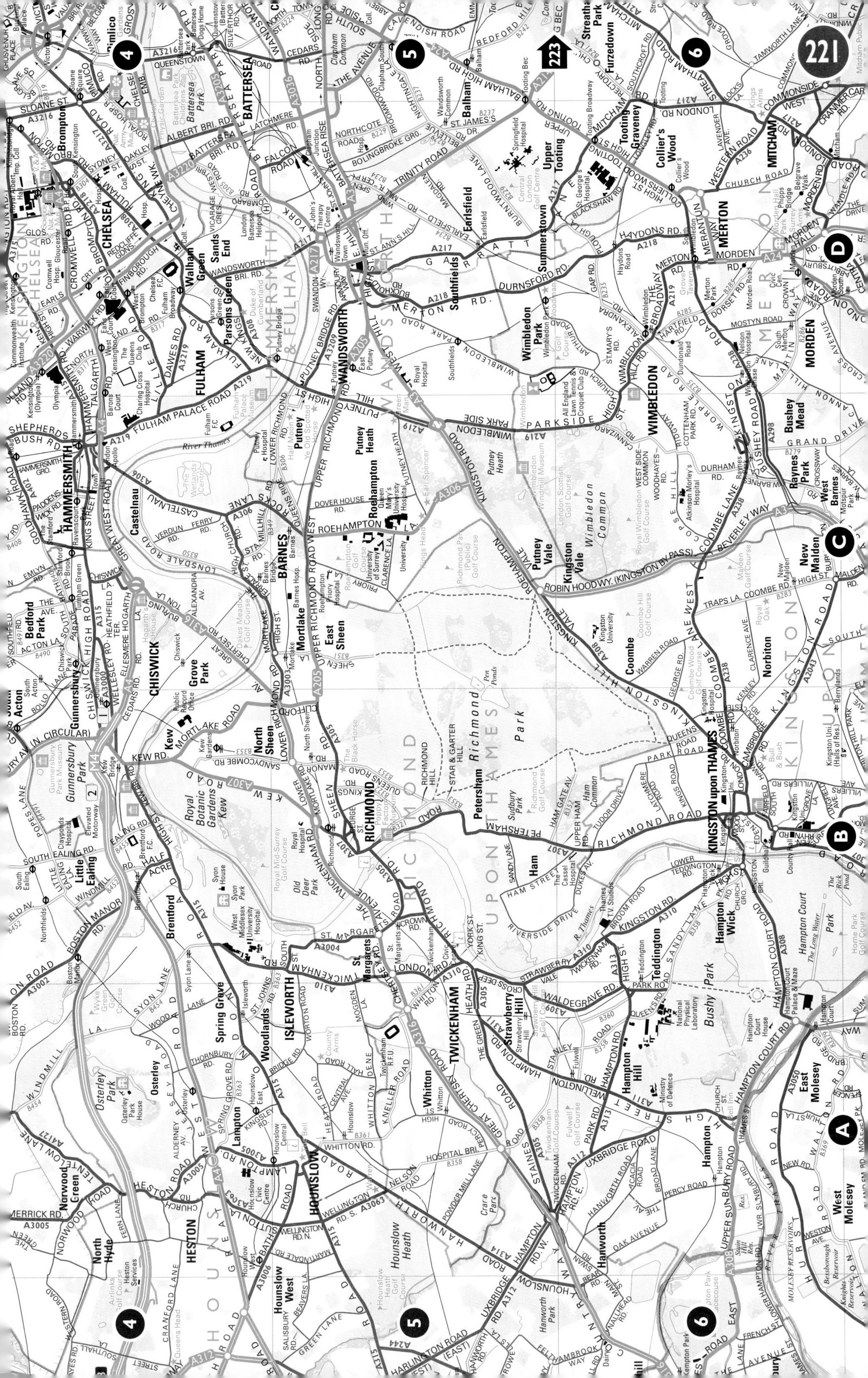
223
CHELSEA
BATTERSEA
Battersea Park
FULHAM
HAMMERSMITH
CHISWICK
BARNES
Putney
WANDSWORTH
Balham
Upper Tooting
Tooting Graveney
Collier's Wood
MITCHAM
MERTON
MORDEN
Summerstown
Earlsfield
Southfields
Wimbledon Park
WIMBLEDON
Wimbledon Common
Putney Heath
Roehampton
East Sheen
Mortlake
Kew
Royal Botanic Gardens Kew
RICHMOND
Richmond Park
Petersham
Ham
KINGSTON upon THAMES
Norbiton
Coombe
Kingston Vale
New Malden
Raynes Park
West Barnes
Bushey Mead
Brentford
ISLEWORTH
TWICKENHAM
Teddington
Hampton Wick
Hampton
Hampton Hill
Bushy Park
Hampton Court Park
East Molesey
West Molesey
Hanworth
HOUNSLOW
Hounslow West
Hounslow Heath
HESTON
Osterley
Lampton
Spring Grove
Woodlands
Whitton
Strawberry Hill
Little Ealing
Gunnersbury
Acton
Bedford Park
Grove Park
Castelnau
Walham Green
Sands End
Parsons Green
Pimlico
Brompton
North Hyde
Norwood Green
RICHMOND UPON THAMES
HAMMERSMITH & FULHAM
KENSINGTON & CHELSEA
WANDSWORTH
KINGSTON UPON THAMES
River Thames

222
GREATER LONDON-EAST
1 mile to 1 inch
0 1 2 mls
0 1 2 3 kms
0.63 km to 1 cm
220
TOTTENHAM
WOOD GREEN
HORNSEY
HARRINGAY
HAMPSTEAD
STOKE NEWINGTON
WALTHAMSTOW
WOODFORD
REDBRIDGE
ILFORD
BARKING
EAST HAM
LEYTON
Leytonstone
Stratford
Hackney
Dalston
Highbury
Barnsbury
Camden Town
Kentish Town
Muswell Hill
Crouch End
Highgate
Stamford Hill
Tottenham Hale
South Tottenham
Upper Edmonton
Higham Hill
South Woodford
Snaresbrook
Gants Hill
Cranbrook
Aldersbrook
Lea Bridge
Lower Clapton
Clapton Park
Hackney Wick
Old Ford
Bow
Mile End
Bethnal Green
Haggerston
Hoxton
Shoreditch
Whitechapel
Stepney
Shadwell
Wapping
Limehouse
Poplar
Bromley
Plaistow
Upton Park
West Ham
Canning Town
Custom House
Beckton
King's Cross
St. Pancras
Finsbury
Bloomsbury
Holborn
Marylebone
Soho
Mayfair
Regent's Park
Westminster
Camden
Islington
Hackney
Haringey
Waltham Forest
Tower Hamlets
Newham

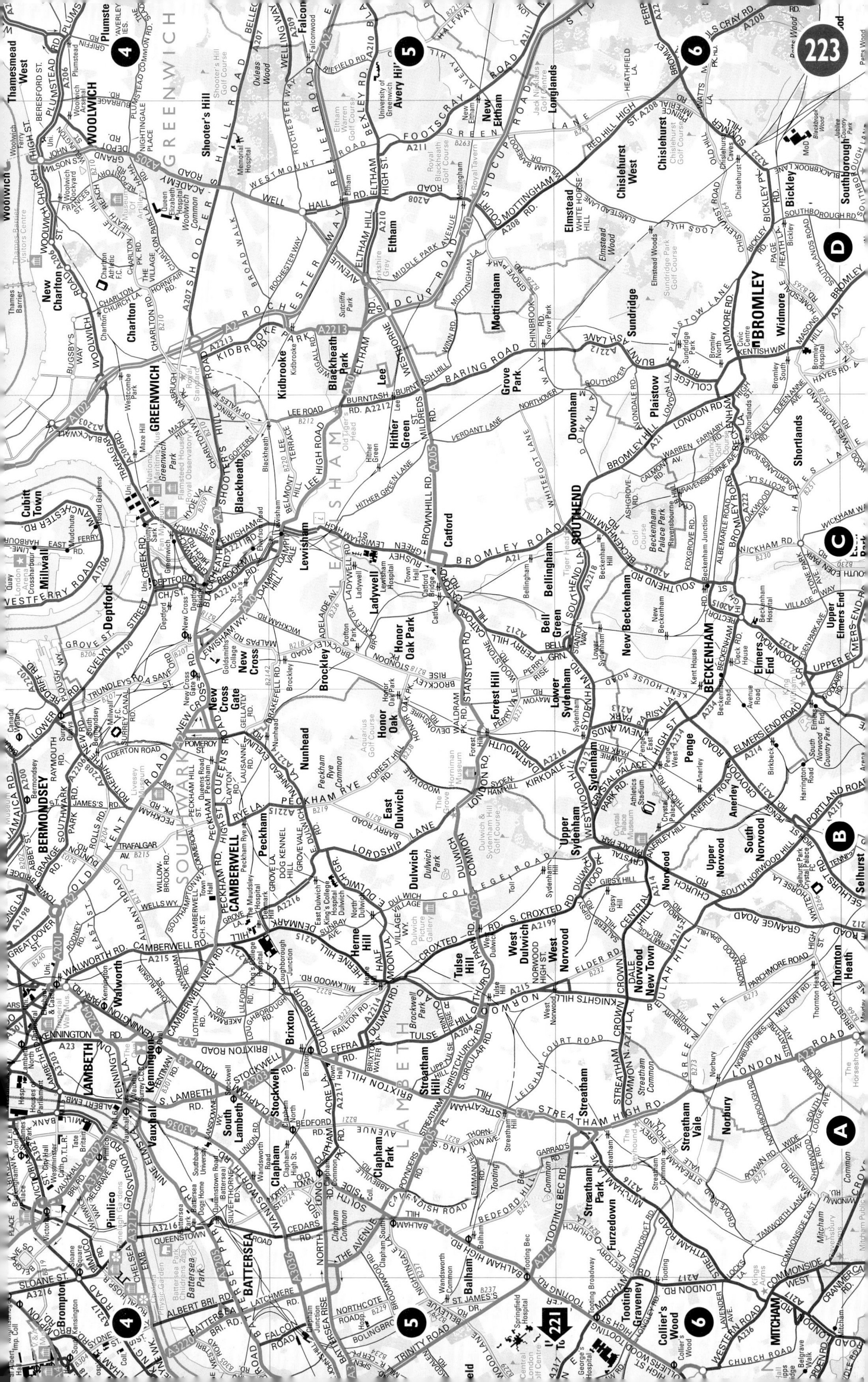

WOOLWICH
Thamesmead West
Plumstead
GREENWICH
Shooter's Hill
Avery Hill
New Eltham
Longlands
Eltham
Charlton
New Charlton
Kidbrooke
Blackheath Park
Lee
Mottingham
Chislehurst West
Chislehurst
Elmstead
Sundridge
BROMLEY
Bickley
Southborough
Widmore
Cubitt Town
Millwall
Deptford
Blackheath
Lewisham
Hither Green
Catford
Grove Park
Downham
Plaistow
Shortlands
BERMONDSEY
New Cross
New Cross Gate
Brockley
Ladywell
Honor Oak Park
Bellingham
SOUTHEND
Beckenham Palace Park
New Beckenham
BECKENHAM
Upper Elmers End
Elmers End
Nunhead
Peckham
Honor Oak
Forest Hill
Bell Green
Lower Sydenham
Sydenham
Penge
CAMBERWELL
East Dulwich
Dulwich
Upper Sydenham
Anerley
Crystal Palace Park
Upper Norwood
South Norwood
Norwood
Walworth
Herne Hill
Tulse Hill
West Dulwich
West Norwood
Dale Norwood
New Town
Thornton Heath
LAMBETH
Kennington
Vauxhall
Brixton
Stockwell
South Lambeth
Streatham Hill
Streatham
Streatham Vale
Norbury
Pimlico
Clapham
Clapham Park
Balham
Streatham Park
Furzedown
Tooting Graveney
Collier's Wood
MITCHAM
BATTERSEA
Brompton
LEWISHAM
SOUTHWARK
GREENWICH
LAMBETH

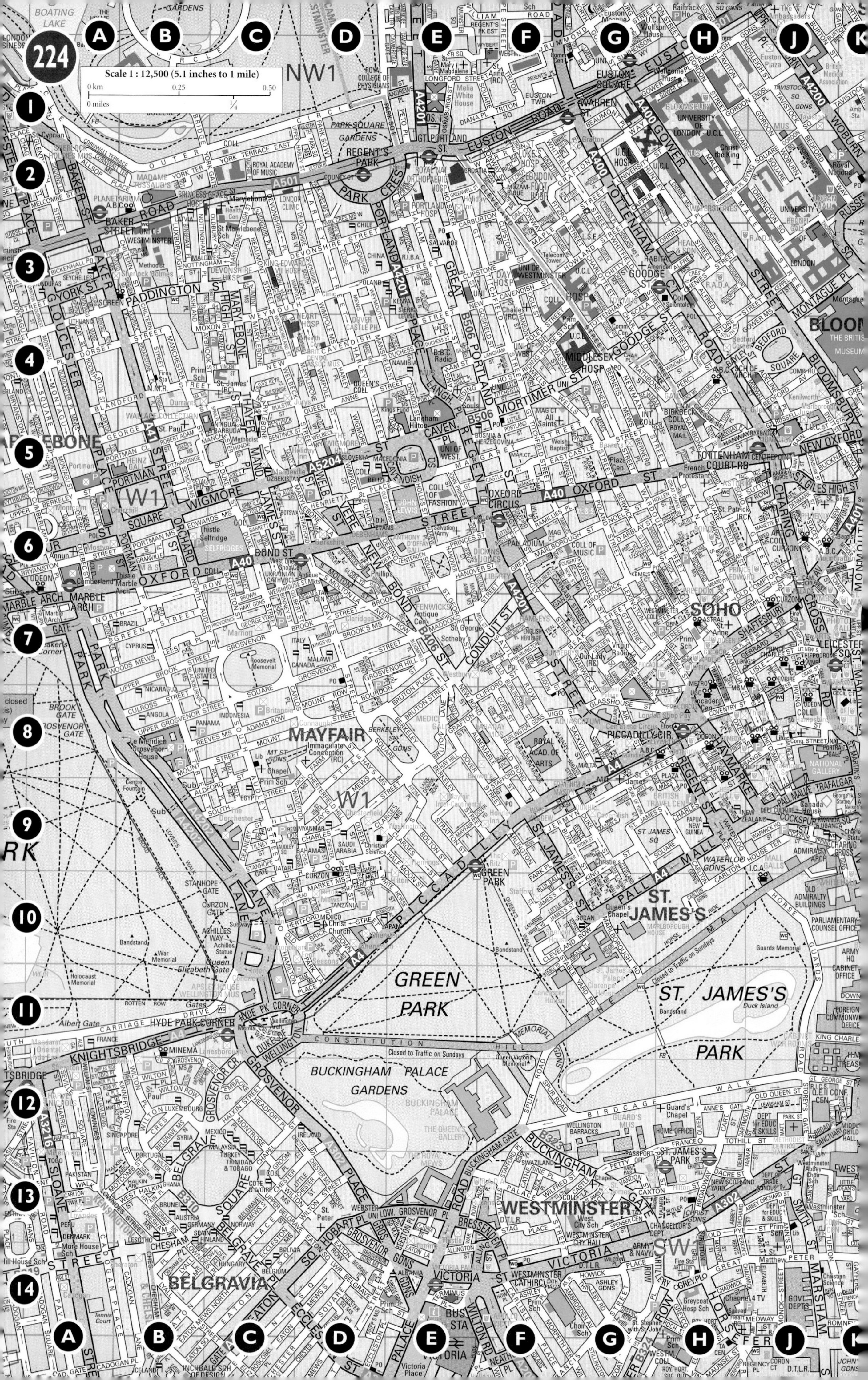
Scale 1 : 12,500 (5.1 inches to 1 mile)
0 km
0.25
0.50
0 miles
1/4
A
B
C
D
E
F
G
H
J
K
1
2
3
4
5
6
7
8
9
10
11
12
13
14
NW1
W1
SW1
MAYFAIR
SOHO
BELGRAVIA
WESTMINSTER
ST. JAMES'S
GREEN PARK
ST. JAMES'S PARK
BUCKINGHAM PALACE GARDENS
BUCKINGHAM PALACE
BOATING LAKE
PARK SQUARE GARDENS
EUSTON ROAD
MARYLEBONE ROAD
OXFORD STREET
PICCADILLY
PARK LANE
KNIGHTSBRIDGE
REGENT STREET
BAKER STREET
TOTTENHAM COURT RD
GOWER ST
CHARING CROSS RD
BLOOMSBURY
HAYMARKET
PALL MALL
THE MALL
CONSTITUTION HILL
BIRDCAGE WALK
VICTORIA ST
HYDE PARK CORNER
MARBLE ARCH
OXFORD CIRCUS
PICCADILLY CIR.
EUSTON SQUARE
GREAT PORTLAND ST.
REGENT'S PARK
WARREN ST.
GOODGE ST.
BOND ST.
GREEN PARK
VICTORIA
ST. JAMES'S PARK
SLOANE STREET
GROSVENOR PLACE
BUCKINGHAM PALACE ROAD
A501
A4201
A40
A4
A41
A5204
A4202
A302
B310
B506
A400
A4200
A3216
B323
Closed to Traffic on Sundays
UNIVERSITY OF LONDON
SELFRIDGES
JOHN LEWIS
NATIONAL GALLERY
ROYAL ACAD. OF ARTS
MADAME TUSSAUD'S
PLANETARIUM
WALLACE COLLECTION

K
L
M
N
P
Q
R
S
T
U
1
2
3
4
5
6
7
8
9
10
11
12
13
14
WC1
EC1
EC4
WC2
SE1
CLERKENWELL
HOLBORN
BARBICAN
STRAND
SOUTHWARK
THE BOROUGH
LAMBETH
ST. LUKE'S
RIVER THAMES
KING'S REACH
BLACKFRIARS
FARRINGDON
CHANCERY LANE
BARBICAN
ST. PAUL'S
MANSION HOUSE
TEMPLE
EMBANKMENT
WATERLOO
WATERLOO INTERNATIONAL
WATERLOO EAST
WESTMINSTER
LAMBETH NORTH
BOROUGH
CITY THAMESLINK
ST. PAUL'S CATHEDRAL
BARTHOLOMEW'S HOSPITAL
MOUNT PLEASANT MAIL CENTRE
LINCOLN'S INN FIELDS
GRAY'S INN GARDENS
ROYAL COURTS OF JUSTICE
SOMERSET HOUSE
HOUSES OF PARLIAMENT
ST. THOMAS' HOSP
TATE MODERN
ROYAL NATIONAL
IMAX
HAYWARD GALLERY
ROYAL FESTIVAL HALL
MILLENNIUM BRIDGE
BLACKFRIARS BRI
WATERLOO BRI
WESTMINSTER BRI
HUNGERFORD BRIDGE
VICTORIA EMBANKMENT
VICTORIA TOWER GARDENS
LAMBETH PALACE
IMPERIAL WAR MUS
GERALDINE MARY HARMSWORTH PARK
SOUTH BANK UNIVERSITY
ELEPHANT & CASTLE
ST. GEORGE'S CIRCUS
KINGSWAY
HOLBORN
FLEET ST
NEW BR ST
CHARTERHOUSE ST
CLERKENWELL RD
THEOBALD'S ROAD
GUILFORD ST
SOUTHAMPTON ROW
STAMFORD STREET
SOUTHWARK STREET
UPPER GROUND
THE CUT
BLACKFRIARS ROAD
WATERLOO ROAD
WESTMINSTER BR ROAD
LAMBETH ROAD
KENNINGTON ROAD
BOROUGH ROAD
BOROUGH HIGH ST
NEWINGTON CAUSEWAY
SOUTHWARK BRIDGE
LONDON WALL
NEWGATE ST
CHEAPSIDE
QUEEN VICTORIA ST
ALDERSGATE ST
GOSWELL RD
FARRINGDON RD
HMS PRESIDENT
H.Q.S. WELLINGTON Master Mariners'
OXO TWR WHARF
LONDON EYE
County Hall
JUBILEE GDNS
MILLBANK
ABINGDON ST
ARCHBISHOP'S PARK
PEABODY SQUARE
LAMBETH PALACE RD

Chandler's Ford
Valley Park
Nutburn
North Baddesley
Fryern Hill
Boyatt Wood
Highbridge
Nob's Crook
Stoke Common
Fish Pond
Crowdhill
Park Hills Wood
Bishopstoke
Pylehill
Lower Upham
EASTLEIGH
Chilworth
Chilworth Old Village
Toothill
M27
M3
ROWNHAMS SERVICES
Rownhams
Chilworth Common
Fair Oak
Itchen Vale
EASTLEIGH DISTRICT
North Stoneham
Southampton International Airport
Horton Heath
Winters
Lord's Wood
Lordswood
Bassett Green
Bassett
Swaythling
Durley
Lord's Hill
Aldermoor
Maybush
Coxford
Shirley Warren
Upper Shirley
Hampton Park
Highfield
Portswood
Bitterne Park
Townhill Park
Midanbury
Moorgreen
West End
Long Common
Boorley Green
Wimpson
Shirley
SOUTHAMPTON
Westwood Park
Bevois Mount
St. Denys
Bitterne
Harefield
Wildern
Curdridge
Millbrook
Freemantle
Banister's Park
Bevois Town
Newtown
Bedford Place
Northam
Thornhill Park
Thornhill
Botley
Kitnocks
Hedge End
Fourposts
Polygon
Merry Oak
Sholing Common
Peartree Green
Itchen
Weston Common
Sholing
Crosshouse
Botany Bay
Pleasant View
Old Netley
Windmill
Curbridge
Power Station
Cracknore Hard
Docks
River Test
Woolston
Town Quay
Platform Rd
Eastern Docks
Weston
Newtown
Lowford
Burridge
Swanwick Wood
Marchwood
Marchwood Park
West Wood
Netley Abbey
Butlocks Heath
Bursledon
Lower Swanwick
Swanwick
Whiteley
Hound
Park Gate
Sarisbury
Hythe Marina Village
Hythe
Dibden
Applemore
Marchwood Inclosure
NEW FOREST DISTRICT
Dibden Bottom
Dibden Purlieu
Langdown
Frostlane
Southampton Water
Holly Hill Woodland Park
Hamble-le-Rice
Locks Heath
Titchfield Common
Warsash
Fleetend
Abshot
Newtown
Hook
Hook Park
FAREHAM DISTRICT
Chilling
Solent Breezes
Brownwich
Fawley
Ashlett
Stonehills
Fawley Power Station
Ower
Calshot
Hillhead
Eaglehurst
THE SOLENT
Stanswood Bay
Stone Points
Stansore Point
St. Leonards Grange
Needs Ore Point
East Cowes ....................1 hours
SOUTHAMPTON
0 400 yds
0 400m
Northam Bridge
Northam Industrial Estate
Combined Courts Centre
YMCA
Royal South Hants. Hospital
Civic Centre
Southampton Central
Mayflower Theatre
Titanic Memorial
East Park
West Park
Civic Centre & Art Gallery
Southampton Institute
Marlands Shopping Centre
Palmerston Park
Houndwell Park
Hoglands Park
Southampton F.C.
West Quay Shopping Centre
Bargate Shopping Centre
East St. Shopping Centre
Southampton City College
Leisure World
The Quays Leisure Centre
Tudor House Museum
Tudor Merchant's Hall
Medieval Merchant's House
Maritime Museum
Mayflower Park
Southampton Hall of Aviation
Ocean Village
The Itchen Bridge (Toll)
Car Ferries to Isle of Wight
Gods House Tower Museum
Royal Pier (Closed)
Town Quay
Foot ferry to Hythe
Harbour Lights Cinema
Marina
River Itchen

## SOUTHAMPTON & PORTSMOUTH

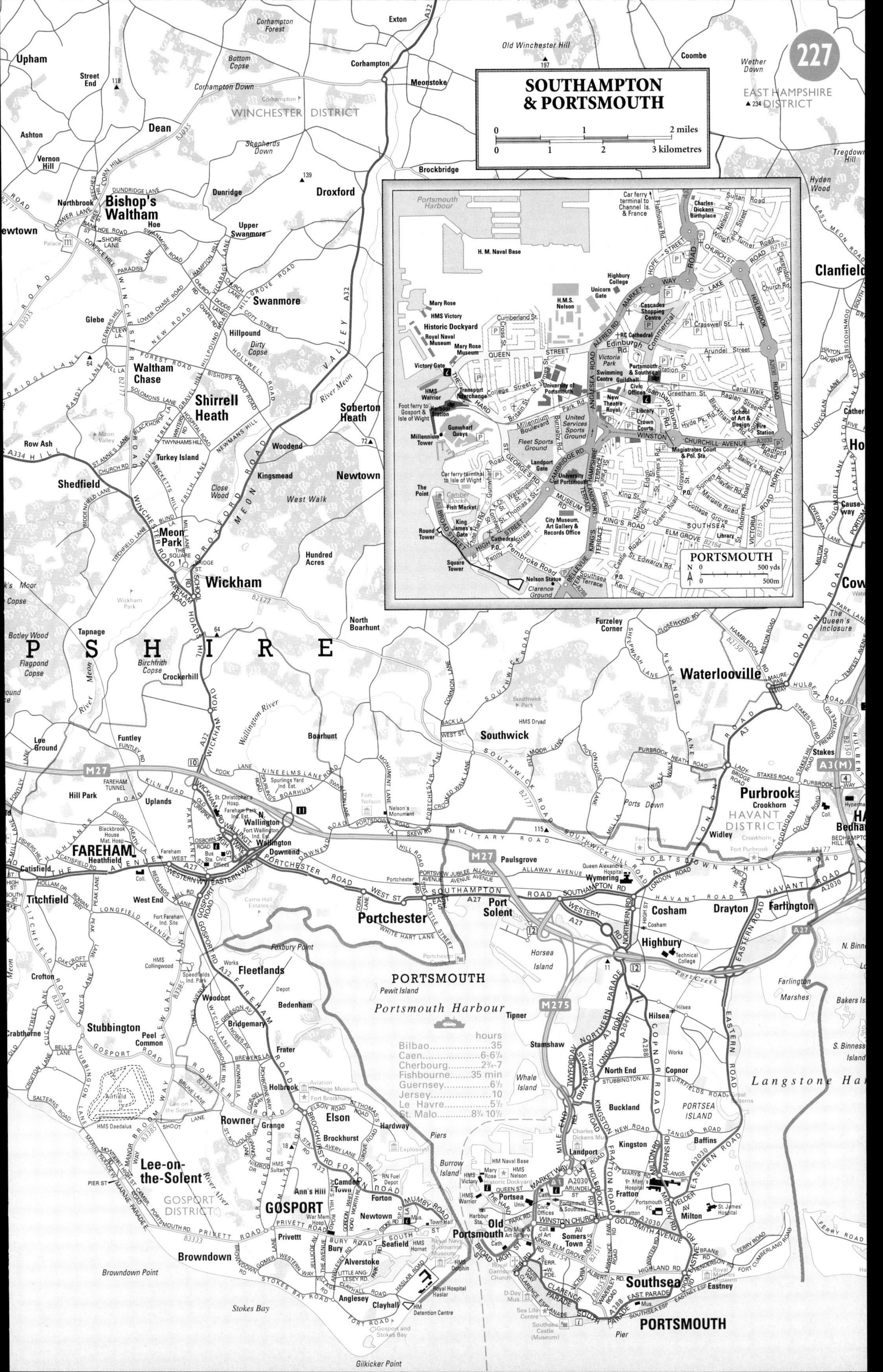

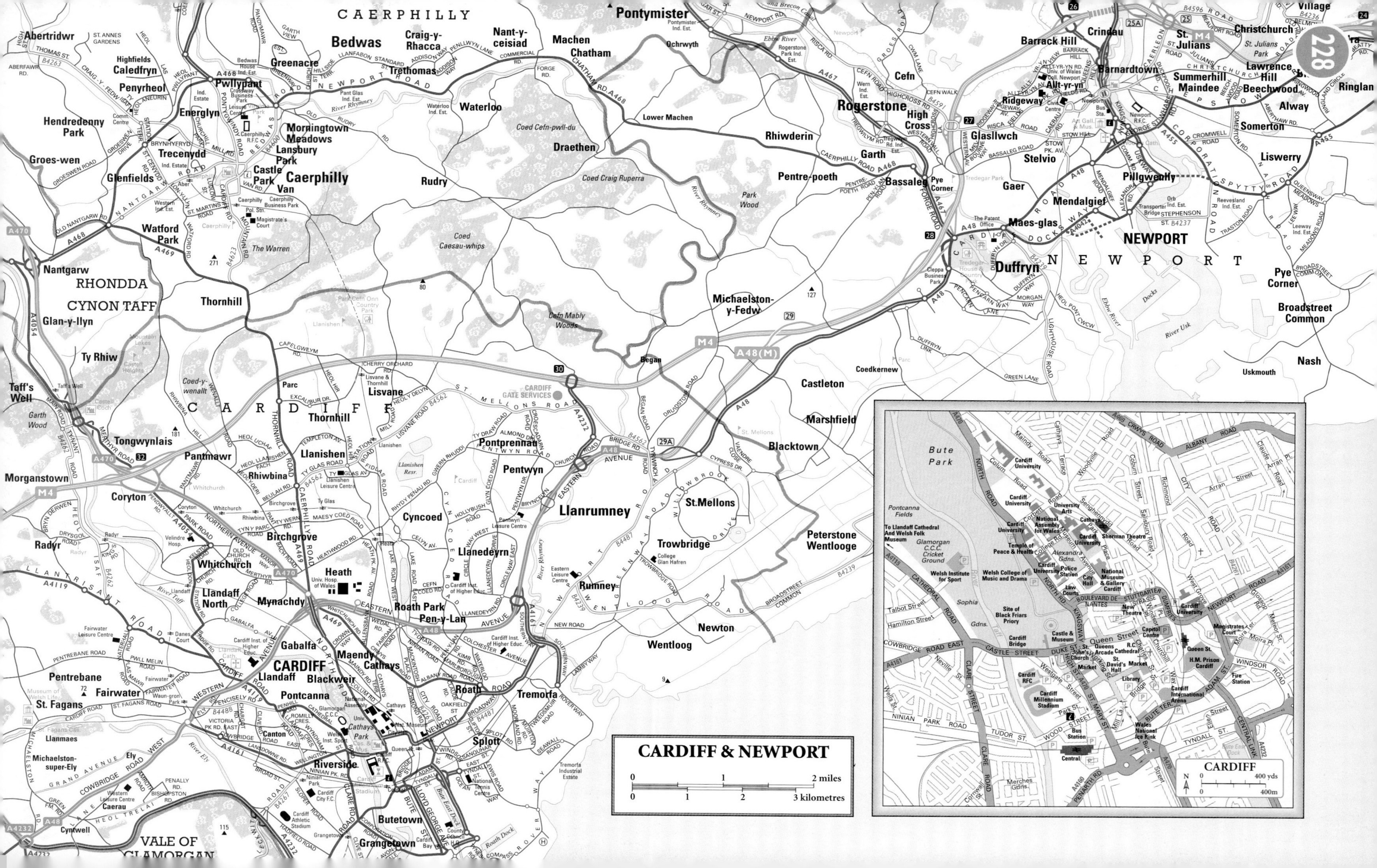
CARDIFF & NEWPORT
0 1 2 miles
0 1 2 3 kilometres
CARDIFF
400 yds
400m
CAERPHILLY
NEWPORT
CARDIFF
RHONDDA CYNON TAFF
VALE OF GLAMORGAN
Caerphilly
Bedwas
Pontymister
Rogerstone
Bassaleg
Maindee
St. Julians
Christchurch
Lliswerry
Pillgwenlly
Maes-glas
Duffryn
Marshfield
Castleton
Michaelston-y-Fedw
St.Mellons
Trowbridge
Llanrumney
Rumney
Pentwyn
Llanedeyrn
Cyncoed
Lisvane
Thornhill
Llanishen
Heath
Birchgrove
Rhiwbina
Whitchurch
Llandaff North
Llandaff
Gabalfa
Cathays
Roath
Splott
Tremorfa
Butetown
Grangetown
Riverside
Canton
Pontcanna
Fairwater
Ely
Caerau
St. Fagans
Radyr
Morganstown
Taff's Well
Tongwynlais
Nantgarw
Coryton
Peterstone Wentlooge
Wentloog
Newton
Blacktown
Coedkernew
Nash
Uskmouth
Broadstreet Common
Pye Corner
Somerton
Alway
Beechwood
Barnardtown
Crindau
Barrack Hill
Allt-yr-yn
Ridgeway
Gaer
Stelvio
Glasllwch
High Cross
Cefn
Garth
Pentre-poeth
Rhiwderin
Machen
Chatham
Draethen
Rudry
Waterloo
Trethomas
Craig-y-Rhacca
Nant-y-ceisiad
Lansbury Park
Van
Trecenydd
Energlyn
Penyrheol
Caledfryn
Abertridwr
Hendredenny Park
Groes-wen
Glenfields
Watford Park
Ty Rhiw
Glan-y-llyn
Pantmawr
Parc
Pontprennau
Roath Park
Pen-y-Lan
Maendy
Blackweir
Mynachdy
Pentrebane
Llanmaes
Michaelston-super-Ely
Cyntwell
Lower Machen
Ochrwyth
Began
Ringland
Lawrence Hill
Summerhill
Bute Park

BRISTOL
0 1 2 miles
0 1 2 3 kilometres
BRISTOL
SOUTH GLOUCESTERSHIRE
NORTH SOMERSET
BATH & NORTH EAST SOMERSET
Avonmouth
Shirehampton
Lawrence Weston
Henbury
Coombe Dingle
Sea Mills
Westbury-on-Trym
Patchway
Bradley Stoke
Little Stoke
Stoke Gifford
Filton
Southmead
Horfield
Henleaze
Westbury Park
Redland
Cotham
Clifton
Hotwells
Bishopston
Ashley Down
Montpelier
Lockleaze
Frenchay
Winterbourne
Frampton Cotterell
Yate
Chipping Sodbury
Westerleigh
Pucklechurch
Downend
Staple Hill
Fishponds
Stapleton
Eastville
Easton
St. George
Hanham
Brislington
Knowle
Bedminster
Ashton Vale
Long Ashton
Flax Bourton
Failand
Leigh Woods
Hengrove
Hartcliffe
Bishopsworth
Withywood
Stockwood
Keynsham
BRISTOL
200 yds
200m
229

230
WOLVERHAMPTON
WOLVERHAMPTON DISTRICT
WALSALL
Compton
Bentley
Birchills
Willenhall
Monmore Green
Moseley
Portobello
Darlaston Green
Pleck
Bradmore
Merry Hill
Stow Lawn
Caldmore
Palfrey
Bescot
Blakenhall
Priestfield
Darlaston
Fallings Heath
Goldthorn Park
Parkfield
Bilston
Woods Bank
Kings Hill
Wood Green
The Delves
Penn
Colton Hills
Ettingshall
Wednesbury
Spring Hill
Lanesfield
Spring Vale
Moxley
The Woods
Yew Tree
Ettingshall Park
Bradley
Lower Bradley
Church Hill
Mesty Croft
Cinder Hill
Friar Park
STAFFORDSHIRE
SOUTH STAFFORDSHIRE DISTRICT
Coseley
Wednesbury Oak
Stone Cross
Gospel End
Sedgley
Hurst Hill
Princes End
Ocker Hill
Balls Hill
Hateley Heath
Wallbrook
Golds Green
Hill Top
Roseville
Summer Hill
Charlemont
Bramford
Bloomfield
Toll End
Black Lake
Wombourn
Upper Gornal
Tipton Green
Harvills Hawthorn
Churchfield
Horseley Heath
Tipton
Ruiton
Swan Village
Lyndon
Himley
Lower Gornal
Guns Village
New Town
West Bromwich
Redhall
Dudley Port
Gornalwood
SANDWELL DISTRICT
Eve Hill
London Fields
Burnt Tree
Tividale
Wall Heath
DUDLEY
Kate's Hill
Brades Village
Russell's Hall
Dixon's Green
Oakham
Darby's Hill
Rounds Green
SANDWELL
Pensnett
Woodside
Oldbury
Langley
Rood End
Kingswinford
Baptist End
Summer Hill
Netherton
Portway
Bromley
Mount Pleasant
Brockmoor
Darby End
The Knowle
Smethwick
Langley Green
Primrose Hill
Rowley Regis
Causeway Green
Wordsley
Buckpool
Brierley Hill
Bowling Green
Ross
Bristnall Fields
Bearwood
Hawbush
Dudley Wood
Old Hill
Blackheath
Audnam
Withymoor Village
Quarry Bank
Cradley Heath
Warley
Amblecote
DUDLEY DISTRICT
Cockshot
Amblecote Bank
Haden Cross
Hurst Green
Dunn's Bank
Netherend
STOURBRIDGE
Overend
Coombeswood
Wollaston
Holloway End
Cradley
Quinton
Ridgacre
Harborne
High Park
Stambermill
Lye
The Hayes
Hawne
Belle Vale
Wollescote
HALESOWEN
Gigmill
Lapal
Hasbury
Spring Hill
Moor Street
California
Lodge
Woodgate
Bartley Green
Weoley Castle
Hunnington
Illey
Shenley Fields
Romsley
Frankley
Northfield
Romsley Hill
Dayhouse Bank
Rubery
Rednal
Longbridge
WORCESTERSHIRE
BROMSGROVE
Turves
Cofton Hackett
Fairfield
BIRMINGHAM
200 yds
200m

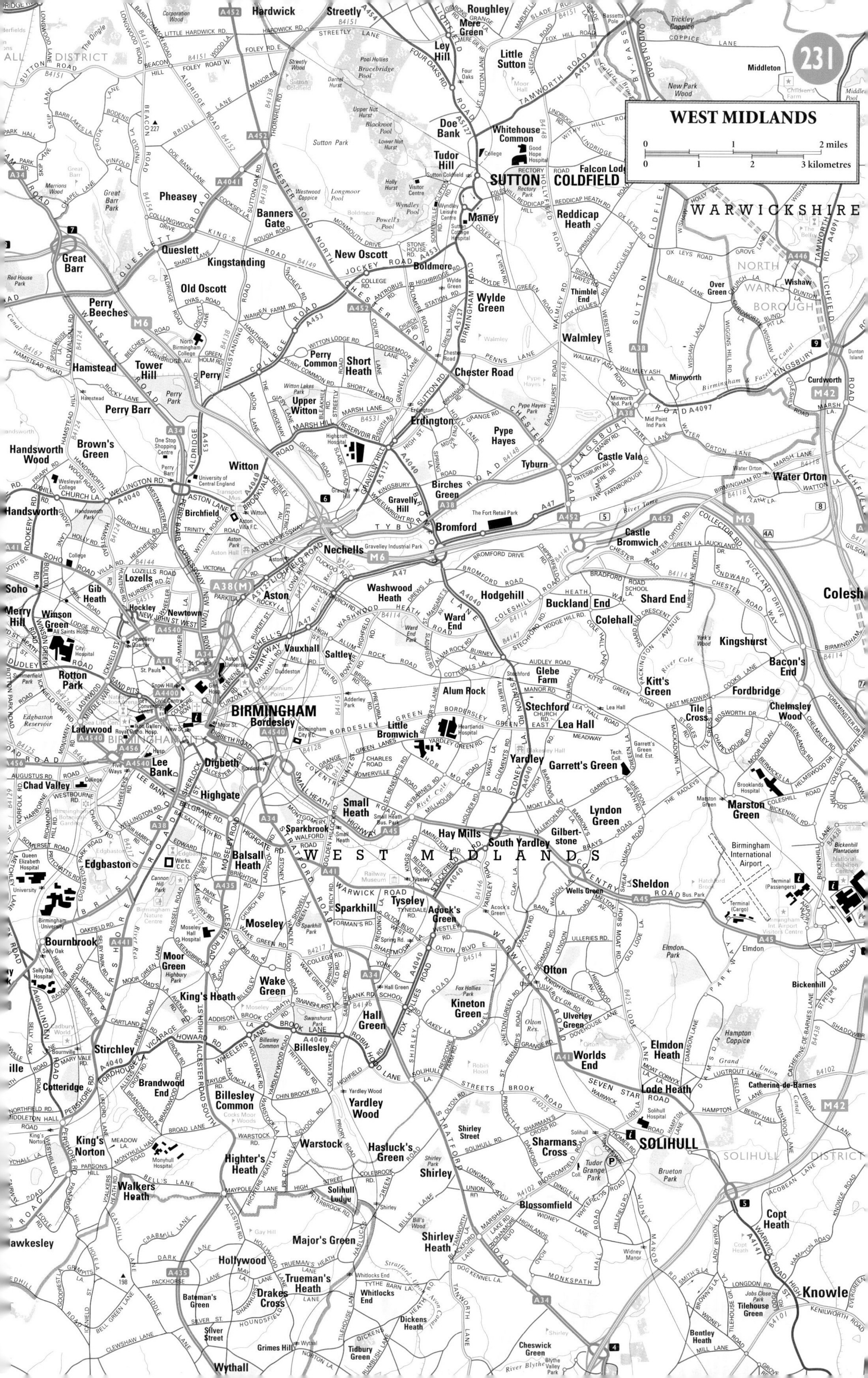
WEST MIDLANDS
0 1 2 miles
0 1 2 3 kilometres
WARWICKSHIRE
NORTH WARKS BOROUGH
SOLIHULL DISTRICT
WEST MIDLANDS
BIRMINGHAM
SUTTON COLDFIELD
SOLIHULL
Hardwick
Streetly
Roughley
Mere Green
Ley Hill
Little Sutton
Middleton
Doe Bank
Whitehouse Common
Tudor Hill
Falcon Lodge
Pheasey
Banners Gate
Maney
Reddicap Heath
Great Barr
Queslett
Kingstanding
New Oscott
Boldmere
Old Oscott
Perry Beeches
Wylde Green
Over Green
Wishaw
Walmley
Hamstead
Tower Hill
Perry
Perry Common
Short Heath
Chester Road
Minworth
Curdworth
Perry Barr
Upper Witton
Erdington
Pype Hayes
Handsworth Wood
Brown's Green
Witton
Tyburn
Castle Vale
Water Orton
Handsworth
Birchfield
Birches Green
Gravelly Hill
Bromford
Castle Bromwich
Soho
Lozells
Nechells
Gib Heath
Aston
Washwood Heath
Hodgehill
Buckland End
Shard End
Coleshill
Winson Green
Merry Hill
Hockley
Newtown
Ward End
Colehall
Kingshurst
Vauxhall
Saltley
Rotton Park
Glebe Farm
Bacon's End
Kitt's Green
Fordbridge
Alum Rock
Stechford
Tile Cross
Chelmsley Wood
Ladywood
Bordesley
Little Bromwich
Lea Hall
Lee Bank
Digbeth
Yardley
Garrett's Green
Chad Valley
Highgate
Small Heath
Marston Green
Sparkbrook
Hay Mills
South Yardley
Lyndon Green
Gilbertstone
Edgbaston
Balsall Heath
Birmingham International Airport
Sheldon
Tyseley
Sparkhill
Acock's Green
Bournbrook
Moseley
Moor Green
Wake Green
Olton
Elmdon
Bickenhill
King's Heath
Hall Green
Kineton Green
Ulverley Green
Stirchley
Billesley
Worlds End
Elmdon Heath
Cotteridge
Brandwood End
Lode Heath
Catherine-de-Barnes
Billesley Common
Yardley Wood
Shirley Street
Sharmans Cross
King's Norton
Warstock
Highter's Heath
Hasluck's Green
Shirley
Walkers Heath
Solihull Lodge
Blossomfield
Copt Heath
Hawkesley
Major's Green
Shirley Heath
Hollywood
Trueman's Heath
Drakes Cross
Whitlocks End
Knowle
Bateman's Green
Tilehouse Green
Dickens Heath
Bentley Heath
Silver Street
Grimes Hill
Tidbury Green
Cheswick Green
Wythall
M6
M42
A38(M)
A38
A452
A34
A45
A41
A435
A441
A4040
A47
A5127
A453

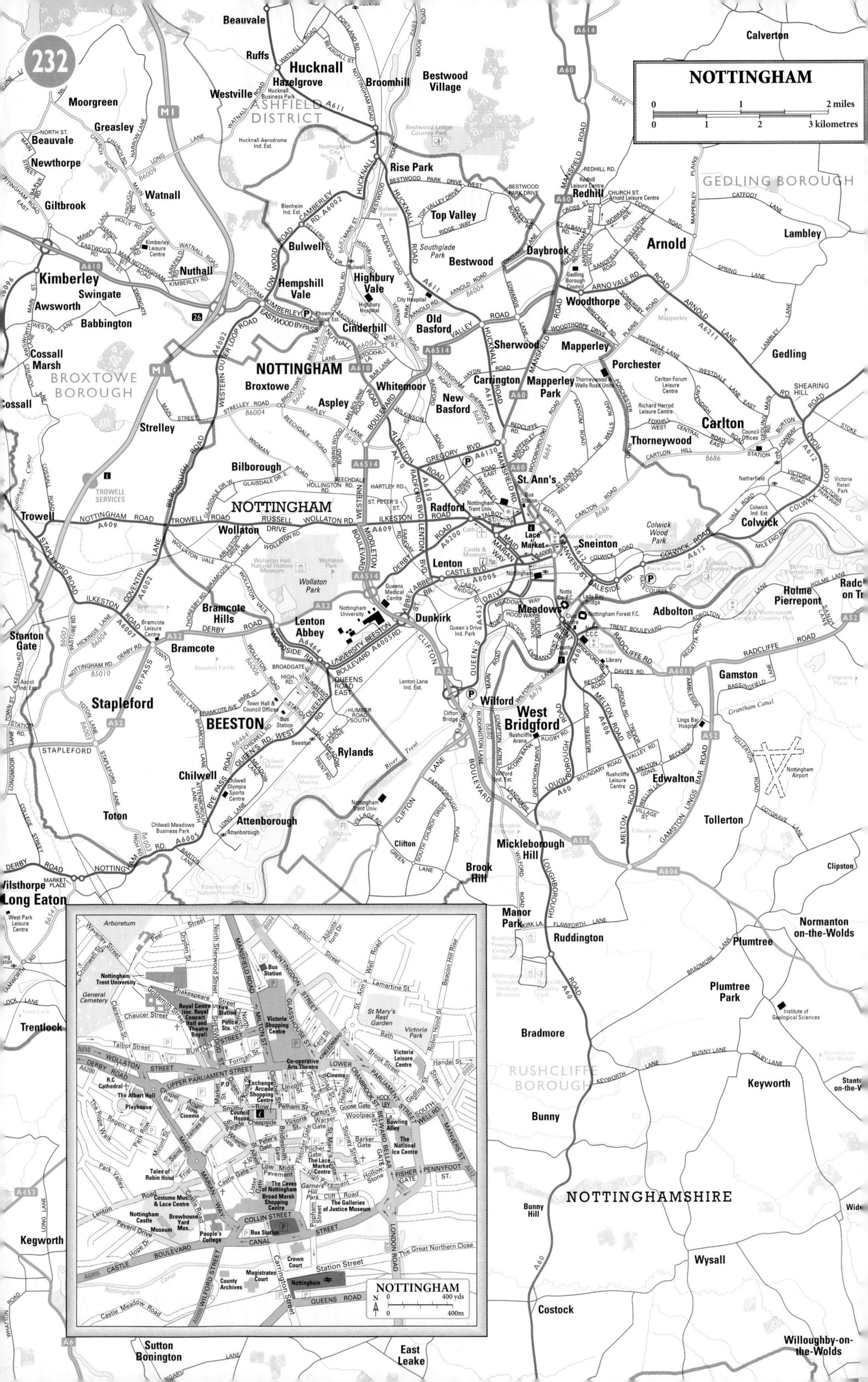
NOTTINGHAM
0 1 2 miles
0 1 2 3 kilometres
Beauvale
Ruffs
Hucknall
Hazelgrove
Westville
Broomhill
Bestwood Village
Calverton
Moorgreen
Greasley
Beauvale
Newthorpe
Watnall
Giltbrook
ASHFIELD DISTRICT
Hucknall Aerodrome Ind. Est.
Bestwood Lodge Country Park
Rise Park
Top Valley
Redhill
GEDLING BOROUGH
Lambley
Arnold
Daybrook
Bestwood
Bulwell
Nuthall
Kimberley
Swingate
Awsworth
Babbington
Hempshill Vale
Highbury Vale
Old Basford
Cinderhill
Woodthorpe
Sherwood
Mapperley
Porchester
Gedling
Cossall Marsh
BROXTOWE BOROUGH
Cossall
NOTTINGHAM
Broxtowe
Whitemoor
Aspley
Carrington
Mapperley Park
New Basford
Carlton
Thorneywood
Strelley
Bilborough
St. Ann's
TROWELL SERVICES
Trowell
Wollaton
Radford
Sneinton
Colwick
Colwick Wood Park
Wollaton Park
Lenton
Lace Market
Holme Pierrepont
Adbolton
Bramcote Hills
Lenton Abbey
Dunkirk
Meadows
Stanton Gate
Bramcote
Gamston
Stapleford
Wilford
West Bridgford
BEESTON
Rylands
Edwalton
Chilwell
Tollerton
Nottingham Airport
Toton
Attenborough
Clifton
Mickleborough Hill
Brook Hill
Clipston
Wilsthorpe
Long Eaton
Manor Park
Ruddington
Normanton on-the-Wolds
Plumtree
Plumtree Park
Trentlock
Bradmore
RUSHCLIFFE BOROUGH
Keyworth
Bunny
NOTTINGHAMSHIRE
Bunny Hill
Kegworth
Wysall
Costock
Sutton Bonington
East Leake
Willoughby-on-the-Wolds
A60
A52
A606
A6005
A6514
A609
A610
A611
A612
A614
A6211
A453
A6
M1
NOTTINGHAM
400 yds
400m
Arboretum
Nottingham Trent University
General Cemetery
Royal Centre (inc. Royal Concert Hall and Theatre Royal)
Victoria Shopping Centre
Bus Station
St Mary's Rest Garden
Victoria Park
Victoria Leisure Centre
Co-operative Arts Theatre
R.C. Cathedral
The Albert Hall
Playhouse
Exchange Arcade Shopping Centre
Council House
The National Ice Centre
The Lace Market Centre
Tales of Robin Hood
Costume Mus. & Lace Centre
Nottingham Castle Museum
Brewhouse Yard Mus.
People's College
The Caves of Nottingham Broad Marsh Shopping Centre
The Galleries of Justice Museum
Crown Court
Magistrates Court
County Archives
Nottingham
Canal
Castle Boulevard
Maid Marian Way
Mansfield Road
Huntingdon Street
Lower Parliament Street
Upper Parliament Street
Wollaton Street
Derby Road
Carrington Street
London Road
Queens Road
Station Street
Collin Street
Wilford Street
Castle Meadow Road
The Great Northern Close

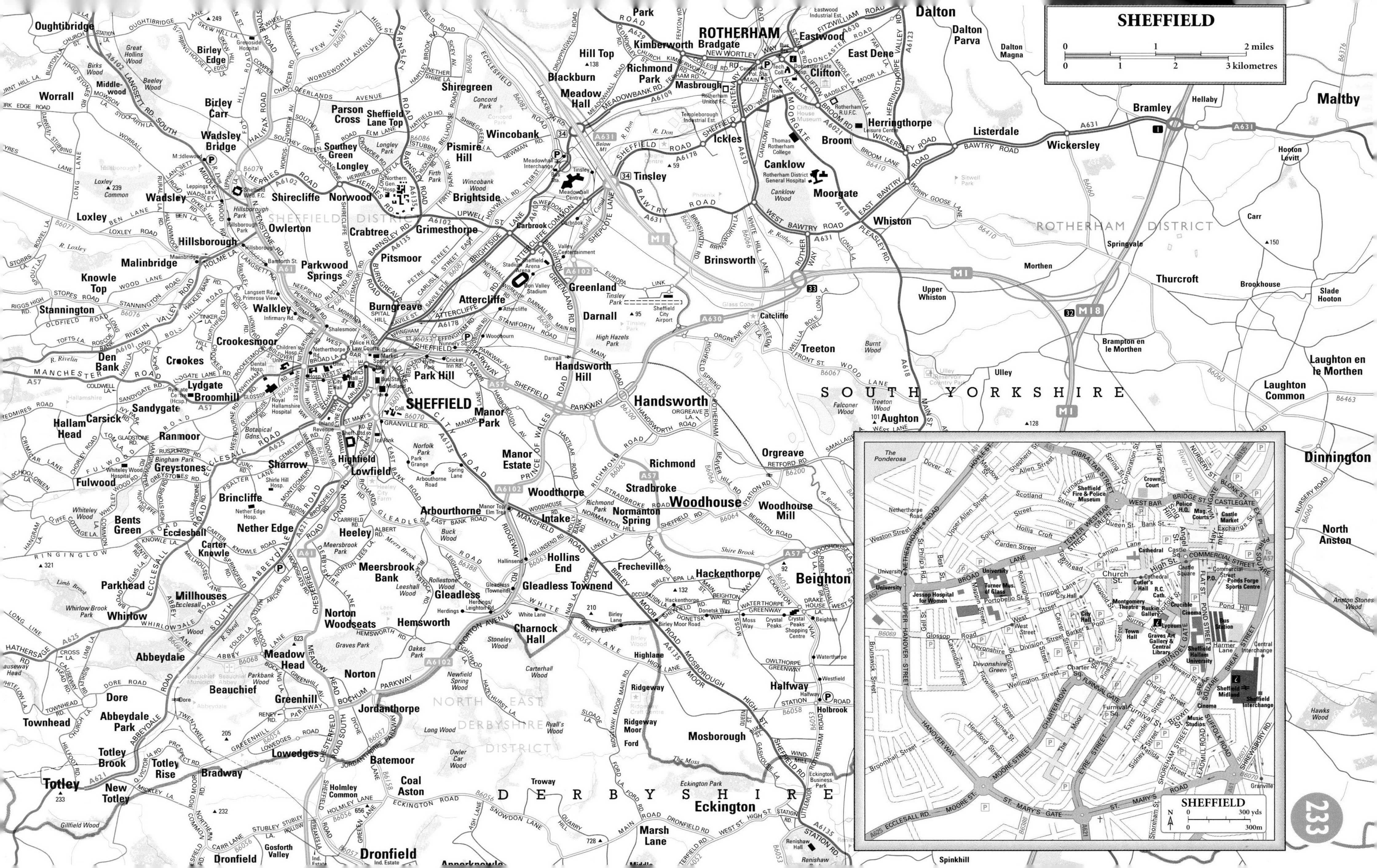
SHEFFIELD
0 1 2 miles
0 1 2 3 kilometres
ROTHERHAM
Dalton
Dalton Parva
Dalton Magna
Maltby
Bramley
Hellaby
Hooton Levitt
Wickersley
Listerdale
Carr
Thurcroft
Brookhouse
Slade Hooton
Laughton en le Morthen
Laughton Common
Brampton en le Morthen
Morthen
Springvale
ROTHERHAM DISTRICT
Upper Whiston
Whiston
Moorgate
Canklow
Broom
Herringthorpe
Clifton
East Dene
Eastwood
Bradgate
Kimberworth
Park
Hill Top
Richmond Park
Masbrough
Blackburn
Meadow Hall
Ickles
Tinsley
Brinsworth
Catcliffe
Treeton
Ulley
Aughton
SOUTH YORKSHIRE
Dinnington
North Anston
Oughtibridge
Worrall
Birley Edge
Birley Carr
Wadsley Bridge
Wadsley
Loxley
Hillsborough
Malinbridge
Knowle Top
Stannington
Shiregreen
Parson Cross
Sheffield Lane Top
Southey Green
Longley
Wincobank
Pismire Hill
Brightside
Shirecliffe
Norwood
Owlerton
Crabtree
Grimesthorpe
Pitsmoor
Parkwood Springs
Walkley
Burngreave
Attercliffe
Greenland
Darnall
Handsworth Hill
Handsworth
Crookesmoor
Crookes
Den Bank
Lydgate
Broomhill
Sandygate
Hallam Head
Carsick
Ranmoor
Park Hill
SHEFFIELD
Manor Park
Manor Estate
Highfield
Lowfield
Sharrow
Greystones
Fulwood
Bents Green
Ecclesall
Brincliffe
Nether Edge
Carter Knowle
Heeley
Arbourthorne
Woodthorpe
Intake
Richmond
Stradbroke
Normanton Spring
Woodhouse
Woodhouse Mill
Orgreave
Beighton
Hackenthorpe
Frecheville
Hollins End
Gleadless Townend
Gleadless
Meersbrook Bank
Norton Woodseats
Hemsworth
Charnock Hall
Millhouses
Parkhead
Whirlow
Abbeydale
Meadow Head
Norton
Beauchief
Greenhill
Jordanthorpe
Dore
Abbeydale Park
Townhead
Totley Brook
Totley Rise
Totley
New Totley
Bradway
Lowedges
Batemoor
Coal Aston
Dronfield
Holmley Common
Gosforth Valley
Mosborough
Halfway
Holbrook
Highlane
Ridgeway
Ridgeway Moor
Ford
Eckington
Marsh Lane
Troway
Spinkhill
NORTH EAST DERBYSHIRE DISTRICT
DERBYSHIRE
SHEFFIELD DISTRICT
SHEFFIELD
0 300 yds
0 300m
233

MERSEYSIDE
0 1 2 miles
0 1 2 3 kilometres
SEFTON DISTRICT
LIVERPOOL DISTRICT
WIRRAL DISTRICT
ELLESMERE PORT AND NESTON DISTRICT
KNOWSLEY DISTRICT
LIVERPOOL BAY
Crosby Channel
River Mersey
hours
Belfast...................7½
Douglas............2½-4
Dublin...............3¾-8
Blundellsands
Great Crosby
CROSBY
Waterloo
Waterloo Park
Litherland
Buckley Hill
Aintree
Kirkby
Westvale
Northwood
Southdene
Seaforth
Orrell
Fazakerley
Gillmoss
Croxteth
Knowsley
BOOTLE
Walton
Dog and Gun
Norris Green
West Derby
New Brighton
Kirkdale
Anfield
Clubmoor
Tuebrook
WALLASEY
Liscard
Egremont
Stoneycroft
Old Swan
Knotty Ash
Woolfall Heath
Fincham
Dovecot
Huyton with Roby
Page Moss
Roby
Swanside
Huyton Park
Everton
Fairfield
LIVERPOOL
Poulton
Seacombe
Court Hey
Bowring Park
Edge Hill
Childwall
Claughton
BIRKENHEAD
Princes Park
Netherley
Belle Vale
Gateacre
Toxteth
Dingle
St Michael's Hamlet
Mossley Hill
Oxton
Tranmere
Prenton
Rock Ferry
Calderstones
Woolton
Aigburth
Allerton
Otterspool
Grassendale
Halewood
Higher Bebington
Woodhey
New Ferry
Hunts Cross
Storeton
BEBINGTON
Bromborough Pool
Lower Bebington
Port Sunlight
Garston
Speke
MERSEYSIDE
Brimstage
Poulton
Liverpool John Lennon Airport
Bromborough
Thornton Hough
Eastham
Brookhurst
Raby
Willaston
Hooton
Childer Thornton
ELLESMERE PORT
Overpool
Little Sutton
Stanlow
Ness
Greater Sutton
Whitby
M53
M57
M62
A5036
A580
A59
A57
A562
A561
A41
A550
A5032

Rainford
Billinge
Chadwick
Garswood
Ashton in Makerfield
WIGAN DISTRICT
Golborn
Mill Lane Ind. Est.
Lion House Wood
Moss Bank
Clinkham Wood
Carr Mill Dam
Haydock Park Race Course
Haydock Ind. Est.
Haydock Park
EAST LANCASHIRE ROAD
St Helen's R.U.F.C
Denton's Green
Newtown
Eccleston
Eccleston Mere
West Park
Victoria Park
ST. HELENS
ST. HELENS DISTRICT
Town Hall
World Of Glass
Blackbrook
Haydock
Parr
Broad Oak
Derbyshire Hill
Newton-le-Willows
Town of Lowton
Newton Lake
Newton-le-Willows
Earlestown
Sankey Valley Industrial Estate
Collins Green
Wargrave
Vulcan Village
SIDE
Grange Park
Toll Bar
Ravenhead
Peasley Cross
Sherdley Ind. Est.
St Helen's Hosp.
Parr Moss
Sutton Moss
Sutton Oak
Knowsley Safari Park
Grange Park
Portico
Thatto Heath
Sutton Park
Sherdley Park
St. Helen's Junction
Bold Power Sta.
Reginald Road Industrial Estate
Eccleston Park
Prescot
Mus. of Clock & Watchmaking
Nutgrove
Sutton Heath
Marshall's Cross
Sutton Leach
Burtonwood
Alder Root
Hollins Park Hosp.
Winwick
Holt
Rainhill
Clock Face
BURTONWOOD SERVICES
Gemini Bus. Park
Winwick Quay
Hulme
Poulton Park
Whiston Cross
Whiston
Whiston Hospital
Stadt Moers Park
Windy Arbor
Rainhill Stoops
Blundells Hill
Sutton Manor
Callands
Longford
Dallam
Bewsey
Bewsey Old Hall
Old Hall
Bold Heath
Lingley Green
WARRINGTON
Sankey for Penketh
Great Sankey
Town End
Cronton
Lunts Heath
Penketh
Sankey Bridges
Warrington Hosp.
Bank Quay
Warrington R.L.F.C
WARRINGTON
Centre Park
Tarbock Green
Farnworth
Crow Wood
Cuerdley Cross
Hough Green
Widnes
Appleton
Power Sta.
River Mersey
Halton
Lower Walton
Ditton
Ball o' Ditton
Kingsway
Widnes R.L.F.C.
Moss Bank
Lugs Dale
St. Helen's Canal (Dis.)
Birch Wood
Hillcliffe
Everite Ind. Estate
St. Michael Jubilee
Municipal Building
Woodend
WIDNES
Manchester Ship Canal
Bridgewater Canal
Higher Walton
Walton Hall Gardens
West Bank Dock Estate
West Bank
Halton Chemical Industry Museum
Hale Road Ind. Estate
Hale Bank
Runcorn Bridge
HALTON
Astmoor
Castlefields
Expressway Ind. Estate
Runcorn
Town Hall
Halton Brook
RUNCORN
Hale
Weston Point
Grange
Runcorn
Weston
Beechwood
Astmoor Ind. Estate
Frodsham Marshes
Frodsham Score
VALE ROYAL BOROUGH
IRE
Ince Marshes
Frodsham
Frodsham Bridge
Marsh Green
Overton
Netherton
Bradley
Acton Bridge
Ince and Elton
Woodhouses
LIVERPOOL
Eaton St.
Gascoyne St.
Naylor Street
Freemasons Row
Paisley St.
Leeds Street
Midghall St.
Addison St.
Police Station
Liverpool John Moores University (JMU)
Liverpool JMU
Mercury Court
Cotton Exchange
Moorfields (Underground)
Municipal Offices
Mersey Tunnel Entrance (Toll)
Liverpool Museum
Walker Art Gallery
Picton Library
William Brown St.
St. Johns Garden
St. George's Hall
Coach Sta.
London Rd.
Empire Theatre
Lime St. (Main Line and Underground)
Mersey Tunnel Exit
Western Approaches Museum
Town Hall
Dublin & Isle of Man Ferry Terminal
Princes Parade
Conservation Centre
Queen's Sq.
Bus Station
Royal Court Theatre
St. John's Precinct
Liverpool Playhouse
The Beacon
Royal Liver Building
Passport Office
Matthew St. Cavern Club
Cunard Building
James St. (U/G)
Port of Liverpool Building
Georges Pierhead
Derby Sq.
Queen Elizabeth II Crown Court
Church Street
Clayton Sq. Shopping Centre
Neptune Theatre
Bluecoat Arts Centre
Central (Underground)
Mersey Ferry Terminal
Bus Station
Chavasse Park
Canning Dock
Graving Docks
Fire Station
Museum of Liverpool Life
Half Tide Dock
Hartley Quay
Maritime Museum & H.M. Customs Museum
Tate Liverpool
Albert Dock
Salthouse Dock
Albert Dock Village
Police H.Q.
River Mersey
Strand Street
Canning Place
Paradise St.
Hanover St.
Duke St.
Bold St.
0 200 yds
0 200m

GREATER MANCHESTER
1 mile to 1 inch
0 1 2 miles
0 1 2 3 kilometres
0.63 km to 1 cm
Deane
Furnhill
Darcy Lever
Burnden
Little Lever
Radcliffe
BURY DISTRICT
Blackford Bridge
Chew Moor
Hunger Hill
Daubhill
Great Lever
Lever Edge
Moses Gate
Harper Green
Water's Nook
Wingates
Westhoughton
Chequerbent
BOLTON DISTRICT
Edge Fold
Hollins
Highfield
Farnworth
New Bury
Nob End
Prestolee
Stoneclough
Kearsley
Cinder Hill
Ringley
Outwood
Chapel Field
Stand
Park Lane
G R E A T E R
Daisy Hill
Greenheys
Little Hulton
Hill Top
Kearsley Moss
Clifton
Philips Park
Atherton
Dangerous Corner
Shakerley
Linnyshaw
Walkden
Clifton Junction
Clifton Green
Wardley
Newtown
Howe Bridge
Hindsford
Tyldesley
Roe Green
Swinton
Pendlebury
Moorside
Leigh
Lilford Park
Gin Pit
Higher Folds
Blackmoor
Parr Brow
Mosley Common
Astley
Ellenbrook
Worsley
Hazelhurst
Swinton Park
Irlams o' th' Height
Boothstown
Lark Hill
Pennington
Bedford
Town Lane
Higher Green
Astley Green
Dales Brow
Alder Forest
Ellesmere Park
Brindle Heath
Seedley
WIGAN DISTRICT
SALFORD DISTRICT
Monton
Winton
Moss Side
Botany Bay Wood
Patricroft
Little Bolton
ECCLES
Lately Common
Worsley Moss
Peel Green
Barton upon Irwell
Barton Airport
Barton Moss
Dumplington
Glazebury
Astley Moss
Trafford Park
The Trafford Centre
Chat Moss
Twiss Green
Fowley Common
Crofts Bank
Davyhulme
Culcheth
Higher Irlam
Larkhill
Irlam Moss
URMSTON
STRETFORD
Little Woolden Moss
Irlam
Flixton
WARRINGTON
Risley Remand Centre
Cadishead Moss
Ashton upon Mersey
Sale Ees
Carrington
Chemical Works
Carrington Moss
TRAFFORD DISTRICT
SALE
Woodhouses
Brooklands
Sinderland Green
Broadheath
Timperley
Oldfield Brow
Dunham Town
Dunham Massey
ALTRINCHAM
Little Bollington
Bowdon
Hale
Well Green
Rosehill
Bowgreen
Ashley Heath
Broomedge
Arthill
Big Wood
Booth Bank
MACCLESFIELD DISTRICT
Halebarns
Warburton Green
Swarton Heath
Ashley
Rostherne Mere
MANCHESTER
0 400 yds
0 400m
STRANGEWAYS
SALFORD
Salford Town Hall
Cathedral (RC)
M.E.N. Arena
Victoria & Metrolink
Manchester Cathedral
Arndale Centre
Royal Exchange Theatre
Manchester Craft Centre
The Pump House
Assize Courts
John Rylands Library
Stock Exchange
Town Hall
Central Library
Art Gallery
County Hall
Opera House
Police Station
Museum of Science & Industry
Air and Space Gallery
Free Trade Hall
G-MEX Centre
Bridgewater Hall
Palace Theatre
Nat. Mus. of Labour History
Piccadilly & Metrolink
U.M.I.S.T.
Castlefield Urban Heritage Park
Deansgate
Oxford Road
B.B.C.
Metropolitan University
Nat. Computing Centre
Royal Northern College of Music
HULME

Middleton
Rhodes
Chadderton
Alkrington
Moston
Blackley
Charlestown
Harpurhey
Crumpsall
Cheetham Hill
Cheetham
Broughton Park
Higher Broughton
Lower Broughton
Pendleton
Strangeways
Collyhurst
Miles Platting
MANCHESTER
Ancoats
Bradford
Beswick
Ardwick
Openshaw
Clayton
Droylsden
Fairfield
Gorton
West Gorton
Abbey Hey
Debdale
Longsight
Brunswick
Hulme
Moss Side
Rusholme
Levenshulme
Whalley Range
Fallowfield
Ladybarn
Withington
Burnage
Didsbury
West Didsbury
East Didsbury
Northenden
Chorlton-cum-Hardy
Barlow Moor
Old Trafford
Ordsall
St. George's
Wallness
Kersal
Lower Kersal
Sedgley Park
Hilton Park
Prestwich
Whitefield
Unsworth
Birch
Langley
Top of Hebers
Hollins
Stanycliffe
Higher Boarshaw
Moor Close
Nimble Nook
White Gate
Chain Bar
New Moston
Hollinwood
Failsworth
Woodhouses
Newton Heath
Clayton Bridge
OLDHAM
Hathershaw
Werneth
Coppice
Busk
Oldham Edge
Mumps
Derker
Higginshaw
Moorside
Watersheddings
Spring Hill
Greenacres
Austerlands
Lees
Springhead
Glodwick
Holts
Alt
Copster Hill
Lime Side
Bardsley
Limehurst
Waterloo
Smallshaw
Hurst
Hazelhurst
Taunton
Crowhill
ASHTON-UNDER-LYNE
Guide Bridge
Audenshaw
Dukinfield
Yew Tree
Newton
Flowery Field
Kingston
Godley
Hyde
Backbower
Gee Cross
Denton
Dane Bank
Haughton Green
Castle Hill
Woodley
Bredbury
Lower Bredbury
Romiley
Cherry Tree
Brinnington
Reddish
North Reddish
South Reddish
Heaton Chapel
Heaton Moor
Heaton Norris
Heaton Mersey
Green End
Lane End
Portwood
STOCKPORT
Stockport Little Moor
Edgeley
Cheadle Heath
Shaw Heath
Offerton Fold
Offerton Green
Foggbrook
Bunkers Hill
Bredbury Green
Marple
Marple Bridge
Ley Hey Park
Marpleridge
Heaviley
Cale Green
Great Moor
Davenport
Woods Moor
Stepping Hill
Adswood
Cheadle
Cheadle Hulme
Bramhall Park
Bramhall Moor
Torkington
Hazel Grove
Norbury Moor
Windlehurst
Bramhall
Kitt's Moss
Smithy Green
Gatley
Sharston
Benchill
Wythenshawe
Peel Hall
Woodhouse Park
Heald Green
Moss Nook
Heyhead
Manchester Airport
Poynton
Higher Poynton
Middlewood
CHESHIRE
MACCLESFIELD DISTRICT
STOCKPORT DISTRICT
TAMESIDE DISTRICT
MANCHESTER DISTRICT
OLDHAM DISTRICT
ROCHDALE DISTRICT
M A N C H E S T E R
M60
M62
M56
M67
M66
A6
A34
A57(M)
A627(M)

LEEDS
BRADFORD
BRADFORD DISTRICT
CALDERDALE DISTRICT
WEST
HALIFAX
HUDDERSFIELD
Bingley
Baildon
Shipley
Saltaire
Oakworth
Harden
Cottingley
Thornton
Allerton
Clayton
Queensbury
Shelf
Brighouse
Elland
Rastrick
Illingworth
Mixenden
Ovenden
Wibsey
Odsal
Low Moor
Wyke
Hipperholme
Southowram
Siddal
Lindley
Birkby
Fartown
Paddock
Golcar
Milnsbridge
Midgley
Mytholmroyd
Midgley Moor
Heaton
Manningham
Great Horton
Little Horton
West Bowling
Frizinghall
Clifton
Bradley
Deighton
Dalton
Moldgreen

LEEDS & BRADFORD
0 1 2 miles
0 1 2 3 kilometres
LEEDS DISTRICT
KIRKLEES DISTRICT
WAKEFIELD DISTRICT
YORKS
Rawdon
Tinshill
Lawnswood
Moor Allerton
Moortown
Dawson Wood
Low Green
Lane Ends
Rawdon Carrs
Cookridge & Ida Hosps.
Claydon Wood
Meanwood Park Hosp.
Tropical World
Roundhay Park
Simpson Green
Apperley Bridge
Calverley Wood
Wellroyd
Horsforth
Horsforth Woodside
West Park
Meanwood Park
Meanwood
Weetwood
Roundhay
Chapel Allerton
Newlay Wood
Hawksworth
Leeds Metropolitan University
Beckett Park
Greengates
Calverley
Gledhow
Bank Top
Round Hood
Ravenscliffe
Whitecote
Rodley
Moorside
Kirkstall
Kirkstall Abbey
Crooked Acres Hosp.
Headingley
Potternewton
Oakwood
Priestthorpe
Bagley
Farsley-Beck Bottom
Stanningley Park
Woodhall Hills
Industrial Museum
Fagley
Farsley
Leeds R.L.F.C. & R.F.C.
Yorkshire C.C.C.
Burley
Burley Park
Woodhouse
Gipton
Harehills
St. James Hosp.
Bramley
Stanningley
Hill Top
Upper Armley
Univ.
Civic Hall
Art Gallery
Infirmary
LEEDS
Burmantofts
Thornbury
Swinnow Moor
New Pudsey
Phoenix Park
Hillfoot
Gamble Hill
St. Mary's Hosp.
Armley
Westgate Police H.Q.
Market
Bus & Coach Sta.
City
Osmondthorpe
East End Park
Chapeltown
Pudsey
Laisterdyke
Upper Moor
Tyresal
Fulneck
Farnley
Wortley
Holbeck
Royal Armouries Museum
Cross Green
Cross Green Industrial Estate
Black Carr
Far Royds
Leeds United F.C.
Hunslet
Beeston Hill
Power Station
Dudley Hill
Holme Shay
Park Wood
New Farnley
Beeston
Stourton
Cockers Dale
Tong
Upper Moor Side
Cottingley
Mill Shaw
Tong Street
Westgate Hill
East Bierley
Toftshaw
Cockersdale
Adwalton Moor 1643
Moor Head
Beeston Park Side
Middleton Railway
Churwell
Middleton Park
Belle Isle
Gildersome
Drighlington
Adwalton
Daisy Hill
Bantam Grove
Rothwell
Moorside
Gildersome Street
New Brighton
Middleton
Birkenshaw
Birkenshaw Bottoms
Robin Hood
Aire Court Hosp.
Hunsworth
Oakwell Hall
Oakwell Ind. Park
Bruntcliffe
Morley
Thorpe on the Hill
Carlton
Norquest Industrial Park
Merchant Fields
Gomersal
Topcliffe
Copley Hill
Tingley
Lofthouse
Red House Museum
Birstall
Spen
Popeley Fields
Upper Green
Woodkirk
East Ardsley
Lofthouse Gate
Wilton Park
Bagshaw Museum
Cleckheaton
Carlinghow
Ardsley Resr.
Howley Hall
Outwood
Spen Valley Industrial Estate
Littletown
Westfield
Batley
Haigh Moor
Beggarington Hill
Carr Gate
Hightown
Healey
Heckmondwike
Clerk Green
Mount Pleasant
Carr Gate Industrial Estate
Liversedge
BMK Industrial Estate
Staincliffe
Batley R.L.F.C.
Hanging Heaton
Dogloitch Wood
Jaw Hill
Outwood
Norristhorpe
Sycamore Industrial Estate
Dewsbury and District Hosp.
Batley Carr
Chidswell
Kirkhamgate
Newton Hill
Roberttown
DEWSBURY
Wrenthorpe
Snow Hill
Dewsbury Moor
Boothroyd
College
Gawthorpe
Fieldhead Hosp.
Moor Top
Crossley
WAKEFIELD
Chickenley
Alverthorpe
Mirfield Moor
Museum & Art Gallery
Riverside Industrial Estate
Earlsheaton
Sandbeds Industrial Estate
Low Laithes
Flanshaw
Flushdyke
Flanshaw Ind. Est.
Wakefield Art Gallery
Longlands Industrial Estate
Ossett
Town Hall
Westgate
Northorpe
Savile Town
Spring Mill
Roundwood Industrial Estate
Battyeford
Mirfield
Ravensthorpe
Lupset
Thornes Park
Ossett Spa
Holmfield Park
Thornhill Lees
Lower Hopton
Healey
South Ossett
Thornes
Monkton Ind. Est.
Combs
Dewsbury District
North Moor
Thornhill
City of Wakefield
Overthorpe
Kirkheaton
Upper Hopton
Whitley Lower
Gregory Spring
Thornhill Edge
Howroyd Beck
Smithy Brook
Calder and Hebble Navigation
River Calder
Horbury
Horbury Bridge
Horbury Junction
Pugneys Country Park
Sandal Castle
Middlestown
Coxley
Houses Hill
Durkar
Overton
Netherton
Calder Grove
Kettlethorpe
National Coal Mining Museum of England
Great Cliff
Crigglestone
Gawthorpe
Cowmes
Fenay Bridge
Lepton
Grange Moor
Painthorpe
Chapelthorpe
Hill Top
M1
M62
M621
A58
A61
A62
A64
A65
A638
A639
A642
A643
A644
A647
A650
A651
A652
A653
A654
A657
A658
A660
A6110
A6120
A6177
A636
A6186
A6029

# NEWCASTLE UPON TYNE

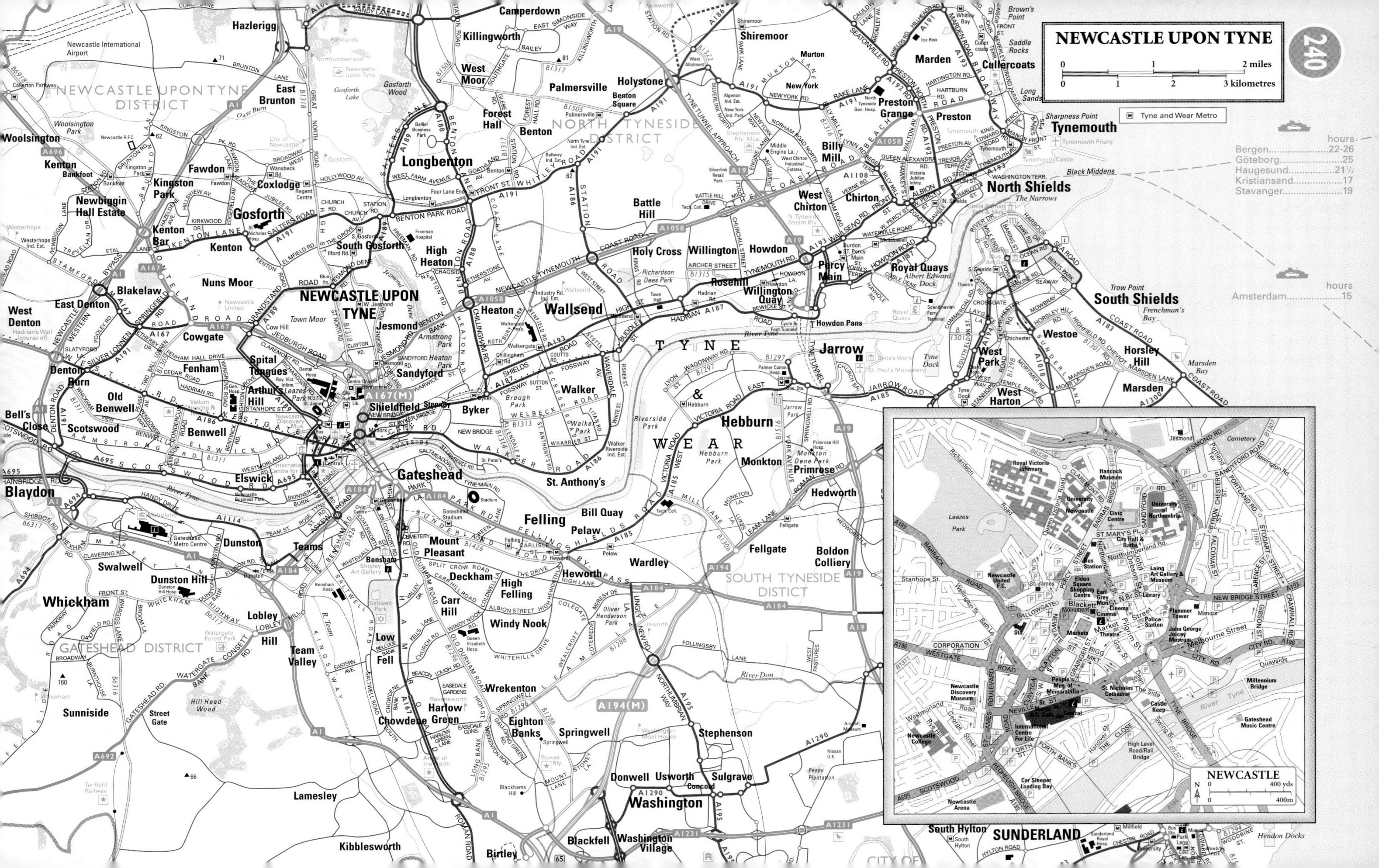

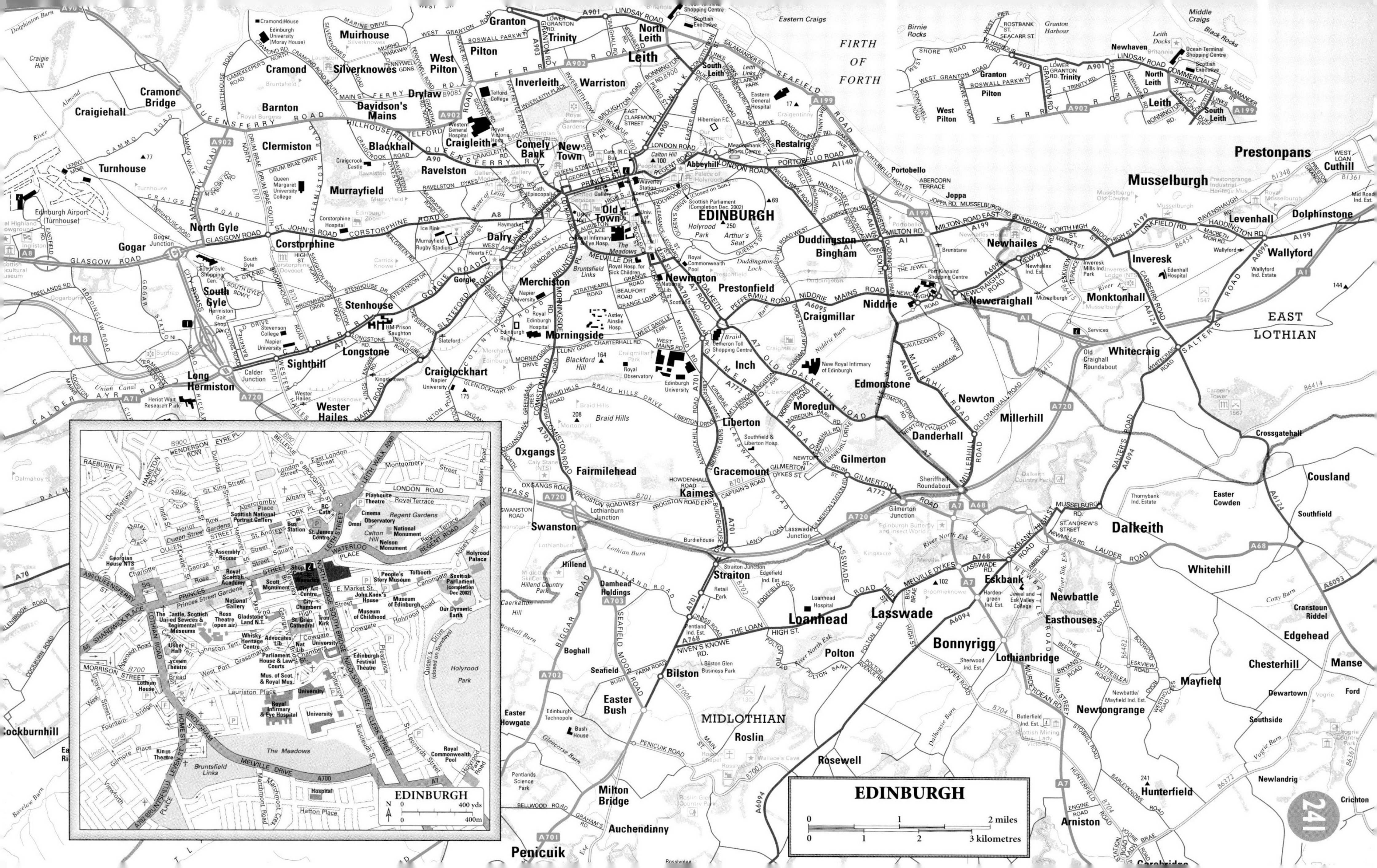
EDINBURGH
0 1 2 miles
0 1 2 3 kilometres
FIRTH OF FORTH
EAST LOTHIAN
MIDLOTHIAN
Granton
Trinity
North Leith
Leith
Newhaven
Muirhouse
Silverknowes
West Pilton
Pilton
Cramond
Cramond Bridge
Craigiehall
Barnton
Davidson's Mains
Drylaw
Inverleith
Warriston
Clermiston
Blackhall
Craigleith
Comely Bank
New Town
Turnhouse
Edinburgh Airport (Turnhouse)
Ravelston
Murrayfield
North Gyle
Gogar
Corstorphine
South Gyle
Stenhouse
Dalry
Gorgie
Merchiston
Morningside
Sighthill
Longstone
Long Hermiston
Wester Hailes
Craiglockhart
Old Town
EDINBURGH
Holyrood Park
Arthur's Seat
Abbeyhill
Restalrig
Portobello
Joppa
Duddingston
Bingham
Newington
Prestonfield
Craigmillar
Niddrie
Newcraighall
Newhailes
Musselburgh
Inveresk
Monktonhall
Whitecraig
Wallyford
Levenhall
Prestonpans
Cuthill
Dolphinstone
Inch
Liberton
Moredun
Edmonstone
Newton
Millerhill
Danderhall
Gilmerton
Gracemount
Kaimes
Fairmilehead
Oxgangs
Swanston
Braid Hills
Blackford Hill
Straiton
Loanhead
Lasswade
Bonnyrigg
Eskbank
Dalkeith
Newbattle
Easthouses
Lothianbridge
Newtongrange
Mayfield
Whitehill
Cousland
Crossgatehall
Polton
Bilston
Roslin
Rosewell
Hillend
Damhead Holdings
Seafield
Easter Bush
Boghall
Milton Bridge
Auchendinny
Penicuik
Easter Howgate
Hunterfield
Arniston
Chesterhill
Edgehead
Manse
Newlandrig
Crichton
Southside
Dewartown
Ford
Cockburnhill
Easter Cowden
Southfield
Cranstoun Riddel
Calder Junction
Gogar Junction
Sheriffhall Roundabout
Gilmerton Junction
Straiton Junction
Lasswade Junction
Lothianburn Junction
Old Craighall Roundabout
The Meadows
Bruntsfield Links
Royal Observatory
New Royal Infirmary of Edinburgh
Scottish Parliament (Completion Dec. 2002)
Palace of Holyroodhouse
Waverley Station
Royal Infirmary & Eye Hosp.
Heriot Watt Research Park
Napier University
Edinburgh University
Queen Margaret University College
Scottish Executive
Ocean Terminal Shopping Centre
Gyle Shopping Centre
Cameron Toll Shopping Centre
Fort Kinnaird Shopping Centre
A1
A7
A68
A70
A71
A8
A90
A199
A702
A703
A720
A701
A902
M8
CITY BYPASS
EDINBURGH
0 400 yds
0 400m
Princes Street
Princes Street Gardens
North Bridge
South Bridge
Nicolson Street
Clerk Street
Leith Walk
Lothian Road
Queensferry St.
Shandwick Place
Regent Road
Waterloo Place
Royal Terrace
Regent Gardens
Calton Hill
National Monument
Nelson Monument
Holyrood Palace
Scottish Parliament (completion Dec 2002)
Our Dynamic Earth
Holyrood Park
Queen's Drive (closed on Sundays)
People's Story Museum
Tolbooth
Museum of Edinburgh
John Knox's House
Museum of Childhood
Scott Monument
National Gallery
Royal Scottish Academy
The Castle, Scottish United Services & Regimental Museums
Ross Theatre (open air)
Gladstone's Land N.T.
St Giles Cathedral
Whisky Heritage Centre
Advocates Lib.
Nat. Lib.
Parliament House & Law Courts
Mus. of Scot. & Royal Mus.
Royal Infirmary & Eye Hospital
University
Edinburgh Festival Theatre
Usher Hall
Lyceum Theatre
Kings Theatre
Royal Commonwealth Pool
The Meadows
Melville Drive
Bruntsfield Links
Georgian House NTS
Playhouse Theatre
Omni
Cinema
Observatory
Bus Station
St. James Centre
Assembly Rooms
Scottish National Portrait Gallery
City Art Centre
City Chambers
Waverley
Hospital
Hatton Place
Marchmont Road

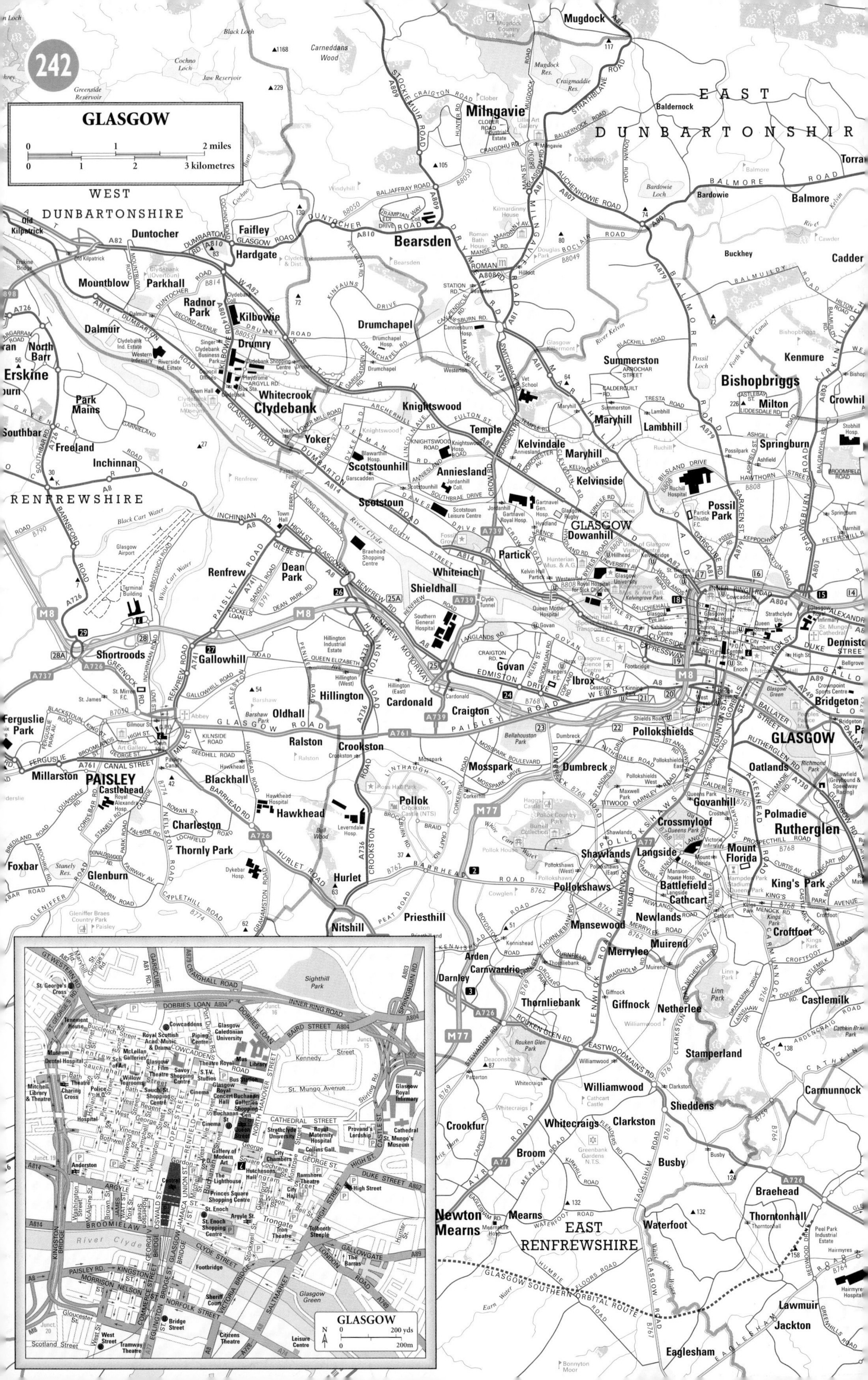
GLASGOW
0 1 2 miles
0 1 2 3 kilometres
WEST DUNBARTONSHIRE
EAST DUNBARTONSHIRE
RENFREWSHIRE
EAST RENFREWSHIRE
Black Loch
Carneddans Wood
Cochno Loch
Jaw Reservoir
Greenside Reservoir
Mugdock
Mugdock Country Park
Mugdock Res.
Craigmaddie Res.
Milngavie
Baldernock
Bardowie
Bardowie Loch
Balmore
Torrance
Old Kilpatrick
Duntocher
Faifley
Hardgate
Bearsden
Mountblow
Parkhall
Radnor Park
Kilbowie
Drumry
Dalmuir
North Barr
Erskine
Park Mains
Southbar
Freeland
Inchinnan
Clydebank
Whitecrook
Drumchapel
Knightswood
Temple
Kelvindale
Maryhill
Summerston
Lambhill
Bishopbriggs
Kenmure
Milton
Crowhill
Springburn
Buckhey
Cadder
Yoker
Scotstounhill
Anniesland
Scotstoun
Kelvinside
Possil Park
Glasgow Airport
Renfrew
Dean Park
Shieldhall
Whiteinch
Partick
GLASGOW Dowanhill
Shortroods
Gallowhill
Hillington
Cardonald
Govan
Ibrox
Craigton
Oldhall
Ralston
Crookston
Mosspark
Dumbreck
Pollokshields
Ferguslie Park
Millarston
PAISLEY
Castlehead
Blackhall
Hawkhead
Pollok
Charleston
Thornly Park
Foxbar
Glenburn
Hurlet
Nitshill
Priesthill
Pollokshaws
Shawlands
Langside
Crossmyloof
Govanhill
Battlefield
Cathcart
Newlands
Mansewood
Muirend
Merrylee
Arden
Carnwadric
Darnley
Thornliebank
Giffnock
Netherlee
Stamperland
Williamwood
Sheddens
Clarkston
Whitecraigs
Crookfur
Broom
Busby
Newton Mearns
Mearns
Waterfoot
Eaglesham
Bridgeton
Dennistoun
Oatlands
Polmadie
Rutherglen
Mount Florida
King's Park
Croftfoot
Castlemilk
Carmunnock
Braehead
Thorntonhall
Lawmuir
Jackton
GLASGOW SOUTHERN ORBITAL ROUTE
M8
M77
A77
A726
A736
A739
A761
A81
A82
A803
A804
A814
River Clyde
River Kelvin
Forth & Clyde Canal
Sighthill Park
Cowcaddens
Royal Scottish Acad. Music & Drama
Glasgow Caledonian University
St. Mungo Avenue
Cathedral Street
Strathclyde University
Glasgow Royal Infirmary
St. Mungo's Museum
Provand's Lordship
Buchanan Galleries
Queen Street
Central
St. Enoch
Argyle St.
Trongate
Tolbooth Steeple
The Barras
Glasgow Green
Gallowgate
Clyde Street
Broomielaw
Kingston Bridge
George V Bridge
Glasgow Bridge
Jamaica Street
Victoria Bridge
Saltmarket
Citizens Theatre
Tramway Theatre
Scotland Street
Paisley Rd.
Morrison St.
Norfolk Street
Anderston
Mitchell Library & Theatre
Charing Cross
GLASGOW
0 200 yds
0 200m

Milton of Campsie
Westerwood
Croy
Twechar
Bar Hill Fort (Antonine Wall)
Carrickstone
Craigmarloch
Kildrum
Birdston
Kirkintilloch
Harestanes
Eastfield
Seafar
Cumbernauld
Balloch
Carbrain
Broadwood
Westfield
Greenfaulds
Lenziemill
Condorrat
Oxgang
Waterside
Gallowhill
Blairlinn
Luggiebank
Lenzie
Strathkelvin Retail Park
Mollinsburn
Bridgend
Moodiesburn
Auchinloch
Gadloch
Annathill
Woodhill
Chryston
Riggend
Wattston
NORTH
LANARKSHIRE
Greenfoot
Rigghead
Marnock
Muirhead
Glenboig
Garnkirk
Stepps
Cardowan
Gartcosh
Stand
Millerston
Glenmavis
Provanmill
Hogganfield Loch
Bishop Loch
Woodend Loch
Gartgill
Townhead
Airdriehill
Riddrie
Ruchazie
Garthamlock
Lochwood
Holehills
Thrashbush
Rawyards
Gartsherrie
Easterhouse
Lochend Loch
Monkland Canal
Carntyne
Springboig
Airdrie
Craigneuk
Coatbridge
Coatdyke
Gartlea
Barlanark
Swinton
Bargeddie
Baillieston
Barrachnie
Garrowhill
Shettleston
Crosshill
Kirkwood
Greenend
Rosehall
Gartness
Carnbroe
Kirkshaws
Shawhead
Woodlands
Old Monkland
Muirhead
Mount Vernon
Calderbank
Braidfauld
Broomhouse
Chapelhall
Carmyle
Birkenshaw
Thorniewood
Tannochside
Viewpark
Newhouse
West
River Clyde
Eastfield
Newton
Kylepark
Fallside
Mossend
Holytown
Uddingston
New Stevenston
Hallside
Bellshill
Yett
Cambuslang
Flemington
Carfin
Kirkfield
Bothwell
Low Blantyre
Forgewood
North Motherwell
Dalton
Cleekhimin
SOUTH
LANARKSHIRE
Barnhill
Motherwell
Blantyre
Springwells
Whitehill
Craigneuk
Nerston
Rogerton
High Blantyre
Burnbank
Stewartfield
Calderwood
Hamilton
Shieldmuir
Hillhouse
Muirhouse
EAST
KILBRIDE
East Mains
Auchentibber
Earnock
West Mains
Laighstonehall
Low Waters
Ferniegair
St. Leonards
Woodhead
Fairhill
Silvertonhill
Cadzow
Allanton
Gowkth
The Murray
Birniehill
Meikle Earnock
Eddlewood
Blantyre Moor
Greenhills
M73
M80
M8
M74
A80
A8
A89
A721
A725
A724
A749
A726
A73
A72

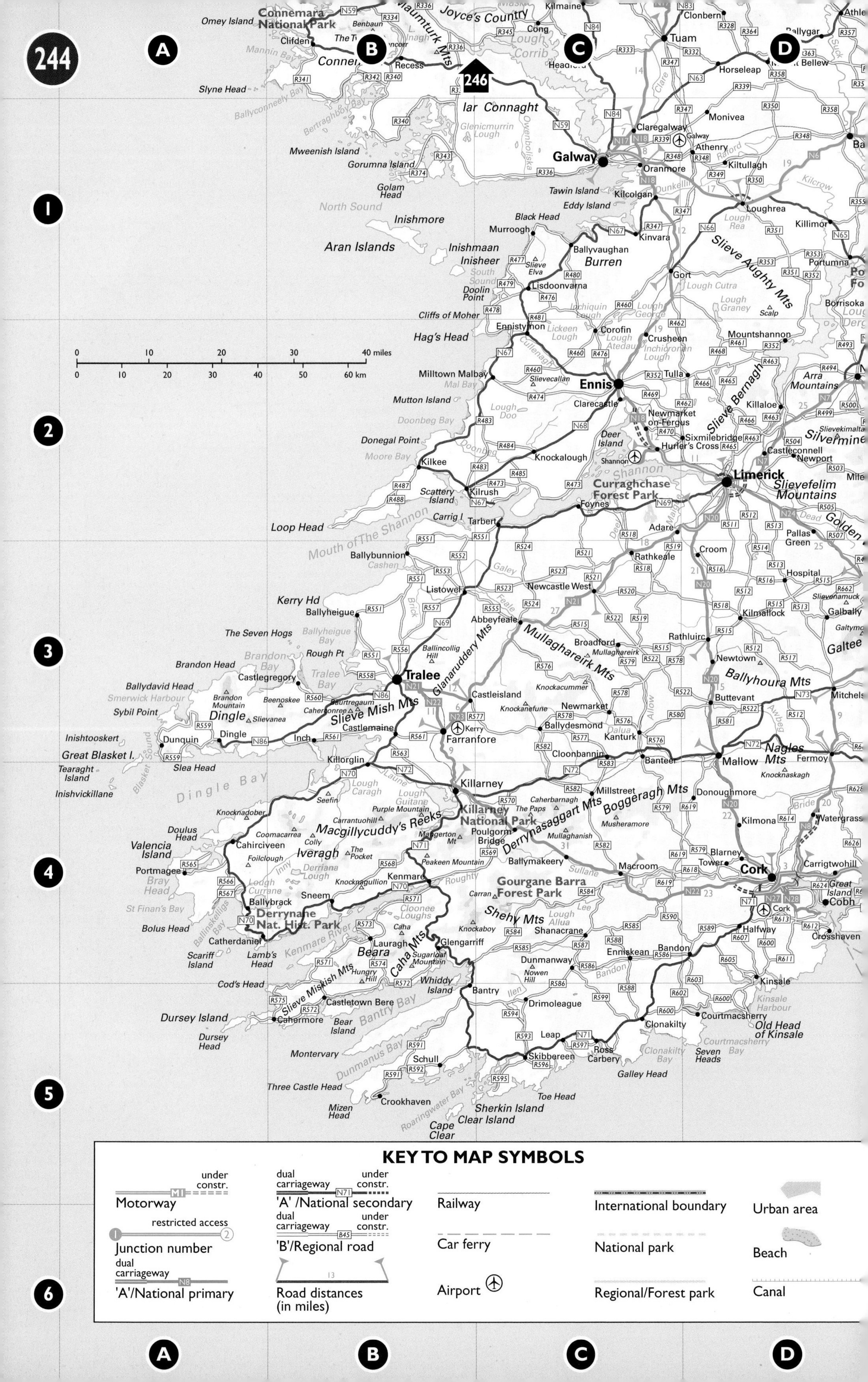

A
B
C
D
1
2
3
4
5
6
246
Connemara National Park
Omey Island
Clifden
Slyne Head
Recess
Joyce's Country
Cong
Lough Corrib
Headford
Tuam
Clonbern
Horseleap
Mount Bellew
Iar Connaght
Monivea
Claregalway
Galway
Athenry
Oranmore
Kiltullagh
Mweenish Island
Gorumna Island
Golam Head
North Sound
Inishmore
Aran Islands
Inishmaan
Inisheer
Tawin Island
Eddy Island
Kilcolgan
Kinvara
Loughrea
Lough Rea
Killimor
Portumna
Black Head
Murrough
Ballyvaughan
Burren
Slieve Elva
Lisdoonvarna
Doolin Point
Gort
Lough Cutra
Slieve Aughty Mts
Lough Graney
Scalp
Borrisokane
Cliffs of Moher
Hag's Head
Ennistymon
Inchiquin Lough
Lickeen Lough
Corofin
Crusheen
Mountshannon
Milltown Malbay
Mal Bay
Slievecallan
Ennis
Tulla
Slieve Bernagh
Arra Mountains
Killaloe
Mutton Island
Clarecastle
Newmarket on-Fergus
Sixmilebridge
Doonbeg Bay
Donegal Point
Moore Bay
Deer Island
Hurler's Cross
Knockalough
Shannon
Castleconnell
Newport
Silvermine
Kilkee
Scattery Island
Kilrush
Curraghchase Forest Park
Limerick
Slievefelim Mountains
Foynes
Loop Head
Carrig I
Tarbert
Mouth of The Shannon
Adare
Ballybunnion
Cashen
Rathkeale
Croom
Pallas Green
Listowel
Newcastle West
Hospital
Kerry Hd
Ballyheigue
Abbeyfeale
Kilmallock
Galbally
The Seven Hogs
Ballyheigue Bay
Mullaghareirk Mts
Broadford
Rathluirc
Rough Pt
Brandon Bay
Brandon Head
Glanaruddery Mts
Newtown
Galtee
Castlegregory
Tralee
Tralee Bay
Ballyhoura Mts
Ballydavid Head
Smerwick Harbour
Castleisland
Knockacummer
Buttevant
Mitchels
Sybil Point
Dingle
Slievanea
Slieve Mish Mts
Newmarket
Castlemaine
Farranfore
Ballydesmond
Kanturk
Inishtooskert
Dunquin
Great Blasket I.
Tearaght Island
Inishvickillane
Slea Head
Dingle Bay
Killorglin
Cloonbannin
Banteer
Mallow
Nagles Mts
Fermoy
Lough Caragh
Killarney
Millstreet
Boggeragh Mts
Donoughmore
Knocknadober
Macgillycuddy's Reeks
Killarney National Park
Carrantuohill
Derrynasaggart Mts
Musheramore
Watergrass
Doulus Head
Valencia Island
Cahirciveen
Iveragh
Poulgorm Bridge
Kilmona
Portmagee
Bray Head
Kenmare
Peakeen Mountain
Ballymakeery
Macroom
Blarney
Tower
Cork
Carrigtwohill
Great Island
Cobh
Lough Currane
Sneem
Gourgane Barra Forest Park
St Finan's Bay
Ballybrack
Derrynane Nat. Hist. Park
Shehy Mts
Crosshaven
Bolus Head
Catherdaniel
Kenmare River
Lauragh
Caha Mts
Glengarriff
Shanacrane
Halfway
Scariff Island
Lamb's Head
Beara
Sugarloaf Mountain
Dunmanway
Enniskean
Bandon
Hungry Hill
Whiddy Island
Kinsale
Cod's Head
Slieve Miskish Mts
Castletown Bere
Bantry
Drimoleague
Kinsale Harbour
Bantry Bay
Dursey Island
Cahermore
Bear Island
Clonakilty
Courtmacsherry
Old Head of Kinsale
Dursey Head
Leap
Ross Carbery
Monterary
Dunmanus Bay
Schull
Skibbereen
Clonakilty Bay
Seven Heads
Galley Head
Three Castle Head
Crookhaven
Toe Head
Mizen Head
Sherkin Island
Clear Island
Cape Clear
Roaringwater Bay
0 10 20 30 40 miles
0 10 20 30 40 50 60 km
KEY TO MAP SYMBOLS
Motorway
under constr.
Junction number
restricted access
'A'/National primary
dual carriageway
'A' /National secondary
'B'/Regional road
Road distances (in miles)
Railway
Car ferry
Airport
International boundary
National park
Regional/Forest park
Urban area
Beach
Canal

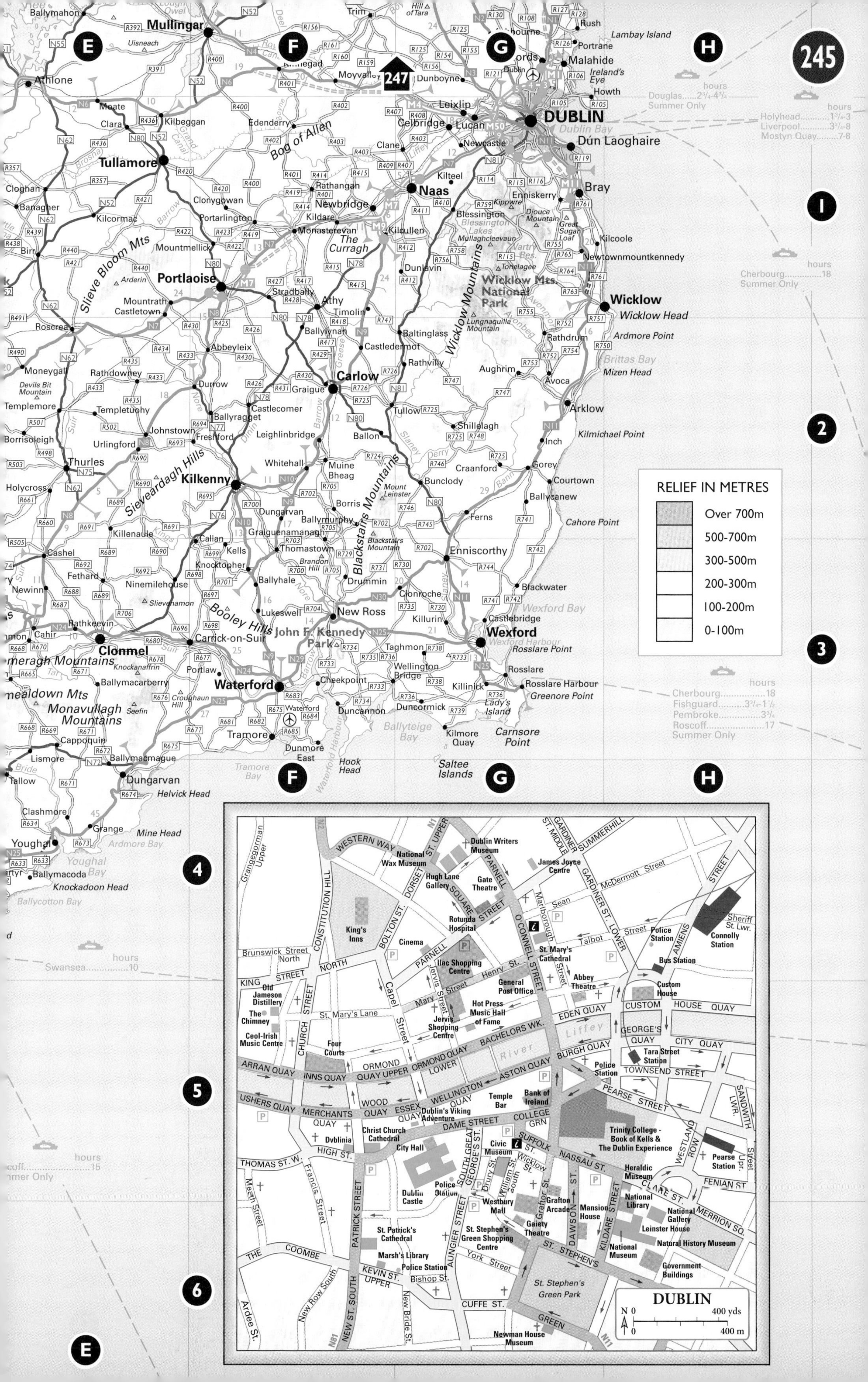
Ballymahon
Mullingar
Uisneach
Athlone
Moate
Clara
Kilbeggan
Tullamore
Edenderry
Bog of Allen
Kinnegad
Moyvalley
247
Trim
Hill of Tara
Dunboyne
Rush
Lambay Island
Portrane
Malahide
Ireland's Eye
Howth
Dublin
Leixlip
Celbridge
Lucan
Newcastle
Clane
DUBLIN
Dublin Bay
Dún Laoghaire
Bray
Douglas 2¾-4¾ Summer Only
hours
Holyhead 1¾-3
Liverpool 3¾-8
Mostyn Quay 7-8
Kilteel
Naas
Rathangan
Newbridge
Kildare
Monasterevan
The Curragh
Kilcullen
Dunlavin
Blessington
Blessington Lakes
Mullaghcleevaun
Kippure
Djouce Mountain
Enniskerry
Great Sugar Loaf
Kilcoole
Newtownmountkennedy
Vartry Res.
Tonelagee
Wicklow Mts. National Park
Wicklow Mountains
Lugnaquilla Mountain
Wicklow
Wicklow Head
Ardmore Point
Rathdrum
Brittas Bay
Mizen Head
Aughrim
Avoca
Arklow
Kilmichael Point
Inch
Gorey
Courtown
Ballycanew
Cahore Point
Cherbourg 18 Summer Only
Cloghan
Banagher
Kilcormac
Birr
Slieve Bloom Mts
Arderin
Portarlington
Clonygowan
Mountmellick
Portlaoise
Mountrath
Castletown
Stradbally
Athy
Timolin
Ballylynan
Baltinglass
Castledermot
Rathvilly
Carlow
Graigue
Roscrea
Abbeyleix
Moneygall
Devils Bit Mountain
Rathdowney
Durrow
Templemore
Templetuohy
Ballyragget
Castlecomer
Johnstown
Freshford
Leighlinbridge
Tullow
Ballon
Shillelagh
Borrisoleigh
Urlingford
Thurles
Holycross
Kilkenny
Slieveardagh Hills
Whitehall
Muine Bheag
Borris
Mount Leinster
Blackstairs Mountains
Bunclody
Craanford
Ferns
Dungarvan
Ballymurphy
Graiguenamanagh
Thomastown
Kells
Callan
Killenaule
Cashel
Fethard
Knocktopher
Ballyhale
Brandon Hill
Blackstairs Mountain
Enniscorthy
Drummin
Clonroche
Killurin
Blackwater
Newinn
Ninemilehouse
Slievenamon
Lukeswell
New Ross
Booley Hills
Cahir
Rathkeevin
Clonmel
Carrick-on-Suir
John F. Kennedy Park
Castlebridge
Wexford Bay
Wexford
Wexford Harbour
Rosslare Point
Taghmon
Knockanaffrin
Comeragh Mountains
Portlaw
Wellington Bridge
Rosslare
Rosslare Harbour
Greenore Point
Ballymacarberry
Croughaun Hill
Seefin
Waterford
Checkpoint
Killinick
Lady's Island
Knockmealdown Mts
Monavullagh Mountains
Waterford
Duncannon
Duncormick
Ballyteige Bay
Kilmore Quay
Carnsore Point
Cappoquin
Tramore
Dunmore East
Hook Head
Saltee Islands
Tramore Bay
Waterford Harbour
Cherbourg 18
Fishguard 3¾-1½
Pembroke 3¾
Roscoff 17
Summer Only
Lismore
Ballymacmague
Tallow
Dungarvan
Helvick Head
Clashmore
Grange
Mine Head
Youghal
Ardmore Bay
Youghal Bay
Ballymacoda
Knockadoon Head
Ballycotton Bay
Swansea 10
RELIEF IN METRES
Over 700m
500-700m
300-500m
200-300m
100-200m
0-100m
E
F
G
H
I
2
3
4
5
6
DUBLIN
Grangegorman Upper
WESTERN WAY
National Wax Museum
Dublin Writers Museum
James Joyce Centre
Hugh Lane Gallery
Gate Theatre
PARNELL SQUARE
Rotunda Hospital
King's Inns
CONSTITUTION HILL
BOLTON ST.
DORSET
ST. UPPER
GARDINER ST. MIDDLE
SUMMERHILL
GARDINER ST. LOWER
McDermott Street
Sean McDermott Street
Marlborough Street
O'CONNELL STREET
Talbot Street
Police Station
AMIENS STREET
Sheriff St. Lwr.
Connolly Station
Bus Station
Cinema
Brunswick Street North
NORTH KING STREET
Old Jameson Distillery
The Chimney
Ceol-Irish Music Centre
PARNELL
Ilac Shopping Centre
Henry St.
General Post Office
St. Mary's Cathedral
Abbey Theatre
Custom House
CUSTOM HOUSE QUAY
Jervis Street
Mary Street
Capel Street
St. Mary's Lane
CHURCH STREET
Jervis Shopping Centre
Hot Press Music Hall of Fame
EDEN QUAY
GEORGE'S QUAY
CITY QUAY
BACHELORS WK.
Liffey
River
Four Courts
ARRAN QUAY
INNS QUAY
ORMOND QUAY UPPER
ORMOND QUAY LOWER
ASTON QUAY
BURGH QUAY
Tara Street Station
Police Station
TOWNSEND STREET
PEARSE STREET
SANDWITH LWR.
USHERS QUAY
MERCHANTS QUAY
WOOD QUAY
ESSEX QUAY
WELLINGTON QUAY
Temple Bar
Bank of Ireland
COLLEGE GRN
Dublin's Viking Adventure
DAME STREET
Christ Church Cathedral
Dvblinia
HIGH ST.
City Hall
Civic Museum
SUFFOLK ST.
Trinity College - Book of Kells & The Dublin Experience
WESTLAND ROW
Pearse Station
Street Upr.
THOMAS ST. W.
Francis Street
PATRICK STREET
SOUTH GREAT GEORGE'S ST.
Wicklow St.
NASSAU ST.
Heraldic Museum
CLARE ST.
FENIAN ST.
Meath Street
Dublin Castle
Police Station
Drury St.
William St. South
Grafton St.
Westbury Mall
Grafton Arcade
DAWSON ST.
Mansion House
KILDARE STREET
National Library
National Gallery
MERRION SQ.
Leinster House
Gaiety Theatre
National Museum
Natural History Museum
Government Buildings
THE COOMBE
St. Patrick's Cathedral
Marsh's Library
AUNGIER STREET
St. Stephen's Green Shopping Centre
York Street
ST. STEPHEN'S
Police Station
KEVIN ST. UPPER
Bishop St.
New Row South
NEW ST. SOUTH
New Bride St.
CUFFE ST.
St. Stephen's Green Park
GREEN
Newman House Museum
Ardee St.
DUBLIN
0 400 yds
0 400 m
N

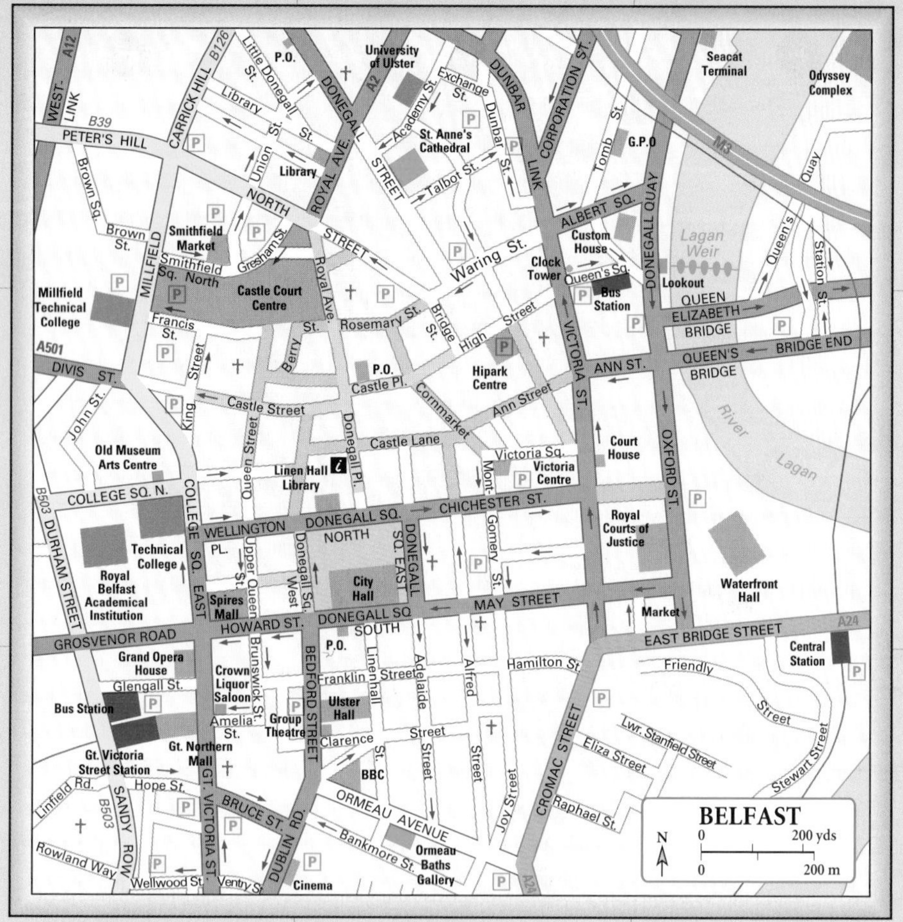
BELFAST
0 200 yds
0 200 m
N
WEST-LINK
A12
B126
CARRICK HILL
Little Donegall St.
P.O.
University of Ulster
DONEGALL ST.
ROYAL AVE.
A2
DUNBAR LINK
CORPORATION ST.
Seacat Terminal
Odyssey Complex
Library
Exchange St.
Academy St.
Dunbar St.
St. Anne's Cathedral
Tomb St.
G.P.O
M3
B39
PETER'S HILL
Union St.
Library
Talbot St.
Quay
Brown Sq.
NORTH STREET
ALBERT SQ.
Queen's
Brown St.
Smithfield Market
Gresham St.
Custom House
DONEGALL QUAY
Lagan Weir
Station St.
MILLFIELD
Smithfield Sq. North
Royal Ave.
Waring St.
Clock Tower
Queen's Sq.
Lookout
Millfield Technical College
Castle Court Centre
Bus Station
QUEEN ELIZABETH BRIDGE
Francis St.
St.
Rosemary St.
Bridge St.
High Street
A501
Berry St.
ANN ST.
QUEEN'S BRIDGE
BRIDGE END
DIVIS ST.
Street
P.O.
Castle Pl.
Hipark Centre
VICTORIA ST.
John St.
Castle Street
Cornmarket
Ann Street
River Lagan
King St.
Queen Street
Donegall Pl.
Castle Lane
Court House
OXFORD ST.
Old Museum Arts Centre
Linen Hall Library
Mont-Gomery St.
Victoria Sq.
Victoria Centre
COLLEGE SQ. N.
COLLEGE SQ. EAST
B503
DURHAM STREET
WELLINGTON PL.
DONEGALL SQ. NORTH
CHICHESTER ST.
Royal Courts of Justice
Technical College
Upper Queen St.
Donegall Sq. West
City Hall
DONEGALL SQ. EAST
Waterfront Hall
Royal Belfast Academical Institution
Spires Mall
MAY STREET
Market
GROSVENOR ROAD
HOWARD ST.
DONEGALL SQ SOUTH
A24
EAST BRIDGE STREET
Grand Opera House
P.O.
BEDFORD STREET
Central Station
Crown Liquor Saloon
Brunswick St.
Franklin Street
Linenhall St.
Adelaide Street
Alfred Street
Hamilton St.
Friendly Street
Glengall St.
Ulster Hall
Bus Station
Amelia St.
Group Theatre
Clarence
Joy Street
Lwr. Stanfield Street
Gt. Victoria Street Station
Gt. Northern Mall
BBC
CROMAC STREET
Eliza Street
Stewart Street
Linfield Rd.
Hope St.
SANDY ROW
GT. VICTORIA ST.
BRUCE ST.
DUBLIN RD.
ORMEAU AVENUE
Raphael St.
Bankmore St.
Ormeau Baths Gallery
Rowland Way
Wellwood St.
Ventry St.
Cinema

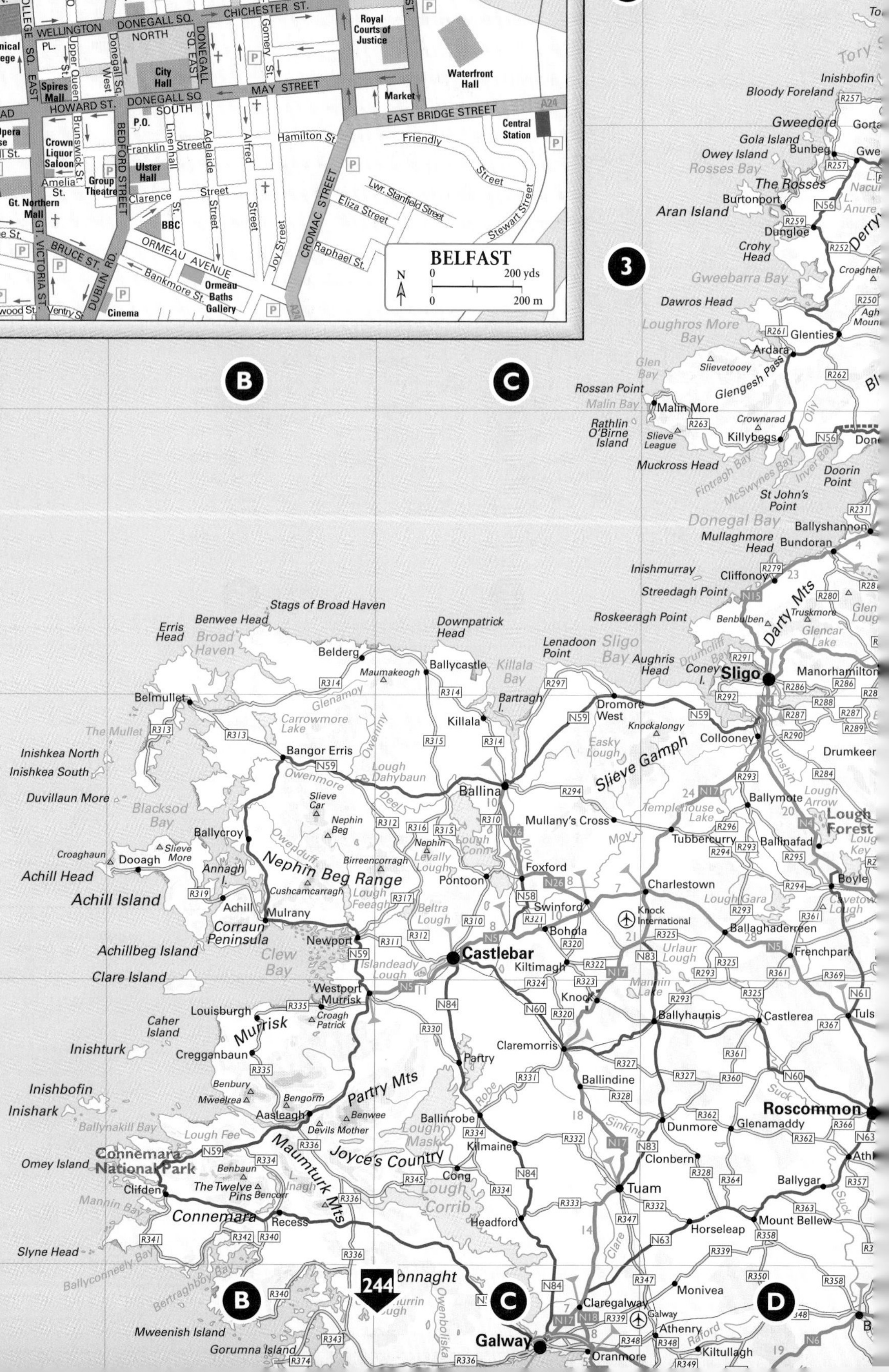
A
B
C
D
1
2
3
4
5
6
Tory
Inishbofin
Bloody Foreland
Gweedore
Gola Island
Owey Island
Bunbeg
Rosses Bay
The Rosses
Aran Island
Burtonport
Dungloe
Crohy Head
Gweebarra Bay
Dawros Head
Loughros More Bay
Glenties
Ardara
Glen Bay
Slievetooey
Glengesh Pass
Rossan Point
Malin Bay
Malin More
Rathlin O'Birne Island
Slieve League
Crownarad
Killybegs
Muckross Head
Fintragh Bay
McSwynes Bay
Inver Bay
Doorin Point
St John's Point
Donegal Bay
Ballyshannon
Mullaghmore Head
Bundoran
Inishmurray
Cliffoney
Streedagh Point
Darty Mts
Truskmore
Benbulben
Glencar Lake
Stags of Broad Haven
Erris Head
Benwee Head
Broad Haven
Downpatrick Head
Roskeeragh Point
Lenadoon Point
Sligo Bay
Aughris Head
Drumcliff Bay
Coney I.
Sligo
Manorhamilton
Belderg
Maumakeogh
Ballycastle
Killala Bay
Belmullet
Glenamoy
Bartragh I.
Dromore West
Knockalongy
Carrowmore Lake
Killala
The Mullet
Collooney
Drumkeeran
Inishkea North
Inishkea South
Bangor Erris
Owenmore
Lough Dahybaun
Easky Lough
Slieve Gamph
Ballina
Ballymote
Lough Arrow
Lough Forest
Duvillaun More
Blacksod Bay
Slieve Car
Nephin Beg
Templehouse Lake
Mullany's Cross
Tubbercurry
Ballinafad
Ballycroy
Nephin
Lough Conn
Lough Key
Croaghaun
Slieve More
Dooagh
Birreencorragh
Levally Lough
Achill Head
Annagh I.
Nephin Beg Range
Pontoon
Foxford
Charlestown
Boyle
Achill Island
Cushcamcarragh
Lough Feeagh
Lough Gara
Achill
Mulranny
Beltra Lough
Swinford
Knock International
Corraun Peninsula
Bohola
Ballaghaderreen
Achillbeg Island
Newport
Clew Bay
Castlebar
Islandeady Lough
Urlaur Lough
Frenchpark
Clare Island
Kiltimagh
Westport
Murrisk
Mannin Lake
Knock
Louisburgh
Croagh Patrick
Caher Island
Murrisk
Ballyhaunis
Castlerea
Inishturk
Cregganbaun
Claremorris
Partry
Inishbofin
Inishark
Benbury
Mweelrea
Bengorm
Partry Mts
Ballindine
Roscommon
Ballynakill Bay
Aasleagh
Benwee
Devils Mother
Ballinrobe
Lough Mask
Dunmore
Glenamaddy
Lough Fee
Maumturk Mts
Joyce's Country
Kilmaine
Sinking
Omey Island
Connemara National Park
Benbaun
The Twelve Pins
Bencorr
Cong
Clonbern
Lough Inagh
Tuam
Ballygar
Clifden
Mannin Bay
Lough Corrib
Connemara
Recess
Headford
Horseleap
Mount Bellew
Slyne Head
Ballyconneely Bay
Bertraghboy Bay
Connaught
Lough Aurrin
Owenboliska
Monivea
Claregalway
Galway
Athenry
Mweenish Island
Gorumna Island
Galway
Oranmore
Kiltullagh
N56
N15
N4
N59
N17
N26
N58
N5
N83
N84
N60
N63
N61
N18
N6
R257
R259
R252
R250
R261
R262
R263
R231
R279
R280
R291
R286
R292
R288
R287
R289
R290
R284
R297
R314
R313
R315
R294
R312
R316
R310
R296
R293
R295
R319
R317
R311
R321
R320
R325
R322
R323
R324
R361
R369
R335
R330
R367
R331
R327
R328
R360
R362
R366
R334
R336
R332
R364
R357
R345
R333
R347
R363
R341
R342
R340
R358
R339
R350
R348
R343
R374
R349

244

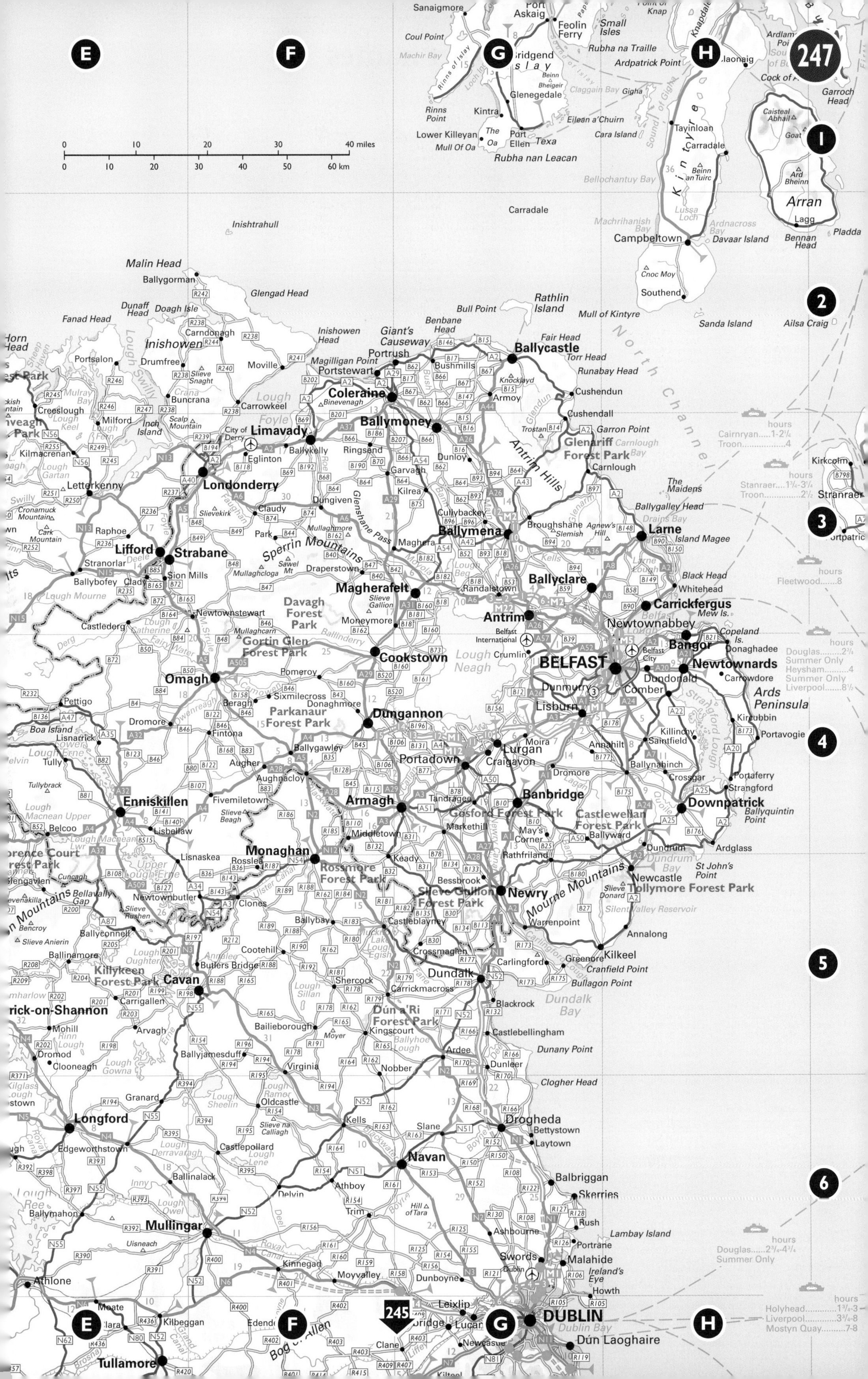

E
F
G
H
I
2
3
4
5
6
0 10 20 30 40 miles
0 10 20 30 40 50 60 km
Sanaigmore
Port Askaig
Feolin Ferry
Small Isles
Coul Point
Machir Bay
Bridgend
Islay
Rinns of Islay
Glenegedale
Kintra
Rinns Point
The Oa
Port Ellen
Texa
Lower Killeyan
Mull Of Oa
Rubha nan Leacan
Rubha na Traille
Ardpatrick Point
Gigha
Claggain Bay
Eilean a'Chuirn
Cara Island
Tayinloan
Carradale
Kintyre
Beinn an Tuirc
Bellochantuy Bay
Machrihanish Bay
Lussa Loch
Ardnacross Bay
Campbeltown
Davaar Island
Cnoc Moy
Southend
Sanda Island
Ailsa Craig
Cock of Arran
Garroch Head
Caisteal Abhail
Goat Fell
Ard Bheinn
Arran
Lagg
Pladda
Bennan Head
Inishtrahull
Malin Head
Ballygorman
Glengad Head
Dunaff Head
Doagh Isle
Fanad Head
Carndonagh
Inishowen
Horn Head
Portsalon
Drumfree
Slieve Snaght
Moville
Buncrana
Lough Foyle
Carrowkeel
Creeslough
Milford
Inch Island
Scalp Mountain
Kilmacrenan
Letterkenny
Lough Swilly
Cronamuck Mountain
Cark Mountain
Raphoe
Lifford
Strabane
Stranorlar
Ballybofey
Clady
Sion Mills
Lough Mourne
Castlederg
Inishowen Head
Giant's Causeway
Benbane Head
Bull Point
Rathlin Island
Mull of Kintyre
North Channel
Fair Head
Ballycastle
Torr Head
Runabay Head
Portrush
Bushmills
Magilligan Point
Portstewart
Coleraine
Knocklayd
Armoy
Cushendun
Cushendall
Garron Point
Ballymoney
Limavady
City of Derry
Eglinton
Londonderry
Ballykelly
Ringsend
Dunloy
Glenariff Forest Park
Carnlough
Antrim Hills
Trostan
Garvagh
Kilrea
Dungiven
Claudy
Slievekirk
Glenshane Pass
Cullybackey
Ballymena
Broughshane
Slemish
Agnew's Hill
Larne
Islandmagee
The Maidens
Ballygalley Head
Sperrin Mountains
Sawel Mt
Park
Maghera
Draperstown
Mullaghcloga
Magherafelt
Slieve Gallion
Randalstown
Ballyclare
Black Head
Whitehead
Antrim
Carrickfergus
Newtownabbey
Belfast International
Crumlin
Lough Neagh
BELFAST
Belfast City
Bangor
Copeland Is.
Donaghadee
Newtownards
Dundonald
Comber
Carrowdore
Ards Peninsula
Kircubbin
Portavogie
Newtownstewart
Davagh Forest Park
Moneymore
Gortin Glen Forest Park
Mullaghcarn
Cookstown
Omagh
Pomeroy
Sixmilecross
Beragh
Donaghmore
Parkanaur Forest Park
Dungannon
Fintona
Dromore
Pettigo
Boa Island
Lisnarrick
Lower Lough Erne
Tully
Ballygawley
Augher
Aughnacloy
Portadown
Lurgan
Craigavon
Moira
Lisburn
Dunmurry
Hillsborough
Annahilt
Saintfield
Killinchy
Strangford Lough
Ballynahinch
Crossgar
Portaferry
Strangford
Downpatrick
Ballyquintin Point
Enniskillen
Fivemiletown
Slieve Beagh
Lisbellaw
Belcoo
Armagh
Tandragee
Banbridge
Gosford Forest Park
Castlewellan Forest Park
Markethill
May's Corner
Ballyward
Dundrum
Dundrum Bay
Ardglass
St John's Point
Newcastle
Slieve Donard
Tollymore Forest Park
Mourne Mountains
Silent Valley Reservoir
Annalong
Kilkeel
Greenore
Cranfield Point
Bullagon Point
Middletown
Monaghan
Rosslea
Lisnaskea
Upper Lough Erne
Keady
Rossmore Forest Park
Bessbrook
Newry
Slieve Gullion Forest Park
Warrenpoint
Carlingford
Carlingford Lough
Newtownbutler
Clones
Castleblayney
Crossmaglen
Dundalk
Dundalk Bay
Blackrock
Castlebellingham
Dunany Point
Ballybay
Cootehill
Ballyconnell
Slieve Rushen
Bencroy
Slieve Anierin
Ballinamore
Killykeen Forest Park
Butlers Bridge
Cavan
Carrigallen
Carrick-on-Shannon
Shercock
Carrickmacross
Lough Sillan
Dún a'Rí Forest Park
Kingscourt
Ballyhoe Lough
Bailieborough
Moyer
Mohill
Dromod
Clooneagh
Arvagh
Lough Gowna
Ballyjamesduff
Virginia
Nobber
Ardee
Dunleer
Clogher Head
Granard
Lough Sheelin
Oldcastle
Lough Ramor
Slieve na Calliagh
Kells
Slane
Drogheda
Bettystown
Laytown
Longford
Edgeworthstown
Lough Derravaragh
Castlepollard
Lough Lene
Navan
Ballinalack
Athboy
Delvin
Hill of Tara
Balbriggan
Skerries
Rush
Lambay Island
Lough Ree
Ballymahon
Mullingar
Lough Owel
Trim
Ashbourne
Portrane
Uisneach
Royal Canal
Swords
Malahide
Dublin
Ireland's Eye
Howth
Athlone
Kinnegad
Moyvalley
Dunboyne
Moate
Kilbeggan
Edenderry
Leixlip
Lucan
DUBLIN
Dublin Bay
Dún Laoghaire
Clane
Newcastle
Tullamore
Bog of Allen
Grand Canal
Kilcock
245
hours
Cairnryan.....1-2¼
Troon.....4
Stranraer.....1¾-3¼
Troon.....2½
Stranraer
Kirkcolm
Fleetwood.....8
Douglas.....2¾
Summer Only
Heysham.....4
Summer Only
Liverpool.....8½
Douglas.....2¾-4¾
Summer Only
Holyhead.....1¾-3
Liverpool.....3¾-8
Mostyn Quay.....7-8

# Index to London street names

## General Abbreviations

| | | | | | | | | | |
|---|---|---|---|---|---|---|---|---|---|
| All | Alley | Circ | Circus | Flds | Fields | Ms | Mews | St | Street |
| App | Approach | Clo | Close | Gdn/Gdns | Garden/Gardens | N | North | St. | Saint |
| Arc | Arcade | Cor | Corner | Grd | Ground | Par | Parade | Ter | Terrace |
| Av/Ave | Avenue | Cres | Crescent | Grn | Green | Pas | Passage | Twr | Tower |
| Bdy | Broadway | Ct | Court | Gro | Grove | Pk | Park | W | West |
| Bldgs | Buildings | Ctyd | Courtyard | Ho | House | Pl | Place | Wf | Wharf |
| Br/Bri | Bridge | Dr | Drive | La | Lane | Rd | Road | Wk | Walk |
| Cen | Central, Centre | E | East | Lo | Lodge | Ri | Rise | Yd | Yard |
| Ch | Church | Embk | Embankment | Mans | Mansions | S | South | | |
| Chyd | Churchyard | Est | Estate | Mkt/Mkts | Market/Markets | Sq | Square | | |

## Post Town Abbreviations

| | | | | | | | | | |
|---|---|---|---|---|---|---|---|---|---|
| Bark. | Barking | Edg. | Edgware | Islw. | Isleworth | Pnr. | Pinner | Twick. | Twickenham |
| Beck. | Beckenham | Felt. | Feltham | Kings.T. | Kingston upon Thames | Rich. | Richmond | Uxb. | Uxbridge |
| Brent. | Brentford | Grnf. | Greenford | | | Ruis. | Ruislip | Walt. | Walton-on-Thames |
| Brom. | Bromley | Har. | Harrow | Mitch. | Mitcham | Stan. | Stanmore | W.Mol. | West Molesey |
| Chig. | Chigwell | Hmptn. | Hampton | Mord. | Morden | Sthl. | Southall | Wdf.Grn. | Woodford Green |
| Chis. | Chislehurst | Houns. | Hounslow | N.Mal. | New Malden | Tedd. | Teddington | Wem. | Wembley |
| E.Mol. | East Molesey | Ilf. | Ilford | Nthlt. | Northolt | Th.Hth. | Thornton Heath | | |


**A**

Abbeville Rd SW4 223 A5
Abbey Orchard St SW1 224 J13
Abbey Rd NW6; NW8 220 D3
Abbey Rd, Bark. IG11 222 D2
Abbey St SE1 223 B4
Abbott Rd E14 222 C3
Abercorn Pl NW8 220 D3
Abingdon St SW1 225 K13
Acacia Rd, Hmptn. TW12 221 A6
Academy Rd SE18 223 D4
Achilles Way W1 224 C10
Acre La SW2 223 A5
Acton La NW10 220 C3
Acton La W3; W4 221 C4
Adam & Eve Ct W1 224 G5
Adam St WC2 225 L8
Adams Row W1 224 C8
Addington St SE1 225 N12
Addle Hill EC4 225 S7
Addle St EC2 225 U4
Adelaide Av SE4 223 C5
Adelaide Rd NW3 220 D2
Adelaide St WC2 225 K8
Adeline Pl WC1 224 J4
Adelphi Ter WC2 225 L8
Aerodrome Rd NW4; NW9 220 C1
Agar St WC2 225 K8
Agdon St EC1 225 R1
Agincourt Rd NW3 220 D2
Air St W1 224 G8
Akerman Rd SW9 223 A4
Alaska St SE1 225 P10
Albany W1 224 F8
Albany Ctyd W1 224 G8
Albany Rd SE5 223 B4
Albany St NW1 222 A3
Albemarle Rd, Beck. BR3 223 C6
Albemarle St W1 224 E8
Albemarle Way EC1 225 R2
Albert Br Rd SW11 221 D4
Albert Embk SE1 223 A4
Albert Gate SW1 224 A11
Albert Rd E16 222 D3
Albert Rd N22 222 A1
Albion Pl EC1 225 R3
Albion Rd N16 222 B2
Albion Way EC1 225 T4
Aldburgh Ms W1 224 C5
Aldermanbury EC2 225 U5
Aldermanbury Sq EC2 225 U4
Alderney Av, Houns. TW5 221 A4
Aldersbrook Rd E11; E12 222 D2
Aldersgate St EC1 225 T5
Aldford St W1 224 B9
Aldwych WC2 225 M7
Alexandra Av W4 221 C4
Alexandra Av, Har. HA2 220 A2
Alexandra Pk Rd N10; N22 222 A1
Alexandra Rd SW19 221 D6
Alfred Ms W1 224 H3
Alfred Pl WC1 224 H3
All Souls Av NW10 220 C3
All Souls Pl W1 224 E4
Allenby Rd, Sthl. UB1 220 A3
Allington St SW1 224 F14
Allsop Pl NW1 224 A2
Alperton La, Grnf. UB6; Wem. HA0 220 B3
Ambassador's Ct SW1 224 G10
Ambrosden Av SW1 224 G14
Amen Cor EC4 225 S6
Amen Ct EC4 225 S5
America St SE1 225 T10
Amhurst Pk N16 222 B2
Amhurst Rd N16 222 B2
Anchor Yd EC1 225 U1
Andrew Borde St WC2 224 J5
Andrewes Ho EC2 225 U4
Andrews Crosse WC2 225 P6
Anerley Hill SE19 223 B6
Anerley Rd SE19; SE20 223 B6
Angel Ct SW1 224 G10
Angel St EC1 225 T5
Ann's Cl SW1 224 A12
Anson Rd NW2 220 C2
Apothecary St EC4 225 R6
Apple Tree Yd SW1 224 G9
Apsley Way W1 224 C11
Aquinas St SE1 225 Q10
Arch St SE1 225 T14
Archer St W1 224 H7
Arches, The WC2 225 L9
Archibald Ms W1 224 C9
Archway Rd N6; N19 220 D1
Argent St SE1 225 S11
Argyle Rd W13; Grnf. UB6 220 B3
Argyll St W1 224 F6
Arlington St SW1 224 F9
Armoury Way SW18 221 D5
Arne St WC2 225 L6
Arneway St SW1 224 J14
Arthur Rd SW19 221 D6
Artillery Pl SW1 224 H14
Artillery Row SW1 224 H14
Arundel Gt Ct WC2 225 N7
Arundel St WC2 225 N7
Ashentree Ct EC4 225 Q6
Ashgrove Rd, Brom. BR1 223 C6
Ashland Pl W1 224 B3
Ashley Gdns SW1 224 G14
Ashley Pl SW1 224 F14
Askew Rd W12 220 C3
Aspen Way E14 222 C3
Audley Sq W1 224 C9
Ave Maria La EC4 225 S6
Avenue, The SW4 223 A5
Avenue, The W4 221 C4
Avenue, The, Hmptn. TW12 221 A6
Avenue, The (Hatch End), Pnr. HA5 220 A1
Avenue, The, Twick. TW1 221 B5
Avenue, The, Wem. HA9 220 B2
Avenue Rd NW8 220 D2
Avery Row W1 224 D7
Avon Pl SE1 225 U12
Avondale Rd, Brom. BR1 223 C6
Avonmouth St SE1 225 T13
Aybrook St W1 224 B4
Aylesbury St EC1 225 R2
Aylmer Rd N2 220 D1
Ayres St SE1 225 U11

**B**

Babmaes St SW1 224 G8
Back Hill EC1 225 P2
Bainbridge St WC1 224 J5
Baird St EC1 225 U1
Baker St NW1 224 A2
Baker St W1 224 A3
Baker's Ms W1 224 B5
Baker's Row EC1 225 P2
Balaam St E13 222 D3
Balderton St W1 224 C6
Baldwin's Gdns EC1 225 P3
Balfour Ms W1 224 C9
Balfour Pl W1 224 C8
Balham High Rd SW12; SW17 223 A5
Balham Hill SW12 223 A5
Ballards La N3; N12 220 D1
Balls Pond Rd N1 222 B2
Baltic St E EC1 225 T2
Baltic St W EC1 225 T2
Banbury Ct WC2 225 K7
Bank End SE1 225 U9
Bankside SE1 225 T8
Banner St EC1 225 U2
Barbican, The EC2 225 T3
Barbon Cl WC1 225 M3
Barge Ho St SE1 225 Q9
Baring Rd SE12 223 D5
Baring St N1 222 B3
Barkham Ter SE1 225 Q13
Barking Rd E6; E13; E16 222 C3
Barlby Rd W10 220 C3
Barley Mow Pas EC1 225 S4
Barlow Pl W1 224 E8
Barnard's Inn EC1 225 Q5
Barnes High St SW13 221 C4
Barons Pl SE1 225 Q12
Barrett St W1 224 C6
Barry Rd SE22 223 B5
Barter St WC1 225 L4
Bartholomew Cl EC1 225 T4
Bartholomew Pl EC1 225 T4
Bartholomew Sq EC1 225 U1
Bartlett Ct EC4 225 Q5
Bartletts Pas EC4 225 Q5
Barton St SW1 224 K13
Bastwick St EC1 225 T1
Bateman St W1 224 H6
Bateman's Bldgs W1 224 H6
Bath Ct EC1 225 P2
Bath Rd W4 221 C4
Bath Ter SE1 225 T14
Battersea Br Rd SW11 221 D4
Battersea Pk Rd SW8; SW11 221 D4
Battersea Ri SW11 221 D5
Bayley St WC1 224 H4
Baylis Rd SE1 225 P12
Bayswater Rd W2 220 D3
Beak St W1 224 G7
Bear All EC4 225 R5
Bear Gdns SE1 225 T9
Bear La SE1 225 S9
Bear St WC2 224 J7
Beauchamp St EC1 225 P4
Beaumont Ms W1 224 C3
Beaumont Pl W1 224 G1
Beaumont St W1 224 C3
Beckenham Hill Rd SE6; Beck. BR3 223 C6
Beckenham La, Brom. BR2 223 C6
Beckenham Rd, Beck. BR3 223 C6
Bedford Av WC1 224 J4
Bedford Ct WC2 225 K8
Bedford Hill SW12; SW16 223 A5
Bedford Pl W1 224 G3
Bedford Pl WC1 225 K3
Bedford Rd SW4 223 A5
Bedford Row WC1 225 N3
Bedford Sq WC1 224 J4
Bedford St WC2 225 K7
Bedford Way WC1 224 J2
Bedfordbury WC2 225 K7
Beech St EC2 225 T3
Beehive La, Ilf. IG1, IG4 222 D1
Beeston Pl SW1 224 E14
Belgrave Ms N SW1 224 B12
Belgrave Ms S SW1 224 C13
Belgrave Ms W SW1 224 B13
Belgrave Pl SW1 224 C13
Belgrave Rd SW1 223 A4
Belgrave Sq SW1 224 B13
Belgrave Yd SW1 224 D14
Bell Grn SE26 223 C5
Bell La NW4 220 C1
Bell Wf La EC4 225 U7
Bell Yd WC2 225 P5
Bellevue Rd SW17 221 D5
Belmont Hill SE13 223 C5
Belmont Rd N15 222 B1
Belsize Rd NW6 220 D3
Belvedere Bldgs SE1 225 S12
Belvedere Pl SE1 225 S12
Belvedere Rd SE1 225 N11
Ben Jonson Rd E1 222 C3
Benjamin St EC1 225 R3
Bennet's Hill EC4 225 S7
Bennett St SW1 224 F9
Bennetts Yd SW1 224 J14
Bentinck Ms W1 224 C5
Bentinck St W1 224 C5
Beresford St SE18 223 D4
Berkeley Ms W1 224 A5
Berkeley Sq W1 224 E8
Berkeley St W1 224 E8
Berkshire Gdns N13 222 A1
Bernard St WC1 225 K2
Berners Ms W1 224 G4
Berners Pl W1 224 G5
Berners St W1 224 G4
Berry St EC1 225 S1
Berwick St W1 224 H6
Bessborough Rd, Har. HA1 220 A2
Bethnal Grn Rd E1; E2 222 B3
Bethune Rd N16 222 B2
Betterton St WC2 225 K6
Beulah Hill SE19 223 A6
Beverley Dr, Edg. HA8 220 B1
Beverley Way (Kingston Bypass) SW20 221 C6
Bexley Rd SE9 223 D5
Bickenhall St W1 224 A3
Bickley Pk Rd, Brom. BR1 223 D6
Bickley Rd, Brom. BR1 223 D6
Billet Rd E17 222 B1
Bilton Rd, Grnf. UB6 220 B3
Bingham Pl W1 224 B3
Binney St W1 224 C7
Bird St W1 224 C6
Birdcage Wk SW1 224 G12
Bishops Av, The N2 220 D2
Bishops Br Rd W2 220 D3
Bishop's Ct EC4 225 R5
Bishop's Ct WC2 225 P5
Bishops Way E2 222 B3
Bishopsgate EC2 222 B3
Bittacy Hill NW7 220 C1
Bittern St SE1 225 T12
Black Friars Ct EC4 225 R7
Black Friars La EC4 225 R7
Blackbrook La, Brom. BR1, BR2 223 D6
Blackburnie's Ms W1 224 B7
Blackfriars Br EC4 225 R7
Blackfriars Br SE1 225 R7
Blackfriars Pas EC4 225 R7
Blackfriars Rd SE1 225 R12
Blackheath Rd SE10 223 C4
Blackhorse La E17 222 B1
Blackshaw Rd SW17 221 D6
Blackstock Rd N4; N5 222 A2
Blackwall La SE10 223 C4
Blackwall Tunnel E14 222 C3
Blake Hall Rd E11 222 D2
Blandford St W1 224 A5
Bleeding Heart Yd EC1 225 Q4
Blenheim St W1 224 D6
Bloomfield Pl W1 224 E7
Bloomsbury Ct WC1 225 L4
Bloomsbury Pl WC1 225 L3
Bloomsbury Sq WC1 225 L4
Bloomsbury St WC1 224 J4
Bloomsbury Way WC1 225 K5
Blore Ct W1 224 H6
Blue Ball Yd SW1 224 F10
Bolingbroke Gro SW11 221 D5
Bollo La W3; W4 221 B4
Bolsover St W1 224 E2
Bolt Ct EC4 225 Q6
Bolton St W1 224 E9
Book Ms WC2 224 J6
Booth Rd NW9 220 C1
Booth's Pl W1 224 G4
Borough High St SE1 225 T12
Borough Rd SE1 225 R13
Borough Sq SE1 225 T12
Boston Manor Rd, Brent. TW8 221 B4
Boston Rd W7 221 A4
Boswell Ct WC1 225 L3
Boswell St WC1 225 L3
Boundary Rd E13 222 D3
Boundary Rd E17 222 C2
Boundary Row SE1 225 R11
Bounds Grn Rd N11; N22 222 A1
Bourchier St W1 224 H7
Bourdon Pl W1 224 E7
Bourdon St W1 224 D8
Bourlet Cl W1 224 F4
Bourne Est EC1 225 P3
Bouverie St EC4 225 Q6
Bow Chyd EC4 225 U6
Bow La EC4 225 U6
Bow Rd E3 222 C3
Bow St WC2 225 L6
Bowland Yd SW1 224 A12
Bowling Grn La EC1 225 Q1
Boxtree La, Har. HA3 220 A1
Boxtree Rd, Har. HA3 220 A1
Boyce St SE1 225 N10
Boyfield St SE1 225 S12
Boyle St W1 224 F7
Brackley St EC1 225 T3
Brad St SE1 225 Q10
Brady St E1 222 B3
Brantwood Rd N17 222 B1
Bread St EC4 225 U6
Bream's Bldgs EC4 225 P5
Brecknock Rd N7; N19 222 A2
Brent St NW4 220 C1
Brentfield NW10 220 C2
Brentfield Rd NW10 220 C2
Bressenden Pl SW1 224 E13
Brewer St W1 224 G7
Brewer's Grn SW1 224 H13
Brewers Hall Gdns EC2 225 U4
Brewhouse Yd EC1 225 R1
Brick Ct EC4 225 P6
Brick La E1; E2 222 B3
Brick St W1 224 D10
Bride Ct EC4 225 R6
Bride La EC4 225 R6
Bridewell Pl EC4 225 R6
Bridford Ms W1 224 E3
Bridge La NW11 220 D1
Bridge Rd, E.Mol. KT8 221 A6
Bridge Rd, Houns. TW3; Islw. TW7 221 A5
Bridge St SW1 225 K12
Bridgewater Rd, Wem. HA0 220 B2
Bridgewater Sq EC2 225 T3
Bridgewater St EC2 225 T3
Bridle La W1 224 G7
Brinton Wk SE1 225 R10
Briset St EC1 225 R3
Britton St EC1 225 R2
Brixton Hill SW2 223 A5
Brixton Rd SW9 223 A4
Brixton Water La SW2 223 A5
Broad Ct WC2 225 L6
Broad La N15 222 B1
Broad La, Hmptn. TW12 221 A6
Broad Sanctuary SW1 224 J12
Broad Wk SE3 223 D4
Broad Wk W1 224 B9
Broad Yd EC1 225 R2
Broadbent St W1 224 D7
Broadmead Rd, Wdf.Grn. IG8 222 D1
Broadstone Pl W1 224 B4
Broadwall SE1 225 Q9
Broadway E15 222 C2
Broadway SW1 224 H13
Broadway, The SW19 221 D6
Broadway, The W5 220 B3
Broadway, The, Grnf. UB6 220 A3
Broadway, The, Sthl. UB1 220 A3
Broadwick St W1 224 G7
Brockham St SE1 225 U13
Brockley Gro SE4 223 C5
Brockley Ri SE23 223 C5
Brockley Rd SE4 223 C5
Broken Wf EC4 225 T7
Bromley Common, Brom. BR2 223 D6
Bromley Hill, Brom. BR1 223 C6
Bromley Pl W1 224 F3
Bromley Rd, Beck. BR3; Brom. BR2 223 C6
Bromley Rd SE6; Brom. BR1 223 C5
Brompton Rd SW1; SW3; SW7 221 D4
Brondesbury Pk NW2; NW6 220 C2
Brondesbury Rd NW6 220 D3
Brook Dr SE11 225 Q14
Brook Gate W1 224 A8
Brook St W1 224 C7
Brooke St EC1 225 P4
Brooke's Ct EC1 225 P3
Brookes Mkt EC1 225 Q3
Brookmill Rd SE8 223 C4
Brook's Ms W1 224 D7
Broom Rd, Tedd. TW11 221 B6
Broomwood Rd SW11 221 D5
Brown Hart Gdns W1 224 C7
Brownhill Rd SE6 223 C5
Browning Ms W1 224 D4
Browning Rd E12 222 D2
Brownlow Ms WC1 225 N2
Brownlow Rd N11 222 A1
Brownlow St WC1 225 N4
Bruce Gro N17 222 B1
Brunswick Cen WC1 225 K1
Brunswick Ms W1 224 A5
Brunswick Rd W5 220 B3
Brunswick Sq WC1 225 L2
Bruton La W1 224 E8
Bruton Pl W1 224 E8
Bruton St W1 224 E8
Brydges Pl WC2 224 K8
Buckhold Rd SW18 221 D5
Buckingham Arc WC2 225 L8
Buckingham Gate SW1 224 F12
Buckingham Ms SW1 224 F13
Buckingham Pl SW1 224 F13
Buckingham St WC2 225 L8
Buckley St SE1 225 P10
Bucknall St WC2 224 J5
Bugsby's Way SE7; SE10 223 D4
Bull Inn Ct WC2 225 L8
Bull Wf La EC4 225 U7
Bulstrode Pl W1 224 C4
Bulstrode St W1 224 C5
Bunns La NW7 220 C1
Burdett Rd E3; E14 222 C3
Burdett St SE1 225 P13
Burges Rd E6 222 D2
Burgon St EC4 225 S6
Burleigh St WC2 225 M7
Burlington Arc W1 224 F8
Burlington Gdns W1 224 F8
Burlington La W4 221 C4
Burlington Rd, N.Mal. KT3 221 C6
Burnt Ash Hill SE12 223 D5
Burnt Ash La, Brom. BR1 223 D6
Burnt Ash Rd SE12 223 C5
Burnt Oak Bdy, Edg. HA8 220 B1
Burntwood La SW17 221 D5
Burrage Rd SE18 223 D4
Burrell St SE1 225 R9
Burrows Ms SE1 225 R11
Bury Pl WC1 225 K4
Bury St SW1 224 F9
Bush Rd E11 222 D2
Bushey Rd SW20 221 C6
Butler Pl SW1 224 H13
Byng Pl WC1 224 H2
Bywell Pl W1 224 F4

**C**

Cable St E1 222 B3
Cadogan La SW1 224 B14
Cadogan Pl SW1 224 A14
Cadogan Sq SW1 224 A14
Cahill St EC1 225 U2
Caleb St SE1 225 T11
Caledonian Rd N1; N7 222 A2
Calmont Rd, Brom. BR1 223 C6
Calthorpe St WC1 225 N1
Camberwell Ch St SE5 223 B4
Camberwell New Rd SE5 223 A4
Camberwell Rd SE5 223 B4
Cambridge Circ WC2 224 J6
Cambridge Heath Rd E1; E2 222 B3
Camden High St NW1 222 A3
Camden Rd N7; NW1 222 A2
Camrose Av, Edg. HA8 220 B1
Candover St W1 224 F4
Cannizaro Rd SW19 221 C6
Cannon St EC4 225 T6
Cannon St Rd E1 222 B3
Canon Row SW1 225 K12
Canonbury Rd N1 222 A2
Canvey St SE1 225 S9
Capel Rd E7; E12 222 D2
Capener's Cl SW1 224 B12
Capper St WC1 224 G2
Capworth St E10 222 C2
Carburton St W1 224 E3
Carey La EC2 225 T5
Carey St WC2 225 N6
Carlisle La SE1 225 N14
Carlisle Pl SW1 224 F14
Carlisle St W1 224 H6
Carlos Pl W1 224 C8
Carlton Gdns SW1 224 H10
Carlton Ho Ter SW1 224 H10
Carlton St SW1 224 H8
Carlton Twr Pl SW1 224 A13
Carmelite St EC4 225 Q7
Carnaby St W1 224 F6
Carpenter St W1 224 D8
Carpenters Rd E15 222 C2
Carr Rd, Nthlt. UB5 220 A2
Carrington St W1 224 D10
Carter La EC4 225 S6
Carteret St SW1 224 H12
Carthusian St EC1 225 T3
Carting La WC2 225 L8
Carton St W1 224 A5
Cassland Rd E9 222 B2
Castelnau SW13 221 C4
Castle Baynard St EC4 225 S7
Castle La SW1 224 G13
Castle Yd SE1 225 S9
Castlebar Hill W5 220 B3
Castlebar Rd W5 220 B3
Catford Hill SE6 223 C5
Catford Rd SE6 223 C5
Cathall Rd E11 222 C2
Cathedral Piazza SW1 224 F14
Cathedral Pl EC4 225 T5
Catherine Griffiths Ct EC1 225 Q1
Catherine Pl SW1 224 F13
Catherine St WC2 225 M7
Catherine Wheel Yd SW1 224 F10
Catton St WC1 225 M4
Cavendish Ms N W1 224 E3
Cavendish Ms S W1 224 E
Cavendish Pl W1 224 E5
Cavendish Rd SW12 223 A5
Cavendish Sq W1 224 E5
Caxton St SW1 224 G13
Cazenove Rd N16 222 B2
Cecil Ct WC2 224 J
Cedars Rd SW4 223 A
Cedars Rd W4 221 B
Centaur St SE1 225 N1
Central Av, Houns. TW3 221 A
Central Hill SE19 223 B
Central Mkts EC1 225 S
Central Pk Rd E6 222 D
Centre Rd E7; E11 222 D
Centrepoint WC1 224 J
Chadwick St SW1 224 J1

Chalk Fm Rd NW1 222 A2
Chamberlayne Rd NW10 220 C3
Chancel St SE1 225 R9
Chancery La WC2 225 P5
Chandos Pl WC2 225 K8
Chandos St W1 224 E4
Chapel Pl W1 224 D6
Chapel St SW1 224 C13
Chaplin Cl SE1 225 Q11
Chapone Pl W1 224 H6
Chapter Ho Ct EC4 225 T6
Charing Cross SW1 224 K9
Charing Cross Rd WC2 224 J5
Charles II St SW1 224 H9
Charles St W1 224 D9
Charlotte Ms W1 224 G3
Charlotte Pl W1 224 G4
Charlotte St W1 224 G4
Charlton Ch La SE7 223 D4
Charlton Pk La SE7 223 D4
Charlton Pk Rd SE7 223 D4
Charlton Rd SE3; SE7 223 D4
Charlton Rd, Har. HA3 220 B1
Charlton Way SE3 223 C4
Charter Rd, The, Wdf.Grn. IG8 222 C1
Charterhouse Bldgs EC1 225 S2
Charterhouse Ms EC1 225 S3
Charterhouse Sq EC1 225 S3
Charterhouse St EC1 225 Q4
Chase, The, Stan. HA7 220 B1
Chase Rd NW10; W3 220 C3
Cheapside EC2 225 U6
Chelsea Embk SW3 223 A4
Chenies Ms WC1 224 H2
Chenies St WC1 224 H3
Chepstow Rd W2 220 D3
Chequer St EC1 225 U2
Cherry Tree Wk EC1 225 U2
Chertsey Rd, Twick. TW1, TW2 221 A5
Chesham Cl SW1 224 B14
Chesham Ms SW1 224 B13
Chesham Pl SW1 224 B14
Chesham St SW1 224 B14
Cheshire Ct EC4 225 Q6
Chester Cl SW1 224 C12
Chester Ms SW1 224 D13
Chester Sq Ms SW1 224 D14
Chester St SW1 224 C13
Chesterfield Gdns W1 224 D9
Chesterfield Hill W1 224 D8
Chesterfield St W1 224 D9
Cheyne Wk SW10 221 D4
Chichele Rd NW2 220 C2
Chicheley St SE1 225 N11
Chichester Rents WC2 225 P5
Chigwell Rd E18; Wdf.Grn. IG8 222 D1
Chiltern St W1 224 B3
Chinbrook Rd SE12 223 D5
Ching Ct WC2 224 K6
Chingford Rd E4; E17 222 C1
Chislehurst Rd Brom. BR1; Chis. BR7 223 D6
Chiswell St EC1 225 U3
Chiswick High Rd W4; Brent. TW8 221 B4
Chiswick La W4 221 C4
Chitty St W1 224 G3
Chobham Rd E15 222 C2
Chrisp St E14 222 C3
Christ Ch Pas EC1 225 S5
Christchurch Av, Har. HA3 220 B1
Christchurch Rd SW2 223 A5
Church Entry EC4 225 S6
Church Gro, Kings.T. KT1 221 B6
Church La E11 222 C2
Church La NW9 220 C1
Church La SW17 223 A6
Church Pl SW1 224 G8
Church Rd E10 222 C2
Church Rd NW10 220 C2
Church Rd SE19 223 B6
Church Rd SW13 221 C4
Church Rd SW19 221 C6
Church Rd W7 220 A3
Church Rd (Heston), Houns. TW5 221 A4
Church Rd, Mitch. CR4 221 D6
Church St, Hmptn. TW12 221 A6
City Rd EC1 222 A3
Clapham Common N Side SW4 223 A5
Clapham Common S Side SW4 223 A5
Clapham Pk Rd SW4 223 A5
Clapham Rd SW9 223 A4
Clapton Common E5 222 B2
Clare Mkt WC2 225 M6
Claremont Rd NW2 220 C2
Clarence Av, N.Mal. KT3 221 C6
Clarence La SW15 221 C5
Clarence Ter NW1 224 A1
Clarges Ms W1 224 D9
Clarges St W1 224 E9
Clarke's Ms W1 224 C3
Clay St W1 224 A4
Clayton Rd SE15 223 B4
Clement's Inn WC2 225 N6
Clement's Inn Pas WC2 225 N6
Clennam St SE1 225 U11
Clerkenwell Cl EC1 225 Q1
Clerkenwell Grn EC1 225 Q2
Clerkenwell Rd EC1 225 P2
Cleveland Ms W1 224 F3
Cleveland Pl SW1 224 G9
Cleveland Row SW1 224 F10
Cleveland St W1 224 F2
Clifford Av SW14 221 B5
Clifford St W1 224 F8
Clifford's Inn Pas EC4 225 P6
Clifton Gdns W9 220 D3
Clink St SE1 225 U9
Clipstone Ms W1 224 F2
Clipstone St W1 224 E3
Cloak La EC4 225 U7
Cloth Ct EC1 225 S4
Cloth Fair EC1 225 S4
Cloth St EC1 225 T3
Coach & Horses Yd W1 224 E7
Cock La EC1 225 R4
Cockpit Steps SW1 224 J12
Cockpit Yd WC1 225 N3
Cockspur Ct SW1 224 J9
Cockspur St SW1 224 J9
Coin St SE1 225 P9
Coldbath Sq EC1 225 P1
Coldharbour La SE5; SW9 223 A5
Cole St SE1 225 U12
Coley St WC1 225 N2
Colindale Av NW9 220 C1
Colindeep La NW4; NW9 220 C1
College Hill EC4 225 U7
College Hill Rd, Har. HA3 220 A1
College Ms SW1 225 K13
College Rd SE19; SE21 223 B5
College Rd, Brom. BR1 223 D6
College Rd, Har. HA1 220 A1
Collinson St SE1 225 T12
Collinson Wk SE1 225 T12
Colnbrook St SE1 225 R14
Colney Hatch La N10; N11 220 D1
Colombo St SE1 225 R10
Colonnade WC1 225 K2
Colville Pl W1 224 G4
Commercial Rd E1; E14 222 B3
Commercial St E1 222 B3
Commercial Way SE15 223 B4
Commonside E, Mitch. CR4 223 A6
Commonside W, Mitch. CR4 221 D6
Compton Pas EC1 225 S1
Compton Pl WC1 225 K1
Compton St EC1 225 R1
Concert Hall App SE1 225 N10
Conduit Ct WC2 225 K7
Conduit St W1 224 E7
Coningham Rd W12 220 C3
Connaught Rd E16 222 D3
Cons St SE1 225 Q11
Constitution Hill SW1 224 D11
Conway Ms W1 224 F2
Conway St W1 224 F2
Cool Oak La NW9 220 C2
Coombe La SW20 221 C6
Coombe La W, Kings.T. KT2 221 B6
Coombe Rd, Kings.T. KT2 221 B6
Coombe Rd, N.Mal. KT3 221 C6
Cooper Cl SE1 225 Q12
Copenhagen St N1 222 A3
Copperfield St SE1 225 S11
Coppetts Rd N10 222 A1
Copse Hill SW20 221 C6
Coptic St WC1 224 K4
Coral St SE1 225 Q12
Coram St WC1 224 K2
Cork St W1 224 F8
Cork St Ms W1 224 F8
Corner Ho St WC2 225 K9
Cornwall Rd SE1 225 P9
Cornwall Ter NW1 224 A2
Cornwall Ter Ms NW1 224 A2
Coronation Rd NW10 220 B3
Corporation Row EC1 225 Q1
Cosmo Pl WC1 225 L3
Cosser St SE1 225 P13
Cotswold Ct EC1 225 T1
Cottenham Pk Rd SW20 221 C6
Cottesloe Ms SE1 225 Q13
County St SE1 225 U14
Court Rd SE9 223 D5
Courtenay Av, Har. HA3 220 A1
Covent Gdn WC2 225 L7
Coventry St W1 224 H8
Cowcross St EC1 225 R3
Cowley St SW1 224 K13
Crab Hill, Beck. BR3 223 C6
Craigs Ct SW1 224 K9
Cramer St W1 224 C4
Cranbourn All WC2 224 J7
Cranbourn St WC2 224 J7
Cranbrook Rd, Ilf. IG1, IG2, IG6 222 D1
Crane Ct EC4 225 Q6
Cranfield Row SE1 225 Q13
Cranley Gdns N10 222 A1
Cranmer Rd, Mitch. CR4 221 D6
Craven Pk NW10 220 C3
Craven Pas WC2 225 K9
Craven St WC2 225 K9
Crawford Pas EC1 225 P2
Creed La EC4 225 S6
Creek Rd SE8; SE10 223 C4
Creighton Av N2; N10 220 D1
Crescent Row EC1 225 T2
Cricklewood Bdy NW2 220 C2
Cricklewood La NW2 220 D2
Cripplegate St EC2 225 T3
Cromwell Rd SW5; SW7 221 D4
Cromwell Twr EC2 225 U3
Cross Deep, Twick. TW1 221 A5
Cross Keys Cl W1 224 C4
Cross Keys Sq EC1 225 T4
Crossway SW20 221 C6
Crouch End Hill N8 222 A2
Crouch Hill N4; N8 222 A1
Crown Ct EC2 225 U6
Crown Ct WC2 225 L6
Crown Dale SE19 223 B6
Crown La SW16 223 A6
Crown La, Mord. SM4 221 D6
Crown Office Row EC4 225 P7
Crown Pas SW1 224 G10
Crown Rd, Twick. TW1 221 B5
Crowshott Av, Stan. HA7 220 B1
Croxted Rd SE21; SE24 223 B5
Croydon Rd SE20 223 B6
Croydon Rd, Beck. BR3 223 C6
Crystal Palace Par SE19 223 B6
Crystal Palace Pk Rd SE26 223 B6
Cubitts Yd WC2 225 L7
Culross St W1 224 B8
Culver Gro, Stan. HA7 220 B1
Currey Rd, Grnf. UB6 220 A2
Cursitor St EC4 225 P5
Curzon Gate W1 224 C10
Curzon Pl W1 224 C10
Curzon St W1 224 C10
Cut, The SE1 225 Q11
Cypress Pl W1 224 G2
Cyrus St EC1 225 S1

**D**

Dacre St SW1 224 H13
Dallington St EC1 225 S1
Dalston La E8 222 B2
Dames Rd E7 222 D2
Dane St WC1 225 M4
Dansey Pl W1 224 H7
D'Arblay St W1 224 G6
Dartmouth Pk Hill N19; NW5 222 A2
Dartmouth Rd SE23; SE26 223 B5
Dartmouth St SW1 224 H12
David Ms W1 224 A3
Davidge St SE1 225 R12
Davies Ms W1 224 D7
Davies St W1 224 D7
Dawes Rd SW6 221 D4
De Walden St W1 224 C4
Dean Bradley St SW1 225 K14
Dean Farrar St SW1 224 H13
Dean Stanley St SW1 225 K14
Dean St W1 224 H5
Dean Trench St SW1 224 K14
Deanery Ms W1 224 C9
Deanery St W1 224 C9
Deans Ct EC4 225 S6
Deans La, Edg. HA8 220 C1
Deans Ms W1 224 E5
Dean's Yd SW1 224 J13
Deansbrook Rd, Edg. HA8 220 B1
Defoe Ho EC2 225 U3
Denman St W1 224 H8
Denmark Hill SE5 223 B5
Denmark Pl WC2 224 J5
Denmark St WC2 224 J6
Deptford Ch St SE8 223 C4
Derby Gate SW1 225 K11
Derby St W1 224 C10
Dering St W1 224 D6
Devas St E3 222 C3
Devereux Ct WC2 225 P6
Devons Rd E3 222 C3
Devonshire Cl W1 224 D3
Devonshire Ms N W1 224 D3
Devonshire Ms S W1 224 D3
Devonshire Ms W W1 224 D2
Devonshire Pl W1 224 C2
Devonshire Pl Ms W1 224 C2
Devonshire Rd NW7 220 C1
Devonshire Rd SE23 223 B5
Devonshire Row Ms W1 224 E2
Devonshire St W1 224 C3
Diadem Ct W1 224 H6
Diana Pl NW1 224 E1
Dickens Sq SE1 225 U13
Disney Pl SE1 225 U11
Disney St SE1 225 U11
Distaff La EC4 225 T7
Dodson St SE1 225 Q12
Dog Kennel Hill SE22 223 B5
Dolben St SE1 225 R10
Dolby Ct EC4 225 U7
Dollis Hill La NW2 220 C2
Dollis Rd N3; NW7 220 D1
Dombey St WC1 225 M3
Domingo St EC1 225 T1
Doon St SE1 225 P10
Dorrington St EC1 225 P3
Dorset Bldgs EC4 225 R6
Dorset Ms SW1 224 D13
Dorset Ri EC4 225 R6
Dorset Rd SW19 221 D6
Dorset St W1 224 A4
Doughty Ms WC1 225 M2
Doughty St WC1 225 M1
Dover Ho Rd SW15 221 C5
Dover St W1 224 E8
Dover Yd W1 224 F9
Down St W1 224 D10
Down St Ms W1 224 D10
Downham Way, Brom. BR1 223 C6
Downhills Way N17 222 B1
Downing St SW1 224 K11
Doyce St SE1 225 T11
Drake St WC1 225 M4
Drakefell Rd SE4; SE14 223 B5
Draycott Av, Har. HA3 220 B1
Drayton Grn Rd W13 220 B3
Drayton Pk N5 222 A2
Drive, The, Ilf. IG1 222 D2
Drummond St NW1 224 F1
Drury La WC2 225 L6
Drury Way NW10 220 C2
Dryden St WC2 225 L6
Duchess Ms W1 224 E4
Duchess St W1 224 E4
Duchy St SE1 225 Q9
Duck La W1 224 H6
Dudden Hill La NW10 220 C2
Dufferin St EC1 225 U2
Dufour's Pl W1 224 G6
Duke of Wellington Pl SW1 224 C11
Duke of York St SW1 224 G9
Duke St SW1 224 G9
Duke St W1 224 C5
Dukes Av, Rich. TW10; Kings.T. KT2 221 B6
Duke's Ms W1 224 C5
Duke's Yd W1 224 C7
Dulwich Common SE21; SE22 223 B5
Dulwich Rd SE24 223 A5
Dulwich Village SE21 223 B5
Dulwich Wd Pk SE19 223 B6
Duncannon St WC2 225 K8
Dunns Pas WC1 225 L5
Dunraven St W1 224 A7
Dunstable Ms W1 224 C3
Dunton Rd SE1 223 B4
Duplex Ride SW1 224 A12
Durham Ho St WC2 225 L8
Durham Rd SW20 221 C6
Durnsford Rd N11 222 A1
Durnsford Rd SW19 221 D5
Durweston Ms W1 224 A3
Durweston St W1 224 A3
Dyer's Bldgs EC1 225 P4
Dyott St WC1 224 K5

**E**

Eagle Ct EC1 225 R3
Eagle Pl SW1 224 G8
Eagle St WC1 225 M4
Ealing Grn W5 220 B3
Ealing Rd, Brent. TW8 221 B4
Ealing Rd, Wem. HA0 220 B2
Earlham St WC2 224 J6
Earls Ct Rd SW5; W8 221 D4
Earlsfield Rd SW18 221 D5
Earnshaw St WC2 224 J5
Easley's Ms W1 224 C5
East Av E12 222 D2
East Cross Route E3 222 C2
East Dulwich Gro SE22 223 B5
East Dulwich Rd SE15; SE22 223 B5
East End Rd N2; N3 220 D1
East Ferry Rd E14 223 C4
East Harding St EC4 225 Q5
East Heath Rd NW3 220 D2
East Hill SW18 221 D5
East India Dock Rd E14 222 C3
East La, Wem. HA0 220 B2
East Pas EC1 225 S3
East Poultry Av EC1 225 R4
East Rd N1 222 B3
East St SE17 223 B4
Eastcastle St W1 224 F5
Eastcote La, Har. HA2 220 A2
Eastcote La, Nthlt. UB5 220 A2
Eastern Av E11; Ilf. IG2, IG4 222 D1
Eastway E9; E10; E15 222 C2
Eaton La SW1 224 E14
Eaton Pl SW1 224 B14
Eaton Ri W5 220 B3
Eaton Row SW1 224 D14
Eaton Sq SW1 224 D13
Eccleston Ms SW1 224 C14
Eccleston St SW1 224 D14
Eden Pk Av, Beck. BR3 223 C6
Eden St, Kings.T. KT1 221 B6
Edgware Rd NW2 220 C2
Edgware Rd NW9 220 C1
Edgware Rd W2 220 D3
Edwards Ms W1 224 B6
Effra Rd SW2 223 A5
Elder Rd SE27 223 B6
Elephant & Castle SE1 225 S14
Elgin Av W9 220 D3
Elizabeth Ct SW1 224 J14
Ellesmere Rd W4 221 C4
Elm Ct EC4 225 P7
Elm St WC1 225 N2
Elmers End Rd SE20; Beck. BR3 223 B6
Elms Rd, Har. HA3 220 A1
Elmstead La, Chis. BR7 223 D6
Eltham High St SE9 223 D5
Eltham Hill SE9 223 D5
Eltham Rd SE9; SE12 223 D5
Ely Ct EC1 225 Q4
Ely Pl EC1 225 Q4
Embankment Pl WC2 225 L9
Emerald St WC1 225 M3
Emerson St SE1 225 T9
Emery Hill St SW1 224 G14
Emery St SE1 225 Q13
Emlyn Rd W12 221 C4
Emmanuel Rd SW12 223 A5
Empire Way, Wem. HA9 220 B2
Endell St WC2 225 K5
Endsleigh Gdns WC1 224 H1
Endsleigh Pl WC1 224 J1
Endsleigh St WC1 224 H1
Endymion Rd N4 222 A2
Englefield Rd N1 222 B2
Errol St EC1 225 U2
Essex Ct EC4 225 P6
Essex Rd N1 222 A3
Essex St WC2 225 P7
Euston Rd NW1 224 E2
Euston St NW1 224 G1
Evelina Rd SE15 223 B4
Evelyn St SE8 223 C4
Evelyn Yd W1 224 H5
Ewer St SE1 225 T10
Excel Ct WC2 224 J8
Exchange Ct WC2 225 L8
Exeter St WC2 225 L7
Exmouth Mkt EC1 225 P1
Exton St SE1 225 P10
Eyre St Hill EC1 225 P2

**F**

Fairfield Rd E3 222 C3
Fairfield S, Kings.T. KT1 221 B6
Falcon Cl SE1 225 S9
Falcon Ct EC4 225 P6
Falcon Rd SW11 221 D4
Falconberg Ct W1 224 J5
Falconberg Ms W1 224 H5
Falloden Way NW11 220 D1
Falmouth Rd SE1 225 U13
Fann St EC1 225 T2
Fann St EC2 225 T2
Fareham St W1 224 H5
Farm St W1 224 D8
Farnaby Rd, Brom. BR1, BR2 223 C6
Farnham Pl SE1 225 S10
Farringdon La EC1 225 Q2
Farringdon Rd EC1 225 P1
Farringdon St EC4 225 R5
Faulkner's All EC1 225 R3
Fentiman Rd SW8 223 A4
Fern La, Houns. TW5 221 A4
Fernhead Rd W9 220 D3
Ferry La N17 222 B1
Ferry Rd SW13 221 C4
Fetter La EC4 225 Q6
Field Ct WC1 225 N4
Finborough Rd SW10; SW17 221 D4
Finchley La NW4 220 C1
Finchley Rd NW2; NW3; NW8; NW11 220 D2
Finck St SE1 225 N12
Fisher St WC1 225 M4
Fitzhardinge St W1 224 B5
Fitzjohns Av NW3 220 D2
Fitzmaurice Pl W1 224 E9
Fitzroy Ct W1 224 G2
Fitzroy Ms W1 224 F2
Fitzroy Sq W1 224 F2
Fitzroy St W1 224 F2
Flaxman Ct W1 224 H6
Fleet St EC4 225 P6
Flitcroft St WC2 224 J5
Floral St WC2 225 K7
Foley St W1 224 F4
Footscray Rd SE9 223 D5
Fore St EC2 225 U4
Fore St N9; N18 222 B1
Forest Dr E12 222 D2
Forest Hill Rd SE22; SE23 223 B5
Forest La E7; E15 222 C2
Forest Ri E17 222 C1
Forest Rd E17 222 B1
Fortess Rd NW5 222 A2
Fortis Grn N2; N10 220 D1
Fortune Grn Rd NW6 220 D2
Fortune St EC1 225 U2
Forty Av, Wem. HA9 220 B2
Forty La, Wem. HA9 220 B2
Forum Magnum Sq SE1 225 M11
Foster La EC2 225 T5
Foubert's Pl W1 224 F6
Foundry Ms NW1 224 G1
Fountain Ct EC4 225 P7
Fourth Av E12 222 D2
Fox & Knot St EC1 225 S3
Foxgrove Rd, Beck. BR3 223 C6
Frances St SE18 223 D4
Francis Rd E10 222 C2
Frazier St SE1 225 P12
Frederic Ms SW1 224 A12
Freemason's Rd E16 222 D3
Friar St EC4 225 S6
Friary Ct SW1 224 G10
Friday St EC4 225 T6
Frith La NW7 220 D1
Frith St W1 224 H6
Fryent Way NW9 220 B1
Fulbourne Rd E17 222 C1
Fulham Palace Rd SW6; W6 221 C4
Fulham Rd SW3; SW10 221 D4
Fulham Rd SW6 221 D4
Fulwood Pl WC1 225 N4
Furnival St EC4 225 P5

**G**

Gabriel's Wf SE1 225 P9
Gage St WC1 225 L3
Galen Pl WC1 225 L4
Galpins Rd, Th.Hth. CR7 223 A6
Gambia St SE1 225 S10
Ganton St W1 224 F7
Gap Rd SW19 221 D6
Garbutt Pl W1 224 C3
Garden Ct EC4 225 P7
Garden Row SE1 225 R14
Gardners La EC4 225 T7
Garlick Hill EC4 225 U7
Garnet St E1 222 B3
Garrad's Rd SW16 223 A6
Garratt La SW17; SW18 221 D5
Garrett St EC1 225 U1
Garrick St WC2 224 K7
Gate St WC2 225 M5
Gaunt St SE1 225 T13
Gayfere St SW1 224 K14
Gaywood Est SE1 225 S14
Gaywood St SE1 225 S14
Gee St EC1 225 T1
Gees Ct W1 224 C6
Gellatly Rd SE14 223 B4
George Ct WC2 225 L8
George Rd, Kings.T. KT2 221 B6
George St W1 224 A5
George St, Rich. TW9 221 B5
George Yd W1 224 C7
Geraldine St SE11 225 R14
Gerrard Pl W1 224 J7
Gerrard St W1 224 H7
Gerridge St SE1 225 Q12
Gervase Rd, Edg. HA8 220 C1
Gilbert Pl WC1 225 K4
Gilbert St W1 224 C7
Gildea St W1 224 E4
Gillespie Rd N5 222 A2
Giltspur St EC1 225 S5
Gipsy Hill SE19 223 B6
Gipsy Rd SE27 223 B6
Gladstone St SE1 225 R13
Glasshill St SE1 225 S11
Glasshouse St W1 224 G8
Glasshouse Yd EC1 225 T3
Glentworth St NW1 224 A2
Globe Rd E1; E2 222 B3
Globe St SE1 225 U13
Globe Yd W1 224 D6
Gloucester Pl W1 224 A3
Gloucester Pl Ms W1 224 A4
Gloucester Rd SW7 221 D4
Gloucester Rd, Kings.T. KT1 221 B6
Goddard Rd, Beck. BR3 223 B6
Godliman St EC4 225 T6
Goffers Rd SE3 223 C4
Golden La EC1 225 T2
Golden La Est EC1 225 T2
Golden Sq W1 224 G7
Golders Grn Rd NW11 220 D1
Goldhawk Rd W6; W12 221 C4
Goldsmith St EC2 225 U5
Goodge Pl W1 224 G4
Goodge St W1 224 G4
Goodwins Ct WC2 224 K7
Gordon Av, Stan. HA7 220 A1
Gordon Sq WC1 224 J2
Gordon St WC1 224 H1
Gosfield St W1 224 F3
Goslett Yd WC2 224 J6
Goswell Rd EC1 225 T2
Gough Sq EC4 225 Q5
Gough St WC1 225 N1
Gower Ct WC1 224 H1
Gower Ms WC1 224 H4
Gower Pl WC1 224 G1
Gower St WC1 224 H2
Grafton Ms W1 224 F2
Grafton St W1 224 E8
Grafton Way W1 224 F2
Grafton Way WC1 224 F2
Graham Rd E8 222 B2
Grahame Pk Way NW7; NW9 220 C1
Granby Pl SE1 225 P12
Grand Av EC1 225 S3
Grand Depot Rd SE18 223 D4
Grand Dr SW20 221 C6
Grange Ct WC2 225 N6
Grange Rd E13 222 C3
Grange Rd SE1 223 B4
Grange Rd SE19; SE25; Th.Hth. CR7 223 B6
Grantham Pl W1 224 D10
Granville Pl W1 224 B6
Grape St WC2 225 K5
Gray St SE1 225 Q12
Gray's Inn WC1 225 N3
Gray's Inn Pl WC1 225 N4
Gray's Inn Rd WC1 222 A3
Gray's Inn Sq WC1 225 N3
Gray's Yd W1 224 C6
Great Cambridge Rd N17 222 B1
Great Castle St W1 224 E5
Great Cen Way NW10; Wem. HA9 220 C2
Great Chapel St W1 224 H5
Great Chertsey Rd W4 221 C4
Great Chertsey Rd (Whitton), Felt. TW13 221 A5
Great College St SW1 224 K13
Great Dover St SE1 225 U12
Great George St SW1 224 J12
Great Guildford St SE1 225 T9
Great James St WC1 225 M2
Great Marlborough St W1 224 F6
Great New St EC4 225 Q5
Great N Rd N2 220 D1
Great N Way NW4 220 C1
Great Ormond St WC1 225 L3
Great Peter St SW1 224 H14
Great Portland St W1 224 E3
Great Pulteney St W1 224 G7
Great Queen St WC2 225 L6
Great Russell St WC1 224 J5
Great St. Thomas Apostle EC4 225 U7
Great Scotland Yd SW1 224 K10
Great Smith St SW1 224 J13
Great Suffolk St SE1 225 S10
Great Sutton St EC1 225 S2
Great Titchfield St W1 224 F5
Great Trinity La EC4 225 U7
Great Turnstile WC1 225 N4
Great W Rd W4; W6 221 C4
Great W Rd, Brent. TW8; Houns. TW5; Islw. TW7 221 A4
Great Western Rd W2; W9; W11 220 D3

Great Windmill St W1 224 H7
Greek Ct W1 224 J6
Greek St W1 224 J6
Greek Yd WC2 224 K7
Green, The, Sthl. UB2 221 A4
Green, The, Twick. TW2 221 A5
Green Arbour Ct EC1 225 R5
Green La SW16 223 A6
Green La SE9; Chis. BR7 223 D5
Green Las N4; N8; N15; N16 222 A1
Green St E7; E13 222 D2
Green St W1 224 B7
Greencoat Row SW1 224 G14
Greenford Av W7 220 A3
Greenford Rd, Grnf. UB6; Sthl. UB1 220 A3
Greengate St E13 222 D3
Greenham Cl SE1 225 P12
Greenhill Way, Har. HA1 220 A1
Greenhill's Rents EC1 225 S3
Green's Ct W1 224 H7
Greenwell St W1 224 E2
Greenwich High Rd SE10 223 C4
Greenwich S St SE10 223 C4
Greet St SE1 225 Q10
Grenville St WC1 225 L2
Gresham St EC2 225 T5
Gresse St W1 224 H4
Greville St EC1 225 Q4
Greycoat Pl SW1 224 H14
Greycoat St SW1 224 H14
Greyfriars Pas EC1 225 S5
Greyhound La SW16 223 A6
Greystoke Pl EC4 225 P5
Grindal St SE1 225 P12
Groom Pl SW1 224 C13
Grosvenor Cres SW1 224 C12
Grosvenor Cres Ms SW1 224 B12
Grosvenor Gdns SW1 224 D13
Grosvenor Gdns Ms E SW1 224 E13
Grosvenor Gdns Ms N SW1 224 D14
Grosvenor Gdns Ms S SW1 224 E14
Grosvenor Gate W1 224 A8
Grosvenor Hill W1 224 D7
Grosvenor Pl SW1 224 C12
Grosvenor Rd N10 222 A1
Grosvenor Rd SW1 223 A4
Grosvenor Sq W1 224 C7
Grosvenor St W1 224 D7
Grotto Pas W1 224 C3
Grove End Rd NW8 220 D3
Grove Grn Rd E11 222 C2
Grove La SE5 223 B4
Grove La, Kings.T. KT1 221 B6
Grove Pk Rd SE9 223 D5
Grove Rd E3 222 C3
Grove Rd E17 222 C1
Grove Rd, Mitch. CR4 223 A6
Grove St SE8 223 C4
Grove Vale SE22 223 B5
Groveland Ct EC4 225 U6
Guilford Pl WC1 225 M2
Guilford St WC1 225 K2
Gunnersbury Av W3; W4; W5 220 B3
Gunnersbury La W3 221 B4
Gunpowder Sq EC4 225 Q5
Gutter La EC2 225 U5

**H**

Ha-Ha Rd SE18 223 D4
Hackney Rd E2 222 B3
Hale End Rd, E4; E17; Wdf.Grn. IG8 222 C1
Half Acre, Brent. TW8 221 B4
Half Moon Ct EC1 225 T4
Half Moon La SE24 223 B5
Half Moon St W1 224 E9
Halkin Arc SW1 224 B13
Halkin Ms SW1 224 B13
Halkin Pl SW1 224 B13
Halkin St SW1 224 C12
Hall Rd, Islw. TW7 221 A5
Hallam Ms W1 224 E3
Hallam St W1 224 E2
Ham Gate Av, Rich. TW10 221 B5
Ham Pk Rd E7; E15 222 C2
Ham St, Rich. TW10 221 B5
Ham Yd W1 224 H7
Hamilton Ms W1 224 D11
Hamilton Pl W1 224 C10
Hammersmith Gro W6 221 C4
Hammersmith Rd W6; W14 221 C4
Hampstead La N6; NW3 220 D2
Hampstead Rd NW1 222 A3
Hampton Ct Rd, E.Mol. KT8; Hmptn. TW12; Kings.T. KT1 221 A6
Hampton Rd, Hmptn. TW12 221 A6
Hampton Rd, Twick. TW2 221 A5
Hampton Rd E, Felt. TW13 221 A6
Hampton Rd W, Felt. TW13 221 A5
Hand Ct WC1 225 N4
Handel St WC1 225 K1
Hanger La W5 220 B3
Hanover Pl WC2 225 L6
Hanover Sq W1 224 E6
Hanover St W1 224 E6
Hans Pl SW1 224 A13
Hans St SW1 224 A14
Hanson St W1 224 F3
Hanway Pl W1 224 H5
Hanway St W1 224 H5
Hanworth Rd, Hmptn. TW12 221 A6
Hanworth Rd, Houns. TW3, TW4 221 A5
Hare Ct EC4 225 P6
Hare Pl EC4 225 Q6
Harewood Pl W1 224 E6
Harlesden Rd NW10 220 C3
Harley Pl W1 224 D4
Harley St W1 224 D4
Harmsworth Ms SE11 225 R14
Harold Rd E13 222 D3
Harold Rd SE19 223 B6
Harp All EC4 225 R5
Harper Rd SE1 225 T13
Harpur Ms WC1 225 M3
Harpur St WC1 225 M3
Harriet St SW1 224 A12
Harriet Wk SW1 224 A12
Harrow Rd E11 222 C2
Harrow Rd NW10; W9; W10 220 C3
Harrow Rd, Wem. HA0 220 B2
Harrow Rd (Tokyngton), Wem. HA9 220 B2
Harrow Vw, Har. HA2, HA3 220 A1
Hartfield Rd SW19 221 D6
Harvist Rd NW6 220 C3
Hat and Mitre Ct EC1 225 S2
Hatfields SE1 225 Q9
Hatton Gdn EC1 225 Q3
Hatton Pl EC1 225 Q2
Hatton Wall EC1 225 P3
Haunch of Venison Yd W1 224 D6
Haven Grn W5 220 B3
Haverstock Hill NW3 220 D2
Hawks Rd, Kings.T. KT1 221 B6
Hay Hill W1 224 E8
Haydons Rd SW19 221 D6
Hayes La, Beck. BR3 223 C6
Hayes Rd, Brom. BR2 223 D6
Haymarket SW1 224 H8
Haymarket Arc SW1 224 H8
Hayne St EC1 225 S3
Hay's Ms W1 224 D8
Hayward's Pl EC1 225 R1
Headfort Pl SW1 224 C12
Headstone Rd, Har. HA1 220 A1
Heath Rd, Houns. TW3 221 A5
Heath Rd, Twick. TW1, TW2 221 A5
Heath St NW3 220 D2
Heathcote St WC1 225 M1
Heathfield Ter W4 221 C4
Heddon St W1 224 F7
Helmet Row EC1 225 U1
Hendon La N3 220 D1
Hendon Way NW2; NW4 220 C1
Henrietta Ms WC1 225 L1
Henrietta Pl W1 224 D6
Henrietta St WC2 225 L7
Herbal Hill EC1 225 Q2
Herbert Cres SW1 224 A13
Herbrand St WC1 224 K1
Hercules Rd SE1 225 N14
Hermit Rd E16 222 C3
Hermitage Rd SE19 223 B6
Hermon Hill E11; E18 222 D1
Herne Hill SE24 223 B5
Hertford Pl W1 224 F2
Hertford St W1 224 D9
Heston Rd, Houns. TW5 221 A4
High Holborn WC1 225 L5
High Rd N2 220 D1
High Rd N15 222 B1
High Rd N22 222 A1
High Rd NW10 220 C2
High Rd, Har. HA3 220 A1
High Rd, Wem. HA0 220 B2
High Rd, Wdf.Grn. IG8 222 C1
High Rd Leyton E10; E15 222 C2
High Rd Leytonstone E11; E15 222 C2
High St E11 222 D1
High St E13 222 D3
High St E15 222 C3
High St N8 222 A1
High St NW10 220 C3
High St SE20 223 B6
High St SE25 223 B6
High St W3 220 B3
High St, Beck. BR3 223 C6
High St, Brent. TW8 221 B4
High St, Brom. BR1 223 D6
High St, Chis. BR7 223 D6
High St, Hmptn. TW12 221 A6
High St (Hampton Wick), Kings.T. KT1 221 B6
High St, N.Mal. KT3 221 C6
High St, Sthl. UB1 220 A3
High St, Tedd. TW11 221 B6
High St, T.Hth. CR7 223 B6
High St (Whitton), Twick. TW2 221 A5
High St Colliers Wd SW19 221 D6
High St N E6; E12 222 D2
High St S E6 222 D3
High St Wimbledon SW19 221 C6
High Timber St EC4 225 T7
Higham Hill Rd E17 222 C1
Highbury Gro N5 222 A2
Highbury Pk N5 222 A2
Highgate High St N6 222 A2
Highgate Hill N6; N19 222 A2
Highgate Rd NW5 222 A2
Highgate W Hill N6 222 A2
Highway, The E1; E14 222 B3
Hill St W1 224 C9
Hillreach SE18 223 D4
Hills Pl W1 224 F6
Hillside NW10 220 C2
Hind Ct EC4 225 Q6
Hinde St W1 224 C5
Hither Grn La SE13 223 C5
Hobart Pl SW1 224 D13
Hoe St E17 222 C1
Hogarth La W4 221 C4
Holborn EC1 225 P4
Holborn Circ EC1 225 Q4
Holborn Pl WC1 225 M4
Holborn Viaduct EC1 225 Q4
Holders Hill Rd NW4; NW7 220 C1
Holland Pk Av W11 221 C4
Holland Rd W14 221 D4
Holland St SE1 225 S9
Hollen St W1 224 H5
Holles St W1 224 E5
Holloway Rd N7; N19 222 A2
Hollybush Hill E11 222 C1
Holmes Ter SE1 225 P11
Holsworthy Sq WC1 225 N2
Homerton High St E9 222 B2
Homerton Rd E9 222 C2
Homesdale Rd, Brom. BR1, BR2 223 D6
Honduras St EC1 225 T1
Honey La EC2 225 U6
Honeypot La NW9; Stan. HA7 220 B1
Honor Oak Pk SE23 223 B5
Hood Ct EC4 225 Q6
Hop Gdns WC2 224 K8
Hopkins St W1 224 G6
Hopton Gdns SE1 225 S9
Hopton St SE1 225 S9
Horn La W3 220 C3
Hornfair Rd SE7 223 D4
Hornsey La N6; N19 222 A2
Hornsey Ri N19 222 A2
Hornsey Rd N7; N19 222 A2
Horse & Dolphin Yd W1 224 J7
Horse Guards Av SW1 225 K10
Horse Guards Rd SW1 224 J10
Horse Ride SW1 224 H10
Horseferry Rd SW1 224 H14
Horsenden La N, Grnf. UB6 220 A2
Horsenden La S, Grnf. UB6 220 B3
Hosier La EC1 225 R4
Hospital Br Rd, Twick. TW2 221 A5
Houghton St WC2 225 N6
Howard Pl SW1 224 F14
Howberry Rd, Edg. HA8; Stan. HA7 220 B1
Howick Pl SW1 224 G14
Howland Ms E W1 224 G3
Howland St W1 224 F3
Huggin Ct EC4 225 U7
Huggin Hill EC4 225 U7
Hungerford Br SE1 225 L9
Hungerford Br WC2 225 L9
Hungerford La WC2 225 K9
Hunter St WC1 225 L1
Huntley St WC1 224 G2
Hunt's Ct WC2 224 J8
Hurst La, E.Mol. KT8 221 A6
Hurst Rd, E.Mol. KT8; W.Mol. KT8 221 A6
Hutton St EC4 225 Q6
Hyde, The NW9 220 C1
Hyde Pk Cor W1 224 C11
Hyde Vale SE10 223 C4

**I**

Ilderton Rd SE15; SE16 223 B4
Ilford La, Ilf. IG1 222 D2
Imperial Dr, Har. HA2 220 A2
India Pl WC2 225 M7
Ingestre Pl W1 224 G6
Inigo Pl WC2 225 K7
Inner Temple La EC4 225 P6
Invicta Plaza SE1 225 R9
Ireland Yd EC4 225 S6
Ironmonger Pas EC1 225 U1
Ironmonger Row EC1 225 U1
Irving St WC2 224 J7
Isabella St SE1 225 R10
Ivybridge La WC2 225 L8

**J**

Jacob's Well Ms W1 224 C5
Jamaica Rd SE1; SE16 223 B4
James St W1 224 C5
James St WC2 225 L7
Jermyn St SW1 224 F9
Jersey Rd, Houns. TW5; Islw. TW7 221 A4
Jerusalem Pas EC1 225 R2
Jervis Ct W1 224 E6
Joan St SE1 225 R10
Jockey's Flds WC1 225 N3
Johanna St SE1 225 P12
John Adam St WC2 225 L8
John Carpenter St EC4 225 R7
John Princes St W1 224 E5
John Ruskin St SE5 223 A4
John St WC1 225 N2
John Wilson St SE18 223 D4
John's Ms WC1 225 N2
Jones St W1 224 D8
Judd St WC1 222 A3
Junction Rd N19 222 A2

**K**

Katherine Rd E6; E7 222 D2
Kean St WC2 225 M6
Keeley St WC2 225 M6
Kell St SE1 225 S13
Kemble St WC2 225 M6
Kemp's Ct W1 224 G6
Kendal Rd NW10 220 C2
Kendall Pl W1 224 B4
Kenley Rd, Kings.T. KT1 221 B6
Kenmore Av, Har. HA3 220 B1
Kenmore Rd, Har. HA3 220 B1
Kennet Wf La EC4 225 U7
Kennington La SE11 223 A4
Kennington Pk Rd SE11 223 A4
Kennington Rd SE1 225 P13
Kennington Rd SE11 225 P14
Kenrick Pl W1 224 B3
Kensington Ch St W8 220 D3
Kensington High St W8; W14 221 D4
Kensington Pk Rd W11 220 D3
Kensington Rd SW7; W8 221 D4
Kent Gdns W13 220 B3
Kent Ho Rd SE26; Beck. BR3 223 B6
Kentish Way, Brom. BR1 223 D6
Kenton La (Belmont), Har. HA3 220 B1
Kenton La (Harrow Weald), Har. HA3 220 A1
Kenton Rd, Har. HA3 220 B1
Kenton St WC1 225 K1
Keppel Row SE1 225 T10
Keppel St WC1 224 J3
Kew Br Rd, Brent. TW8 221 B4
Kew Rd, Rich. KT9 221 B4
Keyworth St SE1 225 S13
Kidbrooke Pk Rd SE3 223 D4
Kilburn High Rd NW6 220 D2
Kilburn La W9; W10 220 D3
Kilburn Pk Rd NW6 220 D3
King Charles St SW1 224 J11
King Edward St EC1 225 T5
King Edward Wk SE1 225 Q13
King James St SE1 225 S12
King St EC2 225 U6
King St SW1 224 G10
King St W6 221 C4
King St WC2 225 K7
King St, Twick. TW1 221 B5
Kinghorn St EC1 225 T4
Kingly Ct W1 224 F7
Kingly St W1 224 F6
King's Av SW4; SW12 223 A5
Kings Bench St SE1 225 S11
Kings Bench Wk EC4 225 Q6
King's Ms WC1 225 N2
Kings Pl SE1 225 T12
King's Reach Twr SE1 225 Q9
King's Rd SW1; SW3; SW6; SW10 221 D4
Kings Rd, Kings.T. KT2 221 B6
Kings Rd, Rich. TW10 221 B5
Kingsbury Rd NW9 220 B1
Kingscote St EC4 225 R7
Kingsfield Av, Har. HA2 220 A1
Kingsland Rd E2; E8 222 B2
Kingsley Rd, Houns. TW3 221 A4
Kingston Hill, Kings.T. KT2 221 B6
Kingston Rd SW15 221 C5
Kingston Rd SW20 221 C6
Kingston Rd, Kings.T. KT1; N.Mal. KT3 221 B6
Kingston Rd, Tedd. TW11 221 B6
Kingston Vale SW15 221 C6
Kingsway WC2 225 M5
Kingsway Pl EC1 225 Q1
Kinnerton Pl N SW1 224 A12
Kinnerton Pl S SW1 224 A12
Kinnerton St SW1 224 B12
Kinnerton Yd SW1 224 A12
Kirby St EC1 225 Q3
Kirkdale SE26 223 B5
Kirkman Pl W1 224 H4
Kneller Rd, Twick. TW2 221 A5
Knightrider Ct EC4 225 T7
Knights Hill SE27 223 A6
Knightsbridge SW1 224 A12

**L**

Ladbroke Gro W10; W11 220 D3
Lady Margaret Rd, Sthl. UB1 220 A3
Ladywell Rd SE13 223 C5
Lake Ho Rd E11 222 D2
Lambeth Hill EC4 225 T7
Lambeth Palace Rd SE1 225 M14
Lambeth Rd SE1 225 N14
Lambeth Rd SE11 225 N14
Lambs Conduit Pas WC1 225 M3
Lamb's Conduit St WC1 225 M2
Lamp Office Ct WC1 225 M2
Lampton Rd, Houns. TW3 221 A5
Lancashire Ct W1 224 E7
Lancaster Pl WC2 225 M7
Lancaster St SE1 225 S12
Lanesborough Pl SW1 224 B11
Langham Pl W1 224 E4
Langham St W1 224 E4
Langley Ct WC2 225 K7
Langley St WC2 225 K6
Lansdowne Rd N17 222 B1
Lansdowne Row W1 224 E9
Lansdowne Ter WC1 225 L2
Lansdowne Way SW8 223 A4
Lant St SE1 225 T11
Larden Rd W3 221 C4
Larkshall Rd E4 222 C1
Lascelles Av, Har. HA1 220 A2
Latchmere Rd SW11 221 D4
Latchmere Rd, Kings.T. KT2 221 B6
Lauderdale Twr EC2 225 T3
Launcelot St SE1 225 P12
Lauriston Rd E9 222 B2
Lausanne Rd SE15 223 B4
Lavender Av, Mitch. CR4 221 D6
Lavington St SE1 225 S10
Lawrence La EC2 225 U6
Lawrie Pk Rd SE26 223 B6
Laxton Pl NW1 224 E1
Laystall St EC1 225 P2
Laytons Bldgs SE1 225 U11
Lea Br Rd E5; E10; E17 222 B2
Leake St SE1 225 N11
Leather La EC1 225 Q4
Lee High Rd SE12; SE13 223 C5
Lee Rd SE3 223 C5
Lee Ter SE3; SE13 223 C5
Lees Pl W1 224 B7
Leicester Ct WC2 224 J7
Leicester Pl WC2 224 J7
Leicester Sq WC2 224 J8
Leicester St WC2 224 J7
Leigh Hunt St SE1 225 T11
Leigh Pl EC1 225 P3
Leigh St WC1 224 K1
Leigham Ct Rd SW16 223 A5
Leighton Rd NW5 222 A2
Leo Yd EC1 225 S2
Leopards Ct EC1 225 P3
Lever St EC1 222 B3
Lewisham High St SE13 223 C5
Lewisham Rd SE13 223 C4
Lewisham St SW1 224 J12
Lewisham Way SE4; SE14 223 C4
Lexington St W1 224 G6
Leyton Grn Rd E10 222 C1
Library St SE1 225 R12
Lilford Rd SE5 223 A4
Lillie Rd SW6 221 C4
Lily Pl EC1 225 Q3
Limeburner La EC4 225 R6
Limeharbour E14 223 C4
Lincoln's Inn WC2 225 N5
Lincoln's Inn Flds WC2 225 M5
Lindsey St EC1 225 S3
Lingfield Av, Kings.T. KT1 221 B6
Links Av, Mord. SM4 221 D6
Lisle St WC2 224 J7
Lisson Gro NW1; NW8 220 D3
Litchfield St WC2 224 J7
Little Albany St NW1 224 E1
Little Argyll St W1 224 F6
Little Britain EC1 225 S4
Little Chester St SW1 224 C13
Little College St SW1 225 K13
Little Dean's Yd SW1 224 K13
Little Dorrit Ct SE1 225 U11
Little Ealing La W5 221 B4
Little Essex St WC2 225 P7
Little George St SW1 224 K12
Little Heath SE7 223 D4
Little Ilford La E12 222 D2
Little Marlborough St W1 224 F6
Little New St EC4 225 Q5
Little Newport St WC2 224 J7
Little Portland St W1 224 F5
Little Russell St WC1 224 K4
Little St. James's St SW1 224 F10
Little Sanctuary SW1 224 J12
Little Smith St SW1 224 J13
Little Titchfield St W1 224 F4
Little Trinity La EC4 225 U7
Little Turnstile WC1 225 M4
Liverpool Rd N1; N7 222 A2
Livonia St W1 224 G6
Loampit Hill SE13 223 C4
Loampit Vale SE13 223 C4
Locks La, Mitch. CR4 223 A6
Logs Hill, Brom. BR1; Chis. BR7 223 D6
Loman St SE1 225 S11
Lombard La EC4 225 Q6
Lombard Rd SW11 221 D4
London La, Brom. BR1 223 C6
London Rd SE1 225 R13
London Rd SE23 223 B5
London Rd SW16 223 A6
London Rd, Brent. TW8; Houns. TW3; Islw. TW7 221 A4
London Rd, Brom. BR1 223 C6
London Rd, Kings.T. KT2 221 B6
London Rd, Mitch. CR4 221 D6
London Rd, Twick. TW1 221 B5
London Wall EC2 225 U4
Long Acre WC2 224 K7
Long La EC1 225 S3
Long La SE1 223 B4
Long Rd SW4 223 A5
Long Yd WC1 225 M2
Longford St NW1 224 E1
Longley Rd SW17 221 D6
Long's Ct WC2 224 H7
Longwood Gdns, Ilf. IG5 222 D1
Lonsdale Av E6 222 D3
Lord N St SW1 224 K14
Lordship La N22 222 A1
Lordship La SE22 223 B5
Lordship Pk N16 222 B2
Lothian Rd SW9 223 A4
Loughborough Rd SW9 223 A4
Love La EC2 225 U5
Lover's Wk W1 224 B9
Lower Belgrave St SW1 224 D14
Lower Boston Rd W7 221 A4
Lower Clapton Rd E5 222 B2
Lower Grosvenor Pl SW1 224 D13
Lower James St W1 224 G7
Lower John St W1 224 G7
Lower Lea Crossing E14; E16 222 C3
Lower Marsh SE1 225 P12
Lower Mortlake Rd, Rich. TW9 221 B5
Lower Richmond Rd SW15 221 C5
Lower Richmond Rd SW14; Rich. TW9 221 B5
Lower Rd SE16 223 B4
Lower Rd, Har. HA2 220 A2
Lower Sunbury Rd, Hmptn. TW12 221 A6
Lower Teddington Rd, Kings.T. KT1 221 B6
Lowlands Rd, Har. HA1 220 A2
Lowndes Cl SW1 224 C14
Lowndes Ct W1 224 F6
Lowndes Pl SW1 224 B14
Lowndes Sq SW1 224 A12
Lowndes St SW1 224 A13
Ludgate Bdy EC4 225 R6
Ludgate Circ EC4 225 R6
Ludgate Hill EC4 225 R6
Ludgate Sq EC4 225 S6
Ludlow St EC1 225 T1
Lumley Ct WC2 225 L8
Lumley St W1 224 C6
Luxborough St W1 224 B3
Lyall Ms SW1 224 B14
Lyall Ms W SW1 224 B14
Lyall St SW1 224 B14
Lygon Pl SW1 224 D14
Lyttleton Rd N8 220 D1

**M**

Macclesfield St W1 224 J7
Macfarren Pl NW1 224 C2
Mackenzie Rd N7 222 A2
Macklin St WC2 225 L5
Maddox St W1 224 E7
Madeley Rd W5 220 B3
Magdalen Rd SW18 221 D5
Magpie All EC4 225 Q6
Maida Vale W9 220 D3
Maiden La SE1 225 U9
Maiden La WC2 225 L8
Maidstone Bldgs SE1 225 U10
Major Rd E15 222 C2
Malden Rd NW5 220 D2
Malet Pl WC1 224 H2
Malet St WC1 224 H2
Mall, The SW1 224 G11
Mall, The W5 220 B3
Mall, The, Har. HA3 220 B1
Malpas Rd SE4 223 C5
Malta St EC1 225 S1
Maltravers St WC2 225 N7
Manchester Ms W1 224 B4
Manchester Rd E14 223 C4
Manchester Sq W1 224 B5
Manchester St W1 224 B4
Mandeville Pl W1 224 C5
Mandeville Rd, Nthlt. UB5 220 A2
Manette St W1 224 J6
Manor Fm Rd, Wem. HA0 220 B3
Manor Pk Rd NW10 220 C3
Manor Rd E16 222 C3
Manor Rd N16 222 B2
Manor Rd, Chig. IG7 222 D1
Manor Rd, Mitch. CR4 223 A6
Manor Rd, Rich. TW9 221 B5
Mansfield Ms W1 224 D4
Mansfield Rd NW3 220 D2
Mansfield St W1 224 D4
Mapesbury Rd NW2 220 D2
Maple Pl W1 224 G2
Maple St W1 224 F3
Marble Arch W1 224 A7
Marchmont St WC1 224 K1
Mare St E8 222 B3
Margaret Ct W1 224 F5
Margaret St W1 224 E5
Marigold All SE1 225 R8
Market Ct W1 224 F5
Market Ms W1 224 D10
Market Pl W1 224 F5
Market Rd N7 222 A2
Markhouse Rd E17 222 C1
Marlborough Ct W1 224 F6
Marlborough Rd SW1 224 G10
Marsh Rd, Pnr. HA5 220 A1
Marsh Wall E14 223 C4
Marshall St W1 224 G6
Marshalsea Rd SE1 225 U11
Marsham St SW1 224 J14
Marshgate La E15 222 C
Mart St WC2 225 L
Martin Way SW20; Mord. SM4 221 D
Martindale Rd, Houns. TW4 221 A
Martlett Ct WC2 225 L
Marylebone High St W1 224 C
Marylebone La W1 224 D
Marylebone Ms W1 224 D
Marylebone Pas W1 224 G
Marylebone Rd NW1 220 D
Marylebone St W1 224 C
Masons Arms Ms W1 224 E
Masons Hill, Brom. BR1 223 D
Mason's Yd SW1 224 G
Matthew Parker St SW1 224 J1
Matthews Yd WC2 225 K
Matthias Rd N16 222 B
Mayes Rd N22 222 A
Mayfair Pl W1 224 E
Mayow Rd SE23; SE26 223 B
Mays Ct WC2 224 K
Maze Hill SE3; SE10 223 C

McAuley Cl SE1 225 P13
McCoid Way SE1 225 T12
Mead Row SE1 225 P13
Meadow Row SE1 225 T14
Meard St W1 224 H6
Mecklenburgh Pl WC1 225 M1
Mecklenburgh Sq WC1 225 M1
Mecklenburgh St WC1 225 M1
Medway St SW1 224 J14
Melbourne Pl WC2 225 N7
Melcombe St NW1 224 A2
Melfort Rd, Th.Hth. CR7 223 A6
Memel Ct EC1 225 T2
Memel St EC1 225 T2
Mepham St SE1 225 N10
Merantun Way SW19 221 D6
Mercer St WC2 224 K6
Merrick Rd, Sthl. UB2 221 A4
Merrick Sq SE1 225 U13
Merton Rd SW18 221 D5
Merton Rd SW19 221 D6
Meymott St SE1 225 R10
Middle La N8 222 A1
Middle Pk Av SE9 223 D5
Middle St EC1 225 T3
Middle Temple EC4 225 P7
Middle Temple La EC4 225 P6
Middlesex Pas EC1 225 S4
Middleton Pl W1 224 F4
Midford Pl W1 224 G2
Milcote St SE1 225 R12
Mildmay Pk N1 222 B2
Mile End Rd E1; E3 222 C3
Milford La WC2 225 N7
Milk St EC2 225 U6
Milkwood Rd SE24 223 A5
Mill Hill Rd SW13 221 C4
Mill La NW6 220 D2
Mill St W1 224 F7
Millbank SW1 225 K14
Miller Wk SE1 225 Q10
Millman Ms WC1 225 M2
Millman St WC1 225 M2
Milroy Wk SE1 225 R9
Mint St SE1 225 T11
Mitcham La SW16 223 A6
Mitcham Rd SW17 221 D6
Mitchell St EC1 225 T1
Mitre Ct EC2 225 U5
Mitre Ct EC4 225 Q6
Mitre Rd SE1 225 Q11
Mogden La, Islw. TW7 221 A5
Monck St SW1 224 J14
Monkwell Sq EC2 225 U4
Monmouth St WC2 224 K6
Montagu Mans W1 224 A3
Montagu Ms N W1 224 A4
Montagu Ms S W1 224 A5
Montagu Ms W W1 224 A5
Montagu Row W1 224 A4
Montagu Sq W1 224 A4
Montagu St W1 224 A5
Montague Pl WC1 224 J3
Montague St EC1 225 T4
Montague St WC1 224 K3
Montreal Pl WC2 225 M7
Montrose Pl SW1 224 C12
Monument Way N17 222 B1
Moor St W1 224 J6
Morden Hall Rd, Mord. SM4 221 D6
Morden Rd SW19 221 D6
Morden Rd, Mitch. CR4 221 D6
Morley St SE1 225 Q13
Morning La E9 222 B2
Mornington Rd, Grnf. UB6 220 A3
Morpeth Ter SW1 224 F14
Mortimer Mkt WC1 224 G2
Mortimer Rd NW10 220 C3
Mortimer St W1 224 F4
Mortlake High St SW14 221 C4
Mortlake Rd, Rich. TW9 221 B4
Morton Pl SE1 225 P14
Morwell St WC1 224 J4
Mostyn Rd SW19 221 D6
Motcomb St SW1 224 A13
Mottingham La SE9; SE12 223 D5
Mottingham Rd SE9 223 D5
Mount Pleasant WC1 225 N2
Mount Pleasant Rd N17 222 B1
Mount Row W1 224 D8
Mount St W1 224 C8
Moxon St W1 224 B4
Mumford Ct EC2 225 U5
Munster Sq NW1 224 E1
Murphy St SE1 225 P12
Museum St WC1 225 K4
Muswell Hill N10 222 A1
Muswell Hill Rd N6; N10 222 A1

**N**

Nag's Head Ct EC1 225 T2
Nassau St W1 224 F4
Neal St WC2 224 K6
Neal's Yd WC2 224 K6
Neasden La NW10 220 C2
Nelson Rd E4 222 C1
Nelson Rd, Houns. TW4; Twick. TW2 221 A5
Nelson Sq SE1 225 R11
Nether St N3; N12 220 D1
New Barn St E13 222 D3
New Bond St W1 224 E7
New Br St EC4 225 R6
New Burlington Ms W1 224 F7
New Burlington Pl W1 224 F7
New Burlington St W1 224 F7
New Cavendish St W1 224 E3
New Change EC4 225 T6
New City Rd E13 222 D3
New Compton St WC2 224 J6
New Ct EC4 225 P7
New Coventry St W1 224 J8
New Cross Rd SE14 223 B4
New Fetter La EC4 225 Q5
New Globe Wk SE1 225 T9
New Inn Pas WC2 225 N6
New Kent Rd SE1 225 T14
New Kings Rd SW6 221 D4
New N Rd N1 222 B2
New N St WC1 225 M3
New Oxford St WC1 224 J5
New Plaistow Rd E15 222 C3
New Quebec St W1 224 A6
New Rd E1 222 B3
New Rd, W.Mol. KT8 221 A6
New Row WC2 224 K7
New Sq WC2 225 N5
New St Sq EC4 225 Q5
New Turnstile WC1 225 M4
New Wanstead E11 222 C2
Newburgh St W1 224 F6
Newbury St EC1 225 T4
Newcastle Cl EC4 225 R5
Newcastle Row EC1 225 Q1
Newgate St EC1 225 S5
Newham Way E6; E16 222 D3
Newington Causeway SE1 225 S14
Newlands Pk SE26 223 B6
Newman Pas W1 224 G4
Newman St W1 224 G4
Newman Yd W1 224 H5
Newman's Row WC2 225 N4
Newnham Ter SE1 225 P13
Newport Ct WC2 224 J7
Newport Pl WC2 224 J7
Newton St WC2 225 L5
Nicholson St SE1 225 R10
Nightingale La SW4; SW12 221 D5
Nightingale Pl SE18 223 D4
Nine Elms La SW8 223 A4
Noble St EC2 225 T5
Noel Rd W3 220 B3
Noel St W1 224 G6
Norbury Cres SW16 223 A6
Norbury Hill SW16 223 A6
Norris St SW1 224 H8
North Acton Rd NW10 220 C3
North Audley St W1 224 B6
North Ct W1 224 G3
North Cres WC1 224 H3
North End Rd NW11 220 D2
North End Rd SW6; W14 221 D4
North Hill N6 222 A1
North Ms WC1 225 N2
North Rd N6 222 A1
North Row W1 224 A7
North St SW4 223 A5
North Woolwich Rd E16 222 D3
Northampton Rd EC1 225 Q1
Northborough Rd SW16 223 A6
Northburgh St EC1 225 S1
Northcote Rd SW11 221 D5
Northern Relief Rd, Bark. IG11 222 D2
Northfield Av W5; W13 220 B3
Northington St WC1 225 N2
Northolt Rd, Har. HA2 220 A2
Northover, Brom. BR1 223 C5
Northumberland Av WC2 224 K9
Northumberland St WC2 225 K9
Northwold Rd E6; N16 222 B2
Northwood Rd, Th.Hth. CR7 223 B6
Norwich St EC4 225 P5
Norwood High St SE27 223 B5
Norwood Rd SE24; SE27 223 A5
Norwood Rd, Sthl. UB2 221 A4
Notting Hill Gate W11 220 D3
Nottingham Ct WC2 225 K6
Nottingham Pl W1 224 B2
Nottingham St W1 224 B3
Nottingham Ter NW1 224 B2
Nunhead La SE15 223 B5

**O**

Oak Av, Hmptn. TW12 221 A6
Oak Hill, Wdf.Grn. IG8 222 C1
Oakey La SE1 225 P13
Oakley St SW3 221 D4
Oakwood Av, Beck. BR3 223 C6
Oat La EC2 225 T5
Odhams Wk WC2 225 K6
Ogle St W1 224 F3
Old Bailey EC4 225 S6
Old Barrack Yd SW1 224 B12
Old Bond St W1 224 F8
Old Brewers Yd WC2 225 K6
Old Brompton Rd SW5; SW7 221 D4
Old Bldgs WC2 225 P5
Old Burlington St W1 224 F7
Old Cavendish St W1 224 D5
Old Compton St W1 224 H7
Old Fish St Hill EC4 225 T7
Old Fleet La EC4 225 R5
Old Ford Rd E2; E3 222 B3
Old Gloucester St WC1 225 L3
Old Hill, Chis. BR7 223 D6
Old Kent Rd SE1; SE15 223 B4
Old N St WC1 225 M3
Old Oak Common La NW10; W3 220 C3
Old Oak La NW10 220 C3
Old Oak Rd W3 220 C3
Old Palace Yd SW1 225 K13
Old Pk La W1 224 C10
Old Pye St SW1 224 H13
Old Quebec St W1 224 A6
Old Queen St SW1 224 J12
Old Seacoal La EC4 225 R5
Old Sq WC2 225 N5
Old St EC1 225 T1
Old Town SW4 223 A5
Oldbury Pl W1 224 C3
Oldfield La N, Grnf. UB6 220 A3
O'Meara St SE1 225 U10
Onslow St EC1 225 Q2
Ontario St SE1 225 S14
Orange St WC2 224 H8
Orange Yd W1 224 J6
Orchard St W1 224 B6
Orde Hall St WC1 225 M2
Ormond Cl WC1 225 L3
Ormond Ms WC1 225 L2
Ormond Yd SW1 224 G9
Osnaburgh St NW1 224 E2
Osnaburgh Ter NW1 224 E1
Ossington Bldgs W1 224 B3
Ossulton Way N2 220 D1
Outer Circle NW1 224 B2
Oxendon St SW1 224 H8
Oxford Circ Av W1 224 F6
Oxford St W1 224 B6
Oxo Twr Wf SE1 225 Q8

**P**

Paddenswick Rd W6 221 C4
Paddington St W1 224 B3
Page Heath La, Brom. BR1 223 D6
Page St NW7 220 C1
Pageantmaster Ct EC4 225 R6
Pakenham St WC1 225 N1
Palace Pl SW1 224 F13
Palace St SW1 224 F13
Pall Mall SW1 224 G10
Pall Mall E SW1 224 J9
Pall Mall Pl SW1 224 G10
Palmer St SW1 224 H12
Palmerston Rd N22 222 A1
Pancras La EC4 225 U6
Pancras Rd NW1 222 A3
Panton St SW1 224 H8
Panyer All EC4 225 T5
Parchmore Rd, Th.Hth. CR7 223 B6
Pardon St EC1 225 S1
Paris Gdn SE1 225 R9
Parish La SE20 223 B6
Park Av N22 222 A1
Park Cres W1 224 D2
Park Cres Ms E W1 224 E2
Park Cres Ms W W1 224 D3
Park La W1 224 C10
Park La, Wem. HA9 220 B2
Park Pl SW1 224 F10
Park Rd N8 222 A1
Park Rd NW1; NW8 220 D3
Park Rd, Hmptn. TW12 221 A6
Park Rd (Hampton Wick), Kings.T. KT1 221 B6
Park Rd, Kings.T. KT2 221 B6
Park Rd, Tedd. TW11 221 A6
Park Royal Rd NW10; W3 220 C3
Park Sq E NW1 224 D1
Park Sq Ms NW1 224 D1
Park Sq W NW1 224 D1
Park St SE1 225 T9
Park St W1 224 B7
Parker Ms WC2 225 L5
Parker St WC2 225 L5
Parkhurst Rd N7 222 A2
Parkside SW19 221 C5
Parkside Way, Har. HA2 220 A1
Parliament Sq SW1 224 K12
Parliament St SW1 225 K12
Parmoor Ct EC1 225 T1
Parnell Rd E3 222 C3
Parson St NW4 220 C1
Passing All EC1 225 S2
Paternoster Row EC4 225 T6
Paternoster Sq EC4 225 S5
Paul's Wk EC4 225 S7
Pavilion Rd SW1 224 A14
Pavilion St SW1 224 A14
Peabody Dws WC1 224 K1
Peabody Est EC1 225 U2
Peabody Est SE1 225 Q10
Peabody Sq SE1 225 R12
Peabody Trust SE1 225 T10
Pear Pl SE1 225 P11
Pear Tree Ct EC1 225 Q1
Pear Tree St EC1 225 S1
Pearman St SE1 225 Q13
Peckham High St SE15 223 B4
Peckham Hill St SE15 223 B4
Peckham Pk Rd SE15 223 B4
Peckham Rd SE5; SE15 223 B4
Peckham Rye SE15; SE22 223 B5
Pemberton Row EC4 225 Q5
Pembroke Cl SW1 224 C12
Pembury Rd E5 222 B2
Penge Rd SE20; SE25 223 B6
Penrhyn Rd, Kings.T. KT1 221 B6
Pentonville Rd N1 222 A3
Pepper St SE1 225 T11
Percival St EC1 225 R1
Percy Ms W1 224 H4
Percy Pas W1 224 G4
Percy Rd, Hmptn. TW12 221 A6
Percy Rd, Twick. TW2 221 A5
Percy St W1 224 H4
Perkin's Rents SW1 224 H13
Perkins Sq SE1 225 U9
Perry Hill SE6 223 C5
Perry Ri SE23 223 C5
Perry Vale SE23 223 B5
Perrys Pl W1 224 H5
Perth Rd, Ilf. IG2 222 D1
Peter St W1 224 G7
Peters Hill EC4 225 T7
Peter's La EC1 225 S3
Petersham Rd, Rich. TW10 221 B5
Peto Pl NW1 224 E1
Petts Hill, Nthlt. UB5 220 A2
Petty France SW1 224 G13
Philip La N15 222 B1
Phipp's Ms SW1 224 D14
Phoenix Pl WC1 225 N1
Phoenix St WC2 224 J6
Piccadilly W1 224 E10
Piccadilly Arc SW1 224 F9
Piccadilly Circ W1 224 H8
Piccadilly Pl W1 224 G8
Pickering Pl SW1 224 G10
Pickwick St SE1 225 T12
Picton Pl W1 224 C6
Pilgrim St EC4 225 R6
Pimlico Rd SW1 223 A4
Pine St EC1 225 P1
Pineapple Ct SW1 224 F13
Pinner Rd, Har. HA1 220 A1
Pinner Rd, Pnr. HA5 220 A1
Pinner Vw, Har. HA1, HA2 220 A1
Pitfield St N1 222 B3
Pitshanger La W5 220 B3
Pitt's Head Ms W1 224 C10
Plaistow La, Brom. BR1 223 D6
Plaistow Rd E13; E15 222 C3
Plashet Gro E6 222 D2
Plashet Rd E13 222 D3
Playhouse Yd EC4 225 R6
Pleydell Ct EC4 225 Q6
Pleydell St EC4 225 Q6
Plough La SW17; SW19 221 D6
Plough Pl EC4 225 Q5
Plough Way SE16 223 B4
Plumstead Common Rd SE18 223 D4
Plumstead Rd SE18 223 D4
Plumtree Ct EC4 225 Q5
Pocock St SE1 225 R11
Poland St W1 224 G6
Pollen St W1 224 E6
Pomeroy St SE14 223 B4
Pontypool Pl SE1 225 R11
Pooles Bldgs EC1 225 P2
Popes La W5 221 B4
Poplar High St E14 222 C3
Poppins Ct EC4 225 R6
Porter St SE1 225 U9
Porter St W1 224 A3
Portland Ms W1 224 G6
Portland Pl W1 224 D2
Portland Rd SE25 223 B6
Portman Cl W1 224 A5
Portman Ms S W1 224 B6
Portman Sq W1 224 B5
Portman St W1 224 B6
Portpool La EC1 225 P3
Portsmouth St WC2 225 M6
Portugal St WC2 225 M6
Pound La NW10 220 C2
Powder Mill La, Twick. TW2 221 A5
Powis Pl WC1 225 L2
Poynders Rd SW4 223 A5
Praed St W2 220 D3
Preston Hill, Har. HA3 220 B2
Preston Rd, Har. HA3; Wem. HA9 220 B2
Prestons Rd E14 223 C4
Priest Ct EC2 225 T5
Primrose Hill EC4 225 Q6
Prince Albert Rd NW1; NW8 220 D3
Prince Imperial Rd, Chis. BR7 223 D6
Prince of Wales Rd SE3 223 C4
Prince Regent La E13; E16 222 D3
Prince's Arc SW1 224 G9
Princes Pl SW1 224 G9
Princes St W1 224 E6
Princess St SE1 225 S14
Princeton St WC1 225 M3
Printer St EC4 225 Q5
Printers Inn Ct EC4 225 P5
Priory La SW15 221 C5
Priory Rd N8 222 A1
Procter St WC1 225 M4
Providence Ct W1 224 C7
Prudent Pas EC2 225 U5
Puddle Dock EC4 225 S7
Pump Ct EC4 225 P6
Pursley Rd NW7 220 C1
Putney Br Rd SW15; SW18 221 D5
Putney Heath SW15 221 C5
Putney High St SW15 221 C5
Putney Hill SW15 221 C5

**Q**

Quadrant Arc W1 224 G8
Quality Ct WC2 225 P5
Quebec Ms W1 224 A6
Queen Anne Av, Brom. BR2 223 C6
Queen Anne Ms W1 224 E4
Queen Anne St W1 224 D5
Queen Anne's Gate SW1 224 H12
Queen Sq WC1 225 L2
Queen Sq Pl WC1 225 L2
Queen St EC4 225 U7
Queen St W1 224 D9
Queen St Pl EC4 225 U8
Queen Victoria St EC4 225 S7
Queenhithe EC4 225 U7
Queens Dr W3; W5 220 B3
Queens Ride SW13; SW15 221 C5
Queens Rd NW4 220 C1
Queens Rd SE14; SE15 223 B4
Queens Rd, Kings.T. KT2 221 B6
Queens Rd, Rich. 221 B5
Queen's Rd, Tedd. TW11 221 A6
Queen's Wk SW1 224 F10
Queens Yd WC1 224 G2
Queensbridge Rd E2; E8 222 B2
Queenstown Rd SW8 223 A4
Quilp St SE1 225 T11

**R**

Railton Rd SE24 223 A5
Ramillies Pl W1 224 F6
Ramillies St W1 224 F6
Rancliffe Rd E6 222 D3
Rathbone Pl W1 224 H5
Rathbone St W1 224 G4
Ravensbourne Av, Beck. BR3; Brom. BR2 223 C6
Ray St EC1 225 Q2
Ray St Br EC1 225 Q2
Raymond Bldgs WC1 225 N3
Raymouth Rd SE16 223 B4
Rayners La, Har. HA2; Pnr. HA5 220 A1
Rectory La SW17 223 A6
Rectory Rd N16 222 B2
Rectory Rd, Beck. BR3 223 C6
Red Hill, Chis. BR7 223 D6
Red Lion Ct EC4 225 Q5
Red Lion Sq WC1 225 M4
Red Lion St WC1 225 M3
Red Lion Yd W1 224 C9
Red Pl W1 224 B7
Redbridge La E, Ilf. IG4 222 D1
Redcliffe Gdns SW5; SW10 221 D4
Redcross Way SE1 225 U11
Redriff Rd SE16 223 B4
Reeves Ms W1 224 B8
Regent Pl W1 224 G7
Regent St SW1 224 H8
Regent St W1 224 E5
Regents Pk Rd N3 220 D1
Regent's Pl NW1 224 F1
Regnart Bldgs NW1 224 G1
Remnant St WC2 225 M5
Rennie St SE1 225 R9
Repository Rd SE18 223 D4
Rex Pl W1 224 C8
Richardson's Ms W1 224 F2
Richbell Pl WC1 225 M3
Richmond Bldgs W1 224 H6
Richmond Hill, Rich. TW10 221 B5
Richmond Ms W1 224 H6
Richmond Rd, Kings.T. KT2 221 B6
Richmond Rd, Twick. TW1 221 B5
Richmond Ter SW1 225 K11
Ridgeway, The (North Harrow), Har. HA2 220 A1
Ridgmount Gdns WC1 224 H2
Ridgmount Pl WC1 224 H3
Ridgmount St WC1 224 H3
Ridgway SW19 221 C6
Riding Ho St W1 224 F4
Risborough St SE1 225 S11
Rising Sun Ct EC1 225 S4
Riverside Dr, Rich. TW10 221 B5
Robert Adam St W1 224 B5
Robert St WC2 225 L8
Roberts Ms SW1 224 B14
Robert's Pl EC1 225 Q1
Robin Hood Way (Kingston Bypass) SW15; SW20 221 C5
Rochester St SW1 224 H14
Rochester Way SE3; SE9 223 D5
Rochester Way Relief Rd SE3; SE9 223 D4
Rockingham Est SE1 225 T14
Rockingham St SE1 225 T14
Rocks La SW13 221 C5
Rodmarton St W1 224 A4
Rodney Rd SE17 223 B4
Roe Grn NW9 220 C1
Roehampton La SW15 221 C5
Roehampton Vale SW15 221 C5
Roger St WC1 225 N2
Rolls Bldgs EC4 225 P5
Rolls Pas EC4 225 P5
Rolls Rd SE1 223 B4
Roman Rd E2; E3 222 C3
Romford Rd E7; E15 222 C2
Romilly St W1 224 H7
Romney Ms W1 224 B3
Romney St SW1 224 J14
Ron Leighton Way E6 222 D3
Roscoe St EC1 225 U2
Rose All SE1 225 U9
Rose & Crown Ct EC2 225 T5
Rose & Crown Yd SW1 224 G9
Rose St WC2 225 K7
Rosebery Av EC1 225 P2
Rosebery Sq EC1 225 P2
Rosoman Pl EC1 225 Q1
Rosslyn Hill NW3 220 D2
Rotary St SE1 225 R13
Rotherham Wk SE1 225 R10
Rotherhithe New Rd SE16 223 B4
Rotherhithe Tunnel E1 222 B3
Rotten Row SW1 224 B11
Roundway, The N17 222 B1
Roupell St SE1 225 Q10
Rowan Rd SW16 223 A6
Roxeth Grn Av, Har. HA2 220 A2
Roxeth Hill, Har. HA2 220 A2
Royal Albert Way E16 222 D3
Royal Arc W1 224 F8
Royal Docks Rd E6 222 D3
Royal Hospital Rd SW3 221 D4
Royal Ms, The SW1 224 E13
Royal Opera Arc SW1 224 H9
Royal St SE1 225 N13
Royalty Ms W1 224 H6
Royston Pk Rd, Pnr. HA5 220 A1
Ruckholt Rd E10 222 C2
Rugby St WC1 225 M2
Ruislip Rd E, W7; W13; Grnf. UB6 220 A3
Rupert Ct W1 224 H7
Rupert St W1 224 H7
Rushey Grn SE6 223 C5
Rushworth St SE1 225 S11
Russell Ct SW1 224 G10
Russell Sq WC1 224 K2
Russell St WC2 225 L7
Russia Ct EC2 225 U5
Russia Row EC2 225 U6
Rutland Pl EC1 225 T2
Ryder Ct SW1 224 G9
Ryder St SW1 224 G9
Ryder Yd SW1 224 G9
Rye La SE15 223 B4

**S**

Sackville St W1 224 G8
Saddle Yd W1 224 D9
Saffron Hill EC1 225 Q2
Saffron St EC1 225 Q3
St. Albans St SW1 224 H8
St. Alphage Gdns EC2 225 U4
St. Andrew St EC4 225 Q4
St. Andrew's Hill EC4 225 S7
St. Andrews Pl NW1 224 E1
St. Anne's Ct W1 224 H6
St. Ann's Hill SW18 221 D5
St. Ann's La SW1 224 J13
St. Ann's Rd N15 222 B1
St. Ann's St SW1 224 J13
St. Anselm's Pl W1 224 D6
St. Bride St EC4 225 R5
St. Bride's Pas EC4 225 R6
St. Christopher's Pl W1 224 C5
St. Clement's La WC2 225 N6
St. Cross St EC1 225 Q3
St. Ermin's Hill SW1 224 H13
St. George St W1 224 E6
St. Georges Circ SE1 225 R13
St. Georges Ct EC4 225 R5
St. Georges Rd E7 222 D2
St. Georges Rd SE1 225 Q13
St. Giles High St WC2 224 J5
St. Giles Pas WC2 224 J6
St. James's Ct SW1 224 G13
St. James's Dr SW12; SW17 221 D5
St. James's Mkt SW1 224 H8
St. James's Palace SW1 224 G11
St. James's Pk SW1 224 H11
St. James's Pl SW1 224 F10
St. James's Rd SE1; SE16 223 B4
St. James's Row EC1 225 Q1
St. James's Sq SW1 224 G9
St. James's St SW1 224 F9
St. James's Wk EC1 225 R1
St. John St EC1 225 S2
St. John's Hill SW11 221 D5
St. John's La EC1 225 R2
St. John's Path EC1 225 R2
St. John's Pl EC1 225 R2
St. John's Rd, Islw. TW7 221 A4
St. John's Sq EC1 225 R2
St. John's Wd Rd NW8 220 D3
St. Margaret's Ct SE1 225 U10
St. Margarets Rd, Twick. TW1 221 B5
St. Margaret's St SW1 225 K12
St. Martin's La WC2 224 K7
St. Martin's Ms WC2 224 K8
St. Martin's Pl WC2 224 K8
St. Martin's St WC2 224 J8
St. Martin's-le-Grand EC1 225 T5
St. Mary's Rd SW19 221 D6
St. Mary's Rd W5 221 B4
St. Matthew St SW1 224 H14
St. Mildreds Rd SE12 223 C5
St. Paul's Chyd EC4 225 S6
St. Paul's Way E3; E14 222 C3
St. Quintin Av W10 220 C3
St. Vincent St W1 224 C4
Salisbury Ct EC4 225 R6
Salisbury Sq EC4 225 Q6
Salmon St NW9 220 B2
Salter Rd SE16 223 B4
Salters Hill SE19 223 B6
Salusbury Rd NW6 220 D3
Sanctuary, The SW1 224 J12
Sanctuary St SE1 225 U12
Sandell St SE1 225 P11
Sanders La NW7 220 C1
Sandland St WC1 225 N4
Sandy La, Kings.T. KT1; Tedd. TW11 221 B6
Sandy La, Rich. TW10 221 B5
Sandycombe Rd, Rich. TW9 221 B5
Sanford St SE14 223 C4
Sans Wk EC1 225 Q1
Sapperton Ct EC1 225 T1
Sardinia St WC2 225 M6
Savile Row W1 224 F7
Savoy Bldgs WC2 225 M8
Savoy Ct WC2 225 L8
Savoy Hill WC2 225 M8
Savoy Pl WC2 225 L8

Savoy Row WC2 225 M7
Savoy St WC2 225 M7
Savoy Way WC2 225 M8
Sawyer St SE1 225 T11
Scala St W1 224 G3
Scoresby St SE1 225 R10
Scotch Common W13 220 B34
Scotland Pl SW1 225 K9
Scotswood St EC1 225 Q1
Scotts La, Brom. BR2 223 C6
Scovell Cres SE1 225 T12
Scovell Rd SE1 225 T12
Scrubs La NW10; W10 220 C3
Secker St SE1 225 P10
Sedley Pl W1 224 D6
Sekforde St EC1 225 R2
Selwyn Av E4 222 C1
Serjeants Inn EC4 225 Q6
Serle St WC2 225 N5
Sermon La EC4 225 T6
Seven Sisters Rd N4; N7; N15 222 A2
Seville St SW1 224 A12
Seward St EC1 225 S1
Seymour Ms W1 224 B5
Shacklewell La E8 222 B2
Shaftesbury Av W1 224 H7
Shaftesbury Av WC2 224 H7
Shaftesbury Av, Har. HA2 220 A2
Shavers Pl SW1 224 H8
Sheen La SW14 221 C5
Sheen Rd, Rich. TW9 221 B5
Sheepcote Rd, Har. HA1 220 A1
Sheffield St WC2 225 M6
Shelton St WC2 224 K6
Shepherd Mkt W1 224 D9
Shepherd St W1 224 D10
Shepherdess Wk N1 222 B3
Shepherds Bush Rd W6 221 C4
Shepherd's Cl W1 224 B7
Shepherds Hill N6 222 A1
Sheraton St W1 224 H6
Sherlock Ms W1 224 B4
Shernhall St E17 222 C1
Sherwood Pk Rd, Mitch. CR4 223 A6
Sherwood St W1 224 G7
Shirland Rd W9 220 D3
Shoe La EC4 225 Q5
Shoot Up Hill NW2 220 D2
Shooter's Hill Rd SE3; SE10; SE18 223 C4
Short St SE1 225 Q11
Shortlands Rd, Brom. BR2 223 C6
Shorts Gdns WC2 224 K6
Shropshire Pl WC1 224 G2
Sicilian Av WC1 225 L4
Sidcup Rd SE9; SE12 223 D5
Siddons La NW1 224 A2
Sidford Pl SE1 225 N14
Sidmouth Rd NW2 220 C2
Sidney St E1 222 B3
Silex St SE1 225 S12
Silk St EC2 225 U3
Silver Pl W1 224 G7
Silverthorne Rd SW8 223 A4
Silvertown Way E16 222 C3
Silvester St SE1 225 U12
Skinners La EC4 225 U7
Slingsby Pl WC2 224 K7
Sloane St SW1 224 A13
Smart's Pl WC2 225 L5
Smith Sq SW1 224 K14
Smithfield St EC1 225 R4
Smith's Ct W1 224 G7
Smokehouse Yd EC1 225 S3
Snakes La E, Wdf.Grn. IG8 222 D1
Snakes La W, Wdf.Grn. IG8 222 D1
Snaresbrook Rd E11 222 C1
Snow Hill EC1 225 R4
Snow Hill Ct EC1 225 S5
Soho Sq W1 224 H5
Soho St W1 224 H5
Somerset Rd, Sthl. UB1 220 A3
South Audley St W1 224 C8
South Circular Rd SW2 223 A5
South Cres WC1 224 H4
South Croxted Rd SE21 223 B5
South Ealing Rd W5 221 B4
South Hill Av, Har. HA1, HA2 220 A2
South Lambeth Rd SW8 223 A4
South La, N.Mal. KT3 221 C6
South Lo Av, Mitch. CR4 223 A6
South Molton La W1 224 D6
South Molton St W1 224 D6
South Norwood Hill SE25 223 B6
South Par W4 221 C4
South Rd, Sthl. UB1 221 A4
South Sq WC1 225 P4
South St W1 224 C9
South St, Islw. TW7 221 B5
South Woodford to Barking Relief Rd, E11; E12; E18; Bark. IG11; Ilf. IG1 222 D1
Southampton Bldgs WC2 225 P5
Southampton Pl WC1 225 L4
Southampton Row WC1 225 L3
Southampton St WC2 225 L7
Southampton Way SE5 223 B4
Southborough Rd, Brom. BR1 223 D6
Southcroft Rd SW16; SW17 223 A6
Southend La SE6; SE26 223 C6
Southend Rd E4; E17; E18 222 C1
Southend Rd, Beck. BR3 223 C6
Southfield Rd W4 221 C4
Southgate Rd N1 222 B3
Southlands Rd, Brom. BR1, BR2 223 D6
Southover, Brom. BR1 223 D6
Southwark Br EC4 225 U9
Southwark Br SE1 225 U9
Southwark Br Rd SE1 225 S13
Southwark Gro SE1 225 T10
Southwark Pk Rd SE16 223 B4
Southwark St SE1 225 S9
Spa Hill SE19 223 B6
Spafield St EC1 225 P1
Spaniards Rd NW3 220 D2
Spanish Pl W1 224 C4
Spencer Pk SW18 221 D5
Spenser St SW1 224 G13
Spring Gdns SW1 224 J9
Spring Gro Rd, Houns. TW3; Islw. TW7 221 A4
Spring Ms W1 224 A3
Spur Rd SE1 225 P11
Spur Rd SW1 224 F12
Stable Yd SW1 224 F11
Stable Yd Rd SW1 224 F10
Stacey St WC2 224 J6
Stafford Pl SW1 224 F13
Stafford St W1 224 F9
Stag La NW9 220 B1
Stag Pl SW1 224 F13
Staines Rd, Twick. TW2 221 A5
Staining La EC2 225 U5
Stamford Hill N16 222 B2
Stamford St SE1 225 P10
Stanhope Gate W1 224 C9
Stanhope Row W1 224 D10
Stanley Rd, Tedd. TW11; Twick. TW2 221 A6
Stansfeld Rd E6 222 D3
Stanstead Rd SE6; SE23 223 B5
Stanton Way SE26 223 C6
Staple Inn WC1 225 P4
Staple Inn Bldgs WC1 225 P4
Star & Garter Hill, Rich. TW10 221 B5
Star Yd WC2 225 P5
Station App SE1 225 N12
Station Rd E12 222 D2
Station Rd NW4 220 C1
Station Rd NW10 220 C3
Station Rd SW13 221 C4
Station Rd, Edg. HA8 220 B1
Station Rd, Har. HA1 220 A1
Stedham Pl WC1 224 K5
Stephen Ms W1 224 H4
Stephen St W1 224 H4
Stephenson St E16 222 C3
Stephenson Way NW1 224 G1
Stepney Grn E1 222 B3
Stepney Way E1 222 B3
Stew La EC4 225 T7
Steyne Rd W3 220 B3
Stockwell Rd SW9 223 A4
Stoke Newington Rd N16 222 B2
Stondon Pk SE23 223 C5
Stone Bldgs WC2 225 N4
Stone Pk Av, Beck. BR3 223 C6
Stonecutter St EC4 225 R5
Stones End St SE1 225 T12
Stopford Rd E13 222 D3
Store St WC1 224 H4
Storey's Gate SW1 224 J12
Strand WC2 225 K8
Strand La WC2 225 N7
Stratford Pl W1 224 D6
Strathyre Av SW16 223 A6
Stratton St W1 224 E9
Strawberry Vale, Twick. TW1 221 B5
Streatfield Rd, Har. HA3 220 B1
Streatham Common N SW16 223 A6
Streatham High Rd SW16 223 A5
Streatham Hill SW2 223 A5
Streatham Pl SW2 223 A5
Streatham Rd, Mitch. CR4 223 A6
Streatham St WC1 224 J5
Streatham Vale SW16 223 A6
Strone Rd E7; E12 222 D2
Stroud Grn Rd N4 222 A2
Strutton Grd SW1 224 H13
Studio Pl SW1 224 A12
Stukeley St WC2 225 L5
Sturge St SE1 225 T11
Sudbury Hill, Har. HA1 220 A2
Sudrey St SE1 225 T12
Suffolk Pl SW1 224 J9
Suffolk St SW1 224 J9
Summer Hill, Chis. BR7 223 D6
Summer St EC1 225 P2
Summers La N12 220 D1
Sumner St SE1 225 S9
Sunray Av SE24 223 B5
Surbiton Rd, Kings.T. KT1 221 B6
Surrey Canal Rd SE14; SE15 223 B4
Surrey Lo SE1 225 P14
Surrey Quays Rd SE16 223 B4
Surrey Row SE1 225 R11
Surrey St WC2 225 N7
Sussex Gdns W2 220 D3
Sutton La, Houns. TW3 221 A5
Sutton Row W1 224 J5
Sutton's Way EC1 225 U2
Swallow Pas W1 224 E6
Swallow Pl W1 224 E6
Swallow St W1 224 G8
Swan Rd (Hanworth), Felt. TW13 221 A6
Swan St SE1 225 U13
Swandon Way SW18 221 D5
Sycamore St EC1 225 T2
Sydenham Hill SE23; SE26 223 B5
Sydenham Rd SE26 223 B6
Sydney St SW3 221 D4
Syon La, Islw. TW7 221 A4

## T

Talgarth Rd W6; W14 221 C4
Tallis St EC4 225 Q7
Tamworth La, Mitch. CR4 223 A6
Tanswell Est SE1 225 Q12
Tanswell St SE1 225 P12
Tarn St SE1 225 T14
Tavistock Pl WC1 224 J1
Tavistock Sq WC1 224 J1
Tavistock St WC2 225 L7
Taviton St WC1 224 H1
Teignmouth Gdns, Grnf. UB6 220 B3
Temple Av EC4 225 Q7
Temple La EC4 225 Q6
Temple Mill La E15 222 C2
Temple Pl WC2 225 N7
Temple W Ms SE11 225 R14
Tenison Ct W1 224 F7
Tenison Way SE1 225 P10
Tennison Rd SE25 223 B6
Tentelow La, Sthl. UB2 221 A4
Tenterden St W1 224 E6
Terminus Pl SW1 224 E14
Terrace, The SW13 221 C4
Tetherdown N10 222 A1
Thames Path SE1 225 Q8
Thavies Inn EC1 225 Q5
Thayer St W1 224 C4
Theed St SE1 225 P10
Theobald's Rd WC1 225 M3
Thicket Rd SE20 223 B6
Thirleby Rd SW1 224 G14
Thomas Doyle St SE1 225 R13
Thornbury Rd, Islw. TW7 221 A4
Thornhaugh Ms WC1 224 J2
Thornhaugh St WC1 224 J3
Thornton Av SW2 223 A5
Thornton Pl W1 224 A3
Thrale St SE1 225 U10
Three Barrels Wk EC4 225 U7
Three Cups Yd WC1 225 N4
Three Kings Yd W1 224 D7
Thurlow Pk Rd SE21 223 A5
Tilney Ct EC1 225 U1
Tilney St W1 224 C9
Timber St EC1 225 T1
Tiverton St SE1 225 T14
Tollgate Rd E16 222 D3
Tollington Pk N4 222 A2
Tolmers Sq NW1 224 G1
Tomswood Hill, Ilf. IG6 222 D1
Tomswood Rd, Chig. IG7 222 D1
Took's Ct EC4 225 P5
Tooting Bec Rd SW16; SW17 223 A5
Tooting High St SW17 221 D6
Topham St EC1 225 P1
Torrington Pl WC1 224 H3
Torrington Sq WC1 224 J2
Tothill St SW1 224 H12
Tottenham Ct Rd W1 224 G2
Tottenham La N8 222 A1
Tottenham Ms W1 224 G3
Tottenham St W1 224 G4
Toulmin St SE1 225 T12
Tower Br Rd SE1 223 B4
Tower Ct WC2 224 K6
Tower Royal EC4 225 U7
Tower St WC2 224 J6
Trafalgar Av SE15 223 B4
Trafalgar Rd SE10 223 C4
Trafalgar Sq SW1 224 J9
Trafalgar Sq WC2 224 J9
Traps La, N.Mal. KT3 221 C6
Trebeck St W1 224 D9
Treveris St SE1 225 R10
Trig La EC4 225 T7
Trinity Ch Sq SE1 225 U13
Trinity Ri SW2 223 A5
Trinity Rd SW17; SW18 221 D5
Trinity St SE1 225 U12
Trio Pl SE1 225 U12
Triton Sq NW1 224 F1
Trott Rd N10 220 D1
Trump St EC2 225 U6
Trundle St SE1 225 T11
Trundleys Rd SE8 223 B4
Tudor Dr, Kings.T. KT2 221 B6
Tudor Pl W1 224 H5
Tudor St EC4 225 Q7
Tufnell Pk Rd N7; N19 222 A2
Tufton St SW1 224 J13
Tulse Hill SW2 223 A5
Tunmarsh La E13 222 D3
Turk's Head Yd EC1 225 R3
Turnagain La EC4 225 R5
Turnmill St EC1 225 Q2
Turnpike La N8 222 A1
Tweezer's All WC2 225 P7
Twickenham Rd (Hanworth), Felt. TW13 221 A5
Twickenham Rd, Islw. TW7 221 B5
Twickenham Rd, Rich. TW9 221 B5
Twickenham Rd, Tedd. TW11 221 B6
Twyford Av W3 220 B3
Twyford Pl WC2 225 M5
Tyburn Way W1 224 A7
Tyler's Ct W1 224 H6

## U

Ufford St SE1 225 Q11
Ulster Pl NW1 224 D2
Ulster Ter NW1 224 D1
Union Rd SW4; SW8 223 A4
Union St SE1 225 S10
University St WC1 224 G2
Upper Belgrave St SW1 224 C13
Upper Brook St W1 224 B8
Upper Clapton Rd E5 222 B2
Upper Elmers End Rd, Beck. BR3 223 C6
Upper Grosvenor St W1 224 B8
Upper Grd SE1 225 P9
Upper Ham Rd, Rich. TW10 221 B6
Upper Harley St NW1 224 C1
Upper James St W1 224 G7
Upper John St W1 224 G7
Upper Marsh SE1 225 N13
Upper N St E14 222 C3
Upper Richmond Rd SW15 221 C5
Upper Richmond Rd W SW14; Rich. TW10 221 C5
Upper Rd E13 222 D2
Upper St. Martin's La WC2 224 K7
Upper St N1 222 A3
Upper Sunbury Rd, Hmptn. TW12 221 A6
Upper Thames St EC4 225 S7
Upper Tooting Rd SW17 221 D6
Upper Tulse Hill SW2 223 A5
Upper Wimpole St W1 224 D3
Upton La E7 222 D2
Uxbridge Rd W3; W5 220 B3
Uxbridge Rd W12 220 C3
Uxbridge Rd, Hmptn. TW12 221 A6
Uxbridge Rd, Har. HA3; Pnr. HA5; Stan. HA7 220 A1
Uxbridge Rd, Sthl. UB1 220 A3

## V

Vale, The NW11 220 C2
Vale, The W3 220 C3
Valentine Pl SE1 225 R11
Valentine Row SE1 225 R12
Vallance Rd E1; E2 222 B3
Valley Rd, Brom. BR2 223 C6
Vanbrugh Pk SE3 223 C4
Vandon Pas SW1 224 G13
Vandon St SW1 224 G13
Vauxhall Br Rd SW1 223 A4
Verdant La SE6 223 C5
Verdun Rd SW13 221 C4
Vere St W1 224 D6
Vernon Pl WC1 225 L4
Verulam Bldgs WC1 225 N3
Verulam St WC1 225 P3
Vicarage Cres SW11 221 D4
Vicarage La E15 222 C2
Vicarage Rd E10 222 C2
Victoria Dock Rd E16 222 D3
Victoria Embk EC4 225 M8
Victoria Embk SW1 225 L11
Victoria Embk WC2 225 M8
Victoria Pk Rd E9 222 B3
Victoria Rd NW10; W3 220 C3
Victoria Sq SW1 224 E13
Victoria St SW1 224 F14
Vigo St W1 224 F8
Village, The SE7 223 D4
Village Way SE21 223 B5
Village Way, Beck. BR3 223 C6
Village Way, Pnr. HA5 220 A2
Villiers Rd, Kings.T. KT1 221 B6
Villiers St WC2 225 K8
Vine Hill EC1 225 P2
Vine St W1 224 G8
Vine St Br EC1 225 Q2
Vine Yd SE1 225 U11
Vineyard Wk EC1 225 P1
Violet Rd E3 222 C3
Virgil St SE1 225 N13
Viscount St EC1 225 T2
Vivian Av NW4 220 C1

## W

Waithman St EC4 225 R6
Wakefield St WC1 225 L1
Waldegrave Rd, Tedd. TW11; Twick. TW1 221 A5
Waldram Pk Rd SE23 223 B5
Wales Fm Rd W3 220 C3
Walkers Ct W1 224 H7
Wallis All SE1 225 U12
Wallside EC2 225 U4
Walm La NW2 220 C2
Walterton Rd W9 220 D3
Walton Rd, E.Mol. KT8; Walt. KT12; W.Mol. KT8 221 A6
Walworth Rd SE1; SE17 223 B4
Wandle Rd, Mord. SM4 221 D6
Wandsworth Br Rd SW6 221 D4
Wandsworth High St SW18 221 D5
Wandsworth Rd SW8 223 A5
Wapping High St E1 222 B3
Wardens Gro SE1 225 T10
Wardour Ms W1 224 G6
Wardour St W1 224 H7
Wardrobe Pl EC4 225 S7
Wardrobe Ter EC4 225 S7
Warner St EC1 225 P2
Warner Yd EC1 225 P2
Warren Av, Brom. BR1 223 C6
Warren Ms W1 224 F2
Warren Rd, Kings.T. KT2 221 C6
Warren St W1 224 F2
Warwick Ct WC1 225 N4
Warwick Ho St SW1 224 J9
Warwick La EC4 225 S6
Warwick Pas EC4 225 S5
Warwick Rd W14 221 D4
Warwick Row SW1 224 E13
Warwick Sq EC4 225 S5
Warwick St W1 224 G7
Warwick Way SW1 223 A4
Warwick Yd EC1 225 U2
Water La E15 222 C2
Water St WC2 225 N7
Waterden Rd E15 222 C2
Watergate EC4 225 R7
Watergate Wk WC2 225 L9
Waterhouse Sq EC1 225 P4
Waterloo Br SE1 225 M8
Waterloo Br WC2 225 M8
Waterloo Pl SW1 224 H9
Waterloo Rd SE1 225 P11
Watermead Way N17 222 B1
Watford Way NW4; NW7 220 C1
Watling Av, Edg. HA8 220 C1
Watling Ct EC4 225 U6
Watling St EC4 225 T6
Watts La, Chis. BR7 223 D6
Waverton St W1 224 C9
Waxwell Ter SE1 225 N12
Webber Row SE1 225 Q13
Webber St SE1 225 Q11
Wedgwood Ms W1 224 J6
Weigall Rd SE12 223 D5
Weighhouse St W1 224 C6
Welbeck St W1 224 D5
Welbeck Way W1 224 D5
Well Ct EC4 225 U6
Well Hall Rd SE9 223 D4
Well St E9 222 B2
Weller St SE1 225 T11
Wellesley Rd W4 221 B4
Wellington Rd NW8 220 D3
Wellington Rd, Hmptn. TW12 221 A6
Wellington Rd N, Houns. TW4 221 A5
Wellington Rd S, Houns. TW4 221 A5
Wellington St SE18 223 D4
Wellington St WC2 225 L7
Wells Ms W1 224 G5
Wells St W1 224 F4
Wells Way SE5 223 B4
Wembley Pk Dr, Wem. HA9 220 B2
Wemborough Rd, Stan. HA7 220 B1
Wesley St W1 224 C4
West Barnes La SW20; N.Mal. KT3 221 C6
West Cen St WC1 225 K5
West End La NW6 220 D2
West Grn Rd N15 222 A1
West Halkin St SW1 224 B13
West Ham La E15 222 C2
West Harding St EC4 225 Q5
West Heath Rd NW3 220 D2
West Hill SW15; SW18 221 D5
West Poultry Av EC1 225 R4
West Side Common SW19 221 C6
West Smithfield EC1 225 R4
West Sq SE11 225 R14
West St WC2 224 J6
Westbourne Gro W2; W11 220 D3
Westbourne Pk Rd W2; W11 220 D3
Westbridge Rd SW11 221 D4
Westbury Av N22 222 A1
Western Av, Grnf. UB6; Nthlt. UB5 220 A3
Western Av W3; W5; Grnf. UB6; Nthlt. UB5; Ruis. HA4; Uxb. UB8, UB10 220 B3
Western Rd SW19; Mitch. CR4 221 D6
Westferry Rd E14 223 C4
Westhorne Av SE9; SE12 223 D5
Westminster Br SE1 225 L12
Westminster Br SW1 225 L12
Westminster Br Rd SE1 225 N12
Westmoreland St W1 224 C4
Westmount Rd SE9 223 D4
Weston Av, W.Mol. KT8 221 A6
Weston Dr, Stan. HA7 220 B1
Westway W2; W9; W10; W12 220 C3
Westwood Hill SE26 223 B6
Weymouth Ms W1 224 D3
Weymouth St W1 224 C4
Wheatley St W1 224 C4
Whetstone Pk WC2 225 M5
Whichcote St SE1 225 P10
Whipps Cross Rd E11 222 C1
Whitchurch La, Edg. HA8 220 B1
Whitcomb St WC2 224 J8
White Horse Hill, Chis. BR7 223 D6
White Horse Ms SE1 225 Q13
White Horse St W1 224 D10
White Lion Hill EC4 225 S7
Whitechapel Rd E1 222 B3
Whitecross St EC1 225 U1
Whitefoot La, Brom. BR1 223 C5
Whitefriars St EC4 225 Q6
Whitehall SW1 224 K9
Whitehall Ct SW1 225 K10
Whitehall Gdns SW1 225 K10
Whitehall Pl SW1 225 K10
Whitehorse La SE25 223 B6
Whitfield Pl W1 224 F2
Whitfield St W1 224 H4
Whittlesey St SE1 225 P10
Whitton Av E, Grnf. UB6 220 A2
Whitton Av W, Grnf. UB6; Nthlt. UB5 220 A2
Whitton Dene, Houns. TW3; Islw. TW7 221 A5
Whitton Rd, Houns. TW3 221 A5
Whitton Rd, Twick. TW1 221 A5
Wick Rd E9 222 B2
Wickham Rd SE4 223 C5
Wickham Rd, Beck. BR3 223 C6
Wickham Way, Beck. BR3 223 C6
Wide Way, Mitch. CR4 223 A6
Widmore Rd, Brom. BR1 223 D6
Wightman Rd N4; N8 222 A1
Wigmore Pl W1 224 D5
Wigmore St W1 224 B6
Wilcox Pl SW1 224 G14
Wild Ct WC2 225 M5
Wild St WC2 225 L6
Wilfred St SW1 224 F13
Willesden La NW2; NW6 220 C2
William Barefoot Dr SE9 223 D6
William IV St WC2 224 K8
William Ms SW1 224 A12
William St SW1 224 A12
Willoughby La N17 222 B1
Willoughby St WC1 224 K4
Willowbrook Rd SE15 223 B4
Wilton Cres SW1 224 B12
Wilton Ms SW1 224 C13
Wilton Pl SW1 224 B12
Wilton Rd SW1 224 E14
Wilton Row SW1 224 B12
Wilton St SW1 224 D13
Wilton Ter SW1 224 B13
Wimbledon Hill Rd SW19 221 C6
Wimbledon Pk Rd SW18; SW19 221 D5
Wimbledon Pk Side SW19 221 C5
Wimpole Ms W1 224 D3
Wimpole St W1 224 D5
Winchelsea Rd NW10 220 C3
Winchester Rd E4 222 C1
Winchester St W3 221 C4
Windmill La, Islw. TW7; Sthl. UB2 221 A4
Windmill Rd SW18 221 D5
Windmill Rd W5; Brent. TW8 221 B4
Windmill St W1 224 H4
Windmill Wk SE1 225 Q10
Windsor Pl SW1 224 G14
Wine Office Ct EC4 225 Q5
Winn Rd SE12 223 D5
Winnett St W1 224 H7
Winsley St W1 224 G5
Winston Way, Ilf. IG1 222 D2
Woburn Pl WC1 224 J1
Woburn Sq WC1 224 J2
Wood La NW9 220 C2
Wood La W12 220 C3
Wood La, Islw. TW7 221 A4
Wood St E17 222 C1
Wood St EC2 225 U6
Wood St, Kings.T. KT1 221 B6
Wood Vale SE23 223 B5
Woodbridge St EC1 225 R1
Woodcock Hill, Har. HA3 220 B1
Woodfield Rd W5 220 B3
Woodford Av, Ilf. IG2, IG4; Wdf.Grn. IG8 222 D1
Woodford New Rd, E1; E18; Wdf.Grn. IG8 222 C1
Woodford Rd E18 222 D1
Woodgrange Rd E7 222 C2
Woodhayes Rd SW19 221 C6
Woods Ms W1 224 A7
Woodstock Ms W1 224 C4
Woodstock St W1 224 D6
Woolstone Rd SE23 223 C5
Woolwich Ch St SE18 223 D4
Woolwich High St SE18 223 D4
Woolwich Manor Way E6; E16 222 D3
Woolwich Rd SE7 223 D4
Wootton St SE1 225 Q11
Worple Rd SW19; SW20 221 C6
Worship St EC2 222 B3
Worton Rd, Islw. TW7 221 A5
Wren St WC1 225 N1
Wrottesley Rd NW10 220 C3
Wybert St NW1 224 E1
Wyndham Rd SE5 223 A4

## Y

Yarmouth Pl W1 224 D10
York Br NW1 224 B1
York Bldgs WC2 225 L8
York Gate NW1 224 B2
York Pl WC2 225 L8
York Rd SE1 225 N11
York Rd SW11; SW18 221 D5
York St W1 224 A3
York St, Twick. TW1 221 B5
York Ter E NW1 224 C2
York Ter W NW1 224 B2
York Way N1; N7 222 A2
Yorkshire Grey Yd WC1 225 M4
Young's Bldgs EC1 225 U1

## Z

Zoar St SE1 225 T9

# Index to place names in Britain

## Use of the Index

The letters and numbers around the page edges of the main map section form the referencing system used in this atlas.
To find a place name first turn to the map page shown in bold type in the index, then locate the grid square indicated by the following letter and number.
The following list of abbreviations shows the counties for England and Wales and the councils for Scotland which appear in this atlas.
Where more than one place has the same name, each can be distinguished by the abbreviated county or council name shown after the place name.

## Abbreviations

| Abbreviation | Name |
|---|---|
| *Aber.* | Aberdeenshire |
| *Arg. & B.* | Argyll & Bute |
| *B'burn.* | Blackburn with Darwen |
| *B. & H.* | Brighton & Hove |
| *B. & N.E.Som.* | Bath & North East Somerset |
| *B.Gwent* | Blaenau Gwent |
| *Beds.* | Bedfordshire |
| *Bourne.* | Bournemouth |
| *Brack.F.* | Bracknell Forest |
| *Bucks.* | Buckinghamshire |
| *Caerp.* | Caerphilly |
| *Cambs.* | Cambridgeshire |
| *Carmar.* | Carmarthenshire |
| *Cere.* | Ceredigion |
| *Chan.I.* | Channel Islands |
| *Ches.* | Cheshire |
| *Cornw.* | Cornwall |
| *Cumb.* | Cumbria |
| *D. & G.* | Dumfries & Galloway |
| *Darl.* | Darlington |
| *Denb.* | Denbighshire |
| *Derbys.* | Derbyshire |
| *Dur.* | Durham |
| *E.Ayr.* | East Ayrshire |
| *E.Dun.* | East Dunbartonshire |
| *E.Loth.* | East Lothian |
| *E.Renf.* | East Renfrewshire |
| *E.Riding* | East Riding of Yorkshire |
| *E.Suss.* | East Sussex |
| *Edin.* | Edinburgh |
| *Falk.* | Falkirk |
| *Flints.* | Flintshire |
| *Glas.* | Glasgow |
| *Glos.* | Gloucestershire |
| *Gt.Lon.* | Greater London |
| *Gt.Man.* | Greater Manchester |
| *Gwyn.* | Gwynedd |
| *Hants.* | Hampshire |
| *Hart.* | Hartlepool |
| *Here.* | Herefordshire |
| *Herts.* | Hertfordshire |
| *High.* | Highland |
| *I.o.A.* | Isle of Anglesey |
| *I.o.M.* | Isle of Man |
| *I.o.S.* | Isles of Scilly |
| *I.o.W.* | Isle of Wight |
| *Inclyde* | Inverclyde |
| *Lancs.* | Lancashire |
| *Leic.* | Leicester |
| *Leics.* | Leicestershire |
| *Lincs.* | Lincolnshire |
| *M.K.* | Milton Keynes |
| *M.Tyd.* | Merthyr Tydfil |
| *Med.* | Medway |
| *Mersey.* | Merseyside |
| *Middbro.* | Middlesbrough |
| *Midloth.* | Midlothian |
| *Mon.* | Monmouthshire |
| *N.Ayr.* | North Ayrshire |
| *N.E.Lincs.* | North East Lincolnshire |
| *N.Lan.* | North Lanarkshire |
| *N.Lincs.* | North Lincolnshire |
| *N.P.T.* | Neath Port Talbot |
| *N.Som.* | North Somerset |
| *N.Yorks.* | North Yorkshire |
| *Norf.* | Norfolk |
| *Northants.* | Northamptonshire |
| *Northumb.* | Northumberland |
| *Nott.* | Nottingham |
| *Notts.* | Nottinghamshire |
| *Ork.* | Orkney |
| *Oxon.* | Oxfordshire |
| *P. & K.* | Perth & Kinross |
| *Pembs.* | Pembrokeshire |
| *Peter.* | Peterborough |
| *Plym.* | Plymouth |
| *Ports.* | Portsmouth |
| *R. & C.* | Redcar & Cleveland |
| *R.C.T.* | Rhondda Cynon Taff |
| *Read.* | Reading |
| *Renf.* | Renfrewshire |
| *Rut.* | Rutland |
| *S'end* | Southend |
| *S'ham.* | Southampton |
| *S.Ayr.* | South Ayrshire |
| *S.Glos.* | South Gloucestershire |
| *S.Lan.* | South Lanarkshire |
| *S.Yorks.* | South Yorkshire |
| *Sc.Bord.* | Scottish Borders |
| *Shet.* | Shetland |
| *Shrop.* | Shropshire |
| *Slo.* | Slough |
| *Som.* | Somerset |
| *Staffs.* | Staffordshire |
| *Stir.* | Stirling |
| *Stock.* | Stockton-on-Tees |
| *Stoke* | Stoke-on-Trent |
| *Suff.* | Suffolk |
| *Surr.* | Surrey |
| *Swan.* | Swansea |
| *Swin.* | Swindon |
| *T. & W.* | Tyne & Wear |
| *Tel. & W.* | Telford & Wrekin |
| *Thur.* | Thurrock |
| *V. of Glam.* | Vale of Glamorgan |
| *W'ham* | Wokingham |
| *W. & M.* | Windsor & Maidenhead |
| *W.Berks.* | West Berkshire |
| *W.Dun.* | West Dunbartonshire |
| *W.Isles* | Western Isles (Na h-Eileanan an Iar) |
| *W.Loth.* | West Lothian |
| *W.Mid.* | West Midlands |
| *W.Suss.* | West Sussex |
| *W.Yorks.* | West Yorkshire |
| *Warks.* | Warwickshire |
| *Warr.* | Warrington |
| *Wilts.* | Wiltshire |
| *Worcs.* | Worcestershire |
| *Wrex.* | Wrexham |

## A


A'Chill **163** F4
Ab Kettleby **82** C5
Abbas Combe **25** E5
Abberley **53** G1
Abberton *Essex* **46** D1
Abberton *Worcs.* **54** B2
Abberwick **137** F5
Abbess Roding **45** E1
Abbey Dore **52** C4
Abbey Hulton **79** G3
Abbey St. Bathans **145** E3
Abbey Village **100** C5
Abbey Wood **45** D5
Abbeycwmhir **63** G5
Abbeystead **100** B2
Abbeytown **117** E1
Abbotrule **136** A5
Abbots Bickington **21** D4
Abbots Bromley **80** B5
Abbots Langley **44** A2
Abbots Leigh **39** E5
Abbots Morton **54** C2
Abbots Ripton **70** A5
Abbot's Salford **54** C2
Abbotsbury **12** B4
Abbotsham **21** E3
Abbotskerswell **9** E1
Abbotsley **58** A2
Abbotts Ann **27** E3
Abbottswood **27** E5
Abdon **65** E4
Aber **50** A3
Aber-banc **49** G3
Aber Bargoed **38** A2
Aber Bowlan **50** C4
Aber-Cywarch **63** E1
Aber-llia **37** F1
Aber-Naint **77** E5
Aber-nant **37** G2
Aberaeron **50** A1
Aberaman **37** G2
Aberangell **63** E2
Aberarad **49** G4
Aberarder **157** G1
Aberarder House **167** F2
Aberargie **151** G3
Aberarth **50** A1
Aberavon **37** D4
Aberbeeg **38** B2
Abercanaid **37** G2
Abercarn **38** B3
Abercastle **48** B4
Abercegir **63** E2
Aberchalder **166** C4
Aberchirder **182** B4
Abercorn **143** E2
Abercraf **37** E1
Abercrombie **152** D4
Abercrychan **51** D4
Abercwmboi **37** G2
Abercych **49** F3
Abercynafon **37** G1
Abercynon **37** G3
Aberdalgie **151** F2
Aberdare **37** F2
Aberdaron **74** A5
Aberdaugleddau (Milford Haven) **34** C2
Aberdeen **171** E4
Aberdeen Airport **171** D3
Aberdesach **74** D2
Aberdour **143** F1
Aberdovey (Aberdyfi) **62** C3
Aberduhonw **51** G2
Aberdulais **37** D3
Aberdyfi (Aberdovey) **62** C3
Aberedw **51** G3
Abereiddy **48** B4
Abererch **74** D4
Aberfan **37** G2
Aberfeldy **159** D5
Aberffraw **74** C1
Aberffrwd **62** C5
Aberford **102** D4
Aberfoyle **150** A4
Abergarw **37** F4
Abergavenny (Y Fenni) **38** C1
Abergele **90** A5
Abergiar **50** B3
Abergorlech **50** B4
Abergwaun (Fishguard) **48** C4
Abergwesyn **51** E2
Abergwili **50** A5
Abergwydol **63** D2
Abergwynant **62** C1
Abergwynfi **37** E3
Abergwyngregyn **89** E5
Abergynolwyn **62** C2
Aberhafesp **63** G3
Aberhonddu (Brecon) **51** G5
Aberhosan **63** E3
Aberkenfig **37** E4
Aberlady **144** B1
Aberlemno **160** D4
Aberllefenni **63** D2
Aberlour (Charlestown of Aberlour) **181** E5
Abermad **62** B5
Abermaw (Barmouth) **62** C1
Abermeurig **50** B2
Abermule **64** A3
Abernant **49** G5
Abernethy **151** G3
Abernyte **152** A1
Aberpergwm **37** E2
Aberporth **49** F2
Aberriw (Berriew) **64** A2
Aberscross **190** C4
Abersky **167** E2
Abersoch **74** C5
Abersychan **38** B2
Abertawe (Swansea) **36** C3
Aberteifi (Cardigan) **49** E3
Aberthin **37** G5
Abertillery **38** B2
Abertridwr *Caerp.* **38** A4
Abertridwr *Powys* **63** G1
Abertysswg **38** A2
Aberuthven **151** E3
Aberyscir **51** F5
Aberystwyth **62** B4
Abhainnsuidhe **184** C3
Abingdon **41** G3
Abinger Common **29** G3
Abinger Hammer **29** F3
Abington **134** A3
Abington Pigotts **58** B3
Abingworth **16** D2
Ablington **40** D2
Abney **93** G5
Aboyne **170** A5
Abram **92** A2
Abriachan **167** E1
Abridge **45** D3
Abronhill **142** B2
Abson **39** F5
Abthorpe **56** B3
Abune-the-Hill **198** A4
Aby **97** E5
Acaster Malbis **103** E3
Acaster Selby **103** E3
Accrington **101** D5
Accurrach **148** D3
Acha **154** A4
Achacha **156** B5
Achadacaie **139** G3
Achadh-chaorrunn **139** F4
Achadh Mòr **187** E5
Achadunan **149** D3
Achagavel **155** G4
Achaglass **139** F5
Achahoish **139** F2
Achalader **159** G5
Achallader **157** F6
Achamore **139** D2
Achandunie **179** F2
Achany **190** A4
Achaphubuil **156** C2
Acharacle **155** F3
Achargary **193** G3
Acharn *Arg. & B.* **148** D1
Acharn *P. & K.* **158** C5
Acharonich **147** D1
Acharosson **140** A2
Achateny **155** E3
Achath **170** C3
Achavanich **195** D4
Achduart **188** C4
Achentoul **194** A5
Achfary **192** B4
Achgarve **188** A5
Achiemore *High.* **192** C2
Achiemore *High.* **194** A3
Achies **194** D3
Achiltibuie **188** C4
Achina **193** G2
Achindown **180** A5
Achinduich **190** A4
Achingills **195** D2
Achintee **177** F5
Achintee House **156** D2
Achintraid **165** E1
Achlean **168** A5
Achleanan **155** E4
Achleek **155** G4
Achlian **148** D2
Achlyness **192** B3
Achmelvich **188** C2
Achmony **167** D1
Achmore *High.* **165** E1
Achmore *High.* **188** C5
Achmore *Stir.* **150** A1
Achnaba **140** A1
Achnabat **167** E1
Achnabourin **193** G3
Achnacairn **148** B1
Achnacarnin **188** C1
Achnaclerach **178** D3
Achnacloich *Arg. & B.* **148** B1
Achnacloich *High.* **164** B4
Achnaclyth **194** C5
Achnacraig **155** D5
Achnacroish **156** A5
Achnadrish **155** D4
Achnafalnich **149** E2
Achnafauld **151** D1
Achnagairn **179** E5
Achnagarron **179** F2
Achnaha *High.* **155** F5
Achnaha *High.* **155** D3
Achnahanat **190** A5
Achnahannet **168** B2
Achnalea **156** A3
Achnamara **139** F1
Achnanellan **155** G3
Achnasaul **157** D1
Achnasheen **178** A4
Achnashelloch **148** A5
Achnastank **169** E1
Achorn **194** D5
Achosnich *High.* **190** C5
Achosnich *High.* **154** D3
Achreamie **194** C2
Achriabhach **156** D3
Achriesgill **192** B3
Achrimsdale **191** E4
Achtoty **193** F2
Achurch **69** F4
Achuvoldrach **193** E3
Achvaich **190** C5
Achvarasdal **194** B2
Achvlair **156** B4
Achvraie **188** C4
Ackergill **195** F3
Acklam *Middbro.* **111** D1
Acklam *N.Yorks.* **103** G1
Ackleton **65** G3
Acklington **129** E1
Ackton **102** D5
Ackworth Moor Top **94** B1
Acle **87** F4
Acock's Green **66** D4
Acol **33** E2
Acomb *Northumb.* **119** F1
Acomb *York* **103** F2
Aconbury **53** E4
Acre **101** D5
Acrefair **77** F3
Acrise Place **33** D4
Acton *Ches.* **78** D2
Acton *Gt.Lon.* **44** A5
Acton *Shrop.* **64** C4
Acton *Suff.* **59** G3
Acton *Worcs.* **54** A1
Acton Beauchamp **53** F2
Acton Bridge **91** G5
Acton Burnell **65** E2
Acton Green **53** F2
Acton Pigott **65** E2
Acton Round **65** F3
Acton Scott **65** D4
Acton Trussell **66** B1
Acton Turville **40** A4
Adamhill **132** C2
Adbaston **79** E5
Adber **24** C5
Adderbury **55** G4
Adderley **79** D4
Adderstone **137** F3
Addiewell **143** D3
Addingham **101** G3
Addington *Bucks.* **56** C5
Addington *Gt.Lon.* **30** C2
Addington *Kent* **31** F3
Addlestone **29** F1
Addlethorpe **84** D1
Adel **102** B4
Adeney **65** F1
Adfa **63** G2
Adforton **64** C5
Adisham **33** E3
Adlestrop **55** E5
Adlingfleet **104** A5
Adlington *Ches.* **92** D4
Adlington *Lancs.* **92** A1
Admaston *Staffs.* **80** B5
Admaston *Tel. & W.* **65** F1
Admington **55** D3
Adsborough **23** F5
Adstock **56** C4
Adstone **56** A2
Adversane **29** F5
Advie **168** D1
Adwalton **102** B5
Adwell **42** B3
Adwick le Street **94** C2
Adwick upon Dearne **94** B2
Ae Village **125** D2
Affleck **171** D2
Affpuddle **13** E3
Afon-wen **90** C5
Afton Bridgend **133** E4
Agglethorpe **109** F4
Aigburth **91** E4
Aignis **187** F4
Aike **104** C3
Aikerness **198** C1
Aikers **197** D3
Aiketgate **118** A3
Aikshaw **117** E2
Aikton **117** F1
Aikwood Tower **135** F3
Ailey **52** C3
Ailsworth **69** G3
Aimster **194** D2
Ainderby Quernhow **110** C4
Ainderby Steeple **110** C3
Aingers Green **47** E1
Ainsdale **91** E1
Ainstable **118** B3
Ainsworth **92** B1
Ainthorpe **111** G2
Aintree **91** E3
Aird **173** F4
Aird a' Mhachair **173** F5
Aird a' Mhulaidh **185** D2
Aird Asaig **184** D3
Aird Dhail **187** F1
Aird Leimhe **184** D5
Aird Mhige **184** D4
Aird Mhighe **184** C5
Aird of Sleat **164** B4
Aird Thunga **187** F4
Aird Uige **186** B4
Airdrie *Fife* **153** D4
Airdrie *N.Lan.* **142** B3
Airidh a' Bhruaich **185** E2
Airieland **124** B5
Airies **122** A4
Airigh-drishaig **165** D1
Airmyn **103** G5
Airntully **151** F1
Airor **164** D4
Airth **142** C1
Airton **101** F2
Airyhassen **115** D2
Aisby *Lincs.* **95** F3
Aisby *Lincs.* **83** F4
Aisgernis **172** C1
Aiskew **110** B4
Aislaby *N.Yorks.* **112** B2
Aislaby *N.Yorks.* **111** G4
Aislaby *Stock.* **110** D1
Aisthorpe **95** G4
Aith *Ork.* **198** A5
Aith *Ork.* **199** E4
Aith *Shet.* **200** C2
Aith *Shet.* **203** F3
Aitnoch **168** B1
Akeld **137** D4
Akeley **56** C4
Akenham **60** C3
Albaston **7** E3
Alberbury **64** C1
Albourne **17** E2
Albrighton *Shrop.* **66** A2
Albrighton *Shrop.* **65** D1
Alburgh **73** D3
Albury *Herts.* **58** C5
Albury *Surr.* **29** F3
Albury Heath **29** F3
Alby Hill **86** C2
Alcaig **179** E4
Alcaston **65** D4
Alcester **54** C2
Alciston **18** A3
Alcombe **22** C3
Alconbury **69** G5
Alconbury Hill **69** G5
Alconbury Weston **69** G5
Aldborough *N.Yorks.* **102** D1
Aldborough *Norf.* **86** C2
Aldbourne **41** E5
Aldbrough **105** E4
Aldbrough St. John **110** A1
Aldburgh **110** B5
Aldbury **43** E1
Aldclune **159** E3
Aldeburgh **61** F2
Aldeby **73** F2
Aldenham **44** A3
Alderbury **26** C5
Alderford **86** C4
Alderholt **14** A1
Alderley **39** G3
Alderley Edge **92** C5
Alderman's Green **67** F4
Aldermaston **27** G1
Aldermaston Soke **28** B1
Aldermaston Wharf **28** B1
Alderminster **55** E3
Alderney Airport **9** F4
Aldersey Green **78** B2
Aldershot **29** D2
Alderton *Glos.* **54** B4
Alderton *Northants.* **56** C3
Alderton *Shrop.* **78** B5
Alderton *Suff.* **61** E3
Alderton *Wilts.* **40** A4
Alderwasley **81** E2
Aldfield **102** B1
Aldford **78** B2
Aldham *Essex* **60** A5
Aldham *Suff.* **60** B3
Aldie *Aber.* **171** F1
Aldie *High.* **179** G1
Aldingbourne **16** B3
Aldingham **107** D5
Aldington *Kent* **32** C5
Aldington *Worcs.* **54** C3
Aldivalloch **169** F2
Aldochlay **149** F5
Aldons **122** C2
Aldreth **70** C5
Aldridge **66** C2
Aldringham **61** F1
Aldro **104** A1
Aldsworth **41** D1
Aldunie **169** F2
Aldville **151** E1
Aldwark *Derbys.* **80** D2
Aldwark *N.Yorks.* **103** D1
Aldwick **16** B4
Aldwincle **69** F4
Aldworth **42** A5
Alexandria **141** E2
Alfardisworthy **20** C4
Alfington **11** E3
Alfold **29** F4
Alfold Crossways **29** F4
Alford *Aber.* **170** A3
Alford *Lincs.* **97** E5
Alford *Som.* **24** D4
Alfreton **81** F2
Alfrick **53** G2
Alfriston **18** A3
Algarkirk **84** A4
Alhampton **24** D4
Alkborough **104** A5
Alkerton **55** F3
Alkham **33** E4
Alkington **78** C4
Alkmonton **80** C4
All Cannings **26** B1
All Saints South Elmham **73** E3
All Stretton **65** D3
Allaleigh **9** E2
Allanaquoich **168** D5
Allancreich **170** A5
Allangillfoot **126** A2
Allanton *D. & G.* **124** D2
Allanton *N.Lan.* **142** C4
Allanton *S.Lan.* **142** B4
Allanton *Sc.Bord.* **145** F4
Allardice **161** G2
Allathasdal **172** B3
Allendale Town **119** E2
Allenheads **119** E3
Allen's Green **45** D1
Allensford **119** G2
Allensmore **53** D4
Allenton **81** E4
Aller **24** A5
Allerby **117** D3
Allerford *Devon* **7** E2
Allerford *Som.* **22** C3
Allerston **112** B4
Allerthorpe **103** G3
Allerton *Mersey.* **91** F4
Allerton *W.Yorks.* **102** A4
Allerton Bywater **102** D5
Allesley **67** E4
Allestree **81** E4
Allexton **68** D2
Allgreave **79** G1
Allhallows **32** A1
Allhallows-on-Sea **32** A1
Alligin Shuas **177** E4
Allimore Green **66** A1
Allington *Lincs.* **83** D3
Allington *Wilts.* **26** D4
Allington *Wilts.* **26** B1
Allithwaite **107** E5
Allnabad **193** D4
Alloa **151** D5
Allonby **117** D2
Alloway **132** B4
Allscot **65** G3
Allt na h-Airbhe **188** D5
Allt-na-subh **165** F2
Alltachonaich **155** G4
Alltan Dubh **188** B3
Alltbeithe **165** G2
Alltforgan **76** C5
Alltmawr **51** G3
Alltnacaillich **193** D4
Alltsigh **167** D3
Alltwalis **50** A4
Alltwen **36** D2
Alltyblaca **50** B3
Almeley **52** C2
Almer **13** F3
Almington **79** D4
Almiston Cross **21** D3
Almondbank **151** F2
Almondbury **93** F1
Almondsbury **39** F4
Alne **103** D1
Alness **179** F3
Alnham **137** D5
Alnmouth **137** G5
Alnwick **137** F5
Alphamstone **59** G4
Alpheton **59** G2
Alphington **10** C3
Alpington **87** D5
Alport **80** D1
Alpraham **78** C2
Alresford **60** B5
Alrewas **67** D1
Alsager **79** E2
Alsagers Bank **79** F3
Alsop en le Dale **80** C2
Alston *Cumb.* **118** D3
Alston *Devon* **11** G2
Alstone **54** B4
Alstonefield **80** C2
Alswear **22** A5
Altanduin **190** D2
Altarnun **5** G1
Altass **190** A4
Altens **171** E4
Alterwall **195** E2
Altham **101** D4
Althorne **46** C3
Althorpe **95** F2
Alticry **123** D5
Altnafeadh **157** E4
Altnaharra **193** E5
Altofts **102** C5
Alton *Derbys.* **81** E1
Alton *Hants.* **28** C4
Alton *Staffs.* **80** B3
Alton Barnes **26** C1
Alton Pancras **12** C2
Alton Priors **26** C1
Altonside **181** E4
Altrincham **92** B4
Altura **157** E1
Alva **151** D5
Alvanley **91** F5
Alvaston **81** E4
Alvechurch **66** C5
Alvecote **67** E2
Alvediston **26** A5
Alveley **65** G4
Alverdiscott **21** F3
Alverstoke **15** F3
Alverstone **15** E4
Alverton **82** C3
Alves **180** D3
Alvescot **41** E2
Alveston *S.Glos.* **39** F4
Alveston *Warks.* **55** E2
Alvie **168** A4
Alvingham **97** D3
Alvington **39** F2
Alwalton **69** G3
Alweston **12** C1
Alwinton **128** B1
Alwoodley Gates **102** C3
Alyth **160** A5
Amalebra **2** B3
Amber Hill **84** A3
Ambergate **81** E2
Amberley *Glos.* **40** A2
Amberley *W.Suss.* **16** C2
Amble **129** E1
Amblecote **66** A4
Ambleside **107** E2
Ambleston **48** D5
Ambrismore **140** B4
Ambrosden **42** B1
Amcotts **95** F1
Amersham **43** E3
Amesbury **26** C3
Amington **67** E2
Amisfield **125** E2
Amlwch **88** C3
Amlwch Port **88** C3
Ammanford (Rhydaman) **36** C1
Amotherby **111** G5
Ampfield **27** E5
Ampleforth **111** E5
Ampleforth College **111** E5
Ampney Crucis **40** C2
Ampney St. Mary **40** C2
Ampney St. Peter **40** C2
Amport **27** E3
Ampthill **57** F4
Ampton **71** G5
Amroth **35** E2
Amulree **151** D1
An T-òb (Leverburgh) **184** C5
An Tairbeart (Tarbert) **185** D3
Anaboard **168** C1
Anaheilt **156** A3
Ancaster **83** E3
Anchor **64** A4
Ancroft **145** G5
Ancrum **136** A4
Ancton **16** B3
Anderby **97** F5
Anderson **13** E3

Anderton 92 A5
Andover 27 E3
Andover Down 27 E3
Andoversford 54 C5
Andreas 98 C2
Anelog 74 A5
Angarrack 2 C3
Angersleigh 11 E1
Angerton 117 F1
Angle 34 B2
Angler's Retreat 62 D3
Angmering 16 C3
Angram 103 E3
Anie 150 A3
Ankerville 180 A2
Anlaby 104 C5
Anmer 85 F5
Anna Valley 27 E3
Annan 125 F4
Annaside 106 B4
Annat *Arg. & B.* 148 C2
Annat *High.* 177 E4
Annbank 132 C3
Annesley 81 G2
Annesley Woodhouse 81 G2
Annfield Plain 120 A2
Annscroft 65 D2
Ansdell 99 G5
Ansford 24 D4
Ansley 67 E3
Anslow 80 D5
Anslow Gate 80 C5
Anstey *Herts.* 58 C4
Anstey *Leics.* 68 A2
Anstruther 153 D4
Ansty *W.Suss.* 17 E1
Ansty *Warks.* 67 F4
Ansty *Wilts.* 26 A5
Anthill Common 15 F1
Anthorn 117 E1
Antingham 87 D2
Anton's Gowt 84 A3
Antony 7 D5
Antrobus 92 A5
Anvil Corner 21 D5
Anwick 83 G2
Anwoth 123 G5
Aoradh 138 A3
Apethorpe 69 F3
Apley 96 B5
Apperknowle 94 A5
Apperley 54 A5
Appin House 156 B5
Appleby 95 G1
Appleby-in-Westmorland 118 C5
Appleby Magna 67 F1
Appleby Parva 67 F2
Applecross 176 D5
Appledore *Devon* 21 E2
Appledore *Devon* 11 D1
Appledore *Kent* 19 E1
Appledore Heath 32 B5
Appleford 42 A3
Appleshaw 27 E3
Applethwaite 117 F4
Appleton 41 G2
Appleton-le-Moors 111 G4
Appleton-le-Street 111 G5
Appleton Roebuck 103 E3
Appleton Thorn 92 A4
Appleton Wiske 110 C2
Appletreehall 135 G4
Appletreewick 101 G1
Appley 23 D5
Appley Bridge 91 G1
Apse Heath 15 E4
Apsley 43 F2
Apsley End 57 G4
Apuldram 16 A3
Arberth (Narberth) 35 E1
Arbirlot 161 D5
Arborfield 28 C1
Arborfield Cross 28 C1
Arborfield Garrison 28 C1
Arbroath 161 E5
Arbuthnott 161 G2
Archdeacon Newton 110 B1
Archiestown 181 E5
Arclid 79 E1
Ard a' Chapuill 140 B2
Ardachearanbeg 140 B1
Ardacheranmor 140 B1
Ardachoil 147 G1
Ardachu 190 B4
Ardachvie 166 A5
Ardailly 139 E4
Ardalanish 146 C3
Ardallie 171 F1
Ardanaiseig 148 C2
Ardaneaskan 165 E1
Ardanstur 148 A3
Ardantiobairt 155 F4
Ardantrive 148 A2
Ardarroch 165 E1
Ardbeg *Arg. & B.* 140 B3
Ardbeg *Arg. & B.* 138 C5
Ardbeg *Arg. & B.* 140 C1
Ardblair 167 D1
Ardbrecknish 148 C2
Ardcharnich 178 A1
Ardchiavaig 146 C3
Ardchonnel 148 B1
Ardchonnell 148 B3
Ardchrishnish 146 D2
Ardchronie 179 F1
Ardchuilk 166 B1
Ardchullarie More 150 A3
Ardchyle 150 A2
Arddlin 64 B1
Ardeley 58 B5
Ardelve 165 E2
Arden 141 E1
Ardencaple House 147 G3
Ardens Grafton 54 D2
Ardentallan 148 A2
Ardentinny 140 C1
Ardeonaig 150 B1
Ardersier 179 G4
Ardery 155 G3
Ardessie 177 G1
Ardfad 147 G3
Ardfern 148 A4
Ardfin 138 C3
Ardgartan 149 E4
Ardgay 190 A5
Ardgenavan 149 D3
Ardgowan 140 D2
Ardgowse 170 B3
Ardgye 180 D3
Ardhallow 140 C2
Ardheslaig 177 D4
Ardiecow 182 A3
Ardinamar 147 G3
Ardindrean 178 A1
Ardingly 17 F1
Ardington 41 G4
Ardintoul 165 E2
Ardkinglas House 149 D3
Ardlair 170 A2
Ardlamont 140 A3
Ardleigh 60 B5
Ardleish 149 F3
Ardler 160 A5
Ardley 56 A5
Ardlui 149 F3
Ardlussa 139 E1
Ardmaddy 148 C1
Ardmair 188 D5
Ardmaleish 140 B3
Ardmay 149 E4
Ardmenish 139 D2
Ardmhór 172 C3
Ardminish 139 E5
Ardmolich 155 G2
Ardmore *Arg. & B.* 138 C5
Ardmore *Arg. & B.* 147 G2
Ardmore *Arg. & B.* 141 E2
Ardmore *High.* 179 G1
Ardnackaig 147 G5
Ardnacross 155 E5
Ardnadam 140 C2
Ardnadrochit 147 G1
Ardnagoine 188 B4
Ardnagowan 148 D4
Ardnagrask 179 E5
Ardnahein 149 E5
Ardnahoe 138 C2
Ardnarff 165 E1
Ardnastang 156 A3
Ardnave 138 A2
Ardno 149 D4
Ardo 171 D1
Ardoch *D. & G.* 133 G5
Ardoch *Moray* 180 D4
Ardoch *P. & K.* 151 F1
Ardochrig 142 A5
Ardoyne 170 B2
Ardpatrick 139 F3
Ardpeaton 140 D1
Ardradnaig 158 C5
Ardrishaig 139 G1
Ardroe 188 C2
Ardrossan 140 D5
Ardscalpsie 140 B4
Ardshave 190 C5
Ardshealach 155 F3
Ardshellach 147 G3
Ardsley 94 A2
Ardslignish 155 E3
Ardtalla 138 C4
Ardtalnaig 150 B1
Ardtaraig 140 B1
Ardteatle 148 D2
Ardtoe 155 F2
Ardtornish 155 G5
Ardtrostan 150 B2
Ardtur 156 B5
Arduaine 148 A4
Ardullie 179 E3
Ardura 147 F1
Ardvar 192 A5
Ardvasar 164 C4
Ardveich 150 B2
Ardverikie 158 A1
Ardvorlich *Arg. & B.* 149 F3
Ardvorlich *P. & K.* 150 B2
Ardwall 123 G5
Ardwell *D. & G.* 114 B2
Ardwell *Moray* 169 F1
Ardwell *S.Ayr.* 122 C1
Areley Kings 66 G5
Arford 28 D4
Argaty 150 C4
Argoed 38 A3
Argoed Mill 51 F1
Argrennan 124 B5
Arichamish 148 B4
Arichastlich 149 E1
Arichonan 147 G5
Aridhglas 146 C2
Arienskill 155 G1
Arileod 154 A4
Arinacrinachd 176 D4
Arinafad Beg 139 F1
Arinagour 154 B4
Arinambane 172 C1
Arisaig 155 F1
Arivegaig 155 F3
Arkendale 102 C1
Arkesden 58 C4
Arkholme 107 G5
Arkleby 117 E3
Arkleside 109 F4
Arkleton 126 B2
Arkley 44 B3
Arksey 94 C2
Arkwright 94 B5
Arlary 151 G4
Arlecdon 116 D5
Arlesey 57 G4
Arleston 65 F1
Arley 92 A4
Arlingham 39 G1
Arlington *Devon* 21 G1
Arlington *E.Suss.* 18 A3
Arlington *Glos.* 40 D2
Arlington Beccott 21 G1
Armadale *High.* 193 G2
Armadale *High.* 164 C4
Armadale *W.Loth.* 142 D3
Armathwaite 118 B3
Arminghall 87 D5
Armitage 66 C1
Armscote 55 E3
Armston 69 F4
Armthorpe 94 D2
Arnabost 154 B4
Arncliffe 109 E5
Arncliffe Cote 109 E5
Arncroach 152 D4
Arne 13 F4
Arnesby 68 B3
Arngask 151 G3
Arngibbon 150 B5
Arngomery 150 B5
Arnhall 161 E3
Arnicle 130 C2
Arnipol 155 G1
Arnisdale 165 E3
Arnish 176 C5
Arniston Engine 144 A3
Arnol 187 E3
Arnold 81 G3
Arnprior 150 B5
Arnside 107 F5
Arowry 78 B4
Arrad Foot 107 E4
Arradoul 181 G3
Arram 104 C3
Arrat 161 E4
Arrathorne 110 A3
Arreton 15 E4
Arrington 58 B2
Arrivain 149 E1
Arrochar 149 F4
Arrow 54 C2
Arscaig 190 A3
Arthington 102 B3
Arthingworth 68 C4
Arthog 62 C1
Arthrath 171 E1
Arthurstone 160 A5
Artrochie 171 F1
Aruadh 138 A3
Arundel 16 C3
Aryhoulan 156 C3
Asby 117 D4
Ascog 140 C3
Ascot 29 E1
Ascott 55 F4
Ascott-under-Wychwood 41 E1
Ascreavie 160 B4
Asenby 110 C5
Asfordby 68 C1
Asfordby Hill 68 C1
Asgarby *Lincs.* 84 B1
Asgarby *Lincs.* 83 G3
Ash *Kent* 33 E3
Ash *Kent* 31 F2
Ash *Som.* 24 B5
Ash *Surr.* 29 D2
Ash Barton 21 F5
Ash Bullayne 10 A2
Ash Magna 78 C4
Ash Mill 22 A5
Ash Priors 23 E5
Ash Thomas 10 D1
Ash Vale 29 D2
Ashampstead 42 A5
Ashbocking 60 C2
Ashbourne 80 C3
Ashbrittle 23 D5
Ashburnham Place 18 B2
Ashburton 9 D1
Ashbury *Devon* 7 F1
Ashbury *Oxon.* 41 E4
Ashby 95 G2
Ashby by Partney 84 C1
Ashby cum Fenby 96 C2
Ashby de la Launde 83 F2
Ashby de la Zouch 67 F1
Ashby Folville 68 C1
Ashby Magna 68 A3
Ashby Parva 68 A4
Ashby Puerorum 96 D5
Ashby St. Ledgers 56 A1
Ashby St. Mary 87 E5
Ashchurch 54 B4
Ashcombe 10 C5
Ashcott 24 B4
Ashdon 59 D3
Ashe 27 G3
Asheldham 46 C2
Ashen 59 F3
Ashenden 32 A5
Ashendon 42 C1
Ashens 139 G2
Ashfield *Arg. & B.* 139 F1
Ashfield *Stir.* 150 C4
Ashfield *Suff.* 60 D1
Ashfield Green 73 D4
Ashfold Crossways 17 E1
Ashford *Devon* 8 C3
Ashford *Devon* 21 F2
Ashford *Hants.* 14 A1
Ashford *Kent* 32 C4
Ashford *Surr.* 43 F5
Ashford Bowdler 65 E5
Ashford Carbonel 65 E5
Ashford Hill 27 G1
Ashford in the Water 80 D1
Ashgill 142 B4
Ashiestiel 135 F2
Ashill *Devon* 11 D1
Ashill *Norf.* 71 G2
Ashill *Som.* 11 G1
Ashingdon 46 B3
Ashington *Northumb.* 129 E3
Ashington *Som.* 24 C5
Ashington *W.Suss.* 16 D2
Ashkirk 135 F3
Ashleworth 54 A5
Ashley *Cambs.* 59 E1
Ashley *Ches.* 92 B4
Ashley *Devon* 21 G4
Ashley *Glos.* 40 B3
Ashley *Hants.* 27 E4
Ashley *Hants.* 14 B3
Ashley *Kent* 33 E4
Ashley *Northants.* 68 C3
Ashley *Staffs.* 79 E4
Ashley *Wilts.* 25 F1
Ashley Green 43 E2
Ashley Heath 14 A2
Ashmanhaugh 87 E3
Ashmansworth 27 F2
Ashmansworthy 20 D4
Ashmore *Dorset* 13 F1
Ashmore *P. & K.* 159 G4
Ashorne 55 F2
Ashover 81 E1
Ashow 67 F5
Ashperton 53 F3
Ashprington 9 E2
Ashreigney 21 G4
Ashtead 29 G2
Ashton *Ches.* 78 C1
Ashton *Cornw.* 2 C4
Ashton *Cornw.* 7 D4
Ashton *Here.* 53 E1
Ashton *Northants.* 69 F4
Ashton *Northants.* 56 C3
Ashton Common 25 F2
Ashton-in-Makerfield 91 G3
Ashton Keynes 40 C3
Ashton under Hill 54 B4
Ashton-under-Lyne 92 D3
Ashton upon Mersey 92 B3
Ashurst *Hants.* 14 C1
Ashurst *Kent* 31 E5
Ashurst *W.Suss.* 17 D2
Ashurstwood 30 D5
Ashwater 7 D1
Ashwell *Herts.* 58 A4
Ashwell *Rut.* 69 D1
Ashwellthorpe 72 C2
Ashwick 24 D3
Ashwicken 71 F1
Ashybank 135 G4
Askam in Furness 106 D5
Askern 94 C1
Askerswell 12 B3
Askett 42 D2
Askham *Cumb.* 118 B5
Askham *Notts.* 95 E5
Askham Bryan 103 E3
Askham Richard 103 E3
Asknish 148 B5
Askrigg 109 E3
Askwith 102 A3
Aslackby 83 F4
Aslacton 72 C2
Aslockton 82 C3
Asloun 170 A3
Aspall 60 C1
Aspatria 117 E2
Aspenden 58 B5
Aspley Guise 57 E4
Aspull 92 A2
Asselby 103 G5
Assington 60 A4
Astbury 79 F1
Astcote 56 B2
Asterby 96 C5
Asterley 64 C2
Asterton 64 C3
Asthall 41 E1
Asthall Leigh 41 F1
Astley *Shrop.* 65 E1
Astley *Warks.* 67 F4
Astley *Worcs.* 53 G1
Astley Abbotts 65 G3
Astley Bridge 92 B1
Astley Cross 54 G1
Astley Green 92 B3
Aston *Ches.* 78 D3
Aston *Ches.* 91 G5
Aston *Derbys.* 93 F4
Aston *Flints.* 78 A1
Aston *Here.* 65 D5
Aston *Herts.* 58 A5
Aston *Oxon.* 41 F2
Aston *S.Yorks.* 94 B4
Aston *Shrop.* 78 C5
Aston *Staffs.* 79 E3
Aston *Tel. & W.* 65 F2
Aston *W'ham* 42 C4
Aston *W.Mid.* 66 C4
Aston Abbotts 42 D1
Aston Botterell 65 F4
Aston-by-Stone 79 G4
Aston Cantlow 54 D2
Aston Clinton 43 D1
Aston Crews 53 F5
Aston Cross 54 B4
Aston End 58 A5
Aston Eyre 65 F3
Aston Fields 66 B5
Aston Flamville 67 G3
Aston Ingham 53 F5
Aston juxta Mondrum 78 D2
Aston le Walls 55 G2
Aston Magna 55 D4
Aston Munslow 65 E4
Aston on Clun 64 C4
Aston on Trent 81 F5
Aston Rogers 64 C2
Aston Rowant 42 C3
Aston Sandford 42 C2
Aston Somerville 54 C4
Aston Subedge 54 D3
Aston Tirrold 42 A4
Aston Upthorpe 42 A4
Astwick 58 A4
Astwood 57 E3
Astwood Bank 54 C1
Aswarby 83 F4
Aswardby 97 D5
Aswick Grange 70 B1
Atch Lench 54 C2
Atcham 65 E2
Athelington 72 D4
Athelney 24 A5
Athelstaneford 144 C2
Atherington 21 F3
Atherstone 67 F3
Atherstone on Stour 55 E2
Atherton 92 A2
Athlinne 185 D2
Atlow 80 D3
Attadale 165 F1
Attenborough 81 G4
Atterby 95 G3
Attleborough *Norf.* 72 B2
Attleborough *Warks.* 67 F3
Attlebridge 86 C4
Atwick 105 D2
Atworth 25 F1
Aubourn 83 E1
Auch 149 F1
Auchairne 122 C2
Auchallater 159 G1
Auchameanach 139 G4
Aucharnie 182 B5
Aucharrigill 189 G4
Auchattie 170 B5
Auchavan 159 G3
Auchbraad 139 G1
Auchbreck 169 E2
Auchenblae 161 F2
Auchenbothie 141 E2
Auchenbrack 124 B1
Auchenbreck 140 B1
Auchencairn 124 C5
Auchencrow 145 F3
Auchendinny 143 G3
Auchendolly 124 B4
Auchenfoyle 141 E2
Auchengray 143 D4
Auchenhalrig 181 F3
Auchenheath 142 C5
Auchenhessnane 124 C1
Auchenlochan 140 A2
Auchenmalg 122 D5
Auchenrivock 126 B3
Auchentiber 141 E5
Auchenvennal 141 D1
Auchessan 149 G2
Auchgourish 168 B3
Auchinafaud 139 F4
Auchincruive 132 B3
Auchindarrach 139 G1
Auchindarroch 156 C4
Auchindrain 148 C4
Auchindrean 178 A1
Auchininna 182 B5
Auchinleck 133 D3
Auchinloch 142 A2
Auchinner 150 B3
Auchinroath 181 E4
Auchintoul *Aber.* 170 A3
Auchintoul *Aber.* 182 B4
Auchintoul *High.* 190 A4
Auchiries 171 F1
Auchleven 170 B2
Auchlochan 133 G2
Auchlunachan 178 A1
Auchlunies 171 D5
Auchlunkart 181 F5
Auchlyne 150 A2
Auchmacoy 171 E1
Auchmair 169 F2
Auchmantle 122 C4
Auchmithie 161 E5
Auchmuirbridge 152 A4
Auchmull 161 D2
Auchnabony 116 A2
Auchnabreac 148 C4
Auchnacloich 150 D1
Auchnacraig 147 G2
Auchnacree 160 C3
Auchnafree 150 D1
Auchnagallin 168 C1
Auchnagatt 183 E5
Auchnaha 140 A1
Auchnangoul 148 C4
Aucholzie 169 F5
Auchorrie 170 B4
Auchraw 150 A2
Auchreoch 149 F2
Auchronie 160 C1
Auchterarder 151 E3
Auchtercairn 177 E2
Auchterderran 152 A5
Auchterhouse 152 B1
Auchtermuchty 152 A3
Auchterneed 179 D3
Auchtertool 152 A5
Auchtertyre *Angus* 160 A5
Auchtertyre *Moray* 181 D4
Auchtertyre *Stir.* 149 F2
Auchtubh 150 A2
Auckengill 195 F2
Auckley 95 D2
Audenshaw 92 D3
Audlem 79 D3
Audley 79 E2
Audley End 58 D4
Auds 182 B3
Aughton *E.Riding* 103 G4
Aughton *Lancs.* 91 E2
Aughton *Lancs.* 100 B1
Aughton *S.Yorks.* 94 B4
Aughton Park 91 F2
Auldearn 180 B4
Aulden 53 D2
Auldhame 144 C1
Auldhouse 142 A4
Aulich 158 B4
Ault a' chruinn 165 F2
Ault Hucknall 81 F1
Aultanrynie 192 C5
Aultbea 177 E1
Aultgrishan 176 D1
Aultguish Inn 178 C2
Aultibea 191 F2
Aultiphurst 194 A2
Aultmore 181 G4
Aultnagoire 167 E2
Aultnamain Inn 179 F1
Aultnapaddock 181 F5
Aulton 170 B2
Aultvoulin 165 D4
Aundorach 168 B3
Aunk 10 D2
Aunsby 83 F4
Auquhorthies 170 D2
Aust 39 E4
Austerfield 95 D3
Austonley 93 F2
Austrey 67 E2
Austwick 101 D1
Authorpe 97 E4
Authorpe Row 97 F5
Avebury 40 C5
Aveley 45 E4
Avening 40 A3
Averham 82 C2
Aveton Gifford 8 C3
Avielochan 168 B3
Aviemore 168 A3
Avington *Hants.* 27 G4
Avington *W.Berks.* 27 E1
Avoch 179 F4
Avon 14 A3
Avon Dassett 55 G2
Avonbridge 142 D2
Avonmouth 39 E5
Avonwick 8 D2
Awbridge 27 E5
Awhirk 122 B5
Awkley 39 E4
Awliscombe 11 E2
Awre 39 G2
Awsworth 81 F3
Axbridge 24 B2
Axford *Hants.* 28 B3
Axford *Wilts.* 41 E5
Axminster 11 F3
Axmouth 11 F3
Aycliffe 120 B5
Aydon 119 G1
Aylburton 39 F2
Ayle 118 D3
Aylesbeare 10 D3
Aylesbury 42 D1
Aylesby 96 C2
Aylesford 31 G3
Aylesham 33 E3
Aylestone 68 A2
Aylmerton 86 C2
Aylsham 86 C3
Aylton 53 F4
Aymestrey 52 D1
Aynho 56 A4
Ayot St. Lawrence 44 A1
Ayot St. Peter 44 B1
Ayr 132 B3
Aysgarth 109 F4
Ayshford 10 D1
Ayside 107 E4
Ayston 69 D2
Aythorpe Roding 45 E1
Ayton *P. & K.* 151 G3
Ayton *Sc.Bord.* 145 G3
Aywick 203 E4
Azerley 110 B5

**B**

Babbacombe 9 F1
Babbinswood 78 A4
Babcary 24 C5
Babel 51 E4
Babell 90 C5
Babeny 7 G3
Babraham 58 D3
Babworth 95 D4
Bac 187 F3
Back of Keppoch 155 F1
Backaland 199 D3
Backaskaill 198 C1
Backbarrow 107 E4
Backburn 170 A1
Backfolds 183 F4
Backford 91 E5
Backhill 170 C1
Backhill of Clackriach 183 E5
Backhill of Trustach 170 B5
Backies *High.* 190 D4
Backies *Moray* 181 G4
Backlass 195 E3
Backside 169 G1
Backwell 24 B1
Backworth 129 E4
Bacon End 45 E1
Baconsthorpe 86 C2
Bacton *Here.* 52 C4
Bacton *Norf.* 87 E2
Bacton *Suff.* 60 B1
Bacup 101 E5
Badachro 177 D2
Badanloch Lodge 193 G5
Badavanich 178 A4
Badbea 191 F3
Badbury 41 D4
Badby 56 A2
Badcall *High.* 192 A4
Badcall *High.* 192 B3
Badcaul 188 C5
Baddeley Green 79 G2
Badden 139 G1
Baddesley Ensor 67 E3
Baddidarach 188 C2
Badenscoth 170 B1
Badenyon 169 F3
Badger 65 G3
Badgerbank 92 C5
Badgers Mount 31 D2
Badgeworth 40 B1
Badgworth 24 A2
Badicaul 165 D2
Badingham 61 E1
Badintagairt 189 G3
Badlesmere 32 C3
Badley 60 B2
Badlipster 195 E4
Badluarach 188 B5
Badminton 40 A4
Badnaban 188 C2
Badnabay 192 B4
Badnafrave 169 E3
Badnagie 195 D5
Badnambiast 158 C2
Badninish 190 C5
Badrallach 188 C5
Badsey 54 C3
Badshot Lea 29 D3
Badsworth 94 B1
Badwell Ash 60 A1
Badyo 159 E3
Bae Cinmel (Kinmel Bay) 90 A4
Bae Colwyn (Colwyn Bay) 89 G5
Bae Penrhyn (Penrhyn Bay) 89 G4
Bag Enderby 97 D5
Bagby 111 D4
Bagendon 40 C2
Baggrave Hall 68 C2
Baggrow 117 E2
Bagh a' Chaisteil (Castlebay) 172 B4
Baghasdal 172 C2
Bagillt 90 D5
Baginton 67 F5
Baglan 37 D3
Bagley 78 B5
Bagnall 79 G2
Bagnor 27 F1
Bagshot *Surr.* 29 E1
Bagshot *Wilts.* 27 E1
Bagstone 39 F4
Bagthorpe *Norf.* 85 F4
Bagthorpe *Notts.* 81 F2
Baguley 92 C4
Bagworth 67 G2
Bagwyllydiart 52 D5
Baildon 102 A4
Baile a' Mhanaich (Balivanich) 173 F4
Baile Ailein 187 D5
Baile an Truiseil 187 E2
Baile Boidheach 139 F2
Baile Gharbhaidh 173 F5
Baile Glas 173 G4
Baile Mhartainn (Balmartin) 173 F2
Baile Mhic Phail 173 G2
Baile Mòr *Arg. & B.* 146 B2
Baile Mòr *W.Isles* 173 F3
Baile-na-Cille 173 G1
Baile nan Cailleach 173 F4
Baile Raghaill 173 F3
Bailebeag 167 E3
Baileguish 168 A5
Bailetonach 155 F2
Bailiesward 169 G1
Bainbridge 109 E3
Bainsford 142 C1
Bainshole 170 B1
Bainton *E.Riding* 104 B2
Bainton *Peter.* 69 F2
Bairnkine 136 A5
Bakebare 169 F1
Baker Street 45 F4
Baker's End 44 C1
Bakewell 80 D1
Bala 76 C4
Balachuirn 176 B5
Balafark 150 B5
Balaldie 180 A2
Balavil 167 G4
Balbeg *High.* 167 D1
Balbeg *High.* 167 D2
Balbeggie 151 G2
Balbirnie 152 A4
Balbithan 170 C3
Balblair *High.* 179 G3
Balblair *High.* 190 A5
Balcharn 190 A4
Balcherry 180 A1
Balchers 182 C4
Balchladich 188 C1
Balchraggan *High.* 179 E5
Balchraggan *High.* 167 E1
Balchrick 192 A2
Balcombe 30 C5
Balcurvie 152 B4
Baldernock 141 G2
Baldersby 110 C5
Balderstone 100 C4
Balderton 82 D2
Baldhu 4 B5
Baldinnie 152 C3
Baldock 58 A4
Baldovie *Angus* 160 B4
Baldovie *Dundee* 152 C1
Baldrine 98 C3
Baldslow 18 C2
Baldwin 98 B3
Baldwinholme 117 G1
Baldwin's Gate 79 E3
Bale 86 B2
Balelone 173 F2
Balemartine 154 A2
Balendoch 160 A5
Balephuil 154 A2
Balerno 143 F3
Balernock 141 D1
Baleromindubh 146 C5
Balerominmore 146 C5
Balevulin 147 D2
Balfield 160 D3
Balfour *Aber.* 170 A5
Balfour *Ork.* 198 C5
Balfron 141 G1
Balfron Station 141 G1
Balgedie 151 G4
Balgonar 151 F5
Balgove 170 D1
Balgowan *D. & G.* 114 B2
Balgowan *High.* 167 F5
Balgown 175 G3
Balgray 152 C1
Balgreen 182 C4
Balgreggan 122 B5
Balgy 177 E4
Balhaldie 150 D4
Balhalgardy 170 C2
Balhary 160 A5
Balhelvie 152 B2
Balhousie 152 C4
Baliasta 203 F2
Baligill 194 A2
Baligrundle 148 A1
Balindore 148 B1
Balintore 180 A2
Balintraid 179 G2
Balintyre 158 B5
Balivanich (Baile a' Mhanaich) 173 F4
Balkeerie 160 B5
Balkholme 103 G5
Balkissock 122 C2
Ball 78 A5
Ball Haye Green 79 G2
Ball Hill 27 F1
Ballabeg 98 A4
Ballacannell 98 C3

Ballacarnane Beg 98 B3
Ballachulish 156 C4
Balladoole 98 A5
Ballafesson 98 A4
Ballagyr 98 A3
Ballajora 98 C2
Ballakilpheric 98 A4
Ballamodha 98 A4
Ballantrae 122 B2
Ballards Gore 46 C3
Ballasalla *I.o.M.* 98 A4
Ballasalla *I.o.M.* 98 B2
Ballater 169 F5
Ballaterach 169 G5
Ballaugh 98 B2
Ballaveare 98 B4
Ballechin 159 E4
Balleich 150 A4
Ballencrieff 144 B2
Ballidon 80 D2
Balliekine 131 D2
Balliemeanoch 148 D4
Balliemore *Arg. & B.* 148 D5
Balliemore *Arg. & B.* 148 A2
Ballig 98 A3
Ballimeanoch 148 C3
Ballimore *Arg. & B.* 140 A1
Ballimore *Stir.* 150 A3
Ballinaby 138 A3
Ballindean 152 A2
Ballingdon 59 G3
Ballinger Common 43 E2
Ballingham 53 E4
Ballingry 151 G5
Ballinlick 159 E5
Ballinluig *P. & K.* 159 E4
Ballinluig *P. & K.* 159 F4
Ballintuim 159 G4
Balloch *Angus* 160 B4
Balloch *High.* 179 G5
Balloch *N.Lan.* 142 B2
Balloch *W.Dun.* 141 E1
Ballochan 170 A5
Ballochandrain 140 A1
Ballochford 169 F1
Ballochgair 130 C3
Ballochmartin 140 C4
Ballochmorrie 122 D2
Ballochmyle 132 D3
Ballochroy 139 F4
Ballogie 170 A5
Balls Cross 29 E5
Ballyaurgan 139 F2
Ballygown 154 D5
Ballygrant 138 B3
Ballyhaugh 154 A4
Ballymeanoch 148 A5
Ballymichael 131 E2
Balmacara 165 E2
Balmaclellan 124 A3
Balmacneil 159 E4
Balmadies 160 D5
Balmae 115 G2
Balmaha 149 G5
Balmalcolm 152 B4
Balmartin (Baile Mhartainn) 173 F2
Balmeanach *Arg. & B.* 155 F5
Balmeanach *Arg. & B.* 147 D1
Balmedie 171 E3
Balmerino 152 B2
Balmerlawn 14 C2
Balminnoch 123 D4
Balmore *E.Dun.* 142 A2
Balmore *High.* 180 A5
Balmore *High.* 166 C1
Balmore *High.* 175 F5
Balmore *P. & K.* 158 C4
Balmullo 152 C2
Balmungie 179 G4
Balmyle 159 F4
Balnaboth 160 B3
Balnabruaich 179 G2
Balnacra 177 F5
Balnafoich 167 F1
Balnagall 180 A1
Balnagown Castle 179 G2
Balnaguard 159 E4
Balnaguisich 179 F2
Balnahard *Arg. & B.* 146 D5
Balnahard *Arg. & B.* 147 D1
Balnain 166 D1
Balnakeil 192 C2
Balnaknock 176 A3
Balnamoon 160 D3
Balnapaling 179 G3
Balnespick 168 A4
Balquhidder 150 A2
Balsall 67 E5
Balsall Common 67 E5
Balscote 55 F3
Balsham 59 D2
Baltasound 203 F2
Balterley 79 E2
Baltersan 123 F4
Balthangie 182 D4
Balthayock 151 G2
Baltonsborough 24 C4
Baluachraig 148 A5
Balulive 138 C3
Balure *Arg. & B.* 148 C1
Balure *Arg. & B.* 148 A1
Balvaird 179 E4
Balvarran 159 F3
Balvicar 147 G3
Balvraid *High.* 165 E3
Balvraid *High.* 168 A1
Bamber Bridge 100 B5
Bamber's Green 59 D5
Bamburgh 137 F3
Bamff 160 A4
Bamford 93 G4
Bampton *Cumb.* 107 G1
Bampton *Devon* 22 C5
Bampton *Oxon.* 41 F2
Banavie 156 D2
Banbury 55 G3
Banc-y-ffordd 50 A4
Bancffosfelen 36 A1
Banchor 180 B5
Banchory 170 C5
Banchory-Devenick 171 E4
Bancyfelin 35 G1
Bandon 152 A4
Banff 182 B3
Bangor 89 D5
Bangor-is-y-coed 78 A3
Bangor Teifi 49 G3
Banham 72 B3
Bank 14 B2
Bank End 106 D4
Bank Newton 101 F2
Bank Street 53 F1
Bankend *D. & G.* 125 E4
Bankend *S.Lan.* 133 G2
Bankfoot 151 F1
Bankhead *Aber.* 170 B3
Bankhead *Aber.* 170 B4
Bankhead *Aberdeen* 171 D4
Bankhead *D. & G.* 116 A2
Bankncok 142 B2
Banks *Cumb.* 118 B1
Banks *Lancs.* 99 G5
Bankshill 125 F2
Banningham 86 D3
Bannister Green 59 E5
Bannockburn 150 D5
Banstead 30 B3
Bantham 8 C3
Banton 142 B2
Banwell 24 A2
Bapchild 32 B2
Baptiston 141 G1
Bar Hill 58 B1
Barabhas (Barvas) 187 E2
Barachander 148 C2
Barassie 132 B2
Barbaraville 179 G2
Barber Booth 93 F4
Barbon 108 B4
Barbrook 22 A3
Barby 68 A5
Barcaldine 156 B5
Barcaple 124 A5
Barcheston 55 E3
Barcombe 17 G2
Barcombe Cross 17 G2
Barden 110 A3
Bardennoch 123 G1
Bardfield End Green 59 E4
Bardfield Saling 59 E5
Bardister 202 C5
Bardney 83 G1
Bardon *Leics.* 67 G1
Bardon *Moray* 181 E4
Bardon Mill 119 D1
Bardsea 107 E5
Bardsey 102 C3
Bardsley 92 D2
Bardwell 72 A4
Barewood 52 C2
Barfad 139 G3
Barford *Norf.* 86 C5
Barford *Warks.* 55 E1
Barford St. John 55 G4
Barford St. Martin 26 B4
Barford St. Michael 55 G4
Barfrestone 33 E3
Bargaly 123 F4
Bargany Mains 132 A5
Bargoed 38 A3
Bargrennan 123 E3
Barham *Cambs.* 69 G5
Barham *Kent* 33 D3
Barham *Suff.* 60 C2
Barharrow 124 A5
Barholm 69 F1
Barholm Mains 123 F5
Barkby 68 B2
Barkby Thorpe 68 B2
Barkestone-le-Vale 82 C4
Barkham 28 C1
Barking *Gt.Lon.* 44 D4
Barking *Suff.* 60 B2
Barking & Dagenham 45 D4
Barkingside 44 D4
Barkisland 93 E1
Barkston *Lincs.* 83 E3
Barkston *N.Yorks.* 103 D4
Barkway 58 B4
Barlae 123 D4
Barlaston 79 F4
Barlavington 16 B2
Barlborough 94 B5
Barlby 103 F4
Barlestone 67 G2
Barley *Herts.* 58 B4
Barley *Lancs.* 101 E3
Barleycroft End 58 C5
Barleyhill 119 G2
Barleythorpe 69 D2
Barling 46 C4
Barlings 96 A5
Barlow *Derbys.* 94 A5
Barlow *N.Yorks.* 103 F5
Barlow *T. & W.* 120 A1
Barmby Moor 103 G3
Barmby on the Marsh 103 F5
Barmer 85 G4
Barmolloch 148 A5
Barmoor Lane End 137 E2
Barmouth (Abermaw) 62 C1
Barmpton 110 C1
Barmston 105 D2
Barnacabber 140 C1
Barnacarry 148 C5
Barnack 69 F2
Barnacle 67 F4
Barnamuc 156 C5
Barnard Castle 109 F1
Barnard Gate 41 G1
Barnardiston 59 F3
Barnard's Green 53 G3
Barnbarroch *D. & G.* 123 E5
Barnbarroch *D. & G.* 124 C5
Barnburgh 94 B2
Barnby 73 F2
Barnby Dun 94 D2
Barnby in the Willows 83 D2
Barnby Moor 95 D4
Barndennoch 124 C2
Barnes 44 B5
Barnet 44 B3
Barnetby le Wold 96 A2
Barney 86 A2
Barnham *Suff.* 71 G5
Barnham *W.Suss.* 16 B3
Barnham Broom 86 B5
Barnhead 161 E4
Barnhill 180 D4
Barnhills 122 A3
Barningham *Dur.* 109 F1
Barningham *Suff.* 72 A4
Barnoldby le Beck 96 C2
Barnoldswick 101 E3
Barns Green 29 G5
Barnsdale Bar 94 C1
Barnsley *Glos.* 40 C2
Barnsley *S.Yorks.* 94 A2
Barnstaple 21 F2
Barnston *Essex* 45 F1
Barnston *Mersey.* 91 D4
Barnstone 82 C4
Barnt Green 66 C5
Barnton 92 A5
Barnwell All Saints 69 F4
Barnwell St. Andrew 69 F4
Barnwood 40 A1
Barr *Arg. & B.* 138 B3
Barr *High.* 155 F4
Barr *S.Ayr.* 123 D1
Barr Hall 59 F4
Barra (Tràigh Mhòr) Airport 172 C3
Barrackan 147 G4
Barraer 123 E4
Barraglom 186 C4
Barrahormid 139 F1
Barran 149 D2
Barrapoll 154 A2
Barrasford 128 B4
Barravullin 148 A4
Barregarrow 98 B3
Barrhead 141 G4
Barrhill 122 D2
Barrington *Cambs.* 58 B3
Barrington *Som.* 11 G1
Barripper 2 D3
Barrisdale 165 E4
Barrmill 141 E4
Barrnacarry 148 A2
Barrock 195 E1
Barrow *Lancs.* 100 D4
Barrow *Rut.* 69 D1
Barrow *Shrop.* 65 F2
Barrow *Som.* 25 E4
Barrow *Suff.* 59 F1
Barrow Gurney 24 C1
Barrow Haven 104 C5
Barrow-in-Furness 99 F1
Barrow Nook 91 F2
Barrow Street 25 F4
Barrow upon Humber 104 C5
Barrow upon Soar 68 A1
Barrow upon Trent 81 E5
Barrowby 83 D4
Barrowden 69 E2
Barrowford 101 E4
Barry *Angus* 152 D1
Barry *V. of Glam.* 23 E1
Barsby 68 C1
Barsham 73 E2
Barskimming 132 C3
Barsloisnoch 148 A5
Barston 67 E5
Bartestree 53 E3
Barthol Chapel 170 D1
Barthomley 79 E2
Bartley 14 C1
Bartlow 59 D3
Barton *Cambs.* 58 C2
Barton *Ches.* 78 B2
Barton *Glos.* 54 C5
Barton *Lancs.* 100 B4
Barton *Lancs.* 91 E2
Barton *N.Yorks.* 110 B2
Barton *Torbay* 9 F1
Barton *Warks.* 54 D2
Barton Bendish 71 F2
Barton Common 87 E3
Barton End 40 A3
Barton Hartshorn 56 B4
Barton in Fabis 81 G4
Barton in the Beans 67 F2
Barton-le-Clay 57 F4
Barton-le-Street 111 G5
Barton-le-Willows 103 G1
Barton Mills 71 F5
Barton on Sea 14 B3
Barton-on-the-Heath 55 E4
Barton St. David 24 C4
Barton Seagrave 69 D5
Barton Stacey 27 F3
Barton Turf 87 E3
Barton-under-Needwood 67 D1
Barton-upon-Humber 104 C5
Barvas (Barabhas) 187 E2
Barway 70 D5
Barwell 67 G3
Barwhinnock 124 A5
Barwick 12 B1
Barwick in Elmet 102 C4
Barwinnock 115 D2
Baschurch 78 B5
Bascote 55 G1
Basford Green 79 G2
Bashall Eaves 100 C3
Bashall Town 100 D3
Bashley 14 B3
Basildon *Essex* 45 G4
Basildon *W.Berks.* 42 B5
Basingstoke 28 B2
Baslow 93 G5
Bason Bridge 24 A3
Bassaleg 38 B4
Bassenthwaite 117 F3
Basset's Cross 21 F5
Bassett 14 D1
Bassingbourn 58 B3
Bassingfield 82 B4
Bassingham 83 E1
Bassingthorpe 83 E5
Basta 203 E3
Baston 69 G1
Bastwick 87 F4
Batavaime 149 G1
Batchworth 43 F3
Batchworth Heath 43 F3
Batcombe *Dorset* 12 C2
Batcombe *Som.* 25 D4
Bate Heath 92 A5
Bath 25 E1
Bathampton 25 E1
Bathealton 23 D5
Batheaston 25 E1
Bathford 25 E1
Bathgate 143 D3
Bathley 82 C2
Bathpool *Cornw.* 5 G2
Bathpool *Som.* 23 F5
Batley 102 B5
Batsford 55 D4
Battersby 111 E2
Battersea 44 B5
Battisborough Cross 8 C3
Battisford 60 B2
Battisford Tye 60 B2
Battle *E.Suss.* 18 C2
Battle *Powys* 51 G4
Battlefield 65 E1
Battlesbridge 45 G3
Battlesden 57 E5
Battleton 22 C5
Battramsley 14 C3
Batt's Corner 28 D3
Bauds of Cullen 181 G3
Baugh 154 B2
Baughton 54 A3
Baughurst 27 G2
Baulds 170 B5
Baulking 41 F3
Baumber 96 C5
Baunton 40 C2
Baveney Wood 65 F5
Baverstock 26 B4
Bawburgh 86 C5
Bawdeswell 86 B3
Bawdrip 24 A4
Bawdsey 61 E3
Bawtry 95 D3
Baxenden 101 D5
Baxterley 67 E3
Baycliff 107 D5
Baydon 41 E5
Bayford *Herts.* 44 C2
Bayford *Som.* 25 E5
Bayfordbury 44 C1
Bayham Abbey 31 F5
Bayles 118 D3
Baylham 60 C2
Baynards Green 56 A5
Baysham 53 E5
Bayston Hill 65 D2
Baythorn End 59 F3
Bayton 65 F5
Beach 155 G4
Beachampton 56 C4
Beacharr 139 E5
Beachborough 33 D5
Beachley 39 E3
Beacon 11 E2
Beacon End 60 A5
Beacon Hill 29 D4
Beacon's Bottom 42 C3
Beaconsfield 43 E3
Beadlam 111 F4
Beadnell 137 G3
Beaford 21 F4
Beal *N.Yorks.* 103 E5
Beal *Northumb.* 137 E2
Bealach 156 B4
Beambridge 78 D2
Beamhurst 80 B4
Beaminster 12 A2
Beamish 120 B2
Beamsley 101 G2
Bean 45 E5
Beanacre 25 F1
Beanley 137 E5
Beaquoy 198 B4
Beardon 7 F2
Beare Green 29 G3
Bearley 55 D1
Bearnie 171 E1
Bearnock 166 D1
Bearnus 154 D5
Bearpark 120 B3
Bearsbridge 119 D2
Bearsden 141 G2
Bearsted 31 G3
Bearwood 13 G3
Beattock 134 B5
Beauchamp Roding 45 E2
Beauchief 94 A4
Beaudesert 55 D1
Beaufort 38 A1
Beaulieu 14 C2
Beauly 179 E5
Beaumaris (Biwmaris) 89 E5
Beaumont *Cumb.* 117 G1
Beaumont *Essex* 60 C5
Beausale 67 E5
Beauworth 27 G5
Beaworthy 7 E1
Beazley End 59 F5
Bebington 91 E4
Bebside 129 E3
Beccles 73 F2
Becconsall 100 A5
Beck Foot 108 B3
Beck Hole 112 B2
Beck Row 71 E5
Beck Side 106 D4
Beckbury 65 G2
Beckenham 30 C2
Beckermet 106 B2
Beckfoot *Cumb.* 106 C2
Beckfoot *Cumb.* 117 D2
Beckford 54 B4
Beckhampton 26 B1
Beckingham *Lincs.* 83 D2
Beckingham *Notts.* 95 E4
Beckington 25 E2
Beckley *E.Suss.* 19 D1
Beckley *Oxon.* 42 A1
Beckton 44 D4
Beckwithshaw 102 B2
Becontree 45 D4
Bedale 110 B4
Bedburn 120 A4
Bedchester 13 E1
Beddau 37 G4
Beddgelert 75 E3
Beddingham 17 G3
Beddington 30 C2
Beddington Corner 30 B2
Bedfield 60 D1
Bedford 57 F3
Bedgebury Cross 31 G5
Bedhampton 15 G2
Bedingfield 60 C1
Bedlington 129 E3
Bedlinog 37 G2
Bedminster 39 E5
Bedmond 44 A2
Bednall 66 B1
Bedol 90 D5
Bedrule 136 G4
Bedstone 64 C5
Bedwas 38 A4
Bedwellty 38 A2
Bedworth 67 F4
Beeby 68 B2
Beech *Hants.* 28 B4
Beech *Staffs.* 79 F4
Beech Hill 28 B1
Beechamwell 71 F2
Beechingstoke 26 B2
Beedon 41 G5
Beeford 104 D2
Beeley 81 D1
Beelsby 96 C2
Beenham 27 G1
Beer 11 F4
Beer Hackett 12 B1
Beercrocombe 24 A5
Beesands 9 E3
Beesby 97 E4
Beeson 9 E3
Beeston *Beds.* 57 G3
Beeston *Ches.* 78 C2
Beeston *Norf.* 86 A4
Beeston *Notts.* 81 G4
Beeston *W.Yorks.* 102 B4
Beeston Regis 86 C1
Beeston St. Lawrence 87 E3
Beeswing 124 C4
Beetham 107 F5
Beetley 86 A4
Began 38 B4
Begbroke 41 G1
Begelly 35 E2
Beggshill 170 A1
Beguildy 64 A5
Beighton *Norf.* 87 E5
Beighton *S.Yorks.* 94 B4
Beith 141 E4
Bekesbourne 33 D3
Belaugh 87 D4
Belbroughton 66 B5
Belchamp Otten 59 G3
Belchamp St. Paul 59 F3
Belchamp Walter 59 G3
Belchford 96 C5
Belford 137 F3
Belgrave 68 A2
Belhaven 145 D2
Belhelvie 171 E3
Belhinnie 169 G2
Bell Bar 44 B2
Bell Busk 101 F2
Bell End 66 B5
Bellabeg 169 F3
Belladrum 179 E5
Bellanoch 148 A5
Bellasize 104 A5
Bellaty 160 A4
Belleau 97 E5
Bellehiglash 169 D1
Bellerby 110 A3
Bellever 7 G3
Belliehill 161 D3
Bellingdon 43 E2
Bellingham 128 A3
Belloch 130 B2
Bellochantuy 130 B2
Bells Yew Green 31 F5
Bellshill *N.Lan.* 142 B4
Bellshill *Northumb.* 137 F3
Bellside 142 C4
Bellsquarry 143 E3
Belluton 24 D1
Belmaduthy 179 F4
Belmesthorpe 69 F1
Belmont *B'burn.* 92 A1
Belmont *Gt.Lon.* 30 B2
Belmont *Shet.* 203 E2
Belowda 5 D3
Belper 81 E3
Belper Lane End 81 E3
Belsay 128 D4
Belsford 9 D2
Belstead 60 C3
Belston 132 B3
Belstone 7 G1
Belstone Corner 7 G1
Belsyde 143 D2
Belthorn 100 D5
Beltinge 33 D2
Beltoft 95 F2
Belton *Leics.* 81 F5
Belton *Lincs.* 83 E4
Belton *N.Lincs.* 95 E2
Belton *Norf.* 87 F5
Belton *Rut.* 68 D2
Beltring 31 F4
Belvedere 45 D5
Belvoir 82 D4
Bembridge 15 F4
Bemersyde 135 G2
Bempton 113 E5
Ben Alder Cottage 157 G3
Ben Alder Lodge 158 A2
Benacre 73 G3
Benbecula (Baile a' Mhanaich) Airport 173 F4
Benbuie 124 B1
Benderloch 148 B1
Bendish 57 G5
Benenden 32 A5
Benfield 123 E4
Bengate 87 E3
Bengeo 44 C1
Benholm 161 G3
Beningbrough 103 E2
Benington *Herts.* 58 A5
Benington *Lincs.* 84 B3
Benington Sea End 84 C3
Benllech 88 D4
Benmore *Arg. & B.* 140 C1
Benmore *Stir.* 149 G2
Bennacott 6 C1
Bennan Cottage 124 A3
Benniworth 96 C4
Benover 31 G4
Benson 42 B3
Benthall *Northumb.* 137 G4
Benthall *Shrop.* 65 F2
Bentham 40 B1
Benthoul 170 D4
Bentley *E.Riding* 104 C4
Bentley *Hants.* 28 C3
Bentley *S.Yorks.* 94 C2
Bentley *Suff.* 60 C4
Bentley *Warks.* 67 E3
Bentley Heath 67 D5
Benton 21 G2
Benton Square 129 F4
Bentpath 126 B2
Bentworth 28 B3
Benvie 152 B1
Benville Lane 12 B2
Benwick 70 B4
Beoley 54 C1
Bepton 16 A2
Berden 58 C5
Bere Alston 8 A1
Bere Ferrers 8 A1
Bere Regis 13 E3
Berea 48 A5
Berepper 3 D4
Bergh Apton 87 E5
Berinsfield 42 A3
Berkeley 39 F3
Berkhamsted 43 E2
Berkley 25 F3
Berkswell 67 E5
Bermondsey 44 C5
Bernera 165 E2
Berners Roding 45 F2
Bernice 148 D5
Bernisdale 176 A4
Berrick Salome 42 B3
Berriedale 191 G2
Berriew (Aberriw) 64 A2
Berrington *Northumb.* 137 E2
Berrington *Shrop.* 65 E2
Berrow 23 F2
Berrow Green 53 G2
Berry Down Cross 21 F1
Berry Hill *Glos.* 39 E1
Berry Hill *Pembs.* 49 D3
Berry Pomeroy 9 E1
Berryhillock 182 A3
Berrynarbor 21 F1
Bersham 78 A3
Berstane 198 C5
Berwick 18 A3
Berwick Bassett 40 C5
Berwick Hill 129 D4
Berwick St. James 26 B4
Berwick St. John 26 A5
Berwick St. Leonard 26 A4
Berwick-upon-Tweed 145 G4
Bescar 91 E1
Besford *Shrop.* 78 C5
Besford *Worcs.* 54 B3
Bessacarr 94 D2
Bessels Leigh 41 G2
Bessingby 105 D1
Bessingham 86 C2
Best Beech Hill 31 F5
Besthorpe *Norf.* 72 B2
Besthorpe *Notts.* 82 D1
Beswick 104 C3
Betchworth 30 B3
Bethania *Cere.* 50 B1
Bethania *Gwyn.* 76 A3
Bethel *Gwyn.* 75 E1
Bethel *Gwyn.* 76 C3
Bethel *I.o.A.* 88 B5
Bethersden 32 B4
Bethesda *Gwyn.* 75 F1
Bethesda *Pembs.* 35 D1
Bethlehem 50 C5
Bethnal Green 44 C4
Betley 79 E3
Betsham 45 F5
Betteshanger 33 F3
Bettiscombe 11 G3
Bettisfield 78 B4
Betton *Shrop.* 64 C2
Betton *Shrop.* 79 D4
Bettws 38 B3
Bettws Bledrws 50 B2
Bettws Cedewain 64 A3
Bettws Evan 49 G3
Bettws Gwerfil Goch 76 D3
Bettws Newydd 38 C2
Bettws-y-crwyn 64 B4
Bettyhill 193 G2
Betws *Bridgend* 37 F4
Betws *Carmar.* 36 C1
Betws Disserth 52 A2
Betws Garmon 75 E2
Betws-y-coed 76 A2
Betws-yn-Rhos 90 A5
Beulah *Cere.* 49 F3
Beulah *Powys* 51 F2
Bevendean 17 F3
Bevercotes 95 E5
Beverley 104 C4
Beverstone 40 A3
Bevington 39 F3
Bewaldeth 117 F3
Bewcastle 127 D4
Bewdley 65 G5
Bewerley 102 A1
Bewholme 105 D3
Bewley Common 26 A1
Bexhill 18 C3
Bexley 45 D5
Bexleyheath 45 D5
Bexwell 71 E2
Beyton 60 A1
Beyton Green 60 A1
Bhalamus 185 E3
Bhaltos 186 B4
Bhatarsaigh (Vatersay) 172 B4
Biallaid 167 G5
Bibury 40 D2
Bicester 56 A5
Bickenhall 11 F1
Bickenhill 67 D4
Bicker 84 A4
Bickerstaffe 91 F2
Bickerton *Ches.* 78 C2
Bickerton *N.Yorks.* 103 D2
Bickford 66 A1
Bickham Bridge 8 D2
Bickham House 10 C4
Bickington *Devon* 21 F2
Bickington *Devon* 10 A5
Bickleigh *Devon* 8 B1
Bickleigh *Devon* 10 C2
Bickleton 21 F2
Bickley 30 D2
Bickley Moss 78 C3
Bickley Town 78 C3
Bicknacre 45 G2
Bicknoller 23 E4
Bicknor 32 A3
Bickton 14 A1
Bicton *Shrop.* 64 D1
Bicton *Shrop.* 64 B4
Bicton Heath 65 D1
Bidborough 31 E4
Biddenden 32 A5
Biddenham 57 F3
Biddestone 40 A5
Biddisham 24 A2
Biddlesden 56 B3
Biddlestone 128 B1
Biddulph 79 F2
Biddulph Moor 79 G2
Bideford 21 E3
Bidford-on-Avon 54 C2
Bidston 91 D3
Bielby 103 G3
Bieldside 171 D4
Bierley *I.o.W.* 15 E5
Bierley *W.Yorks.* 102 A4
Bierton 42 D1
Big Sand 177 D2
Bigbury 8 C3
Bigbury-on-Sea 8 C3
Bigby 96 A2
Bigert Mire 106 C3
Biggar *Cumb.* 99 E1
Biggar *S.Lan.* 134 B2
Biggin *Derbys.* 81 D3
Biggin *Derbys.* 80 C2
Biggin *N.Yorks.* 103 E4
Biggin Hill 30 D3
Biggings 200 A1
Biggleswade 57 G3
Bigholms 126 B3
Bighouse 194 A2
Bighton 28 B4
Biglands 117 F1
Bignor 16 B2
Bigrigg 116 D5
Bigton 200 C5
Bilberry 5 E3
Bilborough 81 G3
Bilbrook *Som.* 22 D3
Bilbrook *Staffs.* 66 A2
Bilbrough 103 E3
Bilbster 195 E3
Bildershaw 120 A5
Bildeston 60 A3
Billericay 45 F3
Billesdon 68 C2
Billesley 54 D2
Billholm 126 A2
Billingborough 83 G4
Billinge 91 G2
Billingford *Norf.* 72 C4
Billingford *Norf.* 86 B3
Billingham 121 D5
Billinghay 83 G2
Billingley 94 B2
Billingshurst 29 F5
Billingsley 65 G4
Billington *Beds.* 57 E5
Billington *Lancs.* 100 D4
Billockby 87 F4
Billy Row 120 A4
Bilsborrow 100 B3
Bilsby 97 E5
Bilsdean 145 E2
Bilsham 16 B3
Bilsington 32 C5
Bilsthorpe 82 B1
Bilston *Midloth.* 143 G3
Bilston *W.Mid.* 66 B3
Bilstone 67 F2
Bilting 32 C4
Bilton *E.Riding* 105 D4
Bilton *N.Yorks.* 103 D2
Bilton *N.Yorks.* 102 C2
Bilton *Northumb.* 137 G5
Bilton *Warks.* 67 G5
Bimbister 198 B5
Binbrook 96 C3

Bincombe 12 C4
Bindal 180 B1
Binegar 24 D3
Bines Green 17 D2
Binfield 42 D5
Binfield Heath 42 C5
Bingfield 128 B4
Bingham 82 C4
Bingham's Melcombe 13 D2
Bingley 102 A4
Binham 86 A2
Binley *Hants.* 27 F2
Binley *W.Mid.* 67 F5
Binniehill 142 C2
Binsoe 110 B5
Binstead 15 E3
Binsted *Hants.* 28 C3
Binsted *W.Suss.* 16 B3
Binton 54 D2
Bintree 86 B3
Binweston 64 B2
Birch *Essex* 46 C1
Birch *Gt.Man.* 92 C2
Birch Green 46 C1
Birch Heath 78 C1
Birch Vale 93 E4
Bircham Newton 85 F4
Bircham Tofts 85 F4
Birchanger 58 D5
Bircher 53 D1
Birchfield 189 G5
Birchgrove *Cardiff* 38 A4
Birchgrove *Swan.* 36 D3
Birchington 33 E2
Birchover 80 D1
Birchwood 92 A3
Bircotes 94 D3
Bird End 66 C3
Birdbrook 59 F3
Birdfield 148 B5
Birdham 16 A4
Birdingbury 55 G1
Birdlip 40 B1
Birdsall 104 A1
Birdsgreen 65 G4
Birdsmoor Gate 11 G2
Birdwell 94 A2
Birdwood 39 G1
Birgham 136 B3
Birichen 190 C5
Birkby 110 C2
Birkdale *Mersey.* 91 E1
Birkdale *N.Yorks.* 109 D2
Birkenhead 91 E4
Birkenhills 182 C5
Birkenshaw 102 B5
Birkhall 169 F5
Birkhill *Angus* 152 B1
Birkhill *Sc.Bord.* 144 C5
Birkhill *Sc.Bord.* 134 D4
Birkin 103 E5
Birkwood 133 G2
Birley 53 D2
Birley Carr 94 A3
Birling *Kent* 31 F2
Birling *Northumb.* 129 E1
Birling Gap 18 A4
Birlingham 54 B3
Birmingham 66 C4
Birmingham International Airport 67 D4
Birnam 159 F5
Birsay 198 A4
Birse 170 A5
Birsemore 170 A5
Birstall 68 A2
Birstall Smithies 102 B5
Birstwith 102 B2
Birthorpe 83 G4
Birtley *Here.* 52 C1
Birtley *Northumb.* 128 A4
Birtley *T. & W.* 120 B2
Birts Street 53 G4
Bisbrooke 69 D3
Bish Mill 22 A5
Bisham 43 D4
Bishampton 54 B2
Bishop Auckland 120 B4
Bishop Burton 104 B4
Bishop Middleham 120 C4
Bishop Monkton 102 C1
Bishop Norton 95 G3
Bishop Sutton 24 C2
Bishop Thornton 102 B1
Bishop Wilton 103 G2
Bishopbridge 96 A3
Bishopbriggs 142 A3
Bishopmill 181 E3
Bishops Cannings 26 B1
Bishop's Castle 64 C4
Bishop's Caundle 12 C1
Bishop's Cleeve 54 B5
Bishop's Frome 53 F3
Bishop's Green 45 F1
Bishop's Hull 23 F5
Bishop's Itchington 55 F2
Bishop's Lydeard 23 E5
Bishop's Nympton 22 A5
Bishop's Offley 79 E5
Bishop's Stortford 58 C5
Bishop's Sutton 28 B4
Bishop's Tachbrook 55 F1
Bishop's Tawton 21 F2
Bishop's Waltham 15 E1
Bishop's Wood 66 A2
Bishopsbourne 33 D3
Bishopsteignton 10 C5
Bishopstoke 15 D1
Bishopston 36 B4
Bishopstone *Bucks.* 42 D1
Bishopstone *E.Suss.* 17 G3
Bishopstone *Here.* 52 D3
Bishopstone *Swin.* 41 E4
Bishopstone *Wilts.* 26 B5
Bishopstrow 25 F3
Bishopswood 11 F1
Bishopsworth 24 C1
Bishopthorpe 103 E3
Bishopton *Darl.* 120 C5
Bishopton *Renf.* 141 F2
Bishton 38 C4
Bisley *Glos.* 40 B2
Bisley *Surr.* 29 E2
Bispham 99 G3
Bissoe 4 B5
Bisterne 14 A2
Bisterne Close 14 B2
Bitchfield 83 E5
Bittadon 21 F1
Bittaford 8 C2
Bittering 86 A4
Bitterley 65 E5
Bitterne 15 D1
Bitteswell 68 A4
Bitton 25 D1
Biwmaris (Beaumaris) 89 E5
Bix 42 C4
Bixter 200 C2
Blaby 68 A3
Black Bourton 41 E2
Black Callerton 120 A1
Black Clauchrie 123 D2
Black Corries Lodge 157 E4
Black Cross 4 D3
Black Dog 10 B2
Black Heddon 128 C4
Black Marsh 64 C3
Black Mount 157 E5
Black Notley 59 F5
Black Pill 36 C3
Black Torrington 21 E5
Blackacre 125 E1
Blackadder 145 F4
Blackawton 9 E2
Blackborough 11 D2
Blackborough End 71 E1
Blackboys 18 A1
Blackbraes *Aber.* 171 D3
Blackbraes *Falk.* 142 D2
Blackbrook 79 E4
Blackburn *Aber.* 170 D3
Blackburn *B'burn.* 100 C5
Blackburn *W.Loth.* 143 D3
Blackbushe 28 C2
Blackcastle 180 A4
Blackchambers 170 C3
Blackcraig *D. & G.* 123 F4
Blackcraig *D. & G.* 124 B2
Blackden Heath 92 B5
Blackdog 171 E3
Blackdown *Devon* 7 F3
Blackdown *Dorset* 11 G2
Blackfield 14 D2
Blackford *Aber.* 170 B1
Blackford *Cumb.* 126 B5
Blackford *P. & K.* 151 D4
Blackford *Som.* 25 D5
Blackford *Som.* 24 B3
Blackfordby 67 F1
Blackgang 15 D5
Blackhall 143 G2
Blackhall Colliery 121 D4
Blackhall Rocks 121 D4
Blackham 31 E5
Blackheath *Essex* 60 A5
Blackheath *Gt.Lon.* 44 C5
Blackheath *Suff.* 73 F4
Blackheath *Surr.* 29 F3
Blackheath *W.Mid.* 66 B4
Blackhill *Aber.* 183 F4
Blackhill *Aber.* 183 F5
Blackhillock 181 G5
Blackhills 181 E4
Blackland 26 B1
Blacklunans 159 G3
Blackmill 37 F4
Blackmoor *Hants.* 28 C4
Blackmoor *Som.* 11 E1
Blackmoor Gate 21 G1
Blackmore 45 F2
Blackmore End *Essex* 59 F4
Blackmore End *Herts.* 44 A1
Blackness *Aber.* 170 B5
Blackness *Falk.* 143 E2
Blackness *High.* 195 E5
Blacknest 28 C3
Blacko 101 E3
Blackpool 99 G4
Blackpool Airport 99 G4
Blackpool Gate 126 D4
Blackridge 142 C3
Blackrock *Arg. & B.* 138 B3
Blackrock *Mon.* 38 B1
Blackrod 92 A1
Blackshaw 125 E4
Blackshaw Head 101 F5
Blacksmith's Corner 60 B4
Blackstone 17 E2
Blackthorn 42 B1
Blackthorpe 60 A1
Blacktoft 104 A5
Blacktop 171 D4
Blacktown 38 B4
Blackwater *Cornw.* 4 B5
Blackwater *Hants.* 29 D2
Blackwater *I.o.W.* 15 E4
Blackwater *Suff.* 73 F4
Blackwaterfoot 131 E3
Blackwell *Darl.* 110 B1
Blackwell *Derbys.* 93 F5
Blackwell *Derbys.* 81 F2
Blackwell *Warks.* 55 E3
Blackwell *Worcs.* 66 B5
Blackwells End 53 G5
Blackwood *Caerp.* 38 A3
Blackwood *D. & G.* 124 D2
Blackwood *S.Lan.* 142 B5
Blackwood Hill 79 G2
Blacon 78 A1
Bladbean 33 D4
Blades 109 E3
Bladnoch 123 F5
Bladon 41 G1
Blaen Dyryn 51 F4
Blaen-y-coed 49 G5
Blaenannerch 49 F3
Blaenau Dolwyddelan 75 F2
Blaenau Ffestiniog 75 F3
Blaenavon 38 B2
Blaenawey 38 B1
Blaencwm 37 F2
Blaenffos 49 E4
Blaengarw 37 F3
Blaengweche 36 C1
Blaengwrach 37 E2
Blaengwynfi 37 E3
Blaenos 51 D4
Blaenpennal 50 C1
Blaenplwyf 62 B5
Blaenporth 49 F3
Blaenrhondda 37 F2
Blaenwaun 49 F5
Blagdon *N.Som.* 24 B2
Blagdon *Torbay* 9 E1
Blagdon Hill 11 F1
Blaich 156 C2
Blaina 38 B2
Blair 141 E5
Blair Atholl 159 D3
Blair Drummond 150 C5
Blairannaich 149 F4
Blairbuie 140 C2
Blairgowrie 159 G5
Blairhall 143 E1
Blairhoyle 150 B4
Blairhullichan 149 G4
Blairingone 151 E5
Blairkip 132 D2
Blairlogie 150 D5
Blairmore *Arg. & B.* 140 C1
Blairmore *High.* 190 C4
Blairmore *High.* 192 A2
Blairnairn 141 E1
Blairnamarrow 169 E3
Blairpark 140 D4
Blairquhan 132 B5
Blairquhosh 141 G1
Blair's Ferry 140 A3
Blairshinnoch 182 B3
Blairuskinmore 149 G4
Blairvadach 141 D1
Blairydryne 170 C5
Blairythan Cottage 171 E2
Blaisdon 39 G1
Blake End 59 E5
Blakebrook 66 A5
Blakedown 66 A5
Blakelaw *Sc.Bord.* 136 B3
Blakelaw *T. & W.* 120 B1
Blakemere 52 C3
Blakeney *Glos.* 39 F2
Blakeney *Norf.* 86 B1
Blakenhall *Ches.* 79 E3
Blakenhall *W.Mid.* 66 B3
Blakeshall 66 A4
Blakesley 56 B2
Blanchland 119 F2
Bland Hill 102 B2
Blandford Camp 13 F2
Blandford Forum 13 E2
Blandford St. Mary 13 E2
Blanefield 141 G2
Blankney 83 F1
Blar a' Chaorainn 156 D3
Blargie 167 F5
Blarglas 141 E1
Blarmachfoldach 156 C3
Blarnalevoch 188 D5
Blashford 14 A2
Blaston 68 D3
Blathaisbhal 173 G2
Blatherwycke 69 E3
Blawith 107 D4
Blaxhall 61 E2
Blaxton 95 D2
Blaydon 120 A1
Bleadney 24 B3
Bleadon 24 A2
Bleak Hey Nook 93 E2
Blean 32 D2
Bleasby 82 C3
Bleatarn 108 C1
Blebocraigs 152 C3
Bleddfa 52 B1
Bledington 55 E5
Bledlow 42 C2
Bledlow Ridge 42 C3
Blencarn 118 C4
Blencogo 117 E2
Blencow 118 A4
Blendworth 15 G1
Blennerhasset 117 E2
Blervie Castle 180 C4
Bletchingdon 42 A1
Bletchingley 30 C3
Bletchley *M.K.* 57 D4
Bletchley *Shrop.* 78 D4
Bletherston 49 D5
Bletsoe 57 F2
Blewbury 42 A4
Blickling 86 C3
Blidworth 81 G2
Blindburn *Aber.* 171 E1
Blindburn *Northumb.* 136 C5
Blindcrake 117 E3
Blindley Heath 30 C4
Blisland 5 F2
Bliss Gate 65 G5
Blissford 14 A1
Blisworth 56 C2
Blithbury 80 B5
Blitterlees 117 E1
Blo Norton 72 B4
Blockley 55 D4
Blofield 87 E5
Blore 80 C3
Blossomfield 66 D5
Blount's Green 80 B4
Bloxham 55 G4
Bloxholm 83 F2
Bloxwich 66 B2
Bloxworth 13 E3
Blubberhouses 102 A2
Blue Anchor *Cornw* 4 D4
Blue Anchor *Som.* 22 D3
Blue Bell Hill 31 G2
Bluewater 45 E5
Blundeston 73 G2
Blunham 57 G2
Blunsdon St. Andrew 40 D3
Bluntisham 70 B5
Blunts 6 D4
Blyborough 95 G3
Blyford 73 F4
Blymhill 66 A1
Blyth *Northumb.* 129 F3
Blyth *Notts.* 94 D4
Blyth Bridge 143 F5
Blythburgh 73 F4
Blythe Bridge 79 G3
Blythe Marsh 79 G3
Blyton 95 F3
Boarhills 153 D3
Boarhunt 15 F2
Boars Hill 41 G2
Boarshead 31 E5
Boarstall 42 B1
Boarzell 18 C1
Boasley Cross 7 F1
Boat o' Brig 181 F4
Boat of Garten 168 B3
Boath 179 E2
Bobbing 32 A2
Bobbington 66 A3
Bobbingworth 45 E2
Bocaddon 5 F4
Bochastle 150 B4
Bockhampton 41 F5
Bocking 59 F5
Bocking Churchstreet 59 F5
Boconnoc 5 F3
Boddam *Aber.* 183 G5
Boddam *Shet.* 201 G4
Boddington 54 A5
Bodedern 88 B4
Bodelwyddan 90 B5
Bodenham *Here.* 53 E2
Bodenham *Wilts.* 26 C5
Bodenham Moor 53 E2
Bodesbeck 134 C5
Bodewryd 88 B3
Bodfari 90 B5
Bodffordd 88 C5
Bodfuan 74 C4
Bodham Street 86 C1
Bodiam 18 C1
Bodicote 55 G4
Bodieve 5 D2
Bodinnick 5 F4
Bodior 88 A5
Bodle Street Green 18 B2
Bodmin 5 E3
Bodney 71 G3
Bodorgan 74 C1
Bodsham Green 32 D4
Bodwen 5 E3
Bogallan 179 F4
Bogbain 179 G5
Bogbrae 171 F1
Bogbuie 179 E4
Bogend 132 B2
Bogfern 170 A4
Bogfields 170 A4
Bogfold 182 D4
Boghead *Aber.* 182 B4
Boghead *E.Ayr.* 133 E3
Boghead *S.Lan.* 142 B5
Boghole Farm 180 B4
Bogmoor 181 F3
Bogniebrae 182 A5
Bognor Regis 16 B4
Bograxie 170 C3
Bogroy 168 B2
Bogside 151 E5
Bogston 169 F4
Bogton 182 B4
Bogue 124 A2
Bohenie 157 E1
Bohortha 3 F3
Bohuntine 157 E1
Boirseam 184 C5
Bojewyan 2 A3
Bolam 120 A5
Bolberry 8 C4
Bold Heath 91 G4
Bolderwood 14 B2
Boldon 120 C1
Boldre 14 C3
Boldron 109 F1
Bole 95 E4
Bolehill 81 D2
Boleigh 2 B4
Boleside 135 F2
Bolfracks 158 D5
Bolgoed 36 C2
Bolham 10 C1
Bolham Water 11 E1
Bolingey 4 B4
Bollington 92 D5
Bolney 17 E1
Bolnhurst 57 F2
Bolshan 161 E4
Bolsover 94 B5
Bolsterstone 93 G3
Bolstone 53 E4
Boltby 111 D4
Bolter End 42 C3
Bolton *Cumb.* 118 C5
Bolton *E.Loth.* 144 C2
Bolton *E.Riding* 103 G2
Bolton *Gt.Man.* 92 B2
Bolton *Northumb.* 137 F5
Bolton Abbey 101 G2
Bolton Bridge 101 G2
Bolton by Bowland 101 D3
Bolton-le-Sands 100 A1
Bolton Low Houses 117 F2
Bolton-on-Swale 110 B3
Bolton Percy 103 E3
Bolton upon Dearne 94 B2
Boltonfellend 118 A1
Boltongate 117 F2
Bolventor 5 F2
Bombie 124 B5
Bomere Heath 65 D1
Bon-y-maen 36 C3
Bonar Bridge 190 B5
Bonawe 148 C1
Bonawe Quarries 148 C1
Bonby 96 A1
Boncath 49 F4
Bonchester Bridge 135 G4
Bonchurch 15 E5
Bondleigh 21 G5
Bonehill 67 D2
Bo'ness 143 D1
Bonhill 141 E2
Boningale 66 A2
Bonjedward 136 A4
Bonkle 142 C4
Bonnington 32 C5
Bonnybank 152 B4
Bonnybridge 142 C1
Bonnykelly 183 D4
Bonnyrigg 144 A3
Bonnyton *Aber.* 170 B1
Bonnyton *Angus* 153 D1
Bonnyton *Angus* 161 E4
Bonnyton *Angus* 152 B1
Bonsall 81 D2
Bont 38 C1
Bont Dolgadfan 63 E2
Bont-goch (Elerch) 62 C4
Bont Newydd 76 A5
Bontddu 62 C1
Bontnewydd 75 D1
Bontuchel 77 D2
Bonvilston 37 G5
Boohay 9 F2
Booker 42 D3
Booley 78 C5
Boor 177 E1
Boosbeck 111 F1
Boot 106 C2
Booth Wood 93 E1
Boothby Graffoe 83 E2
Boothby Pagnell 83 E4
Boothstown 92 B2
Boothtown 101 G5
Boothville 56 C1
Bootle *Cumb.* 106 C4
Bootle *Mersey.* 91 E3
Booton 86 C3
Boquhan 141 G1
Boraston 65 F5
Bordeaux 9 F4
Borden 32 A2
Bordley 101 F1
Bordon 28 C4
Boreham *Essex* 45 G2
Boreham *Wilts.* 25 F3
Boreham Street 18 B2
Borehamwood 44 A3
Boreland *D. & G.* 125 F1
Boreland *D. & G.* 123 E4
Boreland *Stir.* 150 A1
Boreraig 175 E4
Borgh *W.Isles* 184 B5
Borgh *W.Isles* 172 B3
Borghastan 186 C3
Borgie 193 F3
Borgue *D. & G.* 115 G2
Borgue *High.* 191 G2
Borley 59 G3
Bornais 172 C1
Borness 115 G2
Borough Green 31 F3
Boroughbridge 102 C1
Borras Head 78 A2
Borrowash 81 F4
Borrowby *N.Yorks.* 111 G1
Borrowby *N.Yorks.* 110 D4
Borrowdale 117 F5
Borrowfield 170 D5
Borstal 31 G2
Borth 62 C4
Borth-y-Gest 75 E4
Borthwick 144 A4
Borthwickbrae 135 F4
Borthwickshiels 135 F4
Borve 176 A5
Borwick 107 G5
Bosavern 2 A3
Bosbury 53 F3
Boscastle 6 B1
Boscombe *Bourne.* 14 A3
Boscombe *Wilts.* 26 D4
Boscoppa 5 E4
Bosham 16 A3
Bosherston 34 C3
Bosley 79 G1
Bossall 103 G1
Bossiney 5 E1
Bossingham 32 D4
Bossington *Hants.* 27 E4
Bossington *Som.* 22 B3
Bostock Green 79 D1
Boston 84 B3
Boston Spa 102 D3
Boswinger 5 D5
Botallack 2 A3
Botany Bay 44 B3
Botarua 173 F2
Botcheston 67 G2
Botesdale 72 B4
Bothal 129 E3
Bothamsall 95 D5
Bothel 117 E3
Bothenhampton 12 A3
Bothwell 142 B4
Botley *Bucks.* 43 E2
Botley *Hants.* 15 E1
Botley *Oxon.* 41 G2
Botloe's Green 53 G5
Botolph Claydon 56 C5
Botolphs 17 D3
Bottacks 179 D3
Bottesford *Leics.* 82 D4
Bottesford *N.Lincs.* 95 G2
Bottisham 58 D1
Bottom Head 100 C1
Bottomcraig 152 B2
Botusfleming 8 A1
Botwnnog 74 B4
Bough Beech 31 D4
Boughrood 52 A4
Boughspring 39 E3
Boughton *Norf.* 71 E2
Boughton *Northants.* 56 C1
Boughton *Notts.* 82 B1
Boughton Aluph 32 C4
Boughton Green 31 G3
Boughton Lees 32 C4
Boughton Malherbe 32 A4
Boughton Street 32 C3
Boulby 111 G1
Bouldon 65 E4
Boulmer 137 G5
Boulston 34 C1
Boultenstone Hotel 169 G3
Boultham 83 E1
Bourn 58 B2
Bournbrook 66 C4
Bourne 83 F5
Bourne End *Beds.* 57 E3
Bourne End *Bucks.* 43 D4
Bourne End *Herts.* 43 F2
Bournebridge 45 E3
Bournemouth 13 G3
Bournemouth International Airport 14 A3
Bournes Green 40 B2
Bournheath 66 B5
Bournmoor 120 C2
Bournville 66 C4
Bourton *Dorset* 25 E4
Bourton *N.Som.* 24 A1
Bourton *Oxon.* 41 E4
Bourton *Shrop.* 65 E3
Bourton on Dunsmore 67 G5
Bourton-on-the-Hill 55 D4
Bourton-on-the-Water 55 D5
Bousd 154 B3
Boustead Hill 117 F1
Bouth 107 E4
Bouthwaite 110 A5
Bovain 150 A1
Boveney 43 E5
Boveridge 13 G1
Boverton 22 C1
Bovey Tracey 10 B5
Bovingdon 43 F2
Bovinger 45 E2
Bovington Camp 13 E4
Bow *Devon* 10 A2
Bow *Devon* 9 E2
Bow *Ork.* 196 C3
Bow Brickhill 57 E4
Bow of Fife 152 B3
Bow Street 62 C4
Bowbank 119 F5
Bowburn 120 C4
Bowcombe 15 D4
Bowd 11 E4
Bowden *Devon* 9 E3
Bowden *Sc.Bord.* 135 G2
Bowden Hill 26 A1
Bowdon 92 B4
Bower 127 F3
Bower Hinton 12 A1
Bowerchalke 26 B5
Bowerhill 26 A1
Bowermadden 195 E2
Bowers Gifford 45 G4
Bowershall 151 F5
Bowertower 195 E2
Bowes 109 E1
Bowgreave 100 A3
Bowland Bridge 107 F4
Bowley 53 E2
Bowlhead Green 29 E4
Bowling 141 F2
Bowling Bank 78 A3
Bowlish 24 D3
Bowmanstead 107 E3
Bowmore 138 B4
Bowness-on-Solway 126 A5
Bowness-on-Windermere 107 F3
Bowsden 145 G5
Bowside Lodge 194 A2
Bowthorpe 86 C5
Bowtrees 142 D1
Box *Glos.* 40 A2
Box *Wilts.* 25 F1
Box End 57 F3
Boxbush 39 G1
Boxford *Suff.* 60 A3
Boxford *W.Berks.* 41 G5
Boxgrove 16 B3
Boxley 31 G3
Boxmoor 43 F2
Boxted *Essex* 60 A4
Boxted *Suff.* 59 G2
Boxted Cross 60 B4
Boxworth 58 B1
Boxworth End 58 B1
Boyden Gate 33 E2
Boydston 132 C2
Boylestone 80 C4
Boyndie 182 B3
Boynton 104 D1
Boysack 161 E5
Boyton *Cornw.* 6 D1
Boyton *Suff.* 61 E3
Boyton *Wilts.* 26 A4
Boyton Cross 45 F2
Bozeat 57 E2
Braaid 98 B4
Braal Castle 194 D2
Brabling Green 61 D1
Brabourne 32 C4
Brabourne Lees 32 C4
Brabster 195 F2
Bracadale 163 G1
Braceborough 69 F1
Bracebridge 83 E1
Bracebridge Heath 83 E1
Braceby 83 F4
Bracewell 101 E3
Brachla 167 E1
Brackenber 118 D5
Brackenfield 81 E2
Brackens 182 C4
Bracklach 169 F2
Bracklamore 182 D4
Brackletter 157 D1
Brackley *Arg. & B.* 139 G1
Brackley *High.* 180 A4
Brackley *Northants.* 56 A4
Bracknell 29 D1
Braco 150 D4
Bracobrae 182 A4
Bracon Ash 72 C2
Bracora 164 D5
Bracorina 164 D5
Bradbourne 80 D2
Bradbury 120 C5
Bradda 98 A4
Bradden 56 B3
Bradenham 42 D3
Bradenstoke 40 C4
Bradfield *Devon* 10 D2
Bradfield *Essex* 60 C4
Bradfield *Norf.* 87 D2
Bradfield *W.Berks.* 42 B5
Bradfield Combust 59 G2
Bradfield Green 79 D2
Bradfield Heath 60 C5
Bradfield St. Clare 60 A2
Bradfield St. George 60 A2
Bradford *Devon* 21 E5
Bradford *Northumb.* 137 F3
Bradford *W.Yorks.* 102 A4
Bradford Abbas 12 B1
Bradford Leigh 25 F1
Bradford-on-Avon 25 F1
Bradford-on-Tone 23 E5
Bradford Peverell 12 C3
Brading 15 F4
Bradley *Derbys.* 80 D3
Bradley *Hants.* 28 B3
Bradley *N.E.Lincs.* 96 C2
Bradley *Staffs.* 66 A1
Bradley *W.Mid.* 66 B3
Bradley or Low Bradley 101 G3
Bradley Green 54 B1
Bradley in the Moors 80 B3
Bradley Stoke 39 F4
Bradmore *Notts.* 81 G4
Bradmore *W.Mid.* 66 A3
Bradninch 10 D2
Bradnop 80 B2
Bradpole 12 A3
Bradshaw 92 B1
Bradstone 7 D2
Bradwall Green 79 E1
Bradwell *Derbys.* 93 F4
Bradwell *Essex* 59 G5
Bradwell *M.K.* 56 D4
Bradwell *Norf.* 87 G5
Bradwell Grove 41 E2
Bradwell-on-Sea 46 C2
Bradwell Waterside 46 C2
Bradworthy 20 D4
Brae *D. & G.* 124 C3
Brae *High.* 189 G4
Brae *Shet.* 200 C1
Braeantra 179 E2
Braedownie 160 A2
Braefoot 182 C5
Braegrum 151 F2
Braehead *Moray* 181 F5
Braehead *Ork.* 197 E2
Braehead *Ork.* 198 C2
Braehead *S.Lan.* 133 G2
Braehead *S.Lan.* 143 D4
Braehead of Lunan 161 E4
Braehoulland 202 B5
Braeleny 150 B3
Braemar 169 D5
Braemore *High.* 190 A4
Braemore *High.* 194 C5
Braemore *High.* 178 A2
Braenaloin 169 E5
Braes of Enzie 181 F4
Braes of Foss 158 C4
Braes of Ullapool 188 D5
Braeswick 199 E3
Braeval 150 A4
Brafferton *Darl.* 120 B5
Brafferton *N.Yorks.* 110 D5
Brafield-on-the-Green 56 D2
Bragar 187 D3
Bragbury End 58 A5
Bragleenbeg 148 B2
Braichmelyn 75 F1
Braides 100 A2
Braidley 109 F4
Braidwood 142 C5
Braigo 138 A3
Brailsford 81 D3
Braintree 59 F5
Braiseworth 72 C4
Braishfield 27 E5
Braithwaite *Cumb.* 117 F4
Braithwaite *S.Yorks.* 94 D1
Braithwell 94 C3
Bramber 17 D2
Brambletye 30 D5
Bramcote 81 G4
Bramdean 28 B5
Bramerton 87 D5
Bramfield *Herts.* 44 B1
Bramfield *Suff.* 73 E4
Bramford 60 C3
Bramhall 92 C4
Bramham 102 D3
Bramhope 102 B3
Bramley *Hants.* 28 B2
Bramley *S.Yorks.* 94 B3
Bramley *Surr.* 29 F3
Bramling 33 E3
Brampford Speke 10 C3
Brampton *Cambs.* 70 A5
Brampton *Cumb.* 118 B1
Brampton *Cumb.* 118 C5
Brampton *Derbys.* 94 A5

Brampton Lincs. 95 F5
Brampton Norf. 86 D3
Brampton S.Yorks. 94 B2
Brampton Suff. 73 F3
Brampton Abbotts 53 F5
Brampton Ash 68 C4
Brampton Bryan 64 C5
Brampton en le Morthen 94 B4
Bramshall 80 B4
Bramshaw 14 B1
Bramshill 28 C1
Bramshott 28 D4
Bramwell 24 B5
Bran End 59 E5
Branault 155 E3
Brancaster 85 F3
Brancepeth 120 B4
Branchill 180 C4
Brand Green 53 G5
Branderburgh 181 E2
Brandesburton 104 D3
Brandeston 60 D1
Brandis Corner 21 E5
Brandiston 86 C3
Brandon Dur. 120 B4
Brandon Lincs. 83 E3
Brandon Northumb. 137 E5
Brandon Suff. 71 F4
Brandon Warks. 67 G5
Brandon Bank 71 E4
Brandon Creek 71 E3
Brandon Parva 86 B5
Brandsby 111 E5
Brandy Wharf 96 A3
Brane 2 A4
Branksome 13 G3
Branksome Park 13 G3
Bransby 95 F5
Branscombe 11 E4
Bransford 53 G2
Bransford Bridge 54 A2
Bransgore 14 A3
Branson's Cross 66 C5
Branston Leics. 82 D5
Branston Lincs. 83 F1
Branston Staffs. 80 D5
Branston Booths 83 F1
Branstone 15 E4
Brant Broughton 83 E2
Brantham 60 C4
Branthwaite Cumb. 117 F3
Branthwaite Cumb. 117 D4
Brantingham 104 B5
Branton Northumb. 137 E5
Branton S.Yorks. 94 D2
Brantwood 107 E3
Branxholm Bridgend 135 F4
Branxholme 135 F4
Branxton 136 C3
Brassington 80 D2
Brasted 31 D3
Brasted Chart 31 D3
Brathens 170 B5
Bratoft 84 C1
Brattleby 95 G4
Bratton 26 A2
Bratton Clovelly 7 E1
Bratton Fleming 21 G2
Bratton Seymour 25 D5
Braughing 58 B5
Braunston Northants. 56 A1
Braunston Rut. 68 D2
Braunstone 68 A2
Braunton 21 E2
Brawby 111 G5
Brawdy 48 B5
Brawl 194 A2
Brawlbin 194 C3
Bray 43 E5
Bray Shop 6 D3
Bray Wick 43 D5
Braybrooke 68 C4
Brayford 21 G2
Brayshaw 101 D2
Brayton 103 F4
Brazacott 6 C1
Breach 33 D4
Breachwood Green 57 G5
Breacleit 186 C4
Breadsall 81 E4
Breadstone 39 G2
Breage 2 D4
Breakon 203 E2
Bream 39 F2
Breamore 14 A1
Brean 23 F2
Breanais 186 A5
Brearton 102 C1
Breascleit 186 D4
Breaston 81 F4
Brechfa 50 B4
Brechin 161 E3
Brecklate 130 B4
Breckles 72 A2
Brecon (Aberhonddu) 51 G5
Breconside 133 G5
Bredbury 92 D3
Brede 18 D2
Bredenbury 53 F2
Bredfield 61 D2
Bredgar 32 A2
Bredhurst 31 G2
Bredicot 54 B2
Bredon 54 B4
Bredon's Hardwick 54 B4
Bredon's Norton 54 B4
Bredwardine 52 C3
Breedon on the Hill 81 F5
Breibhig 187 F4
Breich 143 D3
Breighton 103 G4
Breinton 53 D3
Bremhill 40 B5
Brenachoille 148 C4
Brenchley 31 F4
Brendon Devon 22 A3
Brendon Devon 21 D4
Brenkley 129 E4
Brent 44 A4
Brent Eleigh 60 A3
Brent Knoll 24 A2
Brent Pelham 58 C4
Brentford 44 A5
Brentingby 68 C1
Brentwood 45 E3
Brenzett 19 F1
Breoch 124 B5
Brereton 66 C1
Brereton Green 79 E1
Brereton Heath 79 F1
Bressingham 72 B3
Bretabister 201 D2
Bretby 81 D5
Bretford 67 G5
Bretforton 54 C3
Bretherdale Head 107 G2
Bretherton 100 A5
Brettenham Norf. 72 A3
Brettenham Suff. 60 A2
Bretton 78 A1
Brewood 66 A2
Briach 180 C4
Briantspuddle 13 E3
Bricket Wood 44 A2
Bricklehampton 54 B3
Bride 98 C1
Bridekirk 117 E3
Bridell 49 E3
Bridestones 79 G1
Bridestowe 7 F2
Brideswell 170 A1
Bridford 10 B4
Bridge Cornw. 4 A5
Bridge Kent 33 D3
Bridge End Lincs. 83 G4
Bridge End Shet. 200 C4
Bridge Hewick 110 C5
Bridge o' Ess 170 A5
Bridge of Alford 170 A3
Bridge of Allan 150 C5
Bridge of Avon 169 D1
Bridge of Balgie 158 A5
Bridge of Bogendreip 170 B5
Bridge of Brewlands 159 G3
Bridge of Brown 168 D2
Bridge of Cally 159 G4
Bridge of Canny 170 B5
Bridge of Craigisla 160 A4
Bridge of Dee Aber. 169 D5
Bridge of Dee Aber. 170 B5
Bridge of Dee D. & G. 124 B4
Bridge of Don 171 E4
Bridge of Dun 161 E4
Bridge of Dye 161 E1
Bridge of Earn 151 G3
Bridge of Ericht 158 A4
Bridge of Feugh 170 B5
Bridge of Forss 194 C2
Bridge of Gairn 169 F5
Bridge of Gaur 158 A4
Bridge of Muchalls 171 D5
Bridge of Muick 169 F5
Bridge of Orchy 149 F1
Bridge of Tilt 159 D3
Bridge of Tynet 181 F3
Bridge of Walls 200 B2
Bridge of Weir 141 E3
Bridge Sollers 52 D3
Bridge Street 59 G3
Bridge Trafford 91 F5
Bridgefoot Cambs. 58 C3
Bridgefoot Cumb. 117 D4
Bridgehampton 24 C5
Bridgemary 15 E2
Bridgemere 79 E3
Bridgend Aber. 170 A1
Bridgend Angus 160 D3
Bridgend Arg. & B. 138 B3
Bridgend Arg. & B. 148 A5
Bridgend (Pen-y-Bont ar Ogwr) Bridgend 37 F5
Bridgend Cornw. 5 F3
Bridgend Cumb. 107 F1
Bridgend Fife 152 B3
Bridgend Moray 169 F1
Bridgend P. & K. 151 G2
Bridgend W.Loth. 143 E2
Bridgend of Lintrathen 160 A4
Bridgerule 20 C5
Bridges 64 C3
Bridgeton 170 A3
Bridgetown Cornw. 6 D2
Bridgetown Som. 22 C4
Bridgeyate 39 F5
Bridgham 72 A3
Bridgnorth 65 G3
Bridgtown 66 B2
Bridgwater 23 F4
Bridlington 105 D1
Bridport 12 A3
Bridstow 53 E5
Brierfield 101 E4
Brierley Glos. 39 F1
Brierley Here. 53 D2
Brierley S.Yorks. 94 B1
Brierley Hill 66 B4
Brig o'Turk 150 A4
Brigehaugh 169 F1
Brigg 96 A2
Brigham Cumb. 117 D3
Brigham E.Riding 104 C2
Brighouse 102 A5
Brighstone 14 D4
Brightgate 81 D2
Brighthampton 41 F2
Brightling 18 B1
Brightlingsea 47 D1
Brighton B. & H. 17 F3
Brighton Cornw. 4 D4
Brightons 142 D2
Brightwalton 41 G5
Brightwell Oxon. 42 A3
Brightwell Suff. 60 D3
Brightwell Baldwin 42 B3
Brignall 109 F1
Brigsley 96 C2
Brigsteer 107 F4
Brigstock 69 E4
Brill Bucks. 42 B1
Brill Cornw. 3 E4
Brilley 52 B3
Brilley Mountain 52 B2
Brimfield 53 E1
Brimington 94 B5
Brimington Common 94 B5
Brimley 10 B5
Brimpsfield 40 B1
Brimpton 27 G1
Brimscombe 40 A2
Brimstage 91 E4
Brind 103 G4
Brindister Shet. 200 D4
Brindister Shet. 200 B2
Brindle 100 B5
Brindley Ford 79 F2
Brineton 66 A1
Bringhurst 68 D3
Brington 69 F5
Brinian 198 C4
Briningham 86 B2
Brinkhill 97 D5
Brinkley 59 E2
Brinklow 67 G5
Brinkworth 40 C4
Brinmore 167 F2
Brinscall 100 C5
Brinsley 81 F3
Brinsop 52 D3
Brinsworth 94 B4
Brinton 86 B2
Brisco 118 A2
Brisley 86 A3
Brislington 39 F5
Bristol 39 E5
Bristol International Airport 24 B1
Briston 86 B2
Britannia 101 E5
Britford 26 C5
Brithdir 63 D1
Brithem Bottom 10 D1
Briton Ferry (Llansawel) 36 D3
Britwell Salome 42 B3
Brixham 9 F2
Brixton 8 B2
Brixton Deverill 25 F4
Brixworth 68 C5
Brize Norton 41 E2
Broad Blunsdon 41 D3
Broad Campden 55 D4
Broad Chalke 26 B5
Broad Green Beds. 57 E3
Broad Green Essex 59 G5
Broad Green Worcs. 53 G2
Broad Haven 34 B1
Broad Hill 71 D5
Broad Hinton 40 D5
Broad Laying 27 F1
Broad Marston 54 D3
Broad Oak Cumb. 106 C3
Broad Oak E.Suss. 18 D2
Broad Oak E.Suss. 18 B1
Broad Oak Here. 53 D5
Broad Street 32 A3
Broad Street Green 46 B2
Broad Town 40 C5
Broadbottom 93 D3
Broadbridge 16 A3
Broadbridge Heath 29 G4
Broadclyst 10 C3
Broadford 164 C2
Broadford Bridge 29 F5
Broadgate 106 C4
Broadgroves 45 F1
Broadhaugh 135 F5
Broadheath Gt.Man. 92 B4
Broadheath Worcs. 53 F1
Broadhembury 11 E2
Broadhempston 9 E1
Broadholme 95 F5
Broadland Row 18 D2
Broadlay 35 G2
Broadley Lancs. 92 C1
Broadley Moray 181 F3
Broadley Common 44 D2
Broadmayne 12 D4
Broadmeadows 135 F3
Broadmere 28 B3
Broadnymett 10 A2
Broadoak Carmar. 50 B5
Broadoak Dorset 12 A3
Broadoak Kent 33 D2
Broadrashes 181 G4
Broadsea 183 E3
Broadstairs 33 F2
Broadstone Poole 13 G3
Broadstone Shrop. 65 E4
Broadstreet Common 38 C4
Broadwas 53 G2
Broadwater Herts. 58 A5
Broadwater W.Suss. 16 D3
Broadway Carmar. 35 G2
Broadway Carmar. 35 F1
Broadway Pembs. 34 B1
Broadway Som. 11 G1
Broadway Suff. 73 E4
Broadway Worcs. 54 C4
Broadwell Glos. 55 E5
Broadwell Glos. 39 E1
Broadwell Oxon. 41 E2
Broadwell Warks. 55 G1
Broadwell House 119 F2
Broadwey 12 C4
Broadwindsor 12 A2
Broadwood Kelly 21 G5
Broadwoodwidger 7 E2
Brobury 52 C3
Brochel 176 B5
Brochloch 123 G1
Brock 154 B2
Brockbridge 15 F1
Brockdish 72 D4
Brockenhurst 14 C2
Brockfield 103 F2
Brockford Street 60 C1
Brockhall 56 B1
Brockham 29 G3
Brockhampton Glos. 54 C5
Brockhampton Here. 53 E4
Brockholes 93 F1
Brockhurst 30 D5
Brocklebank 117 G2
Brocklesby 96 B1
Brockley 24 B1
Brockley Green 59 G2
Brockton Shrop. 65 E3
Brockton Shrop. 65 G2
Brockton Shrop. 64 C2
Brockton Shrop. 64 C4
Brockweir 39 E2
Brockwood Park 28 B5
Brockworth 40 A1
Brocton 66 B1
Brodick 131 F2
Brodsworth 94 C2
Brogborough 57 E4
Brogyntyn 77 F4
Broken Cross Ches. 92 C5
Broken Cross Ches. 92 A5
Brokenborough 40 B4
Bromborough 91 E4
Brome 72 C4
Brome Street 72 C4
Bromeswell 61 D2
Bromfield Cumb. 117 E2
Bromfield Shrop. 65 D5
Bromham Beds. 57 F2
Bromham Wilts. 26 A1
Bromley 30 D2
Bromley Green 32 B5
Brompton Med. 31 G2
Brompton N.Yorks. 110 C3
Brompton N.Yorks. 112 C4
Brompton on Swale 110 B2
Brompton Ralph 23 D4
Brompton Regis 22 C4
Bromsash 53 F5
Bromsberrow Heath 53 G4
Bromsgrove 66 B5
Bromstead Heath 66 A1
Bromyard 53 F2
Bromyard Downs 53 F2
Bron-y-Gaer 35 G1
Bronaber 76 A4
Brongest 49 G3
Bronington 78 B4
Bronllys 52 A4
Bronnant 50 C1
Bronydd 52 B3
Bronygarth 77 F4
Brook Carmar. 35 F2
Brook Hants. 14 B1
Brook Hants. 27 E5
Brook I.o.W. 14 C4
Brook Kent 32 C4
Brook Surr. 29 E4
Brook Street Essex 45 E3
Brook Street Kent 32 B5
Brook Street Suff. 59 G3
Brook Street W.Suss. 17 F1
Brooke Norf. 73 D2
Brooke Rut. 69 D2
Brookend 39 E3
Brookhouse 100 B1
Brookhouse Green 79 F1
Brookland 19 E1
Brooklands 124 C3
Brookmans Park 44 B2
Brooks 64 A3
Brooks Green 29 G5
Brooksby 68 B1
Brookthorpe 40 A1
Brookwood 29 E2
Broom Beds. 57 G3
Broom Warks. 54 C2
Broom Hill 13 G2
Broom of Dalreach 151 F3
Broomcroft 65 E2
Broome Norf. 73 E2
Broome Shrop. 64 C4
Broome Worcs. 66 B5
Broome Wood 137 F5
Broomedge 92 B4
Broomer's Corner 29 G5
Broomfield Aber. 171 E1
Broomfield Essex 45 G1
Broomfield Kent 33 D2
Broomfield Kent 32 A3
Broomfield Som. 23 F4
Broomfleet 104 A5
Broomhaugh 119 G1
Broomhead 183 E3
Broomhill 129 E1
Broom's Green 53 G4
Brora 191 E4
Broseley 65 F2
Brotherlee 119 F4
Brothertoft 84 A3
Brotherton 103 D5
Brotton 121 F5
Broubster 194 C2
Brough Cumb. 108 C1
Brough Derbys. 93 F4
Brough E.Riding 104 B5
Brough High. 195 E1
Brough Notts. 82 D2
Brough Ork. 198 B5
Brough Shet. 201 E3
Brough Shet. 202 D5
Brough Shet. 201 E1
Brough Shet. 203 E5
Brough Lodge 203 E3
Brough Sowerby 108 C1
Broughall 78 C3
Brougham 118 B5
Broughton Cambs. 70 A5
Broughton Flints. 78 A1
Broughton Hants. 27 E4
Broughton Lancs. 100 B4
Broughton M.K. 57 D3
Broughton N.Lincs. 95 G2
Broughton N.Yorks. 111 G5
Broughton N.Yorks. 101 F2
Broughton Northants. 68 D5
Broughton Ork. 198 C2
Broughton Oxon. 55 G4
Broughton Sc.Bord. 134 C2
Broughton V. of Glam. 37 F5
Broughton Astley 68 A3
Broughton Beck 107 D4
Broughton Gifford 25 F1
Broughton Hackett 54 B2
Broughton in Furness 106 D4
Broughton Mills 106 D3
Broughton Moor 117 D3
Broughton Poggs 41 E2
Broughtown 199 E2
Broughty Ferry 152 C1
Browland 200 B2
Brown Candover 27 G4
Brown Edge Lancs. 91 E1
Brown Edge Staffs. 79 G2
Brown Lees 79 F2
Brownhill 183 D5
Brownhills Fife 152 D3
Brownhills W.Mid. 66 C2
Brownieside 137 F4
Brownlow Heath 79 F1
Brownshill Green 67 F4
Brownston 8 C2
Broxa 112 C3
Broxbourne 44 C2
Broxburn E.Loth. 145 D2
Broxburn W.Loth. 143 E2
Broxholme 95 G5
Broxted 59 D5
Broxton 78 B2
Broxwood 52 C2
Bru 187 E2
Bruachmary 180 A5
Bruan 195 F5
Bruera 78 B1
Bruichladdich 138 A3
Bruisyard 61 E1
Bruisyard Street 61 E1
Brund 80 C1
Brundall 87 E5
Brundish 61 D1
Brundish Street 73 D4
Bruntingthorpe 68 B4
Bruntland 169 G2
Brunton Fife 152 B2
Brunton Northumb. 137 G4
Brushford Devon 21 G5
Brushford Som. 22 C5
Bruton 25 D4
Bryanston 13 E2
Brydekirk 125 F3
Brymbo 77 F2
Bryn Carmar. 36 B2
Bryn Gt.Man. 91 G2
Bryn N.P.T. 37 E3
Bryn Shrop. 64 B4
Bryn-côch 36 D3
Bryn Gates 91 G2
Bryn-henllan 48 D4
Bryn-teg 88 C4
Bryn-y-maen 89 G5
Brynamman 36 D1
Brynberian 49 E4
Bryncae 37 F4
Bryncethin 37 F4
Bryncir 75 D3
Bryncroes 74 B4
Bryncrug 62 C2
Bryneglwys 77 E3
Brynford 90 C5
Bryngwran 88 B5
Bryngwyn Mon. 38 C2
Bryngwyn Powys 52 A3
Brynhoffnant 49 G2
Brynmawr 38 A1
Brynmelyn 64 A5
Brynmenyn 37 F4
Brynna 37 F4
Brynog 50 B2
Brynrefail Gwyn. 75 E1
Brynrefail I.o.A. 88 C4
Brynsadler 37 G4
Brynsiencyn 75 D1
Brynteg 78 A2
Buaile nam Bodach 172 C3
Bualintur 164 A2
Bualnaluib 177 E1
Bubbenhall 67 F5
Bubwith 103 G4
Buccleuch 135 E4
Buchan 124 B4
Buchanan Castle 141 F1
Buchanhaven 183 G5
Buchanty 151 E2
Buchlyvie 150 A5
Buckabank 117 G2
Buckby Wharf 56 B1
Buckden Cambs. 57 G1
Buckden N.Yorks. 109 E5
Buckenham 87 E5
Buckerell 11 E2
Buckfast 8 D1
Buckfastleigh 8 D1
Buckhaven 152 B5
Buckholm 135 F2
Buckhorn Weston 25 E5
Buckhurst Hill 44 D3
Buckie 181 G3
Buckies 194 D2
Buckingham 56 B4
Buckland Bucks. 43 D1
Buckland Devon 8 C3
Buckland Glos. 54 C4
Buckland Herts. 58 B4
Buckland Kent 33 E4
Buckland Oxon. 41 F3
Buckland Surr. 30 B3
Buckland Brewer 21 E3
Buckland Common 43 E2
Buckland Dinham 25 E2
Buckland Filleigh 21 E5
Buckland in the Moor 10 A5
Buckland Monachorum 8 A1
Buckland Newton 12 C2
Buckland St. Mary 11 F1
Buckland-tout-Saints 9 D3
Bucklebury 42 A5
Bucklerheads 152 C1
Bucklers Hard 14 D2
Bucklesham 60 D3
Buckley (Bwcle) 77 F1
Buckman Corner 29 F5
Buckminster 83 D5
Bucknall Lincs. 83 G1
Bucknall Stoke 79 G3
Bucknell Oxon. 56 A5
Bucknell Shrop. 64 C5
Buck's Cross 20 D3
Bucks Green 29 F4
Bucks Hill 43 F2
Bucks Horn Oak 28 D3
Buck's Mills 21 D3
Bucksburn 171 D4
Buckspool 34 C3
Buckton E.Riding 113 E5
Buckton Here. 64 C5
Buckton Northumb. 137 E3
Buckworth 69 G5
Budbrooke 55 E1
Budby 82 B1
Buddon 152 D1
Bude 20 C5
Budlake 10 C2
Budle 137 F3
Budleigh Salterton 11 D4
Budock Water 3 E3
Buerton 79 D3
Bugbrooke 56 B2
Bugle 5 E4
Bugthorpe 103 G2
Buildwas 65 F2
Builth Road 51 G2
Builth Wells 51 G2
Buirgh 184 C4
Bulby 83 F5
Buldoo 194 B2
Bulford 26 C3
Bulford Camp 26 C3
Bulkeley 78 C2
Bulkington Warks. 67 F4
Bulkington Wilts. 26 A2
Bulkworthy 21 D4
Bull Bay 88 C3
Bull Green 32 B5
Bulley 39 G1
Bullington 27 F3
Bullpot Farm 108 B4
Bull's Green 44 B1
Bullwood 140 C2
Bulmer Essex 59 G3
Bulmer N.Yorks. 103 F1
Bulmer Tye 59 G4
Bulphan 45 F4
Bulverhythe 18 C3
Bulwark 183 E5
Bulwell 81 G3
Bulwick 69 E3
Bumble's Green 44 D2
Bun Abhainn Eadarra 184 D3
Bun Loyne 166 B4
Bunarkaig 157 D1
Bunbury 78 C2
Bunchrew 179 F5
Bundalloch 165 E2
Buness 203 F2
Bunessan 146 C2
Bungay 73 E3
Bunlarie 130 C2
Bunloit 167 E2
Bunnahabhainn 138 C2
Bunny 81 G5
Buntait 166 C1
Buntingford 58 B5
Bunwell 72 C2
Bunwell Street 72 C2
Burbage Derbys. 93 E5
Burbage Leics. 67 G3
Burbage Wilts. 26 D1
Burchett's Green 42 D4
Burcombe 26 B4
Burcot 42 A3
Burcott 57 D5
Burdale 104 A1
Burdocks 29 F5
Bures 60 A4
Bures Green 60 A4
Burford 41 E1
Burgate 72 B4
Burgess Hill 17 F2
Burgh 60 D2
Burgh by Sands 117 G1
Burgh Castle 87 F5
Burgh Heath 30 B3
Burgh le Marsh 84 C1
Burgh next Aylsham 86 D3
Burgh on Bain 96 C4
Burgh St. Margaret 87 F4
Burgh St. Peter 73 F2
Burghclere 27 F1
Burghead 180 D3
Burghfield 28 B1
Burghfield Common 28 B1
Burghfield Hill 28 B1
Burghill 53 D3
Burghwallis 94 C1
Burham 31 G2
Buriton 28 C5
Burland 78 D2
Burlawn 5 D2
Burleigh 29 E1
Burlescombe 11 D1
Burleston 13 D3
Burley Hants. 14 B2
Burley Rut. 69 D1
Burley Gate 53 E3
Burley in Wharfedale 102 A3
Burley Street 14 B2
Burleydam 78 D3
Burlingjobb 52 B2
Burlow 18 A2
Burlton 78 B5
Burmarsh 32 D5
Burmington 55 E4
Burn 103 E5
Burn Farm 161 E2
Burn Naze 99 G3
Burn of Cambus 150 C4
Burnage 92 C3
Burnaston 81 D4
Burnby 104 A3
Burndell 16 B3
Burnend 182 D5
Burneside 107 G3
Burness 199 E2
Burneston 110 C4
Burnett 25 D1
Burnfoot High. 194 A5
Burnfoot P. & K. 151 E4
Burnfoot Sc.Bord. 135 G4
Burnfoot Sc.Bord. 135 F4
Burnham Bucks. 43 E4
Burnham N.Lincs. 96 A1
Burnham Deepdale 85 G3
Burnham Green 44 B1
Burnham Market 85 G3
Burnham Norton 85 G3
Burnham-on-Crouch 46 C3
Burnham-on-Sea 24 A3
Burnham Overy 85 G3
Burnham Thorpe 85 G3
Burnhaven 183 G5
Burnhead D. & G. 123 G2
Burnhead D. & G. 124 C1
Burnhervie 170 C3
Burnhill Green 65 G2
Burnhope 120 A3
Burnhouse 141 E4
Burniston 112 D3
Burnley 101 E4
Burnmouth 145 G3
Burnopfield 120 A2
Burnsall 101 G1
Burnside Aber. 170 C3
Burnside Angus 160 D4
Burnside E.Ayr. 133 D4
Burnside Fife 151 G4
Burnside Shet. 202 B5
Burnside W.Loth. 143 E2
Burnside of Duntrune 152 C1
Burnstones 118 C2
Burnswark 125 F3
Burnt Houses 120 A5
Burnt Yates 102 B1
Burntcliff Top 79 G1
Burntisland 143 G1
Burnton E.Ayr. 132 C4
Burnton E.Ayr. 132 C5
Burntwood 66 C1
Burntwood Green 66 C2
Burpham Surr. 29 F2
Burpham W.Suss. 16 C3
Burradon Northumb. 128 B1
Burradon T. & W. 129 E4
Burrafirth 203 F1
Burraland 202 C5
Burras 3 D3
Burravoe Shet. 203 E5
Burravoe Shet. 200 C1
Burrells 108 B1
Burrelton 151 G1
Burridge 15 E1
Burrill 110 B4
Burringham 95 F2
Burrington Devon 21 G4
Burrington Here. 64 D5
Burrington N.Som. 24 B2
Burrough End 59 E2
Burrough Green 59 E2
Burrough on the Hill 68 C1
Burrow Bridge 24 A4
Burrowhill 29 E1
Burry Port 36 A2
Burscough 91 F1
Burscough Bridge 91 F1
Bursea 104 A4
Burshill 104 C3
Bursledon 15 D2
Burslem 79 F3
Burstall 60 C3
Burstock 12 A2
Burston Norf. 72 C3
Burston Staffs. 79 G4
Burstow 30 C4
Burstwick 105 E5
Burtersett 109 D4
Burtle 24 B3
Burton Ches. 91 E5
Burton Ches. 78 C1
Burton Dorset 14 A3
Burton Dorset 12 C3
Burton Lincs. 95 G5
Burton Northumb. 137 F3
Burton Pembs. 34 C2
Burton Som. 23 E3
Burton Wilts. 40 A5
Burton Agnes 104 D1
Burton Bradstock 12 A4

Burton Coggles 83 E5
Burton Fleming 113 D5
Burton Green *Warks.* 67 E5
Burton Green *Wrex.* 78 A2
Burton Hastings 67 G3
Burton-in-Kendal 107 G5
Burton in Lonsdale 108 B5
Burton Joyce 82 B3
Burton Latimer 69 E5
Burton Lazars 68 C1
Burton Leonard 102 C1
Burton on the Wolds 81 G5
Burton Overy 68 B3
Burton Pedwardine 83 G3
Burton Pidsea 105 E4
Burton Salmon 103 D5
Burton upon Stather 95 F1
Burton upon Trent 80 D5
Burtonwood 91 G3
Burwardsley 78 C2
Burwarton 65 F4
Burwash 18 B1
Burwash Common 18 B1
Burwash Weald 18 B1
Burwell *Cambs.* 59 D1
Burwell *Lincs.* 97 D5
Burwen 88 C3
Burwick *Ork.* 196 D4
Burwick *Shet.* 200 C3
Bury *Cambs.* 70 A4
Bury *Gt.Man.* 92 C1
Bury *Som.* 22 C5
Bury *W.Suss.* 16 C2
Bury Green 58 C5
Bury St. Edmunds 59 G1
Buryas Bridge 2 B4
Burythorpe 103 G1
Busbridge 29 E3
Busby *E.Renf.* 141 G4
Busby *P. & K.* 151 F2
Buscot 41 E3
Bush Bank 52 D2
Bush Crathie 169 E5
Bush Green 72 D3
Bushbury 66 B2
Bushby 68 B2
Bushey 44 A3
Bushey Heath 44 A3
Bushley 54 A4
Bushton 40 C5
Bussage 40 A2
Busta 200 C1
Butcher's Cross 18 A1
Butcher's Pasture 59 E5
Butcombe 24 C1
Buthill 180 D3
Butleigh 24 C4
Butleigh Wootton 24 C4
Butler's Cross 42 D2
Butler's Hill 81 G3
Butlers Marston 55 F2
Butley 61 E2
Butsfield 120 A3
Butt Green 79 D2
Butt Lane 79 F2
Butterburn 127 E4
Buttercrambe 103 G2
Butterknowle 120 A5
Butterleigh 10 C2
Butterley 81 F2
Buttermere *Cumb.* 117 E5
Buttermere *Wilts.* 27 E1
Butters Green 79 F2
Buttershaw 102 A5
Butterstone 159 F5
Butterton 80 B2
Butterwick *Lincs.* 84 B3
Butterwick *N.Yorks.* 112 C5
Butterwick *N.Yorks.* 111 G5
Buttington 64 B2
Buttonoak 65 G5
Buxhall 60 B2
Buxted 17 G1
Buxton *Derbys.* 93 E5
Buxton *Norf.* 86 D3
Buxton Heath 86 C3
Buxworth 93 E4
Bwcle (Buckley) 77 F1
Bwlch 52 A5
Bwlch-clawdd 49 G4
Bwlch-derwin 75 D3
Bwlch-llan 50 B2
Bwlch-y-cibau 64 A1
Bwlch-y-ddar 77 E5
Bwlch-y-ffridd 63 G3
Bwlch-y-groes 49 F4
Bwlch-y-sarnau 63 G5
Bwlchgwyn 77 F2
Bwlchnewydd 49 G5
Bwlchtocyn 74 C5
Byers Green 120 B4
Byfield 56 A2
Byfleet 29 F1
Byford 52 C3
Bygrave 58 A4
Byker 120 B1
Bylane End 5 G4
Bylchau 76 C1
Byley 79 E1
Bynea 36 B3
Byrness 127 F1
Bythorn 69 F5
Byton 52 C1
Byworth 29 E5

## C

Cabharstadh 187 E5
Cabourne 96 B2
Cabrach *Arg. & B.* 138 C3
Cabrach *Moray* 169 F2
Cackle Street 18 D2
Cacrabank 135 E4
Cadboll 180 A2
Cadbury 10 C2
Cadbury Barton 21 G4
Cadbury Heath 39 F5
Cadder 142 A2
Cadderlie 148 C1
Caddington 43 F1
Caddleton 147 G3
Caddonfoot 135 F2
Cade Street 18 B1
Cadeby *Leics.* 67 G2
Cadeby *S.Yorks.* 94 C2
Cadeleigh 10 C2
Cadgwith 3 E5
Cadham 152 A4
Cadishead 92 B3
Cadle 36 C3
Cadley 26 D1
Cadmore End 42 C3
Cadnam 14 C1
Cadney 96 A2
Cadole 77 F1
Cadover Bridge 8 B1
Cadoxton 23 E1
Cadoxton-Juxta-Neath 37 D3
Cae Ddafydd 75 F3
Caeathro 75 E1
Caehopkin 37 E1
Caen 191 F3
Caenby 96 A4
Caenby Corner 95 G4
Caer-Lan 37 E1
Caer Llan 39 D2
Caerau *Bridgend* 37 E3
Caerau *Cardiff* 38 A5
Caerdeon 62 C1
Caerdydd (Cardiff) 38 A5
Caerfarchell 48 A5
Caerfyrddin (Carmarthen) 36 A1
Caergeiliog 88 B5
Caergwrle 78 A2
Caergybi (Holyhead) 88 A4
Caerhun 89 F5
Caerleon 38 C3
Caernarfon 75 D1
Caerphilly 38 A4
Caersws 63 G3
Caerwent 39 D3
Caerwys 90 C5
Caethle Farm 62 C3
Caggan 168 A3
Caio 50 C4
Cairinis 173 G4
Cairisiadar 186 B4
Cairminis 184 C5
Cairnargat 169 G1
Cairnbaan 148 A5
Cairnbeathie 170 A4
Cairnbrogie 171 D2
Cairnbulg 183 F3
Cairncross 145 F3
Cairncurran 141 E3
Cairndoon 115 D3
Cairndow 149 D3
Cairness 183 F3
Cairney Lodge 152 B3
Cairneyhill 143 E1
Cairnhill *Aber.* 171 E2
Cairnhill *Aber.* 170 B1
Cairnie *Aber.* 170 D4
Cairnie *Aber.* 181 G5
Cairnorrie 183 D5
Cairnryan 122 B4
Cairnsmore 123 F4
Caister-on-Sea 87 G4
Caistor 96 B2
Caistor St. Edmund 86 D5
Caistron 128 B1
Cake Street 72 B2
Calanais (Callanish) 186 D4
Calbost 185 G2
Calbourne 14 D4
Calcot 42 B5
Calcott 33 D2
Caldarvan 141 F1
Caldback 203 F2
Caldbeck 117 G3
Caldbergh 109 F4
Caldecote *Cambs.* 58 B2
Caldecote *Cambs.* 69 G4
Caldecote *Herts.* 58 A4
Caldecote *Warks.* 67 F3
Caldecott *Northants.* 57 E1
Caldecott *Rut.* 69 D3
Calder Bridge 106 B2
Calder Mains 194 C3
Calder Vale 100 B3
Calderbank 142 B3
Calderbrook 92 D1
Caldercruix 142 C3
Calderglen 142 A4
Caldermill 142 A5
Caldhame 160 C5
Caldicot 39 D4
Caldwell *Derbys.* 67 E1
Caldwell *N.Yorks.* 110 A1
Caldy 90 D4
Caledrhydiau 50 A2
Calfsound 199 D3
Calgary 154 C4
Califer 180 C4
California *Falk.* 142 D2
California *Norf.* 87 G4
Calke 81 E5
Callakille 176 C4
Callaly 128 C1
Callander 150 B4
Callanish (Calanais) 186 D4
Callerton Lane End 120 A1
Callestick 4 B4
Calliburn 130 C3
Calligarry 164 C4
Callington 7 D4
Callisterhall 126 A3
Callow 53 D4
Callow End 54 A3
Callow Hill *Wilts.* 40 C4
Callow Hill *Worcs.* 65 G5
Callows Grave 53 E1
Calmore 14 C1
Calmsden 40 C2
Calne 40 B5
Calow 94 B5
Calrossie 179 G2
Calshot 15 D2
Calstock 8 A1
Calstone Wellington 26 B1
Calthorpe 86 C2
Calthwaite 118 A3
Calton *N.Yorks.* 101 F2
Calton *Staffs.* 80 C2
Calveley 78 C2
Calver 93 G5
Calver Hill 52 C3
Calverhall 78 D4
Calverleigh 10 C1
Calverley 102 B4
Calvert 56 B5
Calverton *M.K.* 56 C4
Calverton *Notts.* 82 B3
Calvine 158 D3
Calvo 117 E1
Cam 39 G3
Camasnacroise 156 A4
Camastianavaig 164 B1
Camasunary 164 B3
Camault Muir 179 E5
Camb 203 E3
Camber 19 E2
Camberley 29 D1
Camberwell 44 C5
Camblesforth 103 F5
Cambo 128 C3
Cambois 129 F3
Camborne 4 A5
Cambourne 58 B2
Cambridge *Cambs.* 58 C2
Cambridge *Glos.* 39 G2
Cambridge Airport 58 C2
Cambus 151 D5
Cambus o'May 169 G5
Cambusbarron 150 C5
Cambuskenneth 150 D5
Cambuslang 142 A3
Cambusnethan 142 C4
Camden 44 B4
Cameley 24 D2
Camelford 5 F1
Camelon 142 C1
Camelsdale 29 D4
Camer 31 F2
Cameron 141 E1
Camerory 168 C1
Camer's Green 53 G4
Camerton *B. & N.E.Som.* 25 D2
Camerton *Cumb.* 116 D3
Camghouran 158 A4
Camis Eskan 141 E1
Cammachmore 171 E5
Cammeringham 95 G4
Campbeltown 130 C4
Campbeltown (Machrihanish) Airport 130 B3
Camperdown 129 E4
Camphouse 155 E3
Campmuir 152 A1
Camps End 59 E3
Camps Heath 73 G2
Campsall 94 C1
Campsey Ash 61 E2
Campton 57 G4
Camptown 136 A5
Camquhart 140 A1
Camrose 34 C1
Camserney 158 D5
Camstraddan House 149 F5
Camus Croise 164 C3
Camus-luinie 165 F2
Camusnagaul *High.* 156 C2
Camusnagaul *High.* 177 G1
Camusrory 165 E5
Camusteel 176 D5
Camusterrach 176 D5
Camusurich 150 B1
Camusvrachan 158 B5
Canada 14 B1
Candacraig 169 F5
Candlesby 84 C1
Candy Mill 143 E5
Cane End 42 B5
Canewdon 46 B3
Canford Bottom 13 G2
Canford Cliffs 13 G4
Canford Magna 13 G3
Canisbay 195 F1
Cann 25 F5
Cann Common 25 F5
Cannard's Grave 24 D3
Cannich 166 C1
Cannington 23 F4
Cannock 66 B1
Cannock Wood 66 C1
Cannop 39 F1
Canon Bridge 52 D3
Canon Frome 53 F3
Canon Pyon 53 D3
Canonbie 126 B4
Canons Ashby 56 A2
Canon's Town 2 C3
Canterbury *Aber.* 182 A4
Canterbury *Kent* 32 D3
Cantley *Norf.* 87 E5
Cantley *S.Yorks.* 94 D2
Cantlop 65 E2
Canton 38 A5
Cantray 179 G5
Cantraydoune 179 G5
Cantraywood 179 G5
Cantsfield 108 B5
Canvey Island 45 G4
Canwell Hall 66 D2
Canwick 83 E1
Canworthy Water 6 C1
Caol 156 D2
Caolas *Arg. & B.* 154 B2
Caolas *W.Isles* 172 B4
Caolas Scalpaigh (Kyles Scalpay) 185 E4
Caolasnacon 156 D3
Capel *Kent* 31 F4
Capel *Surr.* 29 G3
Capel Bangor 62 C4
Capel Betws Lleucu 50 C2
Capel Carmel 74 A5
Capel Coch 88 C4
Capel Curig 76 A2
Capel Cynon 49 G3
Capel Dewi *Carmar.* 50 A5
Capel Dewi *Cere.* 62 C4
Capel Dewi *Cere.* 50 A3
Capel Garmon 76 B2
Capel Gwyn *Carmar.* 50 A5
Capel Gwyn *I.o.A.* 88 B5
Capel Gwynfe 50 D5
Capel Hendre 36 B1
Capel Isaac 50 B5
Capel Iwan 49 F4
Capel le Ferne 33 E5
Capel Parc 88 C4
Capel St. Andrew 61 E3
Capel St. Mary 60 B4
Capel St. Silin 50 B2
Capel Seion 62 C5
Capel Tygwydd 49 F3
Capel-y-ffin 52 B4
Capeluchaf 74 D3
Capelulo 89 F5
Capenhurst 91 E5
Capernwray 107 G5
Capheaton 128 C3
Caplaw 141 F4
Cappercleuch 134 D3
Capplegill 134 C5
Capstone 31 G2
Capton 9 E2
Caputh 159 F5
Car Colston 82 C3
Carbellow 133 E3
Carbeth 141 G2
Carbis Bay 2 C3
Carbost *High.* 176 A5
Carbost *High.* 163 G1
Carbrain 142 B2
Carbrooke 86 A5
Carburton 94 D5
Carcary 161 E4
Carclew 3 E3
Carco 133 F4
Carcroft 94 C2
Cardenden 152 A5
Cardeston 64 C1
Cardiff (Caerdydd) 38 A5
Cardiff International Airport 23 D1
Cardigan (Aberteifi) 49 E3
Cardington *Beds.* 57 F3
Cardington *Shrop.* 65 E3
Cardinham 5 F3
Cardno 183 E3
Cardoness 123 G5
Cardow 181 D5
Cardrona 135 D2
Cardross 141 E2
Cardurnock 117 E1
Careby 69 F1
Careston 160 D3
Carew 34 D2
Carew Cheriton 34 D2
Carew Newton 34 D2
Carey 53 E4
Carfrae 144 C3
Carfraemill 144 C4
Cargen 125 D3
Cargenbridge 125 D3
Cargill 151 G1
Cargo 117 G1
Cargo Fleet 121 E5
Cargreen 8 A1
Carham 136 B3
Carhampton 22 D3
Carharrack 4 B5
Carie *P. & K.* 158 B4
Carie *P. & K.* 150 B1
Carines 4 B4
Carisbrooke 15 D4
Cark 107 E5
Carkeel 8 A1
Carlabhagh (Carloway) 186 D3
Carland Cross 4 C4
Carlby 69 F1
Carlecotes 93 F2
Carleton *Cumb.* 118 A2
Carleton *Lancs.* 99 G3
Carleton *N.Yorks.* 101 F3
Carleton *W.Yorks.* 103 D5
Carleton Fishery 122 C2
Carleton Forehoe 86 B5
Carleton Rode 72 C2
Carlin How 111 G1
Carlingcott 25 D2
Carlisle 118 A2
Carlops 143 F4
Carloway (Carlabhagh) 186 D3
Carlton *Beds.* 57 E2
Carlton *Cambs.* 59 E2
Carlton *Leics.* 67 F2
Carlton *N.Yorks.* 103 F5
Carlton *N.Yorks.* 109 F4
Carlton *N.Yorks.* 111 F4
Carlton *Notts.* 82 B3
Carlton *S.Yorks.* 94 A2
Carlton *Stock.* 120 C5
Carlton *Suff.* 61 E1
Carlton *W.Yorks.* 102 C5
Carlton Colville 73 G2
Carlton Curlieu 68 B3
Carlton Husthwaite 111 D5
Carlton-in-Cleveland 111 E2
Carlton in Lindrick 94 C4
Carlton-le-Moorland 83 E2
Carlton Miniott 110 C4
Carlton-on-Trent 82 D1
Carlton Scroop 83 E3
Carluke 142 C4
Carlyon Bay 5 E4
Carmacoup 133 F3
Carmarthen (Caerfyrddin) 36 A1
Carmel *Carmar.* 36 B1
Carmel *Flints.* 90 C5
Carmel *Gwyn.* 75 D2
Carmel *I.o.A.* 88 B4
Carmont 161 G1
Carmore 190 C5
Carmunnock 142 A4
Carmyle 142 A3
Carmyllie 160 D5
Carn 138 A4
Carn Brea 4 A5
Carn Dearg 177 D2
Carnaby 104 D1
Carnach *High.* 165 G2
Carnach *High.* 188 C5
Carnassarie 148 A4
Carnbee 152 D4
Carnbo 151 F4
Carnduncan 138 A3
Carne 3 G3
Carnforth 107 F5
Carnhell Green 2 D3
Carnichal 183 E4
Carnmore 138 B5
Carno 63 F3
Carnoch *High.* 166 C1
Carnoch *High.* 178 B4
Carnoch *High.* 180 A5
Carnock 143 E1
Carnon Downs 4 B5
Carnousie 182 B4
Carnoustie 153 D1
Carnwath 143 D5
Carnyorth 2 A3
Carperby 109 F3
Carr Shield 119 E3
Carr Vale 94 B5
Carradale 130 D2
Carragrich 185 D4
Carrbridge 168 B2
Carrefour Selous 8 C5
Carreg-lefn 88 B4
Carrick *Arg. & B.* 149 D5
Carrick *Arg. & B.* 140 A1
Carrick *Fife* 152 C2
Carriden 143 E1
Carrine 130 B5
Carrington *Gt.Man.* 92 B3
Carrington *Lincs.* 84 B2
Carrington *Midloth.* 144 A3
Carroch 124 A1
Carrog 77 E3
Carroglen 150 C2
Carrol 191 D4
Carron *Arg. & B.* 148 B5
Carron *Falk.* 142 C1
Carron *Moray* 181 E5
Carron Bridge 142 B1
Carronbridge 124 C1
Carronshore 142 C1
Carrot 160 C5
Carrutherstown 125 F3
Carruthmuir 141 E3
Carrville 120 C3
Carry 140 A3
Carsaig 147 E2
Carscreugh 122 D4
Carse 139 F3
Carse of Ardesier 180 A4
Carsegowan 123 F5
Carseriggan 123 E4
Carsethorn 125 D5
Carsgoe 194 D2
Carshalton 30 B2
Carsington 81 D2
Carsluith 123 F5
Carsphairn 123 G1
Carstairs 142 D5
Carstairs Junction 143 D5
Carswell Marsh 41 F3
Carter's Clay 27 E5
Carterton 41 E2
Carterway Heads 119 G2
Carthew 5 E4
Carthorpe 110 C4
Cartington 128 C1
Cartmel 107 E5
Cartmel Fell 107 F4
Carway 36 A2
Cascob 52 B1
Cashel Farm 149 G5
Cashlie 157 G5
Cashmoor 13 F1
Casnewydd (Newport) *Newport* 38 C4
Cassencarie 123 F5
Cassington 41 G1
Cassop 120 C4
Castell Gorfod 49 F5
Castell Howell 50 A3
Castell-Nedd (Neath) 37 D3
Castell Newydd Emlyn (Newcastle Emlyn) 49 G3
Castell-y-bwch 38 B3
Castellau 37 G4
Casterton 108 B5
Castle Acre 71 G1
Castle Ashby 57 D2
Castle Bank 79 G5
Castle Bolton 109 F3
Castle Bromwich 66 D4
Castle Bytham 69 E1
Castle Caereinion 64 A2
Castle Camps 59 E3
Castle Carrock 118 B2
Castle Cary 24 D4
Castle Combe 40 A5
Castle Donington 81 F5
Castle Douglas 124 B4
Castle Eaton 40 D3
Castle Eden 120 D4
Castle End 67 E5
Castle Frome 53 F3
Castle Gresley 67 E1
Castle Heaton 145 G5
Castle Hedingham 59 F4
Castle Hill 60 C3
Castle Kennedy 122 C5
Castle Leod 179 D4
Castle Levan 140 D2
Castle Madoc 51 G4
Castle Morris 48 C4
Castle O'er 126 A2
Castle Rising 85 E5
Castle Stuart 179 G4
Castlebay (Bagh a' Chaisteil) 172 B4
Castlebythe 48 D5
Castlecary 142 B2
Castlecraig *High.* 180 A3
Castlecraig *Sc.Bord.* 143 F5
Castlefairn 124 B2
Castleford 102 D5
Castlemartin 34 C3
Castlemilk *D. & G.* 125 F3
Castlemilk *Glas.* 142 A4
Castlemorton 53 G4
Castleside 119 G3
Castlethorpe 56 D3
Castleton *Aber.* 182 C4
Castleton *Angus* 160 B5
Castleton *Arg. & B.* 139 G1
Castleton *Derbys.* 93 F4
Castleton *Gt.Man.* 92 C1
Castleton *N.Yorks.* 111 F2
Castleton *Newport* 38 B4
Castleton *Sc.Bord.* 126 D2
Castletown *High.* 195 D2
Castletown *High.* 179 G5
Castletown *I.o.M.* 98 A5
Castletown *T. & W.* 120 C2
Castleweary 135 F5
Castlewigg 115 E2
Caston 72 A2
Castor 69 G3
Castramont 123 G4
Cat and Fiddle Inn 93 E5
Catbrain 39 E4
Catchall 2 B4
Catcleugh 127 F1
Catcliffe 94 B4
Catcott 24 A4
Caterham 30 C3
Catesby 56 A2
Catfield 87 E3
Catfirth 200 D2
Catford 44 C5
Catforth 100 A4
Cathedine 52 A5
Catherington 15 F1
Catherton 65 F5
Catlow 101 E4
Catlowdy 126 C4
Catmore 41 G5
Caton *Devon* 10 A5
Caton *Lancs.* 100 B1
Cator Court 7 G3
Catrine 132 D3
Catsfield 18 C2
Catshill 66 B5
Cattadale 138 B4
Cattal 102 D2
Cattawade 60 C4
Catterall 100 B3
Catterick 110 B3
Catterick Camp 110 A3
Catterlen 118 A4
Catterline 161 G2
Catterton 103 E3
Catthorpe 68 A5
Cattistock 12 B2
Catton *N.Yorks.* 110 C5
Catton *Norf.* 86 D4
Catton *Northumb.* 119 E2
Catton Hall 67 E1
Catwick 104 D3
Catworth 69 F5
Caudworthy 6 C1
Caulcott 56 A5
Cauldcots 161 E5
Cauldhame *Stir.* 150 B5
Cauldhame *Stir.* 150 D4
Cauldon 80 B3
Caulkerbush 124 D5
Caulside 126 C3
Caundle Marsh 12 C1
Caunsall 66 A4
Caunton 82 C1
Causeway End *D. & G.* 123 F4
Causeway End *Essex* 45 F1
Causewayhead *Cumb.* 117 E1
Causewayhead *Stir.* 150 D5
Causey Park 129 D2
Causeyend 171 E3
Cautley 108 B3
Cavendish 59 G3
Cavenham 59 F1
Cavens 125 D5
Caversfield 56 A5
Caversham 42 C5
Caverswall 79 G3
Cawdor 180 A4
Cawkwell 96 C5
Cawood 103 E4
Cawsand 8 A2
Cawston 86 C3
Cawthorne 93 G2
Cawthorpe 83 F5
Cawton 111 F5
Caxton 58 B2
Caxton Gibbet 58 A2
Caynham 65 E5
Caythorpe *Lincs.* 83 E3
Caythorpe *Notts.* 82 B3
Cayton 113 D4
Ceallan 173 G4
Ceann a' Bhàigh *W.Isles* 173 F3
Ceann a' Bhàigh *W.Isles* 184 C5
Ceann Loch Shiphoirt 185 E2
Cearsiadar 187 E5
Ceathramh Meadhanach 173 F2
Cedig 76 C5
Cefn-brith 76 C2
Cefn Bycharn (Newbridge) 38 B3
Cefn-caer-Ferch 74 D3
Cefn Cantref 51 G5
Cefn Coch 77 E2
Cefn-coch 77 E5
Cefn-coed-y-cymmer 37 G2
Cefn Cribwr 37 E4
Cefn Cross 37 E4
Cefn-ddwysarn 76 C4
Cefn Einion 64 B4
Cefn-gorwydd 51 F3
Cefn-gwyn 64 A4
Cefn Hengoed 38 A3
Cefn-mawr 77 F3
Cefn-y-bedd 78 A2
Cefn-y-pant 49 E5
Cefndeuddwr 76 A5
Cefneithin 36 B1
Cegidfa (Guilsfield) 64 B1
Ceidio 88 C4
Ceidio Fawr 74 B4
Ceinewydd (New Quay) 49 G2
Ceint 88 C5
Cellan 50 C3
Cellardyke 153 D4
Cellarhead 79 G3
Cemaes 88 B3
Cemmaes 63 E2
Cemmaes Road (Glantwymyn) 63 E2
Cenarth 49 F3
Cennin 75 D3
Ceos 187 E5
Ceres 152 B3
Cerne Abbas 12 C2
Cerney Wick 40 C3
Cerrigceinwen 88 C5
Cerrigydrudion 76 C3
Cessford 136 B4
Chaceley 54 A4
Chacewater 4 B5
Chackmore 56 B4
Chacombe 55 G3
Chad Valley 66 C4
Chadderton 92 D2
Chaddesden 81 E4
Chaddesley Corbett 66 A5
Chaddleworth 41 G5
Chadlington 55 F5
Chadshunt 55 F2
Chadwell 82 C5
Chadwell St. Mary 45 F5
Chadwick End 67 E5
Chaffcombe 11 G1
Chagford 10 A4
Chailey 17 F2
Chainhurst 31 G4
Chalbury Common 13 G2
Chaldon 30 C3
Chaldon Herring or East Chaldon 13 D4
Chale 15 D5
Chale Green 15 D5
Chalfont Common 43 F3
Chalfont St. Giles 43 E3
Chalfont St. Peter 43 F3
Chalford 40 A2
Chalgrove 42 B3
Chalk 45 F5
Challacombe 21 G1
Challoch 123 E4
Challock 32 C3
Chalmington 12 B2
Chalton *Beds.* 57 F5
Chalton *Hants.* 15 G1
Chalvington 18 A3
Champany 143 E2
Chandler's Cross 43 F3
Chandler's Ford 27 F5
Channerwick 200 D5
Chantry *Som.* 25 E3
Chantry *Suff.* 60 C3
Chapel 152 A5
Chapel Allerton *Som.* 24 B2
Chapel Allerton *W.Yorks.* 102 C4
Chapel Amble 5 D2
Chapel Brampton 56 C1
Chapel Chorlton 79 F4
Chapel Cross 18 B1
Chapel-en-le-Frith 93 E4
Chapel End 67 F3
Chapel Fields 67 F5
Chapel Haddlesey 103 E5
Chapel Hill *Aber.* 171 F1
Chapel Hill *Lincs.* 84 A2
Chapel Hill *Mon.* 39 E2
Chapel Lawn 64 C5
Chapel-le-Dale 108 C5
Chapel of Garioch 170 C2
Chapel Rossan 114 B2
Chapel Row 27 G1
Chapel St. Leonards 97 F5
Chapel Stile 107 E2
Chapel Town 4 C4
Chapelbank 151 F3
Chapeldonan 131 G5
Chapelgate 84 C5
Chapelhall 142 B3
Chapelhill *High.* 180 A2
Chapelhill *P. & K.* 152 A2
Chapelhill *P. & K.* 151 F1
Chapelknowe 126 B4
Chapelton *Aber.* 161 G1
Chapelton *Angus* 161 E5
Chapelton *S.Lan.* 142 A5
Chapeltown *B'burn.* 92 B1
Chapeltown *Cumb.* 126 C4
Chapeltown *Moray* 169 E2

Chapeltown S.Yorks. 94 A3
Chapmans Well 7 D1
Chapmanslade 25 F3
Chapmore End 44 C1
Chappel 59 G5
Chard 11 G2
Chard Junction 11 G2
Chardstock 11 G2
Charfield 39 G3
Charing 32 B4
Charing Heath 32 B4
Charingworth 55 D3
Charlbury 41 F1
Charlcombe 25 E1
Charlcutt 40 B5
Charlecote 55 E2
Charles 21 G2
Charles Tye 60 B2
Charlesfield 135 G3
Charleshill 29 D3
Charleston 160 B5
Charlestown Aber. 183 F3
Charlestown Aberdeen 171 E4
Charlestown Cornw. 5 E4
Charlestown Dorset 12 C5
Charlestown Fife 143 E1
Charlestown High. 177 E2
Charlestown High. 179 F5
Charlestown of Aberlour (Aberlour) 181 E5
Charlesworth 93 E3
Charleton 152 C4
Charlinch 23 F4
Charlton Gt.Lon. 44 D5
Charlton Hants. 27 E3
Charlton Herts. 57 G5
Charlton Northants. 56 A4
Charlton Northumb. 128 A3
Charlton Oxon. 41 G4
Charlton Som. 25 D2
Charlton W.Suss. 16 A2
Charlton Wilts. 26 A5
Charlton Wilts. 40 B4
Charlton Wilts. 26 C2
Charlton Worcs. 54 C3
Charlton Abbots 54 C5
Charlton Adam 24 C5
Charlton-All-Saints 26 C5
Charlton Horethorne 25 D5
Charlton Kings 54 B5
Charlton Mackrell 24 C5
Charlton Marshall 13 E2
Charlton Musgrove 25 E5
Charlton-on-Otmoor 42 A1
Charlwood 30 B4
Charminster 12 C3
Charmouth 11 G3
Charndon 56 B5
Charney Bassett 41 F3
Charnock Richard 91 G1
Charsfield 61 D2
Chart Corner 31 G4
Chart Sutton 32 A4
Charter Alley 28 B2
Charterhouse 24 B2
Charterville Allotments 41 F1
Chartham 32 D3
Chartham Hatch 32 C3
Chartridge 43 E2
Charwelton 56 A2
Chase End Street 53 G4
Chase Terrace 66 C1
Chasetown 66 C2
Chastleton 55 E5
Chasty 20 D5
Chatburn 101 D3
Chatcull 79 E4
Chatham 31 G2
Chathill 137 F4
Chattenden 45 G5
Chatteris 70 B4
Chattisham 60 B3
Chatto 136 B5
Chatton 137 E4
Chawleigh 10 A1
Chawley 41 G2
Chawston 57 G2
Chawton 28 C4
Cheadle Gt.Man. 92 C4
Cheadle Staffs. 80 B3
Cheadle Hulme 92 C4
Cheam 30 B2
Cheapside 29 E1
Chearsley 42 C2
Chebsey 79 F5
Checkendon 42 B4
Checkley Ches. 79 E3
Checkley Here. 53 E4
Checkley Staffs. 80 B4
Chedburgh 59 F2
Cheddar 24 B2
Cheddington 43 E1
Cheddleton 79 G2
Cheddon Fitzpaine 23 F5
Chedglow 40 B3
Chedgrave 73 E2
Chedington 12 A2
Chediston 73 E4
Chedworth 40 C1
Chedzoy 24 A4
Cheeklaw 145 E4
Cheesden 92 C1
Cheeseman's Green 32 C5
Cheetham Hill 92 C2
Cheldon 10 A1
Chelford 92 C5
Chellaston 81 E4
Chelmarsh 65 G4
Chelmondiston 60 D4
Chelmorton 80 C1
Chelmsford 45 G2
Chelsfield 31 D2
Chelsham 30 C3
Chelsworth 60 A3
Cheltenham 54 B5
Chelveston 57 E1
Chelvey 24 B1
Chelwood 24 D1
Chelwood Gate 17 G1
Chelworth 40 B3
Cheney Longville 64 D4
Chenies 43 F3
Chepstow 39 E3
Cherhill 40 C5
Cherington Glos. 40 B3
Cherington Warks. 55 E4
Cheriton Devon 22 A3
Cheriton Hants. 27 G5
Cheriton Kent 33 E5
Cheriton Pembs. 34 C3
Cheriton Swan. 36 A3
Cheriton Bishop 10 A3
Cheriton Cross 10 A3
Cheriton Fitzpaine 10 B2
Cherrington 65 F1
Cherry Burton 104 B3
Cherry Hinton 58 C2
Cherry Willingham 96 A5
Chertsey 29 F1
Cheselbourne 13 D3
Chesham 43 E2
Chesham Bois 43 E3
Cheshunt 44 C2
Cheslyn Hay 66 B2
Chessington 29 G1
Chester 78 B1
Chester-le-Street 120 B2
Chesterblade 25 D3
Chesterfield Derbys. 94 A5
Chesterfield Staffs. 66 D2
Chesters Sc.Bord. 136 A5
Chesters Sc.Bord. 136 A4
Chesterton Cambs. 58 C2
Chesterton Cambs. 69 G3
Chesterton Oxon. 56 A5
Chesterton Shrop. 65 G3
Chesterton Staffs. 79 F3
Chesterton Green 55 F2
Chestfield 32 D2
Cheswardine 79 E5
Cheswick 137 E2
Chetnole 12 C2
Chettiscombe 10 C1
Chettisham 70 D4
Chettle 13 F1
Chetton 65 F3
Chetwode 56 B5
Chetwynd Aston 65 G1
Cheveley 59 E1
Chevening 31 D3
Cheverell's Green 43 F1
Chevington 59 F2
Chevington Drift 129 E2
Chevithorne 10 C1
Chew Magna 24 C1
Chew Stoke 24 C1
Chewton Keynsham 24 D1
Chewton Mendip 24 C2
Chicheley 57 E3
Chichester 16 A3
Chickerell 12 C4
Chickering 72 D4
Chicklade 26 A4
Chickney 59 D5
Chicksands 57 G4
Chidden 15 F1
Chiddingfold 29 E4
Chiddingly 18 A2
Chiddingstone 31 D4
Chiddingstone Causeway 31 E4
Chiddingstone Hoath 31 D4
Chideock 12 A3
Chidham 15 G2
Chieveley 41 G5
Chignall St. James 45 F2
Chignall Smealy 45 F1
Chigwell 44 D3
Chigwell Row 45 D3
Chilbolton 27 E3
Chilcomb 27 G5
Chilcombe 12 B3
Chilcompton 24 D2
Chilcote 67 E1
Child Okeford 13 E1
Childer Thornton 91 E5
Childerditch 45 F4
Childrey 41 F4
Child's Ercall 79 D5
Childswickham 54 C4
Childwall 91 F4
Childwick Green 44 A1
Chilfrome 12 B3
Chilgrove 16 A2
Chilham 32 C3
Chillaton 7 E2
Chillenden 33 E3
Chillerton 15 D4
Chillesford 61 E2
Chillingham 137 E4
Chillington Devon 9 D3
Chillington Som. 11 G1
Chilmark 26 A4
Chilson 41 F1
Chilsworthy Cornw. 7 E3
Chilsworthy Devon 20 D5
Chilthorne Domer 12 B1
Chilton Bucks. 42 B1
Chilton Dur. 120 B4
Chilton Oxon. 41 G4
Chilton Candover 27 G4
Chilton Cantelo 24 C5
Chilton Foliat 41 F5
Chilton Polden 24 A4
Chilton Street 59 F3
Chilton Trinity 23 F4
Chilvers Coton 67 F3
Chilworth Hants. 14 D1
Chilworth Surr. 29 F3
Chimney 41 F2
Chineham 28 B2
Chingford 44 C3
Chinley 93 E4
Chinley Head 93 E4
Chinnor 42 C2
Chipchase Castle 128 A4
Chipley Park 23 E5
Chipnall 79 E4
Chippenham Cambs. 59 E1
Chippenham Wilts. 40 B5
Chipperfield 43 F2
Chipping Herts. 58 B4
Chipping Lancs. 100 C3
Chipping Campden 55 D4
Chipping Hill 46 B1
Chipping Norton 55 F5
Chipping Ongar 45 E2
Chipping Sodbury 39 G4
Chipping Warden 55 G3
Chipstable 22 D5
Chipstead Kent 31 D3
Chipstead Surr. 30 B3
Chirbury 64 B3
Chirk 77 F4
Chirmorrie 122 D3
Chirnside 145 F4
Chirnsidebridge 145 F4
Chirton 26 B2
Chisbury 27 D1
Chiscan 130 B4
Chiselborough 12 A1
Chiseldon 41 D4
Chislehampton 42 A3
Chislehurst 44 D5
Chislet 33 E2
Chiswell Green 44 A2
Chiswick 44 B5
Chisworth 93 D3
Chithurst 28 D5
Chittering 58 C1
Chitterne 26 A3
Chittlehamholt 21 G3
Chittlehampton 21 G3
Chittoe 26 A1
Chivelstone 9 D4
Chobham 29 E1
Choicelee 145 E4
Cholderton 26 D3
Cholesbury 43 E2
Chollerford 128 B4
Chollerton 128 B4
Cholsey 42 A4
Cholstrey 53 D2
Cholwell B. & N.E.Som. 24 D2
Cholwell Devon 7 E3
Chop Gate 111 E2
Chopwell 120 A2
Chorley Ches. 78 C2
Chorley Lancs. 91 G1
Chorley Shrop. 65 F4
Chorley Staffs. 66 C1
Chorleywood 43 F3
Chorlton 79 E2
Chorlton-cum-Hardy 92 C3
Chorlton Lane 78 B3
Chowley 78 B2
Chrishall 58 C4
Chrishall Grange 58 C3
Chrisswell 140 D2
Christchurch Cambs. 70 C3
Christchurch Dorset 14 A3
Christchurch Glos. 39 E1
Christchurch Newport 38 C4
Christian Malford 40 B5
Christleton 78 B1
Christmas Common 42 C3
Christon 24 A2
Christon Bank 137 G4
Christow 10 B4
Chryston 142 A2
Chudleigh 10 B5
Chudleigh Knighton 10 B5
Chulmleigh 21 G4
Chunal 93 E3
Church 100 D5
Church Aston 65 G1
Church Brampton 56 C1
Church Broughton 80 D4
Church Common 61 E2
Church Crookham 28 D2
Church Eaton 66 A1
Church End Beds. 57 G4
Church End Beds. 57 E5
Church End Beds. 57 G2
Church End Cambs. 70 B2
Church End Cambs. 58 C2
Church End Cambs. 70 B5
Church End E.Riding 104 C2
Church End Essex 59 D3
Church End Essex 59 F5
Church End Hants. 28 B2
Church End Herts. 44 A1
Church End Lincs. 84 A4
Church End Lincs. 97 E3
Church End Warks. 67 E3
Church End Wilts. 40 C5
Church Enstone 55 F5
Church Fenton 103 E4
Church Green 11 E3
Church Gresley 67 E1
Church Hanborough 41 G1
Church Houses 111 F3
Church Knowle 13 F4
Church Langley 45 D2
Church Langton 68 C3
Church Lawford 67 G5
Church Lawton 79 F2
Church Leigh 80 B4
Church Lench 54 C2
Church Minshull 79 D1
Church Norton 16 A4
Church Preen 65 E3
Church Pulverbatch 64 D2
Church Stoke 64 B3
Church Stowe 56 B2
Church Street 45 G5
Church Stretton 65 D3
Church Village 37 G4
Church Warsop 81 G1
Churcham 39 G1
Churchdown 54 A5
Churchend Essex 46 D3
Churchend Essex 59 E5
Churchend S.Glos. 39 G3
Churchgate 44 C2
Churchgate Street 45 D1
Churchill N.Som. 24 B2
Churchill Oxon. 55 E5
Churchill Worcs. 54 B2
Churchill Worcs. 66 A5
Churchingford 11 F1
Churchover 68 A4
Churchstanton 11 E1
Churchstow 8 D3
Churchthorpe 96 D3
Churchtown Devon 21 G1
Churchtown I.o.M. 98 C2
Churchtown Lancs. 100 A3
Churchtown Mersey. 91 E1
Churnsike Lodge 127 E4
Churston Ferrers 9 F2
Churt 29 D4
Churton 78 B2
Churwell 102 B5
Chute Cadley 27 E2
Chute Standen 27 E2
Chwilog 74 D4
Chwitffordd (Whitford) 90 C5
Chyandour 2 B3
Cilan Uchaf 74 C5
Cilcain 77 E1
Cilcennin 50 B1
Cilfrew 37 D2
Cilfynydd 37 G3
Cilgerran 49 E3
Cilgwyn Carmar. 50 D5
Cilgwyn Pembs. 49 D4
Ciliau-Aeron 50 B2
Cille Bhrighde 172 C2
Cille Pheadair 172 C2
Cilmery 51 G2
Cilrhedyn 49 F4
Cilrhedyn Bridge 48 D4
Ciltalgarth 76 B3
Cilwendeg 49 F4
Cilybebyll 36 D2
Cilycwm 51 D3
Cinderford 39 F1
Cippyn 49 E3
Cirbhig 186 C3
Cirencester 40 C2
City Dulas 88 C4
City of London 44 C5
City of Westminster 44 B4
Clabhach 154 A4
Clachaig 140 C1
Clachan Arg. & B. 149 D3
Clachan Arg. & B. 156 A5
Clachan Arg. & B. 139 F4
Clachan High. 164 B1
Clachan W.Isles 173 F5
Clachan of Campsie 142 A2
Clachan of Glendaruel 140 B1
Clachan-Seil 147 G3
Clachan Strachur 148 D4
Clachandhu 147 D1
Clachaneasy 123 E3
Clachanmore 114 A2
Clachanturn 169 E5
Clachbreck 139 F2
Clachnabrain 160 B3
Clachnaharry 179 F5
Clachtoll 188 C2
Clackmannan 151 E5
Clacton-on-Sea 47 E1
Cladach a' Chaolais 173 F3
Cladach Chircebost 173 F3
Cladich 148 C2
Claggan High. 156 D2
Claggan High. 155 G5
Claigan 175 F4
Claines 54 A2
Clandown 25 D2
Clanfield Hants. 15 G1
Clanfield Oxon. 41 E2
Clannaborough Barton 10 A2
Clanville 27 E3
Claonaig 139 G4
Claonairigh 148 C4
Claonel 190 A4
Clap Gate 102 C3
Clapgate 13 G2
Clapham Beds. 57 F2
Clapham Gt.Lon. 44 B5
Clapham N.Yorks. 100 D1
Clapham W.Suss. 16 C3
Clapham Hill 32 D2
Clappers 145 G4
Clappersgate 107 E2
Clapton 12 A2
Clapton-in-Gordano 39 D5
Clapton-on-the-Hill 41 D1
Clapworthy 21 G3
Clarach 62 C4
Clarbeston 49 D5
Clarbeston Road 48 D5
Clarborough 95 E4
Clardon 194 D2
Clare 59 F3
Clarebrand 124 B4
Clarencefield 125 E4
Clareton 102 C2
Clarilaw 135 G4
Clarkston 141 G4
Clashban 190 B5
Clashcoig 190 B5
Clashgour 157 E5
Clashindarroch 169 G1
Clashmore 190 C5
Clashnessie 188 C1
Clashnoir 169 E2
Clathy 151 E2
Clatt 170 A2
Clatter 63 F3
Clatterford End 45 E2
Clatterin Brig 161 E2
Clatteringshaws 123 G3
Clatworthy 23 D4
Claughton Lancs. 100 B1
Claughton Lancs. 100 B3
Claverdon 55 D1
Claverham 24 B1
Clavering 58 C4
Claverley 65 G3
Claverton 25 E1
Clawdd-newydd 77 D2
Clawfin 132 D5
Clawthorpe 107 G5
Clawton 7 D1
Claxby Lincs. 97 E5
Claxby Lincs. 96 B3
Claxby Pluckacre 84 B1
Claxton N.Yorks. 103 F1
Claxton Norf. 87 E5
Clay Common 73 F3
Clay Coton 68 A5
Clay Cross 81 E1
Clay of Allan 180 A2
Claybrooke Magna 67 G4
Claybrooke Parva 67 G4
Claydene 31 D4
Claydon Oxon. 55 G2
Claydon Suff. 60 C3
Claygate Kent 31 G4
Claygate Surr. 29 G1
Claygate Cross 31 F3
Clayhanger Devon 22 D5
Clayhanger W.Mid. 66 C2
Clayhidon 11 E1
Claylock 195 D3
Claypole 82 D3
Claythorpe 97 E5
Clayton S.Yorks. 94 B2
Clayton Staffs. 79 F3
Clayton W.Suss. 17 E2
Clayton W.Yorks. 102 A4
Clayton-le-Moors 100 D4
Clayton-le-Woods 100 B5
Clayton West 93 G1
Clayworth 95 E4
Cleadale 155 D1
Cleadon 120 C1
Clearbrook 8 B1
Clearwell 39 E2
Cleasby 110 B1
Cleat 197 D4
Cleatlam 110 A1
Cleatop 101 E1
Cleator 116 D5
Cleator Moor 116 D5
Cleckheaton 102 A5
Clee St. Margaret 65 E4
Cleedownton 65 E4
Cleehill 65 E5
Cleethorpes 96 D2
Cleeton St. Mary 65 F5
Cleeve N.Som. 24 B1
Cleeve Oxon. 42 B4
Cleeve Hill 54 B5
Cleeve Prior 54 C3
Cleghorn 142 D5
Clehonger 52 D4
Cleigh 148 A2
Cleish 151 F5
Cleland 142 B4
Clench Common 26 C1
Clenchwarton 85 D5
Clent 66 B5
Cleobury Mortimer 65 F5
Cleobury North 65 F4
Clephanton 180 A4
Clerklands 135 G3
Clestrain 196 C2
Cleuch Head 135 G4
Cleughbrae 125 E3
Clevancy 40 C5
Clevedon 38 D5
Cleveland Tontine 110 D3
Cleveleys 99 G3
Clevelode 54 A3
Cleverton 40 B4
Clewer 24 B2
Clewer Village 43 E5
Cley next the Sea 86 B1
Cliburn 118 B5
Cliddesden 28 B3
Cliff Carmar. 35 G2
Cliff High. 155 F3
Cliff End 19 D2
Cliffe Med. 45 G5
Cliffe N.Yorks. 103 F4
Cliffe Woods 45 G5
Clifford Here. 52 B3
Clifford W.Yorks. 102 D3
Clifford Chambers 55 D2
Clifford's Mesne 53 G5
Cliffs End 33 F2
Clifton Beds. 57 G4
Clifton Bristol 39 E5
Clifton Cumb. 118 B5
Clifton Derbys. 80 C3
Clifton Lancs. 100 A4
Clifton Northumb. 129 E3
Clifton Nott. 81 G4
Clifton Oxon. 55 G4
Clifton Stir. 149 F1
Clifton Worcs. 54 A3
Clifton Campville 67 E1
Clifton Hampden 42 A3
Clifton Reynes 57 E2
Clifton upon Dunsmore 68 A5
Clifton upon Teme 53 G1
Cliftonville 33 F1
Climping 16 C3
Climpy 142 D4
Clint 102 B2
Clint Green 86 B4
Clinterty 170 D3
Clintmains 136 A3
Clippesby 87 F4
Clipsham 69 E1
Clipston Northants. 68 C4
Clipston Notts. 82 B4
Clipstone 81 G1
Clitheroe 100 D3
Clive 78 C5
Clivocast 203 F2
Clocaenog 77 D2
Clochan 181 G3
Clochtow 171 F1
Clock Face 91 G3
Clockhill 183 D5
Cloddach 181 D4
Clodock 52 C5
Cloford 25 E3
Cloichran 150 B1
Clola 183 F5
Clonrae 124 C1
Clophill 57 F4
Clopton 69 F5
Clopton Green 59 F2
Close Clark 98 A4
Closeburn 124 C1
Closworth 12 B1
Clothall 58 A4
Clothan 203 D4
Clotton 78 C1
Clough Cumb. 108 C3
Clough Gt.Man. 92 D1
Clough Foot 101 F5
Cloughton 112 D3
Cloughton Newlands 112 D3
Clounlaid 155 G4
Clousta 200 C2
Clouston 198 B5
Clova Aber. 169 G2
Clova Angus 160 B2
Clove Lodge 109 E1
Clovelly 20 D3
Clovelly Cross 20 D3
Clovenfords 135 F2
Clovenstone 170 C3
Cloverhill 171 E3
Cloves 180 D3
Clovullin 156 C3
Clowne 94 B5
Clows Top 65 G5
Cloyntie 132 B5
Cluanach 138 B4
Clubworthy 6 C1
Cluer 184 D4
Clun 64 B4
Clunas 180 A5
Clunbury 64 C4
Clune High. 167 G2
Clune Moray 182 A3
Clunes 157 D1
Clungunford 64 C5
Clunie Aber. 182 B4
Clunie P. & K. 159 G5
Clunton 64 C4
Cluny 152 A5
Clutton B. & N.E.Som. 24 D2
Clutton Ches. 78 B2
Clwt-y-bont 75 E1
Clydach Mon. 38 B1
Clydach Swan. 36 C2
Clydach Vale 37 F3
Clydebank 141 G3
Clydey 49 F4
Clyffe Pypard 40 C5
Clynder 140 D1
Clynderwen 35 E1
Clynelish 191 D4
Clynfyw 49 F4
Clynnog-fawr 74 D3
Clyro 52 B3
Clyst Honiton 10 C3
Clyst Hydon 10 D2
Clyst St. George 10 C4
Clyst St. Lawrence 10 D2
Clyst St. Mary 10 C3
Cnewr 51 E5
Cnoc 187 F4
Cnwch Coch 62 C5
Coachford 181 G5
Coad's Green 5 G2
Coal Aston 94 A5
Coalbrookdale 65 F2
Coalbrookvale 38 A2
Coalburn 133 G2
Coalburns 120 A1
Coalcleugh 119 E3
Coaley 39 G2
Coalpit Heath 39 F4
Coalpit Hill 79 F2
Coalport 65 G2
Coalsnaughton 151 E5
Coaltown of Balgonie 152 B5
Coaltown of Wemyss 152 B5
Coalville 67 G1
Coast 188 B5
Coat 24 B5
Coatbridge 142 B3
Coate Swin. 41 D4
Coate Wilts. 26 B1
Coates Cambs. 70 B3
Coates Glos. 40 B2
Coates Lincs. 95 G4
Coates W.Suss. 16 B2
Coatham 121 E5
Coatham Mundeville 120 B5
Cobairdy 182 A5
Cobbaton 21 G3
Coberley 40 B1
Cobham Kent 31 F2
Cobham Surr. 29 G2
Cobleland 150 A5
Cobler's Green 45 F1
Cobnash 52 D1
Coburty 183 E3
Cochno 141 F2
Cock Alley 81 F1
Cock Bridge 169 E4
Cock Clarks 46 B2
Cockayne 111 F3
Cockayne Hatley 58 A3
Cockburnspath 145 E2
Cockenzie and Port Seton 144 B2
Cockerham 100 A2
Cockermouth 117 E3
Cockernhoe 57 G5
Cockett 36 C3
Cockfield Dur. 120 A5
Cockfield Suff. 60 A2
Cockfosters 44 B3
Cocking 16 A2
Cockington 9 E1
Cocklake 24 B3
Cockley Beck 107 D2
Cockley Cley 71 F2
Cockpole Green 42 C4
Cockshutt 78 B5
Cockthorpe 86 A1
Cockwood 10 C4
Codda 5 F2
Coddenham 60 C2
Coddington Ches. 78 B2
Coddington Here. 53 G3
Coddington Notts. 82 D2
Codford St. Mary 26 A4
Codford St. Peter 26 A3
Codicote 44 B1
Codmore Hill 16 C2
Codnor 81 F3
Codrington 39 G5
Codsall 66 A2
Codsall Wood 66 A2
Coed Morgan 38 C1
Coed-y-paen 38 C3
Coed-yr-ynys 52 A5
Coed Ystumgwern 75 E5
Coedcae 38 B2
Coedely 37 G4
Coedkernew 38 B4
Coedpoeth 77 F2
Coelbren 37 E1
Coffinswell 9 E1
Cofton Hackett 66 C5
Cogan 38 A5
Cogenhoe 56 D1
Coggeshall 59 G5
Coggeshall Hamlet 59 G5
Coggins Mill 18 A1
Cóig Peighinnean W.Isles 187 E2
Cóig Peighinnean W.Isles 187 G1
Coilantogle 150 A4
Coileitir 156 D5
Coilessan 149 E4
Coillaig 148 C2
Coille Mhorgil 166 A4
Coille-righ 165 F2
Coillore 163 G1
Coity 37 F4
Col 187 F3
Colaboll 190 A3
Colan 4 C3
Colaton Raleigh 11 D4
Colbost 175 F5
Colbury 14 C1
Colby Cumb. 118 C5
Colby I.o.M. 98 A4
Colby Norf. 86 D2
Colchester 60 A5
Colcot 23 E1
Cold Ash 27 G1
Cold Ashby 68 B5
Cold Ashton 39 G5
Cold Aston 54 D5
Cold Blow 35 E1
Cold Brayfield 57 E2
Cold Chapel 134 A3
Cold Hanworth 96 A4
Cold Hesledon 120 D3
Cold Higham 56 B2
Cold Kirby 111 E4
Cold Newton 68 C2
Cold Norton 46 B2
Cold Overton 68 D2
Coldbackie 193 F2
Coldblow 45 E5
Coldean 17 F3
Coldeast 10 B5
Colden Common 27 F5
Coldfair Green 61 F1
Coldham 70 C2
Coldharbour 29 G3
Coldingham 145 F3
Coldrain 151 F4
Coldred 33 E4
Coldrey 28 C3
Coldridge 21 G5
Coldrife 128 C2
Coldstream 136 C3
Coldwaltham 16 C2
Coldwells 183 G5
Cole 25 D4
Cole Green 44 B1
Colebatch 64 C4
Colebrook 10 D2
Colebrooke 10 A2
Coleby Lincs. 83 E1
Coleby N.Lincs. 95 G1
Coleford Devon 10 A2
Coleford Glos. 39 E1
Coleford Som. 25 D3
Colehill 13 G2
Coleman's Hatch 31 D5
Colemere 78 B4
Colemore 28 C4
Colenden 151 G2
Coleorton 67 G1
Colerne 40 A5
Cole's Cross 9 D3
Colesbourne 40 C1
Colesden 57 G2
Coleshill Bucks. 43 E3
Coleshill Oxon. 41 E3
Coleshill Warks. 67 E4
Colestocks 11 D2
Colfin 122 B5
Colgate 30 B5
Colgrain 141 E1
Colinsburgh 152 C4
Colinton 143 G3
Colintraive 140 B2
Colkirk 86 A3

Collace 152 A1
Collafirth *Shet.* 200 D1
Collafirth *Shet.* 202 C4
Collamoor Head 6 B1
Collaton St. Mary 9 E1
Collessie 152 A3
Colleton Mills 21 G4
Collett's Green 54 A2
Collier Row 45 E3
Collier Street 31 G4
Collier's End 58 B5
Colliery Row 120 C2
Collieston 171 F2
Collin 125 E3
Collingbourne Ducis 26 D2
Collingbourne Kingston 26 D2
Collingham *Notts.* 82 D1
Collingham *W.Yorks.* 102 C3
Collington 53 F1
Collingtree 56 C2
Collins Green 91 G3
Colliston 161 E5
Colliton 11 D2
Collmuir 170 A4
Collycroft 67 F4
Collynie 170 D1
Collyweston 69 F2
Colmonell 122 C2
Colmworth 57 G2
Coln Rogers 40 C2
Coln St. Aldwyns 40 D2
Coln St. Dennis 40 C1
Colnabaichin 169 E4
Colnbrook 43 F5
Colne *Cambs.* 70 B5
Colne *Lancs.* 101 E3
Colne Engaine 59 G4
Colney 86 C5
Colney Heath 44 B2
Colney Street 44 A2
Colonsay 146 C5
Colpy 170 B1
Colquhar 144 A5
Colsterdale 110 A4
Colsterworth 83 E5
Colston Bassett 82 C4
Coltfield 180 D3
Coltishall 87 D4
Colton *Cumb.* 107 E4
Colton *N.Yorks.* 103 E3
Colton *Norf.* 86 C4
Colton *Staffs.* 80 B5
Colva 52 B2
Colvend 124 C5
Colvister 203 E3
Colwall Green 53 G3
Colwall Stone 53 G3
Colwell 128 B4
Colwich 80 B5
Colwick 82 B3
Colwinston 37 F5
Colworth 16 B3
Colwyn Bay (Bae Colwyn) 89 G5
Colyford 11 F3
Colyton 11 F3
Combe *Here.* 52 C1
Combe *Oxon.* 41 G1
Combe *W.Berks.* 27 E1
Combe Cross 10 A5
Combe Down 25 E1
Combe Florey 23 E4
Combe Hay 25 E1
Combe Martin 21 F1
Combe Raleigh 11 E2
Combe St. Nicholas 11 F1
Combeinteignhead 10 C5
Comberbach 92 A5
Comberford 67 D2
Comberton *Cambs.* 58 B2
Comberton *Here.* 53 D1
Combpyne 11 F3
Combrook 55 F2
Combs *Derbys.* 93 E5
Combs *Suff.* 60 B2
Combs Ford 60 B2
Combwich 23 F3
Comer 149 F4
Comers 170 B4
Commercial End 59 D1
Commins Coch 63 E2
Common Edge 99 G4
Common Moor 5 G3
Common Side 94 A5
Commondale 111 F1
Commonside 80 D3
Compstall 93 D3
Compton *Devon* 9 E1
Compton *Hants.* 27 F5
Compton *Surr.* 29 E3
Compton *W.Berks.* 42 A5
Compton *W.Suss.* 15 G1
Compton Abbas 13 E1
Compton Abdale 40 C1
Compton Bassett 40 C5
Compton Beauchamp 41 E4
Compton Bishop 24 A2
Compton Chamberlayne 26 B5
Compton Dando 24 D1
Compton Dundon 24 B4
Compton Martin 24 C2
Compton Pauncefoot 24 D5
Compton Valence 12 B3
Comra 167 E5
Comrie 150 C2
Conchra *Arg. & B.* 140 B1
Conchra *High.* 165 E2
Concraigie 159 G5
Conder Green 100 A2
Conderton 54 B4
Condicote 54 D5
Condorrat 142 B2
Condover 65 D2
Coney Weston 72 A4
Coneyhurst 29 G5
Coneysthorpe 111 G5
Coneythorpe 102 C2
Conford 28 D4
Congash 168 C2
Congdon's Shop 5 G2
Congerstone 67 F2
Congham 85 F5
Congleton 79 F1
Congresbury 24 B1
Conicavel 180 B4
Coningsby 84 A2
Conington *Cambs.* 69 G4
Conington *Cambs.* 58 B1
Conisbrough 94 C3
Conisby 138 A3
Conisholme 97 E3
Coniston *Cumb.* 107 E3
Coniston *E.Riding* 105 D4
Coniston Cold 101 F2
Conistone 101 F1
Conland 182 B5
Connah's Quay 77 F1
Connel 148 B1
Connel Park 133 E4
Connor Downs 2 C3
Conon Bridge 179 E4
Cononish 149 F2
Cononley 101 F3
Cononsyth 161 D5
Consall 79 G3
Consett 120 A2
Constable Burton 110 A3
Constantine 3 E4
Contin 179 D4
Contlaw 170 D4
Contullich 179 F2
Conwy 89 F5
Conyer 32 B2
Cooden 18 C3
Coodham 132 B2
Cookbury 21 E5
Cookham 43 D4
Cookham Dean 43 D4
Cookham Rise 43 D4
Cookhill 54 C2
Cookley *Suff.* 73 E4
Cookley *Worcs.* 66 A4
Cookley Green 42 B4
Cookney 171 D5
Cooksbridge 17 G2
Cookshill 79 G3
Cooksmill Green 45 F2
Cookston 171 E1
Coolham 29 G5
Cooling 45 G5
Coombe *Cornw.* 5 D4
Coombe *Cornw.* 20 C4
Coombe *Cornw.* 4 A5
Coombe *Devon* 9 D3
Coombe *Devon* 10 B4
Coombe Bissett 26 C5
Coombe Hill 54 A5
Coombe Keynes 13 E4
Coombes 17 D3
Coombes Moor 52 C1
Cooper's Corner *E.Suss.* 18 C1
Cooper's Corner *Kent* 31 D4
Cooper's Hill 43 E5
Coopersale Common 45 D2
Cootham 16 C2
Cop Street 33 E3
Copdock 60 C3
Copford Green 60 A5
Copgrove 102 C1
Copister 203 D5
Cople 57 G3
Copley 119 G5
Coplow Dale 93 F5
Copmanthorpe 103 E3
Coppathorne 20 C5
Coppenhall 66 B1
Coppenhall Moss 79 E2
Coppingford 69 G5
Coppleridge 25 F5
Copplestone 10 A2
Coppull 91 G1
Coppull Moor 91 G1
Copsale 29 G5
Copster Green 100 C4
Copston Magna 67 G4
Copt Heath 67 D5
Copt Hewick 110 C5
Copt Oak 67 G1
Copthorne 30 C5
Copy Lake 21 G4
Copythorne 14 C1
Coralhill 183 F3
Corbiegoe 195 F4
Corbridge 119 F1
Corby 69 D4
Corby Glen 83 F5
Cordach 170 B5
Coreley 65 F5
Corfcott Green 6 D1
Corfe 11 F1
Corfe Castle 13 F4
Corfe Mullen 13 F3
Corfton 65 D4
Corgarff 169 E4
Corhampton 28 B5
Corley 67 E4
Corley Ash 67 E4
Corley Moor 67 E4
Cornabus 138 B5
Corney 106 C3
Cornforth 120 C4
Cornhill 182 A4
Cornhill on Tweed 136 C3
Cornholme 101 F5
Cornish Hall End 59 E4
Cornquoy 197 E2
Cornriggs 119 E3
Cornsay 120 A3
Cornsay Colliery 120 A3
Corntown *High.* 179 E4
Corntown *V. of Glam.* 37 F5
Cornwell 55 E5
Cornwood 8 C2
Cornworthy 9 E2
Corpach 156 D2
Corpusty 86 C3
Corrachree 169 G4
Corran *Arg. & B.* 149 E5
Corran *High.* 165 E4
Corran *High.* 156 C3
Corranbuie 139 G3
Corranmore 147 G4
Corrany 98 C3
Corrie 140 B5
Corrie Common 126 A3
Corriechrevie 139 F4
Corriecravie 131 E3
Corriedoo 124 A2
Corrielorne 148 A3
Corrievorrie 167 G2
Corrimony 166 C1
Corringham *Lincs.* 95 F3
Corringham *Thur.* 45 G4
Corris 63 D2
Corris Uchaf 62 D2
Corrlarach 156 B2
Corrour Shooting Lodge 157 G3
Corrow 149 D4
Corry 164 C2
Corrychurrachan 156 C3
Corrykinloch 189 F2
Corrylach 130 C3
Corrymuckloch 151 D1
Corsback 195 E2
Corscombe 12 B2
Corse *Aber.* 182 B5
Corse *Glos.* 53 G5
Corse Lawn 54 A4
Corse of Kinnoir 182 A5
Corsebank 133 G4
Corsehill 125 F2
Corsewall 122 B4
Corsham 40 A5
Corsindae 170 B4
Corsley 25 F3
Corsley Heath 25 F3
Corsock 124 B3
Corston *B. & N.E.Som.* 25 D1
Corston *Wilts.* 40 B4
Corstorphine 143 F2
Cortachy 160 B4
Corton *Suff.* 73 G2
Corton *Wilts.* 26 A3
Corton Denham 24 D5
Coruña (Corunna) 173 G3
Corunna (Coruña) 173 G3
Corwar House 123 D2
Corwen 77 D3
Coryton *Devon* 7 E2
Coryton *Thur.* 45 G4
Cosby 68 A3
Coseley 66 B3
Cosford 65 G2
Cosgrove 56 C3
Cosham 15 F2
Cosheston 34 D2
Coshieville 158 C5
Cossall 81 F3
Cossington *Leics.* 68 B1
Cossington *Som.* 24 A3
Costa 198 B4
Costessey 86 C4
Costock 81 G5
Coston *Leics.* 83 D5
Coston *Norf.* 86 B5
Cote *Oxon.* 41 F2
Cote *Som.* 24 A3
Cotebrook 78 C1
Cotehill 118 A2
Cotes *Cumb.* 107 F4
Cotes *Leics.* 81 G5
Cotes *Staffs.* 79 F4
Cotesbach 68 A4
Cotgrave 82 B4
Cothall 171 D3
Cotham 82 C3
Cothelstone 23 E4
Cothercott 64 D2
Cotheridge 53 G2
Cotherstone 109 F1
Cothill 41 G3
Cotleigh 11 F2
Coton *Cambs.* 58 C2
Coton *Northants.* 68 B5
Coton *Staffs.* 79 G4
Coton *Staffs.* 67 D2
Coton Clanford 79 F5
Coton in the Clay 80 C5
Coton in the Elms 67 E1
Cott 9 D1
Cottam *E.Riding* 104 B1
Cottam *Lancs.* 100 A4
Cottam *Notts.* 95 F4
Cottartown 168 C1
Cottenham 58 C1
Cotterdale 108 D3
Cottered 58 B5
Cotteridge 66 C4
Cotterstock 69 F3
Cottesbrooke 68 C5
Cottesmore 69 E1
Cottingham *E.Riding* 104 C4
Cottingham *Northants.* 68 D3
Cottisford 56 A4
Cotton 60 B1
Cotton End 57 F3
Cottown *Aber.* 170 A2
Cottown *Aber.* 182 D5
Cottown *Aber.* 170 C3
Cotwalton 79 G4
Couch's Mill 5 F4
Coughton *Here.* 53 E5
Coughton *Warks.* 54 C1
Cougie 166 B2
Coulaghailtro 139 F3
Coulags 177 F5
Coulby Newham 111 E1
Coull 170 A4
Coulport 140 D1
Coulsdon 30 C3
Coulston 26 A2
Coulter 134 B2
Coultershaw Bridge 16 B2
Coultings 23 F3
Coulton 111 F5
Coultra 152 B2
Cound 65 E2
Coundon 120 B4
Coundon Grange 120 B5
Countersett 109 E4
Countess 26 C3
Countess Wear 10 C3
Countesthorpe 68 A3
Countisbury 22 A3
County Oak 30 B5
Coupar Angus 160 A5
Coupland *Cumb.* 108 C1
Coupland *Northumb.* 136 D3
Cour 139 G5
Court-at-Street 32 C5
Court Barton 10 B3
Court Henry 50 B5
Court House Green 67 F4
Courteenhall 56 C2
Courtsend 46 D3
Courtway 23 F4
Cousland 144 A3
Cousley Wood 31 F5
Coustonn 140 B2
Cove *Arg. & B.* 140 D1
Cove *Devon* 10 C1
Cove *Hants.* 28 D2
Cove *High.* 188 A5
Cove *Sc.Bord.* 145 E2
Cove Bay 171 E4
Covehithe 73 G3
Coven 66 B2
Coveney 70 C4
Covenham St. Bartholomew 96 D3
Covenham St. Mary 96 D3
Coventry 67 F5
Coverack 3 E5
Coverham 109 F4
Covesea 181 D2
Covington *Cambs.* 69 F5
Covington *S.Lan.* 134 A2
Cowan Bridge 108 B5
Cowbeech 18 B2
Cowbit 70 A1
Cowbridge 37 G5
Cowden 31 D4
Cowden Pound 31 D4
Cowdenbeath 151 G5
Cowes 15 D3
Cowesby 111 D3
Cowfold 17 E1
Cowgill 108 C4
Cowie *Aber.* 161 G1
Cowie *Stir.* 142 C1
Cowlam Manor 104 B1
Cowley *Devon* 10 C3
Cowley *Glos.* 40 B1
Cowley *Gt.Lon.* 43 F4
Cowley *Oxon.* 42 A2
Cowling *N.Yorks.* 101 F3
Cowling *N.Yorks.* 110 B4
Cowlinge 59 F2
Cowmes 93 F1
Cowpen 129 E3
Cowpen Bewley 121 D5
Cowplain 15 F1
Cowshill 119 E3
Cowthorpe 102 D2
Cox Common 73 E3
Coxbank 79 D3
Coxbench 81 E3
Coxheath 31 G3
Coxhoe 120 C4
Coxley 24 C3
Coxtie Green 45 E3
Coxwold 111 E5
Coychurch 37 F5
Coylet 140 C1
Coylton 132 C4
Coylumbridge 168 B3
Coynach 169 G4
Coynachie 169 G1
Coytrahen 37 E4
Crabbet Park 30 C5
Crabbs Cross 54 C1
Crabtree *Plym.* 8 B2
Crabtree *W.Suss.* 17 E1
Crackaig 138 D3
Crackenthorpe 118 C5
Crackington 6 B1
Crackington Haven 6 B1
Crackleybank 65 G1
Crackpot 109 E3
Cracoe 101 F1
Craddock 11 D1
Cradhlastadh 186 B4
Cradley *Here.* 53 G3
Cradley *W.Mid.* 66 B4
Crafthole 7 D5
Cragg 101 G5
Craggan *Moray* 169 D1
Craggan *P. & K.* 150 D3
Cragganruar 158 B5
Craggie *High.* 167 G1
Craggie *High.* 191 D2
Craghead 120 B2
Craibstone *Aberdeen* 171 D3
Craibstone *Moray* 181 G4
Craichie 160 C5
Craig *Arg. & B.* 148 C1
Craig *Arg. & B.* 147 E2
Craig *D. & G.* 124 A4
Craig *High.* 177 D3
Craig *High.* 177 G5
Craig *S.Ayr.* 132 B5
Craig-cefn-parc 36 C2
Craig-y-nos 37 E1
Craigans 148 B5
Craigbeg 157 G1
Craigcleuch 126 B3
Craigculter 183 E4
Craigdallie 152 A2
Craigdam 170 D1
Craigdarroch *D. & G.* 124 B1
Craigdarroch *E.Ayr.* 133 E5
Craigdhu *D. & G.* 115 D2
Craigdhu *High.* 179 D5
Craigearn 170 C3
Craigellachie 181 E5
Craigellie 183 F3
Craigencallie 123 G3
Craigend *Moray* 180 D4
Craigend *P. & K.* 151 G2
Craigendive 140 B1
Craigendoran 141 E1
Craigengillan 132 C5
Craigenputtock 124 B2
Craigens 138 A3
Craigglas 139 G1
Craighall 152 C3
Craighat 141 F1
Craighead *Fife* 153 E4
Craighead *High.* 179 G3
Craighlaw 123 E4
Craighouse 138 D3
Craigie *Aber.* 171 E3
Craigie *P. & K.* 159 G5
Craigie *S.Ayr.* 132 C2
Craigie Brae 171 D1
Craigieburn 134 C5
Craigieholm 151 G1
Craiglockhart 143 G2
Craiglug 170 D5
Craigmaud 183 D4
Craigmillar 143 G2
Craigmore 140 C3
Craigmyle House 170 B4
Craignafeoch 140 A2
Craignant 77 F4
Craignavie 150 A1
Craigneil 122 C2
Craignure 147 G1
Craigo 161 E3
Craigoch 132 B5
Craigow 151 F4
Craigrothie 152 B3
Craigroy 180 D4
Craigroy Farm 169 D1
Craigruie 150 A2
Craigsanquhar 152 B3
Craigton *Aberdeen* 170 D4
Craigton *Angus* 152 D1
Craigton *Angus* 160 B4
Craigton *Stir.* 142 A1
Craigtown 194 A3
Craik *Aber.* 169 G2
Craik *Sc.Bord.* 135 E5
Crail 153 E4
Crailing 136 A4
Crailinghall 136 A4
Crakehill 110 D5
Crambe 103 G1
Cramlington 129 E4
Cramond 143 F2
Cranage 79 E1
Cranberry 79 F4
Cranborne 13 G1
Cranbourne 43 E5
Cranbrook 31 G5
Cranbrook Common 31 G5
Cranfield 57 E3
Cranford *Devon* 20 D3
Cranford *Gt.Lon.* 44 A5
Cranford St. Andrew 69 E5
Cranford St. John 69 E5
Cranham *Glos.* 40 A1
Cranham *Gt.Lon.* 45 E4
Crank 91 G2
Cranleigh 29 F4
Cranmer Green 72 B4
Cranmore *I.o.W.* 14 D3
Cranmore *Som.* 25 D3
Cranna 182 B4
Crannach 181 G4
Cranoe 68 C3
Cransford 61 E1
Cranshaws 145 D3
Cranstal 98 C1
Crantock 4 B3
Cranwell 83 F3
Cranwich 71 F3
Cranworth 86 A5
Craobh Haven 147 G4
Crapstone 8 B1
Crarae 148 B5
Crask Inn 190 A2
Crask of Aigas 179 D5
Craskins 170 A4
Craster 137 G4
Craswall 52 B4
Cratfield 73 E4
Crathes 170 C5
Crathie *Aber.* 169 E5
Crathie *High.* 167 E5
Crathorne 110 D2
Craven Arms 64 D4
Craw 139 G5
Crawcrook 120 A1
Crawford *Lancs.* 91 F2
Crawford *S.Lan.* 134 A3
Crawfordjohn 133 G3
Crawfordton 124 B1
Crawick 133 F4
Crawley *Hants.* 27 F4
Crawley *Oxon.* 41 F1
Crawley *W.Suss.* 30 B5
Crawley Down 30 C5
Crawleyside 119 F3
Crawshawbooth 101 E5
Crawton 161 G2
Crawyn 98 B2
Cray *N.Yorks.* 109 E5
Cray *P. & K.* 159 G3
Cray *Powys* 51 E5
Crayford 45 E5
Crayke 111 E5
Cray's Hill 45 G3
Cray's Pond 42 B4
Crazies Hill 42 C4
Creacombe 10 B1
Creag Ghoraidh 173 G5
Creagbheitheachain 156 B3
Creaton 68 C5
Creca 126 A4
Credenhill 52 D3
Crediton 10 B2
Creech Heathfield 23 F5
Creech St. Michael 23 F5
Creed 4 D5
Creedy Park 10 B2
Creekmouth 45 D4
Creeting St. Mary 60 B2
Creeton 83 F5
Creetown 123 F5
Creggans 148 C4
Cregneash 98 A5
Cregrina 52 A2
Creich 152 B2
Creigiau 37 G4
Crelevan 166 C1
Cremyll 8 A2
Cressage 65 E2
Cresselly 35 D2
Cressing 59 F5
Cresswell *Northumb.* 129 E2
Cresswell *Staffs.* 79 G4
Cresswell Quay 35 D2
Creswell 94 C5
Cretingham 60 D2
Cretshengan 139 F3
Crewe *Ches.* 79 E2
Crewe *Ches.* 78 B2
Crewgreen 64 C1
Crewkerne 12 A2
Crewton 81 E4
Crianlarich 149 F2
Cribbs Causeway 39 E4
Cribyn 50 B2
Criccieth 75 D4
Crich 81 E2
Crich Carr 81 E2
Crichie 183 E5
Crichton 144 A3
Crick *Mon.* 39 D4
Crick *Northants.* 68 A5
Crickadarn 51 G3
Cricket Malherbie 11 G1
Cricket St. Thomas 11 G2
Crickheath 77 F5
Crickhowell 38 B1
Cricklade 40 C3
Cridling Stubbs 103 E5
Crieff 151 D2
Criggion 64 B1
Crigglestone 94 A1
Crimdon Park 121 D4
Crimond 183 F4
Crimonmogate 183 F4
Crimplesham 71 E2
Crinan 147 G5
Cringleford 86 C5
Cringletie 143 G5
Crinow 35 E1
Cripplesease 2 B3
Cripp's Corner 18 C1
Crix 45 G1
Croalchapel 124 D1
Croasdale 117 D5
Crock Street 11 G1
Crockenhill 31 E2
Crockernwell 10 A3
Crockerton 25 F3
Crocketford or Ninemile Bar 124 C3
Crockey Hill 103 F3
Crockham Hill 30 D3
Crockhurst Street 31 F4
Crockleford Heath 60 B5
Croes Hywel 38 C1
Croes-lan 49 G3
Croes-y-mwyalch 38 C3
Croes y pant 38 C2
Croesau Bach 77 F5
Croeserw 37 E3
Croesgoch 48 B5
Croesor 75 F3
Croespenmaen 38 A3
Croesyceiliog *Carmar.* 36 A1
Croesyceiliog *Torfaen* 38 C3
Croft *Leics.* 68 A3
Croft *Lincs.* 84 D1
Croft *Warr.* 92 A3
Croft-on-Tees 110 B1
Crofthead 126 B4
Croftmore 159 D3
Crofton *W.Yorks.* 94 A1
Crofton *Wilts.* 27 D1
Crofts 124 B3
Crofts of Benachielt 195 D5
Crofts of Buinach 181 D4
Crofts of Haddo 170 D1
Crofty 36 B3
Crogen 76 D4
Croggan 147 G2
Croglin 118 B3
Croick *High.* 189 G5
Croick *High.* 194 A3
Croig 154 D4
Crois Dughaill 172 C2
Croit e Caley 98 A4
Cromarty 179 G3
Crombie Mill 160 D5
Cromblet 170 C1
Cromdale 168 C2
Cromer *Herts.* 58 A5
Cromer *Norf.* 86 D1
Cromer Hyde 44 B1
Cromford 81 D2
Cromhall 39 F3
Cromhall Common 39 F4
Crompton Fold 93 D2
Cromwell 82 D1
Cronberry 133 E3
Crondall 28 C3
Cronk-y-Voddy 98 B3
Cronton 91 F4
Crook *Cumb.* 107 F3
Crook *Dur.* 120 A4
Crook of Devon 151 F4
Crookedholm 132 C2
Crookham *Northumb.* 136 D3
Crookham *W.Berks.* 27 G1
Crookham Village 28 C2
Crooklands 107 G4
Cropredy 55 G3
Cropston 68 A1
Cropthorne 54 B3
Cropton 111 G4
Cropwell Bishop 82 B4
Cropwell Butler 82 B4
Cros 187 F1
Crosbie 140 D5
Crosbost 187 E5
Crosby *Cumb.* 117 D3
Crosby *I.o.M.* 98 B4
Crosby *Mersey.* 91 E3
Crosby *N.Lincs.* 95 F1
Crosby Court 110 C3
Crosby Garrett 108 C2
Crosby Ravensworth 108 B1
Croscombe 24 C3
Cross 24 B2
Cross Ash 38 D1
Cross-at-Hand 31 G4
Cross Foxes Inn 63 D1
Cross Gates 102 C4
Cross Green *Devon* 7 D2
Cross Green *Suff.* 60 A2
Cross Green *Suff.* 59 G2
Cross Hands *Carmar.* 36 B1
Cross Hands *Pembs.* 35 D1
Cross Hill 81 F3
Cross Hills 101 G3
Cross Houses 65 E2
Cross in Hand 18 A1
Cross Inn *Cere.* 49 G2
Cross Inn *Cere.* 50 B1
Cross Inn *R.C.T.* 37 G4
Cross Keys 40 A5
Cross Lane Head 65 G3
Cross Lanes *Cornw.* 4 B5
Cross Lanes *N.Yorks.* 103 E1
Cross Lanes *Wrex.* 78 A3
Cross o' the Hands 81 D3
Cross of Jackson 170 C1
Cross Street 72 C4
Crossaig 139 G4
Crossapol 154 A4
Crossapoll 154 A2
Crossbush 16 C3
Crosscanonby 117 D3
Crossdale Street 86 D2
Crossens 99 G5
Crossford *D. & G.* 124 C2
Crossford *Fife* 143 E1
Crossford *S.Lan.* 142 C5
Crossgate 84 A5
Crossgatehall 144 A3
Crossgates *Fife* 143 F1
Crossgates *P. & K.* 151 F2
Crossgates *Powys* 51 G1
Crossgill 100 B1
Crosshands 132 C2
Crosshill *Fife* 151 G5
Crosshill *S.Ayr.* 132 B5
Crosshouse 132 B2
Crosskeys 38 B3
Crosskirk 194 C1
Crosslanes *Cornw.* 3 D4
Crosslanes *Shrop.* 64 C1
Crosslee *Renf.* 141 F3
Crosslee *Sc.Bord.* 135 E4
Crosslet 141 F2
Crossmichael 124 B4
Crossmoor 100 A4
Crossroads *Aber.* 170 C5
Crossroads *E.Ayr.* 132 C2
Crossway *Mon.* 38 D1
Crossway *Powys* 51 G2
Crossway Green 54 A1
Crossways *Dorset* 12 D4
Crossways *Glos.* 39 E1
Crosswell 49 E4
Crosthwaite 107 F3
Croston 91 F1
Crostwick 87 D4
Crostwight 87 E2
Crouch 31 F3
Crouch Hill 12 D1
Croughton 56 A4
Crovie 182 D3
Crow 14 A2
Crow Hill 53 F5
Crowan 2 D3
Crowborough 31 E5
Crowcombe 23 E4
Crowdecote 80 C1
Crowdhill 27 F5
Crowfield *Northants.* 56 B3
Crowfield *Suff.* 60 C2
Crowhurst *E.Suss.* 18 C2
Crowhurst *Surr.* 30 C4
Crowhurst Lane End 30 C4
Crowland *Lincs.* 70 A1
Crowland *Suff.* 72 B4
Crowlas 2 C3
Crowle *N.Lincs.* 95 E1
Crowle *Worcs.* 54 B2
Crowle Green 54 B2
Crowmarsh Gifford 42 B4
Crownhill 8 A2
Crownthorpe 86 B5
Crowntown 2 D3
Crows-an-wra 2 A4
Crowthorne 28 D1
Crowton 91 G5
Croxall 67 D1
Croxdale 120 B4
Croxden 80 B4
Croxley Green 43 F3
Croxton *Cambs.* 58 A2
Croxton *N.Lincs.* 96 B1
Croxton *Norf.* 71 G4
Croxton *Staffs.* 79 E4
Croxton Green 78 C2
Croxton Kerrial 82 D5
Croxtonbank 79 E4
Croy *High.* 179 G5
Croy *N.Lan.* 142 B2
Croyde 21 E2
Croydon *Cambs.* 58 B3
Croydon *Gt.Lon.* 30 C2
Cruach 138 B4
Cruchie 182 A5
Cruckmeole 64 D2
Cruckton 64 D1
Cruden Bay 171 F1
Crudgington 65 F1
Crudwell 40 B3
Crug 64 A5

Crugmeer 4 D2
Crugybar 50 C4
Crulabhig 186 C4
Crumlin 38 B3
Crundale *Kent* 32 C4
Crundale *Pembs.* 34 C1
Crutherland 142 A4
Cruwys Morchard 10 B1
Crux Easton 27 F2
Crwbin 36 A1
Cryers Hill 43 D3
Crymlyn 89 E5
Crymych 49 E4
Crynant 37 D2
Crystal Palace 44 C5
Cuaig 176 D4
Cubbington 55 F1
Cubert 4 B4
Cublington 56 D5
Cuckfield 17 F1
Cucklington 25 E5
Cuckney 94 C5
Cuckoo's Nest 78 A1
Cuddesdon 42 A2
Cuddington *Bucks.* 42 C1
Cuddington *Ches.* 92 A5
Cuddington Heath 78 B3
Cuddy Hill 100 A4
Cudham 30 D3
Cudlipptown 7 F3
Cudworth *S.Yorks.* 94 A2
Cudworth *Som.* 11 G1
Cuffley 44 C2
Cuidhaseadair 187 G2
Cuidhir 172 B3
Cuidhtinis 184 C5
Cuidrach 175 G4
Cuil-uaine 148 B1
Cuilmuich 149 D5
Culag 149 F5
Culbo 179 F3
Culbokie 179 F4
Culbone 22 B3
Culburnie 179 D5
Culcabock 179 F5
Culcharan 148 B1
Culcharry 180 A4
Culcheth 92 A3
Culdrain 170 A1
Culduie 176 D5
Culford 59 G1
Culgaith 118 C5
Culgower 191 E3
Culham 42 A3
Culindrach 140 A4
Culkein 188 C1
Culkerton 40 B3
Cullachie 168 B2
Cullen 182 A3
Cullercoats 129 F4
Cullicudden 179 F3
Culligran 178 C5
Cullingworth 101 G4
Cullipool 147 G3
Cullivoe 203 E2
Culloch 150 C3
Culloden 179 G5
Cullompton 10 D2
Culmaily 190 D5
Culmalzie 123 E5
Culmington 65 D4
Culmstock 11 D1
Culnacraig 188 C4
Culnadalloch 148 B1
Culnaknock 176 B3
Culnamean 164 A2
Culpho 60 D3
Culquhirk 123 F5
Culrain 190 A5
Culross 143 D1
Culroy 132 B4
Culsh 169 F5
Culshabbin 123 E5
Culswick 200 B3
Culter Allers Farm 134 B2
Cultercullen 171 E2
Cults *Aber.* 170 A1
Cults *Aberdeen* 171 D4
Cults *D. & G.* 115 E2
Cultybraggan Camp 150 C3
Culverhouse Cross 38 A5
Culverstone Green 31 F2
Culverthorpe 83 F3
Culvie 182 A4
Culworth 56 A3
Cumberhead 133 F2
Cumbernauld 142 B2
Cumberworth 97 F5
Cuminestown 182 D4
Cumloden 123 F4
Cummersdale 117 G1
Cummertrees 125 F4
Cummingstown 180 D3
Cumnock 133 D3
Cumnor 41 G2
Cumrew 118 B2
Cumrue 125 E2
Cumstoun 124 A5
Cumwhinton 118 A2
Cumwhitton 118 B2
Cundall 110 D5
Cunninghamhead 141 E5
Cunnister 203 E3
Cunnoquhie 152 B3
Cupar 152 B3
Cupar Muir 152 B3
Curbar 93 G5
Curbridge *Hants.* 15 E1
Curbridge *Oxon.* 41 F2
Curdridge 15 E1
Curdworth 67 D3
Curland 11 F1
Curload 24 A5
Curridge 41 G5
Currie 143 F3
Curry Mallet 24 A5
Curry Rivel 24 A5
Curteis' Corner 32 A5
Curtisden Green 31 G4
Cury 3 D4
Cushnie 182 C3
Cushuish 23 E4
Cusop 52 B3
Cutcloy 115 E3
Cutcombe 22 C4
Cuthill 179 G1
Cutiau 62 C1
Cutnall Green 54 A1
Cutsdean 54 C4
Cutthorpe 94 A5
Cutts 200 D4
Cuttyhill 183 F4
Cuxham 42 B3
Cuxton 31 G2
Cuxwold 96 B2
Cwm *B.Gwent* 38 A2
Cwm *Denb.* 90 B5
Cwm-Cewydd 63 E1
Cwm Ffrwd-oer 38 B2
Cwm Gwaun 48 D4
Cwm Irfon 51 E3
Cwm-Llinau 63 E2
Cwm-Morgan 49 F4
Cwm-parc 37 F3
Cwm-twrch Isaf 37 D1
Cwm-y-glo 75 E1
Cwm-yr-Eglwys 48 D3
Cwmafan 37 D3
Cwmaman 37 G3
Cwmann 50 B3
Cwmbach *Carmar.* 49 F5
Cwmbach *Powys* 52 A4
Cwmbach *Powys* 51 G2
Cwmbach *R.C.T.* 37 G2
Cwmbelan 63 F4
Cwmbran 38 B3
Cwmbrwyno 62 D4
Cwmcarn 38 B3
Cwmcarvan 39 D2
Cwmcoy 49 F3
Cwmdare 37 F2
Cwmdu *Carmar.* 50 C4
Cwmdu *Powys* 52 A5
Cwmduad 49 G4
Cwmfelin Boeth 35 E1
Cwmfelin Mynach 49 F5
Cwmfelinfach 38 A3
Cwmffrwd 36 A1
Cwmgiedd 37 D1
Cwmgors 36 D1
Cwmgwrach 37 E2
Cwmisfael 36 A1
Cwmllyfri 35 G1
Cwmllynfell 36 D1
Cwmpengraig 49 G4
Cwmsychbant 50 A3
Cwmsymlog 62 C4
Cwmtillery 38 B2
Cwmyoy 52 C5
Cwmystwyth 63 D5
Cwrt 62 C2
Cwrt-newydd 50 A3
Cwrt-y-gollen 38 B1
Cydwelli (Kidwelly) 36 A2
Cyffylliog 77 D2
Cyfronydd 64 A2
Cymmer *N.P.T.* 37 E3
Cymmer *R.C.T.* 37 G3
Cynghordy 51 E4
Cynheidre 36 A2
Cynwyd 77 D3
Cynwyl Elfed 49 G5


## D


Dabton 124 C1
Daccombe 9 F1
Dacre *Cumb.* 118 A5
Dacre *N.Yorks.* 102 A1
Dacre Banks 102 A1
Daddry Shield 119 E4
Dadford 56 B4
Dadlington 67 G3
Dafen 36 B2
Daffy Green 86 A5
Dagenham 45 D4
Daggons 14 A1
Daglingworth 40 B2
Dagnall 43 E1
Dail 148 C1
Dail Beag 186 D3
Dail Bho Dheas 187 F1
Dail Bho Thuath 187 F1
Dail Mòr 186 D3
Dailly 132 A5
Dailnamac 148 B1
Dairsie or Osnaburgh 152 C3
Dalabrog 172 C1
Dalavich 148 B3
Dalballoch 167 F5
Dalbeattie 124 C4
Dalblair 133 E4
Dalbog 161 D2
Dalbreck 190 C3
Dalbury 81 D4
Dalby 98 A4
Dalcairnie 132 C5
Dalchalloch 158 C3
Dalchalm 191 E4
Dalchenna 148 C4
Dalchirach 169 D1
Dalchork 190 A3
Dalchreichart 166 B3
Dalchruin 150 C3
Dalcross 179 G5
Dalderby 84 A1
Daldownie 169 E4
Dale *Derbys.* 81 F4
Dale *Pembs.* 34 B2
Dale Head 107 F1
Dale of Walls 200 A2
Dale Park 16 B3
Dalehouse 111 G1
Dalelia 155 G3
Daless 168 A1
Dalestie 169 D3
Dalfad 169 F4
Dalganachan 194 C4
Dalgarven 141 D5
Dalgety Bay 143 F1
Dalgig 133 D4
Dalginross 150 C2
Dalgonar 133 F5
Dalguise 159 E5
Dalhalvaig 194 A3
Dalham 59 F1
Daligan 141 E1
Dalivaddy 130 B4
Daljarrock 122 C2
Dalkeith 144 A3
Dallas 180 D4
Dallaschyle 180 A5
Dallash 123 F4
Dallinghoo 61 D2
Dallington *E.Suss.* 18 B2
Dallington *Northants.* 56 C1
Dalmadilly 170 C3
Dalmally 149 D2
Dalmarnock 159 E5
Dalmary 150 A5
Dalmellington 132 C5
Dalmeny 143 F2
Dalmichy 190 A3
Dalmigavie 167 G3
Dalmore 179 F3
Dalmunzie Hotel 159 F2
Dalnabreck 155 G3
Dalnacarn 159 F3
Dalnaglar Castle 159 G3
Dalnaha 147 F2
Dalnahaitnach 168 A3
Dalnamain 190 C5
Dalnatrat 156 B4
Dalnavie 179 F2
Dalness 157 D4
Dalnessie 190 B3
Dalnigap 122 C3
Dalqueich 151 F4
Dalreoch 122 C2
Dalriech 150 C1
Dalroy 179 G5
Dalrulzian 159 G4
Dalry 141 D5
Dalrymple 132 B4
Dalserf 142 B4
Dalshangan 123 G2
Dalskairth 124 D3
Dalston 117 G1
Dalswinton 124 D2
Daltomach 167 G2
Dalton *D. & G.* 125 F3
Dalton *Lancs.* 91 F2
Dalton *N.Yorks.* 110 D5
Dalton *N.Yorks.* 110 A2
Dalton *Northumb.* 128 D4
Dalton *Northumb.* 119 F2
Dalton *S.Yorks.* 94 B3
Dalton-in-Furness 106 D5
Dalton-le-Dale 120 D3
Dalton-on-Tees 110 B2
Dalton Piercy 121 D4
Daltote 139 F1
Daltra 180 B5
Dalveich 150 B2
Dalvennan 132 B4
Dalvourn 167 F1
Dalwhinnie 158 B1
Dalwood 11 F2
Damerham 14 A1
Damgate 87 F5
Damnaglaur 114 B3
Damside 151 E3
Danbury 45 G2
Danby 111 G2
Danby Wiske 110 C3
Dandaleith 181 E5
Danderhall 144 A3
Dane End 58 B5
Dane Hills 68 A2
Danebridge 79 G1
Danehill 17 G1
Danesmoor 81 F1
Danestone 171 E3
Danskine 144 C3
Darby Green 28 D1
Darenth 45 E5
Daresbury 91 G4
Darfield 94 B2
Dargate 32 C2
Dargues 128 A2
Darite 5 G3
Darlaston 66 B3
Darley 102 B2
Darley Dale 81 D1
Darlingscott 55 E3
Darlington 110 B1
Darliston 78 C4
Darlton 95 E5
Darnabo 182 C5
Darnall 94 A4
Darnconner 133 D3
Darnford 170 C5
Darngarroch 124 A4
Darnick 135 G2
Darowen 63 E2
Darra 182 C5
Darras Hall 129 D4
Darrington 94 B1
Darsham 61 F1
Dartfield 183 F4
Dartford 45 E5
Dartington 9 D1
Dartmeet 7 G3
Dartmouth 9 E2
Darton 94 A2
Darvel 133 D2
Darvell 18 C1
Darwen 100 C5
Datchet 43 E5
Datchworth 44 B1
Datchworth Green 44 B1
Daubhill 92 B2
Daugh of Kinermony 181 E5
Dauntsey 40 B4
Dava 168 C1
Davaar 130 C4
Davan 169 G4
Davenham 92 A5
Daventry 56 A1
Davidstow 5 F1
Davington 134 D5
Daviot *Aber.* 170 C2
Daviot *High.* 167 G1
Davoch of Grange 181 G4
Dawley 65 F2
Dawlish 10 C5
Dawn 89 G5
Daws Heath 46 B4
Dawsmere 84 C4
Daylesford 55 E5
Ddôl 90 C5
Deadwaters 142 B5
Deal 33 F3
Deal Hall 46 D3
Dean *Cumb.* 117 D4
Dean *Devon* 8 D1
Dean *Dorset* 13 F1
Dean *Hants.* 15 E1
Dean *Oxon.* 55 F5
Dean *Som.* 25 D3
Dean Bank 120 B4
Dean Prior 8 D1
Dean Row 92 C4
Dean Street 31 G3
Deanburnhaugh 135 E4
Deane 27 G3
Deanland 13 F1
Deanscales 117 D4
Deanshanger 56 C3
Deanston 150 C4
Dearham 117 D3
Debach 60 D2
Debate 126 A3
Debden 59 D4
Debden Green 59 D4
Debenham 60 C1
Dechmont 143 E2
Deddington 55 G4
Dedham 60 B4
Deecastle 169 G5
Deene 69 E3
Deenethorpe 69 E3
Deepcar 93 G3
Deepcut 29 E2
Deepdale *Cumb.* 108 C4
Deepdale *N.Yorks.* 109 D5
Deeping Gate 69 G2
Deeping St. James 69 G2
Deeping St. Nicholas 70 A1
Deerhill 181 G4
Deerhurst 54 A5
Defford 54 B3
Defynnog 51 F5
Deganwy 89 F5
Degnish 147 G3
Deighton *N.Yorks.* 110 C2
Deighton *York* 103 F3
Deiniolen 75 E1
Delabole 5 E1
Delamere 78 C1
Delavorar 169 D3
Delfrigs 171 E2
Dell Lodge 168 C3
Delliefure 168 C1
Delnabo 169 D3
Delny 179 G2
Delph 93 D2
Delphorrie 169 G3
Delves 120 A3
Delvine 159 G5
Dembleby 83 F4
Denaby 94 B3
Denaby Main 94 B3
Denbigh (Dinbych) 76 D1
Denbury 9 E1
Denby 81 E3
Denby Dale 93 G2
Denchworth 41 F3
Dendron 107 D5
Denend 170 A1
Denford 69 E5
Dengie 46 C2
Denham *Bucks.* 43 F4
Denham *Suff.* 72 C4
Denham *Suff.* 59 F1
Denham Green 43 F4
Denhead *Aber.* 170 C3
Denhead *Aber.* 183 E4
Denhead *Dundee* 152 B1
Denhead *Fife* 152 C3
Denhead of Arbirlot 161 D5
Denholm 135 G4
Denholme 101 G4
Denholme Clough 101 G4
Denio 74 C4
Denmead 15 F1
Denmill 170 D3
Denmoss 182 B5
Dennington 61 D1
Denny 142 C1
Dennyloanhead 142 C1
Denshaw 93 D1
Denside 170 D5
Densole 33 E4
Denston 59 F2
Denstone 80 B3
Dent 108 C4
Denton *Cambs.* 69 G4
Denton *Darl.* 110 B1
Denton *E.Suss.* 17 G3
Denton *Gt.Man.* 92 D3
Denton *Kent* 33 E4
Denton *Lincs.* 83 D4
Denton *N.Yorks.* 102 A3
Denton *Norf.* 73 D3
Denton *Northants.* 56 D2
Denton *Oxon.* 42 A2
Denver 71 E2
Denvilles 15 G2
Denwick 137 G5
Deopham 86 B5
Deopham Green 72 B2
Depden 59 F2
Deptford *Gt.Lon.* 44 C5
Deptford *Wilts.* 26 B4
Derby 81 E4
Derbyhaven 98 A5
Dererach 147 E2
Deri 38 A2
Derringstone 33 D4
Derrington 79 F5
Derry 150 B2
Derry Hill 40 B5
Derrythorpe 95 F2
Dersingham 85 E4
Dervaig 154 D4
Derwen 77 D2
Derwenlas 62 D3
Derwydd 36 C1
Derybruich 140 A2
Desborough 68 D4
Desford 67 G2
Detchant 137 E3
Detling 31 G3
Deuddwr 64 B1
Deunant 76 C1
Deuxhill 65 F4
Devauden 39 D3
Devil's Bridge (Pontarfynach) 62 D5
Devizes 26 B1
Devonport 8 A2
Devonside 151 E5
Devoran 3 E3
Dewar 144 A5
Dewlish 13 D3
Dewsall Court 53 D4
Dewsbury 102 B5
Dhiseig 147 D1
Dhoon 98 C3
Dhoor 98 C2
Dhowin 98 C1
Dhuhallow 167 E2
Dial Post 17 D2
Dibden 14 D2
Dibden Purlieu 14 D2
Dickleburgh 72 C3
Didbrook 54 C4
Didcot 42 A4
Diddington 57 G1
Diddlebury 65 E4
Didley 52 D4
Didling 16 A2
Didmarton 40 A4
Didsbury 92 C3
Didworthy 8 C1
Digby 83 F2
Digg 176 A3
Diggle 93 E2
Digmoor 91 F2
Digswell 44 B1
Dihewyd 50 A2
Dildawn 124 B5
Dilham 87 E3
Dilhorne 79 G3
Dilston 119 F1
Dilton Marsh 25 F2
Dilwyn 52 D2
Dilwyn Common 52 D2
Dinas *Carmar.* 49 F4
Dinas *Gwyn.* 75 D2
Dinas *Gwyn.* 74 B4
Dinas Cross *Pembs.* 48 D4
Dinas Dinlle 74 D2
Dinas-Mawddwy 63 E1
Dinas Powys 38 A5
Dinbych (Denbigh) 76 D1
Dinbych-y-Pysgod (Tenby) 35 E2
Dinder 24 C3
Dinedor 53 E4
Dingestow 39 D1
Dingley 68 C4
Dingwall 179 E4
Dinlabyre 126 D2
Dinnet 169 G5
Dinnington *S.Yorks.* 94 C4
Dinnington *Som.* 12 A1
Dinnington *T. & W.* 129 E4
Dinorwig 75 E1
Dinton *Bucks.* 42 C1
Dinton *Wilts.* 26 B4
Dinvin 122 B5
Dinwoodie Mains 125 F1
Dinworthy 20 D4
Dippen 130 C2
Dippenhall 28 D3
Dippin 131 F3
Dipple *Moray* 181 F4
Dipple *S.Ayr.* 132 A5
Diptford 8 D2
Dipton 120 A2
Dirdhu 168 C2
Dirleton 144 C1
Discoed 52 B1
Diseworth 81 F5
Dishes 199 E4
Dishforth 110 C5
Disley 93 D4
Diss 72 C3
Disserth 51 G2
Distington 116 D4
Ditcheat 24 D4
Ditchingham 73 E2
Ditchley 55 F5
Ditchling 17 F2
Ditteridge 25 F1
Dittisham 9 E2
Ditton *Halton* 91 F4
Ditton *Kent* 31 G3
Ditton Green 59 E2
Ditton Priors 65 F4
Dixton *Glos.* 54 B4
Dixton *Mon.* 39 E1
Dobcross 93 D2
Dobwalls 5 G3
Doc Penfro (Pembroke Dock) 34 C2
Doccombe 10 A4
Dochgarroch 179 F5
Dockenfield 28 D3
Docking 85 F4
Docklow 53 E2
Dockray 117 G4
Doddinghurst 45 E3
Doddington *Cambs.* 70 B3
Doddington *Kent* 32 B3
Doddington *Lincs.* 95 G5
Doddington *Northumb.* 137 D3
Doddington *Shrop.* 65 F5
Doddiscombsleigh 10 B4
Dodford *Northants* 56 B1
Dodford *Worcs.* 66 B5
Dodington *S.Glos.* 39 G4
Dodington *Som.* 23 E3
Dodington Ash 39 G5
Dodleston 78 A1
Dodworth 94 A2
Doe Lea 81 F1
Dog Village 10 C3
Dogdyke 84 A2
Dogmersfield 28 C2
Dol Fawr 63 E2
Dol-gran 50 A4
Dolanog 63 G1
Dolau 52 A1
Dolbenmaen 75 E3
Dolfach 63 F5
Dolfor 64 A4
Dolgarreg 50 D4
Dolgarrog 76 A1
Dolgellau 62 D1
Dolgoch 62 C2
Doll 191 D4
Dollar 151 E5
Dollarbeg 151 E5
Dolleycanney 52 A3
Dolphinholme 100 B2
Dolphinton 143 F5
Dolton 21 F4
Dolwen *Conwy* 89 G5
Dolwen *Powys* 63 F2
Dolwyddelan 76 A2
Dolybont 62 C4
Dolyhir 52 B2
Dolywern 77 F4
Domgay 64 B1
Doncaster 94 C2
Donhead St. Andrew 26 A5
Donhead St. Mary 26 A5
Donibristle 143 F1
Doniford 23 D3
Donington 84 A4
Donington le Heath 67 G1
Donington on Bain 96 C4
Donisthorpe 67 F1
Donkey Town 29 E1
Donnington *Glos.* 55 D5
Donnington *Here.* 53 G4
Donnington *Shrop.* 65 E2
Donnington *Tel. & W.* 65 G1
Donnington *W.Berks.* 27 F1
Donnington *W.Suss.* 16 A3
Donyatt 11 G1
Dorchester *Dorset* 12 C3
Dorchester *Oxon.* 42 A3
Dordon 67 E2
Dore 94 A4
Dores 167 E1
Dorket Head 81 G3
Dorking 29 G3
Dormans Park 30 C4
Dormansland 30 D4
Dormanstown 121 E5
Dormington 53 E3
Dorney 43 E5
Dornie 165 E2
Dornoch 179 G1
Dornock 126 A5
Dorrery 194 C3
Dorridge 67 D5
Dorrington *Lincs.* 83 F2
Dorrington *Shrop.* 65 D2
Dorsell 170 A3
Dorsington 54 D2
Dorstone 52 C3
Dorton 42 B1
Dorusduain 165 F2
Dosthill 67 E2
Dotland 119 F2
Dottery 12 A3
Doublebois 5 F3
Dougalston 141 G2
Dougarie 131 D2
Doughton 40 A3
Douglas *I.o.M.* 98 B4
Douglas *S.Lan.* 133 G2
Douglas and Angus 152 C1
Douglas Hall 124 C5
Douglas Water 133 G2
Douglastown 160 C5
Doulting 24 D3
Dounby 198 A4
Doune *Arg. & B.* 149 F5
Doune *Arg. & B.* 149 F3
Doune *High.* 168 A3
Doune *High.* 189 G4
Doune *Stir.* 150 C4
Dounepark 182 C3
Douneside 169 G4
Dounie *High.* 179 F1
Dounie *High.* 190 A5
Dounreay 194 B2
Dousland 8 B1
Dovaston 78 A5
Dove Holes 93 E5
Dovenby 117 D3
Dover 33 F4
Dovercourt 60 D5
Doverdale 54 A1
Doveridge 80 C4
Doversgreen 30 B4
Dowally 159 F5
Dowdeswell 54 C5
Dowhill 132 A5
Dowland 21 F4
Dowlands 11 F3
Dowlish Wake 11 G1
Down Ampney 40 D3
Down End 24 A3
Down Hatherley 54 A5
Down St. Mary 10 A2
Down Thomas 8 B3
Downderry 6 D5
Downe 30 D2
Downend *I.o.W.* 15 E4
Downend *S.Glos.* 39 F5
Downend *W.Berks.* 41 G5
Downfield 152 B1
Downfields 71 D5
Downgate 7 D3
Downham *Essex* 45 G3
Downham *Lancs.* 101 D3
Downham *Northumb.* 136 C3
Downham Market 71 E2
Downhead *Cornw.* 5 G1
Downhead *Som.* 25 D3
Downholland Cross 91 E2
Downholme 110 A3
Downies 171 E5
Downing 90 C5
Downley 43 D3
Downside *N.Som.* 24 B1
Downside *Som.* 24 D3
Downside *Surr.* 29 G2
Downton *Devon* 7 F2
Downton *Devon* 9 E2
Downton *Hants.* 14 B3
Downton *Wilts.* 26 C5
Downton on the Rock 64 D5
Dowsby 83 G4
Dowthwaitehead 117 G4
Doynton 39 G5
Draethen 38 B4
Draffan 142 B5
Drakeland Corner 8 B2
Drakes Broughton 54 B3
Drakes Cross 66 C5
Draughton *N.Yorks.* 101 G2
Draughton *Northants.* 68 C5
Drax 103 F5
Draycote 67 G5
Draycott *Derbys.* 81 F4
Draycott *Glos.* 55 D4
Draycott *Som.* 24 B2
Draycott *Worcs.* 54 A3
Draycott in the Clay 80 C5
Draycott in the Moors 79 G4
Drayton *Leics.* 68 D3
Drayton *Lincs.* 84 A4
Drayton *Norf.* 86 C4
Drayton *Oxon.* 55 G3
Drayton *Oxon.* 41 G3
Drayton *Ports.* 15 F2
Drayton *Som.* 24 B5
Drayton *Worcs.* 66 B5
Drayton Bassett 67 D2
Drayton Beauchamp 43 E1
Drayton Parslow 56 D5
Drayton St. Leonard 42 A3
Dre-fach 50 B3
Drebley 101 G2
Dreemskerry 98 C2
Dreenhill 34 C1
Drefach *Carmar.* 49 G4
Drefach *Carmar.* 36 B1
Dreghorn 132 B2
Drellingore 33 E4
Drem 144 C2
Drewsteignton 10 A3
Driby 97 D5
Driffield *E.Riding* 104 C2
Driffield *Glos.* 40 C3
Drigg 106 B3
Drighlington 102 B5
Drimfern 148 C3
Drimlee 148 D3
Drimnin 155 E4
Drimore 162 A1
Drimpton 12 A2
Drimsynie 149 D4
Drimvore 148 A5
Drinan 164 B3
Drinkstone 60 A1
Drinkstone Green 60 A2
Drishaig 149 D3
Drissaig 148 B3
Drointon 80 B5
Droitwich 54 A1
Dron 151 G3
Dronfield 94 A5
Dronfield Woodhouse 94 A5
Drongan 132 C4
Dronley 152 B1
Dropmore 43 E4
Droxford 15 F1
Droylsden 92 D3
Druid 76 D3
Druidston 34 B1
Druimarbin 156 C3
Druimavuic 156 C5
Druimdrishaig 139 F2
Druimindarroch 155 F1
Druimkinnerras 179 D5
Drum *Arg. & B.* 140 A2
Drum *P. & K.* 151 F4
Drumachloy 140 B3
Drumbeg 192 A5
Drumblade 182 A5
Drumblair 182 B5
Drumbuie *D. & G.* 133 F4
Drumbuie *High.* 165 D1
Drumburgh 117 F1
Drumchapel 141 G2
Drumchardine 179 E5
Drumchork 177 E1
Drumclog 133 E2
Drumdelgie 181 G5
Drumderfit 179 F4
Drumeldrie 152 C4
Drumelzier 134 C2
Drumfearn 164 C3
Drumfern 156 B2
Drumgarve 130 C3
Drumgley 160 C5
Drumguish 167 G5
Drumhead 170 B5
Drumin 169 D1
Drumine 179 G4
Drumjohn 123 G1
Drumlamford House 123 D3
Drumlasie 170 B4
Drumlemble 130 B4
Drumlithie 161 F1
Drummond *High.* 179 F3
Drummond *Stir.* 150 B4
Drummore 114 B3
Drummuir Castle 181 F5
Drumnadrochit 167 E1
Drumnagorrach 182 A4
Drumnatorran 156 A3
Drumoak 170 C5
Drumore 130 C3
Drumour 159 E5
Drumrash 124 A3
Drumrunie 189 D4

Drums 171 E2
Drumsturdy 152 C1
Drumuie 176 A5
Drumuillie 168 B2
Drumvaich 150 B4
Drumwhindle 171 E1
Drumwhirn 124 B2
Drunkendub 161 E5
Drury 77 F1
Drws-y-nant 76 B5
Dry Doddington 83 D3
Dry Drayton 58 B1
Dry Harbour 176 C4
Dry Sandford 41 G3
Dry Street 45 F4
Drybeck 108 B1
Drybridge *Moray* 181 G3
Drybridge *N.Ayr.* 132 B2
Drybrook 39 F1
Drygrange 135 G2
Dryhope 135 D3
Drymen 141 F1
Drymuir 183 E5
Drynoch 164 A1
Dryslwyn 50 B5
Dryton 65 E2
Duachy 148 A2
Dubford 182 C3
Dubhchladach 139 G3
Dubheads 151 E2
Dubton 161 D4
Duchal 141 E3
Duchally 189 F3
Duchray 149 G5
Duck End 59 E5
Duckington 78 B2
Ducklington 41 F2
Duck's Cross 57 G2
Duddenhoe End 58 C4
Duddingston 143 G2
Duddington 69 E2
Duddleswell 17 G1
Duddo 145 G5
Duddon 78 C1
Duddon Bridge 106 C4
Dudleston Heath 78 A4
Dudley *T. & W.* 129 E4
Dudley *W.Mid.* 66 B3
Dudley Hill 102 A4
Dudley Port 66 B3
Dudsbury 13 G3
Duffield 81 E3
Duffryn 37 E3
Dufftown 181 F5
Duffus 181 D3
Dufton 118 C5
Duggleby 104 A1
Duiar 168 D1
Duible 191 E2
Duiletter 149 D2
Duinish 158 B3
Duirinish 165 D1
Duisdealmor 164 D3
Duisky 156 C2
Dukestown 38 A1
Dukinfield 92 D3
Dulas 88 C4
Dulax 169 F3
Dulcote 24 C3
Dulford 11 D2
Dull 158 D5
Dullatur 142 B2
Dullingham 59 E2
Dulnain Bridge 168 B2
Duloe *Beds.* 57 G1
Duloe *Cornw.* 5 G4
Dulsie 180 B5
Dulverton 22 C5
Dulwich 44 C5
Dumbarton 141 F2
Dumbleton 54 C4
Dumcrieff 134 C5
Dumeath 169 G1
Dumfin 141 E1
Dumfries 125 D3
Dumgoyne 141 G1
Dummer 27 G3
Dun 161 E4
Dunach 148 A2
Dunalastair 158 C4
Dunan *Arg. & B.* 140 C2
Dunan *High.* 164 B2
Dunans 148 C5
Dunball 24 A3
Dunbar 145 D2
Dunbeath 191 G2
Dunbeg 148 A1
Dunblane 150 C4
Dunbog 152 A3
Duncanston *Aber.* 170 A2
Duncanston *High.* 179 E4
Dunchideock 10 B4
Dunchurch 67 G5
Duncote 56 B2
Duncow 125 D2
Duncraggan 150 A4
Duncrievie 151 G4
Duncroist 150 A1
Duncrub 151 F3
Duncryne 141 F1
Duncton 16 B2
Dundee 152 C1
Dundee Airport 152 B2
Dundon 24 B4
Dundonald 132 B2
Dundonnell 177 G1
Dundraw 117 F2
Dundreggan 166 C3
Dundrennan 116 A2
Dundry 24 C1
Dunearn 143 G1
Dunecht 170 C4
Dunfermline 143 E1
Dunfield 40 D3
Dunford Bridge 93 F2
Dungavel 133 E2
Dunham 95 F5
Dunham-on-the-Hill 91 F5
Dunham Town 92 B4
Dunhampton 54 A1
Dunholme 96 A5
Dunino 152 D3
Dunipace 142 C1
Dunira 150 C2
Dunkeld 159 F5
Dunkerton 25 E2
Dunkeswell 11 E2
Dunkeswick 102 C3
Dunkirk 32 C3
Dunk's Green 31 F3
Dunlappie 161 D3
Dunley 53 G1
Dunlop 141 F5
Dunloskin 140 C2
Dunmere 5 E3
Dunmore *Arg. & B.* 139 F3
Dunmore *Falk.* 142 C1
Dunn 195 D3
Dunnabie 126 A3
Dunnet 195 E1
Dunnichen 160 D5
Dunning 151 F3
Dunnington *E.Riding* 105 D2
Dunnington *Warks.* 54 C2
Dunnington *York* 103 F2
Dunnockshaw 101 E5
Dunoon 140 C2
Dunragit 122 C5
Dunrostan 139 F1
Duns 145 E4
Duns Tew 55 G5
Dunsby 83 G5
Dunscore 124 C2
Dunscroft 95 D2
Dunsdale 111 F1
Dunsden Green 42 C5
Dunsfold 29 F4
Dunsford 10 B4
Dunshelt 152 A3
Dunsinnan 151 G1
Dunsland Cross 21 E5
Dunsley 112 B1
Dunsmore 43 D2
Dunsop Bridge 100 C2
Dunstable 57 F5
Dunstall 80 C5
Dunstall Green 59 F1
Dunstan 137 G4
Dunster 22 C3
Dunston *Lincs.* 83 F1
Dunston *Norf.* 86 D5
Dunston *Staffs.* 66 B1
Dunston *T. & W.* 120 B1
Dunstone *Devon* 9 D3
Dunstone *Devon* 10 A5
Dunstone *Devon* 8 B2
Dunsville 95 D2
Dunswell 104 C4
Dunsyre 143 E5
Dunterton 7 D3
Duntisbourne Abbots 40 B2
Duntisbourne Leer 40 B2
Duntisbourne Rouse 40 B2
Duntish 12 C2
Duntocher 141 F2
Dunton *Beds.* 58 A3
Dunton *Bucks.* 56 D5
Dunton *Norf.* 85 G4
Dunton Bassett 68 A3
Dunton Green 31 E3
Dunton Wayletts 45 F4
Duntulm 176 A2
Dunure 132 A4
Dunure Mains 132 A4
Dunvant 36 B3
Dunvegan 175 F5
Dunwich 73 F4
Dura 152 C3
Durdar 118 A2
Durgates 31 F5
Durham 120 B3
Durinemast 155 F4
Durisdeer 133 G5
Durleigh 23 F4
Durley *Hants.* 15 E1
Durley *Wilts.* 26 D1
Durnamuck 188 C5
Durness 192 C2
Durno 170 C2
Duror 156 B4
Durran *Arg. & B.* 148 B4
Durran *High.* 195 D2
Durrington *W.Suss.* 16 D3
Durrington *Wilts.* 26 C3
Dursley 39 G3
Durston 23 F5
Durweston 13 E2
Dury 201 D1
Duston 56 C1
Duthil 168 B2
Dutlas 64 B5
Duton Hill 59 E5
Dutton 91 G5
Duxford 58 C3
Dwygyfylchi 89 F5
Dwyran 74 D1
Dyce 171 D3
Dyfatty 36 A2
Dyffryn *Bridgend* 37 E3
Dyffryn (Valley) *I.o.A.* 88 A5
Dyffryn *Pembs.* 48 C4
Dyffryn Ardudwy 75 E5
Dyffryn Castell 63 D4
Dyffryn Ceidrych 50 D5
Dyffryn Cellwen 37 E1
Dyke *Devon* 20 D3
Dyke *Lincs.* 83 G5
Dyke *Moray* 180 B4
Dykehead *Angus* 160 B3
Dykehead *N.Lan.* 142 C4
Dykehead *Stir.* 150 A5
Dykelands 161 F3
Dykends 160 A4
Dykeside 182 C5
Dylife 63 E3
Dymchurch 19 F1
Dymock 53 G4
Dyrham 39 G5
Dysart 152 B5
Dyserth 90 B5

**E**

Eadar dha Fhadhail 186 B4
Eagland Hill 100 A3
Eagle 83 D1
Eaglescliffe 110 D1
Eaglesfield *Cumb.* 117 D4
Eaglesfield *D. & G.* 126 A4
Eaglesham 141 G4
Eaglethorpe 69 F3
Eagley 92 B1
Eairy 98 B4
Eakley 56 D2
Eakring 82 B1
Ealand 95 E1
Ealing 44 A4
Eamont Bridge 118 B5
Earby 101 F3
Earcroft 100 C5
Eardington 65 G3
Eardisland 52 D2
Eardisley 52 C3
Eardiston *Shrop.* 78 A5
Eardiston *Worcs.* 53 F1
Earith 70 B5
Earl Shilton 67 G3
Earl Soham 60 D1
Earl Sterndale 80 B1
Earl Stonham 60 C2
Earle 137 D4
Earlestown 91 G3
Earley 42 C5
Earlham 86 C5
Earlish 175 G3
Earls Barton 57 D1
Earls Colne 59 G5
Earl's Common 54 B2
Earl's Croome 54 A3
Earl's Green 60 B1
Earlsdon 67 F5
Earlsferry 152 C4
Earlsford 170 D1
Earlston 135 G2
Earlswood *Mon.* 39 D3
Earlswood *Warks.* 66 D5
Earnley 16 A4
Earsairidh 172 C4
Earsdon 129 F4
Earsdon Moor 129 D2
Earsham 73 E3
Earswick 103 F2
Eartham 16 B3
Earthcott Green 39 F4
Easby 111 E2
Easdale 147 G3
Easebourne 29 D5
Easenhall 67 G5
Eashing 29 E3
Easington *Bucks.* 42 B2
Easington *Dur.* 120 D3
Easington *E.Riding* 97 E1
Easington *Northumb.* 137 F3
Easington *Oxon.* 42 B3
Easington *R. & C.* 111 G1
Easington Colliery 120 D3
Easington Lane 120 C3
Easingwold 103 E1
Easole Street 33 E3
Eassie and Nevay 160 B5
East Aberthaw 22 D1
East Allington 9 D3
East Anstey 22 B5
East Appleton 110 B3
East Ardsley 102 C5
East Ashey 15 E4
East Ashling 16 A3
East Auchronie 170 D4
East Ayton 112 C4
East Barkwith 96 B4
East Barming 31 G3
East Barnby 112 B1
East Barnet 44 B3
East Barsham 86 A2
East Beckham 86 C2
East Bedfont 43 F5
East Bergholt 60 B4
East Bilney 86 A4
East Blatchington 17 G4
East Boldon 120 C1
East Boldre 14 C2
East Bolton 137 F5
East Bradenham 86 A5
East Brent 24 A2
East Bridge 61 F1
East Bridgford 82 B3
East Brora 191 D4
East Buckland 21 G2
East Budleigh 11 D4
East Burrafirth 200 C2
East Burton 13 E4
East Cairnbeg 161 F2
East Calder 143 E3
East Carleton 86 C5
East Carlton 68 D4
East Chaldon or Chaldon Herring 13 D4
East Challow 41 F4
East Charleton 9 D3
East Chelborough 12 B2
East Chiltington 17 F2
East Chinnock 12 A1
East Chisenbury 26 C2
East Clandon 29 F2
East Claydon 56 C5
East Clyth 195 E5
East Coker 12 B1
East Combe 23 E4
East Cornworthy 9 E2
East Cottingwith 103 G3
East Cowes 15 E3
East Cowick 103 F5
East Cowton 110 C2
East Cranmore 25 D3
East Creech 13 F4
East Croachy 167 F2
East Darlochan 130 B3
East Davoch 169 G4
East Dean *E.Suss.* 18 A4
East Dean *Hants.* 27 D5
East Dean *W.Suss.* 16 B2
East Dereham 86 A4
East Down 21 G1
East Drayton 95 E5
East End *Hants.* 27 F1
East End *Hants.* 14 C3
East End *Herts.* 58 C5
East End *Kent* 32 A5
East End *N.Som.* 39 D5
East End *Oxon.* 41 F1
East End *Poole* 13 F3
East End *Suff.* 60 C4
East Farleigh 31 G3
East Farndon 68 C4
East Ferry 95 F3
East Fortune 144 C2
East Garston 41 F5
East Ginge 41 G4
East Goscote 68 B1
East Grafton 27 D1
East Grimstead 26 D5
East Grinstead 30 C5
East Guldeford 19 E1
East Haddon 56 B1
East Hagbourne 42 A4
East Halton 96 B1
East Ham 44 D4
East Hanney 41 G3
East Hanningfield 45 G2
East Hardwick 94 B1
East Harling 72 A3
East Harlsey 110 D3
East Harptree 24 C2
East Hartford 129 E4
East Harting 15 G1
East Hatch 26 A5
East Hatley 58 A2
East Hauxwell 110 A3
East Haven 153 D1
East Heckington 83 G3
East Hedleyhope 120 A3
East Helmsdale 191 F3
East Hendred 41 G4
East Heslerton 112 C5
East Hoathly 18 A2
East Horndon 45 F4
East Horrington 24 C3
East Horsley 29 F2
East Horton 137 E3
East Huntspill 24 A3
East Hyde 44 A1
East Ilsley 41 G4
East Keal 84 B1
East Kennett 26 C1
East Keswick 102 C3
East Kilbride 142 A4
East Kirkby 84 B1
East Knapton 112 B5
East Knighton 13 E4
East Knoyle 25 F4
East Lambrook 12 A1
East Langdon 33 F4
East Langton 68 C3
East Langwell 190 C4
East Lavant 16 A3
East Lavington 16 B2
East Layton 110 A1
East Leake 81 G5
East Learmouth 136 C3
East Learney 170 B4
East Leigh 10 A2
East Lexham 71 G1
East Lilburn 137 E4
East Linton 144 C2
East Liss 28 C5
East Looe 5 G4
East Lound 95 E3
East Lulworth 13 E4
East Lutton 104 B1
East Lydford 24 C4
East Mains 170 B5
East Malling 31 G3
East March 152 C1
East Marden 16 A2
East Markham 95 E5
East Marton 101 F2
East Meon 28 B5
East Mere 10 C1
East Mersea 47 D1
East Mey 195 F1
East Midlands International Airport 81 F5
East Molesey 29 G1
East Morden 13 F3
East Morton 101 G3
East Ness 111 F5
East Norton 68 C2
East Oakley 27 G3
East Ogwell 10 B5
East Orchard 13 E1
East Ord 145 G4
East Panson 7 D1
East Peckham 31 F4
East Pennard 24 C4
East Portlemouth 9 D4
East Prawle 9 D4
East Preston 16 C3
East Putford 20 D4
East Quantoxhead 23 E3
East Rainton 120 C3
East Ravendale 96 C3
East Raynham 85 G5
East Rigton 102 C3
East Rolstone 24 A1
East Rounton 110 D2
East Rudham 85 G5
East Runton 86 C1
East Ruston 87 E3
East Saltoun 144 B3
East Shefford 41 F5
East Sleekburn 129 E3
East Somerton 87 F4
East Stockwith 95 E3
East Stoke *Dorset* 13 E4
East Stoke *Notts.* 82 C3
East Stour 25 E5
East Stourmouth 33 E2
East Stratton 27 G4
East Studdal 33 F4
East Suisnish 164 B1
East Taphouse 5 F3
East-the-Water 21 E3
East Thirston 129 D2
East Tilbury 45 F5
East Tisted 28 C4
East Torrington 96 B4
East Tuddenham 86 B4
East Tytherley 27 D5
East Tytherton 40 B5
East Village 10 B2
East Wall 65 E3
East Walton 71 F1
East Wellow 27 E5
East Wemyss 152 B5
East Whitburn 143 D3
East Wickham 45 D5
East Williamston 35 D2
East Winch 71 E1
East Wittering 16 A4
East Witton 110 A4
East Woodhay 27 F1
East Worldham 28 C4
East Worlington 10 A1
East Youlstone 20 C4
Eastbourne *Darl.* 110 C1
Eastbourne *E.Suss.* 18 B4
Eastburn 104 B2
Eastbury *Herts.* 44 A3
Eastbury *W.Berks.* 41 F5
Eastby 101 G2
Eastchurch 32 B1
Eastcombe 40 A2
Eastcote *Gt.Lon.* 44 A4
Eastcote *Northants.* 56 B2
Eastcote *W.Mid.* 67 D5
Eastcott *Cornw.* 20 C4
Eastcott *Wilts.* 26 B2
Eastcourt 40 B3
Eastend 55 F5
Easter Ardross 179 F2
Easter Balmoral 169 E5
Easter Boleskine 167 E2
Easter Borland 150 B4
Easter Brae 179 F3
Easter Buckieburn 142 B1
Easter Compton 39 E4
Easter Drummond 167 D3
Easter Dullater 150 A4
Easter Ellister 138 A4
Easter Fearn 179 F1
Easter Galcantray 180 A5
Easter Howlaws 145 E5
Easter Kinkell 179 E4
Easter Knox 161 D5
Easter Lednathie 160 B3
Easter Moniack 179 E5
Easter Ord 170 D4
Easter Poldar 150 B5
Easter Quarff 200 D4
Easter Skeld 200 C3
Easter Suddie 179 F4
Easter Tulloch 161 F2
Easter Whyntie 182 B3
Eastergate 16 B3
Easterton 26 B2
Eastertown 24 A2
Eastfield *N.Lan.* 142 C3
Eastfield *N.Yorks.* 112 D4
Eastfield Hall 129 E1
Eastgate *Dur.* 119 F4
Eastgate *Lincs.* 69 G1
Eastgate *Norf.* 86 C3
Eastham 91 E4
Easthampstead 29 D1
Eastheath 28 D1
Easthope 65 E3
Easthorpe *Essex* 60 A5
Easthorpe *Leics.* 82 D4
Easthorpe *Notts.* 82 C2
Easthouses 144 A3
Eastington *Devon* 10 A2
Eastington *Glos.* 40 D1
Eastington *Glos.* 39 G2
Eastleach Martin 41 E2
Eastleach Turville 41 E2
Eastleigh *Devon* 21 E3
Eastleigh *Hants.* 14 D1
Eastling 32 B3
Eastney 15 F3
Eastnor 53 G4
Eastoft 95 F1
Eastoke 15 G3
Easton *Cambs.* 69 G5
Easton *Cumb.* 126 C4
Easton *Cumb.* 117 F1
Easton *Devon* 10 A4
Easton *Dorset* 12 C5
Easton *Hants.* 27 G4
Easton *I.o.W.* 14 C4
Easton *Lincs.* 83 E5
Easton *Norf.* 86 C4
Easton *Som.* 24 C3
Easton *Suff.* 61 D2
Easton *Wilts.* 40 A5
Easton Grey 40 A4
Easton-in-Gordano 39 E5
Easton Maudit 57 D2
Easton on the Hill 69 F2
Easton Royal 26 D1
Eastrea 70 A3
Eastriggs 126 A5
Eastrington 103 G4
Eastry 33 E3
Eastside 197 D3
Eastville 84 C2
Eastwell 82 C5
Eastwick 44 D1
Eastwood *Notts.* 81 F3
Eastwood *S'end* 46 B4
Eastwood *W.Yorks.* 101 F5
Eathorpe 55 F1
Eaton *Ches.* 79 F1
Eaton *Ches.* 78 C1
Eaton *Leics.* 82 C5
Eaton *Norf.* 86 D5
Eaton *Notts.* 95 E5
Eaton *Oxon.* 41 G2
Eaton *Shrop.* 65 E3
Eaton *Shrop.* 64 C4
Eaton Bishop 52 D4
Eaton Bray 57 E5
Eaton Constantine 65 E2
Eaton Ford 57 G2
Eaton Green 57 E5
Eaton Hall 78 B1
Eaton Hastings 41 E3
Eaton Socon 57 G2
Eaton upon Tern 79 D5
Eavestone 102 B1
Ebberston 112 C4
Ebbesborne Wake 26 A5
Ebbw Vale 38 A2
Ebchester 120 A2
Ebford 10 C4
Ebrington 55 D3
Ecchinswell 27 G2
Ecclaw 145 E3
Ecclefechan 125 F3
Eccles *Gt.Man.* 92 B3
Eccles *Kent* 31 G2
Eccles *Sc.Bord.* 145 E5
Eccles Road 72 B2
Ecclesfield 94 A3
Ecclesgreig 161 F3
Eccleshall 79 F5
Ecclesmachan 143 E2
Eccleston *Ches.* 78 B1
Eccleston *Lancs.* 91 G1
Eccleston *Mersey.* 91 F3
Eccup 102 B3
Echt 170 C4
Eckford 136 B4
Eckington *Derbys.* 94 B5
Eckington *Worcs.* 54 B3
Ecton *Northants.* 56 D1
Ecton *Staffs.* 80 B2
Edale 93 F4
Edburton 17 E2
Edderside 117 E2
Edderton 179 G1
Eddington 27 E1
Eddleston 143 G5
Eddlewood 142 B4
Eden Park 30 C2
Edenbridge 30 D4
Edendonich 149 D2
Edenfield 92 C1
Edenhall 118 B4
Edenham 83 F5
Edensor 81 D1
Edentaggart 149 F5
Edenthorpe 94 D2
Edern 74 B4
Edgarley 24 C4
Edgbaston 66 C4
Edgcott 56 B5
Edgcumbe 3 E3
Edge *Glos.* 40 A2
Edge *Shrop.* 64 C2
Edge End 39 E1
Edgebolton 78 C5
Edgefield 86 C2
Edgeley 78 C3
Edgerley 64 C1
Edgeworth 40 B2
Edginswell 9 E1
Edgmond 65 G1
Edgmond Marsh 79 E5
Edgton 64 C4
Edgware 44 B3
Edgworth 92 B1
Edial 66 C2
Edinample 150 B2
Edinbanchory 169 G3
Edinbane 175 G4
Edinbarnet 141 G2
Edinburgh 143 G2
Edinburgh Airport 143 F2
Edinchip 150 A2
Edingale 67 E1
Edingley 82 B2
Edingthorpe 87 E2
Edington *Som.* 24 A4
Edington *Wilts.* 26 A2
Edintore 181 G5
Edinvale 180 D4
Edistone 20 C3
Edith Weston 69 E2
Edithmead 24 A3
Edlaston 80 C3
Edlesborough 43 E1
Edlingham 128 D1
Edlington 96 C5
Edmondsham 13 G1
Edmondsley 120 B3
Edmondthorpe 69 D1
Edmonstone 198 D4
Edmonton 44 C3
Edmundbyers 119 G2
Ednam 136 B3
Ednaston 80 D3
Edney Common 45 F2
Edra 149 G3
Edradynate 159 D4
Edrom 145 F4
Edstaston 78 C4
Edstone 55 D1
Edvin Loach 53 F2
Edwalton 81 G4
Edwardstone 60 A3
Edwinsford 50 C4
Edwinstowe 82 B1
Edworth 58 A3
Edwyn Ralph 53 F2
Edzell 161 D3
Efail Isaf 37 G4
Efailnewydd 74 C4
Efailwen 49 E5
Efenechtyd 77 E2
Effingham 29 G2
Effirth 200 C2
Efford 10 B2
Egbury 27 F2
Egdean 29 E5
Egerton *Gt.Man.* 92 B1
Egerton *Kent* 32 B4
Egerton Forstal 32 A4
Egerton Green 78 C2
Egg Buckland 8 B2
Eggerness 115 E2
Eggesford Barton 21 G4
Eggington 57 E5
Egginton 81 D5
Egglescliffe 110 D1
Eggleston 119 G5
Egham 43 F5
Egleton 69 D2
Eglingham 137 F5
Egloshayle 5 E2
Egloskerry 5 G1
Eglwys-Brewis 22 D1
Eglwys Cross 78 B3
Eglwys Fach 62 C3
Eglwysbach 89 G5
Eglwyswrw 49 E4
Egmanton 82 C1
Egmere 86 A2
Egremont 116 D5
Egton 112 B2
Egton Bridge 112 B2
Egypt 27 F3
Eight Ash Green 60 A5
Eignaig 155 G5
Eil 168 A3
Eilanreach 165 E3
Eilean Darach 178 A1
Eilean Iarmain (Isleornsay) 164 C3
Einacleit 186 C5
Eisgean 185 F2
Eisingrug 75 F4
Eisteddfa Gurig 63 D4
Elan Village 51 F1
Elberton 39 E4
Elburton 8 B2
Elcho 151 G2
Elcombe 40 D4
Eldernell 70 B3
Eldersfield 53 G4
Elderslie 141 F3
Eldrick 123 D2
Eldroth 101 D1
Eldwick 102 A3
Elerch (Bont-goch) 62 C4
Elford *Northumb.* 137 F3
Elford *Staffs.* 67 D1
Elgin 181 E3
Elgol 164 B3
Elham 33 D4
Elie 152 C4
Elilaw 128 B1
Elim 88 B4
Eling 14 C1
Eliock 133 G5
Elishader 176 B3
Elishaw 128 A2
Elkesley 95 D5
Elkstone 40 B1
Elland 102 A5
Ellary 139 F2
Ellastone 80 C3
Ellemford 145 E3
Ellenborough 116 D3
Ellenhall 79 F5
Ellen's Green 29 F4
Ellerbeck 110 D3
Ellerby 111 G1
Ellerdine Heath 78 D5
Elleric 156 C5
Ellerker 104 B5
Ellerton *E.Riding* 103 G3
Ellerton *N.Yorks.* 110 B3
Ellerton *Shrop.* 79 E5
Ellesborough 42 D2
Ellesmere 78 A4
Ellesmere Port 91 E5
Ellingham *Hants.* 14 A2
Ellingham *Norf.* 73 E2
Ellingham *Northumb.* 137 F4
Ellingstring 110 A4
Ellington *Cambs.* 69 G5
Ellington *Northumb.* 129 E2
Ellisfield 28 B3
Ellistown 67 G1
Ellon 171 E1
Ellonby 118 A4
Ellough 73 F3
Elloughton 104 B5
Ellwood 39 E2
Elm 70 C2
Elm Park 45 E4
Elmbridge 54 B1
Elmdon *Essex* 58 C4
Elmdon *W.Mid.* 67 D4
Elmdon Heath 67 D4
Elmesthorpe 67 G3
Elmhurst 66 D1
Elmley Castle 54 B3
Elmley Lovett 54 A1
Elmore 39 G1
Elmore Back 39 G1
Elmscott 20 C3
Elmsett 60 B3
Elmstead Market 60 B5
Elmstone 33 E2
Elmstone Hardwicke 54 B5
Elmswell *E.Riding* 104 B2
Elmswell *Suff.* 60 A1
Elmton 94 C5
Elphin 189 E3
Elphinstone 144 A2
Elrick *Aber.* 170 D4
Elrick *Moray* 169 G2
Elrig 114 D2
Elrigbeag 148 D3
Elsdon 128 B2
Elsecar 94 A2
Elsenham 58 D5
Elsfield 42 A2
Elsham 96 A1
Elsing 86 B4
Elslack 101 F3
Elson 78 A4
Elsrickle 143 E5
Elstead 29 E3
Elsted 16 A2
Elsthorpe 83 F5
Elstob 120 C5
Elston *Lancs.* 100 B4
Elston *Notts.* 82 C3
Elstone 21 G4
Elstow 57 F3
Elstree 44 A3
Elstronwick 105 E4
Elswick 100 A4
Elsworth 58 B1
Elterwater 107 E2
Eltham 44 D5
Eltisley 58 A2
Elton *Cambs.* 69 F3
Elton *Ches.* 91 F5

Elton Derbys. 80 D1
Elton Glos. 39 G1
Elton Here. 65 D5
Elton Notts. 82 C4
Elton Stock. 110 D1
Elvanfoot 134 A4
Elvaston 81 F4
Elveden 71 G5
Elvingston 144 B2
Elvington Kent 33 E3
Elvington York 103 G3
Elwick Hart. 121 D4
Elwick Northumb. 137 F3
Elworth 79 E1
Elworthy 23 D4
Ely Cambs. 70 D5
Ely Cardiff 38 A5
Emberton 57 D3
Embleton Cumb. 117 E3
Embleton Northumb. 137 G4
Embo 190 D5
Embo Street 190 D5
Emborough 24 D2
Embsay 101 G2
Emery Down 14 B2
Emley 93 G1
Emmer Green 42 C5
Emmington 42 C2
Emneth 70 C2
Emneth Hungate 70 D2
Empingham 69 E2
Empshott 28 C4
Emsworth 15 G2
Enborne 27 F1
Enchmarsh 65 E3
Enderby 68 A3
Endmoor 107 G4
Endon 79 G2
Enfield 44 C3
Enford 26 C2
Engine Common 39 F4
Englefield 42 B5
Englefield Green 43 E5
Englesea-brook 79 E2
English Bicknor 39 E1
English Frankton 78 B5
Englishcombe 25 E1
Enham Alamein 27 E3
Enmore 23 F4
Ennerdale Bridge 117 D5
Ennochdhu 159 F3
Ensay 154 C5
Ensdon 64 D1
Ensis 21 F3
Enstone 55 F5
Enterkinfoot 133 G5
Enterpen 111 D2
Enville 66 A4
Eolaigearraidh 172 C3
Eorabus 146 C2
Eorodal 187 G1
Eoropaidh 187 G1
Epperstone 82 B3
Epping 45 D2
Epping Green Essex 44 D2
Epping Green Herts. 44 B2
Epping Upland 44 D2
Eppleby 110 A1
Eppleworth 104 C4
Epsom 30 B2
Epwell 55 F3
Epworth 95 E2
Erbistock 78 A3
Erbusaig 165 D2
Erchless Castle 178 D5
Erdington 66 D3
Eredine 148 B4
Eriboll 192 D3
Ericstane 134 B4
Eridge Green 31 E5
Eriff 132 D5
Erines 139 G2
Eriswell 71 F5
Erith 45 E5
Erlestoke 26 A2
Ermington 8 C2
Erpingham 86 C2
Errogie 167 E2
Errol 152 A2
Errollston 171 F1
Erskine 141 F2
Ervie 122 B4
Erwarton 60 D4
Erwood 51 G3
Eryholme 110 C2
Eryrys 77 F2
Escart 139 G3
Escart Farm 139 G4
Escrick 103 F3
Esgair 49 G5
Esgairgeiliog 63 D2
Esh 120 A3
Esh Winning 120 A3
Esher 29 G1
Eshott 129 E2
Eshton 101 F2
Eskadale 166 D1
Eskbank 144 A3
Eskdale Green 106 C2
Eskdalemuir 126 A2
Eskham 97 D3
Esknish 138 B3
Espley Hall 129 D2
Esprick 100 A4
Essendine 69 F1
Essendon 44 B2
Essich 167 F1
Essington 66 B2
Esslemont 171 E2
Eston 111 E1
Etal 136 D3
Etchilhampton 26 B1
Etchingham 18 C1
Etchinghill Kent 33 D5
Etchinghill Staffs. 66 C1
Ethie Mains 161 E5
Eton 43 E5
Eton Wick 43 E5
Etteridge 167 F5
Ettingshall 66 B3
Ettington 55 E3
Etton E.Riding 104 B3
Etton Peter. 69 G2
Ettrick 135 D4
Ettrickbridge 135 E3
Ettrickhill 135 D4
Etwall 81 D4
Eurach 148 A4
Euston 71 G5
Euxton 91 G1
Evanton 179 F3
Evedon 83 F3
Evelix 190 C5
Evenjobb 52 B1
Evenley 56 A4
Evenlode 55 E5
Evenwood 120 A5
Everbay 199 E4
Evercreech 24 D4
Everdon 56 A2
Everingham 104 A3
Everleigh 26 D2
Everley High. 195 F2
Everley N.Yorks. 112 C4
Eversholt 57 E4
Evershot 12 B2
Eversley 28 C1
Eversley Cross 28 C1
Everthorpe 104 B4
Everton Beds. 58 A2
Everton Hants. 14 B3
Everton Notts. 95 D3
Evertown 126 B4
Evesbatch 53 F3
Evesham 54 C3
Evie 198 B4
Evington 68 B2
Ewart Newtown 137 D3
Ewden Village 93 G3
Ewell 30 B2
Ewell Minnis 33 E4
Ewelme 42 B3
Ewen 40 C3
Ewenny 37 F5
Ewerby 83 G3
Ewerby Thorpe 83 G3
Ewhurst E.Suss. 18 C1
Ewhurst Surr. 29 F3
Ewhurst Green 29 F4
Ewloe 77 F1
Ewood 100 C5
Eworthy 7 E1
Ewshot 28 D3
Ewyas Harold 52 C5
Exbourne 21 G5
Exbury 14 D2
Exebridge 22 C5
Exelby 110 B4
Exeter 10 C3
Exeter Airport 10 C3
Exford 22 B4
Exfords Green 65 D2
Exhall Warks. 54 D2
Exhall Warks. 67 F4
Exlade Street 42 B4
Exminster 10 C4
Exmouth 10 D4
Exnaboe 201 G5
Exning 59 E1
Exton Devon 10 C4
Exton Hants. 28 B5
Exton Rut. 69 E1
Exton Som. 22 C4
Exwick 10 C3
Eyam 93 G5
Eydon 56 A2
Eye Here. 53 D1
Eye Peter. 70 A2
Eye Suff. 72 C4
Eye Green 70 A2
Eyemouth 145 G3
Eyeworth 58 A3
Eyhorne Street 32 A3
Eyke 61 E2
Eynesbury 57 G2
Eynort 163 G2
Eynsford 31 E2
Eynsham 41 G2
Eype 12 A3
Eyre 176 A4
Eythorne 33 E4
Eyton Here. 53 D1
Eyton Shrop. 64 C4
Eyton Wrex. 78 A3
Eyton upon the Weald Moors 65 F1
Eywood 52 C2

F

Faccombe 27 E2
Faceby 111 D2
Fachwen 75 E1
Faddiley 78 C2
Fadmoor 111 F4
Faebait 179 D4
Faifley 141 G2
Fail 132 C3
Failand 39 E5
Failford 132 C3
Failsworth 92 C2
Fain 178 A2
Fair Oak Hants. 15 D1
Fair Oak Hants. 27 G1
Fairbourne 62 C1
Fairburn 103 D5
Fairfield Derbys. 93 E5
Fairfield Worcs. 66 B5
Fairford 40 D2
Fairgirth 124 C5
Fairholm 142 B4
Fairley 171 D4
Fairlie 140 D4
Fairlight 19 D2
Fairlight Cove 19 D2
Fairmile 11 D3
Fairmilehead 143 G3
Fairnington 136 A4
Fairoak 79 E4
Fairseat 31 F2
Fairstead Essex 45 G1
Fairstead Norf. 87 D3
Fairwarp 17 G1
Fairy Cross 21 E3
Fairyhill 36 A3
Fakenham 86 A3
Fala 144 B3
Fala Dam 144 B3
Falahill 144 A4
Faldingworth 96 A4
Falfield Fife 152 C4
Falfield S.Glos. 39 F3
Falkenham 61 D4
Falkirk 142 C2
Falkland 152 A4
Falla 136 B5
Fallgate 81 E1
Fallin 150 D5
Falmer 17 F3
Falmouth 3 F3
Falsgrave 112 D4
Falstone 127 F3
Fanagmore 192 A3
Fanans 148 C2
Fancott 57 F5
Fangdale Beck 111 E3
Fangfoss 103 G2
Fanmore 154 D5
Fans 144 D5
Far Cotton 56 C2
Far Forest 65 G5
Far Gearstones 108 C4
Farcet 70 A3
Farden 65 E5
Fareham 15 E2
Farewell 66 C1
Farforth 96 D5
Faringdon 41 E3
Farington 100 B5
Farlam 118 B2
Farlary 190 C4
Farleigh N.Som. 24 B1
Farleigh Surr. 30 C2
Farleigh Hungerford 25 E2
Farleigh Wallop 28 B3
Farlesthorpe 97 E5
Farleton 107 G4
Farley Shrop. 64 C2
Farley Staffs. 80 B3
Farley Wilts. 26 D5
Farley Green 29 F3
Farley Hill 28 C1
Farleys End 39 G1
Farlington 103 F1
Farlow 65 F4
Farmborough 25 D1
Farmcote 54 C5
Farmington 40 D1
Farmoor 41 G2
Farmtown 182 A4
Farnborough Gt.Lon. 30 D2
Farnborough Hants. 29 D2
Farnborough W.Berks. 41 G4
Farnborough Warks. 55 G2
Farnborough Green 29 D2
Farncombe 29 E3
Farndish 57 E1
Farndon Ches. 78 B2
Farndon Notts. 82 C2
Farnell 161 E4
Farnham Dorset 13 F1
Farnham Essex 58 C5
Farnham N.Yorks. 102 C1
Farnham Suff. 61 E2
Farnham Surr. 28 D3
Farnham Common 43 E4
Farnham Green 58 C5
Farnham Royal 43 E4
Farningham 31 E2
Farnley 102 B3
Farnley Tyas 93 F1
Farnsfield 82 B2
Farnworth Gt.Man. 92 B2
Farnworth Halton 91 G4
Farr High. 193 G2
Farr High. 167 F1
Farr High. 168 A4
Farr House 167 F1
Farraline 167 E2
Farringdon 10 D3
Farrington Gurney 24 D2
Farsley 102 B4
Farthinghoe 56 A4
Farthingloe 33 E4
Farthingstone 56 B2
Farway 11 E3
Fasag 177 E4
Fasagrianach 178 A1
Fascadale 155 E2
Faslane 141 D1
Fasnacloich 156 C5
Fasnakyle 166 C2
Fassfern 156 C2
Fatfield 120 C2
Fattahead 182 B4
Faugh 118 B2
Fauldhouse 142 D3
Faulkbourne 45 G1
Faulkland 25 E2
Fauls 78 C4
Faversham 32 C2
Favillar 169 E1
Fawdington 110 D5
Fawdon 120 B1
Fawfieldhead 80 B1
Fawkham Green 31 E2
Fawler 41 F1
Fawley Bucks. 42 C4
Fawley Hants. 15 D2
Fawley W.Berks. 41 F4
Fawley Chapel 53 E5
Fawsyde 161 G2
Faxfleet 104 A5
Faxton 68 C5
Faygate 30 B5
Fazeley 67 E2
Fearby 110 A4
Fearn 180 A2
Fearnan 158 C5
Fearnbeg 176 D4
Fearnhead 92 A3
Fearnmore 176 D3
Fearnoch Arg. & B. 140 B2
Fearnoch Arg. & B. 140 A2
Featherstone Staffs. 66 B2
Featherstone W.Yorks. 94 B1
Featherstone Castle 118 C1
Feckenham 54 C1
Feering 59 G5
Feetham 109 E3
Feith-hill 182 B5
Feizor 101 D1
Felbridge 30 C5
Felbrigg 86 D2
Felcourt 30 C4
Felden 43 F2
Felindre Carmar. 50 D5
Felindre Carmar. 50 B5
Felindre Carmar. 49 G4
Felindre Powys 64 A4
Felindre Swan. 36 C2
Felinfach 51 G4
Felinfoel 36 B2
Felingwmuchaf 50 B5
Felixkirk 111 D4
Felixstowe 61 D4
Felixstowe Ferry 61 E4
Felkington 145 G5
Felldownhead 7 D2
Felling 120 B1
Fellonmore 147 F2
Felmersham 57 E2
Felmingham 87 D3
Felpham 16 B4
Felsham 60 A2
Felsted 59 E5
Feltham 44 A5
Felthorpe 86 C4
Felton Here. 53 E3
Felton N.Som. 24 C1
Felton Northumb. 129 D1
Felton Butler 64 C1
Feltwell 71 F4
Fen Ditton 58 C2
Fen Drayton 58 B1
Fen End 67 E5
Fen Street 72 A4
Fence 101 E4
Fence Houses 120 C2
Fencott 42 A1
Fendike Corner 84 C1
Fenhouses 84 A3
Feniscowles 100 C5
Feniton 11 E3
Fenny Bentley 80 C2
Fenny Bridges 11 E3
Fenny Compton 55 G2
Fenny Drayton 67 F3
Fenny Stratford 57 D4
Fenrother 129 D2
Fenstanton 58 B1
Fenton Cambs. 70 B5
Fenton Lincs. 95 F5
Fenton Lincs. 83 D2
Fenton Northumb. 137 D3
Fenton Stoke 79 F3
Fenwick E.Ayr. 141 F5
Fenwick Northumb. 128 C4
Fenwick Northumb. 137 E2
Fenwick S.Yorks. 94 C1
Feochaig 130 C4
Feock 3 F3
Feolin 138 D3
Feolin Ferry 138 C3
Feorlan 130 B5
Feorlin 148 B5
Feriniquarrie 175 E4
Fern 160 C3
Ferndale 37 F3
Ferndown 13 G2
Ferness 180 B5
Fernham 41 E3
Fernhill Heath 54 A2
Fernhurst 29 D5
Fernie 152 B3
Fernilea 163 G1
Fernilee 93 E5
Fernybank 160 D2
Ferrensby 102 C1
Ferring 16 C3
Ferrybridge 103 D5
Ferryden 161 F4
Ferryhill 120 B4
Ferryside 35 G1
Fersfield 72 B3
Fersit 157 F2
Ferwig 49 E3
Feshiebridge 168 A4
Fetcham 29 G2
Fetterangus 183 E4
Fettercairn 161 E2
Fetternear House 170 C3
Feus of Caldhame 161 E3
Fewcott 56 A5
Fewston 102 A2
Ffair-Rhos 50 D1
Ffairfach 50 C5
Ffarmers 50 C3
Ffawyddog 38 B1
Ffestiniog 76 A3
Ffordd-las 77 E1
Fforest 36 B2
Fforest-fach 36 C3
Ffos-y-ffin 50 A1
Ffostrasol 49 G3
Ffridd Uchaf 75 E2
Ffrith 77 F2
Ffrwdgrech 51 G5
Ffynnon-ddrain 50 A5
Ffynnon Taf (Taff's Well) 38 A4
Ffynnongroyw 90 C4
Fibhig 187 D3
Fichlie 169 G3
Fidden 146 C2
Fiddington Glos. 54 B4
Fiddington Som. 23 F3
Fiddler's Green 53 E4
Fiddlers Hamlet 45 D2
Field 80 B4
Field Broughton 107 E4
Field Dalling 86 B2
Field Head 67 G2
Fife Keith 181 G4
Fifehead Magdalen 25 E5
Fifehead Neville 13 D1
Fifield Oxon. 41 E1
Fifield W. & M. 43 E5
Fifield Bavant 26 B5
Figheldean 26 C3
Filby 87 F4
Filey 113 E5
Filgrave 57 D3
Filkins 41 E2
Filleigh Devon 21 G3
Filleigh Devon 10 A1
Fillingham 95 G4
Fillongley 67 E4
Filmore Hill 28 B5
Filton 39 E5
Fimber 104 B1
Finavon 160 C4
Fincham 71 E2
Finchampstead 28 C1
Finchdean 15 G1
Finchingfield 59 E4
Finchley 44 B3
Findern 81 E4
Findhorn 180 C3
Findhorn Bridge 168 A2
Findhuglen 150 C3
Findo Gask 151 F2
Findochty 181 G3
Findon Aber. 171 E5
Findon W.Suss. 16 D3
Findon Mains 179 F3
Findrassie 181 D3
Findron 169 D3
Finedon 69 E5
Finegand 159 G3
Fingal Street 60 D1
Fingask 170 C2
Fingerpost 65 G5
Fingest 42 C3
Finghall 110 A3
Fingland Cumb. 117 F1
Fingland D. & G. 134 D5
Fingland D. & G. 133 F4
Finglesham 33 F3
Fingringhoe 46 D1
Finlarig 150 A1
Finmere 56 B4
Finnart Arg. & B. 149 E5
Finnart P. & K. 158 A4
Finningham 60 B1
Finningley 95 D3
Finnygaud 182 B4
Finsbury 44 C4
Finstall 66 B5
Finsthwaite 107 E4
Finstock 41 F1
Finstown 198 B5
Fintry Aber. 182 C4
Fintry Stir. 142 A1
Finzean 170 A5
Fionnphort 146 C2
Fir Tree 120 A4
Fir Vale 94 A4
Firbank 108 B3
Firbeck 94 C4
Firgrove 92 D1
Firs Road 26 D4
Firsby 84 C1
Firth 202 D5
Fishbourne I.o.W. 15 E3
Fishbourne W.Suss. 16 A3
Fishburn 120 C4
Fisherford 170 B1
Fisher's Pond 27 F5
Fisher's Row 100 A3
Fisherstreet 29 E4
Fisherton High. 179 G4
Fisherton S.Ayr. 132 A4
Fisherton de la Mere 26 B4
Fishguard (Abergwaun) 48 C4
Fishlake 95 D1
Fishleigh Barton 21 F3
Fishnish 155 F5
Fishpond Bottom 11 G3
Fishponds 39 F5
Fishpool 92 C1
Fishtoft 84 B3
Fishtoft Drove 84 B3
Fishtown of Usan 161 F4
Fishwick Lancs. 100 B4
Fishwick Sc.Bord. 145 G4
Fiskerton Lincs. 96 A5
Fiskerton Notts. 82 C2
Fittleton 26 C3
Fittleworth 16 C2
Fitton End 70 C1
Fitz 64 D1
Fitzhead 23 E5
Fitzwilliam 94 B1
Fiunary 155 F5
Five Ash Down 17 G1
Five Ashes 18 A1
Five Bridges 53 F3
Five Oak Green 31 F4
Five Oaks Chan.I. 8 C5
Five Oaks W.Suss. 29 F5
Five Roads 36 A2
Five Turnings 64 B5
Five Wents 32 A3
Fivehead 24 A5
Fivelanes 5 G1
Flackwell Heath 43 D4
Fladbury 54 B3
Fladdabister 200 D4
Flagg 80 C1
Flamborough 113 F5
Flamstead 43 F1
Flamstead End 44 C2
Flansham 16 B3
Flasby 101 F2
Flash 80 B1
Flashader 175 G4
Flask Inn 112 C2
Flaunden 43 F2
Flawborough 82 C3
Flawith 103 D1
Flax Bourton 24 C1
Flaxby 102 C2
Flaxley 39 F1
Flaxpool 23 E4
Flaxton 103 F1
Fleckney 68 B3
Flecknoe 56 A1
Fleet Hants. 28 D2
Fleet Lincs. 84 B5
Fleet Hargate 84 B5
Fleetwood 99 G3
Flemingston 22 D1
Flemington 142 A4
Flempton 59 G1
Fleoideabhagh 184 C5
Fletchertown 117 F2
Fletching 17 G1
Flete 8 C2
Fleuchats 169 F4
Fleur-de-lis 38 A3
Flexbury 20 C5
Flexford 29 E2
Flimby 116 D3
Flimwell 31 G5
Flint (Y Fflint) 90 D5
Flint Cross 58 C3
Flint Mountain 90 D5
Flintham 82 C3
Flinton 105 E4
Flishinghurst 31 G5
Flitcham 85 F5
Flitton 57 F4
Flitwick 57 F4
Flixborough 95 F1
Flixton Gt.Man. 92 B3
Flixton N.Yorks. 112 D5
Flixton Suff. 73 E3
Flockton 93 G1
Flockton Green 93 G1
Flodden 136 D3
Flodigarry 176 A2
Flookburgh 107 E5
Floors 181 G4
Flordon 72 C2
Flore 56 B1
Flotterton 128 C1
Flowton 60 B3
Flushing Aber. 183 F5
Flushing Cornw. 3 F3
Flyford Flavell 54 B2
Fobbing 45 G4
Fochabers 181 F4
Fochriw 38 A2
Fockerby 95 F1
Fodderletter 168 D2
Fodderty 179 E4
Foel 63 F1
Foggathorpe 103 G4
Fogo 145 E5
Fogorig 145 E5
Foindle 192 A4
Folda 159 G3
Fole 80 B4
Foleshill 67 F4
Folke 12 C1
Folkestone 33 E5
Folkingham 83 F4
Folkington 18 A3
Folksworth 69 G4
Folkton 113 D5
Folla Rule 170 C1
Follifoot 102 C2
Folly Dorset 12 D2
Folly Pembs. 48 C5
Folly Gate 7 F1
Fonthill Bishop 26 A4
Fonthill Gifford 26 A4
Fontmell Magna 13 E1
Fontwell 16 B3
Foolow 93 F5
Foots Cray 45 D5
Forbestown 169 F3
Force Forge 107 E3
Forcett 110 A1
Forches Cross 10 A2
Ford Arg. & B. 148 A4
Ford Bucks. 42 C2
Ford Devon 8 C2
Ford Devon 21 E3
Ford Devon 9 D3
Ford Glos. 54 C5
Ford Mersey. 91 E2
Ford Midloth. 144 A3
Ford Northumb. 136 D3
Ford Pembs. 48 C5
Ford Shrop. 64 D1
Ford Som. 23 D5
Ford W.Suss. 16 B3
Ford Wilts. 40 A5
Ford End 45 F1
Ford Street 11 E1
Fordcombe 31 E4
Fordell 143 F1
Forden 64 B2
Forder Green 9 D1
Fordham Cambs. 71 E5
Fordham Essex 60 A5
Fordham Norf. 71 E3
Fordham Abbey 59 E1
Fordingbridge 14 A1
Fordon 113 D5
Fordoun 161 F2
Fordstreet 60 A5
Fordwells 41 F1
Fordwich 33 D3
Fordyce 182 A3
Forebrae 151 E2
Foreland 138 A3
Forest Gate 44 D4
Forest Green 29 G3
Forest Hall Cumb. 107 G2
Forest Hall T. & W. 120 B1
Forest Head 118 B2
Forest Hill 42 A2
Forest-in-Teesdale 119 E4
Forest Lodge Arg. & B. 157 E5
Forest Lodge P. & K. 159 E2
Forest Mill 151 E5
Forest Row 30 D5
Forest Town 81 G1
Forestburn Gate 128 C2
Forestside 15 G1
Forfar 160 C4
Forgandenny 151 F3
Forgie 181 F4
Formby 91 D2
Forncett End 72 C2
Forncett St. Mary 72 C2
Forncett St. Peter 72 C2
Forneth 159 F5
Fornham All Saints 59 G1
Fornham St. Martin 59 G1
Fornighty 180 B4
Forres 180 C4
Forrest 142 C3
Forrest Lodge 123 G2
Forsbrook 79 G3
Forse 195 E5
Forsie 194 C2
Forsinain 194 B4
Forsinard 194 A4
Forston 12 C3
Fort Augustus 166 C4
Fort George 179 G4
Fort William 156 D2
Forter 159 G3
Forteviot 151 F3
Forth 142 D4
Forthampton 54 A4
Fortingall 158 C5
Forton Hants. 27 F3
Forton Lancs. 100 A2
Forton Shrop. 64 D1
Forton Som. 11 G2
Forton Staffs. 79 E5
Fortrie 182 B5
Fortrose 179 G4
Fortuneswell 12 C5
Forty Green 43 E3
Forty Hill 44 C3
Forward Green 60 B2
Fosbury 27 E2
Foscot 55 E5
Fosdyke 84 B4
Foss 158 C4
Foss Cross 40 C2
Fossdale 109 D3
Fossebridge 40 C1
Foster Street 45 D2
Foster's Booth 56 B2
Foston Derbys. 80 C4
Foston Lincs. 83 D3
Foston N.Yorks. 103 F1
Foston on the Wolds 104 D2
Fotherby 96 D3
Fotheringhay 69 F3
Foubister 197 E2
Foul Mile 18 B2
Foulbog 134 D5
Foulden Norf. 71 F3
Foulden Sc.Bord. 145 G4
Foulridge 101 E3
Foulsham 86 B3
Foulzie 182 C3
Fountainhall 144 B5
Four Ashes Staffs. 66 B2
Four Ashes Suff. 72 A4
Four Crosses Denb. 76 D3
Four Crosses Powys 64 B1
Four Crosses Powys 63 G2
Four Crosses Staffs. 66 B2
Four Elms 31 D4
Four Forks 23 F4
Four Gotes 70 C1
Four Lanes 3 D3
Four Marks 28 B4
Four Mile Bridge 88 A5
Four Oaks E.Suss. 19 D1
Four Oaks W.Mid. 67 E4
Four Oaks W.Mid. 66 D3
Four Roads 36 A2
Four Throws 18 C1
Fourlane Ends 81 E2
Fourlanes End 79 F2
Fourpenny 190 C5
Fourstones 119 E1
Fovant 26 B5
Foveran House 171 E2
Fowey 5 F4
Fowlis 152 B1
Fowlis Wester 151 E2
Fowlmere 58 C3
Fownhope 53 E4
Fox Lane 29 D2
Fox Street 60 B5
Foxcote 40 C1
Foxdale 98 A4
Foxearth 59 G3
Foxfield 106 D4
Foxham 40 B5
Foxhole Cornw. 5 D4
Foxhole High. 167 E1
Foxholes 112 D5
Foxhunt Green 18 A2
Foxley Here. 52 D3
Foxley Norf. 86 B3
Foxley Northants. 56 B2
Foxley Wilts. 40 A4
Foxt 80 B3
Foxton Cambs. 58 C3
Foxton Dur. 120 C5
Foxton Leics. 68 C3
Foxup 109 D5
Foxwist Green 78 D1
Foy 53 E5
Foyers 167 D2
Frachadil 154 C4
Fraddam 2 C3
Fraddon 4 D4
Fradley 67 D1
Fradswell 79 G4
Fraisthorpe 105 D1
Framfield 17 G1
Framingham Earl 87 D5
Framingham Pigot 87 D5
Framlingham 61 D1
Frampton Dorset 12 C3
Frampton Lincs. 84 B4
Frampton Cotterell 39 F4
Frampton Mansell 40 B2
Frampton on Severn 39 G2
Frampton West End 84 B3
Framsden 60 D2
Framwellgate Moor 120 B3
Franche 66 A5

Frankby 90 D4
Frankley 66 B4
Frankton 67 G5
Frant 31 E5
Fraserburgh 183 E3
Frating 60 B5
Fratton 15 F2
Freathy 7 D5
Freckenham 71 E5
Freckleton 100 A5
Freeby 82 D5
Freefolk 27 F3
Freeland 41 G1
Freemantle 14 D1
Freester 201 D2
Freethorpe 87 F5
Freethorpe Common 87 F5
Freiston 84 B3
Freiston Shore 84 B3
Fremington *Devon* 21 F2
Fremington *N.Yorks.* 109 F3
Frenchay 39 F5
Frenchbeer 7 G2
Frendraught 182 B5
Frenich 149 G4
Frensham 28 D3
Fresgoe 194 B2
Freshfield 91 D2
Freshford 25 E1
Freshwater 14 C4
Freshwater East 34 D3
Fressingfield 73 D4
Freston 60 C4
Freswick 195 F2
Frettenham 86 D4
Freuchie 152 A4
Freystrop Cross 34 C1
Friars Carse 124 D2
Friar's Gate 31 D5
Friarton 151 G2
Friday Bridge 70 C2
Friday Street *E.Suss.* 18 B3
Friday Street *Surr.* 29 G3
Fridaythorpe 104 A2
Friern Barnet 44 B3
Friesthorpe 96 A4
Frieston 83 E3
Frieth 42 C3
Frilford 41 G3
Frilsham 42 A5
Frimley 29 D2
Frimley Green 29 D2
Frindsbury 31 G2
Fring 85 F4
Fringford 56 B5
Frinsted 32 A3
Frinton-on-Sea 47 F1
Friockheim 161 D5
Friog 62 C1
Frisby on the Wreake 68 B1
Friskney 84 C2
Friskney Eaudyke 84 C2
Friston *E.Suss.* 18 A4
Friston *Suff.* 61 F2
Fritchley 81 E2
Frith 32 B3
Frith Bank 84 B3
Frith Common 53 F1
Fritham 14 B1
Frithelstock 21 E4
Frithelstock Stone 21 E4
Frithville 84 B2
Frittenden 32 A4
Fritton *Norf.* 72 D2
Fritton *Norf.* 87 F5
Fritwell 56 A5
Frizington 116 D5
Frocester 39 G2
Frochas 64 B1
Frodesley 65 E2
Frodingham 95 F1
Frodsham 91 G5
Frog End 58 C2
Frog Pool 53 G1
Frogden 136 B4
Froggatt 93 G5
Froghall 80 B3
Frogham 14 A1
Frogmore *Devon* 9 D3
Frogmore *Hants.* 28 D2
Frogmore *Herts.* 44 A2
Frolesworth 68 A3
Frome 25 E3
Frome Market 25 F2
Frome St. Quentin 12 B2
Fromes Hill 53 F3
Fron *Gwyn.* 74 C4
Fron *Powys* 64 B2
Fron *Powys* 51 G1
Fron-goch 76 C4
Froncysyllte 77 F3
Frostenden 73 F3
Frosterley 119 G4
Froxfield 27 D1
Froxfield Green 28 C5
Fryerning 45 F2
Fryton 111 F5
Fugglestone St. Peter 26 C4
Fulbeck 83 E2
Fulbourn 58 D2
Fulbrook 41 E1
Fulford *Som.* 23 F5
Fulford *Staffs.* 79 G4
Fulford *York* 103 F3
Fulham 44 B5
Fulking 17 E2
Full Sutton 103 G2
Fuller Street 45 G1
Fuller's Moor 78 B2
Fullerton 27 E4
Fulletby 96 C5
Fullwood 141 F5
Fulmer 43 E4
Fulmodeston 86 A2
Fulnetby 96 B5
Fulready 55 E3
Fulstow 96 D3
Fulwell *Oxon.* 55 F5
Fulwell *T.&W.* 120 C2
Fulwood *Lancs.* 100 B4
Fulwood *S.Yorks.* 94 A4
Fundenhall 72 C2
Funtington 16 A3
Funtley 15 E2
Funzie 203 F4
Furley 11 F2
Furnace *Arg. & B.* 148 C4
Furnace *Cere.* 62 C3
Furnace *High.* 177 F2
Furness Vale 93 E4
Furneux Pelham 58 C5
Furze Platt 43 D4
Furzehill 22 A3
Fyfett 11 F1
Fyfield *Essex* 45 E2
Fyfield *Glos.* 41 E2
Fyfield *Hants.* 27 D3
Fyfield *Oxon.* 41 G3
Fyfield *Wilts.* 26 C1
Fylingthorpe 112 C2
Fyvie 170 C1

## G

Gabhsunn Bho Dheas 187 F2
Gabhsunn Bho Thuath 187 F2
Gablon 190 C5
Gabroc Hill 141 F4
Gaddesby 68 B1
Gaddesden Row 43 F1
Gaer *Newport* 38 B4
Gaer *Powys* 52 A5
Gaerllwyd 38 D3
Gaerwen 88 C5
Gagingwell 55 G5
Gaich 168 C2
Gaick 167 F1
Gaick Lodge 158 C1
Gailey 66 B1
Gainford 110 A1
Gainsborough 95 F3
Gairloch 177 E2
Gairlochy 157 D1
Gairney Bank 151 G5
Gairnshiel Lodge 169 E4
Gaitsgill 117 G2
Galabank 144 B5
Galashiels 135 F2
Galdenoch 122 C4
Galgate 100 A2
Galhampton 24 D5
Gallanach 148 A2
Gallantry Bank 78 C2
Gallatown 152 A5
Gallchoille 139 F1
Gallery 161 E3
Galley Common 67 F3
Galleyend 45 G2
Galleywood 45 G2
Gallowfauld 160 C5
Gallowstree Common 42 B5
Gallowstree Elm 66 A4
Gallt Melyd (Meliden) 90 B4
Galltair 165 E3
Galmisdale 155 D1
Galmpton *Devon* 8 C3
Galmpton *Torbay* 9 E2
Galphay 110 B5
Galston 132 D2
Galtrigill 175 E4
Gamble's Green 45 G1
Gamblesby 118 C4
Gamelsby 117 F1
Gamlingay 58 A2
Gammaton Moor 21 E3
Gammersgill 109 F4
Gamrie 182 C3
Gamston *Notts.* 95 E5
Gamston *Notts.* 82 B4
Ganarew 39 E1
Ganllwyd 76 A5
Gannochy 161 E2
Ganstead 105 D4
Ganthorpe 111 F5
Ganton 112 C5
Gaodhail 147 F1
Gara Bridge 8 D2
Garabal 149 F3
Garadheancal 188 B4
Garbat 178 D3
Garbhallt 148 C5
Garboldisham 72 B3
Garden 150 A5
Garden City 78 A1
Gardenstown 182 C3
Garderhouse 200 C3
Gardham 104 B3
Gare Hill 25 E3
Garelochhead 149 E5
Garford 41 G3
Garforth 102 D4
Gargrave 101 F2
Gargunnock 150 C5
Gariob 139 F1
Garlies Castle 123 F4
Garlieston 115 E2
Garlogie 170 C4
Garmond 182 D4
Garmony 155 F5
Garmouth 181 F3
Garnant 36 C1
Garndolbenmaen 75 D3
Garneddwen 63 D2
Garnett Bridge 107 G3
Garnfadryn 74 B4
Garnswllt 36 C2
Garrabost 187 G4
Garrachra 140 B1
Garralburn 181 G4
Garras 3 D4
Garreg 75 F3
Garreg Bank 64 B1
Garrick 150 D3
Garrigill 118 D3
Garroch 123 G2
Garrochty 140 B4
Garros 176 B3
Garrow 150 D1
Garryhorn 123 G1
Garrynahine 186 D4
(Gearraidh na h-Aibhne)
Garsdale Head 108 C3
Garsdon 40 B4
Garshall Green 79 G4
Garsington 42 A2
Garstang 100 A3
Garston 91 F4
Garswood 91 G3
Gartachoil 150 A5
Gartally 167 D1
Gartavaich 139 G4
Gartbreck 138 A4
Gartcosh 142 A3
Garth *Bridgend* 37 E3
Garth *Gwyn.* 89 D5
Garth *I.o.M.* 98 B4
Garth *Powys* 51 F3
Garth *Shet.* 200 B2
Garth *Wrex.* 77 F3
Garthbrengy 51 G4
Gartheli 50 B2
Garthmyl 64 A3
Garthorpe *Leics.* 82 D5
Garthorpe *N.Lincs.* 95 F1
Garths 107 G3
Garthynty 50 D3
Gartincaber 150 B4
Gartly 170 A1
Gartmore 150 A5
Gartnagrenach 139 F4
Gartnatra 138 B4
Gartness 141 G1
Gartocharn 141 F1
Garton 105 E4
Garton-on-the-Wolds 104 B1
Gartymore 191 F3
Garvald 144 C2
Garvamore 167 E5
Garvan 156 B2
Garvard 146 C5
Garve 178 C3
Garveld 130 B5
Garvestone 86 B5
Garvie 140 B1
Garvock *Aber.* 161 F2
Garvock *Inclyde* 141 D2
Garvock *P.&K.* 151 F3
Garwald 134 D5
Garwaldwaterfoot 134 D5
Garway 53 D5
Garway Hill 52 D5
Gask *Aber.* 183 F5
Gask *Aber.* 182 C5
Gask *P.&K.* 151 E3
Gaskan 156 A2
Gass 132 C5
Gastard 25 F1
Gasthorpe 72 A3
Gatcombe 15 D4
Gate Burton 95 F4
Gate Helmsley 103 F2
Gate House 139 D2
Gateacre 91 F4
Gatebeck 107 G4
Gateford 94 C4
Gateforth 103 E5
Gatehead 132 B2
Gatehouse 159 D5
Gatehouse of Fleet 124 A5
Gatelawbridge 124 D1
Gateley 86 A3
Gatenby 110 C4
Gateshaw 136 B4
Gateshead 120 B1
Gatesheath 78 B1
Gateside *Aber.* 170 B3
Gateside *Angus* 160 C5
Gateside *Fife* 151 G4
Gateside *N.Ayr.* 141 E4
Gateslack 133 G5
Gathurst 91 G2
Gatley 92 C4
Gattonside 135 G2
Gatwick (London) Airport 30 B4
Gaufron 51 F1
Gaulby 68 B2
Gauldry 152 B2
Gaunt's Common 13 G2
Gautby 96 B5
Gavinton 145 E4
Gawber 94 A2
Gawcott 56 B4
Gawsworth 79 F1
Gawthrop 108 B4
Gawthwaite 107 D4
Gay Street 29 F5
Gaydon 55 F2
Gayhurst 56 D3
Gayles 110 A2
Gayton *Mersey.* 91 D4
Gayton *Norf.* 71 F1
Gayton *Northants.* 56 C2
Gayton *Staffs.* 79 G5
Gayton le Marsh 97 E4
Gayton le Wold 96 C4
Gayton Thorpe 71 F1
Gaywood 85 E5
Gazeley 59 F1
Geanies House 180 A2
Gearach 138 A4
Gearnsary 193 G5
Gearradh 156 B3
Gearraidh Bhailteas 172 C1
Gearraidh Bhaird 187 E5
Gearraidh na h-Aibhne (Garrynahine) 186 D4
Gearraidh na Monadh 172 C2
Gearrannan 186 C3
Geary 175 F3
Gedding 60 A2
Geddington 69 D4
Gedgrave Hall 61 F3
Gedling 82 B3
Gedney 84 C5
Gedney Broadgate 84 C5
Gedney Drove End 84 C5
Gedney Dyke 84 C5
Gedney Hill 70 B1
Gee Cross 93 D3
Geirninis 173 F5
Geisiadar 186 C4
Geldeston 73 E2
Gell *Conwy* 76 B1
Gell *Gwyn.* 75 D4
Gelli Gynan 77 E2
Gelligaer 38 A3
Gellilydan 75 F4
Gellioedd 76 C3
Gelly 35 D1
Gellyburn 151 F1
Gellywen 49 F5
Gelston 124 B5
Gembling 104 D2
Gemmil 147 G4
Genoch 122 C5
Genoch Square 122 C5
Gentleshaw 66 C1
George Green 43 F4
George Nympton 22 A5
Georgeham 21 E2
Georgetown 141 F3
Gerlan 75 F1
Germansweek 7 E1
Germoe 2 C4
Gerrans 3 F3
Gerrards Cross 43 E4
Gerston 194 D3
Gestingthorpe 59 G4
Geuffordd 64 B1
Geufron 63 E4
Gibbshill 124 B3
Gibraltar 85 D2
Gidea Park 45 E4
Gidleigh 7 G2
Giffnock 141 G4
Gifford 144 C3
Giffordland 141 D5
Giggleswick 101 E1
Gilberdyke 104 A5
Gilchriston 144 B3
Gilcrux 117 E3
Gildersome 102 B5
Gildingwells 94 C4
Gileston 22 D1
Gilfach 38 A3
Gilfach Goch 37 F4
Gilfachrheda 50 A2
Gilgarran 116 D4
Gillamoor 111 F3
Gillen 175 F3
Gillenbie 125 F2
Gillfoot 125 D3
Gilling East 111 F5
Gilling West 110 A2
Gillingham *Dorset* 25 F5
Gillingham *Med.* 31 G2
Gillingham *Norf.* 73 F2
Gillivoan 195 D5
Gillock 195 E3
Gillow Heath 79 F2
Gills 195 F1
Gill's Green 31 G5
Gilmanscleuch 135 E3
Gilmerton *Edin.* 143 G3
Gilmerton *P.&K.* 151 D2
Gilmilnscroft 133 D3
Gilmonby 109 E1
Gilmorton 68 A4
Gilsland 118 C1
Gilsland Spa 118 C1
Gilston 144 B4
Gilston Park 44 D1
Gilwern 38 B1
Gimingham 87 D2
Giosla 186 C5
Gipping 60 B1
Gipsey Bridge 84 A3
Girlsta 200 D2
Girsby 110 C2
Girtford 57 G3
Girthon 124 A5
Girton *Cambs.* 58 C1
Girton *Notts.* 82 D1
Girvan 122 C1
Gisburn 101 E3
Gisleham 73 G3
Gislingham 72 B4
Gissing 72 C3
Gittisham 11 E3
Givons Grove 29 G2
Glackour 178 A1
Gladestry 52 B2
Gladsmuir 144 B2
Glaic 140 B2
Glais 36 D2
Glaisdale 111 G2
Glaister 131 E2
Glame 176 B5
Glamis 160 B5
Glan Conwy 76 B2
Glan-Dwyfach 75 D3
Glan Honddu 51 G4
Glan-y-don 90 C5
Glan-y-llyn 38 A4
Glan-y-Wern 75 F4
Glan-yr-afon *Gwyn.* 76 C3
Glan-yr-afon *Gwyn.* 76 D3
Glanaber Terrace 76 A3
Glanadda 89 D5
Glanaman 36 C1
Glanbran 51 D4
Glanderston 170 A2
Glandford 86 B1
Glandwr *B.Gwent* 38 B2
Glandwr *Pembs.* 49 E5
Glangrwyne 38 B1
Glanllynfi 37 E3
Glanmule 64 A3
Glanrhyd 49 E3
Glanton 137 E5
Glantwymyn (Cemmaes Road) 63 E2
Glanvilles Wootton 12 C2
Glapthorn 69 F4
Glapwell 81 F1
Glasahoile 149 G4
Glasbury 52 A4
Glaschoil 168 C1
Glascoed 38 C2
Glascorrie 169 F5
Glascote 67 E2
Glascwm 52 A2
Glasdrum 156 C5
Glasfryn 76 C2
Glasgow 141 G3
Glasgow Airport 141 F3
Glashmore 170 C4
Glasinfryn 75 E1
Glasnacardoch 164 C5
Glasnakille 164 B3
Glaspant 49 F4
Glaspwll 62 D3
Glassburn 166 C1
Glassel 170 B5
Glassenbury 31 G5
Glasserton 115 E3
Glassford 142 B5
Glasshouse Hill 53 G5
Glasshouses 102 A1
Glassingall 150 C4
Glasslie 152 A4
Glasson *Cumb.* 126 A5
Glasson *Lancs.* 100 A2
Glassonby 118 B4
Glasterlaw 161 D4
Glaston 69 D2
Glastonbury 24 B4
Glatton 69 G4
Glazebury 92 A3
Glazeley 65 G4
Gleadless 94 A4
Gleadsmoss 79 F1
Gleann Ghrabhair 187 E5
Gleann Tholastaidh 187 G3
Gleaston 107 D5
Glecknabae 140 B3
Gledhow 102 C4
Gledrid 77 F4
Glemsford 59 G3
Glen *D.&G.* 124 C3
Glen *D.&G.* 123 G5
Glen Auldyn 98 C2
Glen Parva 68 A3
Glen Trool Lodge 123 F2
Glen Vine 98 B4
Glenae 125 D2
Glenaladale 156 A2
Glenald 149 E5
Glenamachrie 148 B2
Glenapp Castle 122 B2
Glenarm 160 B3
Glenbarr 130 B2
Glenbatrick 138 D2
Glenbeg *High.* 178 C1
Glenbeg *High.* 168 C2
Glenbeg *High.* 155 E3
Glenbeich 150 B2
Glenbervie *Aber.* 161 F1
Glenbervie *Falk.* 142 C1
Glenboig 142 B3
Glenborrodale 155 F3
Glenbranter 148 D5
Glenbreck 134 B3
Glenbrittle 164 A2
Glenbuck 133 F3
Glenbyre 147 E2
Glencaple 125 D4
Glencarse 151 G2
Glencat 170 A5
Glenceitlein 157 D5
Glencloy 131 F2
Glencoe 156 D4
Glenconglass 169 D2
Glencraig 151 G5
Glencripesdale 155 F4
Glencrosh 124 B2
Glencruittein 148 A2
Glencuie 169 G3
Glendearg *D.&G.* 134 D5
Glendearg *Sc.Bord.* 135 G2
Glendessary 165 F5
Glendevon 151 E4
Glendoebeg 166 D4
Glendoick 152 A2
Glendoll Lodge 160 A2
Glendoune 122 C1
Glendrissaig 122 C1
Glenduckie 152 A3
Glenduisk 122 D2
Glendye Lodge 161 E1
Gleneagles Hotel 151 E3
Gleneagles House 151 E4
Glenearn 151 G3
Glenegedale 138 B4
Glenelg 165 E3
Glenfarg 151 G3
Glenfeochan 148 A2
Glenfield 68 A2
Glenfinnan 156 B1
Glenfoot 151 G3
Glengalmadale 156 A4
Glengap 124 A5
Glengarnock 141 E4
Glengarrisdale 147 F5
Glengennet 123 D1
Glengolly 194 D2
Glengrasco 176 A5
Glengyle 149 F3
Glenhead 124 C2
Glenhead Farm 160 A3
Glenhurich 156 A3
Glenkerry 135 D4
Glenkiln 131 F2
Glenkin 140 C2
Glenkindie 169 G3
Glenlair 124 B3
Glenlatterach 181 E4
Glenlean 140 B1
Glenlee *Angus* 160 C1
Glenlee *D.&G.* 124 A2
Glenlichorn 150 C3
Glenlivet 169 D2
Glenlochar 124 B4
Glenluce 122 C5
Glenmallan 149 E5
Glenmanna 133 F5
Glenmavis 142 B3
Glenmaye 98 A3
Glenmeanie 178 B4
Glenmore *Arg. & B.* 140 B3
Glenmore *High.* 176 A5
Glenmore Lodge 168 B4
Glenmoy 160 C3
Glenmuick 189 F3
Glennoe 148 C1
Glenochar 134 A4
Glenogil 160 C3
Glenprosen Village 160 B3
Glenquiech 160 C3
Glenramskill 130 C4
Glenrazie 123 E4
Glenridding 117 G5
Glenrisdell 139 G4
Glenrossal 189 G4
Glenrothes 152 A4
Glensanda 156 A5
Glensaugh 161 E2
Glensgaich 179 D3
Glenshalg 170 A4
Glenshellish 148 D5
Glensluain 148 C5
Glentaggart 133 G3
Glentham 96 A3
Glenton 170 B2
Glentress 135 D2
Glentrool 123 E3
Glentruan 98 C1
Glentworth 95 G4
Glenuachdarach 176 A4
Glenuig 155 F2
Glenure 156 C5
Glenurquhart 179 G3
Glenwhilly 122 C3
Glespin 133 G3
Gletness 201 D2
Glewstone 53 E5
Glinton 69 G2
Glooston 68 C3
Glororum 137 F3
Glossop 93 E3
Gloster Hill 129 E1
Gloucester 40 A1
Gloup 203 E2
Gloweth 4 B5
Glusburn 101 G3
Gluss 202 C5
Glympton 55 G5
Glyn 76 A2
Glyn Ceiriog 77 F4
Glyn-Cywarch 75 F4
Glynarthen 49 G3
Glyncoch 37 G3
Glyncorrwg 37 E3
Glynde 17 G3
Glyndebourne 17 G2
Glyndyfrdwy 77 E3
Glynneath 37 E2
Glynogwr 37 F4
Glyntaff 37 G4
Glynteg 49 G4
Gnosall 79 F5
Gnosall Heath 66 A1
Goadby 68 C3
Goadby Marwood 82 C5
Goatacre 40 C5
Goatfield 148 C4
Goathill 12 C1
Goathland 112 B2
Goathurst 23 F4
Gobernuisgeach 194 B5
Gobhaig 184 C3
Gobowen 78 F4
Godalming 29 E3
Godford Cross 11 E2
Godmanchester 58 A1
Godmanstone 12 C3
Godmersham 32 C3
Godolphin Cross 2 D3
Godor 64 B1
Godre'r-graig 37 D2
Godshill *Hants.* 14 A1
Godshill *I.o.W.* 15 E4
Godstone 30 C3
Goetre 38 C2
Goff's Oak 44 C2
Gogar 143 F2
Gogarth 89 F4
Goginan 62 C4
Goirtean a' Chladaich 156 C2
Goirtein 140 A1
Golan 75 E3
Golant 5 F4
Golberdon 6 D3
Golborne 92 A3
Golcar 93 F1
Gold Hill 70 D3
Goldcliff 38 C4
Golden Cross 18 A2
Golden Green 31 F4
Golden Grove 36 B1
Golden Pot 28 C3
Golden Valley 54 B5
Goldenhill 79 F2
Golders Green 44 B4
Goldhanger 46 B2
Goldielea 124 D3
Golding 65 E2
Goldington 57 F2
Goldsborough *N.Yorks.* 112 B1
Goldsborough *N.Yorks.* 102 C2
Goldsithney 2 C3
Goldthorpe 94 B2
Goldworthy 21 D3
Gollanfield 180 A4
Golspie 190 D5
Golval 194 A2
Gomeldon 26 C4
Gomersal 102 B5
Gometra House 154 C5
Gomshall 29 F3
Gonachan Cottage 142 A1
Gonalston 82 B3
Gonfirth 200 C1
Good Easter 45 F1
Gooderstone 71 F2
Goodleigh 21 G2
Goodmanham 104 A3
Goodnestone *Kent* 33 E3
Goodnestone *Kent* 32 C2
Goodrich 39 E1
Goodrington 9 E2
Goodwick (Wdig) 48 C4
Goodworth Clatford 27 E3
Goodyers End 67 F4
Goole 103 G5
Goonbell 4 B5
Goonhavern 4 B4
Goose Green 31 F3
Gooseham 20 C4
Goosewell 8 B2
Goosey 41 F3
Goosnargh 100 B4
Goostrey 92 B5
Gorcott Hill 54 C1
Gorddinog 89 E5
Gordon 144 D5
Gordonbush 190 D4
Gordonstoun 181 D3
Gordonstown *Aber.* 182 A4
Gordonstown *Aber.* 170 C1
Gore Cross 26 B2
Gore Street 33 E2
Gorebridge 144 A3
Gorefield 70 C1
Gorey 8 D5
Goring 42 B4
Goring-by-Sea 16 D3
Gorleston on Sea 87 G5
Gorllwyn 49 G4
Gornalwood 66 B3
Gorrachie 182 C4
Gorran Churchtown 5 D5
Gorran Haven 5 E5
Gors 62 C5
Gorsedd 90 C5
Gorseinon 36 B3
Gorseness 198 C5
Gorsgoch 50 A2
Gorslas 36 B1
Gorsley 53 F5
Gorsley Common 53 F5
Gorstan 178 C3
Gorstanvorran 156 A2
Gorten 147 G1
Gortenbuie 147 E1
Gorteneorn 155 F3
Gorton *Arg. & B.* 154 A4
Gorton *Gt.Man.* 92 C3
Gosbeck 60 C2
Gosberton 84 A4
Goseley Dale 81 E5
Gosfield 59 F5
Gosforth *Cumb.* 106 B2
Gosforth *T.&W.* 120 B1
Gosmore 57 G5
Gospel End 66 B3
Gosport 15 F3
Gossabrough 203 E4
Gossops Green 30 B5
Goswick 137 E2
Gotham 81 G4
Gotherington 54 B5
Gott 200 D3
Goudhurst 31 G5
Goulceby 96 C5
Gourdas 182 C5
Gourdon 161 G2
Gourock 140 D2
Govan 141 G3
Goveton 9 D3
Govilon 38 B1
Gowanhill 183 F3
Gowdall 103 F5
Gowerton 36 B3
Gowkhall 143 E1
Gowthorpe 103 G2
Goxhill *E.Riding* 105 D3
Goxhill *N.Lincs.* 104 D5
Goytre 37 D4
Grabhair 185 F2
Gradbach 79 G1
Grade 3 E5
Graffham 16 B2
Grafham *Cambs.* 57 G1
Grafham *Surr.* 29 F3
Grafton *Here.* 53 D4
Grafton *N.Yorks.* 102 D1
Grafton *Oxon.* 41 E2
Grafton *Shrop.* 64 D1
Grafton *Worcs.* 53 E1
Grafton Flyford 54 B2
Grafton Regis 56 C3
Grafton Underwood 69 E5
Grafty Green 32 A4
Graianrhyd 77 F2
Graig *Conwy* 89 G5
Graig *Denb.* 90 B5
Graig-fechan 77 E2
Graig Penllyn 37 F5
Grain 32 A1
Grainel 138 A3
Grainhow 183 D5
Grainsby 96 C3
Grainthorpe 97 D3
Graiselound 95 E3
Grampound 4 D5
Grampound Road 4 D4
Gramsdal 173 G4
Granborough 56 C5
Granby 82 C4
Grandborough 55 G1
Grandtully 159 E4
Grange *Cumb.* 117 F5
Grange *High.* 166 C1
Grange *Med.* 31 G2
Grange *N.Yorks.* 111 E3
Grange *P.&K.* 152 A2
Grange Crossroads 181 G4
Grange Hall 180 C3
Grange Hill 44 D3
Grange Moor 93 G1
Grange of Lindores 152 A3
Grange-over-Sands 107 F5
Grange Villa 120 B2
Grangemill 80 D2
Grangemouth 142 D1
Grangemuir 152 D4
Grangeston 122 D1
Grangetown *Cardiff* 38 A5
Grangetown *R.&C.* 121 E5
Granish 168 B3
Gransmoor 104 D2

Granston 48 B4
Grantchester 58 C2
Grantham 83 E4
Grantley 110 B5
Grantlodge 170 C3
Granton House 134 B5
Grantown-on-Spey 168 C2
Grantshouse 145 F3
Grappenhall 92 A4
Grasby 96 A2
Grasmere 107 E2
Grasscroft 93 D2
Grassendale 91 E4
Grassholme 119 F5
Grassington 101 G1
Grassmoor 81 F1
Grassthorpe 82 C1
Grateley 27 D3
Gratwich 80 B4
Graveley Cambs. 58 A1
Graveley Herts. 58 A5
Gravelly Hill 66 D3
Gravels 64 C2
Graven 202 D5
Graveney 32 C2
Gravesend 45 F5
Grayingham 95 G3
Grayrigg 107 G3
Grays 45 F5
Grayshott 29 D4
Grayswood 29 E4
Grazeley 28 C1
Greasbrough 94 B3
Greasby 91 D4
Great Abington 58 D3
Great Addington 69 E5
Great Alne 54 D2
Great Altcar 91 E2
Great Amwell 44 C1
Great Asby 108 B1
Great Ashfield 60 A1
Great Ayton 111 E1
Great Baddow 45 G2
Great Bardfield 59 E4
Great Barford 57 G2
Great Barr 66 C3
Great Barrington 41 E1
Great Barrow 78 B1
Great Barton 59 G1
Great Barugh 111 G5
Great Bavington 128 B3
Great Bealings 60 D3
Great Bedwyn 27 D1
Great Bentley 60 C5
Great Billing 56 D1
Great Bircham 85 F4
Great Blakenham 60 C2
Great Bolas 78 D5
Great Bookham 29 G2
Great Bourton 55 G3
Great Bowden 68 C4
Great Bradley 59 E2
Great Braxted 46 B1
Great Bricett 60 B2
Great Brickhill 57 E4
Great Bridgeford 79 F5
Great Brington 56 B1
Great Bromley 60 B5
Great Broughton Cumb. 117 D3
Great Broughton N.Yorks. 111 E2
Great Budworth 92 A5
Great Burdon 110 C1
Great Burstead 45 F3
Great Busby 111 E2
Great Canfield 45 E1
Great Canney 46 B2
Great Carlton 97 E4
Great Casterton 69 F2
Great Chart 32 B4
Great Chatwell 65 G1
Great Chesterford 58 D3
Great Cheverell 26 A2
Great Chishill 58 C4
Great Clacton 47 E1
Great Clifton 116 D4
Great Coates 96 C2
Great Comberton 54 B3
Great Corby 118 A2
Great Cornard 59 G3
Great Cowden 105 E3
Great Coxwell 41 E3
Great Crakehall 110 B3
Great Cransley 68 D5
Great Cressingham 71 G2
Great Crosby 91 E2
Great Cubley 80 C4
Great Dalby 68 C1
Great Doddington 57 D1
Great Dunham 71 G1
Great Dunmow 59 E5
Great Durnford 26 C4
Great Easton Essex 59 E5
Great Easton Leics. 69 D3
Great Eccleston 100 A3
Great Edstone 111 G4
Great Ellingham 72 B2
Great Elm 25 E3
Great Eversden 58 B2
Great Fencote 110 B3
Great Finborough 60 B2
Great Fransham 71 G1
Great Gaddesden 43 F1
Great Gidding 69 G4
Great Givendale 104 A2
Great Glemham 61 E1
Great Glen 68 B3
Great Gonerby 83 D4
Great Gransden 58 A2
Great Green Norf. 73 D2
Great Green Suff. 60 A2
Great Habton 111 G5
Great Hale 83 G3
Great Hallingbury 45 E1
Great Harrowden 69 D5
Great Harwood 100 D4
Great Haseley 42 B2
Great Hatfield 105 D3
Great Haywood 80 B5
Great Heath 67 F4
Great Heck 103 E5
Great Henny 59 G4
Great Hinton 26 A2
Great Hockham 72 A2
Great Holland 47 F1
Great Horkesley 60 A4
Great Hormead 58 C4
Great Horwood 56 C4
Great Houghton Northants. 56 C2
Great Houghton S.Yorks. 94 B2
Great Hucklow 93 F5
Great Kelk 104 D2
Great Kimble 42 D2
Great Kingshill 43 D3
Great Langton 110 B3
Great Leighs 45 G1
Great Limber 96 B2
Great Linford 56 D3
Great Livermere 71 G5
Great Longstone 93 G5
Great Lumley 120 B3
Great Lyth 65 D2
Great Malvern 53 G3
Great Maplestead 59 G4
Great Marton 99 G4
Great Massingham 85 F5
Great Melton 86 C5
Great Milton 42 B2
Great Missenden 43 D2
Great Mitton 100 D4
Great Mongeham 33 F3
Great Moulton 72 C2
Great Munden 58 B5
Great Musgrave 108 C1
Great Ness 64 C1
Great Notley 59 F5
Great Oak 38 C1
Great Oakley Essex 60 C5
Great Oakley Northants. 69 D4
Great Offley 57 G5
Great Ormside 108 C1
Great Orton 117 G1
Great Ouseburn 102 D1
Great Oxendon 68 C4
Great Oxney Green 45 F2
Great Palgrave 71 G1
Great Parndon 44 D2
Great Paxton 58 A1
Great Plumpton 99 G4
Great Plumstead 87 D5
Great Ponton 83 E4
Great Preston 102 C5
Great Raveley 70 A4
Great Rissington 41 D1
Great Rollright 55 F4
Great Ryburgh 86 A3
Great Ryle 137 E5
Great Ryton 65 D2
Great Saling 59 E5
Great Salkeld 118 B4
Great Sampford 59 E4
Great Sankey 91 G4
Great Saxham 59 F1
Great Shefford 41 F5
Great Shelford 58 C2
Great Smeaton 110 C2
Great Snoring 86 A2
Great Somerford 40 B4
Great Stainton 120 C5
Great Stambridge 46 B3
Great Staughton 57 G1
Great Steeping 84 C1
Great Stonar 33 F3
Great Strickland 118 B5
Great Stukeley 70 A5
Great Sturton 96 C5
Great Sutton Ches. 91 E5
Great Sutton Shrop. 65 E4
Great Swinburne 128 B4
Great Tew 55 F5
Great Tey 59 G5
Great Thurlow 59 E3
Great Torrington 21 F4
Great Tosson 128 C1
Great Totham Essex 46 B1
Great Totham Essex 46 B1
Great Urswick 107 D5
Great Wakering 46 C4
Great Waldingfield 60 A3
Great Walsingham 86 A2
Great Waltham 45 F1
Great Warley 45 E3
Great Washbourne 54 B4
Great Welnetham 59 G2
Great Wenham 60 B4
Great Whittington 128 C4
Great Wigborough 46 C1
Great Wilbraham 58 D2
Great Wishford 26 B4
Great Witcombe 40 B1
Great Witley 53 G1
Great Wolford 55 E4
Great Wratting 59 E3
Great Wymondley 58 A5
Great Wyrley 66 B2
Great Wytheford 65 E1
Great Yarmouth 87 G5
Great Yeldham 59 F4
Greatford 69 F1
Greatgate 80 B3
Greatham Hants. 28 C4
Greatham Hart. 121 D5
Greatham W.Suss. 16 C2
Greatstone-on-Sea 19 F1
Greatworth 56 A3
Green End Beds. 57 G2
Green End Herts. 58 B5
Green Hammerton 103 D2
Green Ore 24 C2
Green Street 44 A3
Green Street Green Gt.Lon. 31 D2
Green Street Green Kent 45 E5
Green Tye 44 D1
Greenburn 152 C1
Greencroft 120 A3
Greendams 170 B5
Greendykes 137 E4
Greenfield Beds. 57 F4
Greenfield (Maes-Glas) Flints. 90 C5
Greenfield Gt.Man. 93 E2
Greenfield High. 166 B4
Greenfield Oxon. 42 C3
Greenford 44 A4
Greengairs 142 B2
Greenhalgh 100 A4
Greenhall 170 B2
Greenham Som. 23 D5
Greenham W.Berks. 27 F1
Greenhaugh 127 F3
Greenhead 118 C1
Greenheads 171 F1
Greenhill Gt.Lon. 44 A4
Greenhill High. 191 E4
Greenhill S.Yorks. 94 A4
Greenhithe 45 E5
Greenholm 132 D2
Greenholme 107 G2
Greenhow Hill 102 A1
Greenigo 196 D2
Greenland 195 E2
Greenlands 42 C4
Greenlaw Aber. 182 B4
Greenlaw Sc.Bord. 145 E5
Greenloaning 150 D4
Greenmount 92 B1
Greenmyre 170 D1
Greenock 141 D2
Greenodd 107 E4
Greens Norton 56 B2
Greenscares 150 C3
Greenside 120 A1
Greenstead Green 59 G5
Greensted 45 E2
Greenway Pembs. 49 D4
Greenway Som. 24 A5
Greenwich Gt.Lon. 44 C5
Greenwich Gt.Lon. 44 C5
Greet 54 C4
Greete 65 E5
Greetham Lincs. 96 D5
Greetham Rut. 69 E1
Greetland 101 G5
Greinetobht 173 G2
Greinton 24 B4
Grenaby 98 A4
Grendon Northants. 57 D1
Grendon Warks. 67 E3
Grendon Common 67 E3
Grendon Green 53 E2
Grendon Underwood 56 B5
Grenoside 94 A3
Greosabhagh 185 D4
Gresford 78 A2
Gresham 86 C2
Greshornish 175 G4
Gressenhall 86 A4
Gressingham 107 G5
Greta Bridge 109 F1
Gretna 126 B5
Gretna Green 126 B5
Gretton Glos. 54 C4
Gretton Northants. 69 E3
Gretton Shrop. 65 E3
Grewelthorpe 110 B5
Greygarth 110 A5
Greylake 24 A4
Greys Green 42 C4
Greysouthen 117 D4
Greystoke 118 A4
Greystone Aber. 169 E5
Greystone Angus 160 D5
Greystone Lancs. 101 E3
Greywell 28 C2
Griais 187 F3
Gribthorpe 103 G4
Gribton 124 D2
Gridley Corner 7 D1
Griff 67 F4
Griffithstown 38 B3
Grigadale 154 D3
Grigghall 107 F3
Grimeford Village 92 A1
Grimethorpe 94 B2
Griminis 173 F4
Grimister 203 D3
Grimley 54 A1
Grimmet 132 B4
Grimness 197 D3
Grimoldby 97 D4
Grimpo 78 A5
Grimsargh 100 B4
Grimsbury 55 G3
Grimsby 96 C2
Grimscote 56 B2
Grimscott 20 C5
Grimsiadar 187 F5
Grimsthorpe 83 F5
Grimston Leics. 82 B5
Grimston Norf. 85 F5
Grimstone 12 C3
Grindale 113 E5
Grindiscol 201 D4
Grindle 65 G2
Grindleford 93 G5
Grindleton 101 D3
Grindley 80 B5
Grindlow 93 F5
Grindon Northumb. 145 G5
Grindon Staffs. 80 B2
Gringley on the Hill 95 E3
Grinsdale 117 G1
Grinshill 78 C5
Grinton 109 F3
Griomarstaidh 186 D4
Grishipoll 154 A4
Gristhorpe 113 D4
Griston 72 A2
Gritley 197 E2
Grittenham 40 C4
Grittleton 40 A4
Grizebeck 106 D4
Grizedale 107 E3
Grobister 199 E4
Groby 68 A2
Groes 76 D1
Groes-faen 37 G4
Groes-lwyd 64 B1
Groesffordd 74 B4
Groesffordd Marli 90 B5
Groeslon 75 D2
Grogport 139 G5
Groigearraidh 162 A1
Gromford 61 E2
Gronant 90 B4
Groombridge 31 E5
Grosmont Mon. 52 D5
Grosmont N.Yorks. 112 B2
Grotaig 167 D2
Groton 60 A3
Groundistone Heights 135 F4
Grouville 8 C5
Grove Dorset 12 C5
Grove Kent 33 E2
Grove Notts. 95 E5
Grove Oxon. 41 G3
Grove Park 44 D5
Grovesend 36 B2
Gruids 190 A4
Gruinart Flats 138 A3
Gruline 147 E1
Grundcruie 151 F2
Grundisburgh 60 D2
Gruting 200 B3
Grutness 201 G5
Gualachulain 156 D5
Guardbridge 152 C3
Guarlford 54 A3
Guay 159 F5
Gubbergill 106 B3
Guernsey Airport 9 E5
Guestling Green 19 D2
Guestling Thorn 19 D2
Guestwick 86 B3
Guide Post 129 E3
Guilden Morden 58 A3
Guilden Sutton 78 B1
Guildford 29 E3
Guildtown 151 G1
Guilsborough 68 B5
Guilsfield (Cegidfa) 64 B1
Guisborough 111 F1
Guiseley 102 A3
Guist 86 A3
Guith 199 D3
Guiting Power 54 C5
Gulberwick 200 D4
Gullane 144 B1
Gulval 2 B3
Gulworthy 7 E3
Gumfreston 35 E2
Gumley 68 B4
Gunby E.Riding 103 G4
Gunby Lincs. 83 E5
Gundleton 28 B4
Gunn 21 G2
Gunnerside 109 E3
Gunnerton 128 B4
Gunness 95 F1
Gunnislake 7 E3
Gunnista 201 D3
Gunter's Bridge 29 E5
Gunthorpe Norf. 86 B2
Gunthorpe Notts. 82 B3
Gunville 15 D4
Gunwalloe 3 D4
Gurnard 15 D3
Gurney Slade 24 D3
Gurnos 37 D2
Gussage All Saints 13 G1
Gussage St. Michael 13 F1
Guston 33 F4
Gutcher 203 E3
Guthrie 161 D4
Guyhirn 70 B2
Guynd 161 D5
Guy's Head 84 C5
Guy's Marsh 25 F5
Guyzance 129 E1
Gwaelod-y-garth 38 A4
Gwaenysgor 90 B4
Gwaithla 52 B2
Gwalchmai 88 B5
Gwaun-Cae-Gurwen 36 D1
Gwaynynog 76 D1
Gwbert 49 E3
Gweek 3 E4
Gwehelog 38 C2
Gwenddwr 51 G3
Gwennap 4 B5
Gwenter 3 E5
Gwernaffield 77 F1
Gwernesney 38 D2
Gwernogle 50 B4
Gwernymynydd 77 F1
Gwersyllt 78 A2
Gwespyr 90 C4
Gwinear 2 C3
Gwithian 2 C2
Gwyddelwern 77 D3
Gwyddgrug 50 A4
Gwystre 51 G1
Gwytherin 76 B1
Gyfelia 78 A3
Gyffin 89 F5
Gyre 196 C2
Gyrn Goch 74 D3

## H

Habberley 64 C2
Habrough 96 B1
Haccombe 10 B5
Hacconby 83 G5
Haceby 83 F4
Hacheston 61 E2
Hackenthorpe 94 B4
Hackford 86 B5
Hackforth 110 B3
Hackland 198 B4
Hackleton 56 D2
Hacklinge 33 F3
Hackness N.Yorks. 112 C3
Hackness Ork. 196 C3
Hackney 44 C4
Hackthorn 95 G4
Hackthorpe 118 B5
Hadden 136 B3
Haddenham Bucks. 42 C2
Haddenham Cambs. 70 C5
Haddington E.Loth. 144 C2
Haddington Lincs. 83 E1
Haddiscoe 73 F2
Haddon 69 G3
Hademore 67 D2
Hadfield 93 E3
Hadham Cross 44 D1
Hadham Ford 58 C5
Hadleigh Essex 46 B4
Hadleigh Suff. 60 B3
Hadley 65 F1
Hadley End 80 C5
Hadley Wood 44 B3
Hadlow 31 F4
Hadlow Down 18 A1
Hadnall 78 C5
Hadstock 59 D3
Hadzor 54 B1
Haffenden Quarter 32 A4
Hafod-Dinbych 76 B2
Hafodunos 76 B1
Haggate 101 E4
Haggbeck 126 C4
Haggs 142 B2
Hagley Here. 53 E3
Hagley Worcs. 66 B4
Hagnaby 84 B1
Hagworthingham 84 B1
Haigh 92 A2
Haighton Green 100 B4
Hail Weston 57 G1
Haile 106 B2
Hailes 54 C4
Hailey Herts. 44 C1
Hailey Oxon. 42 B4
Hailey Oxon. 41 F1
Hailsham 18 A3
Haimer 194 D2
Hainault 45 D3
Hainford 86 D4
Hainton 96 B4
Haisthorpe 104 D1
Halam 82 B2
Halbeath 143 F1
Halberton 10 D1
Halcro 195 E2
Hale Gt.Man. 92 B4
Hale Hants. 14 A1
Hale Surr. 28 D3
Hale Bank 91 F4
Hale Street 31 F4
Halebarns 92 B4
Hales Norf. 73 E2
Hales Staffs. 79 E4
Hales Place 32 D3
Halesowen 66 B4
Halesworth 73 E4
Halewood 91 F4
Half Way Inn 11 D3
Halford Shrop. 64 D4
Halford Warks. 55 E3
Halfpenny Green 66 A3
Halfway Carmar. 50 C4
Halfway Powys 51 E4
Halfway S.Yorks. 94 B4
Halfway W.Berks. 27 F1
Halfway House 64 C1
Halfway Houses 32 B1
Halghton Mill 78 B3
Halifax 101 G5
Halistra 175 F4
Halkirk 194 D3
Halkyn 90 D5
Hall 141 F4
Hall Dunnerdale 106 D3
Hall Green 66 D4
Hall of the Forest 64 B4
Halland 18 A2
Hallaton 68 C3
Hallatrow 24 D2
Hallbankgate 118 B2
Hallen 39 E5
Hallin 175 F4
Halling 31 G2
Hallington Lincs. 96 D4
Hallington Northumb. 128 B4
Halloughton 82 B2
Hallow 54 A2
Hallow Heath 54 A2
Hallrule 135 G4
Halls 145 D2
Hall's Green 58 A5
Hall's Tenement 118 B2
Hallsands 9 E4
Hallworthy 5 F1
Halmer End 79 E3
Halmore 39 F2
Halmyre Mains 143 F5
Halnaker 16 B3
Halsall 91 E1
Halse Northants. 56 A3
Halse Som. 23 E5
Halsetown 2 C3
Halsham 105 E5
Halsinger 21 F2
Halstead Essex 59 G4
Halstead Kent 31 D2
Halstead Leics. 68 C2
Halstock 12 B2
Haltham 84 A1
Haltoft End 84 B3
Halton Bucks. 43 D1
Halton Halton 91 G4
Halton Lancs. 100 B1
Halton Northumb. 119 G1
Halton Wrex. 70 A4
Halton East 101 G2
Halton Gill 109 D5
Halton Holegate 84 C1
Halton Lea Gate 118 C2
Halton West 101 E2
Haltwhistle 118 D1
Halvergate 87 F5
Halwell 9 D2
Halwill 7 E1
Halwill Junction 7 E1
Ham Glos. 39 F3
Ham Gt.Lon. 44 A5
Ham High. 195 E1
Ham Kent 33 F3
Ham Shet. 200 B5
Ham Som. 23 F5
Ham Wilts. 27 E1
Ham Green N.Som. 39 E5
Ham Green Worcs. 54 C1
Ham Hill 31 F2
Ham Street 24 C4
Hamble-le-Rice 15 D2
Hambleden 42 C4
Hambledon Hants. 15 F1
Hambledon Surr. 29 E4
Hambleton Lancs. 99 G3
Hambleton N.Yorks. 103 E4
Hambleton Moss Side 99 G3
Hambridge 24 A5
Hambrook S.Glos. 39 F5
Hambrook W.Suss. 15 G2
Hameringham 84 B1
Hamerton 69 G5
Hamilton 142 B4
Hamlet 11 E3
Hammer 29 D4
Hammerpot 16 C3
Hammersmith & Fulham 44 A5
Hammerwich 66 C2
Hammerwood 30 D5
Hammond Street 44 C2
Hammoon 13 E1
Hamnavoe Shet. 200 C4
Hamnavoe Shet. 203 D4
Hamnavoe Shet. 202 B4
Hamnavoe Shet. 203 D5
Hampden Park 18 B3
Hampnett 40 D1
Hampole 94 C2
Hampreston 13 G3
Hampstead 44 B4
Hampstead Norreys 42 A5
Hampsthwaite 102 B2
Hampton Gt.Lon. 29 G1
Hampton Shrop. 65 G4
Hampton Worcs. 54 C3
Hampton Bishop 53 E4
Hampton Heath 78 B3
Hampton in Arden 67 E4
Hampton Lovett 54 A1
Hampton Lucy 55 E2
Hampton on the Hill 55 E1
Hampton Poyle 42 A1
Hamptworth 26 D5
Hamsey 17 G2
Hamstall Ridware 66 D1
Hamstead I.o.W. 14 D3
Hamstead W.Mid. 66 C3
Hamstead Marshall 27 F1
Hamsterley Dur. 120 A4
Hamsterley Dur. 120 A2
Hamstreet 32 C5
Hamworthy 13 F3
Hanbury Staffs. 80 C5
Hanbury Worcs. 54 B1
Hanbury Woodend 80 C5
Hanchurch 79 F3
Handbridge 78 B1
Handcross 17 E1
Handforth 92 C4
Handley 78 B2
Handsacre 66 C1
Handsworth S.Yorks. 94 B4
Handsworth W.Mid. 66 C3
Handy Cross 43 D3
Hanford 79 F3
Hanging Bridge 80 C3
Hanging Langford 26 B4
Hangingshaw 125 F2
Hangleton 17 E3
Hanham 39 F5
Hankelow 79 D3
Hankerton 40 B3
Hankham 18 B3
Hanley 79 F3
Hanley Castle 54 A3
Hanley Child 53 F1
Hanley Swan 54 A3
Hanley William 53 F1
Hanlith 101 F1
Hanmer 78 B4
Hannah 97 E5
Hannington Hants. 27 G2
Hannington Northants. 68 D5
Hannington Swin. 41 D3
Hannington Wick 41 D3
Hanslope 56 D3
Hanthorpe 83 F5
Hanwell Gt.Lon. 44 A5
Hanwell Oxon. 55 G3
Hanwood 64 D2
Hanworth Gt.Lon. 44 A5
Hanworth Norf. 86 C2
Happisburgh 87 E2
Happisburgh Common 87 E3
Hapsford 91 F5
Hapton Lancs. 101 D4
Hapton Norf. 72 C2
Harberton 9 D2
Harbertonford 9 D2
Harbledown 32 D3
Harborne 66 C4
Harborough Magna 67 G5
Harbottle 128 B1
Harbourneford 8 D1
Harbridge 14 A1
Harburn 143 E3
Harbury 55 F2
Harby Leics. 82 C4
Harby Notts. 95 F5
Harcombe 11 E3
Harden 101 G4
Hardenhuish 40 B5
Hardgate 170 C4
Hardham 16 C2
Hardingham 86 B5
Hardings Wood 79 F2
Hardingstone 56 C2
Hardington 25 E2
Hardington Mandeville 12 B1
Hardington Marsh 12 B2
Hardley 14 D2
Hardley Street 87 E5
Hardmead 57 E3
Hardraw 109 D3
Hardstoft 81 F1
Hardway Hants. 15 F2
Hardway Som. 25 E4
Hardwick Bucks. 42 D1
Hardwick Cambs. 58 B2
Hardwick Norf. 72 D2
Hardwick Northants. 57 D1
Hardwick Oxon. 41 F2
Hardwick Oxon. 56 A5
Hardwick Village 94 D5
Hardwicke Glos. 54 B5
Hardwicke Glos. 39 G1
Hardwicke Here. 52 B3
Hardy's Green 46 C1
Hare Green 60 B5
Hare Hatch 42 D5
Hare Street Herts. 58 B5
Hare Street Herts. 58 B5
Hareby 84 B1
Hareden 100 C2
Harefield 43 F3
Harehills 102 C4
Harelaw 142 D5
Haresceugh 118 C3
Harescombe 40 A1
Haresfield 40 A1
Hareshaw 142 A5
Harewood 102 C3
Harewood End 53 E5
Harford 8 C2
Hargate 72 C2
Hargrave Ches. 78 B1
Hargrave Northants. 69 F5
Hargrave Suff. 59 F2
Haringey 44 C4
Harker 126 B5
Harkstead 60 C4
Harlaston 67 E1
Harlaxton 83 D4
Harle Syke 101 E4
Harlech 75 E4
Harlesden 44 B4
Harleston Norf. 72 D3
Harleston Suff. 60 B2
Harlestone 56 C1
Harley 65 E2
Harleyholm 134 A2
Harlington 57 F4
Harlosh 175 F5
Harlow 45 D1
Harlow Hill 119 G1
Harlthorpe 103 G4
Harlton 58 B2
Harman's Cross 13 F4
Harmby 110 A3
Harmer Green 44 B1
Harmer Hill 78 B5
Harmondsworth 43 F5
Harmston 83 E1
Harnham 26 C5
Harnhill 40 C2
Harold Hill 45 E3
Harold Wood 45 E3
Haroldston West 34 B1
Haroldswick 203 F1
Harome 111 F4
Harpenden 44 A1
Harpford 11 D3
Harpham 104 C1
Harpley Norf. 85 F5
Harpley Worcs. 53 F1
Harpole 56 B1
Harprigg 108 B4
Harpsdale 194 D3
Harpsden 42 C4
Harpswell 95 G3
Harpur Hill 93 E5
Harpurhey 92 C2
Harrapool 164 C2
Harrietfield 151 E1
Harrietsham 32 A3
Harrington Lincs. 97 D5
Harrington Northants. 68 C5
Harringworth 69 E3
Harris 163 G5
Harriseahead 79 F2
Harrogate 102 C2
Harrold 57 E2
Harrow Gt.Lon. 44 A4
Harrow High. 195 E1
Harrow on the Hill 44 A4
Harrow Weald 44 A3
Harrowbarrow 7 E3
Harrowden 57 F3
Harston Cambs. 58 C2
Harston Leics. 82 D4
Hart 121 D4
Hartburn Northumb. 128 C3
Hartburn Stock. 110 D1
Hartest 59 G2
Hartfield E.Suss. 31 D5
Hartfield High. 176 D5
Hartford Cambs. 70 A5
Hartford Ches. 92 A5
Hartford End 45 F1
Hartfordbridge 28 C2
Harthill Ches. 78 B2
Harthill N.Lan. 142 D3
Harthill S.Yorks. 94 B4
Hartington 80 C1
Hartland 20 C3
Hartland Quay 20 C3
Hartlebury 66 A5
Hartlepool 121 E4
Hartley Cumb. 108 C2
Hartley Kent 31 F2
Hartley Kent 31 G5

Hartley Northumb. 129 F4
Hartley Wespall 28 C2
Hartley Wintney 28 C2
Hartlip 32 A2
Harton N.Yorks. 103 G1
Harton Shrop. 65 D4
Harton T. & W. 120 C1
Hartpury 53 G5
Hartrigge 136 A4
Hartshill 67 F3
Hartshorne 81 E5
Hartsop 107 F1
Hartwell Bucks. 42 C1
Hartwell E.Suss. 31 D5
Hartwell Northants. 56 C3
Hartwood 142 C4
Harvel 31 F2
Harvington Worcs. 54 C3
Harvington Worcs. 66 A5
Harwell Notts. 95 D3
Harwell Oxon. 41 G4
Harwich 60 D4
Harwood Dur. 119 E4
Harwood Gt.Man. 92 B1
Harwood Dale 112 C3
Harwood on Teviot 135 F5
Harworth 94 D3
Hasbury 66 B4
Hascombe 29 E4
Haselbech 68 C5
Haselbury Plucknett 12 A1
Haseley 55 E1
Haselor 54 D2
Hasfield 54 A5
Hasguard 34 B2
Haskayne 91 E2
Hasketon 60 D2
Hasland 81 E1
Haslemere 29 E4
Haslingden 101 D5
Haslingden Grane 101 D5
Haslingfield 58 C2
Haslington 79 E2
Hassall 79 E2
Hassall Green 79 E2
Hassell Street 32 C4
Hassendean 135 G3
Hassingham 87 E5
Hassocks 17 E2
Hassop 93 G5
Haster 195 F3
Hastigrow 195 E2
Hastingleigh 32 C4
Hastings 18 D3
Hastingwood 45 D2
Hastoe 43 E2
Haswell 120 C3
Hatch Beds. 57 G3
Hatch Hants. 28 B2
Hatch Beauchamp 23 F5
Hatch End 44 A3
Hatch Green 11 F1
Hatching Green 44 A1
Hatchmere 91 G5
Hatcliffe 96 C2
Hatfield Here. 53 E2
Hatfield Herts. 44 B2
Hatfield S.Yorks. 95 D2
Hatfield Broad Oak 45 E1
Hatfield Heath 45 E1
Hatfield Hyde 44 B1
Hatfield Peverel 45 G1
Hatfield Woodhouse 95 D2
Hatford 41 F3
Hatherden 27 E2
Hatherleigh 21 F5
Hathern 81 F5
Hatherop 41 D2
Hathersage 93 G4
Hatherton Ches. 79 D3
Hatherton Staffs. 66 B1
Hatley St. George 58 A2
Hatt 7 D4
Hattingley 28 B4
Hatton Aber. 171 F1
Hatton Derbys. 80 D5
Hatton Gt.Lon. 43 F5
Hatton Lincs. 96 B5
Hatton Shrop. 65 D3
Hatton Warks. 55 E1
Hatton Warr. 91 G4
Hatton Castle 182 C5
Hatton Heath 78 B1
Hatton of Fintray 170 D3
Hattoncrook 170 D2
Haugh Head 137 E4
Haugh of Glass 169 G1
Haugh of Urr 124 C4
Haugham 96 D4
Haughhead 142 A2
Haughley 60 B1
Haughley Green 60 B1
Haughley New Street 60 B1
Haughs 182 A5
Haughton Notts. 95 D5
Haughton Shrop. 65 F3
Haughton Shrop. 65 E1
Haughton Shrop. 78 A5
Haughton Staffs. 79 F5
Haughton Green 92 D3
Haughton Le Skerne 110 C1
Haughton Moss 78 C2
Haultwick 58 B5
Haunn 172 C2
Haunton 67 E1
Hauxley 129 E1
Hauxton 58 C2
Havant 15 G2
Haven 52 D2
Haven Side 105 F5
Havenstreet 15 E3
Haverfordwest (Hwlffordd) 34 C1
Haverhill 59 E3
Haverigg 106 C5
Havering 45 E4
Havering-atte-Bower 45 E3
Haversham 56 D3
Haverthwaite 107 E4
Haverton Hill 121 D5
Hawarden 78 A1
Hawbridge 54 B3
Hawbush Green 45 G1
Hawcoat 106 D5
Hawen 49 G3
Hawes 109 D4
Hawford 54 A1
Hawick 135 G4
Hawkchurch 11 G2
Hawkedon 59 F2
Hawkenbury 31 E5
Hawkeridge 25 F2
Hawkerland 11 D4
Hawkes End 67 F4
Hawkesbury 39 G4
Hawkesbury Upton 39 G4
Hawkhill 137 G5
Hawkhurst 31 G5
Hawkinge 33 E4
Hawkley 28 C5
Hawkridge 22 B4
Hawkshead 107 E3
Hawksland 133 G2
Hawkswick 109 E5
Hawksworth Notts. 82 C3
Hawksworth W.Yorks. 102 A3
Hawkwell Essex 46 B3
Hawkwell Northumb. 128 C4
Hawley Hants. 29 D2
Hawley Kent 45 E5
Hawling 54 C5
Hawnby 111 E3
Haworth 101 G4
Hawstead 59 G2
Hawthorn Dur. 120 D3
Hawthorn Wilts. 25 F1
Hawthorn Hill Brack.F. 43 D5
Hawthorn Hill Lincs. 84 A2
Hawthorpe 83 F5
Hawton 82 C2
Haxby 103 F2
Haxey 95 E3
Haxted 30 D4
Hay Mills 66 D4
Hay-on-Wye 52 B3
Hay Street 58 B5
Haydock 91 G3
Haydon 12 C1
Haydon Bridge 119 E1
Haydon Wick 40 D4
Haye 6 D4
Hayes Gt.Lon. 43 F4
Hayes Gt.Lon. 30 D2
Hayfield Arg. & B. 148 C2
Hayfield Derbys. 93 E4
Hayfield High. 195 D2
Hayhillock 160 D5
Haylands 15 E3
Hayle 2 C3
Haynes 57 G3
Haynes Church End 57 F3
Hayscastle 48 B5
Hayscastle Cross 48 C5
Hayton Cumb. 118 B2
Hayton Cumb. 117 E2
Hayton E.Riding 104 A3
Hayton Notts. 95 E4
Hayton's Bent 65 E4
Haytor Vale 10 A5
Haywards Heath 17 F1
Haywood Oaks 82 B2
Hazel End 58 C5
Hazel Grove 92 D4
Hazelbank Arg. & B. 148 C4
Hazelbank S.Lan. 142 C5
Hazelbury Bryan 12 D2
Hazeleigh 46 B2
Hazeley 28 C2
Hazelside 133 G3
Hazelslade 66 C1
Hazelton Walls 152 B2
Hazelwood Derbys. 81 E3
Hazelwood Gt.Lon. 30 D2
Hazlefield 116 A2
Hazlehead 171 D4
Hazlemere 43 D3
Hazlerigg 129 E4
Hazleton 40 C1
Heacham 85 E4
Head Bridge 21 G4
Headbourne Worthy 27 F4
Headcorn 32 A4
Headington 42 A2
Headlam 110 A1
Headless Cross 54 C1
Headley Hants. 28 D4
Headley Hants. 27 G1
Headley Surr. 30 B3
Headley Down 28 D4
Headon 95 E5
Heads Nook 118 A2
Heage 81 E2
Healaugh N.Yorks. 109 F3
Healaugh N.Yorks. 103 E3
Heald Green 92 C4
Heale 21 G1
Healey Lancs. 92 C1
Healey N.Yorks. 110 A4
Healey Northumb. 119 G2
Healeyfield 119 G3
Healing 96 C1
Heamoor 2 B3
Heanish 154 B2
Heanor 81 F3
Heanton Punchardon 21 F2
Heanton Satchville 21 F4
Heapey 100 C5
Heapham 95 F4
Hearthstane 134 C3
Heasley Mill 22 A4
Heast 164 C3
Heath 81 F1
Heath and Reach 57 E5
Heath End Hants. 27 G1
Heath End Surr. 28 D3
Heath Hayes 66 C1
Heath Hill 65 G1
Heath House 24 B3
Heath Town 66 B3
Heathcot 171 D4
Heathcote Derbys. 80 C1
Heathcote Shrop. 79 D5
Heather 67 F1
Heathfield Devon 10 B5
Heathfield E.Suss. 18 A1
Heathfield Som. 23 E5
Heathton 66 A3
Heatley 92 B4
Heaton Lancs. 100 A1
Heaton Staffs. 79 G1
Heaton T. & W. 120 B1
Heaton Moor 92 C3
Heaverham 31 E3
Heaviley 92 D4
Hebburn 120 C1
Hebden 101 G1
Hebden Bridge 101 F5
Hebden Green 78 D1
Hebing End 58 B5
Hebron Carmar. 49 E5
Hebron Northumb. 129 D3
Heck 125 E2
Heckfield 28 C1
Heckfield Green 72 C4
Heckfordbridge 60 A5
Heckingham 73 E2
Heckington 83 G3
Heckmondwike 102 B5
Heddington 26 A1
Heddle 198 B5
Heddon-on-the-Wall 120 A1
Hedenham 73 E2
Hedge End 15 D1
Hedgerley 43 E4
Hedging 23 F5
Hedley on the Hill 119 G2
Hednesford 66 C1
Hedon 105 D5
Hedsor 43 E4
Heeley 94 A4
Heglibister 200 C2
Heighington Darl. 120 B5
Heighington Lincs. 83 F1
Heights of Brae 179 E3
Heilam 193 D2
Heithat 125 F2
Heiton 136 B3
Hele Devon 21 F1
Hele Devon 10 C2
Hele Bridge 21 F5
Hele Lane 10 A1
Helebridge 20 C5
Helensburgh 141 D1
Helford 3 E4
Helhoughton 85 G5
Helions Bumpstead 59 E3
Helland 5 E2
Hellandbridge 5 E2
Hellesdon 86 C4
Hellidon 56 A2
Hellifield 101 E2
Hellingly 18 A2
Hellington 87 E5
Hellister 200 C3
Helmdon 56 A3
Helmingham 60 C2
Helmsdale 191 F3
Helmshore 101 D5
Helmsley 111 F4
Helperby 110 D5
Helperthorpe 112 C5
Helpringham 83 G3
Helpston 69 G2
Helsby 91 F5
Helston 3 D4
Helstone 5 E1
Helton 118 B5
Helwith Bridge 101 E1
Hemblington 87 E4
Hemborough Post 9 E2
Hemel Hempstead 43 F2
Hemingbrough 103 F4
Hemingby 96 C5
Hemingford Abbots 70 A5
Hemingford Grey 70 A5
Hemingstone 60 C2
Hemington Leics. 81 F5
Hemington Northants. 69 F4
Hemington Som. 25 E2
Hemley 61 D3
Hemlington 111 D1
Hempholme 104 C3
Hempnall 72 D2
Hempnall Green 72 D2
Hempriggs 180 D3
Hempriggs House 195 F4
Hempstead Essex 59 E4
Hempstead Norf. 87 F3
Hempstead Norf. 86 C2
Hempsted 40 A1
Hempton Norf. 86 A3
Hempton Oxon. 55 G4
Hemsby 87 F4
Hemswell 95 G3
Hemsworth 94 B1
Hemyock 11 E1
Henbury Bristol 39 E5
Henbury Ches. 92 C5
Henderland 124 C3
Hendersyde Park 136 B3
Hendon Gt.Lon. 44 B4
Hendon T. & W. 120 C2
Hendy 36 B2
Heneglwys 88 C5
Henfield 17 E2
Henford 7 D1
Henghurst 32 B5
Hengoed Caerp. 38 A3
Hengoed Powys 52 B2
Hengoed Shrop. 77 F4
Hengrave 59 G1
Henham 58 D5
Heniarth 64 A2
Henlade 23 F5
Henley Shrop. 65 E5
Henley Som. 24 B4
Henley Suff. 60 C2
Henley W.Suss. 29 D5
Henley Corner 24 B4
Henley-in-Arden 55 D1
Henley-on-Thames 42 C4
Henley Park 29 E2
Henley's Down 18 C2
Henllan Carmar. 49 G3
Henllan Denb. 76 D1
Henllan Amgoed 49 E5
Henllys 38 B3
Henlow 57 G4
Hennock 10 B4
Henny Street 59 G4
Henryd 89 F5
Henry's Moat 48 D5
Hensall 103 E5
Henshaw 119 D1
Hensingham 116 C5
Henstead 73 F3
Hensting 27 F5
Henstridge 12 D1
Henstridge Ash 25 E5
Henstridge Marsh 25 E5
Henton Oxon. 42 C2
Henton Som. 24 B3
Henwick 54 A2
Henwood 5 G2
Heogan 201 D3
Heol-ddu 36 B1
Heol Lly Goden 52 A5
Heol Senni 51 F5
Heol-y-Cyw 37 F4
Hepburn 137 E4
Hepple 128 B1
Hepscott 129 E3
Heptonstall 101 F5
Hepworth Suff. 72 A4
Hepworth W.Yorks. 93 F2
Herbrandston 34 B2
Herdicott 6 D1
Hereford 53 E3
Heriot 144 A4
Hermiston 143 F2
Hermitage D. & G. 124 C4
Hermitage Dorset 12 C2
Hermitage Sc.Bord. 126 D2
Hermitage W.Berks. 42 A5
Hermitage W.Suss. 15 G2
Hermon Carmar. 49 G4
Hermon I.o.A. 74 C1
Hermon Pembs. 49 F4
Herne 33 D2
Herne Bay 33 D2
Herne Common 33 D2
Herner 21 F3
Hernhill 32 C2
Herodsfoot 5 G3
Herongate 45 F3
Heron's Ghyll 17 G1
Heronsgate 43 F3
Herriard 28 B3
Herringfleet 73 F2
Herring's Green 57 F3
Herringswell 59 F1
Herrington 120 C2
Hersden 33 D2
Hersham Cornw. 20 C5
Hersham Surr. 29 G1
Herstmonceux 18 B2
Herston Dorset 13 G5
Herston Ork. 196 D3
Hertford 44 C1
Hertford Heath 44 C1
Hertingfordbury 44 C1
Hesket Newmarket 117 G3
Hesketh Bank 100 A5
Hesketh Lane 100 C3
Heskin Green 91 G1
Hesleden 120 D4
Hesleyside 128 A3
Heslington 103 F2
Hessay 103 E2
Hessenford 6 D5
Hessett 60 A1
Hessle 104 C5
Hest Bank 100 A1
Heston 44 A5
Heswall 91 D4
Hethe 56 A5
Hetherington 128 A4
Hethersett 86 C5
Hethersgill 118 A1
Hethpool 136 C4
Hett 120 B4
Hetton 101 F2
Hetton-le-Hole 120 C3
Heugh 128 C4
Heugh-head Aber. 169 F3
Heugh-head Aber. 170 A5
Heveningham 73 E4
Hever 31 D4
Heversham 107 F4
Hevingham 86 C3
Hewas Water 5 D5
Hewell Grange 54 C1
Hewell Lane 54 C1
Hewelsfield 39 E2
Hewelsfield Common 39 E2
Hewish N.Som. 24 A1
Hewish Som. 12 A2
Hewton 7 F1
Hexham 119 F1
Hextable 45 E5
Hexton 57 G4
Hexworthy 7 G3
Heybridge Essex 45 F3
Heybridge Essex 46 B2
Heybridge Basin 46 B2
Heybrook Bay 8 B3
Heydon Cambs. 58 C3
Heydon Norf. 86 C3
Heydour 83 F4
Heylipoll 154 A2
Heylor 202 B4
Heysham 100 A1
Heyshaw 102 A1
Heyshott 16 A2
Heyside 92 D2
Heytesbury 26 A3
Heythrop 55 F5
Heywood Gt.Man. 92 C1
Heywood Wilts. 25 F2
Hibaldstow 95 G2
Hickleton 94 B2
Hickling Norf. 87 F3
Hickling Notts. 82 B5
Hickling Green 87 F3
Hickling Heath 87 F3
Hickstead 17 E1
Hidcote Boyce 55 D3
High Ackworth 94 B1
High Balantyre 148 C3
High Beach 44 D3
High Bentham 100 C1
High Bickington 21 F3
High Birkwith 108 D5
High Blantyre 142 A4
High Bonnybridge 142 C2
High Borgue 124 A5
High Bradfield 93 G3
High Bray 21 G2
High Brooms 31 E4
High Bullen 21 F3
High Burton 110 B4
High Buston 129 E1
High Callerton 129 D4
High Catton 103 G2
High Cogges 41 F2
High Coniscliffe 110 B1
High Cross Hants. 28 C5
High Cross Herts. 44 C1
High Cross Bank 67 E1
High Easter 45 F1
High Ellington 110 A4
High Entercommon 110 C2
High Ercall 65 E1
High Etherley 120 A5
High Garrett 59 F5
High Gate 101 F5
High Grange 120 A4
High Green Norf. 86 C5
High Green S.Yorks. 94 A3
High Green Worcs. 54 A3
High Halden 32 A5
High Halstow 45 G5
High Ham 24 B4
High Harrington 116 D4
High Harrogate 102 C2
High Hatton 78 D5
High Hawsker 112 C2
High Heath 79 D5
High Hesket 118 A3
High Hoyland 93 G2
High Hunsley 104 B4
High Hurstwood 17 G1
High Hutton 103 G1
High Ireby 117 F3
High Kilburn 111 E4
High Lane Derbys. 81 F3
High Lane Worcs. 53 F1
High Laver 45 E2
High Legh 92 B4
High Leven 110 D1
High Littleton 24 D2
High Lorton 117 E4
High Melton 94 C2
High Newton 107 F4
High Newton by-the-Sea 137 G4
High Nibthwaite 107 D3
High Offley 79 E5
High Ongar 45 E2
High Onn 66 A1
High Risby 95 G1
High Roding 45 F1
High Salvington 16 D3
High Shaw 109 D3
High Spen 120 A1
High Street Cornw. 5 D4
High Street Kent 31 G5
High Street Suff. 61 F2
High Street Green 60 B2
High Toynton 84 A1
High Trewhitt 128 C1
High Wollaston 39 E3
High Wray 107 E3
High Wych 45 D1
High Wycombe 43 D3
Higham Derbys. 81 E2
Higham Kent 45 G5
Higham Lancs. 101 E4
Higham Suff. 59 F1
Higham Suff. 60 B4
Higham Dykes 128 D4
Higham Ferrers 57 E1
Higham Gobion 57 G4
Higham on the Hill 67 F3
Higham Wood 31 F4
Highampton 21 E5
Highbridge 24 A3
Highbrook 30 C5
Highburton 93 F1
Highbury 25 D3
Highbury Vale 81 G3
Highclere 27 F1
Highcliffe 14 B3
Higher Ansty 13 D2
Higher Ashton 10 B4
Higher Ballam 99 G4
Higher Blackley 92 C2
Higher Brixham 9 F2
Higher Cheriton 11 D2
Higher Gabwell 9 F1
Higher Green 92 B3
Higher Kingcombe 12 B3
Higher Tale 11 D2
Higher Thrushgill 100 C1
Higher Town 4 B1
Higher Walreddon 7 E3
Higher Walton Lancs. 100 B5
Higher Walton Warr. 91 G4
Higher Whatcombe 13 E2
Higher Whitley 92 A4
Higher Wych 78 B3
Highfield E.Riding 103 G4
Highfield N.Ayr. 141 E4
Highfield T. & W. 120 A2
Highfields 58 B2
Highgreen Manor 128 A2
Highlane Ches. 79 F1
Highlane Derbys. 94 B4
Highlaws 117 E2
Highleadon 53 G5
Highleigh 16 A4
Highley 65 G4
Highmead 50 B3
Highmoor Cross 42 B4
Highmoor Hill 39 D4
Highnam 39 G1
Highstead 33 E2
Highsted 32 B2
Highstreet Green 59 F4
Hightae 125 E3
Hightown Ches. 79 F1
Hightown Mersey. 91 D2
Highway 40 C5
Highweek 10 B5
Highworth 41 E3
Hilborough 71 G2
Hilcott 26 C2
Hilden Park 31 E4
Hildenborough 31 E4
Hildersham 58 D3
Hilderstone 79 G4
Hilderthorpe 105 D1
Hilfield 12 C2
Hilgay 71 E3
Hill 39 F3
Hill Brow 28 C5
Hill Chorlton 79 E4
Hill Dyke 84 B3
Hill End Dur. 119 G4
Hill End Fife 151 F5
Hill End N.Yorks. 101 G2
Hill Head 15 E2
Hill of Beath 151 G5
Hill of Fearn 180 A2
Hill Ridware 66 C1
Hill Top Hants. 14 D2
Hill Top W.Yorks. 94 A1
Hill View 13 F3
Hillam 103 E5
Hillbeck 108 C1
Hillberry 98 B3
Hillborough 33 E2
Hillbrae Aber. 182 B5
Hillbrae Aber. 170 C2
Hillbrae Aber. 170 D1
Hillend Aber. 181 G5
Hillend Fife 143 F1
Hillend Midloth. 143 G3
Hillesden 56 B5
Hillesley 39 G4
Hillfarrance 23 E5
Hillhead 9 F2
Hillhead of Auchentumb 183 E4
Hillhead of Cocklaw 183 F5
Hilliard's Cross 67 D1
Hilliclay 195 D2
Hillingdon 43 F4
Hillington 85 F5
Hillmorton 68 A5
Hillockhead Aber. 169 F4
Hillockhead Aber. 169 G3
Hillowton 124 B4
Hillpound 15 E1
Hills Town 81 F1
Hillsford Bridge 22 A3
Hillside Aber. 171 E5
Hillside Angus 161 F3
Hillside Moray 181 D3
Hillside Shet. 200 D1
Hillswick 202 B5
Hillway 15 F4
Hillwell 201 F4
Hilmarton 40 C5
Hilperton 25 F2
Hilsea 15 F2
Hilton Cambs. 58 A1
Hilton Cumb. 118 D5
Hilton Derbys. 80 D4
Hilton Dorset 13 D2
Hilton Dur. 120 A5
Hilton High. 180 B1
Hilton Shrop. 65 G3
Hilton Stock. 111 D1
Hilton Croft 171 E1
Hilton of Cadboll 180 A2
Hilton of Delnies 180 A4
Himbleton 54 B2
Himley 66 A3
Hincaster 107 G4
Hinckley 67 G3
Hinderclay 72 B4
Hinderwell 111 G1
Hindford 78 A4
Hindhead 29 D4
Hindley 92 A2
Hindley Green 92 A2
Hindlip 54 A2
Hindolveston 86 B3
Hindon 26 A4
Hindringham 86 A2
Hingham 86 B5
Hinstock 79 D5
Hintlesham 60 B3
Hinton Hants. 14 B3
Hinton Here. 52 C4
Hinton Northants. 56 A2
Hinton S.Glos. 39 G5
Hinton Shrop. 64 D2
Hinton Admiral 14 B3
Hinton Ampner 27 G5
Hinton Blewett 24 C2
Hinton Charterhouse 25 E2
Hinton-in-the-Hedges 56 A4
Hinton Martell 13 G2
Hinton on the Green 54 C3
Hinton Parva 41 E4
Hinton St. George 12 A1
Hinton St. Mary 13 D1
Hinton Waldrist 41 F3
Hints Shrop. 65 F5
Hints Staffs. 67 D2
Hinwick 57 E1
Hinxhill 32 C4
Hinxton 58 C3
Hinxworth 58 A3
Hipperholme 102 A5
Hirn 170 C4
Hirnant 77 D5
Hirst 129 E3
Hirst Courtney 103 F5
Hirwaen 77 E1
Hirwaun 37 F2
Hiscott 21 F3
Histon 58 C1
Hitcham Bucks. 43 E4
Hitcham Suff. 60 A2
Hitchin 57 G5
Hither Green 44 C5
Hittisleigh 10 A3
Hixon 80 B5
Hoaden 33 E2
Hoaldalbert 52 C5
Hoar Cross 80 C5
Hoarwithy 53 E5
Hoath 33 D2
Hobarris 64 C5
Hobbister 196 C2
Hobbs Lots Bridge 70 B2
Hobkirk 135 G4
Hobland Hall 87 G5
Hobson 120 A2
Hoby 68 B1
Hockering 86 B4
Hockerton 82 C2
Hockley 46 B3
Hockley Heath 67 D5
Hockliffe 57 E5
Hockwold cum Wilton 71 F4
Hockworthy 10 D1
Hoddesdon 44 C2
Hoddlesden 100 D5
Hodgeston 34 D3
Hodnet 78 D5
Hodthorpe 94 C5
Hoe 86 A4
Hoe Gate 15 F1
Hoff 108 B1
Hoffleet Stow 84 A4
Hoggeston 56 D5
Hoggie 182 A3
Hogha Gearraidh 173 F2
Hoghton 100 C5
Hognaston 80 D2
Hogsthorpe 97 F5
Holbeach 84 B5
Holbeach Bank 84 B5
Holbeach Clough 84 B5
Holbeach Drove 70 B1
Holbeach Hurn 84 B5
Holbeach St. Johns 70 B1
Holbeach St. Marks 84 B4
Holbeach St. Matthew 84 C4
Holbeck 94 C5
Holberrow Green 54 C2
Holbeton 8 C2
Holborough 31 G2
Holbrook Derbys. 81 E3
Holbrook Suff. 60 C4
Holburn 137 E3
Holbury 14 D2
Holcombe Devon 10 C5
Holcombe Som. 25 D3
Holcombe Rogus 11 D1
Holcot 56 C1
Holden 101 D3
Holdenby 56 B1
Holdenhurst 14 A3
Holdgate 65 E4
Holdingham 83 F3
Holditch 11 G2
Hole-in-the-Wall 53 F5
Hole Park 32 A5
Hole Street 16 D2
Holford 23 E3
Holker 107 E5
Holkham 85 G3
Hollacombe Devon 21 D5
Hollacombe Devon 21 G4
Holland Ork. 198 C1
Holland Ork. 199 E4
Holland Surr. 30 D3
Holland-on-Sea 47 E1
Hollandstoun 199 F1
Hollee 126 A5
Hollesley 61 E3
Hollingbourne 32 A3
Hollingbury 17 F3
Hollington Derbys. 80 D4
Hollington E.Suss. 18 C2
Hollington Staffs. 80 B4
Hollingworth 93 E3
Hollins 92 C2
Hollins Green 92 A3
Hollinsclough 80 B1
Hollinswood 65 G2
Hollinwood 78 C4
Holloway 81 E2
Hollowell 68 B5
Holly End 70 D2
Holly Green 54 A3
Hollybush Caerp. 38 A2
Hollybush E.Ayr. 132 B4
Hollybush Worcs. 53 G4
Hollym 105 F5
Holm 126 A2
Holm of Drumlanrig 124 C1
Holmbury St. Mary 29 G3
Holmbush Cornw. 5 E4
Holmbush W.Suss. 30 B5
Holme Cambs. 69 G4
Holme Cumb. 107 G5
Holme Notts. 82 D2
Holme W.Yorks. 93 F2
Holme Chapel 101 E5
Holme Hale 71 G2
Holme Lacy 53 E4

Holme Marsh 52 C2
Holme next the Sea 85 F3
Holme-on-Spalding-Moor 104 A4
Holme on the Wolds 104 B3
Holme Pierrepont 82 B4
Holmebridge 13 E4
Holmer 53 E3
Holmer Green 43 E3
Holmes Chapel 79 E1
Holme's Hill 18 A2
Holmesfield 94 A5
Holmeswood 91 F1
Holmewood 81 F1
Holmfield 101 G5
Holmfirth 93 F2
Holmhead *D. & G.* 124 B2
Holmhead *E.Ayr.* 133 D3
Holmpton 105 F5
Holmrook 106 B2
Holmsgarth 201 D3
Holmside 120 B3
Holmston 132 B3
Holmwrangle 118 B3
Holne 8 D1
Holnest 12 C2
Holsworthy 20 D5
Holsworthy Beacon 21 D5
Holt *Dorset* 13 G2
Holt *Norf.* 86 B2
Holt *Wilts.* 25 F1
Holt *Worcs.* 54 A1
Holt *Wrex.* 78 B2
Holt End *Hants.* 28 B4
Holt End *Worcs.* 54 C1
Holt Fleet 54 A1
Holt Heath *Dorset* 13 G2
Holt Heath *Worcs.* 54 A1
Holtby 103 F2
Holton *Oxon.* 42 B2
Holton *Som.* 25 D5
Holton *Suff.* 73 E4
Holton cum Beckering 96 B4
Holton Heath 13 F3
Holton le Clay 96 C2
Holton le Moor 96 A3
Holton St. Mary 60 B4
Holtspur 43 E3
Holtye Common 31 D5
Holwell *Dorset* 12 D1
Holwell *Herts.* 57 G4
Holwell *Leics.* 82 C5
Holwell *Oxon.* 41 E2
Holwell *Som.* 25 E3
Holwick 119 F5
Holworth 13 D4
Holy Cross 66 B5
Holy Island 137 F2
Holybourne 28 C3
Holyhead (Caergybi) 88 A4
Holymoorside 81 E1
Holyport 43 D5
Holystone 128 B1
Holytown 142 B3
Holywell *Cambs.* 70 B5
Holywell *Cornw.* 4 B4
Holywell *Dorset* 12 B2
Holywell *E.Suss.* 18 A4
Holywell *Flints.* (Treffynnon) 90 C5
Holywell Green 93 E1
Holywell Lake 23 E5
Holywell Row 71 F5
Holywood 124 D2
Hom Green 53 E5
Homer 65 F2
Homersfield 73 D3
Homington 26 C5
Honey Hill 32 D2
Honey Tye 60 A4
Honeyborough 34 C2
Honeybourne 54 D3
Honeychurch 21 G5
Honiley 67 E5
Honing 87 E3
Honingham 86 C4
Honington *Lincs.* 83 E3
Honington *Suff.* 72 A4
Honington *Warks.* 55 E3
Honiton 11 E2
Honley 93 F1
Hoo *Med.* 45 G5
Hoo *Suff.* 61 D2
Hooe *E.Suss.* 18 B3
Hooe *Plym.* 8 B2
Hooe Common 18 B2
Hook *E.Riding* 103 G5
Hook *Gt.Lon.* 29 G1
Hook *Hants.* 28 C2
Hook *Pembs.* 34 C1
Hook *Wilts.* 40 C4
Hook-a-Gate 65 D2
Hook Green *Kent* 31 F5
Hook Green *Kent* 31 F2
Hook Green *Kent* 45 F5
Hook Norton 55 F4
Hooke 12 B2
Hookgate 79 E4
Hookway 10 B3
Hookwood 30 B4
Hoole 78 B1
Hooley 30 B3
Hooton 91 E5
Hooton Levitt 94 C3
Hooton Pagnell 94 B2
Hooton Roberts 94 B3
Hopcrofts Holt 55 G5
Hope *Derbys.* 93 F4
Hope *Devon* 8 C4
Hope *Flints.* 78 A2
Hope *Powys* 64 B2
Hope *Shrop.* 64 C2
Hope Bagot 65 E5
Hope Bowdler 65 D3
Hope End Green 45 E1
Hope Mansell 39 F1
Hope under Dinmore 53 E2
Hopehouse 135 D4
Hopeman 180 D3
Hope's Green 45 G4
Hopesay 64 C4
Hopkinstown 37 G3
Hopton *Derbys.* 81 D2
Hopton *Norf.* 87 G5
Hopton *Shrop.* 78 C5
Hopton *Staffs.* 79 G5
Hopton *Suff.* 72 A4
Hopton Cangeford 65 E4
Hopton Castle 64 C5
Hopton Wafers 65 F5
Hoptonheath 64 C5
Hopwas 67 D2
Hopwood 66 C5
Horam 18 A2
Horbling 83 G4
Horbury 93 G1
Horden 120 D3
Horderley 64 D4
Hordle 14 B3
Hordley 78 A4
Horeb *Carmar.* 36 A2
Horeb *Cere.* 49 G3
Horfield 39 E5
Horham 72 D4
Horkesley Heath 60 A5
Horkstow 95 G1
Horley *Oxon.* 55 G3
Horley *Surr.* 30 B4
Horn Hill 43 F3
Hornblotton Green 24 C4
Hornby *Lancs.* 100 B1
Hornby *N.Yorks.* 110 B3
Hornby *N.Yorks.* 110 C2
Horncastle 84 A1
Hornchurch 45 E4
Horncliffe 145 G4
Horndean *Hants.* 15 G1
Horndean *Sc.Bord.* 145 F5
Horndon 7 F2
Horndon on the Hill 45 F4
Horne 30 C4
Horniehaugh 160 C3
Horning 87 E4
Horninghold 68 D3
Horninglow 80 D5
Horningsea 58 C1
Horningsham 25 F3
Horningtoft 86 A3
Horningtops 5 G3
Horns Cross *Devon* 21 D3
Horns Cross *E.Suss.* 18 D1
Hornsby 118 B3
Hornsby Gate 118 B2
Hornsea 105 E3
Hornsey 44 C4
Hornton 55 F3
Horrabridge 8 B1
Horridge 10 A5
Horringer 59 G1
Horse Bridge 79 G2
Horsebridge *Devon* 7 E3
Horsebridge *Hants.* 27 E4
Horsebrook 66 A1
Horsehay 65 F2
Horseheath 59 E3
Horsehouse 109 F4
Horsell 29 E2
Horseman's Green 78 B3
Horseway 70 C4
Horsey 87 F3
Horsford 86 C4
Horsforth 102 B4
Horsham *W.Suss.* 29 G4
Horsham *Worcs.* 53 G2
Horsham St. Faith 86 D4
Horsington *Lincs.* 83 G1
Horsington *Som.* 25 D5
Horsley *Derbys.* 81 E3
Horsley *Glos.* 40 A3
Horsley *Northumb.* 119 G1
Horsley *Northumb.* 128 A2
Horsley Cross 60 C5
Horsley Woodhouse 81 E3
Horsleycross Street 60 C5
Horsmonden 31 G4
Horspath 42 A2
Horstead 87 D4
Horsted Keynes 17 F1
Horton *Bucks.* 43 E1
Horton *Dorset* 13 G2
Horton *Lancs.* 101 E2
Horton *Northants.* 56 D2
Horton *S.Glos.* 39 G4
Horton *Som.* 11 G1
Horton *Staffs.* 79 G2
Horton *Swan.* 36 A4
Horton *W. & M.* 43 F5
Horton *Wilts.* 26 B1
Horton Cross 11 G1
Horton-cum-Studley 42 A1
Horton Grange 129 D4
Horton Green 78 B3
Horton Heath 15 D1
Horton in Ribblesdale 108 D5
Horton Inn 13 G2
Horton Kirby 31 E2
Horwich 92 A1
Horwich End 93 E4
Horwood 21 F3
Hose 82 C5
Hoses 106 D3
Hosh 151 D2
Hosta 173 F2
Hoswick 200 D5
Hotham 104 A4
Hothfield 32 B4
Hoton 81 G5
Houbie 203 F3
Hough 79 E2
Hough Green 91 F4
Hough-on-the-Hill 83 E3
Hougham 83 D3
Houghton *Cambs.* 70 A5
Houghton *Cumb.* 118 A2
Houghton *Devon* 8 C3
Houghton *Hants.* 27 E4
Houghton *Pembs.* 34 C2
Houghton *W.Suss.* 16 C2
Houghton Bank 120 B5
Houghton Conquest 57 F3
Houghton-le-Side 120 B5
Houghton le Spring 120 C3
Houghton on the Hill 68 B2
Houghton Regis 57 F5
Houghton St. Giles 86 A2
Houlsyke 111 G2
Hound 15 D2
Hound Green 28 C2
Houndslow 144 D5
Houndwood 145 F3
Hounsdown 14 C1
Hounslow 44 A5
Hounslow Green 45 F1
Househill 180 A4
Housetter 202 C4
Houston 141 F3
Houstry 195 D5
Houstry of Dunn 195 E3
Houton 196 C2
Hove 17 E3
Hoveringham 82 B3
Hoveton 87 E4
Hovingham 111 F5
How 118 B2
How Caple 53 F4
How End 57 F3
How Man 116 C5
Howden 103 G5
Howden-le-Wear 120 A4
Howe *Cumb.* 107 F4
Howe *High.* 195 F2
Howe *N.Yorks.* 110 C4
Howe *Norf.* 87 D5
Howe Green 45 G2
Howe of Teuchar 182 C5
Howe Street *Essex* 45 F1
Howe Street *Essex* 59 E4
Howell 83 G3
Howey 51 G2
Howgate 143 G4
Howgill 101 G2
Howick 137 G5
Howle 79 D5
Howlett End 59 D4
Howley 11 F2
Hownam 136 B5
Hownam Mains 136 B4
Howpasley 135 E5
Howsham *N.Lincs.* 96 A2
Howsham *N.Yorks.* 103 G1
Howtel 136 C3
Howton 52 D5
Howwood 141 F3
Hoxa 196 D3
Hoxne 72 C4
Hoy 195 E2
Hoylake 90 D4
Hoyland 94 A2
Hoyland Swaine 93 G2
Hubberholme 109 E5
Hubbert's Bridge 84 A3
Huby *N.Yorks.* 103 E1
Huby *N.Yorks.* 102 B3
Hucclecote 40 A1
Hucking 32 A3
Hucknall 81 G3
Huddersfield 93 F1
Huddington 54 B2
Hudscott 21 G3
Hudswell 110 A2
Huggate 104 A2
Hugglescote 67 G1
Hugh Town 4 B1
Hughenden Valley 43 D3
Hughley 65 E3
Hugmore 78 A2
Huish *Devon* 21 F4
Huish *Wilts.* 26 C1
Huish Champflower 22 D5
Huish Episcopi 24 B5
Huisinis 184 B2
Hulcott 43 D1
Hull 104 D5
Hulland 80 D3
Hullavington 40 A4
Hullbridge 46 B3
Hulme End 80 C2
Hulme Walfield 79 F1
Hulver Street 73 F3
Humber 53 E2
Humberside International Airport 96 B2
Humberston 96 D2
Humberstone 68 B2
Humbie 144 B3
Humbleton *E.Riding* 105 E4
Humbleton *Northumb.* 137 D4
Humby 83 F4
Hume 145 E5
Humehall 145 E5
Humshaugh 128 B4
Huna 195 F1
Huncoat 101 D4
Huncote 68 A3
Hundalee 136 A5
Hunderthwaite 119 F5
Hundleby 84 B1
Hundleton 34 C2
Hundon 59 F3
Hundred Acres 15 E1
Hundred End 100 A5
Hundred House 52 A2
Hungarton 68 B2
Hungerford *Hants.* 14 A1
Hungerford *W.Berks.* 27 E1
Hungerford Newtown 41 F5
Hunglader 175 G2
Hunmanby 113 E5
Hunningham 55 F1
Hunny Hill 15 D4
Hunsdon 44 D1
Hunsingore 102 D2
Hunsonby 118 B4
Hunspow 195 E1
Hunstanton 85 E3
Hunstanworth 119 F3
Hunston *Suff.* 60 A1
Hunston *W.Suss.* 16 A3
Hunstrete 24 D1
Hunt End 54 C1
Hunt House 112 B3
Huntercombe End 42 B4
Hunters Forstal 33 D2
Hunter's Inn 21 G1
Hunter's Quay 140 C2
Hunterston 140 C4
Huntford 127 E1
Huntingdon 70 A5
Huntingfield 73 E4
Huntingford 25 F4
Huntington *Here.* 52 B2
Huntington *Staffs.* 66 B1
Huntington *York* 103 F2
Huntingtower 151 F2
Huntley 39 G1
Huntly 182 A5
Huntlywood 144 D5
Hunton *Hants.* 27 F4
Hunton *Kent* 31 G4
Hunton *N.Yorks.* 110 A3
Hunton Bridge 43 F2
Hunt's Cross 91 F4
Huntsham 22 D5
Huntshaw Cross 21 F3
Huntspill 24 A3
Huntworth 24 A4
Hunwick 120 A4
Hunworth 86 B2
Hurdsfield 92 D5
Hurley *W. & M.* 42 D4
Hurley *Warks.* 67 E3
Hurley Bottom 42 D4
Hurlford 132 C2
Hurliness 196 B4
Hurn 14 A3
Hursley 27 F5
Hurst *Gt.Man.* 92 D2
Hurst *N.Yorks.* 109 F2
Hurst *W'ham* 42 C5
Hurst Green *E.Suss.* 18 C1
Hurst Green *Lancs.* 100 C4
Hurst Green *Surr.* 30 C3
Hurstbourne Priors 27 F3
Hurstbourne Tarrant 27 E2
Hurstpierpoint 17 E2
Hurstway Common 52 B3
Hurstwood 101 E4
Hurtmore 29 E3
Hurworth-on-Tees 110 C1
Hury 119 F5
Husabost 175 F4
Husbands Bosworth 68 B4
Husborne Crawley 57 E4
Husthwaite 111 E5
Huthwaite 81 F2
Huttoft 97 F5
Hutton *Cumb.* 118 A5
Hutton *Essex* 45 F3
Hutton *Lancs.* 100 A5
Hutton *N.Som.* 24 A2
Hutton *Sc.Bord.* 145 G4
Hutton Bonville 110 C2
Hutton Buscel 112 C4
Hutton Conyers 110 C5
Hutton Cranswick 104 C2
Hutton End 118 A4
Hutton Henry 120 D4
Hutton-le-Hole 111 G3
Hutton Magna 110 A1
Hutton Roof *Cumb.* 107 G5
Hutton Roof *Cumb.* 117 G3
Hutton Rudby 111 D2
Hutton Sessay 111 D5
Hutton Wandesley 103 E2
Huxley 78 C1
Huxter *Shet.* 200 C2
Huxter *Shet.* 201 E1
Huyton 91 F3
Hwlffordd (Haverfordwest) 34 C1
Hycemoor 106 B4
Hyde *Glos.* 40 A2
Hyde *Gt.Man.* 92 D3
Hyde Heath 43 E2
Hyde Lea 66 B1
Hydestile 29 E3
Hyndford Bridge 142 D5
Hyndlee 135 G5
Hynish 154 A3
Hyssington 64 C3
Hythe *Hants.* 14 D2
Hythe *Kent* 33 D5
Hythe End 43 F5
Hythie 183 F4
Hyton 106 B4


## I


Ianstown 181 G3
Ibberton 13 D2
Ible 80 D2
Ibsley 14 A2
Ibstock 67 G1
Ibstone 42 C3
Ibthorpe 27 E2
Ibworth 27 G2
Icelton 24 A1
Ickburgh 71 G3
Ickenham 43 F4
Ickford 42 B2
Ickham 33 E3
Ickleford 57 G4
Icklesham 19 D2
Ickleton 58 C3
Icklingham 71 F5
Ickwell Green 57 G3
Icomb 55 E5
Idbury 55 E5
Iddesleigh 21 F5
Ide 10 C3
Ide Hill 31 D3
Ideford 10 B5
Iden 19 E1
Iden Green *Kent* 31 G5
Iden Green *Kent* 32 A5
Idlicote 55 E3
Idmiston 26 C4
Idridgehay 81 D3
Idrigil 175 G3
Idstone 41 E4
Idvies 160 D5
Iffley 42 A2
Ifield or Singlewell *Kent* 45 F5
Ifield *W.Suss.* 30 B5
Ifieldwood 30 B5
Ifold 29 F4
Iford 17 G3
Ifton Heath 78 A4
Ightfield 78 C4
Ightham 31 E3
Iken 61 F2
Ilam 80 C2
Ilchester 24 C5
Ilderton 137 E4
Ilford 44 D4
Ilfracombe 21 F1
Ilkeston 81 F3
Ilketshall St. Andrew 73 E3
Ilketshall St. Lawrence 73 E3
Ilketshall St. Margaret 73 E3
Ilkley 102 A3
Illey 66 B4
Illington 72 A3
Illingworth 101 G5
Illogan 4 A5
Illston on the Hill 68 C3
Ilmer 42 C2
Ilmington 55 E3
Ilminster 11 G1
Ilsington 10 A5
Ilston 36 B3
Ilton *N.Yorks.* 110 A5
Ilton *Som.* 11 G1
Imachar 139 G5
Immeroin 150 A3
Immingham 96 B1
Immingham Dock 96 C1
Impington 58 C1
Ince 91 F5
Ince Blundell 91 E2
Ince-in-Makerfield 91 G2
Inch of Arnhall 161 E2
Inchbare 161 E3
Inchberry 181 F4
Inchbraoch 161 F4
Inchgrundle 160 C2
Inchindown 179 F2
Inchinnan 141 F3
Inchkinloch 193 F4
Inchlaggan 166 A4
Inchlumpie 179 E2
Inchmarlo 170 B5
Inchnabobart 160 B1
Inchnacardoch Hotel 166 C3
Inchnadamph 189 E2
Inchock 161 E5
Inchrory 169 D4
Inchture 152 A2
Inchvuilt 166 B1
Inchyra 151 G3
Indian Queens 4 D4
Inerval 138 B5
Ingatestone 45 F2
Ingbirchworth 93 G2
Ingerthorpe 102 B1
Ingestre 79 G5
Ingham *Lincs.* 95 G4
Ingham *Norf.* 87 E3
Ingham *Suff.* 71 G5
Ingleby *Derbys.* 81 E5
Ingleby *Lincs.* 95 F5
Ingleby Arncliffe 110 D2
Ingleby Barwick 110 D1
Ingleby Cross 110 D2
Ingleby Greenhow 111 E2
Inglesbatch 25 D1
Inglesham 41 E3
Ingleton *Dur.* 120 A5
Ingleton *N.Yorks.* 108 B5
Inglewhite 100 B3
Ingmire Hall 108 B3
Ingoe 128 C4
Ingoldisthorpe 85 E4
Ingoldmells 85 D1
Ingoldsby 83 F4
Ingon 55 E2
Ingram 137 E5
Ingrave 45 F3
Ingrow 101 G4
Ings 107 F3
Ingst 39 E4
Ingworth 86 C3
Inistrynich 148 D2
Injebreck 98 B3
Inkberrow 54 C2
Inkhorn 171 E1
Inkpen 27 E1
Inkstack 195 E1
Innellan 140 C3
Innergellie 153 D4
Innerleithen 135 E2
Innerleven 152 B4
Innermessan 122 B4
Innerwick *E.Loth.* 145 E2
Innerwick *P. & K.* 158 A5
Inninbeg 155 G5
Innsworth 54 A5
Insch 170 B2
Insh 168 A4
Inshore 192 C2
Inskip 100 A4
Instow 21 E2
Intake 94 A4
Intwood 86 C5
Inver *Aber.* 169 E5
Inver *Arg. & B.* 156 B5
Inver *High.* 180 A1
Inver *High.* 195 D5
Inver *P. & K.* 159 F5
Inver Mallie 156 D1
Inverailort 155 G1
Inveralligin 177 E4
Inverallochy 183 F3
Inveran 190 A5
Inveraray 148 C4
Inverardoch Mains 150 C4
Inverardran 149 F2
Inverarish 164 B1
Inverarity 160 C5
Inverarnan 149 F3
Inverasdale 177 E1
Inverbain 177 D4
Inverbeg 149 F5
Inverbervie 161 G2
Inverbroom 178 A1
Inverbrough 168 A2
Invercassley 189 G4
Inverchaolain 140 B2
Invercharnan 156 D5
Inverchorachan 149 E3
Inverchoran 178 B4
Invercreran 156 C5
Inverdruie 168 B3
Inverebrie 171 E1
Invereen 168 A1
Invererne 180 C3
Inveresk 144 A2
Inverey 159 F1
Inverfarigaig 167 E2
Invergarry 166 C4
Invergelder 169 E5
Invergeldie 150 C2
Invergloy 157 E1
Invergordon 179 G3
Invergowrie 152 B1
Inverguseran 164 D4
Inverhadden 158 B4
Inverharroch 169 F1
Inverherive 149 F2
Inverhope 193 D2
Inverie 165 D4
Inverinan 148 B3
Inverinate 165 F2
Inverkeilor 161 E5
Inverkeithing 143 F1
Inverkeithny 182 B5
Inverkip 140 D2
Inverkirkaig 188 C3
Inverlael 178 A1
Inverlauren 141 E1
Inverliever 148 A4
Inverliver 148 C1
Inverlochlarig 149 G3
Inverlochy 149 D2
Inverlussa 139 E1
Invermay 151 F3
Invermoriston 166 D3
Invernaver 193 G2
Inverneil 139 G1
Inverness 179 F5
Inverness Airport 179 G4
Invernettie 183 G5
Invernoaden 148 D5
Inveroran Hotel 157 E5
Inverquharity 160 C4
Inverquhomery 183 F5
Inverroy 157 E1
Inversanda 156 B4
Invershiel 165 F3
Inversnaid Hotel 149 F4
Invertrossachs 150 A4
Inverugie 183 G5
Inveruglas 149 F4
Inveruglass 168 A4
Inverurie 170 C2
Invervar 158 B5
Invervegain 140 B2
Invery House 170 B5
Inverythan 182 C5
Inwardleigh 7 F1
Inworth 46 B1
Iochdar 174 A5
Iping 29 D5
Ipplepen 9 E1
Ipsden 42 B4
Ipstones 80 B2
Ipswich 60 C3
Irby 91 D4
Irby in the Marsh 84 C1
Irby upon Humber 96 B2
Irchester 57 E1
Ireby *Cumb.* 117 F3
Ireby *Lancs.* 108 B5
Ireland *Ork.* 196 C2
Ireland *Shet.* 200 C5
Ireleth 106 D5
Ireshopeburn 119 E4
Irlam 92 B3
Irnham 83 F5
Iron Acton 39 F4
Iron Cross 54 C2
Ironbridge 65 F2
Ironside 183 D4
Ironville 81 F2
Irstead 87 E3
Irthington 118 A1
Irthlingborough 69 E5
Irton 112 D4
Irvine 132 B2
Isauld 194 B2
Isbister *Ork.* 198 B5
Isbister *Ork.* 198 A4
Isbister *Shet.* 201 E1
Isbister *Shet.* 202 C3
Isfield 17 G2
Isham 69 D5
Ishriff 147 F1
Islay Airport 138 B4
Islay House 138 B3
Isle Abbotts 24 A5
Isle Brewers 24 A5
Isle of Man Airport 98 A5
Isle of Whithorn 115 E3
Isleham 71 E5
Isleornsay (Eilean Iarmain) 164 C3
Islesburgh 200 C1
Isleworth 44 A5
Isley Walton 81 F5
Islibhig 186 A5
Islington 44 C4
Islip *Northants.* 69 E5
Islip *Oxon.* 42 A1
Isombridge 65 F1
Istead Rise 31 F2
Itchen 14 D1
Itchen Abbas 27 G4
Itchen Stoke 27 G4
Itchingfield 29 G5
Itchington 39 F4
Itteringham 86 C2
Itton 7 G1
Itton Common 39 D3
Ivegill 118 A3
Ivelet 109 E3
Iver 43 F4
Iver Heath 43 F4
Iveston 120 A2
Ivinghoe 43 E1
Ivinghoe Aston 43 E1
Ivington 53 D2
Ivington Green 53 D2
Ivy Hatch 31 E3
Ivy Todd 71 G2
Ivybridge 8 C2
Ivychurch 19 F1
Iwade 32 B2
Iwerne Courtney (Shroton) 13 E1
Iwerne Minster 13 E1
Ixworth 72 A4
Ixworth Thorpe 72 A4


## J


Jack Hill 102 A2
Jackstown 170 C1
Jackton 141 G4
Jacobstow 6 B1
Jacobstowe 21 F5
Jameston 35 D3
Jamestown *D. & G.* 126 B2
Jamestown *High.* 179 D4
Jamestown *W.Dun.* 141 E1
Janefield 179 G4
Janetstown 194 C2
Jarrow 120 C1
Jarvis Brook 18 A1
Jasper's Green 59 F5
Jawcraig 142 C2
Jayes Park 29 G3
Jaywick 47 E1
Jedburgh 136 A4
Jeffreyston 35 D2
Jemimaville 179 G3
Jersay 142 C3
Jersey Airport 8 B5
Jerviswood 142 C5
Jesmond 120 B1
Jevington 18 A3
Jodrell Bank 92 B5
John o' Groats 195 F1
Johnby 118 A4
John's Cross 18 C1
Johnshaven 161 F3
Johnston 34 C1
Johnston Mains 161 F3
Johnstone 141 F3
Johnstone Castle 141 F3
Johnstonebridge 125 E1
Johnstown *Carmar.* 35 G1
Johnstown *Wrex.* 78 A3
Joppa *Edin.* 144 A2
Joppa *S.Ayr.* 132 C4
Jordans 43 E3
Jordanston 48 C4
Jordanstone 160 A5
Jump 94 A2
Juniper Green 143 F3
Jura House 138 C3
Jurby East 98 B2
Jurby West 98 B2


## K


Kaber 108 C1
Kaimes 143 G3
Kames *Arg. & B.* 140 A2
Kames *Arg. & B.* 148 A3
Kames *E.Ayr.* 133 E3
Kea 4 C5
Keadby 95 F1
Keal Cotes 84 B1
Kearsley 92 B2
Kearstwick 108 B4
Kearton 109 F3
Kearvaig 192 B1
Keasden 100 D1
Kebholes 182 B4
Keckwick 91 G4
Keddington 96 D4
Kedington 59 F3
Kedleston 81 E3
Keelby 96 B2
Keele 79 F3
Keeley Green 57 F3
Keeres Green 45 E1
Keeston 34 C1
Keevil 26 A2
Kegworth 81 F5
Kehelland 4 A5
Keig 170 B3
Keighley 101 G3
Keil *Arg. & B.* 130 B5
Keil *High.* 156 B4
Keilhill 182 C4
Keillmore 139 E1
Keillor 100 A5
Keillour 151 E2
Keills 138 C3
Keils 138 D3
Keinton Mandeville 24 C4
Keir House 150 C5
Keir Mill 124 C1
Keisby 83 F5
Keisley 118 D5
Keiss 195 F2
Keith 181 G4
Keithick 152 A1
Keithmore 169 F1
Keithock 161 E3
Kelbrook 101 F3
Kelby 83 F3

Keld Cumb. 107 G1
Keld N.Yorks. 109 D2
Keldholme 111 G4
Keldy Castle 111 G3
Kelfield N.Lincs. 95 F2
Kelfield N.Yorks. 103 E4
Kelham 82 C2
Kellan 155 E5
Kellas Angus 152 C1
Kellas Moray 181 D4
Kellaton 9 E4
Kelleth 108 B2
Kelleythorpe 104 C2
Kelling 86 B1
Kellington 103 E5
Kelloe 120 C4
Kelloholm 133 F4
Kelly Cornw. 5 E2
Kelly Devon 7 D2
Kelly Bray 7 D3
Kelmarsh 68 C5
Kelmscott 41 E3
Kelsale 61 E1
Kelsall 78 C1
Kelsay 138 A4
Kelshall 58 B4
Kelsick 117 E1
Kelso 136 B3
Kelstedge 81 E1
Kelstern 96 C3
Kelston 25 D1
Keltneyburn 158 C5
Kelton 125 D3
Kelton Hill or Rhonehouse 124 B5
Kelty 151 G5
Kelvedon 46 B1
Kelvedon Hatch 45 E3
Kelynack 2 A3
Kemback 152 C3
Kemberton 65 G2
Kemble 40 B3
Kemerton 54 B4
Kemeys Commander 38 C2
Kemeys Inferior 38 C3
Kemnay 170 C3
Kemp Town 17 F3
Kempley 53 F5
Kempley Green 53 F5
Kempsey 54 A3
Kempsford 41 D3
Kempshott 28 B3
Kempston 57 F3
Kempston Church End 57 F3
Kempston Hardwick 57 F3
Kempton 64 C4
Kemsing 31 E3
Kemsley 32 B2
Kenardington 32 B5
Kenchester 52 D3
Kencott 41 E2
Kendal 107 G3
Kenderchurch 52 D5
Kenfig 37 E4
Kenfig Hill 37 E4
Kenilworth 67 E5
Kenknock P.&K. 158 A5
Kenknock Stir. 149 G1
Kenley Gt.Lon. 30 C3
Kenley Shrop. 65 E2
Kenmore Arg. & B. 148 C4
Kenmore High. 177 D4
Kenmore P.&K. 158 C5
Kenmore W.Isles 185 E3
Kenn Devon 10 C4
Kenn N.Som. 24 B1
Kennacraig 139 G3
Kennards House 5 G1
Kennavay 185 E4
Kennerleigh 10 B2
Kennerty 170 B5
Kennet 151 E5
Kennethmont 170 A2
Kennett 59 E1
Kennford 10 C4
Kenninghall 72 B3
Kennington Kent 32 C4
Kennington Oxon. 42 A2
Kennoway 152 B4
Kennyhill 71 E5
Kennythorpe 103 G1
Kensaleyre 176 A4
Kensington & Chelsea 44 B5
Kensworth 43 F1
Kensworth Common 43 F1
Kent Street E.Suss. 18 C2
Kent Street Kent 31 F3
Kentallen 156 C4
Kentchurch 52 D5
Kentford 59 F1
Kentisbeare 11 D2
Kentisbury 21 G1
Kentisbury Ford 21 G1
Kentmere 107 F2
Kenton Devon 10 C4
Kenton Suff. 60 C1
Kenton T.&W. 120 B1
Kentra 155 F3
Kents Bank 107 F5
Kent's Green 53 G5
Kent's Oak 27 E5
Kenwick 78 B4
Kenwyn 4 C5
Kenyon 92 A3
Keoldale 192 C2
Keppanach 156 C3
Keppoch Arg. & B. 141 E2
Keppoch High. 165 E2
Keprigan 130 B4
Kepwick 111 D3
Keresley 67 F4
Kerne Bridge 39 E1
Kerridge 92 D5
Kerris 2 B4
Kerry 64 A4
Kerrycroy 140 C3
Kerry's Gate 52 C4
Kerrysdale 177 E2
Kersall 82 C1
Kersey 60 B3
Kershopefoot 126 C3
Kerswell 11 D2
Kerswell Green 54 A3
Kesgrave 60 D3
Kessingland 73 G3
Kessingland Beach 73 G3
Kestle Mill 4 C4
Keston 30 D2
Keswick Cumb. 117 F4
Keswick Norf. 86 D5
Keswick Norf. 87 E2
Ketsby 97 D5
Kettering 69 D5
Ketteringham 86 C5
Kettins 152 A1
Kettlebaston 60 A3
Kettlebridge 152 B4
Kettlebrook 67 E2
Kettleburgh 61 D2
Kettleholm 125 F3
Kettleness 112 B1
Kettleshulme 93 D5
Kettlesing 102 B2
Kettlesing Bottom 102 B2
Kettlestone 86 A2
Kettlethorpe 95 F5
Kettletoft 199 E3
Kettlewell 109 E5
Ketton 69 E2
Kew 44 A5
Kewstoke 24 A1
Kexbrough 94 A2
Kexby Lincs. 95 F4
Kexby York 103 G2
Key Green 79 F1
Keyham 68 B2
Keyhaven 14 C3
Keyingham 105 E5
Keymer 17 F2
Keynsham 24 D1
Key's Toft 84 C2
Keysoe 57 F1
Keysoe Row 57 F1
Keyston 69 F5
Keyworth 82 B4
Kibblesworth 120 B2
Kibworth Beauchamp 68 B3
Kibworth Harcourt 68 B3
Kidbrooke 44 D5
Kiddal Lane End 102 C4
Kiddemore Green 66 A2
Kidderminster 66 A5
Kiddington 55 G5
Kidlington 41 G1
Kidmore End 42 B5
Kidsdale 115 E3
Kidsgrove 79 F2
Kidstones 109 E4
Kidwelly (Cydweli) 36 A2
Kiel Crofts 148 B1
Kielder 127 E2
Kilbarchan 141 F3
Kilbeg 164 C4
Kilberry 139 F3
Kilbirnie 141 E4
Kilblaan 148 D3
Kilbraur 190 D3
Kilbrennan 154 D5
Kilbride Arg. & B. 148 A2
Kilbride Arg. & B. 140 B3
Kilbride High. 164 B2
Kilbride Farm 140 A3
Kilbridemore 148 C5
Kilburn Derbys. 81 E3
Kilburn N.Yorks. 111 E5
Kilby 68 B3
Kilchattan Arg. & B. 140 C4
Kilchenzie 130 B3
Kilcheran 148 A1
Kilchiaran 138 A4
Kilchoan Arg. & B. 147 G3
Kilchoan High. 155 D3
Kilchoman 138 A3
Kilchrenan 148 C2
Kilchrist 130 B4
Kilconquhar 152 C4
Kilcot 53 F5
Kilcoy 179 E4
Kilcreggan 140 D1
Kildale 111 F2
Kildary 179 G2
Kildavie 130 C4
Kildermorie Lodge 179 E2
Kildonan 131 F3
Kildonan Lodge 191 E2
Kildonnan 155 D1
Kildrochet House 122 B5
Kildrummy 169 G3
Kildwick 101 G3
Kilfinan 140 A2
Kilfinnan 166 B5
Kilgetty 35 E2
Kilgwrrwg Common 39 D3
Kilham E.Riding 104 C1
Kilham Northumb. 136 C3
Kilkenneth 154 A2
Kilkenny 40 C1
Kilkerran Arg. & B. 130 C4
Kilkerran S.Ayr. 132 B5
Kilkhampton 20 C4
Killamarsh 94 B4
Killay 36 C3
Killbeg 155 F5
Killean Arg. & B. 139 E5
Killean Arg. & B. 148 C4
Killearn 141 G1
Killellan 130 B4
Killen 179 F4
Killerby 120 A5
Killichonan 158 A4
Killiechanate 157 E1
Killiechronan 155 E5
Killiecrankie 159 E3
Killiehuntly 167 G5
Killiemor 147 D1
Killilan 165 F1
Killimster 195 F3
Killin High. 191 D4
Killin Stir. 150 A1
Killinallan 138 B2
Killinghall 102 B2
Killington 108 B4
Killingworth 129 E4
Killochyett 144 B5
Killocraw 130 B3
Killunaig 147 D2
Killundine 155 E5
Kilmacolm 141 E3
Kilmaha 148 B4
Kilmahog 150 B4
Kilmalieu 156 A4
Kilmaluag 176 A2
Kilmany 152 B2
Kilmarie 164 B3
Kilmarnock 132 C2
Kilmartin 148 A5
Kilmaurs 141 F5
Kilmelford 148 A3
Kilmersdon 25 D2
Kilmeston 27 G5
Kilmichael 130 B3
Kilmichael Glassary 148 A5
Kilmichael of Inverlussa 139 F1
Kilmington Devon 11 F3
Kilmington Wilts. 25 E4
Kilmington Street 25 E4
Kilmorack 179 D5
Kilmore Arg. & B. 148 A2
Kilmore High. 164 C4
Kilmory Arg. & B. 139 F1
Kilmory Arg. & B. 139 F2
Kilmory High. 163 G4
Kilmory High. 155 E3
Kilmote 191 E3
Kilmuir High. 175 F5
Kilmuir High. 179 F5
Kilmuir High. 179 G2
Kilmuir High. 175 G2
Kilmun 140 C1
Kilmux 152 B4
Kiln Green 42 D5
Kiln Pit Hill 119 G2
Kilnave 138 A2
Kilncadzow 142 C5
Kilndown 31 G5
Kilnhurst 94 B3
Kilninian 154 D5
Kilninver 148 A2
Kilnsea 97 E1
Kilnsey 101 F1
Kilnwick 104 C3
Kiloran 146 C5
Kilpatrick 131 E3
Kilpeck 52 D4
Kilphedir 191 E3
Kilpin 103 G5
Kilrenny 153 D4
Kilsby 68 A5
Kilspindie 152 A2
Kilstay 114 B3
Kilsyth 142 B2
Kiltarlity 179 E5
Kilton R.& C. 111 F1
Kilton Som. 23 E3
Kiltyrie 150 B1
Kilvaxter 175 G3
Kilve 23 E3
Kilverstone 71 G4
Kilvington 82 D3
Kilwinning 141 E5
Kimberley Norf. 86 B5
Kimberley Notts. 81 G3
Kimble Wick 42 D2
Kimblesworth 120 B3
Kimbolton Cambs. 57 G1
Kimbolton Here. 53 E1
Kimcote 68 A4
Kimmeridge 13 F5
Kimmerston 137 D3
Kimpton Hants. 27 D3
Kimpton Herts. 44 A1
Kinaldy 152 D3
Kinblethmont 161 E5
Kinbrace 194 A5
Kinbreack 165 G5
Kinbuck 150 C4
Kincaldrum 160 C5
Kincaple 152 C3
Kincardine Fife 142 D1
Kincardine High. 179 F1
Kincardine O'Neil 170 A5
Kinclaven 151 G1
Kincorth 171 E4
Kincraig Aber. 171 E2
Kincraig High. 168 A4
Kincraigie 159 E5
Kindallachan 159 E5
Kindrogan Field Centre 159 F3
Kinellar 170 D3
Kineton Glos. 54 C5
Kineton Warks. 55 F2
Kineton Green 66 D4
Kinfauns 151 G2
King Sterndale 93 E5
Kingarth 140 B4
Kingcoed 38 D2
Kingerby 96 A3
Kingham 55 E5
Kingholm Quay 125 D3
Kinghorn 143 G1
Kinglassie 152 A5
Kingoodie 152 B2
King's Bromley 66 D1
Kings Caple 53 E5
King's Cliffe 69 F3
King's Coughton 54 C2
King's Green 53 G4
King's Heath 66 C4
Kings Hill 31 F3
Kings Hill 66 B3
Kings Langley 43 F2
King's Lynn 85 E5
Kings Meaburn 118 C5
King's Mills 9 E5
Kings Muir 135 D2
King's Newton 81 E5
King's Norton Leics. 68 B2
King's Norton W.Mid. 66 C5
King's Nympton 21 G4
King's Pyon 52 D2
Kings Ripton 70 A5
King's Somborne 27 E4
King's Stag 12 D1
King's Stanley 40 A2
King's Sutton 55 G4
King's Walden 57 G5
Kings Worthy 27 F4
Kingsand 8 A2
Kingsbarns 153 D3
Kingsbridge Devon 8 D3
Kingsbridge Som. 22 C4
Kingsburgh 175 G4
Kingsbury Gt.Lon. 44 A4
Kingsbury Warks. 67 E3
Kingsbury Episcopi 24 B5
Kingscavil 143 E2
Kingsclere 27 G2
Kingscote 40 A3
Kingscott 21 F4
Kingscross 131 F3
Kingsdale 152 B4
Kingsdon 24 C5
Kingsdown 33 F4
Kingseat 151 G5
Kingsey 42 C2
Kingsfold Pembs. 34 C3
Kingsfold W.Suss. 29 G4
Kingsford Aber. 182 C5
Kingsford Aber. 170 A3
Kingsford Aberdeen 170 D4
Kingsford E.Ayr. 141 F5
Kingsford Worcs. 66 A4
Kingsforth 96 A1
Kingsgate 33 F1
Kingsheanton 21 F2
Kingshouse 150 A2
Kingshouse Hotel 157 E4
Kingskerswell 9 E1
Kingskettle 152 B4
Kingsland Here. 52 D1
Kingsland I.o.A. 88 A4
Kingsley Ches. 91 G5
Kingsley Hants. 28 C4
Kingsley Staffs. 80 B3
Kingsley Green 29 D4
Kingsmuir 160 C5
Kingsnorth 32 C5
Kingsnorth Power Station 32 A1
Kingstanding 66 C3
Kingsteignton 10 B5
Kingsteps 180 B4
Kingsthorne 53 E4
Kingsthorpe 56 C1
Kingston Cambs. 58 B2
Kingston Devon 8 C3
Kingston Dorset 12 D2
Kingston Dorset 13 F5
Kingston E.Loth. 144 C1
Kingston Hants. 14 A2
Kingston I.o.W. 15 D4
Kingston Kent 33 D3
Kingston Moray 181 F3
Kingston W.Suss. 16 C3
Kingston Bagpuize 41 G3
Kingston Blount 42 C3
Kingston by Sea 17 E3
Kingston Deverill 25 F4
Kingston Lisle 41 F4
Kingston near Lewes 17 F3
Kingston on Soar 81 G5
Kingston Russell 12 B3
Kingston St. Mary 23 F5
Kingston Seymour 24 A1
Kingston Upon Hull 104 D5
Kingston upon Thames 44 A5
Kingston Warren 41 F4
Kingstone Here. 52 D4
Kingstone Som. 11 G1
Kingstone Staffs. 80 B5
Kingstown 117 G1
Kingswear 9 E2
Kingswell 141 G5
Kingswells 171 D4
Kingswinford 66 A4
Kingswood Bucks. 42 B1
Kingswood Glos. 39 G3
Kingswood Here. 52 B2
Kingswood Kent 32 A3
Kingswood Powys 64 B2
Kingswood S.Glos. 39 F5
Kingswood Surr. 30 B3
Kingswood Warks. 67 D5
Kingthorpe 96 B5
Kington Here. 52 B2
Kington Worcs. 54 B2
Kington Langley 40 B5
Kington Magna 25 E5
Kington St. Michael 40 A5
Kingussie 167 G4
Kingweston 24 C4
Kinharrachie 171 E1
Kinharvie 124 D4
Kinkell 142 A2
Kinkell Bridge 151 E3
Kinknockie 183 F5
Kinlet 65 G4
Kinloch Fife 152 A3
Kinloch High. 192 C5
Kinloch High. 155 F4
Kinloch High. 164 A5
Kinloch High. 179 E2
Kinloch P.&K. 160 A5
Kinloch P.&K. 159 G5
Kinloch Hourn 165 F4
Kinloch Laggan 158 A1
Kinloch Rannoch 158 B4
Kinlochan 156 A3
Kinlochard 149 G4
Kinlocharkaig 165 F5
Kinlochbeoraid 156 A1
Kinlochbervie 192 B3
Kinlocheil 156 B2
Kinlochetive 156 D5
Kinlochewe 177 G3
Kinlochlaich 156 B5
Kinlochleven 157 D3
Kinlochmoidart 155 G2
Kinlochmorar 165 E5
Kinlochmore 157 D3
Kinlochspelve 147 F2
Kinloss 180 C3
Kinmel Bay (Bae Cinmel) 90 A4
Kinmuck 170 D3
Kinnadie 183 E5
Kinnaird 152 A2
Kinneff 161 G2
Kinnelhead 134 B5
Kinnell Angus 161 E4
Kinnell Stir. 150 A1
Kinnerley 78 A5
Kinnersley Here. 52 C3
Kinnersley Worcs. 54 A3
Kinnerton 52 B1
Kinnesswood 151 G4
Kinnettles 160 C5
Kinninvie 119 G5
Kinnordy 160 B4
Kinoulton 82 B4
Kinrara 168 A4
Kinross 151 G4
Kinrossie 151 G1
Kinsbourne Green 44 A1
Kinsham 52 C1
Kinsley 94 B1
Kinson 13 G3
Kintarvie 185 E2
Kintbury 27 E1
Kintessack 180 B3
Kintillo 151 G3
Kintocher 170 A4
Kinton Here. 64 D5
Kinton Shrop. 64 C1
Kintore 170 C3
Kintour 138 C4
Kintra Arg. & B. 138 B5
Kintra Arg. & B. 146 C2
Kintradwell 191 E4
Kintraw 148 A4
Kinuachdrachd 147 G5
Kinveachy 168 B3
Kinver 66 A4
Kiplaw Croft 171 F1
Kiplin 110 B3
Kiplingcotes 104 B3
Kipp 150 A3
Kippax 102 D4
Kippen P.&K. 151 F3
Kippen Stir. 150 B5
Kippenross House 150 C4
Kippford or Scaur 124 C5
Kipping's Cross 31 F4
Kirbister Ork. 196 C2
Kirbister Ork. 199 E4
Kirbuster 198 A4
Kirby Bedon 87 D5
Kirby Cane 73 E2
Kirby Corner 67 E5
Kirby Cross 47 F1
Kirby Grindalythe 104 B1
Kirby Hill N.Yorks. 110 A2
Kirby Hill N.Yorks. 102 C1
Kirby Knowle 111 D4
Kirby le Soken 60 D5
Kirby Misperton 111 G5
Kirby Muxloe 68 A2
Kirby Row 73 E2
Kirby Sigston 110 D3
Kirby Underdale 104 A2
Kirby Wiske 110 C4
Kirdford 29 F5
Kirk 195 E3
Kirk Bramwith 94 D1
Kirk Deighton 102 C2
Kirk Ella 104 C5
Kirk Hallam 81 F3
Kirk Hammerton 103 D2
Kirk Ireton 81 D2
Kirk Langley 81 D4
Kirk Merrington 120 B4
Kirk Michael 98 B2
Kirk of Shotts 142 C3
Kirk Sandall 94 D2
Kirk Smeaton 94 C1
Kirk Yetholm 136 C4
Kirkabister 201 D4
Kirkandrews 115 G2
Kirkandrews-upon-Eden 117 G1
Kirkbampton 117 G1
Kirkbean 125 D5
Kirkbride 117 F1
Kirkbridge 110 B3
Kirkbuddo 160 D5
Kirkburn E.Riding 104 B2
Kirkburn Sc.Bord. 135 D2
Kirkburton 93 F1
Kirkby Lincs. 96 A3
Kirkby Mersey. 91 F3
Kirkby N.Yorks. 111 E2
Kirkby Bellars 68 C1
Kirkby Fleetham 110 B3
Kirkby Green 83 F2
Kirkby in Ashfield 81 F2
Kirkby la Thorpe 83 G3
Kirkby Lonsdale 108 B5
Kirkby Malham 101 E1
Kirkby Mallory 67 G2
Kirkby Malzeard 110 B5
Kirkby Mills 111 G4
Kirkby on Bain 84 A1
Kirkby Overblow 102 C3
Kirkby Stephen 108 C2
Kirkby Thore 118 C5
Kirkby Underwood 83 F5
Kirkby Wharfe 103 E3
Kirkbymoorside 111 F4
Kirkcaldy 152 A5
Kirkcambeck 118 B1
Kirkcolm 122 B4
Kirkconnel 133 F4
Kirkconnell 125 D4
Kirkcowan 123 E4
Kirkcudbright 124 A5
Kirkdale House 123 G5
Kirkdean 143 F5
Kirkfieldbank 142 C5
Kirkgunzeon 124 C4
Kirkham Lancs. 100 A4
Kirkham N.Yorks. 103 G1
Kirkhamgate 102 B5
Kirkharle 128 C3
Kirkhaugh 118 C3
Kirkheaton Northumb. 128 C4
Kirkheaton W.Yorks. 93 F1
Kirkhill Angus 161 E3
Kirkhill High. 179 E5
Kirkhill Moray 181 F4
Kirkhope 135 E3
Kirkibost High. 164 B3
Kirkibost W.Isles 186 C4
Kirkinch 160 B5
Kirkinner 123 F5
Kirkintilloch 142 A2
Kirkland Cumb. 118 C4
Kirkland Cumb. 117 D5
Kirkland D.&G. 124 C1
Kirkland D.&G. 133 F4
Kirkland D.&G. 125 E2
Kirkland of Longcastle 115 D2
Kirkleatham 121 E5
Kirklevington 110 D1
Kirkley 73 G2
Kirklington N.Yorks. 110 C4
Kirklington Notts. 82 B2
Kirklinton 118 A1
Kirkliston 143 F2
Kirkmaiden 114 B3
Kirkmichael P.&K. 159 F3
Kirkmichael S.Ayr. 132 B5
Kirkmuirhill 142 B5
Kirknewton Northumb. 136 D4
Kirknewton W.Loth. 143 F3
Kirkney 170 A1
Kirkoswald Cumb. 118 B3
Kirkoswald S.Ayr. 132 A5
Kirkpatrick Durham 124 B3
Kirkpatrick-Fleming 126 A4
Kirksanton 106 C4
Kirkstall 102 B4
Kirkstead 83 G1
Kirkstile Aber. 170 A1
Kirkstile D.&G. 126 B2
Kirkton Aber. 170 B2
Kirkton Aber. 182 B4
Kirkton Aber. 170 B3
Kirkton Angus 160 C5
Kirkton Arg. & B. 147 G4
Kirkton D.&G. 125 D2
Kirkton Fife 152 B2
Kirkton High. 167 F1
Kirkton High. 190 C5
Kirkton High. 179 G4
Kirkton High. 194 A2
Kirkton High. 165 E2
Kirkton P.&K. 151 E3
Kirkton Sc.Bord. 135 G4
Kirkton Manor 134 D2
Kirkton of Airlie 160 B4
Kirkton of Auchterhouse 152 B1
Kirkton of Barevan 180 A5
Kirkton of Bourtie 170 D2
Kirkton of Collace 151 G1
Kirkton of Craig 161 F4
Kirkton of Culsalmond 170 B1
Kirkton of Durris 170 C5
Kirkton of Glenbuchat 169 F3
Kirkton of Glenisla 160 A3
Kirkton of Kingoldrum 160 B4
Kirkton of Lethendy 159 G5
Kirkton of Logie Buchan 171 E2
Kirkton of Maryculter 171 D5
Kirkton of Menmuir 160 D3
Kirkton of Monikie 152 D1
Kirkton of Rayne 170 B1
Kirkton of Skene 170 D4
Kirkton of Strathmartine 152 B1
Kirkton of Tealing 152 C1
Kirktonhill 161 E3
Kirktown 183 F4
Kirktown of Alvah 182 B3
Kirktown of Auchterless 182 C5
Kirktown of Deskford 182 A3
Kirktown of Fetteresso 161 G1
Kirktown of Slains 171 F2
Kirkwall 198 C5
Kirkwall Airport 197 D2
Kirkwhelpington 128 B3
Kirmington 96 B1
Kirmond le Mire 96 B3
Kirn 140 C2
Kirriemuir 160 B4
Kirstead Green 73 D2
Kirtlebridge 126 A4
Kirtling 59 E2
Kirtling Green 59 E2
Kirtlington 41 G1
Kirtomy 193 G2
Kirton Lincs. 84 B4
Kirton Notts. 82 B1
Kirton Suff. 61 D4
Kirton End 84 A3
Kirton Holme 84 A3
Kirton in Lindsey 95 G3
Kiscadale 131 F3
Kislingbury 56 B2
Kismeldon Bridge 21 D4
Kites Hardwick 55 G1
Kitley 8 B2
Kittisford 23 D5
Kitwood 28 B4
Kiveton Park 94 B4
Klibreck 193 E5
Knabbygates 182 A4
Knaith 95 F4
Knap Corner 25 F5
Knaphill 29 E2
Knapp P.&K. 152 A1
Knapp Som. 23 F5
Knapton Norf. 87 E2
Knapton York 103 E2
Knapton Green 52 D2
Knapwell 58 B1
Knaresborough 102 C2
Knarsdale 118 C2
Knaven 183 D5
Knayton 110 D4
Knebworth 44 B1
Knedlington 103 G5
Kneesall 82 C1
Kneesworth 58 B3
Kneeton 82 C3
Knelston 36 A4
Knettishall 72 A4
Knightacott 21 G2
Knightcote 55 G2
Knighton Devon 8 B3
Knighton Leic. 68 B2
Knighton Powys 64 B5
Knighton Som. 23 E3
Knighton Staffs. 79 E5
Knighton Staffs. 79 E4
Knighton Wilts. 41 E5
Knightwick 53 G2
Knill 52 B1
Knipoch 148 A2
Knipton 82 D4
Knitsley 120 A3
Kniveton 80 D2
Knock Arg. & B. 147 E1
Knock Cumb. 118 C5
Knock Moray 182 A4
Knock of Auchnahannet 168 C1
Knockalava 148 B5
Knockally 191 G2
Knockaloe Moar 98 A3
Knockan 189 E3
Knockandhu 169 E2
Knockando 181 D5
Knockbain 179 F4
Knockban 178 B3
Knockbreck 179 G1
Knockbrex 115 F2
Knockdamph 189 E5
Knockdee 195 D2
Knockdow 140 C2
Knockdown 40 A4
Knockenkelly 131 F3
Knockentiber 132 C2
Knockfin 166 B2
Knockgray 123 G1
Knockholt 31 D3
Knockholt Pound 31 D3
Knockin 78 A5
Knocklearn 124 B3
Knocknaha 130 B4
Knocknain 122 A4
Knocknalling 123 G2
Knockrome 139 D2
Knocksharry 98 A3
Knockville 123 E3
Knockvologan 146 C3
Knodishall 61 F1
Knolls Green 92 C5
Knolton 78 A4
Knook 26 A3
Knossington 68 D2
Knott End-on-Sea 99 G3
Knotting 57 F1
Knotting Green 57 F1
Knottingley 103 E5
Knotty Ash 91 F3
Knotty Green 43 E3
Knowbury 65 E5
Knowe 123 E3
Knowes of Elrick 182 B4
Knowesgate 128 B3
Knoweside 132 A4
Knowetownhead 135 G4
Knowhead 183 E4
Knowl Green 59 F3
Knowl Hill 42 D5
Knowl Wall 79 F4
Knowle Bristol 39 F5
Knowle Devon 10 A2
Knowle Devon 21 E2
Knowle Devon 11 D4
Knowle Shrop. 65 E5
Knowle W.Mid. 67 D5
Knowle Green 100 C4
Knowle Hall 24 A3
Knowlton Dorset 13 G1
Knowlton Kent 33 E3
Knowsley 91 F3
Knowstone 22 B5
Knucklas 64 B5
Knutsford 92 B5
Knypersley 79 F2
Kuggar 3 E5
Kyle of Lochalsh 165 D2
Kyleakin 165 D2
Kylerhea 165 D2
Kyles Scalpay (Caolas Scalpaigh) 185 E4
Kylesbeg 155 F2
Kylesknoydart 165 E5
Kylesmorar 165 E5
Kylestrome 192 B5
Kyloag 190 B5
Kynnersley 65 F1
Kyre Park 53 F1

**L**

L'Islet 9 F4
Labost 187 D3
Lacasaigh 187 E5
Lacasdal (Laxdale) 187 F4
Laceby 96 C2
Lacey Green 42 D2
Lach Dennis 92 B5
Lackford 71 F5
Lacock 26 A1
Ladbroke 55 G2

Laddingford 31 F4
Lade Bank 84 B2
Ladock 4 C4
Lady Hall 106 C4
Ladybank 152 A3
Ladycross 6 D2
Ladyfield 148 C3
Ladykirk 145 F5
Lady's Green 59 F2
Ladysford 183 E3
Laga 155 F3
Lagalochan 148 A3
Lagavulin 138 C5
Lagg Arg. & B. 139 D2
Lagg N.Ayr. 131 E3
Lagg S.Ayr. 132 A4
Laggan Arg. & B. 138 A4
Laggan High. 166 B5
Laggan High. 167 F5
Laggan Moray 169 F1
Laggan Stir. 150 A3
Lagganulva 155 D5
Lagganvoulin 169 D3
Laglingarten 148 D4
Lagnalean 179 F5
Lagrae 133 F4
Laguna 151 G1
Laid 192 D3
Laide 188 A5
Laig 155 D1
Laight 133 E4
Lainchoil 168 C3
Laindon 45 F4
Lair 159 G3
Lairg 190 A4
Lairg Lodge 190 A4
Lairigmor 156 D3
Laithers 182 B5
Laithes 118 A4
Lake 26 C4
Lakenham 86 D5
Lakenheath 71 F4
Lakesend 70 D3
Lakeside 107 E4
Laleham 29 F1
Laleston 37 E5
Lamancha 143 G4
Lamarsh 59 G4
Lamas 86 D3
Lamb Corner 60 B4
Lamberhurst 31 F5
Lamberhurst Quarter 31 F5
Lamberton 145 G4
Lambeth 44 B5
Lambfell Moar 98 A3
Lambley Northumb. 118 C2
Lambley Notts. 82 B3
Lambourn 41 F5
Lambourn Woodlands 41 F5
Lambourne End 45 D3
Lambs Green 30 B5
Lambston 34 C1
Lamellion 5 G3
Lamerton 7 E3
Lamesley 120 B2
Lamington High. 179 G2
Lamington S.Lan. 134 A2
Lamlash 131 F2
Lamloch 123 G1
Lamonby 118 A4
Lamorran 4 C5
Lampert 127 E4
Lampeter 50 B3
Lampeter Velfrey 35 E1
Lamphey 34 D2
Lamplugh 117 D4
Lamport 68 C5
Lamyatt 25 D4
Lana 6 D1
Lanark 142 C5
Lancaster 100 A1
Lanchester 120 A3
Lancing 17 D3
Landbeach 58 C1
Landcross 21 E3
Landerberry 170 C4
Landewednack 3 E5
Landford 14 B1
Landimore 36 A3
Landkey 21 F2
Landore 36 C3
Landrake 7 D4
Landscove 9 D1
Landshipping 34 D1
Landulph 8 A1
Landwade 59 E1
Landywood 66 B2
Lane-end 5 E3
Lane End Bucks. 42 D3
Lane End Cumb. 106 C3
Lane End Derbys. 81 F1
Lane End Dorset 13 E3
Lane End Kent 45 E5
Lane Green 66 A2
Lane Head Dur. 110 A1
Lane Head Gt.Man. 92 A3
Lane Head W.Yorks. 93 F2
Laneast 5 G1
Laneham 95 F5
Lanehead 127 F3
Laneshawbridge 101 F3
Langais 173 G3
Langamull 154 C4
Langar 82 C4
Langbank 141 E2
Langbar 101 G2
Langcliffe 101 E1
Langdale End 112 C3
Langdon 6 C1
Langdon Beck 119 E4
Langdon Hills 45 F4
Langdon House 10 C5
Langdyke 152 B4
Langenhoe 46 D1
Langford Beds. 57 G3
Langford Devon 10 D2
Langford Essex 46 B2
Langford Notts. 82 D2
Langford Oxon. 41 E2
Langford Budville 23 E5
Langham Essex 60 B4
Langham Norf. 86 B1
Langham Rut. 68 D1
Langham Suff. 60 A1
Langham Moor 60 B4
Langho 100 C4
Langholm 126 B3
Langlands 124 A5
Langlee 136 A5
Langleeford 136 D4
Langley Ches. 92 D5
Langley Derbys. 81 F3
Langley Essex 58 C4
Langley Hants. 14 D2
Langley Herts. 58 A5
Langley Kent 32 A3
Langley Slo. 43 F5
Langley W.Suss. 28 D5
Langley Warks. 55 D1
Langley Burrell 40 B5
Langley Green 81 D4
Langley Heath 32 A3
Langley Marsh 23 D5
Langley Mill 81 F3
Langley Moor 120 B3
Langley Park 120 B3
Langley Street 87 E5
Langney 18 B3
Langold 94 C4
Langore 6 D2
Langport 24 B5
Langrick 84 A3
Langridge B. & N.E.Som. 25 E1
Langridge Devon 21 F3
Langridgeford 21 F3
Langrigg 117 E2
Langrish 28 C5
Langriville 84 A3
Langsett 93 G2
Langshaw 135 G2
Langshawburn 135 D5
Langside 150 C3
Langskaill 198 C2
Langstone 15 G2
Langthorne 110 B3
Langthorpe 102 C1
Langthwaite 109 F2
Langtoft E.Riding 104 C1
Langtoft Lincs. 69 G1
Langton Dur. 110 A1
Langton Lincs. 97 D5
Langton Lincs. 84 A1
Langton N.Yorks. 103 G1
Langton by Wragby 96 B5
Langton Green 31 E5
Langton Herring 12 C4
Langton Long Blandford 13 F2
Langton Matravers 13 G5
Langtree 21 E4
Langwathby 118 B4
Langwell 189 G4
Langwell House 191 G2
Langworth 96 A5
Lanivet 5 E3
Lanlivery 5 E4
Lanner 4 B5
Lanreath 5 F4
Lansallos 5 F4
Lansdown 25 E1
Lanteglos 5 E1
Lanton Northumb. 136 D3
Lanton Sc.Bord. 136 A4
Lapford 10 A2
Laphroaig 138 B5
Lapley 66 A1
Lapworth 67 D5
Larach na Gaibhre 139 F3
Larachbeg 155 F5
Larbert 142 C1
Larden Green 78 C2
Larg 123 E3
Largie 170 B1
Largiemore 140 A1
Largoward 152 C4
Largs 140 D4
Largue 182 B5
Largybaan 130 B4
Largybeg 131 F3
Largymore 131 F3
Lark Hall 59 D2
Larkhall 142 B4
Larkhill 26 C3
Larling 72 A3
Larriston 126 D2
Lartington 109 F1
Lary 169 F4
Lasborough 40 A3
Lasham 28 B3
Lassington 53 G5
Lassintullich 158 C4
Lassodie 151 G5
Lasswade 144 A3
Lastingham 111 G3
Latchford 92 A4
Latchingdon 46 B2
Latchley 7 E3
Lately Common 92 A3
Lathallan Mill 152 C4
Lathbury 57 D3
Latheron 195 D5
Latheronwheel 195 D5
Lathockar 152 C3
Lathones 152 C4
Lathrisk 152 A4
Latimer 43 F3
Latteridge 39 F4
Lattiford 25 D5
Latton 40 C3
Lauchentyre 123 G5
Lauchintilly 170 C3
Lauder 144 C5
Laugharne 35 G1
Laughterton 95 F5
Laughton E.Suss. 18 A2
Laughton Leics. 68 B4
Laughton Lincs. 83 F4
Laughton Lincs. 95 F3
Laughton en le Morthen 94 C4
Launcells 20 C5
Launcells Cross 20 C5
Launceston 6 D2
Launde Abbey 68 D2
Launton 56 B5
Laurencekirk 161 F2
Laurieston D. & G. 124 A4
Laurieston Falk. 142 D2
Lavendon 57 E2
Lavenham 60 A3
Laverhay 125 F1
Lavernock 23 E1
Laversdale 118 A1
Laverstock 26 C4
Laverstoke 27 F3
Laverton Glos. 54 C4
Laverton N.Yorks. 110 B5
Laverton Som. 25 E2
Lavister 78 A2
Law 142 C4
Lawers P. & K. 150 C2
Lawers P. & K. 150 B1
Lawford 60 B4
Lawhitton 7 D2
Lawkland 101 D1
Lawley 65 F2
Lawnhead 79 F5
Lawrenny 34 D2
Laws 152 C1
Lawshall 59 G2
Lawton 52 D2
Laxdale (Lacasdal) 187 F4
Laxey 98 C3
Laxfield 73 D4
Laxfirth Shet. 201 D2
Laxfirth Shet. 200 D3
Laxford Bridge 192 B4
Laxo 200 D1
Laxton E.Riding 103 G5
Laxton Northants. 69 E3
Laxton Notts. 82 C1
Laycock 101 G3
Layer Breton 46 C1
Layer de la Haye 46 C1
Layer Marney 46 C1
Layham 60 B3
Laytham 103 G4
Lazenby 121 E5
Lazonby 118 B4
Lea Derbys. 81 E2
Lea Here. 53 F5
Lea Lincs. 95 F4
Lea Shrop. 64 C4
Lea Shrop. 64 D2
Lea Wilts. 40 B4
Lea Marston 67 E3
Lea Town 100 A4
Lea Yeat 108 C4
Leac a' Li 184 D4
Leachd 148 C5
Leachkin 179 F5
Leadburn 143 G4
Leaden Roding 45 E1
Leadenham 83 E2
Leadgate Cumb. 118 D3
Leadgate Dur. 120 A2
Leadgate T. & W. 120 A2
Leadhills 133 G4
Leafield 41 F1
Leagrave 57 F5
Leake Common Side 84 B2
Leake Hurn's End 84 C3
Lealands 18 A2
Lealholm 111 G2
Lealt Arg. & B. 147 F5
Lealt High. 176 B3
Leamington Hastings 55 G1
Leamington Spa 55 F1
Leanach Arg. & B. 148 C5
Leanach High. 179 G5
Leanaig 179 E4
Leanoch 181 D4
Leargybreck 138 D2
Leasgill 107 F4
Leasingham 83 F3
Leask 171 F1
Leatherhead 29 G2
Leathley 102 B3
Leaton 65 D1
Leaveland 32 C3
Leavenheath 60 A4
Leavening 103 G1
Leaves Green 30 D2
Lebberston 113 D4
Lechlade 41 E3
Leck 108 B5
Leckford 27 E4
Leckfurin 193 G3
Leckgruinart 138 A3
Leckhampstead Bucks. 56 C4
Leckhampstead W.Berks. 41 G5
Leckhampton 40 B1
Leckie High. 177 G3
Leckie Stir. 150 B5
Leckmelm 189 D5
Leckroy 166 C5
Leckuary 148 A5
Leckwith 38 A5
Leconfield 104 C3
Ledaig 148 B1
Ledard 149 G4
Ledbeg 189 E3
Ledburn 57 D5
Ledbury 53 G4
Ledcharrie 150 A2
Ledgemoor 52 D2
Ledicot 52 D1
Ledmore Arg. & B. 155 F5
Ledmore High. 189 E3
Lednagullin 193 G2
Ledsham Ches. 91 E5
Ledsham W.Yorks. 103 D5
Ledston 102 D5
Ledwell 55 G5
Lee Arg. & B. 146 D2
Lee Devon 21 E1
Lee Hants. 14 C1
Lee Lancs. 100 B2
Lee Shrop. 78 B4
Lee Brockhurst 78 C5
Lee Clump 43 E2
Lee Mill Bridge 8 B2
Lee Moor 8 B1
Lee-on-the-Solent 15 E2
Leebotten 200 D5
Leebotwood 65 D3
Leece 99 F1
Leeds Kent 32 A3
Leeds W.Yorks. 102 B4
Leeds Bradford International Airport 102 B3
Leedstown 2 D3
Leegomery 65 F1
Leek 79 G2
Leek Wootton 55 E1
Leeming N.Yorks. 110 B4
Leeming W.Yorks. 101 G4
Leeming Bar 110 B3
Lees Derbys. 81 D4
Lees Gt.Man. 93 D2
Leeswood 77 F2
Legars 145 E5
Legbourne 97 D4
Legerwood 144 C5
Legsby 96 B4
Leicester 68 A2
Leideag 172 B4
Leigh Dorset 12 C2
Leigh Glos. 54 A5
Leigh Gt.Man. 92 A2
Leigh Kent 31 E4
Leigh Shrop. 64 C2
Leigh Surr. 30 B4
Leigh Wilts. 40 C3
Leigh Worcs. 53 G2
Leigh Beck 46 B4
Leigh Common 25 E5
Leigh Delamere 40 A5
Leigh Green 32 B5
Leigh-on-Sea 46 B4
Leigh Sinton 53 G2
Leigh upon Mendip 25 D3
Leigh Woods 39 E5
Leighterton 40 A3
Leighton N.Yorks. 110 A5
Leighton Powys 64 B2
Leighton Shrop. 65 F2
Leighton Som. 25 E3
Leighton Bromswold 69 G5
Leighton Buzzard 57 E5
Leinthall Earls 52 D1
Leinthall Starkes 52 D1
Leintwardine 64 D5
Leire 68 A4
Leirinmore 192 D2
Leiston 61 F1
Leitfie 160 A5
Leith 143 G2
Leitholm 145 E5
Lelant 2 C3
Lelley 105 E4
Lem Hill 65 G5
Lemington 120 A1
Lemnas 182 D3
Lempitlaw 136 B3
Lemsford 44 B1
Lenchwick 54 C3
Lendalfoot 122 C2
Lendrick Lodge 150 A4
Lenham 32 A3
Lenham Heath 32 B4
Lenie 167 E2
Lenimore 139 G5
Lennel 145 F5
Lennox Plunton 124 A5
Lennoxtown 142 A2
Lenton 83 F4
Lenwade 86 C4
Lenzie 142 A2
Leoch 152 B1
Leochel-Cushnie 170 A3
Leominster 53 D2
Leonard Stanley 40 A2
Leorin 138 B5
Lepe 15 D3
Lephinchapel 148 B5
Lephinmore 148 B5
Leppington 103 G1
Lepton 93 G1
Lerags 148 A2
Lerryn 5 F4
Lerwick 201 D3
Lesbury 137 G5
Leschangie 170 C3
Lescrow 5 F4
Leslie Aber. 170 A2
Leslie Fife 152 A4
Lesmahagow 133 G2
Lesnewth 6 B1
Lessendrum 182 A5
Lessingham 87 E3
Lessonhall 117 F1
Leswalt 122 B4
Letchmore Heath 44 A3
Letchworth 58 A4
Letcombe Bassett 41 F4
Letcombe Regis 41 F4
Leth Meadhanach 172 C2
Letham Angus 160 D5
Letham Fife 152 B3
Lethanhill 132 C4
Lethenty 182 D5
Letheringham 61 D2
Letheringsett 86 B2
Lettaford 10 A4
Letter Finlay 166 B5
Letterewe 177 F2
Letterfearn 165 E2
Lettermorar 155 G1
Lettermore Arg. & B. 155 E5
Lettermore High. 193 F4
Letters 178 A1
Lettershaws 134 G3
Letterston 48 C5
Lettoch High. 168 C3
Lettoch High. 168 C1
Letton Here. 64 C5
Letton Here. 52 C3
Letty Green 44 B1
Letwell 94 C4
Leuchars 152 C2
Leumrabhagh 185 F2
Levedale 66 A1
Leven E.Riding 104 D3
Leven Fife 152 B4
Levencorroch 131 F3
Levenhall 144 A2
Levens 107 F4
Levenshulme 92 C3
Levenwick 200 D5
Leverburgh (An T-ób) 184 C5
Leverington 70 C1
Leverstock Green 43 F2
Leverton 84 C3
Leverton Outgate 84 C3
Levington 60 D4
Levisham 112 B3
Levishie 166 D3
Lew 41 F2
Lewannick 5 G1
Lewdown 7 E2
Lewes 17 G2
Leweston 48 C5
Lewisham 44 C5
Lewiston 167 E2
Lewknor 42 C3
Leworthy 21 G2
Lewtrenchard 7 E2
Ley Aber. 170 A3
Ley Cornw. 5 F3
Ley Green 57 G5
Leybourne 31 F3
Leyburn 110 A3
Leycett 79 E3
Leyland 100 B5
Leylodge 170 C3
Leys Aber. 183 F4
Leys Aber. 169 G4
Leys P. & K. 152 A1
Leys of Cossans 160 B5
Leysdown-on-Sea 32 C1
Leysmill 161 E5
Leysters 53 E1
Leyton 44 C4
Lezant 6 D3
Lhanbryde 181 E3
Liatrie 166 B1
Libanus 51 F5
Libberton 143 D5
Liberton 143 G3
Liceasto 184 D4
Lichfield 66 D2
Lickey 66 B5
Lickey End 66 B5
Lickfold 29 E5
Liddel 197 D4
Liddesdale 155 G4
Liddington 41 E4
Lidgate Derbys. 94 A5
Lidgate Suff. 59 F2
Lidlington 57 E4
Lidsing 31 G2
Lidstone 55 F5
Lienassie 165 F2
Lieurary 194 C2
Liff 152 B1
Lifton 7 D2
Liftondown 7 D2
Lighthorne 55 F2
Lightwater 29 E1
Lightwood 79 G3
Lightwood Green Ches. 78 D3
Lightwood Green Wrex. 78 A3
Lilbourne 68 A5
Lilburn Tower 137 E4
Lilleshall 65 G1
Lilley Herts. 57 G5
Lilley W.Berks. 41 G5
Lilliesleaf 135 G3
Lillingstone Dayrell 56 C4
Lillingstone Lovell 56 C3
Lillington 12 C1
Lilliput 13 G3
Lilstock 23 E3
Limbrick 92 A1
Limbury 57 F5
Limefield 92 C1
Limehillock 182 A4
Limekilnburn 142 B4
Limekilns 143 E1
Limerigg 142 C2
Limerstone 14 D4
Limington 24 C5
Limpenhoe 87 E5
Limpley Stoke 25 E1
Limpsfield 30 D3
Linbriggs 128 A1
Linby 81 G2
Linchmere 29 D4
Lincoln 95 G5
Lincomb 54 A1
Lincombe 8 D2
Lindal in Furness 107 D5
Lindale 107 F4
Lindean 135 F2
Lindertis 160 B4
Lindfield 17 F1
Lindford 28 D4
Lindifferon 152 B3
Lindley 93 F1
Lindores 152 A3
Lindridge 53 F1
Lindsaig 140 A2
Lindsell 59 E5
Lindsey 60 A3
Linford Hants. 14 A2
Linford Thur. 45 F5
Lingague 98 A4
Lingdale 111 F1
Lingen 52 C1
Lingfield 30 C4
Lingwood 87 E5
Linhead 182 B4
Linhope 135 F5
Linicro 175 G3
Linkenholt 27 E2
Linkhill 18 D1
Linkinhorne 6 D3
Linklater 197 D4
Linksness Ork. 196 B2
Linksness Ork. 198 D5
Linktown 152 A5
Linley 64 C3
Linley Green 53 F2
Linlithgow 143 D2
Linlithgow Bridge 143 D2
Linn of Muick Cottage 160 B1
Linnels 119 F1
Linney 34 B3
Linshiels 128 A1
Linsiadar 186 D4
Linsidemore 190 A5
Linslade 57 E5
Linstead Parva 73 E4
Linstock 118 A2
Linthwaite 93 F1
Lintlaw 145 F4
Lintmill 182 A3
Linton Cambs. 59 D3
Linton Derbys. 67 E1
Linton Here. 53 F5
Linton Kent 31 G4
Linton N.Yorks. 101 F1
Linton Sc.Bord. 136 B4
Linton W.Yorks. 102 C3
Linton-on-Ouse 103 D1
Lintzford 120 A2
Linwood Hants. 14 A2
Linwood Lincs. 96 B4
Linwood Renf. 141 F3
Lionacleit 173 F5
Lional 187 G1
Liphook 28 D4
Liscombe 22 B4
Liskeard 5 G3
Liss 28 C5
Liss Forest 28 C5
Lissett 104 D2
Lissington 96 B4
Liston 59 G3
Lisvane 38 A4
Liswerry 38 C4
Litcham 71 G1
Litchborough 56 B2
Litchfield 27 F2
Litherland 91 E3
Litlington Cambs. 58 B3
Litlington E.Suss. 18 A3
Little Abington 58 D3
Little Addington 69 E5
Little Alne 54 D1
Little Amwell 44 C1
Little Assynt 188 D2
Little Aston 66 C3
Little Atherfield 15 D5
Little Ayton 111 E1
Little Baddow 45 G2
Little Badminton 39 G4
Little Ballinluig 159 E4
Little Bampton 117 F1
Little Bardfield 59 E4
Little Barford 57 G2
Little Barningham 86 C2
Little Barrington 41 E1
Little Barugh 111 G5
Little Bealings 60 D3
Little Bedwyn 27 D1
Little Bentley 60 C5
Little Berkhamsted 44 B2
Little Billing 56 D1
Little Birch 53 E4
Little Bispham 99 G3
Little Blakenham 60 C3
Little Bollington 92 B4
Little Bookham 29 G2
Little Bowden 68 C4
Little Bradley 59 E2
Little Brampton 64 C4
Little Braxted 46 B1
Little Brechin 161 D3
Little Brickhill 57 E4
Little Bridgeford 79 F5
Little Brington 56 B1
Little Bromley 60 B5
Little Broughton 117 D3
Little Budworth 78 C1
Little Burstead 45 F3
Little Burton 104 D3
Little Bytham 69 F1
Little Carlton Lincs. 97 E4
Little Carlton Notts. 82 C2
Little Casterton 69 F2
Little Catwick 104 D3
Little Cawthorpe 97 D4
Little Chalfont 43 E3
Little Chart 32 B4
Little Chesterford 58 D3
Little Cheverell 26 A2
Little Chishill 58 C4
Little Clacton 47 E1
Little Clifton 117 D4
Little Comberton 54 B3
Little Common 18 C3
Little Compton 55 E4
Little Corby 118 A2
Little Cowarne 53 F2
Little Coxwell 41 E3
Little Crakehall 110 B3
Little Creich 179 F1
Little Cressingham 71 G3
Little Crosby 91 E2
Little Cubley 80 C4
Little Dalby 68 C1
Little Dens 183 F5
Little Dewchurch 53 E4
Little Downham 70 D4
Little Driffield 104 C2
Little Dunham 71 G1
Little Dunkeld 159 F5
Little Dunmow 59 E5
Little Easton 59 E5
Little Eaton 81 E3
Little Ellingham 72 B2
Little End 45 E2
Little Eversden 58 B2
Little Fakenham 72 A4
Little Faringdon 41 E2
Little Fencote 110 B3
Little Fenton 103 E4
Little Finborough 60 B2
Little Fransham 86 G1
Little Gaddesden 43 E1
Little Garway 52 D5
Little Gidding 69 G4
Little Glemham 61 E2
Little Glenshee 151 E1
Little Gorsley 53 F5
Little Gransden 58 A2
Little Green 72 B4
Little Grimsby 96 D3
Little Gruinard 177 F1
Little Habton 111 G5
Little Hadham 58 C5
Little Hale 83 G3
Little Hallingbury 45 D1
Little Hampden 43 D2
Little Harrowden 69 D5
Little Haseley 42 B2
Little Hautbois 87 D3
Little Haven 34 B1
Little Hay 66 D2
Little Hayfield 93 E4
Little Haywood 80 B5
Little Heath 67 F4
Little Hereford 53 E1
Little Holtby 110 B3
Little Horkesley 60 A4
Little Hormead 58 C5
Little Horsted 17 G2
Little Horwood 56 C4
Little Houghton 56 D2
Little Hucklow 93 F5
Little Hulton 92 B2
Little Hungerford 42 A5
Little Idoch 182 C5
Little Kimble 42 D2
Little Kineton 55 F2
Little Kingshill 43 D3
Little Langford 26 B4
Little Laver 45 E2
Little Lawford 67 G5
Little Leigh 92 A5
Little Leighs 45 G1
Little Lever 92 B2
Little Ley 170 B3
Little Linford 56 D3
Little London E.Suss. 18 A2
Little London Hants. 27 E2
Little London Hants. 28 B2
Little London I.o.M. 98 B3
Little London Lincs. 84 C5
Little London Lincs. 84 A5
Little London Lincs. 96 D5
Little London Norf. 85 D5
Little London Norf. 71 F3
Little Longstone 93 F5
Little Malvern 53 G3
Little Maplestead 59 G4
Little Marcle 53 F4
Little Marlow 43 D4
Little Massingham 85 F5
Little Melton 86 C5
Little Mill 38 C2
Little Milton 42 B2
Little Missenden 43 E3
Little Musgrave 108 C1
Little Ness 64 D1
Little Neston 91 D5
Little Newcastle 48 C5
Little Newsham 110 A1
Little Oakley Essex 60 D5
Little Oakley Northants. 69 D4
Little Orton 117 G1
Little Ouseburn 102 D1
Little Parndon 44 D2
Little Paxton 57 G1
Little Petherick 4 D2
Little Plumstead 87 E4
Little Ponton 83 E4
Little Raveley 70 A5
Little Ribston 102 C2
Little Rissington 55 D5
Little Rogart 190 C4
Little Ryburgh 86 A3
Little Ryle 137 E5
Little Salkeld 118 B4
Little Sampford 59 E4
Little Saxham 59 F1
Little Scatwell 178 C4
Little Shelford 58 C2
Little Smeaton 94 C1
Little Snoring 86 A2
Little Sodbury 39 G4
Little Somborne 27 E4
Little Somerford 40 B4
Little Stainton 120 C5
Little Stanney 91 F5
Little Staughton 57 G1
Little Steeping 84 C1
Little Stonham 60 C2
Little Stretton Leics. 68 B3
Little Stretton Shrop. 64 D3
Little Strickland 118 B5
Little Stukeley 70 A5
Little Sutton 91 E5
Little Swinburne 128 B4
Little Tew 55 F5
Little Tey 59 G5
Little Thetford 70 D5
Little Thirkleby 111 D5
Little Thorpe 120 D3
Little Thurlow 59 E2
Little Thurrock 45 F5
Little Torboll 190 C5
Little Torrington 21 E4
Little Totham 46 B1
Little Town 117 F5
Little Urswick 107 D5
Little Wakering 46 C4
Little Walden 58 D3
Little Waldingfield 60 A3
Little Walsingham 86 A2
Little Waltham 45 G1
Little Warley 45 F3

Little Weighton 104 B4
Little Welland 54 A4
Little Welnetham 59 G2
Little Wenham 60 B4
Little Wenlock 65 F2
Little Whittingham Green 73 D4
Little Whittington 119 F1
Little Wilbraham 58 D2
Little Witcombe 40 B1
Little Witley 53 G1
Little Wittenham 42 A3
Little Wolford 55 E4
Little Wratting 59 E3
Little Wymondley 58 A5
Little Wyrley 66 C2
Little Yeldham 59 F4
Littlebeck 112 B2
Littleborough *Gt.Man.* 92 D1
Littleborough *Notts.* 95 F4
Littlebourne 33 D3
Littlebredy 12 B4
Littlebury 58 D4
Littlebury Green 58 C4
Littledean 39 F1
Littleferry 190 D5
Littleham *Devon* 21 E3
Littleham *Devon* 10 D4
Littlehampton 16 C3
Littlehempston 9 E1
Littlehoughton 137 G5
Littlemill *E.Ayr.* 132 C4
Littlemill *High.* 180 B4
Littlemore 42 A2
Littleover 81 E4
Littleport 71 D4
Littlestone-on-Sea 19 F1
Littlethorpe 102 C1
Littleton *Ches.* 78 B1
Littleton *Hants.* 27 F4
Littleton *P. & K.* 152 A1
Littleton *Som.* 24 B4
Littleton *Surr.* 29 F1
Littleton Drew 40 A4
Littleton-on-Severn 39 E4
Littleton Panell 26 A2
Littletown 120 C3
Littlewick Green 42 D5
Littleworth *Oxon.* 41 F3
Littleworth *Staffs.* 66 C1
Littleworth *Worcs.* 54 A2
Littley Green 45 F1
Litton *Derbys.* 93 F5
Litton *N.Yorks.* 109 E5
Litton *Som.* 24 C2
Litton Cheney 12 B3
Liurbost 187 E5
Liverpool 91 E3
Liverpool Airport 91 F4
Liversedge 102 A5
Liverton *Devon* 10 B5
Liverton *R. & C.* 111 G1
Liverton Street 32 A4
Livingston 143 E3
Livingston Village 143 E3
Lixwm 90 C5
Lizard 3 D5
Llaingoch 88 A4
Llaithddu 63 G4
Llan 63 E2
Llan-dafal 38 A2
Llan-faes 89 E5
Llan-y-pwll 78 A2
Llanaber 62 C1
Llanaelhaearn 74 C3
Llanaeron 50 A1
Llanafan 62 C5
Llanafan-fawr 51 F2
Llanafan-fechan 51 F2
Llanallgo 88 C4
Llanarmon 74 D4
Llanarmon Dyffryn Ceiriog 77 E4
Llanarmon-yn-Ial 77 E2
Llanarth *Cere.* 50 A2
Llanarth *Mon.* 38 C1
Llanarthney 50 B5
Llanasa 90 C4
Llanbabo 88 B4
Llanbadarn Fawr 62 C4
Llanbadarn Fynydd 63 G5
Llanbadarn-y-garreg 52 A3
Llanbadoc 38 C2
Llanbadrig 88 B3
Llanbeder 38 C3
Llanbedr *Gwyn.* 75 E5
Llanbedr *Powys* 52 B5
Llanbedr *Powys* 52 A3
Llanbedr-Dyffryn-Clwyd 77 E2
Llanbedr-y-cennin 76 A1
Llanbedrgoch 88 D4
Llanbedrog 74 C4
Llanberis 75 E1
Llanbethery 22 D1
Llanbister 64 A5
Llanblethian 37 F5
Llanboidy 49 F5
Llanbradach 38 A3
Llanbrynmair 63 E2
Llancarfan 37 G5
Llancayo 38 C2
Llancynfelyn 62 C3
Llandaff 38 A5
Llandaff North 38 A5
Llandanwg 75 E5
Llandawke 35 F1
Llanddaniel Fab 88 C5
Llanddarog 36 B1
Llanddeiniol 62 B5
Llanddeiniolen 75 E1
Llandderfel 76 C4
Llanddeusant *Carmar.* 51 D5
Llanddeusant *I.o.A.* 88 B4
Llanddew 51 G4
Llanddewi 36 A4
Llanddewi-Brefi 50 C2
Llanddewi Rhydderch 38 C1
Llanddewi Velfrey 35 E1
Llanddewi Ystradenni 52 A1
Llanddewi'r Cwm 51 G3
Llanddoged 76 B1
Llanddona 89 D5
Llanddowror 35 F1
Llanddulas 90 A5
Llanddwywe 75 E5
Llanddyfnan 88 D5
Llandefaelog 36 A1
Llandefaelog Fach 51 G4
Llandefaelog-tre'r-graig 52 A5
Llandefalle 52 A4
Llandegfan 89 D5
Llandegla 77 E2
Llandegley 52 A1
Llandegveth 38 C3
Llandegwning 74 B4
Llandeilo 50 C5
Llandeilo Abercywyn 35 G1
Llandeilo Graban 51 G3
Llandeilo'r-Fan 51 E4
Llandeloy 48 B5
Llandenny 38 D2
Llandevenny 38 D4
Llandinabo 53 E5
Llandinam 63 G4
Llandissilio 49 E5
Llandogo 39 E2
Llandough *V. of Glam.* 38 A5
Llandough *V. of Glam.* 37 F5
Llandovery 51 D4
Llandow 37 F5
Llandre *Carmar.* 50 C3
Llandre *Carmar.* 49 E5
Llandre *Cere.* 62 C4
Llandrillo 76 D4
Llandrillo-yn-Rhôs 89 G4
Llandrindod Wells 51 G1
Llandrinio 64 B1
Llandudno 89 F4
Llandudno Junction 89 F5
Llandwrog 74 D2
Llandybie 36 C1
Llandyfriog 49 G3
Llandyfrydog 88 C4
Llandygai 89 D5
Llandygwydd 49 F3
Llandyrnog 77 E1
Llandyry 36 A2
Llandysilio 64 B1
Llandyssil 64 A3
Llandysul 50 A3
Llanedeyrn 38 B4
Llanegryn 62 C2
Llanegwad 50 B5
Llaneilian 88 C3
Llanelian-yn-Rhôs 89 G5
Llanelidan 77 E2
Llanelieu 52 A4
Llanellen 38 C1
Llanelli 36 B2
Llanelltyd 62 D1
Llanelly 38 B1
Llanelly Hill *Mon.* 38 B1
Llanelwedd 51 G2
Llanelwy (St. Asaph) 90 B5
Llanenddwyn 75 E5
Llanengan 74 B5
Llanerch-y-medd 88 C4
Llanerfyl 63 G2
Llanfachraeth 88 B4
Llanfachreth 76 A5
Llanfaelog 88 B5
Llanfaelrhys 74 B5
Llanfaes *Powys* 51 G5
Llanfaethlu 88 B4
Llanfaglan 75 D1
Llanfair 75 E5
Llanfair Caereinion 64 A2
Llanfair Clydogau 50 C2
Llanfair Dyffryn Clwyd 77 E2
Llanfair-Nant-Gwyn 49 E4
Llanfair-Orllwyn 49 G3
Llanfair Talhaiarn 90 A5
Llanfair Waterdine 64 B5
Llanfair-yn-neubwll 88 B5
Llanfairfechan 89 E5
Llanfairpwll-gwyngyll 88 D5
Llanfairynghornwy 88 B3
Llanfallteg 35 E1
Llanfallteg West 35 E1
Llanfaredd 51 G2
Llanfarian 62 B5
Llanfechain 77 E5
Llanfechell 88 B3
Llanfendigaid 62 B2
Llanferres 77 E1
Llanfflewyn 88 B4
Llanfigael 88 B4
Llanfihangel ar-arth 50 A4
Llanfihangel Crucorney 52 C5
Llanfihangel Glyn Myfyr 76 C3
Llanfihangel Nant Bran 51 F4
Llanfihangel-nant-Melan 52 A2
Llanfihangel Rhydithon 52 A1
Llanfihangel Rogiet 38 D4
Llanfihangel-Tal-y-llyn 52 A5
Llanfihangel uwch-gwili 50 A5
Llanfihangel-y-Creuddyn 62 C5
Llanfihangel y-pennant *Gwyn.* 75 E3
Llanfihangel-y-pennant *Gwyn.* 62 C2
Llanfihangel-yn Ngwynfa 63 G1
Llanfilo 52 A4
Llanfoist 38 B1
Llanfor 76 C4
Llanfrechfa 38 C3
Llanfrothen 75 F3
Llanfrynach 51 G5
Llanfwrog *Denb.* 77 E2
Llanfwrog *I.o.A.* 88 B4
Llanfyllin 64 A1
Llanfynydd *Carmar.* 50 B5
Llanfynydd *Flints.* 77 F2
Llanfyrnach 49 F4
Llangadfan 63 G1
Llangadog 50 D5
Llangadwaladr *I.o.A.* 74 C1
Llangadwaladr *Powys* 77 E4
Llangaffo 74 D1
Llangain 35 G1
Llangammarch Wells 51 F3
Llangan 37 F5
Llangarron 53 E5
Llangasty-Talyllyn 52 A5
Llangathen 50 B5
Llangattock 38 B1
Llangattock Lingoed 52 C5
Llangattock-Vibon-Avel 39 D1
Llangedwyn 77 E5
Llangefni 88 C5
Llangeinor 37 F4
Llangeitho 50 C2
Llangeler 49 G4
Llangelynin 62 B2
Llangendeirne 36 A1
Llangennech 36 B2
Llangennith 36 A3
Llangenny 38 B1
Llangernyw 76 B1
Llangian 74 B5
Llangiwg 36 D2
Llanglydwen 49 E5
Llangoed 89 E5
Llangoedmor 49 E3
Llangollen 77 F3
Llangolman 49 E5
Llangorse 52 A5
Llangorwen 62 C4
Llangovan 39 D2
Llangower 76 C4
Llangranog 49 G2
Llangristiolus 88 C5
Llangrove 39 E1
Llangua 52 C5
Llangunllo 64 B5
Llangunnor 50 A5
Llangurig 63 F5
Llangwm *Conwy* 76 C3
Llangwm *Pembs.* 34 C2
Llangwm-isaf 38 D2
Llangwnnadl 74 B4
Llangwyfan 77 E1
Llangwyllog 88 C5
Llangwyryfon 62 B5
Llangybi *Cere.* 50 C2
Llangybi *Gwyn.* 74 D3
Llangybi *Mon.* 38 C3
Llangyfelach 36 C3
Llangynhafal 77 E1
Llangynidr 38 A1
Llangyniew 64 A2
Llangynin 35 F1
Llangynog *Carmar.* 35 G1
Llangynog *Powys* 77 D5
Llangynwyd 37 E4
Llanhamlach 51 G5
Llanharan 37 G4
Llanharry 37 G4
Llanhennock 38 C3
Llanhilleth 38 B2
Llanidloes 63 F4
Llaniestyn 74 B4
Llanigon 52 B4
Llanilar 62 C5
Llanilid 37 F4
Llanishen *Cardiff* 38 A4
Llanishen *Mon.* 39 D2
Llanllawddog 50 A5
Llanllechid 75 F1
Llanlleonfel 51 F3
Llanllugan 63 G2
Llanllwch 35 G1
Llanllwchaiarn 64 A3
Llanllwni 50 A3
Llanllyfni 75 D2
Llanllywel 38 C3
Llanmadoc 36 A3
Llanmaes 22 C1
Llanmartin 38 C4
Llanmerewig 64 A3
Llanmihangel 37 F5
Llanmiloe 35 F2
Llanmorlais 36 B3
Llannefydd 90 A5
Llannerch 90 B5
Llannerch-y-Môr 90 C5
Llannon 36 B2
Llannor 74 C4
Llanon 50 B1
Llanover 38 C2
Llanpumsaint 50 A5
Llanreithan 48 B5
Llanrhaeadr 77 D1
Llanrhaeadr-ym-Mochnant 77 E5
Llanrhian 48 B4
Llanrhidian 36 B3
Llanrhos 89 F4
Llanrhyddlad 88 B4
Llanrhystud 50 B1
Llanrothal 39 D1
Llanrug 75 E1
Llanrumney 38 B4
Llanrwst 76 A1
Llansadurnen 35 F1
Llansadwrn *Carmar.* 50 C4
Llansadwrn *I.o.A.* 89 D5
Llansaint 35 G2
Llansamlet 36 C3
Llansanffraid Glan Conwy 89 G5
Llansannan 76 C1
Llansannor 37 F5
Llansantffraed 52 A5
Llansantffraed-Cwmdeuddwr 51 F1
Llansantffraed-in-Elvel 51 G2
Llansantffraid 50 B1
Llansantffraid-ym-Mechain 77 F5
Llansawel *Carmar.* 50 C4
Llansawel (Briton Ferry) *N.P.T.* 36 D3
Llansilin 77 F5
Llansoy 38 D2
Llanspyddid 51 G5
Llanstadwell 34 C2
Llansteffan *Carmar.* 35 G1
Llanstephan *Powys* 52 A3
Llantarnam 38 C3
Llanteg 35 E1
Llanthony 52 B5
Llantilio Crossenny 38 C1
Llantilio Pertholey 38 C1
Llantood 49 E3
Llantrisant *Mon.* 38 C3
Llantrisant *R.C.T.* 37 G4
Llantrithyd 37 G5
Llantwit Fardre 37 G4
Llantwit Major 22 C1
Llantysilio 77 E3
Llanuwchllyn 76 B4
Llanvaches 38 D3
Llanvair-Discoed 38 D3
Llanvapley 38 C1
Llanvetherine 38 C1
Llanveynoe 52 C4
Llanvihangel Gobion 38 C2
Llanvihangel-Ystern-Llewern 38 D1
Llanwarne 53 E5
Llanwddyn 63 G1
Llanwenog 50 A3
Llanwern 38 C4
Llanwinio 49 F5
Llanwnda *Gwyn.* 75 D2
Llanwnda *Pembs.* 48 C4
Llanwnen 50 B3
Llanwnog 63 G3
Llanwonno 37 G3
Llanwrda 50 D4
Llanwrin 63 D2
Llanwrthwl 51 F1
Llanwrtyd 51 E3
Llanwrtyd Wells 51 E3
Llanwyddelan 63 G2
Llanyblodwel 77 F5
Llanybri 35 G1
Llanybydder 50 B3
Llanycefn 49 E5
Llanychaer Bridge 48 C4
Llanycil 76 C4
Llanycrwys 50 C3
Llanymawddwy 63 F1
Llanymynech 77 F5
Llanynghenedl 88 B4
Llanynys 77 E1
Llanyre 51 G1
Llanystumdwy 75 D4
Llanywern 52 A5
Llawhaden 35 D1
Llawnt 77 F4
Llawr-y-dref 74 B5
Llawryglyn 63 F3
Llay 78 A2
Llechcynfarwy 88 B4
Llechfaen 51 G5
Llechryd *Caerp.* 38 A2
Llechryd *Cere.* 49 F3
Llechrydau 77 F4
Lledrod *Cere.* 62 C5
Lledrod *Powys* 77 F4
Llethr 48 B5
Llidiadnenog 50 B4
Llidiardau 76 B4
Llithfaen 74 C3
Lloc 90 C5
Llong 77 F1
Llowes 52 A3
Lloyney 64 B5
Llwydcoed 37 F2
Llwydiarth 63 G1
Llwyn 64 B4
Llwyn-Madoc 51 F2
Llwyn-onn 50 A2
Llwyn-y-brain *Carmar.* 35 F1
Llwyn-y-brain *Carmar.* 50 D4
Llwyncelyn 50 A2
Llwyndafydd 49 G2
Llwynderw 64 B2
Llwyndyrys 74 C3
Llwyngwril 62 B2
Llwynhendy 36 B3
Llwynmawr 77 F4
Llwynypia 37 F3
Llynclys 77 F5
Llynfaes 88 C5
Llys-y-fran 48 D5
Llysfaen 89 G5
Llyswen 52 A4
Llysworney 37 F5
Llywel 51 E4
Loandhu 180 A2
Loanhead *Aber.* 171 E1
Loanhead *Midloth.* 143 G3
Loans 132 B2
Loch Baghasdail (Lochboisdale) 172 C2
Loch Coire Lodge 193 F5
Loch Eil Outward Bound 156 C2
Loch Head *D. & G.* 114 D2
Loch Head *D. & G.* 123 F1
Loch na Madadh (Lochmaddy) 174 C3
Loch Sgioport 162 B1
Lochailort 155 G1
Lochaline 155 F5
Lochans 122 B5
Locharbriggs 125 D2
Lochawe 148 D2
Lochboisdale (Loch Baghasdail) 172 C2
Lochbuie 147 F2
Lochcarron 165 E1
Lochdhu Hotel 194 C4
Lochdon 147 G1
Lochdrum 178 B2
Lochearnhead 150 A2
Lochee 152 B1
Lochend *High.* 195 E2
Lochend *High.* 167 E1
Lochfoot 124 D3
Lochgair 148 B5
Lochgarthside 167 E3
Lochgelly 151 G5
Lochgilphead 139 G1
Lochgoilhead 149 E4
Lochgoin 141 G5
Lochhill *E.Ayr.* 133 E4
Lochhill *Moray* 181 E3
Lochinch Castle 122 C4
Lochinver 188 C2
Lochlair 160 D5
Lochlane 150 D2
Lochlea 132 C3
Lochluichart 178 C3
Lochmaben 125 E2
Lochmaddy (Loch na Madadh) 174 C3
Lochore 151 G5
Lochportain 174 C2
Lochranza 140 A5
Lochside *Aber.* 161 F3
Lochside *High.* 193 D3
Lochside *High.* 194 A5
Lochside *High.* 195 E2
Lochslin 180 A1
Lochton 123 D2
Lochty 152 D4
Lochuisge 155 G4
Lochurr 124 B2
Lochussie 179 D4
Lochwinnoch 141 E4
Lockengate 5 E3
Lockerbie 125 F2
Lockeridge 26 C1
Lockerley 27 D5
Locking 24 A2
Lockington *E.Riding* 104 C3
Lockington *Leics.* 81 F5
Lockleywood 79 D5
Locks Heath 15 E2
Locksbottom 30 D2
Lockton 112 B3
Loddington *Leics.* 68 C2
Loddington *Northants.* 68 D5
Loddiswell 8 D3
Loddon 73 E2
Lode 58 D1
Loders 12 A3
Lodsworth 29 E5
Lofthouse *N.Yorks.* 109 F5
Lofthouse *W.Yorks.* 102 C5
Loftus 111 G1
Logan *D. & G.* 114 A2
Logan *E.Ayr.* 133 D3
Loganlea 143 D3
Loggerheads 79 E4
Logie 188 D5
Logie *Angus* 161 E3
Logie *Angus* 160 B4
Logie *Fife* 152 C2
Logie *Moray* 180 C4
Logie Coldstone 169 G4
Logie Hill 179 G2
Logie Newton 170 B1
Logie Pert 161 E3
Logierait 159 E4
Login 49 E5
Lolworth 58 B1
Lonbain 176 C4
Londesborough 104 A3
London 44 C4
London Beach 32 A5
London City Airport 44 D4
London Colney 44 A2
London Heathrow Airport 43 F5
London Luton Airport 57 G5
Londonderry 110 B4
Londonthorpe 83 E4
Londubh 177 E1
Lonemore 179 G1
Long Ashton 39 E5
Long Bennington 82 D3
Long Bredy 12 B3
Long Buckby 56 B1
Long Clawson 82 C5
Long Common 15 E1
Long Compton *Staffs.* 79 F5
Long Compton *Warks.* 55 E4
Long Crendon 42 B2
Long Crichel 13 F1
Long Ditton 29 G1
Long Downs 3 E3
Long Drax 103 F5
Long Duckmanton 94 B5
Long Eaton 81 F4
Long Gill 101 D2
Long Hanborough 41 G1
Long Itchington 55 G1
Long Lawford 67 G5
Long Load 24 B5
Long Marston *Herts.* 43 D1
Long Marston *N.Yorks.* 103 E2
Long Marston *Warks.* 55 D3
Long Marton 118 C5
Long Melford 59 G3
Long Newnton 40 B3
Long Preston 101 E2
Long Riston 104 D3
Long Stratton 72 C2
Long Street 56 C3
Long Sutton *Hants.* 28 C3
Long Sutton *Lincs.* 84 C5
Long Sutton *Som.* 24 B5
Long Thurlow 60 B1
Long Waste 65 F1
Long Whatton 81 F5
Long Wittenham 42 A3
Longbenton 120 B1
Longborough 55 D5
Longbridge *W.Mid.* 66 C5
Longbridge *Warks.* 55 E1
Longbridge Deverill 25 F3
Longburgh 117 G1
Longburton 12 C1
Longcliffe 80 D2
Longcot 41 E3
Longcroft 142 B2
Longcross *Devon* 7 E3
Longcross *Surr.* 29 E1
Longden 64 D2
Longdon *Staffs.* 66 C1
Longdon *Worcs.* 54 A4
Longdon upon Tern 65 F1
Longdown 10 B3
Longdrum 171 E3
Longfield 31 F2
Longfield Hill 31 F2
Longfleet 13 G3
Longford *Derbys.* 80 D4
Longford *Glos.* 54 A5
Longford *Gt.Lon.* 43 F5
Longford *Shrop.* 78 D4
Longford *Tel. & W.* 65 G1
Longford *W.Mid.* 67 F4
Longforgan 152 B2
Longformacus 145 D4
Longframlington 128 D1
Longham *Dorset* 13 G3
Longham *Norf.* 86 A4
Longhill 183 E4
Longhirst 129 E3
Longhope *Glos.* 39 F1
Longhope *Ork.* 196 C3
Longhorsley 128 D2
Longhoughton 137 G5
Longlands *Aber.* 169 G2
Longlands *Cumb.* 117 F3
Longlane *Derbys.* 81 D4
Longlane *W.Berks.* 42 A5
Longley Green 53 G2
Longmanhill 182 C3
Longmoor Camp 28 C4
Longmorn 181 E4
Longnewton *Sc.Bord.* 135 G3
Longnewton *Stock.* 110 C1
Longney 39 G1
Longniddry 144 B2
Longnor *Shrop.* 65 D2
Longnor *Staffs.* 80 B1
Longparish 27 F3
Longridge *Lancs.* 100 C4
Longridge *W.Loth.* 142 D3
Longridge Towers 145 G4
Longriggend 142 C2
Longrock 2 B3
Longsdon 79 G2
Longside 183 F5
Longslow 79 D4
Longstanton 58 B1
Longstock 27 E4
Longstowe 58 B2
Longstreet 26 C2
Longthorpe 69 G3
Longton *Lancs.* 100 A5
Longton *Stoke* 79 G3
Longtown *Cumb.* 126 B5
Longtown *Here.* 52 C5
Longville in the Dale 65 E3
Longwell Green 39 F5
Longwick 42 C2
Longwitton 128 C3
Longworth 41 F3
Longyester 144 C3
Lonmore 175 F5
Looe 5 G4
Loose 31 G3
Loosegate 84 B5
Loosley Row 42 D2
Lopcombe Corner 27 D4
Lopen 12 A1
Loppington 78 B5
Lorbottle 128 C1
Lorbottle Hall 128 C1
Lorgill 175 E5
Lorn 141 E1
Lornty 159 G5
Loscoe 81 F3
Losgaintir 184 C4
Lossiemouth 181 E2
Lossit 138 A4
Lostock Gralam 92 A5
Lostock Green 92 A5
Lostock Junction 92 A2
Lostwithiel 5 F4
Loth 199 E3
Lothbeg 191 E3
Lothersdale 101 F3
Lothmore 191 E3
Loudwater 43 E3
Loughborough 68 A1
Loughor 36 B3
Loughton *Essex* 44 D3
Loughton *M.K.* 56 D4
Loughton *Shrop.* 65 F4
Lound *Lincs.* 69 F1
Lound *Notts.* 95 D4
Lound *Suff.* 73 G2
Lount 67 F1
Lour 160 C5
Louth 96 D4
Love Clough 101 E5
Lovedean 15 F1
Lover 26 D5
Loversall 94 C3
Loves Green 45 F2
Loveston 35 D2
Lovington 24 C4
Low 107 F4
Low Ballevain 130 B3
Low Barlay 123 G5
Low Bentham 100 C1
Low Bolton 109 F3
Low Bradfield 93 G3
Low Braithwaite 118 A3
Low Brunton 128 B4
Low Burnham 95 E2
Low Burton 110 B4
Low Catton 103 G2
Low Coniscliffe 110 B1
Low Craighead 132 A5
Low Crosby 118 A2
Low Dinsdale 110 C1
Low Eggborough 103 E5
Low Entercommon 110 C2
Low Etherley 120 A5
Low Gate 119 F1
Low Habberley 66 A5
Low Ham 24 B5
Low Hawkser 112 C2
Low Haygarth 108 B3
Low Hesket 118 A3
Low Hesleyhurst 128 C2
Low Hutton 103 G1
Low Laithe 102 A1
Low Leighton 93 E4
Low Marishes 112 B5
Low Mill 111 F3
Low Moor 100 D3
Low Newton-by-the-Sea 137 G4
Low Risby 95 G1
Low Row *Cumb.* 118 B1
Low Row *N.Yorks.* 109 E3
Low Santon 95 G1
Low Stillaig 140 A3
Low Street 87 E3
Low Torry 143 E1
Low Toynton 96 C5
Low Waters 142 B4
Low Wood 107 E4
Low Worsall 110 C1
Lowdham 82 B3
Lower Achachenna 148 C2
Lower Aisholt 23 E4
Lower Apperley 54 A5
Lower Ashton 10 B4
Lower Assendon 42 C4
Lower Auchalick 140 A2
Lower Barewood 52 C2
Lower Beeding 17 E1
Lower Benefield 69 E4
Lower Berry Hill 39 E1
Lower Bockhampton 12 D3
Lower Boddington 55 G2
Lower Boscaswell 2 A3
Lower Bourne 28 D3
Lower Brailes 55 F4
Lower Breakish 164 C2
Lower Broadheath 54 A2
Lower Broughton 92 C3
Lower Brynamman 36 D1
Lower Bullingham 53 E4
Lower Burgate 14 A1
Lower Caldecote 57 G3
Lower Cam 39 G2
Lower Camster 195 E4
Lower Chapel 51 G4
Lower Chute 27 E2
Lower Crossings 93 E4
Lower Darwen 100 C5
Lower Dean 57 F1
Lower Diabaig 177 D3
Lower Dicker 18 A2
Lower Dinchope 64 D4
Lower Down 64 C4
Lower Drift 2 B4
Lower Dunsforth 102 D1
Lower Earley 42 C5
Lower Egleton 53 F3
Lower End 57 D1
Lower Everleigh 26 C2
Lower Failand 39 E5
Lower Farringdon 28 C4
Lower Freystrop 34 C1
Lower Froyle 28 C3
Lower Gabwell 9 F1
Lower Gledfield 190 A5
Lower Godney 24 B3
Lower Green *Kent* 31 F4
Lower Green *Norf.* 86 A2
Lower Green *Staffs.* 66 B2
Lower Green Bank 100 B2
Lower Halstow 32 A2
Lower Hardres 32 D3
Lower Hawthwaite 106 D4
Lower Hayton 65 E4
Lower Hergest 52 B2
Lower Heyford 55 G5
Lower Higham 45 G5
Lower Holbrook 60 C4
Lower Hordley 78 A5
Lower Horsebridge 18 A2
Lower Kilchattan 146 C5
Lower Killeyan 138 A5
Lower Kingcombe 12 B3
Lower Kinnerton 78 A1
Lower Langford 24 B1
Lower Largo 152 C4
Lower Lemington 55 E4
Lower Lovacott 21 F3
Lower Lydbrook 39 E1
Lower Lye 52 D1
Lower Machen 38 B4
Lower Maes-coed 52 C4
Lower Moor 54 B3
Lower Nazeing 44 C2
Lower Oakfield 151 G5
Lower Oddington 55 E5
Lower Ollach 164 B1
Lower Penarth 38 A5
Lower Penn 66 A3

Lower Pennington 14 C3
Lower Peover 92 B5
Lower Quinton 55 D3
Lower Seagry 40 B4
Lower Shelton 57 E3
Lower Shiplake 42 C5
Lower Shuckburgh 55 G1
Lower Slaughter 55 D5
Lower Stanton St. Quintin 40 B4
Lower Stoke 32 A1
Lower Stondon 57 G4
Lower Street 18 C2
Lower Sundon 57 F5
Lower Swanwick 15 D2
Lower Swell 55 D5
Lower Tean 80 B4
Lower Thurlton 73 F2
Lower Thurnham 100 A2
Lower Town *I.o.S.* 4 B1
Lower Town *Pembs.* 48 C4
Lower Tysoe 55 F3
Lower Upham 15 E1
Lower Vexford 23 E4
Lower Wallop 64 C2
Lower Walton 92 A4
Lower Weare 24 B2
Lower Welson 52 B2
Lower Whitley 92 A5
Lower Wield 28 B3
Lower (Nether) Winchendon 42 C1
Lower Withington 79 F1
Lower Woodend 42 D4
Lower Woodford 26 C4
Lower Wraxall 12 B2
Lower Wyche 53 G3
Lowesby 68 C2
Lowestoft 73 G2
Lowestoft End 73 G2
Loweswater 117 E4
Lowfield Heath 30 B4
Lowgill *Cumb.* 108 B3
Lowgill *Lancs.* 100 C1
Lowick *Cumb.* 107 D4
Lowick *Northants.* 69 E4
Lowick *Northumb.* 137 E3
Lownie Moor 160 C5
Lowsonford 55 D1
Lowther 118 B5
Lowther Castle 118 B5
Lowthorpe 104 C2
Lowton 92 A3
Lowton Common 92 A3
Loxbeare 10 C1
Loxhill 29 F4
Loxhore 21 G2
Loxley 55 E2
Loxton 24 A2
Loxwood 29 F4
Lubachoinnich 189 G5
Lubcroy 189 F4
Lubenham 68 C4
Lubfearn 178 C2
Lubmore 177 G4
Lubreoch 157 G5
Luccombe 22 C3
Luccombe Village 15 E5
Lucker 137 F3
Luckett 7 D3
Luckington 40 A4
Lucklawhill 152 C2
Luckwell Bridge 22 C4
Lucton 52 D1
Ludag 172 C2
Ludborough 96 C3
Ludchurch 35 E1
Luddenden 101 G5
Luddenham Court 32 B2
Luddesdown 31 F2
Luddington *N.Lincs.* 95 F1
Luddington *Warks.* 55 D2
Luddington in the Brook 69 G4
Ludford 65 E5
Ludford Magna 96 C4
Ludford Parva 96 B4
Ludgershall *Bucks.* 42 B1
Ludgershall *Wilts.* 27 D2
Ludgvan 2 B3
Ludham 87 E4
Ludlow 65 E5
Ludney 97 D3
Ludstock 53 F4
Ludwell 26 A5
Ludworth 120 C3
Luffincott 6 D1
Luffness 144 B1
Lugar 133 D3
Luggiebank 142 B2
Lugton 141 F4
Lugwardine 53 E3
Luib 164 B2
Luibeilt 157 E3
Lulham 52 D3
Lullington *Derbys.* 67 E1
Lullington *Som.* 25 E2
Lulsgate Bottom 24 C1
Lulsley 53 G2
Lulworth Camp 13 E4
Lumb 101 G5
Lumbutts 101 F5
Lumby 103 D4
Lumphanan 170 A4
Lumphinnans 151 G5
Lumsdaine 145 F3
Lumsden 169 G2
Lunan 161 E4
Lunanhead 160 C4
Luncarty 151 F2
Lund *E.Riding* 104 B3
Lund *N.Yorks.* 103 F4
Lund *Shet.* 203 E2
Lundavra 156 C3
Lunderton 183 G5
Lundie *Angus* 152 A1
Lundie *High.* 166 A3
Lundin Links 152 C4
Lunga 147 G4
Lunna 201 D1
Lunning 201 E1
Lunsford's Cross 18 C2
Lunt 91 E2
Luntley 52 C2
Luppitt 11 E2
Lupton 107 G4
Lurgashall 29 E5
Lurignich 156 B4
Lusby 84 B1
Luss 149 F5
Lussagiven 139 E1
Lusta 175 F4
Lustleigh 10 A4
Luston 53 D1
Luthermuir 161 E3
Luthrie 152 B3
Luton *Devon* 11 D2
Luton *Devon* 10 C5
Luton *Luton* 57 F5
Luton *Med.* 31 G2
Lutterworth 68 A4
Lutton *Devon* 8 B2
Lutton *Lincs.* 84 C5
Lutton *Northants.* 69 G4
Luxborough 22 C4
Luxulyan 5 E4
Lybster *High.* 194 C2
Lybster *High.* 195 E5
Lydacott 21 E5
Lydbury North 64 C4
Lydcott 21 G2
Lydd 19 F1
Lydd Airport 19 F1
Lydd-on-Sea 19 F1
Lydden 33 E4
Lyddington 69 D3
Lydeard St. Lawrence 23 E4
Lydford 7 F2
Lydford-on-Fosse 24 C4
Lydgate 101 F5
Lydham 64 C3
Lydiard Millicent 40 C4
Lydiate 91 E2
Lydlinch 12 D1
Lydney 39 F2
Lydstep 35 D3
Lye 66 B4
Lye Green 43 E2
Lyford 41 F3
Lymbridge Green 32 D4
Lyme Regis 11 G3
Lymekilns 142 A4
Lyminge 33 D4
Lymington 14 C3
Lyminster 16 C3
Lymm 92 A4
Lymore 14 C3
Lympne 32 D5
Lympsham 24 A2
Lympstone 10 C4
Lynaberack 167 G5
Lynchat 167 G4
Lyndhurst 14 C2
Lyndon 69 E2
Lyne *Aber.* 170 C4
Lyne *Sc.Bord.* 143 G5
Lyne *Surr.* 29 F1
Lyne of Gorthleck 167 E2
Lyne of Skene 170 C3
Lyne Station 134 D2
Lyneal 78 B4
Lynedale House 175 G4
Lynegar 195 E3
Lyneham *Oxon.* 55 E5
Lyneham *Wilts.* 40 C5
Lyneholmeford 126 D4
Lynemore *High.* 168 C2
Lynemore *Moray* 168 D1
Lynemouth 129 E2
Lyness 196 C3
Lynford 71 G3
Lyng *Norf.* 86 B4
Lyng *Som.* 24 A5
Lynmouth 22 A3
Lynsted 32 B2
Lynton 22 A3
Lyon's Gate 12 C2
Lyonshall 52 C2
Lyrabus 138 A3
Lytchett Matravers 13 F3
Lytchett Minster 13 F3
Lyth 195 E2
Lytham 99 G5
Lytham St. Anne's 99 G5
Lythe 112 B1
Lythe Hill 29 E4
Lythes 197 D4
Lythmore 194 C2

## M

Mabe Burnthouse 3 E3
Mabie 124 D3
Mablethorpe 97 F4
Macclesfield 92 D5
Macclesfield Forest 93 D5
Macduff 182 C3
Machan 142 B4
Machany 151 E3
Macharioch 130 C5
Machen 38 B4
Machrie *Arg. & B.* 138 A3
Machrie *Arg. & B.* 138 B5
Machrie *N.Ayr.* 131 E2
Machrihanish 130 B4
Machrins 146 C5
Machynlleth 62 D2
Mackworth 81 E4
Macmerry 144 B2
Macterry 182 C5
Madderty 151 E2
Maddiston 142 D2
Madehurst 16 B2
Madeley *Staffs.* 79 E3
Madeley *Tel. & W.* 65 G2
Madeley Heath 79 E3
Madford 11 E1
Madingley 58 B2
Madjeston 25 F5
Madley 52 D4
Madresfield 54 A3
Madron 2 B3
Maen Porth 3 E4
Maenaddwyn 88 C4
Maenclochog 49 D5
Maendy 37 G5
Maentwrog 75 F3
Maer 79 E4
Maerdy *Carmar.* 50 C5
Maerdy *Carmar.* 50 C5
Maerdy *Conwy* 76 D3
Maerdy *Mon.* 38 C2
Maerdy *R.C.T.* 37 F3
Maes-Glas (Greenfield) 90 C5
Maes-glas 38 B4
Maes-Treylow 52 B1
Maesbrook 77 F5
Maesbury Marsh 78 A5
Maesgwynne 49 F5
Maeshafn 77 F1
Maesllyn 49 G3
Maesmynis 51 G3
Maesteg 37 E3
Maesybont 36 B1
Maesycrugiau 50 A3
Maesycwmmer 38 A3
Magdalen Laver 45 E2
Maggieknockater 181 F5
Magham Down 18 B2
Maghull 91 E2
Magor 38 D4
Maiden Bradley 25 E4
Maiden Law 120 A3
Maiden Newton 12 B3
Maiden Wells 34 C3
Maidencombe 9 F1
Maidenhead 43 D4
Maidens 132 A5
Maiden's Green 43 E5
Maidensgrove 42 C4
Maidenwell *Cornw.* 5 F2
Maidenwell *Lincs.* 96 D5
Maidford 56 B2
Maids' Moreton 56 C4
Maidstone 31 G3
Maidwell 68 C5
Mail 200 D5
Mains of Ardestie 152 D1
Mains of Balgavies 160 D4
Mains of Balhall 160 D3
Mains of Ballindarg 160 C4
Mains of Burgie 180 C4
Mains of Culsh 183 D5
Mains of Dillavaird 161 F1
Mains of Drum 170 D4
Mains of Dudwick 171 E1
Mains of Faillie 167 G1
Mains of Fedderate 183 D5
Mains of Glack 170 C2
Mains of Glassaugh 182 A3
Mains of Glenbuchat 169 F3
Mains of Linton 170 C4
Mains of Melgund 160 D4
Mains of Pitfour 183 E5
Mains of Pittrichie 171 D2
Mains of Sluie 180 C4
Mains of Tannachy 181 F3
Mains of Thornton 161 E2
Mains of Tig 122 C2
Mains of Watten 195 E3
Mainsriddle 124 D5
Mainstone 64 B4
Maisemore 54 A5
Makendon 128 A1
Makerstoun 136 A3
Malacleit 173 F2
Malborough 8 D4
Malden Rushett 29 G1
Maldon 46 B2
Malham 101 F1
Maligar 176 A3
Mallaig 164 C5
Mallaigmore 164 D5
Mallaigvaig 164 C5
Malleny Mills 143 F3
Malletsheugh 141 G4
Malling 150 A4
Malltraeth 74 D1
Mallwyd 63 E1
Malmesbury 40 B4
Malmsmead 22 A3
Malpas *Ches.* 78 B3
Malpas *Cornw.* 4 C5
Malpas *Newport* 38 C3
Maltby *S.Yorks.* 94 C3
Maltby *Stock.* 111 D1
Maltby le Marsh 97 E4
Maltman's Hill 32 B4
Malton 111 G5
Malvern Link 53 G3
Malvern Wells 53 G3
Mambeg 140 D1
Mamble 65 F5
Mamhead 10 C4
Mamhilad 38 C2
Manaccan 3 E4
Manafon 64 A2
Manais 184 D5
Manaton 10 A4
Manby 97 D4
Mancetter 67 F3
Manchester 92 C3
Manchester Airport 92 C4
Mancot Royal 78 A1
Mandally 166 B4
Manea 70 C4
Maneight 132 D5
Manfield 110 B1
Mangaster 202 C5
Mangotsfield 39 F5
Mangurstadh 186 B4
Mankinholes 101 F5
Manley 91 G5
Manmoel 38 A2
Mannal 154 A2
Manningford Abbots 26 C2
Manningford Bohune 26 C2
Manningford Bruce 26 C2
Mannings Heath 17 E1
Mannington 13 G2
Manningtree 60 C4
Mannofield 171 E4
Manorbier 35 D3
Manordeifi 49 F3
Manordeilo 50 C5
Manorowen 48 C4
Mansell Gamage 52 C3
Mansell Lacy 52 D3
Mansergh 108 B4
Mansfield 81 G1
Mansfield Woodhouse 81 G1
Mansriggs 107 D4
Manston *Dorset* 13 E1
Manston *Kent* 33 F2
Manswood 13 F2
Manthorpe *Lincs.* 69 F1
Manthorpe *Lincs.* 83 E4
Manton *N.Lincs.* 95 G2
Manton *Rut.* 69 D2
Manton *Wilts.* 26 C1
Manuden 58 C5
Maolachy 148 A3
Maperton 25 D5
Maple Cross 43 F3
Maplebeck 82 C1
Mapledurham 42 B5
Mapledurwell 28 B2
Maplehurst 29 G5
Mapleton 80 C3
Mapperley 81 F3
Mapperton 12 B3
Mappleborough Green 54 C1
Mappleton 105 E3
Mapplewell 94 A2
Mappowder 12 D2
Mar Lodge 168 C5
Marazion 2 C3
Marbhig 185 G2
Marbury 78 C3
March 70 C3
Marcham 41 G3
Marchamley 78 C5
Marchington 80 C4
Marchington Woodlands 80 C5
Marchwiel 78 A3
Marchwood 14 C1
Marcross 22 C1
Marcus 160 D4
Marden *Here.* 53 E3
Marden *Kent* 31 G4
Marden *T. & W.* 129 F4
Marden *Wilts.* 26 B2
Marden Beech 31 G4
Marden Thorn 31 G4
Mardy 38 C1
Mare Green 24 A5
Marefield 68 C2
Mareham le Fen 84 A1
Mareham on the Hill 84 A1
Maresfield 17 G1
Marfleet 104 D5
Marford 78 A2
Margam 37 D4
Margaret Marsh 13 E1
Margaret Roding 45 E1
Margaretting 45 F2
Margate 33 F1
Margnaheglish 131 F2
Margreig 124 C3
Margrove Park 111 F1
Marham 71 F2
Marhamchurch 20 C5
Marholm 69 G2
Marian Cwm 90 B5
Marian-Glas 88 D4
Mariansleigh 22 A5
Marishader 176 A3
Maristow House 8 A1
Mark 24 A3
Mark Causeway 24 A3
Mark Cross 31 E5
Markbeech 31 D4
Markby 97 E5
Markdhu 122 C3
Market Bosworth 67 G2
Market Deeping 69 G1
Market Drayton 79 D4
Market Harborough 68 C4
Market Lavington 26 B2
Market Overton 69 D1
Market Rasen 96 B4
Market Stainton 96 C5
Market Street 87 D3
Market Warsop 81 G1
Market Weighton 104 A3
Market Weston 72 A4
Markethill 152 A1
Markfield 67 G1
Markham 38 A2
Markham Moor 95 E5
Markinch 152 A4
Markington 102 B1
Marks Gate 45 D4
Marks Tey 60 A5
Marksbury 25 D1
Markwell 7 D5
Markyate 43 F1
Marlborough 26 C1
Marldon 9 E1
Marlesford 61 E2
Marley Green 78 C3
Marley Hill 120 B2
Marlingford 86 C5
Marloes 34 A2
Marlow 43 D4
Marlpit Hill 30 D4
Marlpool 81 F3
Marnhull 13 D1
Marnoch 182 A4
Marple 93 D4
Marr 94 C2
Marrel 191 F3
Marrick 109 F3
Marrister 201 E1
Marros 35 F2
Marsden *T. & W.* 120 D1
Marsden *W.Yorks.* 93 E1
Marsett 109 E4
Marsh 11 F1
Marsh Baldon 42 A3
Marsh Benham 27 F1
Marsh Chapel 97 D3
Marsh Gibbon 56 B5
Marsh Green *Devon* 10 D3
Marsh Green *Kent* 30 D4
Marsh Green *Tel. & W.* 65 F1
Marsh Lane 94 B5
Marsh Street 22 C3
Marshall's Heath 44 A1
Marshalsea 11 G2
Marsham 86 C3
Marshaw 100 B2
Marshborough 33 F3
Marshbrook 64 D4
Marshfield *Newport* 38 B4
Marshfield *S.Glos.* 39 G5
Marshgate 6 B1
Marshside 91 E1
Marshwood 11 G3
Marske 110 A2
Marske-by-the-Sea 121 F5
Marston *Ches.* 92 A5
Marston *Here.* 52 C2
Marston *Lincs.* 83 D3
Marston *Oxon.* 42 A2
Marston *Staffs.* 79 G5
Marston *Staffs.* 66 A1
Marston *Warks.* 67 E3
Marston *Wilts.* 26 A2
Marston Green 67 D4
Marston Magna 24 C5
Marston Meysey 40 D3
Marston Montgomery 80 C4
Marston Moretaine 57 E3
Marston on Dove 80 D5
Marston St. Lawrence 56 A3
Marston Stannett 53 E2
Marston Trussell 68 B4
Marstow 39 E1
Marsworth 43 E1
Marten 27 D1
Marthall 92 C5
Martham 87 F4
Martin *Hants.* 13 G1
Martin *Lincs.* 83 G1
Martin Drove End 26 B5
Martin Hussingtree 54 A1
Martinhoe 21 G1
Martinscroft 92 A4
Martinstown 12 C4
Martlesham 60 D3
Martlesham Heath 60 D3
Martletwy 34 D1
Martley 53 G1
Martock 12 A1
Marton *Ches.* 79 F1
Marton *Cumb.* 106 D5
Marton *E.Riding* 105 D4
Marton *Lincs.* 95 F4
Marton *Middbro.* 111 E1
Marton *N.Yorks.* 102 D1
Marton *N.Yorks.* 111 G4
Marton *Shrop.* 64 B2
Marton *Warks.* 55 G1
Marton Abbey 103 E1
Marton-le-Moor 110 C5
Martyr Worthy 27 G4
Martyr's Green 29 F2
Maruig 185 E3
Marwick 198 A4
Marwood 21 F2
Mary Tavy 7 F3
Marybank 179 D4
Maryburgh 179 E4
Maryfield 201 D3
Marygold 145 F3
Maryhill *Aber.* 182 D5
Maryhill *Glas.* 141 G3
Marykirk 161 E3
Marylebone *Gt.Lon.* 44 B4
Marylebone *Gt.Man.* 91 G2
Marypark 169 D1
Maryport *Cumb.* 116 D3
Maryport *D. & G.* 114 B3
Marystow 7 E2
Maryton 161 E4
Marywell *Aber.* 171 E5
Marywell *Aber.* 170 A5
Marywell *Angus* 161 E5
Masham 110 B4
Mashbury 45 F1
Mastrick 171 D4
Matching 45 E1
Matching Green 45 E1
Matching Tye 45 E1
Matfen 128 C4
Matfield 31 F4
Mathern 39 E3
Mathon 53 G3
Mathry 48 B4
Matlaske 86 C2
Matlock 81 E1
Matlock Bank 81 D1
Matlock Bath 81 D2
Matson 40 A1
Matterdale End 117 G4
Mattersey 95 D4
Mattingley 28 C2
Mattishall 86 B4
Mattishall Burgh 86 B4
Mauchline 132 D3
Maud 183 E5
Maufant 8 C5
Maugersbury 55 D5
Maughold 90 C2
Mauld 166 C1
Maulden 57 F4
Maulds Meaburn 108 B1
Maunby 110 C4
Maund Bryan 53 E2
Maundown 23 D5
Mautby 87 F4
Mavesyn Ridware 66 C1
Mavis Enderby 84 B1
Maw Green 66 C3
Mawbray 117 D2
Mawdesley 91 F1
Mawdlam 37 E4
Mawgan 3 E4
Mawla 4 A5
Mawnan 3 E4
Mawnan Smith 3 E4
Maxey 69 G2
Maxstoke 67 E4
Maxton *Kent* 33 E4
Maxton *Sc.Bord.* 136 A4
Maxwellheugh 136 B3
Maxwelltown 125 D3
Maxworthy 6 C1
Maybole 132 B5
Mayen 182 A5
Mayfield *E.Suss.* 18 A1
Mayfield *Midloth.* 144 A3
Mayfield *Staffs.* 80 C3
Mayford 29 E2
Mayland 46 C2
Maylandsea 46 C2
Maynard's Green 18 A2
Maypole *I.o.S.* 4 B1
Maypole *Kent* 33 D2
Maypole Green 73 F2
Maywick 200 C5
Meabhag 185 D4
Mead End 26 B5
Meadle 42 D2
Meadowhall 94 A3
Meadowmill 144 B2
Meadowtown 64 C2
Meal Bank 107 G3
Mealabost 187 F2
Mealasta 186 A5
Meals 97 E3
Mealsgate 117 F2
Meanley 100 D3
Mearbeck 101 E1
Meare 24 B3
Mearns 141 G4
Mears Ashby 56 D1
Measham 67 F1
Meathop 107 F4
Meavy 8 B1
Medbourne 68 D3
Meddon 20 C4
Meden Vale 81 G1
Medmenham 42 D4
Medomsley 120 A2
Medstead 28 B4
Meer End 67 E5
Meerbrook 79 G1
Meesden 58 C4
Meeth 21 F5
Meggethead 134 C3
Meidrim 49 F5
Meifod *Denb.* 76 D2
Meifod *Powys* 64 A1
Meigle 160 A5
Meikle Earnock 142 B4
Meikle Grenach 140 B3
Meikle Kilmory 140 B3
Meikle Rahane 140 D1
Meikle Strath 161 E2
Meikle Tarty 171 E2
Meikle Wartle 170 C1
Meikleour 151 G1
Meinciau 36 A1
Meir 79 G3
Meirheath 79 G4
Melbost 187 F4
Melbourn 58 B3
Melbourne *Derbys.* 81 E5
Melbourne *E.Riding* 103 G3
Melbury 21 D4
Melbury Abbas 13 E1
Melbury Bubb 12 B2
Melbury Osmond 12 B2
Melbury Sampford 12 B2
Melby 200 A2
Melchbourne 57 F1
Melchet Court 27 D5
Melcombe Bingham 13 D2
Melcombe Regis 12 C4
Meldon *Devon* 7 F1
Meldon *Northumb.* 128 D3
Meldreth 58 B3
Melfort 148 A3
Melgarve 167 D5
Melgum 169 G4
Meliden (Gallt Melyd) 90 B4
Melin-y-coed 76 B1
Melin-y-ddol 63 G2
Melin-y-grug 63 G2
Melin-y-Wig 76 D3
Melincourt 37 E2
Melincryddan 37 D3
Melkinthorpe 118 B5
Melkridge 118 D1
Melksham 26 A1
Melksham Forest 26 A1
Melldalloch 140 A2
Melling *Lancs.* 107 G5
Melling *Mersey.* 91 E2
Melling Mount 91 F2
Mellis 72 B4
Mellon Charles 188 A5
Mellon Udrigle 188 A5
Mellor *Gt.Man.* 93 D4
Mellor *Lancs.* 100 C4
Mellor Brook 100 C4
Mells 25 E3
Melmerby *Cumb.* 118 C4
Melmerby *N.Yorks.* 109 F4
Melmerby *N.Yorks.* 110 C5
Melplash 12 A3
Melrose *Aber.* 182 C3
Melrose *Sc.Bord.* 135 G2
Melsetter 196 B4
Melsonby 110 A2
Meltham 93 E1
Melton 61 D2
Melton Constable 86 B2
Melton Mowbray 68 C1
Melton Ross 96 A1
Meltonby 103 G2
Melvaig 176 D1
Melverley 64 C1
Melverley Green 64 C1
Melvich 194 A2
Membury 11 F2
Memsie 183 E3
Memus 160 C4
Menabilly 5 E4
Menai Bridge (Porthaethwy) 89 D5
Mendham 73 D3
Mendlesham 60 C1
Mendlesham Green 60 B1
Menethorpe 103 G1
Menheniot 5 G3
Menie House 171 E2
Mennock 133 G5
Menston 102 A3
Menstrie 150 D5
Mentmore 43 E1
Meoble 155 G1
Meole Brace 65 D1
Meon 15 E2
Meonstoke 15 F1
Meopham 31 F2
Meopham Green 31 F2
Mepal 70 C4
Meppershall 57 G4
Merbach 52 C3
Mercaston 81 D3
Mere *Ches.* 92 B4
Mere *Wilts.* 25 F4
Mere Brow 91 F1
Mere Green 66 D3
Mereworth 31 F3
Mergie 161 F1
Meriden 67 E4
Merkland 124 B3
Merley 13 G3
Merlin's Bridge 34 C1
Merridge 23 F4
Merrifield 9 E3
Merrington 78 B5
Merrion 34 C3
Merriott 12 A1
Merrivale 7 F3
Merrow 29 F2
Merry Hill *Herts.* 44 A3
Merry Hill *W.Mid.* 66 B4
Merrymeet 5 G3
Mersham 32 C5
Merstham 30 B3
Merston 16 A3
Merstone 15 E4
Merther 4 C5
Merthyr 49 G5
Merthyr Cynog 51 F4
Merthyr Dyfan 23 E1
Merthyr Mawr 37 E5
Merthyr Tydfil 37 G2
Merthyr Vale 37 G3
Merton *Devon* 21 F4
Merton *Gt.Lon.* 30 B2
Merton *Norf.* 71 G3
Merton *Oxon.* 42 A1
Mertyn 90 C5
Mervinslaw 136 A5
Meshaw 10 A1
Messing 46 B1
Messingham 95 F2
Metfield 73 D3
Metheringham 83 F1
Methil 152 B5
Methlem 74 A4
Methley 102 C5
Methlick 171 D1
Methven 151 F2
Methwold 71 F3
Methwold Hythe 71 F3
Metrocentre 120 B1
Mettingham 73 E2
Metton 86 C2
Mevagissey 5 E5
Mexborough 94 B3
Mey 195 E1
Meysey Hampton 40 D2
Miabhag 184 C3
Miabhig 186 B4
Mial 177 D2
Michaelchurch 53 E5
Michaelchurch Escley 52 C4
Michaelchurch-on-Arrow 52 B2
Michaelston-le-Pit 38 A5
Michaelston-y-Fedw 38 B4
Michaelstow 5 E2
Micheldever 27 G4
Michelmersh 27 E5
Mickfield 60 C1
Mickle Trafford 78 B1
Mickleby 112 B1
Mickleham 29 G2
Micklehurst 93 D2
Mickleover 81 E4
Micklethwaite 117 F1
Mickleton *Dur.* 119 F5
Mickleton *Glos.* 55 D3
Mickletown 102 C5
Mickley 110 B5
Mickley Square 119 G1
Mid Ardlaw 183 E3
Mid Beltie 170 B4
Mid Cairncross 160 D2
Mid Calder 143 E3
Mid Clyth 195 E5
Mid Lavant 16 A3
Mid Letter 148 C4
Mid Lix 150 A2
Mid Mossdale 108 D3
Mid Sannox 140 B5
Mid Yell 203 E3
Midbea 198 C2
Middle Assendon 42 C4
Middle Aston 55 G5
Middle Barton 55 G5
Middle Claydon 56 C5
Middle Drums 161 D4
Middle Handley 94 B5
Middle Harling 72 A3
Middle Kames 140 A1
Middle Littleton 54 C3

Middle Maes-coed 52 C4
Middle Mill 48 B5
Middle Rasen 96 A4
Middle Rigg 151 F4
Middle Salter 100 C1
Middle Town 4 B1
Middle Tysoe 55 F3
Middle Wallop 27 D4
Middle Winterslow 26 D4
Middle Woodford 26 C4
Middlebie 126 A4
Middleham 110 A4
Middlehill Aber. 182 D5
Middlehill Cornw. 8 C4
Middlehope 65 D4
Middlemarsh 12 C2
Middlesbrough 121 D5
Middleshaw 107 G4
Middlesmoor 109 F5
Middlestone Moor 120 B4
Middlestown 93 G1
Middleton Aber. 170 D3
Middleton Angus 161 D5
Middleton Cumb. 108 B4
Middleton Derbys. 81 D2
Middleton Derbys. 80 C1
Middleton Essex 59 G3
Middleton Gt.Man. 92 C2
Middleton Hants. 27 F3
Middleton Lancs. 100 A2
Middleton Midloth. 144 A4
Middleton N.Yorks. 111 G4
Middleton Norf. 71 E1
Middleton Northants. 68 D4
Middleton Northumb. 128 C3
Middleton Northumb. 137 E3
Middleton P. & K. 151 G4
Middleton P. & K. 159 G5
Middleton Shrop. 64 B3
Middleton Shrop. 65 E5
Middleton Shrop. 78 A5
Middleton Suff. 61 F1
Middleton Swan. 36 A4
Middleton W.Yorks. 102 A3
Middleton W.Yorks. 102 B5
Middleton Warks. 67 D3
Middleton Bank Top 128 C3
Middleton Cheney 55 G3
Middleton Green 79 G4
Middleton Hall 137 D4
Middleton-in-Teesdale 119 F5
Middleton of Potterton 171 E3
Middleton-on-Leven 111 D1
Middleton-on-Sea 16 B4
Middleton on the Hill 53 E1
Middleton-on-the-Wolds 104 B3
Middleton One Row 110 C1
Middleton Park 171 E3
Middleton Priors 65 F4
Middleton Quernhow 110 C5
Middleton St. George 110 C1
Middleton Scriven 65 F4
Middleton Stoney 56 A5
Middleton Tyas 110 B2
Middletown Cumb. 106 A2
Middletown Powys 64 C1
Middlewich 79 E1
Middlewood 92 D4
Middlewood Green 60 B1
Middleyard 132 D2
Middlezoy 24 A4
Middridge 120 B5
Midfield 193 E2
Midford 25 E1
Midge Hall 100 B5
Midgeholme 118 C2
Midgham 27 G1
Midgley W.Yorks. 93 G1
Midgley W.Yorks. 101 G5
Midhopestones 93 G3
Midhurst 29 D5
Midlem 135 G3
Midpark 140 B4
Midsomer Norton 25 D2
Midtown High. 193 E2
Midtown High. 177 E1
Midtown of Barras 161 G1
Midville 84 B2
Migdale 190 B5
Migvie 169 G4
Milarrochy 149 G5
Milber 10 B5
Milbethill 182 B4
Milborne Port 12 C1
Milborne St. Andrew 13 E3
Milborne Wick 25 D5
Milbourne 128 D4
Milburn 118 C5
Milbury Heath 39 F3
Milcombe 55 G4
Milden 60 A3
Mildenhall Suff. 71 F5
Mildenhall Wilts. 41 E5
Mile Elm 26 A1
Mile End Essex 60 A5
Mile End Glos. 39 E1
Milebrook 64 C5
Milebush 31 G4
Mileham 86 A4
Milesmark 143 E1
Milfield 136 D3
Milford Derbys. 81 E3
Milford Devon 20 C3
Milford Shrop. 78 B5
Milford Staffs. 79 G5
Milford Surr. 29 E3
Milford Haven (Aberdaugleddau) 34 C2
Milford on Sea 14 B3
Milkwall 39 E2
Mill Bank 101 G5
Mill End Bucks. 42 C4
Mill End Herts. 58 B4
Mill End Green 59 E5
Mill Green Essex 45 F2
Mill Green Shrop. 79 D5
Mill Hill 44 B3
Mill Houses 100 C1
Mill Lane 28 C2
Mill of Camsail 141 D1
Mill of Colp 182 C5
Mill of Elrick 183 E5
Mill of Fortune 150 C2
Mill of Kingoodie 170 D2
Mill of Monquich 171 D5
Mill of Uras 161 G2
Mill Street 86 B4
Milland 28 D5
Millbank 183 F5
Millbeck 117 F4
Millbounds 199 D3
Millbreck 183 F5
Millbridge 28 D3
Millbrook Beds. 57 F4
Millbrook Cornw. 8 A2
Millbrook S'ham. 14 C1
Millburn Aber. 170 A2
Millburn Aber. 170 B1
Millcombe 9 E3
Millcorner 18 D1
Millden 171 E3
Milldens 160 D4
Millearne 151 E3
Millenheath 78 C4
Millerhill 144 A3
Miller's Dale 93 F5
Millholme 107 G3
Millhouse Arg. & B. 140 A2
Millhouse Cumb. 117 G3
Millhousebridge 125 F2
Millikenpark 141 F3
Millington 104 A2
Millmeece 79 F4
Millness 166 C1
Millom 106 C4
Millport 140 C4
Millthrop 108 B3
Milltimber 171 D4
Milltown Aber. 169 G3
Milltown D. & G. 126 B4
Milltown Derbys. 81 E1
Milltown Devon 21 F2
Milltown High. 180 B5
Milltown High. 178 C4
Milltown of Aberdalgie 151 F2
Milltown of Auchindoun 181 F5
Milltown of Craigston 182 C4
Milltown of Edinvillie 181 E5
Milltown of Rothiemay 182 A5
Milltown of Towie 169 G3
Milnathort 151 G4
Milngavie 141 G2
Milnrow 92 D1
Milnsbridge 93 F1
Milnthorpe 107 F4
Milovaig 175 E4
Milrig 132 D2
Milson 65 F5
Milstead 32 B3
Milston 26 C3
Milton Angus 160 B5
Milton Cambs. 58 C1
Milton Cumb. 118 B1
Milton D. & G. 124 C2
Milton D. & G. 124 C3
Milton Derbys. 81 E5
Milton High. 179 G2
Milton High. 180 B4
Milton High. 176 D5
Milton High. 179 E5
Milton High. 195 F3
Milton High. 167 D1
Milton Moray 182 A3
Milton N.Som. 24 A1
Milton Newport 38 C4
Milton Notts. 95 E5
Milton Oxon. 55 G4
Milton Oxon. 41 G3
Milton P. & K. 151 E1
Milton Pembs. 34 D2
Milton Stir. 150 A4
Milton Stir. 149 G5
Milton Stoke 79 G2
Milton W.Dun. 141 F2
Milton Abbas 13 E2
Milton Abbot 7 E3
Milton Bridge 143 G3
Milton Bryan 57 E4
Milton Clevedon 25 D4
Milton Combe 8 A1
Milton Damerel 21 D4
Milton Ernest 57 F2
Milton Green 78 B2
Milton Hill 41 G3
Milton Keynes 57 D4
Milton Keynes Village 57 D4
Milton Lilbourne 26 C1
Milton Lockhart 142 C5
Milton Malsor 56 C2
Milton Morenish 150 B1
Milton of Auchinhove 170 A4
Milton of Balgonie 152 B4
Milton of Cairnborrow 181 G5
Milton of Callander 150 A4
Milton of Campfield 170 B4
Milton of Campsie 142 A2
Milton of Coldwells 171 E1
Milton of Cullerlie 170 C4
Milton of Cushnie 170 A3
Milton of Dalcapon 159 E4
Milton of Inveramsay 170 C2
Milton of Noth 170 A2
Milton of Tullich 169 F5
Milton on Stour 25 E5
Milton Regis 32 A2
Milton-under-Wychwood 41 E1
Miltonduff 181 D3
Miltonhill 180 C3
Miltonise 122 C3
Milverton 23 E5
Milwich 79 G4
Minard 148 B5
Minard Castle 148 B5
Minchington 13 F1
Minchinhampton 40 A2
Mindrum 136 C3
Minehead 22 C3
Minera 77 F2
Minety 40 C3
Minffordd Gwyn. 62 D1
Minffordd Gwyn. 75 E4
Mingearraidh 172 C1
Miningsby 84 B1
Minions 5 G2
Minishant 132 B4
Minley Manor 28 D2
Minllyn 63 E1
Minnes 171 E2
Minnigaff 123 F4
Minnonie 182 C3
Minskip 102 C1
Minstead 14 B1
Minster Kent 32 B1
Minster Kent 33 F2
Minster Lovell 41 F1
Minsterley 64 C2
Minsterworth 39 G1
Minterne Magna 12 C2
Minting 96 B5
Mintlaw 183 F5
Minto 135 G3
Minton 64 D3
Minwear 34 D1
Minworth 67 D3
Miodar 154 B2
Mirbister 198 B4
Mireland 195 F2
Mirfield 102 A5
Miserden 40 B2
Miskin R.C.T. 37 G4
Miskin R.C.T. 37 G3
Misson 95 D3
Misterton Leics. 68 A4
Misterton Notts. 95 E3
Misterton Som. 12 A2
Mitcham 30 B2
Mitchel Troy 39 D1
Mitcheldean 39 F1
Mitchell 4 C4
Mitchelland 107 F3
Mitcheltroy Common 39 D2
Mitford 129 D3
Mithian 4 B4
Mitton 66 A1
Mixbury 56 B4
Moar 158 A5
Moat 126 C4
Mobberley 92 B5
Moccas 52 C3
Mochdre Conwy 89 G5
Mochdre Powys 63 G4
Mochrum 114 D2
Mockbeggar 31 G4
Mockerkin 117 D4
Modbury 8 C2
Moddershall 79 G4
Modsarie 193 F2
Moelfre I.o.A. 88 D4
Moelfre Powys 77 E5
Moffat 134 B5
Mogerhanger 57 G3
Moin'a'choire 138 B3
Moine House 193 E2
Moira 67 F1
Mol-chlach 164 A3
Molash 32 C3
Mold (Yr Wyddgrug) 77 F1
Molehill Green 59 D5
Molescroft 104 C3
Molesworth 69 F5
Mollance 124 B4
Molland 22 B5
Mollington Ches. 91 E5
Mollington Oxon. 55 G3
Mollinsburn 142 B2
Monachty 50 B1
Monachyle 149 G3
Moncreiffe 151 G3
Monevechadan 149 D4
Monewden 60 D2
Moneydie 151 F2
Moniaive 124 B1
Monifieth 152 C1
Monikie 152 C1
Monimail 152 A3
Monington 49 E3
Monk Fryston 103 E5
Monk Sherborne 28 B2
Monk Soham 60 D1
Monk Street 59 E5
Monken Hadley 44 B3
Monkhill 117 G1
Monkhopton 65 F3
Monkland 53 D2
Monkleigh 21 E3
Monknash 37 F5
Monkokehampton 21 F5
Monks Eleigh 60 A3
Monk's Gate 17 E1
Monks' Heath 92 C5
Monks Kirby 67 G4
Monks Risborough 42 D2
Monkseaton 129 F4
Monkshill 182 C5
Monksilver 23 D4
Monkstadt 175 G3
Monkswood 38 C2
Monkton Devon 11 E2
Monkton Kent 33 E2
Monkton S.Ayr. 132 B3
Monkton T. & W. 120 C1
Monkton Combe 25 E1
Monkton Deverill 25 F4
Monkton Farleigh 25 E1
Monkton Heathfield 23 F5
Monkton Up Wimborne 13 G1
Monkwearmouth 120 C2
Monkwood 28 B4
Monmore Green 66 B3
Monmouth (Trefynwy) 39 E1
Monnington on Wye 52 C3
Monreith 115 D2
Montacute 12 A1
Monteach 183 D5
Montford 64 D1
Montford Bridge 64 D1
Montgarrie 170 A3
Montgomery (Trefaldwyn) 64 B3
Montgreenan 141 E5
Montrave 152 B4
Montrose 161 F4
Monxton 27 E3
Monyash 80 C1
Monymusk 170 B3
Monzie 151 D2
Moodiesburn 142 A2
Moonzie 152 B3
Moor Allerton 102 C4
Moor Cock 100 C1
Moor Crichel 13 F2
Moor End Cumb. 107 G5
Moor End E.Riding 104 A4
Moor Monkton 103 E2
Moor Nook 100 C4
Moor Row 116 D5
Moor Side 84 A2
Moorby 84 A1
Moorcot 52 C2
Moordown 13 G3
Moore 91 G4
Moorends 95 D1
Moorgreen 81 F3
Moorhall 94 A5
Moorhampton 52 C3
Moorhouse Cumb. 117 G1
Moorhouse Notts. 82 C1
Moorland or Northmoor Green 24 A4
Moorlinch 24 A4
Moorsholm 111 F1
Moorside 93 D2
Moortown I.o.W. 14 D4
Moortown Lincs. 96 A3
Morangie 179 G1
Morar 164 C5
Morborne 69 G3
Morchard Bishop 10 A2
Morcombelake 11 G3
Morcott 69 E2
Morda 77 F5
Morden Dorset 13 F3
Morden Gt.Lon. 30 B2
Mordiford 53 E4
Mordington Holdings 145 G4
Mordon 120 C5
More 64 C3
Morebath 22 C5
Morebattle 136 B4
Morecambe 100 A1
Morefield 188 D5
Moreleigh 9 D2
Morenish 150 B1
Moresby 116 C4
Morestead 27 G5
Moreton Dorset 13 E4
Moreton Essex 45 E2
Moreton Here. 53 E1
Moreton Mersey. 91 D4
Moreton Oxon. 42 B2
Moreton Corbet 78 C5
Moreton-in-Marsh 55 E4
Moreton Jeffries 53 F3
Moreton Morrell 55 F2
Moreton on Lugg 53 E3
Moreton Pinkney 56 A3
Moreton Say 78 D4
Moreton Valence 39 G2
Moretonhampstead 10 A4
Morfa Bychan 75 E4
Morfa Glas 37 E2
Morfa Nefyn 74 B3
Morgan's Vale 26 C5
Mork 39 E2
Morland 118 B5
Morley Derbys. 81 E3
Morley Dur. 120 A5
Morley W.Yorks. 102 B5
Morley Green 92 C4
Morley St. Botolph 86 B5
Morningside Edin. 143 G2
Morningside N.Lan. 142 C4
Morningthorpe 72 D2
Morpeth 129 D3
Morphie 161 F3
Morrey 66 D1
Morriston S.Ayr. 132 A5
Morriston Swan. 36 C3
Morroch 155 F1
Morston 86 B1
Mortehoe 21 E1
Mortimer 28 B1
Mortimer West End 28 B1
Mortimer's Cross 52 D1
Mortlake 44 B5
Morton Derbys. 81 F1
Morton Lincs. 83 G5
Morton Lincs. 95 F3
Morton Notts. 82 C2
Morton S.Glos. 39 F3
Morton Shrop. 77 F5
Morton Bagot 54 D1
Morton-on-Swale 110 C3
Morton on the Hill 86 C4
Morvah 2 A3
Morval 5 G4
Morvich High. 165 F2
Morvich High. 190 C4
Morvil 48 D4
Morville 65 F3
Morwellham 8 A1
Morwenstow 20 C4
Morwick Hall 129 E1
Mosborough 94 B4
Moscow 141 F5
Mosedale 117 G3
Moselden Height 93 E1
Moseley W.Mid. 66 C4
Moseley Worcs. 54 A2
Moss Arg. & B. 154 A2
Moss S.Yorks. 94 C1
Moss Wrex. 78 A2
Moss Bank 91 G3
Moss Nook 92 C4
Moss of Barmuckity 181 E3
Moss Side 99 G4
Moss-side High. 180 A4
Moss-side Moray 182 A4
Mossat 169 G3
Mossbank 203 D5
Mossblown 132 C3
Mossburnford 136 A5
Mossdale 124 A3
Mossend 142 B3
Mossgiel 132 C3
Mosshead 170 A1
Mosside of Ballinshoe 160 C4
Mossley 93 D2
Mossley Hill 91 E4
Mosspaul Hotel 126 C2
Mosstodloch 181 F3
Mosston 160 D5
Mosterton 12 A2
Mostyn 90 C4
Motcombe 25 F5
Motherby 118 A5
Motherwell 142 B4
Mottingham 44 D5
Mottisfont 27 E5
Mottistone 14 D4
Mottram in Longdendale 93 D3
Mottram St. Andrew 92 C5
Mouldsworth 91 G5
Moulin 159 E4
Moulsecoomb 17 F3
Moulsford 42 A4
Moulsham 45 G2
Moulsoe 57 E3
Moulton Ches. 79 D1
Moulton Lincs. 84 B5
Moulton N.Yorks. 110 B2
Moulton Northants. 56 C1
Moulton Suff. 59 E1
Moulton Chapel 70 A1
Moulton St. Mary 87 E5
Moulton Seas End 84 B5
Mounie Castle 170 C2
Mount Cornw. 4 B4
Mount Cornw. 5 F3
Mount High. 180 B5
Mount Bures 60 A4
Mount Hawke 4 B5
Mount Manisty 91 E5
Mount Oliphant 132 B4
Mount Pleasant Derbys. 81 E3
Mount Pleasant Suff. 73 F4
Mount Tabor 101 G5
Mountain Ash 37 G3
Mountain Cross 143 F5
Mountain Water 48 C5
Mountbenger 135 E3
Mountblairy 182 B4
Mountfield 18 C1
Mountgerald 179 E3
Mountjoy 4 C3
Mountnessing 45 F3
Mounton 39 E3
Mountsorrel 68 A1
Mousehole 2 B4
Mouswald 125 E3
Mow Cop 79 F2
Mowden 110 B1
Mowhaugh 136 C4
Mowsley 68 B4
Mowtie 161 G1
Moxley 66 B3
Moy High. 157 D1
Moy High. 157 G1
Moy High. 167 G1
Moy House 180 C3
Moyles Court 14 A2
Moylgrove 49 E3
Muasdale 139 E5
Much Birch 53 E4
Much Cowarne 53 F3
Much Dewchurch 53 D4
Much Hadham 44 D1
Much Hoole 100 A5
Much Marcle 53 F4
Much Wenlock 65 F2
Muchalls 171 D5
Muchelney 24 B5
Muchlarnick 5 G4
Muchra 134 D4
Muchrachd 166 B1
Mucking 45 F4
Mucklestone 79 E4
Muckleton 78 C5
Muckletown 170 A2
Muckton 97 D4
Mudale 193 E5
Muddiford 21 F2
Muddles Green 18 A2
Muddleswood 17 E2
Mudeford 14 A3
Mudford 12 B1
Mudgley 24 B3
Mugeary 164 A1
Mugginton 81 D3
Muggleswick 119 G2
Muie 190 B4
Muir 159 F1
Muir of Fowlis 170 A3
Muir of Lochs 181 F3
Muir of Ord 179 E4
Muirden 182 C4
Muirdrum 153 D1
Muirhead Aber. 170 A3
Muirhead Angus 152 B1
Muirhead Fife 152 A4
Muirhead Moray 180 C3
Muirhead N.Lan. 142 A3
Muirhouses 143 E1
Muirkirk 133 E3
Muirmill 142 B1
Muirtack Aber. 171 E1
Muirtack Aber. 182 D5
Muirton 179 G3
Muirton of Ardblair 159 G5
Muirton of Ballochy 161 E3
Muirtown 151 E3
Muiryfold 182 C4
Muker 109 E3
Mulbarton 86 C5
Mulben 181 F4
Mulhagery 185 F3
Mullach Charlabhaigh 186 D3
Mullacott Cross 21 F1
Mullion 3 D5
Mumby 97 F5
Munderfield Row 53 F2
Munderfield Stocks 53 F2
Mundesley 87 E2
Mundford 71 F3
Mundham 73 E2
Mundon 46 B2
Mundurno 171 E3
Munerigie 166 B4
Mungasdale 188 B5
Mungoswells 144 B2
Mungrisdale 117 G3
Munlochy 179 F4
Munnoch 140 D5
Munsley 53 F3
Munslow 65 E4
Murchington 7 G2
Murcott 42 A1
Murdostoun 142 C4
Murkle 195 D2
Murlaganmore 150 A1
Murlaggan High. 165 G5
Murlaggan High. 157 F1
Murra 196 B2
Murroes 152 C1
Murrow 70 B2
Mursley 56 D5
Murston 32 B2
Murthill 160 C4
Murthly 151 F1
Murton Cumb. 118 D5
Murton Dur. 120 C3
Murton Northumb. 145 G5
Murton York 103 F2
Musbury 11 F3
Muscoates 111 F4
Musdale 148 B2
Musselburgh 144 A2
Muston Leics. 82 D4
Muston N.Yorks. 113 E5
Mustow Green 66 A5
Mutford 73 F3
Muthill 151 D3
Mutterton 10 D2
Mybster 195 D3
Myddfai 51 D4
Myddle 78 B5
Myddlewood 78 B5
Mydroilyn 50 A2
Mylor 3 F3
Mylor Bridge 3 F3
Mynachlog-ddu 49 E4
Myndtown 64 C4
Mynydd-bach 39 D3
Mynydd Llandygai 75 F1
Mynytho 74 C4
Myrebird 170 C5
Mytchett 29 D2
Mytholm 101 F5
Mytholmroyd 101 G5
Myton-on-Swale 102 D1


## N


Naast 177 E1
Naburn 103 E3
Nackington 33 D3
Nacton 60 D3
Nafferton 104 C2
Nailbridge 39 F1
Nailsea 39 D5
Nailstone 67 G2
Nailsworth 40 A3
Nairn 180 A4
Nancegollan 2 D3
Nancledra 2 B3
Nanhoron 74 B4
Nannau 76 A5
Nannerch 77 E1
Nanpantan 68 A1
Nanpean 5 D4
Nanstallon 5 E3
Nant-ddu 37 G1
Nant-glas 51 F1
Nant Peris 75 F2
Nant-y-derry 38 C2
Nant-y-dugoed 63 F1
Nant-y-groes 51 G1
Nant-y-moel 37 F3
Nant-y-Pandy 89 E5
Nanternis 49 G2
Nantgaredig 50 A5
Nantgarw 38 A4
Nantglyn 76 D1
Nantlle 75 E2
Nantmawr 77 F5
Nantmel 51 G1
Nantmor 75 F3
Nantwich 78 D2
Nantycaws 36 A1
Nantyffyllon 37 E3
Nantyglo 38 A2
Naphill 43 D3
Nappa 101 E2
Napton on the Hill 55 G1
Narberth (Arberth) 35 E1
Narborough Leics. 68 A3
Narborough Norf. 71 F1
Narrachan 148 B3
Nasareth 75 D2
Naseby 68 B5
Nash Bucks. 56 C4
Nash Here. 52 C1
Nash Newport 38 C4
Nash Shrop. 65 E5
Nash V. of Glam. 37 F5
Nash Lee 42 D2
Nassington 69 F3
Nasty 58 B5
Nateby Cumb. 108 C2
Nateby Lancs. 100 A3
Nately Scures 28 C2
Natland 107 G4
Naughton 60 B3
Naunton Glos. 54 D5
Naunton Worcs. 54 A4
Naunton Beauchamp 54 B2
Navenby 83 E2
Navestock 45 E3
Navestock Side 45 E3
Navidale 191 F3
Navity 179 G3
Nawton 111 F4
Nayland 60 A4
Nazeing 44 D2
Neacroft 14 A3
Neal's Green 67 F4
Neap 201 E2
Near Cotton 80 B3
Near Sawrey 107 E3
Neasham 110 C1
Neath (Castell-Nedd) 37 D3
Neatham 28 C3
Neatishead 87 E3
Nebo Cere. 50 B1
Nebo Conwy 76 B2
Nebo Gwyn. 75 D2
Nebo I.o.A. 88 C3
Necton 71 G2
Nedd 192 A5
Nedderton 129 E3
Nedging Tye 60 B3
Needham 72 D3
Needham Market 60 B2
Needingworth 70 B5
Neen Savage 65 F5
Neen Sollars 65 F5
Neenton 65 F4
Nefyn 74 C3
Neilston 141 F4
Nelson Caerp. 38 A3
Nelson Lancs. 101 E4
Nelson Village 129 E4
Nemphlar 142 C5
Nempnett Thrubwell 24 C1
Nenthall 119 D3
Nenthead 119 D3
Nenthorn 136 A3
Nerabus 138 A4
Nercwys 77 F1
Neriby 138 B3
Nerston 142 A4
Nesbit 137 D3
Ness 91 E5
Ness of Tenston 198 A5
Nesscliffe 64 C1
Neston Ches. 91 D5
Neston Wilts. 25 F1
Nether Alderley 92 C5
Nether Auchendrane 132 B4
Nether Barr 123 F4
Nether Blainslie 144 C5
Nether Broughton 82 B5
Nether Burrow 108 B5
Nether Cerne 12 C3
Nether Compton 12 B1
Nether Crimond 170 D2
Nether Dalgliesh 135 D5
Nether Dallachy 181 F3
Nether End 93 G5
Nether Exe 10 C3
Nether Glasslaw 183 D4
Nether Handwick 160 B5
Nether Haugh 94 B3
Nether Headon 95 E5
Nether Heselden 109 D5
Nether Heyford 56 B2
Nether Kellet 100 B1
Nether Kinmundy 183 F5
Nether Langwith 94 C5
Nether Lenshie 182 B5
Nether Moor 81 E1
Nether Padley 93 G5
Nether Pitforthie 161 G2
Nether Poppleton 103 E2
Nether Silton 111 D3
Nether Stowey 23 E4
Nether Urquhart 151 G4
Nether Wallop 27 E4
Nether Wasdale 106 C2
Nether Wellwood 133 E3
Nether Whitacre 67 E3
Nether (Lower) Winchendon 42 C1
Nether Worton 55 G4
Netheravon 26 C3
Netherbrae 182 C4
Netherbrough 198 B5
Netherburn 142 C5
Netherbury 12 A3
Netherby Cumb. 126 B4
Netherby N.Yorks. 102 C3
Nethercott 55 G5
Netherend 39 E3
Netherfield E.Suss. 18 C2
Netherfield Notts. 82 B3
Netherfield S.Lan. 142 B5
Netherhall 140 D3
Netherhampton 26 C4

Netherley 171 D5
Nethermill 125 E2
Nethermuir 183 E5
Netherseal 67 E1
Nethershield 133 D3
Netherstreet 26 A1
Netherthird *D. & G.* 124 B5
Netherthird *E.Ayr.* 133 D4
Netherthong 93 F2
Netherthorpe 94 C4
Netherton *Angus* 160 D4
Netherton *Ches.* 91 G5
Netherton *Devon* 10 B5
Netherton *Mersey.* 91 E2
Netherton *Northumb.* 128 B1
Netherton *Oxon.* 41 G3
Netherton *P. & K.* 159 G4
Netherton *S.Lan.* 142 D4
Netherton *W.Mid.* 66 B4
Netherton *W.Yorks.* 93 G1
Netherton *W.Yorks.* 93 F1
Netherton *Worcs.* 54 B3
Nethertown *Cumb.* 106 A2
Nethertown *Ork.* 195 F1
Netherwitton 128 D3
Netherwood *D. & G.* 125 D3
Netherwood *E.Ayr.* 133 E3
Nethy Bridge 168 C2
Netley Abbey 15 D2
Netley Marsh 14 C1
Nettlebed 42 C4
Nettlebridge 24 D3
Nettlecombe *Dorset* 12 B3
Nettlecombe *Som.* 23 D4
Nettleden 43 F1
Nettleham 96 A5
Nettlestead *Kent* 31 F3
Nettlestead *Suff.* 60 B3
Nettlestead Green 31 F3
Nettlestone 15 F3
Nettleton *Lincs.* 96 B2
Nettleton *Wilts.* 40 A5
Netton *Devon* 8 B3
Netton *Wilts.* 26 C4
Neuadd *Cere.* 50 A2
Neuadd *I.o.A.* 88 B3
Neuadd *Powys* 51 F3
Nevendon 45 G3
Nevern 49 D4
Nevill Holt 68 D3
New Abbey 125 D4
New Aberdour 183 D3
New Addington 30 C2
New Alresford 27 G4
New Alyth 160 A5
New Arley 67 E3
New Ash Green 31 F2
New Barn 31 F2
New Barnet 44 B3
New Belses 135 G3
New Bewick 137 E4
New Bolingbroke 84 B2
New Bradwell 56 D3
New Bridge 124 D3
New Brighton *Hants.* 15 G2
New Brighton *Mersey.* 91 E3
New Brinsley 81 F2
New Broughton 78 A2
New Buckenham 72 B2
New Byth 182 D4
New Cheriton 27 G5
New Costessey 86 C5
New Cross 62 C5
New Cumnock 133 E4
New Deer 183 D5
New Duston 56 C1
New Earswick 103 F2
New Edlington 94 C3
New Elgin 181 E3
New Ellerby 105 D4
New Eltham 44 D5
New End 54 C1
New England 69 G2
New Farnley 102 B4
New Ferry 91 E4
New Fryston 103 D5
New Galloway 124 A3
New Gilston 152 C4
New Grimsby 4 A1
New Hartley 129 F4
New Haw 29 F1
New Hedges 35 E2
New Holland 104 C5
New Houghton *Derbys.* 81 G1
New Houghton *Norf.* 85 F5
New Houses 108 D5
New Hutton 107 G3
New Hythe 31 G3
New Inn *Carmar.* 50 A4
New Inn *Fife* 152 A4
New Inn *Mon.* 39 D2
New Inn *Torfaen* 38 B3
New Invention *Shrop.* 64 B5
New Invention *W.Mid.* 66 B2
New Lanark 142 C5
New Lane 91 F1
New Leake 84 C2
New Leeds 183 E4
New Leslie 170 A2
New Longton 100 B5
New Luce 122 C4
New Mains 133 G2
New Mains of Ury 161 G1
New Malden 30 B2
New Marske 121 F5
New Marton 78 A4
New Mill *Cornw.* 2 B3
New Mill *Herts.* 43 E1
New Mill *W.Yorks.* 93 F2
New Mill End 44 A1
New Mills *Cornw.* 4 C4
New Mills *Derbys.* 93 D4
New Mills *Mon.* 39 E2
New Mills *Powys* 63 G2
New Milton 14 B3
New Mistley 60 C4
New Moat 49 D5
New Orleans 130 C4
New Park 5 F1
New Pitsligo 183 D4
New Polzeath 4 D2
New Quay (Ceinewydd) 49 G2
New Rackheath 87 D4
New Radnor 52 B1
New Rent 118 A4
New Romney 19 F1
New Rossington 94 D3
New Row 100 C4
New Sawley 81 F4
New Scone 151 G2
New Silksworth 120 C2
New Town *E.Loth.* 144 B2
New Town *E.Suss.* 17 G1
New Town *Glos.* 54 C4
New Tredegar 38 A2
New Tupton 81 E1
New Ulva 139 F1
New Walsoken 70 C2
New Waltham 96 C2
New Winton 144 B2
New Yatt 41 F1
New York *Lincs.* 84 A2
New York *T. & W.* 129 F4
Newark *Ork.* 199 F2
Newark *Peter.* 70 A2
Newark-on-Trent 82 D2
Newarthill 142 B4
Newbarn 33 D4
Newbarns 106 D5
Newbiggin *Cumb.* 118 A5
Newbiggin *Cumb.* 118 C5
Newbiggin *Cumb.* 118 B3
Newbiggin *Cumb.* 99 F1
Newbiggin *Dur.* 119 F5
Newbiggin *N.Yorks.* 109 F4
Newbiggin *N.Yorks.* 109 E3
Newbiggin *Northumb.* 119 F1
Newbiggin-by-the-Sea 129 F3
Newbiggin-on-Lune 108 C2
Newbigging *Aber.* 171 D5
Newbigging *Aber.* 159 G1
Newbigging *Angus* 152 C1
Newbigging *Angus* 152 C1
Newbigging *Angus* 160 A5
Newbigging *S.Lan.* 143 E5
Newbold *Derbys.* 94 A5
Newbold *Leics.* 67 G1
Newbold on Avon 67 G5
Newbold on Stour 55 E3
Newbold Pacey 55 E2
Newbold Verdon 67 G2
Newborough *I.o.A.* 74 D1
Newborough *Peter.* 70 A2
Newborough *Staffs.* 80 C5
Newbottle 56 A4
Newbourne 61 D3
Newbridge (Cefn Bychan) *Caerp.* 38 B3
Newbridge *Cornw.* 2 B3
Newbridge *Cornw.* 7 D4
Newbridge *Edin.* 143 F2
Newbridge *Hants.* 14 C1
Newbridge *I.o.W.* 14 D4
Newbridge *Oxon.* 41 G2
Newbridge *Pembs.* 48 C4
Newbridge *Wrex.* 77 F3
Newbridge-on-Usk 38 C3
Newbridge on Wye 51 G2
Newbrough 119 E1
Newburgh *Aber.* 183 E4
Newburgh *Aber.* 171 E2
Newburgh *Fife* 152 A3
Newburgh *Lancs.* 91 F1
Newburgh *Sc.Bord.* 135 E4
Newburn 120 A1
Newbury 27 F1
Newby *Cumb.* 118 B5
Newby *Lancs.* 101 E3
Newby *N.Yorks.* 111 E1
Newby *N.Yorks.* 108 C5
Newby Bridge 107 E4
Newby East 118 A2
Newby West 117 G1
Newby Wiske 110 C4
Newcastle *Bridgend* 37 F5
Newcastle *Mon.* 38 D1
Newcastle *Shrop.* 64 B4
Newcastle Emlyn (Castell Newydd Emlyn) 49 G3
Newcastle International Airport 129 D4
Newcastle-under-Lyme 79 F3
Newcastle upon Tyne 120 B1
Newcastleton 126 C3
Newchapel *Pembs.* 49 F4
Newchapel *Stoke* 79 F2
Newchapel *Surr.* 30 C4
Newchurch *Carmar.* 49 G5
Newchurch *I.o.W.* 15 E4
Newchurch *Kent* 32 C5
Newchurch *Lancs.* 101 E5
Newchurch *Lancs.* 101 E4
Newchurch *Mon.* 39 D3
Newchurch *Powys* 52 B2
Newcott 11 F2
Newcraighall 144 A2
Newdigate 29 G3
Newell Green 43 D5
Newenden 18 D1
Newent 53 G5
Newerne 39 F2
Newfield *Dur.* 120 B4
Newfield *Dur.* 120 B2
Newfield *High.* 179 G2
Newgale 48 B5
Newgate 86 B1
Newgate Street 44 C2
Newgord 203 E2
Newhall *Ches.* 78 D3
Newhall *Derbys.* 81 D5
Newham *Gt.Lon.* 44 C4
Newham *Northumb.* 137 F4
Newham Hall 137 F4
Newhaven 17 G3
Newhey 92 D1
Newholm 112 B1
Newhouse 142 B3
Newick 17 G1
Newington *Kent* 33 D5
Newington *Kent* 32 A2
Newington *Oxon.* 42 B3
Newington Bagpath 40 A3
Newland *Glos.* 39 E2
Newland *N.Yorks.* 103 F5
Newland *Worcs.* 53 G3
Newlandrig 144 A3
Newlands *Northumb.* 119 G2
Newlands *Sc.Bord.* 126 D2
Newland's Corner 29 F3
Newlands of Geise 194 C2
Newlyn 2 B4
Newlyn East 4 C4
Newmachar 171 D3
Newmains 142 C4
Newmarket *Suff.* 59 E1
Newmarket *W.Isles* 187 F4
Newmill *Aber.* 161 F1
Newmill *Aber.* 183 D5
Newmill *Aber.* 170 D2
Newmill *Moray* 181 G4
Newmill *Sc.Bord.* 135 F4
Newmill of Inshewan 160 C3
Newmills 179 F3
Newmiln *P. & K.* 151 G1
Newmiln *P. & K.* 151 F2
Newmilns 132 D2
Newnham *Glos.* 39 F1
Newnham *Hants.* 28 C2
Newnham *Herts.* 58 A4
Newnham *Kent* 32 B3
Newnham *Northants.* 56 A2
Newnham *Worcs.* 53 F1
Newnham Paddox 67 G4
Newnoth 170 A1
Newport *Cornw.* 6 D2
Newport *Devon* 21 F2
Newport *E.Riding* 104 A4
Newport *Essex* 58 D4
Newport *Glos.* 39 F3
Newport *High.* 191 G2
Newport *I.o.W.* 15 E4
Newport (Casnewydd) *Newport* 38 C4
Newport *Norf.* 87 G4
Newport *Pembs.* 49 D4
Newport *Tel. & W.* 65 G1
Newport-on-Tay 152 C2
Newport Pagnell 57 D3
Newpound Common 29 F5
Newquay 4 C3
Newquay (Cornwall) Airport 4 C3
Newseat 170 C1
Newsham *Lancs.* 100 B4
Newsham *N.Yorks.* 110 A1
Newsham *N.Yorks.* 110 C4
Newsham *Northumb.* 129 E4
Newsholme *E.Riding* 103 G5
Newsholme *Lancs.* 101 E2
Newstead *Northumb.* 137 F4
Newstead *Notts.* 81 G2
Newstead *Sc.Bord.* 135 G2
Newthorpe 103 D4
Newton *Aber.* 181 G5
Newton *Aber.* 183 F5
Newton *Arg. & B.* 148 C5
Newton *Bridgend* 37 E5
Newton *Cambs.* 70 C1
Newton *Cambs.* 58 C3
Newton *Ches.* 78 B2
Newton *Ches.* 91 G5
Newton *Cumb.* 106 D5
Newton *D. & G.* 125 F1
Newton *Gt.Man.* 93 D3
Newton *Here.* 52 C1
Newton *High.* 195 F4
Newton *High.* 179 G5
Newton *High.* 195 F3
Newton *High.* 192 B5
Newton *High.* 179 E4
Newton *High.* 179 G3
Newton *Lancs.* 100 C2
Newton *Lancs.* 107 G5
Newton *Lincs.* 83 F4
Newton *Moray* 181 F3
Newton *N.Ayr.* 140 A4
Newton *Norf.* 71 G1
Newton *Northants.* 69 D4
Newton *Northumb.* 119 G1
Newton *Notts.* 82 B3
Newton *P. & K.* 151 D1
Newton *Pembs.* 48 C5
Newton *Pembs.* 34 C2
Newton *S.Lan.* 134 A2
Newton *Sc.Bord.* 136 A4
Newton *Staffs.* 80 B5
Newton *Suff.* 60 A3
Newton *Swan.* 36 C4
Newton *W.Loth.* 143 E2
Newton *W.Yorks.* 103 D5
Newton *Warks.* 68 A5
Newton *Wilts.* 26 D5
Newton Abbot 10 B5
Newton Arlosh 117 E1
Newton Aycliffe 120 B5
Newton Bewley 121 D5
Newton Blossomville 57 E2
Newton Bromswold 57 F1
Newton Burgoland 67 F2
Newton by Toft 96 A4
Newton Ferrers 8 B3
Newton Flotman 72 D2
Newton Harcourt 68 B3
Newton Kyme 103 D3
Newton-le-Willows *Mersey.* 91 G3
Newton-le-Willows *N.Yorks.* 110 B4
Newton Longville 56 D4
Newton Mearns 141 G4
Newton Morrell 110 B2
Newton Mountain 34 C2
Newton Mulgrave 111 G1
Newton of Affleck 152 C1
Newton of Ardtoe 155 F2
Newton of Balcanquhal 151 G3
Newton of Dalvey 180 C4
Newton of Falkland 152 A4
Newton of Leys 179 F5
Newton-on-Ouse 103 E1
Newton-on-Rawcliffe 112 B3
Newton-on-the-Moor 129 D1
Newton on Trent 95 F5
Newton Poppleford 11 D4
Newton Purcell 56 B4
Newton Regis 67 E2
Newton Reigny 118 A4
Newton St. Cyres 10 B3
Newton St. Faith 86 D4
Newton St. Loe 25 E1
Newton St. Petrock 21 E4
Newton Solney 81 D5
Newton Stacey 27 F3
Newton Stewart 123 F4
Newton Tony 26 D3
Newton Tracey 21 F3
Newton under Roseberry 111 E1
Newton upon Derwent 103 G3
Newton Valence 28 C4
Newtonairds 124 C2
Newtongrange 144 A3
Newtonhill 171 E5
Newtonmill 161 E3
Newtonmore 167 G5
Newtown *B.Gwent* 38 A1
Newtown *Bucks.* 43 E2
Newtown *Ches.* 78 B2
Newtown *Cumb.* 118 B1
Newtown *Derbys.* 93 D4
Newtown *Hants.* 15 F1
Newtown *Hants.* 27 F1
Newtown *Hants.* 14 B1
Newtown *Hants.* 27 E5
Newtown *Hants.* 15 E1
Newtown *Here.* 53 G4
Newtown *Here.* 53 F3
Newtown *High.* 166 C4
Newtown *I.o.M.* 98 B4
Newtown *I.o.W.* 14 D3
Newtown *Northumb.* 128 C1
Newtown *Northumb.* 137 E4
Newtown *Poole* 13 G3
Newtown (Y Drenewydd) *Powys* 64 A3
Newtown *Shrop.* 78 B4
Newtown *Staffs.* 79 G1
Newtown *Staffs.* 80 B1
Newtown *Wilts.* 26 A5
Newtown in St. Martin 3 E4
Newtown Linford 68 A1
Newtown St. Boswells 135 G2
Newtown Unthank 67 G2
Newtyle 160 A5
Neyland 34 C2
Nibley *Glos.* 39 F2
Nibley *S.Glos.* 39 F4
Nicholashayne 11 E1
Nicholaston 36 B4
Nidd 102 C1
Niddrie 143 G2
Nigg *Aberdeen* 171 E4
Nigg *High.* 180 A2
Nightcott 22 B5
Nilig 76 D2
Nimlet 39 G5
Nine Ashes 45 E2
Nine Elms 40 D4
Nine Mile Burn 143 F4
Ninebanks 119 D2
Ninemile Bar or Crocketford 124 C3
Ninfield 18 C2
Ningwood 14 D4
Nisbet 136 A4
Niton 15 E5
Nitshill 141 G3
Nizels 31 E3
No Man's Heath *Ches.* 78 C3
No Man's Heath *Warks.* 67 E2
Noak Hill 45 E3
Noblehill 125 D3
Nobottle 56 B1
Nocton 83 F1
Noddsdale 140 D3
Noke 42 A1
Nolton 34 B1
Nomansland *Devon* 10 B1
Nomansland *Wilts.* 14 B1
Noneley 78 B5
Nonington 33 E3
Nook *Cumb.* 126 C4
Nook *Cumb.* 107 G4
Noonsbrough 200 B2
Noranside 160 C3
Norbiton 29 G1
Norbreck 99 G3
Norbury *Ches.* 78 C3
Norbury *Derbys.* 80 C3
Norbury *Shrop.* 64 C3
Norbury *Staffs.* 79 E5
Norchard 54 A1
Nordelph 71 D2
Norden 13 F4
Nordley 65 F3
Norham 145 G5
Norland Town 101 G5
Norley 91 G5
Norleywood 14 C3
Norman Cross 69 G3
Normanby *N.Lincs.* 95 F1
Normanby *N.Yorks.* 111 G4
Normanby *R. & C.* 111 E1
Normanby-by-Spital 96 A4
Normanby by Stow 95 F4
Normanby le Wold 96 B3
Normandy 29 E2
Normann's Ruh 154 D5
Norman's Bay 18 B3
Norman's Green 11 D2
Normanton *Derby* 81 E4
Normanton *Leics.* 82 D3
Normanton *Lincs.* 83 E3
Normanton *Notts.* 82 C2
Normanton *Rut.* 69 E2
Normanton *W.Yorks.* 102 C5
Normanton le Heath 67 F1
Normanton on Soar 81 G5
Normanton-on-the-Wolds 82 B4
Normanton on Trent 82 C1
Normoss 99 G4
Norrington Common 25 F1
Norris Hill 67 F1
North Anston 94 C4
North Ascot 29 E1
North Aston 55 G5
North Baddesley 27 E5
North Ballachulish 156 C3
North Balloch 123 E1
North Barrow 24 D5
North Barsham 86 A2
North Benfleet 45 G4
North Bersted 16 B3
North Berwick 144 C1
North Boarhunt 15 F1
North Bogbain 181 F4
North Bovey 10 A4
North Bradley 25 F2
North Brentor 7 E2
North Brewham 25 E4
North Buckland 21 E1
North Burlingham 87 E4
North Cadbury 24 D5
North Cairn 122 A3
North Camp 29 D2
North Carlton *Lincs.* 95 G5
North Carlton *Notts.* 94 C4
North Cave 104 A4
North Cerney 40 C2
North Chailey 17 F1
North Charford 26 D5
North Charlton 137 F4
North Cheriton 25 D5
North Cliffe 104 A4
North Clifton 95 F5
North Cockerington 97 D3
North Coker 12 B1
North Connel 148 B1
North Cornelly 37 E4
North Cotes 96 D2
North Cove 73 F3
North Cowton 110 B2
North Crawley 57 E3
North Cray 45 D5
North Creake 85 G4
North Curry 24 A5
North Dallens 156 B5
North Dalton 104 B2
North Dawn 197 D2
North Deighton 102 C2
North Duffield 103 F4
North Elkington 96 C3
North Elmham 86 A3
North Elmsall 94 B1
North End *Bucks.* 56 D5
North End *Essex* 45 F1
North End *Hants.* 27 F1
North End *N.Som.* 24 B1
North End *Norf.* 72 B2
North End *Northumb.* 128 D1
North End *Ports.* 15 F2
North End *W.Suss.* 16 D1
North Erradale 176 D1
North Essie 183 F4
North Ferriby 104 B5
North Frodingham 104 D2
North Gorley 14 A1
North Green 72 D3
North Grimston 104 A1
North Hayling 15 G2
North Hazelrigg 137 E3
North Heasley 22 A4
North Heath 29 F5
North Hill 5 G2
North Hinksey 41 G2
North Holmwood 29 G3
North Huish 8 D2
North Hykeham 83 E1
North Johnston 34 C1
North Kelsey 96 A2
North Kessock 179 F5
North Killingholme 96 B1
North Kilvington 110 D4
North Kilworth 68 B4
North Kyme 83 G2
North Lancing 17 D3
North Lee 42 D2
North Leigh 41 F1
North Leverton with Habblesthorpe 95 E4
North Littleton 54 C3
North Lopham 72 B3
North Luffenham 69 E2
North Marden 16 A2
North Marston 56 C5
North Middleton 144 A4
North Millbrex 182 D5
North Molton 22 A5
North Moreton 42 A4
North Mundham 16 A3
North Muskham 82 C2
North Newbald 104 B4
North Newington 55 G4
North Newnton 26 C2
North Newton 23 F4
North Nibley 39 G3
North Oakley 27 G2
North Ockendon 45 E4
North Ormesby 121 E5
North Ormsby 96 C3
North Otterington 110 C3
North Owersby 96 A3
North Perrott 12 A2
North Petherton 23 F4
North Petherwin 5 G1
North Pickenham 71 G2
North Piddle 54 B2
North Poorton 12 B3
North Queensferry 143 F1
North Radworthy 22 A4
North Rauceby 83 F3
North Reston 97 D4
North Rigton 102 B3
North Rode 79 F1
North Roe 202 C4
North Runcton 71 E1
North Sandwick 203 E3
North Scale 99 E1
North Scarle 83 D1
North Seaton 129 E3
North Shian 156 B5
North Shields 120 C1
North Shoebury 46 C4
North Side 70 A3
North Skelton 111 F1
North Somercotes 97 E3
North Stainley 110 B5
North Stainmore 108 D1
North Stifford 45 F4
North Stoke *B. & N.E.Som.* 25 D1
North Stoke *Oxon.* 42 B4
North Stoke *W.Suss.* 16 C2
North Stoneham 14 D1
North Street *Hants.* 28 B4
North Street *Kent* 32 C3
North Street *W.Berks.* 42 B5
North Sunderland 137 G3
North Tamerton 6 D1
North Tarbothill 171 E3
North Tawton 21 G5
North Third 142 B1
North Thoresby 96 C3
North Tidworth 26 D3
North Togston 129 E1
North Town *Devon* 21 F5
North Town *Hants.* 29 D2
North Tuddenham 86 B4
North Walsham 87 D2
North Waltham 27 G3
North Warnborough 28 C2
North Watten 195 E3
North Weald Bassett 45 D2
North Wheatley 95 E4
North Whilborough 9 E1
North Wick 24 C1
North Widcombe 24 C2
North Willingham 96 B4
North Wingfield 81 F1
North Witham 83 E5
North Wootton *Dorset* 12 C1
North Wootton *Norf.* 85 E5
North Wootton *Som.* 24 C3
North Wraxall 40 A5
North Wroughton 40 D4
North Yardhope 128 B1
Northacre 72 A2
Northall Green 86 B4
Northallerton 110 C3
Northam *Devon* 21 E3
Northam *S'ham.* 14 D1
Northampton 56 C1
Northaw 44 B2
Northay 11 F1
Northborough 69 G2
Northbourne 33 F3
Northbrook 55 G5
Northburnhill 182 D5
Northchapel 29 E5
Northchurch 43 E2
Northcote Manor 21 G4
Northcott 6 D1
Northdyke 198 A4
Northend *B. & N.E.Som.* 25 E1
Northend *Bucks.* 42 C3
Northend *Warks.* 55 F2
Northfield *Aber.* 182 D3
Northfield *Aberdeen* 171 D4
Northfield *High.* 195 F4
Northfield *Sc.Bord.* 145 G3
Northfield *W.Mid.* 66 C5
Northfleet 45 F5
Northhouse 135 F5
Northiam 18 D1
Northill 57 G3
Northington 27 G4
Northlands 84 B2
Northleach 40 D1
Northleigh *Devon* 11 E3
Northleigh *Devon* 21 G2
Northlew 7 F1
Northmoor 41 G2
Northmoor Green or Moorland 24 A4
Northmuir 160 B4
Northney 15 G2
Northolt 44 A4
Northop 77 F1
Northop Hall 77 F1
Northorpe *Lincs.* 84 A4
Northorpe *Lincs.* 95 F3
Northorpe *Lincs.* 69 F1
Northover 24 C5
Northowram 102 A5
Northpunds 200 D5
Northrepps 86 D2
Northton (Taobh Tuath) 184 B5
Northtown 197 D3
Northway 54 B4
Northwich 92 A5
Northwick 39 E4
Northwold 71 F3
Northwood *Gt.Lon.* 43 F3
Northwood *I.o.W.* 15 D3
Northwood *Shrop.* 78 B4
Northwood Green 39 G1
Norton *Glos.* 54 A5
Norton *Halton* 91 G4
Norton *Herts.* 58 A4
Norton *I.o.W.* 14 C4
Norton *N.Yorks.* 111 G5
Norton *Northants.* 56 B1
Norton *Notts.* 94 C5
Norton *Powys* 52 C1
Norton *S.Yorks.* 94 C1
Norton *S.Yorks.* 94 A4
Norton *Shrop.* 65 E2
Norton *Shrop.* 65 G2
Norton *Shrop.* 65 D4
Norton *Stock.* 120 D5
Norton *Suff.* 60 A1
Norton *W.Mid.* 66 A4
Norton *W.Suss.* 16 B3
Norton *W.Suss.* 16 A4
Norton *Wilts.* 40 A4
Norton *Worcs.* 54 A2
Norton *Worcs.* 54 C3
Norton Bavant 26 A3
Norton Bridge 79 F5
Norton Canes 66 C2
Norton Canon 52 C3
Norton Disney 83 D2
Norton Ferris 25 E4
Norton Fitzwarren 23 E5
Norton Green 14 C4
Norton Hawkfield 24 C1
Norton Heath 45 F2
Norton in Hales 79 D4
Norton in the Moors 79 F2
Norton-Juxta-Twycross 67 F2
Norton-le-Clay 110 C5
Norton Lindsey 55 E1
Norton Malreward 24 C1
Norton Mandeville 45 E2
Norton St. Philip 25 E2
Norton sub Hamdon 12 A1
Norton Subcourse 73 F2
Norton Wood 52 C3
Norwell 82 C1
Norwell Woodhouse 82 C1
Norwich 86 D5
Norwich Airport 86 D4
Norwick 203 F1
Norwood Green 44 A5
Norwood Hill 30 B4
Noseley 68 C3
Noss Mayo 8 B3
Nosterfield 110 B4
Nostie 165 E2
Notgrove 54 D5
Nottage 37 E5
Nottingham *High.* 195 E5
Nottingham *Nott.* 81 G3
Notton *W.Yorks.* 94 A1
Notton *Wilts.* 26 A1
Nounsley 45 G2
Noutard's Green 53 G1
Nowton 59 G1
Nox 64 D1
Noyadd Trefawr 49 F3
Nuffield 42 B4
Nun Monkton 103 E2
Nunburnholme 104 A3
Nuneaton 67 F3
Nuneham Courtenay 42 A3
Nunney 25 E3
Nunnington 111 F5
Nunnington Park 23 D5
Nunthorpe 111 E1
Nunton 26 C5
Nunwick *N.Yorks.* 110 C5
Nunwick *Northumb.* 128 A4
Nup End *Bucks.* 43 D1
Nup End *Glos.* 54 A5
Nursling 14 C1
Nursted 28 C5
Nurton 66 A3
Nutbourne *W.Suss.* 16 C2

Nutbourne *W.Suss.* **15** G2
Nutfield **30** C3
Nuthall **81** G3
Nuthampstead **58** C4
Nuthurst *W.Suss.* **29** G5
Nuthurst *Warks.* **67** D5
Nutley *E.Suss.* **17** G1
Nutley *Hants.* **28** B3
Nutwell **94** D2
Nyadd **150** C5
Nybster **195** F2
Nyetimber **16** A4
Nyewood **28** D5
Nymet Rowland **10** A2
Nymet Tracey **10** A2
Nympsfield **40** A2
Nynehead **23** E5
Nythe **24** B4
Nyton **16** B3

## O

Oad Street **32** A2
Oadby **68** B2
Oak Cross **7** F1
Oakamoor **80** B3
Oakbank *Arg. & B.* **147** G1
Oakbank *W.Loth.* **143** E3
Oakdale **38** A3
Oake **23** E5
Oaken **66** A2
Oakenclough **100** B3
Oakengates **65** F1
Oakenhead **181** E3
Oakenshaw *Dur.* **120** B4
Oakenshaw *W.Yorks.* **102** A5
Oakford *Cere.* **50** A2
Oakford *Devon* **22** C5
Oakfordbridge **22** C5
Oakgrove **79** G1
Oakham **69** D2
Oakhanger **28** C4
Oakhill **24** D3
Oakington **58** C1
Oaklands *Conwy* **76** B2
Oaklands *Herts.* **44** B1
Oakle Street **39** G1
Oakley *Beds.* **57** F2
Oakley *Bucks.* **42** B1
Oakley *Fife* **143** E1
Oakley *Hants.* **27** G2
Oakley *Suff.* **72** C4
Oakley Green **43** E5
Oakley Park **63** F4
Oakridge Lynch **40** B2
Oaks **64** D2
Oaksey **40** B3
Oakshaw Ford **126** D4
Oakthorpe **67** F1
Oaktree Hill **110** C3
Oakwoodhill **29** G4
Oakworth **101** G4
Oalinlongart **140** C1
Oare *Kent* **32** C2
Oare *Som.* **22** B3
Oare *Wilts.* **26** C1
Oasby **83** F4
Oatfield **130** B4
Oathlaw **160** C4
Oban **148** A2
Obley **64** C5
Oborne **12** C1
Occlestone Green **79** D1
Occold **72** C4
Occumster **195** E5
Ochiltree **132** D3
Ochr-y-Mynydd **37** G2
Ochtermuthill **150** D3
Ochtertyre *P. & K.* **150** D2
Ochtertyre *Stir.* **150** C5
Ockbrook **81** F4
Ockham **29** F2
Ockle **155** E2
Ockley **29** G4
Ocle Pychard **53** E3
Octon **104** C1
Odcombe **12** B1
Odd Down **25** E1
Oddingley **54** B2
Oddington **42** A1
Oddsta **203** E3
Odell **57** E2
Odie **199** E4
Odiham **28** C2
Odstock **26** C5
Odstone **67** F2
Offchurch **55** F1
Offenham **54** C3
Offerton **92** D4
Offham *E.Suss.* **17** G2
Offham *Kent* **31** F3
Offord Cluny **58** A1
Offord D'Arcy **58** A1
Offton **60** B3
Offwell **11** E3
Ogbourne Maizey **41** D5
Ogbourne St. Andrew **41** D5
Ogbourne St. George **41** D5
Ogden **101** G4
Ogil **160** C3
Ogle **128** D4
Ogmore **37** E5
Ogmore-by-Sea **37** E5
Ogmore Vale **37** F3
Oil Terminal **196** C3
Okeford Fitzpaine **13** E1
Okehampton **7** F1
Okehampton Camp **7** F1
Okraquoy **200** D4
Old **68** C5
Old Aberdeen **171** E4
Old Alresford **27** G4
Old Arley **67** E3
Old Basford **81** G3
Old Basing **28** B2
Old Belses **135** G3
Old Bewick **137** E4
Old Bolingbroke **84** B1
Old Brampton **94** A5
Old Bridge of Urr **124** B4
Old Buckenham **72** B2
Old Burghclere **27** F2
Old Byland **111** E4
Old Cleeve **22** D3
Old Clipstone **82** B1
Old Colwyn **89** G5
Old Craig **171** E2
Old Craighall **144** A2
Old Crombie **182** A4
Old Dailly **122** D1
Old Dalby **82** B5
Old Deer **183** E5
Old Ellerby **105** D4
Old Felixstowe **61** E4
Old Fletton **69** G3
Old Glossop **93** E3
Old Goginan **62** C4
Old Goole **103** G5
Old Gore **53** F5
Old Grimsby **4** A1
Old Hall **96** C1
Old Heath **60** B5
Old Hill **66** B4
Old Hutton **107** G4
Old Kea **4** C5
Old Kilpatrick **141** F2
Old Kinnernie **170** C4
Old Knebworth **58** A5
Old Leake **84** C2
Old Leslie **170** A2
Old Malton **112** G5
Old Micklefield **102** D4
Old Milverton **55** E1
Old Montsale **46** D3
Old Netley **15** D1
Old Newton **60** B1
Old Philpstoun **143** E2
Old Poltalloch **148** A4
Old Radnor **52** B2
Old Rattray **183** F4
Old Rayne **170** B2
Old Romney **19** F1
Old Scone **151** G2
Old Shields **142** C2
Old Sodbury **39** G4
Old Somerby **83** E4
Old Stratford **56** C3
Old Sunderlandwick **104** C2
Old Swarland **129** D1
Old Swinford **66** B4
Old Town *Cumb.* **107** G4
Old Town *I.o.S.* **4** B1
Old Town *Northumb.* **128** A2
Old Tupton **81** E1
Old Warden **57** G3
Old Weston **69** G5
Old Windsor **43** E5
Old Wives Lees **32** C3
Old Woking **29** F2
Old Wolverton **56** D3
Old Woods **78** B5
Oldberrow **54** D1
Oldborough **10** A2
Oldbury *Kent* **31** E3
Oldbury *Shrop.* **65** G3
Oldbury *W.Mid.* **66** B3
Oldbury *Warks.* **67** F3
Oldbury Naite **39** F3
Oldbury-on-Severn **39** F3
Oldbury on the Hill **40** A4
Oldcastle **52** C5
Oldcastle Heath **78** B3
Oldcotes **94** C4
Oldfield *W.Yorks.* **101** G4
Oldfield *Worcs.* **54** A1
Oldford **25** E2
Oldhall *Aber.* **169** G5
Oldhall *High.* **195** E3
Oldham **92** D2
Oldhamstocks **145** E2
Oldhurst **70** A5
Oldland **39** F5
Oldmeldrum **170** D2
Oldmill **170** A4
Oldpark **65** F2
Oldridge **10** B3
Oldshore Beg **192** A3
Oldshore More **192** B3
Oldstead **111** E4
Oldtown of Aigas **179** D5
Oldtown of Ord **182** B4
Oldwalls **36** A3
Oldways End **22** B5
Oldwhat **183** D4
Olgrinmore **194** C3
Oliver **134** C3
Oliver's Battery **27** F5
Ollaberry **202** C4
Ollerton *Ches.* **92** B5
Ollerton *Notts.* **82** B1
Ollerton *Shrop.* **78** D5
Olmstead Green **59** E3
Olney **57** D2
Olrig House **195** D2
Olton **66** D4
Olveston **39** E4
Ombersley **54** A1
Ompton **82** B1
Onchan **98** B4
Onecote **80** B2
Ongar Hill **85** D5
Ongar Street **52** C1
Onibury **64** D5
Onich **156** C3
Onllwyn **37** E1
Onneley **79** E3
Onslow Village **29** E3
Opinan *High.* **188** A5
Opinan *High.* **176** D2
Orange Lane **145** E5
Orbliston **181** F4
Orbost **175** F5
Orby **84** C1
Orcadia **140** C3
Orchard **140** C1
Orchard Portman **23** F5
Orchard Wyndham **23** D4
Orcheston **26** B3
Orcop **53** D5
Orcop Hill **53** D5
Ord **164** C3
Ordhead **170** B3
Ordie **169** G4
Ordiequish **181** F4
Ordsall **95** E5
Ore **18** D2
Oreham Common **17** E2
Oreston **8** B2
Oreton **65** F4
Orford *Suff.* **61** F3
Orford *Warr.* **92** A3
Orgreave **66** D1
Orleton *Here.* **53** D1
Orleton *Worcs.* **53** F1
Orleton Common **53** D1
Orlingbury **69** D5
Ormacleit **162** A1
Ormesby **111** E1
Ormesby St. Margaret **87** F4
Ormesby St. Michael **87** F4
Ormiscaig **188** A5
Ormiston **144** B3
Ormsaigmore **155** D3
Ormsdale **140** B1
Ormskirk **91** F2
Ormwe **194** D2
Orphir **196** C2
Orpington **31** D2
Orrell **91** G2
Orrisdale **98** B2
Orrok House **171** E3
Orroland **116** A2
Orsett **45** F4
Orslow **66** A1
Orston **82** C3
Orton *Cumb.* **108** B2
Orton *Northants.* **68** D5
Orton Longueville **69** G3
Orton-on-the-Hill **67** F2
Orton Waterville **69** G3
Orwell **58** B3
Osbaldeston **100** C4
Osbaldwick **103** F2
Osbaston *Leics.* **67** G2
Osbaston *Tel. & W.* **65** E1
Osborne **15** E3
Osbournby **83** F4
Oscroft **78** C1
Ose **175** G5
Osgathorpe **67** G1
Osgodby *Lincs.* **96** A3
Osgodby *N.Yorks.* **103** F4
Osgodby *N.Yorks.* **113** D4
Oskaig **164** B1
Osmaston *Derby* **81** E4
Osmaston *Derbys.* **80** C3
Osmington **12** D4
Osmington Mills **12** D4
Osmotherley **111** D3
Osnaburgh or Dairsie **152** C3
Osney **42** A2
Ospringe **32** C2
Ossett **102** B5
Ossington **82** C1
Ostend **46** C3
Osterley **44** A5
Oswaldkirk **111** F5
Oswaldtwistle **100** D5
Oswestry **77** F5
Otford **31** E3
Otham **31** G3
Othery **24** A4
Otley *Suff.* **60** D2
Otley *W.Yorks.* **102** B3
Otter **140** A2
Otter Ferry **140** A1
Otterbourne **27** F5
Otterburn *N.Yorks.* **101** E2
Otterburn *Northumb.* **128** A2
Otterburn Camp **128** A2
Otterden Place **32** B3
Otterham **6** B1
Otterhampton **23** F3
Ottershaw **29** F1
Otterswick **203** E4
Otterton **11** D4
Ottery St. Mary **11** D3
Ottinge **33** D4
Ottringham **105** E5
Oughterby **117** F1
Oughtershaw **109** D4
Oughtibridge **94** A3
Oulston **111** E5
Oulton *Cumb.* **117** F1
Oulton *Norf.* **86** C3
Oulton *Staffs.* **79** G4
Oulton *Suff.* **73** G2
Oulton *W.Yorks.* **102** C5
Oulton Broad **73** G2
Oulton Street **86** C3
Oundle **69** F4
Ousby **118** C4
Ousdale **191** F2
Ousden **59** F2
Ousefleet **104** A5
Ouston *Dur.* **120** B2
Ouston *Northumb.* **128** C4
Out Newton **105** F5
Out Rawcliffe **100** A3
Outertown **198** A5
Outgate **107** E3
Outhgill **108** C2
Outlands **79** E5
Outlane **93** E1
Outwell **70** D2
Outwood *Surr.* **30** C4
Outwood *W.Yorks.* **102** C5
Ovenden **101** G5
Over *Cambs.* **58** B1
Over *Ches.* **78** D1
Over *S.Glos.* **39** E4
Over Compton **12** B1
Over End **93** G5
Over Haddon **80** D1
Over Kellet **107** G5
Over Kiddington **55** G5
Over Norton **55** F5
Over Peover **92** B5
Over Rankeilour **152** B3
Over Silton **111** D3
Over Stowey **23** E4
Over Stratton **12** A1
Over Tabley **92** B4
Over Wallop **27** D4
Over Whitacre **67** E3
Over (Upper) Winchendon **42** C1
Over Worton **55** G5
Overbister **199** E2
Overbrae **182** D4
Overbury **54** B4
Overcombe **12** C4
Overleigh **24** B4
Overpool **91** E5
Overscaig Hotel **189** G2
Overseal **67** E1
Oversland **32** C3
Oversley Green **54** C2
Overstone **56** D1
Overstrand **87** D1
Overton *Aber.* **170** C3
Overton *Aberdeen* **171** D3
Overton *Hants.* **27** G3
Overton *Lancs.* **100** A2
Overton *N.Yorks.* **103** E2
Overton *Shrop.* **65** E5
Overton *Swan.* **36** A4
Overton *Wrex.* **78** A3
Overtown **142** C4
Overy Staithe **85** G3
Oving *Bucks.* **56** C5
Oving *W.Suss.* **16** B3
Ovingdean **17** F3
Ovingham **119** G1
Ovington *Dur.* **110** A1
Ovington *Essex* **59** F3
Ovington *Hants.* **27** G4
Ovington *Norf.* **86** A5
Ovington *Northumb.* **119** G1
Ower **14** C1
Owermoigne **13** D4
Owlswick **42** C2
Owmby **96** A2
Owmby-by-Spital **96** A4
Owslebury **27** G5
Owston **68** C2
Owston Ferry **95** F2
Owstwick **105** E4
Owthorpe **82** B4
Oxborough **71** F2
Oxcliffe Hill **100** A1
Oxcombe **96** D5
Oxen End **59** E5
Oxen Park **107** E4
Oxenholme **107** G3
Oxenhope **101** G4
Oxenton **54** B4
Oxenwood **27** E2
Oxford **42** A2
Oxhill **55** F3
Oxley **66** B2
Oxley Green **46** C1
Oxley's Green **18** B1
Oxnam **136** A5
Oxnead **86** D3
Oxnop Ghyll **109** E3
Oxshott **29** G1
Oxspring **93** G2
Oxted **30** C3
Oxton *Mersey.* **91** E4
Oxton *Notts.* **82** B2
Oxton *Sc.Bord.* **144** B4
Oxwich **36** B4
Oxwich Green **36** B4
Oxwick **86** A3
Oykel Bridge **189** F4
Oyne **170** B2
Ozleworth **39** G3

## P

Pabail Iarach **187** G4
Pabail Uarach **187** G4
Packington **67** F1
Padanaram **160** C4
Padbury **56** C4
Paddington **44** B4
Paddlesworth **33** D4
Paddock Wood **31** F4
Paddockhaugh **181** E4
Paddockhole **126** A3
Paddolgreen **78** C4
Padeswood **77** F1
Padiham **101** D4
Padside **102** A2
Padstow **4** D2
Padworth **28** B1
Pagham **16** A4
Paglesham Churchend **46** C3
Paglesham Eastend **46** C3
Paibeil **173** F3
Paible **184** C4
Paignton **9** E1
Pailton **67** G4
Painscastle **52** A3
Painshawfield **119** G1
Painswick **40** A2
Paisley **141** F3
Pakefield **73** G2
Pakenham **60** A1
Pale **76** C4
Palestine **27** D3
Paley Street **43** D5
Palgowan **123** E2
Palgrave **72** C4
Pallinsburn House **136** C3
Palmerscross **181** E3
Palmerstown **23** E1
Palnackie **124** C5
Palnure **123** F4
Palterton **81** F1
Pamber End **28** B2
Pamber Green **28** B2
Pamber Heath **28** B1
Pamington **54** B4
Pamphill **13** F2
Pampisford **58** C3
Pan **196** C3
Panborough **24** B3
Panbride **153** D1
Pancrasweek **20** C5
Pandy *Gwyn.* **62** C2
Pandy *Mon.* **52** C5
Pandy *Powys* **63** F2
Pandy *Wrex.* **77** E4
Pandy Tudur **76** B1
Panfield **59** F5
Pangbourne **42** B5
Pannal **102** C2
Panpunton **64** B5
Pant *Shrop.* **77** F5
Pant *Wrex.* **77** F3
Pant Glas **75** D3
Pant Gwyn **76** B5
Pant-lasau **36** C2
Pant Mawr **63** E4
Pant-pastynog **76** D1
Pant-y-dwr **63** F5
Pant-y-ffridd **64** A2
Pantasaph **90** C5
Pantglas **63** D3
Pantgwyn **49** F3
Panton **96** B5
Pantperthog **62** D2
Pantyffordd **77** F2
Pantyffynnon **36** C1
Panxworth **87** E4
Papcastle **117** E3
Papple **144** C2
Papplewick **81** G2
Papworth Everard **58** A1
Papworth St. Agnes **58** A1
Par **5** E4
Parbold **91** F1
Parbrook **24** C4
Parc **76** B4
Parc-Seymour **38** D3
Parcllyn **49** F2
Parcrhydderch **50** C2
Pardshaw **117** D4
Parham **61** E1
Parish Holm **133** F3
Park **182** A4
Park Corner **42** B4
Park End **128** A4
Park Gate **15** E2
Park Lane **78** B4
Park Street **44** A2
Parkend *Cumb.* **117** F3
Parkend *Glos.* **39** F2
Parkeston **60** D4
Parkford **160** C4
Parkgate *Ches.* **91** D5
Parkgate *D. & G.* **125** E2
Parkgate *S.Yorks.* **94** B3
Parkgate *Surr.* **30** B4
Parkham **21** D3
Parkham Ash **21** D3
Parkhill *Angus* **161** E5
Parkhill *P. & K.* **159** G5
Parkhouse **39** E2
Parkhurst **15** D3
Parkmill **36** B4
Parkmore **181** F5
Parkneuk **161** F2
Parkstone **13** G3
Parley Cross **13** G3
Parracombe **21** G1
Parrog **48** D4
Parson Drove **70** B2
Parsonby **117** E3
Partick **141** G3
Partington **92** B3
Partney **84** C1
Parton *Cumb.* **116** C4
Parton *D. & G.* **124** A3
Partridge Green **17** D2
Parwich **80** C2
Passenham **56** C4
Passfield **28** D4
Passingford Bridge **45** D3
Paston **87** E2
Patcham **17** F3
Patching **16** C3
Patchole **21** G1
Patchway **39** E4
Pateley Bridge **102** A1
Path of Condie **151** F3
Pathe **24** A4
Pathfinder Village **10** B3
Pathhead *Aber.* **161** F3
Pathhead *E.Ayr.* **133** E4
Pathhead *Fife* **152** A5
Pathhead *Midloth.* **144** A3
Patmore Heath **58** C5
Patna **132** C4
Patney **26** B2
Patrick **98** A3
Patrick Brompton **110** B3
Patrington **105** F5
Patrishow **52** B5
Patrixbourne **33** D3
Patterdale **107** G5
Pattingham **66** A3
Pattishall **56** B2
Pattiswick **59** G5
Paul **2** B4
Paulerspury **56** C3
Paull **105** D5
Paulton **24** D2
Pauperhaugh **128** D2
Pavenham **57** E2
Pawlett **23** F3
Pawston **136** C3
Paxford **55** D4
Paxhill Park **17** F1
Paxton **145** G4
Payhembury **11** D2
Paynes Hall **44** C1
Paythorne **101** E2
Peacehaven **17** G3
Peacemarsh **25** F5
Peachley **54** A2
Peak Dale **93** E5
Peak Forest **93** F5
Peakirk **69** G2
Pean Hill **32** D2
Pearsie **160** B4
Pease Pottage **30** B5
Peasedown St. John **25** E2
Peasemore **41** G5
Peasenhall **61** E1
Peaslake **29** F3
Peasmarsh **19** D1
Peaston **144** B3
Peastonbank **144** B3
Peat Inn **152** C4
Peathill **183** E3
Peatling Magna **68** A3
Peatling Parva **68** A4
Peaton **65** E4
Pebble Coombe **30** B3
Pebmarsh **59** G4
Pebworth **54** D3
Pecket Well **101** F5
Peckforton **78** C2
Peckleton **67** G2
Pedmore **66** B4
Pedwell **24** B4
Peebles **143** G5
Peel **98** A3
Pegswood **129** E3
Peighinn nan Aoireann **162** A1
Peinchorran **164** B1
Peinlich **176** A4
Pelaw **120** B1
Pelcomb Bridge **34** C1
Pelcomb Cross **34** C1
Peldon **46** C1
Pelsall **66** C2
Pelton **120** B2
Pelutho **117** E2
Pelynt **5** G4
Pembrey **36** A2
Pembridge **52** C2
Pembroke (Penfro) **34** C2
Pembroke Dock (Doc Penfro) **34** C2
Pembury **31** F4
Pen-bont Rhydybeddau **62** C4
Pen-clawdd **36** B3
Pen-ffordd **49** D5
Pen-groes-oped **38** C2
Pen-llyn **88** B4
Pen-sarn *Gwyn.* **75** E5
Pen-sarn *Gwyn.* **74** D3
Pen-twyn **39** E2
Pen-y-banc **50** C5
Pen-y-bont *Carmar.* **51** D4
Pen-y-bont *Powys* **63** G1
Pen-y-bont *Powys* **77** F5
Pen-y-Bont ar Ogwr (Bridgend) *Bridgend* **37** F5
Pen-y-bryn **62** C1
Pen-y-cae **37** E1
Pen-y-cae-mawr **38** D3
Pen-y-cefn **90** C5
Pen-y-clawdd **39** D2
Pen-y-coedcae **37** G4
Pen-y-fai **37** E4
Pen-y-garn **50** B4
Pen-y-garreg **51** G3
Pen-y-Gwryd Hotel **75** F2
Pen-y-Park **52** B3
Pen-y-sarn **88** C3
Pen-y-stryt **77** E2
Pen-yr-hoel **38** D1
Penallt **39** E1
Penally **35** E3
Penalt **53** E5
Penare **5** D5
Penarth **38** A5
Penboyr **49** G4
Penbryn **49** F2
Pencader **50** A4
Pencaenewydd **74** D3
Pencaitland **144** B3
Pencarreg **50** B3
Pencelli **51** G5
Pencoed **37** F4
Pencombe **53** E2
Pencoyd **53** E5
Pencraig *Here.* **53** E5
Pencraig *Powys* **76** D5
Pendeen **2** A3
Penderyn **37** F2
Pendine **35** F2
Pendlebury **92** B2
Pendleton **101** D4
Pendock **53** G4
Pendoggett **5** E2
Pendomer **12** B1
Pendoylan **37** G5
Penegoes **63** D2
Penfro (Pembroke) **34** C2
Pengam **38** A3
Penge **44** C5
Pengenffordd **52** A4
Pengorffwysfa **88** C3
Pengover Green **5** G3
Pengwern **90** B5
Penhale **3** D5
Penhallow **4** B4
Penhalvean **3** E3
Penhow **38** D3
Penhurst **18** B2
Peniarth **62** C2
Penicuik **143** G3
Penifiler **176** A5
Peninver **130** C3
Penisa'r Waun **75** E1
Penisarcwn **63** G1
Penistone **93** G2
Penjerrick **3** E3
Penketh **91** G4
Penkill **122** D1
Penkridge **66** B1
Penley **78** B4
Penllech **74** B4
Penllergaer **36** C3
Penllyn **37** F5
Penmachno **76** A2
Penmaen **36** B4
Penmaenmawr **89** F5
Penmaenpool **62** C1
Penmark **23** D1
Penmon **89** E4
Penmorfa **75** E3
Penmynydd **88** D5
Penn *Bucks.* **43** E3
Penn *W.Mid.* **66** A3
Penn Street **43** E3
Pennal **62** C2
Pennan **182** D3
Pennance **4** B5
Pennant *Cere.* **50** B1
Pennant *Powys* **63** E3
Pennant Melangell **76** D5
Pennard **36** B4
Pennerley **64** C3
Penninghame **123** E4
Pennington **107** D5
Pennsylvania **39** G5
Penny Bridge **107** E4
Pennyfuir **148** A1
Pennyghael **147** E2
Pennyglen **132** A4
Pennygown **155** F5
Pennymoor **10** B1
Penparc *Cere.* **49** F3
Penparc *Pembs.* **48** B4
Penparcau **62** B4
Penperlleni **38** C2
Penpillick **5** E4
Penpol **3** F3
Penpoll **5** F4
Penpont *D. & G.* **124** C1
Penpont *Powys* **51** F5
Penprysg **37** F4
Penrherber **49** F4
Penrhiw-llan **49** G3
Penrhiw-pal **49** G3
Penrhiwceiber **37** G3
Penrhiwgoch **36** B1
Penrhos *Gwyn.* **74** C4
Penrhos *I.o.A.* **88** A4
Penrhos *Mon.* **38** D1
Penrhos *Powys* **37** E1
Penrhos-garnedd **89** D5
Penrhyn Bay (Bae Penrhyn) **89** G4
Penrhyn-coch **62** C4
Penrhyn-side **89** G4
Penrhyndeudraeth **75** F4
Penrhys **37** G3
Penrice **36** A4
Penrith **118** B4
Penrose **4** C2
Penruddock **118** A5
Penryn **3** E3
Pensarn *Carmar.* **36** A1
Pensarn *Conwy* **90** A5
Pensax **53** G1
Pensby **91** D4
Penselwood **25** E4
Pensford **24** D1
Pensham **54** B3
Penshaw **120** C2
Penshurst **31** E4
Pensilva **5** G3
Pensnett **66** B4
Pentewan **5** E5
Pentir **75** E1
Pentire **4** B3
Pentireglaze **4** D1
Pentlepoir **35** E2
Pentlow **59** G3
Pentney **71** F1
Penton Mewsey **27** E3
Pentraeth **88** D5
Pentre *Powys* **77** D5
Pentre *Powys* **63** G4
Pentre *Powys* **52** B1
Pentre *Powys* **64** B3
Pentre *R.C.T.* **37** F3
Pentre *Shrop.* **64** C1
Pentre *Wrex.* **77** F3
Pentre-bach **51** F4
Pentre Berw **88** C5
Pentre-bont **76** A2
Pentre-bwlch **77** E3
Pentre-celyn *Denb.* **77** E2
Pentre-celyn *Powys* **63** E2
Pentre-chwyth **36** C3
Pentre-cwrt **49** G4
Pentre-Dolau-Honddu **51** F3
Pentre-dwr **36** C3
Pentre Galar **49** E4
Pentre Gwenlais **36** C1
Pentre Gwynfryn **75** E5
Pentre Halkyn **90** D5
Pentre Isaf **76** B
Pentre Llanrhaeadr **77** D
Pentre-Llwyn-Llwyd **51** F
Pentre-llyn-cymmer **76** C
Pentre Maelor **78** A
Pentre-piod **76** B
Pentre-Poeth **38** B
Pentre Saron **76** D
Pentre-tafarn-y-fedw **76** B
Pentre-ty-gwyn **51** E
Pentrebach *M.Tyd.* **37** G
Pentrebach *Swan.* **36** C
Pentrecagal **49** G
Pentreclwydau **37** E
Pentredwr **77** E
Pentrefelin *Carmar.* **50** B
Pentrefelin *Cere.* **50** C
Pentrefelin *Conwy* **89** G
Pentrefelin *Gwyn.* **75** E
Pentrefelin *Powys* **77** E
Pentrefoelas **76** B
Pentregat **49** G
Pentreheyling **64** B
Pentre'r beirdd **64** A
Pentre'r-felin **51** F
Pentrich **81** E
Pentridge **13** G
Pentwyn **38** B
Pentyrch **38** A
Penuwch **50** B
Penwithick **5** E
Penwortham **100** E
Penwyllt **37** E
Penybont **52** A
Penybontfawr **77** D
Penybryn **38** A
Penycae **77** F
Penycwm **48** E

Penyffordd 78 A1
Penygarnedd 77 E5
Penygraig 37 F3
Penygroes *Carmar.* 36 B1
Penygroes *Gwyn.* 75 D2
Penywaun 37 F2
Penzance 2 B3
Penzance Heliport 2 B3
Peopleton 54 B2
Peover Heath 92 B5
Peper Harow 29 E3
Peplow 78 D5
Perceton 141 E5
Percie 170 A5
Perham Down 27 D3
Perivale 44 A4
Perkhill 170 A4
Perkins Beach 64 C2
Perlethorpe 95 D5
Perranarworthal 3 E3
Perranporth 4 B4
Perranuthnoe 2 C4
Perranzabuloe 4 B4
Perry Barr 66 C3
Perry Green 44 D1
Perry Street 45 F5
Pershall 79 F5
Pershore 54 B3
Persie House 159 G4
Pert 161 E3
Pertenhall 57 F1
Perth 151 G2
Perthy 78 A4
Perton 66 A3
Peter Tavy 7 F3
Peterborough 69 G3
Peterburn 176 D1
Peterchurch 52 C4
Peterculter 170 D4
Peterhead 183 G5
Peterlee 120 D3
Peter's Green 44 A1
Peters Marland 21 E4
Petersfield 28 C5
Peterston-super-Ely 37 G5
Peterstone Wentlooge 38 B4
Peterstow 53 E5
Petham 32 D3
Petrockstow 21 F5
Pett 19 D2
Pettaugh 60 C2
Pettinain 143 D5
Pettistree 61 D2
Petton *Devon* 22 D5
Petton *Shrop.* 78 B5
Petty 170 C1
Pettycur 143 G1
Pettymuick 171 E2
Petworth 29 E5
Pevensey 18 B3
Pevensey Bay 18 B3
Pewsey 26 C1
Phesdo 161 E2
Philham 20 C3
Philiphaugh 135 F3
Phillack 2 C3
Philleigh 3 F3
Philpstoun 143 E2
Phoenix Green 28 C2
Phones 167 G5
Phorp 180 C4
Pibsbury 24 B5
Pica 116 D4
Piccadilly Corner 73 D3
Piccotts End 43 F2
Pickerells 45 E2
Pickering 112 B4
Picket Piece 27 E3
Picket Post 14 A2
Pickford Green 67 E4
Pickhill 110 C4
Picklescott 64 D3
Pickletillem 152 C2
Pickmere 92 A5
Pickstock 79 E5
Pickston 151 E2
Pickwell *Devon* 21 E1
Pickwell *Leics.* 68 C1
Pickworth *Lincs.* 83 F4
Pickworth *Rut.* 69 E1
Picton *Ches.* 91 F5
Picton *N.Yorks.* 110 D2
Piddinghoe 17 G3
Piddington *Northants.* 56 D2
Piddington *Oxon.* 42 B1
Piddlehinton 12 D3
Piddletrenthide 12 D3
Pidley 70 B5
Piercebridge 110 B1
Pierowall 198 C2
Pigdon 129 D3
Pikehall 80 C2
Pilgrims Hatch 45 E3
Pilham 95 F3
Pill 39 E5
Pillaton 7 D4
Pillerton Hersey 55 E3
Pillerton Priors 55 E3
Pilleth 52 B1
Pilley *Glos.* 40 B1
Pilley *Hants.* 14 C3
Pilley *S.Yorks.* 94 A2
Pilling 100 A3
Pilling Lane 99 G3
Pillowell 39 F2
Pilning 39 E4
Pilsbury 80 C1
Pilsdon 12 A3
Pilsgate 69 F2
Pilsley *Derbys.* 81 F1
Pilsley *Derbys.* 93 G5
Piltdown 17 G1
Pilton *Devon* 21 F2
Pilton *Northants.* 69 F4
Pilton *Rut.* 69 E2
Pilton *Som.* 24 C3
Pimperne 13 F2
Pinchbeck 84 A5
Pinchbeck Bars 84 A5
Pinchbeck West 84 A5
Pinchinthorpe 111 E1
Pinfold 91 E1
Pinhay 11 G3
Pinhoe 10 C3
Pinkneys Green 43 D4
Pinley Green 55 E1
Pinminnoch 122 C1
Pinmore 122 D1
Pinn 11 E4
Pinner 44 A4
Pinner Green 44 A3
Pinvin 54 B3
Pinwherry 122 C2
Pinxton 81 F2
Pipe and Lyde 53 E3
Pipe Gate 79 E3
Pipe Ridware 66 C1
Piperhall 140 B4
Piperhill 180 A4
Pipers Pool 5 G1
Pipewell 68 D4
Pippacott 21 F2
Pipton 52 A4
Pirbright 29 E2
Pirnmill 139 G5
Pirton *Herts.* 57 G4
Pirton *Worcs.* 54 A3
Pisgah 150 C4
Pishill 42 C4
Pistyll 74 C3
Pitagowan 158 D3
Pitblae 183 E3
Pitcairngreen 151 F2
Pitcairns 151 F3
Pitcaple 170 C2
Pitch Green 42 C2
Pitch Place 29 E2
Pitchcombe 40 A2
Pitchcott 42 C1
Pitchford 65 E2
Pitcombe 25 D4
Pitcot 37 E5
Pitcox 144 D2
Pitcur 152 A1
Pitfichie 170 B3
Pitgrudy 190 C5
Pitinnan 170 C1
Pitkennedy 160 D4
Pitkevy 152 A4
Pitlessie 152 B4
Pitlochry 159 E4
Pitmedden 171 D2
Pitminster 11 F1
Pitmuies 161 D5
Pitmunie 170 B3
Pitnacree 159 E4
Pitney 24 B5
Pitroddie 152 A2
Pitscottie 152 C3
Pitsea 45 G4
Pitsford 56 C1
Pitsford Hill 23 D4
Pitstone 43 E1
Pitstone Green 43 E1
Pitt *Devon* 10 D1
Pitt *Hants.* 27 F5
Pittendreich 181 D3
Pittentrail 190 C4
Pittenweem 152 D4
Pittington 120 C3
Pittodrie House 170 B2
Pitton 26 D4
Pity Me 120 B3
Pityme 4 D2
Pixey Green 72 D4
Place Newton 112 B5
Plaidy 182 C4
Plains 142 B3
Plaish 65 E3
Plaistow 29 F4
Plaitford 14 B1
Plas 50 A5
Plas Gogerddan 62 C4
Plas Gwynant 75 F2
Plas Isaf 77 D3
Plas Llwyd 90 A5
Plas Llwyngwern 63 D2
Plas Llysyn 63 F3
Plas Nantyr 77 E4
Plas-rhiw-Saeson 63 F2
Plas-yn-Cefn 90 B5
Plasisaf 76 C1
Plastow Green 27 G1
Platt 31 F3
Platt Bridge 92 A2
Platt Lane 78 C4
Plawsworth 120 B3
Plaxtol 31 F3
Play Hatch 42 C5
Playden 19 E1
Playford 60 D3
Playing Place 4 C5
Plealey 64 D2
Plean 142 C1
Pleasance 152 A3
Pleasington 100 C5
Pleasley 81 G1
Plenmeller 118 D1
Pleshey 45 F1
Plockton 165 E1
Ploughfield 52 C3
Plowden 64 C4
Ploxgreen 64 C2
Pluckley 32 B4
Pluckley Thorne 32 B4
Plumbland 117 E3
Plumley 92 B5
Plumpton *Cumb.* 118 A4
Plumpton *E.Suss.* 17 F2
Plumpton End 56 C3
Plumpton Green 17 F2
Plumpton Head 118 B4
Plumstead *Gt.Lon.* 44 D5
Plumstead *Norf.* 86 C2
Plumtree 82 B4
Plungar 82 C4
Plush 12 D2
Plwmp 49 G2
Plym Bridge 8 B2
Plymouth 8 A2
Plymouth City Airport 8 B1
Plympton 8 B2
Plymstock 8 B2
Plymtree 10 D2
Pockley 111 F4
Pocklington 104 A3
Pocombe Bridge 10 B3
Pode Hole 84 A5
Podimore 24 C5
Podington 57 E1
Podmore 79 E4
Poffley End 41 F1
Pointon 83 G4
Pokesdown 14 A3
Polanach 156 B4
Polapit Tamar 6 D2
Polbae 123 D3
Polbain 188 B3
Polbathic 7 D5
Polbeth 143 E3
Polchar 168 A4
Poldean 125 F1
Pole Moor 93 E1
Polebrook 69 F4
Polegate 18 A3
Poles 190 C5
Polesworth 67 E2
Polglass 188 C4
Polgooth 5 D4
Polgown 133 F5
Poling 16 C3
Poling Corner 16 C3
Polkerris 5 E4
Poll a' Charra 172 C2
Polla 192 C3
Polldubh 156 D3
Pollie 190 C3
Pollington 94 D1
Polloch 155 G3
Pollokshaws 141 G3
Polmassick 5 D5
Polmont 142 D2
Polnoon 141 G4
Polperro 5 G4
Polruan 5 F4
Polsham 24 C3
Polstead 60 A4
Poltalloch 148 A5
Poltimore 10 C3
Polton 143 G3
Polwarth 145 E4
Polyphant 5 G1
Polzeath 4 D2
Pond Street 58 C4
Ponders End 44 C3
Pondersbridge 70 A3
Ponsanooth 3 E3
Ponsonby 106 B2
Ponsworthy 10 A5
Pont Aber 50 D5
Pont Aberglaslyn 75 E3
Pont Ceri 49 F3
Pont Crugnant 63 E3
Pont Cyfyng 76 A2
Pont Dolgarrog 76 A1
Pont-faen 51 F4
Pont-Henri 36 A2
Pont Nedd Fechan 37 F2
Pont Pen-y-benglog 75 F1
Pont Rhyd-sarn 76 B5
Pont Rhyd-y-cyff 37 E4
Pont-rhyd-y-groes 62 D5
Pont-rug 75 E1
Pont Walby 37 E2
Pont-y-pant 76 A2
Pont yr Alwen 76 C2
Pontamman 36 C1
Pontantwn 36 A1
Pontardawe 36 D2
Pontarddulais 36 B2
Pontarfynach (Devil's Bridge) 62 D5
Pontargothi 50 B5
Pontarsais 50 A5
Pontblyddyn 77 F1
Pontbren Llwyd 37 F2
Pontefract 103 D5
Ponteland 129 D4
Ponterwyd 62 D4
Pontesbury 64 D2
Pontesford 64 D2
Pontfadog 77 F4
Pontfaen 48 D4
Ponthir 38 C3
Ponthirwaun 49 F3
Pontllanfraith 38 A3
Pontlliw 36 C2
Pontllyfni 74 D2
Pontlottyn 38 A2
Pontnewydd 38 B3
Pontnewynydd 38 B2
Pontrhydfendigaid 50 D1
Pontrhydyfen 37 D3
Pontrhydyrun 38 B3
Pontrilas 52 C5
Pontrobert 64 A1
Ponts Green 18 B2
Pontshaen 50 A3
Pontshill 53 F5
Pontsticill 37 G1
Pontwelly 50 A4
Pontyates 36 A2
Pontyberem 36 B1
Pontybodkin 77 F2
Pontyclun 37 G4
Pontycymer 37 F3
Pontygwaith 37 G3
Pontymister 38 B4
Pontypool 38 B2
Pontypridd 37 G4
Pontywaun 38 B3
Pooksgreen 14 C1
Pool *Cornw.* 4 A5
Pool *W.Yorks.* 102 B3
Pool Bank 107 F4
Pool of Muckhart 151 F4
Pool Quay 64 B1
Pool Street 59 F4
Poole 13 G3
Poole Keynes 40 B3
Poolewe 177 E1
Pooley Bridge 118 A5
Poolhill 53 G5
Pope Hill 34 C1
Popeswood 28 D1
Popham 27 G3
Poplar 44 C4
Porchfield 14 D3
Porin 178 C4
Poringland 87 D5
Porkellis 3 D3
Porlock 22 B3
Porlock Weir 22 B3
Port Allen 152 A2
Port Appin 156 B5
Port Askaig 138 C3
Port Bannatyne 140 B3
Port Carlisle 126 A5
Port Charlotte 138 A4
Port Clarence 121 E5
Port Driseach 140 A2
Port e Vullen 98 C2
Port Ellen 138 B5
Port Elphinstone 170 C3
Port Erin 98 A5
Port Erroll 171 F1
Port Eynon 36 A4
Port Gaverne 5 E1
Port Glasgow 141 E2
Port Henderson 177 D2
Port Isaac 5 D1
Port Logan 114 A2
Port Mòr 154 D2
Port Mulgrave 111 G1
Port-na-Con 192 D2
Port na Craig 159 E4
Port nan Giùran (Portnaguran) 187 G4
Port nan Long 173 G2
Port Nis 187 G1
Port o' Warren 124 C5
Port of Menteith 150 A4
Port Penrhyn 89 D5
Port Quin 5 D1
Port Ramsay 156 A5
Port St. Mary 98 A5
Port Solent 15 F2
Port Sunlight 91 E4
Port Talbot 36 D4
Port Wemyss 138 A4
Port William 114 D2
Portachoillan 139 F4
Portavadie 140 A3
Portbury 39 D5
Portchester 15 F2
Portencross 140 C5
Portesham 12 C4
Portessie 181 G3
Portfield 147 G2
Portfield Gate 34 C1
Portgate 7 E2
Portgordon 181 F3
Portgower 191 F3
Porth *Cornw.* 4 C3
Porth *R.C.T.* 37 G3
Porth Colmon 74 A4
Porth Mellin 3 D5
Porth Navas 3 E4
Porth-y-waen 77 F5
Porthaethwy (Menai Bridge) 89 D5
Porthallow *Cornw.* 3 E4
Porthallow *Cornw.* 5 G4
Porthcawl 37 E5
Porthcothan 4 C2
Porthcurno 2 A4
Porthgain 48 B4
Porthkerry 23 D1
Porthleven 2 D4
Porthmadog 75 E4
Porthmeor 2 B3
Portholland 5 D5
Porthoustock 3 F4
Porthpean 5 E4
Porthtowan 4 A5
Porthyrhyd *Carmar.* 50 D4
Porthyrhyd *Carmar.* 36 B1
Portincaple 149 E5
Portington 103 G4
Portinnisherrich 148 B3
Portinscale 117 F4
Portishead 39 D5
Portknockie 181 G3
Portlethen 171 E5
Portlethen Village 171 E5
Portloe 3 G3
Portmahomack 180 B1
Portmeirion 75 E4
Portmore 14 C3
Portnacroish 156 B5
Portnaguran (Port nan Giùran) 187 G4
Portnahaven 138 A4
Portnalong 163 G1
Portnaluchaig 155 F1
Portobello 144 A2
Porton 26 C4
Portpatrick 122 B5
Portreath 4 A5
Portree 176 A5
Portscatho 3 F3
Portsea 15 F2
Portskerra 194 A2
Portskewett 39 E4
Portslade 17 E3
Portslade-by-Sea 17 E3
Portslogan 122 A5
Portsmouth 15 F3
Portsonachan 148 C2
Portsoy 182 A3
Portswood 14 D1
Portuairk 154 D3
Portway *Here.* 52 C3
Portway *Worcs.* 66 C5
Portwrinkle 7 D5
Portyerrock 115 E3
Poslingford 59 F3
Postbridge 7 G3
Postcombe 42 C3
Postling 32 D5
Postwick 87 D5
Potarch 170 B5
Potsgrove 57 E5
Pott Row 85 F5
Pott Shrigley 92 D5
Potten End 43 F2
Potter Heigham 87 F3
Potter Street 45 D2
Potterhanworth 83 F1
Potterhanworth Booths 83 F1
Potterne 26 A2
Potterne Wick 26 A2
Potters Bar 44 B2
Potter's Cross 66 A4
Potters Crouch 44 A2
Potterspury 56 C3
Potterton 171 E3
Potto 111 D2
Potton 58 A3
Poughill *Cornw.* 20 C5
Poughill *Devon* 10 B2
Poulner 14 A2
Poulshot 26 A2
Poulton 40 D2
Poulton-le-Fylde 99 G4
Pound Bank 65 G5
Pound Green 18 A1
Pound Hill 30 B5
Poundffald 36 B3
Poundgate 17 G1
Poundland 122 C2
Poundon 56 B5
Poundsbridge 31 E4
Poundsgate 10 A5
Poundstock 6 C1
Povey Cross 30 B4
Pow Green 53 G3
Powburn 137 E5
Powderham 10 C4
Powerstock 12 B3
Powfoot 125 F4
Powick 54 A2
Powler's Piece 21 D4
Powmill 151 F5
Poxwell 12 D4
Poyle 43 F5
Poynings 17 E2
Poyntington 24 D5
Poynton *Ches.* 92 D4
Poynton *Tel. & W.* 65 E1
Poynton Green 65 E1
Poyntzfield 179 G3
Poys Street 73 E4
Poyston Cross 34 C1
Poystreet Green 60 A2
Praa Sands 2 C4
Pratis 152 B4
Pratt's Bottom 31 D2
Praze-an-Beeble 2 D3
Predannack Wollas 3 D5
Prees 78 C4
Prees Green 78 C4
Prees Higher Heath 78 C4
Preesall 99 G3
Preesgweene 77 F4
Pren-gwyn 50 A3
Prenbrigog 77 F1
Prendergast 34 C1
Prendwick 137 E5
Prenteg 75 E3
Prenton 91 E4
Prescot 91 F3
Prescott 78 B5
Presley 180 C4
Pressen 136 C3
Prestatyn 90 B4
Prestbury *Ches.* 92 C5
Prestbury *Glos.* 54 B5
Presteigne 52 C1
Presthope 65 E3
Prestleigh 24 D3
Prestolee 92 B2
Preston *B. & H.* 17 F3
Preston *Devon* 10 B5
Preston *Dorset* 12 D4
Preston *E.Loth.* 144 C2
Preston *E.Riding* 105 D4
Preston *Glos.* 53 F4
Preston *Glos.* 40 C2
Preston *Herts.* 57 G5
Preston *Kent* 32 C2
Preston *Kent* 33 E2
Preston *Lancs.* 100 B5
Preston *Northumb.* 137 F4
Preston *Rut.* 69 D2
Preston *Sc.Bord.* 145 E4
Preston *Suff.* 60 A2
Preston *T. & W.* 120 C1
Preston *Wilts.* 40 C5
Preston Bagot 55 D1
Preston Bissett 56 B5
Preston Brockhurst 78 C5
Preston Brook 91 G4
Preston Candover 28 B3
Preston Capes 56 A2
Preston Deanery 56 C2
Preston Gubbals 65 D1
Preston on Stour 55 E2
Preston on the Hill 91 G4
Preston on Wye 52 C3
Preston Plucknett 12 B1
Preston-under-Scar 109 F3
Preston upon the Weald Moors 65 F1
Preston Wynne 53 E3
Prestonpans 144 A2
Prestwich 92 C2
Prestwick *Northumb.* 129 D4
Prestwick *S.Ayr.* 132 B3
Prestwick International Airport 132 B3
Prestwold 81 G5
Prestwood 43 D2
Price Town 37 F3
Prickwillow 71 D4
Priddy 24 C2
Priest Hill 100 C4
Priest Hutton 107 G5
Priestland 133 D2
Priestweston 64 B3
Primethorpe 68 A3
Primrose Green 86 B4
Princes End 66 B3
Princes Gate 35 E1
Princes Risborough 42 D2
Princethorpe 67 G5
Princetown *Caerp.* 38 A1
Princetown *Devon* 7 F3
Prior Muir 152 D3
Prior's Frome 53 E4
Priors Hardwick 55 G2
Priors Marston 55 G2
Priory Wood 52 B3
Priston 25 D1
Prittlewell 46 B4
Privett 28 B5
Prixford 21 F2
Proaig 138 C4
Probus 4 C5
Protstonhill 182 D3
Prudhoe 120 A1
Pubil 157 G5
Publow 24 D1
Puckeridge 58 B5
Puckington 11 G1
Pucklechurch 39 F5
Puddinglake 79 E1
Puddington *Ches.* 91 E5
Puddington *Devon* 10 B1
Puddlebrook 39 F1
Puddledock 72 B2
Puddletown 13 D3
Pudleston 53 E2
Pudsey 102 B4
Pulborough 16 C2
Puldagon 195 F4
Puleston 79 E5
Pulford 78 A2
Pulham 12 D2
Pulham Market 72 C3
Pulham St. Mary 72 D3
Pulloxhill 57 F4
Pulrossie 179 G1
Pulverbatch 64 D2
Pumpherston 143 E3
Pumsaint 50 C3
Puncheston 48 D5
Puncknowle 12 B4
Punnett's Town 18 B1
Purbrook 15 F2
Purfleet 45 E5
Puriton 24 A3
Purleigh 46 B2
Purley 30 C2
Purley on Thames 42 B5
Purlogue 64 B5
Purls Bridge 70 C4
Purse Caundle 12 C1
Purslow 64 C4
Purston Jaglin 94 B1
Purton *Glos.* 39 F2
Purton *Wilts.* 40 C4
Purton Stoke 40 C3
Purves Hall 145 E5
Pury End 56 C3
Pusey 41 F3
Putley 53 F4
Putloe 39 G2
Putney 44 B5
Putsborough 21 E1
*Devon*
Puttenham *Herts.* 43 D1
Puttenham *Surr.* 29 E3
Puttock End 59 G3
Putts Corner 11 E3
Puxton 24 B1
Pwll 36 A2
Pwll Trap 35 F1
Pwll-y-glaw 37 D3
Pwllcrochan 34 C2
Pwlldefaid 74 A5
Pwllgloyw 51 G4
Pwllheli 74 C4
Pwllmeyric 39 E3
Pye Corner *Herts.* 45 D1
Pye Corner *Newport* 38 C4
Pye Green 66 B1
Pyecombe 17 E2
Pyle *Bridgend* 37 E4
Pyle *I.o.W.* 15 D5
Pylle 24 D4
Pymore 70 C4
Pyrford 29 F2
Pyrton 42 B3
Pytchley 69 D5
Pyworthy 20 D5

**Q**

Quabbs 64 B4
Quadring 84 A4
Quadring Eaudike 84 A4
Quainton 42 C1
Quarley 27 D3
Quarmby 93 F1
Quarndon 81 E3
Quarr Hill 15 E3
Quarrier's Village 141 E3
Quarrington 83 F3
Quarrington Hill 120 C4
Quarry Bank 66 B4
Quarrybank 78 C1
Quarrywood 181 D3
Quarter 142 B4
Quatford 65 G3
Quatt 65 G4
Quebec 120 A3
Quedgeley 40 A1
Queen Adelaide 71 D4
Queen Camel 24 C5
Queen Charlton 24 D1
Queen Street 31 F4
Queenborough 32 B1
Queen's Head 78 A5
Queensbury 102 A4
Queensferry 78 A1
Queenzieburn 142 A2
Quemerford 40 C5
Quendale 201 F4
Quendon 58 D4
Queniborough 68 B1
Quenington 40 D2
Quernmore 100 B1
Queslett 66 C3
Quethiock 6 D4
Quholm 198 A5
Quidenham 72 B3
Quidhampton *Hants.* 27 G2
Quidhampton *Wilts.* 26 C4
Quilquox 171 E1
Quina Brook 78 C4
Quindry 196 D3
Quine's Hill 98 B4
Quinhill 139 F4
Quinton *Northants.* 56 C2
Quinton *W.Mid.* 66 B4
Quintrell Downs 4 C3
Quoditch 7 E1
Quoig 150 D2
Quoiggs House 150 D4
Quorn 68 A1
Quothquan 134 A2
Quoyloo 198 A4
Quoys 203 F1
Quoys of Reiss 195 F3

**R**

Raby 91 E5
Rachan 134 C2
Rachub 75 F1
Rackenford 10 B1
Rackham 16 C2
Rackheath 87 D4
Racks 125 E3
Rackwick *Ork.* 196 B3
Rackwick *Ork.* 198 C1
Radbourne 81 D4
Radcliffe *Gt.Man.* 92 B2
Radcliffe *Northumb.* 129 E1
Radcliffe on Trent 82 B4
Radclive 56 B4
Radcot 41 E3
Radford *Oxon.* 55 G5
Radford *W.Mid.* 67 F4
Radford Semele 55 F1
Radipole 12 C4
Radlett 44 A2
Radley 42 A3
Radstock 25 D2
Radstone 56 A3
Radway 55 F3
Radway Green 79 E2
Radwell *Beds.* 57 F2
Radwell *Herts.* 58 A4
Radwinter 59 E4
Radyr 38 A4
Raechester 128 B3
Raemoir House 170 B5
Raffin 188 C1
Rafford 180 C4
Ragdale 68 B1
Raglan 38 D2
Ragnall 95 F5
Rahoy 155 F4
Rainford 91 F2
Rainham *Gt.Lon.* 45 E4
Rainham *Med.* 32 A2
Rainhill 91 F3
Rainhill Stoops 91 G3
Rainow 93 D5
Rainton 110 C5
Rainworth 81 G2
Raisbeck 108 B2
Raise 118 D3
Rait 152 A2
Raithby *Lincs.* 84 B1
Raithby *Lincs.* 96 D4
Rake 28 D5
Raleigh's Cross 22 D4
Ram 50 B3
Ram Lane 32 B4
Ramasaig 175 E5
Rame *Cornw.* 3 E3
Rame *Cornw.* 8 A3
Rampisham 12 B2
Rampside 99 F1
Rampton *Cambs.* 58 C1
Rampton *Notts.* 95 F5
Ramsbottom 92 B1
Ramsbury 41 E5
Ramscraigs 191 G2
Ramsdean 28 C5
Ramsdell 27 G2
Ramsden 41 F1
Ramsden Bellhouse 45 G3
Ramsden Heath 45 G3
Ramsey *Cambs.* 70 A4
Ramsey *Essex* 60 D5
Ramsey *I.o.M.* 98 C2
Ramsey Forty Foot 70 B4
Ramsey Heights 70 A4
Ramsey Island 46 C2
Ramsey Mereside 70 A4
Ramsey St. Mary's 70 A4
Ramsgate 33 F2
Ramsgate Street 86 B2
Ramsgill 110 A5
Ramsholt 61 E3
Ramshorn 80 B3
Ramsnest Common 29 E4
Ranachan 155 G3
Ranby *Lincs.* 96 C5
Ranby *Notts.* 95 D4
Rand 96 B5
Randwick 40 A2
Rangemore 80 C5
Rangeworthy 39 F4
Rankinston 132 C4
Rank's Green 45 G1
Rannoch School 158 A4
Ranochan 156 A1
Ranskill 95 D4
Ranton 79 F5
Ranworth 87 E4
Rapness 198 D2
Rascarrel 116 B2
Raskelf 111 D5
Rassau 38 A1
Rastrick 102 A5
Ratby 68 A2
Ratcliffe Culey 67 F3
Ratcliffe on Soar 81 F5
Ratcliffe on the Wreake 68 B1
Ratford Bridge 34 C1
Rathen 183 F3
Rathillet 152 B2
Rathliesbeag 157 E1
Rathmell 101 E1

| | | |
|---|---|---|
| Ratho | 143 | F2 |
| Ratho Station | 143 | F2 |
| Rathven | 181 | G3 |
| Ratley | 55 | F3 |
| Ratlinghope | 64 | D3 |
| Rattar | 195 | E1 |
| Ratten Row | 100 | A3 |
| Rattery | 8 | D1 |
| Rattlesden | 60 | A2 |
| Rattray | 159 | G5 |
| Raughton Head | 117 | G2 |
| Raunds | 69 | F5 |
| Ravenfield | 94 | B3 |
| Ravenglass | 106 | B3 |
| Raveningham | 73 | E2 |
| Ravenscar | 112 | C2 |
| Ravensdale | 98 | B2 |
| Ravensden | 57 | F2 |
| Ravenshaw | 101 | F3 |
| Ravenshayes | 10 | C2 |
| Ravenshead | 81 | G2 |
| Ravensmoor | 78 | D2 |
| Ravensthorpe *Northants.* | 68 | B5 |
| Ravensthorpe *W.Yorks.* | 93 | G1 |
| Ravenstone *Leics.* | 67 | G1 |
| Ravenstone *M.K.* | 57 | D3 |
| Ravenstonedale | 108 | C2 |
| Ravenstruther | 142 | D5 |
| Ravensworth | 110 | A2 |
| Raw | 112 | C2 |
| Rawcliffe *E.Riding* | 103 | F5 |
| Rawcliffe *York* | 103 | E2 |
| Rawcliffe Bridge | 103 | F5 |
| Rawdon | 102 | B4 |
| Rawmarsh | 94 | B3 |
| Rawreth | 45 | G3 |
| Rawridge | 11 | E2 |
| Rawtenstall | 101 | E5 |
| Rawyards | 142 | B3 |
| Raxton | 171 | D1 |
| Raydon | 60 | B4 |
| Raylees | 128 | B2 |
| Rayleigh | 46 | B3 |
| Raymond's Hill | 11 | G3 |
| Rayne | 59 | F5 |
| Reach | 59 | D1 |
| Read | 101 | D4 |
| Reading | 42 | C5 |
| Reading Street | 32 | B5 |
| Reagill | 108 | B1 |
| Rearquhar | 190 | C5 |
| Rearsby | 68 | B1 |
| Rease Heath | 78 | D2 |
| Reaster | 195 | E2 |
| Reaveley | 137 | E5 |
| Reawick | 200 | C3 |
| Reay | 194 | B2 |
| Reculver | 33 | E2 |
| Red Dial | 117 | F2 |
| Red Hill *Hants.* | 15 | G1 |
| Red Hill *Warks.* | 54 | D2 |
| Red Lodge | 71 | E5 |
| Red Oaks Hill | 59 | D4 |
| Red Post *Cornw.* | 20 | C5 |
| Red Post *Devon* | 9 | E1 |
| Red Rock | 91 | G1 |
| Red Roses | 35 | F1 |
| Red Row | 129 | E2 |
| Red Street | 79 | F2 |
| Red Wharf Bay | 88 | D4 |
| Redberth | 35 | D2 |
| Redbourn | 44 | A1 |
| Redbourne | 95 | G2 |
| Redbridge | 44 | D4 |
| Redbrook | 39 | E2 |
| Redbrook Street | 32 | B5 |
| Redburn *High.* | 179 | E3 |
| Redburn *High.* | 180 | B5 |
| Redcar | 121 | F5 |
| Redcastle *Angus* | 161 | E4 |
| Redcastle *High.* | 179 | E5 |
| Redcliff Bay | 38 | D5 |
| Redcloak | 161 | G1 |
| Reddish | 92 | C3 |
| Redditch | 54 | C1 |
| Rede | 59 | G2 |
| Redenhall | 73 | D3 |
| Redesmouth | 128 | A3 |
| Redford *Aber.* | 161 | F3 |
| Redford *Angus* | 161 | D5 |
| Redford *Dur.* | 119 | G4 |
| Redford *W.Suss.* | 29 | D5 |
| Redgrave | 72 | B4 |
| Redheugh | 160 | C3 |
| Redhill *Aber.* | 170 | B1 |
| Redhill *Aber.* | 170 | C4 |
| Redhill *Moray* | 182 | A5 |
| Redhill *N.Som.* | 24 | B1 |
| Redhill *Notts.* | 81 | G3 |
| Redhill *Surr.* | 30 | B3 |
| Redhill *Tel. & W.* | 65 | G1 |
| Redhill Aerodrome & Heliport | 30 | B4 |
| Redhouse *Aber.* | 170 | A2 |
| Redhouse *Arg. & B.* | 139 | G3 |
| Redhouses | 138 | B3 |
| Redisham | 73 | F3 |
| Redland *Bristol* | 39 | E5 |
| Redland *Ork.* | 198 | B4 |
| Redlingfield | 72 | C4 |
| Redlynch *Som.* | 25 | D4 |
| Redlynch *Wilts.* | 26 | D5 |
| Redmarley D'Abitot | 53 | G4 |
| Redmarshall | 120 | C5 |
| Redmile | 82 | D4 |
| Redmire | 109 | F3 |
| Redmoor | 5 | E3 |
| Rednal *Shrop.* | 78 | A5 |
| Rednal *W.Mid.* | 66 | C5 |
| Redpath | 135 | G2 |
| Redpoint | 176 | D3 |
| Redruth | 4 | A5 |
| Redscarhead | 143 | G5 |
| Redshaw | 133 | G3 |
| Redstone Bank | 35 | E1 |
| Redwick *Newport* | 38 | D4 |
| Redwick *S.Glos.* | 39 | E4 |
| Redworth | 120 | B5 |
| Reed | 58 | B4 |
| Reedham | 87 | F5 |
| Reedness | 103 | G5 |
| Reepham *Lincs.* | 96 | A5 |
| Reepham *Norf.* | 86 | C3 |
| Reeth | 109 | F3 |
| Regaby | 98 | C2 |
| Regil | 24 | C1 |
| Regoul | 180 | A4 |
| Reiff | 188 | B3 |
| Reigate | 30 | B3 |
| Reighton | 113 | E5 |
| Reinigeadal | 185 | E3 |
| Reisgill | 195 | E5 |
| Reiss | 195 | F3 |
| Rejerrah | 4 | B4 |
| Relubbus | 2 | C3 |
| Relugas | 180 | B5 |
| Remenham | 42 | C4 |
| Remenham Hill | 42 | C4 |
| Remony | 158 | C5 |
| Rempstone | 81 | G5 |
| Rendcomb | 40 | C1 |
| Rendham | 61 | E1 |
| Rendlesham | 61 | E2 |
| Renfrew | 141 | G3 |
| Renhold | 57 | F2 |
| Renishaw | 94 | B5 |
| Rennington | 137 | G5 |
| Renton | 141 | E2 |
| Renwick | 118 | B3 |
| Repps | 87 | F4 |
| Repton | 81 | E5 |
| Rescobie | 160 | D4 |
| Resipole | 155 | G3 |
| Resolis | 179 | F3 |
| Resolven | 37 | E2 |
| Resourie | 156 | A2 |
| Reston | 145 | F3 |
| Reswallie | 160 | D4 |
| Retew | 4 | D4 |
| Retford | 95 | E4 |
| Rettendon | 45 | G3 |
| Rettendon Place | 45 | G3 |
| Retyn | 4 | C4 |
| Revesby | 84 | A1 |
| Rew | 10 | A5 |
| Rewe | 10 | C3 |
| Reydon | 73 | F4 |
| Reymerston | 86 | B5 |
| Reynalton | 35 | D2 |
| Reynoldston | 36 | A4 |
| Rezare | 7 | D3 |
| Rhandirmwyn | 51 | D3 |
| Rhaoine | 190 | B4 |
| Rhayader | 51 | F1 |
| Rhedyn | 74 | B4 |
| Rhegreanoch | 188 | C3 |
| Rheindown | 179 | E5 |
| Rhelonie | 190 | A5 |
| Rhemore | 155 | E4 |
| Rhes-y-cae | 77 | E1 |
| Rhewl *Denb.* | 77 | E3 |
| Rhewl *Denb.* | 77 | E1 |
| Rhewl *Shrop.* | 78 | A4 |
| Rhian | 190 | A3 |
| Rhicarn | 188 | C2 |
| Rhiconich | 192 | B3 |
| Rhicullen | 179 | F2 |
| Rhidorroch | 189 | D5 |
| Rhifail | 193 | G4 |
| Rhigos | 37 | F2 |
| Rhilochan | 190 | C4 |
| Rhinduie | 179 | E5 |
| Rhireavach | 188 | C5 |
| Rhiroy | 178 | A1 |
| Rhiw | 74 | B5 |
| Rhiwargor | 76 | C5 |
| Rhiwbryfdir | 75 | F3 |
| Rhiwderin | 38 | B4 |
| Rhiwlas *Gwyn.* | 75 | E1 |
| Rhiwlas *Gwyn.* | 76 | C4 |
| Rhiwlas *Powys* | 77 | F4 |
| Rhodes Minnis | 32 | D4 |
| Rhodesia | 94 | C5 |
| Rhodiad-y-Brenin | 48 | A5 |
| Rhodmad | 62 | B5 |
| Rhonadale | 130 | C2 |
| Rhonehouse or Kelton Hill | 124 | B5 |
| Rhoose | 23 | D1 |
| Rhos *Carmar.* | 49 | G4 |
| Rhos *N.P.T.* | 36 | D2 |
| Rhos-berse | 77 | F2 |
| Rhos-ddu | 78 | A2 |
| Rhos-fawr | 74 | C4 |
| Rhos-goch | 88 | C4 |
| Rhos-hill | 49 | E3 |
| Rhôs-on-Sea | 89 | G4 |
| Rhos-y-bol | 88 | C4 |
| Rhos-y-brwyner | 77 | F1 |
| Rhos-y-garth | 62 | C5 |
| Rhos-y-gwaliau | 76 | C4 |
| Rhos-y-llan | 74 | B4 |
| Rhos-y-mawn | 76 | B1 |
| Rhos-y-Meirch | 52 | B1 |
| Rhoscolyn | 88 | A5 |
| Rhoscrowther | 34 | C2 |
| Rhosesmor | 77 | F1 |
| Rhosgadfan | 75 | E2 |
| Rhosgoch | 52 | A3 |
| Rhoshirwaun | 74 | A5 |
| Rhoslan | 75 | D3 |
| Rhoslefain | 62 | B2 |
| Rhosllanerchrugog | 77 | F3 |
| Rhosmaen | 50 | C5 |
| Rhosmeirch | 88 | C5 |
| Rhosneigr | 88 | B5 |
| Rhosnesni | 78 | A2 |
| Rhossili | 36 | A4 |
| Rhosson | 48 | A5 |
| Rhostryfan | 75 | D2 |
| Rhostyllen | 78 | A3 |
| Rhu | 141 | D1 |
| Rhuallt | 90 | B5 |
| Rhubodach | 140 | B2 |
| Rhuddlan | 90 | B5 |
| Rhue | 188 | C5 |
| Rhulen | 52 | A3 |
| Rhumach | 155 | F1 |
| Rhunahaorine | 139 | F5 |
| Rhuthun (Ruthin) | 77 | E2 |
| Rhyd *Gwyn.* | 75 | F3 |
| Rhyd *Powys* | 63 | F2 |
| Rhyd-Ddu | 75 | E2 |
| Rhyd-rosser | 50 | B1 |
| Rhyd-uchaf | 76 | C4 |
| Rhyd-wen | 76 | C5 |
| Rhyd-wyn | 88 | B4 |
| Rhyd-y-clafdy | 74 | C4 |
| Rhyd-y-foel | 90 | A5 |
| Rhyd-y-fro | 36 | D2 |
| Rhyd-y-meirch | 38 | C2 |
| Rhyd-yr-onnen | 62 | C2 |
| Rhydaman (Ammanford) | 36 | C1 |
| Rhydargaeau | 50 | A5 |
| Rhydcymerau | 50 | B4 |
| Rhydd | 54 | A3 |
| Rhydding | 37 | D3 |
| Rhydlanfair | 76 | B2 |
| Rhydlewis | 49 | G3 |
| Rhydlios | 74 | A4 |
| Rhydlydan *Conwy* | 76 | B2 |
| Rhydlydan *Powys* | 63 | G3 |
| Rhydolion | 74 | B5 |
| Rhydowen | 50 | A3 |
| Rhydspence | 52 | B3 |
| Rhydtalog | 77 | F2 |
| Rhydycroesau | 77 | F4 |
| Rhydyfelin *Cere.* | 62 | B5 |
| Rhydyfelin *R.C.T.* | 37 | G4 |
| Rhydymain | 76 | A5 |
| Rhydymwyn | 77 | F1 |
| Rhydywrach | 35 | E1 |
| Rhyl | 90 | B4 |
| Rhymney | 38 | A2 |
| Rhyn | 78 | A4 |
| Rhynd | 151 | G2 |
| Rhynie *Aber.* | 169 | G2 |
| Rhynie *High.* | 180 | A2 |
| Ribbesford | 65 | G5 |
| Ribbleton | 100 | B4 |
| Ribchester | 100 | C4 |
| Ribigill | 193 | E3 |
| Riby | 96 | B2 |
| Riccall | 103 | F4 |
| Riccarton | 132 | C2 |
| Richard's Castle | 53 | D1 |
| Richings Park | 43 | F5 |
| Richmond | 110 | A2 |
| Richmond upon Thames | 44 | A5 |
| Rickarton | 161 | G1 |
| Rickford | 24 | B2 |
| Rickinghall | 72 | B4 |
| Rickling | 58 | C4 |
| Rickling Green | 58 | D5 |
| Rickmansworth | 43 | F3 |
| Riddell | 135 | G3 |
| Riddings | 81 | F2 |
| Riddlecombe | 21 | G4 |
| Riddlesden | 101 | G3 |
| Ridge *Dorset* | 13 | F4 |
| Ridge *Herts.* | 44 | B2 |
| Ridge *Wilts.* | 26 | A4 |
| Ridge Green | 30 | C4 |
| Ridge Lane | 67 | E3 |
| Ridgebourne | 51 | G1 |
| Ridgeway | 94 | B4 |
| Ridgeway Cross | 53 | G3 |
| Ridgewell | 59 | F3 |
| Ridgewood | 17 | G1 |
| Ridgmont | 57 | E4 |
| Riding Mill | 119 | G1 |
| Ridley | 31 | F2 |
| Ridleywood | 78 | A2 |
| Ridlington *Norf.* | 87 | E2 |
| Ridlington *Rut.* | 69 | D2 |
| Ridsdale | 128 | B3 |
| Riechip | 159 | F5 |
| Rievaulx | 111 | E4 |
| Rigg *D. & G.* | 126 | A5 |
| Rigg *High.* | 176 | B4 |
| Riggend | 142 | B3 |
| Rigmaden Park | 108 | B4 |
| Rigsby | 97 | E5 |
| Rigside | 133 | G2 |
| Rileyhill | 66 | D1 |
| Rilla Mill | 5 | G2 |
| Rillington | 112 | B5 |
| Rimington | 101 | E3 |
| Rimpton | 24 | D5 |
| Rimswell | 105 | F5 |
| Rinaston | 48 | C5 |
| Ringford | 124 | A5 |
| Ringland | 86 | C4 |
| Ringles Cross | 17 | G1 |
| Ringmer | 17 | G2 |
| Ringmore | 8 | C3 |
| Ringorm | 181 | E5 |
| Ring's End | 70 | B2 |
| Ringsfield | 73 | F3 |
| Ringsfield Corner | 73 | F3 |
| Ringshall *Herts.* | 43 | E1 |
| Ringshall *Suff.* | 60 | B2 |
| Ringshall Stocks | 60 | B2 |
| Ringstead *Norf.* | 85 | F3 |
| Ringstead *Northants.* | 69 | E5 |
| Ringwood | 14 | A2 |
| Ringwould | 33 | F4 |
| Rinloan | 169 | E4 |
| Rinmore | 169 | G3 |
| Rinnigill | 196 | C3 |
| Rinsey | 2 | C4 |
| Ripe | 18 | A3 |
| Ripley *Derbys.* | 81 | F2 |
| Ripley *Hants.* | 14 | A3 |
| Ripley *N.Yorks.* | 102 | B1 |
| Ripley *Surr.* | 29 | F2 |
| Riplingham | 104 | B4 |
| Ripon | 110 | C5 |
| Rippingale | 83 | G5 |
| Ripple *Kent* | 33 | F3 |
| Ripple *Worcs.* | 54 | A4 |
| Ripponden | 93 | E1 |
| Risabus | 138 | B5 |
| Risbury | 53 | E2 |
| Risby | 59 | F1 |
| Risca | 38 | B3 |
| Rise | 105 | D3 |
| Risegate | 84 | A4 |
| Riseley *Beds.* | 57 | F1 |
| Riseley *W'ham* | 28 | C1 |
| Rishangles | 60 | C1 |
| Rishton | 100 | D4 |
| Rishworth | 93 | E1 |
| Risley *Derbys.* | 81 | F4 |
| Risley *Warr.* | 92 | A3 |
| Risplith | 102 | B1 |
| Rispond | 192 | D2 |
| Rivar | 27 | E1 |
| Rivenhall | 46 | B1 |
| Rivenhall End | 46 | B1 |
| River | 29 | E5 |
| River Bank | 58 | D1 |
| River Bridge | 24 | A3 |
| Riverford Bridge | 9 | D1 |
| Riverhead | 31 | E3 |
| Rivington | 92 | A1 |
| Roa Island | 99 | F1 |
| Roade | 56 | C2 |
| Roadhead | 126 | D4 |
| Roadside *High.* | 195 | D2 |
| Roadside *Ork.* | 199 | E2 |
| Roadside of Kinneff | 161 | G2 |
| Roadwater | 22 | D4 |
| Roag | 175 | F5 |
| Roath | 38 | B5 |
| Roberton *S.Lan.* | 134 | A3 |
| Roberton *Sc.Bord.* | 135 | F4 |
| Robertsbridge | 18 | C1 |
| Robertstown | 181 | E5 |
| Roberttown | 102 | A5 |
| Robeston Cross | 34 | B2 |
| Robeston Wathen | 35 | D1 |
| Robin Hood *Derbys.* | 93 | G5 |
| Robin Hood *W.Yorks.* | 102 | C5 |
| Robin Hood's Bay | 112 | C2 |
| Robins | 28 | D5 |
| Roborough *Devon* | 21 | F4 |
| Roborough *Plym.* | 8 | B1 |
| Roby | 91 | F3 |
| Roby Mill | 91 | G2 |
| Rocester | 80 | C4 |
| Roch | 48 | B5 |
| Rochallie | 159 | G4 |
| Rochdale | 92 | C1 |
| Roche | 5 | D3 |
| Rochester *Med.* | 31 | G2 |
| Rochester *Northumb.* | 128 | A2 |
| Rochford *Essex* | 46 | B3 |
| Rochford *Worcs.* | 53 | F1 |
| Rock *Caerp.* | 38 | A3 |
| Rock *Cornw.* | 4 | D2 |
| Rock *Northumb.* | 137 | G4 |
| Rock *Worcs.* | 65 | G5 |
| Rock Ferry | 91 | E4 |
| Rockbeare | 10 | D3 |
| Rockbourne | 14 | A1 |
| Rockcliffe *Cumb.* | 126 | B5 |
| Rockcliffe *D. & G.* | 124 | C5 |
| Rockfield *Arg. & B.* | 139 | G4 |
| Rockfield *High.* | 180 | B1 |
| Rockfield *Mon.* | 39 | D1 |
| Rockhampton | 39 | F3 |
| Rockhead | 5 | E1 |
| Rockingham | 69 | D3 |
| Rockland All Saints | 72 | A2 |
| Rockland St. Mary | 87 | E5 |
| Rockland St. Peter | 72 | A2 |
| Rockley | 41 | D5 |
| Rockside | 138 | A3 |
| Rockwell End | 42 | C4 |
| Rockwell Green | 11 | E1 |
| Rodborough | 40 | A2 |
| Rodbourne | 40 | B4 |
| Rodbridge Corner | 59 | G3 |
| Rodd | 52 | C1 |
| Roddam | 137 | E4 |
| Rodden | 12 | C4 |
| Rode | 25 | F2 |
| Rode Heath | 79 | F2 |
| Rodeheath | 79 | F1 |
| Rodel (Roghadal) | 184 | C5 |
| Roden | 65 | E1 |
| Rodhuish | 22 | D4 |
| Rodington | 65 | E1 |
| Rodley | 39 | G1 |
| Rodmarton | 40 | B3 |
| Rodmell | 17 | G3 |
| Rodmersham | 32 | B2 |
| Rodney Stoke | 24 | B2 |
| Rodsley | 80 | D3 |
| Rodway | 23 | F3 |
| Roe Green | 58 | B4 |
| Roecliffe | 102 | C1 |
| Roehampton | 44 | B5 |
| Roesound | 200 | C1 |
| Roffey | 29 | G4 |
| Rogart | 190 | C4 |
| Rogate | 28 | D5 |
| Rogerstone | 38 | B4 |
| Roghadal (Rodel) | 184 | C5 |
| Rogiet | 39 | D4 |
| Roker | 120 | D2 |
| Rollesby | 87 | F4 |
| Rolleston *Leics.* | 68 | C2 |
| Rolleston *Notts.* | 82 | C2 |
| Rolleston *Staffs.* | 80 | D5 |
| Rollestone | 26 | B3 |
| Rolston | 105 | E3 |
| Rolvenden | 32 | A5 |
| Rolvenden Layne | 32 | A5 |
| Romaldkirk | 119 | F5 |
| Romanby | 110 | C3 |
| Romannobridge | 143 | F5 |
| Romansleigh | 22 | A5 |
| Romford *Dorset* | 13 | G2 |
| Romford *Gt.Lon.* | 45 | E4 |
| Romiley | 92 | D3 |
| Romney Street | 31 | E2 |
| Romsey | 27 | E5 |
| Romsley *Shrop.* | 65 | G4 |
| Romsley *Worcs.* | 66 | B4 |
| Ronachan | 139 | F4 |
| Ronague | 98 | A4 |
| Ronnachmore | 138 | B4 |
| Rookhope | 119 | F3 |
| Rookley | 15 | E4 |
| Rooks Bridge | 24 | A2 |
| Rookwith | 110 | B4 |
| Roos | 105 | E4 |
| Roosecote | 99 | F1 |
| Rootpark | 143 | D4 |
| Ropley | 28 | B4 |
| Ropley Dean | 28 | B4 |
| Ropley Soke | 28 | B4 |
| Ropsley | 83 | E4 |
| Rora | 183 | F4 |
| Rorandle | 170 | B3 |
| Rorrington | 64 | B2 |
| Rosarie | 181 | F4 |
| Rose | 4 | B4 |
| Rose Ash | 22 | A5 |
| Rose Green | 59 | G5 |
| Roseacre | 100 | A4 |
| Rosebank | 142 | C5 |
| Rosebrough | 137 | F4 |
| Rosebush | 49 | D5 |
| Rosedale Abbey | 111 | G3 |
| Roseden | 137 | E4 |
| Rosehall | 189 | G4 |
| Rosehearty | 183 | E3 |
| Rosehill *Aber.* | 170 | A5 |
| Rosehill *Shrop.* | 79 | D4 |
| Roseisle | 180 | D3 |
| Rosemarket | 34 | C2 |
| Rosemarkie | 179 | G4 |
| Rosemary Lane | 11 | E1 |
| Rosemount *P. & K.* | 159 | G5 |
| Rosemount *S.Ayr.* | 132 | B3 |
| Rosepool | 34 | B1 |
| Rosewarne | 2 | D3 |
| Rosewell | 143 | G3 |
| Roseworthy | 2 | D3 |
| Rosgill | 107 | G1 |
| Roshven | 155 | G2 |
| Roskhill | 175 | F5 |
| Rosley | 117 | G2 |
| Roslin | 143 | G3 |
| Rosliston | 67 | E1 |
| Rosneath | 141 | D1 |
| Ross *D. & G.* | 115 | G2 |
| Ross *Northumb.* | 137 | F3 |
| Ross *P. & K.* | 150 | C2 |
| Ross-on-Wye | 53 | F5 |
| Ross Priory | 141 | F1 |
| Rossdhu House | 141 | E1 |
| Rossett | 78 | A2 |
| Rossie Farm School | 161 | E4 |
| Rossie Ochill | 151 | F3 |
| Rossie Priory | 152 | A1 |
| Rossington | 94 | D3 |
| Rosskeen | 179 | F3 |
| Roster | 195 | E5 |
| Rostherne | 92 | B4 |
| Rosthwaite *Cumb.* | 117 | F5 |
| Rosthwaite *Cumb.* | 106 | D4 |
| Roston | 80 | C3 |
| Rosyth | 143 | F1 |
| Rothbury | 128 | C1 |
| Rotherby | 68 | B1 |
| Rotherfield | 18 | A1 |
| Rotherfield Greys | 42 | C4 |
| Rotherfield Peppard | 42 | C4 |
| Rotherham | 94 | B3 |
| Rothersthorpe | 56 | C2 |
| Rotherwick | 28 | C2 |
| Rothes | 181 | E5 |
| Rothesay | 140 | B3 |
| Rothiebrisbane | 170 | C1 |
| Rothienorman | 170 | C1 |
| Rothiesholm | 199 | E4 |
| Rothley *Leics.* | 68 | A1 |
| Rothley *Northumb.* | 128 | C3 |
| Rothwell *Lincs.* | 96 | B3 |
| Rothwell *Northants.* | 68 | D4 |
| Rothwell *W.Yorks.* | 102 | C5 |
| Rotsea | 104 | C2 |
| Rottal | 160 | B3 |
| Rottingdean | 17 | F3 |
| Rottington | 116 | C5 |
| Roud | 15 | E4 |
| Roudham | 72 | A3 |
| Rough Close | 79 | G4 |
| Rough Common | 32 | D3 |
| Rougham *Norf.* | 85 | G5 |
| Rougham *Suff.* | 60 | A1 |
| Rougham Green | 60 | A1 |
| Roughburn | 157 | F1 |
| Roughlee | 101 | E3 |
| Roughley | 66 | D3 |
| Roughton *Lincs.* | 84 | A1 |
| Roughton *Norf.* | 86 | D2 |
| Roughton *Shrop.* | 65 | G3 |
| Roundhay | 102 | C4 |
| Roundstreet Common | 29 | F5 |
| Roundway | 26 | B1 |
| Rous Lench | 54 | C2 |
| Rousdon | 11 | F3 |
| Rousham | 55 | G5 |
| Rousham Gap | 55 | G5 |
| Routenburn | 140 | D3 |
| Routh | 104 | C3 |
| Row *Cornw.* | 5 | E2 |
| Row *Cumb.* | 107 | F4 |
| Row *Cumb.* | 118 | C4 |
| Row Heath | 47 | E1 |
| Row Town | 29 | F1 |
| Rowanburn | 126 | C4 |
| Rowardennan Lodge | 149 | F5 |
| Rowberrow | 24 | B2 |
| Rowchoish | 149 | F4 |
| Rowde | 26 | A1 |
| Rowen | 89 | F5 |
| Rowfoot | 118 | C1 |
| Rowhedge | 60 | B5 |
| Rowhook | 29 | G4 |
| Rowington | 55 | E1 |
| Rowington Green | 67 | E5 |
| Rowland | 93 | G5 |
| Rowland's Castle | 15 | G1 |
| Rowlands Gill | 120 | A2 |
| Rowledge | 28 | D3 |
| Rowley *Devon* | 10 | A1 |
| Rowley *Dur.* | 119 | G3 |
| Rowley *E.Riding* | 104 | B4 |
| Rowley *Shrop.* | 64 | C2 |
| Rowley Regis | 66 | B4 |
| Rowlstone | 52 | C5 |
| Rowly | 29 | F3 |
| Rowner | 15 | E2 |
| Rowney Green | 66 | C5 |
| Rownhams | 14 | C1 |
| Rowrah | 117 | D5 |
| Rowsham | 43 | D1 |
| Rowsley | 81 | D1 |
| Rowstock | 41 | G4 |
| Rowston | 83 | F2 |
| Rowthorne | 81 | F1 |
| Rowton *Ches.* | 78 | B1 |
| Rowton *Shrop.* | 64 | C1 |
| Rowton *Tel. & W.* | 65 | F1 |
| Roxburgh | 136 | A3 |
| Roxby *N.Lincs.* | 95 | G1 |
| Roxby *N.Yorks.* | 111 | G1 |
| Roxton | 57 | G2 |
| Roxwell | 45 | F2 |
| Royal British Legion Village | 31 | G3 |
| Royal Leamington Spa | 55 | F1 |
| Royal Tunbridge Wells | 31 | E5 |
| Roybridge | 157 | E1 |
| Roydon *Essex* | 44 | D1 |
| Roydon *Norf.* | 72 | B3 |
| Roydon *Norf.* | 85 | F5 |
| Roydon Hamlet | 44 | D2 |
| Royston *Herts.* | 58 | B3 |
| Royston *S.Yorks.* | 94 | A1 |
| Royton | 92 | D2 |
| Ruabon | 78 | A3 |
| Ruaig | 154 | B2 |
| Ruan Lanihorne | 4 | C5 |
| Ruan Major | 3 | D5 |
| Ruan Minor | 3 | E5 |
| Ruanaich | 146 | B2 |
| Ruardean | 39 | F1 |
| Ruardean Woodside | 39 | F1 |
| Rubery | 66 | B5 |
| Ruckcroft | 118 | B3 |
| Ruckinge | 32 | C5 |
| Ruckland | 96 | D5 |
| Ruckley | 65 | E2 |
| Rudbaxton | 48 | C5 |
| Rudby | 111 | D2 |
| Rudchester | 120 | A1 |
| Ruddington | 81 | G4 |
| Ruddlemoor | 5 | E4 |
| Rudford | 53 | G5 |
| Rudge | 25 | F2 |
| Rudgeway | 39 | F4 |
| Rudgwick | 29 | F4 |
| Rudhall | 53 | F5 |
| Rudheath | 92 | A5 |
| Rudley Green | 46 | B2 |
| Rudry | 38 | A4 |
| Rudston | 104 | C1 |
| Rudyard | 79 | G2 |
| Rufford | 91 | F1 |
| Rufforth | 103 | E2 |
| Ruffside | 119 | F2 |
| Rugby | 68 | A5 |
| Rugeley | 66 | C1 |
| Ruilick | 179 | E5 |
| Ruishton | 23 | F5 |
| Ruisigearraidh | 184 | B5 |
| Ruislip | 43 | F4 |
| Rumbling Bridge | 151 | F5 |
| Rumburgh | 73 | E3 |
| Rumford | 4 | C2 |
| Rumney | 38 | B5 |
| Rumwell | 23 | E5 |
| Runacraig | 150 | A3 |
| Runcorn | 91 | G4 |
| Runcton | 16 | A3 |
| Runcton Holme | 71 | E2 |
| Rundlestone | 7 | F3 |
| Runfold | 29 | D3 |
| Runhall | 86 | B5 |
| Runham | 87 | F4 |
| Runnington | 23 | E5 |
| Runsell Green | 45 | G2 |
| Runswick | 112 | B1 |
| Runtaleave | 160 | A3 |
| Runwell | 45 | G3 |
| Ruscombe | 42 | C5 |
| Rush Green | 45 | E4 |
| Rushall *Here.* | 53 | F4 |
| Rushall *Norf.* | 72 | C3 |
| Rushall *W.Mid.* | 66 | C2 |
| Rushall *Wilts.* | 26 | C2 |
| Rushbrooke | 59 | G1 |
| Rushbury | 65 | E3 |
| Rushden *Herts.* | 58 | B4 |
| Rushden *Northants.* | 57 | E1 |
| Rushford | 72 | A3 |
| Rushlake Green | 18 | B2 |
| Rushmere | 73 | F3 |
| Rushmere St. Andrew | 60 | C3 |
| Rushmoor *Surr.* | 29 | D3 |
| Rushmoor *Tel. & W.* | 65 | F1 |
| Rushock | 66 | A5 |
| Rusholme | 92 | C3 |
| Rushton *Ches.* | 78 | C1 |
| Rushton *Northants.* | 68 | D4 |
| Rushton *Shrop.* | 65 | F2 |
| Rushton Spencer | 79 | G1 |
| Rushwick | 54 | A2 |
| Rushyford | 120 | B5 |
| Ruskie | 150 | B4 |
| Ruskington | 83 | F2 |
| Rusko | 123 | G5 |
| Rusland | 107 | E4 |
| Rusper | 30 | B5 |
| Ruspidge | 39 | F1 |
| Russel | 177 | E5 |
| Russell's Water | 42 | C4 |
| Rusthall | 31 | E4 |
| Rustington | 16 | C3 |
| Ruston | 112 | C4 |
| Ruston Parva | 104 | C1 |
| Ruswarp | 112 | B2 |
| Rutherend | 142 | A4 |
| Rutherford | 136 | A4 |
| Rutherglen | 142 | A3 |
| Ruthernbridge | 5 | E3 |
| Ruthin (Rhuthun) | 77 | E2 |
| Ruthrieston | 171 | E4 |
| Ruthven *Aber.* | 182 | A5 |
| Ruthven *Angus* | 160 | A5 |
| Ruthven *High.* | 168 | A1 |
| Ruthven *High.* | 167 | G5 |
| Ruthvoes | 4 | D3 |
| Ruthwaite | 117 | F3 |
| Ruthwell | 125 | F4 |
| Ruyton-XI-Towns | 78 | A5 |
| Ryal | 128 | C4 |
| Ryal Fold | 100 | C5 |
| Ryall | 12 | A3 |
| Ryarsh | 31 | F3 |
| Rydal | 107 | E2 |
| Ryde | 15 | E3 |
| Rydon | 20 | D5 |
| Rye | 19 | E1 |
| Rye Foreign | 19 | D1 |
| Rye Harbour | 19 | E2 |
| Rye Park | 44 | C2 |
| Ryhall | 69 | F1 |
| Ryhill | 94 | A1 |
| Ryhope | 120 | D2 |
| Ryland | 96 | A4 |
| Rylstone | 101 | F2 |
| Ryme Intrinseca | 12 | B1 |
| Ryther | 103 | E4 |
| Ryton *Glos.* | 53 | G4 |
| Ryton *N.Yorks.* | 111 | G5 |
| Ryton *Shrop.* | 65 | G2 |
| Ryton *T. & W.* | 120 | A1 |
| Ryton-on-Dunsmore | 67 | F5 |
| **S** | | |
| Sabden | 101 | D4 |
| Sackers Green | 60 | A4 |
| Sacombe | 44 | C1 |
| Sacriston | 120 | B3 |
| Sadberge | 110 | C1 |
| Saddell | 130 | C2 |
| Saddington | 68 | B3 |
| Saddle Bow | 71 | E1 |
| Sadgill | 107 | F2 |
| Saffron Walden | 58 | D4 |
| Sageston | 35 | D2 |
| Saham Toney | 71 | G2 |
| Saighdinis | 173 | G3 |
| Saighton | 78 | B1 |
| St. Abbs | 145 | G3 |
| St. Agnes | 4 | B4 |
| St. Albans | 44 | A2 |
| St. Allen | 4 | C4 |
| St. Andrews | 152 | D3 |
| St. Andrews Major | 38 | A5 |
| St. Anne | 9 | G4 |
| St. Anne's | 99 | G5 |
| St. Ann's | 125 | E1 |
| St. Ann's Chapel *Cornw.* | 7 | E3 |
| St. Ann's Chapel *Devon* | 8 | C3 |
| St. Anthony *Cornw.* | 3 | E4 |
| St. Anthony *Cornw.* | 3 | F3 |
| St. Arvans | 39 | E3 |
| St. Asaph (Llanelwy) | 90 | B5 |
| St. Athan | 22 | D1 |
| St. Aubin | 8 | C5 |
| St. Audries | 23 | E3 |
| St. Austell | 5 | E4 |
| St. Bees | 116 | C5 |
| St. Blazey | 5 | E4 |
| St. Blazey Gate | 5 | E4 |
| St. Boswells | 135 | G2 |
| St. Brelade | 8 | B5 |
| St. Breock | 5 | D2 |
| St. Breward | 5 | E2 |
| St. Briavels | 39 | E2 |
| St. Brides | 34 | B1 |
| St. Brides Major | 37 | E5 |
| St. Brides Netherwent | 38 | D4 |
| St. Bride's-super-Ely | 37 | G5 |
| St. Brides Wentlooge | 38 | B4 |
| St. Budeaux | 8 | A2 |
| St. Buryan | 2 | B4 |
| St. Catherine | 39 | G |
| St. Catherines | 148 | D |
| St. Clears | 35 | F |
| St. Cleer | 5 | G |
| St. Clement | 4 | C |
| St. Clether | 5 | G |
| St. Columb Major | 4 | D |
| St. Columb Minor | 4 | C |
| St. Columb Road | 4 | D |
| St. Combs | 183 | F |
| St. Cross South Elmham | 73 | D |
| St. Cyrus | 161 | F |
| St. Davids *Fife* | 143 | F |
| St. David's *P. & K.* | 151 | E |
| St. David's (Tyddewi) *Pembs.* | 48 | A |
| St. Day | 4 | B |
| St. Decumans | 23 | D |
| St. Dennis | 5 | D |
| St. Dogmaels | 49 | E |
| St. Dogwells | 48 | C |
| St. Dominick | 8 | A |
| St. Donats | 22 | C |
| St. Edith's Marsh | 26 | A |
| St. Endellion | 5 | D |
| St. Enoder | 4 | C |
| St. Erme | 4 | C |
| St. Erth | 2 | C |
| St. Erth Praze | 2 | C |
| St. Ervan | 4 | C |
| St. Eval | 4 | C |
| St. Ewe | 5 | D |
| St. Fagans | 38 | A |
| St. Fergus | 183 | G |
| St. Fillans | 150 | B |
| St. Florence | 35 | D |
| St. Gennys | 6 | E |
| St. George | 90 | A |
| St. Georges *N.Som.* | 24 | A |

St. George's *V. of Glam.* 37 G5
St. Germans 7 D5
St. Giles in the Wood 21 F4
St. Giles on the Heath 7 D1
St. Harmon 63 F5
St. Helen Auckland 120 A5
St. Helena 86 C3
St. Helen's *E.Suss.* 18 D2
St. Helens *I.o.W.* 15 F4
St. Helens *Mersey.* 91 G3
St. Helier 8 C5
St. Hilary *Cornw.* 2 C3
St. Hilary *V. of Glam.* 37 G5
St. Hill 30 C5
St. Illtyd 38 B2
St. Ippollitts 58 A5
St. Ishmael 35 G2
St. Ishmael's 34 B2
St. Issey 4 D2
St. Ive 6 D4
St. Ives *Cambs.* 70 B5
St. Ives *Cornw.* 2 C2
St. Ives *Dorset* 14 A2
St. James South Elmham 73 E3
St. John *Chan.I.* 8 C4
St. John *Cornw.* 8 A2
St. John's *I.o.M.* 98 A3
St. John's *Surr.* 29 E2
St. John's *Worcs.* 54 A2
St. John's Chapel *Devon* 21 F3
St. John's Chapel *Dur.* 119 E4
St. John's Fen End 70 D1
St. Johns Hall 119 G4
St. John's Highway 70 D1
St. John's Kirk 134 A2
St. John's Town of Dalry 124 A2
St. Judes 98 B2
St. Just 2 A3
St. Just in Roseland 3 F3
St. Katherines 170 C1
St. Keverne 3 E4
St. Kew 5 E2
St. Kew Highway 5 E2
St. Keyne 5 G3
St. Lawrence *Cornw.* 5 E3
St. Lawrence *Essex* 46 C2
St. Lawrence *I.o.W.* 15 E5
St. Leonards *Bucks.* 43 E2
St. Leonards *Dorset* 14 A2
St. Leonards *E.Suss.* 18 D3
St. Leonards Grange 14 D3
St. Leonard's Street 31 F3
St. Levan 2 A4
St. Lythans 38 A5
St. Mabyn 5 E2
St. Margaret South Elmham 73 E3
St. Margarets *Here.* 52 C4
St. Margarets *Herts.* 44 C1
St. Margaret's at Cliffe 33 F4
St. Margaret's Hope 196 D3
St. Mark's 98 B4
St. Martin *Chan.I.* 9 F5
St. Martin *Chan.I.* 8 C5
St. Martin *Cornw.* 5 G4
St. Martin *Cornw.* 3 E4
St. Martins *P. & K.* 151 G1
St. Martin's *Shrop.* 78 A4
St. Mary Bourne 27 F2
St. Mary Church 37 G5
St. Mary Cray 31 D2
St. Mary Hill 37 F5
St. Mary in the Marsh 19 F1
St. Marychurch 9 F1
St. Mary's 197 D2
St. Mary's Airport 4 B1
St. Mary's Bay 19 F1
St. Mary's Croft 122 B4
St. Mary's Grove 24 B1
St. Mary's Hoo 45 G5
St. Mawes 3 F3
St. Mawgan 4 C3
St. Mellion 7 D4
St. Mellons 38 B4
St. Merryn 4 C2
St. Mewan 5 D4
St. Michael Caerhays 5 D5
St. Michael Penkevil 4 C5
St. Michael South Elmham 73 E3
St. Michaels *Kent* 32 A5
St. Michaels *Worcs.* 53 E1
St. Michael's on Wyre 100 A3
St. Minver 5 D2
St. Monans 152 D4
St. Neot 5 F3
St. Neots 57 G2
St. Nicholas *Pembs.* 48 C4
St. Nicholas *V. of Glam.* 37 G5
St. Nicholas at Wade 33 E2
St. Ninians 150 C5
St. Osyth 47 E1
St. Ouen 8 B5
St. Owen's Cross 53 E5
St. Paul's Cray 31 D2
St. Paul's Walden 57 G5
St. Peter 8 B5
St. Peter Port 9 F5
St. Peter's 33 F2
St. Petrox 34 C3
St. Pinnock 5 G3
St. Quivox 132 B3
St. Sampson 9 F4
St. Saviour 9 E5
St. Stephen 4 D4
St. Stephens *Cornw.* 8 A2
St. Stephens *Cornw.* 6 D2
St. Stephens *Herts.* 44 A2
St. Teath 5 E1
St. Tudy 5 E2
St. Twynnells 34 C3
St. Veep 5 F4
St. Vigeans 161 E5
St. Wenn 5 D3
St. Weonards 53 D5
Saintbury 54 D3
Salachail 156 C4
Salcombe 8 D4
Salcombe Regis 11 E4
Salcott 46 C1
Sale 92 B3
Sale Green 54 B2
Saleby 97 E5
Salehurst 18 C1
Salem *Carmar.* 50 C5
Salem *Cere.* 62 C4
Salem *Gwyn.* 75 E2
Salen *Arg. & B.* 155 E5
Salen *High.* 155 F3
Salesbury 100 C4
Salford *Beds.* 57 E4
Salford *Gt.Man.* 92 C3
Salford *Oxon.* 55 E5
Salford Priors 54 C2
Salfords 30 B4
Salhouse 87 E4
Saline 151 F5
Salisbury 26 C4
Salkeld Dykes 118 B4
Sall 86 C3
Sallachan 156 B3
Sallachry 148 C3
Sallachy *High.* 190 A4
Sallachy *High.* 165 F1
Salmonby 96 D5
Salmond's Muir 153 D1
Salperton 54 C5
Salph End 57 F2
Salsburgh 142 C3
Salt 79 G5
Salt Hill 43 E5
Saltash 8 A2
Saltburn 179 G2
Saltburn-by-the-Sea 121 F5
Saltby 83 D5
Saltcoats 140 D5
Saltcotes 99 G5
Saltdean 17 F3
Salterforth 101 E3
Saltergate 112 B3
Salterhill 181 E3
Salterswall 78 D1
Saltfleet 97 E3
Saltfleetby All Saints 97 E3
Saltfleetby St. Clements 97 E3
Saltfleetby St. Peter 97 E4
Saltford 25 D1
Salthaugh Grange 105 E5
Salthouse 86 B1
Saltley 66 C4
Saltmarshe 103 G5
Saltney 78 A1
Salton 111 G4
Saltwick 129 D3
Saltwood 33 D5
Salvington 16 D3
Salwarpe 54 A1
Salwayash 12 A3
Sambourne 54 C1
Sambrook 79 E5
Samhla 173 F3
Samlesbury 100 B4
Samlesbury Bottoms 100 C5
Sampford Arundel 11 E1
Sampford Brett 23 D3
Sampford Courtenay 21 G5
Sampford Peverell 10 D1
Sampford Spiney 7 F3
Samuelston 144 B2
Sanaigmore 138 A3
Sancreed 2 B4
Sancton 104 B4
Sand 200 C3
Sand Hole 104 A4
Sand Hutton 103 F2
Sand Side 106 D4
Sandaig *Arg. & B.* 154 A2
Sandaig *High.* 164 D4
Sandaig *High.* 165 D3
Sandbach 79 E1
Sandbank 140 C1
Sandbanks 13 G4
Sandend 182 A3
Sanderstead 30 C2
Sandford *Cumb.* 108 C1
Sandford *Devon* 10 B2
Sandford *Dorset* 13 F2
Sandford *I.o.W.* 15 E4
Sandford *N.Som.* 24 B2
Sandford *S.Lan.* 142 B5
Sandford-on-Thames 42 A2
Sandford Orcas 24 D5
Sandford St. Martin 55 G5
Sandfordhill 183 G5
Sandgarth 198 D5
Sandgate 33 E5
Sandgreen 123 G5
Sandhaven 183 E3
Sandhead 122 B5
Sandhills *Dorset* 12 C1
Sandhills *Surr.* 29 E4
Sandhoe 119 F1
Sandholme *E.Riding* 104 A4
Sandholme *Lincs.* 84 B4
Sandhurst *Brack.F.* 28 D1
Sandhurst *Glos.* 54 A5
Sandhurst *Kent* 18 C1
Sandhutton 110 C4
Sandiacre 81 F4
Sandilands 97 F4
Sandiway 92 A5
Sandleheath 14 A1
Sandleigh 41 G2
Sandling 31 G3
Sandness 200 A2
Sandon *Essex* 45 G2
Sandon *Herts.* 58 B4
Sandon *Staffs.* 79 G5
Sandown 15 E4
Sandplace 5 G4
Sandquoy 199 F2
Sandridge *Herts.* 44 A1
Sandridge *Wilts.* 26 A1
Sandringham 85 E5
Sandrocks 17 F1
Sandsend 112 B1
Sandside House 194 B2
Sandsound 200 C3
Sandtoft 95 E2
Sanduck 10 A4
Sandway 32 A3
Sandwich 33 F3
Sandwick *Cumb.* 107 F1
Sandwick *Shet.* 200 D5
Sandwick (Sanndabhaig) *W.Isles* 187 F4
Sandwith 116 C5
Sandy 57 G3
Sandy Haven 34 B2
Sandy Lane *W.Yorks.* 102 A4
Sandy Lane *Wilts.* 26 A1
Sandycroft 78 A1
Sandygate *Devon* 10 B5
Sandygate *I.o.M.* 98 B2
Sandylands 100 A1
Sandyway 53 D5
Sangobeg 192 D2
Sanna 155 D3
Sannaig 138 D3
Sanndabhaig (Sandwick) 187 F4
Sanquhar 133 F5
Santon Bridge 106 C2
Santon Downham 71 G4
Sapcote 67 G3
Sapey Common 53 G1
Sapiston 72 A4
Sapperton *Glos.* 40 B2
Sapperton *Lincs.* 83 F4
Saracen's Head 84 B5
Sarclet 195 F4
Sardis 34 C2
Sarisbury 15 E2
Sarn *Bridgend* 37 F4
Sarn *Powys* 64 B3
Sarn Bach 74 C5
Sarn Meyllteyrn 74 B4
Sarnau *Carmar.* 35 G1
Sarnau *Cere.* 49 G2
Sarnau *Gwyn.* 76 C4
Sarnau *Powys* 64 B1
Sarnesfield 52 C2
Saron *Carmar.* 36 C1
Saron *Carmar.* 49 G4
Saron *Gwyn.* 75 E1
Sarratt 43 F3
Sarre 33 E2
Sarsden 55 E5
Sarsgrum 192 C2
Sartfield 98 B2
Satley 120 A3
Satterleigh 21 G3
Satterthwaite 107 E3
Sauchen 170 B3
Saucher 151 G1
Sauchie 151 D5
Sauchieburn 161 E3
Sauchrie 132 B4
Saughall 78 A1
Saughall Massie 90 D4
Saughtree 127 D2
Saul 39 G2
Saundby 95 E4
Saundersfoot 35 E2
Saunderton 42 C2
Saunton 21 E2
Sausthorpe 84 B1
Savalbeg 190 A4
Savalmore 190 A4
Sawbridgeworth 45 D1
Sawdon 112 C4
Sawley *Derbys.* 81 F4
Sawley *Lancs.* 101 D3
Sawley *N.Yorks.* 102 B1
Sawston 58 C3
Sawtry 69 G4
Saxby *Leics.* 68 D1
Saxby *Lincs.* 96 A4
Saxby All Saints 95 G1
Saxelbye 82 C5
Saxilby 95 F5
Saxlingham 86 B2
Saxlingham Green 72 D2
Saxlingham Nethergate 72 D2
Saxlingham Thorpe 72 D2
Saxmundham 61 E1
Saxon Street 59 E2
Saxondale 82 B1
Saxtead Green 61 D1
Saxtead Little Green 60 D1
Saxthorpe 86 C2
Saxton 103 D4
Sayers Common 17 E2
Scackleton 111 F5
Scadabhagh 105 D4
Scaftworth 95 D3
Scagglethorpe 112 B5
Scalasaig 146 C5
Scalby *E.Riding* 104 A5
Scalby *N.Yorks.* 112 D4
Scaldwell 68 C5
Scale Houses 118 B3
Scaleby 118 A1
Scalebyhill 118 A1
Scales *Cumb.* 117 G4
Scales *Cumb.* 107 D5
Scalford 82 C5
Scaling 111 G1
Scallasaig 165 E3
Scallastle 147 G1
Scalloway 200 C4
Scamblesby 96 C5
Scammadale 148 A2
Scamodale 156 A2
Scampston 112 B5
Scampton 95 G5
Scaniport 167 F1
Scapa 196 D2
Scar 199 E2
Scarborough 112 D4
Scarcewater 4 D4
Scarcliffe 81 F1
Scarcroft 102 C3
Scardroy 178 B4
Scarff 202 B4
Scarfskerry 195 E1
Scargill 109 F1
Scarinish 154 B2
Scarisbrick 91 E1
Scarning 86 A4
Scarrington 82 C3
Scarth Hill 91 F2
Scartho 96 C2
Scatraig 167 G1
Scaur *D. & G.* 124 C3
Scaur or Kippford *D. & G.* 124 C5
Scawby 95 G2
Scawton 111 E4
Scayne's Hill 17 F1
Scealascro 186 C5
Scethrog 52 A5
Schaw 132 C3
Scholar Green 79 F2
Scholes *W.Yorks.* 102 C4
Scholes *W.Yorks.* 93 F2
Sciberscross 190 C3
Scleddau 48 C4
Sco Ruston 87 D3
Scofton 94 D4
Scole 72 C4
Scolpaig 173 F2
Scones Lethendy 151 G2
Sconser 164 B1
Scoor 146 D3
Scopwick 83 F2
Scoraig 188 C5
Scorborough 104 C3
Scorrier 4 B5
Scorriton 8 D1
Scorton *Lancs.* 100 B3
Scorton *N.Yorks.* 110 B2
Scotby 118 A2
Scotch Corner 110 B2
Scotforth 100 A2
Scothern 96 A5
Scotland Gate 129 E3
Scotlandwell 151 G4
Scotnish 139 F1
Scots' Gap 128 C3
Scotsburn 179 G2
Scotston *Aber.* 161 F2
Scotston *P. & K.* 159 E5
Scotstown 156 A3
Scotter 95 F2
Scotterthorpe 95 F2
Scottlethorpe 83 F5
Scotton *Lincs.* 95 F3
Scotton *N.Yorks.* 110 A3
Scotton *N.Yorks.* 102 C2
Scottow 87 D3
Scoulton 86 A5
Scourie 192 A4
Scourie More 192 A4
Scousburgh 201 F4
Scrabster 194 C1
Scrainwood 128 B1
Scrane End 84 B3
Scraptoft 68 B2
Scratby 87 G4
Scrayingham 103 G1
Scredington 83 F3
Scremby 84 C1
Scremerston 137 E2
Screveton 82 C3
Scriven 102 C2
Scrooby 95 D3
Scropton 80 C4
Scrub Hill 84 A2
Scruton 110 B3
Sculthorpe 85 G4
Scunthorpe 95 F1
Scurlage 36 A4
Sea Palling 87 F3
Seabank 156 B5
Seaborough 12 A2
Seacombe 91 D3
Seacroft *Lincs.* 85 D1
Seacroft *W.Yorks.* 102 C4
Seafield *Arg. & B.* 139 F1
Seafield *S.Ayr.* 132 B3
Seafield *W.Loth.* 143 E3
Seaford 17 G4
Seaforth 91 E3
Seagrave 68 B1
Seaham 120 D3
Seahouses 137 G3
Seal 31 E3
Sealand 78 A1
Seale 29 D3
Seamer *N.Yorks.* 111 D1
Seamer *N.Yorks.* 112 D4
Seamill 140 D5
Searby 96 A2
Seasalter 32 C2
Seascale 106 B2
Seathwaite *Cumb.* 117 F5
Seathwaite *Cumb.* 106 D3
Seatoller 117 F5
Seaton *Cornw.* 6 D5
Seaton *Cumb.* 116 D3
Seaton *Devon* 11 F3
Seaton *Dur.* 120 D3
Seaton *E.Riding* 105 D3
Seaton *Northumb.* 129 F4
Seaton *Rut.* 69 E3
Seaton Burn 129 E4
Seaton Carew 121 E4
Seaton Delaval 129 F4
Seaton Junction 11 F3
Seaton Ross 103 G3
Seaton Sluice 129 F4
Seatown *Aber.* 183 G4
Seatown *Dorset* 12 A3
Seatown *Moray* 181 G3
Seatown *Moray* 182 A3
Seave Green 111 E2
Seaview 15 F3
Seaville 117 E1
Seavington St. Mary 12 A1
Seavington St. Michael 12 A1
Seawick 47 E1
Sebastopol 38 B3
Sebergham 117 G2
Seckington 67 E2
Second Coast 188 B5
Sedbergh 108 B3
Sedbury 39 E3
Sedbusk 109 D3
Sedgeberrow 54 C4
Sedgebrook 83 D4
Sedgefield 120 C5
Sedgeford 85 F4
Sedgehill 25 F5
Sedgley 66 B3
Sedgwick 107 G4
Sedlescombe 18 C2
Sedlescombe Street 18 C2
Seend 26 A1
Seend Cleeve 26 A1
Seer Green 43 E3
Seething 73 E2
Sefton 91 E2
Seghill 129 E4
Seifton 65 D4
Seighford 79 F5
Seilebost 184 C4
Seion 75 E1
Seisdon 66 A3
Seisiadar 187 G4
Selattyn 77 F4
Selborne 28 C4
Selby 103 F4
Selham 29 E5
Selkirk 135 F3
Sellack 53 E5
Sellafield 106 B2
Sellafirth 203 E3
Sellindge 32 C5
Selling 32 C3
Sells Green 26 A1
Selly Oak 66 C4
Selmeston 18 A3
Selsdon 30 C2
Selsey 16 A4
Selsfield Common 30 C5
Selside 108 C5
Selstead 33 E4
Selston 81 F2
Selworthy 22 C3
Semblister 200 C2
Semer 60 A3
Semington 25 F1
Semley 25 F5
Send 29 F2
Send Marsh 29 F2
Senghenydd 38 A3
Sennen 2 A4
Sennen Cove 2 A4
Sennybridge 51 F5
Senwick 115 G2
Sequer's Bridge 8 C2
Sessay 111 D5
Setchey 71 E1
Setley 14 C2
Setter *Shet.* 201 E3
Setter *Shet.* 200 C2
Settiscarth 198 B5
Settle 101 E1
Settrington 112 B5
Seven Bridges 40 D3
Seven Kings 45 D4
Seven Sisters 37 E2
Seven Springs 40 B1
Sevenhampton *Glos.* 54 C5
Sevenhampton *Swin.* 41 E3
Sevenoaks 31 E3
Sevenoaks Weald 31 E3
Severn Beach 39 E4
Severn Stoke 54 A3
Sevington 32 C4
Sewards End 59 D4
Sewardstone 44 C3
Sewerby 105 E1
Seworgan 3 E3
Sewstern 83 D5
Sexhow 111 D2
Sgarasta Mhòr 184 C4
Sgiogarstaigh 187 G1
Sgodachail 189 G5
Shabbington 42 B2
Shackerley 66 A2
Shackerstone 67 F2
Shackleford 29 E3
Shadfen 129 E3
Shadforth 120 C3
Shadingfield 73 F3
Shadoxhurst 32 B5
Shadwell 72 A3
Shaftesbury 25 F5
Shafton 94 A1
Shalbourne 27 E1
Shalcombe 14 D4
Shalden 28 B3
Shaldon 10 C5
Shalfleet 14 D4
Shalford *Essex* 59 F5
Shalford *Surr.* 29 F3
Shalford Green 59 F5
Shallowford 22 A3
Shalmsford Street 32 C3
Shalmstry 194 D2
Shalstone 56 B4
Shalunt 140 B2
Shambellie 125 D4
Shamley Green 29 F3
Shandon 141 D1
Shandwick 180 A2
Shangton 68 C3
Shankend 135 G5
Shankhouse 129 E4
Shanklin 15 E4
Shannochie 131 E3
Shantron 141 E1
Shantullich 179 F4
Shanzie 160 A4
Shap 107 G1
Shapwick *Dorset* 13 F2
Shapwick *Som.* 24 B4
Shardlow 81 F4
Shareshill 66 B2
Sharlston 94 A1
Sharnbrook 57 F2
Sharnford 67 G3
Sharoe Green 100 B4
Sharow 110 C5
Sharpenhoe 57 F4
Sharperton 128 B1
Sharpham House 9 E2
Sharpness 39 F2
Sharpthorne 30 C5
Sharrington 86 B2
Shatterford 65 G4
Shaugh Prior 8 B1
Shavington 79 D2
Shaw *Gt.Man.* 92 D2
Shaw *Swin.* 40 D4
Shaw *W.Berks.* 27 F1
Shaw *Wilts.* 25 F1
Shaw Mills 102 B1
Shawbury 78 C5
Shawclough 92 C1
Shawell 68 A4
Shawford 27 F5
Shawforth 101 E5
Shawhead 124 C3
Shawtonhill 142 A5
Sheanachie 130 C4
Sheandow 169 E1
Shear Cross 25 F3
Shearington 125 E4
Shearsby 68 B3
Shebbear 21 E5
Shebdon 79 E5
Shebster 194 C2
Shedfield 15 E1
Sheen 80 C1
Sheepscombe 40 A1
Sheepstor 8 B1
Sheepwash *Devon* 21 E5
Sheepwash *Northumb.* 129 E3
Sheepway 39 D5
Sheepy Magna 67 F2
Sheepy Parva 67 F2
Sheering 45 E1
Sheerness 32 B1
Sheet 28 C5
Sheffield 94 A4
Sheffield Bottom 28 B1
Sheffield City Airport 94 B4
Sheffield Green 17 G1
Shefford 57 G4
Shefford Woodlands 41 F5
Sheigra 192 A2
Sheinton 65 F2
Shelderton 64 D5
Sheldon *Derbys.* 80 C1
Sheldon *Devon* 11 E2
Sheldon *W.Mid.* 66 D4
Sheldwich 32 C3
Shelf 102 A5
Shelfanger 72 C3
Shelfield 66 C2
Shelford 82 B3
Shellachan *Arg. & B.* 148 A3
Shellachan *Arg. & B.* 148 C2
Shellbrook Hill 78 A3
Shelley *Essex* 45 E2
Shelley *Suff.* 60 B4
Shelley *W.Yorks.* 93 G1
Shellingford 41 F3
Shellow Bowells 45 F2
Shelsley Beauchamp 53 G1
Shelsley Walsh 53 G1
Shelton *Beds.* 57 F1
Shelton *Norf.* 72 D2
Shelton *Notts.* 82 C3
Shelton *Shrop.* 65 D1
Shelton Green 72 D2
Shelve 64 C3
Shelwick 53 E3
Shenfield 45 F3
Shenington 55 F3
Shenley 44 A2
Shenley Brook End 56 D4
Shenley Church End 56 D4
Shenleybury 44 A2
Shenmore 52 C4
Shennanton 123 E4
Shenstone *Staffs.* 66 D2
Shenstone *Worcs.* 66 A5
Shenstone Woodend 66 D2
Shenton 67 F2
Shenval 169 E2
Shepeau Stow 70 B1
Shephall 58 A5
Shepherd's Green 42 C4
Shepherdswell (Sibertswold) 33 E1
Shepley 93 F2
Sheppardstown 195 E5
Shepperdine 39 F3
Shepperton 29 F1
Shepreth 58 B3
Shepshed 67 G1
Shepton Beauchamp 12 A1
Shepton Mallet 24 D3
Shepton Montague 25 D4
Shepway 31 G3
Sheraton 120 D4
Sherborne *Dorset* 12 C1
Sherborne *Glos.* 41 D1
Sherborne St. John 28 B2
Sherbourne 55 E1
Sherburn *Dur.* 120 C3
Sherburn *N.Yorks.* 112 C5
Sherburn in Elmet 103 D4
Shere 29 F3
Shereford 85 G5
Sherfield English 27 D5
Sherfield on Loddon 28 B2
Sherford 9 D3
Sheriff Hutton 103 F1
Sheriffhales 65 G1
Sheringham 86 C1
Sherington 57 D3
Shernborne 85 F4
Sherramore 167 E5
Sherrington 26 A4
Sherston 40 A4
Sherwood Green 21 F3
Shettleston 142 A3
Shevington 91 G2
Shevington Moor 91 G1
Sheviock 7 D5
Shiel Bridge 165 F3
Shieldaig *High.* 177 E4
Shieldaig *High.* 177 E2
Shieldhill 142 C2
Shielfoot 155 F2
Shielhill 160 C4
Shiels 170 B4
Shifford 41 F2
Shifnal 65 G2
Shilbottle 129 D1
Shildon 120 B5
Shillingford *Devon* 22 C5
Shillingford *Oxon.* 42 A3
Shillingford St. George 10 C4
Shillingstone 13 E1
Shillington 57 G4
Shillmoor 128 A1
Shilstone 21 F5
Shilton *Oxon.* 41 E2
Shilton *Warks.* 67 G4
Shimpling *Norf.* 72 C3
Shimpling *Suff.* 59 G2
Shimpling Street 59 G2
Shincliffe 120 B3
Shiney Row 120 C2
Shinfield 28 C1
Shingay 58 B3
Shingle Street 61 E3
Shinner's Bridge 9 D1
Shinness Lodge 190 A3
Shipbourne 31 E3
Shipdham 86 A5
Shipham 24 B2
Shiphay 9 E1
Shiplake 42 C5
Shipley *Northumb.* 137 F5
Shipley *Shrop.* 66 A3
Shipley *W.Suss.* 29 G5
Shipley *W.Yorks.* 102 A4
Shipley Bridge *Devon* 8 C1
Shipley Bridge *Surr.* 30 C4
Shipmeadow 73 E2
Shippon 41 G3
Shipston on Stour 55 E3
Shipton *Glos.* 40 C1
Shipton *N.Yorks.* 103 E2
Shipton *Shrop.* 65 E3
Shipton Bellinger 26 D3
Shipton Gorge 12 A3
Shipton Green 16 A4
Shipton Moyne 40 A4
Shipton-on-Cherwell 41 G1
Shipton-under-Wychwood 41 E1
Shiptonthorpe 104 A3
Shira 149 D3
Shirburn 42 B3
Shirdley Hill 91 E1
Shire Oak 66 C2
Shirebrook 81 G1
Shirehampton 39 E5
Shiremoor 129 F4
Shirenewton 39 D3
Shireoaks 94 C4
Shirl Heath 52 D2
Shirland 81 E2
Shirley *Derbys.* 80 D3
Shirley *Gt.Lon.* 30 C2
Shirley *Hants.* 14 A3
Shirley *S'ham.* 14 D1
Shirley *W.Mid.* 66 D5
Shirrell Heath 15 E1
Shirwell 21 F2
Shirwell Cross 21 F2
Shiskine 131 E3
Shobdon 52 C1
Shobrooke 10 B2
Shocklach 78 B3
Shoeburyness 46 C4
Sholden 33 F3
Sholing 15 D1
Shoot Hill 64 D1
Shooter's Hill 44 D5
Shop *Cornw.* 4 C2
Shop *Cornw.* 20 C4
Shop Corner 60 D4
Shoreditch 44 C4
Shoreham 31 E2
Shoreham-by-Sea 17 E3
Shoremill 179 G3
Shoresdean 145 G5
Shoreswood 145 G5
Shoretown 179 F3
Shorncote 40 C3
Shorne 45 F5
Shorne Ridgeway 45 F5
Short Cross 64 B2
Short Green 72 B3

Short Heath *Derbys.* 67 F1
Short Heath *W.Mid.* 66 C3
Shortacombe 7 F2
Shortgate 17 G2
Shortgrove 58 D4
Shortlanesend 4 C5
Shorwell 15 D4
Shoscombe 25 E2
Shotesham 72 D2
Shotgate 45 G3
Shotley 60 D4
Shotley Bridge 119 G2
Shotley Gate 60 D4
Shotleyfield 119 G2
Shottenden 32 C3
Shottermill 29 D4
Shottery 55 D2
Shotteswell 55 G3
Shottisham 61 E3
Shottle 81 E2
Shottlegate 81 E3
Shotton *Dur.* 120 D4
Shotton *Flints.* 78 A1
Shotton *Northumb.* 136 C3
Shotton Colliery 120 C3
Shotts 142 C3
Shotwick 91 E5
Shoughlaige-e-Caine 98 B3
Shouldham 71 E2
Shouldham Thorpe 71 E2
Shoulton 54 A2
Shover's Green 31 F5
Shrawardine 64 C1
Shrawley 54 A1
Shrewley 55 E1
Shrewsbury 65 D1
Shrewton 26 B3
Shripney 16 B3
Shrivenham 41 E4
Shropham 72 A2
Shroton (Iwerne Courtney) 13 E1
Shrub End 60 A5
Shucknall 53 E3
Shudy Camps 59 E3
Shurdington 40 B1
Shurlock Row 42 D5
Shurrery 194 C3
Shurrery Lodge 194 C3
Shurton 23 E3
Shustoke 67 E3
Shut Heath 79 F5
Shute 11 F3
Shutford 55 F3
Shuthonger 54 A4
Shutlanger 56 C2
Shuttington 67 E2
Shuttlewood 94 B5
Shuttleworth 92 C1
Siabost 187 D3
Siadar Iarach 187 E2
Siadar Uarach 187 E2
Sibbaldbie 125 F2
Sibbertoft 68 B4
Sibdon Carwood 64 D4
Sibertswold (Shepherdswell) 33 E4
Sibford Ferris 55 F4
Sibford Gower 55 F4
Sible Hedingham 59 F4
Sibsey 84 B2
Sibson *Cambs.* 69 F3
Sibson *Leics.* 67 F2
Sibster 195 F3
Sibthorpe 82 C3
Sibton 61 E1
Sicklesmere 59 G2
Sicklinghall 102 C3
Sidbury *Devon* 11 E3
Sidbury *Shrop.* 65 F4
Sidcot 24 B2
Sidcup 45 D5
Siddington *Ches.* 92 C5
Siddington *Glos.* 40 C3
Sidemoor 66 B5
Sidestrand 87 D2
Sidford 11 E3
Sidlesham 16 A4
Sidley 18 C3
Sidlow 30 B4
Sidmouth 11 E4
Sigford 10 A5
Sigglesthorne 105 D3
Sigingstone 37 F5
Silchester 28 B1
Sileby 68 B1
Silecroft 106 C4
Silfield 72 C2
Silian 50 B2
Silk Willoughby 83 F3
Silkstone 93 G2
Silkstone Common 93 G2
Silksworth 120 C2
Silloth 117 E1
Sills 128 A1
Sillyearn 182 A4
Silpho 112 C3
Silsden 101 G3
Silsoe 57 F4
Silton 25 E5
Silver End 46 B1
Silver Hill *E.Suss.* 18 C1
Silverburn 143 G3
Silvercraigs 139 G1
Silverdale *Lancs.* 107 F5
Silverdale *Staffs.* 79 F3
Silverhill 18 D2
Silverley's Green 73 D4
Silvermoss 170 D1
Silverstone 56 B3
Silverton 10 C2
Silvington 65 F5
Silwick 200 B3
Simonburn 128 A4
Simonsbath 22 A4
Simonstone 101 D4
Simprim 145 F5
Simpson 57 D4
Sinclair's Hill 145 F4
Sinclairston 132 C4
Sinderby 110 C4
Sinderhope 119 E2
Sindlesham 28 C1
Singdean 135 G5
Singleton *Lancs.* 99 G4
Singleton *W.Suss.* 16 A2
Singlewell or Ifield 45 F5
Sinnahard 169 G3
Sinnington 111 G4
Sinton Green 54 A1
Sipson 43 F5
Sirhowy 38 A1
Sisland 73 E2
Sissinghurst 31 G5
Siston 39 F5
Sithney 2 D4
Sittingbourne 32 B2
Siulaisiadar 187 G4
Six Ashes 65 G4
Six Mile Bottom 59 D2
Sixhills 96 B4
Sixmile Cottages 32 D4
Sixpenny Handley 13 F1
Sizewell 61 F1
Skail 193 G4
Skaill *Ork.* 198 A5
Skaill *Ork.* 197 E2
Skares *Aber.* 170 B1
Skares *E.Ayr.* 132 D4
Skarpigarth 200 A2
Skateraw 145 E2
Skaw 201 E1
Skeabost 176 A5
Skeabrae 198 A4
Skeeby 110 A2
Skeffington 68 C2
Skeffling 97 D1
Skegby 81 G1
Skegness 85 D1
Skelberry 201 G4
Skelbo 190 C5
Skeldon 132 B4
Skeldyke 84 B4
Skellingthorpe 95 G5
Skellister 201 D2
Skellow 94 C1
Skelmanthorpe 93 G1
Skelmersdale 91 F2
Skelmonae 171 D1
Skelmorlie 140 C3
Skelmuir 183 E5
Skelton *Cumb.* 118 A4
Skelton *E.Riding* 103 G5
Skelton *N.Yorks.* 109 F2
Skelton *N.Yorks.* 102 C1
Skelton *R. & C.* 111 F1
Skelton *York* 103 E2
Skelton Green 111 F1
Skelwick 198 C2
Skelwith Bridge 107 E2
Skendleby 84 C1
Skenfrith 53 D5
Skerne 104 C2
Skeroblingarry 130 C3
Skerray 193 F2
Sketty 36 C3
Skewen 36 D3
Skewsby 111 F5
Skeyton 86 D3
Skidbrooke 97 E3
Skidby 104 C4
Skilgate 22 C5
Skillington 83 E5
Skinburness 117 E1
Skinflats 142 D1
Skinidin 175 F5
Skinnet 194 D2
Skinningrove 121 G5
Skipness 140 A4
Skipsea 105 D2
Skipton 101 F2
Skipton-on-Swale 110 C4
Skipwith 103 F4
Skirbeck 84 B3
Skirlaugh 104 D4
Skirling 134 B2
Skirmett 42 C4
Skirpenbeck 103 G2
Skirwith *Cumb.* 118 C4
Skirwith *N.Yorks.* 108 C5
Skirza 195 F2
Skulamus 164 C2
Skullomie 193 F2
Skye of Curr 168 B2
Slack 170 A1
Slackhall 93 E4
Slackhead 181 G3
Slad 40 A2
Slade 21 F1
Slade Green 45 E5
Slaggyford 118 C2
Slaidburn 100 D2
Slains Park 161 G2
Slaithwaite 93 E1
Slaley 119 F2
Slamannan 142 C2
Slapton *Bucks.* 57 E5
Slapton *Devon* 9 E3
Slapton *Northants.* 56 B3
Slate Haugh 181 G3
Slatenber 108 C5
Slattadale 177 E2
Slattocks 92 C2
Slaugham 17 E1
Slaughden 61 F2
Slaughterford 40 A5
Slawston 68 C3
Sleaford *Hants.* 28 D4
Sleaford *Lincs.* 83 F3
Sleagill 107 G1
Sleapford 65 F1
Sledge Green 54 A4
Sledmere 104 B1
Sleights 112 B2
Slepe 13 F3
Slickly 195 E2
Sliddery 131 E3
Sliemore 168 C2
Sligachan 164 A2
Slimbridge 39 G2
Slindon *Staffs.* 79 F4
Slindon *W.Suss.* 16 B3
Slinfold 29 G4
Slingsby 111 F5
Slioch 170 A1
Slip End *Beds.* 43 F1
Slip End *Herts.* 58 A4
Slipton 69 E5
Slochd 168 A2
Slockavullin 148 A5
Slogarie 124 A4
Sloley 87 D3
Slongaber 124 C3
Sloothby 97 E5
Slough 43 E5
Sluggan 168 A2
Slyne 100 A1
Smailholm 136 A3
Small Dole 17 E2
Small Hythe 32 A5
Smallbridge 92 D1
Smallburgh 87 E3
Smallburn *Aber.* 183 F5
Smallburn *E.Ayr.* 133 E3
Smalley 81 F3
Smallfield 30 C4
Smallridge 11 F2
Smallthorne 79 F2
Smallworth 72 B3
Smannell 27 E3
Smardale 108 C2
Smarden 32 A4
Smaull 138 A3
Smeale Farm 98 C1
Smeatharpe 11 E1
Smeeth 32 C5
Smeeton Westerby 68 B3
Smelthouses 102 A1
Smerral 195 D5
Smethwick 66 C4
Smirisary 155 F2
Smisby 67 F1
Smith End Green 53 G2
Smithfield 118 A1
Smithincott 11 D1
Smith's Green 59 D5
Smithton 179 G5
Smithy Green 92 B5
Smug Oak 44 A2
Smyrton 122 C2
Smythe's Green 46 C1
Snailbeach 64 C2
Snailwell 59 E1
Snainton 112 C4
Snaith 103 F5
Snape *N.Yorks.* 110 B4
Snape *Suff.* 61 E2
Snape Green 91 E1
Snarestone 67 F2
Snarford 96 A4
Snargate 19 E1
Snave 32 C5
Sneachill 54 B2
Snead 64 C3
Sneaton 112 B2
Sneatonthorpe 112 C2
Snelland 96 A4
Snellings 106 A2
Snelston 80 C3
Snetterton 72 A2
Snettisham 85 E4
Snibston 67 G1
Snishival 162 A1
Snitter 128 C1
Snitterby 95 G3
Snitterfield 55 E2
Snitton 65 E5
Snodhill 52 C3
Snodland 31 G2
Snowshill 54 C4
Soar *Carmar.* 50 C5
Soar *Devon* 8 D4
Soberton 15 F1
Soberton Heath 15 F1
Sockburn 110 C2
Sodylt Bank 78 A4
Soham 71 D5
Solas 173 G2
Soldon Cross 20 D4
Soldridge 28 B4
Sole Street *Kent* 32 C4
Sole Street *Kent* 31 F2
Solihull 67 D5
Solihull Lodge 66 C5
Sollers Dilwyn 52 D2
Sollers Hope 53 F4
Sollom 91 F1
Solsgirth 151 E5
Solva 48 A5
Solwaybank 126 B4
Somerby 68 C1
Somercotes 81 F2
Somerford Keynes 40 C3
Somerley 16 A4
Somerleyton 73 F2
Somersal Herbert 80 C4
Somersby 96 D5
Somersham *Cambs.* 70 B5
Somersham *Suff.* 60 B3
Somerton *Oxon.* 55 G5
Somerton *Som.* 24 B5
Somerton *Suff.* 59 G2
Sompting 17 D3
Sonning 42 C5
Sonning Common 42 C4
Sonning Eye 42 C5
Sopley 14 A3
Sopworth 40 A4
Sorbie 115 E2
Sordale 194 D2
Sorisdale 154 B3
Sorn 133 D3
Sornhill 132 D2
Soroba 148 A2
Sortat 195 E2
Sotby 96 C5
Sots Hole 83 G1
Sotterly 73 F3
Soudley 79 E5
Soughton 77 F1
Soulbury 57 D5
Soulby 108 C1
Souldern 56 A4
Souldrop 57 E1
Sound *Ches.* 78 D3
Sound *Shet.* 201 D3
Sound *Shet.* 200 C2
Soundwell 39 F5
Sourhope 136 C4
Sourin 198 C3
Sourton 7 F2
Soutergate 106 D4
South Acre 71 G1
South Allington 9 D4
South Alloa 151 D5
South Ambersham 29 E5
South Anston 94 C4
South Ascot 29 E1
South Ballachulish 156 C4
South Balloch 123 E1
South Bank 121 E5
South Barrow 24 D5
South Beddington 30 B2
South Bellsdyke 142 D1
South Benfleet 45 G4
South Bersted 16 B4
South Blackbog 170 C1
South Bowood 12 A3
South Brent 8 C1
South Brentor 7 E2
South Brewham 25 E4
South Broomhill 129 E2
South Burlingham 87 E5
South Cadbury 24 D5
South Cairn 122 A4
South Carlton 95 G5
South Cave 104 B4
South Cerney 40 C3
South Chard 11 G2
South Charlton 137 F4
South Cheriton 25 D5
South Cliffe 104 A4
South Clifton 95 F5
South Cockerington 97 D4
South Common 17 F2
South Cornelly 37 E5
South Corrygills 131 F2
South Cove 73 F3
South Creagan 156 B5
South Creake 85 G4
South Croxton 68 B1
South Dalton 104 B3
South Darenth 31 E2
South Duffield 103 F4
South Elkington 96 C4
South Elmsall 94 B1
South End *Bucks.* 57 D5
South End *Cumb.* 99 F1
South End *N.Lincs.* 96 B1
South Erradale 176 D2
South Fambridge 46 B3
South Fawley 41 F4
South Ferriby 104 B5
South Flobbets 170 C1
South Garth 203 E3
South Godstone 30 C4
South Gorley 14 A1
South Green *Essex* 45 F3
South Green *Norf.* 86 B4
South Hall 140 B2
South Hanningfield 45 G3
South Harting 15 G1
South Hayling 15 G3
South Hazelrigg 137 E3
South Heath 43 E2
South Heighton 17 G3
South Hetton 120 C3
South Hiendley 94 A1
South Hill 6 D3
South Hinksey 42 A2
South Hole 20 C4
South Holmwood 29 G3
South Hornchurch 45 E4
South Hourat 141 D4
South Huish 8 C3
South Hykeham 83 E1
South Hylton 120 C2
South Kelsey 96 A3
South Kessock 179 F5
South Killingholme 96 B1
South Kilvington 110 D4
South Kilworth 68 B4
South Kirkby 94 B1
South Kirkton 170 C4
South Kyme 83 G3
South Lancing 17 D3
South Ledaig 148 B1
South Leigh 41 F2
South Leverton 95 E4
South Littleton 54 C3
South Lopham 72 B3
South Luffenham 69 E2
South Malling 17 G2
South Marston 41 D4
South Milford 103 D4
South Milton 8 D3
South Mimms 44 B2
South Molton 22 A5
South Moor 120 A2
South Moreton 42 A4
South Mundham 16 A3
South Muskham 82 C2
South Newbald 104 B4
South Newington 55 G4
South Newton 26 B4
South Normanton 81 F2
South Norwood 30 C2
South Nutfield 30 C4
South Ockendon 45 E4
South Ormsby 97 D5
South Otterington 110 C4
South Oxhey 44 A3
South Park 30 B4
South Perrott 12 A2
South Petherton 12 A1
South Petherwin 6 D2
South Pickenham 71 G2
South Pool 9 D3
South Queensferry 143 F2
South Radworthy 22 A4
South Rauceby 83 F3
South Raynham 85 G5
South Redbriggs 182 C5
South Reston 97 E4
South Runcton 71 E2
South Scarle 82 D1
South Shian 156 B5
South Shields 120 C1
South Somercotes 97 E3
South Stainley 102 C1
South Stoke *Oxon.* 42 B4
South Stoke *W.Suss.* 16 C3
South Street *E.Suss.* 17 F2
South Street *Kent* 31 F2
South Tawton 7 G1
South Thoresby 97 E5
South Tidworth 26 D3
South Town 28 B4
South Upper Barrack 183 E5
South Walsham 87 E4
South Warnborough 28 C3
South Weald 45 E3
South Weston 42 C3
South Wheatley *Cornw.* 6 C1
South Wheatley *Notts.* 95 E4
South Whiteness 200 C3
South Widcombe 24 C2
South Wigston 68 A3
South Willesborough 32 C4
South Willingham 96 B4
South Wingate 120 D4
South Wingfield 81 E2
South Witham 69 E1
South Wonston 27 F4
South Woodham Ferrers 46 B3
South Wootton 85 E5
South Wraxall 25 F1
South Yardley 66 D4
South Zeal 7 G1
Southall 44 A5
Southam *Glos.* 54 B5
Southam *Warks.* 55 G1
Southampton 14 D1
Southampton International Airport 15 D1
Southbar 141 F3
Southborough 31 E4
Southbourne *Bourne.* 14 A3
Southbourne *W.Suss.* 15 G2
Southburgh 86 B5
Southburn 104 B2
Southchurch 46 C4
Southcott 7 F1
Southdean 127 E1
Southease 17 G3
Southend *Aber.* 182 C5
Southend *Arg. & B.* 130 B5
Southend *W.Berks.* 42 B5
Southend-on-Sea 46 B4
Southerndown 37 E5
Southerness 125 D5
Southery 71 E3
Southfleet 45 F5
Southgate *Gt.Lon.* 44 B3
Southgate *Norf.* 86 C3
Southgate *Norf.* 85 E4
Southgate *Swan.* 36 B4
Southill 57 G3
Southington 27 G3
Southleigh 11 F3
Southminster 46 C3
Southmuir 160 B4
Southoe 57 G1
Southolt 60 C1
Southorpe 69 F2
Southowram 102 A5
Southport 91 E1
Southrepps 87 D2
Southrey 83 G1
Southrop 41 D2
Southrope 28 B3
Southsea *Ports.* 15 F3
Southsea *Wrex.* 77 F2
Southstoke 25 E1
Southtown *Norf.* 87 G5
Southtown *Ork.* 197 D3
Southwaite *Cumb.* 108 C2
Southwaite *Cumb.* 118 A3
Southwark 30 C1
Southwater 29 G5
Southway 24 C3
Southwell *Dorset* 12 C5
Southwell *Notts.* 82 C2
Southwick *Hants.* 15 F2
Southwick *Northants.* 69 F3
Southwick *T. & W.* 120 C2
Southwick *W.Suss.* 17 E3
Southwick *Wilts.* 25 F2
Southwold 73 G4
Southwood *Norf.* 87 E5
Southwood *Som.* 24 C4
Sowerby *N.Yorks.* 110 D4
Sowerby *W.Yorks.* 101 G5
Sowerby Bridge 101 G5
Sowerby Row 117 G2
Sowton 10 C3
Soyal 190 A5
Spa Common 87 D2
Spadeadam 127 D4
Spalding 84 A5
Spaldington 103 G4
Spaldwick 69 G5
Spalefield 153 D4
Spalford 82 D1
Spanby 83 F4
Sparham 86 B4
Spark Bridge 107 E4
Sparkford 24 D5
Sparkwell 8 B2
Sparrowpit 93 E4
Sparrow's Green 31 F5
Sparsholt *Hants.* 27 F4
Sparsholt *Oxon.* 41 F4
Spartylea 119 E3
Spaunton 111 G3
Spaxton 23 F4
Spean Bridge 157 E1
Speddoch 124 C2
Speen *Bucks.* 42 D2
Speen *W.Berks.* 27 F1
Speeton 113 E5
Speke 91 F4
Speldhurst 31 E4
Spellbrook 45 D1
Spelsbury 55 F5
Spen Green 79 F1
Spencers Wood 28 C1
Spennithorne 110 A4
Spennymoor 120 B4
Spetchley 54 A2
Spetisbury 13 F2
Spexhall 73 E3
Spey Bay 181 F3
Speybridge 168 C2
Speyview 181 E5
Spilsby 84 C1
Spindlestone 137 F3
Spinkhill 94 B5
Spinningdale 190 B5
Spirthill 40 B5
Spital *High.* 195 D3
Spital *W. & M.* 43 E5
Spital in the Street 95 G3
Spitalbrook 44 C2
Spithurst 17 G2
Spittal *D. & G.* 123 F4
Spittal *D. & G.* 123 E5
Spittal *E.Loth.* 144 B2
Spittal *Northumb.* 137 E1
Spittal *Pembs.* 48 C5
Spittal of Glenmuick 160 B1
Spittal of Glenshee 159 G3
Spittalfield 159 G5
Spixworth 86 D4
Spofforth 102 C2
Spondon 81 F4
Spooner Row 72 B2
Spoonley 79 D4
Sporle 71 G1
Sportsman's Arms 76 C2
Spott 145 D2
Spratton 56 C1
Spreakley 28 D3
Spreyton 7 G1
Spridlington 96 A4
Springburn 142 A3
Springfield *Arg. & B.* 140 B2
Springfield *D. & G.* 126 B5
Springfield *Fife* 152 B3
Springfield *Moray* 180 C4
Springfield *P. & K.* 151 G1
Springfield *W.Mid.* 66 C4
Springholm 124 C4
Springkell 126 A4
Springleys 170 C1
Springside 132 B2
Springthorpe 95 F4
Springwell 120 B2
Sproatley 105 D4
Sproston Green 79 E1
Sprotbrough 94 C2
Sproughton 60 C3
Sprouston 136 B3
Sprowston 86 D4
Sproxton *Leics.* 83 D5
Sproxton *N.Yorks.* 111 F4
Spurstow 78 C2
Square Point 124 B3
Squires Gate 99 G4
Sròndoire 139 G2
Sronphadruig Lodge 158 C2
Stableford 79 F4
Stackhouse 101 E1
Stackpole 34 C3
Stacksteads 101 E5
Staddiscombe 8 B2
Staddlethorpe 104 A5
Stadhampton 42 B3
Stadhlaigearraidh 162 A1
Staffield 118 B3
Staffin 176 A3
Stafford 79 G5
Stagden Cross 45 F1
Stagsden 57 E3
Stagshaw Bank 119 F1
Stain 195 F2
Stainburn 102 B3
Stainby 83 E5
Staincross 94 A2
Staindrop 120 A5
Staines 43 F5
Stainfield *Lincs.* 83 F5
Stainfield *Lincs.* 96 B5
Stainforth *N.Yorks.* 101 E1
Stainforth *S.Yorks.* 94 D1
Staining 99 G4
Stainland 93 E1
Stainsacre 112 C2
Stainton *Cumb.* 107 G4
Stainton *Cumb.* 118 A5
Stainton *Dur.* 109 F1
Stainton *Middbro.* 111 D1
Stainton *N.Yorks.* 109 F3
Stainton *S.Yorks.* 94 C3
Stainton by Langworth 96 A5
Stainton le Vale 96 B3
Stainton with Adgarley 107 D5
Staintondale 112 C3
Stair *Cumb.* 117 F4
Stair *E.Ayr.* 132 C3
Staithes 111 G1
Stake Pool 100 A3
Stakeford 129 E3
Stalbridge 12 D1
Stalbridge Weston 12 D1
Stalham 87 E3
Stalham Green 87 E3
Stalisfield Green 32 B3
Stalling Busk 109 E4
Stallingborough 96 C1
Stalmine 99 G3
Stalybridge 93 D3
Stambourne 59 F4
Stamford *Lincs.* 69 F2
Stamford *Northumb.* 137 G5
Stamford Bridge 103 G2
Stamfordham 128 C4
Stanborough 44 B1
Stanbridge *Beds.* 57 E5
Stanbridge *Dorset* 13 G2
Stanbridge Earls 27 E5
Stanbury 101 G4
Stand 142 B3
Standburn 142 D2
Standeford 66 B2
Standen 32 A4
Standford 28 D4
Standish 91 G1
Standlake 41 F2
Standon *Hants.* 27 F5
Standon *Herts.* 58 B5
Standon *Staffs.* 79 F4
Stane 142 C4
Stanfield 86 A3
Stanford *Beds.* 57 G3
Stanford *Kent* 32 D5
Stanford Bishop 53 F2
Stanford Bridge 53 G1
Stanford Dingley 42 A5
Stanford in the Vale 41 F3
Stanford-le-Hope 45 F4
Stanford on Avon 68 A5
Stanford on Soar 81 G5
Stanford on Teme 53 G1
Stanford Rivers 45 E2
Stanghow 111 F1
Stanground 70 A3
Stanhoe 85 G4
Stanhope *Dur.* 119 F4
Stanhope *Sc.Bord.* 134 C3
Stanion 69 E4
Stanley *Derbys.* 81 F3
Stanley *Dur.* 120 A2
Stanley *P. & K.* 151 G1
Stanley *Staffs.* 79 G2
Stanley *W.Yorks.* 102 C5
Stanley *Wilts.* 40 B5
Stanley Common 81 F3
Stanmer 17 F3
Stanmore *Gt.Lon.* 44 A3
Stanmore *W.Berks.* 41 G5
Stannersburn 127 F3
Stanningfield 59 G2
Stannington *Northumb.* 129 E4
Stannington *S.Yorks.* 94 A4
Stansbatch 52 C1
Stansfield 59 F2
Stanstead 59 G3
Stanstead Abbotts 44 C1
Stansted 31 F2
Stansted Airport 58 D5
Stansted Mountfitchet 58 D5
Stanton *Derbys.* 67 E
Stanton *Glos.* 54 C
Stanton *Northumb.* 128 D
Stanton *Staffs.* 80 C
Stanton *Suff.* 72 A
Stanton by Bridge 81 E
Stanton by Dale 81 F
Stanton Drew 24 C
Stanton Fitzwarren 41 D
Stanton Harcourt 41 G
Stanton Hill 81 F
Stanton in Peak 80 D
Stanton Lacy 65 D
Stanton Long 65 E
Stanton-on-the-Wolds 82 B
Stanton Prior 25 D
Stanton St. Bernard 26 B
Stanton St. John 42 A
Stanton St. Quintin 40 B
Stanton Street 60 A
Stanton under Bardon 67 G
Stanton upon Hine Heath 78 C
Stanton Wick 24 D
Stanwardine in the Fields 78 B
Stanway *Essex* 60 A
Stanway *Glos.* 54 C
Stanwell 43 F
Stanwell Moor 43 F
Stanwick 69 E
Stanwix 118 A
Stanydale 200 B
Staoinebrig 162 A
Stape 111 G
Stapehill 13 G
Stapeley 79 D
Staple 33 E
Staple Fitzpaine 11 F
Staplecross 18 C
Staplefield 17 E
Stapleford *Cambs.* 58 C
Stapleford *Herts.* 44 C
Stapleford *Leics.* 68 D
Stapleford *Lincs.* 83 D
Stapleford *Notts.* 81
Stapleford *Wilts.* 26 E
Stapleford Abbotts 45 D
Stapleford Tawney 45 E
Staplegrove 23
Staplehurst 31 C
Staplers 15 E
Stapleton *Bristol* 39 E
Stapleton *Cumb.* 126 D
Stapleton *Here.* 52 C
Stapleton *Leics.* 67 C
Stapleton *N.Yorks.* 110

Stapleton *Shrop.* 65 D2
Stapleton *Som.* 24 B5
Stapley 11 E1
Staploe 57 G1
Staplow 53 F3
Star *Fife* 152 B4
Star *Pembs.* 49 F4
Star *Som.* 24 B2
Starbotton 109 E5
Starcross 10 C4
Starkigarth 200 D5
Starling's Green 58 C4
Starr 123 F1
Starston 72 D3
Startforth 109 F1
Startley 40 B4
Statham 92 A4
Stathe 24 A5
Stathern 82 C4
Station Town 120 D4
Staughton Green 57 G1
Staughton Highway 57 G1
Staunton *Glos.* 39 E1
Staunton *Glos.* 53 G5
Staunton Harold Hall 81 E5
Staunton on Arrow 52 C1
Staunton on Wye 52 C3
Staveley *Cumb.* 107 F3
Staveley *Derbys.* 94 B5
Staveley *N.Yorks.* 102 C1
Staveley-in-Cartmel 107 E4
Staverton *Devon* 9 D1
Staverton *Glos.* 54 A5
Staverton *Northants.* 56 A1
Staverton *Wilts.* 25 F1
Staverton Bridge 54 A5
Stawell 24 A4
Stawley 23 D5
Staxigoe 195 F3
Staxton 112 D5
Staylittle 63 E3
Staynall 99 G3
Staythorpe 82 C2
Stean 109 F5
Steane 56 A4
Stearsby 111 F5
Steart 23 F3
Stebbing 59 E5
Stebbing Green 59 E5
Stedham 29 D5
Steel Cross 31 E5
Steele Road 126 D2
Steen's Bridge 53 E2
Steep 28 C5
Steep Marsh 28 C5
Steeple *Dorset* 13 F4
Steeple *Essex* 46 C2
Steeple Ashton 26 A2
Steeple Aston 55 G5
Steeple Barton 55 G5
Steeple Bumpstead 59 E3
Steeple Claydon 56 B5
Steeple Gidding 69 G4
Steeple Langford 26 B4
Steeple Morden 58 A3
Steeton 101 G3
Stein 175 F4
Steinmanhill 182 C5
Stella 120 A1
Stelling Minnis 32 D4
Stemster *High.* 195 D2
Stemster *High.* 195 D4
Stemster House 195 D2
Stenalees 5 E4
Stenhousemuir 142 C1
Stenigot 96 C4
Stenness 202 B5
Stenscholl 176 A3
Stenton *E.Loth.* 144 D2
Stenton *P. & K.* 159 F5
Steornabhagh (Stornoway) 187 F4
Stepaside 35 E2
Stepney 44 C4
Steppingley 57 F4
Stepps 142 A3
Sternfield 61 E1
Sterridge 21 F1
Stert 26 B2
Stetchworth 59 E2
Stevenage 58 A5
Stevenston 141 D5
Steventon *Hants.* 27 G3
Steventon *Oxon.* 41 G3
Stevington 57 E2
Stewartby 57 F3
Stewarton *D. & G.* 115 E2
Stewarton *E.Ayr.* 141 F5
Stewkley 57 D5
Stewton 97 D4
Steyning 17 D2
Steynton 34 C2
Stibb 20 C4
Stibb Cross 21 E4
Stibb Green 26 D1
Stibbard 86 A3
Stibbington 69 F3
Stichill 136 B3
Sticker 5 D4
Stickford 84 B1
Sticklepath 7 G1
Stickney 84 B2
Stiffkey 86 A1
Stifford's Bridge 53 G3
Stillingfleet 103 E3
Stillington *N.Yorks.* 103 E1
Stillington *Stock.* 120 C5
Stilton 69 G4
Stinchcombe 39 G3
Stinsford 12 D3
Stirchley *Tel. & W.* 65 G2
Stirchley *W.Mid.* 66 C4
Stirkoke House 195 F3
Stirling *Aber.* 183 G5
Stirling *Stir.* 150 C5
Stirton 101 F2
Stisted 59 F5
Stithians 3 E3
Stittenham 179 F2
Stivichall 67 F5
Stix 158 C5
Stixwould 83 G1
Stoak 91 F5
Stobo 134 C2
Stoborough 13 F4
Stoborough Green 13 F4
Stobwood 143 D4
Stock 45 F3
Stock Green 54 B2
Stock Lane 41 E5
Stock Wood 54 C2
Stockbridge *Hants.* 27 E4
Stockbridge *Stir.* 150 C4
Stockbury 32 A2
Stockcross 27 F1
Stockdalewath 117 G2
Stockerston 68 D3
Stocking Pelham 58 C5
Stockingford 67 F3
Stockland 11 F2
Stockland Bristol 23 F3
Stockleigh English 10 B2
Stockleigh Pomeroy 10 B2
Stockley 26 A1
Stocklinch 11 G1
Stockport 92 C4
Stocksbridge 93 G3
Stocksfield 119 G1
Stockton *Here.* 53 E1
Stockton *Norf.* 73 E2
Stockton *Shrop.* 65 G3
Stockton *Warks.* 55 G1
Stockton *Wilts.* 26 A4
Stockton Heath 92 A4
Stockton-on-Tees 120 D5
Stockton on Teme 53 G1
Stockton on the Forest 103 F2
Stockwood 12 B2
Stodday 100 A2
Stodmarsh 33 E2
Stody 86 B2
Stoer 188 C2
Stoford *Som.* 12 B1
Stoford *Wilts.* 26 B4
Stogumber 23 D4
Stogursey 23 F3
Stoke *Devon* 20 C3
Stoke *Hants.* 27 F2
Stoke *Hants.* 15 G2
Stoke *Med.* 32 A1
Stoke *W.Mid.* 67 F5
Stoke Abbott 12 A2
Stoke Albany 68 D4
Stoke Ash 72 C4
Stoke Bardolph 82 B3
Stoke Bliss 53 F1
Stoke Bruerne 56 C2
Stoke by Clare 59 F3
Stoke-by-Nayland 60 A4
Stoke Canon 10 C3
Stoke Charity 27 F4
Stoke Climsland 7 D3
Stoke D'Abernon 29 G2
Stoke Doyle 69 F4
Stoke Dry 69 D3
Stoke Ferry 71 E3
Stoke Fleming 9 E3
Stoke Gabriel 9 E2
Stoke Gifford 39 F5
Stoke Golding 67 F3
Stoke Goldington 56 D3
Stoke Hammond 57 D5
Stoke Heath 79 D5
Stoke Holy Cross 86 D5
Stoke Lacy 53 F2
Stoke Lyne 56 A5
Stoke Mandeville 42 D2
Stoke Newington 44 C4
Stoke on Tern 78 D5
Stoke-on-Trent 79 F3
Stoke Orchard 54 B5
Stoke Poges 43 E4
Stoke Prior *Here.* 53 E2
Stoke Prior *Worcs.* 54 B1
Stoke Rivers 21 G2
Stoke Rochford 83 E5
Stoke Row 42 B4
Stoke St. Gregory 24 A5
Stoke St. Mary 23 F5
Stoke St. Michael 25 D3
Stoke St. Milborough 65 E4
Stoke sub Hamdon 12 A1
Stoke Talmage 42 B3
Stoke Trister 25 E5
Stoke Wake 13 D2
Stokeford 13 E4
Stokeham 95 E5
Stokeinteignhead 10 C5
Stokenchurch 42 C3
Stokenham 9 E3
Stokesay 64 D4
Stokesby 87 F4
Stokesley 111 E2
Stolford 23 F3
Ston Easton 24 D2
Stonar Cut 33 F2
Stondon Massey 45 E2
Stone *Bucks.* 42 C1
Stone *Glos.* 39 F3
Stone *Kent* 45 E5
Stone *Kent* 19 E1
Stone *Staffs.* 79 F4
Stone *Worcs.* 66 A5
Stone Allerton 24 A2
Stone Cross *E.Suss.* 10 D3
Stone Cross *Kent* 32 C5
Stone Cross *Kent* 31 E5
Stone House 108 C4
Stone Street *Kent* 31 E3
Stone Street *Suff.* 73 E3
Stonebridge *E.Suss.* 18 A1
Stonebridge *Warks.* 67 E4
Stonebroom 81 F2
Stoneferry 104 D4
Stonefield *Arg. & B.* 139 G2
Stonefield *S.Lan.* 142 A4
Stonegate 18 B1
Stonegrave 111 F5
Stonehaugh 127 F4
Stonehaven 161 G1
Stonehouse *D. & G.* 124 C4
Stonehouse *Glos.* 40 A2
Stonehouse *Northumb.* 118 C2
Stonehouse *Plym.* 8 A2
Stonehouse *S.Lan.* 142 B5
Stoneleigh 67 F5
Stonely 57 G1
Stoner Hill 28 C5
Stones Green 60 C5
Stonesby 82 D5
Stonesfield 41 F1
Stonestreet Green 32 C5
Stonethwaite 117 F5
Stoney Cross 14 B1
Stoney Middleton 93 G5
Stoney Stanton 67 G3
Stoney Stoke 25 E4
Stoney Stratton 25 D4
Stoney Stretton 64 C2
Stoneyburn 143 D3
Stoneygate 68 B2
Stoneyhills 46 C3
Stoneykirk 122 B5
Stoneywood 171 D3
Stonganess 203 E2
Stonham Aspal 60 C2
Stonnall 66 C2
Stonor 42 C4
Stonton Wyville 68 C3
Stony Houghton 81 F1
Stony Stratford 56 C3
Stonybreck 200 A5
Stoodleigh 10 C1
Stopham 16 C2
Stopsley 57 G5
Stoptide 4 D2
Storeton 91 E4
Stornoway (Steornabhagh) 187 F4
Stornoway Airport 187 F4
Storridge 53 G3
Storrington 16 C2
Storth 107 F4
Storwood 103 G3
Stotfield 181 E2
Stotfold 58 A4
Stottesdon 65 F4
Stoughton *Leics.* 68 B2
Stoughton *Surr.* 29 E2
Stoughton *W.Suss.* 16 A2
Stoul 165 D5
Stoulton 54 B2
Stour Provost 25 E5
Stour Row 25 F5
Stourbridge 66 A4
Stourpaine 13 E2
Stourport-on-Severn 66 A5
Stourton *Staffs.* 66 A4
Stourton *Warks.* 55 E4
Stourton *Wilts.* 25 E4
Stourton Caundle 12 D1
Stove 199 E3
Stoven 73 F3
Stow *Lincs.* 95 F4
Stow *Sc.Bord.* 144 B5
Stow Bardolph 71 E2
Stow Bedon 72 A2
Stow cum Quy 58 D1
Stow Longa 69 G5
Stow Maries 46 B3
Stow-on-the-Wold 55 D5
Stowbridge 71 E2
Stowe *Glos.* 39 E2
Stowe *Shrop.* 64 C5
Stowe *Staffs.* 80 B5
Stowell *Glos.* 40 C1
Stowell *Som.* 25 D5
Stowey 24 C2
Stowford 7 E2
Stowlangtoft 60 A1
Stowmarket 60 B2
Stowting 32 D4
Stowupland 60 B2
Stracathro 161 E3
Strachan 170 B5
Stradbroke 72 D4
Stradishall 59 F2
Stradsett 71 E2
Stragglethorpe 83 E2
Straiton *Edin.* 143 G3
Straiton *S.Ayr.* 132 B5
Straloch *Aber.* 171 D2
Straloch *P. & K.* 159 F3
Stramshall 80 B4
Strang 98 B4
Strannda 184 C5
Stranraer 122 B4
Strata Florida 50 D1
Stratfield Mortimer 28 B1
Stratfield Saye 28 B1
Stratfield Turgis 28 B2
Stratford 54 A4
Stratford St. Andrew 61 E2
Stratford St. Mary 60 B4
Stratford sub Castle 26 C4
Stratford Tony 26 B5
Stratford-upon-Avon 55 D2
Strath 195 E3
Strathan *High.* 188 C2
Strathan *High.* 185 F5
Strathaven 142 B5
Strathblane 141 G2
Strathcarron 177 F5
Strathdon 169 F3
Strathgirnock 169 F5
Strathkanaird 188 D4
Strathkinness 152 C3
Strathmiglo 152 A4
Strathpeffer 179 D4
Strathrannoch 178 C2
Strathtay 159 E4
Strathwhillan 131 F2
Strathy 194 A2
Strathyre 150 A3
Stratton *Cornw.* 20 C5
Stratton *Dorset* 12 C3
Stratton *Glos.* 40 C2
Stratton Audley 56 B5
Stratton-on-the-Fosse 25 D2
Stratton St. Margaret 41 D4
Stratton St. Michael 72 D2
Stratton Strawless 86 D3
Stravanan 140 B4
Stravithie 152 D3
Streat 17 F2
Streatham 44 B5
Streatley *Beds.* 57 F5
Streatley *W.Berks.* 42 A4
Street *Lancs.* 100 B2
Street *N.Yorks.* 111 G2
Street *Som.* 24 B4
Street Dinas 78 A4
Street End *Kent* 32 D3
Street End *W.Suss.* 16 A4
Street on the Fosse 24 D4
Streethay 66 D1
Streetlam 110 C3
Streetly 66 C3
Strefford 64 D4
Strensall 103 F1
Strensham 54 B3
Stretcholt 23 F3
Strete 9 E3
Stretford 92 B3
Stretford Court 52 D2
Strethall 58 C4
Stretham 70 D5
Strettington 16 A3
Stretton *Ches.* 78 B2
Stretton *Derbys.* 81 E1
Stretton *Rut.* 69 E1
Stretton *Staffs.* 66 A1
Stretton *Staffs.* 81 D5
Stretton *Warr.* 92 A4
Stretton en le Field 67 F1
Stretton Grandison 53 F3
Stretton Heath 64 C1
Stretton-on-Dunsmore 67 G5
Stretton-on-Fosse 55 E4
Stretton Sugwas 53 D3
Stretton under Fosse 67 G4
Stretton Westwood 65 E3
Stribers 107 E4
Strichen 183 E4
Stringston 23 E3
Strixton 57 E1
Stroat 39 E3
Stromeferry 165 E1
Stromemore 165 E1
Stromness 196 B2
Stronachlachar 149 G4
Strone *Arg. & B.* 140 C1
Strone *High.* 167 E2
Strone *High.* 156 D1
Strone *Stir.* 149 G3
Stronechrubie 189 E3
Stronenaba 157 E1
Stronlonag 140 C1
Stronmilchan 149 D2
Strontian 156 A3
Strontoiller 148 B2
Stronvar 150 A3
Strood 31 G2
Strood Green 29 F5
Stroquhan 124 C2
Stroud *Glos.* 40 A2
Stroud *Hants.* 28 C5
Stroud Common 29 F3
Stroud Green 40 A2
Stroul 141 D1
Stroxton 83 E4
Struan *High.* 163 G1
Struan *P. & K.* 158 D3
Strubby 97 E4
Strumpshaw 87 E5
Struthers 152 B4
Struy 178 D5
Stryt-issa 77 F3
Stryt-yr-hwch 78 A3
Stuartfield 183 E5
Stub Place 106 B3
Stubbington 15 E2
Stubbins 92 B1
Stubhampton 13 F1
Stubley 94 A5
Stubton 83 D3
Stuck *Arg. & B.* 140 B3
Stuck *Arg. & B.* 148 D5
Stuckbeg 149 E5
Stuckgowan 149 F4
Stuckindroin 149 F3
Stuckreoch 148 C5
Stuckton 14 A1
Stud Green 43 D5
Studdon 119 E2
Studfold 108 D5
Studham 43 F1
Studholme 117 F1
Studland 13 G4
Studley *Warks.* 54 C1
Studley *Wilts.* 40 B5
Studley Common 54 C1
Studley Roger 110 B5
Stuggadhoo 98 B4
Stump Cross 58 D3
Stuntney 71 D5
Stunts Green 18 B2
Sturbridge 79 F4
Sturmer 59 F3
Sturminster Common 13 D1
Sturminster Marshall 13 F2
Sturminster Newton 13 D1
Sturry 33 D2
Sturton by Stow 95 F4
Sturton le Steeple 95 E4
Stuston 72 C4
Stutton *N.Yorks.* 103 D3
Stutton *Suff.* 60 C4
Styal 92 C4
Styrrup 94 D3
Suainebost 187 G1
Suardail 187 F4
Succoth *Aber.* 169 G1
Succoth *Arg. & B.* 149 E4
Succothmore 148 D4
Suckley 53 G2
Sudborough 69 E4
Sudbourne 61 F2
Sudbrook *Lincs.* 83 E3
Sudbrook *Mon.* 39 E4
Sudbrooke 96 A5
Sudbury *Derbys.* 80 C4
Sudbury *Gt.Lon.* 44 A4
Sudbury *Suff.* 59 G3
Sudgrove 40 B2
Suffield *N.Yorks.* 112 C3
Suffield *Norf.* 86 D2
Sugarloaf 32 B5
Sugnall 79 E4
Suie Lodge Hotel 149 G2
Sulby 98 B2
Sulgrave 56 A3
Sulham 42 B5
Sulhamstead 28 B1
Sullington 16 C2
Sullom 202 C5
Sullom Voe Oil Terminal 202 C5
Sully 23 E1
Sumburgh 201 G5
Sumburgh Airport 201 G5
Summer Bridge 102 B1
Summercourt 4 C4
Summerfield 85 F4
Summerhill 78 A2
Summerhouse 110 B1
Summerleaze 38 D4
Summerseat 92 B1
Summertown 42 A2
Summit 92 D1
Sunadale 139 G5
Sunbury 29 G1
Sundaywell 124 C2
Sunderland *Cumb.* 117 E3
Sunderland *T. & W.* 120 C2
Sunderland Bridge 120 B4
Sundhope 135 E3
Sundon Park 57 F5
Sundridge 31 D3
Sundrum Mains 132 C3
Sunhill 40 D2
Sunipol 154 C4
Sunk Island 96 C1
Sunningdale 29 E1
Sunninghill 29 E1
Sunningwell 41 G3
Sunniside *Dur.* 120 A4
Sunniside *T. & W.* 120 B2
Sunny Bank 107 D3
Sunnylaw 150 C5
Sunnymead 42 A2
Sunnyside *Aber.* 171 D5
Sunnyside *Northumb.* 119 F1
Sunnyside *W.Suss.* 30 C5
Sunwick 145 F4
Surbiton 29 G1
Surfleet 84 A5
Surfleet Seas End 84 A5
Surlingham 87 E5
Sustead 86 C2
Susworth 95 F2
Sutcombe 20 D4
Suton 72 B2
Sutors of Cromarty 180 A3
Sutterton 84 A4
Sutton *Beds.* 58 A3
Sutton *Cambs.* 70 C5
Sutton *Gt.Lon.* 30 B2
Sutton *Kent* 33 F4
Sutton *Lincs.* 83 D2
Sutton *Norf.* 87 E3
Sutton *Notts.* 82 C4
Sutton *Notts.* 95 D4
Sutton *Oxon.* 41 G2
Sutton *Pembs.* 34 C1
Sutton *Peter.* 69 G3
Sutton *S.Yorks.* 94 C1
Sutton *Shrop.* 65 G4
Sutton *Shrop.* 79 D4
Sutton *Shrop.* 65 E1
Sutton *Staffs.* 79 E5
Sutton *Suff.* 61 E3
Sutton *W.Suss.* 16 B2
Sutton Abinger 29 G3
Sutton at Hone 45 E5
Sutton Bassett 68 C4
Sutton Benger 40 B5
Sutton Bonington 81 G5
Sutton Bridge 84 C5
Sutton Cheney 67 G2
Sutton Coldfield 66 D3
Sutton Courtenay 42 G3
Sutton Crosses 84 C5
Sutton Grange 110 B5
Sutton Green 29 F2
Sutton Holms 13 G1
Sutton Howgrave 110 C5
Sutton in Ashfield 81 F2
Sutton-in-Craven 101 G3
Sutton in the Elms 68 A3
Sutton Lane Ends 92 D5
Sutton le Marsh 97 F4
Sutton Leach 91 G3
Sutton Maddock 65 G2
Sutton Mallet 24 A4
Sutton Mandeville 26 A5
Sutton Montis 24 D5
Sutton-on-Hull 104 D4
Sutton on Sea 97 F4
Sutton-on-the-Forest 103 E1
Sutton on the Hill 80 D4
Sutton on Trent 82 C1
Sutton Poyntz 12 D4
Sutton St. Edmund 70 B1
Sutton St. James 70 C1
Sutton St. Nicholas 53 E3
Sutton Scarsdale 81 F1
Sutton Scotney 27 F4
Sutton-under-Brailes 55 E4
Sutton-under-Whitestonecliffe 111 D4
Sutton upon Derwent 103 G3
Sutton Valence 32 A4
Sutton Veny 25 F3
Sutton Waldron 13 E1
Sutton Weaver 91 G5
Sutton Wick 41 G3
Swaby 97 D5
Swadlincote 67 F1
Swaffham 71 G2
Swaffham Bulbeck 59 D1
Swaffham Prior 59 D1
Swafield 87 D2
Swainby 111 D2
Swainshill 53 D3
Swainsthorpe 86 D5
Swainswick 25 E1
Swalcliffe 55 F4
Swalecliffe 32 D2
Swallow 96 B2
Swallow Beck 83 E1
Swallowcliffe 26 A5
Swallowfield 28 C1
Swalwell 120 B1
Swampton 27 F2
Swan Street 59 G5
Swanage 13 G5
Swanbach 79 D3
Swanbourne 56 D5
Swanbridge 23 E1
Swancote 65 G3
Swanland 104 B5
Swanlaws 136 B5
Swanley 31 E2
Swanmore 15 E1
Swannington *Leics.* 67 G1
Swannington *Norf.* 86 C4
Swanscombe 45 F5
Swansea (Abertawe) 36 C3
Swanton Abbot 87 D3
Swanton Morley 86 B4
Swanton Novers 86 B2
Swanwick *Derbys.* 81 F2
Swanwick *Hants.* 15 E2
Swarby 83 F3
Swardeston 86 C5
Swarkestone 81 E5
Swarland 129 D1
Swaton 83 G4
Swavesey 58 B1
Sway 14 B3
Swayfield 83 E5
Swaythling 14 D1
Swaythorpe 104 C1
Sweetshouse 5 E3
Sweffling 61 E1
Swell 24 A5
Swepstone 67 F1
Swerford 55 F4
Swettenham 79 F1
Swffryd 38 B3
Swiftsden 18 C1
Swilland 60 C2
Swillbrook 100 A4
Swillington 102 C4
Swimbridge 21 G3
Swimbridge Newland 21 G2
Swinbrook 41 E1
Swincliffe 102 B2
Swinderby 83 D1
Swindon *Staffs.* 66 A3
Swindon *Swin.* 41 D4
Swindon Village 54 B5
Swine 104 D4
Swinefleet 103 G5
Swineshead *Beds.* 57 F1
Swineshead *Lincs.* 84 A3
Swineshead Bridge 84 A3
Swiney 195 E5
Swinford *Leics.* 68 A5
Swinford *Oxon.* 41 G2
Swingfield Minnis 33 E4
Swinhoe 137 G4
Swinhope 96 C3
Swining 201 D1
Swinithwaite 109 F4
Swinscoe 80 C3
Swinside Hall 136 B5
Swinstead 83 F5
Swinton *Gt.Man.* 92 B2
Swinton *N.Yorks.* 111 G5
Swinton *N.Yorks.* 110 B4
Swinton *S.Yorks.* 94 B3
Swinton *Sc.Bord.* 145 F5
Swintonmill 145 F5
Swithland 68 A1
Swordale 179 E3
Swordland 165 D5
Swordle 155 E3
Swordly 193 G2
Sworton Heath 92 A4
Swyddffynnon 50 C1
Swyncombe 42 B3
Swynnerton 79 F4
Swyre 12 B4
Syde 40 B1
Sydenham *Gt.Lon.* 44 C5
Sydenham *Oxon.* 42 C2
Sydenham Damerel 7 E3
Syderstone 85 G4
Sydling St. Nicholas 12 C3
Sydmonton 27 F2
Syerston 82 C3
Syke 92 C1
Sykehouse 94 D1
Sykes 100 C2
Sylen 36 B2
Symbister 201 E1
Symington *S.Ayr.* 132 B2
Symington *S.Lan.* 134 A2
Symonds Yat 39 E1
Symondsbury 12 A3
Synod Inn 50 A2
Syre 193 F4
Syreford 54 C5
Syresham 56 B3
Syston *Leics.* 68 B1
Syston *Lincs.* 83 E3
Sytchampton 54 A1
Sywell 56 D1


## T


Taagan 177 G3
Tabost *W.Isles* 185 F2
Tabost *W.Isles* 187 G1
Tacher 195 D4
Tackley 41 G1
Tacleit 186 C4
Tacolneston 72 C2
Tadcaster 103 D3
Tadden 13 F2
Taddington 93 F5
Taddiport 21 E4
Tadley 28 B1
Tadlow 58 A3
Tadmarton 55 F4
Tadworth 30 B3
Tafarn-y-bwlch 49 D4
Tafarn-y-Gelyn 77 E1
Tafarnaubach 38 A1
Taff's Well (Ffynnon Taf) 38 A4
Tafolwern 63 E2
Tai-bach 77 E5
Tai'n Lôn 74 D2
Taibach 37 D4
Taicynhaeaf 62 C1
Tain *High.* 195 E2
Tain *High.* 179 G1
Tai'r Bull 51 F5
Tairgwaith 36 D1
Tairlaw 132 C5
Takeley 59 D5
Takeley Street 58 D5
Tal-sarn 50 B2
Tal-y-bont *Conwy* 76 A1
Tal-y-bont *Gwyn.* 75 E5
Tal-y-bont *Gwyn.* 89 E5
Tal-y-Cae 75 F1
Tal-y-cafn 89 F5
Tal-y-llyn 62 D2
Tal-y-wern 63 E2
Talachddu 51 G4
Talacre 90 C4
Talardd 76 B5
Talaton 11 D3
Talbenny 34 B1
Talbot Green 37 G4
Talerddig 63 F2
Talgarreg 50 A2
Talgarth 52 A4
Taliesin 62 C3
Talisker 163 G1
Talke 79 F2
Talkin 118 B2
Talla Linnfoots 134 C3
Talladale 177 F2
Talladh-a-Bheithe 158 A4
Tallarn Green 78 B3
Tallentire 117 E3
Talley 50 C4
Tallington 69 F2
Talmine 193 E2
Talog 49 G5
Talsarnau 75 F4
Talskiddy 4 D3
Talwrn *I.o.A.* 88 C5
Talwrn *Wrex.* 77 F3
Talybont 62 C4
Talybont-on-Usk 52 A5
Talyllyn 52 A5
Talysarn 75 D2
Tamavoid 150 A5
Tamerton Foliot 8 A1
Tamworth 67 E2
Tan-lan 75 F3
Tan-y-fron 76 C1
Tan-y-graig 74 C4
Tan-y-groes 49 F3
Tan-y-pistyll 77 D5
Tandridge 30 C3
Tanerdy 50 A5
Tanfield 120 A2
Tangiers 34 C1
Tanglandford 171 D1
Tangley 27 E2
Tangmere 16 B3
Tangwick 202 B5
Tangy 130 B3
Tankerness 197 E2
Tankersley 94 A2
Tannach 195 F4
Tannachie 161 F1
Tannachy 190 C4
Tannadice 160 C4
Tannington 60 D1
Tannochside 142 B3
Tansley 81 E2
Tansor 69 F3
Tantobie 120 A2
Tanton 111 E1
Tanworth in Arden 66 D5
Tanygrisiau 75 F3
Taobh a' Deas Loch Baghasdail 172 C2
Taobh Siar 184 D3
Taobh Tuath (Northton) 184 B5
Tapeley 21 E3
Taplow 43 E4
Taraphocain 156 C5
Tarbat House 179 G2
Tarbert *Arg. & B.* 139 G3
Tarbert *Arg. & B.* 139 E4
Tarbert *Arg. & B.* 139 E1
Tarbert *High.* 155 F3
Tarbert (An Tairbeart) *W.Isles* 185 D3
Tarbet *Arg. & B.* 149 F4
Tarbet *High.* 165 D5
Tarbet *High.* 192 A4
Tarbolton 132 C3
Tarbrax 143 E4
Tardebigge 54 B1
Tardy Gate 100 B5
Tarfside 160 C1
Tarland 169 G4

Tarleton 100 A5
Tarlscough 91 F1
Tarlton 40 B3
Tarnbrook 100 B2
Tarnock 24 A2
Tarporley 78 C1
Tarr 23 E4
Tarrant Crawford 13 F2
Tarrant Gunville 13 F1
Tarrant Hinton 13 F1
Tarrant Keyneston 13 F2
Tarrant Launceston 13 F2
Tarrant Monkton 13 F2
Tarrant Rawston 13 F2
Tarrant Rushton 13 F2
Tarrel 180 A1
Tarring Neville 17 G3
Tarrington 53 F3
Tarrnacraig 131 E2
Tarsappie 151 G2
Tarskavaig 164 B4
Tarves 171 D1
Tarvie *High.* 178 D4
Tarvie *P. & K.* 159 F3
Tarvin 78 B1
Tarvin Sands 78 B1
Tasburgh 72 D2
Tasley 65 F3
Taston 55 F5
Tatenhill 80 D5
Tatham 100 C1
Tathwell 96 D4
Tatsfield 30 D3
Tattenhall 78 B2
Tatterford 85 G5
Tattersett 85 G5
Tattershall 84 A2
Tattershall Bridge 83 G2
Tattershall Thorpe 84 A2
Tattingstone 60 C4
Tatworth 11 G2
Tauchers 181 F4
Taunton 23 F5
Tavelty 170 C3
Taverham 86 C4
Tavernspite 35 E1
Tavistock 7 E3
Taw Bridge 21 G5
Taw Green 7 G1
Tawstock 21 F3
Taxal 93 E5
Tayburn 141 G5
Taychreggan 148 C2
Tayinloan 139 E5
Taylors Cross 20 C4
Taynafead 148 C3
Taynish 139 F1
Taynton *Glos.* 53 G5
Taynton *Oxon.* 41 E1
Taynuilt 148 C1
Tayock 161 E4
Tayovullin 138 A2
Tayport 152 C2
Tayvallich 139 F1
Tealby 96 B3
Team Valley 120 B1
Teanamachar 173 F3
Teangue 164 C4
Teasses 152 C4
Tebay 108 B2
Tebworth 57 E5
Tedburn St. Mary 10 B3
Teddington *Glos.* 54 B4
Teddington *Gt.Lon.* 44 A5
Tedstone Delamere 53 F2
Tedstone Wafre 53 F2
Teesside International Airport 110 C1
Teeton 68 B5
Teffont Evias 26 A4
Teffont Magna 26 A4
Tegryn 49 F4
Teigh 69 D1
Teigngrace 10 B5
Teignmouth 10 C5
Telford 65 F2
Telham 18 C2
Tellisford 25 E2
Telscombe 17 G3
Telscombe Cliffs 17 G3
Tempar 158 B4
Templand 125 E2
Temple *Cornw.* 5 F2
Temple *Midloth.* 144 A4
Temple Bar 50 B2
Temple Cloud 24 D2
Temple Ewell 33 E4
Temple Grafton 54 D2
Temple Guiting 54 C5
Temple Hirst 103 F5
Temple Normanton 81 F1
Temple Sowerby 118 C5
Templecombe 25 E5
Templeton *Devon* 10 B1
Templeton *Pembs.* 35 E1
Templeton Bridge 10 B1
Templewood 161 E3
Tempsford 57 G2
Ten Mile Bank 71 D3
Tenbury Wells 53 E1
Tenby (Dinbych-y-Pysgod) 35 E2
Tendring 60 C5
Tenga 155 E5
Tenterden 32 A5
Tepersie Castle 170 A2
Teralty 114 B2
Terling 45 G1
Ternhill 78 D4
Terregles 124 D3
Terrington 111 F5
Terrington St. Clement 85 D5
Terrington St. John 70 D1
Tervieside 169 E1
Teston 31 G3
Testwood 14 C1
Tetbury 40 A3
Tetbury Upton 40 A3
Tetchill 78 A4
Tetcott 6 D1
Tetford 96 D5
Tetney 96 D2
Tetney Lock 96 D2
Tetsworth 42 B2
Tettenhall 66 A2
Tettenhall Wood 66 A3
Tetworth 58 A2
Teuchan 171 F1
Teversal 81 F1
Teversham 58 C2
Teviothead 135 F5
Tewel 161 G1
Tewin 44 B1
Tewkesbury 54 A4
Teynham 32 B2
Thainston 161 E2
Thainstone House 170 C3
Thakeham 16 D2
Thame 42 C2
Thames Ditton 29 G1
Thames Haven 45 G4
Thamesmead 45 D4
Thanington 32 D3
Thankerton 134 A2
Tharston 72 C2
Thatcham 27 G1
Thatto Heath 91 G3
Thaxted 59 E4
The Apes Hall 71 D4
The Bage 52 B3
The Balloch 150 D3
The Banking 170 C1
The Bar 29 G5
The Belfry 67 D3
The Birks 170 C4
The Bog 64 C3
The Bourne 28 D3
The Bratch 66 A3
The Bryn 38 C2
The Burf 54 A1
The Burn 161 D2
The Camp 40 B2
The Chequer 78 B3
The City 42 C3
The Common 27 D4
The Craigs 189 G5
The Cronk 98 B2
The Den 141 E4
The Dicker 18 A3
The Drums 160 B3
The Eaves 39 F2
The Flatt 127 D4
The Folly 44 A1
The Grange *Shrop.* 78 A4
The Grange *Surr.* 30 C4
The Green *Arg. & B.* 154 A2
The Green *Wilts.* 25 F4
The Haven 29 F4
The Headland 121 E4
The Hermitage 30 B3
The Howe 98 A5
The Isle 65 D1
The Knowle 31 F4
The Laurels 73 E2
The Leacon 32 B5
The Lee 43 E2
The Lhen 98 B1
The Lodge 149 D5
The Marsh 64 C3
The Moor *E.Suss.* 18 D2
The Moor *Kent* 18 C1
The Mumbles 36 C4
The Mythe 54 A4
The Neuk 170 C5
The Node 44 B1
The Oval 25 E1
The Rhos 34 D1
The Rowe 79 F4
The Sands 29 D3
The Shoe 40 A5
The Smithies 65 F3
The Stocks 19 E1
The Vauld 53 E3
The Wrythe 30 B2
The Wyke 65 G2
Theakston 110 B4
Thealby 95 F1
Theale *Som.* 24 B3
Theale *W.Berks.* 42 B5
Thearne 104 C4
Theberton 61 F1
Thedden Grange 28 B4
Theddingworth 68 B4
Theddlethorpe All Saints 97 E4
Theddlethorpe St. Helen 97 E4
Thelbridge Barton 10 A1
Thelnetham 72 B4
Thelveton 72 C3
Thelwall 92 A4
Themelthorpe 86 B3
Thenford 56 A3
Therfield 58 B4
Thetford 71 G4
Theydon Bois 44 D3
Thickwood 40 A5
Thimbleby *Lincs.* 96 C5
Thimbleby *N.Yorks.* 110 D3
Thirkleby 111 D5
Thirlby 111 D4
Thirlestane 144 C5
Thirn 110 B4
Thirsk 110 D4
Thistleton *Lancs.* 100 A4
Thistleton *Rut.* 69 E1
Thistley Green 71 E5
Thixendale 104 A1
Thockrington 128 B4
Tholomas Drove 70 B2
Tholthorpe 103 D1
Thomas Chapel 35 E2
Thomastown 170 A1
Thompson 72 A2
Thomshill 181 E4
Thong 45 F5
Thoralby 109 F4
Thoresby 94 D5
Thoresway 96 B3
Thorganby *Lincs.* 96 C3
Thorganby *N.Yorks.* 103 F3
Thorgill 111 G3
Thorington 73 F4
Thorington Street 60 B4
Thorlby 101 F2
Thorley 45 D1
Thorley Street *Herts.* 45 D1
Thorley Street *I.o.W.* 14 C4
Thormanby 111 D5
Thorn Falcon 23 F5
Thornaby-on-Tees 111 D1
Thornage 86 B2
Thornborough *Bucks.* 56 C4
Thornborough *N.Yorks.* 110 B4
Thornbury *Devon* 21 E5
Thornbury *Here.* 53 F2
Thornbury *S.Glos.* 39 F4
Thornby 68 B5
Thorncliff 80 B2
Thorncombe 11 G2
Thorncombe Street 29 F3
Thorncote Green 57 G3
Thorndon 60 C1
Thorndon Cross 7 F1
Thorne 95 D1
Thorne St. Margaret 23 D5
Thorner 102 C3
Thornes 66 C2
Thorney *Bucks.* 43 F5
Thorney *Notts.* 95 F5
Thorney *Peter.* 70 A2
Thorney *Som.* 24 B5
Thorney Hill 14 B2
Thornford 12 C1
Thorngrove 24 A4
Thorngumbald 105 E5
Thornham 85 F3
Thornham Magna 72 C4
Thornham Parva 72 C4
Thornhaugh 69 F2
Thornhill *Cardiff* 38 A4
Thornhill *D. & G.* 124 C1
Thornhill *Derbys.* 93 F4
Thornhill *S'ham.* 15 D1
Thornhill *Stir.* 150 B4
Thornhill *W.Yorks.* 93 G1
Thornholme 104 D1
Thornicombe 13 E2
Thornley *Dur.* 120 C4
Thornley *Dur.* 120 A4
Thornliebank 141 G4
Thorns 59 F2
Thornsett 93 E4
Thornthwaite *Cumb.* 117 F4
Thornthwaite *N.Yorks.* 102 A2
Thornton *Angus* 160 B5
Thornton *Bucks.* 56 C4
Thornton *E.Riding* 103 G3
Thornton *Fife* 152 A5
Thornton *Lancs.* 99 G3
Thornton *Leics.* 67 G2
Thornton *Lincs.* 84 A1
Thornton *Mersey.* 91 E2
Thornton *Middbro.* 111 D1
Thornton *Northumb.* 145 G5
Thornton *P. & K.* 159 F5
Thornton *Pembs.* 34 C2
Thornton *W.Yorks.* 102 A4
Thornton Curtis 96 A1
Thornton Hough 91 E4
Thornton-in-Craven 101 F3
Thornton-le-Beans 110 C3
Thornton-le-Clay 103 F1
Thornton-le-Dale 112 B4
Thornton le Moor *Lincs.* 96 A3
Thornton-le-Moor *N.Yorks.* 110 C4
Thornton-le-Moors 91 F5
Thornton-le-Street 110 D4
Thornton Park 145 G5
Thornton Rust 109 E4
Thornton Steward 110 A4
Thornton Watlass 110 B4
Thorntonhall 141 G4
Thorntonloch 145 E2
Thornwood Common 45 D2
Thornyhill 161 E2
Thornylee 135 F2
Thoroton 82 C3
Thorp Arch 102 D3
Thorpe *Derbys.* 80 C2
Thorpe *E.Riding* 104 C3
Thorpe *Lincs.* 97 E4
Thorpe *N.Yorks.* 101 G1
Thorpe *Norf.* 73 F2
Thorpe *Notts.* 82 C2
Thorpe *Surr.* 29 F1
Thorpe Abbotts 72 C4
Thorpe Acre 81 G5
Thorpe Arnold 82 C5
Thorpe Audlin 94 B1
Thorpe Bassett 112 B5
Thorpe Bay 46 C4
Thorpe by Water 69 D3
Thorpe Constantine 67 E2
Thorpe Culvert 84 C1
Thorpe End Garden Village 87 D4
Thorpe Green 60 A2
Thorpe Hall 111 E5
Thorpe Hesley 94 A3
Thorpe in Balne 94 C1
Thorpe in the Fallows 95 G4
Thorpe Langton 68 C3
Thorpe Larches 120 C5
Thorpe-le-Soken 60 C5
Thorpe le Street 104 A3
Thorpe Malsor 68 D5
Thorpe Mandeville 56 A3
Thorpe Market 86 D2
Thorpe Morieux 60 A2
Thorpe on the Hill *Lincs.* 83 E1
Thorpe on the Hill *W.Yorks.* 102 C5
Thorpe St. Andrew 87 D5
Thorpe St. Peter 84 C1
Thorpe Salvin 94 C4
Thorpe Satchville 68 C1
Thorpe Thewles 120 C5
Thorpe Tilney Dales 83 G2
Thorpe Underwood 103 D2
Thorpe Waterville 69 F4
Thorpe Willoughby 103 E4
Thorpeness 61 F2
Thorpland 71 E2
Thorrington 47 D1
Thorverton 10 C2
Thrandeston 72 C4
Thrapston 69 F5
Threapland 101 F1
Threapwood 78 B3
Three Bridges 30 B5
Three Burrows 4 B5
Three Chimneys 32 A5
Three Cocks 52 A4
Three Crosses 36 B3
Three Cups Corner 18 B1
Three Holes 70 D2
Three Leg Cross 31 F5
Three Legged Cross 13 G2
Three Mile Cross 28 C1
Threekingham 83 F4
Threemilestone 4 B5
Threlkeld 117 G4
Threshers Bush 45 D2
Threshfield 101 F1
Threxton Hill 71 G2
Thriepley 152 B1
Thrigby 87 F4
Thringarth 119 F5
Thringstone 67 G1
Thrintoft 110 C3
Thriplow 58 C3
Throcking 58 B4
Throckley 120 A1
Throckmorton 54 B2
Throphill 128 D3
Thropton 128 C1
Throwleigh 7 G1
Throwley 32 B3
Throws 59 E5
Thrumpton 81 G4
Thrumster 195 F4
Thrunton 137 E5
Thrupp *Glos.* 40 A2
Thrupp *Oxon.* 41 G1
Thrushelton 7 E2
Thrussington 68 B1
Thruxton *Hants.* 27 D3
Thruxton *Here.* 52 D4
Thrybergh 94 B3
Thulston 81 F4
Thundergay 139 G5
Thundersley 46 B4
Thunderton 183 F5
Thundridge 44 C1
Thurcaston 68 A1
Thurcroft 94 C4
Thurdistoft 195 E2
Thurgarton *Norf.* 86 C2
Thurgarton *Notts.* 82 B3
Thurgoland 93 G2
Thurlaston *Leics.* 68 A3
Thurlaston *Warks.* 67 G5
Thurlbear 23 F5
Thurlby *Lincs.* 69 G1
Thurlby *Lincs.* 83 E1
Thurleigh 57 F2
Thurlestone 8 C3
Thurloxton 23 F4
Thurlstone 93 G2
Thurlton 73 F2
Thurmaston 68 B2
Thurnby 68 B2
Thurne 87 F4
Thurnham 32 A3
Thurning *Norf.* 86 B3
Thurning *Northants.* 69 F4
Thurnscoe 94 B2
Thurrock Lakeside 45 E5
Thursby 117 G1
Thursford 86 A2
Thursley 29 E4
Thurso 194 D2
Thurstaston 90 D4
Thurston 60 A1
Thurstonfield 117 G1
Thurstonland 93 F1
Thurton 87 E5
Thurvaston 80 D4
Thuster 195 E3
Thuxton 86 B5
Thwaite *N.Yorks.* 109 D3
Thwaite *Suff.* 60 C1
Thwaite Head 107 E3
Thwaite St. Mary 73 E2
Thwing 104 C1
Tibbermore 151 F2
Tibberton *Glos.* 53 G5
Tibberton *Tel. & W.* 79 D5
Tibberton *Worcs.* 54 B2
Tibbie Shiels Inn 134 D3
Tibenham 72 C2
Tibertich 148 A4
Tibshelf 81 F1
Tibthorpe 104 B2
Ticehurst 31 F5
Tichborne 27 G4
Tickencote 69 E2
Tickenham 39 D5
Tickhill 94 C3
Ticklerton 65 D3
Ticknall 81 E5
Tickton 104 C3
Tidcombe 27 D2
Tiddington *Oxon.* 42 B2
Tiddington *Warks.* 55 E2
Tidebrook 18 B1
Tideford 7 D5
Tidenham 39 E3
Tidenham Chase 39 E3
Tideswell 93 F5
Tidmarsh 42 B5
Tidmington 55 E4
Tidpit 13 G1
Tidworth 26 D3
Tiers Cross 34 C1
Tiffield 56 B2
Tifty 182 C5
Tigerton 160 D3
Tigh a' Gearraidh 173 F2
Tighachnoic 155 F5
Tighnablair 150 C3
Tighnabruaich 140 A2
Tighnacomaire 156 B3
Tigley 9 D1
Tilbrook 57 F1
Tilbury 45 F5
Tile Cross 67 D4
Tile Hill 67 E5
Tilehurst 42 B5
Tilford 29 D3
Tillathrowie 169 G1
Tillers' Green 53 F4
Tillery 171 E2
Tilley 78 C5
Tillicoultry 151 E5
Tillingham 46 C2
Tillington *Here.* 53 D3
Tillington *W.Suss.* 29 E5
Tillington Common 53 D3
Tillyarblet 160 D3
Tillybirloch 170 B4
Tillycairn Castle 170 B3
Tillycorthie 171 E2
Tillydrine 170 B5
Tillyfar 183 D5
Tillyfour 170 A3
Tillyfourie 170 B3
Tillygreig 171 D2
Tillypronie 169 G4
Tilmanstone 33 E3
Tilney All Saints 71 D1
Tilney High End 71 D1
Tilney St. Lawrence 71 D1
Tilshead 26 B3
Tilstock 78 C4
Tilston 78 B2
Tilstone Fearnall 78 C1
Tilsworth 57 E5
Tilton on the Hill 68 C2
Tiltups End 40 A3
Timberland 83 G2
Timberland Dales 83 G1
Timbersbrook 79 F1
Timberscombe 22 C3
Timble 102 A2
Timperley 92 B4
Timsbury *B. & N.E.Som.* 25 D2
Timsbury *Hants.* 27 E5
Timsgearraidh 186 B4
Timworth Green 59 G1
Tincleton 13 D3
Tindale 118 C2
Tingewick 56 B4
Tingley 102 B5
Tingrith 57 F4
Tingwall 198 C4
Tinhay 7 E2
Tinney 6 C1
Tinshill 102 B4
Tinsley 94 B3
Tinsley Green 30 B5
Tintagel 5 E1
Tintern Parva 39 E2
Tintinhull 12 A1
Tintwistle 93 E3
Tinwald 125 E2
Tinwell 69 F2
Tippacott 22 A3
Tipperty *Aber.* 161 F1
Tipperty *Aber.* 171 E2
Tiptoe 14 B3
Tipton 66 B3
Tipton St. John 11 D3
Tiptree 46 B1
Tiptree Heath 46 B1
Tir-y-dail 36 C1
Tirabad 51 E3
Tirdeunaw 36 C3
Tiree Airport 154 B2
Tirindrish 157 E1
Tirley 54 A5
Tirphil 38 A2
Tirril 118 B5
Tisbury 26 A5
Tissington 80 C2
Tister 195 D2
Titchberry 20 C3
Titchfield 15 E2
Titchmarsh 69 F5
Titchwell 85 F3
Tithby 82 B4
Titley 52 C1
Titsey 30 D3
Titson 20 C5
Tittensor 79 F4
Tittleshall 85 G5
Tiverton *Ches.* 78 C1
Tiverton *Devon* 10 C1
Tivetshall St. Margaret 72 C3
Tivetshall St. Mary 72 C3
Tixall 79 G5
Tixover 69 E2
Toab *Ork.* 197 E2
Toab *Shet.* 201 G5
Tobermory 155 E4
Toberonochy 147 G4
Tobha Mòr 162 A1
Tobson 186 C4
Tocher 170 B1
Tockenham 40 C5
Tockenham Wick 40 C4
Tockholes 100 C5
Tockington 39 F4
Tockwith 103 D2
Todber 25 E5
Toddington *Beds.* 57 F5
Toddington *Glos.* 54 C4
Toddington *W.Suss.* 16 C3
Todenham 55 E4
Todhills *Angus* 152 C1
Todhills *Cumb.* 126 B5
Todlachie 170 B3
Todmorden 101 F5
Todwick 94 B4
Toft *Cambs.* 58 B2
Toft *Lincs.* 69 F1
Toft *Shet.* 202 D5
Toft Hill 120 A5
Toft Monks 73 F2
Toft next Newton 96 A4
Toftcarl 195 F4
Toftrees 85 G5
Tofts 195 F2
Toftwood 86 A4
Togston 129 E1
Tokavaig 164 C3
Tokers Green 42 C5
Tolastadh 187 G3
Tolastadh a' Chaolais 186 C4
Tolastadh Ùr 187 G3
Toll of Birness 171 F1
Tolland 23 E4
Tollard Royal 13 F1
Tollcross 142 A3
Toller Down Gate 12 B2
Toller Fratrum 12 B3
Toller Porcorum 12 B3
Toller Whelme 12 B2
Tollerton *N.Yorks.* 103 E1
Tollerton *Notts.* 82 B4
Tollesbury 46 C2
Tollesby 111 E1
Tolleshunt D'Arcy 46 C1
Tolleshunt Knights 46 C1
Tolleshunt Major 46 B1
Tolpuddle 13 D3
Tolvah 168 A5
Tolworth 29 G1
Tom an Fhuadain 185 F2
Tomatin 168 A2
Tombreck 167 F1
Tomchrasky 166 B3
Tomdoun 166 A4
Tomdow 180 C5
Tomich *High.* 166 C2
Tomich *High.* 179 F2
Tomich *High.* 190 B4
Tomintoul 169 D3
Tomnacross 179 E5
Tomnamoon 180 C4
Tomnaven 169 G1
Tomnavoulin 169 E2
Tomvaich 168 C1
Ton Pentre 37 F3
Ton-teg 37 G4
Tonbridge 31 E4
Tondu 37 E4
Tonfanau 62 B2
Tong 65 G2
Tong Norton 65 G2
Tong Street 102 A4
Tonge 81 F5
Tongham 29 D3
Tongland 124 B5
Tongue 193 E3
Tongue House 193 E3
Tongwynlais 38 A4
Tonna 37 D3
Tonwell 44 C1
Tonypandy 37 F3
Tonyrefail 37 G4
Toot Baldon 42 A2
Toot Hill 45 E2
Toothill 14 C1
Top End 57 F1
Topcliffe 110 C5
Topcroft 73 D2
Topcroft Street 73 D2
Toppesfield 59 F4
Toppings 92 B1
Topsham 10 C4
Topsham Bridge 8 D2
Torastan 154 B3
Torbain 169 D3
Torbeg *Aber.* 169 F4
Torbeg *N.Ayr.* 131 E3
Torbryan 9 E1
Torcastle 156 D2
Torcross 9 E3
Tordarroch 167 F1
Tore 179 F4
Toreduff 180 D3
Toremore *High.* 168 D1
Toremore *High.* 195 D5
Torgyle 166 C3
Torksey 95 F5
Torlum 173 F4
Torlundy 156 D2
Tormarton 39 G5
Tormisdale 1138 A4
Tormore 131 D2
Tormsdale 194 D3
Tornagrain 179 G4
Tornahaish 169 E4
Tornaveen 170 B4
Torness 167 E2
Torpenhow 117 E3
Torphichen 143 D2
Torphins 170 B4
Torpoint 8 A2
Torquay 9 F1
Torquhan 144 B5
Torr 8 B2
Torran *Arg. & B.* 148 A4
Torran *High.* 179 G2
Torran *High.* 176 B5
Torrance *E.Dun.* 142 A2
Torrance *S.Lan.* 142 A4
Torrancroy 169 F3
Torrich 180 A4
Torridon 177 F4
Torrin 164 B2
Torrisdale *Arg. & B.* 130 C2
Torrisdale *High.* 193 F2
Torrish 191 E3
Torrisholme 100 A1
Torroble 190 A4
Torry *Aber.* 181 G5
Torry *Aberdeen* 171 E4
Torryburn 143 E1
Torsonce 144 B5
Torterston 183 F5
Torthorwald 125 E3
Tortington 16 B3
Tortworth 39 G3
Torvaig 176 A5
Torver 107 D3
Torwood 142 C1
Torworth 95 D4
Tosberry 20 C3
Toscaig 164 D1
Toseland 58 A1
Tosside 101 D2
Tostarie 154 C5
Tostock 60 A1
Totaig 175 F4
Totamore 154 A4
Tote 176 A5
Totegan 194 A2
Totford 27 G4
Tothill 97 E4
Totland 14 C4
Totley 94 A4
Totnes 9 E1
Toton 81 G4
Totronald 154 A4
Tottenham 44 C3
Tottenhill 71 E1
Totteridge 44 B3
Totternhoe 57 E5
Tottington *Gt.Man.* 92 B1
Tottington *Norf.* 71 G3
Totton 14 C1
Touchen-End 43 D5
Toulton 23 E4
Toux 183 E4
Tovil 31 G3
Tow Law 120 A4
Toward 140 C3
Towcester 56 B3
Towednack 2 B3
Tower Hamlets 44 C4
Towersey 42 C2
Towie *Aber.* 183 D3
Towie *Aber.* 170 A2
Towie *Aber.* 169 G3
Towiemore 181 F5
Town End *Cambs.* 70 C3
Town End *Cumb.* 107 F4
Town Green 91 F2
Town Row 31 E5
Town Street 71 F4
Town Yetholm 136 C4
Townend 141 F2
Townhead 115 G2
Townhead of Greenlaw 124 B4
Townhill 143 F1
Townshend 2 C3
Towthorpe *E.Riding* 104 B1
Towthorpe *York* 103 F2
Towton 103 D4
Towyn 90 A5
Toynton All Saints 84 B1
Toynton Fen Side 84 B1
Toynton St. Peter 84 C1
Toy's Hill 31 D3
Trabboch 132 C3
Traboe 3 E4
Tradespark *High.* 180 A4
Tradespark *Ork.* 197 D2
Trafford Centre 92 B3
Trafford Park 92 B3
Trallong 51 F5
Trallwn *Swan.* 36 C3
Tranch 38 B2
Tranent 144 B2
Trantlebeg 194 A3
Trantlemore 194 A3
Tranwell 129 D3
Trap 36 C1
Traprain 144 C2
Traquair 135 E2
Trawden 101 F4
Trawsfynydd 76 A4
Tre-ddiog 48 B5
Tre-groes 50 A3
Tre-Rhys 49 E3
Tre-vaughan 50 A5
Trealaw 37 F3
Treales 100 A4
Trearddur 88 A5
Treaslane 175 G4
Trebanog 37 G3
Trebanos 36 D2
Trebarrow 6 C1
Trebartha 5 G2
Trebarwith 5 E1
Trebetherick 4 D2
Treborough 22 D4
Trebudannon 4 C3
Trebullett 6 D3
Treburley 7 D3
Trebyan 5 E3
Trecastle 51 E5
Trecwn 48 C4
Trecynon 37 F2
Tredavoe 2 B4
Tredegar 38 A2
Tredington *Glos.* 54 B5
Tredington *Warks.* 55 E3
Tredinnick *Cornw.* 4 D2
Tredinnick *Cornw.* 5 G4
Tredomen 52 A4
Tredrissi 49 D3
Tredunnock 38 C3
Treen 2 A4
Treeton 94 B4
Trefaldwyn (Montgomery) 64 B3
Trefasser 48 B4
Trefdraeth 88 C5
Trefecca 52 A4
Trefeglwys 63 F3
Trefenter 50 C1
Treffgarne 48 C5
Treffynnon (Holywell) *Flints.* 90 C5

Treffynnon *Pembs.* 48 B5
Trefgarn Owen 48 B5
Trefil 38 A1
Trefilan 50 B2
Treflach 77 F5
Trefnanney 64 B1
Trefnant 90 B5
Trefonen 77 F5
Trefor *Gwyn.* 74 C3
Trefor *I.o.A.* 88 B4
Treforest 37 G4
Treforest Industrial Estate 38 A4
Trefriw 76 A1
Trefynwy (Monmouth) 39 E1
Tregadillett 6 D2
Tregaian 88 C5
Tregare 38 D1
Tregaron 50 C2
Tregarth 75 F1
Tregavethan 4 B5
Tregear 4 C4
Tregeare 5 G1
Tregeiriog 77 E4
Tregele 88 B3
Tregidden 3 E4
Treglemais 48 B5
Tregolds 4 C2
Tregole 6 B1
Tregonetha 5 D3
Tregony 4 D5
Tregoyd 52 A4
Treguff 37 G5
Tregurrian 4 C3
Tregynon 63 G3
Trehafod 37 G3
Treharris 37 G3
Treherbert 37 F3
Trekenner 6 D3
Treknow 5 E1
Trelash 6 B1
Trelassick 4 C4
Trelawnyd 90 B5
Trelech 49 F4
Trelech a'r Betws 49 G5
Treleddyd-fawr 48 A5
Trelewis 38 A3
Treligga 5 E1
Trelights 5 D2
Trelill 5 E2
Trelissick 3 F3
Trelleck 39 E2
Trelleck Grange 39 D2
Trelogan 90 C4
Trelystan 64 B2
Tremadog 75 E3
Tremail 5 F1
Tremain 49 F3
Tremaine 5 G1
Tremar 5 G3
Trematon 7 D5
Tremeirchion 90 B5
Tremethick Cross 2 B3
Trenance 4 C3
Trenarren 5 E5
Trench *Tel. & W.* 65 F1
Trench *Wrex.* 78 A4
Treneglos 5 G1
Trenewan 5 F4
Trent 12 B1
Trentham 79 F3
Trentishoe 21 G1
Treoes 37 F5
Treorchy 37 F3
Tre'r-ddol 62 C3
Trerulefoot 6 D5
Tresaith 49 F2
Trescott 66 A3
Trescowe 2 C3
Tresham 39 G3
Treshnish 154 C5
Tresillian 4 C5
Tresinney 5 F1
Tresinwen 48 C3
Treskinnick Cross 6 C1
Tresmeer 5 G1
Tresparrett 6 B1
Tresparrett Posts 6 B1
Tressait 158 D3
Tresta *Shet.* 203 F3
Tresta *Shet.* 200 C2
Treswell 95 E5
Trethurgy 5 E4
Tretio 48 A5
Tretire 53 E5
Tretower 52 A5
Treuddyn 77 F2
Trevalga 5 E1
Trevalyn 78 A2
Trevanson 5 D2
Trevarren 4 D3
Trevarrick 5 D5
Trevaughan 35 F1
Trevellas 4 B4
Trevelmond 5 G3
Treverva 3 E3
Trevescan 2 A4
Trevethin 38 B2
Trevigro 6 D4
Trevine *Arg. & B.* 148 C2
Trevine *Pembs.* 48 B4
Treviscoe 4 D4
Trevone 4 C2
Trevor 77 F3
Trewalder 5 E1
Trewarmett 5 E1
Trewarthenick 4 D5
Trewassa 5 F1
Trewellard 2 A3
Trewen 5 G1
Trewern 64 B1
Trewidland 5 G4
Trewilym 49 E3
Trewint 6 B1
Trewithian 3 F3
Trewoon 5 D4
Trewornan 5 D2
Treyarnon 4 C2
Treyford 16 A2
Triangle 101 G5
Trickett's Cross 13 G2
Trimdon 120 C4
Trimdon Colliery 120 C4
Trimdon Grange 120 C4
Trimingham 87 D2
Trimley St. Martin 61 D4
Trimley St. Mary 61 D4
Trimpley 65 G5
Trimsaran 36 A2
Trimstone 21 F1
Trinafour 158 C3
Trinant 38 B3
Tring 43 E1
Trinity 161 E3
Trislaig 156 C2
Trispen 4 C4
Tritlington 129 E2
Trochry 159 E5
Troedyraur 49 G3
Troedyrhiw 37 G2
Trondavoe 202 C5
Troon *Cornw.* 3 D3
Troon *S.Ayr.* 132 B2
Trosaraidh 172 C2
Troston 71 G5
Troswell 6 C1
Trottiscliffe 31 F3
Trotton 28 D5
Troughend 128 A2
Troustan 140 B2
Troutbeck 107 F2
Troutbeck Bridge 107 F2
Trow Green 39 E2
Trowbridge 25 F2
Trowle Common 25 F2
Trowley Bottom 43 F1
Trows 136 A3
Trowse Newton 86 D5
Trudernish 138 C4
Trudoxhill 25 E3
Trull 23 F5
Trumaisge Arraidh 173 G2
Trumpan 175 F3
Trumpet 53 F4
Trumpington 58 C2
Trunch 87 D2
Trunnah 99 G3
Truro 4 C5
Trusham 10 B4
Trusley 81 D4
Trusthorpe 97 F4
Truthan 4 C4
Trysull 66 A3
Tubney 41 G3
Tuckenhay 9 E2
Tuckingmill 4 A5
Tuddenham *Suff.* 60 C3
Tuddenham *Suff.* 71 F5
Tudeley 31 F4
Tudhoe 120 B4
Tudweiliog 74 B4
Tuffley 40 A1
Tufton *Hants.* 27 F3
Tufton *Pembs.* 48 D5
Tugby 68 C2
Tugford 65 E4
Tughall 137 G4
Tuirnaig 177 E1
Tulchan 151 E2
Tullibody 151 D5
Tullich *Arg. & B.* 148 C3
Tullich *Arg. & B.* 148 A3
Tullich *High.* 180 A2
Tullich *High.* 167 F2
Tullich *Moray* 181 F5
Tullich *Stir.* 150 A1
Tullich Muir 179 G2
Tulliemet 159 E4
Tulloch *Aber.* 170 D1
Tulloch *High.* 190 B5
Tulloch *Moray* 180 C4
Tullochgorm 148 B5
Tullochgribban High 168 B2
Tullochvenus 170 A4
Tulloes 160 D5
Tullybannocher 150 C2
Tullybelton 151 F1
Tullyfergus 160 A5
Tullymurdoch 159 G4
Tullynessle 170 A3
Tumble 36 B1
Tumby 84 A2
Tumby Woodside 84 A2
Tummel Bridge 158 C4
Tunbridge Wells 31 E5
Tundergarth Mains 125 F2
Tunga 187 F4
Tunstall *E.Riding* 105 F4
Tunstall *Kent* 32 A2
Tunstall *Lancs.* 108 B5
Tunstall *N.Yorks.* 110 B3
Tunstall *Norf.* 87 F5
Tunstall *Stoke* 79 F2
Tunstall *Suff.* 61 E2
Tunstead 87 E3
Tunworth 28 B3
Tupsley 53 E3
Tupton 81 E1
Tur Langton 68 C3
Turbiskill 139 F1
Turclossie 183 D4
Turgis Green 28 B2
Turin 160 D4
Turkdean 40 D1
Turnastone 52 C4
Turnberry 132 A5
Turnchapel 8 A2
Turnditch 81 D3
Turner's Green 67 D5
Turners Hill 30 C5
Turners Puddle 13 E3
Turnford 44 C2
Turnworth 13 E2
Turret Bridge 166 C5
Turriff 182 C4
Turton Bottoms 92 B1
Turvey 57 E2
Turville 42 C3
Turville Heath 42 C3
Turweston 56 B4
Tutbury 80 D5
Tutnall 66 B5
Tutshill 39 E3
Tuttington 86 D3
Tuxford 95 E5
Twatt *Ork.* 198 A4
Twatt *Shet.* 200 C2
Twechar 142 A2
Tweedmouth 145 G4
Tweedsmuir 134 B3
Twelveheads 4 B5
Twenty 83 G5
Twerton 25 E1
Twickenham 44 A5
Twigworth 54 A5
Twineham 17 E1
Twinhoe 25 E2
Twinstead 59 G4
Twiss Green 92 A3
Twitchen *Devon* 22 A4
Twitchen *Shrop.* 64 C5
Twizell House 137 F4
Two Bridges 7 G3
Two Dales 81 D1
Two Gates 67 E2
Twycross 67 F2
Twyford *Bucks.* 56 B5
Twyford *Derbys.* 81 E5
Twyford *Dorset* 13 E1
Twyford *Hants.* 27 F5
Twyford *Leics.* 68 C2
Twyford *Norf.* 86 B3
Twyford *Oxon.* 55 G4
Twyford *W'ham* 42 C5
Twyford Common 53 E4
Twyn-y-Sheriff 38 D2
Twyn-yr-odyn 38 A5
Twynholm 124 A5
Twyning 54 A4
Twyning Green 54 A4
Twynllanan 51 D5
Twywell 69 E5
Ty-hen 74 A4
Ty-Mawr 76 C3
Ty-mawr 77 E3
Ty-nant *Conwy* 76 C3
Ty-nant *Gwyn.* 76 C5
Ty-uchaf 76 C5
Tyberton 52 C4
Tyburn 66 D3
Tycroes 36 C1
Tycrwyn 64 A1
Tydd Gote 70 C1
Tydd St. Giles 70 C1
Tydd St. Mary 70 C1
Tyddewi (St. David's) 48 A5
Tye Common 45 F3
Tye Green 59 F5
Tyldesley 92 A2
Tyle-garw 37 G4
Tyler Hill 32 D2
Tylers Green *Bucks.* 43 E3
Tyler's Green *Essex* 45 E2
Tylorstown 37 G3
Tylwch 63 F5
Tyn-y-cefn 77 D3
Tyn-y-Cwm 63 E4
Tyn-y-ffridd 77 E4
Tyn-y-graig 51 G3
Ty'n-y-groes 89 F5
Tyndrum 149 F1
Tyneham 13 E4
Tynehead 144 A4
Tynemouth 120 C1
Tynewydd 37 F3
Tyninghame 144 D2
Tynribbie 156 B5
Tynron 124 C1
Tynygraig 50 C1
Tyringham 57 D3
Tythegston 37 E5
Tytherington *Ches.* 92 D5
Tytherington *S.Glos.* 39 F4
Tytherington *Som.* 25 E3
Tytherington *Wilts.* 26 A3
Tytherleigh 11 G2
Tytherton Lucas 40 B5
Tywardreath 5 E4
Tywardreath Highway 5 E4
Tywyn 62 B2


## U


Uachdar 173 G4
Uags 164 D1
Ubbeston Green 73 E4
Ubley 24 C2
Uckerby 110 B2
Uckfield 17 G1
Uckinghall 54 A4
Uckington 54 B5
Uddingston 142 A3
Uddington 133 G2
Udimore 19 D2
Udny Green 171 D2
Udny Station 171 E2
Udstonhead 142 B5
Uffcott 40 D5
Uffculme 11 D1
Uffington *Lincs.* 69 F2
Uffington *Oxon.* 41 F4
Uffington *Shrop.* 65 E1
Ufford *Peter.* 69 F2
Ufford *Suff.* 61 D2
Ufton 55 F1
Ufton Nervet 28 B1
Ugborough 8 C2
Uggeshall 73 F4
Ugglebarnby 112 B2
Ugley 50 D5
Ugley Green 58 D5
Ugthorpe 111 G1
Uig *Arg. & B.* 154 A4
Uig *Arg. & B.* 140 C1
Uig *High.* 175 G3
Uig *High.* 175 E4
Uigen 186 B4
Uiginish 175 F5
Uigshader 176 A5
Uisgebhagh 173 G5
Uisken 146 C3
Ulbster 195 F4
Ulcat Row 118 A5
Ulceby *Lincs.* 97 E5
Ulceby *N.Lincs.* 96 B1
Ulceby Cross 97 E5
Ulcombe 32 A4
Uldale 117 F3
Uldale House 108 C3
Uley 39 G3
Ulgham 129 E2
Ullapool 188 D5
Ullenhall 54 D1
Ullenwood 40 B1
Ulleskelf 103 E3
Ullesthorpe 68 A4
Ulley 94 B4
Ullingswick 53 E3
Ullinish 163 G1
Ullock 117 D4
Ulpha 106 C3
Ulrome 105 D2
Ulsta 203 D4
Ulting 46 B2
Uluvalt 147 E2
Ulverston 107 D5
Ulwell 13 G4
Ulzieside 133 F5
Umberleigh 21 G3
Unapool 192 B5
Underbarrow 107 F3
Underhoull 203 E2
Underriver 31 E3
Underwood *Newport* 38 C4
Underwood *Notts.* 81 F2
Undy 38 D4
Unifirth 200 B2
Union Croft 170 D5
Union Mills 98 B4
Unstone 94 A5
Unthank 118 A4
Up Cerne 12 C2
Up Exe 10 C2
Up Hatherley 54 B5
Up Holland 91 G2
Up Marden 15 G1
Up Nately 28 C2
Up Somborne 27 E4
Up Sydling 12 C2
Upavon 26 C2
Upchurch 32 A2
Upcott *Devon* 7 E1
Upcott *Here.* 52 C2
Upend 59 E2
Uphall *Dorset* 12 B2
Uphall *W.Loth.* 143 E2
Uphall Station 143 E2
Upham *Devon* 10 B2
Upham *Hants.* 27 G5
Uphampton 54 A1
Uphill 24 A2
Uplawmoor 141 F4
Upleadon 53 G5
Upleatham 121 F5
Uplees 32 C2
Uploders 12 B3
Uplowman 10 D1
Uplyme 11 G3
Upminster 45 E4
Upottery 11 E2
Upper Affcot 64 D4
Upper Ardroscadale 140 B3
Upper Arley 65 G4
Upper Arncott 42 B1
Upper Aston 66 A3
Upper Astrop 56 A4
Upper Basildon 42 B5
Upper Beeding 17 D2
Upper Benefield 69 E4
Upper Bighouse 194 A3
Upper Boat 38 A4
Upper Boddington 55 G2
Upper Borth 62 C4
Upper Boyndlie 183 E3
Upper Brailes 55 F3
Upper Breakish 164 C2
Upper Breinton 53 D3
Upper Broughton 82 B5
Upper Bucklebury 27 G1
Upper Burgate 14 A1
Upper Burnhaugh 170 D5
Upper Caldecote 57 G3
Upper Camster 195 E4
Upper Catshill 66 B5
Upper Chapel 51 G3
Upper Chute 27 D2
Upper Clatford 27 E3
Upper Coberley 40 B1
Upper Cound 65 E2
Upper Cwmbran 38 B3
Upper Dallachy 181 F3
Upper Dean 57 F1
Upper Denby 93 G2
Upper Derraid 168 C1
Upper Diabaig 177 E3
Upper Dicker 18 A2
Upper Dovercourt 60 D5
Upper Dunsforth 102 D1
Upper Eastern Green 67 E4
Upper Eathie 179 G3
Upper Elkstone 80 B2
Upper End 93 E5
Upper Farringdon 28 C4
Upper Framilode 39 G1
Upper Froyle 28 C3
Upper Gills 195 F1
Upper Glendessarry 165 F5
Upper Godney 24 B3
Upper Gornal 66 B3
Upper Gravenhurst 57 G4
Upper Green *Essex* 58 C4
Upper Green *Mon.* 38 C1
Upper Green *W.Berks.* 27 E1
Upper Gylen 148 A2
Upper Hackney 81 D1
Upper Halliford 29 F1
Upper Halling 31 F2
Upper Hambleton 69 E2
Upper Hardres Court 32 D3
Upper Hartfield 31 D5
Upper Hawkhillock 171 F1
Upper Hayton 65 E4
Upper Heath 65 E4
Upper Helmsley 103 F2
Upper Hergest 52 B2
Upper Heyford 55 G5
Upper Hill 53 D2
Upper Hopton 93 F1
Upper Horsebridge 18 A2
Upper Hulme 80 B1
Upper Inglesham 41 E3
Upper Kilchattan 146 C5
Upper Killay 36 B3
Upper Knockando 181 D5
Upper Lambourn 41 F4
Upper Langwith 81 G1
Upper Largo 152 C4
Upper Lochton 170 B5
Upper Longdon 66 C1
Upper Longwood 65 F2
Upper Ludstone 66 A3
Upper Lybster 195 E5
Upper Lydbrook 39 F1
Upper Maes-coed 52 C4
Upper Midhope 93 G3
Upper Minety 40 C3
Upper Mitton 66 A5
Upper Muirskie 170 D5
Upper North Dean 43 D3
Upper Norwood 44 C5
Upper Obney 151 F1
Upper Oddington 55 E5
Upper Ollach 164 B1
Upper Poppleton 103 E2
Upper Quinton 55 D3
Upper Ridinghill 183 F4
Upper Rissington 55 E5
Upper Rochford 53 F1
Upper Sanday 197 E2
Upper Sapey 53 F1
Upper Scolton 48 C5
Upper Seagry 40 B4
Upper Shelton 57 E3
Upper Sheringham 86 C1
Upper Skelmorlie 140 D3
Upper Slaughter 55 D5
Upper Sonachan 148 C2
Upper Soudley 39 F1
Upper Stoke 67 F4
Upper Stondon 57 G4
Upper Stowe 56 B2
Upper Street *Hants.* 14 A1
Upper Street *Norf.* 87 E4
Upper Street *Suff.* 60 C4
Upper Sundon 57 F5
Upper Swell 55 D5
Upper Tean 80 B4
Upper Thurnham 100 A2
Upper Tillyrie 151 G4
Upper Tooting 44 B5
Upper Town 24 C1
Upper Tysoe 55 F3
Upper Upham 41 E5
Upper Upnor 45 G5
Upper Victoria 152 D1
Upper Wardington 55 G3
Upper Weald 56 D4
Upper Weedon 56 B2
Upper Welson 52 B2
Upper Wield 28 B4
Upper (Over) Winchendon 42 C1
Upper Woodford 26 C4
Upper Wootton 27 G2
Upper Wraxall 39 G5
Upper Wyche 53 G3
Uppermill 93 D2
Upperthong 93 F2
Upperton 29 E5
Uppertown 195 F1
Uppingham 69 D3
Uppington *Dorset* 13 G2
Uppington *Shrop.* 65 E2
Upsall 110 D4
Upsettlington 145 F5
Upshire 44 D2
Upstreet 33 E2
Upton *Bucks.* 42 C1
Upton *Cambs.* 69 G5
Upton *Ches.* 78 B1
Upton *Cornw.* 5 G2
Upton *Devon* 11 D2
Upton *Devon* 8 D3
Upton *Dorset* 13 F3
Upton *Hants.* 27 E2
Upton *Hants.* 14 C1
Upton *Lincs.* 95 F4
Upton *Mersey.* 91 D4
Upton *Norf.* 87 E4
Upton *Northants.* 56 C1
Upton *Notts.* 95 E5
Upton *Notts.* 82 C2
Upton *Oxon.* 42 A4
Upton *Peter.* 69 G2
Upton *Slo.* 43 E5
Upton *Som.* 22 C5
Upton *W.Yorks.* 94 B1
Upton Bishop 53 F5
Upton Cheyney 25 D1
Upton Cressett 65 F3
Upton Cross 5 G2
Upton End 57 G4
Upton Green 87 E4
Upton Grey 28 B3
Upton Hellions 10 B2
Upton Lovell 26 A3
Upton Magna 65 E1
Upton Noble 25 E4
Upton Pyne 10 C3
Upton St. Leonards 40 A1
Upton Scudamore 25 F3
Upton Snodsbury 54 B2
Upton upon Severn 54 A3
Upton Warren 54 B1
Upwaltham 16 B2
Upware 58 D1
Upwell 70 D2
Upwey 12 C4
Upwood 70 A4
Uradale 200 D4
Urafirth 202 C5
Urchany 180 A5
Urchfont 26 B2
Urdimarsh 53 E3
Ure 202 B5
Urgha 185 D4
Urlay Nook 110 C1
Urmston 92 B3
Urquhart *High.* 179 E4
Urquhart *Moray* 181 E3
Urra 111 E2
Urray 179 E4
Ushaw Moor 120 B3
Usk 38 C2
Usselby 96 A3
Utley 101 G3
Uton 10 B3
Utterby 96 D3
Uttoxeter 80 B4
Uwchmynydd 74 A5
Uxbridge 43 F4
Uyeasound 203 E2
Uzmaston 34 C1


## V


Valley (Dyffryn) 88 A5
Valley Truckle 5 F1
Valleyfield *D. & G.* 124 A5
Valleyfield *Fife* 143 E1
Valsgarth 203 F1
Vange 45 G4
Vardre 36 C2
Varteg 38 B2
Vatersay (Bhatarsaigh) 172 B4
Vatten 175 F5
Vaul 154 B2
Vaynor 37 G1
Vaynor Park 64 A2
Veaullt 52 A2
Veensgarth 200 D3
Velindre *Pembs.* 49 E4
Velindre *Powys* 52 A4
Vellow 23 D4
Veness 199 D4
Venn 8 D3
Venn Ottery 11 D3
Vennington 64 C2
Ventnor 15 E5
Vernham Dean 27 E2
Vernham Street 27 E2
Vernolds Common 65 D4
Verwood 13 G2
Veryan 3 G3
Vicarage 11 F4
Vickerstown 99 E1
Victoria 5 D3
Vidlin 201 D1
Viewfield 194 C2
Viewpark 142 B3
Vigo 66 C2
Vigo Village 31 F2
Villavin 21 F4
Vinehall Street 18 C1
Vine's Cross 18 A2
Viney Hill 39 F2
Virginia Water 29 E1
Virginstow 7 D1
Virley 46 C1
Vobster 25 E3
Voe *Shet.* 200 D1
Voe *Shet.* 202 C4
Vowchurch 52 C4
Voy 198 A5


## W


Wackerfield 120 A5
Wacton 72 C2
Wadborough 54 B3
Waddesdon 42 C1
Waddingham 95 G3
Waddington *Lancs.* 100 D3
Waddington *Lincs.* 83 E1
Waddingworth 96 B5
Wadebridge 5 D2
Wadeford 11 G1
Wadenhoe 69 F4
Wadesmill 44 C1
Wadhurst 31 F5
Wadshelf 94 A5
Wadsley Bridge 94 A3
Wadworth 94 C3
Wadworth Hill 105 E5
Waen 77 E1
Waen-fach 64 B1
Waen-wen 75 E1
Wag 191 F2
Wainfleet All Saints 84 C2
Wainfleet Bank 84 C2
Wainhouse Corner 6 B1
Wainscott 45 G5
Wainstalls 101 G5
Waitby 108 C2
Wakefield 102 C5
Wakerley 69 E3
Wakes Colne 59 G5
Walberswick 73 F4
Walberton 16 B3
Walcot *Lincs.* 83 F4
Walcot *Lincs.* 83 G2
Walcot *N.Lincs.* 104 A5
Walcot *Shrop.* 64 C4
Walcot *Tel. & W.* 65 E1
Walcot Green 72 C3
Walcote *Leics.* 68 A4
Walcote *Warks.* 54 D2
Walcott 87 E2
Walcott Dales 83 G2
Walden 109 F4
Walden Head 109 E4
Walden Stubbs 94 C1
Walderslade 31 G2
Walderton 15 G1
Walditch 12 A3
Waldley 80 C4
Waldridge 120 B2
Waldringfield 61 D3
Waldron 18 A2
Wales 94 B4
Walesby *Lincs.* 96 B3
Walesby *Notts.* 95 D5
Walford *Here.* 64 C5
Walford *Here.* 53 E5
Walford *Shrop.* 78 B5
Walgherton 79 D3
Walgrave 68 D5
Walhampton 14 C3
Walk Mill 101 E4
Walkden 92 B2
Walker 120 B1
Walker Fold 100 C3
Walkerburn 135 E2
Walkeringham 95 E3
Walkerith 95 E3
Walkern 58 A5
Walker's Green 53 E3
Walkhampton 8 B1
Walkington 104 C4
Walkwood 54 C1
Wall *Northumb.* 119 F1
Wall *Staffs.* 66 D2
Wall Bank 65 E3
Wall Heath 66 A4
Wall under Heywood 65 E3
Wallacehall 126 A4
Wallacetown 132 A5
Wallasey 91 D3
Wallbottle 120 A1
Wallend 32 A1
Waller's Green 53 F4
Wallingford 42 B4
Wallington *Gt.Lon.* 30 B2
Wallington *Hants.* 15 E2
Wallington *Herts.* 58 A4
Wallis 48 D5
Wallisdown 13 G3
Walliswood 29 G4
Walls 200 B3
Wallsend 120 C1
Wallyford 144 A2
Walmer 33 F3
Walmer Bridge 100 A5
Walmersley 92 C1
Walmley 66 D3
Walpole 73 E4
Walpole Cross Keys 70 D1
Walpole Highway 70 D1
Walpole St. Andrew 70 D1
Walpole St. Peter 70 D1
Walsall 66 C3
Walsall Wood 66 C2
Walsden 101 F5
Walsgrave on Sowe 67 F4
Walsham le Willows 72 B4
Walsoken 70 C1
Walston 143 E5
Walsworth 57 G4
Walterstone 52 C5
Waltham *Kent* 32 D4
Waltham *N.E.Lincs.* 96 C2
Waltham Abbey 44 C2
Waltham Chase 15 E1
Waltham Cross 44 C2
Waltham Forest 44 C3
Waltham on the Wolds 82 D5
Waltham St. Lawrence 42 D5
Walthamstow 44 C4
Walton *Bucks.* 42 D1
Walton *Cumb.* 118 B1
Walton *Derbys.* 81 E1
Walton *Leics.* 68 A4
Walton *M.K.* 57 D4
Walton *Mersey.* 91 E3
Walton *Peter.* 69 G2
Walton *Powys* 52 B2
Walton *Som.* 24 B4
Walton *Staffs.* 79 F4
Walton *Suff.* 61 D4
Walton *Tel. & W.* 65 E1
Walton *W.Yorks.* 94 A1
Walton *W.Yorks.* 102 D3
Walton *Warks.* 55 E2
Walton Cardiff 54 B4
Walton East 48 D5
Walton-in-Gordano 38 D5
Walton-le-Dale 100 B5
Walton-on-Thames 29 G1
Walton-on-the-Hill *Staffs.* 79 G5
Walton on the Hill *Surr.* 30 B3
Walton on the Naze 60 D5
Walton on the Wolds 68 A1
Walton-on-Trent 67 E1
Walton Park 124 B3
Walton West 34 B1
Walwen *Flints.* 90 C5
Walwen *Flints.* 90 D5
Walwick 128 B4
Walworth 110 B1
Walwyn's Castle 34 B1
Wambrook 11 F2
Wanborough *Surr.* 29 E3
Wanborough *Swin.* 41 E4
Wandel 134 A3
Wandon 137 E4
Wandsworth 44 B5
Wandylaw 137 F4
Wangford *Suff.* 73 F4
Wangford *Suff.* 71 F4
Wanlip 68 B1
Wanlockhead 133 G4
Wannock 18 A3
Wansford *E.Riding* 104 C2
Wansford *Peter.* 69 F3
Wanstead 44 D4
Wanstrow 25 E3
Wanswell 39 F2
Wantage 41 F4
Wapley 39 G5

Wappenbury 55 F1
Wappenham 56 B3
Warblebank 117 F2
Warbleton 18 B2
Warborough 42 A3
Warboys 70 B5
Warbstow 6 C1
Warburton 92 A4
Warcop 108 C1
Ward End 66 D4
Ward Green 60 B1
Warden *Kent* 32 C1
Warden *Northumb.* 119 F1
Wardgate 81 D3
Wardhouse 170 A1
Wardington 55 G3
Wardle *Ches.* 78 D2
Wardle *Gt.Man.* 92 D1
Wardley 68 D2
Wardlow 93 F5
Wardy Hill 70 C4
Ware *Herts.* 44 C1
Ware *Kent* 33 E2
Wareham 13 F4
Warehorne 32 B5
Waren Mill 137 F3
Warenford 137 F4
Warenton 137 F3
Wareside 44 C1
Waresley 58 A2
Warfield 43 D5
Wargrave 42 C5
Warham 86 A1
Wark *Northumb.* 128 A4
Wark *Northumb.* 136 C3
Warkleigh 21 G3
Warkton 69 D5
Warkworth *Northants.* 55 G3
Warkworth *Northumb.* 129 E1
Warlaby 110 C3
Warland 101 F5
Warleggan 5 F3
Warley 66 C4
Warley Town 101 G5
Warlingham 30 C3
Warmfield 102 C5
Warmingham 79 E1
Warminghurst 16 D2
Warmington *Northants.* 69 F3
Warmington *Warks.* 55 G3
Warminster 25 F3
Warmlake 32 A3
Warmley 39 F5
Warmsworth 94 C2
Warmwell 13 D4
Warndon 54 A2
Warnford 28 B5
Warnham 29 G4
Warningcamp 16 C3
Warninglid 17 E1
Warren *Ches.* 92 C5
Warren *Pembs.* 34 C3
Warren House 7 G2
Warren Row 42 D4
Warren Street 32 B3
Warrenby 121 E5
Warrington *M.K.* 57 D2
Warrington *Warr.* 92 A4
Warroch 151 F4
Warsash 15 D2
Warslow 80 B2
Warter 104 A2
Warthill 103 F2
Wartle 170 A4
Wartling 18 B3
Wartnaby 82 C5
Warton *Lancs.* 107 G5
Warton *Lancs.* 100 A5
Warton *Northumb.* 128 C1
Warton *Warks.* 67 E2
Warwick *Cumb.* 118 A2
Warwick *Warks.* 55 E1
Warwick Bridge 118 A2
Wasbister 198 B3
Wash Common 27 F1
Washaway 5 E3
Washbourne 9 D2
Washfield 10 C1
Washfold 109 F2
Washford 22 D3
Washford Pyne 10 B1
Washingborough 96 A5
Washington *T. & W.* 120 C2
Washington *W.Suss.* 16 D2
Washmere Green 60 A3
Wasing 27 G1
Waskerley 119 G3
Wasperton 55 E2
Wass 111 E5
Watchet 23 D3
Watchfield *Oxon.* 41 E3
Watchfield *Som.* 24 A3
Watchgate 107 G3
Watendlath 117 F5
Water 101 E5
Water Eaton 42 A1
Water End *Herts.* 44 B2
Water End *Herts.* 43 F1
Water Newton 69 G3
Water Orton 67 D3
Water Stratford 56 B4
Water Yeat 107 D4
Waterbeach 58 C1
Waterbeck 126 A4
Waterfall 80 B2
Waterfoot *E.Renf.* 141 G4
Waterfoot *Lancs.* 101 E5
Waterford 44 C1
Waterhead *Cumb.* 107 E2
Waterhead *D. & G.* 124 B2
Waterhill of Bruxie 183 E5
Waterhouses *Dur.* 120 A3
Waterhouses *Staffs.* 80 B2
Wateringbury 31 F3
Waterloo *Aber.* 171 F1
Waterloo *Mersey.* 91 E3
Waterloo *N.Lan.* 142 C4
Waterloo *Norf.* 86 D4
Waterloo *P. & K.* 151 F1
Waterloo *Pembs.* 34 C2
Waterloo *Poole* 13 G3
Waterloo Cross 11 D1
Waterloo Port 75 D1
Waterlooville 15 F1
Watermeetings 134 A4
Watermillock 118 A5
Waterperry 42 B2
Waterrow 22 D5
Waters Upton 65 F1
Watersfield 16 C2
Waterside *Aber.* 169 F3
Waterside *Aber.* 171 F2
Waterside *Bucks.* 43 E2
Waterside *E.Ayr.* 132 C5
Waterside *E.Ayr.* 141 F5
Waterside *E.Dun.* 142 A2
Waterstock 42 B2
Waterston 34 C2
Waterthorpe 94 B4
Watford *Herts.* 44 A3
Watford *Northants.* 56 B1
Wath *N.Yorks.* 110 C5
Wath *N.Yorks.* 102 A1
Wath Brow 116 D5
Wath upon Dearne 94 B2
Watlington *Norf.* 71 E1
Watlington *Oxon.* 42 B3
Watnall 81 G3
Watten 195 E3
Wattisfield 72 B4
Wattisham 60 B2
Watton *E.Riding* 104 C3
Watton *Norf.* 86 A5
Watton at Stone 44 C1
Watton Green 86 A5
Wattston 142 B3
Wattstown 37 G3
Wattsville 38 A3
Waun Fawr 62 C4
Waun y Clyn 36 A2
Waunarlwydd 36 C3
Waunclynda 50 C4
Waunfawr 75 E2
Wavendon 57 E4
Waverbridge 117 F2
Waverton *Ches.* 78 B1
Waverton *Cumb.* 117 F2
Wawne 104 C4
Waxham 87 F3
Waxholme 105 F5
Way Gill 101 F1
Way Village 10 B1
Wayford 12 A2
Waytown 12 A3
Wdig (Goodwick) 48 C4
Weachyburn 182 B4
Weald 41 F2
Wealdstone 44 A4
Weare 24 B2
Weare Giffard 21 E3
Wearhead 119 E3
Wearne 24 B5
Weasenham All Saints 85 G5
Weasenham St. Peter 85 G5
Weathercote 108 C5
Weatheroak Hill 66 C5
Weaverham 92 A5
Weaverthorpe 112 C5
Webheath 54 C1
Webton 52 D4
Wedderlairs 171 D1
Weddington 67 F3
Wedhampton 26 B2
Wedmore 24 B3
Wednesbury 66 B3
Wednesfield 66 B2
Weedon 42 D1
Weedon Bec 56 B2
Weedon Lois 56 B3
Weeford 66 D2
Week 10 A1
Week Orchard 20 C5
Week St. Mary 6 C1
Weekley 69 D4
Weeley 60 C5
Weeley Heath 47 E1
Weem 158 D5
Weeping Cross 79 G5
Weethley 54 C2
Weeting 71 F4
Weeton *E.Riding* 105 F5
Weeton *Lancs.* 99 G4
Weeton *N.Yorks.* 102 B3
Weir *Essex* 46 B4
Weir *Lancs.* 101 E5
Weirbrook 78 A5
Welbeck Abbey 94 C5
Welborne 86 B5
Welbourn 83 E2
Welburn 103 G1
Welbury 110 C2
Welby 83 E4
Welches Dam 70 C4
Welcombe 20 C4
Weldon 69 E4
Welford *Northants.* 68 B4
Welford *W.Berks.* 41 G5
Welford-on-Avon 54 D2
Welham *Leics.* 68 C3
Welham *Notts.* 95 E4
Welham Green 44 B2
Well *Hants.* 28 C3
Well *Lincs.* 97 E5
Well *N.Yorks.* 110 B4
Well End 43 D4
Well Hill 31 D2
Well Town 10 C2
Welland 53 G3
Wellbank 152 C1
Wellesbourne 55 E2
Wellhill 180 B3
Welling 45 D5
Wellingborough 57 D1
Wellingham 85 G5
Wellingore 83 E2
Wellington *Cumb.* 106 B2
Wellington *Here.* 53 D3
Wellington *Som.* 23 E5
Wellington *Tel. & W.* 65 F1
Wellington Heath 53 G3
Wellington Marsh 53 E3
Wellow *B. & N.E.Som.* 25 E2
Wellow *I.o.W.* 14 C4
Wellow *Notts.* 82 B1
Wells 24 C3
Wells-next-the-Sea 86 A1
Wellsborough 67 F2
Wellwood 143 E1
Welney 70 D3
Welsh Bicknor 39 E1
Welsh End 78 C4
Welsh Frankton 78 A4
Welsh Hook 48 C5
Welsh Newton 39 E1
Welsh St. Donats 37 G5
Welshampton 78 B4
Welshpool (Y Trallwng) 64 B2
Welton *B. & N.E.Som.* 25 D2
Welton *Cumb.* 117 G2
Welton *E.Riding* 104 B5
Welton *Lincs.* 96 A4
Welton *Northants.* 56 A1
Welton le Marsh 84 C1
Welton le Wold 96 C4
Welwick 105 F5
Welwyn 44 B1
Welwyn Garden City 44 B1
Wem 78 C5
Wembdon 23 F4
Wembley 44 A4
Wembury 8 B3
Wembworthy 21 G5
Wemyss Bay 140 C3
Wenallt 76 C3
Wendens Ambo 58 D4
Wendlebury 42 A1
Wendling 86 A4
Wendover 43 D2
Wendron 3 D3
Wendy 58 B3
Wenhaston 73 F4
Wenlli 76 B1
Wennington *Cambs.* 70 A5
Wennington *Gt.Lon.* 45 E4
Wennington *Lancs.* 108 B5
Wensley *Derbys.* 81 D1
Wensley *N.Yorks.* 109 F3
Wentbridge 94 B1
Wentnor 64 C3
Wentworth *Cambs.* 70 C5
Wentworth *S.Yorks.* 94 A3
Wentworth Castle 94 A2
Wenvoe 38 A5
Weobley 52 C2
Weobley Marsh 52 D2
Wepham 16 C3
Wepre 77 F1
Wereham 71 E2
Wergs 66 A2
Wernyrheolydd 38 C1
Werrington *Cornw.* 6 D2
Werrington *Peter.* 69 G2
Werrington *Staffs.* 79 G3
Wervil Brook 49 G2
Wervin 91 F5
Wesham 100 A4
Wessington 81 E2
West Aberthaw 22 D1
West Acre 71 F1
West Allerdean 145 G5
West Alvington 8 D3
West Amesbury 26 C3
West Anstey 22 B5
West Ashby 96 C5
West Ashling 16 A3
West Ashton 25 F2
West Auckland 120 A5
West Ayton 112 C4
West Bagborough 23 E4
West Barkwith 96 B4
West Barnby 112 B1
West Barns 144 D2
West Barsham 86 A2
West Bay 12 A3
West Beckham 86 C2
West Benhar 142 C3
West Bergholt 60 A5
West Bexington 12 B4
West Bilney 71 F1
West Blatchington 17 E3
West Boldon 120 C1
West Bradenham 86 A5
West Bradford 100 D3
West Bradley 24 C4
West Bretton 93 G1
West Bridgford 81 G4
West Bromwich 66 C3
West Buckland *Devon* 21 G2
West Buckland *Som.* 23 E5
West Burrafirth 200 B2
West Burton *N.Yorks.* 109 F4
West Burton *W.Suss.* 16 B2
West Butterwick 95 F2
West Byfleet 29 F1
West Cairncake 182 D5
West Caister 87 G4
West Calder 143 E3
West Camel 24 C5
West Cauldcoats 142 A5
West Challow 41 F4
West Charleton 9 D3
West Chelborough 12 B2
West Chevington 129 E2
West Chiltington 16 C2
West Chiltington Common 16 C2
West Chinnock 12 A1
West Chisenbury 26 C2
West Clandon 29 F2
West Cliffe 33 F4
West Clyne 191 D4
West Coker 12 B1
West Compton *Dorset* 12 B3
West Compton *Som.* 24 C3
West Cross 36 C4
West Curry 6 C1
West Curthwaite 117 G2
West Dean *W.Suss.* 16 A2
West Dean *Wilts.* 27 D5
West Deeping 69 G2
West Derby 91 E3
West Dereham 71 E2
West Ditchburn 137 F4
West Down 21 F1
West Drayton *Gt.Lon.* 43 F5
West Drayton *Notts.* 95 E5
West Dullater 150 A4
West Dunnet 195 E1
West Edington 129 D3
West Ella 104 C5
West End *Beds.* 57 E2
West End *E.Riding* 104 C1
West End *Hants.* 15 D1
West End *Kent* 32 D2
West End *Lancs.* 100 A1
West End *Lincs.* 97 D3
West End *N.Som.* 24 B1
West End *N.Yorks.* 102 A2
West End *Norf.* 87 F4
West End *Oxon.* 41 G2
West End *S.Lan.* 143 D5
West End *Suff.* 73 F3
West End *Surr.* 29 G1
West End *Surr.* 29 E1
West End Green 28 B1
West Farleigh 31 G3
West Farndon 56 A2
West Felton 78 A5
West Firle 17 G3
West Fleetham 137 F4
West Garforth 102 C4
West Ginge 41 G4
West Glen 140 B2
West Grafton 26 D1
West Green 28 C2
West Grimstead 26 D5
West Grinstead 29 G5
West Haddlesey 103 E5
West Haddon 68 B5
West Hagbourne 42 A4
West Hagley 66 B4
West Hall 118 B1
West Hallam 81 F3
West Halton 104 B5
West Ham 44 D4
West Handley 94 A5
West Hanney 41 G3
West Hanningfield 45 G3
West Hardwick 94 B1
West Harptree 24 C2
West Harting 28 C5
West Hatch 23 F5
West Heath *Hants.* 29 D2
West Heath *W.Mid.* 66 C5
West Helmsdale 191 F3
West Hendred 41 G4
West Heslerton 112 C5
West Hill *Devon* 11 D3
West Hill *N.Som.* 39 D5
West Hoathly 30 C5
West Holme 13 E4
West Horndon 45 F4
West Horrington 24 C3
West Horsley 29 F2
West Horton 137 E3
West Hougham 33 E4
West Huntspill 24 A3
West Hyde 43 F3
West Hythe 32 D5
West Ilsley 41 G4
West Itchenor 16 G2
West Keal 84 B1
West Kennett 26 C1
West Kilbride 140 D5
West Kingsdown 31 E2
West Kington 40 A5
West Kirby 90 D4
West Knapton 112 B5
West Knighton 12 D4
West Knoyle 25 F4
West Kyloe 137 E2
West Lambrook 12 A1
West Langdon 33 F4
West Langwell 190 B4
West Lavington *W.Suss.* 29 D5
West Lavington *Wilts.* 26 B2
West Layton 110 A1
West Leake 81 G5
West Lexham 71 G1
West Lilling 103 F1
West Lingo 152 C4
West Linton 143 F4
West Littleton 39 G5
West Lockinge 41 G4
West Looe 5 G4
West Lulworth 13 E4
West Lutton 104 B1
West Lydford 24 C4
West Lyng 24 A5
West Lynn 71 E1
West Mains 137 E2
West Malling 31 F3
West Malvern 53 G3
West Marden 15 G1
West Markham 95 E5
West Marsh 96 C2
West Marton 101 E2
West Melton 94 B2
West Meon 28 B5
West Meon Hut 28 B5
West Mersea 46 D1
West Milton 12 B3
West Minster 32 B1
West Molesey 29 G1
West Monkton 23 F5
West Moors 13 G2
West Mostard 108 C3
West Muir 161 D3
West Ness 111 F5
West Newton *E.Riding* 105 E4
West Newton *Norf.* 85 E5
West Norwood 44 C5
West Ogwell 10 B5
West Orchard 13 E1
West Overton 26 C1
West Park *Aber.* 170 C5
West Park *Mersey.* 91 G3
West Parley 13 G3
West Peckham 31 F3
West Pennard 24 C4
West Pentire 4 B3
West Perry 57 G1
West Porlock 22 B3
West Putford 21 D4
West Quantoxhead 23 E3
West Rainton 120 C3
West Rasen 96 A4
West Raynham 85 G5
West Rounton 110 D2
West Row 71 E5
West Rudham 85 G5
West Runton 86 C1
West Saltoun 144 B3
West Sandwick 203 D4
West Scrafton 109 F4
West Shinness Lodge 190 A3
West Somerton 87 F3
West Stafford 12 D4
West Stockwith 95 E3
West Stoke 16 A3
West Stonesdale 109 D2
West Stoughton 24 B3
West Stour 25 E5
West Stourmouth 33 E2
West Stow 71 G5
West Stowell 26 C1
West Stratton 27 G3
West Street 32 B3
West Tanfield 110 B5
West Taphouse 5 F3
West Tarbert 139 G3
West Tarring 16 D3
West Thorney 15 G2
West Thurrock 45 E5
West Tilbury 45 F5
West Tisted 28 B5
West Tofts *Norf.* 71 G3
West Tofts *P. & K.* 151 G1
West Torrington 96 B4
West Town *Hants.* 15 G3
West Town *N.Som.* 24 B1
West Tytherley 27 D4
West Walton 70 C1
West Walton Highway 70 C1
West Wellow 27 D5
West Wemyss 152 B5
West Wick 24 A1
West Wickham *Cambs.* 59 E3
West Wickham *Gt.Lon.* 30 C2
West Williamston 34 D2
West Winch 71 E1
West Winterslow 26 D4
West Wittering 15 G3
West Witton 109 F4
West Woodburn 128 A3
West Woodhay 27 E1
West Woodlands 25 E3
West Worldham 28 C4
West Worlington 10 A1
West Worthing 16 D3
West Wratting 59 D2
West Wycombe 42 D3
West Yell 203 D4
Westbere 33 D2
Westborough 83 D3
Westbourne *Bourne.* 13 G3
Westbourne *W.Suss.* 15 G2
Westbrook 41 G5
Westbury *Bucks.* 56 B4
Westbury *Shrop.* 64 C2
Westbury *Wilts.* 25 F2
Westbury Leigh 25 F2
Westbury-on-Severn 39 G1
Westbury on Trym 39 E5
Westbury-sub-Mendip 24 C3
Westby 99 G4
Westcliff-on-Sea 46 B4
Westcombe 25 D4
Westcote 55 E5
Westcott *Bucks.* 42 C1
Westcott *Devon* 10 D2
Westcott *Surr.* 29 G3
Westcott Barton 55 G5
Westdean 18 A4
Westdowns 5 E1
Wester Aberchalder 167 E2
Wester Badentyre 182 C4
Wester Culbeuchly 182 B3
Wester Dechmont 143 E2
Wester Fintray 170 D3
Wester Foffarty 160 C5
Wester Greenskares 182 C3
Wester Gruinards 190 A5
Wester Lealty 179 F2
Wester Lonvine 179 G2
Wester Newburn 152 C4
Wester Ord 170 D4
Wester Quarff 200 D4
Wester Skeld 200 B3
Westerdale *High.* 194 D3
Westerdale *N.Yorks.* 111 F2
Westerfield *Shet.* 200 C2
Westerfield *Suff.* 60 C3
Westergate 16 B3
Westerham 30 D3
Westerleigh 39 F5
Westerton *Aber.* 170 C5
Westerton *Angus* 161 E4
Westerton *Dur.* 120 B4
Westerton *P. & K.* 151 D3
Westerwick 200 B3
Westfield *Cumb.* 116 C4
Westfield *E.Suss.* 18 D2
Westfield *High.* 194 C2
Westfield *Norf.* 86 A5
Westfield *W.Loth.* 142 D2
Westgate *Dur.* 119 F4
Westgate *N.Lincs.* 95 E2
Westgate *Norf.* 86 A1
Westgate *Northumb.* 128 D4
Westgate Hill 102 B5
Westgate on Sea 33 F1
Westhall *Aber.* 170 B2
Westhall *Suff.* 73 F3
Westham *Dorset* 12 C5
Westham *E.Suss.* 18 B3
Westham *Som.* 24 A3
Westhampnett 16 A3
Westhay 24 B3
Westhead 91 F2
Westhide 53 E3
Westhill *Aber.* 170 D4
Westhill *High.* 179 G5
Westhope *Here.* 53 D2
Westhope *Shrop.* 65 D4
Westhorpe *Lincs.* 84 A4
Westhorpe *Suff.* 60 B1
Westhoughton 92 A2
Westhouse 108 B5
Westhouses 81 F2
Westhumble 29 G2
Westing 203 E2
Westlake 8 C2
Westleigh *Devon* 21 E3
Westleigh *Devon* 11 D1
Westleigh *Gt.Man.* 92 A2
Westleton 61 F1
Westley *Shrop.* 64 C2
Westley *Suff.* 59 G1
Westley Heights 45 F4
Westley Waterless 59 E2
Westlington 42 C1
Westlinton 126 B5
Westloch 143 G4
Westmarsh 33 E2
Westmeston 17 F2
Westmill 58 B5
Westmuir 160 B4
Westness 198 B4
Westnewton *Cumb.* 117 E2
Westnewton *Northumb.* 136 C3
Weston *B. & N.E.Som.* 25 E1
Weston *Ches.* 79 E2
Weston *Devon* 11 E4
Weston *Dorset* 12 C5
Weston *Halton* 91 G4
Weston *Hants.* 28 C5
Weston *Herts.* 58 A4
Weston *Lincs.* 84 A5
Weston *Moray* 181 G3
Weston *N.Yorks.* 102 A3
Weston *Northants.* 56 A3
Weston *Notts.* 82 C1
Weston *Shrop.* 78 C5
Weston *Shrop.* 65 E3
Weston *Staffs.* 79 G5
Weston *W.Berks.* 41 G5
Weston Beggard 53 E3
Weston by Welland 68 C3
Weston Colville 59 E2
Weston Corbett 28 B3
Weston Coyney 79 G3
Weston Favell 56 C1
Weston Green *Cambs.* 59 E2
Weston Green *Norf.* 86 C4
Weston Green *Surr.* 29 G1
Weston Heath 65 G1
Weston Hills 84 A5
Weston-in-Gordano 38 D5
Weston Jones 79 E5
Weston Longville 86 C4
Weston Lullingfields 78 B5
Weston-on-the-Green 42 A1
Weston-on-Trent 81 F5
Weston Patrick 28 B3
Weston Point 91 F4
Weston Rhyn 77 F4
Weston Subedge 54 D3
Weston-super-Mare 24 A1
Weston Turville 43 D1
Weston-under-Lizard 66 A1
Weston under Penyard 53 F5
Weston under Wetherley 55 F1
Weston Underwood *Derbys.* 81 D3
Weston Underwood *M.K.* 57 D3
Westonbirt 40 A4
Westoning 57 F4
Westonzoyland 24 A4
Westow 103 G1
Westport *Arg. & B.* 130 B3
Westport *Som.* 11 G1
Westrigg 142 D3
Westruther 144 D4
Westry 70 B3
Westside 171 D5
Westward 117 F2
Westward Ho! 21 E3
Westwell *Kent* 32 B4
Westwell *Oxon.* 41 E1
Westwell Leacon 32 B4
Westwick *Cambs.* 58 C1
Westwick *Dur.* 109 F1
Westwick *Norf.* 87 D3
Westwood *Devon* 10 D3
Westwood *Wilts.* 25 F2
Westwood Heath 67 E5
Westwoodside 95 E3
Wether Cote Farm 111 F4
Wetheral 118 A2
Wetherby 102 D3
Wetherden 60 B1
Wetheringsett 60 C1
Wethersfield 59 F4
Wethersta 200 C1
Wetherup Street 60 C1
Wetley Rocks 79 G3
Wettenhall 78 D1
Wettenhall Green 78 D1
Wetton 80 C2
Wetwang 104 B2
Wetwood 79 E4
Wexcombe 27 D2
Weybourne 86 C1
Weybread 72 D3
Weybridge 29 F1
Weycroft 11 G2
Weydale 194 D2
Weyhill 27 E3
Weymouth 12 C5
Whaddon *Bucks.* 56 D4
Whaddon *Cambs.* 58 B3
Whaddon *Glos.* 40 A1
Whaddon *Wilts.* 26 C5
Whaddon Gap 58 B3
Whale 118 B5
Whaley 94 C5
Whaley Bridge 93 E4
Whaligoe 195 F4
Whalley 100 D4
Whalton 128 D3
Wham 101 D1
Whaplode 84 B5
Whaplode Drove 70 B1
Whaplode St. Catherine 70 B1
Wharfe 101 D1
Wharles 100 A4
Wharncliffe Side 94 A3
Wharram le Street 104 A1
Wharram Percy 104 A1
Wharton *Ches.* 79 D1
Wharton *Here.* 53 E2
Whashton 110 A2
Whatcote 55 E3
Whatfield 60 B3
Whatley 25 E3
Whatlington 18 C2
Whatstandwell 81 E2
Whatton 82 C4
Whauphill 115 E2
Whaw 109 E2
Wheatacre 73 F2
Wheatenhurst 39 G2
Wheathampstead 44 A1
Wheathill 65 F4
Wheatley *Hants.* 28 C4
Wheatley *Oxon.* 42 B2
Wheatley Hill 120 C4
Wheatley Lane 101 E4
Wheaton Aston 66 A1
Wheddon Cross 22 C4
Wheedlemont 169 G2
Wheelerstreet 29 E3
Wheelock 79 E2
Wheelton 100 C5
Wheen 160 B2
Wheldrake 103 F3
Whelford 41 D3
Whelpley Hill 43 F2
Whelpo 117 G3
Whenby 103 F1
Whepstead 59 G2
Wherstead 60 C3
Wherwell 27 E3
Wheston 93 F5
Whetley Cross 12 A2
Whetsted 31 F4
Whetstone 68 A3
Whicham 106 C4
Whichford 55 F4
Whickham 120 B1
Whiddon Down 7 G1
Whifflet 142 B3
Whigstreet 160 C5
Whilton 56 B1
Whim 143 G4
Whimple 10 D3
Whimpwell Green 87 E2
Whin Lane End 99 G3
Whinburgh 86 B5
Whinnyfold 171 F1
Whippingham 15 E3
Whipsnade 43 F1
Whipton 10 C3
Whisby 83 E1
Whissendine 68 D1
Whissonsett 86 A3
Whistley Green 42 C5
Whiston *Mersey.* 91 F3
Whiston *Northants.* 57 D1
Whiston *S.Yorks.* 94 B4
Whiston *Staffs.* 80 B3
Whiston *Staffs.* 66 A1
Whitbeck 106 C4
Whitbourne 53 G2
Whitburn *T. & W.* 120 D1
Whitburn *W.Loth.* 142 D3
Whitby *Ches.* 91 E5
Whitby *N.Yorks.* 112 B1
Whitchurch *B. & N.E.Som.* 24 D1
Whitchurch *Bucks.* 56 D5
Whitchurch *Cardiff* 38 A5
Whitchurch *Devon* 7 E3
Whitchurch *Hants.* 27 F3
Whitchurch *Here.* 39 E1
Whitchurch *Pembs.* 48 B5
Whitchurch *Shrop.* 78 C3
Whitchurch Canonicorum 11 G3
Whitchurch Hill 42 B5
Whitchurch-on-Thames 42 B5
Whitcombe 12 D4

Whitcott Keysett 64 B4
White Colne 59 G5
White Coppice 92 A1
White Cross Cornw. 4 C4
White Cross Devon 10 D3
White Cross Here. 53 D3
White End 54 A5
White Lackington 12 D3
White Ladies Aston 54 B2
White Mill 50 A5
White Moor 81 E3
White Notley 45 G1
White Pit 97 D5
White Roding 45 E1
White Waltham 43 D5
Whiteacen 181 E5
Whiteash Green 59 F4
Whitebog 183 E4
Whitebridge High. 195 E1
Whitebridge High. 167 D3
Whitebrook 39 E2
Whiteburn 144 C5
Whitecairn 122 D5
Whitecairns 171 E3
Whitecastle 143 E5
Whitechapel 100 B3
Whitechurch 49 E4
Whitecraig 144 A2
Whitecroft 39 F2
Whitecrook 122 C5
Whitecross 2 C3
Whiteface 179 G1
Whitefield Aber. 170 C2
Whitefield Gt.Man. 92 C2
Whitefield High. 167 E2
Whitefield High. 195 E3
Whitefield P. & K. 151 G1
Whiteford 170 C2
Whitegate 78 D1
Whitehall 199 E4
Whitehaven 116 C5
Whitehill Hants. 28 C4
Whitehill Kent 32 B3
Whitehill N.Ayr. 141 D4
Whitehills 182 B3
Whitehouse Aber. 170 B3
Whitehouse Arg. & B. 139 G3
Whitekirk 144 C1
Whitelackington 11 G1
Whitelaw 145 F4
Whiteleen 195 F4
Whitelees 132 B2
Whiteley 15 E2
Whiteley Bank 15 E4
Whiteley Village 29 F1
Whiteleys 122 B5
Whitemans Green 17 F1
Whitemire 180 B4
Whiteparish 27 D5
Whiterashes 171 D2
Whiterow 195 F4
Whiteshill 40 A2
Whiteside Northumb. 118 D1
Whiteside W.Loth. 143 D3
Whitesmith 18 A2
Whitestaunton 11 F1
Whitestone Aber. 170 B5
Whitestone Arg. & B. 130 C2
Whitestone Devon 10 B3
Whitestripe 183 E4
Whiteway 40 B1
Whitewell Aber. 183 E3
Whitewell Lancs. 100 C3
Whiteworks 7 G3
Whitewreath 181 E4
Whitfield Here. 52 D4
Whitfield Kent 33 E4
Whitfield Northants. 56 B3
Whitfield Northumb. 119 D2
Whitfield S.Glos. 39 F3
Whitford Devon 11 F3
Whitford (Chwitffordd) Flints. 90 C5
Whitgift 104 A5
Whitgreave 79 F5
Whithorn 115 E2
Whiting Bay 131 F3
Whitkirk 102 C4
Whitlam 171 D2
Whitland 35 F1
Whitland Abbey 35 F1
Whitletts 132 B3
Whitley N.Yorks. 103 E5
Whitley Read. 28 C1
Whitley Wilts. 25 F1
Whitley Bay 129 F4
Whitley Chapel 119 F2
Whitley Lower 93 G1
Whitley Row 31 D3
Whitlock's End 66 D5
Whitminster 39 G2
Whitmore Dorset 13 G2
Whitmore Staffs. 79 F3
Whitnage 10 D1
Whitnash 55 F1
Whitney 52 B3
Whitrigg Cumb. 117 F1
Whitrigg Cumb. 117 F3
Whitsbury 14 A1
Whitsome 145 F4
Whitson 38 C4
Whitstable 32 D2
Whitstone 6 C1
Whittingham 137 E5
Whittingslow 64 D4
Whittington Derbys. 94 A5
Whittington Glos. 54 C5
Whittington Lancs. 108 B5
Whittington Norf. 71 F3
Whittington Shrop. 78 A4
Whittington Staffs. 67 D2
Whittington Staffs. 66 A4
Whittington Worcs. 54 A2
Whittle-le-Woods 100 B5
Whittlebury 56 B3
Whittlesey 70 A3
Whittlesford 58 C3
Whitton N.Lincs. 104 B5
Whitton Northumb. 128 C1
Whitton Powys 52 B1
Whitton Shrop. 65 E5
Whitton Stock. 120 C5
Whitton Suff. 60 C3
Whittonditch 41 E5
Whittonstall 119 G2
Whitway 27 F2
Whitwell Derbys. 94 C5
Whitwell Herts. 57 G5
Whitwell I.o.W. 15 E5
Whitwell N.Yorks. 110 B3
Whitwell Norf. 86 C3
Whitwell Rut. 69 E2
Whitwell-on-the-Hill 103 G1
Whitwick 67 G1
Whitwood 102 D5
Whitworth 92 C1
Whixall 78 C4
Whixley 102 D2
Whorlton Dur. 110 A1
Whorlton N.Yorks. 111 D2
Whygate 127 F4
Whyle 53 E1
Whyteleafe 30 C3
Wibdon 39 E3
Wibsey 102 A4
Wibtoft 67 G4
Wichenford 53 G1
Wichling 32 B3
Wick Bourne. 14 A3
Wick High. 195 F3
Wick S.Glos. 39 G5
Wick V. of Glam. 37 F5
Wick W.Suss. 16 C3
Wick Wilts. 26 C5
Wick Worcs. 54 B3
Wick Airport 195 F3
Wick Hill Kent 32 A4
Wick Hill W'ham 43 D5
Wick St. Lawrence 24 A1
Wicken Cambs. 71 D5
Wicken Northants. 56 C4
Wicken Bonhunt 58 C4
Wickenby 96 A4
Wickerslack 108 B1
Wickersley 94 B3
Wickford 45 G3
Wickham Hants. 15 E1
Wickham W.Berks. 41 F5
Wickham Bishops 46 B1
Wickham Heath 27 F1
Wickham Market 61 D2
Wickham St. Paul 59 G4
Wickham Skeith 60 B1
Wickham Street Suff. 59 F2
Wickham Street Suff. 60 B1
Wickhambreaux 33 E3
Wickhambrook 59 F2
Wickhamford 54 C3
Wickhampton 87 F5
Wicklewood 86 B5
Wickmere 86 C2
Wickwar 39 G4
Widdington 58 D4
Widdop 101 F4
Widdrington 129 E2
Wide Open 129 E4
Widecombe in the Moor 10 A5
Widegates 5 G4
Widemouth Bay 20 C5
Widewall 196 D3
Widford Essex 45 F2
Widford Herts. 44 D1
Widmerpool 82 B5
Widnes 91 G4
Widworthy 11 F3
Wigan 91 G2
Wiggaton 11 E3
Wiggenhall St. Germans 71 E1
Wiggenhall St. Mary Magdalen 71 E1
Wiggenhall St. Mary the Virgin 71 D1
Wiggenhall St. Peter 71 E1
Wiggington 103 F2
Wigginton Herts. 43 E1
Wigginton Oxon. 55 F4
Wigginton Staffs. 67 E2
Wigglesworth 101 E2
Wiggonby 117 F1
Wiggonholt 16 C2
Wighill 103 D3
Wighton 86 A2
Wightwizzle 93 G3
Wigmore Here. 52 D1
Wigmore Med. 32 A2
Wigsley 95 F5
Wigsthorpe 69 F4
Wigston 68 B3
Wigston Parva 67 G3
Wigthorpe 94 C4
Wigtoft 84 A4
Wigton 117 F2
Wigtown 123 F5
Wilbarston 68 D4
Wilberfoss 103 G2
Wilburton 70 C5
Wilby Norf. 72 B2
Wilby Northants. 57 D1
Wilby Suff. 72 D4
Wilcot 26 C1
Wilcott 64 C1
Wilcrick 38 D4
Wildboarclough 79 G1
Wilden Beds. 57 F2
Wilden Worcs. 66 A5
Wildhern 27 E2
Wildhill 44 B2
Wildsworth 95 F3
Wilford 81 G4
Wilkesley 78 D3
Wilkhaven 180 B1
Wilkieston 143 F3
Willand 10 D1
Willaston Ches. 91 E5
Willaston Ches. 79 D2
Willen 57 D3
Willenhall W.Mid. 66 B3
Willenhall W.Mid. 67 F5
Willerby E.Riding 104 C5
Willerby N.Yorks. 112 D5
Willersey 54 D3
Willersley 52 C3
Willesborough 32 C4
Willesborough Lees 32 C4
Willesden 44 B4
Willesley 40 A4
Willett 23 E4
Willey Shrop. 65 F3
Willey Warks. 67 G4
Williamscot 55 G3
Williamthorpe 81 F1
Willian 58 A4
Willimontswick 119 D1
Willingale 45 E2
Willingdon 18 A3
Willingham Cambs. 58 C1
Willingham Lincs. 95 F4
Willington Beds. 57 G3
Willington Derbys. 81 D5
Willington Dur. 120 A4
Willington T. & W. 120 C1
Willington Warks. 55 E4
Willington Corner 78 C1
Willisham 60 B2
Willitoft 103 G4
Williton 23 D3
Willoughby Lincs. 97 E5
Willoughby Warks. 56 A1
Willoughby-on-the-Wolds 82 B5
Willoughby Waterleys 68 A3
Willoughton 95 G3
Willows Green 45 G1
Willsworthy 7 F2
Wilmcote 55 D2
Wilmington Devon 11 F2
Wilmington E.Suss. 18 A3
Wilmington Kent 45 E5
Wilmslow 92 C4
Wilnecote 67 E2
Wilpshire 100 C4
Wilsden 101 G4
Wilsford Lincs. 83 F3
Wilsford Wilts. 26 C3
Wilsford Wilts. 26 B2
Wilsill 102 A1
Wilsley Green 31 G5
Wilson 81 F5
Wilstead 57 F3
Wilsthorpe 69 F1
Wilstone 43 E1
Wilton Cumb. 116 D5
Wilton N.Yorks. 112 B4
Wilton R. & C. 121 E5
Wilton Sc.Bord. 135 F4
Wilton Som. 23 F5
Wilton Wilts. 27 D1
Wilton Wilts. 26 B4
Wimbish 59 D4
Wimbish Green 59 E4
Wimblebury 66 C1
Wimbledon 44 B5
Wimblington 70 C3
Wimborne Minster 13 G2
Wimborne St. Giles 13 G1
Wimbotsham 71 E2
Wimpole 58 B3
Wimpstone 55 E3
Wincanton 25 E5
Wincham 92 A5
Winchburgh 143 E2
Winchcombe 54 C5
Winchelsea 19 E2
Winchelsea Beach 19 E2
Winchester 27 F5
Winchet Hill 31 G4
Winchfield 28 C2
Winchmore Hill Bucks. 43 E3
Winchmore Hill Gt.Lon. 44 C3
Wincle 79 G1
Wincobank 94 A3
Windermere 107 F3
Winderton 55 F3
Windhill 179 E5
Windlesham 29 E1
Windley 81 E3
Windley Meadows 81 E3
Windmill Hill E.Suss. 18 B2
Windmill Hill Som. 11 G1
Windrush 41 D1
Windsor 43 E5
Windy Yet 141 F4
Windygates 152 B4
Wineham 17 E1
Winestead 105 F5
Winewall 101 F3
Winfarthing 72 C3
Winford 24 C1
Winforton 52 B3
Winfrith Newburgh 13 E4
Wing Bucks. 57 D5
Wing Rut. 69 D2
Wingate 120 D4
Wingates Gt.Man. 92 A2
Wingates Northumb. 128 C2
Wingerworth 81 E1
Wingfield Beds. 57 F5
Wingfield Suff. 72 D4
Wingfield Wilts. 25 F2
Wingham 33 E3
Wingmore 33 D4
Wingrave 43 D1
Winkburn 82 C2
Winkfield 43 E5
Winkfield Row 43 D5
Winkhill 80 B2
Winkleigh 21 G5
Winksley 110 B5
Winksley Banks 110 B5
Winkton 14 A3
Winlaton 120 A1
Winlaton Mill 120 A1
Winless 195 E3
Winmarleigh 100 A3
Winnards Perch 4 D3
Winnersh 42 C5
Winscombe 24 B2
Winsford Ches. 79 D1
Winsford Som. 22 C4
Winsh-wen Swan. 36 C3
Winsham 11 G2
Winshill 81 D5
Winskill 118 B4
Winslade 28 B3
Winsley 25 E1
Winslow 56 C5
Winson 40 C2
Winsor 14 C1
Winster Cumb. 107 F3
Winster Derbys. 80 D1
Winston Dur. 110 A1
Winston Suff. 60 C1
Winstone 40 B2
Winswell 21 E4
Winterborne Came 12 D4
Winterborne Clenston 13 E2
Winterborne Houghton 13 E2
Winterborne Kingston 13 E3
Winterborne Monkton 12 C4
Winterborne Stickland 13 E2
Winterborne Whitechurch 13 E2
Winterborne Zelston 13 E3
Winterbourne S.Glos. 39 F4
Winterbourne W.Berks. 41 G5
Winterbourne Abbas 12 C3
Winterbourne Bassett 40 C5
Winterbourne Dauntsey 26 C4
Winterbourne Earls 26 C4
Winterbourne Gunner 26 C4
Winterbourne Monkton 40 C5
Winterbourne Steepleton 12 C4
Winterbourne Stoke 26 B3
Winterburn 101 F2
Wintercleugh 134 A4
Winteringham 104 B5
Winterley 79 E2
Wintersett 94 A1
Wintershill 15 E1
Winterslow 26 D4
Winterton 95 G1
Winterton-on-Sea 87 F4
Winthorpe Lincs. 85 D1
Winthorpe Notts. 82 D2
Winton Bourne. 13 G3
Winton Cumb. 108 C1
Wintringham 112 B5
Winwick Cambs. 69 G4
Winwick Northants. 68 B5
Winwick Warr. 92 A3
Wirksworth 81 D2
Wirswall 78 C3
Wisbech 70 C2
Wisbech St. Mary 70 C2
Wisborough Green 29 F5
Wiseton 95 E4
Wishaw N.Lan. 142 B4
Wishaw Warks. 67 D3
Wisley 29 F2
Wispington 96 C5
Wissett 73 E4
Wissington 60 A4
Wistanstow 64 D4
Wistanswick 79 D5
Wistaston 79 D2
Wiston Pembs. 34 D1
Wiston S.Lan. 134 A2
Wistow Cambs. 70 A4
Wistow N.Yorks. 103 E4
Wiswell 100 D4
Witcham 70 C5
Witchampton 13 F2
Witchburn 130 C4
Witchford 70 D5
Witcombe 24 B5
Witham 46 B1
Witham Friary 25 E3
Witham on the Hill 69 F1
Withcote 68 D2
Witherenden Hill 18 B1
Witherhurst 18 B1
Witheridge 10 B1
Witherley 67 F3
Withern 97 E4
Withernsea 105 F5
Withernwick 105 E3
Withersdale Street 73 D3
Withersfield 59 E3
Witherslack 107 F4
Witherslack Hall 107 F4
Withiel 5 D3
Withiel Florey 22 C4
Withington Glos. 40 C1
Withington Gt.Man. 92 C3
Withington Here. 53 E3
Withington Shrop. 65 E1
Withington Staffs. 80 B4
Withington Green 92 C5
Withleigh 10 C1
Withnell 100 C5
Withybrook 67 G4
Withycombe 22 D3
Withycombe Raleigh 10 D4
Withyham 31 D5
Withypool 22 B4
Witley 29 E4
Witnesham 60 C2
Witney 41 F1
Wittering 69 F2
Wittersham 19 D1
Witton 161 D3
Witton Bridge 87 E2
Witton Gilbert 120 B3
Witton-le-Wear 120 A4
Witton Park 120 A4
Wiveliscombe 23 D5
Wivelsfield 17 F1
Wivelsfield Green 17 F2
Wivenhoe 60 B5
Wiveton 86 B1
Wix 60 C5
Wixford 54 C2
Wixoe 59 F3
Woburn 57 E4
Woburn Sands 57 E4
Wokefield Park 28 B1
Woking 29 F2
Wokingham 28 D1
Wolborough 10 B5
Wold Newton E.Riding 112 D5
Wold Newton N.E.Lincs. 96 C3
Woldingham 30 C3
Wolfelee 135 G5
Wolferlow 53 F1
Wolferton 85 E5
Wolfhampcote 56 A1
Wolfhill 151 G1
Wolfpits 52 B2
Wolf's Castle 48 C5
Wolfsdale 48 C5
Woll 135 F3
Wollaston Northants. 57 E1
Wollaston Shrop. 64 C1
Wollaston W.Mid. 66 A4
Wollerton 78 D5
Wolsingham 119 G4
Wolstenholme 92 C1
Wolston 67 G5
Wolvercote 41 G2
Wolverhampton 66 B3
Wolverley Shrop. 78 B4
Wolverley Worcs. 66 A5
Wolverton Hants. 27 G2
Wolverton M.K. 56 D3
Wolverton Warks. 55 E1
Wolvesnewton 39 D3
Wolvey 67 G4
Wolviston 120 D5
Wombleton 111 F4
Wombourne 66 A3
Wombwell 94 B2
Womenswold 33 E3
Womersley 94 C1
Wonastow 39 D1
Wonersh 29 F3
Wonson 7 G2
Wonston 27 F4
Wooburn 43 E4
Wooburn Green 43 E4
Wood Burcote 56 B3
Wood Dalling 86 B3
Wood End Beds. 57 F3
Wood End Herts. 58 B5
Wood End Warks. 67 E3
Wood End Warks. 66 D5
Wood Enderby 84 A1
Wood Green 44 C3
Wood Hayes 66 B2
Wood Norton 86 B3
Wood Street Village 29 E2
Woodale 109 F5
Woodbastwick 87 E4
Woodbeck 95 E5
Woodbine 34 C1
Woodborough Notts. 82 B3
Woodborough Wilts. 26 C1
Woodbridge 61 D3
Woodbury 10 D4
Woodbury Salterton 10 D4
Woodchester 40 A2
Woodchurch Kent 32 B5
Woodchurch Mersey. 91 D4
Woodcote Oxon. 42 B4
Woodcote Tel. & W. 65 G1
Woodcott 27 F2
Woodcroft 39 E3
Woodcutts 13 F1
Woodditton 59 E2
Woodeaton 42 A1
Woodend Aber. 170 B3
Woodend Cumb. 106 C3
Woodend High. 167 G2
Woodend High. 155 G3
Woodend Northants. 56 B3
Woodend P. & K. 158 C5
Woodend W.Suss. 16 A3
Woodfalls 26 D5
Woodford Cornw. 20 C4
Woodford Glos. 39 F3
Woodford Gt.Lon. 44 D3
Woodford Gt.Man. 92 C4
Woodford Northants. 69 E5
Woodford Bridge 44 D3
Woodford Green 44 D3
Woodford Halse 56 A2
Woodgate Norf. 86 B4
Woodgate W.Mid. 66 B4
Woodgate W.Suss. 16 B3
Woodgate Worcs. 54 B1
Woodgreen 14 A1
Woodhall 109 E3
Woodhall Spa 83 G1
Woodham Dur. 120 B5
Woodham Surr. 29 F1
Woodham Ferrers 45 G3
Woodham Mortimer 46 B2
Woodham Walter 46 B2
Woodhaven 152 C2
Woodhead 170 C1
Woodhill 65 G4
Woodhorn 129 E3
Woodhouse Cumb. 107 G4
Woodhouse Leics. 68 A1
Woodhouse S.Yorks. 94 B4
Woodhouse Eaves 68 A1
Woodhouses 67 D1
Woodhuish 9 F2
Woodhurst 70 B5
Woodingdean 17 F3
Woodland Devon 9 D1
Woodland Dur. 119 G5
Woodlands Dorset 13 G2
Woodlands Hants. 14 C1
Woodlands Shrop. 65 G4
Woodlands Park 43 D5
Woodleigh 8 D3
Woodlesford 102 C5
Woodley 42 C5
Woodmancote Glos. 40 C2
Woodmancote Glos. 54 B5
Woodmancote W.Suss. 17 E2
Woodmancote W.Suss. 15 G2
Woodmancott 27 G3
Woodmansey 104 C4
Woodmansterne 30 B3
Woodminton 26 B5
Woodmoor 64 B2
Woodnesborough 33 E3
Woodnewton 69 F3
Woodplumpton 100 B4
Woodrising 86 A5
Woodseaves Shrop. 79 D4
Woodseaves Staffs. 79 E5
Woodsend 41 E5
Woodsetts 94 C4
Woodsford 13 D3
Woodside Aberdeen 171 E4
Woodside Brack.F. 43 E5
Woodside D. & G. 125 E3
Woodside Fife 152 C4
Woodside Fife 152 B4
Woodside Herts. 44 B2
Woodside N.Ayr. 141 E4
Woodside P. & K. 151 G1
Woodside Shrop. 64 C5
Woodside W.Mid. 66 B4
Woodstock 41 G1
Woodstock Slop 48 D5
Woodston 69 G3
Woodthorpe Derbys. 94 B5
Woodthorpe Leics. 68 A1
Woodton 73 D2
Woodtown 21 E3
Woodville 67 F1
Woodwalton 70 A4
Woodyates 13 G1
Woofferton 53 E1
Wookey 24 C3
Wookey Hole 24 C3
Wool 13 E4
Woolacombe 21 E1
Woolaston 39 E3
Woolavington 24 A3
Woolbeding 29 D5
Wooler 137 D4
Woolfardisworthy Devon 10 B2
Woolfardisworthy Devon 20 D3
Woolfords Cottages 143 E4
Woolhampton 27 G1
Woolhope 53 F4
Woollage Green 33 E4
Woolland 13 D2
Woollard 24 D1
Woollaton 21 E4
Woolley B. & N.E.Som. 25 E1
Woolley Cambs. 69 G5
Woolley W.Yorks. 94 A1
Woolmer Green 44 B1
Woolmere Green 54 B1
Woolmersdon 23 F4
Woolpit 60 A1
Woolscott 55 G1
Woolstaston 65 D3
Woolsthorpe Lincs. 82 D4
Woolsthorpe Lincs. 83 E5
Woolston S'ham. 14 D1
Woolston Shrop. 78 A5
Woolston Shrop. 64 D4
Woolston Warr. 92 A4
Woolston Green 9 D1
Woolstone M.K. 57 D4
Woolstone Oxon. 41 E4
Woolton 91 F4
Woolton Hill 27 F1
Woolverstone 60 C4
Woolverton 25 E2
Woolwich 44 D5
Woonton 52 C2
Wooperton 137 E4
Woore 79 E3
Wootton Beds. 57 F3
Wootton Hants. 14 B3
Wootton Kent 33 E4
Wootton N.Lincs. 96 A1
Wootton Northants. 56 C2
Wootton Oxon. 41 G1
Wootton Oxon. 41 G2
Wootton Shrop. 65 D5
Wootton Staffs. 79 F5
Wootton Staffs. 80 C3
Wootton Bassett 40 C4
Wootton Bridge 15 E3
Wootton Common 15 E3
Wootton Courtenay 22 C3
Wootton Fitzpaine 11 G3
Wootton Green 57 F3
Wootton Rivers 26 C1
Wootton St. Lawrence 27 G2
Wootton Wawen 55 D1
Worcester 54 A2
Worcester Park 30 B2
Wordsley 66 A4
Wordwell 71 G5
Worfield 65 G3
Work 198 C5
Workington 116 D4
Worksop 94 C5
Worlaby 96 A1
Worlds End Hants. 15 F1
World's End W.Berks. 41 G5
Worle 24 A1
Worleston 79 D2
Worlingham 73 F2
Worlington 71 E5
Worlingworth 60 D1
Wormbridge 52 D4
Wormegay 71 E1
Wormelow Tump 53 D4
Wormhill 93 F5
Wormiehills 153 E1
Wormingford 60 A4
Worminghall 42 B2
Wormington 54 C4
Worminster 24 C3
Wormiston 153 E4
Wormit 152 B2
Wormleighton 55 G2
Wormley Herts. 44 C2
Wormley Surr. 29 E4
Wormshill 32 A3
Wormsley 52 D3
Worplesdon 29 E2
Worrall 94 A3
Worsbrough 94 A2
Worsley 92 B2
Worstead 87 E3
Worsted Lodge 58 D2
Worsthorne 101 E4
Worston 101 D3
Worswell 8 B3
Worth Kent 33 F3
Worth W.Suss. 30 C5
Worth Matravers 13 F5
Wortham 72 B4
Worthen 64 C2
Worthenbury 78 B3
Worthing Norf. 86 B4
Worthing W.Suss. 16 D3
Worthington 81 F5
Wortley Glos. 39 G3
Wortley S.Yorks. 94 A3
Worton 26 A2
Wortwell 73 D3
Wotherton 64 B2
Wotton 29 G3
Wotton-under-Edge 39 G3
Wotton Underwood 42 B1
Woughton on the Green 57 D4
Wouldham 31 G2
Wrabness 60 C4
Wrae 182 C4
Wrafton 21 E2
Wragby 96 B5
Wragholme 97 D3
Wramplingham 86 C5
Wrangham 170 B1
Wrangle 84 C2
Wrangle Lowgate 84 C2
Wrangway 11 E1
Wrantage 24 A5
Wrawby 96 A2
Wraxall N.Som. 39 D5
Wraxall Som. 24 D4
Wray 100 C1
Wray Castle 107 E2
Wraysbury 43 F5
Wrea Green 99 G4
Wreay Cumb. 118 A5
Wreay Cumb. 118 A3
Wrecclesham 28 D3
Wrecsam (Wrexham) 78 A3
Wrekenton 120 B2
Wrelton 111 G4
Wrenbury 78 C3
Wreningham 72 C2
Wrentham 73 F3
Wrenthorpe 102 C5
Wrentnall 64 D2
Wressle 103 G4
Wrestlingworth 58 A3
Wretham 72 A3
Wretton 71 E3
Wrexham (Wrecsam) 78 A3
Wrexham Industrial Estate 78 A3
Wribbenhall 65 G5
Wrightington Bar 91 G1
Wrightpark 150 B5
Wrinehill 79 E3
Wrington 24 B1
Writhlington 25 D2
Writtle 45 F2
Wrockwardine 65 F1
Wroot 95 E2
Wrotham 31 F3
Wrotham Heath 31 F3
Wrotham Hill 31 F2
Wrotham Park 44 B3
Wroughton 40 D4
Wroxall I.o.W. 15 E5
Wroxall Warks. 67 E5
Wroxeter 65 E2
Wroxham 87 E4
Wroxton 55 G3
Wstrws 49 G3
Wyaston 80 C3
Wyberton 84 B3

Wyboston 57 G2
Wybunbury 79 D3
Wych Cross 30 D5
Wychbold 54 B1
Wyck 28 C4
Wyck Rissington 55 D5
Wycliffe 110 A1
Wycoller 101 F4
Wycomb 82 C5
Wycombe Marsh 43 D3
Wyddial 58 B4
Wye 32 C4
Wyke *Dorset* 25 E5
Wyke *Shrop.* 65 F2
Wyke *W.Yorks.* 102 A5
Wyke Regis 12 C5
Wykeham *N.Yorks.* 112 C4
Wykeham *N.Yorks.* 112 B5
Wyken 65 G3
Wykey 78 A5
Wylam 120 A1
Wylde Green 66 D3
Wyllie 38 A3
Wylye 26 B4
Wymering 15 F2
Wymeswold 82 B5
Wymington 57 E1
Wymondham *Leics.* 69 D1
Wymondham *Norf.* 86 C5
Wyndham 37 F3
Wynford Eagle 12 B3
Wynnstay Park 78 A3
Wynyard 120 D5
Wyre Piddle 54 B3
Wyresdale Tower 100 C2
Wysall 82 B5
Wyson 53 E1
Wythall 66 C5
Wytham 41 G2
Wythburn 117 G5
Wyton 70 A5
Wyverstone 60 B1
Wyverstone Street 60 B1
Wyville 83 D5
Wyvis Lodge 179 D2

**Y**
Y Bryn 76 B5
Y Drenewydd (Newtown) 64 A3
Y Fan 63 F4
Y Felinheli 75 E1
Y Fenni (Abergavenny) 38 C1
Y Fflint (Flint) 90 D5
Y Ffôr 74 C4
Y Trallwng (Welshpool) 64 B2
Yaddlethorpe 95 F2
Yafford 15 D4
Yafforth 110 C3
Yalding 31 F4
Yanworth 40 C1
Yapham 103 G2
Yapton 16 B3
Yarburgh 96 D3
Yarcombe 11 F2
Yardley 66 D4
Yardley Gobion 56 C3
Yardley Hastings 57 D2
Yardro 52 B2
Yarkhill 53 F3
Yarlet 79 G5
Yarley 24 C3
Yarlington 25 D5
Yarm 110 D1
Yarmouth 14 C4
Yarnacott 21 G2
Yarnbrook 25 F2
Yarnfield 79 F4
Yarnscombe 21 F3
Yarnton 41 G1
Yarpole 53 D1
Yarrow 135 E3
Yarrow Feus 135 E3
Yarrowford 135 F3
Yarsop 52 D3
Yarwell 69 F3
Yate 39 G4
Yateley 28 D1
Yatesbury 40 C5
Yattendon 42 A5
Yatton *Here.* 52 D1
Yatton *N.Som.* 24 B1
Yatton Keynell 40 A5
Yaverland 15 F4
Yaxham 86 B4
Yaxley *Cambs.* 69 G3
Yaxley *Suff.* 72 C4
Yazor 52 D3
Yeading 44 A4
Yeadon 102 B3
Yealand Conyers 107 G5
Yealand Redmayne 107 G5
Yealmpton 8 B2
Yearby 121 F5
Yearsley 111 E5
Yeaton 64 D1
Yeaveley 80 C3
Yedingham 112 B5
Yelford 41 F2
Yelland *Devon* 21 E2
Yelland *Devon* 7 F1
Yelling 58 A1
Yelvertoft 68 A5
Yelverton *Devon* 8 B1
Yelverton *Norf.* 87 D5
Yenston 25 E5
Yeo Vale 21 E3
Yeoford 10 A3
Yeolmbridge 6 D2
Yeomadon 20 D5
Yeovil 12 B1
Yeovil Marsh 12 B1
Yeovilton 24 C5
Yerbeston 35 D2
Yesnaby 198 A5
Yetlington 137 E5
Yetminster 12 B1
Yettington 11 D4
Yetts o'Muckhart 151 F4
Yielden 57 F1
Yiewsley 43 F5
Ynys 75 E4
Ynysboeth 37 G3
Ynysddu 38 A3
Ynyshir 37 G3
Ynyslas 62 C3
Ynysmeudwy 36 D2
Ynystawe 36 C2
Ynysybwl 37 G3
Yockenthwaite 109 E5
Yockleton 64 C1
Yokefleet 104 A5
Yoker 141 G3
Yonder Bognie 182 A5
York 103 F2
Yorkletts 32 C2
Yorkley 39 F2
Yorton 78 C5
Youldon 20 D5
Youldonmoor Cross 20 D5
Youlgreave 80 D1
Youlthorpe 103 G2
Youlton 103 D1
Young's End 45 G1
Yoxall 66 D1
Yoxford 61 E1
Yr Wyddgrug (Mold) 77 F1
Ysbyty Cynfyn 63 D5
Ysbyty Ifan 76 B3
Ysbyty Ystwyth 62 D5
Ysceifiog 90 C5
Ysgubor-y-coed 62 C3
Ystalyfera 37 D2
Ystrad 37 F3
Ystrad Aeron 50 B2
Ystrad Meurig 50 D1
Ystrad Mynach 38 A3
Ystradfellte 37 F1
Ystradffin 51 D3
Ystradgynlais 37 D1
Ystradowen *N.P.T.* 36 D1
Ystradowen *V. of Glam.* 37 G5
Ythanwells 170 B1
Ythsie 171 D1

**Z**
Zeal Monachorum 10 A2
Zeals 25 E4
Zelah 4 C4
Zennor 2 B3


# Index to place names in Ireland

**Abbreviations**
*Ant.* Antrim
*Dub.* Dublin
*Kilk.* Kilkenny
*Tipp.* Tipperary
*Tyr.* Tyrone
*Water.* Waterford
*Wexf.* Wexford


**A**
Aasleagh 246 B6
Abbeyfeale 244 C3
Abbeyleix 245 F2
Achill 246 B5
Adare 244 C2
Annahilt 247 G4
Annalong 247 H5
Antrim 247 G3
Ardara 246 D3
Ardee 247 G5
Ardglass 247 H4
Arklow (An tinbhear Mór) 245 G2
Armagh 247 G4
Armoy 247 G2
Arvagh 247 E5
Ashbourne 247 G6
Athboy 247 F6
Athenry 244 D1
Athleague 246 D6
Athlone (Baile Átha Luain) 247 E6
Athy 245 F1
Augher 247 F4
Aughnacloy 247 F4
Aughrim 245 G2
Avoca 245 G2

**B**
Bailieborough 247 F5
Balbriggan 247 G6
Ballaghaderreen 246 D5
Ballina (Béal an Átha) 246 C5
Ballinafad 246 D5
Ballinalack 247 E6
Ballinamore 247 E5
Ballinasloe (Béal Átha na Sluaighe) 244 D1
Ballindine 246 C6
Ballinrobe 246 C6
Ballon 245 F2
Ballybay 247 F5
Ballybofey 247 E3
Ballybrack 244 A4
Ballybunnion 244 B3
Ballycanew 245 G2
Ballycastle *Ant.* 247 G2
Ballycastle *Mayo* 246 C4
Ballyclare 247 G3
Ballyconnell 247 E5
Ballycroy 246 B5
Ballydesmond 244 C3
Ballygar 246 D6
Ballygawley 247 F4
Ballygorman 247 F2
Ballyhale 245 F3
Ballyhaunis 246 D6
Ballyheigue 244 B3
Ballyjamesduff 247 F5
Ballykelly 247 F3
Ballylynan 245 F2
Ballymacarberry 245 E3
Ballymacmague 245 E4
Ballymacoda 245 E4
Ballymahon 247 E6
Ballymakeery 244 C4
Ballymena 247 G3
Ballymoney 247 G3
Ballymote 246 D5
Ballymurphy 245 F2
Ballynahinch 247 H4
Ballyragget 245 F2
Ballyshannon 246 D4
Ballyvaughan 244 C1
Ballyward 247 G4
Baltinglass 245 G2
Banagher 245 E1
Banbridge 247 G4
Bandon 244 D4
Bangor 247 H4
Bangor Erris 246 B5
Banteer 244 C3
Bantry 244 B5
Belcoo 247 E4
Belderg 246 B4
Belfast 247 H4
Belfast City Airport 247 H4
Belfast International Airport 247 G4
Belmullet 246 B5
Beragh 247 F4
Bessbrook 247 G5
Bettystown 247 G6
Birr 245 E1
Blackrock 247 G5
Blackwater 245 G3
Blarney 244 D4
Blessington 245 G1
Bohola 246 C5
Borris 245 F2
Borrisokane 244 D1
Borrisoleigh 245 E2
Boyle 246 D5
Bray (Bré) 245 G1
Broadford 244 C3
Broughshane 247 G3
Bunbeg 246 D3
Bunclody 245 G2
Buncrana 247 E2
Bundoran 246 D4
Burtonport 246 D3
Bushmills 247 G2
Butlers Bridge 247 F5
Buttevant 244 D3

**C**
Cahermore 244 B5
Cahir 245 E3
Cahirciveen 244 A4
Callan 245 F3
Cappoquin 245 E3
Carlingford 247 G5
Carlow (Ceatharlach) 245 F2
Carndonagh 247 F2
Carnlough 247 G3
Carraroe 244 B1
Carrick-on-Shannon 247 E5
Carrick-on-Suir (Carraig na Siúire) 245 F3
Carrickfergus 247 H3
Carrickmacross 247 F5
Carrigallen 247 E5
Carrigtwohill 244 D4
Carrowdore 247 H4
Carrowkeel 247 F2
Cashel 245 E3
Castlebar (Caisleán an Bharraigh) 246 C5
Castlebellingham 247 G5
Castleblayney 247 F5
Castlebridge 245 G3
Castlecomer 245 F2
Castleconnell 244 D2
Castlederg 247 E3
Castledermot 245 F2
Castlegregory 244 B3
Castleisland 244 B3
Castlemaine 244 B3
Castlemartyr 245 E4
Castlepollard 247 F6
Castlerea 246 D6
Castletown 245 E1
Castletown Bere 244 B5
Catherdaniel 244 A4
Cavan 247 F5
Celbridge 245 G1
Charlestown 246 D5
Cheekpoint 245 F3
City of Derry Airport 247 F3
Clady 247 E3
Clane 245 G1
Clara 245 E1
Clarecastle 244 C2
Claregalway 244 C1
Claremorris 246 C6
Clashmore 245 E4
Claudy 247 F3
Clifden 246 B6
Cliffonoy 246 D4
Cloghan 245 E1
Clogheen 245 E3
Clonakilty 244 C5
Clonbern 246 D6
Clones 247 F5
Clonmel (Cluain Meala) 245 E3
Clonroche 245 G3
Clonygowan 245 F1
Cloonbannin 244 C3
Clooneagh 247 E5
Cobh (An Cóbh) 244 D4
Coleraine 247 F2
Collooney 246 D5
Comber 247 H4
Cong 246 C6
Cookstown 247 F4
Cootehill 247 F5
Cork (Corcaigh) 244 D4
Cork Airport 244 D4
Corofin 244 C2
Courtmacsherry 244 D5
Courtown 245 G2
Craanford 245 G2
Craigavon 247 G4
Creeslough 247 E2
Cregganbaun 246 B6
Crookhaven 244 B5
Croom 244 D3
Crossgar 247 H4
Crosshaven 244 D4
Crossmaglen 247 G5
Crumlin 247 G4
Crusheen 244 C2
Cullybackey 247 G3
Cushendall 247 G3
Cushendun 247 G2

**D**
Delvin 247 F6
Dingle 244 A3
Donaghadee 247 H4
Donaghmore 247 F4
Donegal 246 D4
Donoughmore 244 D4
Dooagh 246 B5
Downpatrick 247 H4
Draperstown 247 F3
Drimoleague 244 C5
Drogheda (Droichead Átha) 247 G6
Dromod 247 E5
Dromore *Down* 247 G4
Dromore *Tyr.* 247 E4
Dromore West 246 C5
Drumfree 247 E2
Drumkeeran 246 D5
Drummin 245 F3
Dublin (Baile Átha Cliath) 245 G1
Dublin Airport 247 G6
Dún Laoghaire 245 G1
Dunboyne 247 G6
Duncannon 245 F3
Duncormick 245 G3
Dundalk (Dún Dealgan) 247 G5
Dundonald 247 H4
Dundrum 247 H4
Dungannon 247 F4
Dungarvan *Kilk.* 245 F2
Dungarvan (Dún Garbhán) *Water.* 245 E4
Dungiven 247 F3
Dungloe 246 D3
Dunlavin 245 G1
Dunleer 247 G5
Dunloy 247 G3
Dunmanway 244 C4
Dunmore 246 D6
Dunmore East 245 F3
Dunmurry 247 G4
Dunquin 244 A3
Durrow 245 F2

**E**
Edenderry 245 F1
Edgeworthstown 247 E6
Eglinton 247 F3
Ennis (Inis) 244 C2
Enniscorthy (Inis Córthaidh) 245 G3
Enniskean 244 C4
Enniskerry 245 G1
Enniskillen 247 E4
Ennistymon 244 C2

**F**
Farranfore 244 B3
Fermoy 244 D3
Ferns 245 G2
Fethard 245 E3
Fintona 247 F4
Fintown 246 D3
Fivemiletown 247 F4
Foxford 246 C5
Foynes 244 C2
Frenchpark 246 D5
Freshford 245 F2

**G**
Galbally 244 D3
Galway (Gaillimh) 244 C1
Galway Airport 244 C1
Garvagh 247 F3
Glenamaddy 246 D6
Glengarriff 244 B4
Glengavlen 247 E5
Glenties 246 D3
Gorey 245 G2
Gort 244 C1
Gortahork 246 D2
Graigue 245 F2
Graiguenamanagh 245 F2
Granard 247 E6
Grange 245 E4
Greenore 247 G5
Gweedore 246 D3

**H**
Halfway 244 D4
Headford 246 C6
Holycross 245 E2
Horseleap 246 D6
Hospital 244 D3
Howth 247 G6
Hurler's Cross 244 C2

**I**
Inch *Kerry* 244 B3
Inch *Wexf.* 245 G2

**J**
Johnstown 245 E2

**K**
Kanturk 244 C3
Keady 247 F5
Kells *Kilk.* 245 F3
Kells (Ceanannus Mór) *Meath* 247 F6
Kenmare 244 B4
Kerry Airport 244 B3
Kilbeggan 245 E1
Kilcolgan 244 C1
Kilcommon 245 E3
Kilcoole 245 G1
Kilcormac 245 E1
Kilcullen 245 F1
Kildare 245 F1
Kilkee 244 B2
Kilkeel 247 G5
Kilkenny (Cill Chainnigh) 245 F2
Killala 246 C5
Killaloe 244 D2
Killarney (Cill Airne) 244 B4
Killenaule 245 E2
Killimor 244 D1
Killinchy 247 H4
Killinick 245 G3
Killorglin 244 B4
Killurin 245 G3
Killybegs 246 D4
Kilmacrenan 247 E3
Kilmaine 246 C6
Kilmallock 244 D3
Kilmona 244 D4
Kilmore Quay 245 G3
Kilrea 247 G3
Kilrush 244 B2
Kilteel 245 G1
Kiltimagh 246 C5
Kiltullagh 244 D1
Kingscourt 247 F5
Kinnegad 247 F6
Kinsale 244 D4
Kinvara 244 C1
Kircubbin 247 H4
Knock 246 C6
Knock International Airport 246 C5
Knockalough 244 C2
Knocktopher 245 F3

**L**
Lanesborough 247 E6
Larne 247 H3
Lauragh 244 B4
Laytown 247 G6
Leap 244 C5
Leighlinbridge 245 F2
Leixlip 245 G1
Letterkenny 247 E3
Lifford 247 E3
Limavady 247 F3
Limerick (Luimneach) 244 D2
Lisbellaw 247 E4
Lisburn 247 G4
Lisdoonvarna 244 C1
Lismore 245 E3
Lisnarrick 247 E4
Lisnaskea 247 E5
Listowel 244 B3
Londonderry (Derry) 247 F3
Longford 247 E6
Loughrea 244 D1
Louisburgh 246 B6
Lucan 245 G1
Lukeswell 245 F3
Lurgan 247 G4

**M**
Macroom 244 C4
Maghera 247 G3
Magherafelt 247 G3
Malahide 247 G6
Malin More 246 D3
Mallow (Mala) 244 D3
Manorhamilton 246 D4
Markethill 247 G4
May's Corner 247 G4
Middletown 247 F4
Midleton 244 D4
Milestone 245 E2
Milford 247 E3
Millstreet 244 C4
Milltown Malbay 244 C2
Mitchelstown 244 D3
Moate 245 E1
Mohill 247 E5
Moira 247 G4
Monaghan (Muineachán) 247 F5
Monasterevan 245 F1
Moneygall 245 E2
Moneymore 247 G3
Monivea 244 D1
Mount Bellew 246 D6
Mountmellick 245 F1
Mountrath 245 E1
Mountshannon 244 D2
Moville 247 F2
Moyvalley 247 F6
Muine Bheag 245 F2
Mullany's Cross 246 C5
Mullingar (Án Muileann gCearr) 247 F6
Mulrany 246 B5
Murrisk 246 B6
Murroogh 244 C1

**N**
Naas (An Nás) 245 G1
Navan (An Uaimh) 247 G6
Nenagh (An tAonach) 244 D2
New Ross 245 F3
Newbridge (Droichead Nua) 245 F1
Newcastle *Down* 247 H5
Newcastle *Dub.* 245 G1
Newcastle West 244 C3
Newinn 245 E3
Newmarket 244 C3
Newmarket-on-Fergus 244 C2
Newport *Mayo* 246 B5
Newport *Tipp.* 244 D2
Newry 247 G5
Newtown 244 D3
Newtownabbey 247 H4
Newtownards 247 H4
Newtownbutler 247 F5
Newtownmount-kennedy 245 G1
Newtownstewart 247 F3
Ninemilehouse 245 E3
Nobber 247 F5

**O**
Oldcastle 247 F6
Omagh 247 F4
Oranmore 244 C1

**P**
Pallas Green 244 D2
Park 247 F3
Partry 246 C6
Pettigo 247 E4
Pomeroy 247 F4
Pontoon 246 C5
Portadown 247 G4
Portaferry 247 H4
Portarlington 245 F1
Portavogie 247 H4
Portlaoise 245 F1
Portlaw 245 F3
Portmagee 244 A4
Portrane 247 G6
Portrush 247 G2
Portsalon 247 E2
Portstewart 247 F2
Portumna 244 D1
Poulgorm Bridge 244 C4

**R**
Randalstown 247 G3
Raphoe 247 E3
Rathangan 245 F1
Rathdowney 245 E2
Rathdrum 245 G2
Rathfriland 247 G5
Rathkeale 244 C3
Rathkeevin 245 E3
Rathluirc (Charleville) 244 D3
Rathvilly 245 G2
Recess 246 B6
Ringsend 247 F3
Roscommon 246 D6
Roscrea 245 E2
Ross Carbery 244 C5
Rosslare 245 G3
Rosslare Harbour 245 G3
Rosslea 247 F5
Rush 247 G6

**S**
Saintfield 247 H4
Schull 244 B5
Shanacrane 244 C4
Shannon Airport 244 C2
Shercock 247 F5
Shillelagh 245 G2
Sion Mills 247 E3
Sixmilebridge 244 D2
Sixmilecross 247 F4
Skerries 247 G6
Skibbereen 244 C5
Slane 247 G6
Sligo (Sligeach) 246 D4
Sneem 244 B4
Strabane 247 E3
Stradbally 245 F1
Strangford 247 H4
Stranorlar 247 E3
Strokestown 246 D6
Swinford 246 C5
Swords 247 G6

**T**
Taghmon 245 G3
Tallow 245 E4
Tandragee 247 G4
Tarbert 244 C2
Templemore 245 E2
Templetuohy 245 E2
Thomastown 245 F3
Thurles (Durlas) 245 E2
Timolin 245 F1
Tipperary 244 D3
Tower 244 D4
Tralee (Trá Lí) 244 B3
Tramore (Trá Mhór) 245 F3
Trim 247 F6
Tuam 246 C6
Tubbercurry 246 D5
Tulla 244 D2
Tullamore (Tulach Mhór) 245 E1
Tullow 245 F2
Tully 247 E4
Tulsk 246 D6

**U**
Urlingford 245 E2

**V**
Virginia 247 F5

**W**
Warrenpoint 247 G5
Waterford (Port Láirgé) 245 F3
Waterford Airport 245 F3
Watergrasshill 244 D4
Wellington Bridge 245 F3
Westport 246 B6
Wexford (Loch Garman) 245 G3
Whitehall 245 F2
Whitehead 247 H3
Wicklow (Cill Mhantáin) 245 H1

**Y**
Youghal (Eochaill) 245 E4

# U.K. distance chart

## DISTANCE IN KILOMETRES

| | ABERDEEN | ABERYSTWYTH | AYR | BIRMINGHAM | BRADFORD | BRISTOL | CAMBRIDGE | CARDIFF | CARLISLE | COVENTRY | DERBY | DONCASTER | DOVER | EDINBURGH | EXETER | FISHGUARD | FORT WILLIAM | GLASGOW | GLOUCESTER | HARWICH | HOLYHEAD | HULL | INVERNESS | KENDAL | LEEDS | LEICESTER | LINCOLN | LIVERPOOL | MANCHESTER | NEWCASTLE UPON TYNE | NORWICH | NOTTINGHAM | OXFORD | PENZANCE | PERTH | PLYMOUTH | PORTSMOUTH | SALISBURY | SHEFFIELD | SHREWSBURY | SOUTHAMPTON | SOUTHEND-ON-SEA | STOKE-ON-TRENT | STRANRAER | THURSO | WORCESTER | YORK | LONDON |
|---|---|---|---|---|---|---|---|---|---|---|---|---|---|---|---|---|---|---|---|---|---|---|---|---|---|---|---|---|---|---|---|---|---|---|---|---|---|---|---|---|---|---|---|---|---|---|---|---|
| ABERDEEN | | 689 | 288 | 652 | 525 | 779 | 772 | 787 | 348 | 678 | 631 | 554 | 943 | 208 | 896 | 776 | 253 | 235 | 723 | 869 | 679 | 566 | 169 | 420 | 531 | 660 | 624 | 531 | 533 | 377 | 789 | 628 | 779 | 1069 | 135 | 977 | 904 | 866 | 584 | 628 | 872 | 858 | 592 | 370 | 365 | 689 | 509 | 816 |
| ABERYSTWYTH | | | 492 | 179 | 285 | 217 | 319 | 187 | 341 | 211 | 224 | 278 | 476 | 489 | 335 | 87 | 681 | 494 | 164 | 444 | 175 | 366 | 761 | 269 | 293 | 235 | 306 | 158 | 228 | 447 | 417 | 248 | 238 | 507 | 554 | 407 | 340 | 274 | 251 | 121 | 307 | 396 | 174 | 507 | 958 | 153 | 335 | 340 |
| AYR | | | | 455 | 328 | 583 | 571 | 591 | 151 | 481 | 435 | 385 | 734 | 127 | 700 | 579 | 227 | 53 | 526 | 682 | 483 | 402 | 333 | 224 | 335 | 470 | 449 | 335 | 336 | 238 | 613 | 436 | 554 | 872 | 153 | 772 | 681 | 634 | 388 | 423 | 668 | 666 | 388 | 82 | 529 | 484 | 340 | 621 |
| BIRMINGHAM | | | | | 182 | 138 | 161 | 161 | 304 | 32 | 66 | 153 | 285 | 452 | 256 | 267 | 64 | 457 | 82 | 265 | 232 | 209 | 787 | 232 | 175 | 68 | 142 | 142 | 125 | 331 | 249 | 84 | 98 | 428 | 517 | 328 | 225 | 179 | 122 | 69 | 201 | 232 | 68 | 470 | 903 | 45 | 206 | 171 |
| BRADFORD | | | | | | 309 | 249 | 333 | 177 | 190 | 117 | 55 | 426 | 323 | 439 | 372 | 517 | 330 | 253 | 354 | 254 | 106 | 578 | 100 | 15 | 162 | 119 | 100 | 56 | 156 | 283 | 122 | 270 | 599 | 389 | 499 | 397 | 352 | 61 | 164 | 377 | 351 | 114 | 343 | 774 | 217 | 51 | 312 |
| BRISTOL | | | | | | | 235 | 72 | 431 | 148 | 204 | 288 | 338 | 579 | 117 | 248 | 771 | 584 | 56 | 311 | 368 | 348 | 832 | 359 | 314 | 185 | 264 | 261 | 253 | 470 | 328 | 222 | 108 | 290 | 644 | 190 | 146 | 82 | 261 | 167 | 117 | 259 | 195 | 597 | 1028 | 100 | 346 | 196 |
| CAMBRIDGE | | | | | | | | 286 | 425 | 129 | 146 | 179 | 185 | 549 | 340 | 404 | 752 | 565 | 193 | 105 | 383 | 201 | 826 | 348 | 228 | 101 | 134 | 270 | 240 | 381 | 93 | 127 | 127 | 497 | 637 | 425 | 200 | 225 | 179 | 232 | 211 | 101 | 191 | 591 | 1022 | 166 | 256 | 85 |
| CARDIFF | | | | | | | | | 439 | 185 | 227 | 314 | 351 | 587 | 190 | 175 | 779 | 592 | 93 | 364 | 343 | 370 | 840 | 367 | 336 | 222 | 301 | 261 | 275 | 491 | 380 | 245 | 161 | 362 | 652 | 262 | 217 | 150 | 286 | 167 | 185 | 299 | 220 | 605 | 1036 | 116 | 367 | 237 |
| CARLISLE | | | | | | | | | | 330 | 283 | 233 | 582 | 148 | 549 | 428 | 340 | 153 | 375 | 531 | 331 | 251 | 401 | 72 | 183 | 319 | 298 | 183 | 185 | 90 | 460 | 285 | 402 | 721 | 212 | 621 | 529 | 483 | 237 | 272 | 517 | 515 | 237 | 166 | 597 | 333 | 187 | 470 |
| COVENTRY | | | | | | | | | | | 72 | 151 | 253 | 497 | 265 | 304 | 669 | 483 | 92 | 233 | 262 | 183 | 731 | 257 | 187 | 37 | 116 | 174 | 151 | 330 | 219 | 77 | 76 | 438 | 542 | 338 | 203 | 162 | 134 | 100 | 179 | 200 | 93 | 496 | 927 | 66 | 204 | 138 |
| DERBY | | | | | | | | | | | | 87 | 309 | 431 | 322 | 311 | 623 | 436 | 150 | 251 | 248 | 146 | 684 | 211 | 109 | 45 | 82 | 129 | 90 | 264 | 217 | 24 | 148 | 494 | 496 | 394 | 272 | 235 | 56 | 103 | 251 | 240 | 56 | 449 | 880 | 116 | 140 | 187 |
| DONCASTER | | | | | | | | | | | | | 364 | 346 | 417 | 365 | 573 | 286 | 237 | 303 | 267 | 74 | 607 | 161 | 50 | 106 | 64 | 130 | 80 | 179 | 228 | 72 | 217 | 578 | 418 | 478 | 344 | 314 | 27 | 158 | 320 | 280 | 105 | 399 | 803 | 203 | 53 | 262 |
| DOVER | | | | | | | | | | | | | | 718 | 396 | 581 | 932 | 745 | 312 | 188 | 533 | 386 | 996 | 517 | 420 | 264 | 319 | 426 | 404 | 566 | 262 | 306 | 209 | 554 | 808 | 460 | 201 | 256 | 365 | 352 | 220 | 116 | 346 | 748 | 1192 | 296 | 441 | 114 |
| EDINBURGH | | | | | | | | | | | | | | | 697 | 576 | 225 | 69 | 523 | 661 | 480 | 357 | 261 | 220 | 330 | 476 | 415 | 331 | 333 | 167 | 579 | 418 | 570 | 869 | 72 | 769 | 697 | 658 | 383 | 420 | 665 | 650 | 385 | 200 | 457 | 481 | 301 | 608 |
| EXETER | | | | | | | | | | | | | | | | 365 | 888 | 702 | 174 | 399 | 486 | 449 | 949 | 476 | 431 | 303 | 381 | 378 | 370 | 587 | 430 | 340 | 212 | 158 | 761 | 69 | 203 | 140 | 378 | 285 | 171 | 344 | 312 | 715 | 1146 | 217 | 463 | 282 |
| FISHGUARD | | | | | | | | | | | | | | | | | 768 | 581 | 269 | 537 | 262 | 423 | 829 | 356 | 383 | 322 | 393 | 254 | 315 | 534 | 504 | 335 | 335 | 537 | 640 | 438 | 394 | 330 | 338 | 208 | 365 | 475 | 261 | 594 | 1025 | 238 | 422 | 430 |
| FORT WILLIAM | | | | | | | | | | | | | | | | | | 187 | 715 | 871 | 671 | 591 | 108 | 412 | 523 | 658 | 637 | 523 | 525 | 415 | 801 | 624 | 742 | 1061 | 171 | 961 | 869 | 822 | 576 | 612 | 856 | 855 | 576 | 309 | 285 | 673 | 526 | 810 |
| GLASGOW | | | | | | | | | | | | | | | | | | | 528 | 684 | 484 | 404 | 280 | 225 | 336 | 471 | 451 | 336 | 338 | 228 | 615 | 438 | 555 | 874 | 100 | 774 | 882 | 636 | 389 | 425 | 669 | 668 | 389 | 135 | 476 | 486 | 340 | 623 |
| GLOUCESTER | | | | | | | | | | | | | | | | | | | | 277 | 282 | 275 | 776 | 303 | 257 | 129 | 208 | 212 | 196 | 414 | 286 | 171 | 74 | 346 | 587 | 246 | 171 | 106 | 211 | 119 | 143 | 232 | 138 | 541 | 972 | 43 | 290 | 175 |
| HARWICH | | | | | | | | | | | | | | | | | | | | | 497 | 306 | 922 | 462 | 352 | 206 | 238 | 368 | 341 | 486 | 129 | 232 | 203 | 557 | 734 | 468 | 253 | 259 | 293 | 333 | 264 | 97 | 288 | 697 | 1118 | 290 | 361 | 117 |
| HOLYHEAD | | | | | | | | | | | | | | | | | | | | | | 346 | 732 | 259 | 262 | 274 | 299 | 148 | 198 | 397 | 465 | 272 | 325 | 658 | 544 | 528 | 457 | 389 | 191 | 162 | 425 | 463 | 191 | 497 | 929 | 238 | 306 | 402 |
| HULL | | | | | | | | | | | | | | | | | | | | | | | 620 | 200 | 88 | 146 | 68 | 198 | 148 | 190 | 232 | 132 | 257 | 637 | 431 | 537 | 385 | 346 | 105 | 216 | 360 | 303 | 162 | 417 | 816 | 277 | 64 | 278 |
| INVERNESS | | | | | | | | | | | | | | | | | | | | | | | | 473 | 584 | 713 | 677 | 584 | 586 | 430 | 842 | 681 | 832 | 1122 | 188 | 1030 | 958 | 919 | 637 | 681 | 925 | 911 | 645 | 415 | 196 | 742 | 562 | 869 |
| KENDAL | | | | | | | | | | | | | | | | | | | | | | | | | 111 | 246 | 225 | 111 | 121 | 138 | 383 | 220 | 330 | 649 | 285 | 549 | 457 | 410 | 161 | 200 | 444 | 451 | 164 | 238 | 669 | 261 | 142 | 406 |
| LEEDS | | | | | | | | | | | | | | | | | | | | | | | | | | 154 | 114 | 114 | 64 | 154 | 278 | 114 | 265 | 603 | 396 | 504 | 393 | 354 | 53 | 172 | 360 | 343 | 116 | 349 | 780 | 212 | 37 | 304 |
| LEICESTER | | | | | | | | | | | | | | | | | | | | | | | | | | | 79 | 162 | 135 | 291 | 182 | 40 | 111 | 475 | 525 | 375 | 238 | 200 | 101 | 114 | 214 | 195 | 82 | 484 | 909 | 103 | 159 | 150 |
| LINCOLN | | | | | | | | | | | | | | | | | | | | | | | | | | | | 195 | 151 | 248 | 164 | 58 | 190 | 554 | 489 | 454 | 317 | 278 | 74 | 185 | 303 | 235 | 134 | 463 | 874 | 174 | 122 | 211 |
| LIVERPOOL | | | | | | | | | | | | | | | | | | | | | | | | | | | | | 50 | 249 | 346 | 148 | 249 | 550 | 396 | 451 | 383 | 320 | 110 | 93 | 341 | 357 | 80 | 349 | 780 | 171 | 150 | 325 |
| MANCHESTER | | | | | | | | | | | | | | | | | | | | | | | | | | | | | | 219 | 307 | 100 | 227 | 542 | 397 | 443 | 351 | 311 | 61 | 108 | 331 | 330 | 58 | 351 | 782 | 161 | 108 | 303 |
| NEWCASTLE UPON TYNE | | | | | | | | | | | | | | | | | | | | | | | | | | | | | | | 412 | 251 | 402 | 760 | 241 | 660 | 529 | 491 | 208 | 307 | 505 | 483 | 270 | 256 | 626 | 380 | 125 | 441 |
| NORWICH | | | | | | | | | | | | | | | | | | | | | | | | | | | | | | | | 193 | 220 | 587 | 653 | 515 | 296 | 319 | 235 | 296 | 304 | 164 | 274 | 626 | 1038 | 259 | 286 | 171 |
| NOTTINGHAM | | | | | | | | | | | | | | | | | | | | | | | | | | | | | | | | | 157 | 512 | 492 | 417 | 278 | 240 | 61 | 127 | 254 | 228 | 80 | 451 | 877 | 122 | 125 | 192 |
| OXFORD | | | | | | | | | | | | | | | | | | | | | | | | | | | | | | | | | | 397 | 644 | 298 | 127 | 97 | 209 | 162 | 103 | 156 | 169 | 568 | 1028 | 87 | 277 | 95 |
| PENZANCE | | | | | | | | | | | | | | | | | | | | | | | | | | | | | | | | | | | 933 | 125 | 360 | 298 | 576 | 443 | 328 | 502 | 484 | 887 | 1318 | 375 | 636 | 439 |
| PERTH | | | | | | | | | | | | | | | | | | | | | | | | | | | | | | | | | | | | 842 | 769 | 731 | 449 | 492 | 737 | 723 | 457 | 235 | 385 | 554 | 373 | 681 |
| PLYMOUTH | | | | | | | | | | | | | | | | | | | | | | | | | | | | | | | | | | | | | 272 | 209 | 451 | 354 | 240 | 414 | 385 | 787 | 1226 | 286 | 536 | 351 |
| PORTSMOUTH | | | | | | | | | | | | | | | | | | | | | | | | | | | | | | | | | | | | | | 64 | 336 | 290 | 32 | 191 | 293 | 695 | 1154 | 214 | 397 | 124 |
| SALISBURY | | | | | | | | | | | | | | | | | | | | | | | | | | | | | | | | | | | | | | | 306 | 225 | 35 | 204 | 246 | 649 | 1115 | 150 | 373 | 142 |
| SHEFFIELD | | | | | | | | | | | | | | | | | | | | | | | | | | | | | | | | | | | | | | | | 130 | 307 | 290 | 77 | 402 | 834 | 171 | 84 | 253 |
| SHREWSBURY | | | | | | | | | | | | | | | | | | | | | | | | | | | | | | | | | | | | | | | | | 262 | 301 | 53 | 438 | 877 | 76 | 214 | 240 |
| SOUTHAMPTON | | | | | | | | | | | | | | | | | | | | | | | | | | | | | | | | | | | | | | | | | | 200 | 280 | 682 | 1122 | 171 | 380 | 130 |
| SOUTHEND-ON-SEA | | | | | | | | | | | | | | | | | | | | | | | | | | | | | | | | | | | | | | | | | | | 274 | 681 | 1107 | 220 | 357 | 63 |
| STOKE-ON-TRENT | | | | | | | | | | | | | | | | | | | | | | | | | | | | | | | | | | | | | | | | | | | | 402 | 842 | 97 | 161 | 245 |
| STRANRAER | | | | | | | | | | | | | | | | | | | | | | | | | | | | | | | | | | | | | | | | | | | | | 612 | 499 | 352 | 636 |
| THURSO | | | | | | | | | | | | | | | | | | | | | | | | | | | | | | | | | | | | | | | | | | | | | | 938 | 758 | 107 |
| WORCESTER | | | | | | | | | | | | | | | | | | | | | | | | | | | | | | | | | | | | | | | | | | | | | | | 256 | 171 |
| YORK | | | | | | | | | | | | | | | | | | | | | | | | | | | | | | | | | | | | | | | | | | | | | | | | 315 |

## DISTANCE IN MILES

| | ABERDEEN | ABERYSTWYTH | AYR | BIRMINGHAM | BRADFORD | BRISTOL | CAMBRIDGE | CARDIFF | CARLISLE | COVENTRY | DERBY | DONCASTER | DOVER | EDINBURGH | EXETER | FISHGUARD | FORT WILLIAM | GLASGOW | GLOUCESTER | HARWICH | HOLYHEAD | HULL | INVERNESS | KENDAL | LEEDS | LEICESTER | LINCOLN | LIVERPOOL | MANCHESTER | NEWCASTLE UPON TYNE | NORWICH | NOTTINGHAM | OXFORD | PENZANCE | PERTH | PLYMOUTH | PORTSMOUTH | SALISBURY | SHEFFIELD | SHREWSBURY | SOUTHAMPTON | SOUTHEND-ON-SEA | STOKE-ON-TRENT | STRANRAER | THURSO | WORCESTER | YORK |
|---|---|---|---|---|---|---|---|---|---|---|---|---|---|---|---|---|---|---|---|---|---|---|---|---|---|---|---|---|---|---|---|---|---|---|---|---|---|---|---|---|---|---|---|---|---|---|---|
| ABERYSTWYTH | 428 | | | | | | | | | | | | | | | | | | | | | | | | | | | | | | | | | | | | | | | | | | | | | | |
| AYR | 179 | 306 | | | | | | | | | | | | | | | | | | | | | | | | | | | | | | | | | | | | | | | | | | | | | |
| BIRMINGHAM | 405 | 111 | 283 | | | | | | | | | | | | | | | | | | | | | | | | | | | | | | | | | | | | | | | | | | | | |
| BRADFORD | 326 | 177 | 204 | 113 | | | | | | | | | | | | | | | | | | | | | | | | | | | | | | | | | | | | | | | | | | | |
| BRISTOL | 484 | 135 | 362 | 86 | 192 | | | | | | | | | | | | | | | | | | | | | | | | | | | | | | | | | | | | | | | | | | |
| CAMBRIDGE | 480 | 198 | 355 | 100 | 155 | 146 | | | | | | | | | | | | | | | | | | | | | | | | | | | | | | | | | | | | | | | | | |
| CARDIFF | 489 | 116 | 367 | 100 | 207 | 45 | 178 | | | | | | | | | | | | | | | | | | | | | | | | | | | | | | | | | | | | | | | | |
| CARLISLE | 216 | 212 | 94 | 189 | 110 | 268 | 264 | 273 | | | | | | | | | | | | | | | | | | | | | | | | | | | | | | | | | | | | | | | |
| COVENTRY | 421 | 131 | 299 | 20 | 118 | 92 | 80 | 115 | 205 | | | | | | | | | | | | | | | | | | | | | | | | | | | | | | | | | | | | | | |
| DERBY | 392 | 139 | 270 | 41 | 73 | 127 | 91 | 141 | 176 | 45 | | | | | | | | | | | | | | | | | | | | | | | | | | | | | | | | | | | | | |
| DONCASTER | 344 | 173 | 239 | 95 | 34 | 179 | 111 | 195 | 145 | 94 | 54 | | | | | | | | | | | | | | | | | | | | | | | | | | | | | | | | | | | | |
| DOVER | 586 | 296 | 456 | 177 | 265 | 210 | 115 | 218 | 362 | 157 | 192 | 226 | | | | | | | | | | | | | | | | | | | | | | | | | | | | | | | | | | | |
| EDINBURGH | 129 | 304 | 79 | 281 | 201 | 360 | 341 | 365 | 92 | 309 | 268 | 215 | 446 | | | | | | | | | | | | | | | | | | | | | | | | | | | | | | | | | | |
| EXETER | 557 | 208 | 435 | 159 | 273 | 73 | 211 | 118 | 341 | 165 | 200 | 259 | 246 | 433 | | | | | | | | | | | | | | | | | | | | | | | | | | | | | | | | | |
| FISHGUARD | 482 | 54 | 360 | 166 | 231 | 154 | 251 | 109 | 266 | 189 | 193 | 227 | 361 | 358 | 227 | | | | | | | | | | | | | | | | | | | | | | | | | | | | | | | | |
| FORT WILLIAM | 157 | 423 | 141 | 400 | 321 | 479 | 467 | 484 | 211 | 416 | 387 | 356 | 579 | 140 | 552 | 477 | | | | | | | | | | | | | | | | | | | | | | | | | | | | | | | |
| GLASGOW | 46 | 307 | 33 | 284 | 205 | 363 | 351 | 368 | 95 | 300 | 271 | 240 | 463 | 43 | 436 | 361 | 116 | | | | | | | | | | | | | | | | | | | | | | | | | | | | | | |
| GLOUCESTER | 449 | 102 | 327 | 51 | 157 | 35 | 120 | 58 | 233 | 57 | 93 | 147 | 194 | 325 | 108 | 167 | 444 | 328 | | | | | | | | | | | | | | | | | | | | | | | | | | | | | |
| HARWICH | 40 | 276 | 424 | 165 | 220 | 193 | 65 | 226 | 330 | 145 | 156 | 188 | 117 | 411 | 248 | 334 | 541 | 425 | 172 | | | | | | | | | | | | | | | | | | | | | | | | | | | | |
| HOLYHEAD | 22 | 109 | 300 | 144 | 158 | 229 | 238 | 213 | 206 | 163 | 154 | 166 | 331 | 298 | 302 | 163 | 417 | 301 | 175 | 309 | | | | | | | | | | | | | | | | | | | | | | | | | | | |
| HULL | 52 | 209 | 250 | 130 | 66 | 216 | 125 | 230 | 156 | 114 | 91 | 46 | 240 | 222 | 279 | 263 | 367 | 251 | 171 | 190 | 215 | | | | | | | | | | | | | | | | | | | | | | | | | | |
| INVERNESS | 05 | 473 | 207 | 439 | 359 | 517 | 513 | 522 | 249 | 454 | 425 | 377 | 619 | 162 | 590 | 515 | 67 | 174 | 482 | 573 | 455 | 385 | | | | | | | | | | | | | | | | | | | | | | | | | |
| KENDAL | 61 | 167 | 139 | 144 | 62 | 223 | 216 | 228 | 45 | 160 | 131 | 100 | 321 | 137 | 296 | 221 | 256 | 140 | 188 | 287 | 161 | 124 | 294 | | | | | | | | | | | | | | | | | | | | | | | | |
| LEEDS | 30 | 182 | 208 | 109 | 9 | 195 | 142 | 209 | 114 | 116 | 68 | 31 | 261 | 205 | 268 | 238 | 325 | 209 | 160 | 219 | 163 | 55 | 363 | 69 | | | | | | | | | | | | | | | | | | | | | | | |
| LEICESTER | 10 | 146 | 292 | 42 | 101 | 115 | 63 | 138 | 198 | 23 | 28 | 66 | 164 | 296 | 188 | 200 | 409 | 293 | 80 | 128 | 170 | 91 | 443 | 153 | 96 | | | | | | | | | | | | | | | | | | | | | | |
| LINCOLN | 88 | 190 | 279 | 88 | 74 | 164 | 83 | 187 | 185 | 72 | 51 | 40 | 198 | 258 | 237 | 244 | 396 | 280 | 129 | 148 | 186 | 42 | 421 | 140 | 71 | 49 | | | | | | | | | | | | | | | | | | | | | |
| LIVERPOOL | 30 | 98 | 208 | 88 | 62 | 162 | 168 | 162 | 114 | 108 | 80 | 81 | 265 | 206 | 235 | 158 | 325 | 209 | 132 | 229 | 92 | 123 | 363 | 69 | 71 | 101 | 121 | | | | | | | | | | | | | | | | | | | | |
| MANCHESTER | 31 | 142 | 209 | 78 | 35 | 157 | 149 | 171 | 115 | 94 | 56 | 50 | 251 | 207 | 230 | 196 | 326 | 210 | 122 | 212 | 123 | 92 | 364 | 75 | 40 | 84 | 94 | 31 | | | | | | | | | | | | | | | | | | | |
| NEWCASTLE UPON TYNE | 34 | 278 | 148 | 206 | 97 | 292 | 237 | 305 | 56 | 205 | 164 | 111 | 352 | 104 | 365 | 332 | 258 | 142 | 257 | 302 | 247 | 118 | 267 | 86 | 96 | 181 | 154 | 155 | 136 | | | | | | | | | | | | | | | | | | |
| NORWICH | 90 | 259 | 381 | 155 | 176 | 204 | 58 | 236 | 286 | 136 | 135 | 142 | 163 | 360 | 267 | 313 | 498 | 382 | 178 | 80 | 289 | 144 | 523 | 238 | 173 | 113 | 102 | 215 | 191 | 256 | | | | | | | | | | | | | | | | | |
| NOTTINGHAM | 90 | 154 | 271 | 52 | 76 | 138 | 79 | 152 | 177 | 48 | 15 | 45 | 190 | 260 | 211 | 208 | 388 | 272 | 106 | 144 | 169 | 82 | 423 | 137 | 71 | 25 | 36 | 92 | 62 | 156 | 120 | | | | | | | | | | | | | | | | |
| OXFORD | 34 | 148 | 344 | 61 | 168 | 67 | 79 | 100 | 250 | 47 | 92 | 135 | 130 | 354 | 132 | 208 | 461 | 345 | 46 | 126 | 202 | 160 | 517 | 205 | 165 | 69 | 118 | 155 | 141 | 250 | 137 | 94 | | | | | | | | | | | | | | | |
| PENZANCE | 64 | 315 | 542 | 266 | 372 | 180 | 309 | 225 | 448 | 272 | 307 | 359 | 344 | 540 | 98 | 334 | 659 | 543 | 215 | 346 | 409 | 396 | 697 | 403 | 375 | 295 | 344 | 342 | 337 | 472 | 365 | 318 | 247 | | | | | | | | | | | | | | |
| PERTH | 4 | 344 | 95 | 321 | 242 | 400 | 396 | 405 | 132 | 337 | 308 | 260 | 502 | 45 | 473 | 398 | 106 | 62 | 365 | 456 | 338 | 268 | 117 | 177 | 246 | 326 | 304 | 246 | 247 | 150 | 406 | 306 | 400 | 580 | | | | | | | | | | | | | |
| PLYMOUTH | 07 | 253 | 480 | 204 | 310 | 118 | 264 | 163 | 386 | 210 | 245 | 297 | 286 | 478 | 43 | 272 | 597 | 481 | 153 | 291 | 328 | 334 | 640 | 341 | 313 | 233 | 282 | 280 | 275 | 410 | 320 | 259 | 185 | 78 | 523 | | | | | | | | | | | | |
| PORTSMOUTH | 52 | 211 | 423 | 140 | 247 | 91 | 124 | 135 | 329 | 126 | 169 | 214 | 125 | 433 | 126 | 245 | 540 | 424 | 106 | 157 | 284 | 239 | 595 | 284 | 244 | 148 | 197 | 238 | 218 | 329 | 184 | 173 | 79 | 224 | 478 | 169 | | | | | | | | | | | |
| SALISBURY | 38 | 170 | 394 | 111 | 219 | 51 | 140 | 93 | 300 | 101 | 146 | 195 | 159 | 409 | 87 | 205 | 511 | 395 | 66 | 161 | 242 | 215 | 571 | 255 | 220 | 124 | 173 | 199 | 193 | 305 | 198 | 149 | 60 | 185 | 454 | 130 | 40 | | | | | | | | | | |
| SHEFFIELD | 63 | 156 | 241 | 76 | 38 | 162 | 111 | 178 | 147 | 83 | 35 | 17 | 227 | 238 | 235 | 210 | 358 | 242 | 131 | 182 | 149 | 65 | 396 | 100 | 33 | 63 | 46 | 69 | 38 | 129 | 146 | 38 | 130 | 358 | 279 | 280 | 209 | 190 | | | | | | | | | |
| SHREWSBURY | 90 | 75 | 263 | 43 | 102 | 104 | 144 | 104 | 169 | 62 | 64 | 98 | 219 | 261 | 177 | 129 | 380 | 264 | 74 | 207 | 101 | 134 | 423 | 124 | 107 | 71 | 115 | 58 | 67 | 203 | 184 | 79 | 101 | 275 | 306 | 220 | 180 | 140 | 81 | | | | | | | | |
| SOUTHAMPTON | 42 | 191 | 415 | 125 | 234 | 73 | 131 | 115 | 321 | 111 | 156 | 199 | 137 | 413 | 106 | 227 | 532 | 416 | 89 | 164 | 264 | 224 | 575 | 276 | 224 | 133 | 188 | 212 | 206 | 314 | 189 | 158 | 64 | 204 | 458 | 149 | 20 | 22 | 191 | 163 | | | | | | | |
| SOUTHEND-ON-SEA | 83 | 246 | 414 | 144 | 218 | 161 | 63 | 186 | 320 | 124 | 149 | 174 | 72 | 404 | 214 | 295 | 531 | 415 | 144 | 60 | 288 | 188 | 566 | 280 | 213 | 121 | 146 | 222 | 205 | 300 | 102 | 142 | 97 | 312 | 449 | 257 | 119 | 127 | 180 | 187 | 124 | | | | | | |
| STOKE-ON-TRENT | 68 | 108 | 241 | 42 | 71 | 121 | 119 | 137 | 147 | 58 | 35 | 65 | 215 | 239 | 194 | 162 | 358 | 242 | 86 | 179 | 119 | 101 | 401 | 102 | 72 | 51 | 83 | 50 | 36 | 168 | 170 | 50 | 105 | 301 | 284 | 239 | 182 | 153 | 48 | 33 | 174 | 170 | | | | | |
| STRANRAER | 0 | 315 | 51 | 292 | 213 | 371 | 367 | 376 | 103 | 308 | 279 | 248 | 465 | 124 | 444 | 369 | 192 | 84 | 336 | 433 | 309 | 259 | 258 | 148 | 217 | 301 | 288 | 217 | 218 | 159 | 389 | 280 | 353 | 551 | 146 | 489 | 432 | 403 | 250 | 272 | 424 | 423 | 250 | | | | |
| THURSO | 7 | 595 | 329 | 561 | 481 | 639 | 635 | 644 | 371 | 576 | 547 | 499 | 741 | 284 | 712 | 637 | 177 | 296 | 604 | 695 | 577 | 507 | 122 | 416 | 485 | 565 | 543 | 485 | 486 | 389 | 645 | 545 | 639 | 819 | 239 | 762 | 717 | 693 | 518 | 545 | 697 | 688 | 523 | 380 | | | |
| WORCESTER | 8 | 95 | 301 | 28 | 135 | 62 | 103 | 72 | 207 | 41 | 72 | 126 | 184 | 299 | 135 | 148 | 418 | 302 | 27 | 180 | 148 | 172 | 461 | 162 | 132 | 64 | 108 | 106 | 100 | 236 | 161 | 70 | 54 | 233 | 344 | 178 | 133 | 93 | 106 | 47 | 106 | 137 | 60 | 310 | 583 | | |
| YORK | 6 | 208 | 211 | 128 | 32 | 215 | 159 | 228 | 116 | 127 | 87 | 33 | 274 | 187 | 288 | 262 | 327 | 211 | 180 | 224 | 190 | 40 | 349 | 88 | 23 | 99 | 76 | 93 | 67 | 78 | 178 | 78 | 172 | 395 | 232 | 333 | 247 | 232 | 52 | 133 | 236 | 222 | 100 | 219 | 471 | 159 | |
| LONDON | 7 | 211 | 386 | 106 | 194 | 122 | 53 | 147 | 292 | 86 | 116 | 163 | 71 | 378 | 175 | 267 | 503 | 387 | 109 | 73 | 250 | 173 | 540 | 252 | 189 | 93 | 131 | 202 | 188 | 274 | 106 | 119 | 59 | 273 | 423 | 218 | 77 | 88 | 157 | 149 | 81 | 39 | 152 | 395 | 662 | 106 | 196 |